WORKING WOMEN AND CHILDREN

WORKING WOMEN AND CHILDREN

WORKING WOMEN AND CHILDREN

Volume - 6

Exploitation of Children and Welfare Measures

Editor-in-Chief
C. P. RAI

LAXMI SHIKSHAN SANSTHAN
LUCKNOW

&

ANMOL PUBLICATIONS PVT. LTD.
NEW DELHI - 110 002 (INDIA)

ANMOL PUBLICATIONS PVT. LTD.
4374/4B, Ansari Road, Daryaganj
New Delhi - 110 002

First Edition, 2000

ISBN 81-261-0658-1 (Set)

PRINTED IN INDIA

Published by J.L. Kumar for Anmol Publications Pvt. Ltd., New Delhi -110 002 and Printed at Mehra Offset Press, Delhi.

CONTENTS

22

THE ECONOMIC ROLES OF CHILDREN: ISSUES FOR ANALYSIS

TOWARDS A TYPOLOGY OF CHILD ACTIVITY PATTERNS

To analyse the determinants of children's activity patterns and to explore their implications, it is necessary to devise: an appropriate typology of child activities. The lack of such a conceptualisation has greatly contributed to the dearth of information on the economic roles of children. However, the desirable typology depends on the analytical focus of the research. In this chapter we are primarily concerned with interactions between child roles and production structures, the extent and nature of inequality and exploitation, and patterns of household or individual behaviour. The main purpose is to assess the implications of these relationships for personal and social development and welfare. Later sections of the chapter develop these issues in some detail; but it is essential to start by considering the range and nature of child activities.

The major analytical problem in devising a valid typology is that the desirable categories depend crucially on the nature of the social system and prevailing mode of production. That means that certain concepts are irrelevant or inadequate in some environments but essential in others. In particular, the conventional labour force approach by which sharp distinctions are drawn between "economic" and "non-economic" activities is even more unsatisfactory for the analysis of child activity patterns than it is for the analysis of those of adults. Not only is the distinction between "economic" and "non-economic" activity hard to apply in many environments, but it also aggregates analytically separate categories of activity, while frequently distinguishing between activities which have similar social functions. Moreover, such simple distinctions are liable to be misleading guides to actual behaviour when many people are engaged in multiple activity patterns.

The typology suggested in the following paragraphs attempts to distinguish the analytically most important categories of child activity. In so doing, it is intended to facilitate the task of investigating the determinants and impact of child employment, as well as to provide the nucleus of a methodology for data collection.

1. Domestic Work

Cleaning, cooking, child-care and other domestic chores are undertaken by children to some extent in all societies. In general, these tasks tend to be sex-typed, with girls taking a disproportionate share of the total, and in the process internalising the set-typing of adult roles (see; for example, Zerdoumi, 1968, for a description of this process in Algeria). They comprise an important category of activity to be carefully conceptualised and measured. One difficulty is that some tasks may take place over an extended period, involve rather little effort or active involvement, and be compatible with other activities. This is. particularly the case with "child-care", which many surveys have reported as accounting for a significant proportion of the working day of children (see, for example, Mueller, 1979, on Botswana; Mummert, 1,979, on Mexico; and studies by Cain and White cited below).

An example of the type of data generated on children's domestic work is the pattern found in a village study in Bangladesh (Cain, 1977a). This study indicated. that even young children under 7 years old did about an hour's housework per day, while girls aged 13 to 15 did seven hours a day (table 22.1). In a somewhat comparable survey in rural Indonesia, the time devoted to housework was much less in the case of girls, and somewhat more in the case of boys (White, 1975; table 22.2). Such findings suggest that, even in comparable rural societies, the contribution of children to domestic activities may vary markedly. But it also raises the issue of statistical measurement, for a closer inspection of the Indonesia and Bangladesh data reveals that in the former the definition of housework was a little more restrictive, highlighting the pitfalls of interpretation.

TABLE 22.1

Hours Per Day in Housework by Age Group and Sex: Rural Bangladesh, 1976

Sex	*Age*					
	4-6	*7-9*	*10-12*	*13-15*	*16-21*	*22-29*
Male	0.9	1.1	0.6	0.7	0.7	1.1
Female	1.2	3.7	5.4	7.0	7.8	7.5

Source: Cain (1977a).

TABLE 22.2

Hours Per Day in Housework by Age Group and Sex: Rural Indonesia, 1972

Sex	*Age*					
	4-6	*7-9*	*10-12*	*13-15*	*16-18*	*19-29*
Male	NA	1.0	1.4	1.4	0.7	0.2
Female	NA	2.6	3.1	4.3	3.0	3.8

Source: White (1975).

Although hard to identify clearly and, measure, the collective category of domestic, work deserves to be separated from those activities producing marketable goods and services. In effect it encompasses tasks associated with family and personal services. One purpose in making a distinction between domestic and non-domestic work is to analyse the intra-household division of labour and the process of substitution of different groups in the labour force as the nature of the labour process changes.

2. Non-domestic, Non-monetary Work

This category of work is a major form of chile activity in subsistence economies, and encompasses farm work and such tasks as hunting and gathering. Time-use surveys have suggested that in agrarian economies children spend a great deal of time in such activities, particularly those that are highly time-intensive such as tending livestock, protecting crops from birds and animals, weeding, and other tasks associated with subsistence production. Such tasks form a continuum with domestic work, and the attribution of,. say, winnowing to this category while treating food preparation as domestic work reflects current conventions rather than a functional distinction.

For analytical purposes, this category of activity could be sub-divided. One should if possible distinguish between work contributing to subsistence production and work contributing to production for the market (though this may be difficult in practice). A differentiation according to the exploitative mechanism involved is also desirable—the child may be working for himself or herself, for or with parents, for kin (e.g. treated as a foster child), or for strangers, the implications being different in each case. Thus we suggest the following breakdown:

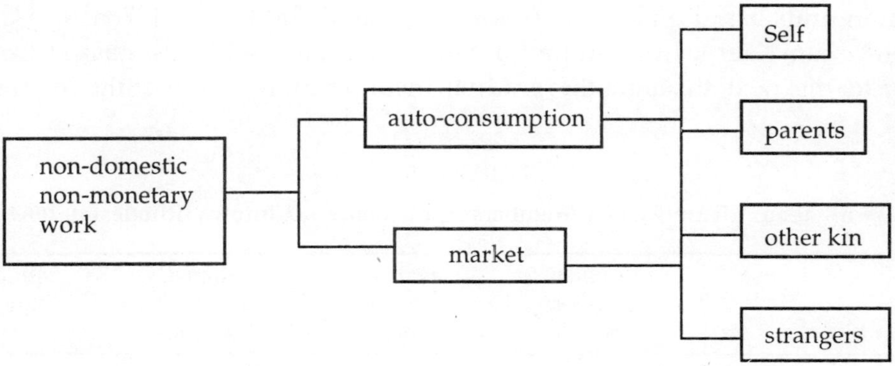

A number of rural time-use surveys in Africa cited in Cleave (1974) have shown a common pattern. In a study of a village in. Gambia it was found that 75 per cent of the boys and about. 50 per cent of the girls aged 11 to 15 did farm work more or less regularly (Haswell, 1953). A survey conducted in south-western Nigeria found considerable farm work being done by children aged 7 to 15, but there was considerable variation by village and by season—in one village, for instance, children worked for about four hours per week over the whole year, in another 16 hours, and in the latter village children worked an average of 45 hours per week in the busiest five weeks of the year (Upton, 1967). In a survey carried out in Rhodesia (now Zambia and Zimbabwe) in 1963-1964, children were recorded as working in farming for about a quarter of the time worked by women, who did somewhat more work than the men (table 22.3), while paid labourers worked about 9 per cent of total working, hours (Johnson, 1965). In a survey of smallholders in two districts of Zambia in 1968-69 it was reported that while children under 8 years old did relatively little farm work they did considerably more off-farm work, and children of both sexes over the age of 8 did a considerable amount of both farm and off-farm work (Elliot, *et al.*, 1970).

A more disaggregated picture of time allocation is given by data from a small farm survey conducted in Uganda in 1965-66 (table 22.4). Despite data deficiencies, the figures highlight both the intra-household division of labour and the flexibility of the family labour force, with almost all activities being done to some extent by men, women and children (Pudsey, 1967).

Although quantitative evidence is scarce, there is no doubt that children make similar contributions to household production in non-agrarian environments. Urban household production, particularly in trade and services, but also in artisanal manufacturing and the like, offers ample scope for time-intensive work in running errands, fetching and carrying, looking after goods for short periods, marketing domestic produce, and so on—work which may be indirectly highly productive, in permitting a more efficient allocation of the time of adults. Thus there may be a complementarity between child and adult activities in small-scale production in units based on kinship in small-scale production in units based on kinship (see for instance Schildkrout, 1978a, and Chapter 3 below on urban Kano). In addition, of course, artisanal skills are passed from one generation to the next through the gradual incorporation of the child in the adult activity.

TABLE 22.3

Hours Worked on A Farm: Family Members and Labourers, Chitowa (Rhodesia), 1963-64

	Annual days per person	*Hours per working day*	*Annual hours per person*	*Annual hours per family*
Men	146	6.2	900	2,157
Women	156	6.6	1,020	3,006
Children (7-15)	42	5.8	242	889
Labourers	226	6.7	1,500	586

Source: Johnson (1965, p. 6).

TABLE 22.4

Average Hours Per Year in Family Work in Kahangi, Toro (Uganda), 1965-66

Activity	*15 farmers*	*22 wives*	*20 other women*	*Aged 10-15*	
				11 boys	*11 girls*
Clearing bush	66	4	1	4	4
Cultivation	98	355	274	7	176
On bananas	325	216	132	17	113
Brewing	44	31	25	11	24
On arable crops	213	455	269	26	193
On livestock	290	47	128	820	279
Total farm hours/day*	3.6	.3.7	2.7	2.9	2.6

Source: Pudsey (1967), cited in Cleave (1974, p. 49).

*Assuming 307 days available for work per year.

3. Tied or Bonded Labour

"Feudal" and "semi-feudal" modes of exploitation impose labour services of various kinds on peasants and other lower-class groups.[1] As children are often induced to work in the process, this category of activity should be incorporated in any realistic typology. The activities concerned often, form part of a set of obligations to a landlord, with children having to contribute a specified amount of work as part of a peasant family's feudal rent. One common arrangement entails children working as unpaid household servants for the landlord, usually for some minimal board and lodging (Marla, 1977). Another common practice is the pledging of children as workers in part-payment of a debt. Indeed, intergenerational bonded labour, with children being bonded virtually for life by the age of 8, has recently been documented by a national survey in India (Marla and Maharaj, 1978). And in most cases the nature of the contract between the exploiting group and the family induced to provide their children's labour makes it hard to assess the full extent of the practice, especially as laws in many countries have ostensibly outlawed it. Thus in India the Children (Pledging of Labour) Act was passed as early as 1933, and amended in 1950 and 1951. Under its regulations parents or guardians were forbidden from pledging their children's labour in return for any payment or benefit. Indeed, all bonded labour was "abolished" by the Bonded Labour System (Abolition) Act, 1976. But few would doubt that such practices have continued, and not only in India.

It should also be noted that certain types of apprenticeship system, discussed below, although not part of a classic feudal system, have implications similar to those of bondage of child labour.

4. Wage Labour

Wage labour is a major type of work activity for children, with analytical implications quite unlike those of domestic or even non-domestic family work. Conceptually, child wage labour should be classified by a series of characteristics. Probably the most basic distinction is between those working as part of a family labour force and those working as individual wage workers. Wage employment of the youngest children typically involves work as part of a family group; this has often characterised agricultural field labour where it is common for employers to hire a family work-group; as illustrated in a recent ILO report from Argentina (Centre for Labour Studies and Research, in ILO, 1979b). However, similar patterns are possible in manual work in industry e.g. the case of carpet-making in Pakistan, reported by Hafeez (also in ILO, 1979b), and brick-making, reported by S. Banerjee (1979). In domestic service, a common pattern has involved women taking their daughters as assistants. Another system involves the wage labour of children as domestic servants of distant kin, with the extent of exploitation being inversely related to the closeness of kinship (Oppong, 1975; Dzidzienya, 1978). The "co-exploitation" of children by employers and older relatives is also observed in industrial firms in industrialising economies. A study of Santiago, for instance, noted the very low wages received by children working as assistants to adults in factories and shops (de la Luz Silva, 1978).

Several other classifications are also important: first, those workers on a piece-rate or sharecropping basis should be distinguished from time-rate workers; second, an attempt should be made to distinguish wage employment that involves some training content from that involving no such content; third, "regular" employment should be distinguished from irregular, casual work, and those in permanent, or potentially permanent jobs should be clearly delineated; fourth, some attempt should be made to identify those in illegal wage employment, since this category may. well comprise the majority; and fifth, a distinction should be made between wage employment that is essentially complementary to or compatible with schooling and that which is essentially competitive.

Probably child wage labour is more frequent in small than in large industrial enterprises, because the latter can less easily ignore legal restrictions. But confirmation of this is difficult, because of an obvious reluctance to report child employment among employers, parents and children alike. Moreover, there is evidence of the use of child labour in some large enterprises, as in Morocco. where extensive employment of young girls in large carpet factories has been reported (Anti-Slavery Society, 1978).

Another major aspect of child wage labour is the widespread system of apprenticeship contracts. Such employment is often sought by children as a means of labour market entry (Callaway, 1973). But the training content of many apprenticeships is minimal, and in some cases the net effect is to tie child workers for long periods to a highly exploitative system. Many 'apprentices' are little more than disguised wage labour, with the added disadvantages of little or no bargaining power, pitifully low wages, and frequently lack of freedom to take other work. In some industries in Nigeria Callaway's data show that virtually the entire wage labour force consists of apprentices (e.g. leather, 85 per cent), suggesting that the apprenticeship system is merely a means of lowering the wage and increasing control over the workforce.

5. Marginal Economic Activities

In addition to activities which can be clearly interpreted as domestic. work, unpaid family labour, bonded labour, and wage employment, there is a set of activities widely undertaken by children which do not fit into such categories. They are typically characterised by their irregularity and short-term nature, though some of those individuals practising the activities may do so on a regular., long term basis. Marginal, semi—economic activities of this type include the. selling of newspapers; "looking after" earnings shoeshining; selling of sweets and other small items; running of errands; and the sorting of garbage for usable objects. Work of this type is graphically described by de la Luz Silva (1978) for Santiago and Bromley (1978) for Cali, and other accounts are to be found in many places in the literature. The sources of child work of this type lie in the impoverishment of their families, but the children concerned are frequently working independently or on commission. Such work typically does not contribute to capital accumulation, and could be described as the activities of a lumpenproletariat.

In this marginal category should be included theft, prostitution, and other activities which are typically illegal or semi-legal. For some purposes it is useful to distinguish between legitimate and illegitimate marginal activities, but analytically that may not be appropriate because an activity which is illegitimate in one place may be legitimate in another. Another point is that child participation in legitimate street-side marginal activities easily leads to various forms of crime. Prostitution tends to fall in a similar category in many societies, where ambivalent and often hypocritical attitudes lead to its association with crime and semi-legitimate activities. Under such circumstances, impoverishment and unemployment push many very young girls into an early life of prostitution.[2] But prostitution is also widely regarded as a socially acceptable and even relatively well paid form of work. However perceived, it tends to reflect wider patterns of inequality and exploitative social relations.

In Santiago children undertaking marginal activities are often in contact with "delinquent" groups, or with more organised systems of theft and racketeering. Evidence tends to be scarce and qualitative, but this is probably a very widespread phenomenon, in large, cities. Desai and Pillai (1972), for instance, note that in Bombay there is a difference in child activities between non-slum areas (where children work in hotels, in canteens, as shoeshine boys. etc.) and slum areas (where the children are "delinquent", "deviant", or "idle").

Analytically, Interest in participation in marginal economic activities is primarily due to the need to trace its effect on subsequent behaviour and experience. Empirically, such activities are extremely hard to measure. Anecdotal information is inadequate, as would be the practice of treating them as some sort of residual after all other forms of activity had been measured. Indeed, one criticism of data collection on time-use and activity distribution in general is that there is a tendency to distort reality by omitting 'deviant' activities I which are rarely if ever admitted and unlikely to be observed. The consequence is that measured use of time tends to cluster unrealistically around a perceived normal pattern.

6. Schooling

This is an activity that is harder to assess than conventional statistics suggest. Typically census and survey data present children as being "at school" or not at school. But such are the ambiguities that the conventional index of educational attainment, namely 'years of schooling', may be thoroughly misleading. In analysing child activity patterns the first distinction is between school enrolment, which in most countries is supposedly compulsory, at least at the primary level, and school attendance. But even the notion of attendance is fraught with difficulties, involving questions of regularity, daily duration and seasonality. In addition to the daily-weekly-yearly time in school, some allowance must be made for time spent in travelling, to and from school, and the time required for schooling outside school hours. Moreover, school may well be combined with other activities, which no doubt reflects on the regularity and value of school attendance. For instance, in a survey in rural Chile, 66 per cent of those aged 9 to 15 were said to be attending school full-time, and a further 12 per cent were full—time in economic activity; but 22 per cent were combining school and work.[3]

To conceptualise the activity of schooling adequately it is also necessary to consider the question of the children's ability to learn, not in terms of their native faculties, but in terms of their nutritional-energy levels and access to facilities. Attending a chronically overcrowded, ill-equipped school while suffering from malnutrition or fatigue due to other work is very different from attending small classes in a state of full health. It is also necessary to consider the anticipated duration of schooling, in terms of attendance through. the year and the expected number of years and grades. In many cases school attendance is little more than a token exercise of short duration. Finally, it is important not to confuse schooling with education. Many other activities contribute to education, and some forms of economic activity are among them.

Data on schooling or education are therefore to be handled with care. However, figures such as a 34 per cent school enrolment rate of scheduled caste children aged 6 to 11 in Bihar in 1973 (Sarna, 1975) can only be regarded as low, however they are interpreted. In this case póverty, opportunities for child employment, and a lack of perceived value in schooling (together with reported caste discrimination in school) combine to ensure early drop-out even if there is an initial period of regular school attendance.

7. Idleness and Unemployment

Few children lees than 14 years of age are classified as unemployed in conventional labour force statistics, which makes recorded labour force participation rates for, say, 10 to 14 year olds thoroughly misleading. In many low-income countries, especially in urban areas, any realistic measure of the youth unemployment rate would be very high: for unemployment is the only valid way of describing the idleness frequently observed among the young. Out of school at an early age, they have no real income-earning opportunities, though the unemployment they experience is liable to be interspersed with marginal, irregular activities that provide a modicum of income. But the essence of unemployment is the induced sense of passivity, anomie and, if prolonged, surely something like unemployability for many forms of regular employment. This is the crucial difference between unemployment and recreation, which can be depicted as having a beneficial effect.

The vicious circle of poverty and unemployment has often been demonstrated. Thus low nutritional intake, and the consequent energy deficit, are certainly major causes of the widespread inactivity observed in, for example, Indian villages when there is no income-producing work that could be done, and sometimes even when there is. Equally, inadequate physical development leads to young teenagers being unable to secure a niche in the labour market, or it means that having acquired a job, they are unable to maintain the effort demanded and revert to further unemployment. Such unemployment should not be measured by some job-seeking criterion, for discouragement is pervasive. It should be assessed in terms of needs and aspirations, as well as in terms of the lack of alternative options. Some effort should be directed to assessing the extent and form of unemployment among children of school-going age. The practical difficulties in measuring child and youth unemployment are legion, but that is no excuse for statistics ignoring it altogether.

8. Recreation and Leisure

Recreation or leisure is an essential activity for all age groups and has often been presented as the objective of economic life. For children it is widely regarded as the primary activity along with schooling, which in turn is often ideally presented as combining learning and play. The category of recreation is again more complex than is implied by some discussions, since the socialisation content of any given play activity may be merely facilitating a subsequent lifetime of exploitation, or developing an appropriate attitude to work and social relations, depending on your point of view. Even the separation of play and work is not necessarily easy—Schildkrout, gives some examples of the difficulties from urban Nigeria. If the intention is to analyse the effects of child activity patterns on subsequent social and economic behaviour, and to analyse. the function of those activity. patterns in the prevailing socio-economic system, this issue has to be faced.

9. Reproductive Activities

To make the typology comprehensive in terms of time allocation, there should be a separate category embracing physiological activities, the most important in terms of time being sleep. Time taken or available for other reproductive activities, such as eating or cleaning and related personal care, should also be included in this category and be separated from recreation and from household work.

Clearly, these various activities are not mutually incompatible, and various combinations will exist. In some cases, one activity will dominate, as in the case of girls engaged for seven or eight hours a day in domestic work. In other cases, time will be divided—children in the urban slums; for instance, may divide their time between domestic work, marginal and illegitimate activities, schooling and idleness. It is useful to develop "stereotypes" of frequently recurring activity patterns. There will be many such stereotypes corresponding to different socioeconomic settings, though there will of course be many children who cannot be readily classified in any given stereotype, The development of a statistical method for combining stereotypes with the typology far activities seems a necessary task in the analysis of child employment and its relationship to the socioeconomic structure. One activity may of course imply another; a case in point is travel, an important use of time and energy in most low-income countries, and one that is not explicitly distinguished in the proposed typology.

One evident aspect of child activity patterns is their demographic variation, notably with respect to age, sex, and family structure. Several of the rural time-allocation studies cited earlier give evidence on this (Cain, 1977a; Mueller, 1979; White, 1975). Wage and other types of non-household labour are usually sharply differentiated by age, but even in peasant agriculture age specialisation is common. Sex-specialisation is equally widespread, usually with a progression towards the conventional adult activities of the child's sex.

In urban areas, the progressive integration of children into adult activities may also occur in household production. Apprenticeship systems sometimes serve that function, though as we have noted they may merely be disguised forms of exploitation. However, the entry of children to non-domestic economic activity is bath more generally necessary and more difficult than in rural areas. Commonly children drift out of school, and, between the age of about 8 and 12 or 14, drift into marginal economic activities, leading to a *working* life of intermittent labour force activity and unemployment.

A final comment is worth making on the implications of this typology for data collection. Clearly, the appropriate data collection technique is some sort of time-use survey. However, the implementation of such a survey requires an appreciation of the activities comprising the crucial alternative uses of time and energy. For children the focus should be on the annual distribution of time to different activities, as well as on the relationship of current and past activity patterns to subsequent behaviour, experience and status. Accordingly, time—use data related to a specific day or even week would have little analytical value, and may indeed be quite misleading. Moreover, it is not only time devoted to particular activities that matters. It is also necessary to consider the effort expended and the intensity of time use, issues which are far harder to conceptualise or measure, but which are crucial for the analysis of the implications of different activity patterns. And even time, effort and intensity are not necessarily sufficient to identify the structural social context yet this is critical for understanding the nature, sources and consequences of different types of child activities.

STRUCTURAL SOCIO-ECONOMIC DETERMINANTS OF CHILD EMPLOYMENT

1. Modes of Production: Situations and Transitions

Among the structural influences on the extent and nature of the economic roles of children in low-income countries, two sets of factors can be identified: first, the mode of production; and second, the associated structure of the labour market. Briefly, by a mode of production is meant a specific set of social relations of production and distribution combined with a related development of the forces of production. It can be expected that the economic roles of children will vary systematically according to the nature of the mode of production, and that these roles will undergo systematic change in the transition from one mode of production to another. Several such transitions are possible, but the one of most immediate relevance to current patterns of development in low-income countries concerns the transition from various types of what are usually called "pre-capitalist" modes to a capitalist mode of production. In the following, therefore, most reference is made to this type of change. Other transitions, notably towards various types of socialism, are little discussed in the present chapter. Any complete analysis of the economic roles of children, and particularly of policy towards children, would have to remedy this omission.

(a) The Role of Children in Agrarian Societies

In technologically primitive, pastoral, or hunting-and-gathering societies almost all those capable of contributing to the daily and annual cycles of survival and social cohesion do so, although in such societies the amount of daily work is often remarkably small.[4] The social division of labour is therefore limited and related to age, sex, and personal capacities. There is a tendency for "prime-age" adults to take primary responsibility for those activities involving relatively *effort—intensive* tasks, while children, and (to the extent that they are present) the elderly, take the more *time—intensive* tasks. But to call these high and low productivity activities respectively would be somewhat misleading, since the very complementarity of the various tasks makes such distinctions dubious. If there is a general rule governing the division of labour, it might be that distance of the site of the activity from the site of residence determines the relative probability of different age groups participating in the activity in question, but this is at most an hypothesis.

Despite low levels of work, and the correspondingly large amount of time devoted to 'rest' and social leisure activities, exploitative relations have existed in such societies, whether relations of production correspond to the independent peasant family model of

Chayanov[5] or to the lineage mode of production recently presented as characteristic of large parts of Africa, in which identifiable groups receive surplus product from the direct producers. Perhaps the most common form of exploitation in the latter type of society is based on age, involving the socially sanctioned relationships between communal elders and youths.[6] In such cases tributary labour services are performed by the younger members of the compound or village community for the elders. Another common feature is debt bondage in various guises, arising typically from the exercise of judicial powers by the elders. Where adults have been put into debt, it is a common practice for elders to take a child or other young relative as a servant until the debt has been paid off.[7] The prevalence of such practices is impossible to estimate, but exploitation of this type is almost certainly widespread, albeit difficult to quantify, and—according to Bekombo, in previous chapters—also hard to conceptualise adequately. While it is particularly characteristic of many rural areas, there is also evidence of similar relationships in urban areas. A case in point is the use of children of distantly related kin as domestic servants in urban Ghana (Dzidzienya, 1978).

In a peasant family production system, whether or not there is significant inequality between production units, there may be considerable intra-household exploitation, similarly based on socially sanctioned age, sex or kin relationships.[8] For instance, in parts of Africa residential units consist of compounds in which systems of duolocal or parallel residence have meant children living apart from one or both parents. In such circumstances the pressure for children to be integrated into the productive system must be considerable. Systems of fostering of children by non-parental kin, as among the Hausa in Nigeria, have meant that one way or another a substantial proportion of children have lived apart from kin. But even in rural areas of many Asian countries, where family residence is more typical, children are viewed essentially as producers. Although the conventional model is one of parents "investing" in children in order to be assured of support in their old age, another model may fit at least as well of parents producing labour power, to be set to work and exploited at as early an age as possible.

Historically, where there has been a growth of feudal relations of production there has been an increase in work intensity and exploitation, as feudal obligations have systematically transferred surplus product from peasants to landlords or other beneficiary classes. The classic feudal relationship involves peasant families providing labour services to landlords or their ilk, often including specific obligations to bodies such as religious organisations, or local political and judicial authorities[9] Commonly children have had to contribute, and indeed in many cases there is evidence of feudal rent being calculated on the assumption that all members of peasant families would work. There is even anecdotal evidence of peasants with relatively large families being taken as tenants in place of those with a smaller capacity to provide such rental services; even if rents were calculated as a percentage of output, the landlord would gain from the latter practice. Typically the children would be expected to work under the immediate direction of their parents. And while this conjures up a picture of members of peasant families working alongside one another in the fields, it can also apply to certain types of domestic and craft work. It is a particularly common feature of sharecropping arrangements.

With the pattern of work sharing and steady assimilation, of children to more adult tasks and obligations, the role of schooling in such pre-capitalist economies is minimal, its socialisation function almost certainly not required and its provision of literacy or related skills scarcely in the interests of the dominant groups. As for the peasant families themselves, continuing rental obligations are likely to force them to employ all their domestic labour resources, while the potential return to what little schooling has been made available is negligible. Indeed, the net return to schooling might even be negative, in that the skills the peasants need for survival are those gained in work rather than through schooling.

Of course, there have been many variants of "feudal" relations. In some countries, peasants have been tied into what might be described as semi-feudal relations of production, in which peasant-worker families are exploited through various rental and wage obligations relying on non-market power. Thus, one or more family members may be working for a wage that is less than the cost of reproducing their or their family's labour power. They can do so only because of the subsistence contribution of other family members. Debt is the most common mechanism for enforcing such patterns of behaviour. In some such cases, especially where children are involved, little or no wage is paid. Thus in India children of peasant or bonded labour families have often been put out or pledged as servants and labourers in the households of richer peasants and landlords in lieu of debt repayment (Maria and Maharaj, 1978). In other cases the family has been able to meet its obligations to landlords only through some member migrating temporarily to earn the necessary income. Though usually involving young men or women, there are many cases of teenage or even pre-teenage children being sent to work for long hours in poor conditions and for meagre wages.

(b) Transitions to Industrial Capitalism

The growth of capitalist relations of production in many parts of the world has been associated with a set of interrelated phenomena—an increase in industrial production, a shift to cash-crop farming and a general commercialisation of agriculture, the growth of a landless population, migration and urbanisation, the progressive monetisation of domestic activities, and a growth of unemployment in its various forms. With the growth of wage labour, the increasing division of labour has been associated with various types of labour market segmentation. And in place of primitive, subsistence-oriented skills the emphasis has been placed, on specific labour market skills associated with on-the-job training, literacy and schooling. Not all these changes are occurring, and there are conspicuous examples of countries following different types of development paths. But patterns of this type recur frequently. Since they clearly generate changes in the economic role of children, it is essential to examine the more important effects of such changes.

The growth of wage labour and capitalist relations of production has been associated, in the industrialised countries, with a long-run decline in child employment. But in the early stages children were used in many guises to further capital accumulation and intensify exploitation. Thus in the early part of the Industrial Revolution in the United Kingdom agricultural employers commonly hired whole families for a "family wage", based on the expected output of the different family members. As a result of the task-work wage system, single men and old men whose children had grown tip found it difficult to obtain employment (Pinchbeck, 1930, p. 101). Indeed, one conclusion of a famous report on women and children in agriculture in 1843 was that men feared children's employment more than women's, because a boy "worked more regularly, and he at once brought down the price of labour and made it more difficult to obtain employment". Such situations were by no means reserved to the agricultural labour market.

In most low-income countries today large industrial firms and other sizeable capitalist enterprises do not seem to make extensive use of child labour, perhaps because of the need to respect legislation, or possibly because adult and youth labour is in ample supply to regular jobs. However, at least one exception was noted earlier, and the extent of child employment is probably much greater than official statistics suggest because of the obvious incentive to under-report child labour. In small manufacturing enterprises children are used as cheap, "sweated" labour, frequently working alongside older relatives and possibly not paid directly but indirectly through a "supplementary wage" paid to the parent worker. Such practices have been reported from Chile (de la Luz Silva, 1978), Pakistan (Hafeez, in ILO, 1979b), and Jamaica (Standing, 1978a), among others. In all such cases the employment of relatively cheap child labour has helped to accelerate the process of capital accumulation by raising the over-all rate of exploitation. Child employment can also contribute indirectly to exploitation by introducing a relatively easily disciplined segment of a nascent proletariat, thereby forcing adult workers into greater labour commitment, in addition to directly substituting cheap labour for workers with higher wage expectations.

The substitution of capitalist for feudal and semi-feudal relations of production is strongly felt in rural areas. Where urban wage employment grows, or, where rural families require wage income to pay taxes or to purchase new or newly monetised commodities, youths often young children are encouraged to leave the rural domestic production unit,. notably the peasant farm. Several Indian studies have traced large numbers of "runaway" child workers, many being below 10 years old (Kapadai and Pillai, 1971; Gangrade, 1979). Where the farming system is dominated by male workers, as in Latin America and the Caribbean, there has been a considerable out-migration of girls and young women, often very young teenagers. In many other countries—and in most rural areas experiencing an expansion of wage employment generally—young men have been the first to shift into the wage labour market, whether or not this has involved migration. In such cases women and children have usually been required to perform more of the domestic income-earning and agricultural work. In Africa and the Middle East, for example, surveys have repeatedly shown this pattern of adaptation. In Egypt a rural employment survey in 1964-65, undertaken by the INP (Cairo) and the ILO, recorded that children (aged 6 to 15), and to a lesser extent women, were hired by small-scale farmers to do the cotton picking and weeding so that the men could take higher-paying, non-agricultural seasonal work (Hansen, 1969).

Another correlate of the growth of capitalist relations is increasing landlessness, itself usually the precursor of the growth of a rural proletariat, and closely associated with rural class differentiation.

With such changes the social division of labour is modified, in that the children of the landless or near landless are forced into the labour market to a greater extent than is typically the case for any social category of children where class differentiation is less advanced. Labour force participation of children from poor and medium strata of peasants is likely to be particularly high because the pressure of subsistence requirements remains considerable, while the possibilities for work are increased by small-scale ownership of means of production. However, evidence on these relationships is mixed. In Bangladesh, Cain found little difference in over-all child "productive" work-time between the landless and small landowners. Child work among large landowners was also similar for children up to the age of 12, but was distinctly lower beyond that up to the age of 21, probably reflecting full-time secondary school attendance. Mueller in Botswana found the non-linear relationship expected (child labour supply highest at intermediate land ownership levels) but statistical reliability was low (Mueller, 1979). Rosenzweig and Evenson (1977), using aggregate data, found child labour supply in India to be positively associated with land holding and negatively with wage levels; however, there were no strong income effects on school enrolment. But in Rosenzweig's paper in this volume, using a micro-data set, these relationships are not reproduced—indeed, the results are almost the reverse of those in the earlier paper. This highlights the, difficulty of replicating research findings, and underlines the dearth of reliable empirical research.

2. Unemployment, Poverty and the Labour Market

With the growth of capitalist relations of production the structure of labour demand and labour utilisation is radically changed. Increasing proletarianisation is associated with the growth of labour market segmentation, by which the labour force is separated into submarkets with different employment conditions and wages.[10] This helps raise the rate of exploitation by reducing class unity and weakening bargaining power, allowing relatively strong groups of workers to improve their working conditions without all workers benefiting. One common result is the creation of a "labour aristocracy", whereby high wages are maintained for small numbers of workers despite considerable excess labour supply.

Children can affect and be affected by this type of labour market in many different ways. Most crucially, their availability may permit employers to rely on a particularly intensely exploited group of workers. Unorganised, with low dependency rates, a need for income, and vulnerable by nature of their age, children are more readily exploited than other labour groups. As argued in Section 1.4, many so-called apprenticeship schemes have been little more than devices for concealing this type of labour. The use of child workers, nominally as apprentices, helps to reinforce labour market segmentation. At the same time, by permitting children to enter the fully-fledged labour force through a clear, if limited, career structure, such a system induces greater labour force commitment on their part and indirectly increases the over-all level of commitment to wage labour.

The employment of children also puts indirect pressure on wage rates. Where adult wages are determined by conventional subsistence criteria, child work reduces the wage required for subsistence (or the reproduction of the labour force) and thereby permits increased exploitation.

Segmentation is also a means of stratifying the labour he force. Higher-status, higher-paid jobs are differentiated from the mass of unskilled work. And, in general, career paths do not lead vertically through segments. Access to the high-level jobs is largely determined by the entry point to the system, not by performance at lower levels. A screening process, based on educational and social qualifications, ensures that higher-level jobs are effectively excluded by the performance of child labour, which tends to be incompatible with the acquisition of the necessary educational qualifications. Thus a contradiction emerges between the formal educational system preparing children for clerical, managerial and related jobs and the opportunities for unskilled child labour, increasing incipient class consciousness and accentuating the divergence in class interests, and attitudes.

This issue of schooling and its functions is clearly critical for analysing the joint processes of differentiation in the labour market and the distribution of child activity between schooling and labour. The role of schooling in non-industrial economies is negligible except among tiny elites. But the growth of a wage labour market, particularly for manufacturing and clerical jobs, greatly increases its significance. In many low-income economies, schooling can be seen to have two functions, that of socialisation and inculcating a commitment to stable wage labour, and that of providing the nucleus of labour market skills. In almost all labour markets, schooling is a means of selecting workers, schooling credentials being a signal not only of a capacity to acquire technical skills but also of a malleability. to the concentrated discipline of wage jobs.

Differentiation in job access associated with schooling is paralleled by differentiation in access to schooling itself. In rural areas, the growth of a subclass of capitalist farmers tends to promote educational differentiation, as these relatively prosperous farmers substitute hired for family labour, thereby reducing the pressure on their children to substitute economic activity for schooling At the same time, the increasing use of hired labour draws mare adults and sometimes children into the labour market. Even where children are not directly hired, their work levels are likely to increase if they have to substitute for those who have started working outside the domestic unit of production. There are similar effects where the household "head" migrates in search of employment, either seasonally or for longer periods, as is widely observed in Africa and Latin America (UNICEF, 1970). In any case, impoverished, landless families can rarely afford the direct costs of schooling, and see little benefit from making major sacrifices in order to permit children to attend school. In addition, the very experience of poverty is likely to induce a set of fatalistic attitudes and behavioural attributes inimical to regular and useful school attendance. The outcome is differential access to schooling across social groups, reflected in differential enrolment rates. An example from India gives enrolment rates varying from 43 per cent among the landless. to 75 per cent among larger cultivators (Government of India, 1965).

A similar differentiation can be observed in urban areas. Drop-out from school among the urban poor is associated with the low perceived advantage from schooling, its high direct and indirect cost, as well as the pressing need for the income children might be able to earn. The urban bourgeoisie, including civil servants and other administrative workers, face no such constraints. They, can therefore at least partially control both the supply of and the demand for qualified workers. In such circumstances it is almost useless trying to impose a system of compulsory school enrolment and attendance; the problem is structural.

Thus the growth of a labour market, and particularly of jobs requiring literacy, makes schooling an increasingly important determinant of labour market entry and subsequent career patterns. But while lack of schooling makes access to attractive segments of the labour market unlikely, the inverse does not necessarily hold. Rising qualifications are required for access to specific rungs of the job ladder, and while this has been associated with higher average schooling levels in the labour force, the increasing capacity of the formal education systems of most low-income countries has also been associated with more educated unemployment. [11] In consequence, an analysis of schooling and the labour force activity of children and youths would be incomplete if it were not set in the more general context of labour market structure and levels, of unemployment.

The drift to urban areas in the early stages of capitalist industrialisation is usually associated with widespread unemployment. Whether or not children in peasant—type economies progress by stages into the adult labour force, no such easy process of assimilation is found in urban environments. In most low-income industrialising countries urban unemployment levels are persistently and even chronically high, in some cases conservatively reaching 20 to 25 per cent. In addition, many workers are forced to eke out an existence of casual employment interspersed with long periods of unemployment and economic inactivity. The highest. rates of open unemployment despite the statistical ambiguities associated with such measures are observed among teenagers. In Latin

American and Caribbean cities, for instance, youth unemployment rates as high as 40 to 50 per cent have been recorded. Such figures have to be treated cautiously, as there is a tendency for the denominator to be artificially deflated by labour force withdrawal among teenagers. But there is no denying the enormity of the phenomenon.

High levels of unemployment have two opposite effects on activity patterns corresponding to the much analysed "discouraged worker" and "additional worker" effects. In the case of the young the net effect of high over-all unemployment on labour force participation is particularly hard to assess. Among the "discouraged worker" effects, there is the tendency for teenagers to drift out of the labour force into crime. Many girls are forced to take up prostitution as almost the only means of survival, the number involved sometimes being strikingly high (Bamberger, 1973, p. 3). Some case studies from Santiago are discussed by de la Luz Silva. Occasional paid sexual relationships may or may not be regarded as prostitution: one recent study of girls from rural elementary schools in Ghana estimated that 61.6 per cent of those who had boyfriends did so primarily to get money. (Akuffo, 1978, p. 7), without this involving any social disapproval.[12] But typically child prostitution is demeaning and oppressive, often involving virtual imprisonment (for example in. Thailand, see Banerjee, 1981.

On the demand side of the labour market, high unemployment can lead to a substitution of older for younger workers in many wage jobs, which may then be formalised by worker organisations encouraging employers and governments to impose minimum age restrictions on hiring practices. High levels of unemployment facilitate the growth of labour market segmentation, making some jobs the preserve of particular categories of workers, while more marginal groups such as children and the elderly are restricted to the least stable and lowest paid jobs. This in itself may weaken their attachment to the labour force.

One form of discouragement of young workers is worth emphasising. In several industrialised and industrialising countries for instance Colombia (Walter, 1970)—high youth unemployment has encouraged teenagers with intermediate educational qualifications to stay in or return to schooling. The most discussed case is that of Indian youth. There is little doubt that the bleak job prospects of those with poor educational credentials have induced many young Indians to pursue successively higher levels of schooling,[13] especially in lower middle-class families where perception of the returns to schooling is strong but control over labour market access is weak. Elsewhere, teenagers attending primary or secondary school have been induced to pursue more schooling for the same reason. What is particularly interesting is that the process may produce a non-linear relationship between age and labour force participation. Thus children and teenagers who leave school and enter the labour force before the age of 15 find themselves unqualified to obtain anything but casual low-income forms of work. After a period spent in dispiriting unemployment, some of them return to school or resort to informal schooling to seek the credentials needed for wage employment. In Kingston, Jamaica, where this phenomenon has been common, the return to school has proved largely unsuccessful (Standing, 1978a), but its effect has been that teenagers have withdrawn wholly or partially from the labour force following initial discouragement.

The reason many of these teenagers or children enter the labour force initially is that the poverty or unemployment of their parents or parent obliges them to become secondary workers. For certain casual forms of work, and for such quasi-economic activities as begging-with-services, children may well have a higher opportunity income thaw adults. Indeed, whereas high unemployment has a strong discouragement effect on the urban labour force participation rate of teenagers, it is likely that there is often a net additional worker effect for children under the age of about 12.

Much of the employment of children aged 12 or less, other than within the household or as domestic servants, occurs in small enterprises for which they constitute by far the cheapest form of labour for unskilled jobs not requiring heavy labour, such as providing sales assistance, running errands, or helping in various tasks. Those who cannot obtain even these types of jobs turn to marginal, legitimate or illegitimate activities or end up unemployed. Tire search by children for income-earning opportunities is typically part of a family survival strategy—a response to extreme poverty, or to major household crises (e.g. death, departure or unemployment of principal income-earner). When households rely for survival only on their own labour, and especially where the work available is irregular, casual, and poorly paid, there is an obvious need to mobilise all family labour resources. In this, wage-labour households are no different from the peasant or artisan household which mobilises domestic labour for production; the difference lies in the greater difficulty faced by urban working-class households in finding jobs. Failure accelerates the drift into poverty, idleness, and illegitimate activities. For undesirable as this form of child labour is from the perspective of ILO labour standards, or of the macro-economist analysing its contribution to an exploitative system, it may be viewed somewhat differently by the children concerned, and even more so by their families, to whom the bulk of the income is likely to be transferred.

Thus while discouragement is likely to be widespread, the need for child labour is almost certain to mean that high levels of adult unemployment and widespread poverty push children into the labour market.

CULTURAL AND BEHAVIOURAL ASPECTS OF CHILD ACTIVITY PATTERNS

In addition to structural socio-economic factors, at least two sets of determinants of child work should be considered: (1) the social and cultural framework attitudes to children and their roles, cultural constraints, and the social institutions which govern the processes of acculturation and socialisation; and (2) the nature of decision-making at the household or other micro-unit level, and the employment of children as an outcome of the trade-offs between alternatives in economic behaviour.

1. The Social and Cultural Framework

Child employment not only reflects economic processes but depends on normative attitudes towards children in society, the culturally determined roles and functions of children, the values by which the activities of children are judged, and the nature of socialisation processes. In most of Europe, there is general disapproval of formal labour force participation of children below the age of 14 or so; on the other hand, participation of children in housework is approved, by parents at least (though the extent to which the attitude is sex-differentiated varies from one class and country to another). Elsewhere, by, contrast, participation in various types of economic activity from an early age is considered an essential part of socialisation (Oppong, 1973; Schildkrout, 1978a, and Bekombo).

The process of socialisation, and the cultural objectives to which it responds, are clearly interdependent with the structural economic system within which socialisation occurs. There is much debate about whether cultural values are the causes, or consequences of economic needs. Kozak (1978), surveying some of the literature on child socialisation, argues strongly that economic needs are the basic causes. In his model, the nature of, the child's socialisation is associated with the class position of his or her parents. Personality development, role acceptance, and the internalisation of social norms are thereby transmitted in a way which reflects and perpetuates the existing stratification of society. The basic argument is convincing; but to treat culture only as a dependent variable is too extreme. One comment on Kozak's model is that in so far as economic changes generate lifetime experiences for individuals which differ from those of their parents, conditioning will be imperfect. There is therefore a lag in the transmission of cultural values behind the needs of the economic system. This suggests that cultural variables tend to slow the process of economic change. There are also independent effects of any given cultural heritage which affect the nature of economic change, as well as its pace. Thus while many aspects of culture, and its internalisation by children, may be conditioned by the needs of the economic system, this does not permit us to neglect the independent effects of the socio-cultural framework.

The effects of the prevailing modes of domestic organisation and of the system of kinship and marriage are a case in point. Their related sets of rights and obligations clearly influence the development of child activities. In some contexts delegation of aspects of parental roles, and the institutionalised practice of fostering of children by non-parental kin, involve widespread transfers of the obligations to train and maintain children, and the rights to enjoy the services of the young. Such practices may involve an element of apprenticeship and specialist training, as among the Dagomba of West Africa (Oppong, 1973). There is evidence that such practices in peasant settings do not necessarily entail any material or emotional changes in the kinds and content of relationships established with parental figures. Foster children and own children may be treated with just the same kind of care and attention.[14] A broadly based family with a wide and complex obligation structure may nevertheless imply a greater variety of child activities, merely because it presents a wider range of options and obligations. In such family systems socialisation occurs largely through contact with the economic activities of kin, while reciprocal obligations induce the child to start many of these activities at an early age. Independence is attained late, if at all, and activities continue to be regulated by the needs and possibilities of the family.

By contrast, kinship systems in which the nuclear family is functionally individuated and residentially isolated, and in which parental and filial rights and obligations are, not shared, may provide a less flexible and less secure system. They provide an economic and social framework to support the child through a formal education process, and perhaps also through initial labour market entry, before the child becomes independent. The obligation network is narrower, as are the possibilities for child work. Provided that household income is adequate for perceived household needs, child labour supply will be lower. However, there are fewer or no available substitutes in case of crisis. Death or incapacity of a parent will lead to single parents attempting to supply a range of conflicting needs of children. In such cases, very high child employment rates are probable, whereas in more broadly based family structures, kin obligations provide an alternative source of subsistence.

Another example of the independent effects of socio-cultural variables is the attribution of sex roles among children. Some aspects of these roles clearly, consist of preparation, for the adult sexual division of labour. Thus it seems almost universal that child-care and housework fall more to girls than to boys, in keeping with the traditional view of the domestic role of women. However, there is much more variability in the extent to which girls work outside the home, which cannot be fully explained by socio-economic factors. For instance, Islamic traditions arguably restrict female labour force participation rates, and indeed, among Arab countries the prevalence of restrictions on female activity, presumably reflecting cultural orthodoxy rather than economic needs, is statistically associated with lower female labour supply.[15] The net effect is that at puberty a decline in girls. extra-domestic activity is frequently observed, while for boys the reverse is the case. Schildkrout's contribution to this volume documents similar tendencies in Kano, where children have roles which contribute to the maintenance of the *adult* division of labour. They undertake many fetching and carrying chores which would otherwise fall to women, but which would be incompatible with the institution of purdah.

So with respect to both family structure and sex roles, cultural factors have an independent effect. But their influence should not be exaggerated. There is much evidence that family structure changes in response to economic needs, however slowly; this is brought out by Goode (1963), in his classic analysis of changing family patterns. Even the role of women in Islamic countries is not immutable—Hansen (1969) reports that in the Delta region of Egypt, where agricultural labour needs are relatively high, women work outside the home much more than do women in Upper Egypt where labour demand is lower. In short, any examination of cultural variables has to consider their interaction with structural economic phenomena.

At a broader level, the roles of children are associated with the values attached to children by parents, with the images of the future which parents perceive, and with the objectives underlying particular levels of fertility. Several "value of children" studies have explored the psychological factors underlying fertility. Though many factors are cited by parents as reasons for having children, the work of children, domestic or otherwise, recurs frequently. In the Philippines, for instance, among the reasons the 'financial contribution' of children was cited by 39 per cent of households, 'help in housework' by 42 per cent. The latter figure rose to 71 per cent for daughters, the former figure to 54 per cent for sans in rural areas (Bulatao, 1975). The implication is that parents see the 'production' of children as a means of adding to the household labour force. However, in the conventional jargon, children are also viewed as if they were 'consumption goods', providing happiness, companionship, and psychological benefits. The balance of these different objectives, and their social respectability, determine to a great extent parental attitudes to their children, and the nature of their socialisation.

2. Micro-behavioural Determinants

The pattern of child activities reflects choices among a limited number of alternative possibilities, the latter being defined by the socio-economic, cultural and legal context. A widespread practice is to analyse these choices as deriving from a complex decision-making process by a composite unit such as a "household" or "family". Indeed, many recent empirical analyses of child activity patterns have been concerned with the household as an optimising, rational decision-making unit, in which children are depicted as both consumption and investment "goods" (Willis, 1973; Schultz, 1974). This neo-classical approach, known popularly as the "new home economics, also depicts the determinants of fertility in terms of the relative utilities of children and other goods or services, with children involving the investment of time and income.

Applications of this model to the determinants of child employment tend to focus on the trade-off between time devoted to schooling and labour force activity. The neo-classical model represents parents as choosing between "quantity" and "quality" of children; if they have more children they cannot afford to invest as much in the quality, or in practical terms schooling, of their children. If we neglect the "consumer good" aspect of children, this quality-quantity trade-off maps directly on to a child labour force activity relationship. At least three factors are directly involved: (i) the opportunity cost of schooling which mainly concerns the returns to child labour: (ii) the returns to schooling, in terms of the effects on the potential wage (and the share of parents in the wage); and (iii) life expectancy of children. High mortality, by reducing the expected duration of a child's work activity, reduces, the returns to schooling, and therefore makes early child labour force activity more likely. This in turn reduces the expected investment cost of children and increases the probability of high fertility. Indeed, many economic analyses of fertility have made fertility a positive function, inter alia, of the opportunities for child employment. Analogously, if there is effective compulsory school enrolment and attendance over a wide age range, then the costs of children in terms of schooling and related factors, and in terms of income forgone, will be relatively high, making the desired number of children correspondingly smaller.

Complex micro-behavioural functions can be formulated for child labour force participation. This is not the place to propose any particular model. However, it may be helpful to review the major stages of analysis implied by the construction of such a model. Firstly, and most abstractly, the probability of labour force participation, p(L), can be depicted as

$$p(L) = f(A, I, d^*, Z) \qquad \ldots 1$$

where A is the cost of economic activity, I the gains from that activity, d* the demand or perceived need for income, and Z represents the series of socio-economic, legal and cultural constraints discussed In previous sections. L might be regarded as a vector of alternative activities, along the lines of the typology in Section I, in which case corresponding vectors would have to be defined for the Independent variables. More commonly, however, the simpler approach is adopted of classifying certain activities as labour force participation, and analysing a dichotomous dependent variable. In the latter case, the partial derivatives of A, I and d* are negative, positive and positive, respectively. This formulation is of course trite, in the sense that It merely says that children participate in, the labour force according to the advantages and disadvantages of doing so. More theoretical content is implied when we consider the determinants of A, I and d* (and of course Z, but this we have treated qualitatively above).

$$A = g_1 (y^*, c_h, c_n, c_d, c_p, c_r, c_u \ldots) \qquad \ldots 2$$

The major determinants of A can be fairly easily described, although measurement is often difficult. Firstly, y* is the present value of the expected net income stream differential associated with foregone schooling. Secondly, c is the cost of activity in terms of the. effect on, the health of the child. To the extent that the work endangers the child's health, or leaves him or her debilitated and incapable of learning or developing manual or mental strength, A will be raised. Thirdly, c_n is the cost of the additional food required to replenish the energy expended in work. Fourthly, c_d is the cost or opportunity cost of alternative domestic labour made necessary by the non-domestic labour force participation of the child; this may be negligible, or it may be considerable if the alternative to economic activity is, say, caring for younger children. Fifthly, c is the cost of the activity in terms of the loss of prestige involved in having young children working; again this may be negligible, but in some instances having children clearly outside the labour force entails a certain gain of status. Sixthly, c_r is the cost of the activity In terms of loss of recreational time. Seventhly, c_u is a measure of the "disutility" of work, although it should be remarked that in practice it is extremely difficult to, operationalise such a concept.

These factors, in turn, have a complex set of determinants. In particular, y* depends on wage structure and employment opportunities at different education levels, and on the degree of incompatibility between different forms of work and school attendance. It also depends on the perceptions of those involved: y* could be interpreted as Income received by parents, by a household unit, or by the child concerned, or indeed by some weighted combination of all of these, depending on how and by whom the labour force participation decision is taken. The importance of mortality was noted above. It is also worth noting that y*, c_d and e_r interact, in that they reflect substitutable activity patterns; taking account of such interactions requires a, more complex model specification. The factors c_u, c_h, c_n, and c_p, all depend on the nature, conditions and duration of the work undertaken, indicating that a better specification of the dependent variables is required to allow for their effects.

The gains from economic activity can be expressed as a positive function of three sets of determinants:

$$I = g_2 (W^e, Y_{exp}, c_q) \qquad ...3$$

where W^e is expected income, Y_{exp} is the full income accruing in subsequent periods attributable to labour force experience as a child worker, and c measures related prestige and satisfaction associated with early progression to adult activities. In turn, the expected Income can be expressed as follows:

$$W^e = h_1 (W_1, W_2, W_3, ..., W_n; p_1, p_2, ..., p_n) \qquad ...4$$

where W_i is the wage or other form of income the employed child would earn in job i, and p_i is the probability of employment or work opportunity in job i. W_i should, be interpreted as the present value of a lifetime stream of income, and $(1-\Sigma_i p_i)$ is the probability of unemployment. Without going further into this function it is clear that both W and p will vary systematically with other household variables—an example is the effect of land ownership, which Increases the probability of work and raises the return to such work.

The second subset of factors is encompassed by the impact of early labour force experience on subsequent opportunities. This can be expressed by a function such as:

$$Y_{exp} = h_2 (c_{sk}, c_s, c_i) \qquad ...5$$

where c_{sk} represents the lost opportunity to obtain, maintain or develop labour force skills through early work, c_s allows for the opposite effect, namely increased ability to develop physical strength or manual dexterity in work, and c_i is a somewhat broader variable, in that it represents theopportunity to develop the ability to interact with other workers, extending to the comprehension of the nature of the labour process and the capacity to survive in it subsequently as an adult worker. Some of these points may seem somewhat nebulous and are hard to define and operationalise in any satisfactory manner. But they are certainly relevant. The third factor in equation 3, c_q, reflects the possibility that, from the perspective of the child at least, there will, be a gain in status relative to his or her school-going peers from labour force activity.

The demand-for-income function is complicated because it necessarily includes taste formation, a variable economists habitually ignore. Thus we could postulate,

$$d^* = g_3 (Y, B, F, C) \qquad \ldots 6$$

where Y is the current income of the household or "consumption unit" to which the child is attached, less any contribution of the child, B the level of assets or wealth, F the family size expressed in some per equivalent adult form, and C an index of the (subjective) socio-economic status of the household, which can be regarded as a proxy for "tastes". This set of factors is probably not comprehensive and for present purposes can be left at this level of abstraction. However, the behavioural implications should be apparent. Thus the higher the income or wealth per equivalent adult, the less the perceived need for additional income, and the less the importance for labour supply of the direct and opportunity costs of economic activity and inactivity. In sum, the implicit demand for income affects labour force participation not by changing the costs of activity or inactivity, but by modifying their perceived importance.

Many of the issues noted above have received scant attention in empirical studies; indeed, relatively little empirical work has been devoted to the micro-behavioural determinants of child economic activity. A major reason has been the lack of appropriate data. The few available studies are notable for their necessarily tentative nature and limited findings. Thus in a study of 1960 census data from Chile, regression results suggested that labour force participation of those aged 12 to 14 was positively related to fertility and the female wage rate, and negatively related to the male wage. The meaningfulness of these observed partial correlations depends on the reliability of the interpretation of the independent variables, for the fertility rate and male wage rate were interpreted as determinants of the need for income, while the female wage was treated as a proxy, for the child wage. These variables had the opposite signs in a school attendance function for 10 year olds, in line with the expectation of substitution between labour force activity and schooling (DaVanzo, 1972). In another study, in which a somewhat fuller model was constructed to explain the activity patterns of children aged 5 to 14 in India, it was concluded that employment opportunities raised the extent of labour force participation and lowered school attendance (Rosenzweig and Evenson, 1977). In a review of evidence from Asia, school enrolment was shown to be inversely related to the income status of households (Leonor and Richards, 1980). In a comparative study of child activity patterns in San Salvador and Khartoum, the statistical analysis suggested labour force activity was inversely related to household income and to the father's schooling (Peek, 1978).

Apart from the last-mentioned study, most empirical work has been restricted to straightforward trade-offs between "schooling" and "employment", essentially because of the nature of the available data. Subsequent research in this behavioural tradition will have to be extended into more complex substitution possibilities, considering in particular various cross-elasticities between a broader set of activities. One approach would be to use the elements of the typology outlined in Section I. While some elements in the typology (recreation, illegitimate activities) are difficult to treat, a minimal requirement would seem to be that the model should explain the allocation of child time between schooling, domestic work, labour in household enterprise, wage labour, recreation, and idleness. If this is done, one could also expect an increase in the explanatory power of fertility models in which child activity plays a significant part (Schultz, 1974; Sarma, 1978).

The dependent variable should be disaggregated not only into types of activities, but also into their duration and intensity. Though this may be impractical, serious empirical and analytical difficulties follow if the point is ignored. Thus school attendance is compatible with some types of labour force activity, and indeed with several other types of activities, depending on their nature and intensity. Another point about model design, partially taken into account in some of the empirical work, is that household decisions interact. The relationships involved in child labour supply have been discussed in cascade fashion, as if the whole model were recursive. In reality this is doubtful, especially as several of the determining variables are in their turn functions of child activity patterns. In principle, this sort of problem can be solved with appropriate specification and good data. But another theoretical difficulty, of even more importance, concerns the nature of the utility function underlying the structure of models of this type. There tends to be an assumption that the 'household' or "family" has a single utility function. Such an assumption is dubious, especially where the behavioural unit consists of a loosely structured kin group. In any case, where the earnings of a labour force participant are partly retained by that person, the model's assumptions are undermined. Logically it is also incorrect to treat a fertility decision (in which the child has no say) as depending on the same utility function as a child labour force participation decision, since even if the child has no direct say in the decision his or her presence in the family is bound to modify perceptions of family welfare.

A third theoretical difficulty concerns the conventional assumption that behaviour is based on some form of optimisation by individuals or households. A more realistic assumption would have to take account of the social network in which the children have to develop. In particular this would mean taking account of the nature and extent of relationships of "structured reciprocity" within kinship and community groups. Introducing such parameters greatly reduces the sense of neat cohesion associated with conventional micro-economic models.

As a concluding comment to this section, it is worth dwelling briefly on the problem of the link between micro-behavioural processes and the socio-economic structures shaping the available behavioural options. Clearly it is inadequate to attempt to explain child activity patterns in micro-behavioural terms without considering the nature of the social formation, the cultural constraints, the nature of household, kinship and community obligations, the structure of the labour market, and the access to it of different socio-economic groups. In conventional micro-models these factors generate constraints, exogenous variables or "tastes" which are omitted from the analysis. Such an approach sharply limits the range of phenomena micro-level analysis can address. It is therefore essential to incorporate these societal conditions into micro-economic analysis, just as it is to incorporate an understanding of micro-level behaviour into analyses of structural change. Unless both are taken into account, structural analyses risk degenerating into descriptions of processes which are rarely understood and never foreseen, while behavioural models continue to give cautious empirical support to the obvious.

IMPLICATIONS OF CHILD WORK ACTIVITIES

Various implications of child activities have been noted in earlier sections—indeed, the determinants of child activity patterns could not be understood without at the same time considering their effects. Here we try to bring together some of the more important of these effects. However, this section is relatively speculative and undocumented, for it is frequently very difficult to isolate the effects of particular types of activity. Nevertheless, this is in a sense the core of any analysis, and the fact that it is inadequately treated here highlights the apparent dearth of research. Below the main socio-economic and demographic effects are discussed under seven headings, starting with the personal and ending with the societal.

1. Health, Physical Development and Mortality

These are unquestionably among the most tendentious issues associated with child work activity, for it is generally assumed that there are deleterious effects on the health, stature and life expectancy of the children involved. First, it seems common for children to have a low priority claim on the meagre food available to poor rural and urban families. To the extent that children are required to perform work activities that use up scarce reserves of energy, a disequilibrium arises between their energy needs and the calorific value of the food available (UNICEF, 1969). Work by children can weaken their resistance to debilitating illnesses and decrease life expectancy. Some of the working conditions observed—e.g. a 72-hour week reported from two carpet-making establishments in Morocco (Anti-Slavery Society, 1978), including one employing many 9 or 10 year olds—could scarcely fall to have adverse effects on health and physical development. It is well known that during the Industrial Revolution working children suffered permanent disadvantages as a direct consequence of their early experience. As a famous 1843 report noted, children of framework knitters, an industrial group of workers whose children worked long hours for little or nothing, were generally weaker and smaller than children of agricultural labourers (Levine, 1977, p. 29). Thus, it is not only the effect of working which deserves to be considered, but the differential effect of different types of work as well.

There are, however, many situations in which some work by children may make a positive contribution to the health and physical capacity of themselves and other family members—in situations of extreme poverty, the mobilisation of all household labour available, including that of children, may be necessary if basic consumption needs are to be met. Also it is conceivable that some work is beneficial to the health and physical development of children, if it is not too strenuous and develops muscular and related physical powers, thereby increasing fitness and strengthening resistance to certain types of illness. This is likely to be particularly important where the alternative to work is not schooling but idleness, which in itself is debilitating. In societies where there is a gradual assimilation of children to adult work roles, notably domestic and subsistence roles, there will often be no adverse effects on children that do not equally apply to adults, and economically productive work may then contribute to physical development in much the same way as sport or other recreational activities do in other societies. Objective criteria for differentiating between these effects are of course difficult to devise.

2. Education and Intellectual Development

In this case we have to be careful not to make an automatic assumption that work by children impairs education and intellectual development. It will generally do so, particularly in so far as energy-consuming and tiring work leaves them with neither energy, time nor inclination to attend school or learn while in school. But this is not a universal sequel, for three reasons. First, work itself may be an important component of "education" especially in household-based production systems, but also in various apprenticeship arrangements. This is one reason for not confusing education with schooling. Second, it is often claimed that the type of schooling provided for the poor and working-class population is primarily concerned not with developing and refining the creative faculties of children, but with providing malleable, committed workers or docile citizens who acquiesce in diverse forms of exploitation. Third, there is some suggestion that formal schooling may be dysfunctional in that it weakens rather than strengthens the child's ability to survive in an environment of poverty, high unemployment, and malnutrition. It is also often argued that schooling leads youths to refuse many forms of employment, and thereby leads them to become "voluntarily" unemployed and subsequently almost unemployable for many jobs. This type of reasoning can and has been used to argue that the poor should be denied access to schooling but to our mind it should be used to demonstrate the need to alter the structure not only of the educational system, but, more fundamentally, of the labour market to make work and education more compatible (Standing, 1978b, pp. 127-35). A similar point could be made about the interpretation of findings that many parents in low-income families themselves question the value of schooling. One recent review (Bamberger, 1973) cited examples of people in Latin America taking such views:

> "In this type of school they create in children from—let us say—humble classes, certain needs which are not real needs, but which are needs of people in the upper classes."

> "I have thought of taking my children out of the school as they teach habits which we can't keep up at home, because we don't have the money."

"Sometimes they (the children) go to ask for money in the houses of the rich so they have money to satisfy the habits that they have learnt at school."

Similar attitudes have been reported from Bombay (Desai and Pillai, 1972), and in many other places.

However, whatever the quality and role of schooling, there can be little doubt that child participation in labour force activity tends to reduce the potential for educational development, the more so the greater the, degree of drudgery of the work and the less the children are able to acquire knowledge and skills through their work. But it is noteworthy that a limited amount of certain specific types of work may be compatible with and even complementary to education and intellectual development, particularly if timed to fit the schooling calendar, and if providing children with a sense of the links between what they learn and adult work roles. There is indeed some appeal in making labour force activity one component of the process of education—that is, making economic work of various types part of the school curriculum—and this is an approach being implemented in a few countries such as Tanzania and Cuba (Carnoy and Wertheim, 1979).

3. Demographic Behaviour

There are reasons for believing that child labour has a positive influence on fertility; indeed, much of the rationalisation of high fertility in agrarian societies has been in these terms. Moreover, changes in fertility differentials over time and between groups have coincided with changing patterns of child labour. Commonly, though not always, fertility is lower in urban than in rural areas; higher among the landed than among the landless; and lower where educational enrolment is higher.[16] And although attempts have been made (e.g. Mueller, 1976) to show that the return to parents of childbearing is negative even with extensive use of child labour, the partial relationship between child labour and fertility remains positive. This of course assumes the existence of sufficiently strong intergenerational obligations for one or both parents to benefit from child production activities, but such obligations are widely observed.

The effects of child work on marriage and family formation patterns are more complex. In so far as child labour implies contribution to parental income only prior to marriage, the age of marriage may well be deferred. However, with a multi-generational family structure and contributions to production at an early age, there is an advantage to short 'intervals between generations and thus early family formation. Moreover, sex differentiation, dowry Systems, and inheritance patterns are all likely to play a role. So there can be no general conclusion about the likely effect of child activity patterns.

The extent of child labour in rural areas also has potential implications for rural emigration. As noted in an earlier section, the potential use of child workers in domestic and farm, activities may well allow other family members to migrate in search of seasonal or longer-term employment. Conversely, a lack of opportunities for child work, or a lack of adequate schooling facilities, encourages the emigration of children themselves.

4. Sex Roles and the Intra-household Division of Labour

The activity patterns of children affect the age-sex division of labour in several ways. In particular, the tendency for girls to be set the quasi-domestic tasks while boys are given tasks such as herding encourages the growth of "sexual dualism", in the adult labour force, with men having access and commitment to non-domestic wage and other jobs, while women are relegated to domestic and related subsistence activities. However, it is interesting that time-use surveys in various parts of the world have shown that the sexual division of tasks done by children varies considerably. In a small Indonesian study, for example, it was reported that girls aged 6 to 14 spent much more time on child-care, housework and food preparation than boys of comparable ages, whereas boys spent much more time on firewood collection and animal care (White, 1975, p. 285). Yet in the village studied it was also noticeable that girls were acquiring non-domestic skills through the large amount of time they devoted to handicrafts and to agricultural wage labour; they spent much more time than boys in both activities. Moreover girls aged 12 to 14 did much more work than the boys in the sample. In Kano, Schildkrout noted relatively little sex differentiation between girls and boys in economic activities until approaching the age of puberty. But although both sexes undertook most activities as young children, there was a gradual transition to role differentiation as adulthood approached. Several other chapters in this book comment on this issue, and Cain.

5. Unemployment and Labour Force Stratification

Child activity patterns influence both the extent of labour force stratification and the level and incidence of unemployment. But empirically it is hard to disentangle the various strands of the relationships or identify the independent effects of child activity.

The effects on the development of the labour market are best understood in terms of several differentiating tendencies identified in earlier sections. Thus it is clear that the manual work done by the children of the poor is liable to leave them permanently disadvantaged in the labour market, in so far as it results in educational shortcomings and perhaps also nutritional-health inadequacies not shared by children of more affluent families who are not required to work. Similarly, as noted earlier, sexual dualism in the labour market may be strongly intensified by patterns of sex roles among children.

Levels of unemployment may be raised by the labour force participation of young workers reducing the work opportunities of adults, though work experience of adults is likely to help them to resist such competition.[17] But high unemployment also contributes to the growth of labour. force stratification through educational differentiation. Thus in urban-industrial labour markets the existence of high and rising youth unemployment encourages the more affluent families to invest more time and money in schooling, as higher qualifications are required to have a reasonable chance of obtaining a high-status, high-wage job. Conversely, among the working class, high unemployment may well have the perverse. effect of discouraging families from sending children to school, not only because children and youths are required as secondary workers to supplement low and uncertain family incomes, but because parents perceive that the amount of schooling their children could reasonably expect to obtain would be insufficient to provide access to most school—requiring jobs. Indeed, work experience may be more valuable than schooling as qualifications for the jobs they can hope to obtain. To the extent that there is such a "class" divergence in schooling, the growth of labour force stratification will strengthened and perpetuated. The vast majority of the poor are cut off from higher-status, higher-wage jobs, and, in competing for the jobs for which there are no credentialist barriers, they drive relatively low wages down further. So the pattern of supply of workers to different types of job can be expected to strengthen labour market segmentation.

6. Social Attitudes and Cultural Responses

As child work is often an important aspect of socialisation, the development of attitudes and of normative behaviour in employment is likely to contribute significantly to the perpetuation of patterns of social behaviour. We have already noted some aspects of these embedded cultural patterns, notably with respect to sex roles Similar processes lead to a division of labour and responsibility by age—a socially stabilising phenomenon where a well defined transition with age can be identified. One cultural outcome of child employment patterns is their impact on kin commitment and the interpersonal obligation structure. Child employment frequently occurs within a social framework in which the work reflects personal commitment to kin, and in which the production or income is not an individual but a household or kin group benefit. The behavioural norms which the child internalises over the years of integration into work reinforce social patterns of obligation, generating positive attitudes towards particular patterns of exploitation, social organisation, and labour utilisation. This is particularly noticeable in stable, traditional societies, and any breakdown in these, patterns, however induced, surely presages a transition in mode of production and social framework.

Another, related issue is the impact of child activities on the extent of labour force commitment. The gradual development of a work ethic characterises production in which there is a gradual integration of child workers, whether this is based on the survival needs of a proletariat or on subsistence production within a household unit. Where high unemployment or credentialist barriers limit access to jobs, there is likely to be a negative impact on the work ethic, with lifetime implications for job satisfaction and perception of the relationship between work and society. Bekombo, describes the processes whereby school drop-out leads to various marginal or illegitimate activities. Much has been made of the "culture of poverty". Whether or not one accepts this as a useful analytical concept, some of its elements are dearly valid and related to distorted patterns of socialisation. Inadequate social opportunities lead to anomie or aimlessly violent responses by Individuals or groups, to the rejection of conventional social norms, and the formation of new norms of "delinquent" or illegitimate behaviour. Such responses can be destructive both for the individual and for social relationships

7. Poverty and Socio-economic Inequality

In so far as children of poor families in low-income countries are required to work to a greater extent than those belonging to more wealthy families, it could be argued that child labour is a means of marginally improving the distribution of income. This conclusion might be valid as seen from the perspective of individual households in many situations poverty is dearly alleviated by the work of children. A macro-level view, however, suggests that child employment is associated with greater inequality of income, wealth and material standards of living.

There are several reasons for this. The first concerns the effects of child work on the total incomes of the wage labour force. As noted above, there are indications that child labour helps to maintain low wages for the labour force as a whole, notably because as a low-cost form of labour they can be substituted for more expensive adults, and because they can reduce the cost of producing wage-goods. It is questionable whether withdrawal of child workers (into the education system, for instance) would lower the wage share. In so far as they were replaced by higher-paid adults, the tendency would be the reverse. It follows that the total incomes of labour households are unlikely to be higher as a consequence of the wage employment of children. Secondly, there are effects on the ownership of wealth and means of production. High fertility among the poor is stimulated by the need for and use of child labour, leading in the longer term to increased division on inheritance of such assets as are possessed, which is one route to landlessness. Within the peasantry there may simultaneously be class differentiation if the wealthier peasants are able to consolidate their position by having larger numbers of children who can help to operate an expanded area of land.[18] Thus the marginal landholders may. suffer most from this type of dynamic process, while the middle and upper groups suffer less or not at all.

A third factor increasing this differentiation is inequality of access to schooling. The higher rates of child work among low-income families tend t& be at the expense of schooling, despite the increasing importance of education as a means of gaining income, wealth, and access to high-status jobs. This type of process greatly accelerates incipient class differentiation.

POLICY ISSUES AND RESEARCH DESIGN

The objective of this introductory chapter is to raise questions which need to be researched. But its rationale is that certain of the activities undertaken by children in most low-income countries have unacceptable effects, both for the personal development of the children concerned, and on the societies in which they live. Accordingly, before we comment on research priorities it is worth briefly considering the issue of policy formulation and implementation.

1. Child Employment Policies

In considering issues of policy design, it is crucial to recognise that the application of policies is not independent of the social formation which the State represents. In analysing any policy, it is necessary to consider whose interests it serves, and the influence of those interests on the political, cultural, and social structure of the country concerned. Thus effective policy to control child labour in a feudal society is quite unlikely. The interests at stake would be too strong, and benefit too much from the exploitation of child labour. In countries experiencing a transition to capitalism, various patterns can emerge, depending on the size of the capitalist sector and its influence in the State, the structure of production, the extent of state intervention in production, the effectiveness of administrative structures and the mix of conservatism, liberalism and socialism in the prevailing political ethos. Each situation must be analysed in its historical and contemporary context. There is no need to labour this. point; but too often one sees lists of policy prescriptions which pay no regard to issues of this type.

Among direct child employment policies, three main groups can be identified: those which, through legislation, attempt to control the age from which different types of work can be done, as well as the wage and the working conditions; those attempting to control marginal and "delinquent" activities; and those relating to schooling and training. The first group, involving labour legislation, are effective only where there is determined implementation, a capable administration, relative difficulty in hiding the employment of children; and relatively little advantage from child employment. These conditions are essentially a function of the level and nature of development. While legislation may help to control the more obvious forms of exploitation, legislation designed to eliminate child employment is, on its own, not enough. Indeed, it is one of the ironies of child labour that, where it is prohibited by law, the law is likely to leave child workers unprotected, since legally they do not exist. Nevertheless, two situations should be distinguished—those where the law exists but is not enforced, and others where the activity is not covered by existing laws.

The second group of policies may well be more effective, if only because the interests behind marginal activities and delinquency are weak; strong governments can therefore control them. On the whole, however, they do not need to do so, and where they are induced to do so through pressure to "clean the streets", the effect is essentially to eliminate the symptoms with little effect on the more fundamental issues underlying poverty and unemployment.

It is possible to be more positive about the potential of education, training, and apprenticeship policies. After all, school enrolment rates have leapt upward in low—income countries, and there is a complementarity between compulsory school enrolment and labour legislation. One should not be too sanguine about the impact of compulsory school enrolment policies, and it is pertinent to note that some rigorous statistical analyses have concluded that historically child labour laws have had little impact on raising the extent of schooling, even where school attendance has been compulsory (Landes and Salmon, 1972). However, possibilities exist in terms of more relevant curriculum design, integration of work and school (e.g. timing of schooling. to avoid peak agricultural seasons, or integration of schooling and apprenticeship), and the like. Still, the practice is widely disillusioning. Schooling often becomes an instrument of class differentiation rather than of integration; apprenticeships effectively become forms of exploitation; and compulsory enrolment is not and cannot be enforced because the poverty-stricken parents see no gains from schooling and something, if not much, as a return to child work.

Perhaps we are too pessimistic; one should not neglect the real gains which policies in these three categories have achieved. But most of them are faced with structural constraints which limit their potential beneficial effects, while others have merely legitimated changes that have already occurred.

In critically assessing the impact of policies, not only, those addressed specifically to children should be considered. The indirect effects of policies with other objectives may be larger than the direct impact of child employment. Examples of government policies having indirect effects, beneficial or otherwise, include land reform, the undermining of feudal relationships and the promotion of capitalistic farming with capital-intensive production techniques, anti-natalist policies of various types, employment creation schemes such as, public works programmes, investment programmes aimed at rapid industrialisation, informal sector promotion policies, creation of co-operatives, and social security programmes. The relevance of such policies is that they modify the set of socio-economic relationships which are primarily responsible for the work of children. Thus public works programmes might attract male workers from small farms, leading to increased agricultural labour inputs by women and children. Anti-natalist policies might indirectly affect child work by affecting family size and structure. Informal sector promotion involves expanding a sector which in some places relies heavily on fake apprenticeship. Clearly, many of the relationships discussed in the body of this chapter may be involved.

2. Some Research Suggestions

The employment of children is a complex issue. There exists a rapidly growing literature on the subject, as the bibliography at the end of this book indicates (though it is very incomplete, especially in languages other than English). But ascertained facts are less in evidence than gaps in our knowledge. Part of this is purely a data problem. It is difficult to obtain accurate information on the economic activities of children, even when the conceptual framework is well defined, which is rarely the case. Conscious or unconscious concealment of child work makes formal interview techniques highly unreliable. Small-scale surveys designed to clarify concepts and analytical approaches should be strongly encouraged, including actual observation of the behaviour patterns of children by means of participant-observer techniques and other anthropological data-collecting methods. Large-scale surveys of time allocation also have a role, especially as they permit the application of econometric techniques. But they risk hiding more than they reveal if used alone, without complementary data permitting the estimation of misreporting, the assessment of work intensity and productivity, and the depiction of the structural context within which child work occurs. In particular, it is essential to identify the social relations of production and modes of exploitation which condition the activities of children. Some of these issues are taken up by Hull in the next chapter.

Useful data collection must be based on a realistic typology of child activities, involving an extension and refinement of the approach outlined in Section I. In addition to refining the typology itself, the distribution of activities of children across different categories of the typology—what might be called activity portfolios—will identify further subgroups. Particular activity portfolios recur; which and to what extent are empirical questions. If they are answered, a more adequate understanding of the extent, incidence and significance of child work will be possible.

Besides the research problems posed by description and measurement, several crucial but under-researched analytical issues can be identified:

1. Historical analyses of the evolution of child activities through transitions in the mode of production are essential. These should not be directed so much towards the industrialised countries—a reasonable literature exists in France, the United Kingdom, the United States, and no doubt elsewhere, on the eighteenth, nineteenth and early twentieth centuries (though Morice, argues that more work is needed). It would be more interesting to track the evolution of child activities in the course of more recent (Argentina, India) or rapid (Brazil, Republic of Korea) cases of development of industrial capitalism, or in the course of the development of capitalist or socialist agriculture.
2. More needs to be known about many structural issues: the effects of entry of children into labour markets, in terms of segmentation and stratification; the personal effects on skill development and subsequent career patterns; the interaction between work and school; the effect of child work on intellectual and physical development, sex roles, kin obligations and family structure; the nature of the relationship between child work and fertility; and more generally, the interactions between child work, inequality and poverty. The framework for such studies should be dynamic, in the sense of analysing the social roles of children and how their integration into adult roles forms part of the process by which societies are reproduced or modified.
3. At the micro-level, there exist possibilities for improving the usefulness of time-allocation data by relating each use of time to its socio-economic context, along the lines of the typology presented in Section I. Neo-classical models of household resource allocation and human capital development can, to a limited extent, give indications on the strength and direction of individual or

household responses to external intervention. While they rarely give much assistance in analysing in the over-all structure of behaviour, their ability to predict and analyse derivatives and marginal behaviour makes them a useful tool. Micro-level socio-cultural models are also needed not only as a complement to neo-classical approaches, but (as argued in Section III) because cultural variables have independent effects on child activities. Micro-level work of this type tends to require specially designed data sets, and is costly. One major shortcoming of the type of time-use data gathered in past behavioural research has been the absence of information on the social, relations of production within which any particular activity occurs. As a consequence the data have been unable to reveal much about patterns and levels of exploitation. Only if such information is gathered along with time-use data can a link be forged between micro—behavioural models and structural analysis.

4. Finally, much more work is required on the impact of different types of policy in controlling, reducing or redirecting the economic activities of children, whether these effects be direct or indirect.[19] In a sense, this type of work is not independent of the previous topics mentioned. Except in controlled experiments, the impact of policies cannot even be measured without same underlying model of the relationships involved. Thus the impact of policy is best analysed in the context of one of the research areas identified earlier. But at the same time, those research areas themselves lose much of their interest unless they are related to policy issues.

CONCLUDING REMARKS

Some child work is clearly highly exploitative, and particularly so by virtue of children's weakness as a group. This is true of bonded child labour, for example, or of the employment for many years of minimally paid "apprentices" who receive-little or no training. But to regard this as the only aspect of the problem would be an error. In the sense of appropriation of surplus value, children engaged in wage labour are exploited, but not necessarily much more than adults in similar situations. Many forms of child work are a source of interest and possibly creative activity for the children concerned, and contribute significantly to family incomes or to family subsistence. Conventional views of the normal duration of childhood, or of the desirability of formal schooling tend to obscure these points. In low-income countries, many if not most children combine some form of schooling with some form of non-school work. It is the incompatibility of the one with the other that must be carefully considered. The value of the type of schooling generally available should be regarded as a matter of debate. It should not be presumed that it is clearly preferable to the type of work the children would be doing. That is not to glamourise child work, only to try to correct the view that simply regards child work as the obstacle to effective learning.

Child labour which is a subset of child work, that involving social relations of production extending beyond the family unit—should be a vital concern, of all workers' organisations, for where it exists it weakens the working population generally. Children are highly exploitable, and it is right to be concerned to focus on those circumstances in which their vulnerability is manipulated to their lasting disadvantage.

Where child labour does have adverse effects—and in terms of personal development and social differentiation these are often serious—they can usually be traced to the socio-economic framework within which children work, as much as to the work itself. Thus the suppression of child wage labour opportunities is unlikely to increase the welfare of the children concerned unless substitute income sources and alternative possibilities for personal development are developed at the same time. Compulsory schooling will not help much if it neither develops creative faculties nor provides a meaningful basis for subsequent labour market entry.

Action towards child work must be sympathetically oriented towards the needs and perceptions of the children themselves. It must also be based on a thorough understanding of the motivations behind child work, its functions, and the individual gains from it, whether for the children themselves or for others who benefit from their work. There is no substitute for adequate data collection and thorough research on these issues in specific settings.

NOTES

1. This is not the place to discuss the enormous literature on what constitute "feudal relations of production", and whether the term can validity be applied in differing social and cultural contexts. Here we refer generally to social relations whereby surplus product is extracted by various forms of rent, typically supported by the use of extra-economic power, without necessarily separating the direct producers from the means of production. The term "semi-feudal" is used to refer to production relations in which the direct producers are exploited through wage labour as well as through feudal rent and usury, again typically involving extra-economic coercion. See also Section II.1.
2. For discussion of this in French-speaking Africa see UNESCO, 1972.
3. Quoted in de la Luz Silva (1978).
4. M. Sahlins: *Stone age economics* (London, Tavistock Press, 1974).
5. D. Thorner, B. Kerblay and R.E.F. Smith (eds.): *A.V. Chayanov on the theory of peasant economy* (Homewood, Ill., American Economic Association, 1966).
6. D. Seddon (ed.): *Relations of production* (London, Frank Cass, 1978); E. Terray: *Maxism and "primitive" societies* (London, Monthly Review Press, 1972); inter alia.
7. *Ibid.*, p. 116.
8. This points to the danger of using the household as the basic unit of analysis, an issue to which we will return in discussing the micro-behavioural determinants of the economic roles of children.
9. See, for instance, E.J. Hobsbawn, "A case of neo-feudalism: La Convencion, Peru", in *Journal of Latin American Studies*, Vol. 1, No. 1, 1969.

10. The extensive literature on this subject includes C. Kerr: "The Balkanisation of labour markets", in G.W. Bakke (ed.): *Labour Mobility and Economic Opportunity* (New York, Wiley, 1954); M. Reich, D.M. Gordon and R.C. Edwards: "A theory of labour market segmentation", in *The American Economic Review*, Papers and Proceedings, May 1973.
11. ILO: *Matching Employment Opportunities and Expectations: A Programme of Action for Ceylon* (Sri Lanka) (Geneva, 1971).
12. Prostitution is, of course, regarded as something approaching a normal occupation in some societies. In those cases the entry of children to such work should be analysed in terms of income, health and career structure, level of exploitation and implications for personal development, as would be the case for other forms of work.
13. M. Blaug, R. Layard and M. Woodhall: *Graduate unemployment in India* (London, Oxford University Press, 1969).
14. E. Goody: *Contexts of socialisation* (Cambridge University Press, 1974); idem: "Some theoretical and empirical aspects of parenthood in West Africa", in C. Oppong et al (eds.): *Marriage, fertility and parenthood in West Africa* (Canberra, Australian University Press, 1978).
15. On these issues see, inter-alia, Anker (1978); also H. Azzam: *The participation of Arab women in the labour force: Development factors and policies* (Geneva, ILO, 1979; mimeographed World Employment Programme research working paper; restricted).
16. United Nations: *The determinants and consequences of population trends* (New York, 1973; Sales No.: 71. XIII. 5).
17. For evidence from Sri Lanka see P. Richards: "Job mobility and unemployment in the Ceylon urban labour market", in *Oxford Bulletin of Economic and Statistics*, 1973, Vol. 35, No. 1.
18. Compare the non-linear relationship between assets and fertility discussed in Section I.
19. For one approach to policy analysis, see G. Standing: *State policies and child labour: Accumulation versus legitimation?*, paper presented to a conference on child labour organised by the Anti-Slavery Society and the Institute of Development Studies, University of Sussex, 5-8 January 1981.

23

PERSPECTIVES AND DATA REQUIREMENTS FOR THE STUDY OF CHILDREN'S WORK

This chapter examines some of the perspectives that have guided research on child employment and suggests grounds for adopting broader, more comprehensive conceptual frameworks. Then, drawing on recent field studies, it briefly reviews methodological issues, including problems of defining such concepts as "child", "work", and "family", dilemmas encountered in data collection, and a number of points to be considered in the tabular presentation or statistical analysis of the results. Finally, it discusses the importance of reporting the assumptions and methodology used, of validating concepts and of placing data on children's work in the appropriate institutional setting.

PERSPECTIVES FOR THE STUDY OF CHILDREN'S WORK

> An only son preserves his father's name. And keeps the fortune growing in one house: If you have two, you'll need to have more wealth And live a longer time. But Zeus can find Ways to enrich a larger family: More children mean more help and greater gains.
>
> Hesiod, eighth Century BC.

In many places at various times Hesiod's advice in *Works and days* has been the standard perspective on children's employment. Its bias is clearly towards the parent, with emphasis on the benefits expected to flow from children rather than on the costs borne by parents. This perspective relates to an agrarian economy facing little competition for land and using fairly primitive technology. Such societies have tended to hold a highly unified view of life that sees no basic divisions, and certainly no conflict between the economic, social and psychological value of children.

It was not until the spread of commerce, and later the rise of industry, that questions were raised on the economic roles of children and their roles as family members. The prodigal had, of course, existed in agrarian communities, as the Bible describes on many occasions, but the growth of towns in Europe, the great expansion of trade and the development of the apprenticeship system increased children's mobility with the result that parents recognised "economic" values in their offspring; a value that could be readily converted into cash.

The decline of family-based systems of production occurred *gradually* in Europe. By the end of the eighteenth century, however, the pace of change had quickened to such an extent that only the term "revolution" could adequately describe the technological innovations and new social organisations that characterised the dawn of the industrial age. A key factor in this transformation was the exploitation of child labour in factories, mines and mills (Hammond and Hammond, 1948). The economic activity of children, while often vital to the family budget, was generally independent of the employment of the parents. In addition, long working hours, and in some cases shift work, widened the gap between the lives of parents and their children.[1]

Reaction against the exploitation of child labour came through lengthy debate, government inquiries and attempts to initiate reforms. Out of these grew the first attempts to study children's employment using surveys, government records and direct observation. The British Parliament received a series of reports on the employment of children in factories (1816, 1818, 1819, 1832, 1833), as chimney sweeps (1817, 1818, 1834) and as handloom weavers (1834, 1835). Numerous scholars of the period included the issue of children's employment in their research into poverty and the principles of political economy.[2]

While scientific methods transformed research on the subject of children's work into a more objective, inductive exercise that placed great stress on the collection of valid data, the perspective that directed the inquiries maintained essentially the same normative orientation taken by earlier writers. The guiding question was: what is the impact of work on the welfare of the child and the family? For most academic researchers the *a priori* orientation was that child work was harmful, and research design often leaned toward proving this point rather than weighing alternative interpretations. However, in the early part of the nineteenth century, there were numerous "pro—manufacturing" writers who argued that children were better off in factories than in the streets or working as apprentices for artisans, as family labourers, or in mines. By the 1830s public opinion and the weight of evidence were against such arguments, and laws controlling children's participation in paid employment were gradually enacted. At the same time, the spread of schooling offered an increasingly legitimate alternative to children's employment and an additional{ argument for its control. Working children, it was said, were denied the opportunities offered by literacy, numeracy, and a broadened world-view. New official personalities such as the truant officer and writers such as Horatio Alger in the United States reflected a shift in the socialisation of young people. Compulsory schooling brought mass literacy, and the mass production of 'stories for boys and girls' inculcated the virtues of thrift, diligence and industry.

If we look back to the beginning of the twentieth century, the crucial generalisation would seem to be that exploitation of child workers in the industrial nations of the world was gradually becoming limited to special areas, industries or racial groups. At the same time the non-industrial world was receiving more attention from social scientists as European colonial powers attempted to understand native societies in order to make were effective use of them. One intellectual stream of particular interest for our purposes is the study of socialisation undertaken by anthropologists throughout the world in the first half of this century. In the course of discovering how individuals acquired the characteristics and behaviour of a given culture, these researchers found themselves considering the vital period of late infancy and adolescence. During this period active participation in adult types of employment was initiated, and this was recognised by anthropologists as a major element in cultural transmission and socialisation.[3] This type of study produced a remarkably different picture of children's employment from that painted by nineteenth-century social reformers, and only part of the difference can be attributed to the differing economic systems considered. The reformer seldom paused to ask whether factory discipline passed on cultural norms and values to young children, and anthropologists seldom remarked on the effect of repetitive activities on children's intellectual development, or evaluated the danger of accident or illness attributable to child work. Hence the horrifying accounts of the former, and the rather romantic renderings of the latter.

In retrospect it is interesting to note that the normative orientations of these two intellectual streams were associated with very different empirical approaches. The survey techniques and urban-oriented community investigation of Charles Booth and associates fit firmly in the tradition which later produced "Middletown"—type studies. Using census data analysis, large-scale surveys and industry investigations, the emphasis here is on quantification. The ethnographic approach, and in particular the emergence of the "participant—observer" produces results that are characteristically small—scale and highly detailed, and focus on "typical" behaviour.

There is no reason to argue that the normative orientations of these two branches of the literature on children's employment either determined or were produced by the empirical approaches taken by their respective practitioners. After all, there is something of the participant-observer in Engels report on the plight of the residents of Manchester (1844), and many an anthropologist has puzzled over contingency tables showing rates of children's participation in harvesting and weeding. However, since the social sciences developed with quantifiers mainly in industrial societies and anthropologists mainly sent to the tribal or peasant societies of the colonies, the methodologies were dictated primarily by the nature of the object of the research; the subject of the research—be it welfare or socialisation—was dictated by the researcher's interest, or the interests of his or her patrons.

The preceding paragraphs take no account of a number of other traditions of research into children's labour, most notably those followed by various groups interested in children's employment in the cottage industries of non-industrial nations. Some of these date back to the last century. It is not our purpose here to undertake an exhaustive review of such studies. The two streams of thought described above illustrate the important influence of the normative orientation — or what might be called research perspective on the course and results of research. Essentially, researchers seldom find much more than they set out to discuss.

If this is the case, then research design must be prefaced by a clear statement of perspective, outlining the researcher's conception of the nature of the problem. Some researchers set this out in terms of a hypothesis designed to be rejectable, or as a guiding question designed to be answerable according certain criteria. Either approach is preferable to an 'investigation" of a general topic. The researcher who sets out to discover the "nature of children's work in village x" is much more liable to produce spurious results than one who aims test a well formed hypothesis.

While clarity of purpose is, an over-riding requirement for any social research, breadth, of purpose is also important in studies of children and employment. The literature on this subject dramatically illustrates how concern with a narrow aspect of behaviour—be it the effect of working on child welfare or the transmission of culture through job training—can blind the investigator to alternative concerns. If the purpose of the research is purely academic, this might be excused as part of the step-wise approach researchers follow to undertake inquiries. However, even purely academic uni-dimensional research may be used in the determination of social and economic policies, with ramifications far beyond the research process *per se*. Expenditure planning, regulations and the design of government programmes inevitably have multi-dimensional effects.[4]

The criticism of research projects that take only on perspective on the work of children is largely prompted by the fact that so many such projects have been found to be incomplete. For example, there has recently been considerable interest in studying children's work as an element in parents desire for high fertility (the so-called "Value of Children studies) and as a contribution to the family labour force; these investigations, while unquestionably of great value, suffer from a general failure to note the techniques and, more tellingly, the substantive results of other types of studies.

In the remainder of this chapter a variety of techniques for the study of children's work will be reviewed. Some methods, like time-budget analysis, are associated in the literature with particular theoretical concerns while others, like census and, survey analysis, are used by people who view the problem very differently. It will be argued that while there may be a link between perspective and method in particular cases, in general methods can be discussed independently from perspective. Moreover, the fact that studies sharing a common theoretical or moral orientation have not taken advantage of a particular type of data or technique of analysis may in itself raise suspicion about the validity of the results. For example, studies of children's work in particular industries may be used to support broad generalisations. But if they are based on data obtained through participant observation techniques, rather than analysis of survey or census data, they are likely to be questioned on the grounds of "unrepresentativeness". On the, other hand, a researcher who quotes a labour force participation rate for children aged 10 to 14 as being "5.3 per cent" might equally be challenged to provide verification from data based on observation or intensive Survey. Repeated use of one technique may reliably reproduce similar results, hut normally it is only through the use of a variety of approaches which yield consistent results that the validity of conclusions can be established.[5]

RESEARCH STRATEGY AND THE INFORMATION BASE

1. Finding a Basis for Collaborative Studies

The analytical framework proposed by Rodgers and Standing derives primarily from the, tradition of concern over children's welfare discussed above, but explicitly takes notice of other perspectives which focus on patterns of exploitation, socialisation, fertility, labour force structure, and such issues as poverty, the role of women and socio-cultural institutions. The eclectic nature of the framework welcomes research designs of great breadth and variety, and the participation of investigators from many disciplines. While this move toward a holistic approach is fully in line with important recent developments in the philosophy of social science research, it does carry some dangers. A broad, comprehensive framework is often difficult to put into operation, both as a whole, and as separate units. The assumptions, definitions, and research orientation of the various relevant disciplines are often at variance, and sometimes in contradiction, so investigators nominally using a common framework of analysis may find it hard to co-ordinate efforts satisfactorily. Presumably, though, this is a problem that can be overcome through extended collaboration and compromise.

The first step in any such collaboration is agreement on the scope of the study, including the identification of a common perspective. Implicitly the papers in this volume, and other recent research noted in the bibliography, can be seen to fit comfortably in one or another section of the Rodgers-Standing framework. This is to be expected, given its eclectic nature. However, the papers' individual approaches serve to isolate them and make it difficult to draw together the results as an intelligible unity.

To overcome this difficulty researchers studying the problem of children and employment should attempt to relate their particular topics to several main themes:

(i) The impact of work on the welfare of children
(ii) The role of work on the socialisation of children
(iii) The inter-relation of schooling and employment
(iv) Children's productive contribution to the family and society.

(v) The socio-economic determinants of children's participation in the workforce
(vi) Patterns of exploitation.

Some studies lend themselves more readily to broad interpretation than others. Schildkrout's chapter on Kano addresses all these perspectives to some extent, because it takes a comprehensive ethnographic approach. On the other hand, Morice deals with the informal sector and is more explicitly concerned with welfare issues, so the task of examining his proposals in terms of socialisation is more difficult, though none the less worthwhile.

The second step is the definition of basic concepts that are at least translatable, and if possible common, to all members of a collaborative effort. What is a "child"? This question appears simple, but is especially vexing when one attempts to standardise concepts. Researchers have used such definitions as "those under 16", "age 1 to 15", or "unmarried workers", but in practice, in societies with little concept of calendar age, the data on age are really based on interviewers' evaluations of physique.[6] Similar problems arise in defining such apparently simple concepts as "work", "employment", "leisure" and other activities; "income group", social class", "education", and other dimensions of socio-economic difference; "employer", "head of family", and other relationships which describe the nature of authority and subordination in the economy. Unless researchers share a common understanding of the phenomena, and correctly perceive the relations between each other's assumption, data, analysis and findings, there can be little hope of effective collaboration.

The third task to be faced in a collaborative research programme is a more narrow problem of definition, and deals with operational specification of units of analysis. The villages, or other social groups. Whatever unit is used, it is the researcher's prime responsibility to specify clearly the definition of the unit, and where possible to describe and relations of this unit to other commonly used units of analysis. The importance of this requirement is underscored by Leach in his critique of a social survey in Ceylon.[7] The investigators bad used a "common cooking-pot" definition of a household and produced the striking statistic that over three in five households were landless. Leach, drawing on anthropological data, noted that it is common in Sinhalese society for different married couples living under the same roof (in extended or joint families) to have separate cooking-pots but to work land together, legal ownership of the land being with the senior family member until his death. Thus, Leach concludes, the true statistic on landlessness is probably much lower than that found in the survey. Had the surveyors paid more attention to the units chosen for their analysis, they could have avoided such inaccurate results.

This point is all the more important when one considers the work of children. Dangers of bias arise because of the potential mobility of children. Village surveys using families as the unit of analysis may miss large numbers of youngsters who have left home to go to the city or to distant schools, to serve apprenticeships or to live with relatives. Studies focusing on particular agricultural practices or industries may ignore great numbers of children who do not participate in these activities, and, of course, studies of school-children invariably fail to describe the lives of drop-outs.

The final step in establishing a basis for collaboration is the design of research instruments and plans of analysis which can effectively operationalise the decisions made as to perspective, basic concepts and units of analysis. Superficially, this seems to be a natural by-product of the previous steps, but the frustrations of researchers coming to grips with the conventions and techniques of other disciplines are most likely to emerge, here.[8] There are three typical approaches to the problem of operationalising study designs.

First, the purists acknowledge the contribution of other disciplines to the identification of research problems and definitions, but insist on disciplinary autonomy in the development of analysis plans, and implicitly claim central importance for their own disciplines through their habit of regarding other disciplines as providers of "important background information" or "useful data for testing our models" or "interesting alternative ways of interpreting our data".[9]

The second approach is more avowedly interdisciplinary in that collaborators acknowledge the essential equality of disciplines but maintain nevertheless a certain degree of autonomy in the development of separate segments of the research plan in order better to exploit the comparative advantages enjoyed by disciplines in handling different types of data collection or analysis problems. An interesting example of this type of approach is documented in the report of a project studying the commercialisation of agriculture in Buganda where it is clear that the co-investigators were strongly committed to their different research techniques, but modified their approaches in the light of their partners' experiences.[10]

The third approach is that of people who have training in methods and theories that are not traditional to their nominal discipline and for whom issues of disciplinary equality or autonomy are of only marginal interest. Techniques of analysis are designed and applied according to the needs of the research problem, and with little regard to the boundaries of disciplines.[11] Myrdal exemplifies this approach on a grand scale in *Asian drama* where he strongly argues for a removal of "the barriers hampering the transmission of ideas". But even he hesitates at the boundaries of "behavioural research" and hopes that his study "can stimulate researchers in other disciplines" to follow lines of inquiry suggested by results of economic research.

2. General Approaches to Collection Data on Children's Work

The history of research on children and employment contains a wide variety of methods of data collection, from the standard procedures of historians to quite specialised forms of inquiry designed specifically to overcome problems inherent in studying children. In the following discussion emphasis will be placed on direct data collection methods, since methods of handling secondary data are fairly well known, and in any case very dependent on the nature and availability of records in particular societies. Moreover, this discussion will focus on the relevance of primary data collection techniques to the specific issues of children and employment. Readers interested in attaining a general understanding of these techniques are referred to manuals prepared for this purpose.

Several techniques are discussed below, starting with the most directly observational, and proceeding along a continuum of increasingly structured mass-interview methods to national censuses. This sequence is arbitrary, but is not without importance. Good censuses are grounded in knowledge of the nature of socio-economic conditions, derived from observational studies and surveys however, it is also true that the researcher is likely to interpret observations more acutely if informed about the general patterns revealed in surveys and censuses. Thus the order of exposition does not seek to suggest a temporal pattern when it comes to applying the techniques; they should be regarded as interactive, with research methods evolving as broader understanding of the nature of the research problems is achieved. No one technique should necessarily be used first; but the researcher's initial step should be to review the experience of others in applying a variety of methods.

(a) Direct Observation

Epitomised by the method of participant observation[12] developed in anthropology, the researcher using direct observation techniques would normally reside in the study area, participate in daily activities, observing the behaviour of a (probably small) group of children, and systematically record these observations. There are a number of problems inherent in this approach, the most vexing of which is the issue of obtrusiveness; children's work patterns may change in response to a researcher's presence. To overcome this source of bias a system of "random visits" may be arranged on various days and at different times, with the researcher recording only what the child was doing immediately prior to the researcher's arrival (Johnson, 1975, pp. 301-303). There are also various times of day and certain activities during which even a brief visit from the researcher would be considered ill mannered. To cover these occasions some anthropologists have relaxed the principle of personal observation and either interviewed the child about the activities of the preceding 24 hours, or asked the child (if literate) to keep a diary of activities for given periods. The fact that the researcher is resident in the area offers many opportunities for such indirect data to be validated through "accidental" observations made during the course of daily life.

Direct observation provides the researcher with opportunities to refine continuously the basic concepts of investigation with increasing understanding of the social, economic, and psychological context of particular behaviour. Take for example the concept of "work". At first glance small boys may appear to be playing as they fashion slings, but when the sling is later used to hunt birds around rice fields, the researcher may reinterpret this behaviour as being a form of work. This new interpretation may alter again as it is learned that the boys have not been ordered to hunt birds, and may be dramatically reversed of their father suddenly confiscates the sling and berates them for killing birds which are natural predators of grain-eating rodents. This example shows that a great variety of studies undertaken in different socio-economic environments are required in order to develop and refine a set of concepts about the meaning of children's work. The studies may be "pure descriptions" of activities observed by researchers or perceptions and description contributed by children and other members of the study population.

When societies are undergoing rapid and dramatic changes the direct observation method runs the danger of misinterpreting current behaviour as representing a timeless pattern. This is exacerbated if reports are written in the "ethnographic present" tense characterised by statements such as: "The Javanese do..." or "The Javanese believe..." with no acknowledgement that behaviour in the past was different.

History may be injected into direct observation if the researcher can find informants who are able accurately to relate the changing patterns of children's activities, preferably in detail, and with as comprehensive a coverage of family members, neighbours or schoolmates as possible. These oral histories have the advantage that information is provided by respondents who are reflective and can articulate experiences in a meaningful fashion, but of course there is always a danger that such talented people have untypical experience and perception that cannot be taken to represent the "average".[13] However, if the experience of Oscar Lewis (especially as reported in Lewis (1963)) during his various compilations of oral history is any guide, patience, skilful probing and careful translation and editing can reveal eloquence in respondents whose natural language may be crude.

(b) Community-level Studies

Among the major pitfalls of observation techniques is the problem of discovering what is happening outside the field of observation. This is particularly important in the case of children's work since the accessibility of children to the observer will depend on the nature of the job, and it is common to find that the most conspicuous children are those who are working in fields, in fairly large shops, or on outdoor household tasks. Many other jobs are less conspicuous, hence more likely to escape observation. The same problem is inherent in the observation of different types of leisure or schooling behaviour. As mentioned above, one solution is for the researcher to collect work diaries, or detailed life histories to supplement observation. Another is to expand the coverage gradually, relax the requirement of direct observation, and utilise such indirect tools as surveys, official records, and key informants. Such a shift tends to refocus the researcher's attention from the level of the individual child or small group (family) to larger social organisations and institutions. Then the purpose of research becomes the comprehensive study of children's work *within* the broader social framework, normally defined as a *community.*

Arensberg has classified community-level studies as a type of "observational method" through which the researcher undertakes a "massive immersion... in [the community's] internal realities and complexities".[14] This style of research which he and others call *in vivo* is contrasted with social surveys and experimental designs, both of which involve greater detachment on the part of the investigator, While this is a useful definition, it could as well be argued that the distinction between direct observation and "community" studies is that, practically speaking, a researcher cannot directly observe *all* behaviour in a community and hence must rely on some form of structured, indirect data-collection techniques. The type of community studies we are considering here are thus not *in vivo*, grounded in experience, but rather attempts to extract key elements of information from all sections of the community.[15]

The use of indirect data collection techniques in community studies introduces a series of problems for survey researchers, whether they study a relatively small village or plan a national census. Whereas the direct observer may enter the field without a systematic conceptual framework and absorb information as it naturally enters his or her field of perception, the survey researcher must predetermine the type of data sought, with clear, operational definitions of terms and standard procedures for obtaining, recording and manipulating the data. Preferably, of course, the definitions are based on some prior understanding of the community under study, perhaps from previous direct observation. However, one of the most frequent criticisms of the survey approach is that the basic concepts included in the survey schedules sometimes have little relation to social reality, and the results therefore lack a vital dimension.

Community surveys have a number of strengths that make them particularly useful for studies of children's work. First, because they are inclusive, the researcher is assured of obtaining comparable data on all children of the community, and thus avoids the biases mentioned above which arise out of selection problems. Second, since all children are studied, it is normally feasible to study social and economic factors causing differences in work patterns (e.g. Hull, 1975; Hart, 1978; Cain). Third, given the relative compactness of communities in rural (and some urban) societies, the researcher can reasonably undertake surveys in stages, with each round serving as the basis for refining definitions and concepts to be used in later rounds. This is particularly useful in the context of children's work because relatively little is known about cultural variations. Fourth, within each community there are normally particular groups of children with unusual work patterns who can be studied through direct observational techniques, thus providing rich additional data and the basis for verifying survey results.

As community-level studies become more detailed, include more respondents and consequently require more research team-members, the task of the principal investigator is increasingly that of administrator rather than observer. Those steeped in the anthropological tradition[16] of Malinowski, Evans-Pritchard, Morgan, Murdock and other pioneer participant-observers often find the demands of creating a research bureaucracy frustrating if not altogether stifling; but unless these demands are met the project may fail. Questionnaire design and testing, interviewer selection and training, mapping, record-keeping, checking and re-checking, coding and tabulating are vital steps requiring careful planning and execution.[17] This is not to say that the researcher should approach the task with the mentality of a clerk; each stage requires creative thought that must, however, be complemented by thoroughness.

Village studies of employment are increasingly common and many of them have looked in some detail at children's work (e.g. Dasgupta, 1977, pp. 23-33; Nag, White and Peet, 1978; Hart, 1978, pp. 131-135; Hull, 1975; and Khuda, 1978). Connell and Lipton (1976, pp. 46-53), in reviewing the literature, call for greater efforts to be put into studies of the relation of household composition to labour use with special attention to the nature of labour force participation at young ages. Such issues are likely to be most effectively studied at the community level.

At this point it might also be mentioned that community—level studies include not only those social aggregates normally termed communities—villages, neighbourhoods, towns, squatter settlements, and so forth—but might also refer to studies of industries, occupational groups or schools. The major criteria for inclusion is that the individuals studied share some experience which the researcher (and presumably the individuals) regard as a force binding them into a community. Such a description may open the way to debate on precise definitions—are there "communities" of pickpockets, street vendours, high school students?—but as long as researchers are careful to demonstrate how their defined communities fir into the broader society, both in terms of proportions (quantitative) and functions (qualitative), such debate should be useful in advancing our understanding of children's work.

Two major criticism of community-level surveys frequently arise. One is that, since they are generally carried out intensively over a relatively short period of time, they represent only a "snapshot" of the situation. Such a view might be distorted if the community is experiencing rapid socio-economic change. Researchers may then be looking for explanations of behaviour in cross-sectional patterns, when what is really needed is an understanding of historical development. This criticism can be partially overcome by designing surveys to collect retrospective data (analogous to the oral histories described above), or by restudies, longitudinal (monitoring) studies or periodic surveys (to be discussed in the next section).

The other major criticism is that community-level surveys are representative of a particular geographical or social isolate only, and cannot be taken to reflect the behaviour of a broader population. From a purely statistical viewpoint this criticism is undeniable. However, researchers who have used the approach point out that statistical standards refer to only one rather rigid notion of representativeness, and that normally the selection of communities for study follows criteria which the investigator regards as being of *a priori* importance in the conduct of the research. The community is thus "representative" of broader social groups displaying the same characteristics according to these criteria. Further, the depth attained by community studies in understanding the processes of children's work is important. Children may display different work patterns in other communities, but researchers often find that the logic of behaviour found in one community is applicable to other, quite different situations, if not by analogy then often by contrast.

(c) Periodic or Continuous Monitoring, and Restudies

Multiple rounds increase both the depth and richness of survey results by testing issues such as seasonality, chance variations, and the validity and reliability of data.

Periodic monitoring is especially valuable in studies of children's work in agrarian economies because of the high variability of children's participation during the agricultural cycle. When the school calendar and religious observances are taken into account, one often finds that children's work is highly irregular and best measured through frequent revisits. In his study of a Javanese village, White visited households every sixth day. This period was regarded as being short enough to catch major variations due to season, school calender and holidays, but long enough to avoid pestering respondents. More importantly, since the Javanese week has five days, and the Gregorian seven, the use of a six-day interval eliminated any potential bias from activities that were undertaken in weekly patterns such as marketing (which follows the Javanese week) and mosque attendance (each Friday).

If visits are made daily, or if recording is simple enough for families to keep activity, diaries, monitoring becomes a virtually continuous operation. It is doubtful whether continuous monitoring offers any real advantages over the sort of a regular visits undertaken by White (1975) and referred to by Cain, and it has the serious drawback of being extremely intrusive, thus most likely to influence the very activity patterns it is meant to study.

Budget and time restrictions generally limit the duration of even the most ambitious attempts at periodic monitoring to one, or two years; while this is sufficient to account for various short—term changes such as seasonality, it cannot encompass the broad transformations that have been occurring around the world over the past decades and centuries. For this purpose the restudy of a community can be particularly enlightening. Epstein has, discussed the advantages and drawbacks of such endeavours, pointing out that a second study or survey may be carried out by the same people who did the first, or another group entirely.[18] One of the problems raised by restudies is to decide whether observed differences are due to true social change, different investigative techniques or simply different perspectives that yield two visions of the truth. If the initial investigator presents clear descriptions of study concepts and methods, these problems should not arise. Of course, scientific methods develop and there is often a case for modifying data collection procedures to account for improvements. None the less, restudies that aim to examine change should not depart so far from the original methods as to cast doubt on the comparability of findings. In any case they should repeat enough of the original method to establish some common basis of understanding before applying alternative approaches.

Apart from examining change, researchers may use restudies to test the validity and reliability of the original study,[19] intentionally applying quite different, and far them more relevant, methodologies. Mamdani (1972) provides one of the most effective examples of this in his critique of the Khanna Family Planning Study[20] where, using an anthropological approach backed by a strong theoretical framework, he reinterpreted the meaning of villagers' responses to a survey, explaining the "rationality" of their high fertility in terms of their economic conditions. More studies of this type are needed, although they do not always have to oppose "anthropologists and surveyors". It is worth noting that Mamdani's data on the work of children are extremely patchy, leaving numerous open questions about the nature, organisation and productivity of children's work; the influence of schooling on children's propensity to work and the life-cycle pattern of children's participation in family enterprises. There is scope here for a further restudy using approaches such as those developed by Johnson, White, Cain or Hart. While this could theoretically be done in any village in the region of the Khanna Study, it would be particularly useful to restudy Manupur, where Mamdani worked, to establish a vivid basis for comparison.

(d) Sample Surveys

Despite anthropologists' arguments supporting various non-statistical notions of representativeness, researchers would often like to obtain results that accurately reflect the behaviour of people in large regions. To obtain data through full enumerations would be prohibitively expensive, time-consuming and ultimately futile since scientific sampling procedures allow the investigator to select, a small group, of respondents whose behaviour, within narrow margins of error, is representative of the behaviour of all members of the population.[21]

Sample surveys are another step along the continuum away from direct observation, and because of their geographical dispersion they offer fewer opportunities for the principal investigator to become "participant-observer" than are available in community studies. Mapping, construction of a sampling frame, transport and lodging of interviewers and other logistic questions are extremely time-consuming in the sample survey. Mitchell argues forcefully that the survey technique makes great demands on back ground information, personnel qualifications and organisational skill, which are difficult if not impossible to attain in developing countries.[22] Moreover, whereas the team members of a community survey generally have fairly close relations among themselves and with their respondents, sample survey teams are scattered, with perhaps days or weeks elapsing between meetings. When problems, arise, either with respondents or with the questionnaires, community-level researchers can handle them quickly, but sample surveyors often find that time-lags in reaching interview teams prevent changes in questionnaires. Because of this, sample surveys are generally most successful in collecting hard data, where basic concepts and collection techniques are very clear. They are not as successful in exploratory ventures that demand an iterative research strategy.

At the present stage of research on children's employment, sample surveys have most to offer in collecting relatively straightforward data on age, sex and participation in various types of activities, and in relating these to a wide range of independent and background variables, such as residence, family structure, income, schooling, marital status, parents' characteristics, etc.[23] Only after much greater refinement of concepts and methods will sample surveys be useful in collecting data on children's marginal economic pursuits, participation in the informal sector, and irregular involvement in what might be called "traditional" activities, such as village night-watch, service in ceremonies and artistic endeavours. These aspects of children's work are often important, but they are so complex or culture-specific that the (often westernised) researcher does not know how to ask valid questions about them.

One area of particular importance that has commanded relatively little attention in the literature is housework. Children are often very active from young ages in various tasks in and around the house and in many countries have prime responsibility for collecting fuel and water and tending animals. Surveys directed specifically at this issue might shed new light on co-operation among household members in matters of mutual welfare. One tactic is to ask all individuals what housework, they do, but also ask a key informant to report on which members regularly do various basic household tasks such as cooking, sweeping, washing, gardening, etc. By alternately directing specific attention to individuals and tasks, a survey can be designed to collect hard data on a relatively under-researched topic (Hull and Hull, 1977).

As more observational and community studies are reported and reviewed, the list of children's employment topics suitable for investigation through sample surveys will grow. Specialised sample surveys, designed to ensure maximum data validity and reliability, and addressing very narrow, clearly defined topics, have an important role to play. However, they should be focused and well planned to avoid becoming misguided, encyclopaedic attempts to give empirical vestments to the Rodgers-Standing framework.

(e) Census

Censuses, and by implication the huge labour force, agriculture and industry surveys regularly conducted by governments, present a particular challenge to researchers on children's employment. For many of the same reasons why sample surveys were criticised above, we might feel that censuses do not collect data on children's work effectively. But while it is the researcher (and the funding agency) who decides whether or not to conduct a specialised survey, censuses are *faits accomplis* like it or not, governments conduct them, and there are usually a number of variables relevant to children's work. The researcher's task is thus to evaluate the validity and, reliability of these data, and to suggest improvements in census procedures to ensure better data quality. Where data are found to be of acceptable quality the field is open for all manner of analyses.

However, census or other government survey data tend to cover only organised and regular activities, and even for these topics the data normally deal only with participation in activities and not intensity of work, productivity or changes over time.

The issue of children's participation in economic activity is important in understanding the total labour force, but it has been overshadowed recently by the concern most analysts have shown for adult and particularly female, participation.[24] In quantitative terms there is no doubt that variations of participation derived from differences in female labour force participation are the largest component in rates as a whole. However children's participation (looking here at people aged 5 to 20) way be a sensitive, barometer of changes in labour force structure, and in any case will reveal a great deal about future labour quality. Adolescents' experiences in schooling, work in industry, agriculture, or family enterprises, unemployment or none of these activities are indicators of likely later participation in organised economic pursuits.

The dilemma facing the analyst is that the stringent definitions needed to collect census data may be too narrow to capture much of the activity of children.[25] To relax the definitions, though, is to run the risk of obtaining less valid or less reliable data. This is not to say that current practices are properly balanced, for there is evidence (Standing, 1978b, p. 26) that standard labour force definitions might be, considerably relaxed without affecting data quality.

A starting point for deeper analysis of census data on children's work has been provided by Durand (1975, pp. 15-45, 218-223) in his international review of census labour force data. Much more work must be done on the particular problems of data validity and reliability in census analyses of children's work, through a number of country case studies. This would allow sufficient attention to be paid to the socio-economic, demographic and cultural factors that are assumed to play determining roles in children's participation. A major goal of research should be to examine census definitions and interviewing procedures carefully, so as to ensure that data on children's work, however defined, are accurately obtained.

SPECIAL ISSUES IN THE STUDY OF CHILDREN'S WORK

The approaches we have described face a number of common issues surrounding the study of children's employment; as they cannot all be fully developed here, we will concentrate on the most important.

1. Determination of Ages and the Definition of a "Child"

While different cultures have their own notions of childhood, and many take no notice of passing solar years in the measurement of human transitions, researchers must rely on chronological age as the basic unit of any operational definition for a study (but cf. Schildkrout). To do otherwise would almost certainly exclude comparison with research from other cultures. Moreover, the standards used in many cultures are often subjective ("When a boy is strong enough... when a girl is skilled") and could vary among individuals and over time, thus becoming sliding criteria of little value in measurement, whatever intrinsic interest they might have as a reflection of indigenous concepts.

Some researchers are lucky enough to study people who have long experience with the Gregorian calendar, who document births, baptisms, marriages and deaths, and annually celebrate birth anniversaries with special food and gift exchanges. In these societies, children and adults may be able to recite not only their own birthdate and age accurately, but also those of their siblings, parents, friends and perhaps a bevy of extended kin. Researchers in most of Africa, west, south and south east Asia have no such luck and, sometimes unsure even of their own birthday, have no expectation that respondents will be able to report accurate chronological age.

When studies focus specifically on current patterns of children's work they tend to benefit from some recent social trends. First, as schooling spreads, many children find themselves "assigned" an age when they are around 5 or 6 years old, and this is generally within a year or two of their real age. As they progress through school, years are regularly "assigned", and by the late teens are still likely to be enumerated within two years of actual age, well within the margins sought by most studies. As children go through this process parents begin to take note of the timing of subsequent births, and the margin of error of estimation on entry to school is reduced (if it is not manipulated by parents seeking to give their child an advantage by saying that a 7 year old child is, only 5, in the hope that the child will perform better than younger classmates).

Second, radio, newspapers, urban employment, government regulations and all the other accoutrements of modernism that follow schedules are making calendar watchers out of increasing numbers of the world's people. When asked about dates, they at least understand the reference point of the question, and; can frequently give an answer which, though unfounded in fact, feels right. Brightly coloured calendars are also favourite wall decorations in homes the world over.

Various gadgets are used by survey interviewers to estimate people's ages. Wheels and sliding scales can be devised to convert local to Gregorian calendars, event lists are compiled to jog the memory ("was x born before or after the war"?), and elaborate schedules designed to order births (see Scott and Sabagh, 1970; Caldwell and Igun, 1971; Hull, 1976). It is safe to say that when such devices are necessary, truly accurate age reporting is impossible, although improved age reporting can be achieved.

Researchers planning to collect their own data should not regard the impossibility of attaining fully accurate age data as a licence to record ages in arbitrary groupings (such as "under 5, 5-10, 10-15"). Instead interviewers should be trained to scale the most accurate estimate of a respondent's age possible, record this in *completed* years (not rounded to the nearest year) and note all supporting information used in making the estimate (such as birth certificates). The researcher should examine the distribution of ages before choosing the age groups to be used in the analysis. If there are anomalies such as disproportionately high frequencies of certain ages, the groupings can be chosen to maximise the probability of people failing within the range of their real age. For example, if heaping occurs at 10, 15 and 20, these ages can be put at the centre of the groups 8-12, 13-17, 18-22, since the people mistakenly recorded as being, say, 15 are most likely to actually be 15 plus or minus one or two years. So long as the ages are recorded in exact completed years the researcher can experiment with different grouping that best suit the current analytical purpose, and data can easily be regrouped to conform with results published by other investigators, or with the standard five year classifications used in censuses (10-14; 15-19; 20-24).

Researchers are frequently at a loss when it comes to deciding on upper and lower age limits to their definition of "children", and sometimes make arbitrary cut-off points with little thought as to how the decision will affect their analysis or the comparability of their results with other studies. In the data collection process, a good rule of thumb is to take the broadest limits, and then make decisions about narrowing boundaries during the tabulation of results. In deciding whether to interview or observe 5, 8, 10 or 12 year-olds for example, the researcher should consider the receptivity of the different age groups to be examined and, whenever possible, test the questionnaire or observation procedures on a few young children to discover where problems might arise. The studies by White (1975) and Cain (1977a), for instance, have shown that some quite young children work in lower-income countries, so the researcher is best advised to err on the young side in selecting a minimum age.

The maximum age in defining a child is more difficult. Social definitions often consider puberty, marital status, schooling, male or female circumcision, and various social and religious ceremonies as criteria of adulthood. When census data are tabulated according to standard five-year age groups, the investigator is forced to select 19 or 24 as maximum ages. There is no obvious age or social status that can be suggested as a definitive upper limit to childhood across cultures. One benefit of choosing a rather high chronological year of age as a cut-off point is that it extends analytical possibilities. Either 19 or 24 would be possible choices, with the former preferred in societies with young age at marriage and low levels of schooling, and the latter where periods of dependence on parents tend to be long.

2. Classification of Activities

A precise scheme for classifying the activities of children depends on the purpose of the particular study, hut there area number of issues that frequently arise and deserve consideration here.[26]

First, in low-income countries children's participation in various household tasks is sometimes regarded as being economically productive, and sometimes not. The argument for treating it as an economic activity is supported by the fact that it often frees adults to undertake directly productive tasks. Moreover, many household duties, such as sewing and mending, food processing, fuel and water gathering and waste disposal, are clearly productive constituents of subsistence economies. Researchers need to think carefully about such tasks, considering analogous situations in advanced economies, before assigning them to "productive", "economic" or other value-premised categories.

Second, children's involvement in child-care presents some problems since older siblings may be "caring" for younger sibs, or simply playing with them. The researcher is forced to form a consistent interpretation of the nature of the activity. An examination of the intrinsic qualities of children's behaviour the degree of authority of the older over the younger, the degree of dependency of the younger, the desire of the older to pursue other activities may reveal no clear criteria for distinguishing work from play. On the other hand, if account is taken of external factors, such as the parents' evaluation of the activity, or whether it is associated with parents leaving the house for marketing, work or leisure, there is a danger that some children will be regarded as working and others not, even though they are doing the same thing. On the whole it seems preferable in cases like this to adopt clear criteria relating to intrinsic characteristics of activities. Even if these criteria are later found to be wrong in detail, the data will be more valuable than if they were collected on the basis of vague and shifting definitions.

Third, given the enormous variety of tasks and work patterns found in even the most simple village economy, researchers have tried to measure multiple-participation through time-budgets and work histories. These show the number and duration of jobs done by children during given periods of time. A dimension of importance that is seldom measured directly is work intensity. Normally job classification is intended to reflect the difficulty of tasks, and for some activities, such as sweeping, weaving or weeding, this is achieved in rough measure. But other tasks, like fetching water, gardening and gathering fuel, can vary greatly in terms of difficulty, even over similar durations. In very small-scale observational studies efforts can be made to estimate intensity of work, or respirometers can be used to measure energy expenditure during representative work sessions. In larger studies the classification of activities should be made so as to recognise and codify varying work intensities. Preferably, such evaluations should be based on the findings of intensive studies, but if these are not available, time should be spent observing work pattern before deciding on the classification scheme.

As with data on age, the general rule in classifying activities is to collect as much detail as possible within the chosen criteria, and delay any summarising of material until the analysis phase.

3. Calculation of Appropriate Descriptive Statistics

Researchers collecting quantitative data soon learn to think in terms of the *shape* of frequency distributions of variables. Age distributions are shown as pyramids, while hours worked at a given task may take the shape of a hell (the so-called "normal" distribution), and other distributions may be hyperbolic, double-humped, or straight lines parallel to the axis.

To graph or even tabulate the distribution of all variables in the average study would take an enormous amount of space, and would present the reader with a bewildering array of numbers. Instead, the researcher chooses summary statistics that describe various aspects of the distributions; these are divided into measures of central tendency and measures of dispersion. The problem faced in studies of children's work is the establishment of a proper basis for the calculation of such statistics.

Data on participation are most often presented in terms of the proportions of children of each age undertaking given activities. Should the denominator of the proportion be *all* children of the age group, or only children who participated in at least one activity and were thus "workers", or those children who could be defined as being "at risk" of participating? In the latter case, the researcher may decide to exclude from calculations of proportions fetching water, for example, those children living in houses with piped water. Likewise, children of landless artisans may be excluded from calculations of proportions farming.

Similarly, in summarising durations of work the researcher may wish to calculate the average number of hours worked by *all* children, or limit the denominator to those children who worked. The impression gained will be very different. Activities with low participation rates but high hours worked will have low averages if all children are in the denominator, and high if only working children are included.

The exclusive use of means in presenting results is often misleading and researchers are well advised to calculate standard deviations, medians and modes to demonstrate more fully the shape of distributions. This is particularly important in the analysis of data on age of first participation in economic activities. To say that "children as young as 8 years of age hoe in the fields" is misleading if it is found that only two out of 1,000 children begin at that age; the mean age for beginning hoeing may be 15 (for those who ever hoe), the median 18, and a quarter of all children may never hoe. This example is hypothetical but not unreasonable. When similar information is presented about the full range of children's activities in any society it will be seen that simple generalisations are impossible. Instead, analysts must grapple with descriptions and explanations that reflect the diversity of children's occupations.

4. Reporting of Assumptions and Methodology

Connell and Lipton (1976, p. 124) have complained that a major drawback of Indian village studies has been lack of detail concerning research methodology. The problem is not confined to India, nor to village studies. Sometimes the methodology is omitted for space reasons and presented in a separate, less widely distributed publication. Economists, in particular, abbreviate discussions of methodology because they assume their audience will be disciplinary colleagues who are aware of standard analytical techniques. Definitions and assumptions used in studies are often not presented because researchers regard them as cumbersome or merely mundane, hence not worth reporting. Such reasons are understandable, but none the less unacceptable.

The need for clear reporting of assumptions and methodologies used in studies of children's work has three aspects: the complexity of the subject itself, the variety of disciplines involved, and the lack of an accepted set of standard definitions and methodologies. Readers must be given enough information to evaluate the study critically and researchers the material with which to design follow-up studies to verify the results.

One desirable by-product to be anticipate from a more systematic collaborative study, guided by a conceptual framework such as that presented by Rodgers and Standing, is the development of more standard concepts and methodologies. Initially these will necessarily be based on various culture-specific case studies, but eventually it should be possible for groups of investigators to collaborate on the identification of definitions relevant to specific types of economy. They might also want to prepare methodology handbooks for different research strategies. These could take the form of model formats for classifying activities; descriptions of techniques for measuring children's participation and duration and intensity of work; sample questionnaires and code schemes; caveats in the design of scientific samples for the study of children's work; and suggestions for the tabulation of research results. Such manuals would presumably be of some interest to researchers currently working on the topic of children's work, but more importantly they would encourage others to enter the field in ways which will avoid both naive errors and unnecessary duplication of efforts.

5. Validation of Basic Concepts

A constantly recurring theme of research on children's work is the vital need to review and validate the basic conceptual framework of our studies. This is the key to defining a "child", classifying activities, and selecting descriptive statistics, and it is the major justification for demanding full reports of research methodology. Some methods of testing the validity of concepts have been mentioned above, but it is well to reiterate them.

First, concepts can be established through literature reviews and analytical procedures of verification. For example, "work" may be defined as any activity undertaken for wage or profit (excess of material returns over costs) in a particular body of literature. When examined in the light of our understanding of a particular subsistence economy, this definition may appear highly restrictive and unspecific. Many activities are found to bring no wage or material return to the child, and some, such as child-care, produce no material return at all. On this basis the concept can be broadened to include activities undertaken as part of a specific subsistence production process.

Second, concepts can be tested against direct observation of children's attributes and behaviour. To verify that child-care is work rather than play, the researcher can observe a number of pairs of siblings (of various combinations of ages) to see how child-care is initiated (by self, or by other), the nature of the child-care relationship, responses to crises (when the younger child becomes hungry, restless, angry or demanding, or when the older sib is tempted by alternative activities), and whether the parents are thus enabled to carry out alternative productive activities. When these and other aspects of behaviour are analysed the researcher may be able to reformulate the concept of child-care to establish it more firmly within the concepts of "work" or "play", or perhaps identify certain types of child-care (sibs of particular ages) that fit clearly in one or the other of these categories.

Third, the concepts can be operationalised so as to be included in formal social survey questions. This may involve simplification and perhaps modification of the definition to make it acceptable to interviewers and respondents. The survey method involves a number of stages at which concepts are modifiable: compilation of the questionnaire, selection of a community or sample group, coding of responses, summarises and tabulation of codes, and the interpretation of results. Validation of the integrity of basic concepts is necessary at each of these stages. For example, the researcher may operationalise the definition of a "child" as being a person between exact ages 5 and 20 (i.e. *completed* ages 4 and 19). On the questionnaire, space may be provided for noting a number of estimates of age, with a final box for the interviewer to choose a "most likely age". Intrusion of the interviewer's judgement amounts to a modification of the original definition based on true age. If, during coding, it is found that some interviewers left the evaluation box blank, the coders may be instructed to insert any estimate based on documents; during tabulation the researcher, faced with a very uneven age distribution, may decide to group the ages as 5-9, 10-14, 15-19 and analyse the results according to these categories. Each of these changes modifies the original concept slightly but if it is then found that no people aged 5-9 undertook any activity defined as "work", the researcher might decided to change the operational definition of a child entirely to 10-19—thus revising the basic concept. Alternatively, the result might throw the operational definition of "work" into question, opening the way to even more extensive attempts to validate basic research concepts.

Questions of validity are seldom settled, even with the formulation of "standard" classifications, questionnaires and procedures. Exposure to new situations reveals weaknesses in accepted concepts and children's work is particularly likely to raise new issues.

SETTING CHILDREN'S WORK IN INSTITUTIONAL PERSPECTIVE

In reviewing general approaches and special issues we emphasised that socio-economic and cultural variations account for many of the difficulties experienced in research design and analysis. For this reason it was argued that such variations should not be isolated from the structure and functioning of the society. For example, an understanding of children's participation in goat-herding demands an understanding of the institution from methods of breeding (or the process of obtaining young animals) through general care, feeding and methods of slaughter to the sale of goat products. Moreover, in considering each stage, the focus is not on how that individual relates to institutions such as agricultural extension offices, other goat-herders, veterinarians, storekeepers who sell goat's milk, abattoirs and retail meat sellers.

Most studies focus on individuals rather than social institutions.[27] This is especially true of surveys where the individual respondent is the major unit for data collection and presentation. Institutional variables are then relegated to uni-dimensional indices, such as "years of schooling", "income", "father's occupation", each of which is taken to represent an important aspect of the individual's place in the social structure. In itself, this is unobjectionable, because there are generally very good reasons for thinking that when these variables are compared with others whose vagueness or complexity prevents easy inclusion on a survey questionnaire (e.g. social class, skill, economic status) they will be found to provide useful approximations of the latter qualities. They then become indicators of institutional setting and data on, say, work according to father's occupation are interpretable as showing the way in which a family's economic status can affect the likelihood of children working.

Since the operationalised variables commonly used in surveys have individual meaning, sometimes quite separate from their roles as indicators of broader concepts, there is a danger that analysts may wrongly restrict interpretations and be misled by apparent consistencies in data. Thus, the finding in Indonesian fertility studies that mothers with high education have more children than those with low or no education has sometimes led readers to conclude that increased levels of schooling will lead to increased fertility. In fact as detailed analysis of the data shows, schooling *per se* has little or nothing to do with the determination of fertility levels. Factors such as marital disruption, infecundity, and differences in patterns of breastfeeding and post-partum abstinence set levels of childbearing, and these factors are determined by such things as nutritional standing, adherence to traditional norms, husband-wife economic relationships and relative female autonomy in decision-making, all of which in turn are aspects of what might generally be termed social class. The availability of schooling to women was for many decades a function of class in that only the fairly well-to-do could afford, and were motivated, to send their daughters to school. Thus the high fertility of the well schooled women was less a matter of curriculum than class, and further increases of schooling throughout the society cannot be expected to increase fertility.[28]

By analogy, studies of children's work face the difficulty of properly interpreting variables having both literal and representative meanings. However, many economists are used to searchers think of schooling as education, and that in turn purely as a matter of acquired intellectual skills; both groups ignore the institutional setting from which these variables are abstracted and within these and other factors interact to influence children's working behaviour.

Studies that seek to set children's work in an institutional setting will require much more data than can be obtained through surveys of individuals. Relevant social institutions will have to be identified and analysed. Questions will have to be asked about the nature of power in societies: Who decides whether a child will work? Who bears the costs? Who gains the benefits? How are protests registered? By what standards are hierarchical relationships governed? How does the child develop independence from parents? The answers are contained in an understanding of how institutions shape individual behaviour. Some means will have to be found for marshalling the great variety of such analyses, and the mass of information about individuals, into a coherent whole which will clearly delineate the causes and consequences of children's work in low-income countries. The approach will have to be particularistic; case by case, study by study, gradually refining concepts, describing situations, developing typologies, testing hypotheses. To propose sweeping general theories at the outset would be blatantly to ignore the importance of seeing children's work in the context of institutions. If such theories are tested against the limited data of surveys of individuals, and if variables of deep social meaning are interpreted only in their literal form, there is a risk that the results will be totally misunderstood. Investigators will have to exercise great caution and patience in the conduct of collaborative research aimed at describing the institutional setting of children's work, but they should be rewarded with much richer results than could be obtained by grand theoretical leaps through obscure masses of data.

SUMMARY

A long tradition of academic interest in the study of children's work has produced a number of research perspectives, including concern for child welfare, the view of work as an element in socialisation, the role of children in the household economy, the inter-relation of schooling and employment and the socio-economic determinants of children's work. None the less, the literature has yet to provide a set of commonly accepted concepts, and research methodologies have yet to be standardised.

Spurred partially by the International Year of the Child, there is a growing awareness that researchers of different disciplines should co-operate on this topic. At the least there should be a general exchange of information and discussion of value premises, methods and results. Preferably, though, there should be greater co-ordination of efforts through collaborative projects where researchers are forced to make joint decisions as to the structure and conduct of a research programme.

The Rodgers-Standing conceptual framework presented of this volume provides a starting point for such collaborative efforts. It is eclectic, and fairly comprehensive. While taking primarily the "child welfare" perspective, it is broad enough to admit studies from different viewpoints. However, experience in other areas indicates that researchers frequently misunderstand the assumptions and methods of other disciplines. Collaboration, then, must begin with a concerted disciplines. Collaboration, then, must begin with a concerted search for a common basis of understanding through standardised definitions and compatible methodologies.

The general approaches used in studies of children's work to date include direct observation, community-level studies, periodic or continuous monitoring, restudies, sample surveys and analysis of census data. Each approach demands careful formulation of research design and operationalistion of basic variables.

Researchers face a number of special issues in the study of children's work in low-income countries. To ensure a commonly accepted operational definition of a "child" it is necessary to adopt criteria based on chronological age rather than social notions of childhood. These data are difficult to obtain in cultures which do not have solar calendars. Activity patterns of children must be thoroughly studied, and consistent criteria adopted to determine what constitutes "work"; and summary statistics must be calculated on the basis of an appropriately selected base—be it all children, only children who work at all, or only children at risk of undertaking particular activities. Because the study of children's work is such a complex matter, it is important that researchers provide full reports of their concepts and methods which are intelligible to professionals from other disciplines. This provides the opportunity for concepts and methods to be validated, both on evidence of internal logic, and through comparison with other approaches.

Above all, children's work must be set in an institutional context, to portray accurately the socio-cultural dimensions of the behaviour, and to avoid simplistic interpretations of variables which have been greatly narrowed and formalised for purposes of analysis.

The institutional setting, the inherent complexity of the topic, the special need for care in defining and validating concepts and developing methodologies, and the incongruous obscurity of a topic of such long-standing interest to researchers and policy-makers, combine to place the study of children's work high on the agenda of all social science disciplines. There is a promise that, in seeking an understanding of this rather special area of human behaviour, we shall gain deeper insights into the nature of the societies of low-income countries. That is a promise we can ill afford to ignore.

NOTES

* Australian National University, Canberra, Australia. The author is grateful to Benjamin White and Mead Cain for sharing their experiences with me over the various stages of their research. Murray Chapman, Barry Popkin and Pat Quiggin have been helpful in directing me to references, and Valerie Hull made a number of useful criticism of earlier expressions of these ideas. Above all, I thank Gerry Rodgers, Guy Standing and other participants at the workshop for stimulating me to formalise some of the thoughts I have had about research on children's work.

1. Gaskell noted in 1833 that it was "absurd" to use the term "family" when parents and children saw each other in the home only one day a week (cited in Inglis, 1972, p. 424).
2. Inglis (1972), pp. 474-483) provides a good bibliography for the period up to 1835, while for the late 1800s the reader is referred to the works of Charles Booth, Sidney and Beatrice Webb, and Seebohm Rowntree.
3. For a review of this literature, see Middleton (1970, pp. xvii-xx). Mayor (1970) has collected a series of essays on the contribution of (largely British) social anthropology to the study of

socialisation. A recent project of interest is the cross-cultural study of child-rearing organised by Whiting and Child (1953), though they play remarkably little attention to children's work or work-related play.

4. One example of note is the series of international Labour Conventions on children's employment which derive from the "welfare" perspective noted above. Because of their unidimensional character they encourage law-makers to undertake actions which ignore a wide variety of aspects of children's work—such as its socialisation function, contribution to family economy and in some cases its purely recreational aspect. The result is that the Conventions once adopted are commonly ignored where the economic environment is vastly more complex than that assumed. Effective attempts to control exploitation must take this complexity into account.

5. Charles Booth, at the end of his monumental studies of poverty in London, commented: "I have relied first and chiefly on mere average and consensus resulting from the great number and variety of my sources of information. Statements on which reliance could be placed would tend to enforce themselves, and errors balance each other and drop out of count...it was all the more necessary that there should be no persistent bias at the centre at which all this varied information was assorted and assimilated. On this the entire value of the work depended" (cited in A. Fried and R. Elman (eds.): *Charles Booth's London: a portrait of the poor at the turn of the century drawn from his life and labour of the people in London.* (London, Hutchinson, 1969; Harmondsworth, Penguin Books, 1971). In contrast many researchers today use a single data source (usually a survey) and a single analytical technique (e.g. regression analysis) in their studies, pleading lack of time or lack of expertise as excuses for not having undertaken alternative approaches in verifying their results.

6. Connell and Lipton (1976, p. 77) report that in a sample of Indian village studies over 54 distinct age classification schemes were used in tabulations.

7. E.R. Leach: "An anthropologist's reflections on a social survey", in *Ceylon Journal of Historical and Social Studies*, 1958, No. 1, p. 9-20.

8. The following comments draw on personal experience in workshops on Costs of Children, Household Models of Economic-Demographic Decision-Making, Value of Children, Children's Work, and Nutrition and Fertility. Despite differences in topic format, participants and venue, some common problems arose as people from different disciplines attempted to communicate.

9. Economists, and particularly orthodox neo-classicists, have gained a reputation among those interested in children's employment as being esoteric and chauvinistic, but these same characteristics are found in professionals of all disciplines at one time or another. Social anthropologists are vociferous in defence of their discipline. Nadel argues that there are good reasons for specialisation in disciplines relating to totally different aspects of social phenomena, or in his terms "the transition from one (discipline) to the other appears to be more than merely a deepening of analysis; it gives at least the illusion of stepping into another order of existence, governed by the regularities peculier to it and only there established". By implication disciplines arise not as accidents in the history of science but as outgrowths of the nature of societies under consideration. S.F. Nadel: *The foundations of social anthropology* (London, Cohen and West, 1951).

10. A.I. Richards, F. Sturrock and J.M. Fortt (eds.): *Subsistence to commercial farming in present day Buganda* (Cambridge, Cambridge University Press, 1973).

11. Some recent methodology textbooks have included "primer" selections on a variety of quantitative and qualitative techniques, apparently in an attempt to "arm" the researcher for any eventuality. For an excellent example, see P.J. Pelto and G.H. Pelto: *Anthropological research: The structure of inquiry* (Cambridge, Cambridge University Press, 2nd ed., 1978).

12. For discussions of the method of participant observation see Pelto and Pelto, op. cit.; M.S.

Schwartz and C.G. Schwartz: "Problems in participant observation", in *American Journal of Sociology*, 1955, No. 4, pp. 343-353; and H.S. Becker: "Problems of inference and proof in participant observation", in *American Sociological Review*, 1958, No. 6, pp. 652-600. R.H. Janes: "A note on phases of the community role of the participant-observer", in *American Sociological Review*, 1961, No. 3, pp. 446-450, probes the issue of the researcher's establishment of a role within a community, and distinguishes various phases of acceptance. G.D. Berreman: *Behind many masks: Ethnography and impression management in a Himalayan village*, Monograph No. 4 (Ithaca, NY, Society for Applied Anthropology, 1962) analyses the interaction of researcher and study community in terms of "impression management", asserting that the researcher is "inevitably an outsider and never becomes otherwise... The nature of his data is largely determined by his identity as seen by his subjects" (p. 21). Clark goes further to argue that an integral part of fieldwork—and ultimately analysis—is the personal involvement of the researcher, and that this should be reported and analysed with the other information collected in the research. M. Clarke: "Survival in the field: Implications of personal experience in field work", in *Theory and Society*, 1975, No. 2, pp. 59-123.

13. For a good over-all manual and an excellent bibliography on oral (or life) history techniques, see L.L. Langness: *The life history in anthropological science* (New York, Holt, Rinehart and Winsteon, 1965).

14. C. Arensberg: "The community as object and as sample", in *American Anthropologists*, 1961, No. 63, pp. 241-264.

15. An early, but still relevant, discussion of the need for indirect data collection instruments in community studies is Richards presentation of methods of conducting a village census: A. Richards: "The village census in the study of contact", in *Africa*, 1935, Vol. 8, pp. 20-33. Also of interned are R. Firth: "Census and sociology in a primitive is and community (Tikopia)", in *Proceedings of the World Population Conference 1954*, Vol. 6 (New York, United Nations, 1955), pp. 117-125; and E. Colson: "The intensive study of small sample communities", in R.F. Spencer (ed.): *Method and Perspective in anthropology* (Minneapolis, University of Minneeapolis Press, 1954), pp. 43-59. For a more recent treatment, see Carroll, especially Chapters 1, 2 and 10, which deal with general issues of analysing population data of relatively small communities: V. Carroll (ed.): *Pacific atoll populations* (Honolulu, University Press of Hawaii, 1975).

16. A taste of that tradition can be obtained five collections of articles edited by S.T. Kimball and J.B. Watson: *Crossing cultural boundaries: The anthropological experience* (San Francisco, Chandler, 1972); D. Hymes: *Reinventing anthropology* (New York, Random House, 1969), and R. Fox: *Encounter with anthropology* (New York, Harcourt Brace Jovanovich, 1968).

17. Texts of interest are C.A. Moser and G. Kalton: *Survey methods in social investigation* (London, Heinemann, 2nd ed., 1971); A.N. Oppenheim: *Questionnaire design and attitude measurement* (London, Heinemann, 1966); and especially E.R. Babbie: *Survey research methods* (Belmont, Wadsworch, 1973). The novice fieldworker on the verge of undertaking a project should also read some of the essays collected in B. Dasgupta (ed.): *Village studies in the Third World* (Delhi, Hindustan Publishing Corporation, 1978), especially those or Srinivas, Norman, Lipton and Moore and Lipton.

18. T.S. Epstein: "Re-surveys and re-studies of rural societies", in B. Dasgupta (ed.): *Village studies in the Third World*, op. cit., pp. 127-131.

19. In one of the classic examples, Oscar Lewis undertook a restudy of Robert Redfield's study community in Mexico to describe change but ended up writing a stinging reinterpretation of Redfield's findings. See O. Lewis: *Life in a Mexican village: Tepoztlan restudied* (Urbana, Ill., University of Illinois Press, 1951); R. Redfield: *Tepoztlan: A Mexican village* (Chicago, University of Chicago Press, 1930).

20. J. Wyon and J.E. Gordon: *The Khanna study: Population problems in the rural Punjab* (Cambridge, Mass., Harvard University Press, 1971).
21. The fact that an investigator has instituted some form of randomness in selecting a sample does not make it scientific. The basic criterion for a scientific sample is that is should be designed in such a way that standard errors of sample estimates can be computed.
22. R.E. Mitchell: "Survey materials collected in the developing countries: Sampling, measurement, and interviewing obstacles to intra—and inter-national comparisons", in *International Social Science Journal*, 1965, No. 4, pp. 665-685.
23. This being said, it is important to note that the Laguna study in the Philippines surveyed 573 rural households from 34 rural *barrios*, and collected somewhat more detailed data than listed here (see Boulier, 1976, for one report of the results). However, experience suggests that most survey researchers cannot obtain budgets, staff (professional, managerial and field) and background data comparable to the Laguna project. In any case, by most measures, a survey of around 600 households is fairly small. National samples are more often drawn in the thousands or tens of thousands. One is tempted to wonder whether the Laguna project might not have obtained equally interesting results had it been a community study rather than a sample survey, and in the process saved both money and effort.
24. Standing (1978b, p. viii) concentrates on female participation because it "has been most sensitive to economic and social influences". See also the articles in Standing and Sheehan (1978).
25. A somewhat dated review of definitions is presented in Y. Miura: "A comparative analysis of operational definitions of the economically active population in African and Asian statistics", in *World Population Conference, 1965*, Vol. 4, (New York, United Nations, 1967), pp. 372-379; while Standing (1978b, Chapter 2) provides a critique of a variety of measures of work.
26. Neale (1964) discusses problems of classifying activities from a cross-disciplinary perspective. His comments serve as a useful starting point for a deeper analysis of what constitutes an "economic activity".
27. The term "institutions" in this context does not refer only to formal legitimised groupings (like banks, governments and marriage) but also to patterns of group behaviour, such as the "institutions" of football-fan rowdiness, patron-client relationships, and "machismo".
28. Fuller discussions of this point are found in Hull and Hull (1977) and T.H. Hull, V.J. Hull, and M. Singarimbun: "Indonesia's family planning story: Success and challenge", in *Population Bulletin*, 1977, No. 6.

24

HANDICRAFT CHILD LABOUR

General information about the strength of child labour in India is available through the Census of Population data and the National Sample Survey Reports. However, we do not have detailed information about children working in some of the sectors of the economy. Fortunately some data relating to child labour employed in handicraft and handloom activities are available for Jammu and Kashmir which were collected under the first and the only handicraft census undertaken in the state in 1978-79. Though the census does not include government training and production centres where a large number of persons work and also excludes Kargil and Zanskar (their schedules did not reach in time) the data do throw useful light on the children working in this sector.

Magnitude and Status

Handicraft manufacture contributed 4.74 per cent of the net state domestic product in 1978-79. The production of craft gods increased from Rs. 30.79 crores in 1978-79 to Rs. 81.37 crores in 1983 and to Rs. 100 crores in 1987, while the employment increased from 99,990 to 1.65 lakh during 1978-79 to 1983.

Child labour is an important segment of the total work-force engaged in crafts. As per the census, 27,221 workers (27.77 per cent) were under 15 years of age. Though the break up of child labour employed in different crafts is not available, it has been estimated that embroidery and carpet are the major crafts in the state and, about 78 per cent of craft workers are engaged in these activities. Carpet weaving is particularly dominated by child workers with a large number of carpet weaving centres manned exclusively by children. Requirements of fixed capital in handicrafts being nominal, production of craft goods is undertaken mainly at the household type level. About 89.28 per cent of handicraft units are of household and most of the non-household units are operated by self-employed persons. Only 2.95 per cent of the units are classified as work centres where work is carried out on behalf of entrepreneurs and proprietors.

Of the 27,221 handicraft child workers, 16,964 were employed in the household units, 4,322 in non-household units and 5,935 in work centres. The first two types of units accounted for 70.70 and 15.41 per cent of child workers respectively. The census shows that 16,437 child workers (60 per cent) are hired workers and 10,784 are 'own family members'. It is worth noting that family workers are not less exploited. History is full of instances where parents themselves turn out to be the most ruthless exploiters of their own children. Hired persons may work for stipulated hours, but the working day for 'own family members' may extend beyond these hours.

Age and Sex

Data relating to child labour in the handicraft and handloom sectors together (96.02 per cent of the child workers are in handicraft sector) show that over 10,000 workers in these sectors are in the age group of five to nine years and about 18,257 are in the 10 to 14 age group. Together they account for 64.39 per cent of the workers under 15 years. Females accounted for 11.36 per cent of the child labour in the age group of five to nine years and 19.81 per cent in the 10 to 14 age group.

Work-force employed in handicrafts and handlooms in the state, is dominated by males. As per the census, a total of 1,15,559 workers were employed in these activities in 1978-79, of which only 27,636 were females. It follows that females constitute less than one-fourth (24 per cent) of craft work-force. In the case of child labour it is observed that of the 28,348 child workers employed 19,513 were males (68.83 per cent) and 8,835 females (31.17 per cent). It appears that the share of females in child labour is higher than their share in the total work-force. This is quite expected as a good number of female workers may give up work after getting married in non-artisan households. Females have acquired proficiency in all crafts. A survey of the employment pattern in major crafts shows females working side by side with males. However, they outnumber men in only one craft, namely, *zari* embroidery. They are concentrated in carpet, *namda* and *gabba* trades.

Levels of Literacy

Majority of working children, including the children of master craftsmen who dominate craft employment, are not economically well off. As per the census data, 97.41 per cent of children in the state were drawn to craft employment by poverty. Only 2.59 per cent of such workers sought employment due to lack of interest in studies. Obviously these children who work to support their families cannot be expected to be literate and educated as they have neither the resources nor the time to enroll in formal schools for a couple of years. In 1978-79, 40.81 per cent of handicraft child labour in the state were totally illiterate and another 28.65 per cent had below primary education (any child having attended a school even for a few months is considered below primary.) In other words, nearly seven-tenths of the working children were illiterate at the time of the handicraft census. Of the literates most had reached up to middle school level.

Working Hours and Wage Rates

Handicraft manufacture is primarily a household activity, undertaken on part time or full time basis, or even on a seasonal basis. Small and marginal farmers work as artisans mainly during lean agricultural seasons. As per the handicraft census, 78.5 per cent workers were engaged on full time basis, and the rest on part time basis. Nearly 28 per cent of the workers were employed on seasonal basis. It has been estimated that children are mostly employed on full time and full year basis though some of the children may work on seasonal and part time basis.

Child labour employed in handicrafts can be classified under four groups on the basis of working hours: below four hours; between four and six hours; form six to eight hours; and above eight hours. The largest number of workers (48.06 per cent) work for four to six hours, while about 31.29 per cent work for more than eight hours. The corresponding percentages for 'below four hours' and 'six to eight' hours groups, work out to be 16.45 and 4.20 per cent, respectively. Most of the child workers are employed near their residences, as 85.48 per cent of them travel less than 2 km. (sometimes a negligible distance) to reach their unit, while 1.36 per cent travel four to five km and the remaining 13.16 per cent travel 2 to 4 km to reach their work-place. Since most child workers belong to very poor households, the distances are covered on foot.

What compensation is obtained by child workers for their usually long working hours? It may be noted that there is no distinction between the work undertaken by child and adult workers as craft manufacturing involves mostly skilled work and children cannot be expected to be engaged in simpler and lighter aspects of craft manufacture. In the case of *sozni* embroidery, 87.7 per cent workers are embroiderers, 9.4 per cent are designers and the rest are dyers and washermen. In the case of carpet manufacture, 80.4 per cent workers are weavers, 16.1 per cent designers, 1.7 per cent script writers and 1.8 per cent dyers and washermen.

These workers can be classified under four wage groups, besides the category of 'unpaid' workers (12.63 per cent of the total) who are not paid any wages as these are mostly children without much experience and skill. These children work with master craftsmen till they acquire proficiency in craft work. The largest number of working children who constitute 37.47 per cent of the total child labour earn the daily wage rate between Rs. 2 and Rs. 2.50. About 16.92 per cent workers earn between Rs. 1 to Rs. 1.99 a day, 20.44 per cent earn between Rs. 2.50 to Rs. 5 a day, and the remaining 12.54 per cent workers earn less than a rupee a day. None earns more than Rs. 5 a day. It is worth noting that most adult workers also earn a low wage rate of Rs. 10 a day.

The daily earnings of these child workers are stated to have gone up appreciably after the conduct of the census in 1978-79. Fast growth of the handicraft sector is believed to have influenced wage rates very favourably. A sample survey of the carpet trade conducted recently reveals that the average daily earning of 48 per cent of the child workers exceeds Rs. 5, and 16 per cent of such workers earned more than Rs. 9 a day. However, the conditions of workers will not improve significantly as long as middlemen pocket most of the profits.

Legal actions taken so far against the system of child labour are not adequate, and we would like to put forward some suggestions in this context; First there is a need to conduct interdisciplinary studies to estimate the strength of child labour and to identify hazardous operations which should be banned for children. Secondly, craft training programmes should be conducted in regular schools only and stipend should be paid to those children who opt for craft training on a part-time basis. This will ensure primary education to the working children. These long duration programmes (four to five years) would also help in increasing the age of entry in craft employment. Thirdly, working conditions and working hours of children need to be regulated which could be done by constructing separate handicraft centres in each locality where the working conditions can be regulated. And fourthly, non-formal education should be provided to these working children and facilities like midday meals, weekly holidays and short breaks should also be ensured to them. Extending social welfare facilities to these children will go a long way in improving their condition.

REFERENCES & NOTES

1. Jolly, Richard. et al. (eds.), *Third World Employment Problems and Strategy*, (Penguin, Education) p. 10 1973. See also D. Turnhan and I. Jaeger, *The Employment Problem in less developed countries.* OECD, 1971.
2. For some implications of child labour see Klaus Voll. "Child Labour in the late 18th and 19th Centuries in Germany and some Theoretical Considerations". The paper was presented at a Seminar on "Child Labour in India and the New Legislation", organised by Friedrich Ebert Foundation at Srinagar from 4 to 7 May, 1987.
3. Burra, Neera. "On Preparing Action Plans for Child Labour Concentration Areas: Some Reflections", Ibid, p. 2.
4. For details relating to scope, coverage and findings of the census, see *Handicraft Census 1978-79* (Directorate of Handicrafts, Jammu and Kashmir Govt., Srinagar). 1981.
5. *Indicators of Economic Development: Jammu and Kashmir State* (Planning and Development Department, Directorate of Economies and Statistics, Govt. of Jammu and Kashmir) p. 9, 1984.
6. Pandit M.L. "Child Labour in Handicrafts of Kashmir". Paper presented at the seminar on "Child Labour in India and the New Legislation", op. cit., pp. 13-15.
7. *Report the Evaluation Study on Massive Carpet Training Programme*, (Directorate of Economics and Statistics, Govt. of Jammu and Kashmir, Srinagar) p. 15, 1979.

25

EXPLOITATION OF CHILD WORKERS IN THE LOCK INDUSTRY OF ALIGARH

Some 7,000 to 10,000 children below the age of 14 years work in the traditional lock industry in Aligarh in breach of the Factories Act and the more recently enacted Child Labour (Prohibition and Regulation) Act. Earning Rs. 5 to 10 a day, the children often work more than 20 hours at a stretch, inhaling vast quantities of metal dust and emerging powder. This industry is over 100 years old and is considered to be the traditional occupation of the people of Aligarh district Uttar Pradesh. It is concentrated, however, in Aligarh city and its adjoining areas.

Of the total population of 25,74,625 (1981) of Aligarh district, about 80,000 to 90,000 workers are involved directly or indirectly, in the lock industry. Of these approximately 7,000 to 10,000 are children below the age of 14 years. However, these are only estimates and no one is sure of the actual figures. According to the factory owners and government officials, there are only 5,000 child workers who comprise 8 per cent of the total labour force. It is also claimed that these children are working only as part of family labour. The actual facts are, however, different. This paper discusses these facts which are based upon a three-month study of the lock industry of Aligarh.

Lock Industry: Historical Background

The lock industry of Aligarh was started in 1860 by the Postal Department. In the early years, the making of locks was a village industry and locks or components of locks were made by the artisan in his home, using his family labour.[1] Many families, who found it difficult to support themselves only by agriculture or whose lands were usurped by the Thakurs and landlords also worked in it. As the demand for locks increased some families sold their lands and shifted to the city.

After the partition of India in 1947, there was a sudden shift in the social composition of lock makers. Many of the traditional lock makers in Aligarh city who were Muslims, and who were master craftsmen and the backbone of the industry, went away to

* We would like to express our sincere thanks to Mr. Krishna Raj, Editor of *Economic and Political Weekly* to allow us to publish this paper. Editors.

Pakistan. Gradually, however, Punjabi Hindus migrated to Aligarh and set up small units by hiring labour. This led to the mass production of locks.

The present lock industry at Aligarh comes largely under small scale and cottage industry sectors. Locks or parts of locks are made in almost every home in the old city. It is estimated that about 80 per cent of the country's locks are made in Aligarh district.

There are two methods of making padlocks. One is the traditional method where the lock maker designs a lock and gets an order from the trader who is usually also the financier. Once an order is placed, the lock maker gives the raw material, namely brass or iron, to the *dhalai* or moulder (who usually belongs to a scheduled caste) along with a model. The *dhalai* casts all the pieces according to specifications and returns them to the lock maker who then files them. The components like the handle, springs, and keys are brought from the market. The lock is assembled and sent to the trader who polishes it, gets his brand name engraved and sells it. Well known locks such as Harrison, Plaza and Parker are made thus.

The smaller and less expensive locks are mass produced in factories. In this process, the manufacturers have their own production units where they cut scrap iron sheets (MSA) on power presses, for the outer cover of locks, the lid, flat keys, etc. Other parts of the lock like the handle, are also cut and bent in big factories. Once this is done, the work shifts to the hand-presses where the components are smoothened, holes pierced in keys or key holes pierced in lock cases. These rusted components of locks are either sent for *dhol* or drum polishing on buffing machines and are then electroplated. It is worth noting that all the processes (of which there are approximately 45) are not carried out in the same premises. Most of the factories get some parts made outside on a contract basis and it is the responsibility of the contractor to get the work done. All workers are paid on a piece-rate basis and work up to 48 hours at a stretch when the work load is heavy.

In the big factories, components are cut and then farmed out to artisans to do the filling, finishing, etc. There are different contractors for different jobs. Some people are paid by the gross, others are given a weekly wage and still others are remunerated according to lots. Ninety-five per cent of the workers have no protection as they are piece-rate workers. Normally workers do not own any machines.

Participation of Children

Children are employed to work on hand-presses which cut different components of locks. They are also engaged in electroplating, polishing pieces on buffing machines, in spray panting units, in the assembling and packing of locks, etc. Of all the processes, polishing, electroplating, spray painting and working on hand-presses are the most hazardous processes, particularly for child workers. The hand presses become particularly dangerous because children work for 12 to 14 hours a day on them. Children frequently meet with accidents and lose the tips of their fingers which get caught in the machines. Also, polishing process of rusted metal on a buffing machine is equally hazardous because the bobs are covered with emery powder. The piece is held by hand against the bob and the rusted portion is polished off with the face of the worker within 10 inches of the machine. The worker is bent over and directly inhales the emery powder and metal dust which covers him from head to toe. If a piece slips from the hand of the worker, it severely injures another worker. More than 60 per cent of the workers here are less than 14 years of age. Children of eight to nine years can be seen working very late at night. Those who are too young to work on the machine, work on polishing with gum discs and then cover them with "the black *masala*". The process of polishing generates a lot of dust and therefore the buffing machines are kept in a separate place.

Most of the buff polishing work is done in the Upper Kote *mohallas* where there is maximum concentration of unregulated units. There is no control over hours of work, wages, etc. in these units, and more than 70 per cent of the workers here are children below the age 14 years.

Electroplating is another extremely hazardous process in which more than 70 per cent of workers are children. These children are engaged in trying polished metal pieces on cooper wires, which are then strung on roads and submerged in acid and alkaline baths. It is not possible to enter the units because of the noxious fumes. Electroplating work is hazardous because the chemicals used are potassium cyanide, trisodium phosphate, sodium silicate, hydrochloric acid, sulfuric acid, sodium hydroxide, chromic acid and barium hydroxide which are extremely dangerous. The hands of children remain in these solutions for the better part of 12 hours a day. Moreover, an electric current passes through these chemical tanks and children often get shocks. The wet floors also cause accidents. Although most units have converters, which transform AC current into DC, and though this does not exceed 10 volts, the illegal connections taken from street lights sometimes lead to electrocution. In none of the units workers wear gloves or aprons, and there are no exhaust fans. Many units work through the night.

At least 50 per cent of the total labour force in the spray painting units is below 14 years. They carry pieces of metal to the painting table and pass them on to the man who holds the spray gun. In this process, they inhale substantial quantities of paint and paint thinners with grave consequences on their lungs.

Child Labour, But Adult Unemployment

A recent study done by the inter disciplinary group of the Aligarh Muslim University (AMU) revealed that while there is a demand for child labour, there is also high adult underemployment. The study observed that as against 1,560 children below 15 years of age there were more than 2000 adults between 16-59 years and 62 persons above 60 years of age in these families. Employers prefer children because children can be paid less and exploited more. Adults may revolt at least in principle if not so far in practice.

Wage Structure

There is no uniform wage structure in the lock industry. In one assembling unit, the man said he paid children Rs. 25 a month for a 10-hour day while children in the polishing unit earn up to Rs. 15 a day if they work 12 to 15 hours a day. In electroplating, children earn Rs. 5 to 10 a day depending upon the number of working hours. Two children reported that they sometimes work for 36 hours at a stretch and earn 60 paise an hour as overtime. Many children work without wages particularly in the polishing units. After training they earned Rs. 50 a month. A man is able to earn Rs. 600 a month only after working 10 to 15 years at 14 hours a day.

There is no fixed wage rate for different jobs. For example, for cutting a keyhole in the lock case with a pointed chisel and fitting the key, a child earns Rs. 3 per thousand. He can complete 500 to 1000 holes in a day. Sometimes, a child is paid 30 to 35 paise per gross also. Likewise, in an electroplating unit a child could tie 1,000 to 1,500 locks/ handles on copper wires and is paid at the rate of Rs. 2 to 3 per 1000. The rate was also fixed at 30 paise per gross. ON an average a child earns Rs. 50 a month after an initial period of apprenticeship (up to one year) during which he earns nothing. After a few years, he earns between Rs. 125 and Rs. 150 per month plus on overtime depending upon the urgency of the order and the mood of the contractor. He is not entitled to any other benefit like casual leave, medical assistance and provident fund.

Health Hazards

Those who work on buffing machines for long periods, tend to suffer from chest disorders, particularly tuberculosis. Polishers inhale vast quantities of metal dust and emery powder in the course of their work and consequently they have difficulty in swallowing and breathing. I met two boys working as polishers aged eight and 12 years respectively, both suffering from tuberculosis. Those working in electroplating units tend to suffer from asthmatic condition. However, even though they know the dangers of the work, they are forced to employ their children on the same work later on. As Nabi Ahmed, a worker, put it, this is *'duniya dari'* or the 'way of the world'.

Children sometimes taste the liquid in the chemical tanks out of curiosity and either get seriously ill or even die. But there is no accurate information about deaths or accidents. The case of Gyan Prakash, a 35 year old worker in the Tiger Lock Factory near Marris Road, is indeed very shocking. He was responsible for mixing chemicals in the tanks with his gloves on. One morning, he made a solution with potassium cyanide using his hands. Though he washed his hands before eating, he started vomiting blood after lunch. He was rushed to the Employees State Insurance Corporation (ESIC) hospital. He was ill for a long time and never went back to work. He thinks that perhaps the gloves he used while mixing was slightly torn, which caused the accident. He thinks that electroplating is very dangerous, particularly to children. But as a worker put it: "the owner is only interested in the profit. What difference does it make to him if the worker lives or dies?" One adolescent youth complained of breathlessness ever since he received an electric shock. Another electroplating worker was saved in the nick of time and a young worker of about 15 to 16 years of age was unconscious for a long time after he received a shock.

Painting units are very hot due to the combined impact of paint thinners, the bright lights, the ovens and long hours of work. All these have an adverse effect on workers' physical and mental health. But a worker who left this work after 15 years wants to send his son into it!

Occupational Diseases

Doctors, workers as well as unit owners believe that except for electrocution or consumption of dangerous chemicals, there is no immediate health hazard to children. However, no systematic medical survey has ever been made, and therefore, the exact nature of the health problems children are affected by is not known. The common ailments like cough, cold, temperature and breathlessness are generally ignored. However, one can see signs of pneumoconiosis, tuberculosis and bronchitis after the child has worked for five to six years. Figures of pneumoconiosis, vary from 5 to 40 per cent but details are not available. The capacity of the lungs of the workers in the polishing units gets greatly reduced causing breathlessness, but nobody knows the extent of this or the deaths caused by it. Everywhere in the Upper Kote area, people talked of death and diseases directly related to their work, but no one could give me exact numbers or percentages. Doctors say that almost all the workers, adults and children, who work in these units get tuberculosis.

While pneumoconiosis is an occupational disease which exists amongst workers in buff polishing and electroplating units, no doctor knows what happens to these patients. Pneumoconiosis, is caused by dust particles within the size range of 0.5 to 0.3 microns. After a period of exposure to these dust particles, fibrosis is caused in the lungs which may cripple a man and reduce his working capacity. There is no cure for it and the only thing that can be done is to prevent secondary infection by removing the person from the place of work. The workers however, are not in a position to take long-term treatment and leave their jobs. Children, being illegal workers, cannot avail of the facility of the ESIC hospital. The other occupational diseases prevalent amongst lock makers, particularly those working in electroplating and painting units, are occupational dermatitis, eczema and perhaps even cancer. Occupational dermatitis is caused, amongst other things, by chemicals such as acids, alkalies and dyes etc.[2] Workers in electroplating plants are likely to suffer from lung cancer which is an occupational hazard for nickel and chromium workers.[3]

Only a few studies have been made on the health status of lock workers. One important study is that of Mohammad Anees (1978)[4] who concentrated on chest disorders amongst adult and child workers. Anees' study says that exposure to vapours of lead, copper, zinc, brass and iron, etc., may produce metal fume fever, an acute febrile illness that clinically resembles bacterial infection of the lungs[5]. The inhalation of nickel in the form of carbonyl or dust, gives rise to bronchopneumonia or cancer of the lungs and nasal sinuses.[6] The study also points out that the worker in the industry is exposed to mineral dusts, specially to dusts of iron and brass. While polishing he may get an additional exposure to chrome mist, nickel and other inorganic and organic dusts. Since the majority of workers are employed in ill-ventilated and overcrowded premises, the likelihood of chest diseases is very high. It was also noticed that the proportion of workers from small factories had a higher percentage (40 per cent) of chest disease against 23.6 per cent from the bigger factories. Annes's research showed that pulmonary tuberculosis, chronic bronchitis and short respiratory illnesses were the common chest diseases suffered by lock workers.

All the health hazards have an adverse impact on the life of the workers. The interdisciplinary study by the Aligarh Muslim University sited earlier observed that the poor living and working conditions cause so much damage to health that living beyond 50 years becomes difficult.[7] Unfortunately, the lock industry is not a forbidden occupation either under the Employment of Children Act, 1938 (now repealed) or under the new Child Labour (Prohibition and Regulation) Act, 1986. However, this industry clearly is hazardous to children and as per Article 24 of the Constitution, their employment must be banned.

When we examine the provisions of the Factories Act of 1948, it becomes apparent that they are being blatantly violated in the lock industry of Aligarh. The act unambiguously lays down (section 67) that children below the age of 14 are prohibited from working in a factory. But the evidence collected in this study points to the fact that this provision is implemented largely in the breach. Some factory owners evade the law by circumventing it. For example, they partition their premises into small units and isolate the areas where work is being done with power, and thereby escape the definition of a 'factory'. Their workers therefore do not receive the benefits of paid leave, medical assistance, provident funds, etc. By this device, they also evade excise duty as their units are then considered small-scale units or cottage units. The regulations under the Factories Act to protect the interests of children above 14 years of age are also not followed. All children above 14 are supposed to be registered but no one maintains any register. Also, children are not supposed to work for more than four and a half hours a day or during the night, but in reality they commonly do.

The escape clause that unit owners may employ their own children has come in very handy for them. Our investigation showed that frequently many children reported as children of the owners, are not their children. For example, in one unit the owner started by saying that the children working there were his brothers. But after talking for about 15 minutes, he came around to saying that the boys were actually *mohalla* brothers or brothers of the locality.

Some Recommendations

In order to oversee the ban and make it possible to regulate working conditions, the first step necessary is to shift the units doing the hazardous jobs of polishing, electroplating and spray painting from the city centre and the *mohalla* to an area like the industrial estate. To facilitate this shift, government may consider offering plots of land at concessional rates to small entrepreneurs provided they do not employ children. Other incentives like cheaper electricity tariffs and subsidised raw materials, could be given to the units not using child labour. Along with the carrot of such facilities, the stick of stringent penal action should be kept in readiness. Those units that continue to employ children in these processes should be severely fined and closed down, if necessary. Every unit must be registered even if it is not getting any aid from the government and owners must not be allowed to engage even their own children in these obviously hazardous processes.

The advantages of bringing these widely dispersed units out of the city centre and homes are many. Apart from giving loans to install exhaust fans and adopt other safety measures to prevent undue health hazards to workers, exercising proper control over working conditions will become much easier. Moreover, centralised facilities for recreation, toilets, drinking water and rest rooms could be provided for the community of workers rather than making each entrepreneur individually responsible. Medical care could also be given to those workers not covered by the ESIC scheme.

Keeping in mind the poverty of the children we do not recommend banning of child labour in the short run. These children however should be employed in filing, assembling and packing, which are not hazardous to their health. However, children should not be allowed to enter the factory as it is difficult to control their work once they enter it. Such activities should be organised in outside centres where non-formal education and feeding programmes also can be organised. To the extent possible, the small entrepreneur who just about manages to stay afloat should not be displaced. Sudden and drastic changes are likely to make child labour even more unregulated and exploited.

Changes also need to be made in the new Child Labour (Prohibition and Regulation) Act, 1986. Firstly, the provision which allows children to work in hazardous processes if they are a part of family labour needs to be deleted. Secondly, the processes of electroplating, polishing, spray painting and working on hand-presses should be included in the schedule of hazardous operations attached to the act. Thirdly, the act allows only the Child Labour Technical Advisory Committee to determine whether any processes/industries are harmful for the health of children. It will be useful if individuals or organisations are allowed to bring to the notice of the competent authority the health hazards in any unit or industry. The advisory committee may call the complainant and receive his evidence and investigate the veracity of the charges made. It will not then be possible to dismiss the complaints of the concerned industries/groups without investigation. Such an amendment will allow it to become more broad-based and provide an opportunity to the journalist, the social worker or the voluntary agency to put to good use his or her findings.

In conclusion, one may say that the need of the hour is to investigate different industries from the point of view of their impact upon the health of children and whenever necessary, take steps to see that the children of the poor are protected against the entrepreneur in search of profit.

REFERENCES AND NOTES

1. See "Inter-Disciplinary Study on Muslim Entrepreneurs in Aligarh" (draft), nd., Aligarh Muslim University, Aligarh, p. 20.
2. *Ibid.*, p. 501
3. *Ibid.*, p. 500
4. See Anees Mohammad (1978), "Epidemiology of the Chest Disease in Lock Workers in Aligarh (Uttar Pradesh)", thesis for MD Department of Preventive and Social Medicine, Jawaharalal Nehru Medical College, Aligarh Muslim University, Aligarh.
5. *Ibid.*, p. 7
6. *Ibid.*, p. 8
7. *Inter-Disciplinary Study*, op. cit., p. 20

26

CHILD LABOUR IN THE CARPET INDUSTRY

"We cut our fingers but no blood falls. . . ."

Carpet weaving was introduced in India in the sixteenth century by the Mughal Emperors. During the reign of Akbar and Shahjahan, imperial carpet factories were established in Agra, Delhi and Lahore. With the departure of the Mughals, however, the factories experienced a decline. The rebirth of the Indian carpet industry dates back to the first half of the twentieth century, when carpet production for export was launched on a commercial scale. Today India exports about 95 per cent of its carpets, as the expensive floor covering is beyond the reach of all but the small, higher income segment of the population.

Carpet making has spread from Kashmir to the Southern tip of India. But Uttar Pradesh produces 80 per cent of the total carpets and has 80 per cent of the weavers. Rajasthan produces fine and medium quality carpets ranging from 100 to 280 knots per square inch. Jaipur, Tonk, Sikar and Bikaner are the main centres for carpet manufacture. There are about 6,000 carpet looms employing about 30,000 people in the state. It is estimated that there will be an annual increase of 10 per cent in the market for carpets, which means there will be 3,000 new entrants every year.

Rajasthan, having a sheep population of about 10 million, is a leading wool producing state in the country with 14 million tons of wool production per year. Of this 60 per cent is suitable for carpet weaving. The nomadic tribes in Rajasthan had been traditionally weaving *namadas,* roughly finished carpets, for their own domestic use. It is only in the mid twentieth century that carpet production on a large organised scale started in the state because of its export potential. Entrepreneurs from Uttar Pradesh and Punjab established factories with 25 to 200 looms for carpet weaving in Rajasthan. Today, however, entrepreneurs prefer to subcontract the work into smaller units with three to ten looms employing less than 20 persons to escape labour laws. Looms are now spread in weavers' homes where children work on a large scale. Carpets are woven in the small sheds or in weavers' homes and then taken to the main exporter/entrepreneur who has a centralised work site for the finishing process.

The weavers are mostly Muslims or belong to Scheduled Castes who either own small pieces of land where they barely manage to produce some coarse grain, or own no land and practice their traditional crafts such as slaughtering animals making shoes and weaving cloth. Most of these families took to carpet weaving 12 to 15 years ago when there was a need in the industry.

It is estimated that roughly 30,000 workers are employed in this industry of whom about 40 per cent are children below 15 years. Accurate data are difficult because most of the looms are in houses or in small sheds not registered, and hence technically, do not exist. Labour inspectors never bother to visit them and they maintain no records of the labour employed by them.

Manufacturers commission knotters in distant villages and supply them with dyed woollen yarn and a specific design and size. Some knotters own their looms, while others are provided with looms by middlemen or contractors who act as a link between dealers/exporters and knotters. Sometimes, large carpet manufacturers/exporters in towns and cities lend weavers money for purchasing looms. The exporter pays the middleman for the goods and the middleman pays the weaver according to the work produced. Usually the exporter has no direct contract with the knotter. In rural areas, children and adults work in their free time, while in urban areas they work full time. Children employed on the looms work from 8 a.m. to 6 p.m. with an hour's break for lunch and if working in a factory, get a day off per week. They earn Rs 8 to 15 per day and Rs 150 to 300 per month. After the contractor's commission (14 to 15 per cent) the rest is paid to the parents. For the same work done, an adult is paid one to one and a half times more. The labour component is usually 43 per cent of the total cost, though for high quality carpets it may go up to 60 to 70 per cent.

The cost per sq. ft. for carpet with 14 × 10 knots per sq. inch will be about Rs. 115 (for 4 × 6 carpet). The selling price of FRG customers comes to Rs. 293.36 per sq. ft. This fetches 75 per cent profit after the deduction of all costs of transport, freight etc. it is interesting to note that the selling price of the carpet is Rs. 111.53 against the cost of Rs. 115. The loss is borne by the government as it provides an incentive of 17 per cent (Rs. 20) which gives an approximate profit of 14.5 per cent (Rs. 17). In other words, the industry's savings are mainly because of the government incentives for exports. This implies that India's tax payers are subsidising the German importers.

It has been estimated that two workers on an average, earn about Rs. 1200 (at the rate of Rs. 50 per sq. ft.) in two months, that is, each earns Rs. 300 per month. A carpet for which a German customer pays Rs 7041, gives only Rs. 600 to the workers, while the manufacturer gets Rs. 400 as profit. For poorer quality carpets the labour component is only 40 per cent and hence earnings from weaving are also much less.

Working Environment in Family Units

It is observed that the houses in which family units operate are small, consisting of a small verandah, one or two rooms and a small courtyard at the back. The loom is set up in the front verandah or in the courtyard. All the male members work on the loom whenever they can get time. A five ft loom will take three workers while a 7 ft loom takes 4 workers. They work from 8 a.m. to 5 p.m. with a lunch break. A male child is taught to knot the carpets as early as at the age of five to six years. After one year he starts working on his own. It is the responsibility of adult male members to work on the loom in family units. There is less pressure on children. Some children go to school also. However, women/girls do not work on the loom. Most of them make *bandhini* (tie and dye). The wage payment by the contractor is made to the head of the family at a rate agreed upon earlier. The child gets no wage separately.

Carpet knitting demands complete concentration and therefore is a tremendous strain on the eyes. The children work almost eight hours a day with the wool fluff constantly getting into their lungs. The children as well as adults therefore look very weak. One hardly sees male children playing or laughing in the colonies. The only sound one hears is of the knotter counting the knots softly.

Factory Units

In factory type units the looms and other equipment are set up under a shed. The employer recruits labourers through contractors each of whom takes the responsibility of one or more loom. The contractor learns the design and explains it to the weavers who then know the craft well.

At least three quarters of the knotters are children, of whom some are as young as five or six years old. We noticed three or four children who were barely four years old, who were not weaving but would start after a few months after observing their brothers at work. The work begins at 8 a.m. There is no question of being late as the contractor will see to it that they are on time. The children work non-stop till 5 p.m. or 5.30 p.m. with a break of 45 minutes to one hour for lunch during which they eat a frugal meal of *rotis.* onion and, may be some *dal* brought from home. Running water is available, because the carpets have to be washed, but there are no toilet facilities. In case of accidents or ill health, the employer takes no responsibility. If at all, it is the contractor who might take the child to a doctor or usually just send him home. There were no first aid boxes to be seen. The sheds are dark and poorly ventilated. The floors are usually of mud. The looms are surface looms and the child sits crouched on the platform which is barely one to one and a half feet wide with his eyes fixed on the loom for hours at a stretch breathing wool fluff which gets into his lungs. Most of the children have an unhealthy and resigned look about them as the joys and fun of childhood are denied to them.

During the training period, they only get 25 to 50 paise per day as pocket money and the parent is given Rs 25 to 30 per month. After learning for one year, they earn Rs. 7 to 8 per day. The adults are paid Rs. 55 to 20 per day. Children with 'nimble fingers' work faster and are able to produce more in comparison with adults, but they make mistakes also. Wages are paid to the parents by the contractor, who takes a part as his commission. Often large advances and loans are taken by parents and then the child becomes almost a bonded labourer, never able to break away from the clutches of the contractor. It is observed that organised carpet units are gradually closing down and work is given to individuals working in their homes so as to avoid labour laws.

Children in factories live in awe of the contractor. They have to produce a given amount of work every day, and if they weave less, their wages are cut. The parents and the Seth (the owner) also will be angry. They live under constant dread. They therefore take a holiday on the slightest excuse and work for about 15 to 16 days a month. The physical strain of weaving also is too much as they have to sit on their haunches to be able to knot, with the stomach muscles constantly pressed, legs and knee joints suffering intense pain, and eyes feeling the strain. Any distraction invariably means a mistake in the knotting. According to the older children the body soon gets used to these discomforts. It is argued that as adults cannot do so, children are preferred for this work.

What about first aid or medical treatments in the events of accidents? The normal answer would be a sarcastic laugh "If fingers get cut we put some tumeric paste or *mehendi* paste and go back to work. Our fingers are bloodless—no blood falls". These children do not grow well physically. Their legs lose their strength and they become incapable of doing any other work. Their body remains small, but the face looks old. They remain anaemic and suffer from constant colds due to inhaling dust and wool fluff. Most children seem to have weak eyes. No medical surveys have been conducted by the Rajasthan government to assess the affect of carpet weaving on the health of the children and therefore no information is available on this.

Legal Position

Carpet weaving is banned for children under the "Employment of Children Act, 1938" and under the Child Labour Act of 1986. However, in Rajasthan, the government is running 35 grant-in-aid training centres with trainees between the ages of eight and fifteen years. These children work from 8 a.m. to 5 p.m. with an hour's lunch break and earn Rs. 60 as monthly stipend. The work place is dark, dingy and small. It has been found that almost 42 per cent of the trained children continue to practice the craft and about 58 per cent trainees come mainly for stipend. Carpets produced here are sold through the Rajasthan Government Emporium. This is indeed a typical example of a government violating an act which has been in existence since 1938 and been reinforced in 1986.

Our investigation showed that parents send their children for carpet weaving mainly because they need children's income for survival and there are no other job opportunities around.

What is the Solution?

What is the solution to this glaring exploitation of children? According to one view, as expressed by Prof. R. Champakalakshmi, "it would be neither feasible nor fair to prevent the children from working in the present economic situation", because their families will suffer if they do not work. According to her the approach should be to improve their working conditions on one hand and to extend the facilities of education, nutrition and health care on the other. She suggests that:

1. Carpet weaving should be encouraged as a cottage industry and the craft should be taught to children in schools.
2. The Government should encourage cooperatives of weaving families by giving them loans and by helping them in procuring raw material and in marketing so that they get out of the clutches of the big manufacturers. The benefits then would reach the poor weaver who will send his children to school instead of putting them out to work at an early age.
3. Every school-going child should be given a stipend along with one free nutritional meal. The stipend will somewhat offset the loss in income and the free meal will ensure healthy growth of the child.
4. The working conditions of the children in this industry must be improved. In the factory sheds, the lighting and ventilation should be improved. The flooring should be cemented so that it could be swept clean after a day's work so that the dust or fluff is not inhaled by children. The bench on which the children sit should be made wider so that even in a crouched position, they must be slightly more comfortable and the working hours are regulated.
5. It should be made compulsory for all shed owners to see that the children working for them are given at least the basic education within or outside the premises, and the daily schedule should be planned in such a way that afternoons are free for schooling.
6. The shed owner should be asked to provide a simple, nutritious midday meal with a glass of milk. Regular medical check ups should be done at all factory sites in the weaving colonies in towns and villages.
7. The exporters who get a cash incentive from the government for carpet exports should create a fund for improving the educational, nutritional and health care of the children working in their industries.
8. Women should be encouraged to take to carpet weaving and to set up small units of their own in urban areas. State governments should provide loans and training facilities for the purpose.
9. Child Labour Laws must be effectively implemented at least in organised units. Also, a time limit must be set so that factory owners replace all child workers with adult labour.
10. Consciousness should be created in the minds of politicians, parents, labour contractor and employers about this abhorrent practice, and the government should be persuaded to take suitable legal actions. Trade unions should take

up the cause of child labour and gradually work towards the abolition of this practice. They must realise that every child worker can be replaced by an adult and this will lead to increase in adult employment.

The problem of child labour in India is of immense magnitude and of complex nature. It is seen that a child worker by the time he becomes 35 years of age is a total physical wreck and he cannot earn much. The survivor then sends his child to work, and this cycle goes on. There is a need to create more awareness and consciousness in our society so that parents, employers and the government realise the harm which is done to the child by stifling his natural instincts, by forcing him to work and by denying him the freedom to laugh, play and educate himself.

APPENDIX-1

The Carpet Manufacturing Process

1. Wool is procured from wholesalers as undyed yarn in banks. It is cleaned and dyed and made into balls by first unravelling the woolen yarn and making it into a single strand. The ball is made according to the play.
2. The loom which is basically a wooden frame is set up with the required tension and the balls of wool placed on top according to the design.
3. Threads of yarn are stretched from the upper beam to the lower beam as warp threads.
4. The knotting is done between the cotton yarn with the woollen strand according to the design. Each knot is cut off with a knife as per the required length.
5. When a row of knots is complete the weft thread is beaten into position with a heavy metal comb to pack it tight.
6. Once the weaving is complete the carpet is taken off the loom and the binding of the edges is done.
7. The carpets are then washed in a solution of caustic soda and other chemicals and hung up to dry.
8. While still a little damp the carpets are stretched on a frame to give them complete symmetry in shape.
9. The carpets are then spread out for clipping which is done with long sharp scissors by trained adults. The carpet is now ready for the market.

APPENDIX-2

SALES FROM HANDMADE WOOLEN CARPETS FROM RAJASTHAN*

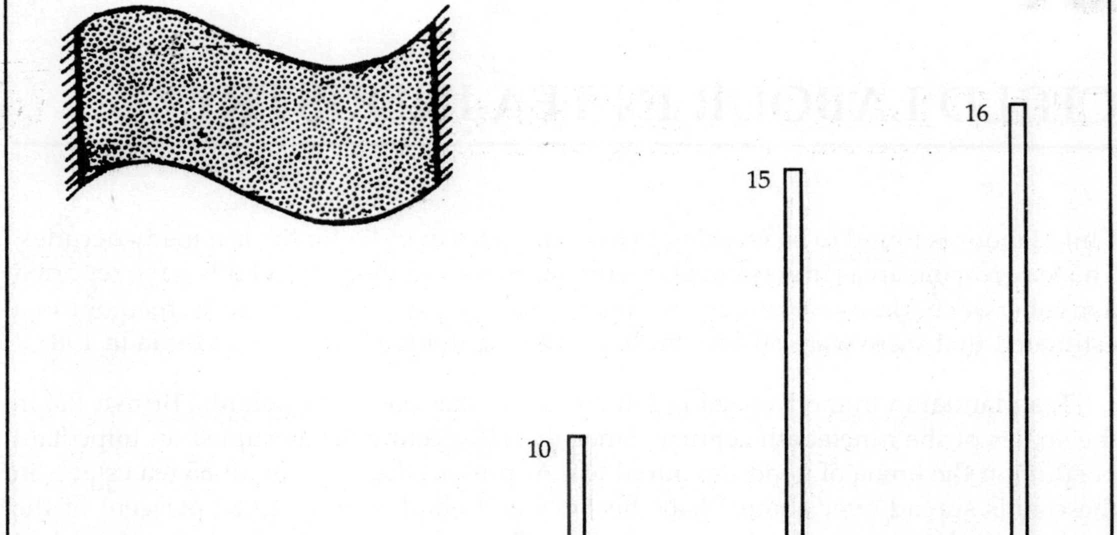

*Courtesy: Rajasthan Carpet Manufacturers and Exporters Association, Jaipur

Figures in crores (Rs.)

27

CHILD LABOUR IN TEA INDUSTRY

Child labour is found to be working in the tea estates in India for the last many decades. The tea growing areas in Assam, Darjeeling, Dooars and the Nilgiri Hills have reported a number of children working regularly in the tea gardens. The Labour Bureau of India estimated that there were 80,499 children working in tea plantations in India in 1980.

Tea plantation in the Darjeeling hill areas was started by the colonial British Raj in the sixties of the nineteenth century. Since then Darjeeling has occupied an important position in the arena of good flavoured tea. At present there are about 85 tea estates in these hills spread over about 14,400 hectares and employing 70 to 80 per cent of the workers in the region directly or indirectly. Darjeeling produces between 11 and 13 million kg. of tea annually which still fetches the highest price in the world tea market.

Child Labour: A Numerical Estimate

The British advocated the employment of families rather than individuals, thus absorbing women and children in their labour force. This practice was continued by the Indian tea planters also in the early post-Independence period. We do not have an accurate estimate of the strength of child labour in Darjeeling as the available estimates vary widely. The micro-level employment study of 76 estates conducted by the Indian Institute of Hill Economy, Darjeeling, show that on an average tea estates employed about 470 local children and many more outside children. The average number of children employed in an estate varied from zero to 38. The estimate of the number of child labour made by the Tea Board in Tea Statistics (1982-83) however, is much lower. These vast differences in the estimated numbers is itself is an issue which needs thorough scrutiny.

Nature of Occupation

Both the estimates show that: (a) child labour is prevalent mainly in the field operations and not in the factory operations; (b) the number of child labour coming from outside the respective tea estates is quite significant; and (c) most of the child labourers are not permanent employees of the tea estates, but are employed as casual or temporary workers. Children perform field operations like replanting, pruning, plucking, sowing, manuring and weed control, as well as non-field operations like carrying firewood from the godowns to the allotted houses and carrying plucked tea leaves to the factory or to the weighing centres. Some of these are too strenuous for children. The number of child labour on tea estates increases during March and September when there is maximum work on the estates. As the regular workers are not able to cope with this rush, child labour both from within and outside are put into services. Labourers consider this season to be an earning season to buy some household durable items, and therefore offer as many children as possible for work.

The payments to child labour are mainly made on piece-rate basis. The two main basis for payments are known as *hazira* and *ticca*. The *hazira* is daily wage paid to each workers on completion of a particular task which has been allotted to him for the day. A worker is paid *hazira* for the operations like plucking, sorting and withering. *Ticca* refers to overtime work as well as extra plantation work given on contract.

Wage Issues

The wage payments system in the Darjeeling tea industry is not satisfactory at all. The profit making philosophy which has strictly guided the colonial tea planters has not changed so far. Though a new set of planters mainly with a merchant's background have emerged in the last three decades, they are no less in deriving the legitimate share of the tea workers. Being the most vulnerable section of the labour force, child labourers are the worst suffers. Children received 12 paise per day *hazira* rate till 1950. However, in 1951 when the Plantation Labour Act was passed, there was a marginal improvement in the average money earnings for children. The second Minimum Wage Fixation Committee for Tea Plantation in 1973 once again increased wages for child labour to Rs. 1.50 per day. In 1985, the daily wage of a child labour was Rs. 4.57, which was utterly inadequate in the context of the high cost of living in the hills.

Social Issues

The adverse effects on the mental and physical development of the child labourers on tea plantations are indeed very alarming. These children are deprived of basic education as the nature of the work does not allow children to continue in the school. The main teaching period in the schools coincides with the peak plucking season, when school-going children are either withdrawn permanently or are made to remain absent for two to three months. This lack of education has naturally an adverse affect on the employment and productivity of children in future.

The physical development of these children also causes a deep concern. Many of these children suffer from impaired health caused by malnutrition or by chronic diseases like tuberculosis and goitre. Very few tea estates have basic health amenities or a permanent doctor. As most of the parents are drunkards their children also imbide the same habits at a very early age. Tables 27.1 and 27.2 show that the recommended food intake in the hills is much higher than on the plains. But despite the higher requirements of the calories and other vital elements, the intakes of these children are much lower than the recommended levels for the plains. It is suggested therefore that the fixation of need-based minimum wages should not bypass the calorie requirements and other amenity requirements by the hill children, such as, warm clothing and shoes. The nutritional requirement of child labour in the hills should be re-examined taking into account the most authoritative scientific data on the subject. In this context the estimate made by the National Nutritional Advisory Committee is quite supportive. As per its estimate a child of six to fourteen years of age requires 2,010 calories in general and higher in the hills. Darjeeling tea industry should also formulate its wage policies with this perspective in view. Another important requirement is to give permanency of employment to children after six months or so, so that, he is entitled to a house, a monthly salary and other benefits.

TABLE 27.1

Recommended Consumption of Food Items for Children in Hills

(in gm)

	Age Groups		*13-15 yrs*	
Food Items	*Boys*	*Girls*	*Boys*	*Girls*
Cereals	420	380	510	470
Pulses	45	45	45	40
Vegetables	100	100	90	120
Roots and tubers	30	30	50	30
Milk	250	250	200	200
Oil and fat	40	35	40	30
Sugar and jaggery	45	45	40	30

Source: *Handbook of Food and Nutrition Statistics*, pp. 32-33, 1982.

TABLE 27.2

Food Intake of Child in West Bengal and Sikkim

	Protein (gm)	*Calories (K. cal)*	*Iron (mg)*	*Vitamin A (mg)*
West Bengal	34.8	1231	18.00	453
Sikkim	38.0	1504	21.0	304

Source: *Ibid.*, pp. 47-48.

The trade unions is the region have so far shown very little awareness and interest in this crucial area of child labour. However, some voluntary agencies in the region like Hayden hall, have done some work to provide literacy, better employment, better health and recreational facilities to child labour. There is a need to intensify these efforts.

28

CHILD LABOUR IN DIAMOND PROCESSING UNITS

Diamond cutting industry has emerged as one of the major industrial sectors in the Indian economy. The diamond processing and allied activities have proliferated quite dramatically during the last two decades or so. The growth has been particularly marked during the last decade. Paucity of exact information does not permit precise measurement, but it is estimated that in the early seventies the industry employed about 20,000 workers but by the early eighties it was employing around 3 lakh workers.

Diamond cutting and polishing industry is highly export oriented and can generate substantial employment. Huge capital and high technical skills are not needed to start it. Consequently, entry into the industry is easy and often it is possible for a worker to own his enterprise in a short span of time (about five years). The industry is largely constituted by small size (unregistered) enterprises.

Different studies relating to the industry have paid attention to its global ramifications as well its emergence in India as a major processing centre of rough diamonds.[1] The purpose of this paper is however limited. We aim at understanding the income profile and the future prospects of the work-force that must have entered the industry as child labour. Our inferences are based on a case study of Surat (1978-79) where information was collected from 204 firms and 500 workers.[2] It must be confessed at the outset that our main intention was to portray the functioning of firms and study the working conditions and levels of living of the work-force engaged in the industry. Child labour was not directly focussed on but we did discover that 7 per cent of the work-force (35 out of 500), who gave their work experience must have entered the industry as child labour. In the following account we delineate the earning profile of those who entered as child labour and assess their prospects for future growth. It may be added that, since the study was not directly addressed to child labour, most of our conclusions are based on circumstantial evidence rather than direct appeal to facts.

Wage Differentials and Wage Levels of Child Labour

It was noted that the industry presented a picture of rising money wages and the workers' primary motive for interfirm mobility was to enhance their earnings. Firms, irrespective of the size, showed keenness to retain their workers by giving them, to the extent possible, benefits of loan and stay facilities. Given this and the fact that skills in the industry were not highly differentiated, it was realistic to expect the earning differentials in the industry to the narrow and amenable to easy explanation.

This, however, was not the case. There was no clustering of workers in a narrow income range. Only less than half of the work-force was concentrated within a somewhat broad income range of Rs. 250 to Rs. 350, and the rest had monthly earnings ranging from Rs. 150 to more than Rs. 500 a month (Table 28.1).

This deserved further probing. One possible explanation was that workers' earnings rose along with their experience and education. Earnings, to an extent were a function of learning, would tend to rise as a worker was to put in more years of service till a plateau was reached and after that the earnings would not longer rise with time. Similarly, education might facilitate learning. Also, more educated a worker, more keen he would be to enhance his financial prospects until the possibilities were fully exhausted. Thus we would expect earnings to rise with education. The possibility was investigated but no significant relationship was established.

TABLE 28.1

Percentage of Workers in Each Income Range

Monthly income range (Rs.)	*Percentage of workers*
150-250	11.2
251-350	47.0
351-400	21.0
401-450	8.4
451-500	6.8
Greater than 500	5.6

Source: S.P. Kashyap, and R.S. Tiwari, *op. cit.*, p. 92.

Table 28.2 arranges workers' earnings by experience. There indeed is a tendency for earnings to rise with the experience, specially for the first six years of work experience in the industry, where we had sufficient number of observations for each category of experience. Beyond this we did not have enough observations and earnings by experience showed wide fluctuations. However, even during the first six years the relationship was marked by some unusual features. In the initial phase (up to first two years) earnings rose at a snail's pace with experience, there was then a rapid increase during the third year and subsequently there was a gradual improvement in the earnings. Further, within each group of workers by experience, there were wide variations. It was possible for a worker to earn Rs. 700 a month within two years of learning this craft, or Rs. 800 a month within three years. The coefficient of variation, which gives importance to each observation within a group, also showed no tendency to decline with time. Thus, though learning over a period of time tended to enhance earnings, the variations within the group could not be explained merely by the time factor.

TABLE 28.2

Workers by Earnings and Experience

Experience years	*Number of workers*	*Monthly earnings Rs./ month*	*Highest earnings Rs./ month*	*Lowest earnings Rs./ month*	*Coefficient of variation*
Up to 1 year	57	327.3	562	150	23.5
Up to 2 year	106	336.7	700	200	26.3
Up to 3 year	99	361.7	800	250	25.4
Up to 4 year	76	357.1	750	200	23.2
Up to 5 year	47	381.5	700	250	25.0
Up to 6 year	46	403.5	800	200	28.7
Up to 7 year	12	433.1	504	300	13.8
Up to 8 year	15	386.0	473	200	25.3
Up to 9 year	2	325.0	350	300	10.9
Up to 10 year	12	406.2	500	325	14.2
Up to 11 year	8	337.8	462	250	25.2
Up to 12 year	3	450.0	550	300	29.4
Up to 13 year	4	398.5	624	250	41.8
Up to 14 year	4	411.2	600	220	41.5
Up to 15 year	2	423.3	600	350	22.2
Up to 16 year	4	481.2	625	300	32.7
Up to 18 year	2	337.5	420	255	34.6
Up to 19 year	1	300.0	300	—	—

Source: S.P. Kashyap and R.S. Tiwari, *op. cit.*, p. 99.

Could education explain why some workers attain high levels of income in a short time in the industry or why earnings varied within groups of workers arranged in a hierarchy of experience? Unfortunately there did not seem to be any relationship between education and earnings (Table 28.3). Workers with three years of education did as well as those with seven years or 10 years of education and better than those with nine years of education. Wide variations between minimum and maximum earnings also persisted within groups of workers arranged in the hierarchy of educational levels. Thus experience explained, though not fully, the variations in earnings, while education did not seem to influence income differentials. The analysis unfortunately gave no inkling as to why some workers despite sending quite a few years in the industry continued to get meagre rewards for their toils, while others attained high earning levels within a short time.

TABLE 28.3

Workers by Education and Earnings

Education	*Number of workers*	*Average earnings Rs/month*	*Minimum earnings within group Rs./month*	*Maximum earnings within group Rs./month*
Up to 0 level	18	342.1	200	624
Up to 1 level	1	325.0	—	—
Up to 2 level	5	274.2	150	312
Up to 3 level	18	361.5	200	500
Up to 4 level	48	348.1	200	650
Up to 5 level	30	370.7	250	624
Up to 6 level	31	334.3	250	500
Up to 7 level	90	360.3	250	800
Up to 8 level	83	372.7	250	750
Up to 9 level	64	350.9	250	575
Up to 10 level	66	360.7	200	700
Up to 11 level	26	374.8	250	700
Up to 12 level	4	363.5	300	450
Up to 13 level	4	435.0	330	600
Up to 14 level	3	605.3	300	700
Total	491	360.4		

Source: S.P. Kashyap and R.S. Tiwari *op. cit.*, p. 100.

In order to understand these earnings differentials we hypothesised that perhaps wage earners belonged to the disadvantaged classes in the society. We assumed that a group of workers who previous work experience was as agriculture labour or who had an entry into the industry as child labour were likely to belong to the economically depressed classes compared to the rest. Since there was no overlapping between these categories, but for three workers, we could examine their attributed separately. Table 28.4 arranges workers by sub-groups and their attributes. The Table shows that the workers who started as child labour or as farm labour, in that order, were less educated, earned less and had more experience. That these sub-groups of workers despite being more experienced earned less than an average worker showed that where one belonged was not inconsequential even in a fast expanding enterprise, and where, at least at the firm level, the relations between the workers and the management appeared to be cordial, and unlike the plight of the child labour in some other industries,[3] free from gross exploitation.[4]

TABLE 28.4
Workers by Sub-groups and Their Attributes

Sr. No.	*Categories of work-force*	*Age*	*Education*	*Earning*	*Experi-ence*	*No. of ob-servations*
1.	Previous work experience as agricultural labourer	26.1	6.3	348.9	6.0	23
2.	Those who entered as child labour	19.5	5.1	326.8	6.6	35
3.	All workers	24.2	7.2	360.4	4.6	91

Source: S.P. Kashyap and R.S. Tiwari *op. cit.*, p. 105.

It may be mentioned that earning differentials between child labour and an average worker in the industry, though significant can be misleading, although compared with an average worker earnings of child labour are lower by Rs. 35. Workers belonging to child labour category on an average had spent more than six years in the industry and workers with similar work experience on an average were able to have much higher earnings (ranging from Rs. 76 to 106, Table 28.2). Thus, the true differentials range from 23 to 32 per cent.[5] There are perhaps other reasons about which, for want of an in-depth analysis, we can only speculate. It is possible that given their background child workers have limited horizons and are satisfied with whatever they are able to earn. It is also possible that because of their upbringing they do not have enough physical strength to put in extra hours of work. There may be problems associated with adjusting to an alien industrial culture. Pathak cites several examples indicating the serious socio-cultural and psychological problems faced by workers of somewhat younger age. "Their transition to an industrial life is marked by many problems of quick adjustments. The anxiety and tension through which they pass arise out of a new environment, hard work, training, lack of support and friendship."[6]

Future Prospects

We have noted above that the category of workers who entered as child labour on an average earn much less than workers with similar experience. It would be relevant to examine their prospects of owing their enterprise, because our study showed that about 65 per cent of the entrepreneurs in the industry had been initiated in the industry as workers. Some clue to workers graduation to the entrepreneurship can be had by comparing their age profile with those of entrepreneurs themselves (Table 28.5). Concentration of workers was in the first age group (less than 25 years) and then there was a sharp decline of the percentage of workers in the higher age brackets. The same was true of entrepreneurs starting with the very next age group (25 to less than 30 years). The evidence suggested that roughly five years' work experience was enough for a worker to set up his own unit. This is not unusual. In fact, experience of some of the countries where small scale factories have had a rapid growth was almost parallel to our case study.[7]

TABLE 28.5

Percentage of Workers and Entrepreneurs in Different Age Groups

Age group	*Percentage*	
	Entrepreneurs	*Workers*
Less than 25	13	71
25 to less than 30	35	20
30 to less than 35	25	6
35 to less than 40	14	2
40 to less than 45	6	1
45 and above	5	—
Total	100	100

Source: S.P. Kashyap and R.S. Tiwari *op. cit.*, p. 33.

TABLE 28.6

Educational Attainments: "Wage Earner to Entrepreneurs" Versus The Rest of The Entrepreneurs and The Workers

Level of education	*Wage earner to entrepreneurs*	*Rest of the entrepreneurs*	*Workers employed in the industry*
1. Up to primary	20	14	121
	(15)	(19)	(24)
2. Up to 8th	39	33	207
	(30)	(44)	(42)
3. Up to 11th	68	25	160
	(53)	(33)	(32)
4. Degree or Diploma	2	3	12
	(2)	(4)	(2)

Note: Figures in parentheses indicate percentage to the column total.

Source: S.P. Kashyap and R.S. Tiwari *op. cit.*, p. 31.

The upward mobility from wage earner to entrepreneur would perhaps be a function of several factors, such as, asset base, contacts,[8] family background, psychological attributes (achievement motivation) and education. It was not possible to uncover all the factors but we did consider the role of education because is often considered as an essential for upward mobility. Table 28.6 compares the educational attainment of entrepreneurs who initially joined the industry as wage earners with the rest of the entrepreneurs. More than half of the "wage earners to entrepreneurs" had education up to 11th standard as compared to one-third in the rest of the set. The same was true if we compared the educational attainments of 'wage earner to entrepreneurs' with those of the wage earners in the industry. In fact wage earners and the 'rest of the entrepreneurs' had almost similar distribution of educational attainments. Thus, being somewhat better educated than the class of their origin as well as the class to which they become a part seemed to have helped the process of upward mobility. Given the above facts, it would seem that workers who entered as child labour are too young and have low educational qualifications. As they earn low earnings compared to the other workers when they enter, it is unlikely that they would have access to financial assets that are needed to set up an industrial enterprise.

Concluding Observations

Workers who entered the diamond processing industry as child labour emerge as the most unfavourable placed group in the industry. This is despite the industry having grown quite rapidly, which should ordinarily imply, workers with long association with the industry should be able to improve their fortunes over time. That this has not happened in the case of workers entering as child labour tends to suggest that the initial start in life, exceptions apart, crucially determines the earning profile over time.

ACKNOWLEDGEMENT

The author's is grateful to Prof. Devendra Kothari for his useful suggestions

REFERENCES AND NOTES

1. See for instance, Timothy Green, *The World of Diamonds,* London: Weidenfeld and Nicolson, 1981 for global perspective, and for Indian case studies, S.P. Kashyap, and R.S. Tiwari, *Shaping of Diamonds in Surat: Some Passes (Facets)* Sardar Patel Institute of Economic and Social Research, Monograph No. 12 (Distributed by Allied Publishers), 1986, and H.N. Pathak *Diamond Trade and Industry in India,* Ahmedabad: Indian Institute of Management, 1984 (mimeo).
2. Kashyap, S.P. and R.S. Tiwari *op. cit.,* for detailed account.
3. For instance, S. Kothari, There is Blood on Those Matchsticks: Child Labour in Sivakasi, Economic and Political Weekly, pp. 1191-1202, 1983 and N. Burra, "Glass Factories of Firozabad, "*Economic and Political Weekly*", pp. 1983-1985 and 2033-2036, 1986.
4. Kashyap, S.P. and R.S. Tiwari *op. cit.,* noted that the industry was organised on caste lines. The entrepreneur and the workers in a firm often belonged to the same caste. Indeed, it was possible in the industry to draw a close parallel to patron-client relationship as had been observed in the farm sector of some of the South-east Asian villages. Elaborating the concept of patron-client relationship, Y. Hayami mentions: "The traditional moral principle of mutual help and income sharing in South-east Asian villages and its erosion due to modernisation forces are often exaggerated....there is no denying that principle does exist and does survive. To violate the principle involves cost in the form of social approbrium...village communities in South-east Asia are homogeneous socially if not economically. Many landless labourers are

relatives, employers and employees are tied in a patron-client bond of mutual trust....". Agrarian problem in India: An East and South-east Asian Perspective, Economic and Political Weekly, p. 709, 1981.

5. It may be mentioned that about 14 per cent of the workers (mostly those who were without families) were noticed to be staying in the place of work. S.P. Kashyap, and R.S. Tiwari, *op cit.*, p. 111.
6. *Op. cit.*, Vol. 2, p. 289.
7. Ho, Sam P.S., Small Scale Enterprises in Korea and Taiwan, World Bank Working Staff Paper No. 384, Washington, 1980. Consider the statement; "In fact, one-third of the proprietors, before becoming owners, work in the same line of business and most of them at least for five years. This reflects the well-known fact, that in many industries, e.g. furniture, the aim of most apprentices and journeymen is to go into business for themselves." p. 84.
8. It was noticed that given the nature of the product, contacts based on trust played an important role in establishing a unit. In fact trust factor pervaded the industry from units to sightholders through the commission agents. S.P. Kashyap, and R.S. Tiwari, *op. cit.*, Chapter 2.

29

CHILD LABOUR IN FIROZABAD, UTTAR PRADESH

'Indispensability' of Child Labour

"If you propose a ban on child labour in the glass industry here in Firozabad, let me tell you, the whole township will be out in the streets protesting against the ban. There will be agitations, violence, because you will be depriving thousands of their livelihood." A senior government official in Firozabad instructed me, when I re-visited Firozabad last year. Beneath the facade of this matter of fact statement suppurates a macabre world of absent values and crushed spirits trapped in glittering glass.

The senior government official is right that a ban on child labour will disturb the peace of the town. Yes, if children will not work, the town will not survive, the industry will die, the economy would be debilitated, the power structure would be deprived of the cantilevers that uphold it and tension would pervade of the lives of the people who control the economy. If the children do not work, they would play, sing and be children. They will not be premature adults, beasts of burden, or *bonasaied* labourers who accept, exploitative work conditions and repressive master servant relationship, as normal. They will be acceding to and building up the valueless culture of survival.

Risking Lives to Earn A Living Wage

What must the children do to keep the glass industry in glittering health? They must work in the most hazardous environment, in self-destructive strenuous ways, at the cost of their future. They must destroy their future and risk their lives to earn a meagre wage.

There are three major types of glass works in Firozabad. The glass product moulding factories, the bangle industry and the bead-making unit. The children work near furnaces as helpers and semi-skilled workers in glass blowing factories. In the bangle industry, they handle *jhalai* (bringing two ends of the are together to prepare the unjoined bangle for joining), *judai* (joining the two ends to form a ring), *katai* (cutting grooves to fill in golden tint), *pakai* (baking the sealed and cut bangle), *hil* work (painting the grooves in bangles with a chemical containing minute proportion of gold), and *chhatai* (sorting out difference colours and sizes). They also carry molten glass loams stuck on to tips of iron rods. All child workers are barefooted, they wear cheap clothes and are poorly nourished. They work for eight hours at a stretch without break for tea or meals. Most factories do not having drinking water facility and only a few keep a locally prepared ointment in the first aid box.

In the glass blowing factories the children work near furnaces. There the giant pot furnaces are kept smouldering every minute of the day for more than a year. Adult workers keep shovelling tons of coal into these to keep the temperature around 1400°C. Sillica sand and soda ash, emitting hazardous fumes blazes inside the belly of the furnace. The heat too polutes the workers' bodies causing heat strokes. Soot, dust and fumes saturate the air. Broken glass litters the floor. Teenaged and adult workers stand close to the windows of the furnaces, pull out of the belly a pound of blazing glass with the tip of a long and heavy iron rod, *labia* and throw these rods at child workers between seven and 12 years of age, over the heads of other labourers working around the furnace on different processes. The child catches the rod thrown at him and rushes it to the moulding furnace making his way through a crowd of other child workers moving to and fro with *labias.* While moving and breathing in chemical fumes and heat, the children may step on broken glass or, accidentally get scalded by the burning looms on the *labias.* Adolescent children sit on the platform and handle the semi-skilled job of cooling a freshly blown mould on the *labia.* They hold the mould a foot and half away and pour cold water on the rim so that the mould shrinks to grip the *labia.* If water drops fall on the body of the mould, it splinters injuring the child and other workers around. A smaller child then carries the mould to a stone and separates it from the labia. There are moulding furnaces which are of the size of a small cupboard. A child worker sits right next to them and cools the rim of the mould on the *labia.*

The furnaces in which glass is manufactured for making heads are smaller and have shorter life. The skilled adult worker sitting right next to the window of the furnace, blows narrow pipes of different designs which are then cut into beads. A child worker sits next to the furnace to separate the bead pipe from its blower. *Jhalai* and *judai* of the bangles are done on an acetelyene or kerosene flame placed in the centre of a mud *chulha.* The child leans over the flame to do his work and thus constantly inhales fumes, dust and other pollutants. The worker must sit in a crouching position for hours to do this work. The *pakai* furnace is like an open shelf. Silica sand is spread on a steaming hot plate on which a child worker deftly arranges rows of single bangles for *pakai.*

Minor and major accidents and disease and death stalk the glass factories of Firozabad, daily, silently and dramatically. However, the permanent presence of the hazards is ignored by all, including the parents of the children.

The Employers' Philosophy

The employers' attitude was pithily stated to me by a Darshan Bihari Gupta, President of Bangle Marketeers' Association. "Why should cancel business bother if twenty workers die? There will be another twenty ready to work." The businessman's objective is his comfort. According to another prominent citizen, R.N. Mittal, President of Glass Industrialists' syndicate, the entrepreneurs' priority must be to keep the cost low, even if it means exposing the workers to dangers. He insisted that the way of minimising workers' suffering is to expose them to the hazardous work environment early in life as child workers. He argued that the industry will survive only if workers are acclamatised to the excessive heat and dangerous chemical fumes from childhood.

The confidence with which the industrialists talk of using workers as raw material for the industrial produce, has its roots in the assured support to them of various government agencies. The labour department classifies glass bangle industry as a cottage industry by virtue of which it is out of the purview of the Factory Act. The labour department insists that unless a victim or a relative of the victim approaches them they cannot legally take cognizance of the accident or even a death at work site. The regional labour officers pretend to be blind to the existence of thousands of child workers.

The Doctor's Oath of Allegiance

Since the child workers have no legal existence, the medicos working for the employee's State Insurance Scheme have evolved their own schemes one of which is to ignore the injured or dying child worker. They may, rarely though, treat the child by entering his age as above 16 or giving him medicare on the care of the adult worker. Some of the employers have a regular contract with the ESIS doctor under which the doctor visits the factory to treat the injured workers and no record of the treatment is made at the government clinic. Majority of the child workers foot their own bill though the government hospital is supposed to give free services to the poor.

Medico-legal cases may not be recorded as such by the doctors and if recorded, about 75 per cent patients are usually discharged almost immediately without informing the police (as required by law). If police are informed after a long delay, the site of the accident vital in the case of a medico-legal injury may even be shifted away from the factory.

The 'Premier' Administrative Services Premier Role

The police simply copy the vague medical entries in the hospital register. "If we record cases of injuries acquired by workers at work at under the IPC section dealing with injuries caused by negligence, we will have to open a separate department which will do no other work." A senior police officer informed me. "Why don't you open a separate wing then?" I asked. The reply was, "We won't be allowed to."

In Firozabad, the administrative chief is Addition District Magistrate (ADM) (as Firozabad is not a district) who is the controller of the police. I learnt that the businessmen did not want Firozabad to be declared a district because then, senior officers would be posted there and some of them may not be amenable to corruption and political gamesmanship. My theory is that the bureaucrats themselves may have opposed upgradation of Firozabad as a district so that they do not have to live in the highly polluted town and manoeuvre their way out of money power politics. Be that as it may, no a accidents at work sites result in prosecution and no worker is paid adequate compensation. I know this for a fact. Two adolescent boys got killed when the chimney of a factory under construction collapsed on them. The factory owner, saluted the ADM daily while the local hospital did not even treat the boys. They were taken to Agra hospital for treatment where they died.

If the worker dies in Firozabad itself, the sub-divisional magistrate (SDM) has to get his dying declaration. In the several dying declarations I read, the worker blames himself. It is sufficient enough reason for the SDM never to visit the work site or make any enquiry whatsoever. The dying declaration is sent to the office of the district judge (DJ) in Agra. So that the worker's relative may file a petition with the DJ. The workers do not even know of this provision and of course have no means to visit Agra. Consequently no one approaches the DJ whose office is a morgue of dying declarations.

Adult and Child Workers

Unprotected by laws and by the concerned officers, the adult labourers of Firozabad are docile, unorganised and willing to work under the most wretched conditions. In other words, they are like child labour. Then, why do not the industrialist employ adults instead of children? The answer lies in the vested interests of various people. The parents have vested interests in a child's capacity to earn-the culture of survival teaches them to. The governance, which comprises the political executive and the bureaucracy, has vested interest in appeasing the moneyed class, who have vested interest in perpetuating child labour. The net result is that child labour depresses wages of adult workers and also sustains underdevelopment. The children who start life as child labour mostly stay in the casual labour market and thus breed another generation of child labour.

Yet, if some one proposes a ban on child labour, the whole township will be out in the street in protest. But nobody comes out in the street to demand children's right to childhood to education and to a bright future.

Concrete Steps Needed

What concrete steps can we take to reduce the incidence of child labour and eventually eradicate this system? In this paper, I am going to mention only one point which is more important than it seems.

My insistence is that we must be very careful about who takes interest in researching and acquiring expertise in the phenomenon of child labour. I see a number of career researches and career activists crowding, but the commitment of these careerists is that of butterflies in a flower. So when the chips are down and the establishment wants 'experts' and 'activist' with a trail of research papers, studies and reports to support them the careerists will help them rationalise police decisions. Let us not help create such a lethal lobby. How do we, then start moving towards the eradication of child labour?

Conscientising: Any programme for eradication of child labour must begin by conscientising the people about the rights of children. Dissemination of information on hazards faced by the working children and their exploitation may provoke quick reaction but what is needed is the awareness of children's plight in the large context of his right to childhood, growth and future.

Widening the Bases: The most important people to reach out first should be the persons and organisation already active as socially responsible individuals and entities. They should be involved in the issue of children by linking their concerns and goals with those of the organisations working for child labour. Some of the link areas are education, human rights, eradication of exploitation and general development.

Creches. Creches may set up in schools, offices and urban slums, so that, the children who look after the siblings are freed of the responsibilities.

Compulsory Education and Schooling Linked Credit: The government, the social organisations and the community may be inspired to intensity their efforts to realise the Constitutional goal of making education compulsory up to the age of 14 years (Article 45 of the Constitution). My preference is for the limit of 18 years, because: (1) the children from deprived environment start schooling late; and (2) their education is likely to get interrupted due to frequent illnesses, farm activities or family crises. The impoverished families who cannot afford to send their children to schools may be supported through education grants and schooling-linked credits. *Ashramshalas* or residence schools may be set up in areas where child labour is intensive. A counselling cell may be attached to schools in areas where the incidence of child labour is high, to guide parents and motivate them to send their children to school.

Postage Stamp Funding: A special fund may be raised through a 'Care for the Child' postage stamp to finance the above programmes. Another source of funds could be a Rs. 1 excess on every train ticket bought.

30

CHILD LABOUR IN JARI INDUSTRY

This paper is a by-product of our study[1] in Surat (South Gujrat) undertaken at Sardar Patel Institute of Economic and Social Research, Ahmedabad. The main purpose of the study was to understand the functioning of the *jari* industry and to examine the socio-economic conditions of the workers of the industry at Surat. The study was conducted during June to August 1980. It covered a sample of 300 firms and 500 workers in the industry. Apart from structured questionnaires, the study also relied on discussions and meetings with the leading *jari* manufacturers, office bearers of *Jari* Merchants' Association of Surat and some enlightened citizens.

It may be pointed out that the study's objective did not include an in-depth analysis of child labour. However, during our field visit we came across a number of household units employing children as labourers. It was observed that 52.% per cent of the labourers in our sample were family members while 48 per cent were hired labour (Table 30.1). Of the family labour around 53 per cent were males, 35 per cent females and

TABLE 30.1

Composition of Labour Force in *Jari* Industry

Sr. No.	*Employment size of the unit*	*Family workers (numbers)*	*Hired workers (numbers)*	*Total workers (numbers)*
1	2	3	4	5
1.	1-5	151 (51)	243 (49)	294 (100.00)
2.	6-10	581 (54)	491 (46)	1072 (100.00)
3.	11-15	387 (52)	361 (48)	748 (100.00)
4.	Above 15	339 (50)	340 (50)	679 (100.00)
	Total	1458 (52)	1335 (48)	2793 (100.00)

Note: Figures in parentheses denote percentage.

around 12 per cent children (below the age of 15 years). In case of hired labour, however, 62 per cent were males 34 per cent females and the remaining 4 per cent were children. For the industry as a whole about 8 per cent of the labour force consisted of children (Table 29.2). The proportion of child labour was observed to be varying across the size of the unit. In very small units the proportion of child labour was insignificant, while with the expansion of the unit, their proportion increased.

TABLE 30.2

Composition of Labour Force Across Sex

Sr. No.	*Employment size of the unit*	*Number of units*	*Family employment*				*Hired employment*				*Total labour force*			
			Male (No.)	*Female (No.)*	*Children (No.)*	*Total (No.)*	*Male (No.)*	*Female (No.)*	*Children (No.)*	*Total (No.)*	*Male (No.)*	*Female (No.)*	*Children (No.)*	*Total (No.)*
1.	1-5	71	97	49	5	151	94	49	—	143	191	98	5	294
2.	6-10	141	333	199	49	581	290	181	20	491	623	380	69	1072
3.	11-15	59	202	144	41	387	215	124	22	361	417	268	63	748
4	Above 15	29	137	120	82	339	233	95	12	340	370	215	94	679
5	Total	300	769	512	177	1458	832	449	54		1601	961	231	2793
			(52.74)	(35.12)	(12.14)	(100.00)	(62.32)	(33.63)	(4.05)	(100)	(57.32)	(34.40)	(8.28)	(100)

Note: Figures in brackets denote percentage.

An interesting observation regarding the concentration of child labour was related to the nature of processes of the unit. It was noticed that a majority of the units were engaged in more than one process or activity. (It may be mentioned that the *jari* manufacturing can be composed into 10 different processes/activities.) There were 141 units engaged in a single activity, 118 units engaged in two activities and 41 units engaged in more than two activities (Table 30.3). It was observed that a higher proportion of child labour was engaged in units carrying out two activities that is, flattening and winding (Table 30.4), which do not require any specific skills.

Most of the processes of the industry are quite safe from the point of view of health of the workers except for the gold gilding process in which *jari* threads are passed through the solution of gold and potassium cynide. The chemical reaction between these two affects adversely the health and the life span of the workers.

The study estimated that the annual average wage rate paid in the industry was Rs. 3,084. The female wage rate was nearly 60 per cent and the child wage rate was nearly 40 per cent of the average male rate. It was seen that wage rates varied not only across different activities but also across the different categories of units demarcated by size and number of activities. While discussing with some of the entrepreneurs, it was gathered that in many cases, the wages were paid according to the work done by the workers irrespective of the number of hours worked. Therefore, it is quite possible that the child labour was paid less because their low productivity per hour and/or less number of hours worked.

TABLE 30.3

Distribution of Units According to Number of Activities

Sr. No.	Employment size of the unit	No. of units engaged in: Single activities (Category-I)	Two activities (Category-II)	More than 2 activities (Category-III)	Total
1.	1-5	46	22	3	71
		(65)	(31)	(4)	
2.	6-10	74	49	18	141
		(52)	(35)	(13)	
3.	11-15	16	31	12	59
		(27)	(52)	(21)	
4.	Above 15	5	16	8	29
		(17)	(55)	(28)	
	Total	141	118	41	300
		(47)	(39)	(14)	

Note: Figures in parentheses denote percentage.

TABLE 30.4

Estimated Wage Rate for *Jari* Workers

Sr. No.	Employment size of the unit	Wage rate per annum (Rs.): Male	Female	Children	Average
1.	1-5	3600.60	2112.20	—	3090.50
2.	6-10	3890.98	2202.01	2553.80	3213.90
3.	11-15	3498.87	2393.10	952.73	2963.89
4.	Above 15	3560.63	1964.84	939.67	3022.25
	Total	3664.33	2194.80	1542.81	3084.27

What are the possible explanations for the existence of child labour in the *jari* industry? Let us understand the working of the industry for this purposed. Jari manufacturing is an old craft of Surat going back to the sixteenth century.

It may not be contributing significantly to the national or the state economy but its importance to the civic life of Surat cannot be ignored. According to an estimate by *Jari* Merchants' Association of Surat more than 40,000 persons were directly or indirectly connected with this industry. More than 80 per cent of the total *jari* production is manufactured at Surat. For real *jari*, silver and gold are important raw material while for the artificial *jari* the important raw materials are copper and gold. It was estimated that the majority of entrepreneurs (90 per cent) and workers (73 per cent) were from the Rana community which is firmly rooted in Surat. The intracommunity cordial relationship has led to industrial peace in the industry which is very important for the health of the industry.

The average size of a family is quite high in this community. The industry is basically a household industry—employing quite a sizeable proportion of family labour. A majority of the unites sampled were observed to be having children more than sixteen years of age (see Table 30.5). The craft of *jari* making is transferred from one generation to another in family units. Around 90 per cent of the entrepreneurs revealed that they had inherited this craft from their fathers (Table 30.6), and 85 per cent of them took over the units as managers/proprietors. The high proportion of family labour among child labour in the industry is due to the fact that parents train their children in this craft from their young age. Another reason is the large family size of the entrepreneurs and workers in this industry—(12) in the case of entrepreneurs and seven in the case of workers.) Entry from other communities as workers is not welcomed in the industry. In other words the Rana community produces, the work-force for the industry and trains them from childhood so that their hold on this craft is not diluted over time. The Rana community trains young girls also in the craft. It was reported that the knowledge of the craft is an important qualification for a girl in the marriage market as women participate in this work even after marriage.

TABLE 30.5

Distribution of Units According to Age

Sr. No.	*Age of the units (in years)*	*Number of units*
1.	1-5	40
2.	6-10	54
3.	11-15	33
4.	16-20	43
5.	Above 20	130
	Total	300

It is usually believed that poverty induces the phenomenon of child labour. According to our survey estimate, however, only 12.50 per cent of the sample households were below the poverty line. On the basis of our observation regarding hired child labour it may be argued that the children were sent to work not merely for wages but also for learning the craft. It was observed that in most cases children were initiated to work in units where the unit holders (entrepreneurs) were their intimate relatives so that skill formation could be facilitated irrespective of the wages received. The phenomenon of child labour in this industry may therefore be considered as a seed-bed for entrepreneurial development.

TABLE 30.6

Distribution of Units According to the Age

Sr. No.	*Age of the units (in years)*	*Number of units*
1.	1-5	40
2.	6-10	54
3.	11-15	33
4.	16-20	43
5.	Above 20	130
	Total	300

Our study thus indicates that it is not the economic factors alone that induce child labour in the *jari* industry. Factors like demographic characteristics of the work-force, community needs, nature of industry and social and economic environments may also explain the existence of child labour in the *jari* industry.

ACKNOWLEDGEMENTS

Thanks are the due to Prof. S.P. Kashyap for the comments and suggestions. Miss Alka Dave rendered valuable help in arranging information base for the paper.

Rohit D. Desai, Associate Professor, Sardar Patel Institute of Economic and Social Research, Ahmedabad.

REFERENCES

1. Rohit D. Desai, *The Problem of Household Sector- A Study of Jari Industry of Surat*, Sardar Patel Institute of Economic and Social Research, Ahmedabad 380 054, 1985.
2. Desai, Rohit D., *The Problem of Household Sector: A Study of the Jari Industry of Surat*, Sardar Patel Institute of Economic and Social Research, Ahmedabad, 1985.

31

HOW PROTECTED INDIAN CHILDREN ARE?

A Child does not come to the world by its own volition. A child is brought to this world by a pair of man and woman, who want to perpetuate the lineage; family or species. In India, a child is brought to the world with the expectation, that when the parents become old, the son or daughter will look after them in the old age. A child is taken as an insurance policy for them, against any eventuality. In general, it is expected that a son will definitely look after the parents. The child is supposed to have a moral obligation to provide for the parents in their old age. But the parents, who are responsible for bringing a child to the world also have some sort of moral obligation to the child. In most of the societies, conception of moral and social obligations are so interwoven, that it is not always possible to isolate the two. In India, specially in the rural set up, it is seldom assured that a child is to be protected from the ravages of the cruel world, so that it can finally become both mentally and physically a healthy adult. A healthy and well adjusted adult, always can look after the parents in much better way than a handicapped one. All animals protect their offsprings for a certain length of period, depending on the period required for development. Man is the most developed animal and no doubt, "man" guided by the natural instinct of preservation of the species, protect his children to a certain length of time. But the question one would like to ask here, is "how much protection a child needs, and how much it is getting." Are the Indian children as much protected as in the developed countries? If not, why? What are the reasons, which compels, some Indian children to work for subsistance from a very young age?

The concept of child care and need for protection of the children in changing from the primitive hunting-gethering stage to the modern world. The child had to look after himself in the hunting—gathering society as soon as he was able to do it. In the simple agrarian society the child is required to help the parents in the field from very early age. The idea that the child has equal right for protection as an adult developed only very recently. But as industrialisation increased, fertility rate decreased and population of some nations exhibited negative growth rate of total population, the necessary for child-protection was found in human society. After the industrial revolution, to decrease the growth of population, several measures were taken in West European countries to ensure better health of the children. As infant mortality and child mortality were found to be associated with high fertility, prohibition of employment of children in certain categories of work was enforced. Britain was the first country of prohibit employment of children under 15 years to work in mines. Gradually, different industrialised countries enforced prohibition employment of children in different types of jobs and introduced compulsory schooling upto a certain age.

The population below the age of 15 years are treated as children. A child labour is a working child who is employed in a gainful occupation and in the process of work, may be exposed to injurious work and also may be deprived of developmental opportunities. At present, the incidence of child labour is almost negligible in the developmental industrialised countries but in the development countries the incidence of child labour is considerably high.

Most children, at different times, help the family in doing different types of household chores as unpaid workers. According to the International Labour Organisations Bureau of Statistics Report of 1980, nearly 95 per cent of the world's children in the age group of 10 years of 15 years help their family at different times as unpaid workers. The unpaid child family worker is usually not considered and enumerated as child labour through they contribute labour to the family. As family is an economic unit, all the members are responsible for maintaining family and in the process contribute towards the upkeep of the whole family, a child may be required to work in the house. In the present context, usually the unpaid child family workers is not considered as a child labour.

Most of the child labour of the world are between 10 years and 15 years, though occasionally children below 10 years are also employed. Major proportion of the child workers of the world are from the developing countries. 80 per cent of them live in Asia, 58 per cent are from South Asia and 30.9 per cent in India. Proportion of child worker is also high in Africa and Latin America Country-wise it is highest in Sri Lanka (5.3 per cent). It is totally absent in U.S.S.R. and Australia. In North America, the proportion of child labour is high among the non-white population.

In India, according to 1981 census, 4.76 per cent of the total working population are child workers. The proportion of child worker is decreasing from 1961; when it was 7.66 per cent and in 1971 this was 5.05 per cent. Among different States, Kerala has the lowest proportion of child workers and Sikkim has highest. It has to be mentioned here, that during census operation, only a child labour who earns some money is enumerated as child labour. As a girl in most of the States in India not allowed to go outside her native place and work, the proportion of male child worker is much higher than the female child worker. Female child are mostly unpaid family worker.

According to 1981 Census of India, there are 2,22,517 thousand main workers in the whole country, and out of them 11,69 thousands are below 15 years of age. There are 22,089 thousand marginal workers of which 2,424 thousands are children. Majority of the child worker in India are employed in primary sector. Employment of children is not found at present in organised sector, though earlier children in very low proportion (less that 1 per cent) were employed in factories. In the rural areas, among main workers male child workers are higher in proportion than the female child workers; but among the marginal workers, female child workers are higher than the male child workers. In urban areas, female child workers are much lower in proportion than the male child workers, both among the main and marginal workers. In urban areas, most of the child workers are employed in construction, trade and commerce, household industries or work as domestic help. They are also employed in small hotels.

In most of the census data, the child workers are shown as the proportion of the total workers. As such in 1981, 5.02 per cent of the main workers and 1.09 per cent of the marginal workers were below 15 years of age. But when we try to find out what proportion of children are working, we get a slightly different picture, Among all the children in India, 5.16 per cent are working, in rural areas 6.11 per cent of children are working and in urban areas 1.80 per cent of children are workers. The proportion of children working does not appear to be very high. But here the total universe is all the children below 15 years. Every body knows that children below 5 years can not work and the children between 5 years to 10 years seldom work as paid worker. In India almost all the children working are within 10 years to 14 years.

It we assume that all the child workers are above 5 years, then we find that 7.58 per cent of children from 5 years to 14 years are workers. In rural areas, their proportion is 8.79 per cent and in urban areas, they are 2.64 per cent. If we assume that all child workers are between 10 years to 14 years, then we find a dismal picture. Among all the children between 10 years and 14 years, 15.86 per cent are workers. In rural areas their proportion is 18.93 per cent and in urban areas, they are 5.36 per cent. The increase in proportion, both in rural and urban areas exhibit the same gradient. Proportion of child workers is much low in urban areas, because in the urban areas, employment opportunities in unorganised sector is rather low and children all over India are generally employed in unorganised sector.

A large number of studies, had been undertaken in different parts of India, on the problem of child labour. Most of them have paid enough attention to find out how many children are working and what proportion of total workers are represented by children. Few of the studies have been devoted to explore why in a country like India, where a large section of the adult population is unemployed or underemployed, a child has to work and earn.

In the tribal society, a child has to work in different capacities to help their parents and at times to add to the family income. Here, the income of one adult is not sufficient to maintain the whole family and the child has to work. In rural society, almost the same idea prevail though may be less in degree. In a society with less develop technology, the working hands required will be always more and a child is always there to help. In the developed countries, the children mainly work to earn some pocket money and mostly in vacation. But in rural India, schooling less important when agricultural help is needed in the field. Therefore, in rural India, bulk of the child workers are the schooling drop-outs in the age group of 10 years to 14 years. Poor economic condition and less developed technology compel the parents to allow their children to work. In the urban areas, there may be some more added reasons, which encourage the child workers. In the cities, the migrant population may not always earn sufficient to look after their family properly and the children are forced to look after themselves. Because of this factor, there are more child workers among the migrants than the residents.

There are several causes for continuation of child labour in India. But main causes are poor economic condition, traditional authority of father, lack of status of the child in the society, low level of adult literacy, lack of social security and cheapness of human labour. But at the same time the lack of vigilance of the society to see that all the laws enacted for betterment of the children are really enforced properly is not less responsible for continuation of child labour in India.

Thirty years back, on 20.11.1959, United Nations declared 9 principles on the Rights of the children. Of these 4 important principles are:—

(a) The child shall enjoy special protections to enable him to develop physically, mentally, morally, spiritually and socially in a healthy and normal manner.
(b) The child shall be entitled from his birth to a name and a nationality.
(c) The child shall enjoy the benefits of social security.
(d) Physically, mentally and socially handicapped children will be given special treatment.

After almost two decades, in 1977, United Nations declared 1979 as the International Year of the Children. Certain number of protective measures for the children were adopted. They are mainly:—

(a) Prohibition of child labour below 15 years of age.
(b) Protection of child workers.
(c) Protection of night work of the children.
(d) Prohibitions of hazardous and dangerous work for persons below 18 years of age.
(e) Medical examinations of the child workers.
(f) Vocational guidance and training for the children, so that they are better equipped to select jobs.

India as a member nation of the United Nations also adopted different measures for protection of children. There are several Articles in the Constitution which are beneficial to the children. Article 15, empowers the State to make any type of special provision for women and children, who are treated as weaker section. Article 24 prohibits employment of children below 14 years of age in any factory or mines or in any kind of hazardous job Article 45 states that "the State shall endeavour to provide, within a period of ten years from the commencement of Constitution, for free and compulsory education for all children until they complete the age of 14 years."

Apart from the constitutional safeguards, there are several acts and rules, which govern the child labour. These acts were made from 1919 onwards. There are several acts governing, minimum age of employment, minimum wages, working hours, working conditions, etc. Our legislators deserve all the credits for enactment of different acts safeguarding the interest and welfare of the child labour. But these acts and constitutional provisions have not improved the condition of the children and the child labour. To an ordinary man, it is not clear, why in spite of all these provisions child labour exist in India. Recently Swami Agnibesh had released some bonded child labour from an area near Delhi, the youngest one being only 7 year old.

The International Year of Children was observed with high enthusiasm and after a decade we find the child labour still exists in India. Only there is slight drop in the proportion of child labour in the total labour force in every State. This decrease may not be decrease in the proportion of child working among the total children. This decrease may also be due to two factors, decrease in proportion of children in the total population and increase in the longivity of the Indian population in recent past.

The multi-dimentional problem of child labour cannot be solved in India unless one examines thoroughly the main causes of child labour. Apart from poor economic condition, low literacy rate both among the adult and children, there are other factors which encourage child labour. The indifferent altitude of the people to child abuse or hardship of the children are primarily responsible for encouraging persistence of child labour in India. As most of the child labour force comprises of the non-school going children between 10 years and 14 years of age, strict enforcement of compulsory schooling of everybody below 15 years will stop child labour. Kerala has highest literacy rate and highest proportion of school going children from 5 years and above and it has lowest proportion of child labour.

At the time of making the Constitution, it was envisaged that within 10 years, all the States will make primary education compulsory. But unfortunately till 1983, the following States had no act or rule in favour of compulsory primary education—Bihar, Manipur, Meghalaya, Nagaland, Orissa, Sikkim, Tripura, Arunachal Pradesh and Mizoram. In Orissa, the State is empowered to declare any area for introduction of compulsory education under section 4(i) of Orissa Basic Education Act of 1951, but no such declaration has been made so far regarding any area. In the States of Andhra Pradesh, Gujarat, Haryana, Himachal Pradesh, Karnataka, Maharashtra, Punjab Rajasthan, Tamil Nadu, Uttar Pradesh and West Bengal, penal action for not sending the children to school is also provided in the act, but till 1983, there was not single case of prosecution in whole of India for not sending the children to school and never any penal action was enforced. The guardians of the low are very superficial regarding the rights of the children. It seems that only the vocal groups get advantage and the children will have to be vocal. In Uttar Pradesh, Compulsory Primary Education Act came into existence in 1926 (excluding few districts), but in 1981, the literacy rate among the persons who are more than 10 years is as low as 33.59 per cent. It is quite obvious that simply by enacting an act, one cannot remove a malady or provide security to anybody. A section of responsible public will have to keep watchful eye that enacted acts and laws are observed fully. The law enforcement processes and machinary should be more vigilant to see that children below 14 years really attend school.

The collousness and apathy of the Indian society is also observed from the report of the Labour Bureau, Simla. From the report, it is observed that till 1980, children were employed in some factories. But more important fact is that nearly 50 per cent of the registered factories in India, did not submit any return about their labour to the Labour Bureau. Among different plantation, the plantation engaged the maximum proportion of children among total workers, i.e., nearly 10 per cent of children on average till 1981 in spite of all the acts prohibiting employment of children under the age of 15 years.

It is very unfortunate that though the Indian Children and also the child labour are protected legally, in fact there is no mechanism operating properly in the State level or in national level to look after the welfare of the children. We the Indians, are very much vociforus of our different types of moral values but at no time majority of us considered that protection of children is moral duty and obligation of our social and communal life. There are several legislative measures to protect the children of the country but any numbers of legislative measures will be useless the adult members of the society and the guardians of the children are conscious of their duty and obligation to the children, who were brought to this world without considering their option. The children cannot be treated as a piece of property. The common man of the country should be made aware of their obligation to the children and they should be brought to a stage, where they can consciously accept these protective measures. Just like Sardar Act, all the protective measures will simply remain in books and archives without achieving any goal. In spite of Sardar Act for nearly 70 years, *i.e.,* till 1981 girls were married between the age of 10 years and 14 years (Rajasthan had 18 per cent of child marriage of female and all the States, except the States of North-East India and Himachal Pradesh had married girls between 19 years and 14 years).

While trying to remove a social malady, *i.e.,* child labour, we must try to motivate first a section of society who are affected by this malady. The parents when have too many mouth to feed and do not have sufficient means to provide food for them, with despair engage the children to earn something. The State and the country along with volunteers should keep an watchful eye. The members of the society should be made aware of the social evil and should try to protect the future generation of the country.

Because of negligence of the society, the fertility rate cannot be brought down to the ideal level and hence the people of lower economic condition depend on the income of the children. Even today, we find that girls hardly 8 or 9 years old are brought and sold in the brothels with the knowledge of their parents.

In India, almost all the child workers are employed with full knowledge of their parents. In a country with high fertility, low technological level of development and poor economic condition, the child will be forced to earn for his family or atleast for himself. The sorry plight of the children who have to work from a tender age can only be improved by developing social awareness, moral obligation and proper enforcement of all the acts provided for the protection of the children, with more watchful eyes.

TABLE 31.1

Percentage Proportion of Children in India (0-14 years)

Period	Per cent
1901	38.05
1911	37.84
1921	38.68
1931	38.50
1941	39.14
1951	38.42
1961	41.04
1971	42.03
1981	39.70

TABLE 31.2

Proportion of Child Workers to Different Age Categories (Based on 1981 Census Data)

	Total	*Rural*	*Urban*
Total Children (0-14 years)	26,30,65,000	20,54,61,000	5,76,04,000
Total child workers	1,35,93,000	1,25,54,000	10,39,000
Total Child Workers as			
(a) P.C. of total children	5.16	6.11	1.80
(b) P.C. of children of 5 to 14 years.	7.58	8.97	2.64
(c) P.C. of children of 10 to 14 years.	15.86	18.93	5.36

TABLE 31.3

Literacy Rate and School Drop-out in Different States

	Literacy Rate in 10 years and above (1981)	*Non-School going children in 10 to 14 years (1981)*	*School Drop-out in primary stage in (1974-78)*
India	43.52	49.45	62.7
Andhra Pradesh	34.91	58.88	62.2
Bihar	32.07	58.56	65.7
Gujarat	51.70	39.37	60.7
Haryana	43.43	45.11	28.9
Karnataka	45.57	51.93	67.5
Kerala	80.99	14.04	9.4
Madhya Pradesh	34.70	58.75	65.8
Maharashtra	55.22	37.41	56.6
Orissa	41.18	56.54	70.9
Punjab	46.78	37.14	46.5
Rajasthan	30.67	60.01	57.0
Tamil Nadu	53.54	44.53	43.7
Uttar Pradesh	33.59	56.40	76.0
West Bengal	49.52	47.14	72.3

REFERENCES

Barooah, P.P., Working Children in Urban Delhi (Research Project) Indian Council of Child Welfare, 1977.

Kapoor, Anup K., "Child Labour in Himalayas" *Himalayas Man in Nature,* Vol. 3 (8-9), Jan.-Feb. 1980.

Kulashreshtha, J.C., Child Labour in India.

Mahapatra, L.K., Problem of Child Labour in Unorganised Sectors and Their Social Service Needs in Cuttack District (Research Project) Ministry of Social Welfare, 1980.

Menon, S., "Sivakasi, The Little Japan of India" The Times of India, 7.10.1979.

Mitra, A., "Employment of children under fifteen" in India's Population Aspect and Quality Control. Abhinav, New Delhi, 1978.

Raza Moonis and Sudesh Nangia, Atlas of the Child in India, Concept Publishing Company, 1986.

Pandhe, M.K., Child Labour in India (ed.), India Book Exchange, 1979.

Patnaik, M., "Child Labour in India: Size and Occupational Distribution" *The Journal of Public Administration,* 24 (3), July-Sept. 1979.

Tripathy, S.K., Child Labour in Orissa (Unpublished), M. Phil Thesis. Department of Labour Welfare, Utkal University.

Government of India, Child in India: A Statistical Profile, Govt. of India, Ministry of Welfare, 1985.

32

EXPLOITATION OF CHILD LABOUR

Child labour is one of the oldest profession of the world and has remained as the most neglected phenomenon for the last few centuries. Towards the mid-twentieth century social reformers, jurists and the like conveyancers began to bring reforms against such neglected and exploited class of human labour considering their tender age.

The most vulnerable areas of child labour are found in the categories of agricultural field workers in the rural areas and they may be found as agricultural/ forest labourers or cultivators; workers engaged in livestock, fishing, plantation and orchards, pottery, carpentary, black-smithing, household industries, domestic work (serventing). They are also found in various trade, commerce, transportation services, storage, construction, maintenance, works and other developmental schemes or projects.

According to the National Sample Survey the country's child labour force has been estimated to be reaching 36.25 million currently. A State-wise survey reveals that 'Andhra Pradesh has the largest child labour force of 11.2 per cent of the total child labour force in the country, followed by Karnataka with 8.7 per cent. The number of child workers in Orissa is estimated to be 7.23 lakhs. Most of the children are employed in hotels, restaurants, sweet ships, tea-stalls, road-side *dhabas,* automobile repair shops, foundries, recognised and unrecognised engineering units, cinema halls, as cleaners for buses and taxies, a few are also employed as domestic servants, as usual the other traditional field of work such as pottery, black-smithy, gold smithy, weaving, *Kalam Kari,* cobblery, carpentary, sculpture making, stone cutting, grafficking, brick-clins, tannerying, etc. Quite a sizeable number of children are also found as rag-pickers.

The working condition of these child workers is not uniform and varies according to the avocations. There is no standard guide-line nor any yardstick for their work. These children are required to work to the satisfaction of their masters which occasionally (now-a-days quite frequently) goes beyond their capacities. Quite often the children are ruthlessly exploited to work and innocently fall prey to the meagre allurement promised by their masters, which is seldom fulfilled. There is no time schedule for rendering services by children working in hotels, restaurants, sweet stalls, tea stalls, roadside *Dhabas,* etc., and quite often it is seen that children are working round the clock, in such organisations. They even receive mercyless beatings for showing unwilful latches in performance of their duties and are forced to work with their woes and worries remaining untold, unheared and un-redressed. The child labourers in the organised and unorganised industrial sector face similar hardship in rendering services to their employers since most of the workers are engaged in job works and are paid poorly for each completed job and often not paid on one pretext or the other. In the private sector the story is altogether different where the children are denied even the minimal liberties for a human living and are treated mostly as sub-bonded labourers.

The grave situation of exploitation of child labourer affected a many, among the social thinkers, philosophers, jurists, legislators *et. al.* To combat against such exploitation effective legislations were deployed into the society to arrest, avoid or modify child labour in the society. This chapter aims to aggrandize the semantics of problems and perspectives of child labour in India.

Recognition of Rights of Children Under International Law

The Geneva Declaration of the Rights of the Child, 1924 is the first convention adopted by the League of Nations in which Rights to children was considered. The Universal Declaration of Human Rights as adopted by the Untied Nations General Assembly in 1948 incorporated within it certain basic rights for children. Article 24 of the International Covenant of Civil and Political Rights and Article 10 of the International Covenant on Economic, Social and Cultural Rights deal particularly with the rights of the children Directly emphasising the needs for 'Rights of Children' an independent 'Declaration on the Rights of Child' was passed by the United Nations in 1959.

The U.N. Declarations proclaim principles of child welfare, having application to every social condition, by conferring specific rights to children through Social Security Legislation prohibiting any discrimination[1] There are also some new concepts manifested in the Declaration which ensures the child a right to a name of nationality[2] and to adequate nutrition, housing, recreation and medical service.[3] It further says that a child shall not be admitted to employment before an appropriate minimum age.[4] and in no case be caused or permitted to be engaged in any occupation or employment which would prejudice his education or interfere with his physical, mental or moral development[5] and in case of physically handicapped child a special treatment, education and care are provided.[6]

The U.N. Declaration is an International document with great potential for improving the social and legal status of children in the world. But all children are not born free and cannot claim equal status by their natural order because they are distincted to the social, economic and political factors in which they are born or are living. They may also be another difficulty that these U.N. Declarations are merely a proclamation of general principles and have less binding nature upon the State Signatories, even after ratification as because most of the countries face difficulties in accepting the legal obligations due to their economic and social conditions. However, in 1978 the Polish Representative introduced a draft on an International Convention on the Rights of the Child in the U.N. Commission on Human Rights,[7] which seeks to transform the proclamation of 1959 U.N. Declaration into a legally binding Instrument.

By virtue of the said conventions children below the age of fifteen are not usually considered part of the work force. However, a large number of children in the developing world are forced to work. It is evident from the above discussion, therefore, that notwithstanding the International Concern for the children the responsibility of implementing the international standards falls upon the respective countries who are required to practically carry it out for the protection and safeguarding the interests of the children at the global level.

Constitutional Safeguards Against Child Labour in India

The Constitution carries important expression of the government policies against the abuse of child labour. Fundamentally the Constitution provides that 'no child below the age of fourteen (as against the U.N. Declaration of fifteen) years shall be employed to work in any factory or mines or engaged in any hazardous employment,[8] It further proclaims that the State shall, in particular, direct its policy towards securing that the health and strength of the tender age of children are not forced by economic necessity to enter avocation unsuited to their age or strength.[9] It further enjoins that childhood and youth are to be protected against exploitation against moral and material abandonment.[10] Apart from that the Constitution also endeavours to provide free and compulsory education for all children until they complete the age of fourteen years.[11]

Besides the above mentioned provisions there are also certain other provisions contained in Part IV, dealing with the Directive Principles of State Policy, which although do not lay emphasis on the child welfare directly, yet the children are bound to be the beneficiaries if these provisions are implemented. Article 38, 41, 42, 43, 46 and 47 contain such provisions, which *inter alia* provides strategy for indirectly promoting the welfare of the children.

Article 38(1) provides that State shall strive to promote the welfare of the people by securing and protecting as effectively as it may secure a social order in which justice, social economic and political shall inform all institutions of national life. Naturally, an effective implmentation fro this principle resulting in promoting the welffare of the people through social, economic and political justice, is expected to promote proportionately the child welfare.

Similarly according to the provisions of Article 41, it is required that the State shall within the limits of its economic capacity and development; make effective provision for securing, *inter-alia,* the right to education and to public assistance in cases of unemployment and other cases of undeserved want. Implementation of such provision is expected to promote the welfare of the children proportionately.

According to the provisions of Article 42 of the Constitution the State is required to secure just and humane conditions of work besides some maternity benefit. This provision envisages a healthy psychological environment to the child particularly during the significant period when the child requires a normal bringing-up.

Article 43 of the Constitution lays emphasis that the State shall endeavour to secure, by suitable legislation, to all workers agricultural, industrial or otherwise; not only work but also living wage with specified conditions of work ensuring a decent standard of life and full enjoyment of leisure and social and cultural opportunities. This provision also includes child labourers in its widest interpretation.

Article 46 of the Constitution, similarly lays down that the State shall promote with special care the educational and economic interests of the Scheduled Castes and Scheduled Tribes and other workers sections of the Society. The children belonging to such category are the worst affected and need to be constitutionally protected.

Similarly Article 47 of the Constitution lays emphasis that it shall be the primary duty of the State to raise the standard of living of its people which includes children.

However, in spite of the foregoing discussions of the Constitutional Provisions the assessment of progress made against child labour exploitation or the welfare measures provided to them appears to be disappointing.[12] However, basing on the I.L.O. Conventions and recommendations and the Declaration of the Rights of the Child adopted by the General Assembly of the United Nations more than 250 Central and State Laws were enacted pertaining to children. A broad classification in which these enactments fall is—marriage, legitimacy, guardianship, maintenance, adoption, criminal law, reformatory services, probation, prohibition of smoking, supression of immoral traffic, child welfare, prevention of vagrancy and beggary, transfer of property, education of children, child health and child labour and many other miscellaneous matters.

In regard to child employment several laws were passed with an objective of improving working conditions of such children and in protecting them against abuse, exploitation and health hazardous. One such law, the Employment of Children Act was passed in 1938 and was amended as many as five times during the years 1939, 1948, 1949, 1951 and 1978 only to ameliorate better working conditions to such children. Several other Acts such as the Factories Act, 1948, State Shops and Commercial Establishment Acts, Plantation Labour Act,, 1951, Motor Transport Workers, Act, 1951. The Mines Act, 1952, Merchant Shipping Act, 1961, Atomic Energy Act, 1962, etc. regulate the conditions of work that affect children. Many such laws are honoured more in the breach than in observance. It would be appropriate to undertake comprehensive review of all existing laws aimed at either prohibiting children from being employed in dangerous occupations or protecting them from being crudely exploited. It would also be desirable to discuss the recommendations of the National Committee on Child Labour set up by Government of India in 1972, who were entrusted the task of examining the existing laws, their adequacy and the corrective actions required to improve the implementation of such laws. Considering firstly, the overall recommendations of the National Committee it can be stated that the economic problems involved in the employment of children are very much significant. The poverty resulting with inadequate family income and the desire to supplement the family needs compel the children to work. Indeed the parents of many of low income group cannot afford to educate their children even if education is free or compulsory. For them an uneducated child is an asset because an educated becomes a double liability because of : (a) Loss of earning if the child did not work; and (b) Additional expenditure on child's education, however, small.

Secondly, in the legislative field, the socio-legal problems vested in the employment of children frustrate the objectives of child labour exploitation because of the following (a) children who are orphans, destitutes, neglected and abandoned are required to work for a living are circumvented to work; and (c) children belonging to the migrant families are compelled to work for a living.

Major Fields of Child Labour in India

The evil of employment of children in agriculture and industrial sectors in India is a product of economic, social and among others, inadequate legislative measures. The social evil involved in the employment of children may be due to illiteracy and occasionally shifting towards lack of development of child's personality which continues beyond his childhood and/or adulthood. There may also be yet another cause which may force children to employment particularly when the society neglects the child indifferent attitude towards him. The most common cause of child labour in this regard perhaps due to the sinister attitude or improper appreciation on the part of the parents in respect of child's education, capabilities, intelligence; or that education could help in stabilising or improving their economic conditions, or would become significant in the future earnings of their children. Also the parents show an improper appreciation of their child's educational attainments which may benefit their employment prospectus or otherwise help in their standard of living through such education and employment.[13]

Economic problems compel children to work to supplement the family needs even in spite of free education facilities offered to children. Considering all these factors it can be stated that the indifference attitude of legislatures to provide adequate legislation or proper of implementation of such legislation, if any, is not there in order to regular the child labour, or in case it is possible, in order to prohibit children to work no formula has been devised to minimise exploitation of such child labour.

Owing to abject poverty, the children have never enough to eat and lack clothings and medical care and are forced themselves in the labour market to have minimal subsistance. And legislation totally prohibiting child labour, would virtually amount to inflicting on these children an unbearable suffering and in the absence of possible alternatives, such a measure would likely aggravate rather than mitigate their misery and hardships.[14] Thus, the total eradication of child labour is neither feasible nor desirable in the foreseable future.

It may be suggested here that in order to meet the said impediments on child labour certain effective policies may be implemented which may be (a) short term policy or may be (b) long term policy. In the short term policy it is necessary to see that suitable legislations are provided which would eliminate and minimise the impact of adverse conditions affecting child labour,[15] and improve their working conditions which can be done by (i) regulating hours of work, (ii) allowing weekly holidays and leave, (iii) providing health, safety and welfare measures. In the long run policy it is necessary to create feasible facilities by providing proper climate of work, social security, non-formal educational training and such other facilities which would gradually eradicate forced child labour, giving scope for exploitation.

Legislative Attempts to Protect Child Labour in India

There was no statutory provisions regulating the employment of the children in industry till 1881, the year in which First Indian Law defining child was passed,[16] besides prescribing prohibitory regulations for employment of children below seven years of age. But the said Factories Act, 1881 was insufficient to control child labour as a result of which the Act was amended by virtue of Indian Factories (Amendment) Act 1891; which too failed to achieve its' objectives prompting to re-enact a fresh law known as Factories Act, 1911, *Inter alia* providing prohibitory regulation for employing children in certain dangerous occupations or working during the night hours. But the formation of International Labour Organisation, after the First World War, necessitated a fresh amended Factory Act, 1922 which raised the minimum age of the child to 15 years. However, children below the age of 12 years were only prohibited to employment prescribing an obligatory condition that, for employment, such children are required to produce certificate of age and certificate of fitness from a qualified Medical Practitioner. Subsequently the Factories Act, 1934 raised the minimum age of employment of children from 12 to 13 years, besides providing other protection relating to their employment in certain occupations, prescribed hours of work including intervals of rest. The present Factories Act, 1948 however, prescribes prohibitory regulations for employment of children in any factory who have not completed 14 years, an adolescent as a person who has competed 15 years but is less than 18 years and a young person includes both children and adolescent.[18]

The Indian Mines Act, 1951 defines a child to be a person who has not completed the age of 15[19] years and an adolescent means who has completed 15 years of age but is less than 18 years of age[20] and puts an embargo that an adolescent who has completed the age of 16 years can only be employed in an part of the mine which is under ground.[21]

In the Motor Transport Worker's Act, 1961 employment of the children in motor transport undertakings in any capacity is absolutely prohibited,[22] however, an adolescent can only be employed if a certificate of fitness is granted to him to work as a worker in a motor transport undertaking.[23]

A child who has completed 12 years of age can be employed to work in any plantation according tot he Plantations Labour act, 1951.[24]

Thus, all these enactments says that a young person can be employed either in a factory, mine, motor transport organisation or in a plantation, provided the said young person is medically examined and found fit to bear strain of different work and such certificate should always be kept in the custody of the manager of the factory; while a reference of such certificate of fitness being kept in the custody of the said child-worker, so that it can be checked at any time without any inconvenience.[25]

It may be pointed out that there may be doubtless questions as to whether children in such organisations know the age restrictions imposed upon them? And a certificate of fitness is a mandatory condition before being employed in such organisations? Perhaps the answer is a big No. The reasons for such ignorance on the part of a job seeker in multifarious, moving from posts to pillars for knowing the rules and regulations is a hazardous task, nor that the child is so much educated to get acquainted with the legal framework of the Factories Act. They in turn depend upon some middle men, under a brokerage, and learn how to get exploited financially. It may be noted that such young persons seek job mostly on the ground of economic necessity and the initial exploitation, if not digested, is at least borne because of possibilities for future redemption of debts. In the process many suffer untold allurements and hopes remaining fervent they submit to further exploitations.

Legally speaking, the procedure for fitness certificate with or without conditions, by a certifying Surgeon is cumbersome and quite often depends upon his (certifying surgeon's) personal satisfaction as to the completion of statutory age by the said young person, which is further subjected to revokation in case the young person is no longer found fit to hold that certificate. All these provisions give a wide discretionary powers on the certifying surgeon to enable a young person to work in a factory for which he had to resort to be exploited financially for a fervent hope of getting employment.

After crossing these hurdles, a child out of ignorance may not know that the is required only to work for not more than four and a half hours, nor that his shifts are only limited to two, barring night hours between 10 p.m. to 8 a.m.[26] In spite of the fact that there are spelled responsibilities of the management and there are survelliance agents (Inspectors) to scrutinise the same, a good deal of child labourers are exploited in the private sector entrepreneurs, if not in the public sector organisations. Helplessly the child worker submits to such exploitation, undermining his health, for a hope that he can earn a little more, if he can achieve an extra target of finished products.

Notwithstanding the above facts, a special Article for India fixing a minimum age i.e., thirteen years for the employment of children in the transportation of passengers, goods or mail by rail or in the handling of goods at docks, wharves or quays was included in a convention adopted in the 23rd Session of International Labour Conference, on the basis of which the employment of children Act, 1938 was passed. This Act prohibits employment of children under 15 years of age in occupations connected with the transport of goods, passengers or mail by railways or handling goods in books.[27] The Act further envisages that a child below the age of 15 years shall not be employed and the period of work for such child should be so fixed as to enable him to have rest for at least twelve consecutive hours and to ensure that he is not required to work between 10 p.m. to 7 a.m.[28] But the above mentioned restrictions are not applicable as against an apprentice or any person receiving vocational training in any of the aforesaid occupations. The competent authority may also waive the application of the said provisions in the public interest, possibly, allowing child labour exploitation.

The fifty year old Child Labour Employment Act, 1938 (as amended in 1978) prohibit children below the age of 14 years in *beedi* making,[29] carpet weaving; cement manufacture including bagging of cement; cloth printing: dyeing and weaving; cotton spinning, manufacture of matches, explosives and fire works; mica-cutting and splitting; shellac manufacture; soap manufacture, tanning, wool cleaning; utensil making' bangle making; etc.[30] But has such restrictions or prohibitions really worked out? The answer will no doubt, be a big NO. On the contrary, it would be seen that in most of such units only few adults are employed to supervise the 90 per cent child labour available in such organisations. No Inspector or Medical Officer can restrict or prohibit nor any other authority can close such units, because of organised racketeering and further socio-politically also it is impossible, else majority of such children will be thrown to embrace vagrancy or beggary.

Conclusion

The Directive Principles of State Policy embodied in the Constitution of India provides policy of protection of children with a self-imposing direction towards securing the health and strength of workers, particularly to see that the same in the children of tender age is not abused, nor they are forced by economic necessity to enter into avocations unsuited to their age or strength, and are only protected against exploitation but also from moral or material abandonment. Notwithstanding the pious promises of the law markers, the profile on eradication of child labour is not too assuring. The only solution there, is to minimise the child labour exploitation.

The government agency principally responsible for abolition of child labour exploitation through it's Social Welfare Departments, should set up a separate monitoring unit to maintain a continuing review of the adequacy of existing legislation.

The existing laws relating to minimum age for the employment of children should be uniform and should be in tune with the latest Children's Act and should be consolidated into a comprehensive law covering the minimum pre-conditions for the employment of child labour to ensure that their early start in a vocation does not cripple them for life. There is also no uniformity in the labour legislation in regard to working hours, duration of night work and rest interval for a child labor. They vary from Act to Act. Small industries, cottage industries, rural oriented production units, private sectors in industry and agriculture and some unrecognised sectors do not have any provision to regulate working hours of children nor there are any means to prevent the child from being exploited or is subjected to unregulated working hours or committed to hazardous conditions of work. There is, therefore, necessary to have a uniform legislation in regard to working hours of children.

The constitutional frame work and national policy for child welfare take into account very well all phases of child development. But a large number of legally uncovered gaps due to administrative hindrances frustrate the objective of child welfare. In order to avoid the same comprehensive secular law on child, placing the 'child' in the Concurrent List, by amending the Constitution, would help in proper implementation of welfare programmes for the children and the comfortable co-operation between Centre and States would render quick administrative actions.

Denial of opportunity to the Children due to economic difficulties would necessarily hinder the social progress of the child forced to fate employment. Therefore, it is necessary that the hours of work of child labour be fixed in such a manner as to enable him to attend the schooling and if the number of child labourers are more, than an organised non-formal education system if imparted at the child's working place, possibly it would help educating him.

The penal provision in various labour legislations is inadequate in respect of violation of working hours and thereby the employer remains undeterred. It is, therefore, desirable to prescribe certain deterrent punishment (serve penalty and cancellation of licence) so that the commission of similar offence is not repeated and such punishment may also set an example to other employers not to violated the legal prescriptions. Such laws should not only concentrate on organised sectors but also should be more meticulous to look after the unorganised sector.

In the search for alternatives to minimise child labour exploitation, it is necessary to encourage programme of social action groups, like voluntary organisations to serve public good and the government should allow them competent leadership and considerable flexibility aiding them financially in such operations. It may also be helped to organise Legal-Aid Camps through Law students and social workers to impart de-professionalised justice to these child victims so that exploitation of child labour can be considerably reduced.

REFERENCES

1. U.N. Declaration of the Rights of the Child, Art. I. Quoted from *Chanleu, Elisha* and *Morier, G.M.*, Declaration of the Rights of the Child, Vol. XXII, International Child Welfare Review, 1968 Edn.
2. *Id.*, Article III.
3. *Id.*, Article IV.
4. *Id.*, Article IX.

5. *Id.*, Article IX (2).
6. Declaration of the Rights of the Child, 1959, Article V.
7. Bulletin of Human Rights, No. 19, Jan.-Mar. 1978.
8. Article 24.
9. Article 39 (e).
10. Article 39 (F), by virtue of Constitution 42nd Amendment Act, 1976, S. 7, w.e.f. 3.1.1977.
11. Article 45.
12. Upadhyaya, M.L., Constitutional Prescription, Planning Perspective and Profile of Children, Kurukshetra Law Journal, V. 7, p. 11' (1981).
13. See, Pandia, M.K., Child Labour in India, 1979 Edn., p. 54.
14. See, Report of the National Commission of Labour, 1969, p. 386.
15. Recommendation of the National Seminar on Employment of children, 25-28, Nov. 1975, New Delhi: quoted from Child and the Law, *Supra citt.*
16. Factories act, 1881 prescribes a person below twelve years of age to be called as a child.
17. Sec. 67.
18. Sec. 2 (b), (c) and (d).
19. Sec. 2 (i) (e).
20. Sec. (i) (a).
21. Sec. 40.
22. Sec. 21.
23. Sec. 22
24. Sec. 24.
25. Section 68 of the Factories Act, 1948 read with Section 27 of the Plantations Labour Act, 1951, Section 23 of the Motor Transport Worker's Act 1951 and Section 40 of the Mines Act, 1952: See also Merchant Shipping Act, 1961, Atomic Energy Act, 1962 and State Shops and Commercial Establishment Acts.
26. Sec. 71 of the Factories Act, 1948.
27. The minimum age limit of 14 years is prescribed under Section 6 (1-A) of the Indian Ports Act, 1908.
28. Section 3 of Employment of Children Act, 1938.
29. See Beedi and Cigar Workers (Conditions of Employment) Act, 1966.
30. Section 3 (3) of Employment of Children Act, 1938.

33

WORKING CONDITIONS AND ENVIRONMENT OF CHILD LABOUR

A child can be defined as someone who needs adult care and protection for physical, psychological and intellectual development until he/she is able to become independently integrated into the adult world.

1. The Concept of Child in Relation to Labour

The concept of child labour begins with the working child himself/herself who is often deprived of his childhood opportunities for all round personality development. The conflict between economic pursuits and those of growth and education give rise to the problem of child labour.

The child labour refer to both as economic practice as well as an attendant social evil. Its perception as a social evil and a need of protection against it is a relatively recent development. The concept of child has two fold relation to labour, on one hand, they are incapable of performing the physical or mental work, until reaching a minimum age, in the production world of labour. On the other hand educational requirement, as understood in law and ILO recommendations depends on the stage of economic development. Technological progress widens the gap between family's ability to educate and the requirements of the productive system.

As children are subject to the responsibility and authority of their family, only factors affecting the whole family and preventing it from fulfilling its function can explain the persistence of child work. This is what causes work to be classed as irregular, as it is neither 'deviant conduct' nor appropriate to their age.

The irregular character of work poses the questions of forms of exploitation. When children have to work because the family is so over exploited that it can not care for them properly they are exploited indirectly as well as directly as workers.

2. Statutory Provisions Regulating Working Conditions and Environment: An Analysis

On November 20, 1959 the general assembly of United Nations declared the *basic rights* of the child and children's charter number 16 says "for every child, protection against labour that stunts growth, either, physical or mental, that limits education that deprives children of the rights of comradeship, of play and of joy" is a basic right.

International Labour organisation policy programmes are based on the following principal phases:

1. Prohibition of child labour.
2. Protection of children at work.
3. Attacking the basic causes of child labour.
4. Provision of vocational preparation for all children.

Constitutional Mandate: Indian Scanario

Keeping in view the U.N. and ILO standards and recommendations, India is one of the few countries in the world that has adopted a comprehensive 'National Policy for Children' in 1974, which recognises the children as the "nation's supreme important asset" and declares that the nation is responsible for their nurture and solicitude, as well as for provision of free and compulsory education for children, also the prohibition of child labour and to protect them against neglect, cruelty, hazards and exploitation by promoting effective implementation of existing legislation.

Wide array of acts eg. Factories Act 1948, Employment of Children Act 1938, Plantation Labour Act 1951, Mines Act 1952, Children (pledging of labour) Act 1933, Apprentices Act 1961, Shops and Establishment Act etc. are supposed to regulate the employment of children with a purpose to protect the health and well being of children. These basically cover three-major aspects—minimum age of employment, prohibition of night work and medical examination. The laws, however, are not at par with the international standards laid down by the ILO because of various reasons viz. poverty, lack of educational facilities, traditions, unorganised nature of various economic sectors and smallness of the manufacturing units etc.

Minimum Age

To project some of the deficiencies in the matter of minimum age, it may be pointed out that there is no law fixing any age for employment in agriculture. Factories Act and in cases of non-industrial employment stipulated minimum age ranges from 12 to 14 years, whereas ILO convention requires minimum age for any employment (except hazardous occupations) to be 15 years.

Medical Examination

The Indian laws are deficient in the matter of medical examination of children as compared to ILO standards. Only Factories Act and Mines Act require medical examination upto the age of 18 years where as ILO stipulates medical examination upto 21 years in hazardous jobs. No law covers unorganised sector in this regard.

Night Work

Indian laws only cover industry in this regard., Non industrial occupations have been ignored so far.

The ILO recommendations lay down higher standards than the conventions. For instance, it has been suggested that minimum age for employment should be 16 and that there should be the same minimum age for all employment except hazardous jobs. There should be satisfactory standards of safety and health for employment of children. There should be compulsory medical examination for workers upto the age of 21 years. There should be other suitable occupations to give them the advantage of financial aid during the period of medical treatment, schooling or vocational training.

3. Working Conditions: Projections from Research

Minimum Age

The author carried out in the year 1983 "A Study of Child Labour in Baroda City." Research findings reveal that 44% are in Domestic service and 2% in apprentice. A comparison with "the Shops and Commercial Establishment Act of Gujarat" which stipulates the age of working child between 12 to 17 years reflect violation of law in the establishment category.

A survey of child labour in Delhi (ICCW) projects that 60% children belonged to age group of 13-14, 24 to 35% in the age group of 11 to 12 years and remaining were below 10 years of age. A study in Bombay revealed that 39% were in the age group of 9 to 12 years and 78% in the age group of 12 to 15 years. Most of the children joined the labour force by the age of 10 years. Irrespective of sex, eldest child in the family had to work (96% boys and 90% girls).

This shows the violation of the related laws as well as exploitation of tender innocent children even below 12 years of age.

House of Work

In the survey of child labour in Baroda queries were made on hours of work which is presented in the tabular form.

An inter -category comparison of the figures shows that the mean working hours are high in establishment and apprentice category 10.03 and 9.4 hours respectively; whereas only an average of 4.87 hours in domestic service (intermittent job not covered by any law). A comparison with state laws reveals that working hours in establishment are on an average 4.03 hours more than the standard and out of which 44% of children were below 12 years of age. Further scrutiny of the data reveals that length of work hours was 7.00 a.m. to 9.00 p.m. as compared to the GSIEA standard 6.00 a.m. to 7.00 p.m.

A study at Delhi (ICCW) also reveals that daily work hours were excessive often more than 10 hours a day. In "A study on working children in Hissar" by C.K. Sharma and R. Singh it was found that 56% children had to work for 15 to 18 hours/day.

The review indicates beyond doubt that hours of work are excessive and violation of laws seems to be a rule than an exception.

TABLE 33.1

Frequency and Percentage Distribution of Spread Over of Working Hours in Different Jobs

Spread over of work hours	*Establishment n = 33 F*	*%*	*Domestic service n = 12 F*	*%*	*Apprentice n = 5 F*	*%*
2-4	—	—	4	33.33	—	—
4-6	1	3.03	6	50.00	—	—
6-8	1	3.03	2	16.67	—	—
8-10	14	42.42	—	—	4	80
10-12	14	42.42	—	—	1	20
12-14	3	9.08	—	—	—	—
Total	33	100	12	100	5	100
X		10.3		4.67		9.4
Md		10.7		4.67		9.25
Mo		10.15		5.0		9.0
SD		1.65		1.37		8.0

Rest Interval and Holidays

GSCEA stipulates ½ an hour rest after every 3 hours of work and one day weekly off. But in establishment category 42.42% of the children were getting ½ an hour rest interval between 12 noon to 3 p.m. 24.24% were not getting weekly off, 36.36% got ½ a day weekly off with pay and 9.09% without pay. 12.12% were having one day off with pay where as 15.15% without pay. So the infringement of law was common. It was same for apprentice. Domestic service being a part time job rest interval is out of question but they too were not getting any regular weekly off.

Wage and Pay Period

Table No. 33.2 presents the wages and the period of payment as found in the survey of child labour at Baroda.

Average wage earning was 109.84 for establishment which is Rs. 60/- less than prescribed law and for 72.73% cases pay period was daily and in domestic service means income was Rs. 100/- on monthly basis for all. Only 2 apprentices were getting stipend.

Studies carried out in Delhi and Bombay also report the same flouting of law. In some jobs child workers are paid both in cash and in kind (food, clothing, shelter etc.)

child workers, generally pay a large part to their parents retaining only a small sum for their personal expenditure.

TABLE 33.2

Frequency and Percentage of Distribution of Respondents on Basis of Wages and Pay Periods

	Establishment *N* = 33		*Apprentice* *n* = 5		*Domestic Service* *n*-12	
	F	%	*F*	%	*F*	%
I Pay Period						
Daily	24	73.73	—	—	—	—
Monthly	9	27.27	2	40	12	100
Total	33	100	2*	40	12	100
II Wages Rs/Month						
0-50	—	—	—	—	6	50
50-100	13	39.39	1	20	6	50
100-150	17	51.52	1	20	—	—
150-200	3	9.09	—	—	—	—
Total	33	100	2	40	12	100
	X	109.81	* 3 were	50		
	Md	109.41	not	50		
	Mo	125	getting	50		
	Sd	31.42	stipend	50		

4. An Overview of Environment Where Children Work

The environment of the work place i.e. location, structure, light and ventilation and the continued association with adult workers have significant impact on the growth and development of the child-perhaps more significant than the working conditions.

Field observations and survey in a few cities viz Delhi, Madras, Bombay, Baroda and Hissar and study of labour bureau of the ministry of labour portray horrifying picture of the working environment in which children live and work. There is no doubt that it is in the urban unorganised sector only child workers are treated the worst, exploited most and undergo greatest privations.

They may be forced to work in awkward positions in badly lit and ventilated, noisy or unhygienic premises in terms of gases, dust or dampness, crammed together with other workers, exposed to vagaries of weather without adequate clothing or footwear without adequate means of security etc. These children are often devoid of medical facilities, proper place for rest and toilet facilities, educational or training facilities, they are often victims of ill treatment by employers or adult co-workers, so on an so forth.

In electro plating workshops children of tender age were doing routine and repetitive tasks like polishing or mixing 'masalas' with their entire body covered with black soot.

The most unhygienic conditions were observed in the case of children collecting rags and waste material. Their physique and clothing reveal the extent of their poverty and deprivation. Research surveys in Baroda and other cities reveal that parents and working children including employers were utterly ignorant of the laws regulating different working conditions and environment of child labour.

5. Repercussions of Child Labour on H.R.D.

In order to find out the effects of child labour in terms of physical and behavioural changes as perceived by parents and children different statements were prepared. Parents and working children were interviewed.

Changes as perceived by Parents

Parents view regarding behavioural changes after the child has joined work force reveals that parents perceived positive behavioural traits in the personality of the child. Any how 18.18% respondents indicated less desirable characteristics, 70.46% medium and only 11.36% perceived highly desirable characteristics. "Now he does not obey us" is the negative change with which 70.45% parents partially agreed.

Regarding effect of job on child's health only 8% children had fallen sick after they had joined the labour force, it was ordinary fever, 36% of the parents noted changes in health. Out of these 44.44% accepted he has become healthy, 55.55% felt he has become weak, 66.66% of the respondents complained about body aches. 2 children had accident at place of work. One was a minor finger burn and in other case child's stomach was burnt, but the family got free medical compensation from employer.

Changes: as Perceived by Child

52% children found the "Job tiring." Further probe in the date showed 62.5% out of them were employed in catering lari working more than 10 hours per day. 9% children employed in production work said because of continuous bending and pasting work their neck and back ached. Only 5.38% found the work hazardous 34.65% felt job is "monotonous," as many as 53.85% children were disgusted with the `employers' behaviour. Regarding effect of job 64% children felt "tired and fatigued" specially those who returned late, 24% reported' Now I often do not keep well. 50% of respondents expressed Now I feel very elderly." 60% of them said `I want to play more with children."

Consequence of Child Labour — On the Child and the Labour Force

It may lead to distaste for regular employment and many remain unskilled casual labour throughout life. As a general rule, when child performs precarious and insignificant work from an early age, it leads to intertia for acquisition of any genuine qualifications for more skilled work. Immaturity may lead to inclination to learn something which may end his chances of improving scio-economic status. At the macro level child labour weakens the working population by having two fold depressing effects, firstly, it deprives an adult of the job in question. Secondly, upon the wage level of adult workers at lest in that particular sector because he does the job at low rates, thus reducing bargaining power of adult workers which may influences the pattern of employment significantly, unproductively.

Physical Consequences

Working conditions and environment which has already been discussed at length earlier has long lasting effects on a child's health. Researches reveal that excessive heat bad weather, dust, noise, poor light and ventilation, harmful gases, overcrowdedness may lead to skin troubles, bronchitis, tuberculosis and many other diseases.

An inquiry concerning children under 12 years of age working on plantations showed that 25.6% of the children were in an advanced stage of vit. A deficiency. One in ten of the children showed signs of riboflavin deficiency. Anaemic and chronic bronchitis are common among child workers in the bidi industry.

Physical growth retardation or deformities may result because of heavy loads, awkward body positions, chronic fatigue. Over exertion coupled with unbalanced diet may lead to malnutrition. Lack of concentration may result in accidents in hazardous jobs.

Thus it is a scientifically established fact that depending upon working conditions and environment the child workers may be harmed directly or indirectly and its result may be carried over into adult life.

Mental and Psychological Consequences

Adolescence and puberty is a period of profound mental and emotional changes in a child. Child's inadequate comprehension and imitation of adult world may lead to "pseudo" maturity. Creativeness and fantasies which characterise children are promptly replaced by the practical harsh realities that mark the world of work i.e. production and services. These inturn impoverish the whole mental world of working children. It has already been reported that many children felt elderly after joining labour force. These premature economic worries are unhealthy for the present and future well-being of child. As already reported 53.85% children were disgusted with the ill treatment by employer. Employer may use different forms of abuses as physical punishment, humiliation or deduction of wags etc. or could be protective and affectionate or some where in these two extremes. If children do not get consideration or respect and because they lack understanding they take criticism to heart. It may affect their behaviour, attitude, expressions of childhood and their mental, psychological faculties may remain undeveloped.

Moral and Social Consequences

According to Edward Clopper the following "moral deterioration" may be noted: the child may be encouraged to play truant, he may show independence and defiance of parental control; he may develop weaknesses cultivated by the formation of bad habits; he may from a linking for "petty excitements of the streets," Opportunities may arise for him to drift into delinquency; and street work furnishes a large percentage of the recruits to the criminal population.

The child may become hostile, aggressive, drug addicted and may indulge in alcoholism, sexual pervession, robbery and violence. Thus working children are under constant moral danger.

Consequences on the Family and Nation

The working conditions of work place in a different unusual set of relationship poses new problems of adjustment for the child as well as many a times it replaces the affectionate and emotional relationship of child and his family with a commercial interaction. Since the child stays out of home whole day devoid of love and care, the family will have less control on the child; this may treat on the very institution of family.

Lastly child labour stiffles the human potentials, it is a drain on human resource development of any country if the children remain uneducated and unskilled labour. A country rich in material capital but lacking in good human capital would remain poor and vice versa. A child is the 'basement of society' as rightly pointed out by Danois. Experts argue that child labour is inefficient power, hence it is a premature expenditure rather than a saving to a nation.

Concluding Remarks

An overview of working conditions and environment and its impact on human resource development suggests that socially and ethically it is unsound, but it exists in inverse relation to the degree of economic advancement of a society or country. The exploitation of children is one of the consequences of complex situations of insufficient progress. It is neither feasible nor desirable to eliminate child labour at the present state of our economic development. Child work being illegal child labour cannot form organisations to protect their interests. In informal sector nature of work makes unions practically impossible. Final irony is that the most vulnerable group of workers has the least opportunity to protect their interests. The government should implement a series of short term revision of law to remove the adverse and unhealthy conditions attending child labour and its complete abolition as a progressive goal to be achieved, since "the protection and preparation of the human factor is at the same time a means of achieving development and the ultimate goal of development."

REFERENCES

1. ..... 'Child and Work' An ILO policy frame work for the international year of children 1979. ILO Genea February 1978.
2. Desai, Morarji: 'Children a cherished and valued trust' (A message for international year of children from Prime Minister) *Social Welfare* Vol. XXV No. 11 February 1979 p. 3.
3. Dwivedi S., "A study of child labour in Baroda. A multi dimensional approach" Unpublished Masters thesis, Faculty of Home Science, M.S. University, Baroda, 1983.
4. Justice Iyer Krishna V.R., The child and the law, *Social Welfare* Vol. XXVI Nov. 1979 Nov. 1979.
5. Mendelienich Elias, *"Children at work"* International Labour office, Geneva 1980.
6. Naidu A.N., "Child labour participation in India. A Statewise census analysis" *Journal of family welfare,* Vol. XXVII No. 4, June 1981.
7. Pandey M.K., *"Child labour in India"* India book exchange, Calcutta 1979.
8. ...... Report on child labour in Indian Industries, by Labour Bureau, Ministry of Labour, Government of India 1981.
9. Rodgers G. and Standing G., *"Child work, poverty and under employment"* ILO Geneva 1981.
10. Sharma C.K. Singh R., "Working Children in Hissar" *Social Welfare* Vol. XXIX No. 4 July 1982.

34

SUPPORTIVE MEASURES AND CHILD LABOUR[1]

The paper presents perspective on child labour. It highlights the inter-relatedness of long term measures such as family planing improved technologies, enhanced productivity, raid industrialisation and urban pressures on demand for labour, along with supportive services. The problem of child labour being multi-dimensional, an integrated development approach is recommended. Examples of experiments in Maharashtra, based on the needs of children are narrated.

Introduction

The question of child labour often tends to be viewed as one of total abolishment of all economically-related work of a child. Hence the often repeated lament about its prevalence. It is described as a necessary social evil, to be tolerated on account of the economic realities. By and large, the goals in respect of child labour remain unclear and the distinction between negative, exploitative aspects and non-exploitative work done by child to support the family remains poorly understood.

While there is much to deplore and clecry about the child labour that is exploitative in nature, there are on the other hand positive aspects of child being a partner in economic endeavours of the family that deserve appreciation and support.

Dignity of Labour as a Value

At one time in the history of this nation, there was a deliberate and a concentrated effort to establish the dignity of labour and of the values of self-reliance. Mahatma Gandhi's fight for the change of value systems included dignity of labour as of central importance. These values have to from a part of the socialisation process itself of a child if it were to take roots in the cultural soil of the nation. As such, work done by the child under certain non-competitive economic circumstances needs to be viewed more positively and as a constructive input in the struggle against poverty. The support of working child in a situation that is non-exploitative and its legitimisation will, in fact, only help improve the status of the working child and to assure to it certain minimum entitlements such as health, education and welfare. Since the working child whether at home or outside s fulfiling basic felt needs, it is desirable that rather than preventing the child from working, adequate safeguards should be introduced to protect it from being exploited, abused, underpaid or overworked. Emphasis in Article 24 of the Indian Constitution on prevention of exploitation needs to be underscored in this context.

Youth and Societal Roles

A significant observation which has relevance to this discussion is made in the report on 'Social Welfare in Development' of the Expert Group that met late last year under the aegis of United Nations Centre for Social Development and Humanitarian Affairs (UNCSDHA). It observes that "....in all parts of the world, there is awareness of the presence of everlarger numbers of youth who do not grow into readily available and acceptable labour force and societal roles. Their lack of work, and their subsequent alienation, threatens the social fabric. Their lack of preparation for necessary roles in the economic sector constitutes an important deprivation of resources for society, on the one hand; and a serious threat to development plans on the other. The group concluded that there is need, here, as elsewhere for much ingenuity in social and economic policy."

Reading deeper into this trend, one could hardly miss the message of caution for today's working children. Unless there are clear, acceptable roles for these children in the future economic life of the community they belong to, any drastic shifts in the orientation and life expectations to-day could lead to negative future consequences. Individual instances of most placed importance placed on provision of formal services to replace work for an individual child abound. Sometimes unrelated and inappropriate systems hold out but a dubious future for the child. This enthusiasm is carried from individuals to groups. The zeal of the promoters in these cases only leads to unmindful swapping of one evil for another that is more distressing for the individual as well as for the society.

Alternatives

It does not take a scholarly analysis to understand the consequences of non-availability of a rule in the economic activities for children whose families live below subsistence level. Given the high unemployment and underemployment rate it is logical to conclude that the whole group of families below the poverty line must suffer the consequences of exclusion from work force participation. To that extent of toiling child is one notch favourably placed than a non-working child of a poverty-striken family in a social context where developmental services are either not available or are not adequate.

Children in Need

"Children present a powerful numerical obligation to any society which decides to pledge itself to their well-being and universal care. This point has somewhere been missed in planning welfare interventions for providing welfare and developing services to children in predominantly deprived societies such as India. As the social work and welfare tools generally have been evolved and sophisticated in the West where the needy children are much less numerous, there is a certain practicability and even a credibility gap in applying those methods and the accompany norms to the much more sizeable needy in India. Where the major chunk of a society is operating outside the mainstream of development, development and welfare of children cannot be allowed the luxury of remaining either a peripheral or an eventual function of development planning. By the same virtu, the criteria for supportive and welfare assistance and its *modus operandi* need automatically to be geared to service a clientele that is both substantially and substantively different from that obtaining in the primarily affluent societies."[2]

Differences arise on several accounts. Here, as welfare thinkers have repeatedly wailed, we are confronting not 'pockets of poverty amidst affluence' but 'pockets of affluence amidst wide and deep-set poverty. This, combined with the demographic effect of high birth rate, accounts for more children and at the same time more needy children. Together of course, this is formidable combination of need with numbers that makes for distinction and with difference.

For years we have suffered under two dogmas namely legislation and insitutionalisation which was inherited from colonial rulers. This attitude resulted in large scale statutory institutionalisation, without realising that institutional treatment tends to give diminishing returns. It also overlooked the basic right of every child to belong to a family.

What does it really mean to belong? Is it not total sharing, giving according to needs of each one and taking from everyone according to his capacity. In this sense if the child works on the family farm without being exploited is it to be condemned as child labour?

An urban child dropping newspapers copies in the neighbourhood in the morning does help to upgrade the family income indirectly supporting his own health and educational requirements. Are there not innumerable children and youth in Bombay who earn and learn? How do we then achieve a balance between child labour and working child?

The Demographic Pressures

The pressures of demography bears heavily on the socio-economic life of a nation. A large base of fertility, a high population growth rate, both lead to a large number of new entrants into the labour market, and prior to that into schools and educational institutions. Increasing numbers also bring along corresponding numbers of new claimants or clients of social welfare as well as of nutritional and other services. The pressure of rising demands from these younger segments in the population places unprecedented strain on socio-economic services available or likely to be available. That leads to short-falls of services and resources (both material and human) and causes a crisis of frustrated aspirations, in turn constituting a threat to the stability of a society. While this chain reaction is observed, perhaps even comprehended, and routinely talked of, it is a matter of some doubts whether its policy and action implications have been sufficiently concretised. In other words, just as the social implications of the context of poverty have remained on the periphery of the planners' and the policy-makers' consciousness in India, we feel that similarly, the social ramifications of the demographic process on labour market in general and on child labour in particular have either eluded or been ignored by the development planner.

The second ramification to which we would like to refer is attitudinal. Among Indian planners and demographers, there has been a tendency to treat population always as a constraint or a pressure, in other words, to view it as a liability. This need not always be so. In China, for instance, the vast population is reportedly looked upon as potential manpower or work force and as a human resource. That approach necessitates of course an efficient manpower planning, training and utilisation policy and socio-economic thinking that can harmonise inter-generational claims and pay-off; and review the dimensions and social implications of working child's as a phenomenon.

Towards Integrated Services

Conceptual problems arise from ambiguities of ideas, of terms and objectives. In child welfare, for instance, the terminological pendulum has swung certainly between child welfare and child development but the transition whatever it is on the conceptual plane, has barely touched the programmes. Another concept with difficult translatability is that of integration of service. In many child welfare forums, the point has often been discussed as to how to integrate and what. The latter querry is not meant to be facetious since there is some pith in the contention that in order for integration to take place, there must be entities or activities to integrate! Yet, for many years, integration was being promoted as a concept in the absence of even rudimentary programmatic units. The one positive development towards the integrated approach has recently taken place in the from of the I.C.D.S. (Integrated Child Development Services), which has a great significance for supportive services.

Multi-Dimensional Problem

The problem of child labour is thus multi-dimensional. Since children form a large segment of the total population, it is expected that the number involved within or outside labour force would be massive. According to the estimations the proportion of child workers among the total work force in India ranges between 2 per cent to 9 per cent. It varies from state to state; and appears to be related to the variations in the socio-economic and educational level obtaining in a particular state.[3]

The variations are also found in the rural-urban areas. Compared to the child labour engaged in rural areas, the proportional rate for urban areas is significantly low. According to an estimate based on the 1971 census figures. 93 per cent of all child labour occurred in the rural areas.

The extent of child labour is again closely related to the extent of the implementation of the policy of free, compulsory education and the type of economy obtained in a particular region.

Rule Scene

A large multitude of children are employed in agriculture, plantations and allied village industries. By an large, these are informal sectors and completely unorganised.

According to the report[4] of a Rural Labour Enquiry Committee the rural child gets an employment 224 full days in a year. For the rest of the three months no work is available either to children or to adults. Payments to children, notwithstanding the same hours of work they put in is usually half or less than half the wages paid to adults. The minimum wags legislation for agricultural workers, where in existence, are hardly enforced.

The children of small, marginal farmers, and landless labourers work along side their parents and their contribution is what brings the family to survival level.

Exploitation: Definition

The definition of young and tender aged children has to extend to include the family as a unit. The child alone in the above cited situations is not the only victim of exploitation. What is true for him is equally true for the whole family. It is exploitative socio-economic system that denies the adults a guaranteed income with which to support the family. From one standpoint the child's working alongside the parents appear to be the only mitigating factor, in this situation.

Children Working in Unorganised Sector

As against the agricultural and live stock activities, condition of children engaged in other unorganised sectors is even worst. The latest sample survey carried out by the Labour Bureau, Govt. of India, included *inter alia* spot studies in five industries in the unroganised sector.[5] The conditions range from fair to extremely harsh. Instances in this study reveal that the children employed in plantations are assigned light jobs; given subsidised ration and free medical aid. On the other hand, children in fish peeling centres in Kerala are put to work for 15 hours.

Matching of Supportive Services With Needs

The range of work that children are engaged in; working hours, environmental condition, moral and physical health hazards they are exposed to vary from one scene to another. The nature and extent of the mitigative measures should also vary with the total condition obtaining in a particular set up. Therefore in the considerations of the supportive measures, directly affecting the concerned children it is possible only to outline the broad principles governing the choice of intervention.

The Odd Age Group

A side observation concerning children in the age group 6 to 15 years consists the comparative lack of attention and concern received by this group compared to the different age groups named in the development planning. While there is solicitude for the maternal and infant health care, immunisation, nutrition, prenatal and post natal services for the age bracket of 0 to 6 years and emphasis on promotion of services for the pre-school age child, (Balwadis), what appears to be assumed for the age group of 6 to 12 years is the only activity, namely formal education. Here is a case of imbalance in services. Dismal record of enrolment and drop-out figures in the primary schools notwithstanding the preoccupation for this group is confined mainly to the extension of implementation of free and compulsory primary education to cover an ever wider percentage of this population. (Under 14 years of age). The accent could shift from formal to informal functional education and other health and welfare services to suit the needs of the vast number of working children in this age group.

Integrated Services

If children working in the rural areas were to be provided a minimum of nutritional, health, education and recreational services to alleviate the rigours of their work-life, it has to be centered round their work-life. It should contain attractive elements not only to motivate the child but also the family to prompt them to benefit of it. Accessibility would be among the essential characteristic of such a service. Thus any supportive service to be effective has to be in tune with economic and social life of the family, has to be integrated in approach, developmental in content and accessible.

Some Examples

There are scattered examples of such experiments. In the state of Maharashtra for example School for Rural Boys and Girls run by Anutai Wagh at Kosabad is among the noteworthy ones. The basic educational approach is informal based on Gandhian approach to education as developed by Late Mrs. Tarabai Modak. The child is considered in the totality of his/her environment and the content of instruction related directly to his day to day life. The educational content comprises subjects such as health, hygiene, nutrition, sanitation, practical education related to agricultural practices, simple training in crafts and rural technologies. The educational aids and equipment are completely indigenous. The sessions are held in the open and time and place-wise, they are located in convenient areas.

Another experiment of "One hour School" run by Community Aid and Sponsorship Programme (CASP) in collaboration with Sarvoday workers at `Urali Kanchan' is also unique in this respect. It provides teaching as and when it is needed and the contents are directly related to day to day life and needs of people.

Urban Child

The incidence of child labour in urban areas is proportionately small. However, in terms of rigours of work and environmental condition the working child in urban areas is not much better off. The urban working children engaged in unorganised sectors more frequently are employed in restaurants and hotels, cotton ginning and weaving, carpet weaving, stone-breaking, brick-kiln, handicraft, construction work, domestic help, car-cleaning, distribution services like milk and paper, employments in shops and establishments, self-employment such as vending, boot-polishing and score of other such odd services.

There have been surveys conducted on working conditions of children working in powerloom and handlooms industries. For example, according to the sot studies made under the survey carried out by the Labour Bureaus and referred to earlier, in Machipuram in Tamil Nadu, nearly 75 per cent of the population is employed in the handloom industry, of which about a third of workers are children below 14. Similar study conducted in Maharashtra State by the Labour Institute revealed that children as young as 7 years of age enter work, and their working hours stretch to 12 hours. They are engaged mostly in filling bobbins and drawing work on the looms.

Among the urban child labour force should be counted a large fleet of children employed in antisocial activities such as carriers in the trade of drugs and narcotics, begging, crime and who are mercilessly exploited.

Mitigative Measures for an Urban Child

Among the measures that could be supportive of these children's educational recreational and health needs would be the establishment of multi-purpose centres located in school or public buildings, during the evening hours. These multi-purpose centres located in low economic areas and slum localities could play the role of a recreational cum educational centres, with periodic health check-up camps.

Some Examples

Interventions on behalf of the urban working children could also include sponsorship help of the kind undertaken by the Community Aid and Sponsorship Programme (CASP). With the initial grant from the Maharashtra State, Welfare Department under the IYC Programmes the Sponsorship programme was started for 3 months to begin with. Now it is extended to 75 working children on a long term basis. The sponsorship amount is supplementary income administered under social workers' supervision to met the neglected needs of the working child. They include scholarship to attend special training or evening school provision towards health and nutritional needs of the child. CASP started this programme for working children of unorganised sector with the tripartite support of restaurant owners (where children are employed as hotel boys. Trade Unions or community support and that of Government. This unorganised sector project covers domestic aids, hotel boys and shoe shine boys.

The other experiment relates to 'Anand Kendra,' a centre started for children living on the streets without family shelter. Education, health and welfare components of support are well cared for and professional skills injected in both these programmes which are yielding satisfactory results.

There is an obvious need for enforcement of laws regulating the hours of work, conditions of work, and protection against health hazards that children engaged in some of the small manufacturing units in the so-called unorganised sectors face. Progressive enforcement of legislation however, should be coupled with state and community interventions through supportive and development programmes if it were to achieve even the very modest goals.

Developmental Strategies and Child Labour

In the developmental thinking the trend that is slowly emerging is towards socio-economic development, motivated by social justice. Such social development warrants investment in human capital and human resource development in the manner that investments made heretofore were thought of only in economic activity.

As the problem of child labour is multi-dimensional so are the remedies. They are closely intertwined with the several interrelated aspects of total development.

Poverty and Unemployment

These are the twin critical factories that affect the prevalence of child labour under damaging conditions. There are no short-term solutions to this twin problem. The knowledge and experience gained through the three decades of development process is cumulatively available to the countries of he world at different levels of development. In this, three is not much ambiguity left about the single most critical element, namely political will which determines whether these lessons would be put to use or ignored.

Ensuring Minimum Wages

This measure could have a direct, positive effect in reducing the incidence of child labour. The question is not really only of legislation; it is one of progressive enforcement of the legislation that already exists. Further, creation of public awareness, of raising the level of participation of those who are affected are identified as ingredients of bringing about the social change.

Thus on the one hand we have social protective forces and on the other pressing economic compulsions of an unplanned labour market, an impact on size and quality of child labour. The value systems of each society provide a kind of philosophical context to questions relating to working child.

Summing Up

Child Labour as well as Working Child are the grim realities in developing countries which needs to be reviewed more positively and as a constructive input in the struggle against poverty. The supportive services for working child and its legitimisation will in fact only help improve the status of the working child and to assure to it certain minimum working conditions as well as entitlements. The authors on child welfare legislation and child labour evidently affirm this belief. The economic value of a child is fully acknowledged in our society and indeed sometimes serves as a motivating factor for parents to have children in the first place. As soon as the child grows up, it serves either as an extra hand in the family occupation and a source of extra earning, or as an alternate mother or father to help in the rearing of the younger ones at home. In either case, it is expected to perform maturer tasks than its age should allow. Yet, since the working child whether at home or outside, is fulfilling basic felt needs, it is desirable that rather than preventing the child from working, adequate safeguards should be introduced to protect it from being exploited, abused, under paid or over worked.[6] At the same time, provisions aimed at equipping such children with both work skills and domestic know-how as well as functional literacy need to be introduced. Some such preparation for girls is already being aimed at through I.C.D.S. and related-activity. But more comprehensive and systematic facilities need to be provided so that children are able to learn while they earn and to improve their performance both as present and potential workers.

This could best be achieved by providing supportive services as discussed earlier through state interventions in areas in nutritions, health, education and welfare.

By definition, the 'Supportive' or complementary function of social welfare is fulfilled when certain social welfare activities are designed to help in achievement of the planning objectives of some other sector rather than that of social welfare *per se.*

Thus the major functions of welfare activity may be identified broadly as (a) providing assistance to those with problems (remedial); (b) predicting the emergence of social problems and taking measures against their occurrence (preventive)'; (c) helping to create conditions conductive to development (developmental) and (d) contributing to achieve objectives of other sectors of service (supportive).

A study of the welfare programmes developed in India, indicates a clear relationship between the status of development in each state and the quantum of preventive, remedial and developmental action. A review of the state welfare budgets, spread of programmes by Social Welfare Boards and the type of coverage of international assistance can provide enough data to support this statement. In states like Bihar, UP and Madhya Pradesh, a greater emphasis is still on remedial action, while an awareness of developmental action seems evident in Tamil Nadu, Punjab, Bengal and Maharashtra. The level of preventive services however seems to be at a similar, if not the same level in most of the states. It is not possible to provide detailed comparisons due to limitations of space. But this area needs to be explored further.

The foregoing discussion suggests that the question of child labour is intrinsically related to the long-term developmental issues; that its remedies lie in the amelioration of the total socio-economic situation of the country.

If any appreciable difference is to be made in the life of the working children, who are a legion; piece-meal, *ad hoc* steps on an intermitent basis will not do.

A voluntary organisation here, or a charitable trust there sponsoring a few children could reach only an infinitesimal proportion of the needy. On the principle that every bit counts, these bits do help. But they do not measure up fully to the task.

That way the cause is being attended to by different set of agencies. Working child is a concern of health, education, labour, child-welfare, and allied agencies; and it should continue to remain so to that extent. But to make it an effective concern, no less than a full-scale movement is required. The cause of child-labour which is non-exploitative and which contributes to his health, education, welfare needs a champion, an espouser, whose total, sole and exclusive concern would be working child.

For a sustained, emphatic and effective movement an appropriate set-up needs to emerge. Whose devotion can naturally flow into the problems of the working child? Whole patronage could naturally get aligned to its cause? These are important questions, but not too difficult to answer.

The Trade Union movement (apart from welfare organisations) could be a natural espouser of the cause of the working child. It has to take the cause up in a big way. A natural adjunct to it should be the commerce organisations like Chamber of Commerce and Industry; who have a direct stake in the work of the child. Their conscientisation is of critical importance.

In the urban centres, where manufacturer's guilds and Trade Union activity is already alive, the strategy of tripartite set-up could work. The rural masses through by the large unorganised are no longer completely outside the mainstream system.

Our experience of drawing Trade Unions into the welfare measures for children through sponsorship programme has met with a somewhat cold response; but that could not be taken as a sign of their disinterestedness. We are convinced that a well thought out strategy needs to be kindled; a thruster for the movement has to be found. Probably an essential first step is the acknowledgment of child work as acceptable activity within the clearly spelt out conditions.

Recommendations of the Seminar

The recommendations of the Seminar were presented by Dr. (Mrs.) U.S. Naidu and after the discussion, were adopted by the participants.

It was emphasised that abolition of child labour is not possible in the near future and, therefore, we should think of protection of minimum working hours and improvement in conditions of work for children. Thus, it is necessary to identify the occupations in which the children are engaged and also the risks which they face.

For the development of children at work, services pertaining to health, education and recreation should reach them. For the health services, it was recommended that arrangements have to be made to provide the basic health care in slum pockets, and also to the children at their work laces in urban areas. In rural areas the strengthening of Primary Health Centres is essential in order to enable them to extend their services to working child. Community Health Worker, should particularly, be oriented to the developmental needs of working child.

Provisions should be made for the educational, vocational and recreational services for the working children at their work places and home. Flexibility of content of education as well as hours of school should be made. Educating working children and providing them the opportunities to develop skills of the trade in which children are employed are some of the issues to be dealt with without any further delay to reinforce the concept of "earn and learn."

Another important aspect of educating the working children is to make them aware of their own needs. Here, different models for different situations may be followed.

Through the minimum age of employment is kept at 14 years, the Government should be given the powers to make some exceptions in certain occupations where the need is felt. Further, legislation should be enacted to give to the working children facilities and concessions on similar basis as to the adults workers. At the same time a persuasive approach should be made towards the employers and organisations employing children for seeking their cooperation in future development of working children.

The salient themes identified for research were: the impact of work on the health and personality-development of children, the role of work in the socialisation of children, the inter-relation of schooling and employment and patterns of exploitation.

It was felt by the participants that the problems pertaining to child labour deserve an eclectic approach and, therefore, the attempt should be made to develop research designs of great breadth and variety involving investigators from various disciplines. However, individual researchers working in the field might attempt to relate their topic to some of the themes mentioned above.

Further, it was recommended that action-cum-research should be encouraged for the welfare of working children.

Finally, it was recommended strongly that till the economic condition of the country improves, immediate attempts will have to be made to organise better conditions of work that will eradicate abuse, exploitation and health hazards emerging from child labour.

REFERENCES

1. Paper presented by Dr. S.D. Gokhale at ESCAP Meeting on Child Labour 1980.
2. Ms. Neera Sohini and S.D. Gokhale in *Adoption and Foster Care*, ICSW Publication, 1976.
3. Based on the article 'Demographic Profile of an Indian Child' by J.R. Rele and Tara Kanetkar in *Child in India* 1979, Somaiya Publications Pvt. Ltd.
4. Paper prepare by Mrs. Vaidya for the Indian Councilof Social Welfare Seminar, 'Child in India': 1979.

35

CHILD WELFARE NEEDS AND SERVICES: A THEORETICAL PERSPECTIVE

"Every child is an experiment, an adventure into noble life, an opportunity to change the old pattern and make it new".

Dr. S. Radha Krishnan

Undoubtedly, in human society child enjoys a very important position. Without the child, men are neither appreciated nor given better status. Manusmiriti opines that the man is imperfect in itself, but when he commits himself with wife and child, he becomes perfect. But the personality of the child as shaped by heredity as well as environment of the early years of childhood. Therefore, maximum facilities should be made available for the proper growth and development of the child. Deficiencies of any kind, during childhood cause handicap to the child. Therefore, any investment on the child development project rightly deserves to be considered as investment in the future of the nation. According to 1981 census, the total children under 14 years of age in India was 271.0 million which constitutes nearly 38.8 per cent of total population of the country. The break-up of the rural-urban population was 78 per cent and 22 per cent respectively. Projection made for 1991 and 2001 are 304.4 million and 377.0 million respectively.

Welfare Needs

Since the population of children is on the increase from one decade to another in almost every state of the country, the problem of their growth and development remains unsolved inspite of increasing governmental efforts in the form of providing welfare services for them. The main concern is to take into account the welfare needs of children upto 14 years of age. An attempt is made in the following paragraphs to bring into focus the important needs of children:

Needs of Children

It is almost an article of faith with the civilised countries that children should have opportunities for their proper development and growth through physical, emotional, mental and spiritual well-being. Some of the basic needs of a child are as follows:

1. Healthful and nutritional food, comfortable clothing and a home that offers protection and safety.
2. Immunisation against diseases and health and medical measures.
3. Love and understanding are the emotional needs of all children which are easy to state but difficult to fulfil in practice. If a child feels that the people around him are loving and understanding, he, in turn, will feel friendly, develop trust and feel emotionally secure.
4. A child also needs occasional affectionate pat on the back which means recognition and appreciation.
5. A child needs to grow at his own pace without being pushed ahead of his capacity or held back by being 'babied' and over-protected.
6. A child also needs constructive and creative activity both physical and mental.

Human beings are basically alike, though individuals differ and so do children. Therefore, every child must be allowed to grow in his own way.

Child Welfare

In fact, the objective of child welfare has became wider. There are not restricted to preventive goals; only the objectives are to help in achieving the fullest possible growth of the mind, body, and personality of every child irrespective of class, creed, race or nationality. In fact, our understanding of the process of child development has deepened. We no longer refer to childhood as necessarily a blissful state. It can be blissful state for every child if its physical and emotional needs are met. But if they are not, the life of the child can be a continued state of tension and anxiety. As a matter of fact, a child suffers much more under these strains than an adult who has developed the ability to manage and control them. The physical needs of the child are simple and easily perceived. The emotional needs are also simple, but not easily perceived. They are same fundamental needs of every child: affection, physical and emotional security, acceptance as an individual, self-respect, and achievement. The simplicity of these needs, however, should not make us lose right of their crucial significance. The non-satisfaction of these needs means frustration which in its own term would have consequences that would vary in their gravity depending upon a number of other factors characterising the life situation of the child.

The capacity of the parents to meet these needs of children is much dependent upon their own personalities. It used to be considered enough for a parent to be found of his child. Now we know that fondness or love is not enough it is important to know how to love one's child wisely. A possessing, a doting love can be harmful for the growth of a child's personality. Overprotection and rejection of a child on the part of the parents can both be equally harmful for the child's personality growth.

While frustrations are painful. There is an inevitable part of the life of every person.

The growing child has also to be helped to accept the limitations of life around him and to overcome his frustrations. Thus, he becomes equipped to meet such situations in adult life. Physical punishment is considered largely unnecessary. It is felt that a parent who can be consistent in his dealings with the child and remains firm on his do's and don'ts without resorting to punishment or pampering, he will really be able to help his child grow normally without unnecessary anxieties.

The child is the father of man. It is during childhood that foundations of the personality of an individual are laid. It will require a generation of thinking, courageous, democratic, and socially responsible citizens. He will have to begin rearing them in our nurseries, schools and playgrounds.

The role of the parents in the growth of a child's personality is an important one. Similar is the-role of a teacher. The teacher will not make the child learn his lessons. In fact, the very concept of learning has changed. Learning is by-product of acting, thinking and experiencing. It is, therefore, necessary to provide an opportunity to children to do and think in a meaningful manner.

Play and recreational activities are not to be regarded as wasteful but are to be looked upon as necessary and wholesome. Play is now ween to have a great variety of significance. In the first place, it is an activity enjoyable in itself and in so far as it is enjoyable, it does not require justification on any other grounds. But play can also become a medium through which the child can tide over his anxieties and worries. The new insight that science has given us into the process of child development, has thus necessitated a re-orientation of our attitudes to child upbringing in respect of education and play. Child welfare is, therefore, not limited to only the physically, mentally and socially handicapped but also to the normally growing children in general. "The ICDS programmes and many such other programmes cater to the growing needs of every child. The concept of welfare has changed from preventive, curative and rehabilitative services to the developmental and promotive aspects of population in general because of the belief and thinking that the handicapped are the product of our prevailing social system. Welfare services, therefore, should be a regular feature and part of our social services and not accidental and casual services to a few unfortunate ones. In the following paragraphs an attempt is made to review the programme specially for the handicapped children who deserve batter attention from us and Government.

Day Care

The Government has launched various programmes for children who, for some social, economic and psychological reasons are not given proper care by their families or who need care and protection outside their homes. The problem of child care has become more important because urbanisation and industrialisation which has changed the status of women who are getting opportunities to go outside their homes for learning or earning to meet increasing family expenses. The need for day-care of children is mainly related to the working mothers in various occupations outside their homes who have infants and children of pre-school age for whom they find it difficult to make arrangements at home. Moreover, a large number of women are engaged in agriculture. They can not take kue care of their children. A study (Singh RK, Gopal AK, 1980) conducted on this aspect has revealed that more than 64 per cent of the family labour force listed in 1971 census and 94 per cent employed in unorganised sectors are in need of day-care facilities for their pre-school children.

Nutrition

Nutrition plays a significant role in the physical, mental and emotional development of the child. Therefore, proper nutrition should be available to the expectant and nursing mothers and children in adequate quantity. Malnutrition or under-nutrition is directly related to the growth and development of the child.* Malnutrition is responsible for higher rates of deaths of children. An estimated account shows that 6,600 children upto 5 years of age die every day in India due to malnutrition. About 7 per cent deaths of children in 0 to 5 years age-group has been reported due to malnutrition. A normal healthy child is expected to be of a particular weight at the time of birth. This weight is dependent upon the level of nutrition given to the pregnant mother. Therefore, nutrition during pregnancy assumes more significance and deserves priority.

In India, a large number of children are not given adequate amount of vitamins, minerals and proteins needed for their growth and development. These children are, therefore, found with vitamin and protein deficiency and anaemia. A seminar report** estimates that 80-90 per cent Indian children do not receive adequate protein. The acute diarrheal diseases are found requantly among the malnourished children in comparison with normal children. According to a special estimate, about 22 per cent of school-going children are found with one or more signs of nutritional deficiency. They suffer from analiusia due to istaucise 'A' and istauise 'B' coueplex deficiency 56 per cent are in low-socio-economic groups. While 15 per cent show severe nutrition deficiency as reflected in their body weights. It is estimated that out of 3 million disabled children in the country, about 2 million are mentally retarded 5,00,000 are orthopedically handicapped and 2,00,000 deaf.

Health Care

For the proper growth and development of a child especially in infancy, congenial environment is essential. Therefore, a proper environment free from infections and full of fresh air and sun should be available for every newly born baby. This is important because infectious and communicable diseases are common among the Indian children. As a result, children especially below 5 years after die. According to a study,*** out of total deaths in the country, about 40 per cent occurred among children below 5 years of age and 50 per cent among children of one year age-group. The causes responsible for

* Profill of child in India, 1980.

** National Institute of Public Cooperation and Child Development, 1982.

*** Study Conducted by R.K. Gupta in 1968.

these deaths are stated to be nutritional disorders and infections and communicable diseases. Bhatta (1979) found that, especially in the developing countries like India the child abuse is seen in the forms of diseases which exist with poverty, mal-nutrition, etc.

A higher birth rate and infant mortality are found more in the poor rural and slum areas. Illiteracy, ignorance and traditional system have given rise to the tendency to beget more children to compensate for the prevailing infant mortality and also for increasing family income. Their idea is that more children mean more earnings whereas in a rich and educated family, one healthy child is considered better then hundred problem children. In fact, nutrition food, fresh air, clean water, exercise, adequate sleep, good housing, non-polluted environment and medical facilities essential for the healthy development of body and issued.

Education

Education provides new skills and new knowledge of each occupation. With the bulk of our work force either illiterate or semi-literate, we can not hope to achieve full production, efficiency and capacity utilisation of our plants to the same extent as in the developed countries. Education also enhances the social and national cohesion. But uneven speed of education, particularly education devoid of values, perception and sensitivities towards suffering and poverty, lack of values of equality and social justice lead to undesirable results while the idea of child education has become neither very popular among the rural, slum people nor has the govt. adequately provided facilities all over the country. Even in some of the areas with such facilities the aim of teacher-parents co-ordination has not been achieved so far due to poor finance and lack of proper coordination. A study conducted by V.K. Singh in 1983 reveals that about 36 per cent parents do not send their children to schools because of the fear to lose the monetary support, 34 per cent parents use children in domestic work and child care and 26 per cent for placing their children in gainful employment in Rajasthan. The condition of female children is worst. Their birth, education and employment in some of the castes and social classes are not treated to be welcome signs. As per 1961 census, female literacy rate in the age group of 10-14 years was 20.7 per cent in rural India compared to 49.1 per cent for males. In 1971, it was 30 per cent compared to 54.6 per cent for males.

Physical Abuse

As population is on the increase, child abuse is also increasing among different castes and classes. However, this figure varies from state to state and from nation to nation. The 2nd International Conference (1978) held in U.K. and the 3rd Conference (1981) held at Amsterdam realised that the problem of child abuse had assumed an alarming proportion all over the world. According to a survey conducted in USA, the physical abuse of children was about 6 per 1000, numbering 300 cases per million in a year. In India, it can be seen in various forms such as rape, kidnapping, etc. A study conducted by an expert on raped, kidnapped and abandoned children brought to the care of a hospital during 4 years revealed that of the 18 children treated at a paediatric clinic, most of them were of less than 4 weeks of age and were predominantly females. These babies were also mostly premature and malnourished, deserted and later on, picked up by the police or social workers from gutters, dustbins, garbage tins, railway platforms, etc. The spectrum of abuse includes new-born babies with intact placenta, at times lacerated strangling marks on the throat, multiple bruises of bleeding from the umbilicus, avulsion of scalp with severe bleeding and shocks and evidence of infection, rat-bite marks, fracture, etc. the related morbidity of these cases if almost 100 per cent over varying periods of time, maximum survival being for 22 days only.

A study of 100 cases of kidnapped children including 96 per cent girls between 3 and 16 years of age reveals that 3.4 per cent children were kidnapped for prostitution purposes, 4.5 per cent for sale, 51.6 per cent for employment and boot-legging, 3.5 per cent for vengeance, 29.1 per cent for sexual gratification and 3.4 per cent for using as domestic servants and 4.5 per cent for begging. Another study of 130 cases of rape victious between 6 and 18 years of age indicated that all of them came predominantly from the slum areas. About 51.33 per cent offenders were neighbours who brought them and the rest were employers, relatives, friends and known persons from the locality.

Vagrant Children

The problem of vagrant children has become common due to urbanisation and industrialisation. One often comes across children who commit thefts, take to begging or are loafing about in cities. They are not looked after by their family members and feel the absence of love and security in the homes. They come out and try to earn their bread, but when they fail in their efforts, they adopt unlawful methods for their existence. When the child is not looked after and guided by his parents, he develops unsocial tendencies for becoming a delinquent. It is, therefore, essential to organise non-institutional services for these children who are deprived of the family care and protection.

Orphan and Destitute Children

Home is the place where all the needs of children such as physical, mental and emotional are fulfilled. But due to long illness, desertion, divorce, imprisonment and death of the parents or adult members of the family, sometimes a child has to be removed from his home. It is, therefore, always advisable to place him in an environment which like a home. The United States Children's Bureau (1939) found broken homes as causes of destitution in 36 per cent of boys cases and 50 per cent in girls' cases, disposed of in sixty-four juvenile courts in 1936. Similarly, in the Indian setting, the two follow-up studies in Maharashtra by the Indian Council of Social Welfare revealed that out of 229 and 305 non-delinquents traced and interviewed, 55 per cent and 61 per cent respectively had belonged to broken homes prior to their institutionalisation. The collateral evidence on this point is also available from the research as based on Juvenile Court records, (Sheth). According to these researches, the incidence of broken,, homes was to the tune of 47.4 per cent among the offenders brought before the juvenile court, Bombay, during the period 1941-56, one fifth of these offenders from broken homes who had lost both the parents. Further, from a study of 300 cases of delinquents, if was found that only in 120 cases both parents were alive, in 60 cases both mother and father were dead. The criminologists like Sutherland and Creasey pointed out on the basis of various research reports that delinquents coming from broken homes range from 30 to 60 per cent.

Juvenile Delinquency

A child requires proper food, clothing education, recreation, love, affection and guidance, which are very essential for him to cope up with the social problems. But due to the lack of parental affection, over protection, bad company, economic insufficiency, poor-group sub-culture, impact of violent and sexy movies the child comes in conflict with law. He has to be protected and all effects are to be made to prevent him from going astray.

Child Labour

It may be mentioned here that the total urban and rural population below poverty line is reported to be 36 per cent of the total population of India as per the statement of the Govt. in 1985. This shows the reduced percentage of people below the poverty line because of the Govt. anti-poverty programmes. In brief, it may be said that the poor in rural and urban areas due to illiteracy, traditional system to employ children rather than to send them to schools, unemployment of adult members in families, tremendous increasing population and large family size, deaths, disease of parents, low income of the families and lack of opportunity to employ them and employers' preference, a bulk of children found to be working in different unorganised sectors (ORG 1983). The said circumstances force their parents to send them into the labour market. In the labour market children are put to work for long hours in ill-ventilated and unhygienic conditions which is harmful for their growth and development. Accidents are not uncommon. The Statutory welfare services are grossly lacking. The 1981 census shows that in India 13.6 million children were at work while the operations research group estimated 44 million in 1983.

Handicapped Children

Every society has children who are physically and mentally handicapped. Current statistics about the population of all types of handicaps and their state wise distribution are not available. They are in need of institutional and non-institutional care, opportunities of education and programmes to rehabilitate them. To make it move explicit all these problems of the children where welfare is needed, can be presented in the following order to give a comprehensive view:

Children in Need of Welfare Services

I. Handicapped children
    A. Physically handicapped
    B. Mentally handicapped

C. Socially handicapped
 (i) Orphans
 (ii) Deserted Children
 (iii) Neglected children
 (iv) Victimised children
 (v) Begging, immoral and used for anti-social purposes
 (vi) Children in slums
 (vii) Children in poor families
 (viii) Children in socially exploited classes, such as the Harijans, Girijans, Industrial labour, etc.

II. Children with behavioural problems or emotionally disturbed children.
III. Physically sick children
IV. Children who fail to benefit from school and other social institutions.
V. Delinquent children.
VI. Children of deviant or handicapped parents.
 A. Children of Delinquent parents.
 B. Children of prisoners
 C. Children of beggers
 D. Children of prostitutes
 E. Children of handicapped parents
 F. Children of broken families
 G. Gifted children.

Child Welfare Services

A satisfactory rearing of the child was ensured by social institutions like joint family, caste and close-knit rural community. These institutions lay stress on corporate responsibility of members towards dependents and thus provide care and protection to the needy children and other members of the family, caste and community. Rapid changes in consequence of industrialisation, urbanisation, emergence of highly individualistic and competitive influences, decreasing dependence on agricultural economy and increasing poverty have, in the last hundred and fifty years, weakened the traditional social organisation giving rise to the need for different services. Another fact contributes to the need for services to children can be traced to the changing position and role of women, in our present day society. The most common form of service to children so far, has been institutionalisation for the orphan, destituted blind and orthopaedically handicapped children. Historically, in 1920 the first children's organisation was set up which is now called Balkunji Ban in Bombay. In 1924, the guild of service started its excellent child welfare services in Madras. In 1927 the children's aid society, Bombay, took vagrant children for residential care. The constitution was adopted in 1950 with the

Directive Principles of State Policy emphasing the welfare concept of a state.

The Planning Commission was set up in the same year under the chairmanship of the late Prime Minister Jawahar Lal Nehru. The five year plans were formulated. Shri P.N. Luthra, the then secretary to the Govt. of India said in 1975," since India has the ultimate aim of a socialist society, the ultimate aim of economic development is the welfare of the family. And in the family, the most precious asset is the child". Therefore, in the strategy of the planned development India focussed its foremost interest on the young child. The First Five Year Plan was launched in 1951 to mobilise the voluntary activity in every state in favour of children's need. The Indian Council of Child Welfare was formed in 1952. Another unique organisation, the Central Social Welfare Board, an autonomous body was set up in 1953 by the Govt. to encourage the voluntary agencies working in the field of family and child welfare through State Advisory Boards in every state. For the planned development of the future services, the welfare extension projects were launched in 1959 by the Central Social welfare services like Balwadi, Craft training for women, maternity services and general medical and social education services in the rural areas where voluntary organisations were not operative.

In the Second Five Year Plan, the Central and the State Govts took initiative to start programmes for the socially handicapped children, i.e., those who were neglected, destitute or came into conflict with law, and disabled children. However, the emphasis was more on control and rehabilitation of delinquents through enactments of children Acts in different states which were to establish a large number of institutions with correctional services. In this plan maternity and child health programmes did not receive proper attention. The Indian Council for Child welfare made a representation to the Govt. to make a specific plan for child welfare in 1958. An official letter was issued by the Ministry of Education to formulate this plan. The Planning Commission, however, created a special cell for social welfare in the Third Five Year Plan with seven sub committees covering social defence, women welfare, child welfare, etc. During this five year plan an important scheme called Demonstration Project was introduced for the welfare of children upto 16 years with a view to integrating all services of education, health, nutrition, etc. and it was set up in a block where it did not exist. In 1962-63, a scheme of pilot projects to experiment on foster care was also introduced. However, on the recommendation of the Evaluation Committee, it was decided to revise the services already existing in the rural areas under different patterns of the scheme like Welfare Extension Projects and Demonstration Projects, and also to develop a country-wide programme in terms of integrated welfare services for children with particular reference to the preschool children. Thus, a new scheme called Family and Child Welfare Project was introduced in 1967 with the aim to provide health care, nutrition non-formal education to the children upto 6 years, training handicrafts and family life education to women. The Welfare Extension Projects used to provide different services for women and children whereas the Demonstration Projects aimed at integrated development of pre-school children and provided training to young mothers in hone-craft, handicraft and health education. These were replaced by Family Child Welfare. These various services were being run without any administrative involvement of the Govt. Therefore, it was not possible to run services properly by the Balsevikas at the village level because of their low status and poor knowledge. They were found to be ineffective to run and maintain its services.

In August, 1974, the Govt. adopted the National Policy for Children because of the realisation that children are the nation's "supremely important asset". It stressed that children's programmes should form an important part of our national plan and that it should be the policy of the state to provide adequate care to children both before and after birth and throughout the period of growth to insure their physical, mental and social development. The policy lays down 15 measures for the balanced growth such as, comprehensive health programme for children, nutrition services, nutrition and health programmes for the nursing and expectant mothers, formal and non-formal education, special assistance to children belonging to the weaker section of the society, socially and physically handicapped children, etc. It also adds that the voluntary agencies engaged in the field of child welfare will continue their activities either on their own or with state assistance.

The National Children's Board was also set up under the chairmanship of the Prime Minister. Similar boards are also existing in different state and Union Territories (except Himachal Pradesh and Chandigarh) under the chairmanship of the Chief Ministers for planning, reviewing and coordinating all available essential services for children at different levels. The year 1979 was declared 'as the International year of the child. Accordingly, a national plan of action under the guidance of the National Children's Board for the International year of the child was formulated by the Govt. which included provision of proper health, nutrition, environmental sanitation, safe drinking water, education including pre-school, elementary and community education, social welfare legislation for children and publicity and fund raising for the care and welfare of children. To meet the targets, various programmes were implemented, such as, health programmes, promotive, preventive, curative and rehabilitative programmes health care services for mothers and children, immunisation against different communicable and chronic diseases at maternity and child health services centres, school health services and mobile health care units.

To tackle the problem of malnutrition and to meet the minimum nutritional needs, two programmes have been launched. The first programme is known as special nutrition programme for children upto the age of 0-6 years and nursing and expectant mothers. Under this scheme, supplementary feeding to the extent of 300 calories and 10-12 grams of protein to children and 500 calories and 20-25 grams of protein for mothers is provided for 300 days in a year. The second scheme is the midday meal programme which is meant for the school children of 6 to 11 years for 200 days in a year.

In the field of education, pre-school centres (Balwadies) have been set-up for children in the age-group of 3-6 especially in backward areas where children receive pre-primary school education. This scheme operates through voluntary organisations with two aims, first, to provide for school education and secondly, supplementary nutrition. As per the Constitutional Directives, compulsory and free education upto 14 years of age is the responsibility of the states. Elementary education was accorded high priority in the Sixth Five Year Plan (1980-85). At present, all schools in the country are implementing this directive except in Uttar Pradesh. This Constitutional Objective is likely to be achieved by 1989-90. The measures to reduce drop-our rates have been suggested through the steps like concersion of single-teacher primary schools into two-teacher schools, provision of setting up of early education centres in addition to primary schools and a provision of incentive such as free books, free uniforms, mid-day meals, etc.

The foundation of individuals, development, physical, mental and social are significantly based on early childhood care and training. To meet all the needs physical, mental and social. The Integrated Child Development Services were launched II years ago in 1975, with a view to providing services to pre-school children, pregnant women and nursing mothers in an integrated manner so as to ensure proper growth and development of children in the rural and slum areas. Until 1976, infant mortality rate was alarmingly high and morbidity and prevalence of malnutrition children was also guite high. The Integrated Child Development Services Project as a part of the total development programmes are struggling to change the picture of development and health in early years of life. The scheme has following objectives:

1. To improve the nutritional and health status of children in the age group of 0-6 years.
2. To lay the foundation for proper physical, psychological and social development of the child.
3. To reduce the incidence of mortality, morbidity, and school drop-outs.
4. To achieve effective coordination of the policy and its implementation amongst the various development programme for children.
5. To enhance the capability of mother to look after the normal health and nutritional needs of the child through supplementary nutrition and health education.

To achieve all the above mentioned objectives the following services are being given to different groups of target population to create an integrated approach to the development of the child:

Target group	Package of services
1. Expectant and nursing mothers	(i) Health check-ups (ii) Immunisation of expectant mothers against tetanus. (iii) Supplementary nutrition (iv) Nutrition and health education.

2.	Other women (15-44 years)		Nutrition and health education.
3.	Children below 3 years	(i)	Supplementary nutrition
		(ii)	Im-munisation
		(iii)	Health check-ups
		(iv)	Referral services.
4.	Other children (3 years and above but below 6 years)	(i)	Supplementary nutrition
		(ii)	Immunisation
		(iii)	Health check-ups
		(iv)	Referral services
		(v)	Non-formal pre-school education.

The Integrated Child Development programmes have been evaluated by Programme Evaluation Cell of the Planning Commission. Its findings show that it has overcome the initial difficulties such as, recruitment of staff, training and equipment. However, the success of the programme has been greater with regard to children in the age group of 3-6 years. The periodic assessment made by the all India Institute of Medical Sciences has indicated that the nutrition status and health standards of children have been remarkable improved in the project areas.

The institutional and non-institutional centres are being run by voluntary agencies with some or more financial assistance of Govt. for children in need of care and protection as well as for the setting up of creches, balwadies, recreational centres, etc. Similarity, for the physically and mentally handicapped children, there are institutional and non-institutional services which are being provided by voluntary organisations and Govt. agencies for treatment and rehabilitation of the handicapped children. The physically handicapped children are now given two special types of services, first, award of scholarships for pursuing education and professional or vocational training, and second, integrated education under which, they are placed in normal schools where this appears to be the most practical way for enlarging educational opportunities for the handicapped children and promoting their integration. The handicapped children are also benefited under other schemes like assistance to the disabled persons for purchase fitting of aids and appliances, etc. Recently, the Union Minister for Welfare has identified about a dozen types of group A and B posts in the Ministries, Departments and public sectors that can be manned by the blind. The Union Public Service Commission has also agreed to the recruitment of the blind persons. With this opening, the blind will be eligible for appointment as teacher, translators, office assistant and section officer. There are 22 special employment exchanges in the country for the benefit of the blind and other handicapped. In addition, special cells have been opened in 42 other employment exchanges for their placement. A Placement Officer has been appointed in each of these cells to help the handicapped job-seekers.

In the field of social defence, various correctional services have been introduced under the children acts now the Juvenile Justice Act, 1986 and various institutional and non-institutional services, for development of children are currently available in the country. The major child welfare programmes now under the State plan are balwadies, creches, child welfare centres, family counselling centres, foundling homes, children's homes, foster care services, child guidance clinics, scholarships for the handicapped children, etc. These are either run by the State Govt. or by the voluntary agencies with or without assistance from the Govt.

The television is playing an important role in creating awareness of the children's problems, their abilities, required services for them, role of parents, teachers, society and the nation for their growth and development. Features and documentary films and programmes for them on television and radio is also helpful for their education. Through television programmes in the last Five Year Plans some 16,500 classes were held. Education through television is available for children from first grade class to those in 13-17 years of age-group. The number of pupils rose considerably over the years. By 1986, it is expected that all children of 6-11 age-group would be receiving television education. All services given to the concerned persons for welfare and development of children can be presented in the following manner:

Personnel for Direct Services	To children To parents and substitute parents To others in the community, e.g., teachers.
Personnel for Indirect services	Administrative Planning Training Research.

Child Labour Welfare Services Under Seventh Five Year Plan

Under the Seventh Five Year Plan, 1985-90 the Govt. of India, Planning Commission decided to pay attention to making the working condition of the Child labour better and more acceptable socially. Improved legislation and better enforcement machinery are called for. Association of Voluntary Organisations for providing child workers with health care, nutrition and education will be desirable. Efforts can be made to bring non-formal education to the child workers in the large number of small factories and workshops in which child workers are working. The ultimate goal of abolition of child labour can only be achieved when there is sufficient improvement in the condition of families whose children are compelled to work under the Sixth and the Seventh plans to meet the various objectives including grants-in-aid to the voluntary agencies for identification of bonded labour and also for the project for improvement of the conditions of the child labour through a package provision of non-formal education, health care, nutrition and recreation. The Govt. has made a plan outlay of Rs. 199.64 crores for the Sixth Five Year plan which in distributed as Rs. 78.50 crores for the centre, Rs. 11.93 crores for the states and Rs. 9.22 crores for the union Territories while for the Seventh Five year Plan a sum of Rs. 333.72 crores has been provided of which Rs. 95.44 crores are ear-marked for the centre, 219.0 crores for the States and the rest 18.83 crores for the union Territories.

Legislation for Children

The Govt. has enacted several laws to promote proper growth and development of children and made provisions for their proper care, protection, maintenance, welfare, training, education and rehabilitation. Some of the Acts are the Children Act, 1960 (Amendment 1978) (now the juvenile Justice Act, 1986). Suppression of Immoral Traffic in women and Girls Act, 1956 (now amended as the Immoral Traffic [Prevention] Act). Prevention of Begging Acts, Children, students and Youth (Rights and Welfare) Bill, 1975, Laws relating to children's education, Vaccination Act, 1880. Prevention of Smoking Act, the Sharda Act, 1929 (Amended in 1949), Hindu Marriage Act, 1955, Child Marriage Restraint (Amendment) Act, 1978, Special Marriage Act, 1954, Evidence Act, 1972, Marriage Laws (Amendment) Act, 1976, Hindu Succession Act, 1956, Hindu Adoptions and Maintenance Act, 1956, Hindu Minority and Guardianship Act, 1956; Adoption of Children Bill, 1972, Criminal Procedure Code, 1973, Indian Divorce Act, 1869 Young Persons Harmful Publications Act, 1956, etc. The services to children can be summarised in the following tabular form:

Child Development services

1. Integrated Child Development Services
2. Feeding Programmes
3. Parents' education
4. Bal Bhavan, Balvikash centres

Child Care (institutional care).

Statutory

1. Institutions under children etc.
2. Institutions under Borstal Schools Act.

Non-Statutory

1. Orphanages
2. Destitute children's Home
3. SOS children village/Bal Sadans
4. After Care hostels
5. Institutions for the Handicapped children.

Child Welfare Services

Other Child Welfare service (non institutional services)

1. Multipurpose community Centres.
2. Juvenile Guidance Bureau
3. Jouvenile Aid Police Units and recreational centres.
4. Child Guidance clinic
5. Foster Care
6. Adoption
7. Sponsorship
8. Education, training and rehabilitation of Handicapped children.

36

SOCIO-ECONOMIC CONDITIONS OF WORKING CHILDREN AND THEIR LABOUR USE

We studied the socio-economic background of the 492 families which send their children to work. We saw the socio-economic status of the families, the health and educational status of their members and heads, and the general environment in which the children live. Why these households supply their children as labour to earn wages in the labour market, is also discussed in the foregoing chapter.

In this chapter we shall study the status of the child in his work and his use as labour. As we already know, all the 492 children work in carpet industry of Mirzapur. The workers are of both the sexes and are between the age group of 7 to 14 years. Most of them are illiterate and in poor health, and a very few of them have attended schools, but they work because of the poor socio-economic status of their families. Most of the children live with their parents and are grossly underpaid by their employers. But since they are illiterate and needy they work for meagre wages. Most of the children have no past experience of work but they like working because it means, to them, some pocket money which they can spend on entertainment, snacks and movies. Female workers in the industry are few and illiterate because of the conservative attitude of the parents. We shall now study the status of the child workers, their labour use, and the perception and attitude of the working children concerning the supply and use of their labour.

Age Sex-Wise Distribution, Educational and Occupation Characteristics

Table 36.1 shows the age and sex wise distribution of child workers in the sample of the carpet industry workers of Mirzapur. The maximum number of child workers are in the age group of 11-14 years while no children in the very small age group of 4-7 years work as child labour. As can be seen clearly from the table, the number of male workers far exceed the number of female workers in the sample. The female workers constitute just 5 per cent of the total.

Table 36.2 shows the age of entry of the working child in the present job. The table shows that of the total 492 children of the sample, 381 centered the job between the age group of 7-11 years while only 20 per cent of the workers in the sample entered the job at the age group of 11-14 years. Thus it can be seen clearly that most of the children in the sample entered the present job between the age group of 7-11 years. Female workers in the sample are few and most of them entered the present job between 7-11 years of age.

TABLE 36.1

Age and Sex-wise Distribution of Child Workers

Age Group	*Male*	*Female*	*Total*
4-7	—	—	—
7-11	51 (10.87)	10 (43.48)	61 (12.40)
11-14	418 (89.13)	13 (46.52)	431 (87.60)
All Groups	469 (100.00)	23 (100.00)	492 (100.00)

Note: Figures within brackets refer to percentage.

TABLE 36.2

Distribution of Working Children According to Age of Entry into The Present Job

Age Entry Group	*Male*	*Female*	*Total*
4-7	11 (3.30)	—	11 (2.40)
7-11	362 (77.19)	19 (82.61)	381 (77.44)
11-14	96 (19.51)	4 (17.39)	100 (20.36)
All Groups	469 (100.00)	23 (100.00)	492 (100.00)

Note: Figures within brackets refer to percentages.

Table 36.3 shows the educational status of the working children according to age and sex. There are no children below the age of 6 years in the sample. Only 17 children in the 7-11 years age group and 138 children in the 11-14 years group are educated. About 69 per cent of the children in the sample are illiterate. Of the literate children, only 17 have been educated upto the secondary level. The rest of them are educated below or upto the primary education level. Among female workers only 4 out of the 23 have been educated at levels below the primary level.

Table 36.4 shows the schooling status of the working children in the sample. The table reflects clearly the illiteracy of the children working in the industry and a non-serious attitude towards education. About 69 per cent of the child workers in the sample have never attended school, while about 24 per cent of them have dropped out from the school. It means less of time which can be utilised for work and thus less of money. Again going to school would mean no profit bearing expenditure education from the point of view the parents, because of their poverty to meet the expenditure. Only a small number (8 per cent of the child workers) are receiving formal education.

TABLE 36.3

Educational Status of Working Children According to Age and Sex

Age and Sex	*Illiterate*	*Primary Level and Below*	*Upto Secondary level*	*Beyond Secondary level*	*Total*
Upto 6 years					
Male	—	—	—	—	—
Female	—	—	—	—	—
Total	—	—	—	—	—
7-11 years					
Male	37	15	—	—	52
Female	8	2	—	—	10
Total	45	17	—	—	62
11-14 years					
Male	281	119	17	—	417
Female	11	2	—	—	13
Total	292	121	17	—	430
All Groups					
Male	318	134	17	—	469
Female	19	4	—	—	23
Total	337	138	17	—	492

TABLE 36.4

Schooling Status of Working Children

Schooling Status	*Number*	*Percentage*
Still attending school	38	7.72
Never attending school	337	68.50
Attended but dropped out	117	23.78
Total	492	100.00

Table 36.5 shows the details of past work experience of the sample child workers. As is evident from the table, no female worker has any work experience, while among the male workers only 29 have experience. About 94 per cent of the children have no past work experience at all.

TABLE 36.5

Details of Past Work Experience of Sample Child Workers

Age Groups	*Worked*			*Not Worked*			*Total*		
	Male	*Female*	*Total*	*Male*	*Female*	*Total*	*Male*	*Female*	*Total*
4-7 years	—	—	—	—	—	—	—	—	—
7-11 years	1	—	1	51	10	61	3.45	—	3.45
11-14 years	28	—	28	389	13	402	96.55	—	96.55
All Groups	29	—	29	440	23	463	100.00	—	100.00

Table 36.6 tells us why the child workers in the sample left their past jobs. Of the 492 workers in the sample, only 29 left their jobs to join the carpet industry. The most popular reasons with the workers for leaving their past jobs seem to be the low wages paid to them in their previous jobs and the long distance involved in going to their workplaces. Other reasons for leaving the job are: advance money was not given, wages were not paid for work done and the industry where the child worked was closed down.

TABLE 36.6

Reason-wise Distribution of Working Children Related to Past Job

Reasons for leaving the past job	*Number*	*Percentage*
1. Work was not always available	—	—
2. Started to go to school	—	—
3. The industry was closed	1	3.45
4. Low wages were given	9	31.05
5. Work was too much	—	—
6. Wages were not being paid	5	17.24
7. Work place was at a long distance	8	27.59
8. Work was not given	1	3.45
9. The advance money was not given	5	17.24
Total	29	100.00

When we look at the work status of the working children in Table 36.7, we find that of the total 492 child workers interviewed, all are paid wages but just about 12 per cent of them are currently receiving training while on the job.

Most of the children (about 98 per cent) live in the secure home environment with their parents. Only 10 children live with their relatives.

TABLE 36.7

Status of Child Workers

1. Total Number of Child Workers in the Sample	492
2. Number of Child Workers under Training	57
3. Percentage of Workers under training	11.59
4. Number of Child Workers who are paid	492
5. Percentage of workers paid	100.00

Data regarding the distance from the working place and mode of transport used by the working children reveal that most of them (i.e. 405 out of 492) do not commute to work as they are working at home (Table 36.9). As has been mentioned some where else, that the carpet weaving process is carried out at the household level and the children work mostly at homes. There are only 55 and 28 children, who go on foot to their respective work places by covering distance of from less than 1 km. to 3 km. away from their houses. There are only three children who go by bicycles to covering a distance of 3 km. and above.

TABLE 36.8

Housing/A Accommodation Facilities for The Working Children

Working Children Living with	*Number*	*Percentage*
Parents	482	97.97
Relatives	10	2.03
Shelter/Children's Home	—	—
Staying alone	—	—
Total	492	100.00

TABLE 36.9

Distance From Place of Work and Mode of Transport Used by The Children

Distance (kms.)	*Number of working children*				
	Working at Home	*Walk*	*Bicycle*	*Bus*	*Others*
Zero distance (working at home)	405	—	—	—	—
Less than one km.	—	55	1	—	—
1 km. to 3 kms.	—	28	1	—	—
3 kms. and above	—	1	1	—	—
Total	405	84	3	—	—

Pattern of Wage Income and Child Labour Use

The income size-wise distribution of the working children shows that 88.43 per cent of the total children get income ranging from Rs. 75 to Rs. 400 per month. There are only about 10 per cent and 1.01 per cent working children whose income levels fall in the income size-groups of Rs. 400 to Rs. 500 and Rs. 500-600. There are also four children whose monthly income is less than Rs. 75 per month. The monthly income per child worker work out to about Rs. 300 and so the daily income per child worker is about Rs. 10. Table 36.10 shows a wide range of variations in the monthly and daily wage per working child, from Rs. 61.25 to Rs. 590 and from Rs. 2 to about Rs. 20 respectively in the carpet industry of Mirzapur. The same table also reflects gross under-payment to the working children in the carpet industry of Mirzapur.

TABLE 36.10

Size-wise Income Distribution Pattern of Working Children and Level of Monthly and Daily Income Per Child Worker

Income Group (Rs.)	*No. of Children*	*Total Monthly (absolute) (Rs.)*	*Total Average Monthly Income (Rs.)*	*Average Salary per Child (Rs.)*
0-75	4 (0.80)	245	61.25	2.04
75-150	54 (10.98)	7200	133.33	4.44
150-200	95 (19.31)	19000	200.00	6.67
200-300	182 (37.00)	53266	292.67	9.76
300-400	104 (21.14)	40821	392.51	13.09
400-500	48 (9.76)	23898	497.88	16.60
500-600	5 (1.01)	2950	590.00	19.67
600-700	—	—	—	—
700-800	—	—	—	—
800 +	—	—	—	—
Total	492 (100.00)	147380	299.55	9.99

The level of wage income among the working children depends on the duration of work, level of skill, nature work, age of the child and the establishment where the child gets employment.

Table 36.11 indicates that the child labour employed in the carpet industry at Mirzapur is clearly an overtaxed lot. Out of the total 40.05 per cent have to suffer from working for inhumanly long 8-10 hours a day. About 9.75 per cent of them work even longer, more than 10 hours a day. The inhuman and unjust attitude of the employers infringe upon the child's right to a healthy and dignified existence. The seriousness and impropriety of the problem depends further as more than eighty per cent (82.32 per cent) of these children contribute their labour to family owned firms. For these children charity does not begin at home. Such in considerate business practices are contemptuous and merit stringent action. There appear to be very few employers who make the children employed by them work for shorter hours. Just 2.23 per cent work for 2-4 hours a day but none for less than 2 hours. Moreover, there seems to be a parallelism between duration of work and exploitation. With the increasing working hours, there is a corresponding increase in the number of working children.

TABLE 36.11

Distribution of Working Children According to Working Hours Per Day

Hours Worked Per Day (Number)	*No. of Children*	*Percentage*
0-2	—	—
2-4	11	2.23
4-6	69	14.02
6-8	167	33.95
8-10	197	40.05
10 +	48	9.75
Total	492	100.00

TABLE 36.12

Classification of Working Children According to Working Hours Per Day and Its Relationship With Income Levels

No. of Hours Worked Per Day	*Monthly Income of the working child (Rs.)*										
	0-75	*75-150*	*150-200*	*200-300*	*300-400*	*400-500*	*500-600*	*600-700*	*700-800*	*800 and Above*	*Total*
0-2	—	—	—	—	—	—	—	—	—	—	—
2-4	—	3	7	1	—	—	—	—	—	—	11
		(5.36)	(6.36)	(0.56)							(2.24)
4-6	2	21	14	18	5	8	—	—	—	—	69
	(33.33)	(37.50)	(12.73)	(10.61)	(5.26)	(19.51)					(14.02)
6-8	1	22	37	51	31	22	3	—	—	—	167
	(16.67)	(39.29)	(33.64)	(28.49)	(32.63)	(53.66)	(60.00)				(33.94)
8-10	1	6	33	92	52	11	2	—	—	—	197
	(16.67)	(10.71)	(30.00)	(51.40)	(54.74)	(26.83)	(40.00)				(40.04)
10 +	2	4	19	16	7	—	—	—	—	—	48
	(33.33)	(7.14)	(17.27)	(8.94)	(3.37)						(9.76)
Total	6	56	110	179	95	41	5	—	—	—	492
	(100.00)	(100.00)	(100.00)	(100.00)	(100.00)	(100.00)	(100.00)				(100.00)

Note: Figures in parentheses refer to percentages.

Given different income groups (i.e. assuming constant income), observe from Table 36.12 that a large number of the working children have to sweat for longer hours per day for the same income. About of 90 per cent of the 110 working children belonging to the income group of Rs. 150 to 200 put in 6 hours to over 10 hours per day for the same income level. A little more than 47 per cent of the same number of working children work more than 8 hours per day. Similarly, 60.35 per cent of the 179 working children in the income size group of Rs. 200 to 300 work from 8 hours to over 10 hours per day for the same income. A little more than 62 per cent of the 95 working children with income size of Rs. 300 to 400 put in more than 8 hours of work per day for the same income. Table 36.12 by and large, reflects that in most cases large number of the working children work for longer hours per day in order to get a give income level. In other words, it also measures the exploitation of child labour in terms of lengthening the duration of work by the employer.

TABLE 36.13

Classification of Working Children According to Different Levels of Monthly Income and Its Relationship Working Hours Per Day

No. of Hours Worked Per Day	*Monthly Income of the working child (Rs.)*										
	0-75	*75-150*	*150-200*	*200-300*	*300-400*	*400-500*	*500-600*	*600-700*	*700-800*	*800 and Above*	*Total*
0-2	—	—	—	—	—	—	—	—	—	—	—
2-4	—	3	7	1	—	—	—	—	—	—	11
		(27.28)	(63.63)	(9.09)							(100.00)
4-6	2	21	14	19	5	8	—	—	—	—	69
	(2.89)	(30.44)	(20.29)	(27.54)	(7.25)	(11.59)					(100.00)
6-8	1	22	37	51	31	22	3	—	—	—	167
	(0.59)	(13.18)	(22.15)	(30.54)	(18.57)	(13.18)	(1.79)				(100.00)
8-10	1	6	33	92	52	11	2	—	—	—	197
	(0.05)	(3.05)	(16.76)	(46.70)	(26.39)	(5.59)	(1.01)				(100.00)
10 +	2	4	19	16	7	—	—	—	—	—	48
	(4.16)	(8.33)	(39.59)	(33.33)	(14.59)						(100.00)
Total	6	56	110	179	95	41	5	—	—	—	492
	(1.21)	(11.39)	(22.36)	(36.39)	(19.20)	(8.34)	(1.01)				(100.00)

Note: Figures in parentheses refer to percentages.

Table 36.13 also reveals that the working children are underpaid and exploited. In this table the duration of workers is kept constant and the income is held as a variable. We observe here that a large number of the working children get less payment for the same number of working hours. The working children, numbered 197, work for 8 to 10 hours per day; but 63.45 per cent of them get in income between Rs. 150 to 300. Similarly, about 4 per cent and about 33 per cent of them get an income for the same working hours between Rs. 0 to 150 and Rs. 300 to 600 respectively. In this way, the figures in the horizontal rows of Table 36.13 indicate how a large number of the working children get less income by putting in the same number of working hours in their work process. All this reflects the extent of under payment and exploitation of child labour in the carpet industry.

The status of working children can be also reflected by the pattern of wage collection among them to some extent. Similarly, it gives some clue about the exploitation and attitude of parents towards their children. It is an irony that the working children do not enjoy the right to the income earned by them on the one hand and the keen concern of parents for the earnings of their children as well as the economic condition of the households on the other. Table 36.14 shows that about 18 per cent of the children get their wages themselves from the employers while 76 per cent of them reported that their wages are collected by their parents. A little more than 6 per cent of them also mentioned that their local guardians collect their wages on their behalf from the employers. Such a mode of wage collection in fact veils other exploitative practices which may be in operation due to the advance of money to their parents in order to make them bonded to debts as a security to ensure the supply of child labour for the employers.

TABLE 36.14

Pattern of Collection of Wages by Child Workers

Collection of Wages by	*Number of Child Workers*	*Percentage*
Self	88	17.88
Parents	374	76.02
Local Guardians	30	6.10
Others	—	—
Total	492	100.00

Let us see how much of the wage income earned by the working children is spent by them as pocket money. It is observed that the child workers in the sample earn an average of Rs. 300 per month but they get a mere Rs. 25 on an averages as pocket money. The money is given or taken away by parents, due to extreme poverty, to meet basic needs.

Table 36.15 indicates that, 420 child workers out of the total sample of 492 get pocket money. A little more than 25 per cent of them get between Rs. 31 to Rs. 40, while 23 per cent get between Rs. 11 to Rs. 20, showing the meagre amount parents give to their children on account of extreme poverty of the household.

Data are also collected from the working children about the items on which they generally spend their pocket money. A large majority of them, 87 per cent, spend most of their money on snacks, while 28 per cent spend mostly on entertainment. A part of the pocket money is also spent on smoking and tobacco, as reported by 13.41 per cent of the working children.

TABLE 36.15

Distribution of Child Workers According to Level of Pocket Money

Level of Pocket Money	*Number of Child Workers*	*Percentage*
Upto Rs. 10	75	17.86
Rs. 11 to Rs. 20	115	27.38
Rs. 21 to Rs. 30	102	24.28
Rs. 31 to Rs. 40	4	0.96
Rs. 41 and above	124	29.52
Total	420	100.00

It is also observed that saving habits have not been inculcated in the child workers taken in the sample. The workers simply living from hand to mouth and spend all they earn.

Children's Perception and Attitude Towards Their Work and Use As Child Labour

The foregoing analysis has thrown light on the status, use and exploitation of child labour in the carpet industry of Mirzapur. In this section, the perception and attitude of the working children towards their work and use as child labour is discussed on the basis of our relevant field data.

During the discussions with the working children, it was observed that the work is not liked by many of the working children. They do not like to work in their childhood. But their dislike for the work in which they are engaged is subordinated to their family conditions. Therefore, many of them are not in position to be categorical in this regard, as they do not have any scale of preference. That is why only about 35 per cent of the total working children reported a dislike for work and the rest of them liked it.

TABLE 36 16

Attitude of Child Towards Work

Attitude of Child	*Number of Child Workers*	*Percentage*
Number of Child Workers in the sample	492	100.00
Number of Child Workers who like to work	322	65.45
Number of Child workers who do not like to work	170	34.55

Among those who did not like the job, about 88 per cent of them reported low wages but more work as the cause for their dislike. A little more than 8 per cent of them mentioned the dangerous-cum-injurious nature of work as the cause for disliking the job. A new of them (3.6 per cent) also reported the nature of work having injurious effects to their bodies as the cause for their dislike. All this is what Table 36.17 reflects.

TABLE 36.17

Reasons for Not-liking Work

Reasons for not liking work	*Number of Child Workers*	*Percentage*
Dangerous or injurious work	15	8.29
Low wages and more work	148	87.57
Work is being done at night	—	—
Wants to go to school	1	0.59
Work leads to body pain	6	3.55
Work leads to deterioration to health	—	—
Total	170	100.00

There were 322 working children who expressed their liking for the present job. Table 36.18 indicates that about 90 per cent of them like to work because they want to earn money. Some children have other reasons for working. They work because the work is not dangerous or because they are eager to work or because the work is easily available in their locality or at home.

TABLE 36.18

Reasons for Liking Work

Reasons for liking work	*Number of Child Workers*	*Percentage*
To earn money	290	90.06
Not dangerous	16	4.97
Eager to work	3	0.93
Work is easily available in the locality or at home	13	4.04

The 170 working children who expressed their dislike for the present job were questioned to understand the reasons for their working at the present jobs, despite their disliking for it. Table 36.19 indicates the existence of poverty among them as the most important reason for working them in the present occupation. The rest of them reported some other reasons but all of them are related to the socio-economic conditions in which they have to work for subsistence. In other words, ameliorating their poor socio-economic lot is the main cause for them to work.

TABLE 36.19

Socio-Economic Compulsions for Working

Work Compulsion	*Number of Child Workers*	*Percentage*
Poverty	148	87.06
Parents sickness or death	8	4.71
Coercion by parents	5	2.94
To supplement household income	9	5.29
Total	170	100.00

As evident from the foregoing discussion, it becomes clear that the working children do not have any scale of preference or choice because of their socio-economic conditions. Table 36.19 shows the socio-economic compulsions to work and earn for supporting their families to maintain a subsistence level of existence. However, we wanted to comprehend the perception or preference of the working children about their work. About 62 per cent of the total working children reported that they would like to continue the work. There were only 12 children who expressed their preference for education. The rest of them desired more training or switching over to some other job.

TABLE 36.20

Aspiration/Preference of Working Child Regarding Work

Discription	*Number of Child Workers*	*Percentage*
Likes to continue work	309	62.80
Likes to get more training	76	15.45
Wants to switch over	95	19.31
Wants to go back to school	12	2.44
Total	492	100.00

None of the children working in carpet weaving industry gets weekly holidays. Working for 30 days in a month spoils their health. It is, therefore, apt to say here that "all work and no play makes Jack a dull boy". Carpet weaving is a complex and complicated job which is done best in day light. All the children working in this industry work during the day.

Day time working without any holidays is in practice because the carpet weaving work is done at the household and the children have to work for wages at a given rate or on piece-meal basis, depending upon the nature of contract with the manufacturer negotiated through the middle men. Table 36.22 shows that as many as 72.15 per cent of the children spend leisure hours on playing. Quite a few (47.35 per cent) like to roam around either alone or with friends in the fields and around the village and some (34.34 per cent) take rest. A few like to spend this time gossiping with friends and only two of them spend their leisure in reading. In fact, having put in a long duration of work they rarely avail leisure except in case of having no work given to them by the manufacturer.

TABLE 36.21

Timings of Work and Weekly Holidays

Discription	*Working Children*	
	Number	*Percentage*
Child labour reporting provision of weekly holidays	—	—
Child workers working during day time	492	100.00
Child workers working during night time	—	—
Child Workers working during other time	—	—

TABLE 36.22

Ways of Spending Leisure Time

Nature of Work	*Working Children*	
	Number	*Percentage*
Playing	355	72.15
Walking/Roaming	233	47.35
Taking Rest	169	34.34
Reading	2	0.40
Gossiping	6	1.21

Note: Multi-responses are given by the working children so far ways of spending leisure time is concerned.

Besides bringing home their share of the family income many children help their parents with household chores too. Maximum (29.67 per cent) assist in the fields, taking active part in clearing, weeding etc. and grazing the cattle. Some (14.43 per cent) collect water and cooking fuel while 7.11 per cent of them help by bringing things from the market (Table 36.23).

In Mirzapur only 7.12 per cent of the children attended school while working. This low percentage reflects a lack of awareness regarding benefits of education among families. Most of the employed children were trained (88.42 per cent) while about 8 per cent of them were under training, leaving only 3.65 per cent untrained. This high rate of skilled workers is a must as carpet weaving is a highly specialised industry.

TABLE 36.23

Nature of Household Work Done by Child Labour

Nature of Work	*Working Children*	
	Number	*Percentage*
To brings things from the market	35	7.11
To collect water and cooking fuel	71	14.43
Working related with agriculture and animal husbandry	146	29.67

TABLE 36.24

Skill and Vocational Status of Working Children

Discription	*Working Children*	
	Number	*Percentage*
Total number of working children	492	100.00
Child Workers till attending school while working	38	7.72
Untrained child workers	18	3.66
Child workers under training	39	7.92
Trained child workers	435	88.42

The Main Points

The present chapter is a most crucial part of the study. The age-sex-wise distribution of the working children shows that about 88 per cent of the total working children belong to the age-group of 11-14 years and most of them are male children. A little more than 77 per cent of them have entered the present job at the age group of 7 to 11 years. About 3 per cent of them have entered the job at the age group of 4-7 years.

About 69 per cent of the total 492 working children are illiterate and 138 of them are semi-literates in the sense that they have education upto the primary level. Thus, the majority is illiterate.

About 67 per cent of them never attended the school and about 24 per cent of them were school drop outs. Only 38 of the total children were attending the school while on the job.

Only 29 children (out of 492) have past work experience most of these children reported the closure of the industry, a long distance and non-payment of wages as the main causes for leaving the past job.

All the working children in the sample are paid and about 12 per cent of them are still under training. Most of them live with their parents in their own houses. Only a few live with their relatives. Given the nature and form of production in the carpet industry, most of the children work at home and they do not commute. There are 87 children who do not work at their own houses/villages and so most of them walk to their work places.

The income size (or level) wise distribution of the working children shows that a majority of the working children (i.e. 88.43 per cent) get monthly income ranging from Rs. 7 to 400. The are few whose monthly income falls in the category of Rs. 400-500 and Rs. 500-600. The monthly income per working child works out to be on an average of Rs. 300 and the daily wage income is about Rs. 10. About 50 per cent of the total working children have to work for more than 8 hours to earn such incomes. About 34 per cent of them work for 6 to 8 hours per day. In this way, it is observed that most of the working children work for a duration varying from 6 to 10 + hours per day in order to earn their wages.

The relationship between the working hours and income of the working children reflects two things , first, in most cases a large number of children work for longer hours per day in order to earn a give wage income and secondly, a large number of them get less income by putting in the same working hours per day. Tables 36.12 and 36.13 shows the extent of underpayment and exploitation of child labour in the carpet industry.

The children work for a longer duration but are paid less. At the same time, they do not have control of their own wage income as the wages earned by them are not collected by themselves from the employers. In most cases, their parents and relatives collected their wages for the employers on their behalf. On an average, they earn Rs. 300 per month but 420 children in the total sample get Rs. 25 per child as a monthly pocket money from their parents. However, the distribution of the working children according to different levels of pocket money received shows that about 30 per cent of them are given more than Rs. 40 as monthly pocket money and most of them get a sum varying from less than Rs. 10 to Rs. 30. Most of them reported spending their pocket money on snacks and some of them also mentioned the spending of their pocket money on smoking and gambling.

The perception and attitude of the working children about their work and use reveals that they do not have preference or choice, except to work for wages on account of their poverty and socio-economic compulsions from which they suffer. However, we made an attempt to show those who dislike the work and those who like it, and to comprehend the causes for their respective dislikes and likes for the work. A synthetic analysis of both (i.e. those who like and those who dislike the work) indicates that the extent of poverty and the socio-economic compulsions prevailing among the working children and their families make them work for wages.

Briefly speaking, the supply of child labour is a product of socio-economic compulsions from which the working children and their families suffer; and the exploitation of child labour appears to be a product of the socio-economic structure of production in which it is used and employed.

37

PHYSICAL DEVELOPMENT, HEALTH HAZARDS AND SOCIAL INFRASTRUCTURE

The overburdened children engaged in carpet weaving industry of Mirzapur are devoid of a healthy atmosphere. Malnutrition and overwork are leading to their steady and silent physical degeneration. Disease and illnesses resulting from poor diet and occupational hazards have far reaching consequences for these children i.e. weak child labour graduates to a weaker adult labour force further reducing its efficiency and thereby its remuneration. To counter these problems the government has started welfare schemes and programmes in good faith. But the response to these well meaning efforts has left most of the targeted population untouched and will become clear as we proceed with the chapter. Labour laws and their clauses are known just to a handful of the sample respondents. Ignorance for them is not bliss as it makes way for easy exploitation by employers. In a way, this chapter makes an attempt to discuss the implications of the abuse of child labour on the physical development and health of the working children, the availability of social infrastructures and their beneficial utilisation at Mirzapur.

Physical Development

Let us begin with the case of physical development of the working children. Weight and height are taken to be good enough to measure the physical development of the working children. The age-wise medically prescribed standard norms of weight and height were taken from Davison's Principles and Practice of Medicine, edited by John Macleod, 1975 for presenting the children with or below standard weight and height, having their actual weights and heights through the field surveys.

Classification of the working children according to weights in the sample taken from Mirzapur indicates that only 15 working children of both sexes have standard weight and 54 them of both the sexes have more than standard weight belonging to their respective age groups. Table 37.1 also shows that the working children of a large number (i.e. 423 of 492), constituting about 86 per cent of the total sample, are having weights below the standard norm, belonging to their respective age groups. This means that a majority of them are underweight that reflects their poor physical development.

TABLE 37.1

Classification of Working Children According to Age-Sex Wise Standard Weights

Age (Yrs.)	*Sex*	*Standard Weight (kgs.)*	*No. of Working Children*			
			With Standard Weight	*Less Than Standard Weight*	*More Than Standard Weight*	*Total*
6	M	22	—	—	—	—
	F	21	—	—	—	—
7	M	25	—	—	—	—
	F	25	—	—	—	—
8	M	26	—	7	3	10
	F	26	—	3	—	3
9	M	30	—	8	4	12
	F	27	—	—	2	2
10	M	32	—	24	6	30
	F	33	—	5	—	5
11	M	35	4	34	10	48
	F	37	—	2	—	2
12	M	39	1	111	17	129
	F	43	—	7	—	7
13	M	42	10	208	12	230
	F	49	—	4	—	4
14	M	45	—	10	—	10
	F	54	—	—	—	—
Total			15	423	54	492

Table 37.2 presents the distribution of working children according to their respective age sex-wise standard heights in Mirzapur. The table indicates that there are only four children of both the sexes who possess normal height and 23 children have more the than normal height. About 94 per cent of the total sample of 492 are under height, belonging to their respective age groups (these figures include both the sexes).

A majority of the working children being under-weight and under-height, in fact, present the case of their physical under-development which enfolds the kind of health they process.

TABLE 37.2

Classification of Working Children According to Age-Sex Wise Standard Heights

Age (Yrs.)	*Sex*	*No. of Working Children*	*Standard Height (Cms.)*	*Working Children*		
				No. of Children with Standard Height	*No. of Children Below Standard Height*	*No. of Children Above Standard Height*
6	M	—	46.85	—	—	—
	F	—	46.06	—	—	—
7	M	—	48.43	—	—	—
	F		48.43	—	—	—
8	M	10	50.39	—	10	—
	F	3	50.00	—	3	—
9	M	12	52.76	—	12	—
	F	2	51.97	—	2	—
10	M	30	54.33	—	30	—
	F	5	54.72	—	5	—
11	M	48	56.30	2	45	1
	F	2	56.69	—	2	—
12	M	129	58.66	—	113	16
	F	7	59.06	1	6	—
13	M	230	60.63	—	224	6
	F	4	61.02	1	3	—
14	M	10	62.99	—	10	—
	F	—	62.99	—	—	—
Total		492		4	465	23

Health Hazards

Table 37.3 presents the level of immunisation among the children (below 6 years) in the sample households.

Discriminatory attitude of parents towards male and female children is reflected by the sex-wise immunisation status of children. In absolute terms fewer females than males were immunised against various diseases. The status in percentages is slightly different. Except D.P.T. which has lower percentage of males immunised (12.20 per cent) to total male children as compared to female children (14.80 per cent), the rest have a higher percentage of immunised males over females against them (Table 37.3). Polio drops have been given to 49.77 per cent children in the sample households. However, this percentage is recorded higher among the male children.

TABLE 37.3

Children Below Six Years of Age and Their Immunisation Status

Item	*Level of Immunisation*								
	No. of Children Below 6 Years			*Children Immunised*			*Percentage of Immunised Children*		
	Male	*Female*	*Total*	*Male*	*Female*	*Total*	*Male*	*Female*	*Total*
D.P.T.	246	196	442	30	29	59	12.20	14.80	13.35
Polio				124	96	220	50.41	48.98	49.77
B.C.G.				62	45	107	25.20	22.96	24.21
Meales				37	29	66	15.04	14.80	14.93

It has been found that about 92.47 per cent household reported sickness of their family members during the last 6 months. In this context data pertaining to centre of treatment against sickness in the sample households revealed that out of the total households reporting sickness, 88.35 per cent visited private practitioners for treatment (Table 37.4). PHCs rank as centres of treatment with 17.14 per cent accepting their services. They were followed by dispensaries and district hospitals. The respondents reported that due to ill treatment of workers in district hospitals and non-availability of medicine they do not prefer to go to hospital for treatment.

TABLE 37.4

Illness and Centre of Treatment

Description	*Number*	*Percentage*
Sample households	492	
Households reporting in the last six months	455	92.47
Centre of Treatment		
(i) PHCs	78	17.14
(ii) Dispensaries	5	1.09
(iii) Private practitioners	402	88.35
(iv) ESI dispensaries	—	—
(v) District hospitals	2	0.43
(vi) Not taken treatment in above mentioned places	5	1.09
(vii) Other		

Out of 492 households, 92.47 per cent reported sickness among the family members in the last six-months (Table 37.4). Of these 99.12 per cent took allopathic medicines. Homeopathic treatment was taken by just 0.66 per cent households. Fewer still went in for Ayurvedic cure (Table 37.5).

TABLE 37.5

Illness and Method of Treatment in The Households

Description	*Number*	*Percentage*
Number of sample households	492	
Number of households reported sickness in the last six months	455	92.48
System of medicine availed		
(i) Allopathic	451	99.12
(ii) Ayurvedic	1	0.22
(iii) Homeopathic	3	0.66
(iv) Unani	—	—
(v) Native	—	—
(vi) Home remedies	—	—

The health problems related to external part of the body of the working children revealed that 9.15 per cent of the children in the sample have health related problems, with a maximum number of children having cracks in the lip or mouth. Some children also suffer from problems like dispigmented hairs, bleeding gums, dental caries and ulcers of the skin or scabies. Among the above mentioned problems about 24.24 per cent of the total 45 children are suffering from dental caries. Crack in the lip is reported by 55.56 per cent of them (Table 37.6).

TABLE 37.6

Health Status of The Working Children

Problems Related to Health	*Working Children having Problems*	
	Number	*Percentage*
Dispigmented hair	1	2.43
Bleeding gums	·6	13.33
Dental caries	11	24.24
Cracked lips/soar mouth	25	55.56
Ulcer on skin/scabies	2	4.44
Total	45	100.00 (9.15)

Note: Figure within bracket refer to percentage of the total sample of 492 children.

In Mirzapur district more than three-fourth (75.81 per cent) of the working children in hand-made carpet industry fell prey to some kind of sickness or the other in the past 12 months from the date of the survey. Most of the sick were those who fell sick occasionally. This preponderance of sick working children is a direct consequence of overwork and inadequate nutrition. More than 19 per cent of the total working children reported that they fell sick more than 5 times during the last one year (Table 37.7). There were working children who did not fall sick during the last 12 months as reported by 24.18 per cent of the working children (Table 37.7).

Different types of sickness were reported by the working children who fell ill during the last 12 months. The types of morbidity among the working children indicate that fever plagues 94.36 per cent of the sick 373 children. The cause being overwork which is not supplemented by adequate nutrition (Table 37.8). As many as 21.98 per cent children complained of stomach disorder and 0.53 per cent of jaundice reflecting an improper sanitation of the work place and impure drinking water. These little carpet weavers work in dingy ill ventilated rooms where woollen/cotton strands and dust accumulate leading to cold, cough and asthma among 12.60 per cent children and in extreme case TB (0.26 per cent). A few developed skin problems too (Table 37.8).

TABLE 37.7

Morbidity Among Working Children During Past Twelve Months

Frequency of Sickness (in the last 12 months)	*Working Children*	
	Number	*Percentage*
Often sick (more than 5 times)	95	19.30
Occasionally sick (less than 5 times)	278	56.52
No sickness	119	24.18
Total	492	100.00

TABLE 37.8

Type of Morbidity Among Working Children

Type of Sickness	*Working Children*	
	Number	*Percentage in Total Children reporting Morbidity during Past 12 Months*
Fever	352	94.36
Diseases related with the stomach pain, cholera, etc.	82	21.8
Skin diseases	3	0.80
Jaundice	2	0.53
Small pox	—	—
Cold and cough (Asthma)	47	12.60
Polio	—	—
T.B.	1	0.26

Sickness was also reported by the working children due to their working in the industry. Of the 492 child workers in the sample 4.67 per cent were sick due to the nature of work they were made to do in the industry. The environment the work place was found unhygienic in most of the cases. As a result, the workers suffered from various diseases, particularly the child workers became sick.

Social Infrastructure and Awareness

Data were collected from the working children about the facilities of education, health and welfare near their homes and work places. Most of the working children have reported that these facilities are not provided near their work places. However these facilities are available near their homes; it was found that a small proportion of the child workers use them. Although 97.56 per cent of the working children reported that educational institutions are located near their homes, but these educational facilities were used by only 9.76 per cent of the working children (Table 37.9). Due to poverty, the educational facilities are not used by the working children. Similarly 95.53 per cent of the working children admitted that the health facilities are provided near their homes. The proper attention is not paid by the staff of health centres. As a result, the benefits of health facilities are not reaching to the common mass. Only 9.96 per cent of the working children use the health facilities. The welfare measures for child development near their homes was reported by 9.35 per cent of the working children but these welfare measure were availed by only one child worker.

TABLE 37.9

Level of Facilities of Health, Education and Welfare and Their Utilisation

Description	*No. of Child Workers Reporting Facilities*	*Percentage of Child Workers Giving Posi-tive Answer about the utilisation*
Education Facilities Provided		
(i) Near home	480	97.56
(ii) Near factory	1	0.20
Child Workers Used Education Facilities	48	9.76
Health Facilities Provided		
(i) Near home	470	95.53
(ii) Near factory/work place	5	1.02
Child Workers Used the Health Facilities	49	9.96
Welfare Facilities Provided		
(i) Near home	46	9.35
(ii) Near factory	—	—
Child Workers Use the Welfare Facilities	1	0.20

The child workers in the sample have various reasons for not availing the facilities of education, health and welfare. A large number of children, 43.9 per cent, do not avail the educational facilities due to extreme poverty, which makes working essential and does not give the child time to study. Some children do not avail of the education facilities because their parents are ill or dead. They were not interested in studying, parents compel children to work, schools are far from home or lack of learning environment. Similarly 11.38 per cent of the children do not avail medical facilities because medical facilities are not available (Table 37.10). However, these facilities are available in some places but the medicine is not provided.

TABLE 37.10

Reasons for Not Using the Educational, Health and Welfare Facilities

Reasons for Not Using Facilities	*Child Workers*	
	Number	*Percentage*
Medicine does not give relief	30	6.10
Medicine not available	56	11.38
Due to poverty, work becomes essential	216	43.90
Parents are ill/dead	15	3.05
No child welfare programme	—	—
Nobody cares in Govt. hospital	15	3.05
Not interested in studying	46	9.35
Parents compel the children to do work	14	2.85
Schools are too far from home	11	2.29
Hospitals are too far	30	6.10
No learning environment	99	9.96
Others	1	0.20

Various rehabilitation programmes are launched to eradicate the practice of child labour. Welfare measures are also taken for the protection of child labour. The government agencies and voluntary organisations are engaged in the rehabilitation of child labour. In district of Mirzapur, where the survey was conducted, the number of rehabilitation centres are very little. However, some non-government organisations have established the rehabilitation centres for children who have been removed from employment. There are about 12 such centres in Mirzapur which provide education, food and shelter to such children.

The government in its well meaning effort has established rehabilitation centres through voluntary agencies for needy children in villages. But there appears to be a gap between establishing a concrete structure and spreading the message of the facilities provided. This is evident from the handful number (8.74 per cent) of children who reported being aware of such institutions engaged in rehabilitation of child labour. This fact highlights that working children are not aware of rehabilitation programme on the one hand and that there is an urgent need of rehabilitation centres in the district on the other so that the children engaged in handmade carpet industry may be removed from work and rehabilitated. The rehabilitation centres established by the voluntary organisations in the district are hardly working very smoothly according to their capacity. They are not in a position to cater to more children with the limited existing infrastructure.

TABLE 37.11

Awareness of Rehabilitation Centres Among Working Children

Number of Child Workers	*Rehabilitation Centres*		*Percentage of Child Workers Aware*
	Aware	*Unaware*	
492	43	449	8.74

Among the small number of (43) children aware of the existence of rehabilitation centres in the vicinity, merely 2.33 per cent among them availed the benefits (Table 37.12). It can be said that both the government and the masses require concentrated efforts for a better interaction to make government schemes/programmes fruitful. Similarly, it seems that the number of such centres are not enough to appreciate the magnitude of problem in the district.

TABLE 37.12

Utilisation of Facilities Provided by The Rehabilitation Centres

Description	*Working Children*	
	Number	*Percentage*
Facilities being used	1	2.33
Facilities not being used	42	97.67
Facilities were used but dropped	—	—
Total	43	100.00

TABLE 37.13

Type of Facilities in The Rehabilitation Centres Reported by Child Workers

Type of Facilities	*No. of Children Reporting the Facilities*	*Percentage of Child Workers Reported the Facilities*
Health and medical facilities	43	8.74
Education and school	43	8.74
Shelter and home	20	4.07
Food and nutrition	43	8.74
Entertainment and recreation	43	8.74
Other facilities	43	8.74

Few child workers in the sample are aware of the facilities provided by the rehabilitation centres. About 9 per cent working children have the knowledge of facilities such as health, education, food and entertainment provided by rehabilitation centres (Table 37.13). The facilities of shelter and home in these centres is known to 4.07 per cent of the working children. It is suggested that attention should be given to establish rehabilitation centres and at the same time the child workers and their parents should be made aware about the programmes and facilities, so that they can be motivated to join the rehabilitation centres.

As far as the level of utilisation of facilities by the working children and level of satisfaction among them from the rehabilitation centres is concerned it is found that only one child has availed of the facilities provided by the rehabilitation centres and he is satisfied with the facilities.

Of the 43 working children (8.74 per cent of the total sample) were aware about the facilities extended by the rehabilitation centres, 42 did not use the facilities. Data pertaining to reasons for not using the facilities reveals that about half (47.63 per cent) of the children were not admitted to these centres (Table 37.14). In some cases the centres were recently opened as reported by 28.57 per cent of the working children who were aware of the rehabilitation centres. Poverty remains as one of the reasons for not using the facilities, because the working children (14.38 per cent) have no alternative but that of earning. About 4.76 per cent of these working children were not interested in availing of the facilities.

TABLE 37.14

Reasons for Non-Utilisation of Facilities Provided by Rehabilitation Centres

Reasons for Not Using Facilities by child workers aware of the centres	*Child Workers*	
	Number	*Percentage*
Not interested	2	4.76
Due to poverty and compulsion to earn money	6	14.28
No knowledge about centre	—	—
Not admitted	20	47.63
Recent opening of centres	12	28.57
Compulsion to work from the parents' side	1	2.38
Centre Non-approachable	1	2.38
Total	42	100.00

Several development programmes are initiated by the government to remove poverty and to improve the economic conditions of the poor households. The analysis of data regarding the awareness of the programmes and the level of benefits indicates that only few in our sample are aware and a lesser number have been benefited from the various programmes run by the government. Only half of the people in our sample are aware of the IRDP and out of them a mere 13.31 per cent have been benefited. TRYSEM is known to 4.27 per cent with beneficiaries equalling zero per cent. The Jawahar Rozgar Yojana is known to comparatively more people than the other programmes. About 63 per cent of the people were aware of the programmes but only 26.77 per cent of them have received benefits from it. The awareness of the ICDS was found among 22.15 per cent households and only one household received its benefits. It seems that adult education is futile since only 46.54 per cent were aware of the programme. Merely 1.75 per cent of the aware households have been benefited from adult education programme. Data regarding the awareness of various laws and legislative measures about labour and wage rates among the sample households reveals that very few number of households have the knowledge of these laws and acts. Most of the households in the sample are in the dark regarding labour laws. Minimum wage rate is known to only 10.37 per cent of the households (Table 37.16). The proportion of households is found to be 12.60 per cent which are aware of the Accident Compensation Act. Provision of Provident Fund is known to only 9.96 per cent households. The child Labour Act is known to 39.84 per cent household (Table 37.16). The analysis suggests that the people should be made aware of various laws and acts so that they can be benefited and workers' protection is assured.

TABLE 37.15

Awareness and Benefit of Government Programmes in The Sample Households

Government Programmes	*Household Aware*		*Benefited*	
	Number	*Percentage*	*Number*	*Percentage*
IRDP	278	56.50	37	13.31
TRYSEM	21	4.27	—	—
Jawahar Rozgar Yojana (JRY)	310	63.01	83	26.77
ICDS	109	22.15	1	0.92
Adult Education	229	46.54	4	1.75

Data regarding the role and participation of sample household shows that the credit societies are in-effective in mobilising the financial support as it is evident from the data that a negligible proportion (0.41 per cent) of the total households are members and they are not availing any kind of loaning facilities from these societies.

All this presents a picture about the availability of social infrastructure facilities and awareness among the households in utilising them for their benefit.

The Main Highlights

The first implication that arises from the abuse of child labour in the carpet industry is the physical underdevelopment of the working children. Most of them are under-weight and under-height. However, the percentage of immunised children below 6 years of age appears to be high.

TABLE 37.16

Awareness of Labour Laws Among Households

Legislation	*No. of Household*		*Percentage*	
	Aware	*Not Aware*	*Aware*	*Not Aware*
Minimum wages	51	441	10.37	89.63
Accident compensation	62	430	12.60	87.40
ESI	110	382	22.36	77.64
Provident fund	49	443	9.96	90.04
Child labour	196	296	39.84	60.16
Others	2	490	0.41	99.59

A little more than 92 per cent of the sample households reported sickness of their family members during the last six months. The households, numbering 402 of the total households reporting sickness consulted private practitioners for treatment and most of them took allopathic medicines. There were 45 working children who reported to their health problems.

About 56 per cent of them reported suffering from crack in the lip or soared mouth and 22.24 per cent of them reported suffering from dental caries. The rest of them were suffering from dispigmented hair, bleeding gums and ulcers on their skin or scabies.

Except 24 per cent of the total working children the rest (about 76 per cent) of them fell sick often or occasionally. The 352 sick children of the total sample suffered from fever. About 35 per cent of the working children in the sample suffered from cough and cold, and the diseases related to stomach pain, cholera etc. Some of them also suffered from skin diseases, jaundice and T.B. Almost all the working children reported to have suffered from one disease or the other.

Most of the working children were aware of availability of the social infrastructure facilities relating to medical and health, and education. But all of them could not use them or derive benefits from the existing social infrastructures. The reasons for non-utilisation of those infrastructural facilities were reported by many of the working children. Notable among them was the existence of poverty among them non-availability of medicines, and no interest in education. In other words, their socio-economic conditions and apathetic attitude of the concerned officials, or personnel attached to the infrastructural facilities, seem to be the responsible factor for their non-utilisation.

In Mirzapur, only 43 working children were aware of the existence of rehabilitation centres and only one among them availed of the facilities provided by the rehabilitation centres. Despite being aware of the different facilities available at these centres, among the causes for their non-utilisation, as reported by the 42 working children, the most notable are recent opening of the centres, poverty and their non-admissibility. The situation highlights the apathy of the concerned persons of the centres in benefiting the children from the programmes which are meant for their (child's) welfare.

The Government has launched a package of anti-poverty programmes in order to improve the socio-economic lot of the poor. About 57 per cent and 63 per cent of the total households are found to be aware of the IRDP and JRY programmes respectively; but only 13.31 per cent and about 27 per cent of those aware of the IRDP and JRY programmes could benefit them respectively. Similarly, there exists a big gap between the number of the households which are aware of other programmes and the households which actually derive benefits from them. In other words, there is a big difference between awareness among the people regarding different anti-poverty programmes and the benefits they actually derive from them.

Data regarding the awareness of various laws and legislative measures regarding labour and wages among the sample households reveals that very few number of the sample households have knowledge of these laws and measures. For instance, the Minimum Wage Act is known to 10.37 per cent, P.F. Act to about 10 per cent, Child Labour Act to about 40 per cent, Accident Compensation to 13 per cent and ESI to 22 per cent of the total sample households. All this presents a pitiable picture not only about the awareness of these laws, measures and programmes among the households and people in Mirzapur but also the apathetic role of bureaucracy and the government in the present democratic set-up of the state and society.

38

HEALTH HAZARDS OF WORKING CHILDREN

This paper deals with the determinants and consequences of child labour and the existing child health services. Risks of injury, silicosis of lungs, bronchitis, anaemia, tuberculosis, etc., are highlighted. Possible strategies for correction and prevention of health hazards are suggested.

Introduction

The practice of children's working is economically unsound, psychologically disastrous and physically as well as morally dangerous and harmful for any society or even for the individual child. It involves the use of labour at its point of lowest productivity and as such an inefficient utilisation of labour power. It precludes the full unfoldment of child's potentialities. It deprives him of education, training and skills which are the necessary prerequisities of earning power and economic development.

Children are the most vulnerable group in any population and in need of greatest social care. On account of their vulnerability and dependence, they can be exploited, ill-teated and directed into undesirable channels by unscrupulous elements in the community. The State has the duty of according proper care and protection children at all times as it is on their physical and mental well-being that the future of the nation depends. Existing legislation covering child workers in factories and establishments is not adequately enforced. There are also areas where no legislative coverage exists, and others where the laws themselves permit early childhood employment. As a result, owing to unhygienic working condition, several jobs expose the children to various kinds of health hazards emanating from the extensive use of chemicals and poisonous substances in industries, and the pollutants discharged by them, to long hours work in the plantations in both fair and foul weather—in the scorching summer sun and in the driving rain of the monsoon. Such working environments obviously endanger children's physical health and mental growth.

Prevalence of Working Children in India

In India, millions of children instead of going to school, go to work to earn to support themselves or their parents. However, lack of data makes it difficult to arrive at a reliable figure of the number of children pushed into the labour force by economic pressures. No less than 10.79 million children were returned as workers in 1971 Census, consisting of 7.9 million boys and 2.8 million girls in the age group 0.14, giving an activity rate of 4.67 (Table 38.1). It is estimated that about 10 to 30 million children, i.e. about 5 to 10 per cent of India's children take up jobs, giving India the largest* child labour force in the world. These children constitute about 6 per cent of the labour force in the country. Table 38.1 shows the number of workers and the activity rate among children of age group 0-14. These data, however, do not seem to adequately reflect the role of girls in the family-based economy, although the proportion of girls to female adult workers has been found to be about 10 per cent higher than the proportion of boys to male adult workers.

Major Sectors and States Where Children Work

The 1971 Census also reveled that there were about 230 million children in the age group 0-14 years. They constituted 42 per cent of the total population. The number of child workers, below 15 years of age, was placed at 10.79 million representing 4.7 per cent of the total child population and 5.9 per cent of the total labour force. The Census operations also revealed that occupationwise, nearly 42.7 per cent of the child labour was employed in agriculture mainly as agricultural workers, i.e., as much as 9.7 per cent of the total labour force in agriculture in the country. About 8.2 per cent of the total child workers were engaged in livestock, forestry, fishing, hunting, plantations, orchards, etc. Thus the child labour constituted 20.6 per cent of the total labour force employed in these activities. Only 6 per cent of the child labour approximately was engaged in manufacturing and processing services and another 6 per cent in household and other industries. Trade, Commerce, Transport, Storage, Communication, etc. engaged about 2.4 per cent of the total working children.

It was also evident, as further revealed by Census, that child labour was more prevalent in *rural* areas than in urban areas—5.5 per cent of the children were working in rural areas as compared to 0.4 per cent in urban areas. In absolute numbers, out of 180 million total workers in the country, 148 million, i.e. 82.2 per cent were in rural areas and the rest 32 million or 17.8 per cent in urban areas. Amongst the working children, out of their total strength of 10.7 million, nearly 10 million or 93 per cent were in rural areas and 0.7 million or 7 per cent in urban areas, Sex-wise the male children constituted 6.6 per cent and female children constituted 2.6 per cent of the child population.

---

* This has been disputed by Natarajan (1979). Although a substantial proportion of children are working in India, he thinks that the proportion cannot be considered highest in the world. According to labour statistics of 1976 published by I.L.O., there were countries like Nepal, Thailand in Asia, Turkey in Europe, Papua New Guinea in Oceania, Benin, Egypt and Tanganyika in Africa, Brazil, Columbia, Dominican and Haiti in America where the percentage of children working is higher than that of India. However, the fact that a substantial proportion of children are engaged as workers seem to be common to all developing countries.

TABLE 38.1
Number of Workers and Their Participation rate in Economic Activity for Age-group 0-14, 1971 Census

India/States/U.T.s	*Workers in 0-14 Age Group*	*Activity Rate*
India	10,753,985	4,67
States		
Andhra Pradesh	1,627,492	9.24
Assam	239,349	3.41
Bihar	1,059,359	4.42
Gujarat	518,061	4.51
Haryana	137,826	2.97
Himachal Pradesh	71,384	5.01
Jammu and Kashmir	70,489	3.56
Kerala	111,801	1.30
Madhya Pradesh	1,112,319	6.11
Maharashtra	988,357	4.74
Manipur	16,380	3.59
Meghalaya	30,440	6.91
Mysore (Karnataka)	808,719	6.50
Nagaland	13,726	7.02
Orissa	492,477	5.30
Punjab	232,774	4.16
Rajasthan	587,389	5.16
Sikkim	15,661	19.37
Tamil Nadu	713,305	4.58
Tripura	17,490	2.54
Uttar Pradesh	1,326,726	3.59
West Bengal	511,443	2.69
Union Territories		
A. and N. Islands	572	1.31
Arunachal Pradesh	17,925	10.02
Chandigarh	1,086	1.21
D. and N. Haveli	3,102	9.19
Delhi	17,120	1.09
G. D. and Diu	7,391	2.26
Lakshadweep	97	0.75
Pondicherry	3,725	2.00

Source: Indian Association for the Study of Population. Proceedings of the Conference on Child in India. *New Delhi*, April, 1979, p. 56.

The number of children employed in the unorganised sector is not reflected in Census data and therefore it can only be guessed at best. This sector accounts for children working as domestic servants, helpers in hotels, restaurants, wayside shops and similar establishments; hawkers, newspaper vendors, porters, shoe-shine boys, sweepers, and scavengers, children employed in small workshops, and repair shops, and helpers at construction sites engaged in breaking stones, loading and unloading goods, etc. The working hours of these children in this sectors are long, their wages low and uncertain, and their working and living conditions are bad. They are at the mercy of their employers. It will thus be seen that the majority are in agriculture of farm related work, or in the unorganised sector. Only those working in the organised sector of the economy are expected to benefit from various child protection laws. Most child workers are therefore outside the scope of such protective legislation.

Similarly, the incidence of child labour was highest in Andhra Pradesh—9 per cent of the total labour force and 3.7 per cent of the total population in the State. In fact, Andhra Pradesh alone accounted for 15.2 per cent of the total child workers in the country, followed by Madhya Pradesh where child labour constituted 7.3 per cent of the total labour force and 2.7 per cent approximately of the total population in the State. In Orissa, the percentage of the child labour to total workers was placed at 7.2 per cent. Karnataka, Meghalaya, Nagaland, Rajasthan, Arunachal Pradesh and Dadra and Nagar Haveli are also other States and Union Territories where proportions are higher than the national average.

Detemrinants and Consequences of Child Labour

Children are mostly engaged as additional help, both at home as well as in agriculture, business or industry. The employment of children may be understood mainly from two points of view: first, to supplement the family income, when the income from the main bread-earners is inadequate to meet the family needs (in extreme cases the death or incapacity of the adult members to earn a living even makes the child's earning as the only or main source of income for the sustenance of the family); secondly, it is to pick up the technical know-how by doing the job so that proficiency could be achieved at an early stage. It is the stage of child apprenticeship. Since children remain unprotected, they are exposed to all sorts of exploitation. Thus, the child labour gets associated with two different yet related factors, i.e. one, the economic feature, and the other, a social evil. As an economic feature, it refers to the employment of children in gainful occupations normally away from the family and in return for wages. Such a feature has to be treated as unavoidable last resort and as such it has to be tolerated by the society. The second aspect, however, is becoming a point of universal concern. It is not necessary to take into account only the dangers or hazards to which the child is exposed but also the opportunities of development, physical, moral and cultural, that are denied to him. For, a child labourer is as much a child as any other child and needs all opportunities for the growth of his personality. It is only when the unavoidable necessity to engage himself in an economic pursuit conflicts directly or indirectly with his development and education that the social evil manifests itself. In rural areas, for example, employment of children as wage-paid labour is mainly to supplement the meagre income of chronically poverty-striken rural households. During agricultural season, child labour, which is cheaper than adult labour, is in demand, because of the general labour shortage. Irrespective of the motives of employing children, whether for earning larger profits as child labour is cheaper or from the sense of charity to engage children from poor sections of the society, or from the point of view of "catching them young" to train them as better workers when they become adults, the society, and for that matter, the State, cannot shirk its responsibility to crush this social evil.

Also, frequent migration seems to encourage early employment of children. Several studies indicate that as many as 80 per cent of the children of migrants are workers. This is four times higher than the rate among settled populations. In fact, a heavy load of dependent children per adult workers, coupled with rising cost of living, eventually contracts their saving in investment.

Apart from its economic implications (which obviously are indicative of unproductive and inefficient utilisation of labour power) the problem of child labour has its social implications and consequences too. The most frequently cited social aspect is directly related to child health, wherein there is interference in normal family life, and education comes to a standstill.

Child Labour, Health Status and Existing Child Health Services

The endogenic and exogenic factors determine the pattern of child mortality in a country. The endogenic factors include genetic causes affecting growth of organism, damages during gestation and risks of delivery. These have little or remote relationship with mortality and morbidity patterns of working children. The exogenic factors, on the other hand, cover infections, respiratory and digestive disorders, etc., including the neglect and faulty health care and as such are more related to health condition of working children who have to face many health hazards, and many die young for lack of timely health care due to illiteracy, ignorance of parents, lack of support from employees and adverse working conditions, etc.

It is estimated that 40 per cent of all deaths in India occur among children below five years of age. Of these deaths, about half are of children less than a year old. In the lowest age group (0-12 months), 50 per cent of deaths are due to dysentery, diarrhoea, respiratory diseases and gastro-intestinal disorders. Among the grown up children 56 per cent are reported to be related to intestinal infections, respiratory complaints and nutritional disorders. Tuberculosis is widespread in working children. In the rural areas where children are engaged in agriculture sector, the average distance between the village and the health centre is about 8 Kms., and about 87 per cent of people attending the Primary Health Centres (PHCs) are from villages within a 6.4 Kms. radius. Many children do not get family attention because 50 per cent of the village women are daily wage earners and most often children also being wage earners, cannot be carried to the PHC without losing family earning.

The health services for children are also inadequate. The number of hospital beds for children—about 9,300—is barely 50 per cent of the minimum requirement, and the country has only 25 children's hospitals and 424 paediatric wards to met the need of nearly 250 million children. Most of these are located far from the villages. There are major regional disparities: Bihar, Gujarat and Haryana do not have any children's hospitals at all. Thus the existing maternal and the child health services reach only a small proportion of the children who need them and the health needs of a majority of working children remain unmet. In the rural areas water-borne and water related diseases create greatest health hazards. About 163 million children (0-14 years) in rural India do not have access to safe drinking water, and are thus exposed to infection which can prove fatal. In 113,000 villages, the drinking water supply is either more than 1.6 K.M. away, or is sub-standard, and is responsible for diseases like Cholera and Guinea-worm or problems related to a mineral content too high for health. In another 214,000 villages, the water supplied from wells, streams, tanks, ponds and rivers is not only inadequate in quality, but is also open to the risk of pollution. In brief there are atleast 185,00 villages where the supply of water is both inadequate and unprotected. As a result, about 15.2 per cent of deaths in the 5-15 group are due to diarrhoea.

Malnutrition is another killer and/or creates health hazard for the children in India. Their poor diet having made them susceptible to infection and vulnerable during their occupational work. They survive malnourishment depending on the degree of deficiency due to inadequate amounts of key vitamins and minerals. Acute diarrhoeal diseases are more frequent and serious among malnourished working children. Signs of moderate protein-calorie malnutrition are in higher proportion among working children from low socio-economic group (56%) while 15 per cent show severe malnutrition.

Health Hazards of Working Children

The practice of child labour does not assure the working children healthy conditions of work and protect them from exploitation and hazardous occupations. Although a set of 13 major enactments having a bearing on working children, besides fixing the age limits and hours of work, do provide protection to children from adverse working conditions that might affect their health and growth, these provisions are inadequate for want of their proper enforcement. Furthermore, with the advancement of technology and increasing mechanisation, the occupational health hazards have increased which need to be identified and evaluated against their ill-effects.

A number of surveys conducted by the Labour Bureau and other agencies indicate that generally the work assigned to child labour has been comparatively of a *light* nature. For example, in agriculture, the children are mainly said to be employed as helpers, during sowing, weeding, harvesting and thrashing operations, etc. In factories, they are usually employed on packing, pasting, labelling etc. Other industries in which child labour is prevalent are Tea, Bidi manufacturing, Mica factories, Wood and Cork, Furniture and Fixtures, Printing, Publishing and allied Trades, Leather and leather products, Rubber and rubber products, Machinery, Transport equipment and personal services such as laundries, dyeing and cleaning. In plantations of tea and coffee, the light work entrusted to the children includes weeding, manuring, the care of nurseries, harvesting, plucking tea leaves and picking coffee, etc. In Bidi industry they roll bidis are assist the adult workers. In Handloom and Carpet Weaving, the children assist the weavers by working in the middle of the loom. In Glass Bangle Industry in U.P. (Ferozabad) children are employed for doing light duties in the process of manufacturing the bangles or assist the adult workers as helpers.

The findings of these surveys, conducted by official agencies, in terms of the so called *light assignment* of work to children should not be taken too lightly. The implications from the point of view of health hazards are indeed serious. In fact, a recent investigation entitled "A sub-proletariat in Short Trousers" (published in "India," My 1979) has shown that despite the legislation prohibiting young people from working below the age of 14 (and in exceptional cases — 12 years), the exploitation of child labour has been a common practice. In some parts of the city of Bombay, 24.7 per cent of children had begun working between the ages of six and nine years, and 48.4 per cent between 10 and 12; while another 26.4 per cent had found their way on the labour market between 13 and 15 years. This is inspite of the very high adult unemployment rate, which is over 40 per cent of the working population if strict criteria for full employment are applied. Similarly, in Agra, boys of 12 years and above work with their fathers to make shoes for sale to dealers and help to increase the day's output. Also, almost all over the world, specially in many developing countries, girls are sent to middle class homes as maids, who may develop eye injuries while working in the kitchen, etc. Like-wise, girls who make carpets in Kashmir, U.P., etc. develop bone deformities in their lower limbs due to squatting on planks for long hours and many of them later on face difficult pregnancies or even sterility. In the match factories of Tamil Nadu, children are employed from the age of six. Many of them who live in out-lying villages, have to get up as early as three a.m. to be picket up by a bus and taken to the factories returning home late at night. The above investigation also includes a case study of the brick kiln industry in Satwari Gaon near Delhi, where poor rural families come to work during the dry season from September to June when there is no agricultural work to be had. The labourers bring their whole families with them and live in shacks and tents on the site, without education, health facilities or clean drinking water. Families are paid on a piece work basis, as low as Rs. 17/- per 1,000 bricks, with the result that they have to use their children to increase their production. The family gets only one day off per fortnight. The children risk injury from the work, as well as *silicosis* of the lungs after three or four years of exposure to brick dust.

Of all other sectors, magnitude of problems for the health of working children in much greater in agricultural sector where child agricultural labourers are paid not in cash but in kind mostly. For example, most recently, (last week) the newspapers have exposed such a malpractice in Madhya Pradesh where labourers are being paid in *Khesari dal* which is a toxic pulse (Indian Express, April 9, 10, 11, 12, 1982). It is a known fact that regular eating of *Khesari* as a staple for two to six months causes incurable paralysis of the legs (lathyrism). Such a *criminal* practice had been noted even more than 60 years ago by Major H.W. Acton, a professor of pathology in the school of Tropical Medicines, Calcutta. However, in Rewa and Satna districts of the Vindhya region of Madhya Pradesh, the poisonous *Khesari* is still being given by landlords to bonded labour in lieu of their wages. It is usually accepted that "Khesari, after all, is the poor man's grain and lathyrism is his funeral."

In plantations, the sanitary conditions of labour lines, where children under 8 years are hired to work as baby sitters in tea gardens, are far from satisfactory. Absence of adequate arrangements for domiciliary or specialised treatment has been recommended in almost all the estates by the Committee on Labour Welfare (1969). According to a Survey, only about 5 per cent of the estates in tea plantations, 14 per cent in rubber plantations and 1 per cent in coffee plantations provide latrines at workplaces; however, urinals have been provided by a negligible percentage of estates

A study of 300 working children from slum facilities in Bombay conducted by National Institute of Public Co-operation and Child Development (1978) has shown that working children engaged in different occupation were provided very meagre facilities for protection of health. For example, protection against sun and rain was not available to 20 per cent of the wage employed children; separate rest place to 79 per cent; proper lighting to 11 per cent; medical facilities to 59 per cent; drinking and bathing water facilities to 21 per cent; protection against job hazards to 47 per cent; proper ventilation to 16 per cent; and toilet facilities to 43 per cent. Twenty-two per cent of the parents also felt that the work had affected the health of their children.

One of the worst health hazards for the working children is conspicuous in the bidi manufacturing industry in which children roll bidis and assist the adult workers by cleaning and cutting the leaf and closing the ends. About 200,000 children were working in bidi making alone according to a survey done in 1959 and they have to work under very insanitary and unhygienic conditions. The survey conducted by Labour Bureau (1954) in Murshidabad alone revealed that about 9 per cent of bidi workers between the ages of 10 and 14 years showed definite signs of *Chronic Bronchitis* and 10 per cent of the boys suffered from *Anaemia.* There is also sufficient indication to suspect a higher incidence of *Tuberculosis* among the bidi workers and this is due to starting the work at a tender age, very long hours of work, excessive over-crowding and the peculiar posture during the work which impedes the healthy development of the lungs of the working children. Employers also pay to the children much less than adults on the pretext that the productions did not come upto the required standard of quality.

Ferozabad, which is the home of the Glass Bangle Industry in the country and where children between 8-14 years of age from one-fifth of the total labour force employed in the industry, ranks first as far as *Tuberculosis* incidence in concerned., The factories, run for about eight months in the year, work only at night. Children are paid only Rs. 3/- a day for eight hours of work. The temperature inside the factory is 40-50° Centigrade which makes working in summer most miserable. Seven out of ten factories have no first-aid box and cases of *Asthma* and *Bronchitis* are many. In fact, working children in glass industries have to work amidst wretched and sordid surroundings so much so that they are not only emaciated, anaemic myopic and gloomy but also stunted in their physical growth.

Children of about 8—10 years of age are forced to work eight hours a day just for Rs. 80/- per month to assist the weavers in the Handloom and Carpet Weaving Industries specially in Jammu and Kashmir where they are packed into sheds in long rows behind giant looms feverishly picking warp and woof as a master draftsman gives instruction. The air is thick with particles of cotton fluffs and wool and 60 per cent of the children are *asthmatic* or have *primary tuberculosis.*

The *Unorganised* and *Self-employment* sectors account for a larger number of child employment where countless number of children are working as domestic servants or as workers in hotels, restaurants, canteens wayside tea-stalls and establishments, hawkers, newspaper sellers, coolies, shoe-shining boys, vendors, helpers in repair shops and in service stations, or as construction workers, rag pickers, and casual labourers, etc. They are also hired, along with their parents, in construction work and take part in loading, unloading and breaking of stones, etc. where, by and large, even basic minimum welfare amenities are not available to them. For example, a child construction worker digs the earth, carries headloads of mud and mortar, removes, debris, prepares mortar, breaks stones, straightens, bends, and solders, heavy iron rods and yet he has to do such a hard labour in the open exposed to the vagaries of weather, giving a profile of an unclean, ill-clad and barefooted sad victim of sordid exploitation. These children specially those engaged in the job of scrap-collecting or rag-picking, hail from poverty-stricken scheduled caste families residing in slums and they develop several kinds of *skin-diseases.* While collecting rusted iron pieces, they run the risk of receiving cuts on their hands and become susceptible to *Tatanus.* The sharp glass pieces lying hidden in the garbage may injure their bare feet and injury and develop into festering wounds.

Such is the pitiable plight of working children exposed to continuous health hazards. Apart from their health being impaired, the problem of delinquency also arises. It is well known that children working in street trades and in domestic service come before the courts more often than do children employed in other occupations.

Possible Strategies for Correction and Prevention

In view of our contemporary economic situation, the total eradication of child labour through legislation does not seem to be an immediate possibility. A better strategy would therefore be to assure healthy conditions of work for the working children and protect them from exploitation and hazardous occupations rather than to legally prevent them from joining the workforce. For this purpose, some suggestions are offered as given below:

1. It is necessary first to determine the extent of child labour precisely in various sectors before suitable actions are proposed to control this menace to child development. Work participation of children is best measured by the percentage of working children (5—14) among total number of children (5—14). Such a rate should be defined as "Child Labour Participation Rate (CLPR)" as distinguished from "Labour Force Participation Rate (LFPR)," Empirical evidence suggests that CLPR as revealed by 1971 Census data is grossly underestimated. Therefore, such approaches need to be refined.

2. Empirical evidence reveals that rural-urban migration of children is bound to continue. The more unfavourable impact of this is naturally on towns and cities. Proper corrective steps through appropriate welfare measures should be taken to arrest the exploitation of migrant child labour specially in towns and cities.

3. Education has the most dominant, effective and constructive role to play in reducing CLPR. The emphasis in this regard should clearly lie in rural areas where education should be made more attractive to children of poor family and their parents should be given adult and non-formal education to make them conscious about educating not only their own but all children.

4. An integrated child development approach should be adopted for children entering into the labour force with the following components:

(a) Children (0-6) should receive child care and adequate health and nutrition support,
(b) Children (7-11) should receive compulsory education, and
(c) Children 12-14) should receive vocational and specialised training along with non-formal education and health and welfare services.

5. In the various enactments that we already have, a good deal of change and augmentation is necessary from the point of view of safeguarding the health of child labour against occupational health hazards which are many more in several other industries which might not have been identified so far. As such, they call for urgent attention of all concerned to evaluate adequacy or otherwise of the existing legislative and non-legislative measures in this regard so that some administrative measures could be adopted to identify the problem with a view to mitigating its rigours against the health and development of working children.

6. Child employment in factories, as compared to the total working children is almost negligible. In the vast sea of unorganised sector, a good deal of positive work in ameliorating the lot of the working children can be done by *non-legislative* efforts of social organisation and even by trade unions, if they take up the challenge. But will they

do so is a big question mark specially in the case of trade unions.

7. Realistically, in order to make the education subserve the future work needs of children, there is a need to vocationalise school education.

8. There is a great need to educate the employers as well as the public about the legal provisions made to protect the interests of children. An educational brochure giving detailed information as to the rationale of passing protective labour laws with regard to employment of children and how the violation of such legislation would be harmful to children, should be prepared and widely circulated among all the concerned parties—the employers, the trade union leaders and the general public. The brochure should be supplemented by information collected through systematic research studies about the health hazards, economic and social consequences of taking up employment at an early age, etc. In the rural areas, all possible materials of mass-media should be employed in disseminating information on: prevention of accidents on the roads, in factories, and mechanised farms; checking damages from unhealthy working conditions in small scale industries employing children; promoting early detection and treatment of physical and mental disabilities, etc.

9. It should be recognised that there are four channels of health to children. The *first* is the family in which the child is found. The *second*, is the community in which the family is located. The third is the system of government services available to both. The *fourth* is the outside assistance. The first thing is that a family should be aware of need; aware of choice; aware of the value of preventive health hazards. A mother is most suitable target audience for giving the right information on all the precautions. Similarly, among the poor, the concern for the well being of one another is so strong that it extends beyond immediate family. In fact, the concept of the primary health care cannot succeed without its central component, namely, *the full involvement of the community.* Unfortunately, the health problems have been "successfully" medicalised—to the detriment of the general health of the people. The medical profession is at the *centre* of the health stage, and those who need health services are at the *periphery.* Although modern medical science is all good for the people, its benefits do not reach most of the people, obviously because they are not involved. Similarly, the government services alone should not be relied upon. Control of health hazards will be possible not through uni-sectoral approach but through multi-sectoral approaches involving a number of government ministries and coordination of outside assistance from voluntary agencies.

Conclusion

Finally, we need a change in attitudes. On a threshold of a new perspective plan for *Health for All* by 2000 A.D., India seeks to mobiles the people's vast potential to accelerate the pace of needed change. They Key—as always in social development—is *Motivation.* The people must be made aware that they have something to give — and only then enabled to give of their best. The administrators and planers must motivate and generate local leadership. For this, they must themselves have the conviction that those whom we now call "beneficiaries" can be partners. Their participation can help to change today's pockets of inequity into tomorrow's islands of hopes. Lastly, if we wish to accomplish what we appear to agree today is necessary, we would need the *political will* to so — and less pious rhetoric. We would also need to have *practical propolsals* — and not repetitive resolutions. And more importantly, we would finally need personal commitment and practice—and not the recommendations for others to implement.

REFERENCES

1. India, 1954, *Child Labour in India.* Simla: Labour Bureau, Ministry of Labour.
2. India, 1969, *Report of the National Commission on Labour,* Simla. p. 386.
3. *Indian Express,* 1982 News Item published on April 9, 10, 11, 12, in Delhi Edition.
4. Natarajan, K.S., 1979. *Child in India: A demographic profile.* Paper presented in Conference on Child in India, New Delhi, March 22-24. Organised by Indian Association for the Study of Population.
5. Singh, M., Kaura, V.D. and Khan, S.A., 1978, *Working Children in Bombay: A Study.* New Delhi: National Institute of Public Cooperation and Child Development.

39

ERADICATING CHILD LABOUR FROM THE WORLD

The problem of child labour as faced by the developing economies today, has indeed taken on serious dimensions. However, this problem can neither be understood nor resolved without bringing the developed countries into the picture. This is because the roots of the problem lie in the exploitative systems prevailing not only at the national level but also the international level. At the national level the lopsided development process in the background of exploitative socio-economic structures results in marginalisation of the poor, who are left with no option but to use child labour as a survival strategy. And at the international level the need for foreign exchange on one hand and stiff competition for markets in the developed world on the other encourage the producers of export industries in the third world to use cheap and vulnerable child labour. Also, powerful multinational corporations use child labour directly or indirectly, to minimise cost of production and to maximise profits. Consequently, it becomes inevitable to discuss eradication of child labour in the context of the world rather than only the third world.

It is also observed that some industrialised economies are not yet fully out of the phenomenon of child labour. Some of them do have some child labour, originating from social problems, educational systems and poverty. The main theme of the seminar was not therefore limited to the problem of child labour in the third world countries, but it was also to discuss the problem in the context of developed economies.

It was realised right form the inception of the seminar that not much would be achieved merely by repeating grim stories of exploitation of child labour in different sectors and different countries. It was decided therefore to focus the seminar on: (a) understanding the root causes of the emergence of child labour system in the context of the dynamics of the forces operating at the national and international levels, (b) drawing lessons for policies and programmes for eradicating child labour from the experiences of developed economies, (c) formulating an indicative action plan towards abolition of child labour from the world, and (d) evolving strategy for effective implementation of policies and programmes pertaining to child labour.

Child Labour in the Third World Countries

The first paper on "Child Labour in the Developing Economies Today" by Indira Hirway starts by giving broad estimates of child labour in the world. Though there are no accurate data available it can be said that the population of child labour is around 100 million today (50 million by ILO and 145 million by a UN study and 75 million to 100 million by other studies). Of these more than half live in South Asian countries. This incidence of child labour (the number of child labour per 1000 population) however, is the highest in some African countries like Rwanda (55.6(, Benin (53.8), Botswana (53.0) and Mali (50.0), followed by Asian countries (25 to 35) and other countries.

Though the ILO adopted the first Convention on Minimum Age (Industry) way back in 1919 and though it was followed by a number of other Conventions and Recommendations including the Comprehensive Convention of 1973, the problem of child labour remains a pressing problem in much of the world today. It seems that the problem has defied most of the solutions implemented at national and international levels largely because on one hand there is a limited understanding of the dynamics of the problem, as well as limited political will to resolve the problem, while on the other, the policies and programmes have not been implemented well.

The root causes for the emergence of the problem, are extreme poverty and unemployment; lack of proper educational factories for children (in fact Hirway, on the basis of the data of 34 developing countries, shows that the per capita income and the incidence of illiteracy together explain about 50 per cent of the variations in the incidence of child labour across countries); and, inadequate formulation and implementation of legal measures. There is, however, a circular casual relationship here in the sense that the prevalence of child labour system is a cause as well as the result of poverty and unemployment. The exploitative system therefore not only supports child labour but also gets strengthened by it. The same kind of circular relationship prevails at the international level also as the exploitative North-South relationship supports and gets supported—at least partly—by the child labour system.

Unfortunately the efforts made at the national and international levels have not been able to break these vicious circles, because: (a) national government have relied more on legal measures and less on other measures such as poverty alleviation, improving primary education systems which supported legal measures; (b) instead of adopting a multi-pronged well integrated approach they have tried out various measures in an isolated fashion; (c) the enforcement of the legal measures by national governments has been very poor; and (d) at the international level the efforts have relied more on controls and regulations, which are not implemented effectively. Hirway suggests that instead of postponing the goal of complete ban on child labour on the ground that "the time is not yet ripe," there is a need to accept it as a short-term goal to be achieved within five to ten years and a time-bound programme should be formulated for the purpose.

Child Labour in European Countries

Can the present developing economies learn something from the experiences of some of the European countries which have been able to eradicate the child labour system to a considerable extent form their own societies? Experiences of Germany, the U.K., Norway, Sweden, France, Belgium, Portugal, Cyprus and Malta are presented and analysed by the experts form these respective countries.

Kalus Voll's paper on the German experience shows that though some forms of child labour (mainly in orphanages and work houses) existed in the sixteenth and the seventeenth century Germany, the problem acquired dangerous dimensions in the eighteenth and the nineteenth centuries when industrial revolution advanced in the country. Accounts of their exploitation soon became known to all. The government of Germany, however, took the first step only in 1853 when the first law regarding the health and safety of child labour was passed. These regulations were not implemented well initially. Later on however, trade unions pressurised the government to formulate more progressive legislations and to see to their effective implementation under the influence of Karl Marx who strongly protested against "the transformation of immature human beings into mere machines." In the later part of the nine-tenth century child labour in factories was banned in the country.

The German experience shows that child labour is an integral part of the early stages of development of the capitalist mode of production, and for a considerable extent its incidence depends on the socio-cultural and religion-based values of the society. Consequently, its eradication can be brought about not only by legal measures alone but by social awareness and people's movements including trade union movement. The process of eradication therefore, is a long process frequently spread over decades.

E. Kostal and K. Baklund's paper on the Norwegian experience notes that child labour was prevalent in Norway in the eighteenth and nineteenth century (early part) mainly in farming, herding and fishing. With the industrial revolution in the country, however, the problem acquired serious dimensions not only because it spread to industries, such as, textiles, glass and match, but also because the working and living conditions of child labour in these sectors deteriorated considerably. The paper shows that the main force that worked for the eradication of child labour from the country came from trade unions who protested against this system and indulged in a long struggle for its eradication because it reduced their employment and also affected adversely the overall development of their children. Also the demand for better wages and social security measures by trade unions, (which motivated them not to send their children for work), less children per family, overall socio-economic development in the country and more machines in the industrial process were the major factors that helped in removing the child labour system from the country.

The papers by Wastyn Bert on the Belgium experience, Philippe Girad's paper on the French experience, the Swedish report by the Swedish IFM-SEI, and the British experience by Woodcraft Folk have more or less the same line of approach to the problem. Swedish experience shows that technological and economic development of the country (which raised the productivity and wages of workers, along with a strong trade union movement and legal support from the government contributed towards eradication of child labour from Sweden, while in the case of Belgium, legal measures adopted in the last part of the nineteenth century and the introduction of compulsory education for children up to the age of 18 years played an important role. Development of the country and trade union movement also supported this process. Philippe Girand shows that in the case of France, legal protection for the welfare of child labour was first introduced in 1841, however, child labour in factories was banned only in 1936. This is because, according to the author, trade union movement, general awareness and overall development took some time to become strong enough to attack the evil. Britain was the first country to experience the industrial revolution. Consequently, the problems of child labour in factories showed up first in this country. The tales of their exploitation were incorporated even in the contemporary literature. The British government started formulating legislations for the welfare of children form 1802. However, the system of child labour was abolished satisfactorily only in the twentieth century when laws regarding compulsory education for children below 16 (1920) and minimum age for work at 16 (1933) were passed.

Though, Malta, Portugal and Cyprus still have some child labour, the size is not very significant. According to Joseph Agius, in the case of Malta the credit goes to the socialist labour movement that pressurised the government to take the necessary steps, while in the cases of Cyprus and Portugal national governments and trade unions are still trying to regulate the child labour system. It is argued by both CERA (Cyprus) as well as APCC (Portugal) that the evil will be removed from their respective countries only when their economies develop and general awareness about the problem is created.

The papers regarding the European (Western) situation make a few points very clear; Firstly, not all these countries have been successful yet in eradicating the child labour system. Inadequate primary education (leading to drop outs), poverty and some socio-cultural factors seem to be supporting the system (though the incidence is very low) in some of the countries even now. Secondly, the process of eradication of child labour is indeed very time-consuming as it requires not only legal action which also takes time, but also awareness of trade unions and general public and a reasonably high level of economic development. Thirdly, there is some evidence that suggests that two new problems of child labour have emerged in some of the developed countries, namely, the unemployment of youth between 16 to 18 years of ages and the increasing burden of studies on children, some times leading to suicides in these highly competitive societies. Both these problems need urgent attention of the respective national governments.

The restoration of the conference on Child Labour in Europe held in January 1990, which is presented at the end of the chapter on the European experiences reveals the concern of these countries regarding the existence of Child Labour in Europe. It shows that in spite of economic developments a relatively strong trade union movement and legal support of the government these countries have not been able to eradicate the evil of child labour satisfactorily. It seems that ratification of the ILO Convention 138 is equally desirable in these developed countries. Also, more intensive efforts are needed in the areas of primary education, employment planing for the youth and general awareness and interest taken by the trade unions.

Major lessons that can be learnt by the developing economies from the European experiences are fairly clear. To start with, historically speaking, the problem of child labour seems to be an integral part of early stages of development of the capitalist mode of production. However, how much time a country will take to eradicate the evil depends not merely on the rate of economic growth but also on the socio-cultural-economic values of the country as well as on the political will of the national government. In other words, there is no need to wait till the economy develops and poverty is eradicated. After all, a firm commitment to abolition of child labour will pressurise the national government to take suitable steps in the area of poverty alleviation and education. The second lesson that can be learnt from the experiences of these developed countries is that legal measures are not enough to eradicate the child labour system from a country. These measures must be supported by non-governmental actions on the part of trade unions, voluntary agencies and the general public.

In the context of the present developing economies, there is a newly emerged additional factor supporting eradication of child labour. This is the forum of international organisations, such as ILO, WHO, UNICEF which can not only guide the national governments, but can also put an indirect pressure on them to take firm steps for the eradication of child labour.

Child Labour in Asian Countries

There are five papers which discuss the child labour situation in Philippines, Sri Lanka, Thailand, Nepal and Indonesia.

Elvis Santos's papers on Philippines states that there are about 20 million child labour in the Philippines engaged in agriculture, fishing, small trade, manufacturing and service sectors. Some young girls are engaged in prostitution also. The root causes of the problem are poverty and unemployment as well as lack of adequate concern by the national government. These working children earn extremely low wages, live in acute poverty and also suffer from serious health problems. Santos is of the opinion that scattered efforts of the present government will never deliver the goods and that international cooperation may help in creating awareness and in pressuring the government.

According to Ananda Senavirative the system of child labour is a part of the survival strategy of the poor in Sri Lanka. Child labour are predominant mainly in agriculture, industries, domestic service and other services. Some children, however, are also engaged in drug selling, smuggling and prostitution. It is observed that legal measures relating to child labour have failed miserably so far. One very interesting observation in Sri Lanka is that though the government has expanded educational facilities for children, introduced midday meal programmes and provided free text books and other facilities, the poor are forced to send their children for work for making two ends meet.

Pimol Sintawlanni's paper on the Thailand situation points out that the strength of child labour has be an increasing in Thailand during the past decade or so. This is largely because of the exploitative attitude of industrialists and traders who bring children form rural areas on a large scale through middlemen, brokers or friends/ relation of the poor. Extreme poverty on one hand and inadequate concern of the government on the other fail to help working children in any significant manner. Sintawlanni therefore emphasises the need for international cooperation on this issue. Gauri Pradhan's paper on Nepal draws attention to about 60 per cent of the children in Nepal having to work in some form of economic activity the major activities being agriculture, handicrafts, hotels and restaurants, and small scale industries. Pardhan argues that this problem cannot be resolved without strong commitment at the national level. In the case of Indonesia the problem of child labour is not as serious as in other developing economies because, as Yudotome argues, the government of Indonesia has taken some strong steps to control the working of children. With economic development the situation is likely to improve further.

These five papers show that in spite of some differences, the nature and characteristics of the problems of child labour are similar in the countries covered. The national governments in these countries have opted for soft options of undertaking some scattered and low key programmes for child labour—all of which have not made much of a dent on the problem so far. The way things stand today there does not seem to be any hope for the working children in these countries in the near future.

Child Labour in India

The papers on India are basically of two types: sectorial papers dealing with sectorial studies of child labour, and, macro-level papers which discuss the macro dimensions of the problem. Suctorial papers include M.L. Pandit's paper on "Handicrafts in Jammu and Kashmir," Neera Burra's paper on "Lock Industry in Aligarh" (Uttar Pradesh), S.P. Kashyap's paper on "Diamond cutting Industry in South Gujarat," Rohit Desai's paper on "Brocade Industry in Gujarat," M. Lama's paper on "Tea Gardens in Darjeeling" (West Bengal), Sheela Barse's paper in "Glass Industry in Ferozabad" (Uttar Pradesh) and Manju Gupta's paper on Carpet Industry in Rajasthan."

M.L. Pandit's paper on handicrafts in Jammu and Kashmir shows that this sector contributed 4.74 per cent of net state domestic product in 1978-79, and that the total production as well as the share have increased over the years. About 28% per cent of the work-force in this sector consists of child labour, of whom 35% per cent belong the five to nine-year age group. The main crafts where children work are embroidery and carpet manufacturing where they work either as helpers (family units) or hired workers (non-household units). Pandit's study shows that abut one-third of the children work for more than eight hours a day, about one-tenth of the children do not earn anything at all as they are 'learning,' while the majority of them earn Rs. 2 to Rs. 2.50 per day. None earns more than Rs. 5 a day. These crafts are mainly for exports and the trade is in the hands of middlemen who make huge profits. Pandit observes that state legislations are inadequate and implemented indifferently.

Tea is another export item in the production of which child labour are employed. Mahendra Lama's paper on tea industry in Darjeeling shows that the practice of employing children on tea estates was started by the Britishers in the pre-Independence era; which continues even today. Children perform mainly field operations like pruning, plucking, sowing, manuring and weeding. Long working hours and low wages (about Rs. 4.57 per day) as well as cold climate have affected their health and overall development adversely.

The lock industry in Aligarh, again an export industry produces 80 per cent of the locks produced in the country and employs about 7,000 to 10,000 children who constitute 10 per cent of the total workers working in the industry in Aligarh. Lock factories farm out some processes to household workers on piece-rated basis. Children work in household units as well as in factories and perform hazardous operations like pressing, polishing and electroplating. Neera Burra points out that legal measures exclude household workers and therefore do not touch these young workers. Burra recommends that all these units should be shifted to industrial estates so that regulations are enforced effectively.

Carpet industry in Rajasthan also exploits 'nimble fingers' of children to minimise costs and maximise profits. Manju Gupta observes that sometimes very young children of four to five years of age also work in the industry, in cottage units as well as in factories. Gupta's study shows that these children, suffer from serious health risks, such as, strain lung problem, malnutrition, stunted growth and general weakness. The worst part of these children is that they frequently work under constant fear of contractors, employers and even parents which affects their psychological development adversely. It is estimated by Gupta that a carpet that fetches Rs. 7041 in West Germany gives only Rs. 600 to two workers who work on it for 60 days.

Sheela Barse's paper on children trapped in the glittering glass industry of Firozabad under lines the extremely hazardous working conditions of child labour on one hand and the helplessness of these children in the midst of extreme poverty, exploitative employers and indifferent (or perhaps sympathetic to employers) government machinery on the other. Her account of the conspiracy of government officials, medical staff and employers against the vulnerable child labour clearly shows that the legal measures are openly violated or ignored by them. Public awareness and mass movement are inevitable for helping these children, who are trapped in the glitter of glass which is exported to earn foreign exchange for the country.

Child labour in diamond cutting industry earn relatively good wages and therefore do not suffer from acute poverty. However, as S.P. Kashyap's study points out, this fast growing industry treats child labour very unfavourably. Those who enter the industry as child labour earn lower wages as adult workers and enjoy poor vertical mobility as the initial poor start determines their earning profile over time adversely. The story of the broade industry, also in south Gujarat, is not very different in the sense that child labour in this industry de earn good wages. The problem, however, is basically about their early adulthood which deprives them of their childhood. Rohit Desai, however, points out very correctly that passing on skills to the next generation does involve child labour, which is not always undesirable.

These sectoral papers reveal the dynamics of the exploitation of working children very clearly: extreme poverty and unemployment force the poor to send their children to work as a part of their survival strategy; greed for profits and desperate competition for markets in the developed world encourage employers to use their economic (and also political) advantage to exploit these meek labourers; and lack of firm commitment to the goal of eradication of child labour result in haphazard and ineffective intervention from the government. Trade unions and voluntary agencies are the only agencies who could be expected to break this deadlock.

Macro-level papers on the Indian scene are written by B.B. Patel Patel's and S.S. Mehta. B.B. Patel's paper discusses dimensions of the problem of child labour in India and comments on the issues pertaining to the policy of the Government of India in historical perspective. Patel shows that though the strength of child labour has increased form 16.33 million in 1972-73 to 17.36 million in 1983, their percentage share in the total labour force has declined marginally. He also shows with the help of the data that though child labour work as unpaid workers, helpers or wage earners, their exploitation is maximum in the manufacturing sector where apart form getting low wages they also suffer in terms of physical and mental strain and an extreme kind of exploitation. While tracing the historical developments in the government's approach towards child labour, Patel observes that there is better understanding of the problems and more willingness to help working children over the years. The latest Child Labour (Prohibition and Regulation) Act, 1986 has adopted 'a realistic approach" towards the problem by prohibiting child labour in hazardous industries and processes. Patel is of the opinion that the economy is not yet ready to ban child labour completely and therefore there is no point in preparing a time-bound programme for the eradication of child labour form the country.

S.S. Mehta in his paper "Why child labour?" Argues that the available estimates of child labour exclude subsidiary workers and therefore do not give a correct picture of the situation. If these "subsidiary workers" are included, there are 20.5 million child labour in India (1985). On the other hand, if one tries to estimate child labour on the basis of school enrolment data, it becomes clear that out of the total idles of 66.75 million in age group of five to fourteen many would be part time or full time workers working as family helpers or as wage earners outside the family. As regards the casual aspects of child labour, Mehta observes that state-wise variations in the incidence of poverty, extent of unemployment and the literacy rates are closely associated with the state-wise variations in the incidence of child labour. An important policy implication of this is that child labour cannot be eradicated by legal measures alone. The legal measures will have to be supported by other measures like alleviation of poverty, expansion of employment opportunities and spread of primary education for children.

Issues Pertaining to Health and Education

Working children are prone to serious problems in the areas of health and education. These problems are highlighted by G.R. Ramachandran, S.H. Clerk and Kamala Srinivasan.

Ramachandran's paper gives a broad view of the problems of health and safety of working children. While using the various studies on these problems, the author observes that working children are likely to suffer specific problems of occupational health and safety, because: (a) the working condition of these children are invariably poor, (b) machines on which they work are meant for the adults and are not meant for them, (c) easy fatigability and lesser attention span of them coupled with long hours of monotonous work can make them more accident prone, and (d) children have a high susceptibility to specific toxics and chemicals, such as, lead and synthetic resins. He also adds that child labour suffer from poor nutrition because of their low wages and the poverty at home, as well as or availability of food at the work site. In addition, there are psychological and social problems, originating from their deprivation of education and forced adulthood. Consequently when they become adults, their health status is poor education is nil or limited, and they are incapable of getting work with a reasonable level of remuneration. In fact, frequently these adults are thrown out of their old jobs. They are then forced to join the long army of the unemployed.

Dr. Clerk's paper examines health hazards of child labour in three industries, namely, petrol pumps, agate industry and bangle industry (glass). On the basis of his micro-level surveys based on medical check-ups in three industries in India, he shows that all the three industries create heavy health risks for children. In the case of petrol pumps the children were exposed to gases which resulted in headache, lachrymatin (watering of the eyes), threat congestion, coated tongue, and urine infection. Some children also exhibited abnormal behaviour at work which reflected the psychological impact of the physical factors. In the case of agate industry young workers were found to be suffering from a higher incidence of lung diseases which frequently led to tuberculosis. And in the case of glass (bangle) industry the production processes were observed to be affecting children's health and safety severely. Clerk observed that in all the three industries children were more prone to health hazards than the adults. Kamala Srinivasan's study of child labour in hotels, restaurants, garages, domestic services, etc. in Baroda city show that working children shared a higher incidence of deficiencies in Vitamin B complex, calcium and protein, and consequently they showed a higher incidence of raw tongue, angular stomatitis and diffused pigmentation than non-working children. Shrinivasan observes that poor socio-economic background and surroundings of their residence intensify health problems of working children.

Pravin Nangia's paper entitled "Elementary education and child worker in India" starts by emphasising the need for primary education for a healthy and normal development of children. In spite of growth of educational facilities in India, however, children's education has not performed very well specially rural children and female children have been left behind the urban male children. Nangia shows that inadequate education facilities, in quantitative and qualitative terms, as well as socio-economic factors are responsible for this low enrolment and high drop out rates, which, in urn, support and strengthen the child labour system in the country. Interestingly, the causes of child labour are also the consequences of the system. The cause-effect syndrome of child labour can be broken by the spread of elementary education. However, this requires qualitative and quantitative improvement in the elementary education in the country in the areas of non-formal education and craft training.

International Agencies, National Government and Child Labour

It is the primary duty of a national government to eradicate child labour form the country. International organisations and international agencies are expected to guide them and, if necessary, create moral pressure on national governments more towards this goal.

R.K.A. Subrahmanya's paper, "A Critical Evaluation of Policies and Programmes of the International Organisations" starts with quoting the declaration of the rights of the child by the UN General Assembly which accepts eradication of child labour as an important objective for the children of the world. Subrahamanya reviews the ILO's approach as reflected in various Conventions and Recommendations starting from the year 1919 to the comprehensive convention of 1973 which aims at elimination of child labour from all the major sectors of an economy. He argues that eradication of total child labour is not a practical proposition for the third world countries because a high incidence of poverty on one hand and how level of political will of the national governments on the other hand will not allow and effective implementation of any such move. He therefore suggests, gradual move in the direction through expansion of schooling facilities, faster rate of economic development etc.

Ashok Narayan expresses similar views in the context of a national government, namely the Government of India. He points out that the problem of child labour in India stems from poverty and unemployment, lack of adequate education and lack of awareness of parents on one hand, and the exploitative approach of the employes on the other. Government of India has taken up various steps, including the latest 1986 Child Labour (Prohibition and Regulation) Act, and the proposed 10 specific projects in problem areas each of which covers specific problem areas and aims at eradication of child labour from the area by undertaking rehabilitation work of child labour and eradication of poverty of their parents through employment generating activities. Narayan is of the opinion that a complex problem like child labour cannot be resolved by legislation alone, it calls for a close cooperation of the government with voluntary agencies, social groups, trade unions and general public. Narayan also is against the ratification of the ILO Convention (138) by the Government of India as 'the time is not yet ripe' for such a step.

Both the papers are thus against any radical legal action or adoption of any time-bound programme for eradicating child labour from the developing economies. This view though "sounds practical" does not seem to be accepted as the time will never be ripe if such an approach continues. In fact, it seems that once a time-bound programme is chalked out there will be pressure to take suitable actions.

Voluntary Agencies and Child Labour

Though it is clear that voluntary agencies should play an important role in resolving the problem, what precise role can they play?

Vidyut Joshi defines the role of NGOs in the context of the concept of child labour. According to him child labour is the labour put in by children which directly or indirectly comes into conflict with their opportunities for mental and physical development. These opportunities, however are determined by the socio-economic background, institutional frame work and political goals of a nation's society. Eradication of child labour therefore can be brought about not by legal action, but by the efforts of non-governmental agencies which try to change the social milieu in which child labour work. Social activists can contribute significantly by organising child labour and by relating the issue of child labour to larger issues, such as, the type of society and the level of technological and economic development they want.

Brij Mohan Toofan believes that child labour should not be considered as a "necessary evil" by trade unions because apart from anything else, the existence of child labour is against the interests of adult workers themselves. Experiences of the past show that Government of India is neither interested in, nor capable of, eradicating child labour from the country. Trade unions therefore have no alternative but to put up a collective demand for banning child labour, at least through a time-bound programme from the country. Unfortunately trade unions have shown utter apathy to this issue. It is high time they changed in the interest of their own welfare and collectively demanded: (a) a time-bound programme for eradicating child labour an immediate ratification of the ILO Convention 138 by the government of India, (b) an employment guarantee programme for adult workers so that parents are not forced to send their children to work, (c) effective enforcement of the laws pertaining to child labour, and (d) a comprehensive programme for rehabilitation of child labour their parents in problem industries/areas.

M.K. Patra's paper supports the demand for providing employment guarantee to the poor. Patra is very clear that welfare measures for child labour can only be a temporary solution to the problem. Patra suggests that international organisations, such as UNICEF, ILO, WHO should be involved in helping child labour in strengthening the demand for eradicating the system.

Ranana Jhabwala's, Joseph Gathia's and Aruna Mehta's papers are based on experiences of voluntary agencies in helping working children. Jhabwala's paper, which is based on SEWA's work among urban unorganised women workers shows that SEWA started working with young girls mainly because their mothers were organised by SEWA. SEWA's experiences reveal the multiple exploitation of young girl labourers in the urban surroundings of Ahmedabad. Though traditional parents were not very cooperative with SEWA's efforts in the initial stages, Jhabwala feels that a voluntary agency can do a lot in terms of literacy and skill formation of child labour. Jhabwala however is of the opinion that fundamental problems of child labour cannot be tackled only by helping the children; ensuring minimum income to each family also is inevitable if child labour is to be abolished. Gathia's paper is based on the action research on child labour working in carpet weaving industry in Mirzapur, lock industry in Aligarh and Nepali child workers working in Delhi Gathia observes that these children are "silent sufferers" because they are neglected by the `conspiracy" of officials as well as by trade unions and voluntary agencies. CCFCL (Centre For Concern For Child Labour) is an organisation that works for : (a) improvement of health and education of child labour (b) raising public opinion about the plight of working children, (c) involving trade unions and voluntary agencies in helping working children, and (d) pressurising the national government to take appropriate action for rehabilitation of child labour; and (e) for pressuring the government to adopt the ILO Convention No. 138. Gathia sees a great potential of the actions initiated by CCFCL.

Nandana Reddy's paper documents noteworthy efforts of her voluntary agency in the area of organising child labour as well as pressurising the Indian Government in taking legal action to resolve the problem of child labour. Reddy's experiences show that child labour can be organised and can be involved in formulating programmes for their own benefits. Organised child labour by her organisation clearly specified their demands as: (1) legal ban on child labour in hazardous activities, immediately; (2) welfare activities for child labour in the areas of health, education, nutrition and entertainment; and (3) strict monitoring of the implementation of regulations pertaining to child labour. Reddy therefore recommends that child labour should be organised wherever they are working and should be involved in the activities in their own interest. Such organised children can be effective as pressure groups also.

Aruna Mehta's paper which attempts to identify the role of voluntary agencies, argues that non-formal education, development programmes on various skills, medical check up, and other welfare activities may help working children considerably. Bhaskar Vyas and Aruna Lakhani's paper is "a modest attempt at formulating an action plan for eradication of child labour from urban Gujarat." The author's approach is based on : (a) introduction of compulsory primary education; (b) midday meals to children in schools; and (c) setting up an infrastructure for non-formal education of children when required. It is suggested that a pilot programme on these lines should be initiated to start with.

Renu Bhanot emphasises the need for providing employment at minimum wages to adult workers so that they are not forced to send their children for work. This should be accompanied by compulsory primary education for children. Bhanot argues that voluntary agencies can contribute significantly towards achieving this goal firstly by pressurising national governments to take appropriate legal action and programmes, and secondly by getting involved in these activities themselves.

It seems that voluntary agencies, including trade unions have adopted broadly three kinds of approaches. Some voluntary agencies consider child labour as "a necessary evil" at least for the time being and therefore, get involved mainly in welfare activities like health and education. Some others, however do not agree with this soft approach and ask for banning child labour at least within a reasonable period of time. They demand that the government should ratify the ILO convention 138 and adopt a time-bound programme for abolition of child labour. Some more radical ones go a step further and demand for an employment guarantee programme for adults so that the poor and not forced to send their children for work. One thing is very clear, however, that all these agencies have not yet played this kind of role effectively in India or in most developing economies.

Voluntary agencies and trade unions will have to adopt a different approach if they really want eradication of child labour. Firstly, they will have to interact with each other to put up a collective demand on the basis of their common approach. Secondly, they will have to lobby to pressurise the government to accept the time-bound goal of banning child labour from all activities and to ratify the ILO convention No. 138 for the purpose. Thirdly, they will have to be vigilant about the enforcement of government regulations regarding child labour. And fourthly, they will have to join hands with other outside organisations to create a pressure group at the international level. They will have a shake away their apathy and take up the challenge 'boldly' as Toofan puts it, "in their own selfish interest."

Administrative Support

Less than satisfactory implementation of the regulations on child labour seems to be a common feature of most developing countries. What can be done in this regard?

Covering scattered unorganised sectors seems to be an important challenge in this context. One can suggest a number of measures for the purpose: Firstly, all workers working inside their houses should be brought out to work in work sheds or work centres which can be set up in their neighbourhood. This will allow for easy supervision of regulations. Secondly, all those working in the production units at home or in factories should be given an identity card and nobody should be allowed to work without the card. Thirdly, district level, block level and industry level vigilance cells should be set up and representatives of voluntary agencies/trade unions should be nominated on these cells. And fourthly, strict punishment should be laid down for violating the laws pertaining to child labour. In addition, steps should be taken for improving the efficiency of the administration Proper staffing, better supervision and training of the staff, are some of the measures which are likely to help.

Concluding Observation

It is very clear that the problem of child labour is a highly complex problem as it is a consequence of the system under which the national economies are functioning. The problem has so far defied all kinds of solutions tried out at various levels. Even in industrialised countries the problem is not fully resolved. In fact, some new forms of the problem seem to be emerging in these economies. However, a solution to this problem is possible if there is enough commitment on the part of the policy makers.

Prof. D.T. Lakdawala put it very aptly, when he observed in the valedictory session that child labour is not a necessary evil, firstly, because child labour is playing at best a very marginal role in any developing economy today, and secondly because there is a great degree of substitutability between child labour and adult labour at the national level, if not at the family level. Child labour can easily be dispensed with without any negative impact on a national economy.

A time-bound action strategy is a must for abolishing child labour because if we wait for "a ripe time," it will never come. Each nation therefore will have to formulate a time-bound action plan for eradicating the system. Such a plan may start with a firm commitment in the form of ratifying the ILO Convention 138. It should, however, be supported by speedy programmes of poverty alleviation, educational reforms and creation of awareness of parents.

The detailed action strategy prepared on these lines is the result of the efforts of the participants of the seminar.

40

TOWARDS ELIMINATION OF CHILD LABOUR

The conclusions that emerge from various research studies on child labour both in urban and rural societies, the experience gained so far in enforcement of numerous legislations preventing the employment of children, the exploitative working conditions, and the inadequacy or the absence of the measures to provide for health care, protection against employment injuries, education, vocational training, and career development, etc., reveal that child labour, however objectionable it may be, will continue to persist so long as low incomes, high dependency ratios, and limited socio-economic opportunities prevail, and so long as children are required to contribute, even if modestly, to the inadequate family income. This harsh reality suggests that child labour policies must proceed along two fronts: first, the improvement of the conditions under which the children are employed and work, their protection from exploitation, and provision for education and skill training, etc.; and second, adopting measures such as improved health care and supplementary nutrition, career planning, socio-economic programmes for the families of the working children and others who sooner or later would force their children into labour market so that the problem could be controlled and gradually eliminated. While the first kind of measures call for a comprehensive legislation which we have proposed and discussed in the previous chapter, the second type of measures underline the need for adopting a developmental approach to the problem and help the children themselves and their families through action projects.

In fact, various Committees and Commissions appointed by the Government of India and some States in the past have suggested measures to control and gradually eliminate child labour. But the Governments have not taken any action on such recommendations. It was only in 1985 that the Union Ministry of Labour formulated a pilot project for working children to be implemented with the assistance of donor agencies in two regions having a high concentration of child labour — the carpet weaving belt of Varanasi-Bhadoi in Uttar Pradesh and match and fire-works industry in Sivakasi of Tamil Nadu; but implemented the project only in Sivakasi in April 1986. Before going to consider any action project, let us know what have been the recommendations of different Commissions and Committees.

The National Commission on Labour (1969) observed that "while the economic difficulties are real, a way has to be found to give the child the necessary education in his more receptive years." The Commission felt that `this can be ensured by fixing the employment hours of children so as to enable them to attend to schooling. Where the number of children is adequate, the employers, with the assistance of the State Governments, should make arrangements to combine work with education" (P 387).

The Working Group on Child Labour (1974) was more elaborate in recommending protective measures besides the legal ones. The Working Group recommended; (1) to promote cottage and small scale industries in rural areas to help the poor parents in improving their economic conditions and desisting from sending their children to work, (2) the Department of Education, Department of Rural Development, and the Ministry of Information and Broadcasting should make concerted efforts to retain the children in the school system to educating and motivating their parents to enroll them in schools rather than in the employment market and to take suitable measures to prevent school drop-out. With a view to improving and regulating the working conditions of the children, the Working Group recommended that the non-governmental organisations should be involved in educating the child workers and employers so that the working conditions of young domestic servants were made as conducive as possible. The Government should adopt some regulatory and promotional measures in small and cottage industries to improve the working and living conditions of child labour and minimise the health hazards to which they are exposed. The Working Group felt that a beginning could be made in this regard in industrial estates.

One of the terms of references of the National Committee on Child Labour (1979) was to "suggest welfare measures, training and other facilities which could be introduced to benefit children in employment. Hence, the Committee after examining the issue in detail recommended several long term measures to eliminate child labour. These recommendations include: (1) the Planning Commission should be asked to work out the feasibility of taking away all children below the age of 15 years from the labour market in order to find employment for the unemployed able-bodied persons in the age group 15 to 60 in the country and to work out a cost-benefit analysis of this proposition; (2) to make accelerated effects in national planning to improve the earnings of adult workers by stricter enforcement of the Minimum Wages Act, 1948: (3) to evolve a more meaningful educational requirements with local crafts, allow greater involvement of voluntary agencies, and provide for changes in the schedule of vacations and holidays to coincide with environmental requirements; (4) to evolve comprehensive statutory provisions for providing educational facilities for the child workers and to include education as a part of the labour welfare measures to be adopted by the employers; (5) to make arrangements for non-formal education in areas where here is no concentration of working children; (6) to establish in rural areas creches/child-care centres at the school premises, or at the community centres, so as to encourage girls, who have to take care of young siblings in the family, to attend schools; (7) to link periodical medical check-up with national health schemes in respect of child workers; (8) to pay constant attention to keep the working environment hygienically free especially in places where the children are employed; (9) to require the employers with suitable subsidy to provide supplementary nutrition to the working children (10) to examine the possibility of imposing access or alternatively to allow concessions in taxes, etc., to employers who undertaken to implement the development and welfare schemes; (11) to introduce housing schemes and basic amenities in areas where large number of children are working; (12) to provide the liberty and reading facilities linked with special teaching classes for working children as well as arrangements for recreational and cultural activities. (13) the better enforcement of the Apprentices Act and setting up of separate vocational guidance clinics and employment bureaux for children; (14) to make systematic efforts to identify hazardous occupations and for detecting the occupational diseases and their treatment; and (15) to persuade and induce the media to make more purposeful efforts to create greater awareness in respect of the evils of child labour.

The Government of Tamil Nadu in May 1976 had appointed a Committee under the Chairmanship of Sri Harbans Singh to conduct an indepth study of the problem of child labour in fire and match works industry in Sivakasi. The recommendations of this Committee were every much similar to the recommendations of the Working Group on Child Labour that was appointed in 1976 by the Ministry of social Welfare, Government of India. The Government of Tamil Nadu appointed another committee in March 1984 under the Chairmanship of Sri. N. Hari Bhaskar to review the present working conditions and measures taken to mitigate the sufferings of the children employed in the industries in Sivakasi. The observations and recommendations to this Committee were similar to those of the Sanat Mehta Committee on Child Labour appointed by the State Labour Ministers sub-committee in 1983.

The Sanat Mehta Committee strongly felt that a time bound action plan should be taken up by the Government for gradual elimination of child labour. This action should be comprehensive covering legislation, welfare arrangements including education and economic development with a declaration of the ultimate goal of eliminating child labour in some time frame. The Committee, however, recommended that the Government should enact a legislation covering the non-formal education of the working children, compulsory medical check-up and health care, skill development training, transport of working children to restrict their working hours, and contributions to provident fund by the employers, etc.

The Sanat Mehta Committee also recommended to provide suitable organisational support for non-formal education, compulsory medical check-up, skill development training, and transport of working children. The Committee felt that arrangements for formal education and skill development training should be made by the Government through its own agencies or by the voluntary agencies or others. The wage compensation for the period the children spend in these programmes should be the liability of the employers in all the organised industries. The employers engaging child workers in the production of goods for export market should be given subsidy only on the condition that they provide non-formal education, skill development training, and compulsory health check-up for the children employed by them. The Committee urged the Government to secure active involvement of the trade unions in the matter of providing welfare services to the child workers, particularly in the unorganised sector; they could even be entrusted with the planning and execution of the welfare activities and persuaded to play an effective role in arousing a sense of consciousness in society about the exploitation of child workers by the employers.

Finally, the Sanat Mehta Committee suggested that the Government should endeavour to integrate the child labour welfare activities with the on-going development programmes. The Committee observed that in order to achieve the ultimate objective of abolishing child labour, it would be necessary to have an overall improvement in the economic conditions of the families whose children are compelled to work. The Committee recommended that wherever there is concentration of child workers, it should be the endeavour of the government to provide adequate attention in mobilising resources to undertake developmental activities on a suitable scale. The Committee, more importantly, observed that even the existing schemes of Government could be utilised fruitfully in this regard. The Committee felt that the priorities of Tribal Plans, Integrated Rural Development Projects, Droughtprone Area Development Programmes, etc., could be profitably linked with the question of elimination of child labour and providing welfare service for them where they must continue to work. The Committee rightly noted that such a linkage will become more fruitful during the Seventh Plan period because the Plan lays increased emphasis on such of the programmes.

Incorporating these observations and recommendations an action project for the development of working children should be formulated and implemented urgently. Such a project would help us to control and regulate the problem and prevent the exploitation of children employed in many industries in the unorganised sector not only in the short term but also in the intermediate period. But to eliminate child labour an action project with a long term perspective primarily meant to improve the economic conditions of the disadvantaged families who ordinarily force their children to wage labour need to be formulated and implemented both by the Governmental and non-governmental agencies. The two types of programmes, however, should be introduced simultaneously if we are interested in effective control and elimination of the problem.

The immediate concern of all of us is to control the growing problem of child labour and to enable the child workers to get education and training in vocations of their interest so that they develop into productive and efficient labour force for the industries and agriculture of the 21st century. Hence, the action project first and foremost, must make suitable provisions for education, skill development training, and secondly, for all other needs of the child worker and his family.

I. Formal and Non-Formal Education

A vast majority of the working children are either illiterates or only semiliterates, and almost all of them have a desire to get educated as the study conducted by us in Bangalore revealed. At the same time, many of the working children do not want, and cannot afford, to take up education on a full-time and formal basis in view of the family conditions, while others want to continue simultaneously their education and work. Therefore, arrangements for formal and non-formal education for the working children should be made by way of establishing evening and week-end schools both in the urban and rural communities where there is a concentration of working children. These schools should have enough flexibility in educational programmes and timings of the schools. The schools should be equipped with adequate staff trained in non-formal methods of teaching materials and teaching aids essentially required for non-formal education.

II. Vocational Training for Skill Development

Over a period of time the child employed in industrial and other occupations learns to do the job and even may become a good worker. But he always feels that there is some deficiency in him in terms of the job knowledge. He would not be able to become a skilled technical worker. He normally continues in the low paying unorganised sector, for his employability as an industrial worker in the modern sophisticated industries remains low. This deficiency and drawback could be overcome only if the child worker is provided with vocational training in the trades in which either he is interested or in which he is already employed. Therefore, along with the arrangements for formal and non-formal education, the provisions for vocational training in different trades and vocations should be made. The vocational training schools should be established wherever a school for formal and non-formal education is started. These schools should function similar to the educational ones. In fact, it is more proper and effective if both the educational and vocational training schools are housed in the same complex with additional provisions for recreation, supplementary nutrition, and health care facilities, etc.

III. Career Planning

Many child workers take to one or the other job out of compulsion. Sooner or later they find the jobs in which they are employed disinteresting and monotonous. Some other children develop a desire to become self-employed, or would like to change to a large scale industrial establishment on becoming adults. In such cases, there is a need to identify the interests of the child and enable him to plan for his career and help him to realise his career goals. Therefore, any action project for the development of child workers should have a provision for helping them to plan their career and work towards the achievement of those goals. Under this programme even arrangements need to be made to help them financially. Accordingly, a contributory fund could be created out of which the children could be granted financial assistance to set up their own trade/calling/workshops.

IV. Health Care Supplementary Nutrition, and Welfare

The employment of children from poor families for long hours in fatiguing job conditions affect the normal physical growth of the child leading to stunted physical growth and other health problems. As a matter of fact, an action project must provide for health care and periodical medical check-up and treatment, if necessary, for all the working children. As a preventive step, the children need to be provided with supplementary nutrition, the arrangements for which should be made in the premises of the educational complex. In addition to health care, provision for recreation, reading facilities also need to be made.

V. Counselling and Guidance Services

A child goes to work in the formative years of his life and often works in an environment that it detrimental to his normal physical and mental development. His tender age is abused and his labour exploited. More often than not, he is ill-treated not only by the employer but also by his fellow adult workers. All these factors may have an ill effect on his mind and personality development. Besides, he may also have problems at home and in the neighbourhood. Therefore, he needs guidance and counselling in confronting his problems and tackling them. Counselling is also needed for the families of the working children as well as those who are on the verge of sending their children to labour market. Counselling and guidance are also needed for those children who are poor in their studies and are truants so that they are prevented from dropping out of the school and entering into the labour market. As a matter of fact, an action project should have adequate provision for counselling and guidance services for the child workers. Qualified counsellors and psychiatrists need to be appointed for these purposes.

VI. Documentation, Research, Training and Publication

The success of an on-going project for the development of working children depends to a great extent on action research, documentation, dissemination of information, and sharing of experiences among the activists and the agencies involved in the welfare of the working children. The personnel engaged in educational training tasks need to be trained and retained. This means that suitable provisions for these services and activities need to be made along with others.

VII. Socio-Economic and Anti-Poverty Programmes

The most important component of an action project for the control and elimination of child labour is the socio-economic and anti-poverty programmes meant for the families of the working children and also the socially and economically disadvantaged ones living in the same community or elsewhere but who are likely to send their children to earn for the family. If the economic status of such families is improved, it would certainly prevent the employment of children not only in the intermediate period but also in the long run. Therefore, an action project should simultaneously make provision for some kind of socio-economic projects for the benefit of the families of working children and others living below the poverty line. These programmes could be contributory to make them more effective and meaningful. On a small scale, a non-governmental organisation can provide for these programmes, which may not help to tackle the problem on a large scale and effectively. Hence, it should be the responsibility of the Government and the governmental organisations to make provision for specially designed socio-economic and anti-poverty programmes preferably by linking with the larger developmental and anti-poverty programmes already in existence or which may be introduced by the Government from time to time. Only such a step by the Government would help to control and eliminate the child labour.

VII. Involvement of the Employers

The task of educating training and providing better employment opportunities or jobs to the working children is a stupendous one. It could be shared by the governmental and non-governmental agencies with the employers of children in particular and all the employers in general. Therefore, efforts must be made to actively involve the employers not only for training the children but also in getting them better jobs after their training is complete and they reach the age of employment.

These last two components of this action project are necessarily beyond the capabilities of the non-governmental organisations though they may be very much interested in the welfare and development of the working children. It is, therefore, imperative that state should come forward to provide for these programmes. At the same time, it is important to note that if the Government of India enacts a comprehensive legislation on child labour, the non-governmental organisations can undertake these programmes to some extent with the help of the Child Labour Boards to be constituted under the provisions of the new. Act and which are required to provide financial assistance to the non-governmental organisations endeavouring to promote the welfare and development of the working children.

The action project implemented by the Union Ministry of Labour in Sivakasi, viz., "The National Child Labour Programme: A Pilot Project," is developed with the technical assistance and guidance from the International Labour Organisation. This Project is intended to carry out five principal activities in the pursuit of improving the conditions under which the children work, protecting them from exploitation, and enabling them to have an access to nutrition and minimum levels of education and health protection; and more importantly, the gradual elimination of child labour by adopting measures that bear on the factors that generate and sustain child labour. These activities are as follows:

1. The project seeks to provide for essential social and welfare services for working children in order to effect improvements in their working and living conditions.
2. It provides for the upgrading of the existing governmental programmes and the introduction of new ones in order to bring about improvements in the economic life of the community in general and of low income and the disadvantaged groups in particular.

3. The project intends to carry out a series of activities for promoting and ensuring the active involvement and participation of the communities concerned, in particular the working children and women. Women are being encouraged to organise; and working children and their families are expected, inter alia, to make contribution to the cost of the programmes. The active participation of women and working children is an especially critical component in this programme in order to stimulate gross-root development on a sustained basis, to ascertain project accountability and relevance, to establish the principle and the bases for self-reliant community development by requiring them to share in the financing of project cost and in determining its shape.
4. The programme anticipates the employers contribution and involvement in at least two areas. Firstly, the employers are being encouraged and involved in decisions concerning the implementation of the overall programmes, particularly in facilitating the improvements at the work place. Secondly, they are expected to play a major role in the financing of the project by making a regular contribution from the exports proceeds.
5. Finally, as a support for these activities, the Project assigns an important role for various types of training, media support, self-evaluation by Project staff and the community, and policy oriented research as an integral part of the entire planning and implementation process.

This project (in Sivakasi region) covers about forty thousand children employed in the match and fireworks industries. The beneficiaries of this project also include: (i) the parents of the working children, and (ii) low income and disadvantaged groups who will have benefitted directly or indirectly from the accelerated provision of employment and income generating schemes and social services. In view of the long term objective of gradual reduction and final elimination of child labour, The programme anticipates, and the Government is committed to, the intensification, on a priority basis, of the on-going and planned developmental activities in the areas of health, education, welfare, credit, employment and income-generation.

It was hoped that this project would enhance the capability of Central and the State Governments in policy formulation, implementation and management of child labour programmes on a wider scale. It was further hoped that the project programmes would be replicated in other regions where there is heavy concentration of child labour and that the non-governmental organisations would be allowed to strengthen the Governmental efforts. It was also claimed that this project is of more than national importance to the extent it is likely to serve as a model for the third world countries where child labour has been a problem of similar nature and magnitude. But so far (November 1988) the Project has not made any impact.

41

CHILD LABOUR: AN ALLEVIATION CUM ERADICATION MODEL

Child Labour is an issue of great concern to all Home-Economists of Home Scientists since all our disciplines are focussed on the family and its well being with special emphasis on women are children. From human resource development and management perspectives child labour is misuse of the precious potential human resource of a society. Its effect on the child is total: the compulsion of a child to assume an adult's role and enter the labour market for the purpose of fulfilling the family's basic needs stunts and distorts the physical, mental, moral and social development of the child. It is deprived of its right to education, play, rest, leisure childhood fantasies, all of which are sine que non for the all round development of the child. Several studies have adequately substantiated the vicious association of child labour with other macro problems; adult unemployment, accentuation of poverty, high fertility and population explosion migration, mushrooming of urban slums etc. Child Labour is positively related to high fertility rate and poverty which in turn adversely affect women's power and status. Women who constitute nearly fifty percent of the nation's human potential are forced by child labour phenomenon and poverty into roles of submission subordination and economic dependence as well as under-utilisation as a human resource, a fact well-documented in various studies. This Child Labour is a drag on all developmental efforts. At a recently held international Seminar on Child Labour it was also pointed out that child labour can pose a threat to world piece since it is a factor which widens the gap between the rich and the poor nations of the world. From this perspective it is an issue of global concern.

India has the dubious distinction of having the largest number of working children. Several factors—demographic, social, psychological, economic and cultural factors—that mutually reinforce themselves have been identified as cause for the persistence of this scourge in India and other developing countries of the world. The present government of India is also seriously concerned about this issue. A National Child Labour Programme (NCLP) has been devised and the state governments have been directed to take effective steps for regulating the working conditions of children in labour force as also for initiating programmes for total eradication of child labour. In the task of achieving this national goal higher educational institutions can contribute significantly both by generating a sound data based on this problem as well as through guidance and consultancy in planning and implementing action programmes.

The paper presented here reports on a modest research* survey undertaken with this orientation, in the year 1986 on working children in Baroda City. The sample consisted of 180 working children, 150 of them selected from households in randomly selected slum pockets of the city and 30 selected purposively from the different hostel canteens of M.S.U. with the intention that any model of alleviation could be tried and tested readily with this group.

The major goal of the research was to design an alleviation cum eradication model which will encompass the economic, psychological, health and nutritional aspects of child labour. The interview schedule was geared towards this purpose. Before presenting the model I would like to highlight briefly the major findings of the study.

The following table presents in a nutshell the salient demographic and socio-economic profile of the households of the working children:

TABLE 41.1

Profile of Child Labour Family (n = 180)

	Family size	*Family income p.m. in Rs.*	*Per-capita Income of*	*income in working*	*Literacy of parents (%)*	
			Rs. p.m.	*child p.m. Rs.*	*Father Literate*	*Mother Literate*
Mean	5.71	849.02	148.69	151.97	34	18
s.d.	1.92	521.900	—	143.89	—	—

Fifty two out of 180 families were migrants from outside the state. Poverty and adult unemployment were given as primary reasons for migration, and 55 per cent of the sample children belonged to scheduled castes or tribes. The fact that the mean wage of the working child is Rs. 152 approximately—nearly 21 per cent of the total earnings of the other members of the family— and slightly more than the per capita income of the family shows how crucial the earning of the working child is for the family's survival. But at what cost? The family is not concerned about this because its concern is with day to day survival.

Profile of the Working Child

The sample children were distributed between six occupational categories: domestic servants (majority girls), garage workers, construction workers, small scale industries, errand workers in restaurants and way-side-catering laris and miscellaneous (covering

*The Study was sponsored by the Gandhi Labour Institute, Ahmedabad.

self-employed in petty trades or hired by intermediaries as pig catchers, rag pickers etc.). The following table gives the profile of the working child.

TABLE 41.2
Profile of the working Child (n = 180)

Age mean	*Attending school with work*	*Age of Entry into Labour Market*	*Wage p.m. Rs.*	*Pocket Allowance given by parents*
12.82	24.44%	below 12 years (70%)	151.97 s.d. (143.89)	Rs. 20/- approx

There were 150 boys and 30 girls in the sample. Boys spent their allowance on sweetmeats, gambling, movies, while girls spent on sweetmeats, trinkets and movies. Significant variations were found in wage between occupational groups. Domestic servants received the lowest. Employees exploited children working in garages by not paying stipend during their so called apprenticeship under the guise of giving them training. Girls were roped in to the labour market much earlier than boys. An explicit gender discrimination was found among parents regarding the need and importance of skill training and education for girls—an offshoot of traditional outlook regarding the role of women.

Work of Children

As far as the nature of the work, environment, conditions etc. are concerned the following features stood out:

— mean number of working hours 9.08 per day (25% more than 12 hours per day!)

— significant variations in the number of working hours among the different occupations (Max.: garage workers and errand workers)

— provision of basic amenities at work place; rated fair by the children though observed to be poor by the investigators.

Forty one children (23%) had no rest interval while 37 (21%) had irregular rest intervals, while the remaining 102 (50%) had one hour rest interval. Holidays were given only for religious festivals, causal and sick leave were frowned upon and in most cases not granted. In any case it was without pay.

Level of General Knowledge of the Working Children

Working ability identifying colours, naming animals, and basic general knowledge were very poor. Reading ability in Gujarati decreased steeply when one proceeded from alphabets (107/180) to simple words (83/180) to a long sentence (40/180).

Considering their low ability in reading and general knowledge their ability in doing arithmetical sums was almost spectacular. Addition was done correctly by about 78% of the children, subtraction by 70%, while multiplication and division were found to be more difficult (58 and 54?% respectively). Only 20% were not able to do any of the operations. The above clearly shows that the children have the innate capacity to learn when they have the motivation. It is a pity that they are being denied the opportunities.

Health and Nutritional Status

Simple field techniques, namely anthropometric measurements, clinical examination and daily dietary intake were used to assess the health and nutritional status of the working children. It was found that 64% of the children had indications of anaemia, while 36% exhibited symptoms of deficiencies such an angular stomatitis, raw tongue, diffused pigmentation indicating deficiency of vitamin B complex. Only 8% had normal weight, 20% showed signs of malnutrition while 72% belonged to the category of moderate to severe malnutrition.

Comparison with another study made on non-working children, showed some significant differences. Working children had significantly lower means in respect of energy (Kcal), calcium and protein. Only in respect of iron (mg) were the working children found to have a better mean. Analysis revealed gender discrimination. Girls were found to be consuming significantly lower amounts of calcium, iron and protein than boys. Though the comparison has been done with previous study on school-going non-working children this aspect has to be assessed with a control group of non-working children having a similar background.

Role of Employees

Fifty of the employees were interviewed to have an idea of their opinions, attitude and perception of the employees with regard to child labour. The importance of training was admitted only by garage owners who did not pay any stipend to the working children. Majority of the employers viewed child labour positively-vested interests? And they also held the view that government would not be effective in implementing the child labour law. A Redeeming feature was that some employees expressed willingness to cooperate with any outside agency willing to offer training programmes to working children. A few also suggested their own work place or the open space in the community temple compound where vocational training could be imparted to the children.

Hypotheses

Excepting for family size as a positive determinant of child labour at 0.05 level none of the other variables, viz. income of family, wage of mother of working children, caste, migration emerged as significant explanatory variables. Income variation was perhaps not sufficient enough to exert any negative impact on child labour. Further the perennial inflationary pressure erodes any impact which income increase can have on child labour. The positive effect of family size on child labour confirmed the micro-economic theory of fertility.

Future Course of Action—A Model Plan

The National Workshop on Child Labour held at Delhi in 1986, appeared to divide the participants into two groups, those who wanted to introduce alleviatory measures in child labour and those who were against it because they subscribed to the view that any alleviatory measure is a tacit support for continuance of child labour. Considering the fact that, there are atleast 11 million children engaged in child labour, to take the most conservative estimate, any scheme to abolish child labour must provide atleast the same amount of input as the income earned by the children. Since the child earns about Rs. 150 p.m. the government must invest a massive amount of atleast 2,000 crores annually. While agreeing with those who held the view firmly that there should be no compromise on the issue of child labour we suggest as an interim measure a multipronged approach related to the three target groups:

(i) School-going children of slum families at primary and secondary level.
(ii) Working children of slum families (of less than 15 years of age) living in slums.
(iii) Mothers of children living in slums.

The strategy suggested is based on the following principles;

1. A slum child retained at school is possibly a child saved from the labour market.
2. The deficits of a working child at various level (Health and nutrition, recreation and skill, education/training) must be compensated.
3. Increasing the value of mother's time through gainful employment will have a depressing effect on child labour.

Alleviation Cum Abolition Model

1. Identification of Slums for the Programme

Clusters of slums where there is concentration of working children under the age ot 15 years may be identified for implementing the programme. Proximity to Primary Health Centre and Corporation School/Anganwadi) as well as playground would assist in implementing the programme with existing infrastructure.

2. Target Groups

IA-School going children (Primary and Secondary Level)" Child Labour Weaning Technique"

(i) Under this concept, education should be made attractive so that it discourages dropouts. The schooling will be subsidised through exemption of school fees, free uniform books and notebooks.
(ii) Mid-day meals or snacks (balanced diet)

(iii) Incentives for sports, cultural and other activities; slum children should be sent for coaching camps, etc. with stipends. This is important as slum children, are not likely to shine in studies but they may have potential for development in sports and other types of skills. It is necessary to test each child's aptitude for this purpose.

(iv) Regular check up of health and nutritional status; any deficiencies should be corrected through supply of vitamin A, iron and other tablets.

(v) Immunisation status of the children should be checked.

IB. Working Children

(i) Social Workers and functionaries must ensure that minimum working conditions are adhered to.

(ii) Employers who are well disposed towards the programme may be identified and their cooperation sought for ensuring that working children are provided with an environment that is conducive to them, i.e. humanise the work environment. The action of such employers will hopefully have a 'demonstration effect' on the other employers.

(iii) Working children must get instruction in the 3R's through non-formal education. Training should be in mother tongue. Elementary level Hindi and English should also be imparted.

(iv) They should get technically oriented training based on their aptitude, e.g. watch repairing, automobile repairing as well as making consumer products like soap etc.) Girls also should be given technical training if they show aptitude. The courses should be part-time, say thrice a week.

(v) Working child should be encouraged to take part in cultural and sports activities. Employers who release children for training and who cooperate in other ways may be given incentives by way of loan, licence and subsidy.

IC. Mothers of Children Living in Slums

(i) Mothers should be trained in income generating activities and the other necessary inputs should be given to them (soap making, garment making, quilt making, kite making etc., repairing of various gadgets, tailoring etc.) Market outlets should be provided in the from of orders from government and semi government agencies.

(ii) The lead bank credit scheme should cover this target group.

(iii) Non-formal education in health and nutrition child care, housing, hygiene, sanitation, population, education and family planning, role of trade union, labour laws and consumer education etc. should be imparted.

Agencies which are to be involved in non-formal education are viz. the university departments in the Faculty of Home Science, Institutions giving training in polytechnic, students of NSS as well as medical students, voluntary agencies such as Friends Society, Lions Club, Jaycees may also be involved.

A community TV set should be installed at one or more places so that Doordarshan educative programmes can be availed of.

Funding and Overall Coordinating and Monitoring Agencies

A Comprehensive programme covering just 1000 children alone would need the support of numerous organisations. The support of UNICEF, WHO and ILO may be sought for certain aspects of the programme (health and nutrition). At the central level, the ministries of Human Resource Development, Health Education and Labour may be involved for offering stipends for attending sports coaching campus, organising non-formal training courses). At the state level premier institutions like Gandhi Labour institute, who have been specifically working for labour welfare and training, public sector firms such as IPCL, GSFC, GNFC, (for funding recreational and educational programmes), may be involved.

A number of voluntary organisations such as Baroda Citizen's Council are doing dedicated work. Also research-oriented institutions such as ORG should be involved, so that their expertise is taken advantage for designing, analysing quantitative cum qualitative research.

Monitoring of the Programme

A number of well intentioned schemes have not produced the results anticipated because evaluation procedures have been unsatisfactory. Evaluation is often done by those who implement so that there is a built-in tendency to cover up deficiencies. If the programme is to succeed then it is necessary that as much importance is given to evaluation as to planning and implementation.

In order to ensure the success of the programme there must be an autonomous monitoring cum evaluation committee consisting of individuals concerned with this problem.

Data Base

If slum children are to be identified and helped it is necessary to have a data base on these children. These children should be given identity cards and their data should be stored for future electronic data processing. Their health and nutritional status may be checked periodically at the primary health centre and recorded. The children might be induced to participate in such activities through say screening of a film. The data base will assist in monitoring the health of the children over the year or years and also provide researchers with valuable primary data.

42

HOW CHILD LABOUR CAN BE ERADICATED

Child Labour is both an economic and social problem. The term "child labour" today brings before ones eyes images of exploitation of little children, weak, under-developed bodies, illiteracy, physical abuse in the from of beatings, by employers and accidents, often fatal, at worksites. However, child labour in some form has existed from earliest times. Children were employed to supplement the family income and to help the family in their traditional crafts by acquiring necessary skills at a very early age. The situation became really bad with the advent of industrialisation in India when factory owners found it far more profitable to employ children at low wages who could be made to work uncomplainingly for long hours.

Taking a global view of the situation, in which India features prominently, the ILO came to the conclusion: The problem with child labour is that it can hardly be legislated away, for its roots lie in the abject poverty. Where social and economic conditions have improved, children go to school and child labour has virtually disappeared. So any society which wants its children to be free to learn and play must first free its entire population from fear of want. This means ensuring basic human needs of all people. They include such essentials as food, shelter, clothing, water, education, training and provision of gainful employment.[1]

Rehabilitation of working children has to be viewed on two fronts. Even with the strongest of legislation and the most efficient implementation machinery, child labour cannot be eradicated overnight. It is too deep-rooted a problem to be whisked away by mere legislation. All rehabilitation programmes will therefore have to be undertaken in two phases. The first phase would be directed towards improving the working conditions and introducing health, nutrition and education programmes for all working children. Children working in occupations and processes which are banned under the Child Labour Act, 1986 would have to be gradually removed from all worksites, whether they be in organised units or in the relative security of their homes. How can a process or occupation which is hazardous in a factory be considered safe if performed at home? This is a phenomenal task for which the Government machinery will prove inadequate, as has already been seen in the last 48 years, since most of these occupations were banned even in the Child Labour act of 1938. Trade Unions, voluntary agencies and society on the whole have to be made conscious of their role in assisting the Government in this task.

The second phase in the programmes would be the rehabilitation of children 'displaced' from these hazardous industries. This is again a complex problem. What can happen to children who are not gainfully occupied in any activity, not only economically but also without any facilities for education and recreation? It is said "an idle mind is a devil's workshop." These children must not be pushed into idleness, vagrancy and other subcultures of the street. Our objective therefore has to be to remove children from working in hazardous occupations and to create conditions to gradually eliminate children labour altogether.

Any programme for eradication of child labour must begin with creating a consciousness about the evils of this practice in society, in the minds of parents, labour contractors, entrepreneurs, politicians, labour leader et al. As Shela Barse has rightly pointed out, "The designers of the blue print for conscientising strategies must concern themselves with heightening people's sensitivity to the total issue of the child. There must be absolute clarity that the child labour issue is always kept in the larger context of the child's right to childhood, growth and future."[2]

1. Parental apathy is always a great constraint. The low family incomes, and hence the necessity of supplementing this income to eke out a bare existence, forces parents to send their children to work by closing their eyes to the fact that they are denying their child a childhood : a childhood where education can help them to have a brighter future, a childhood of healthy mental and physical growth. Adult education programmes imparting knowledge of sanitation, nutrition and health care as well as creating an awareness that pushing children to work is detrimental to the mental and physical growth of their child will go a long way in overcoming parental apathy. Voluntary agencies who are specialising in the field should be given complete Governmental support and financial aid. Relevant educational material should be prepared for this purpose.

2. According to the 1981 Census of India, only 9.17% of the main male child workers in rural areas had attained the primary education level while only 4.95% main girl child workers in rural areas had studied upto primary level. The education level among the child worker in urban areas is only slightly better. Article 45 of the Directive Principles of State Policy (Part IV of the Constitution) asks the State to provide free and compulsory education for children upto the age of 14 years and this was to be achieved within 10 years from the commencement of the Constitution. So, we have a long way to go. It is clear that because of economic necessity children are sent to work instead of being sent to school. If every school going child were to be given a stipend along with one free nutritional meal, it would act as a great incentive for the parents. The money from the

stipend will somewhat offset the loss in income and the free meal will ensure a better, healthy growth of the child. The educational programme will have to take into account various factors, for instance, it must coincide with the learn period in agriculture so that in the rural areas children can help their parents during the sowing and harvesting seasons. The rigid school curriculum must change so that it comprises of training in crafts, reading, writing, basic mathematics—all of which will help him in his adult life. The education programme will have to be different for children who are displaced from working units. Many of these children may be in the age group of 11.14 years who have not attained even primary education. These children cannot automatically be brought into the main-stream of education at this age. Hence education programmes for them have to be specially planned. Here organisations like the National Council for Educational Research and Training could be entrusted with the task of formulating a relevant educational syllabus. The second category of children will be the ones who will continue to work because their occupation is not hazardous and hence not banned. It should be compulsory for employers to see that children working for them are given at least a basic education. They could either go to an afternoon school or, in case the shed employs more than 15 children, classes with one teacher could be organised within their own premises. The daily schedule of the child could be planned in such a way that he works from 8 a.m. to 1 p.m., has an hour and a half break for lunch and goes to school from 2.30 p.m. to 5.00 p.m. or goes to school 8 a.m. to 10.30 a.m., works from 11 a.m. to 1 p.m., has a break for one hour, and works again from 2 p.m. to 5 p.m. Even with two and a half hours of schooling, if the curriculum is properly planned, the children need not remain illiterate.

3. It has been seen that the health of working children suffers because of the long hours of work in unhealthy conditions, often on extremely hazardous work tasks. These children need special attention because a frail child will remain a frail adult. He will not have the physical strength to do labourious work; to survive he will send his child to work and this cycle will go on. Regular medical check-ups must be done at all worksites and a similar exercise undertaken in the rural areas where children are working in family run units or as agricultural labour. Special medical centres dealing in occupational illnesses must be set up near the worksites and organisations like the Indian Council of Medical Research, the Nutrition Foundation of India and the National Institute of Occupational Diseases, Ahmedabad given the task of doing research and identifying diseases closely associated with certain occupations and finding their remedies. Primary Health Centres must be set up in areas where there is a high concentration of child labour. In the rural areas, it has been seen that often villagers have to go long distances for basic medical aid. During the agricultural season, a number of cases are reported of accidents due to threshing machines, chemicals, pesticides, etc. Mobile Health Vans which could travel in the rural areas during these seasons would be of great help.

4. The food which a working child eats has no nutritional value. Coming from such poor families, their diet comprises of chapaties, pieces of onion and salt. They may have

a spoon of the cheapest vegetable available in the market. Is it any wonder that most of these children suffer from malnutrition? A supplementary daily meal must be provided either at their work-sites or at their school.

In industries where child labour is not yet banned, the working environment must be improved. Lighting and ventilation should be improved. Care should be taken to let in as much of natural sunlight as possible. Health care, sanitation and drinking water facilities must be provided. Care must be taken that accidents do not occur at work-sites. Machinery and tools must be improved with the help of modern technology, such as designing of a new look for carpet weaving. The working hours must be adjusted to suit the climate. In summer work could start earlier and in winter work could stop early before the cold of the evening sets in.

5. It is an accepted fact that one of the reasons for sending children to work is that of economic necessity. Most of the working children belong to landless labourers, marginal farmers or the poor rural artisan classes. The income brought in by these children is very necessary for their families to survive. The Government must provide alternative sources for income generation within these affected families. In the rural areas, investment in better irrigation, credit and marketing facilities should be made available so that the rural poor can get more out of their land. Programmes of dairy development and fisheries must be started. Rural cooperative must play a more vital role by giving loans, help in procuring raw material and in marketing so that the rural poor can get out of the clutches of middlemen and big manufacturers. With more income coming in, they can then be persuaded to sand their children to school instead of putting them out to work at an early age.

6. It will be a slow process to remove children from industries where child labour has existed since many years. The reasons for this are entrenched in the socio-political environment of the country. Parental apathy is on great drawback. But more important is the children strength of the vested interests who will perpetuate this evil only for their own private gain. "The coercive `malik-mazdoor' (lord-serf) relation that governed the agrarian structure has been transposed in industrial relations. As in the field of agriculture, higher productivity and profits, have only intensified the coercive character of the relationship."[3] Mafia gangs on the pay roll of big factory owners forcibly bring children to work in horrendous conditions and no from of protest is allowed. There have been many cases in Mirzapur-Bhadohi and Firozabad where complaining labour and social activists have been eliminated.' Child labour is a part of the political economy of the country. It is a really the creation of a class of labour which can be forced into work and discarded at will. One of the main reasons why child labour cannot be stopped is because of a lack of political will. The employers have a clout with the politically powerful persons of the area and hence can violate labour laws with impunity. There has to be a conscientisation progamme to create an atmosphere where parents, employers and politicians feel guilty and are made to realise their duty in giving back to children their basic right of a carefree childhood. The children themselves can be motivated to

protest and demand their rights. In the CREDA programme in Mirzapur-Bhadohi region children took out peaceful processions with slogans and banners demanding education and recreational facilities.

7. There has to be more effective implementation of labour laws. This task cannot be left to the Government alone. Under the Child Labour Act of 1986, any person can file a complaint for an offence under the Act. These complaints must be enquired into in all good faith and not lightly dismissed. Trade unions must realise that every child worker takes the place of an adult and this leads to adult unemployment and lower wages. Trade unions and voluntary organisations must take up the cause of child labour and help the Government in implementing labour laws and welfare programmes for working children.

Child labour should be discussed as a topic in the Joint Consultative Committee of the big national trade union federations irrespective of their ideological differences. There should be articles in trade union newspapers and journals highlighting the harmful effect of child labour on the physical and mental development of a child. There should be a periodic dialogue between trade unions and voluntary agencies for formulating action plans for solving this problems.

8. Funds for rehabilitation programmes could be collected either through voluntary donations by private individuals, companies and charitable organisations of through a 'postage stamp' drive whereby an additional 5 paise stamp is affixed on all mail, as well as additional cess of Re. 1.00 on every train and air ticket which is brought.

9. A fact which needs to be emphasised is that unless we can control our population growth all social, economic and welfare programmes will come to nought because of the expanding numbers of human beings involved. We will never be able to provide enough food, enough jobs, enough medical and educational facilities to the expanding millions within our country. So family planning programmes have to be intensified especially amongst the urban and rural poor whose children, due to economic want, are pushed into the labour market.

However, care must be taken that all rehabilitation programmes take into account regional and occupational variations. Every area has its own peculiar problems and each one has to be dealt with separately. More research must be undertaken and each child labour concentration area studied separately in its particular context and local setting. It is only after such detailed studies are conducted that rehabilitation programmes can be formulated and effectively implemented.

APPENDIX-I

To understand the categories of workers mentioned in the following tables we give a brief explanation from the Census of Indian Report 1981, Series I, Part II p. 93.

"Workers are mainly considered on the basis of work as main workers and marginal workers. Main workers, are those who have worked for the major part of the year proceeding the date of enumeration and whose main activity was in either cultivation or as an agricultural labourer or in household industry or in other work. Marginal workers are those who have not worked for the major part of the preceding year concerned but nevertheless have don some work during any time in the reference period. In other words, such workers while not being capable of being classified as main workers, nevertheless perform some work.

A person is treated as a cultivator if he or she is engaged either as an employer, single workers or family worker in cultivation of land owned or held from Government or held from private persons or institutions for payment in money, kind or share. Cultivation would include supervision and direction of cultivation. However, those engaged in fruit growing or keeping of orchards or groves or working in plantations are not classified as cultivators but are classified as "other workers."

A person who works in another person's land for wages, in money, kind or share is an agricultural labourer. An agricultural labourer has no risk in the cultivation and merely works in another person's land for wags and has no right of lease or contract on such land.

If a person works in production, processing, servicing or repair of articles or goods in an industry, he or she is classified as working in the household industry sector. A household industry is defined as an industry conducted by the head of the household himself or herself or members of the household at home or within the village in rural areas or within the precincts of the house in which the household lives in the urban areas.

The larger proportion of workers in a household industry must consist of members of the household. A household industry should not be run on the scale of registered factory. All workers who are not cultivators or agricultural labourers or in household industry are 'other workers' (OW)."

TABLE I

Comparison of the Number of Main Child Workers by Nature of Activity in Rural/Urban Areas-1971 and 1981

(Figures in Thousands)

	Child Workers					
	1971			*1981*		
Nature of Activity	*Rural*	*Urban*	*Total*	*Rural*	*Urban*	*Total*
1. Cultivators	3,827	45	3,872	3,961	51	4,012
Males	3,086	39	3,125	2,869	42	2,911
Females	741	6	747	1,092	9	1,101
2. Agricultural Labourers	4,473	133	4,586	4,629	145	4,774
Males	2,929	75	3,004	2,694	89	2,783
Females	1,544	58	1,582	1,935	56	1,991
3. Livestock, Forestry, Fishing, Hunting, Plantations, etc.	854	31	885	674	30	704
Males	716	27	743	537	26	563
Females	138	4	142	137	4	141
4. Mining, Quarrying	20	4	24	25	1.6	26.6
Males	12	3	15	14	1	15
Females	8	1	9	11	6	11.6
5. Manufacturing Processing Servicing and Repairs, etc.						
(a) Household Industry	260	79	339	323	101	424
Males	151	49	200	171	58	229
Females	109	30	139	152	43	195
(b) Others	141	174	315	259	281	540
Males	93	148	241	170	229	399
Females	48	26	74	89	52	141
6. Construction	35	24	59	48	31	79
Males	24	18	42	28	23	51
Females	11	6	17	20	8	28
7. Trade and Commerce	82	129	211	98	147	245
Males	73	124	197	84	140	224
Females	9	5	14	14	7	21

8.	Transport, Storage, Communication	14	28	42	10	23	33
	Males	11	25	36	9	22	31
	Females	3	3	6	1	1	2
9.	Other Services	258	148	406	163	163	326
	Males	183	100	283	105	98	203
	Females	75	48	123	58	65	123
Total		10,739			11,163.6		

Source: Census of India, 1971,—Series 1, India, paper 3 of 1972—Economic Characteristics of Populations (Selected Tables), Registrar General and Census Commissioner, India, New Delhi, 1972. pp: 2-73. Census of India 1981 Series 1 Part II Special, Table B-3.

TABLE II

Child Workers (0.14 years) Classified by Industrial Category and Sex, 1981

Sl. no.	*Category of workers*	*Main workers*		*Marginal workers*	
		Males	*Females*	*Males*	*Females*
1	2	3	4	5	6
1.	Cultivators	2,911,613	1,101,195	351,796	831,367
2.	Agricultural labourers	2,783,209	1,990,821	239,740	767,046
3.	Livestock, forestry, fishing, hunting and plantations, orchards and allied activities	562,704	141,212	33,717	33,493
4.	Mining and quarrying	15,705	11,285	864	1,729
5.	Manufacturing, processing and repairs				
	(a) Household industry	229,455	195,327	17,211	51,742
	(b) Other than household industry	399,514	141,106	14,254	25,585
6.	Construction	51,586	28,011	3,519	6,633
7.	Trade and commerce	224,410	21,194	12,558	7,371
8.	Transport, storage and communication	31,142	2,573	1,372	486
9.	Other services	203,601	123,156	8,544	14,519
	Total	7,412,939	3,755,880	683,574	1,739,972
	Grand total		13,592,365		

Source: India Registrar General and Census Commissioner, Census of India 1981, Series-1, India, Part II. Special Report and Tables Based on 5 Per cent Sample Data p. 6 and 24 (Part II) New Delhi, 1981.

TABLE III

Main Child Workers, Marginal Child Workers and Non-workers Classified by Age and Sex

(Figures in millions)
(Percentages are in brackets)

Total	*Age*	*Population*			*Main Workers*			*Marginal workers*			*Non-workers*		
Rural Urban	*Group*	*Total*	*Male*	*Female*	*Total*	*Male*	*Female*	*Total*	*Male*	*Female*	*Total*	*Male*	*Female*
Total	0-14	263	135.8	127.2	11.2	7.4	3.8	2.4	0.7	1.7	249.4	127.7	121.7
					(4.3)	(5.4)	(3.0)	(0.9)	(0.5)	(1.3)	(94.8)	(94.0)	(95.7)
Rural	-14	205.4	106.1	99.3	10.2	6.7	3.5	2.4	0.7	1.7	192.9	98.8	94.1
					(5.0)	(6.3)	(3.5)	(1.2)	(0.7)	(1.7)	(93.9)	(93.1)	(94.8)
Urban	0-14	57.6	29.7	27.9	1.0	0.7	0.3	0.06	0.02	0.04	56.5	28.9	27.6
					(1.7)	(2.3)	(1.1)	(0.1)	(0.0)	(0.1)	(98.1)	(97.3)	(98.9)

Source: Census of India 1981 Report.

TABLE IV

Distribution (Per Cent) of Child Workers (Main Plus Marginal) By Industrial Categories and by Broad Age Groups, 1981

	Industrial Category	*Persons 0-14*	*Males 0-14*	*Females 0-14*
I-IX	Total workers	5.55	4.47	8.65
I	Cultivators	5.05	4.13	8.11
II	Agricultural labourers	8.98	8.42	9.69
III	Livestock, forestry, fishing, etc.	14.21	13..90	15.36
IV	Mining and quarrying	2.30	1.49	7.47
V	Manufacturing, processing, servicing and repairs:			
	(a) Household industry	5.76	4.29	8.77
	(b) Other than household industry	3.22	2.58	8.35
VI	Construction	2.42	1.68	8.06
VII	Trade and Commerce	1.86	1.80	2.58
VIII	Transport, storage and communications	0.58	0.54	1.68
IX	Other services	1.76	1.28	4.05

Source: Census of India Report, 1981.
Figures exclude Assam.

TABLE V

Comparison of Child Population of India (in Percentages) in 1971 and 1981 (Age Group 0-14 Years)

1971		1981	
Males	41.86	Males	39.49
Females	42.19	Females	39.59
Total	42.02	Total	39.54

Source: Census of India 1981 Report, Statement 3.

5.55 per cent of total work force is in the age group 0-14. Among males 4.47 per cent are in the age group 0-14. Among females 8.65 per cent of workers are in the age group 0-14. In category III, 15.36 per cent of female works are 13.90 per cent of male workers are in the age group 0-14. Similarly, cultivators, agricultural labourers and household industry account for a lot of children in this age group. Among females the proportion of child in the age group 0-14 is much higher compared to males in categories I to VI.

The proportion of population in age group 0-14 has shown a decline of 2.48 per cent in 1981 as compared to 1971.

Table I shows that the proportion of working children to total population has also decreased from 1.96% in 1971 to 1.63% in 1981 although the total numbers of child workers have increased from 10.7 million to 11.2 million though the national Sample Survey gives the figure in 1983 as 17.36 million.

TABLE VI

Proportion of Child Workers to Total Child Population.
(In Millions)

Total no. of children between 0-14 yrs.	263
Total no. of main child workers	11.2
Percentage of child workers to total child population	4.3%

Source: Census of India, 1981.

TABLE VII

Proportion (Per Cent) of Main Child Workers in the Agricultural Sector, 1971 and 1981

Age Group	*1971*		*1981*	
	Males	*Females*	*Males*	*Females*
All ages	69.68	82.61	65.60	81.23
0-14	87.14	86.73	84.41	86.08

Source: Census of India Report, 1981, Statement 57.

Note: Figures exclude Assam.

TABLE VIII

Distribution (Per Cent of Main Child Workers in Primary, Secondary and Tertiary Sectors, 1971 and 1981

Sector	*Age group*	*1971*		*1981*	
		Males	*Females*	*Males*	*Females*
Primary	All ages	70.22	83.01	66.22	81.59
	0-14	87.33	87.05	84.63	86.39
Secondary	All ages	11.48	7.66	13.91	8.94
	0-14	6.23	8.08	9.18	9.70
Tertiary	All ages	18.30	9.33	19.87	9.47
	0-14	6.44	4.87	6.19	3.91

Note: 1. Figures exclude Assam.
2. The proportions in each age group and calculated on the basis of the respective workers population in that particular age group.

Source: Census of India Report, 1981 Statement 58.

TABLE IX

Literacy Rate (Per Cent) by Age, Sex, and Strata in India

Age Group	*Stratum*	*Persons* 1971	*Persons* 1981	*Males* 1971	*Males* 1981	*Females* 1971	*Females* 1981
5-9	Total	23.21	30.56	27.27	35.05	18.90	25.79
	Rural	18.29	25.03	22.76	30.09	13.54	19.63
	Urban	44.93	50.93	47.09	53.35	42.62	48.36
10-14	Total	49.79	56.59	60.06	66.90	38.16	44.85
	Rural	43.16	50.16	54.89	62.42	29.83	36.44
	Urban	76.18	78.09	80.85	82.35	70.97	73.39

Source: Census of India 1981, Report.

(i) Declaration by the Director General of the ILO Concerning the International Year of the Child*

Resolution 31/169 adopted by the General Assembly on 21 December 1976 proclaimed 1979 the International Year of the Child, with the general objectives of promoting the well-being of children, drawing attention to their special needs and encouraging national action on behalf of children, particularly for the least privileged and those who are at work.

This International Year is of special importance to the ILO, which ever since its foundation in 1919, has sought to restrict child labour and provide protection for children. In doing so, the ILO has acted in accordance with the principle set forth in the Untied Nations Declaration of the Rights of the Child—that a child has a right to protection against exploitation. Despite the efforts made by the ILO and by many countries which have laid down regulations on the minimum age for admission of children employment and on the conditions of employment of children, child labour is still widespread and a disturbing problem in many parts of the world where poverty and tradition have precluded its elimination.

In the light of ILO standards, the International Year should enable governments and employers' and workers' organisation the world over to assess the situation of children at work and also give the competent national bodies and the ILO an opportunity and the means to strengthen their action programmes for children. For that purpose the ILO urgently appeals to them to apply its standards on the minimum age for admission to employment and the conditions of employment of children. Action should be based on the following principles: (a) a child is not a "small adult" but a person entitled to self-

*Declaration endorsed by the ILO Governing Body at its 209th Session, February-March 1979.

fulfilment through learning and play so that his adult life is not jeopardised by his having had to work at an early age; (b) governments should, in co-operation with all the national organisations concerned, take all necessary social and legislative action for the progressive elimination of child labour; (c) pending the elimination of child labour, it must be regulated and humanised.

I therefore declare the ILO's endorsement of the aims of the International year of the Child and its pledge to make every effort and lend all support to member States for their earliest possible fulfilment.

(ii) Resolution Concerning the International year of the Child and the Progressive Elimination of Child Labour and Transitional Measures*

The General Conference of the International Labour Organisation.

Recalling resolution, 31/169 adopted by the United Nations General Assembly, proclaiming 1979 as the International Year of the Child, with the general objectives of promoting the well-being of children, drawing attention to their special needs and encouraging national action on behalf of children, particularly for the lest, privileged and those who are at work,

Noting the activities that were undertaken at the national regional and international levels in preparation for the International year of the Child and the progress made since,

Convinced that the International Year of the Child provides for all members States an opportunity to review their economic and social policies concerning child welfare and to formulate guidelines in this sphere,

Considering that a new and fair international economic order would greatly contribute towards genuine economic and social development, primarily of benefit to children,

Recalling the endorsement by the ILO of the aims of the International Year of the Child and its pledge to make every effort and lend all support to member States for their earliest possible fulfilment,

Recalling the United Nations Declaration of the Rights of the Child, 1959, and particularly Principle 9, which stipulates that the child should be protected against all forms of neglect, cruelty and exploitation; that he should not be admitted to employment before an appropriate minimum age; and that he should in no case be caused or permitted to engage in any occupation or employment which would prejudice his health or education, or interfere with his physical, mental or moral development,

Considering that since its foundation the International Labour Organisation has sought to eliminate child labour and to provide protection of children,

*Adopted by the International Labour Conference at its 65th Session in June 1979.

Noting with approval the Director-General's Declaration on the International Year of the Child,

Deeply concerned that child labour still remains widespread in many parts of the world and that working children frequently work under conditions including those of exploitation detrimental to their health and welfare,

Recognising the need to ensure that the health and strength and the tender age of children are not abused and that children are not permitted to enter avocations unsuited to their age or strength,

Considering that the International year of the Child should be an occasion to reaffirm with practical measures and deeds that the well-being of today's children is the concern of all people everywhere,

Recalling the decision of the Governing Body of the International Labour Office, taken at its 208th Session (November 1978), to request the member States to supply a report in 1980 under article 19 of the Constitution on the extent to which effect has been given or is proposed to be given to the Minimum Age Convention (No. 138) and Recommendation (No. 146) of 1973:

1. Calls upon member States to strengthen their efforts for the elimination of child labour and for the protection of children, and in this context—

(a) to implement the provisions of the Minimum Age Convention, 1973 (No. 138), and, where they have not already done so, to ratify this Convention as early as practicable;

(b) to ensure in particular full recognition of the principle that any work undertaken by children who have not completed their compulsory education shall not be such as would prejudice their education or development;

(c) to apply the Minimum Age Recommendation, 1973 (No. 146), and the Minimum Age (Underground Work) Recommendation, 1965 (No. 124);

(d) to report in detail in 1980 under the procedure of article 19 of the Constitution on the progress reached in the implementation of the Minimum Age Convention (No. 138) and Recommendation (No. 146), 1973;

(e) pending the elimination of child labour, to take all necessary social and legislative action for the progressive elimination of child labour and, during the transitional period until the elimination of child labour, to regulate and humanise it and to give particular attention to the implementation of special standards for children relating to medical examination, night work, underground work, working hours, weekly rest, paid annual leave and certain types of hazardous and dangerous work embodied in a number of ILO instruments;

(f) to make every effort to extend the provisions of appropriate educational facilities, in order fully to apply compulsory education and to introduce it where it does not exist and, where education is compulsory, to make if effective;

(g) to ensure that appropriate protective labour legislation applies to all children at work in the sectors of activity in which they are employed;

(h) to ensure that special attention is given to the provision of fair remuneration and to its protection for the benefit of the child;

(i) to strengthen, where appropriate, labour inspection and to undertake all other measures conducive to the elimination of child labour;

(j) (i) to identify the special needs of children, to strengthen efforts to improve the general economic and social well-being of the family, and to launch a national campaign aimed at creating awareness among the general public of the adverse effects of child labour on his/her development;

(ii) to develop international solidarity and co-operation with the developing countries and to activate efforts to establish a new and fair international economic order so as to respond more effectively to the basic measures undertaken by each State for better child protection.

2. Calls upon governments and employers' and workers' organisations to assess the situation of child work and to assist the competent bodies and the ILO to strengthen their action programme for children.

3. Invites the Governing Body of the International Labour Office to instruct the Direct-General to continue and reinforce the ILO's action through such means as factual surveys of national situations and practices for the elimination of child labour and for the protection of children at work, and to make the necessary preparations for a global revision of the relevant ILO instruments.

(iii) List of ILO Conventions Ratified by India

Sl. No.		*Title and No. of Convention*	*Date of Ratification*
1		2	3
1.	No. 1	Hours of Work (Industry) Convention, 1919	14-7-1921
2.	No. 2*	Unemployment Convention, 1919	14.7.1921
3.	No. 4	Night Work (Women) Convention, 1919	14.7.1921
4.	No. 5	Minimum Age (Industry) Convention, 1919	9-9-1955
5.	No. 6	Night Work of Young Persons (Industry) Convention, 1919	14-7-1921

6.	No. 11	Right of Association (Agriculture) Convention 1921	11-5-1923
7.	No. 14	Weekly Rest (Industry) Convention, 1921	11-5-1923
8.	No. 15	Minimum Age (Terminers and Stockers) Convention, 1921	20-11-1922
9.	No. 16	Medical Examination of Young Persons (Sea) Convention, 1921	20-11-1922
10.	No. 18	Workmen's Compensation (Occupational Diseases) Convention, 1925	30-9-1927
11.	No. 19	Equality of Treatment (Accident Compensation) Convention, 1925	30-9-1927
12.	No. 21	Inspection of Emigrants' Convention, 1926	14-1-1928
13.	No. 22	Seemen's Article of Agreement Convention, 1928	31-10-1932
14.	No. 26	Minimum Wage-fixing Machinery Convention, 1928	10-1-1955
15.	No. 27	Marking of Weight (Packages Transported by Vesels) Convention 1929	7-9-1931
16.	No. 29	Forced Labour Convention, 1930	30-11-1954
17.	No. 32	Protection against Accidents (Dockers) Convention (Revised), 1932	10-2-1947
18.	No. 41	£Night Work (Women) Convention (Revised) 1934	22-11-1935
19.	No. 42	Workmen's Compensation (Occupational Diseases) Convention (Revised) 1934	13-1-1964
20.	No. 45	Underground Work (Women) Convention, 1935	25-3-1938
21.	No. 80	Final Articles Revision Convention 1946	17-11-1947
22.	No. 81	Labour Inspection Convention, 1947	7-4-1949
23.	No. 88	Employment Service Convention, 1948	24-6-1959
24.	No. 89	Night Work (Women) Convention (Revised), 1948	27-2-1950
25.	No. 90	Night Work of Young Persons (Industry) Convention (Revised), 1948	27-2-1950
26.	No. 100	Equal Remuneration Convention, 1951	25-9-1958
27.	No. 107	Indigenous and Tribal Population Convention, 1957	29-9-1958

28.	No. 111	Discrimination (Employment and Occupation) Convention, 1958	3-6-1962
29.	No. 116	Final Articles Revision Convention, 1916	22-6-1962
30.	No. 118	Equality of Treatment (Social Security) Convention, 1962	19-8-1964
31.	No. 123	Minimum Wage (Underground Work) Convention, 1965	20-3-1975
32.	No. 115	Radiation Protection Convention, 1960	17-11-1975
33.	No. 141	Rural Worker's Organisation Convention, 1975	18-8-1977
34.	No. 144	Tripartite Consultations (International Labour Standards) Convention, 1975	27-2-1978

* Ratification denounced.

£ Is no longer in force as the later Convention (No. 89) on the subject has been ratified by India.

Source: Indian Labour Year Book 1984, Labour Bureau, Simla.

Registered No. D-(D)-72

THE GAZETTE OF INDIA

EXTRAORDINARY

PART II-SECTION 1

Published By Authority

No. 75, New Delhi, Tuesday, December, 23, 1986/Pausa 2. 1908

Separate paging is given to this Part in order that it may be filed as a separate compilation

MINISTRY OF LAW AND JUSTICE

(Legislative Department)

New Delhi, the 23rd December, 1986/Pausa 2, 1908 (Saka)

The following Act of Parliament received the assent of the President on the 23rd December, 1986, and is hereby published for general information:

THE CHILD LABOUR (PROHIBITION AND REGULATION) Act, 1986

No. 61 of 1986

(23rd December, 1986]

An Act to prohibit the engagement of children in certain employments and to regulate the conditions of work of children in certain other employments.

Excepts from the Act

2. In this Act, unless the context otherwise requires—

(i) "appropriate Government" means, in relation to an establishment under the control of the Central Government or a railway administration or a major port or a mine or oilfield, the Central Government, and in all other cases, the State Government.

(ii) "child" means a person who has not completed his fourteenth year of age,.......

PART II

Prohibition of Employment of Children in certain Occupations and Processes

3. *Prohibition of employment of children in certain occupations and processes.* No child shall be employed or permitted to work in any of the occupations set forth in Part A of the Schedule or in any workshop wherein any of the processes set forth in Part B of the Schedule is carried on:

Provided that nothing in this section shall apply to any workshop wherein any process is carried on by the occupier with the aid of his family or to any school established by, or receiving assistance or recognition from, Government.

4. *Power to amend the Schedule.* The Central Government, after giving by notification in the Official Gazette, not less than three months' notice of its intention so to do, may, by like notification, add any occupation or process to the Schedule and thereupon the Schedule shall be deemed to have been amended accordingly.

5. *Child Labour Technical Advisory Committee.* (1) The Central Government may, by notification in the Official Gazzette, constitute an advisory committee to be called the Child Labour Technical Advisory Committee (hereafter in this section referred to as the Committee) to advice the Central Government for the purpose of addition of occupations and processes to the Schedule. —— ..... ——

PART III

Regulations of Conditions of Work of Children

6. *Application of Part.* The provisions of this Part shall apply to an establishment or a class of establishments in which none of the occupation or processes referred to in section 3 is carried on.

7. *Hours and period of work.* (1) No child shall be required or permitted to work in any establishment in excess of such number of hours as may be prescribed for such establishment or class of establishments.

(2) The period of work on each day shall be so fixed that no period shall exceed three hours and that no child shall work for more than there hours before he has had an interval for rest for at least one hour.

(3) The period of work of a child shall be so arranged that inclusive of his interval for rest, under sub-section (2) it shall not be spread over more than six hours, including the time spent in waiting for work on any day.

(4) No child shall be permitted or required to work between 7 p.m. and 8 a.m.

(5) No child shall be required or permitted to work overtime.

(6) No child shall be required or permitted to work in any establishment on any day on which he has already been working in another establishment.

8. *Weekly Holidays.* Every child employed in an establishment shall be allowed in each week, a holiday of one whole day, which day shall be specified by the occupier in a notice permanently exhibited in a conspicuous place in the establishments and the day so specified shall not be altered by the occupier more than once in three months.

13. *Health and safety.* (1) The appropriate Government may, by notification in the Official Gazette, make rules for the health and safety of the children employed or permitted to work in any establishment or class of establishments.

(2) Without prejudice to the generality of the foregoing provisions, the said rules may provide for all or any of the following matters, namely:

(a) cleanliness in the place of work and its freedom from nuisance;
(b) disposal of wastes and effluents;
(c) ventilation and temperature;
(d) dust and fume;
(e) artificial humidification;
(f) lighting;
(g) drinking water;
(h) latrine and urinals;
(i) spittoons;
(j) fencing of machinery;
(k) work at or near machinery in motion;
(l) employment of children on dangerous machines,
(m) instructions, training and supervision in relation to employment of children on dangerous machines;
(n) devices for cutting off power;
(o) self-acting machines;
(p) easing of new machinery;
(q) floor, stairs and means of access;
(r) its, sumps, openings in floors, etc.;
(s) excessive weights;

(t) protection of eyes;
(u) explosive or inflammable dust, gas, etc.'
(v) precautions in case of fire;
(w) maintenance of buildings; and
(x) safety of buildings and machinery.

PART IV

Miscellaneous

14. *Penalties.* (1) Whoever employs any child or permits any child to work in contravention of the provisions of section 3 shall be punishable with imprisonment for a term which shall not be less than three months but which may extend to one your or with fine which shall not be less than ten thousand rupees but which shall not be less than ten thousand rupees but which may extent to twenty thousand rupees or with both.

(2) Whoever, having been convicted of an offence under section 3, commits a like offence afterwards, he shall be punishable with imprisonment for a term which shall not be less than six months but which may extend to two years. ——.....——

16. (1) Any person, police officer or Inspector may file a complaint of the commission of an offence under this Act in any court of competent jurisdiction.——.....——

20. Subject to the provisions contained in section 15, the provisions of this Act and the rules made thereunder shall be in addition to, and not in derogation of, the provisions of the Factories, Act, 1948, the Plantations Labour Act, 1951 and the Mines Act, 1952.——....——

22. (1) The Employment of Children Act, 1938 is hereby repealed.——....——

THE SCHEDULE
(See Section 3)

PART A

Occupations

Any occupations connected with—

(1) Transport of passengers, goods or mails by railway;
(2) Cinder picking, clearing of an ash pit or building operation in the railway premises;
(3) Work in catering establishment at a railway station, involving the movement of a vendor or any other employee of the establishment from one platform to another or into or out of a moving train;

(4) Work relating to the construction of a railway station or with any other work where such work is done in close proximity to or between the railway lines;

(5) A port authority within the limits of any port.

PART B

Processes

(1) Bidi-making.

(2) Carpet-weaving.

(3) Cement manufacture, including bagging of cement.

(4) Cloth printing, dyeing and weaving.

(5) Manufacture of matches, explosives and fire-works.

(6) Mica-cutting and splitting.

(7) Shellac manufacture.

(8) Soap manufacture.

(9) Tanning.

(10) Wool-cleaning.

(11) Building and construction industry.

C. Raman Menon
Additional Secy. to the Govt. of India:

(ii) Special Provisions Relating to Hours of Work, etc., for Young Persons in different State Shops and Commercial Establishments Acts

State	*Age Definition of young persons*	*Employment to young persons permitted during*	*Hours of work for young persons*	*Rest intervals for young persons*
1	2	3	4	5
Andhra Pradesh	14-17	6 A.M. to 7 P.M.	7 per day and 42 per week, overtime work not allowed.	—
Bihar	12-18	7 A.M. to 7 P.M.	Children* 5 per day and 30 per week. Young persons 7 per day and 42 per week.	One hour after 4 hours work.
Gujarat	12-17	6 A.M. to 7 P.M.	6 per day.	Half an hour after 3 hours continuous work.
Himachal Pradesh	14	to be fixed by an order of the Govt.	5 per day and 30 per week,	Half an hour after 3 hours continuous work.
Haryana	18	Do.	Do.	Do .
Jammu and Kashmir	12-18	7 A.M. to 9 P.M.	6 per day.	½ an hour after 3 hours continuous work.
Maharashtra	12-17	6 A.M. to 7 P.M.	Do.	—
Kerala	14-17	6 A.M. to 7 P.M.	—	—
Madhya Pradesh	12-17	7 A.M. to 9 P.M.	5 per day.	—
Karnataka	12-15	6 A.M. to 8 P.M.	5 per day.	—
Orissa	12-15	Employment prohibited during night (between 10 P.M. and 6 A.M.	5 per day.	—
Punjab	14-18	To be fixed by an order of the Govt.	6 per day and 40 per week.	Half an hour after 3 hours continuous work.

Rajasthan	12-15	Employment prohibited during night (between 10 P.M. and 6 A.M.)	3 per pay.	—
Tamil Nadu	14-17	6 A.M. to 7 P.M.	7 per day and 42 per week. Overtime work prohibited.	—
Tripura	12-15	Not after 8 P.M.	7 per day and 40 per week.	One hour after 4 hours work.
Uttar Pradesh	14-17	—	6 per day.	—
West Bengal	12-15	Not after 8 P.M.	7 per day and 40 per week.	One hour after 4 hours work.
Chandigarh	14-18	to be fixed by an order	5 per day and 30 per week.	Half an hour after 3 hours continu-ous work
Delhi	12-18	8 A.M. to 8 P.M. during winter and between 7 A.M. to 9 P.M. during summer	6 per day.	½ an hour after 3 hours continuous work.
Pondicherry	14-18	6 A.M. to 7 P.M.	7 per day or 42 a week.	1 hour.

— Indicates that no special provisions other than those given in Table 9.04 are made for young persons.

* In Bihar Act the term 'Children' means persons between the ages of 12 and 14 and the term 'Young persons' means persons between the ages of 14 and 18.

Source: Indian Labour Year Book 1984. Labour Bureau, Simla.

LIST OF INSTITUTIONS AND ORGANISATIONS CONCERNED WITH CHILD LABOUR

1. Action Aid
   28, Adyar Club Grate Road, Adyar
   Madras 28

2. Ankur
   B-41, Nizamuddin East
   New Delhi 110013

3. Ankar Bharati (Gujarat)
   C/o Jeevan Sadhana
   Navi Dharti
   Baroda 390001

4. Banwasi Sewa Ashram
   Govindpur (via Turra)
   Mirzapur U.P.

5. Bihar Jan Uthan Parishad
   Salimpur Ahra, Kadamkuan
   Patna 3

6. Bonded Labour Liberation Front
   7, Jantar Mantar Road
   New Delhi 110001

7. Centre for Informal Education and
   Development Studies
   No. 7, Balaji Layout
   Wheeler Road Extention
   Bangalore 560084

8. Centre for Concern for Child Labour
   Kapoor's House, 15, Maitri Apartments,
   A/3, Paschim Vihar
   New Delhi 110063

9. Central Social Welfare Board
   Jeevan Deep Building
   Parliament Street
   New Delhi 110001

10. Child Labour Rehabilitation Centre
    55, Bhimsen Garden Road, Mylapore
    Madras 1

11. Children's Aid Society
    83th, Katharia Marg
    Opp. Matunga Railway Station, Mahim
    Bombay.

12. Child Labourer's Welfare Project
    Thirupathur
    Tamil Nadu

13. Child in Need Institute
    Daulatpur, P.O. Amgachi, via Joka
    24 Parganas, West Bengal

14. Concerned for Working Children
    58, St. Mark's Road
    Bangalore 560001

15. C.R.E.D.A.
    Sherkhan Lane
    Mirzapur, U.P.

16. Delhi Council of Child Welfare
    Qudsia Gardens, Alipur Road Delhi 110054

17. Gandhi Peace Foundation
    Deen Dayal Upadhyay Marg
    New Delhi 110002

18. Gandhian Labour Institute
    Ahmedabad
    Gujarat

19. Ganbdhian Institute of Studies
    P.O. Box 1116,
    Rajghat
    Varanasi, U.P. 221001

20. Gramodaya
    P.O. Nageruntari
    Distr. Palamau
    Bihar

21. International Labour Organisation (ILO)
7, Sardar Patel Marg,
New Delhi 110021

22. Indian Council for Child Welfare
4, Deen Dayal Upadhyay Marg,
New Delhi 110002

23. Indian Council of Social Welfare
175, Dadabhai Naoroji Road
Bombay 400001

24. Indian Institute of Rural Workers
Khadkeshwar
Aurangabad

25. Institute of Psychological and
Education Research
27, Circus Avenue
Calcutta 700017

26. Karnataka State Council for
Child Welfare "Shishuraksha"
135, III Cross, Nadidrug Road Jayamahal
Bangalore

27. Little Brothers of the Oppressed
3, Auxilium College Road, Gandhinagar
Vellore 632006

28. Madurai Multipurpose
Social Service Society
De Nobili Press, P.O. Madurai
Tamil nadu 625008

29. National labour Organisation
Gandhi Majdoor Sevalaya
P.O. No. 110 Bhadra
Ahmedabad 38001

30. National Institute of Public
Cooperation and Child Development
5, Siri Institutional Area, Khelgaon Marg
New Delhi 110016

31. National Labour Institute
AB 6, Safdarjang Enclave
New Delhi

32. Self-Employed Women's Association
SEWA Reception Centre
Ahmedabad 380017

33. Sisters of the Cross Society for Education
and Development Holy Cross Convent, Tiruchirapalli
Tamil Nadu 620001

34. Tata Institute of Social Sciences
(Dept. of Family and Child Welfare)
Deonar/Bombay 400088

35. World Health Organisation
World Health House, Ring Road
New Delhi

REFERENCES

1. Report of Child Labour in Indian Industries, Labour Bureau, Ministry of Labour, Government of India, Simla 1981, p. 7.
2. Barse, Sheela: Towards Eradication of Child Labour: Labyrinth of Feudal Systems (An AWDI/FES Seminar Paper, 14th May, 1987), p. 6.
3. Juyal, B.N. "Child Exploitation in Carpet Industry—A Mirzapur-Bhadohi Case Study," ISI Seminar 1986.

ANNEXURE-I

CHILDREN AND WORLD PEACE

Jacqui Cottyn

(IFM - SEI)

Dear comrades, friends and participants of this seminar: World peace—taste that word: Have you ever heard a nicer word? Have you ever thought that there will be such a peace? I hope so—if we are not striving for it, thinking of it, discussing it—then it will never come through.

What do we mean by peace? In IFM-SEI we have described it in our "Democratic Socialist Declaration of the Rights of Children," which was adopted at the congress 1979. Let me remind you of something which we have said in that:

A society where all the children's rights have become a reality is a society:

1. where satisfactory nutrition, shelter and education is provided;
2. where all people's right to live in freedom and peace are safeguarded;
3. where all human rights are guaranteed and where all exploitation of man by man is abolished;
4. where the means and results of production lie in the hands of the people;
5. where people of all ages organise themselves in mass movements to take care of their common social, cultural and political interests and to develop awareness and self-reliance;
6. where all citizens have full and active role in society and where full employment is guaranteed;
7. where relations between people are based on freedom, equality and solidarity, and where all forms of racism and discrimination are abolished;
8. where the society provides an environment where free and democratic citizens can grow.

Those were eight points—each of them worthy of a seminar to discuss pros and cons.

Then our IFM-SEI-declaration continues:

> The main reason why most children in the developing countries are denied their basic human rights is the present international economic order, which also affects working class children in industrialised countries who are hindered in their self-realisation. Therefore, a new international economic order must replace the present one, and ensure an adequate production system and a just distribution of wealth.

In a later chapter the declaration states:

(a) "All children, regardless of their parents, social and economic situation, must be seen as equal members of society, entitled to the satisfaction of basic needs such as an adequate nutrition, housing, clear water close at hand, medical care and recreation.

(b) Regardless of their economic, social and cultural situation, all children shall have the right to equal education which gives them equal possibilities to determine their future life....Education shall promote understanding, tolerance and friendship among people and further activities which aim is of the establishment and maintenance of *peace.*

Let me now go to our PEACE EDUCATION CHARTER, which was adopted by our congress 1982. In the preamble it is said:

Peace education is achieved:

- through family and friends,
- through learning,
- through work,
- through play,
- through fair sharing of power to affect what happens,
- through the fair sharing of resources, money, land, food, medicines and other basic necessities, and
- through a spirit of international understanding and cooperation.

It is important that we explain all this to our groups, so that our children understand that we have to do something for peace. It is not what they should do — it is what *we* shall do. Even a common member in a falcon group — he or she has to do something for the peace. It can never be enough to claim, that others should behave in a good — and better way — we have to do it ourselves — you have to do it yourself.

This is the fundamental base for our work for peace education, in which we have to behave as responsible people ourselves. If *we* cannot behave in a peaceful manner - how could we then ask others to do that? This is also a fundamental part in our socialist education; you can never promote solidarity, if you do not show solidarity yourself.

In 1983 we had a seminar about the North-South dialogue in Bombay. This was the first time many of our organisations really realised the situation of children living not only in Asia, but also in Africa, Latin America, North America and Europe. Working children or child labour became for many an issue very important for IFM-SEI to deal with.

In 1989 United Nations decided about the "Convention for the child's rights" IFM-SEI was in the forefront to take action when child labour was put on the agenda. We will do it as a continuing part of our work for peace. There will never be a peace worth the name if there still should be exploitation of the child as a cheap labour. World peace -

will not happen with child labour. We have gathered here to find the ways to reach the solution of the problem — the peace problem and the child problem.

Dear participants, you have really a big task — children around the world are waiting for your results.

Then there might be a world peace.

Thanking you!

ACTION STRATEGY FOR ERADICATION OF CHILD LABOUR FROM THE WORLD

An important outcome of the seminar was the formulation of the Action Strategy For Eradication of Child Labour From The World. The draft of the strategy which was prepared by Indira Hirway was discussed in the last session of the seminar and was finalised on the basis of the discussions and recommendations made by the participants in the session. The following is the text of the action strategy:

(1) The phenomenon of child labour, which is a consequence of the exploitative systems operating at the national and international levels, not only closes the future of millions of children in the third world countries, but it also restricts the developmental prospects of these countries drastically. The existence of child labour is a threat to overall world development, and to the solidarity and peace in the world. Eradication of child labour from the world is therefore a goal which must be achieved at the earliest.

(2) The problem of child labour cannot be viewed in isolation, because it is a symptom of the disease which is spread at various levels. At the national level, the lopsided development process in the background of exploitative socioeconomic structure results in the marginalisation of the poor who are left with no option but to use child labour as a survival strategy. Inequitable distribution of land, poor access of the weaker sections to resources, gradual destruction of the environment, existing socio-political systems — all put so many constrainsts on the poor that they are forced to use the meagre incomes of children to support themselves. At the international level, the need for foreign exchange on one hand and the stiff competition for markets in the developed world on the other, encourage the producers of export goods in the third world to use cheap and vulnerable child labour. In addition, powerful multinational corporations use child labour, directly or indirectly, to minimise costs and maximise profits.

(3) Efforts made in the direction of eradicating child labour have not given concrete results because; (a) the policies and programmes designed for the purpose have proved inadequate, and (b) their implementation suffers from a number of shortcomings. What is needed now therefore is a bold action strategy which aims at eradication of child labour, not in the long run, but in the near foreseeable future.

(4) Eradication of child labour system is primarily a responsibility of the national

government. But it also calls for a multidimensional approach, the major dimensions being economic, educational and legal. It must be accepted that the problem cannot be solved by legislations alone.

(5) To start with, all the national governments should ratify the ILO Convention (No. 138) on Minimum Age for Admission to Employment, which aims at total abolition of child labour, without delay. Ratification of the convention will imply: (a) immediate ban on using child labour in certain sectors, and (b) gradual expansion of the coverage of the ban to all the sectors which use child labour. The implementation of the convention will therefore call for two strategies: short-term strategy and long-term strategy. The latter will aim at the goals like poverty eradication, overhauling the education, system, creation of general awareness about the problem, and creation of a pressure group at national and international levels; while the short- term strategy will aim at regulation of the working and living conditions of child labour and at improving their health, nutrition, skill and education levels.

(6) The process of eradication of poverty from the third world countries should be accelerated. This calls for corrections in the developmental process. However what must be emphasised as an immediate step is the right to work or the guarantee of work to the poor. If the poor are not ensured of a minimum level of living, they are likely to use children as earners for their survival.

(7) On the education front there is a need to reinforce compulsory primary education for all the children below the ages of 14 years. .To pragmatise this, however, the following steps should be taken:

(a) Contents of primary education should include skill formation training relevant to the needs of the labour market.
(b) These should also include education for cooperation and for socio-economic aspects of change, including awareness building among the exploited children themselves.
(c) Designing of the syllabus and courses should be done at the regional level to incorporate the specific needs of the region.
(d) In order to attract female children, facilities like a creche and day care centres should be provided.
(e) Training programmes for working children should be designed in such a fashion that they are not deprived of primary education, and their upward mobility in work later on is also ensured.

(8) Administration of national government should be geared to implement the long-term and short-term programmes successfully. This calls for the following:

(a) Ban on child labour in any sector should be accompanied with planned rehabilitation of children as well as of their families.

(b) Ban should start with hazardous occupations which should be identified carefully by proper investigations. The concept of hazard should also include occupations which have extreme forms of exploitation of child labour.

(c) Comprehensive area planning approach should be adopted for eradicating child labour from the areas where child labour is concentrated. A special machinery should be set up for this purpose. A special officer should also be appointed for each such area who will be entrusted with the overall powers to plan and implement the programmes.

(d) Special care should be taken for migrant child workers and for street children while formulating and implementing these programmes.

(e) A multi-disciplinary group (which should include local trade unions and NGOs) should be appointed in each industry/region who should be authorised to inspect workshops, factories etc., and it should have an access to all relevant information.

(f) All the units of child labour using industries should be registered with the national government.. The list of these units should be published annually so that this information is available to all those who are concerned.

(g) At present national governments are finding it difficult to cover the scattered units of the unorganised sector under government regulations and controls. It is suggested that the methods which could he help are: (i) organising the units in cooperatives, (ii) setting up work centres/work sheds in neighbourhood areas to bring the units together and (iii) issuing work cards to all the workers who take work home from the employers.

(h) Legislations which aim at abolition of child labour from hazardous occupations should be made applicable to family workers also.

(i) Stringent punishment should be incorporated in national legislations on child labour so as to discourage employers from violating them.

(j) Appropriate budget allocations should be made to implement the programmes and legislations pertaining to child labour successfully.

(k) Subsidies from national governments to industry (in India most specifically) should be looked into, as they often simply add to the profits of exploiters of child labour.

(9) The health of child labour deserves special attention of all those who are concerned. Major actions needed in this area are:

(a) Careful investigation of health conditions of child workers in different occupations on a regular basis.

(b) Collecting data on accidents, burns and diseases of child labour regularly.

(c) Designing appropriate measures to improve their health conditions.

(10) About 89 to 90 per cent child workers in the third world countries are engaged in agriculture and allied activities. Though most of them are not working in unhealthy or unsafe surroundings, some of them are working as bonded or mortgaged workers or are working for long hours. It is therefore, necessary that:

(a) An extreme kind of exploitation of these workers is removed.
(b) The working hours of others are reduced.
(c) They are all covered under primary education which is designed carefully as discussed above. National government should expand the coverage of primary education to cover all these children, and if necessary should provide financial incentives to the children and their families to send their children to schools.

(11) The problem of child labour is prevailing in European countries also thou, though the nature and the extent of the problem are different. Employment of child labour in certain sectors is observed to be due to the drop outs from the schools. It is necessary to strengthen the educational system (that is, the syllabus) to prevent this. In addition, it is also observed that there is relatively a high incidence of unemployment among adult workers, and specially among the youth in these countries which use child labour. It is worth noting that eradication of child labour from the third world countries will help adult employment in developing countries also.

(12) Non-government-organisations, or independent people's organisations have very important roles to play in achieving the goal of abolition of child labour in the third world countries:

(a) Campaigns should be organised to combat the use of sex tourism as seen in some countries, and to boycott the travel agencies engaged in this.
(b) Campaigns should also be launched to demand employment of adults to replace child labour. Should such campaigns prove ineffective, boycott of such products should be encouraged. It is important, however, that these campaigns are initiated by people in the producers' countries and are supported internationally as and when asked.
(c) International campaigns should be developed when multinational corporations exploit children directly or indirectly (for example, Swedish Match or Brooke Bond).

(13) Promoting a meeting of independent people's organisation to act as a catalyst in the formation of the regional, national and international network is proposed as a long-term objective. IFM-SEI is charged with this responsibility.

(14) Independent people's organisation should also campaign for all countries to become signatories to the ILO Convention No. 138. It is the duty of every national government to implement this convention in its respective country.

(15) Independent people's organisations should work for the ecological improvement of rural areas as well as for the development of total human resources.

(16) Independent people's organisations should continue to exchange information about specific situations that continue to exist, and use the good offices of IFM-SEI to publicise the situation of children in the world. They should continue to apply pressures through the mass media on the issue of child labour as long as the evil exists.

(17) Trade union movement at the national and international levels has a major role to play in achieving the goal of abolition of child labour. Within the trade union movement the following should be taken up:

(a) The inclusion of the issue of child labour in all agreements, manifestos and national executives.
(b) The replacement of child workers by adults supported by vocational education, nutrition, health and recreation.
(c) The education and development of cadres to deal with this problem.
(d) The unionisation of the urorganised and agricultural sectors.
(e) The strengthening of the trade unions.
(f) Study and analysis of areas of child work and policies affecting child labour leading to the drawing up of alternative strategies.

(18) In addition, trade unions should take up the following, with the cooperation of the independent people's organisations:

(a) The dissemination of information about child labour.
(b) Work with NGOs around child labour problems.
(c) The calling of a Child Labour Day.

(19) Trade union organisation at the international level can take up the following:

(a) Direct action for example, organising boycotts by trade unionists in developed countries of goods produced by child labour. This should be initiated by trade unions in the producer country only, and should get supported by others as and when called for.
(b) Sharing of experience between trade unions and other progressive organisation through IFM-SEI.
(c) Investigation and action by international trade union organisations of multinational subcontracts using child labour.

(20) It is recognised that the national aspect of child labour cannot be seen in isolation from the international context. The terms of trade between North and South need to be more favourable to developing countries than is presently the case. There are

also problems of indirect interference as in the case of selling arms to developing countries.

(21) Nevertheless, there are some measures which could be taken up to ease and solve the problem of child labour at the international level. Within European countries, greater emphasis is needed upon development and peace education, and also upon education for solidarity. The consciousness of the European public is not great with regard to awareness that they should not simply be concerned for the sake of the plight of children in other countries, but they should realise that their vested interests have been responsible for the plight. Also, it is their problem too, as we are all interdependent. More specific publicity is therefore needed, in a range of areas and in many languages, to be widely accessible:

(a) To heighten awareness of the child labour situation within particular industries, along with case studies, to bring the message home to people more directly. (Industries like carpet weaving, art and filigree, wood carving.)

(b) To make people related to the issue and to focus upon what people want for their children in the future, say by 2001?

(c) Aim the message not only at men, but very specifically at mothers to achieve success.

(d) Linked in with publicity is the task of awareness building among the exploited children themselves, so that they become conscious of their rights.

(22) It is suggested that trade unions or independent people's organisations could take up projects based upon needs felt in particular areas where the problem exists, to try and find possible ways to solutions of the problem. IFM-SEI could finance such experimental projects.

(23) Several international organisations, institutions and agencies in the world connected with children, in some way or the other should take up the following:

(a) UNICEF takes up child labour form the perspective of children rights. We ask form the seminar for IFM-SEI-UNICEF to be the lead agency for implementation of the convention of children rights.

(b) UNICEF as the UN-agency for education take up programmes in the member countries where there is child labor and try to give them the right emphasis for working children.

(c) ILO is already responsible for the implementation of the convention about child labour. It should try harder to do that, and also come with additional guide-lines about working conditions.

(d) ICFTU increase its activities to get the trade unions in the concerned countries involved.

(e) WHO, responsible UN-agency for the health related questions, take up everything related to working conditions for child labour forming some kinds of hazard to health.

(f) NGO-group in Geneva continue their efforts regarding the rights of the child with more emphasis on child labour.

(g) IPA--the international association for the child's right to play—has to be involved in helping recreation of child labour.

(h) Different European countries--in their international aid—should include projects for abolishing child labour in certain areas. This is specially a task for Nordic countries, the Netherlands and Austria.

(i) IFM-SEI's task must be opinion oriented through its member organisations and directed both to the members and to the government in the respective countries and to the labour movement in these countries.

(j) Peace institutions all over the world should get the IFM-SEI task force to put up the case of child labour as a threat to the world peace--and try to do something about it.

(24) IFM-SEI and its member organisations can do the following:

(a) Looking after countries who have not signed the ILO convention and encouraging them to do so.

(b) Encouraging countries to sign the convention on children's rights.

(c) Collect information on several trades where child labour is involved—wood carving, carpet, *jari* industry etc. and give all the details to the member organisations to show how the developed countries are using child labour in the developing countries.

(d) Taking up the question of child labour at the Human Rights commission of Socialist International and to try to get it in the agenda of the next SI-Congress 1989.

(25) The action strategy for eradication of child labour should also include the actions needed in the area of research at the national and international levels:

(a) Studies should be conducted to identify various employments where children are working, and information should be collected about their working and living conditions.

(b) The second area is of documenting experiences of the interventions of NGOs and trade unions in helping child labour. A number of such experiences are scattered and are not studied systematically.

(c) It is also necessary to carry out evaluation studies of national government programmes in the area of child labour. Such studies are likely to throw useful light on the problems of enforcement of the programmes.

(d) There is ample scope for action-research in this area. The problem of child labour is complex and the solutions not easy. It will be useful therefore if innovative experiments are made as action-research projects.

(e) Study of national legislations on child labour and comparing them with the ILO conventions on child labour. Such a study will throw useful light on the gaps in the two and the causes thereof.

(26) It is decided that appropriate follow up actions emerging from this action strategy will be taken by all the participants who come from different walks of life, such as trade unions, independent people's organisations, academicians and officials. This action strategy provides a broad guide-line, which can be implemented after making minor adjustments as per the specific needs of various countries.

WORKING WOMEN AND CHILDREN

WORKING WOMEN AND CHILDREN

Volume - 4

Child Labour: A Reality

Editor-in-Chief

C. P. RAI

LAXMI SHIKSHAN SANSTHAN
LUCKNOW

&

ANMOL PUBLICATIONS PVT. LTD.
NEW DELHI - 110 002 (INDIA)

ANMOL PUBLICATIONS PVT. LTD.
4374/4B, Ansari Road, Daryaganj
New Delhi - 110 002

Working Women and Children

First Edition, 2000

ISBN 81-261-0658-1 (Set)

PRINTED IN INDIA

Published by J.L. Kumar for Anmol Publications Pvt. Ltd., New Delhi -110 002 and Printed at Mehra Offset Press, Delhi.

CONTENTS

VOLUME II

CONTENTS

VOLUME II

24

CHILD LABOUR WELFARE LEGISLATION

I. PRELUDE

The child has been subject of special laws and legal provisions. Because of its tender years, weak physique, and inadequately developed mind and understanding, it needs protection against moral and physical harm and exploitation by others. In the formative years of its life, the child needs special care service to realise its full potential for growth and development. There are about 300 central and state statutes concerning children. These have been enacted with an intention to protect and help children and achieve the goal of child labour welfare enshrined in our National Charter.[1]

The constitution-makers were conscious of the need for special care for children and, therefore, provisions to the welfare of children dealing specially with the protection of child labour have been envisaged in our National Charter.[2] Accordingly, our National Policy resolution for children, 1974, lays special stress on the responsibility of the national for physical, mental, moral and special development of children. All this calls for great deal of legislative activity. The subject of "child" does not fall exclusively either in the Union (Central) or the State field. Different matters related to child care and development are distributed among the Union; state and concurrent list of the constitution. It is not only in India but in other industrialised countries including those developed ones that the present labour legislation is aimed to provide legal protection to child labour who constitute an important section of wage-earning population. The underlying conviction of all labour legislations is that it is one of the principal duties of the state to protect and safeguard the interest and well-being of workers. Irrespective of their age, caste, creed and colours.[3]

The welfare state, as the modern 'patria potestas[4] is required to see that childhood is not abused. The dignity of the individual, the basis of the democratic society has been assumed by the constitution by declaring the fundamental rights of the individual on the one hand, and by forbidding the traffic in human beings, begar and exploitation of youth and childhood on the other. The traffic in human beings, means buying and selling wrongfully of human beings, and includes slavery, *bandhak Mazdoor* and immoral traffic in women.[5]

It may be submitted that the labour legislation in India including protective legislation for children has been greatly influenced and is the result of various conventions[6] and recommendations adopted by international Labour Organisation. Besides constitutional provisions, there are at present 13 major legislative enactments which provides legal protection to children in various occupations. These are:

(i) The Children (Pleading of Labour) Act, 1933;
(ii) The Employment of Children Act, 1938;
(iii) The minimum Wages Act, 1948; and rules made thereunder by the government;
(iv) The Factories Act, 1948;
(v) The Plantations Labour Act, 1951;
(vi) The Mines Act, 1952;
(vii) The Merchant Shipping Act, 1958;
(viii) The Motor Transport Workers Act, 1961;
(ix) The Apprentices Act, 1961;
(x) The Atomic Energy Act, 1962;
(xi) The Beedi and Cigar Workers (Conditions of Employment) Act, 1966;
(xii) The shops and Establishments Act in various states.
(xiii) Child Labour (Prohibition and Regulation) Act, 1986.

From time to time, amendments have been made in most of the above statutes, because of the progressive outlook of the governments for improving the conditions of the important legislations which regulate the working conditions of child workers and mitigate the adverse effect of employment on their health, education and training, etc.[7]

II. TEXT OF LEGISLATION

(i) The Children) (Pledging of Labour) Act, 1933

The main object of this Act is to eradicate the evils arising from the pledging of labour of young children by their parents employers in lieu of loans or advances.

Previously, the Act extended to whole of India except Jammu and Kashmir, but after September 1, 1971, it has been extended to the Jammu and Kashmir also.[8]

The Act declares an agreement, oral or written, to pledge the labour of children, whereby the parents or the guardian of child, in return of any payment or benefit to be received, undertakes to cause or allow the services of a child to be utilised in any employment, to be void.[9] "However, an agreement made without detriment in a child and not made in consideration of any benefit other than reasonable wages to be paid for the child's service and terminable at more than a weak's notice is not to be deemed to be an illegal agreement.[10] A person who knowingly enters into an agreement with a parent or guardian of a child whereby such parent or guardian pledges the labour of child, or an employer who knowingly employs such a child is liable to a fine upto Rs. 200. A parent or a guardian who knowingly pledges the labour of his child is liable to be wished with a find which may extend upto Rs. 50.[11]

Child means, under this Act, a person who has not complete the age of 15 years.[12]

(ii) The Employment of Children Act, 1938

This Act is also applied to the whole of India. To prevent employment of children in hazardous employment and certain categories of unhealthy occupations, the Act prohibits the employment of children below 15 years of age in any occupation connected with the transport of passengers, goods or mail by railway, or a port authority within the limits of a port.[13]

With the exception of children employed as apprentices or trainees, no child between the age of 15-17 can be employed or permitted to work in these occupations unless he is allowed a rest interval of at least 12 consecutive hours in a day. The period of rest is to include at least 7 such consecutive hours between 10 P.M. and 7 A.M. as may be prescribed by the appropriate government.[14]

The Act also prohibits the employment of children below the age of 14 in workshops connected with bidi-making; carpet-weaving; cement manufacture including bagging of cement, cloth printing; dyeing and weaving; manufacture of matches; explosives and fire works; mica cutting and splitting; shellac manufacture; soap manufacture tanning and wool cleaning.[15] These provisions, however, do not apply to workshops where the work is done by the occupier with the aid of his family only or to any school established, aided or recognised by any state government. The State governments are empowered to extend the scope of this provision of the Act to any other employment also.[16] In exercise of this power the government of Madras has extended the Act to children working as cleaners in workshops attached to motor transport companies. The Government of Uttar Pradesh has also extended this provision of the Act to brassware and glass bangle industries. The penalty for the breach of the Act is imprisonment upto one month or fine upto Rs. 500 or both.[17] The Act also require the Railway and port authorities to maintain registers showing names, date of birth, rest intervals, etc. of children under 17.[18] It is however imperative to mention here that this Act has been repeated to the extent it is in consistent with the child labour (Prohibition and Regulation) Act, 1986.

(iii) The Factory Act, 1948

The Act extends to the whole of India except the state of Jammu and Kashmir.[19] It applies to establishments employing 10 or more workers with power or 20 or more workers without power.[20] A child under the Act., is defined as a person who has not completed the fifteen years of age.[21] A 'young person' is defined as either a child or an adolescent,[22] who has completed his fifteen years but not eighteen years.[23] Thus, "young person" may be divided into three categories:

(i) Those who are under fourteen years. They are totally prohibited by this Act from entering into employment in factory.[24]

In *Walker T. Ltd. v. Martindale*,[25] it was held that the prohibition is absolute and not restricted to employment in one of manufacturing processes; thus a child employed as a sweeper to clean the floor of a factory is in contravention of the 'provisions of the section, even though he is not employed in any of the manufacturing processes.

The following employments are also prohibited by the court:

(a) Shorting of groundnuts in a courtyard near the machinery rook for decorticating *Ramanathan* v. *K.E.*[26]
(b) To employ children under 7 years in plating straw in a workroom, the benefit of which goes to the mother, was held liable to penalty—*Beedon* v. *Parrot*.[27]
(c) Oiling of parts of machinery of the spinning mill by a young person during meal time, though done without orders and for workers own amusement was held in *Prior* v. *Slaith-Waite Spinning Co.*[28]

Violation of law making the occupier liable to fine.

(ii) Persons who are between 14 and 15 years, they can be employed under the following restrictions provided under Sections 68, 69 and 71 to 75 of the Act:

(i) Such persons should have a certificate of fitness issued by a surgeon and should carry a token of such certificate.[29]
(ii) The certifying surgeon should follow the procedure laid down in Section 69.
(iii) They should not work at night, i.e., twelve consecutive hours including the period from 10 P.M. To 6 A.M.[30]
(iv) They should work not more than four and half hours a day.[31]
(v) The period of work is to be limited to two shifts.[32]
(vi) The shift should not overlap.[33]
(vii) Each child has to be employed in one relay.[34]
(viii) The spread over is not to exceed five hours and should also not change except once in 30 days.[35]
(ix) They should not be employed in two separate factories on the same day.[36]
(x) The employer should display a notice regarding the periods of work for such children.[37]
(xi) The manager of the factory should maintain a register in respect of such child-workers.[38]
(xii) No such child be employed except in accordance with the notice of periods of work displayed at the entries against his name in register of child workers.[39]

Section 75 empowers the inspectors to require any such person for re-examination by surgeon and he may prohibit the employment till the examination is made.

Person between 15 and 18: They are employed as adults if they possess a certificate of physical fitness issued by the certifying surgeon and they also carry a token of such certificate.[40] The adolescents under 17 are not allowed to work at night.[41]

The object of those statutory restriction over the employment of young person is to prevent exploitation of young labourers and to provide for their safety. This was the view expressed by Chief Justice Narasimha. Orissa High Court in *Jhunjhunwalla* v. *B.K. Patnaik,*[42] where the occupier of a glass factory was severely punished for employing 14 adolescent in blowing section of the factory, which is a hazardous occupation, without a certificate of fitness required under sections 68 and 69 of the Factories Act.

In *Mechnitosh* v. *First Brook Book Co.,*[43] it was observed that it was the duty of the employer to ascertain by reasonable means that the applicant was a requisite age and merely the statement of child about his age should not be treated as correct.

The Act also prohibits the employment of children to any part of the factory for pressing cotton in which a cotton opener is at work, except where the feed end of a cotton opener is in a room separated from the delivery end.[44]

The state government is empowered by this Act to make rules prescribing the maximum weights which may be lifted by adolescents and children.[45] Besides a weekly day of rest, every child worker who has worked for a period of 240 days or more in a factory during a calendar year is entitled during the subsequent year of leave with wages at the rate of one day for every 15 days of work as against every 20 days in the case of an adult worker.[46] Rest-shelters, canteens, etc. are also to be provided to all workers including children.[47]

(iv) The Plantation Labour Act, 1951

The Act covers in the first instance all tea, coffee, rubber, cinchona, cordamom plantation and areas 10.117 hectares or more, in which 30 or more persons are employed,[48] or were employed on any day of the preceding 12 months. Further the state government is, however, empowered to extend, all or any of the provisions of this Act to any land used or intended to be used for growing and plantation even if it measures less than 10.117 hectares and the number of persons employed therein is less than thirty. provided that land which measured less than 10.117 hectares or in which measured less than 30 persons are employed immediately before the commencement of the Act would not be covered.

The Act prohibits the employment of children under 12 years.[49] An adolescent between 15-18 years cannot be employed for work unless he is certified fit for work by a surgeon.[50] Such certificate is valid only for one year.[51] Use of a false certificate of fitness is punishable by imprisonment which may extend to one month, or with fine or both.[52]

This Act is, however, more comprehensive in the sense that this Act alone makes the provisions for education as a responsibility of the employer and so is for the housing and medical and recreational facilities.[53] Perhaps the legislators were moved to make all these provisions in this Act because of the fact that plantation labour is commonly known as "family labour" as against `individual' child labour.

(v) The Mines Act, 1952

This Act also extends to the whole of India[54] and includes all excavations where any operation for the purpose of searching for or obtaining minerals is carried out.[55] This Act also defines child as a person who has not completed his fifteen years.[56] This Act not only prohibits the employment of children in mines, but also prohibits the presence of children in any part of a mine which is below ground or in any open cast working in which any mining operation is being carried on.[57] Even an adolescent is not allowed to work in part of a mine which is below ground, unless he has completed his 16th year and has a medical certificate of fitness for work.[58] A certificate is valid only for 12 months.[59] The act also says that adolescent is allowed to be employed in any mine except between 6 A.M. and 6. P.M. This act also includes:

(i) All bearing, bore holes and oil well;

(ii) all shafts, in or adjacent to and belonging to mine, whether in the course of being sunk or not;

(iii) all levels and inclined planes in the course of being driven;

(iv) all converse or alrial railways provided for the bringing into or removal from mine of minerals or other articles or for the removal of refuse thereform;

(v) all adits, level, planes, machinery, works, railways, tramways, and riding;

(vi) in or adjacent to and belonging to a mine;

(vii) all workshops situated within the precinct of a mine and under the same management and used solely for purposes connected with that mine or a number of mines under the same management;

(viii) all power stations for supplying solely for the purpose of working the mines or a number of mines under the same management;

(ix) any premise exclusively occupied by the owner of the mines and for the time being used for depositing refused from a mine or in which any operation in connection with such refuse is being carried on; and

(x) unless exempted by the central government by notification in the official gazette, any premises for part thereof in or adjacent to and belonging to a mine, on which any process ancillary to getting, dressing or preparation for sale of minerals[60] or of coke is carried on.

(vi) The Merchant Act, 1958

The Act prohibits the employment of children in any capacity, who are below 15 years of age, on sea-going ships. This Act applied to ships registered in India. It also prohibits the employment of young persons under 15 as trimmers and stakers except under certain specific conditions. Such persons, if employed, are required to produce a certificate of fitness. Further the Act empowers the government to make necessary rules regarding employment of young persons as and when the occasion demands.

(vii) The Apprentices Act, 1961

The main object of the Act is to provide for the regulation and control of training of apprentices in trades and for matters connected therewith. The Act extends to the whole of India[61] and provides for the regulations and control of training of apprentices in trade and for matters connected therewith.[62] Under the Act. an apprentice has been defined "as person who is undergoing apprenticeship training in a designated trade in pursuance of control of apprenticeship." The Act provides that no person shall be qualified for engaged as an apprentice or to undergo apprenticeship training in any designated trade unless he is atleast 14 years of age and satisfies such standards of education and physical fitness as may be prescribed.[63] If he is a minor. His guardian is required to enter into a contract of apprenticeship with the employer[64] and it shall be registered with the Apprenticeship Advisor.[65]

Initially the Act was enforced in 12 industries but in order to met the growing and changing demands of all skilled workers in other industries, the coverage of the Act has been extended to 1995 industries. The central government has also specified 56 designated trades for the purpose of the Act.[66]

(viii) The Motor Transport Workers Act, 1961

This act applies to the whole of India,[67] it covers every motor transport undertaking employing 5 or more transport workers. The state governments are authorised to apply all or any of the provisions of this Act to any motor transport undertakings employing less than 5 workes.[68] This Act also prohibits the employment of children under 15 in any capacity in the motor transport undertakings[69] The adolescents are prohibited to work unless a certificate of fitness is granted,[70] which is valid only for 12 months.[71] An adolescent can work only for 6 hours including a rest interval of half an hour and between 10 A.M. and 6 P.M. only.

(ix) Bidi and Cigar Works (Conditions of Employment) Act, 1966

The Act also extends to whole of India.[72] The Act provides that no child should be required or allowed to work in any industrial premises;[73] the Act defines the child as a person who has not completed his fourteen years of age.[74] The employment of young persons between 14 to 18 years is prohibited between 7 P.M. to 6 A.M.[75] The Administration of Act rests with the state who appoint Chief Inspectors or Inspectors for the purpose. The Act provides the penalties for breach which may be imprisonment upto three months or a fine upto Rs. 500 or both.[76]

(x) Contract Labour (Regulations and Abolition) Act, 1970

The Act also extends to the whole of India.[81] The Act applies to establishments and contractors employing 20 or more workers.[82] It is not applied to establishment in which work only of an intermittent or casual nature is performed.[83] There are no specific provisions under the Act pertaining to employment of children.

(xi) Shops and Commercial Establishment Act, 1969

Provisions relating to minimum age also exists in different state shops and commercial establishments Act. These acts applied to shops, commercial establishments, restaurants and hotels and place of amusement and notified urban areas, to which the Factories Act does not apply. Further the state governments are empowered to extend the coverage of the Act in any establishment.

The minimum age of employment in shops and commercial establishment is 12 years in Bihar, Gujarat, J and K, Madhya Pradesh, Karnataka, Orissa, Rajasthan, Tripura, Uttar Pradesh, West Bengal, Goa, Daman and Diu and Manipur, and 14 years in Andhra Pradesh, Assam, Haryana, Himachal Pradesh, Kerala, Tamil Nadu, Punjab, Delhi, Chandigarh, Pondicherry and Meghalaya. The minimum age of employment is 15 years in Maharashtra. There is no separate Shops and Commercial Establishment Act in Andaman and Nicobar, Arunachal Pradesh, Dadra and Nagar Haveli Lakshdweep, Nagaland and Sikkim.[84]

(xii) The Child Labour (Prohibition and Regulation) Act, 1986

The Act states right in the beginning that its aim is to prohibit the engagement of children in certain employments and to regulate the conditions of work of children in certain other employments.

According to this Act, the Employment of Children Act, 1938 is repealed. All rules made in this Act will be in addition to the provisions of the Factories Act, 1948, the Plantations Labour Act, 1951 and Mines Act, 1952:

(i) According to this Act "Child" means a person who has not completed his fourteen years of age.[85]

(ii) Again, family units and training centres are not included in the purview of the Act.

(iii) The Act provides for the setting up of "Child Labour Technical Advisory Committee" for the purpose of addition of occupations and processes to the schedule. A notice of at least three months will be given by the Central Government before adding any occupation or process to the schedule.[86]

(iv) The Act clearly lays down that no child will be allowed to work for more than six hours per day[87] with a rest period of one hour after three hours of work. Once a week he will be given a holiday.[88]

(v) No child will be allowed to work between 7 P.M. and 8 A.M.[89] No over time will be permitted.[90]

(vi) The Act clearly states that the government can make rules for the health and safety of children who are permitted to work in any establishment.[91] These rules can provide for matters such as cleanliness,[92] ventilation.[93] dust and fumes,[94] lighting,[95] drinking water,[96] and sanitary facilities, etc. But there is no mention of nutrition or medical facilities.

(vii) The penalty of violation of the Act will range from three months to one year of imprisonment with a fine of Rs. 10,000 to Rs. 20,000.[97]

(viii) If a person is found guilty he will be liable for punishment under the clauses given in Section 14 (1 and 2) and not under any of the previous Acts.

(ix) Any person, policy officer or an inspector can file a complaint of an offence under this Act in any Court of Competent jurisdiction.[89]

(x) Part 'B" of the schedule has added one more process into existing list and that is "building and construction industry." All other provisions are similar to the ones already existing in the Act of 1938.[99]

The government proposes to bring in amendment to The Child Labour (Prohibition Regulation) Act, 1986, to make it more effective.[100]

III. NATIONAL POLICY ON CHILD LABOUR

The implementation of child labour in our country is very ineffective. The main reasons for this are lack of adequate enforcement machinery, lack of political will, deliberate attempt of employers to flout the legal provisions and the lack of consciousness within the minds of parents themselves who obtain false age and medical certificate to enable their children to work. The number of labour inspectors is pitifully low. They can barely visit all the factories in their jurisdiction. Keeping in view the pitiable conditions of child labour in India, the government of India has endeavoured to expound national policy on Child Labour Welfare. New Projects are on the anvil for checking child labour in our country. A two day's 42nd State Labour Minister's Conference was held at New Delhi.[101] State Labour Minister's Conference was the national child labour policy. Other topic that came up at the conference was the enforcement of legal provisions for prohibition and regulation of child labour, developmental schemes for child labour and association of the non-governmental agencies in implementation of such projects.[102]

The conference deliberated on the recommendations made at the meeting of the employers of child labour with Union Labour Minister P.A. Sangma. Both the government and the employers had resolved at the meeting to co-operate on the move for eradication of child labour. The employers had endorsed the government move to amount the Minimum Wage Act to ensure payment of wages to child labour at a par with adult workers.[103]

It had also been announced by the Labour Minister Child Labour Act would be amended to bring more industries under the category banned of child labour. The employment of child labour in all industries would be regulated.[104]

In the recent past the practice of child labour in India has evoked world-wide criticism. On the lines of the action taken by the US Senate, the German Parliament also has before it a Bill seeking a ban on import of Indian goods produced by child labour.[105]

Besides the Child Labour (Prohibition and Regulation). Act, 1986, provisions against the employment of children exist in other labour laws also such as the Factories Act, the Mines Act, the Plantation Labour Act as well as the Shops and Establishments Acts of the State Governments.

The project was implemented through registered project societies constituted. Under the chairmanship of district collectors and through voluntary agencies. Two of the existing projects identified for the elimination of child labour within one year pertain to those employed by the title manufactures in Jaggampet (Andhra Pradesh) and those working in the state pencil industry in Mandsaur (Madhya Pradesh).[106]

Moreover, the Central Advisory Board for Child Labour has identified ten states and union territories for which a target of three years for the elimination of child labour has been set. They are: Mizoram, Meghalaya, Manipur, Nagaland, Arunachal Pradesh, Tripura, Goa, Pondicherry, Chandigarh and Sikkim.[107] Besides, a National Policy on child labour has been formulated in conjunction with the legal measures to address the socio-economic issues having a bearing on child labour and to provide a framework for a concrete programme of action. The policy encompasses action in the fields of education, health, nutrition, integrated child development and employment., The discussion on the various issues concerning child labour welfare contains the following resolution:

(i) Education Programmes

A National Policy on Education, 1986, sets a target whereby all children who attained the age of 11 years by 1990 will have received five years of schooling, or its equivalent in a non-formal system of education. With this goal in view, 490,000[108] non-formal education centres are proposed to be opened nationally to supplement the formal education system. Since non-formal education is to be planned and organised at the local level, centres for child labour will be set up in both urban and rural areas with the involvement of local voluntary agencies and Panchayati Raj Institutions (the latter being self-governing organisations with the participation of the people's elected representatives). Funds from the National Rural Employment Programme and the Rural Landless Employment Guarantee Programme will be used on a priority basis to create the infrastructure for these centres. Efforts will be made to link the non-formal educational institutions with the formal educational system, so as to enable child workers who have completed the formal to continue their schooling in the latter.[109]

Special attention will be given to attracting and retaining working girls at these centres. Part-time vocational courses will also be provided after work and during holidays. The centres would aim to educate children upto Class V level, with arrangements for continuing upto Class VII wherever feasible.

Details of scheme of incentives and assistance for families who are forced to involve their children in wages or quasi-wages employment are to be worked out in consultation with state governments. Scholarships will be given to working children who come from especially deprived families engaged in occupations like scavenging, to ensure that they are enrolled successfully and complete the non-formal education course.[110]

(ii) Health Programmes

Responsibility for carrying out medical inspections of children lies with the 'state governments. Progress among the various states is uneven and while a few have good programmes, others are lagging behind. In these states where a school health service exists, many, and in some cases all rural primary school pupils receive regular health checks. However, working children unable to attend schools are not covered by such schemes. The Ministry of Health and Family Welfare will recommend to the state governments that intensive medical inspection of children should be taken up in areas where child labour is prevalent, and that the school health service should include working children. It should also be possible to arrange for health screening of working children at the non-formal education centres[111]

(iii) Anti-Poverty Programmes

The Central Government has developed a number of income and employment generating programmes for poor families, many of whom contain; child workers—in rural areas. The most disadvantaged families will be given assistance to raise themselves above the poverty line and this, in conjunction with the provision of non-formal education, is expected to go long way towards tackling a major underlying cause of child labour.[112]

(iv) Project-based Plan of Action

The policy anticipates and provides for specific pilot projects which could establish the basis for a more vigorous national programme of action. In India, there are certain sectors where the incidence of child labour is particularly high. These include the match industry of Sivakasi, Tamil Nadu, the diamond-polishing industry of Surat Gujarat, the precious stone polishing industry of Jaipur, Rajasthan; the glass industry of Ferozabad, Uttar Pradesh; the brass ware industry of Moradabad, Uttar Pradesh, the carpet industry of Mirzapur-Bhadohi, U.P., the lock-making industry of Aligarh, Uttar Pradesh; the carpet industry of Jammu and Kashmir and the salt industry of Mandsour, Madhya Pradesh, and Markapur. Andhra Pradesh. Children engaged in these occupations and areas deserve priority attention because the employment processes which they work are prohibited by law and the work is very likely to seriously effective their welfare.[113]

The plan is to mount pilot projects in each of these areas of high concentrations of child labour. The strategy will be to evolve a model comprising a number of key elements. The first of these entails stepping up the enforcement of the Factories Act, 1948, the Mines Act, 1952, and the Child Labour (Prohibition and Regulation) Act, 1986. If necessary, special enforcement staff will be employed for this purpose. The second involves the inclusion of families of child workers in the income, and employment-generating schemes which form part of existing anti-poverty programmes. The third lays down special component and tribal sub-plans[114] by the state governments in each project areas where there is a concentration of such families with child workers. The fourth consists in the provision of both formal and nonformal education, the setting up of special schools providing vocational training and supplementary nutrition for child workers, and a programme of adult education for the parents of working children. The policy also anticipates a stipend for children withdrawn for prohibited employment. The final element involves co-ordinating the activities of different departments and ministries of the central and state governments to the benefit of child workers.[115]

Existing infrastructures run by the departments of education and health will be suitably modified and incorporated into these schemes. Special funds will be allocated in order to ensure intensive coverage in the project areas of the anti-poverty, health and nutrition programmes and to provide for special schools and stipends. The additional funds will be channelled through the Ministry of Labour, which will be responsible for planning and co-ordinating the projects in close consultation with the state government and the appropriate ministers of the central government. The first phase of the special projects is expected to cover upto 30,000 child workers.[116]

There will be a Chief Executive Officer in-charge of each project area, who will work under the general super-vision and direction of the administrative head of the district in which the project is situated. A Child Labour Project Board will be created with representatives from the district educational, health and nutrition authorities and the voluntary agencies and Panchayat Raj instructions active in the area. This will ensure co-ordination among the various bodies executing schemes in the project area. In view of the fact that voluntray organisations have made a major contribution to research and action-orient programmes for working children, they are to part an important role in future projects, particularly those aimed at rehabilitating children removed from profited employment and those providing welfare facilities or working children.[117]

The child labour projects will be monitored to a Committee of the Central Government with representatives from the ministries and departments concerned and from the state governments in areas here child labour projects are being implemented. The committee will meet as often as in necessary to ensure the smooth functioning of the project.

IV. TEXT OF CHILD LABOUR DETERRENCE BILL 1992

A serious push seems to be coming in the share of Child Labour Deterrence Bill, moved in the United States Senate to link international trade with children's right. The Bill has been moved by Senator Harkin and In-Sponsored by Conrad, Inouye. Wofford, Cranson. Grassley, Rockefeller and Matzenboum. It defines and valid as one who is below the age of 15 years. This is important for India because the constitution makes of a "fundamental duty," of governance by any political party to ensure free and compulsory primary education for the children till the age of 14 years. Further, the Supreme Court in *Unnikrishnan case*[118] has declared that his is not only a fundamental duty but a fundamental right which can enforce through Court of law.

The proposed Bill requires that the U.S. Labour Secretary to compile and maintain a list of foreign industries and their respective host countries that use child labour in the production of goods exported to the United States. The identification process can be initiated at the instance of any one filing a petition with the Labour Secretary. Prior to identifying the industry and the country the Secretary of State, Commerce and Treasury. After this a notice shall be published in the Federal Register and objections invited to the industry and the country being listed.[119]

Once a country and its industry have been identified as using child labour, the Treasury Secretary is directed to prohibit the entry of any manufactured article from such industry and country. The ban will not apply if the U.S. importers can certify that the product from the industry and its country is not made by the child labour. The importer would be required to sign a certificate to affirm that they took reasonable steps to ensure that the products imported from the industries identified by the Labour Secretary do not employ child labour. Companies importing wilfully and knowingly importing the banned products will be subject to penalties.

The Bill urges the President of the United States to seek an agreement with other governments to secure an international ban on trade in the products of child labour. This directly links trade negotiations of human rights.

India is a signatory to a whole gamut of international conventions prohibiting the use of children in industry at the cost of their education and health. Its own constitution mandate a government budget and an economy that will give "social, economic and political justice" to children. Since the enforcement of the constitution in 1949, the Union and State Finance Ministers have got away with a violation of the constitution by actively promoting unconstitutional economics.[120]

May be the U.S. Bill will force politicians here to function according to the Indian constitution.

V. SUM UP

The sum up, it is revealed from the foregoing chapter that many labour welfare legislations have been enacted from time to time to promote and improve the working conditions of child labour. Even the British Government enacted child welfare legislation in the early 1930 under the title "The Child (Pleading of Labour) Act, 1933 to eradicate the evil arising from pleding of young children by their parents in lieu of Iran taken in advance. Similarly, it is shown in the foregoing chapter that the British Government enacted employment of Children Act, 1938, to prevent the employment of children in hazardous employment and certain categories of unhealthy occupation. It also prohibits the employment of children below 14 years of age.

Even after Independence numerous welfare legislations have been enacted by the both centre and state governments, in the light of the philosophy contained in our National Charter. More than 250 legislations have been enacted with a zeal of promote the welfare of child workers and improve their working conditions in various establishments. It is quite evident from the survey of various Articles of constitution. Our founding fathers had in their mind and intensive care to safeguard the child workers from exploitation and improve their working conditions in various occupations. The subject of child welfare, child care and development have been enlisted in concern list in concurrent list of our constitution. Our National Charter imposes a duty on centre as well as state government to create an healthy environment for their all-round development. The dignity of individual, the basis of democratic set up of our society has been assured by our National Charter by declaring the fundamental rights of individual on the one hand and by forbidding the traffic in human beings. begar and exploitation of youth and childhood on the other hand.

After Independence our legislature has enacted the Minimum Wages Act, 1948; Factories Act. 1948; the Plantation Labour Act, 1951; the Mines Act, 1952; the Merchant Shipping Act 1958; The Motor Transport Workers' Act, 1961; The Apprentice Act, 1961; The Automic Energy Act, 1962; The Beedi and Cigar Conditions of Employment) Act, 1966; The Shop and Establishments Act in various States; and Child Labour (Prohibition and Regulation) Act, 1986 to meet the requirements of child labour from time to time.

Besides these legislative enactments, the government has also adopted a National Policy of Child Labour in 1974. The policy resolution has evolved guidelines in the field of education, health. Nutrition integrated child development etc. Both the Governments, i.e. Centre Government and State Governments are errected to carry out the guidelines of National policy to ensure the improvement of the working conditions of the child workers.

It is also revealed that the child labour welfare legislation in India has been influenced ti a great extent by the conventions and recommendations adopted by International Labour Organisations from time to time. Besides Constitutional Provisions there are at present thirteen major enactments which provide legal protection to our children in various occupations. For making them more effective and progressive, numerous amendments have also been made in most of thee legislations. Moreover, the Child Labour Deterrence Bill, 1992 which was introduced in the United States Senate recently open a new era in the field of child labour welfare. It defines a child as one who is below the age of 5 years. It is important for India because the Constitution makes it a 'fundamental duty' of the government to ensure free and compulsory primary education to all children till the age of 14 years. The Bill prohibits the import of product in which the child labour is involved. India is a signatory to a whole gamut of international conventions prohibiting the use of the children in industries at the cost of their education and health.

REFERENCES

1. See, *Encyclopaedia of Social Work in India,* (1987), Vol. I, 69.
2. See, Articles, 15(3), 14, Clauses (e) and (f) of Articles 39 and 45 of the constitution.
3. See, B.D. Rawat, *Labour Welfarism in India,* (1988), p. 185.
4. See, M.C. J. Kazi, *Constitution of India,* (1984), Vol. II. p. 858.
5. *Ibid.,* 859.
6. India has ratified 4 conventions, namely, Minimum Age (Industry) Convention, 1919, Minimum Age (Trimmers and Stockers) Convention 1921; Medical Examination of Young Persons (Sea) Convention, 1921; and Night Work of young Persons (Industry) Convention, 1948.
7. See, Jinesh Chandra Kulshreshtha, (1978), p. 76.
8. See, The children (Pledging of Labour) Act, 1933, Section 1(2).
9. *Ibid.,* Section 3.
10. *Ibid.,* Section 2.
12. *Ibid.,* Section 4.
12. *Ibid.,* Section 2.
13. The Employment of Children Act. 1938, Section 3(3).
14. *Ibid.,* Section 3(2).
15. *Ibid.,* Section 3(3).
16. *Ibid.,* Section 3-A.
17. *Ibid.,* Section 4.
18. *Ibid.,* Section 3-E.
19. The Factory Act, 1948, Section 1(2).
20. *Ibid.,* Section 2(m).
21. *Ibid.,* Section 2(c).
22. *Ibid.,* Section 2(d).
23. *Ibid.,* Section 2(b).
24. *Ibid.,* Section 67.
25. *Ibid.,* (1916) 85 J.L.K.B. 1543.
26. See AIR 1927 Mad. . 435.
27. See (1871) L.R.Q.B. 718.
28. See (1898), I.O.B. 881.
29. See, Factory Act, 1948, Section 68.
30. *Ibid.,* Section 71(i) (6).
31. *Ibid.,* Section 71(i) (a).
32. *Ibid.,* Section 7(2).
33. *Ibid.*

34. *Ibid.*
35. *Ibid.*
36. *Ibid.*, Section 71(4).
37. *Ibid.*, Section 72.
38. *Ibid.*, Section 73.
39. *Ibid.*, Section 74.
40. The Factory Act, 1948, Section 68.
41. *Ibid.*, Section 70.
42. See, 11 L.L.J. Orissa, 551 (1964).
43. See (1904) 34 C.L.T. 370.
44. The Factory Act, 1948, Section 27.
45. *Ibid.*, Section 34(2).
46. *Ibid.*, Section 79.
47. *Ibid.*, Chapter 5.
48. See, The *Plantation Labour Act*, 1951, Section 4(a).
49. *Ibid.*, Section 24.
50. *Ibid.*, Section 26.
51. *Ibid.*, Section 27(2).
52. *Ibid.*, Section 34.
53. *Ibid.*, *Section* 5, 6, 7.
54. Mines act, 1952, Section 1(2).
55. *Ibid.*, Section 2(j).
56. *Ibid.*, Section 2(e).
57. *Ibid.*, Section 45(i).
58. *Ibid.*, Section 40(i)
59. *Ibid.*, Section 4.(i).
60. See, *The Indian Labour Year Book* (1974), p. 175.
61. See, *The Apprentices Act*, 1961, Section (2).
62. *Ibid.*, Preamble.
63. *Ibid.*, Section 3.
64. *Ibid.*, Section 4(a).
65. *Ibid.*, Section 4(b).
66. See, Suresh C. Srivastava, "Labour Laws Relating to Children in Employment: Their Impact and implementation," *Punjab University Law Review*, (1980), p. 335.
67. The Motor Transport Workers Act, 1961, Section 14.
68. *Ibid.*, Section 1(4).
69. *Ibid.*, Section 21.
70. *Ibid.*, Section 22.
71. *Ibid.*, *Section 23(2).*
72. See, Bidi and Cigar Works (Conditions and Employment) Act, 1966, Section 1(2).

73. *Ibid.*, Section 24(b).
74. *Ibid.*, Section 2(b).
75. *Ibid.*, Section 25.
76. *Ibid.*, Section 32.
77. *Ibid.*, Section 16.
78. *Ibid.*, Section 15.
79. *Ibid.*, Section 8.
80. *Ibid.*, Section 9.
81. The Contract Labour (Regulation and Abolition) Act, 1970, Section 1(2).
82. *Ibid.*, Section 1(4).
83. *Ibid.*, Section 1(5)(4).
84. See Child Labour in India, Document 4, (1979), *The Indian Journal of Public Administration*, Vol. XXV (No. 3). p. 933.
85. See, The Child Labour (Prohibition and Legislation) Act, 1986, Section 2(ii).
86. *Ibid.*, Section 5.
87. *Ibid.*, Section 7(3).
88. *Ibid.*, Section 8.
89. *Ibid.*, Section 7(4).
90. *Ibid.*, Section 7(4).
91. *Ibid.*, Section 13(1).
92. *Ibid.*, Section 13(a).
93. *Ibid.*, Section 13(c).
94. *Ibid.*, Section 13(d).
95. *Ibid.*, Section 13(f).
96. *Ibid.*, Section 13(g).
97. *Ibid.*, Section 14.
98. *Ibid.*, Section 16(1).
99. *Ibid.*, Part B(ii).
100. See, *The Tribune*, August 7, 1993, p. 14.
101. See, *The Tribune*, July 7, 1993, p. 4.
102. *Ibid.*
103. *Ibid.*
104. *Ibid.*
105. *Ibid.*
106. *Ibid.*
107. *Ibid.*
108. Ashok Narayan, "Child Labour Policy and Programme: The Indian Experience," Assefe Bequele and Jo Bovden (ed.) *Combating Child Labour*, (1988), p. 147.
109. *Ibid.*
110. *Ibid.*
111. *Ibid.*

112. *Ibid.*
113. *Ibid.*
114. Components of the overall plan intended for the scheduled castes and tribals population respectively.
115. *Ibid.*
116. *Ibid.*
117. *Ibid.*
118. See, Krishan Mahajan, "US Bill Seek to Strike at Child Labour." *Indian Express*, March 29, 1993, p. 15.
119. *Ibid.*
120. *Ibid.*

25

GENESIS OF CHILD LABOUR

Child Labour was in practice in Indian society from time immemorial. Children gave helping hands to their parents in the household chores and also in family occupations. Various Sanskrit books have described how children in Indian families shared the work-load of their parents and of their gurus during their Brahmachary period (study-life). The famous story of Krishna and Sudama clearly establishes that children (students) were used by their gurus for carrying out certain household chores. In the modern period with the advent of new industrial culture, this practice has assumed an alarming proportion only to attract the attention of social workers, philanthropists and social activists to its various negative aspects. It was never a problem till children were used as helping hands. The need for more production at cheaper costs and the motive to earn more and more resulted in using the helping hands as working hands. Various social organisations and leaders took serious notice of this practice and made hue and cry. Consequently, it attracted attention of the gout, Parliamentarians and social scientist who made several attempts to understand this problem from different angles. This chapter will make a modest attempt to review all such efforts and link these findings with the present study on child labour in the Carpet Industry. The studies available on the subject can be categorised broadly into four areas.

Prevalence of Child Labour

The study on the working children in urban Delhi (1977) tried to examine the extent, causes and consequences of child labour in urban Delhi. The study estimated 21,000 child workers in Delhi in 1973. Out of 1,992 household surveyed, only 60 families had working children numbering 18. Most of the local children were employed in the workshops. Children working in tea stalls, dhabas and as domestic servants came from the eastern and north-eastern parts of Uttar Pradesh and Bihar. The average size of their household was 5.5 and the average monthly income including the earning of working children was Rs. 321.5 per month (approx.). Another study by the Committee on Child Labour (1979) appointed by the Ministry of Labour, Govt. of India examined various dimensions of child labour in different occupations. The study revealed that the incidence of child labour was highest in Andhra Pradesh where it accounted for about 9.0 per cent of the total labour force, 9.2 per cent of the total child population and 3.7 per cent of the total population of state in 1971. The Child labour was more prevalent in rural areas than in urban areas. A higher percentage of children (5.31 per cent) in rural area were workers whereas this ratio in urban areas was only 1.82 per cent. The participation of children in the labour force in the age-group of 10-14 years was very high (28.9 per cent) for males as compared to females (20 per cent).

The census figures (1971) also reveal that out of 10.74 million working children, 36.03 per cent are cultivators, 42.70 per cent agricultured labours and 8.24 per cent are engaged in live-stock, forestry, fishing, etc., 0.22 per cent in mining, and quarrying and 6.08 per cent in manufacturing process, 0.54 per cent in construction, 1.95 per cent in trade and commerce, 0.39 per cent in transport and 3.7 per cent in other services. Another study of child workers conducted in rural Haryana (1979) was based on a sample of 200 child labour families in four villages. It was found that 89 per cent parents of child labour were illiterate, about 49 per cent working children had never gone to school, 40 per cent had discontinued schooling and only 11 per cent child workers were regular in carrying on the burden of schooling and earning of both. In Rewari Tehsil, under study, 70.7 per cent were boys and the rest were girls; 19.4 per cent were between 6 and 8 years of age and 47.6 per cent were of 11-14 years of age; 30.5 per cent of them belonged to Rajput casts and Yadav each and the largest group of child workers consisted of Chamar (Scheduled Caste). The family size of the majority of these workers was 6 to 8. The greater load was on the shoulders of children belonging to nuclear families (70 per cent) than to those (30 per cent) of the joint families. The maximum number (66.0 per cent) of children came from the most prevalent family size of 6 to 8 member whereas the small size of families of 3 to 5 members contributed 34 per cent only. Due to limited coverage, it did not present the working conditions, perception of child labour by their parents, relationship between children and employers and the Child Labour Laws in different working settings.

Another study on Problems and Social Services Needs of Child Labour in Agriculture in Uttar Pradesh (Singhs, 1982) revealed that the average age of the child workers was 13.6 years while the majority of child workers (70.2 per cent) belonged to the age-group of 13-18 years. The majority of the child workers were from non-tribal Hindus and Scheduled Castes. The maximum number of child workers who discontinued the studies were in the age group of 8-12 years.

Similarly, another study on the working condition of children employed in unorganised sector (CSIR 1984) which was based on a sample of 900 male and female child workers below the age of 16 years, indicated that the majority of children employed in match units in Sivakasi were girls (67 per cent). Only 8 per cent were children below 8 years of age and a majority of the child workers (71 per cent) were in the age-group of 13-16 years. Another study on the working children in Bombay (Singh M., 1980) in the age-group of 6-15 years found that most of the working children belonged to low income groups in urban centres who generally reside in slums and depressed areas. This study was conducted on 203 boys (67.7 per cent) and 97 girls (32.3 per cent): three per cent of them belonged to the age-group of 6-9 years, 25.7 per cent to the age-group of 9-12 years and 71.3 per cent to the age-group of 12-15 years. Out of these 300 working children 211 (70.3 per cent) worked under the employer and 89 (29.7 per cent) were self-employed, 287 lived with their parents and 13 with guardians and relatives. The majority of the families of the working children (63.8 per cent) had 5 to 8 members, the average being 5.8 per family. There were more male members than female members in these families. Out of 703 children in the age-group of 6-15 years, as many as 319 (45.4 per cent) were found working. Out of these 703, 403 (57.39 per cent) were boys and 300 (42.7 per cent) girls. Out of 319 working children, 200 (62.7 per cent) were boys and 119 (37.3 per cent) girls. The working children from Hindu families were more than those from Muslim families. The percentage of the working children increased with age, 9 per cent were in the age-group of 6-9 years; 39 per cent in 9-12 years; 78 per cent were in 12-15 Years. Most of the children joined the labour force by the time they were 10 years. Male children shouldered the family's economic responsibility to a large extent than the female. Irrespective of sex, the eldest child in the family invariably had to work, the percentage being 96 per cent boys and 90 per cent girls.

A study on the problem of the working children in the state of Himachal Pradesh had revealed that about 1/3rd of the children of the age-group of 10-14 years in rural and 1/8th of those in urban areas were at work in India. Children working in agriculture and in households on an average worked for 280 days in a year. In villages, children were used as bonded labour and as contract labour in urban areas. Of the working children, 36.79 per cent belonged to Schedule Castes and Scheduled Tribes, and 20.75 per cent to lower castes. Thus, incidence of child labour is much higher in economically backward communities. As regards their literacy, 71.52 per cent were illiterate. A majority (80.35 per cent) of them belonged to agriculture and 16.75 per cent to households. Most of them owned houses but a majority lived in Katcha houses. Regarding income, 5.44 per cent were getting less than Rs. 900, 24.78 per cent between Rs. 901-1800 and 34.71 per cent between Rs. 1801-3600 as their annual income. Another report (Gangrade, 1983) reveals that the states like Uttar Pradesh, Jammu and Kashmir and Tamil Nadu have flourishing centres of carpet weaving. Varanasi, Bhodhi, Mirjapur are also big centres of carpet weaving. It is in Mirjapur where 50,000 workers are engaged in carpet weaving of which nearly 20 per cent are children. Similarly, a survey (Gerry, 1981) shows that carpet weaving is flourishing in the states of Madras, Travancore, Uttar Pradesh and Kashmir. Employment of children in activities suited to them keeps the cost of production low. They also work as apprentices. In household carpet weaving enterprises children are considered indispensable as helpers and as trainees who continue the craft.

Factors Responsible for Child Labour

The survey of children at work (Mendelvich, 1979) tried to highlight the problem of child labour in India and its causes. In fact, the problem of child labour in India may be seen as the result of traditional attitudes, urbanisation, industrialisation, migration, lack of schools or the reluctance of parents to send their children to schools, etc. In the ultimate analysis, main causes are extreme poverty and agriculture being the main occupation of the majority of population requiring more hands.

Child labour is essentially a problem of the poor and destitute families, where parents can not afford to provide education to their children. A study of the working children in Bombay (Singh M. 1980) found that 20.6 per cent of the interviewed employers were employing children because they were quick and efficient, 12.6 per cent preferred them because they were more amenable to discipline, some found them better suited for some types of jobs, 30.5 per cent said that their plight had greater sentimental appeal, 9.3 per cent were in favour of them as they were cheap and 1.9 per cent favoured because of their honesty. Out of 287 respondents (parents), the majority (170 i.e. 69.2 per cent) mentioned economic compulsions as the main factor. As many as 74 (25.8 per cent) mentioned that the child was idle and doing nothing. Therefore, he was put to work to save him from the demoralising effects of idleness. There were 69 (24 per cent) respondents who said that the child had left the school and there was no alternative but to put him at work at keep him busy. Sixty two of them (21.6 per cent) attributed the early entry to work on the part of their children to death, disease or loss of job of the earning member of the family. A few did not mention any special reason or circumstances and said that child labour was their family tradition. Seventeen of the respondents (6.0 per cent) said that their children were keeping bad company and slipping into delinquency so they had to put them on some job so that they might inculcate a sense of discipline. Twelve of the respondents mentioned that the child himself was keen to earn; so they did not stop him from working. A few (10 per cent) said that the child was alone at home and, therefore, he was not safe to ensure his safety, they put him on same job.

Another study on the working children in Hissar (Sharma 1982) revealed that a majority of the child workers joined the labour force due to acute poverty of their family, death and chronic illness of the earning members and there was no source to supplement their family income. Children came from different States. About 4/5 of the children came from the families whose average monthly income was less than Rs. 300 and the size of the family was 8 on an average. The social circumstances which also motivated the child workers to seek jobs were company of friends, rude behaviour of fathers and lack of affection in the family, etc.

One more study on the working conditions of Children employed in unorganised sector, in Sivakasi (CSR, 1984) found that children were the main bread winners in most of the families there. A large number of families depended on the income from match units either as main source or as supplementary source of family income. About 36 per cent of the families had more than two children employed in match units. Most of the children were under compulsion to work due to poverty. A majority (95 per cent) of them took up jobs in match units because of the poor financial conditions of their families. Another 6 per cent of them were interested to continue their studies but were forced by their parents to work to support their families or to supplement the family income. Similarly, another study on Child labour in Himachal Pradesh found that it was the economic necessity which compelled the families to send their children to work. Increasing incidence of debts created more pressure for sending all possible hands to work for wages.

Employers preferred child labour, because it was easy to manage them and also they had to pay less wages to them. About 14.67 per cent employers expressed their opinion that children should be employed but 82.67 per cent replied in the negative. It was also found that in certain handicrafts like Zaribrocade, carpets which need training at the early ages children are preferred to adults.

Working Conditions

A study conducted (Singh M, 1980) in Bombay City presents the working conditions of both self-employed and employed children. Self-employed child workers were found to be working for 10 hours a day who earned around Rs. 82 per month on an average. The Lack of fixed place of shelter, inadequacy of equipment and harassment by officials were the main problems in carrying out the job smoothly. According to me parents, work developed a sense of responsibility in their children made them sober, considerate and well-behaved. The findings about the employed children revealed that none was asked to produce a certificate of medical fitness by the employer nor the employer got him/her medically examined. A majority of the children (68.2 per cent) were getting a monthly salary of Rs. 100 and below. The Children engaged in construction work, arts and crafts and production received the highest payments whereas those in households and restaurants were paid the lowest emoluments in terms of hard cash.

Out of 205 children who were earning, as many as 133 (64.9 per cent) received pocket money, 64.9 per cent, i.e., 133 children worked on regular basis and the rest on daily wages. The minimum number of hours a child worked was 4 hours and the maximum was 14 hours, the average being 8.7 hours. Out of the total sample, 5.10 per cent working children had no fixed rest interval. Similarly, 35 per cent of the children did not get an off-day during the week. Nearly 33 per cent of the parents did not visit the work places of their children.

According to employers, protection against sun and rain was available to 79.9 per cent of the working children, separate rest places to 20.6 per cent, proper lighting to 88.7 per cent, medical facilities to 41.2 per cent, drinking' water and bath facilities to 79.4 per cent, protection against job hazards to 52.9 per cent, proper ventilation to 83.8 per cent, recreational facilities to 17.2 per cent and toilet facilities to 57.4 per cent. As many as 54 per cent children did not express any difficulties in the performance of their jobs. Another 88.60 per cent of the children were satisfied with the treatment accorded to them their employers and only 11.4 per cent were not satisfied.

So far as the employers satisfaction is concerned, 68.1 per cent of the employers were satisfied with the work behaviour of the children and 6.4 per cent were not satisfied.

According to the parents, none of the employed children ever met with any accident at the work place. It was further that 47.3 per cent were satisfied with their salaries, 66.6 per cent were satisfied with the length of their working hours, 13.7 per cent with the physical conditions of their work, 5.9 per cent with the facilities and benefits available, 10.2, per cent with the security to their jobs, 3.9 per cent with the treatment of their employers and 2.4 per cent with the treatment of their colleagues. Another 36 per cent of the children had to do household chores also in addition to the regular job. The study under discussion covered most of the aspects of child labour which were not found in other studies. However, due to limitations of its coverage, it could not present the acute problems, of the children working in the carpet weaving industry.

Statistics show that the total employed children in two units of the carpet industry in Srinagar, wages varied from Rs. 2 to Rs. 10 per day for weavers. The wages were Rs. 2 to Rs. 4 per day when full skill of the trade was obtained. In both the units, children were required to work for the same hours as fixed for adult workers. There 'were no special provisions for education, recreation, social security and other welfare amenities for children.

Another study was conducted to find out various dimension of child labour and occupations where children are employed. The study revealed that chronic poverty was a stronger factor than tradition in respect of child labour. The income accruing from child labour might be a pittance but it played a crucial role in saving the family from a shipwreck. Accordingly to this report, children, too in many cases had the fear of being discarded by their parents, if they failed to earn and prove that they were useful to the family. In case of parental incapacitation, children become the sole bread winners. The child workers are not organised on the lines of trade unions which can fight for their causes. Child labour is also justified on the ground that it trains the child's fingers for the required skill. This study, though conducted on an all-India basis, does not throw light on all the aspects of the problem. Moreover, there is hardly any meaningful preferences to the child labour in weaving industry.

A study (Gopunjkar 1980) on the working children in the tribal areas of Maharashtra, conducted with a view to preparing a detailed note on different types of work children did, revealed that children participated in all the occupations/jobs available to them and activities of home/family occupations and kept themselves engaged through-out the year. The child starts working from about 5 to 6 years of age. The income from the work of the child is of two types in cash and in kind. Wages in cash are governed to some extent, by the Minimum wages (amendment) Act of 1979. But in many cares labourers are paid less than what is due to them. The wages in kind are given at rates in accordance with the local practice.

Except for a few activities like Saldari, children enjoy real free life and do not feel the constraints of work. They are not overburdened and feel free in the working atmosphere. However, proper education and health facilities are not available in the country. Diseases resulting from malnourishment and unhygienic conditions and practices are very common.

Another study on child labour in Himachal Pradesh based on a sample of 438 children, 419 parents and 337 employers highlighted that most of the children worked for less than a year but those engaged in tea plantations (Kangra) were more stable. Similarly, agricultural jobs appeared to be more stable than non-agricultural jobs. As reported, 41.10 per cent children were having temporary jobs whereas 30.14 per cent had sessional jobs and 42.85 per cent of child workers lived within one kilometer from their places of work. Others had travel 1 to 5 Kilometre. They procured their jobs on the basis of personal contracts and a few through newspapers, etc. Less than half (37.59 per cent) conceded that the working children were getting better treatment at home in the form of better food, clothes, etc. A majority of the children were working for long hours, e.g., 5.26 per cent for more than 15 hours and 18.31 per cent for 10-15 hours. In Kangra 76 per cent of the children worked for 7-8 hours. About 9.07 per cent reported about the poor safety conditions; but most of them felt no problems. One complained that their work affected their lungs.

A survey report revealed the working conditions of children working in industries were unhygienic and deplorable. The work places in most cases were overcrowded, dark and dingy. The workers were poor and hard-pressed and had to work for long hours to earn their livelihood, especially in view of the prevailing low wage rates.

Another study (Singh S. 1982) on problems of social service needs of child labour in agriculture in U.P. showed that an average monthly income of the child worker had been Rs. 68, Rs. 86 which came to about Rs. 2 per day. A majority of child workers were engaged in carrying water, house watching, buying domestic things, cattle grazing, working in night on irrigation and crop watching, etc. Mean monthly income of the child workers was Rs. 60.86 and in the majority of cases, payment of wages was made directly by the employers and received directly by the child workers. Child workers were suffering from minor ailments only caused by seasonal variations though they were exposed to various serious diseases. A majority of the child workers stated that employers did not exploit them for undue work. The health of the majority of the child workers was poor and their guardians were illiterate without any technical knowledge. The entire monthly earning was between Rs. 200 to Rs. 400 only.

Another study by Sharma (1982) on the working children to examine the extent of exploitation and socio-economic background of child labour found that 56 per cent respondents had to work for 15 to 18 hours per day for earning their livelihood and 44 per cent for 10-15 hours per day. The average daily working hours was 16 hours. As for the payment of wages, 81 per cent of the respondents were receiving upto Rs. 50 per month whereas 16 per cent were paid Rs. 50 to Rs. 100 per month while only 3 per cent respondents received more than Rs. 100. The respondent contributed the maximum of their earnings to support their families.

Another study (CSR 1984) conducted on working conditions of children employed in unorganised sector in Sivakasi reported that about 53 per cent of the child workers had been working for more than two years. They worked for more than 10 hours per day in ill-ventilated places without basic amenities and rest which affected their health and retarded their physical and mental growth and development at this age. The employers were found to be very strict with the employed child workers. Thus, 11 per cent of the children stated that they were treated harshly by their employers, 88 per cent stated that they were scolded when mistakes were committed and the rest were beaten on such occasions. Primarily, this study was based on a sample of 900 child workers only. Therefore, the required information could not be verified by the parents and the employers of the child workers. Secondly, the study did not cover the problem of those children who were found to be working under carpet units.

A study (Juyal 1985) conducted on Child Labour in Varanasi at the suggestion of a Committee on Child Labour appointed by the Govt. of India, indicated that wages paid to the Child Workers varied from occupation to occupation. Similarly, the mode of payment of wages also varied from occupation to occupation. About 36.56 per cent employers said that they had child workers because they are cheaper, 27.13 per cent employed them due to easy availability. The hours of work and employers' behaviour varied from occupation to occupation and depended on the nature of activities. However, in most of the activities, the working hours ranged from 9 hours to 15 hours. The environment of 198 work units was generally clear but dirty in 73 units. Out of 258 employers, as many as 206 (80 per cent) answered that they had not ever encountered any representative of the labour laws enforcement agencies coming to the unit for an inspection. Similarly, a survey (Khatu, 1983) in carpet weaving industry in Kashmir shows that about 80,000 to one lakh children between 6-14 years of age were engaged in carpet weaving. They work about 10-12 hours a day and earn a total of Rs. 10-15 daily.

Legal Measures

So far as the implementation of various laws for the working conditions and welfare of child labour is concerned, a study, (Singh M, 1980) revealed that employers had colossal ignorance about the existing laws. Only 20 were in favour of legislation regulating employment of children. Out of 159 employers owing establishments, only 9 mentioned that officials visited their establishments for inspection purpose. Similarly, another study had found that to remove the legal binding, the employers did not enter the name of the working—children in the register maintained by them. Children disappeared as soon as the inspector arrived in the factory. The record did not reflect child employment.

Another survey report revealed that the working hour of the child workers were very lengthy in the most of the factories. It was observed in 44 cases that the daily working hours varied between 6-8 hours as against 4-1/2 hours prescribed under the factory Act, 1948. Practically, there was no much difference between working hours of the child workers and the adult workers in 30 units. Thus, the weekly hours of work for children were more than 41 in 17 plantation units. There is no uniformity of age for employment of children as prescribed under the employment of Children Act, 1938, the Plantation Labour Act, 1951, Mines Act, 1952, etc. Wages paid to children varied from state to state and also industry to industry. Analysis of results showed that the daily wages of the working children in different industries was upto Rs. 5 only. There is no statutory provision for providing educational facilities under labour laws except in the Plantation Labour Act, 1951. Welfare, recreational and other facilities were also not available to the child workers. Another study (Sharma, 1982) conducted in Hisar in Haryana revealed that the problem of child labour was on the increase inspite of legal enactments to prevent the practice. Hence, in the organised sector the problem of child labour practice is on the decrease whereas in the unorganised sector it is on the increase.

A study conducted in Sivakasi in 1984 found a big contrast in the statement given by the employers. For instance, according to match units 35 per cent to 50 per cent more than the minimum wages fixed by the Govt. was paid to the child workers while an analysis showed less than what was stated. According to another statement of the employers of the match units, almost all the child workers were provided with facilities as available under the Insurance Act, Providend Fund Act, etc., but in actual practice, these were not made available. The toilet facilities were almost non-existent in their places of work as well as in their homes. There were no recreational facilities except movies.

Indeed, it is true that apart from a number of studies conducted in both urban and rural areas in different occupations, a few Enquiry Committees, Commissions were set up by the State and the Central Govts. Economic books dealing with labour problems which are based only on secondary data and a few articles in different journals have been published. Surveys were also conducted to assess the working conditions and effects on child labour. But the reports were often casual, sketchy, impressionistic and limited in scope which did not give a comprehensive and integrated picture of the problems. Therefore, in the present study, an attempt has been made to evaluate the problems such as extent, pre-work life, situational factors motivating them to join labour force, working conditions, work effect on child labour, perception of parents, their employers, about child labour, child labour laws, its practical implementation especially in the Carpet weaving Industry in Varanasi District of Uttar Pradesh.

26

GENESIS OF CHILD LABOUR IN INDIA

Introduction

This chapter attempts to analyse from historical perspective, the multi-dimensional problem of child labour, causes of child labour and its magnitude, as demonstrated in India.

A Brief History of Child Labour in India

The phenomenon of child labour has existed in one form or another in all historical times. The problem of child labour has been prevalent in India since long and it constitutes an ugly feature of the social life of our country.

Child Labour in Ancient India

As regards Child Labour in Ancient India, it can be said that it existed in the forms of child slaves. The children of less than 8 years were purchased as slaves like articles of trade for doing low and dishonourable works. Children of slave took birth as slaves, live and died as slaves unless the master liked to release them from slavery.[1]

Kautilya pointed out that the trade of children as slaves was not prohibited in Mlechchas, because they were backward and uncivilised. On the other hand, Arya child was prohibited to become a slave.[2] Thus, though there is little evidence of the employment of children for wages, but if child slavery could be regarded as that, the existence of child labour in ancient India cannot be denied.[3]

However, later on Kautilya realised that children were not physically fit to do ignoble work. Therefore, the first reform, in the field of slavery, that Kautilya sought to bring about was to impose a ban upon the sale and purchase of children as slaves. Any person pledging or selling his own minor children or children of his relatives as slaves was heavily fined.[4]

Child Labour—The Product of Indebtedness and Industrialisation

The economic practice of child labour in India, dates back to the Industrial Revolution in the country. Since then the demand of Industry for cheap labour grow so rapidly and the poverty of the masses become so acute that the tendency to exploit child labour

among the employers increased in an unprecedented manner. As a result, children began to be employed in organised factories and other industrial establishments in large number.[5]

The British Policy of Land Settlement and Industry

In Introduction of 'Permanent Settlement' by Lord Cornwallis in March 1793 resulted in the collection of land revenue which for exceeded the volume collected in the past.[6] The small holdings and landlordism were factors which were directly responsible for increasing indebtedness of the rural population.[7] The British Land Policy made deadly assult on the Indian handicrafts. The handicrafts of ancient India, had provided jobs to the surplus population and controlled pressure on land. Industries like Saltpetre, glass-making, paper making, handlooms etc., were the worst hit by the British Policy on Industry and tariff. The industries started declining, the cities started shrinking and this led to the increasing pressure on the land. It was this policy which put the vicious circle of poverty operating in India, as it resulted in the pressure of population on the soil, mass indebtedness in rural Indian and created conditions unfavourable to the health of the rural economy. This was the story of small holdings and indebtedness, the two great evils of the agrarian economy in the modern times, resulting in the problems of child labour which continued unabated.

Thus, with the advent of the industrialisation and urbanisation, children become subject to economic and social exploitation by employers whose main consideration was maximisation of profits. This was pointed out by the Royal Commission on Labour (1929—31) which described at length the extremely unsatisfactory employment and working conditions of child workers.

Disintegration of Traditional Indian Economy

The plunder of the wealth and resources of this vast territory and the life and labour of its people and finally absolute domination for the last two centuries by the Britishers, reduced Indian people to a miserably impoverished mass. East India Company acted as the vehicle for draining India's wealth into Britain. The sweat and blood of the Indian people, reduced to money, became one of the principal sources of the primitive accumulation of capital in Britain.[8]

Wages, working hours, employment of child labour, housing and in all other spheres the extent of exploitation was appallingly excessive. But the nature of that exploitation on the Indian Labour during its germinating period and for a long time therefore, for reasons of its being under a rupacious colonial rule, was more terrifying.[9]

Exploitation of Women and Children

Fifteen to sixteen hours of working at a stretch was a most common practice during the early phase. Even the women and children as little as between five and six years of age were also inhumanly tied to the grinding wheels of the factory. The exploitation of

Indian working class was expressed chiefly in the fact both British and Indian Capitalists secured absolute surplus value. Working hours of maximum length, from dawn to dusk and often longer was the most striking indication of the brutal manner in which labour was exploited.[10]

The British Capitalists owning the jute mills of Calcutta set the record making the weavers of these mills work for 15 hours and also from 15½ to 16 hours in some cases.[11]

Indian Factory Labour Commission of 1908

The employer did not show any sense of proportion or any human consideration in exploiting female and child labour children even of such tender age as between 5 and 7 were worked most cruely everywhere.[12] Investigations conducted by the Indian Factory Labour Commission of 1908 revealed that half of the time, 30 to 40 per cent of these employed in the factories were tender aged children. The Commission while narrating the mode of work of a jute mill in Bengal stated that the workers lived three to four miles away from the mill. But when the siren struck at 3 O'clock in the night, the child labourers below 7 years of age attended the factory travelling on foot that distance of three to four miles in the darkness of night.[13] Regarding female labourers also the commission pointed out that their health break down under the strain of working whole of the night. Many of these women labourers attended the factory with suckling babies in arms. When the workers physically broke down under the strain of his labour unbearable for any human being, one set was replaced by another of new recruits just like replacing a broken cog of a wheel by a fresh one.

Brutal and Inhuman Exploitation

Dewan Chamanlal noted down a heart-rendering story about the brutal exploitation on child labour as reproduced below:

Slavery is the key note of Industrial life of India. We do not have to look to countries like Libenia or Abyssinia to find forms of child slavery. We have it here in the heart of India. Not long ago a well-known public man, in the days when he was working as a school-master, disclosed that in the house adjoining his own, a large number of children used to be drafted in everyday and that sometimes at night he used to hear their pitiable cries, which gave him no rest. He thought that the adjoining house was a school and that it was his duty as a school-master to report to the authorities regarding the crucities that were being inflicted upon innocent children. When enquiries were made, it was discovered that the adjoining house was a Lace Factory in which little children of tender age were made to work unheard of hours and it was when they were tired and when their heads bent in sleep over their work that the kind-hearted factory owner would cane with his wheep and make them up thinking that their cries and their tears were an aid to their industrial education. The name of this public man was the right Hon'ble Srinivas Sastri.

The foregoing evidence brought tot he fore the inhuman character of exploitation perpetrated upon the workers by way of abnormally long working hours in the modern capitalist factories of colonial India.

Stronger than tradition is the factor of chronic poverty responsible for the prevalence and perpetuation of child labour. Nearly half of India's population subsists below poverty line. In the country side, the distribution of land is most iniquitous. The lower 50 per cent households own only 4 per cent of the land.[14] Thus, the problem of child labour is the by-product of exploitation by a few socially and economically powerful persons trading on the misery and suffering of large number of poverty-striken labourers. Economic exploitation of child labourers is the result of the concentration of national wealth in a fewer hands who enjoy all the privileges of affluent living, condemning the under-privileged to a living of distress and despair.

Poverty and Indebtedness the Twin Vital Factors

The social customs and obligations like births, marriages, death in the families and drinking habits play an important role in compelling the poor to resort to borrowing. The money lenders use to take advantage of the deteriorating economic conditions of the poor. They advance small loans from time to time in lieu of binding them to work as agricultural labourers till the final payment of loans.[15] Indebtedness becomes an economic inevitability and child labour and exploitation a way of life to many of them. thus, one of the potent causes of child labour in India is the poverty of landless agricultural labourers. Poverty forced them to incur loans for consumption and their inability to repay the loans lead to their children to work in industrial and non-industrial occupations.

The fate of many child labourers were sealed by forces of socio-economic nature due to poverty, low-birth or degraded nature of occupation.[16] The Scheduled Tribes, the Scheduled Castes and other backward classes are the main victims of the child labour problem.

Thus, socio-economic, demographic factors like size of the family, poverty, indebtedness and illiteracy compelled the children from the poor families to participate in the labour force. With limited or total absence of skill and training, a traditional society with conservative and fatallistic outlook provides congenial ground for employment of children.

Studies on Incidence of Child Labour

The studies of Ashok Mitra, Kulshreshtha, Pandhe, Jain and Chand have attempted to identify the reasons for the large scale incidence of child labour. The large-size of the families, poverty, illiteracy of the parents, their ignorance about the importance of education as well as about the impact of labour on the health of the child, infirmities of state protection programmes, and poor implementation of universal primary education programmes are considered to be the important causes of child labour in India. Besides, the economic benefits accuring from child employment are also high as it generates an income which is higher than what they actually consume in the family.

These factors contribute the reasons for prevalence of child labour in India. In brief, the problem of child labour is undoubtedly very complex as historical, sociological political and economic considerations come into play.

Why Employer Prefer to Child Labour

Employer generally prefer children to adults because of various reasons. Children are less egoistically developed, less status conscious and they are affected by the feelings of guilt and shame. They are more agile, active and feel less tired and can put up with even more demanding works. They are more amenable for discipline, are cheaper to buy and by employing children the employers avoid many a labour problem. They are better candidates for tasks of helper in a grocer's shop or an auto-garage. They can be coaxed, admonished, pulled up and punished for defaults without jeopardising relations.[17] Thus, children are employed because they are available at cheaper wages and they are exploited because they are poor. All this explains why children are liked more for jobs.

Demographic Profile of Children in India

As per 1971 census, there were 230.3 million children in India accounting for 42.02 per cent of the total population. The distribution of child population varies from 34.76 per cent in Haryana to 46.86 per cent in Assam.

The factor behind these variations are quite numerous. It is observed that 41.86 per cent of the male population and 42.19 per cent of the female population belong to the child age-group (i.e., less than 14 years). Of the total child population, 14.94 per cent belongs to the Scheduled Caste while 6.94 per cent belongs to be Scheduled Tribes. The ratio of the Scheduled Caste/Scheduled Tribe child population to the total population is depending upon the general distribution of Scheduled Caste/Scheduled Tribe population in a particular administrative division. Of the total population 17.55 per cent in estimated to be migrant population. The percentage varies from as high as 35.11 in West Bengal to as low as 9.63 in Bihar. The analysis of migration data revealed that migration rates have been higher amongst the rural children than the urban children. The child population has increased by 27.9 per cent between 1961 and 1971. The change has been as high as 67.1 per cent in Delhi and as low as 4.87 in Pondicherry.

Child Work Force

Out of 230.3 million children in India, 10.7 million were enumerated as workers by the census in 1971 of these nearly three-fourths were males. The child workers constitute 5.95 per cent of the total work force of the country. There are 7.9 million male child workers and 2.8 million female child workers in the country. Earlier study has revealed that child work force is low is areas where literacy level is high, and where urban and industrial development is high. In rural and backward regions, or in areas where Scheduled Caste/Scheduled Tribe concentration is high, child workers also tend to be high.

The proportion of male child workers varies from 0.56 per cent in Alleppy district of Kerala to 14.1 per cent in Kalahandi district of Orissa. The proportion of female child workers varies from 1.05 per cent in Ganganagar district to 25.9 per cent in Dungarpur district (Rajasthan) during 1971.

The participation rate of children in the work force is 2.42 per cent in the urban areas while it is three times of it in the rural areas. Owing to the large rural population in the country, a high proportion of children (92.78 per cent) are engaged as workers in the rural areas. Nearly 87.23 per cent of the child workers are engaged in primary sector, that is, agriculture and allied activities. Secondary and tertiary sectors employ 6.67 per cent and 6.13 per cent respectively.

It is observed that where literacy is low, child workers is high. In Kerala, where literacy rate is the number of high (69.75 per cent), the proportion of child work force is low (1.79 per cent) and in Rajasthan where literacy is low (22.57 per cent) the proportion of child workers is high (7.29 per cent). The development of the region generally leads to the reduction of the size of the child work force.

State-wise Information on Child Labour

Extent of child labour and its magnitude has been discussed in the first chapter. It is, however, necessary to discuss in brief, the dimensions of child labour in Indian States.

According to 1981 census Jammu and Kashmir had the highest number of Child labourer that is 10.3 per cent. The figures for the other states are as follows.

Madhya Pradesh 7.9 per cent. Sikkim 6.8 per cent, Himachal Pradesh 5.8 per cent, Rajasthan 5.6 per cent, Bihar 3.7 per cent, Manipur 3.6 per cent, Tripura 3.0 per cent, West Bengal 2.8 per cent. Meghalaya 7.9 per cent, Karnataka 7.6 per cent, Maharashtra 6.4 per cent. Nagaland 5.6 per cent, Gujarat 4.7 per cent, Haryana 3.6 per cent, Punjab 3.6 per cent. Uttar Pradesh 3.0 per cent, Kerala 1.0 per cent. The figure for whole of India was 5.1 per cent. For some states the 1981 figures are not available and hence the findings of 1971 census, Andhra Pradesh 9.2 per cent. Assam 3.4 per cent, Orissa 5.3 per cent. Tamil Nadu 4.5 per cent. According to one report the trend during the last decade (1971—81) has been such that the work participation by boys of 0-14 years has decreased by 3.5 per cent while that for girls has increased by 3.2 per cent.[18] (Further statistics on child labour are given in Annexures).

Inadequacy of Actual Data

However, data relating to the extent of employment of child labour are inadequate. The number of children reported as employed varies greatly from the number actually at work. Besides, 'here are several lacunae in the statistics regarding the estimation of child labour. Some of these defects are the man-power statistics very often do not include persons under 15 years and such statistics take into account only children with permanent or regular jobs. A large proportion of them are in fact, employed in casual work for irregular time-periods or as part of family labour under contract or like arrangements. Moreover, child labourers employed in unorganised industries and commercial establishments are not included in such statistics.

Types of Child Labour

The number and types of occupations in which children are being employed in endless and includes almost every aspect of human work and life. Generally, children are employed in the argicultural sector helping in agricultural operations like sowing, weeding, harvesting and threshing. Their activities also include looking after animals, collecting firewoods, carrying water, spreading manure and fertilisers in the farm land. In urban areas, they are engaged in more diversified activities such as loading-unloading hawking, looking after parked vehicles, shoe-shining. Besides, they are also employed as helpers in tea shops and auto-repair shops or are engaged as domestic servants, house and road construction works, brick-kiln, stone breaking, carpet-weaving, beedi making, match making etc. Quite a large number of child labour is in existence in unorganised sector including small scale and cottage industries viz., handlooms weaving, leather tannery, glass bangles, mat-making, tailoring pottery, fireworks.[19]

Spectrum of Child Labour in Indian Industries

The labour investigation committee (1946) remarked that "one black spot of labour conditions in India is illegal employment of children in certain industries."[20]

Some case studies on the plight of child labour by social workers and researchers have contributed a lot for the raising consciousness about the problem. The more horrible features of exploitation of child labour are found in the match-box industry and printing presses of Sivakasi (Tamil Nadu) lead mines and state pencil factories of Mandsaur (Madhya Pradesh), glass factories of Ferozabad (Uttar Pradesh), the carpet industry in Mirzapur-Bhadohi (Uttar Pradesh).

The Match-Box Industry in Sivakasi (Tamil Nadu)

In recent years, several write ups in news papers and periodicals have focussed light on the deplorable position of child labour employed in the match and fireworks industry in Sivakasi. The Gurupadaswamy Committee (1979) had estimated about 50,000 child labourers employed in Sivakasi area. In these match factories, child workers in the age group of 5 to 15 work about 12 hours in a day and receive wages in the range of Rs. 1 to 8. Because, the wages are determined on the basis of piece rates, the child workers work feverishly in time available to them to show the maximum output. This results in a complete neglect of their own requirements and many of the children were found rather frail and anaeomic in their looks. There was no medical assistance available to them, and children even in sick conditions had no option except to sit in the factory and work on box making, frame filling, labelling and band role pasting. In spite of their best efforts for the day, their return was very meagre one.

Kanchipuram Handloom Weaving

In the state of Tamil Nadu, in Kanchipuram a large number of children in the age group of 7 to 14 are working on looms. It was pointed out that, because of their nimble fingers, they were particularly deft in weaving designs and borders. Most of them had never been to school. They were getting a wave between Rs. 60 and 100 per month. Some of the very young children were being paid as low as Rs. 15 per month.[21] In some cases, it was also observed that children had been pledged into work by the guardians on a long term basis.

The Carpet Industry in Mirzapur-Bhadohi (U.P.)

One of the largest employers of children is the carpet-weaving industry. In Kashmir, this sector employs more than one million children. The carpet industry utilises child labour in Bhadohi Mirzapur, Allahabad and Varanasi. The carpet industry has only increased oppression and reinforced the feudalistic structure of social relations.[22] Dr. B.N. Juyal has observed, "Indulging in physical violence and other abuses on child labour becomes a matter of routine and ordinary occurrences which may not disturb anybody.[23]

At a rough estimate, 1.5 lakh children work in the carpet industry and they do the major part of the work.[24] The Industry could not survive without the children. A carpet is not woven; it is knotted and each individual knot has to be made by hand. Eighty per cent of the knotting work is done by children under the age of sixteen. They work long hours without protest, are easily coerced and will also do a lot of unpaid work for the owner willingly. The difference in the earnings of a weaver boy and the final seller tells the whole story. A square yard of carpet which a boy may weave in a day can sell for anything between Rs. 100-400 in the export market. For that, the boy who actually made it, is paid the princely sum of Rs. 5-10. And from it is loom owner will deduct the expense of food, medicines and clothes.[25]

Inhuman Exploitation

Dr. Juyal has studied the inhuman exploitation inflicted upon child labourers and pointed out, "The Child Labourers rescued in the Famous Bilwaria incident bore visible marks of physical torture, such as branching with hot iron, bruises and lathi blows. They were severely beaten with iron rods if they were slow at work, made mistakes in weaving, asked for adequate food, or even if they went to case themselves without the master's permission. At night, they were all locked up in a small room. This happened to them daily. But once they were caught in the act of escaping, their feet were fied together and they were slung upside down from the branch of a tree and then, to "Properly" drive the lesson home, they were branded with hot irons."[26]

It has been found that about 50 per cent of child labourers are anaemic and/or suffering from the worst infestation. The evil consequences of remaining cramped in damp pit looms, resulting in boils, the swelling of the lower limbs and aching joints, etc. have been frequently observed.

The Bidi-Rolling Industry in Madhya Pradesh

The bidi-rolling industry is located at various places but in Madhya Pradesh alone it employs about 2 lakh children. In such industries, child workers roll bidies and assist the adult workers by cleaning and cutting the leaf and closing the ends. Employers pay the children much less than the adults on the pretext that the products do not come upto the required standard of quality. There was sufficient indication to suspect a high incidence of tuberculosis among the bidi workers and this, was due to starting work at a tender age, very long hours of work.[26]

The Glass Bangle Industry in Ferozabad

The glass industry is another important child employer. Children are employed in Jurai (joining of ends), Chhatai (Sorting), Katai (engraving of different patterns with the help of abrasive wheels), Pakai (heating) and then in counting and packing. The decoration of bangles with hill (liquid gold) is done by girls and women. The factories run for about 8 months in the year and work only at night. In Ferozabad alone, there are about 250 such factories which employ about 60,000 children out of a total labour force of 1 lakh.[28] Many of these children have to stand about 4 feet away from furnaces and ovens with temperatures as high as 800-1200 F. Seven out of 10 factories have no first-aid box. The cases of asthma and bronchitis are many. Workers suffer from various eye diseases. Ferozabad ranks first as far as tuberculosis is concerned.

Pottery Industry in Khurja

In Khurja (Uttar Pradesh) out of the 20,000 pottery workers, about 50,000 are children below the age of 14. Here, children carry lamps of clay for cutting and moulding. They clay is fitted in the moulds and then taken out into the open for drying. They then return with empty moulds. All this work is done at a very fast pace as the employer aims at a rapid output with the maximum profit. The total weight to be carried per trip is about 8 kgs. Thus in his 8 hours of work a child has to reach a distance of virtually 5 kms with this load, thus making about 1000 trips.[29] Despite such harsh and hard work, the child workers are labelled as mere helpers and therefore, paid a negligible amount of money.

Zari Making Industry in Lucknow

Children are also employed in the zari-making and embroidery industry. About 7000 child workers in the age group 8-15 were employed in Lucknow with an average monthly Rs. 50 payment towards waves.[30] They sit and work in over-crowded rooms with poor lighting and ventilation. Many of them suffer from eye diseases.

Stone-polishing Industry in Jaipur

The precious stone-polishing industry of Jaipur employs 10,000 children, all of whom work in slums or miserable hovels. The work is done through middle-men who procure children for a pittance.

Similarly, in the diamond-polishing industry of Surat, the child workers develops eye defects very soon. They are ruthlessly retrenched with the first early signs of eye fatigue. Many are jobless in their teens.

A Varanasi Case Study

The Gandhian Institute of Studies did a study of the magnitude and employment pattern of child labour in the Varanasi City area only.

The study was focussed on the unorganised sector. With regard to the magnitude of the problem of child labour, taking the 1971 census as the norm (which is 4.27 per cent of the total workers in the Varanasi Municipal Corporation area), it appeared to be many times higher. The activity-wise survey revealed that the proportion of child workers was around 40 per cent or even more in some prominent activities, namely food products, repair services, silk products and construction, specifically sand filling from the river bed.[31]

Child Labour in Calcutta

It is Calcutta and its surroundings that can safely claim having the biggest contingent of teen-age workers 90 per cent of the children in Calcutta hail from different rural districts, 30 per cent of these children come from Midnapur alone, with Howrah occupying the second position.[32] There is also a sizeable migration from Bihar, Orissa and Uttar Pradesh. Agricultural Labour families, owning a bit of land or absolutely landless, are migrating to the cities in large numbers.

According to physicians' estimate, 100 per cent of the City's child workers suffer from Vitamin deficiencies, 52 per cent from worm infections, 32 per cent from skin diseases, 22 per cent from eye complaints, 23 per cent from asthma and respiratory infections and quite a good number from T.B. and lung cancer.[33]

Child Labour in the Unorganised Sectors of Bombay

Thousands of children work like robots in the various hotels and restaurants in Bombay despite the civic fathers' pretence that child labour does not exist in their dream city. With an estimated 50,000 of the 3 lakh people employed in the City's nearly 12,000 food shops of various nature, Bombay has the largest number of working children among the Indian Cities, next only to Calcutta.[34] A team of the All India Guild of Law Graduates and the Bombay Labour Union, that jointly conducted a survey in the recent past, found a majority of the kids belonging to the migrant families hailing from the Souther States, for whom 12 to 13 hours labour against a monthly pittance of Rs. 100 to Rs. 150 is the order of the day.[35] A study made by Kumar Ketkar in 1977 reveals that children and women work beyond 12 hours, in filthy working conditions, all safety measures being ignored, not to speak of bonus or exgratia payments.[36] Thus, child labour is essentially a problem of poor and destitute families, where parents cannot afford the education of their children. It is not uncommon to find especially in the urban areas, that families below the poverty line depend on the earnings of their children. Moreover, in the majority of cases, there is no liability on the part of the employer to give any service benefits such as provident fund, gratuity, leave, promotion and annual increments.[37]

A Survey of Employed Children in Bombay

A recent survey of employed children in Bombay has been able to identify the following reasons :

(*i*) they are quick and efficient, 20.5 per cent;
(*ii*) they are amenable to discipline, 12.6 per cent;
(*iii*) they are better suited for some type of jobs, 12.6 per cent;
(*iv*) their plight has greater sentimental appeal, 30.5 per cent; and
(*v*) others (who are cheap, 9.3 per cent, and honest, 1.9 per cent) 23.8 per cent.[38]

In urban areas the reasons advocated for child labour are migration, urbanisation, industrialisation etc. The circumstances under which a child has to start working are :

(*i*) economic compulsion, 40.1 per cent;
(*ii*) the child was idle and doing nothing, 17.5 per cent; had to leave school; 16.3 per cent; and
(*iii*) others, 11.5 per·cent.[39]

There is a definite co-relation between poverty and child labour, between the school drop-out rate and the increase in the numbers of the children employed.[40] It has been found that the employers with impunity violate the laws meant to protect children from the various hazardous jobs. The children are neither paid adequate wages nor provided healthy working conditions.[41]

Child Labour in Delhi

There are over 2.5 lakh of child workers on the Capital's streets who have to work for long hours just for two square meals a day. From Bihar, Uttar Pradesh, Rajasthan and Madhya Pradesh about 15-20 of them arrive in the Capital each day in search of jobs.[42] A majority of these children sleep on the pavements near the New Delhi and Old Delhi railway stations, the Inter-State Bus Terminus, Jama Masjid, Connaught Place and the Walled City areas. Sexual harassment is the major problem among girls. A large number of children are sent from the Uttar Pradesh villages by their parents during weekends to work in Delhi. Those who join dhabas and shops are found to be exploited most, as they have to work for 14 to 16 hours daily and due to the accommodation and food provided by the owners, such children are not in a position to bargain for better wages.[43].

Study by Dr. Nangia

A recent study by Dr. Parveen Nangia of the Jawaharlal Nehru University reveals that there are over 50,000 children in the Capital who live on the streets.[44] "Their condition is more pathetic than that of those working in dhabas and other places, as they don't even have a roof over their heads and are left to the mercy of the weather gods and anti-social elements." Dr. Nangia observes,"....adults have lured these children into gambling, knowing well that they are bound to lose consistently, to pocket their little earnings." A recent estimate in Delhi reveals that there are no less than 60,000 children who are employed in small eating houses.

According to a study on working children in urban Delhi made in 1977, the majority of the children employed in the dhabas of Delhi come from Bihar and Uttar Pradesh. They work for more than 12 hours a day and get Rs. 26 to Rs. 50 a month, and free board and lodging.[45]

There are between 2,00,000 and 3,00,000 registered shops and establishments in Delhi according to the Labour Commissioner of the Delhi Administration. But they are Categorised'.[46]

Child Pledging in Tamilnadu

There are innumerable cases where unfortunate children are being exploited both by their parents and the agents for their own selfish needs. These innocent little ones an being treated like cattle, pledged and mortgaged at the will of their masters. In their case, the masters are the parents and, later, the agents. In the society of around one lakh people subsiding on the Bidi Industry located mainly in the district of Vellore and its suburbs. The deep-rooted traditons and customs among bidi workers together with the strong and cut culture of this community has made child pledging an accepted practice. The ironical fact is that they perceive the agents as their saviours who provide work to their children and the subsequent meal to the family. But in reality children are abused, pledged, redeemed and repledged to different agents for a higher amount from the agents.

In the bidi industry of Vellore, child pledging has become an organised trade where the term 'Pledging' refers to the bondage of children by their parents to an employer or his agent against a loan on an agreement, written or oral, that the child would work till the repayment of the debt. The term 'Child' means the son or daughter of a migrant who has not completed 15 years of age involved in bidi rolling. Due to continuous drought, economic compulsions or death of the main head earner, the landless labourers were forced to take up employment elsewhere, preferably in the Bidi industry since the whole family could be employed by it. The migrant families became squatters on the road side or any other 'Promoke' land in these villages. Except their children, they had nothing at hand to rely upon. As a last resort, to feed themselves they preferred to pledge their children for survival.

A study reveals about the ill-treatment and the stories of exploitation meted out to these children, the pledged children work 12 hours a day and are paid a daily sum of Rs. 1 to Rs. 4, depending upon the amount pledged, if the contractual obligations are not violated by the child.[47] It was reported that the parents have to provide another family member to replace the pledged boy. The children have no recreation, no freedom and no basic human rights. They are like caged birds. Their only world is their work spot and their home which is place only to sleep. At an early stage in their lives, they have frustrations resulting in a high rate of alcohclism and smoking.

They study further reveals that excessive hours of work and over exertion results in back pain, hip pain and nervous problems among the pledged children. Their normal growth is shunted and the tobacco strack inside their nails causes infection and pain.

Child Bonded Labourers in Other States

There are reports about child bonded labour in Andhra Pradesh especially in the Medak district. All the villages in Sidipet, Medak and Gogipet Taluqs that have been surveyed had child labourers chained by leand lords and money lenders. A substantial number of child bonded labourers in every village without exception has been manifested. In some villages of the Medak district, land lords were found thriving upon child labourers, known as Jute Gadus. It has been noticed that once a jute gadu (child bonded labourer) complained to the police inspector about the cruelties committed against him by his master. He was beaten up and thrown out of the police station.[48] It is obvious that such illegal actions made the child labourers silent and they did not dare to approach any government agency or raise their voice against their masters.

It is a deplorable fact that the annual wage for a child bonded labour on the verge of starvation and aged between 7-15, ranges between Rs. 25 and Rs. 250. In some parts of Madhya Pradesh[49] and Bihar, the situation is even more pitiable. In these areas, the annual wage ranges between Rs. 70 and Rs. 175 for the same age group.

Several studies indicate that the plight of working children has some relationship with Industrial capitalism. The gradual shift to cash crops and the growing number of landless labourers also adds to the exploitation of child labour.[50]

Many of the children are exploited by being trapped in pilferage, the blackmarketing of cinema tickets, the selling of alcohol, gambling and the life.[51] In riots, bus and vehicle burning, harassment of women in buses and lonely places, and in bank robberies, criminal elements make use of this frustrated youth power, while political parties use them for their dirty works departments'. Mafia elements in the Bengal Coal Fields, Matka elements in the Bombay slums and smugglers on the Punjab Circuit are only some constituents of a manpower group spawned from the harsh realities of neglected childhood. For the child who could not tolerate abundonment, who grew up with no habit of responsibility or concern for others, drifting into the easiest path available to him, stress and fear have inevitably created the anti-social personality.[52]

The children inteviewed in the carpet industry in the Mirzapur-Badoli area, or in the matchworks in Sivakasi and countless other industrial centres that exploit child labour, demonstrate how they have cheerfully accepted abysonal working conditions, long hours of work and health hazards. They have nowhere to sleep, no education or opportunity to train for employment as adults. Many such children are bonded and slave on year after year as the family's continuing poverty cannot release them.

A countless number of children are working in the unorganised and self-employed sectors in towns as servants and in machine-tools and repair shops. A significant proportion of child labourers are found in the handloom industry of Kashmir, in the private mines of Meghalaya, in the Sugar factory of Lucknow, in the fish industries of Kerala, in the tea gardens and industries of Assam and in innumerable unorganised industries.

The aforesaid analysis present a broad description of the nature and extent of child labour found in India. The study brings into light the fact that children are often exploited and underpaid and made to work for long hours. Child Labourers must be protected from inhuman exploitation and from hazardous working conditions which threaten their physical and mental development.

NOTES

1. Kulshreshtha, J.C. *Child Labour in India*, Ashish Publishing House, New Delhi, 1978, p. 49.
2. *Ibid.*
3. Saran, K.M.
4. *Ibid.*, p. 27.
5. Bhagoliwala, T.N. (Dr.), *'Economics of Labour and Industrial Relations'*, Chapter-31, Sahitya Bhavan, Agra, 1982, p. 196.
6. Raya Choudhary, S.C. *'Social Cultural and Economic History of India'* (Modern Times), Surjeet Publications, Delhi, 1978, p. 50.
7. *Ibid.*, p. 53.
8. Sen Sukomal, *Working Class of India, History of Emergence and Movement* (1830-1970), K.P. Bagchi and Company, 1977, p. 18.
9. *Ibid.*, p. 37.
10. *Ibid.*
11. Report of the Indian Factory Labour Commission, 1908, Vol. I, pp. 6, 7, 11.
12. Sen, Sukomal *Op. Cit.* p. 40.
13. *Ibid.*
14. Report of the Committee on Child Labour (Gurupadaswamy Committee) Ministry of Labour, Government of India, December, 1979, p. 10.
15. Tripathy, S.N. (Dr), *Bonded Labour in India*, Discovery Publishing House, New Delhi, p. 32.
16. Lorenzo, A.M., *'Agricultural Conditions in Northern India'*, New Book Company Ltd., Bombay, p. 58.
17. Report of the Committe on Child Labour (Gurupadaswamy Committee) *Op. cit.*, p. 11.
18. Khan, A.M. (Dr), 'Child Labour, Causes and Remedy', *Yojana*, December 16-31, 1988, p. 18.
19. Report of Child Labour in Indian Industries Labour Bureau, Ministry of Labour, Government of India, Simla, p. 7.
20. Bhuguliwala, T.N. (Dr), *op. cit.* Chapter 31, p. 197.

21. *Report of the Committee on Child Labour (Gurupadaswamy Committee) op. cit.* p. 19.
22. Juyal, B.N. (Dr), *'Child Labour and Exploitation in the Carpet Industry'*, Indian Social Institute, New Delhi, p. 33.
23. *Ibid.*, p. 43.
24. *The Indian Express*, September 4, 1988.
25. *Ibid.*
26. Juyal, B.N. (Dr), Child Labour and Exploitation in Carpet Industry, *op. cit.*, p. 43.
27. Punekar, S.D., 'Child Labour in Unorganised Industries'. Rural Vocation paper presented at the National Seminar on the Exployment of Children in India, New Delhi, November 25-28, 1975.
28. Khan, A.M. (Dr), *op. cit.*, p. 18.
29. *Ibid.*
30. Report of the Committee on Child Labour (Gurupadaswamy Committee) *op. cit.*, p. 18.
31. Juyal, B.N. (Dr), Kumari Sudarshan Chandola, L.M. 'Child Labour : The twice exploited' Gandhian Institute of Studies, Varanasi, 1985.
32. Sinha, Swapan Kumar, 'A Profile of Child Labour in Calcutta' *Social Welfare*, Vol. XXXII, November-December, 1985, p. 24.
33. Mukhopadhyaya, Ashim, 'Children Without Childhood', *Frontier*, June 24, 1989, p. 23.
34. *Ibid.*, p. 14.
35. *Ibid.*
36. Ketkar, Kumar (1977) 'Bombay Workers up in Arms', *Economic Times*, 26 May, 1977.
37. Seal, K.C., *'Profile of the Child in India'* Ministry of Social Welfare, Government of India, New Delhi, 1980, p. 181.
38. *'Working Children in Bombay'*, National Institute of Public Cooperation and Child Development, New Delhi, 1978, p. 110.
39. *Ibid.*
40. Nigam, Sevanti, Child Labour and Education, *Voluntary Action*, Vol. 24, No. 7, February 1982, pp. 286-287.
41. Gangrade, K.D Gathia, J.A. (edited), *'Women and Child Workers in Unorganised Sector'*. Concept Publishing Company, New Delhi, 1983, p. 60.
42. 'They are Nobody's Children'. *NIPCCD News letter*, May-June 1988, p. 5.
43. *Ibid.*
44. *Ibid.*
45. Gathia, J.A., 'Child Workers in the Informal Sector' in *Women and Child Workers in Unorganised Sector* (1983). Concept Publishing Company, New Delhi, p. 77.
46. *Ibid.*
47. Panwar, Brijendra Singh, 'Pledged for Rs. 100, *Free Press Journal*, September 1988, p. 11.
48. The Dark World of 'Jeeta Gadus', National Labour Institute Bulletin, December 1977, p. 543.
49. *Ibid.*, p. 544.
50. Marla and Mahajan, *'Bonded Labour'*, 1981
51. Sinha, Swapan Kumar, *op. cit.*, p. 24.
52. Baig, Tara Ali, 'The Child: The Trauma of a Change' *Social Welfare*, August 1988, pp. 7 and 39.

27

FEATURES OF CHILD LABOUR

Introduction

This chapter makes an attempt to explore the socio-economic and historical factors responsible for child labour in Orissa and particularly in the tribal and backward district of Phulbani.

Genesis and Evolution of the Problem

Orissa became a separate state on 1st April, 1936. Before that, portions of the state had been tagged to the erstwhile Indian Provinces of Madras, Central Provinces, Bengal and Bihar from time to time according to the administrative convenience of the East India Company and the Crown. A number of princely states merged with the newly created Orissa state in 1948.

In fact, the origin of the child labour problem is deep-rooted in the socio-economic and historical factors that prevailed during the 19th Century and the early 20th Century Orissa.

Maratha Misrule and Rural Indebtedness

In the Orissa economy rural indebtedness became an imperative necessity not because of the advent of British rule but because of the Maratha misrule between 1751 and 1803 which destroyed the saving capacity of the peasant holding.[1] The process was only accelerated by the early British rule. The role of village money lenders in the peasant economy of Orissa was indispensable in view of the non-existence of any other credit agencies which could provide the loans vitally necessary for the agricultural process in the way they did.[2]

The Mahalwari land system gave rise to many evils in the agrarian system in Orissa after 1837. It also produced the new elements of landlordism which had been non-existent since 1818. From an organic part of the social and political structure of rural Orissa, the landed proprietors, were transformed into an alien rent collecting agency. They paid regular land taxes to the colonial government and purchased imported colonial goods (which supported the foreign manufacturers but not the rural industries). The rural credit net-work also developed and intensified its exploitation in response to the increasing dependence of ryits on money lenders who were dependent on the urban Mahajans and indigenous banking houses.[3]

Judicial Machinery and Indebtedness

The new judicial regulation and machinery for setting land disputes, which gave birth to a class for urban labourers, drained away the agrarian surplus income to the towns. Moreover, if the evidence collected in Hunter's Statistical Accounts is to be relied upon, it appears proper that in many cases rents rose faster than prices in the 19th century.[4]

In the second half of the 19th Century the deepening crisis in the agrarian economy of Orissa made the position of the cultivators still more deplorable. In the absence of rapid industrialization, the unchanged ratio of the rural-urban population, the urban market for agricultural products remained static. Orissa throughout the century remained predominantly rural. Its expanding grain trade was constrained by the poverty of the villagers. It was this under development of the rural economy of Orissa throughout the 19th century which exposed the exploitative nature of the British Raj and ultimaterly led to Child labour problem.

Princely States of Orissa

Orissa formed a Division in the province of Bengal from 1803 to 1912 and in the province of Bihar and Orissa from 1912 to 1936. The separate province of Orissa came into being on 1st April, 1936.

Upto 1905, Orissa mainly consisted of the three districts of Balasore, Cuttack and Puri. As a result of the language agitation in the district of Sambalpur, which was hitherto with Central Provinces it was merged with Orissa in 1905. The Utakal Union Movement led to the amalgamation of the Koraput and Ganjam districts included till then within Madras Presidency, with Orissa in 1936. Thus Orissa came to contain the six districts, of Cuttack, Puri, Balasore, Sambalpur, Ganjam and Koraput.

Upto 1940, there were nineteen princely states of Orisa. Banki and Angul were annexed to British Orissa in 1840 and 1847 respectively.[5] Then onwards Angul and Banki remained under the direct administration of the British. The princely states, also known as Tributary Mahals and formerely 19 in number, got reduced to 17. They were: Athgarh, Athmallik, Baud, Baramba, Daspalla, Dhenkanal, Hindole, Khandpara, Keonjhar, Mayurbhanj, Narsinghpur, Nayagarh, Nilgiri, Patlahera, Talcher, Tigiria and Ranpur. In 1905, five Orissa speaking states of Central Provinces, i.e, Patna, Kalahandi, Sonepur, Rairakhol and Bamra and two Orissa speaking states of Chhotanagpur, i.e, Gangpur and Bonai were transferred to the Orissa Division. There were still two other Oriya states namely: Saraikella and Kharswan, which were still left with the commissioner of Chhotanagpur. In 1916, they were transferred to Orissa Division. Thus the number of the princely states of Orissa rose to 26. All these Orissa-speaking states, except Saraikella and Kharswan, were integrated with the province of Orissa in 1948-49.[6] These two states were merged with the province of Bihar in 1948. The princely states referred to by the

British as tributary or feudatory states, were ruled indirectly by the British through the Princes themselves. They were completely subordinate to the British Authorities. The history of the 19th century Orissa of the Princely states significantly responsible for the evils of Child labour and exploitation.

Growing Poverty and Indebtedness

The exploitative land revenue policy of the British caused untold sufferings to the poor peasants of Orissa under the Princely states. The exploitation of the Zamindars and the exactions of the Zamindari amalas led to the steady impoverishment of the peasantry of Orissa. Their improverished condition became a great obstacle in the way of their agricultural pursuits.[7]

Decay of Industries

The decay of traditional industries along with illegal and exorbitant Land Revenue contributed to the growth of poverty and the consequently, to the problem of child labour. The importation of foreign goods led to the decay of traditional industries like weaving, spinning, and salt manufacture finally stopped in 1899-1900; it has been a source of income and employment to a large number of people.[8] Spinning, weaving and salt making were alternative and supplementary sources of income but the British policy was detrimental to such indigenous industries. In fact, thousands of rural artisans lost their traditional livelihood and become agricultural labourers or petty tenants holding tiny plots. This added to the general pressure on the land. The increasing pressure on agriculture was one of the major causes of the extreme poverty and of the growth of child labour under the British rule.

The exploitation of the distressed peasants by the money lenders was a paramount cause of the rapid impoverishment of Oriya peasants. More often, the inability to pay revenue drove the peasant to borrow money at high rates of interest from the money lender. The money lender charged high rates of interest and, through cunning and deceitful measures, such as false accounting, forged signatures and making the debtor sign for larger amounts than he had borrowed, got the peasants deeper and deeper into debt till he parted with his land. Thus, landless poverty-stricken farmers sent their children to work for a bare survival.

The Historical Factors Responsible for Child Labour

Gradually, the cultivators sank deeper and deeper into the hands of money lenders, merchants, rich peasants and other moneyed classes. It was also found that the tenants lost their tenancy rights and were ejected from the land or became the subtenants of the money lender.[9]

The process of the transfer of land from the cultivators was intensified during the periods of scarcity and famine. The Oriya peasants hardly had any savings for critical times and whenever crop failed he fell back upon the money lender not only to pay the land revenue but also to feed himself and his family under this exploitative background, the problem of child labour was the sequel. The poverty and indebtedness of the people reached its omega in a series of famines which ravaged all parts of Orissa during 1866-1947.

The plight of agricultural labourers and child labourers was horrible during the British rule in Orissa. The women and children of the family could obtain small earnings from occasional employment in the fields in busy seasons, and from collecting jungle roots, fruits and fuel.[10]

Thus, the princely rule had a terrible economic impact on the people of the state which ultimately compelled the landless labourers and their children to toil hard and to fight tooth and nail for mere survival.

Peasant's Discontent

The growing poverty of the people made them desperate and led them to revolt several times against the oppressive feudal system. Several factors were attributed to the growth of peasant's discontent in the Orissa State. The factors like the maladministration of the chiefs, the overassessment of land revenue, heavy taxation, the enforcement of arbitrary laws, the imposition of Bethi and Begari, the collection of illegal dues like magan and rasad led to the wide-spread discontent among the peasants of the states, which ultimately burst forth in the form of open revolts.[11] Child labour was the product of these oppressive and exploitative factors mainly due to British maladministration.

Child Labour in the Tribal Districts of Koraput, Kalahandi, Bolangir and Phulbani

It was during the British rule in Orissa that the introduction of modern economy into the tribal area produced the back wash effects of exploitation and land alienation by traders and money lenders. The introduction of land settlement by the British rulers similarly helped the increase of the non-tribal population, which again led to the increasing alienation of tribal lands by them. The traditional power, position and authority of the Khand leaders tended to decline in proportion to the prosperity of the non-tribal settlers. Thus, the unequal distribution of the land holdings favoured the interest of the non-tribals who emerged as prosperous peasants and powerful money-lenders. This inturn, forced the landless tribals to employ their children for a bare subsistence.[12]

Land Alienation and Poverty in Koraput

The relative ignorance of the hill people and the craftiness of the money lenders who settled in Koraput was the vital factor of their economic misery. By the process of mortgage and sale, the non-tribals took possession of most of the fertile land belonging to the tribals. The law prohibiting the transfer of land from the hill tribe to the non-tribals came much latter. The tribals had very little opportunity left for gainful employment. Heavy expenses on account of social ceremonies and illness made men to fall into the hands of the money lenders who advanced money at a very high rate of interest.[13] The district of Koraput is inhabited mostly by the scheduled tribes and backward classes with distressed economic conditions. Indebtedness has been a common feature with them. They frequently borrow at usurious rates to buy the necessaries. Standing crops are pledged to the money lenders in advance. They are thereby deprived of a fair price for their produce.[14]

Thus, the indebtedness of the tribals and land alienation by non-tribals led to untold misery and poverty and caused the problem of child labour in Koraput.

Child Labour in Bolangir

In the Bolangir district, the exploitation of tribal agricultural labourers is a common feature in Patnagarh because of the low income and seasonal employment of such labourers. The economic plight drives them almost to the point of starvation, leading them to pledge the services of their family including children to the money lenders.[15] Recent reports reveal that the prevailing drought condition has affected a population of about 14 lakh, including 5 lakh belonging to scheduled tribes and scheduled castes.[16] Reports of starvation deaths in the affected areas are pouring in and the affected people have started migrating to the neighbouring states in search of work. Thus, failure of crop is an important factor which plays a havoc in the lives of the tribals and causes the acute problem of child labour.

Incidence of Poverty in Kalahandi

One of the three most backward districts of Orissa is Kalahandi with heavy concentration of tribal population. According to the 1971 Agricultural census, Kalahandi is extremely poor with about 46 per cent of cultivating households. About 35 per cent of the workers of the district belonged to the category of agricultural labourers in 1981, compared to the state average of 27 per cent. The incidence of poverty is the highest among the scheduled tribes and scheduled castes, which constitute 47 per cent of the district population.[17]

Heavy Land Revenue During British Rule in Kalahandi

The survey reports and recorded evidence exhibit the continuous increase in the revenue collected from the peasantry and the tribal people of Kalahandi during the British period. The first summary settlement was introduced in the district as early as in 1833 followed by the second in 1888. The first and the second regular settlement had been introduced in 1904-1905 and in 1911-1912 respectively. During these settlements, land revenue was excessively enhanced and that gave a heavy blow to the tribal people of Kalahandi leading to the perpetuation of poverty. The last British settlement was made in 1946 which has resulted in a rise in the revenue by 62 per cent, from Rs. 3 lakhs during the 1922-23 settlement to about Rs. 5 lakhs in 1946.[18] Excessive high land revenue left nothing surplus with the tribal-dominated population of Kalahandi, leading to their indebtedness and forcing them into the army of unskilled labourers and child labourers. Landless agricultural labourers in search of daily wages are available in large numbers in the rural areas of the Kalahandi district.[19]

Sale of Children in Kalahandi

The economic plight often forces the landless labour to sell their children during the days of distress. In the Junagarh block of Kalahandi, it was observed that boys and girls were purchased at a tender age by rich landlords. The services of these children were utilised till the attainment of their adolescence; in agricultural and non-agricultural work, and then they were married off by the purchasers. With the marriage, the contract of service used to cease. Abject poverty and social disabilities were responsible for such sale of children. Landless labourers with big families, when unable to make both ends meet, are forced to sell their children to rich persons in the neighbourhood. It was a common custom among the rich Gountias in the Junagarh locality of the Kalahandi district, to present a purchased girl to their daughters at the time of their marriage as a part of the dowry.[20] After independence, with the amalgamation of the princely states of Kalahandi with Orissa, the sale/purchase of children was declared illegal. However, reports of severe drought, exploitation of tribal labourers and the sale of their children and the high incidence of child labour, figure in news paper even to-day.[21] The sale of female child labour and children in the Khariarh block during April 1985 for a meagre sum of Rs. 40 reveals tale of poverty and starvation.[22]

Recurring Droughts in Kalahandi

The drought situation played havoc in the district of Kalahandi in the different phases of the 20th century. Shortage and irregular rainfall in the hilly regions were some of the natural factors responsible for severe droughts experienced during the years 1954-55, 1964-66 and 1985-86. Recent reports reveal that during 1988-89 crop loss in Kalahandi has affected about 13.10 lakh people, of whom the scheduled castes and scheduled tribes account for about 6 lakh.[23] In other words, 47 per cent of the total affected population of the district are mainly tribals and Harijans who are living below the poverty line. Under such precarious conditions of drought, uncertain rainfall, indebtedness and landlessness, the problem of child labour is the outcome.

Child Labour in Phulbani

The district of Phulbani represents a backward region in the state of Orissa. The concentration of the tribal population is high in the district of Phulbani (38.9 per cent) as per 1981 census report. The poverty-striken population, the marginal farmers, landless labourers and the tribals constitute the vast majority of the population of the district. Exploitation and lack of employment opportunities are the realities of everyday life for the bulk of the tribals of Phulbani.

The System of Headmanship

The village headman, known as the 'PADHAN', the Sarbarakar and the Gaontia had occupied a distinctive place in the princely states. Not only did they form an elitist background for the rulers but they also served as the only link between the state and tenants (individual holders of the land assessed for rent). Since the earliest times, the village was taken as the unit of revenue administration and the headman used to remain in charge of rent collection and to discharge all his duties in respect of the management of the village.[24]

These muthaheads were all Oriyas. They owened extensive lands which the Adivasis had to cultivate free of remuneration on Bethi or the forced labour system[25] The income of these muthaheads consisted partly of mamools (Customary Requisites) of money and of kind and partly of Inam lands or revenue free lands.[26]

The Mamool System

In the Khond Agency, the mamools were not very exorbitant but towards the South, mamools went an increasing in quantity and value till almost nothing was left to the Adivasi for himself. Alongwith the payments listed among mamools and the articles that went under the name, there was free service to be rendered by the Adivasis to the Mutha-head and his subordinates. Besides, the hill-tribe people were required to maintain roads, construct buildings and carry the luggage of the officers on tour on payment for below the normal. This was known as the Bethi system. On the whole, the system of mamools and Bethi brought untold sufferings to the tribals.

Most of the people of the Agency Areas were tribals like Khonds and Savars. Both hill officials known as Muthaheads and the people of the plains also exploited them in numerous ways. This was the primary cause of the rapid improverishment of the tribal peasantry.[27]

The extreme poverty compelled many tribals to sell or mortgage their lands to the people of the plains. To put a stop to such alienation, the Agency Tracts Interests and Land Transfer Act I of 1917 was passed, prohibiting all transfer from hillmen to non-hillmen without the express permission of the authorities.[28]

Mamools, Gothi and Bethi

The hill-tracts of South Orissa known as agency tracts were predominantly inhabited by the tribals such as Khonda, Savaras and Gandas etc. As elsewhere, they were exploited by the well-to-do agriculturists or Sahears, village headmen or Naiks, rent Collectors or mustajars and certain Government officials in several ways; taking advantage of their poverty and utter ignorance. The exaction of the largest possible customary dues, Gothi labour and Bethi labour not only demoralised the tribal peasants but also broke down their economic back-bone. As remarked by R.C.S. Bell of the Indian Civil Service, the intolerable burden imposed on them by the systems of mamools, Gothi and Bethi led to their large-scale emigration to Assam and other places in search of livelihood.

Agents of 'New Order'

In the course of time, the tribals of the region were driven to inaccessible forests and hilly areas where they maintained their simple life style and survival-oriented culture. The agents of the 'new order' represented by traders, money lenders and contractors did not leave them there either. The outcome of this oppressive 'new order' is that the 'tribal poor' have found themselves exceedingly indebted and alienated from most of their land except for a few pieces of eroded land strips.[29]

Unorganised Labour and Child Labour

Agriculture not being an organised industry, the labour employed on small farms lacks the bargaining power. The abundant and unorganised supply of man power, the availability of women and children for field work and their lack of bargaining strength result in bewildering range of low wages. Another factor responsible for low wages is the prevalence of the system of payment in kind which is governed by the traditions and customs beset with exploitative factors.[30] The barriers posed by the mountains in the field of human mobility and transportation, lack of irrigation potential, scarcity of cultivable lands and extreme climatic conditions have all served to keep the Khondmals isolated to a very great degree from the neighbouring plains of Orissa.[31]

On the whole, it can be said that the backwardness of agriculture, almost complete absence of machine industries, the decay of the weaving industry, arbitrary and burdensome taxation the imposition of variety ceases, illegal exactions, and Bethi has led to the growing impoverishment of the people and the problem of child labour.[32]

In addition to these historical factors, the unprecedented drought conditions during these years, and the erratic behaviour of the monsoon, coupled with the state Government's callous attitude towards providing irrigation facilities have added fuel to the fire. Reports in the newspaper bring to light that Kantamal, Boudh and Khajuripada are the three blocks of Phulbani district which have sustained the maximum crop loss.[33] Most of the people in Phulbani suffer from malnutrition, an agony they suffer for a long time, and are forced to discontinue the studies of their children for employment.

Child Workers in Orissa

According to the census of 1971, the total population of the State is 219 millions, of which 43 per cent belong to the age group of 0-14 years. Out of 6851 thousands workers, child workers constitute 492,000. In Orissa, child workers constitute 2.24 per cent of the total population as compared to 1.96 per cent in Punjab, 1.73 per cent in Tamil Nadu, 1.5 per cent in Uttar Pradesh and 1.15 in West Bengal as per the 1971 census. The total population of Orissa, as per the 1981 census was 26,370,271 out of which child labourers constitute 515,000.

In Orissa, about 77 per cent of the population is engaged in agriculture while the rest of it is engaged in works such as mining, trade, manufacturing labour and Government service etc.

The Economic Classification of Workers, 1981

The agriculture is the primary occupation of the people of Orissa and Orissa's economy is, therefore, agriculture dominated. The economic classification of workers as per the 1981 census is represented in Table 27.1.

TABLE 27.1

Economic Classification of Workers, 1981

(in percentage)

Occupation	*Percentage in Total Workers*	*Percentage to Total ST Workers*	*Percentage to Total SC Workers*
Cultivators	49.16	52.38	27.45
Agricultural Labourers	28.28	36.72	49.21
Live stock Forestry, Fishing, Hunting Plantation and others	2.14	1.87	2.50
Mining and Quarrying	0.76	1.38	0.70
Manufacturing Processing, Servicing and Repairs	6.93	2.40	6.89
Construction	0.55	0.24	0.51
Trade and Commerce	3.31	0.58	1.63
Transport and Communication	1.45	0.67	1.57
Other Services	8.42	3.82	9.54
Total workers in million 8.6, male : 7.2, female : 1.4,			

Source: Economic Survey of Orissa', 1980-81, Bureau of Statistics and Economics Orissa.

The distribution of main workers in different districts of Orissa according to 1981 census has been represented in Table 27.2.

The Distribution of Child Workers in Orissa

The districtwise distribution of child-workers in different sectors in Orissa as per 1971 census is stated in Table 27.3

Table 27.3 and 3.4 reveal that most of the main workers and child workers in Orissa are employed in Primary sector i.e., agriculture. It is clear that there is non-industrialisation and absence of secondary source of employment in Orissa.

Land reforms and land ceiling measure have not been effective and they have hardly helped in changing the agrarian structure of the State. Orissa is still gripped by semi-feudalism, small farmers and agricultural labourers by and large, are still attached to their landlords. In spite of the vast industrial potential in the forests, mines and other natural resources, Orissa remains an industrially backward state.

TABLE 27.2

Number of Main Workers in the Different Districts of Orissa, According to the 1981 Census

(in '000)

Name of the District	*Culti-vator*	*Agricul-tural Labourers*	*House-hold Industry*	*Others*	*Margi-nal Workers*	*Total*
	No. of different categories of workers					
Balasore	328	157	17	117	41	654
Bolangir	260	157	22	71	90	599
Cuttack	572	303	40	364	72	1352
Dhenkanal	230	135	17	118	80	579
Ganjam	391	301	31	204	195	1123
Kalahandi	244	171	12	54	79	560
Keonjhar	182	82	9	88	73	434
Koraput	512	278	18	152	233	1198
Mayurbhanj	284	203	32	39	65	344
Phulbani	148	82	9	39	65	344
Puri	377	190	26	250	54	905
Sambalpur	354	253	47	176	166	996
Sundargarh	163	79	11	181	88	522
Orissa	4053	2397	285	1900	138	10022

Source: *Statistical Outline of Orissa*, 1985. Bureau of Statistics and Economics, Orissa, pp. 78-79.

TABLE 27.3

Distribution of Child Workers in Different Sectors

Sectors	*Total*	*Male*	*Female*
Cultivators	33.06	39.10	18.80
Agricultural labourers	49.60	43.54	61.14
Livestock, Forestry Plantation, Hunting and Fishing	6.07	6.90	3.98
Mining and Quarrying	0.27	0.17	0.69
Manufacturing, Processing etc.			
(a) At Household Works	2.81	2.08	5.46
(b) Other than Household Works	2.03	2.03	2.04
Construction Works	0.30	0.22	0.01
Trade and Commerce	1.70	2.17	1.07
Transport, Storage and Communication Works	0.14	0.18	0.07
Other Services	4.02	3.61	5.74

Source: *Census of India Series'*-16 Orissa Part-II, 1981.

TABLE 27.4

District-wise Percentage, Distribution of Child Workers in Different Sectors in Orissa 1971

Districts	*Primary*	*Secondary*	*Tertiary*
Orissa	86.93	4.06	9.01
Sambalpur	87.07	7.46	5.47
Sundargarh	85.69	3.45	10.86
Keonjhar	85.78	2.63	11.59
Mayurbhanj	84.17	5.36	10.47
Balasore	86.71	2.76	10.53
Cuttack	75.42	6.78	17.80
Dhenkanal	88.42	5.47	6.11
Boudh-Khondmals	89.48	3.17	7.35
Bolangir	93.47	3.05	4.48
Kalahandi	91.57	2.08	6.35
Koraput	92.53	1.87	5.60
Ganjam	82.95	4.40	12.65
Puri	79.11	5.10	15.79

Source: *Atlas of the Child in India*, Moonis Raza, Sudesh Nangia, Concept Publishing Company 1986, p. 366.

Participation Rate of Child Workers in Orissa

The Table 27.5 reveals that participation rate of child workers in Orissa is 5.97 per cent whereas the male and female participation rates are 5.36 per cent and 9.13 per cent respectively. In Kalahandi, the rate of child workers participation is higher than any other districts of the state, which is followed by Koraput and Phulbani. With concentration of tribal population these three are the backward districts. In such tribal and backward districts children belonging to culturally isolated and socially segregated group are found to be in disadvantaged position, in various educational institutions. Therefore, it is found in India and particularly in Orissa most of the children from lower caste and tribal groups are disadvantaged. The tribal children are economically poor, materially they are deprived due to lack of basic necessities, socially and economically deprived due to lack of parental interest, unhygienic living conditions and pathological living environment. The advanced coastal districts like Cuttack, Balasore and Puri the participation rate of children is comparatively lower due to better facilities of education, health, irrigation and industrialisation. However, child labour is pervaded in all areas of the State.

TABLE 27.5

Participation Rate of Child Workers in Orissa

District	*Total*		*Total*
	Male	*Female*	
Sambalpur	5.32	8.72	5.98
Sundargarh	4.85	9.83	5.60
Keonjhar	4.29	7.50	4.84
Mayurbhanj	6.04	9.29	6.92
Balasore	3.02	6.09	3.23
Cuttack	2.42	5.17	2.61
Dhenkanal	5.20	8.10	5.56
Phulbani	7.18	11.25	8.14
Bolangir	7.24	8.29	6.67
Kalahandi	10.93	13.19	11.30
Koraput	8.48	10.99	9.03
Ganjam	6.59	8.98	7.22
Puri	3.46	6.93	3.74
All Orissa	5.36	9.13	5.97

Source: *Census* of India, Part-II (A) and (B), Series 16 Orissa, 1981.

TABLE 27.6

Scheduled Caste and Scheduled Tribe Population in Different Districts as per 1981 Census.

Name of the District	*Scheduled Caste Population (000)*	*Percentage of SC Population to Total Population*	*Scheduled Tribe lation (000)*	*Percentage of ST Popu lation to Total Population*
Balasore	404	17.94	154	6.84
Bolangir	228	17.67	280	19.22
Cuttack	318	15.64	145	3.13
Dhenkanal	251	15.83	194	12.26
Ganjam	401	15.02	253	9.48
Kalahandi	211	15.76	419	31.28
Keonjhar	124	11.16	500	44.82
Koraput	349	14.06	1372	55.27
Mayurbhanj	104	6.58	912	57.67
Phulbani	133	18.55	279	38.94
Puri	378	12.93	101	3.45
Sambalpur	350	15.35	621	27.21
Sundargarh	114	8.52	686	51.26
Orissa	3865	14.66	5915	22.43

Source: Census Report, 1981.

The Distribution of S.T. and S.C. Population in Orissa

An interesting feature of Orissa is the large percentage of the Scheduled castes (S.C.) and Scheduled Tribes (S.T.) in its population. The S.T. and S.C. constitute about 38 per cent of the total population, of which 22.43 per cent are S.T. and 14.66 per cent are S.C. The district of Mayurbhanj has got the largest number of S.T. constituting about 57.67 per cent. On the other hand, the district of Cuttack has the lowest number of S.T. constituting 3.13 per cent of its population. Table 27.6 analyses the Scheduled Caste (S.C.) and Scheduled Tribe (S.T.) population of different districts of Orissa.

District-wise Distribution of Male-Female, Rural-Urban Ratio of Child Workers in Orissa

Table 27.7 reveals the district-wise distribution of male-female and rural-urban ratio of child workers in Orissa as per 1971 census. The table shows that next to Mayurbhanj, the district Boudh-Khandmals (Phulbani) has the highest percentage of female child labourers. (With 22.30 per cent of female child workers). Next to Phulbani is the district Ganjam with 22.20 per cent of female child workers occupies the third position among the Districts.

TABLE 27.7

District-wise Distribution of Male-Female and Rural-Urban Ratio of Children Workers in Orissa 1971

Districts	*Male*	*Female*	*Rural*	*Urban*
Orissa	85.97	14.03	96.53	3.47
Sambalpur	83.37	16.63	95.73	4.27
Sundargarh	84.64	15.36	93.49	6.51
Keonjhar	86.78	13.22	96.07	3.93
Mayurbhanj	76.55	23.45	98.90	1.10
Balasore	91.72	8.78	94.77	5.23
Cuttack	91.95	8.05	92.59	7.41
Dhenkanal	91.94	8.06	98.47	1.53
Boudh-Khandmal	78.70	22.30	98.68	1.32
Bolangir	92.64	7.36	98.03	1.97
Kalahandi	91.63	8.37	98.31	1.69
Koraput	95.56	14.44	97.65	2.35
Ganjam	77.80	22.20	95.47	4.53
Puri	91.10	8.90	93.30	6.70

Source: *Atlas of the Child in India*, Moonis Raza, Sudesh Nangia. Concept Publishing Company 1986, p. 368.

District-wise Analysis of Literacy Rate of Child Workers

Table 27.8 reveals that the literacy rate of child labour in general and female children in particular in lower. In the tribal districts of Koraput, Mayurbhanj and Kalahandi the literacy rate is significantly lower than other districts of Orissa.

TABLE 27.8

District-wise and Sex-wise Distribution of Literacy Rate of Child Workers.

District	*Male*	*Female*	*Total*
Sambalpur	30.67	11.92	25.38
Sundargarh	17.93	6.62	14.91
Keonjhar	16.53	5.04	13.64
Mayurbhanj	10.48	3.42	7.92
Balasore	29.31	4.41	26.08
Cuttack	34.12	7.95	29.31
Dhenkanal	32.66	8.95	28.69
Phulbani	28.99	5.83	21.46
Bolangir	21.93	3.91	20.92
Kalahandi	13.46	1.42	11.14
Koraput	8.86	1.41	6.85
Ganjam	26.52	6.30	19.86
Puri	43.04	9.81	38.32
Orissa	22.64	4.87	17.93

Source: Census of India, Part-III (A) and (B), Series-16 Orissa, 1981

A General Note on Child Labour in Orissa

In Orissa, about 80 per cent of child workers are involved in agricultural operations. As per 1981 census, the child population was 10.45 million, out of which 0.52 million children are found working. In tribal areas, where parents have taken loan from the land owners, the children are to work as a bonded labour until the loan is repaid. But this is a continuous process which is mostly found in Kalahandi, Phulbani and Mayurbhanj districts of Orissa. Employment of children is extensive and in agricultural construction projects, bidi making, kendu leaf collection, bamboo forest operations, salt fields and the like.[34] The farmers of Orissa are mostly engaged in a year and the rest of the period they go out of the village in search of employment elsewhere. Either they engage themselves in construction projects, bamboo forest organisations, kendu leaf collections, bidi making and other alternative occupations or go out of the state of dadan labouers to work in construction projects in other Indian states and even in neighbouring countries like Iraq, Iran and other Arabian countries, Bhutan, Nepal etc. It is estimated that out of the dadan labouers go outside the state 10 per cent of them are within the age group of 12 to 15, which came to more than 4 lakhs.[35] These dadan child workers engage themselves in various operations in different period of time. In addition to this, poverty and economic backwardness of the state being the primary factor for the employment of children, children and young persons are also employed in hotels and domestic service in urban areas. They are mostly drugged for brought from the rural sector. The total employment of children in these operations will be much more since the Orissa Shops and Commercial Establishments Act, 1956 only extends to the municipal and notified areas of the state. Children are also employed in these establishments in other small towns and villages in the state. Besides, no appropriate statistics are available with regard to the enactment of child labour in the domestic services.

Employment of Children in Organised Sector

The employment of children in the organised factories and other industrial establishments is very meager because of two reasons. First, child labour being mostly unskilled, adult labourers are available in plenty in state and the employers do not prefer to employ children because of their, marginal outturn in the organised sector. Secondly, the existing labour laws regulate the employment of children in these sectors.

Problems of Child Labour in Orissa

The problem of child labour are manifold. These problems mostly relate to the nature of work in which they are engaged and quantum of wages they are paid. Truely speaking, in agricultural operations, they do not have any problem with regard to the nature of engagements. But, the question arises in case of their remuneration. Generally, a child labourer is paid half of the wages of an adult worker.

The plight of child labourers in Orissa is most acute. In case of dadan labourers young persons being fascinated by the sardars and khatadars, leave their native land and go to the distant lands of Kashmir, Assam Nagaland, Manipur, U.P. and other states and engaged in most difficult, jobs or earth cutting and road making in billacks amidst snow and other gloomy weather. The children of Orissa are generally not accustomed to cold as a result of this, either they die out of cold or suffer from severe cold diseases. In many cases, these children have come to distant places without the knowledge of their parents and ultimately meet to untold miseries un-noticed.[36]

Formation of a High Land Committee

The state government on receipt of numerous complaints with regard to the plights of dadan labourers have constituted a high level committee with the Welfare Commissioner, Eastern Zone as Chairman, and Deputy Labour Commissioner, Orissa and a nominee of the concerned state Labour Commissioner as members. The committee went around the effected areas and rescued many child labourers from their untold miseries and also processed compensation claims in accordance with the provisions of the Workmen's Compensation Act, 1923.

Child Bonded Labourers in Orissa

A still distressing feature of the engagement of child labour in Orissa is the employment of young scheduled tribe population in the form of bonded labourers. The tribals incur loans from money lenders generally for their marriage and other social celebrations. Excepting their human labour, they have no other source of repayment. As a result of this, they engage themselves as bonded labourer. They also engage their children for such purposes. In consequence, the tribals serve as bonded labourers for generations together. The Debt Bondage Abolition Act, 1948 and the Bonded Labour (Abolition) Act, 1976 though came as rescue stations to the vagories of bonded labourers in Orissa yet, the tribal children are still under the clutches of village landlords in different forms and garbs in the will tracks of Koraput, Kalahandi, Phulbani and Ganjam and other hilly areas of the state.

Employment of Children in Kendu-Leaf Collection

The condition of employment of child labour in Kendu Leaf collection is also miserable. Because of their low height their services are effectively utilised in kendu leaf plucking. They are also more useful in drying kendu leaves on river beds and rocks under hot sun in base foots. In course of kendu leaf plucking, they are subjected to frequent attacks of wild animals in the drying process, they become the victims of stone-strokers. While cutting the kendu leaves, the leaf edges prick their eyes which results in eye infection. Despite this, because of this ignorance they do not come forward with their grievances to the proper authorities of the Forest Department and as such face the miseries un-noticed. The tribal children engaged in sal seed collection in interior forests also face identical problems.

Again in bidi rolling operations, the child labourers are also engaged, from the very childhood they are subjected to the evil smell of 'Zarda' and suffer from lungs trouble.

In construction activities, the child labour also do the work of earth cutting, road making, stone breaking chips making, sand carrying etc. Though these operations are really painful, yet because of their poverty, they are compelled to engage themselves in these works. Though the minimum wages act make no discrimination in fixing wages for the child labourers as compared to the adult workers. Yet, the contractors of their own accord make discrimination in payment of wages in all these operations.

Substance of the Analysis

In the light of the above analysis, it can be concluded that the magnitude and miseries of child labourers in the state of Orissa are vast and extensive. Since, it is the outcome of economic necessity no social law can abolish or regulate the employment of children and when there is any strict regulation, the child workers will be thrown out of their employment adding fuel to the fire of economic hardships to their parents. The Government can did solution to this problem may be to provide un-employment allowances to the parents of child workers and to create better employment opportunities to them in order to strengthen their economic conditions. This will ensure enrollment of children in schools for better education and thereby the talent of such child workers can effectively be engaged for the development of the country in future. The planners and policy makers should chart out of the details to uplift the children of our country in this direction to prevent their early employment and wastage of future human resources.

Trade Unions could also play important role in both improvement of conditions of work and also in gradual elimination of child labour. Their working conditions could be improved-if trade unions extend their activities also to unorganised sector. They could help in gradual elimination of child labour by educating the employers and also adult workers of the harmful effects of child labour. The problem of child labour could also be minimised by extending the scope of social security measures so that large number of people could be brought within its purview. This will prevent especially orphans from entering into labour market. They have concentrated solely on rural poverty, because most of the child labour in Orissa are concentrated in rural areas-child labourers in urban centres are invariably the children of the migrants who came from obscure rural areas to the city in search of a job. Thus it's the widespread poverty and destitution of the rural population that lies at the root of the problem. High incidence of employment of children and non-schooling amongst this 4-14 age group almost go hand in hand.

To enforce a law forbidding child labour which would cause the child and its parents to go hungry would not be feasible. The only feasible solution would be to enforce a minimum wages act more strictly for the parents so that children will not be forced to work for subsistence sake.

Feasibility of Prohibiting Child Labour

The child labour being more an economic problem in India. Its total prohibition may have far reaching consequences. Its prohibition without concrete alternative arrangements may shake the very foundation of the poor. Many young persons having no alternative in the event of prohibition of child labour, may resort to theft, pick-pocketing etc. Many may adopt beggary for survival at the first instant and may subsequently accept it as a profession. All these may contribute towards social disorganisation, various forms of unrest, large scale unemployment and add to the problem of juvenile, delinquency. In India where a significantly number of people live below the poverty line, it is difficult to prohibit employment of child labour unless there is adequate economic growth.

Conclusion

The analysis brings into light that owing to historical causes Orissa remained exploited and underdeveloped for a long period of time. The backwardness of agriculture, the increasing dependence of the people on agriculture, complete neglect of industrialisation, excessive land revenue, the exploitation of the poor peasants by the zamindars and money lenders reduced the people of Orissa to extreme poverty. The land alienation, indebtedness, lack of irrigation and callous attitude of the Government, recurring drought and failure of crops, dominances of tribal and weaker sections—all contributed to the growth of child labour problem in Orissa.

NOTES

1. Das, Binod, S., *'Studies in Economic History of Orissa'* (From Ancient time to 1833), Calcutta, 1978, p. 207.
2. *Ibid.*, p. 212.
3. *Ibid.*, p. 222.
4. *Ibid.*
5. Samal, J.K., *Princely States of Orissa (1905-1947)*, Vora Publishers and Distributors, Allahabad, 1988, p. ix.
6. *Ibid.*, p.x.
7. *Report on the Land Revenue Administration of Lower Provinces, 1903-1904*, p. 8.
8. Bhola, S.C., *British Economic Policy in Orissa*, Discovery Publishing House, New Delhi, p. 145.
9. *Ibid.*, p. 147.
10. *Indian Annual Register*, 1943, Vol. II, pp. 19-20.
11. Final Report on the *Survey and Settlement of the Province of Orissa*, Vols. 2, 1890-1900 S.L. Maddox, Calcutta, 1900.
12. Tripathy, S.N., *Bonded Labour in India*, Discovery Publishing House. New Delhi, p. 63.
13. A Study of Gothi System of Koraput, *Adivasi*, Vol. VIII, Tribal Research Bureau, Government of Orissa, 1976-77, p. 4.
14. Behuria, N.C., *Final Report on the Major Settlement Operations in Koraput District, 1938-64*, p. 52.
15. Senapati, Nilaman, (Ed.), *Orissa District Gazetteer*, 1968, Bolangir, Chapter XVII, p. 446.
16. *The Blitz*, Volume XIXX, Number 8, February 25, 1989, p. 9.
17. *Ibid.*
18. Orissa—'Drought and Poverty' — A Report from Kalahandi, *Economic and Political Weekly*, Nov. 2, 1985, p. 1857.
19. *Orissa District Gazetteer Kalahandi Gazetteer of India*, 1980, p. 297.
20. Rao, B.S., "Bonded labour in Orissa", *Man in India*, Vol. 52 March, 1972, pp. 64-72.
21. *The Dainik Asha*, dated 25.7.1985, p. 2.
22. *The Samaj*, dated 1-1-1986, p. 6, dated 21.1.1986, p. 6, 26.1.1986, p. 8 and 14.9.1986, p. 8.
23. *The Blitz*, February 25, 1989 Opp. Cit., p. 9.
24. Rath, Bijoy Chandra, "The System of Headmanship in Princely States of Orissa". *The Journal of Orissan History*, Volume IX, June 1989, p. 131.
25. *Reports of the Administrative Enquiry Committee*, Vol, 1, 1958, p. 31.
26. *Ibid.*
27. Taylor, H.D. *Memoir on the Ganjam Maliaha in the Madras Presidencey*, Madras 1969, p. 10.

28. Report of the Administrative Enquiry Committee, Vol. I, 1958, pp. 461-462.
29. Tripathy, S.N., *Bonded Labour in India, op. cit.*, p. 73.
30. *Yojana*, May 16, 1971, p. 23.
31. Bailey, F.G., *'Caste and Economic Frontier'* (A village in Highland Orissa), Oxford University Press, 1962, p. 19.
32. Samal, J.K. *Princely States of Orissa (1905-1947), op. cit.*, p. 204.
33. *The Blitz*, February 25, 1989, p. 9.
34. Das, Prafulla Chandra (Dr.) Labour Directorates, Orissa, 'Child Labour in Orissa: its Problems and Prospects' (Seminar Paper), p. 2.
35. *Ibid.*, p. 3
36. *Ibid.*, pp. 506.

28

CHILD LABOUR IN INDIA: MYTH AND REALITY

A child labourers is differentiated from an adult worker on the basis of age. Usually a child worker is someone below the age of 14 or 15 years who is involved in any productive activity where paid or unpaid, with the family or outside. Children are involved in all types of work. They work in agricultural activities, looking after cattle and sheep, scaring away birds from the fields, helping at the time of sowing and harvesting. In their homes, they look after the younger siblings, collect fire-wood and water, and participate in other domestic and non-domestic work as in a cottage industry. In the urban sector, they work in a wide variety of activities from organised factories to roadside cafes, motor repairing workshops, street, vending, shoe-shining, selling of newspapers, fruits and peanuts, domestic help in homes and even in organised beggary. Parents put their children to work at a very early age, sometimes when they are only 6-7 years old. As the child grows older, he gains more expertise in the tasks he has been performing since early childhood.

A large percentage of children start working because of being orphaned, rejected by parents or because of broken families and other domestic problems. These children go into the streets totally abandoned with no one to care for them. They have no option but to take to work for their bare survival. It is in these unfortunate circumstances that young girls are drawn into prostituion and young boys and girls have been forced into organised beggary, even being maimed in the process.

In the case of agricultural labour, it has been seen that when the family head moves from one area to another depending on the agricultural cycle, his wife and young children will either move with him or stay back to look after the small family plot in his absence. In both cases, it is traumatic experience for the young children. Moving around constantly, they feel insecure and unsettled and being without their father for long periods often makes them indisciplined and irresponsible.

In the urban areas, the case is similar. When whole families move from their village to the cities, they face the traumas of lack of shelter, hunger, joblessness, etc. Staying back in the village along for long periods is again not a happy situation. In the cities, young children start to work by helping their father in petty jobs on the streets, usually without payment. Later they start to work on their own or for somebody else. The type of jobs they do are cleaning cars, polishing shoes, selling magazines and newspapers, selling fruit and peanuts, guarding parked cars, carrying messages, etc. In the bigger cities, children have been caught selling drugs. It is a common sight to see them begging. In Delhi, on a cold winter evening or in the hot summer afternoon, one sees these children braving the weather in their scanty clothes. On often reads of the police catching gangs which deliberately maim young children for the purpose of begging. In the cities again, children work as domestic help with no set hours of work. They provide various kinds of services in workshops, dhabas (roadside cafes), petrol pumps, etc. Their hours of work are irregular and often they do not even go home—if they have at home at all and sleep in the place of work itself. Their day starts early in the morning and goes on till late at night. In the organised sector, there are various manufacturing units and processes where children are preferred, such as the glass and bangle industry, matchbox and fireworks manufacture, carpet, weaving, etc. The reason given by the entrepreneurs is that they have soft, nimble fingers and are hence able to do the job better than adults. But this has been found to be only partially true. The same work can easily be done by women and even men. It is convenient to have children because they constitute a cheap, silent, uncomplaining workforce.

Children begin work in family undertakings from an early age alongside their parents. Later parents, relatives or friends taken them to their future employers. The treatment meted out to the working child depends entirely on the temperament of the employer. Some children may be ill-treated and humiliated, even beaten; while others are looked after with parental care. Most of the work they do is monotonous, repetitive and dull and is often not suited to their physical and mental capabilities. The child continues to work in appalling conditions because he expects very little from his job, knowing that at least he is employed and can earn some money.

Normally, the child who works in a family undertaking, whether in agriculture, manufacturing, commerce or handicrafts, is exploited less than the wage-earning child. Certainly, "the stress, fatigue and harmful effects to which he is exposed are partly compensated for by the personal attention and affection which his parents can give him during both work and rest periods".

The number of hours spent in working varies considerably from 6 to 8 hours per day to even 12 or 14 hours, much more than their young bodies can stand. Often they have no fixed hours at all as in roadside cafes, workshops or domestic work. To this one should add the time spent in travelling to and from home.

In the unorganised urban sector, the wages of the child depend entirely on the importance of the work done by him. In any case, the child is paid much less than what an adult earns for the same work. Employers will explain this discrimination by stating that the children are inexperienced, the quality and quantity of work produced by them is not the same as adults, they have to be trained and a lot of time and effort is involved in this. Even in the organised sector, children are hardly ever paid the legal minimum wage. They are supposed to be on training for long periods of time during which they are not paid at all even though they have gained expertise and are really working while being trained. The child may have secured his job through a labour contractor as in the case of carpet weaving. Here the contractor will take his commission, often as much as 25%, on the wages earned by the child. Where the children are paid on a piece-rate, they are again at a disadvantage. Being illiterate, they are unable to calculate how much work they produce in month and hence have no way to check what payment is due to them. Parents of working children often take large advances and loans from their employers. These advances are slowly deducted from the child's wages, which means that his monthly takings get reduced. It takes years to repay their loans by which time the family needs a fresh load and this cycle goes on. The children in this way get 'bonded' to work. There is no getting away for them. There have been a few cases where children are pledged to work while still in the mother's womb and advances taken against this pledge.

Whatever the occupation, the element of risk is always there as far as a child is concerned. Some occupations like firework and match-making, glass and bangle manufacture, and carpet weaving are extremely hazardous and yet children continue to be employed in them. Because their bodies are young, they get tired easily and fatigue sets in. They work in unhygienic conditions, with little or no ventilation and bad light. Their bodies are often in uncomfortable positions for long periods of time and they have to concentrate on minutes detailed work. In carpet waving, they sit in a crouched position for eight hours a day because of which their legs and joints become stiff and their growth gets retarded. The intense concentration on the loom all the time leads to eye strain and fatigue. Inhaling wool fluff constantly gives them breathing problem. In the match and fireworks industry, the children inhale lungfulls of toxic fumes from the chemicals, suffer intense heat, run the risk of being badly injured and suffer intense strain from lifting heavy frames. Working in the glass and bangle factories, the workers are affected by the silica dust which causes silicosis, a killing disease of the lungs; the intense heat near the furnaces affects the body cells and the blazing glass can result in accidental burns and other injuries. Accidences often occur at the worksites and there are usually no first aid facilities available. The employer does not even bother to take them to a doctor, and the children learn to look after one another. Social security and accident insurance schemes hardly exist. The machinery, tools, etc. are designed for adults and not for children. Some of the chemicals can be extremely dangerous. In agricultural work, contact with pesticides and fertilizers leads to skin problems and poisoning. Agricultural work is, in any case, strenuous and puts a great strain on the young body of a child. Self employed children working in street trades have no health security at all. They are exposed to extreme weather conditions, traffic hazards, besides becoming victims of unhealthy habits like smoking, drinking, etc. They continue to work even when they are ill because the daily earnings are so important to meet their basic needs in life.

The living conditions of working children are appalling. Families, though extremely poor, are large in size. Family planning had not been very successful with the illiterate working classes. In any case, the general opinion is that many children mean many more hands to work and earn. Their homes are congested and overcrowded with hardly any ventilation or sanitary facilities. The entire 'Basti', (living area with a cluster of houses or huts) is unhygienic with water logging, dirt, insects and flies. This in itself results in illness of all types like typhoid, malaria, hepatitis, etc. The pressure of life is so intense that the adult males spend their evenings drinking and have no time or inclination to look after or supervise the children. The children roam the streets unattended and uncared for. Working children have very little contact with their parents because they spend a greater part of the day at work away from home and come back only late at night. Children who leave their village home and come away to the cities to work face acute housing problems. Most of them either sleep on the pavements, in corridors or market places or in a corner in the 'dhaba' or the workshop where they work. Their diet is frugal, comprising of dal, chapati or rice, often just dry chapati, sliced onion and salt. They suffer from malnutrition and hunger. They continue to work even when they are ill and hence weaken their bodies further. Vitamin deficiency, anaemia, bronchitis and tuberculosis are common diseases which working children suffer from.

The mental and physical development working children suffer. The child has no time to play or take part in any healthy exercise which is so important for the proper physical development of his body. He has no time to go to school because the hours clash with his time at work and hence his mental faculties are not developed. Since he starts working at such an early age, he remains illiterate and unskilled for the rest of his life and this hinders any progress or advancement in his life, and "he spends his whole life at the bottom of the social ladder, performing routine, unskilled jobs, when he is not out of job altogether."

Working children can be divided broadly into three categories, education-wise. First, those who do not go and have never been to school. Second, those who have spent a few years in school and have left school to start working. Third, those who work and still spend a few hours in school everyday. The greatest percentage of working children in India came from the first category. The reason for this is that parents feel that educating the child will not help to feed them whereas a working child brings money into the home to take care of certain basic needs. Secondly, our curriculum does not take into consideration their actual requirements in daily life. It is rigid and examination-oriented. If it was non-formal, with more emphasis on vocational training, then it would be of far greater use to the child. Thirdly, in the agriculture sector children are needed when there is pressure of work during sowing and harvesting. At this time, it is impossible to spare them for school. "What comes through loud and clearly is that children are working in almost every sphere of economic life, they are exploited both by their parents and by the employer, and above all that the child is deprived. This deprivation is of two types; one related to the impact on its health, the second concerns its educational status ... (they are) unable to go to school".

The reason for employing children has been two-fold. First, to supplement the family income when it has not been sufficient to meet the requirements of the family. This is the main reason for child labour in India today, where more than 37% of people live below the poverty line. Any addition to the family income helps to case the burden of a very tedious existence. "Child labour exists in inverse relation to the degree of economic advancement of a society, country of region." In most developing countries having more children is considered a great advantage because every child means two extra hands to work, which means more income for the family. Children are not sent to school mainly because preparing them for a brighter future is unimportant when the immediate present is so bleak. The child by working is able to reduce to a great extent the poverty in which he lives and hence satisfies some of his basic needs. Even the smallest payments in cash or kind are welcome in his poor home and he shares in the maintenance of his family.

The second reason is that children were taught a traditional craft at a very early age to make them proficient in a job which would then be a source of income to them on gaining adulthood. It is a recognised fact that in childhood the body is more flexible and pliable and can hence bend, twist, stretch more easily to acquire postures requires for particular jobs. It is both a physical and mental adjustment which is required in the learning process. Even musicians and dancers start to train their children at the early age of 5 or 6. It is for the same reason that craftsmen train their children in their hereditary crafts because the nimble fingers and keen eye-sight of early childhood are an asset in the learning process. Carpet weaving, pottery, silk and cotton weaving, wood carving, etc. are some of the traditional crafts taught to young children within their homes. In the villages, the boys at a young age are made to handle a plough, reap the harvest, cut and bring fuel from the forest, catch fish from the village ponds, graze the cattle, guard the crops against birds and monkeys, etc. While the girls help i weeding the fields, looking after younger siblings, sweeping the house, etc. They may not be viewed as 'gainful' activities. However, they do free the mother or older siblings for working in the fields or in other wage earning activities.

Children form an integral part of the household economy. They are trained while still young and gradually start contributing individually to the family's income. There is an obvious oppression and they learn mainly through observation, imitation and assistance to elders. Soon parents find that children cannot only assist in the household activities but can even be made to work for others in return for wages in cash or kind. In family run businesses the children are relatively much happier but we find that children who are made to work outside their homes are far more exploited by having to work long hours in arduous and often hazardous tasks, at low wages, and often in unhygenic worksites with hardly any facilities. Most of these jobs are "monotonous, strenuous, harmful or unduly prolonged", and "the very many children who are engaged on them grow up prematurely and sadly, instead of leading a carefree existence with their friends during what could be the happiest days of their lives."

The family is not the only one to blame, it is society as a whole that is at fault. Besides the parents, it is the employers who are responsible for perpetuating this terrible practice. Even in family-run units, where the child is generally better looked after by his parents and may not suffer from any physical hardship, he goes through mental strain because of problems and anxieties regarding the undertaking which he shares with his parents.

SOME LIFE STORIES

DELHI

1. Riazuddin

At the time of this study, 13 year old Riazuddin was new to Delhi. He ran away from his home in Agra after a bitter fight with his father. Riazuddin had enjoyed a carefree life until 6 years back, when his father took the decision to pull him out of school (he was studying in 2nd standard) and put him to work. At the age of 7, Riazuddin joined the ranks of thousands of child workers in the country who are all in it, not out of choice but out of necessity. He has no quarrel about it, but what hurt him most was his father's constant bickering about how little he earned. Riazuddin worked in a shop that sold ladies purses and handbags and earned about Rs. 15 a day. His father's dissatisfaction with him became more pronounced after his sister's marriage for which his father had taken a huge loan. What sparked the bitter right was his father's demand that he earn at least Rs. 250 a week. Riazuddin's eyes filled up with tears when he said : "I tried my best to earn more, it was hard work and very tiring. The maximum I could earn was about Rs. 140 a week. My eyes and fingers ached stitching leather bags and tiny purses." Not being able to bear the pressure at home Riazuddin left home to come to a city hoping to get a better paying job so that he could send more money to home.

Riazuddin realises his responsibility and his father's financial problem; he wants to help him. While in Agra his father used to receive his wages. He did not get any pocket money. When asked if he would like to continue his studies, his eyes lit up with hope. Riazuddin is keen to finish his schooling as well as upgrade his skill in manufacturing purses. Riazuddin has not lotched on to any job having just arrived at the time of this interview. For the moment Riazuddin sleeps on the footpath until he finds better shelter—the question is, will he?

2. Raju

Twelve year old Raju left his home in Delhi as he was constantly pressurized to work. He has been on the streets for the past 3 years. Initially he took on any odd job that came his way—coolie, shop help, etc. when one day every thing changed and a nightmare began—an ordeal that lasted for two years. One evening as he was loitering around the railway station two policemen started rounding up boys near the station. He too was taken to the station and beaten up on the charges that he was using smack and was a courier for a peddler. The policemen demanded money from them; those who would pay were let off with a stern warning but Raju and another child who could not pay were further beaten and sent to jail on a false charge.

Raju is today very bitter about his prison experience and he hates the police. He kept saying that if government or any voluntary organisation wants to help street children, the greatest service they could do is to see that police harassment is topped. Raju works in an unregistered wayside restaurant and gets about Rs. 100 per month with meals and shelter. He visits his home every month to give his earnings to his parents but does not intend to live at home. Raju would be interested in learning the 3 R's and is keen to learn a trade skill that would fetch him, him a better job, pay and security.

3. Sheikh Farid

Sheikh Farid is a refugee from Bangladesh. His parents migrated to India in the wake of Bangaldesh-Pakistan War. Since then they are living on a pavement in north Delhi. In fact Sheikh Farid was born on the street. Adjoining the pavement is a whole cluster of Bangladeshi migrant families — quite a large community. Farid did go to school for two years but then the school teacher stopped coming to school. Meanwhile his father, a rickshaw puller, wanted him to work and placed him with his maternal uncle who is a tailor to teach him the trade so that eventually he could start tailoring. Farid has been an apperentice to his uncle for the past four years. He gets paid very little most of which his uncle takes back on some pretext or the other. Farid works eight and half hours a day with one hour lunch break. He also does most of the housework in his uncle's place, which amounts to a total of 15 hours of work every day. With no money on hand to spend on bidis, gambling and movies like other children, the only recreation he has is resting or watching cars and trucks go by. Farid's father would have loved to educate his son but does not have the means. He needs his son to acquire a skill so as to start earning and supplement the family income. Farid himself would like to learn higher grades of tailoring and expressed his dream to get bank loan someday to buy a sewing machine and enough capital to start his business.

4. Alam

Thirteen-year old Alam works as a coolie and lives on the platform on New Delhi Railway Station. He came to Delhi from Pune leaving his family behind. Alam's father, a heavy drinker, is an auto-rickshaw driver. He married six times to make a family of 25 members, including 10 children below 15 years of age. His father deserted Alam's mother, leaving her to fend for her three children. She tried to do so by stitching clothes for others but this only brought her Rs. 10 per day. This was not enough for a family of four; so Alam was forced to drop out of school when he was in Class III. He started to earn a living for himself, his mother and his younger brother and sister by working in a bakery at Pune for four years. There he was beaten up frequently by by his employer over minor mistakes. He was miserable. One day he decided he could not bear it any more, so he left for Delhi, all on his own. He had no place to stay, so he took refuge on the railway platform.

Today, Alam works for 12 to 13 hours daily to earn 20 to 30 rupees. He spends all the money he earns as he has no place to keep it safely. He cannot deposit it anywhere because he does not trust anybody. For his entertainment he watches video movies in a nearby street center where he spends one rupee on the entrance fee. On the platform, danger luks in the form of policemen. But he is not scarced because he keeps them happy by washing their clothes and doing odd jobs for them.

Alam's desire is to take up a job in bakery and learn more about baking.

5. Mukesh

Mukesh, a friend of Alam on the other hand, wants to go back home to his mother. Mukesh's eyes filled up with tears when he spoke of his mother and sister. His face registered emotions of fear and distress as he could not recall his sister's name.

Mukesh had a miserable family life. He was ill-treated by his father who later deserted the family. His mother married again and history repeated itself. His stepfather was cruel and did not treat him well. When the family move to Calcutta, they left Mukesh behind—all alone.

Only 10 years old and lame, Mukesh had nowhere to go. He moved to the railway platform at New Delhi railway station. He sells newspapers and earn four to five rupees a day. He deposits his savings with a shopkeepers who charges one rupee a day for keeping money.

Mukesh wants to be a policeman when he grows up so that he can take revenge on his father.

6. Pehani

At the Tibetan Monastery Market, 13 year old Pehani, a Tibetan girl sell-woollens in a stall. She stays there with her employer who owns the stall. She looks after his stall and a one year old child. She has been in this employment for six years and working at the stall for one year. She does not know her income. Her pay is sent to her parents. Sometimes she is given 5 to 10 rupee as pocket money. Pehani's master scolds or beats her when some things are missing or if the child gets hurt or she breaks things accidentally.

Pehani's father is in Darjeeling and her mother in Manali. She does not know what they do. She has no met them for a long time. She wants to see them and be with them. Pehani also wants to study and learn some thing. But she has no time to study or play, no time for rest. She sits at the stall from 8 a.m. to 8 p.m., takes a break for lunch, looks after the child and does household work when required. When asked if she liked to sit at the stall, she shrugged her little shoulders, as if to say, "Do I have a choice" ?

7. Seemabai

Seemabai and her family live in a lane behind the New Delhi Railway Station. They are nomadic tribals from Rajasthan. Seema has four sisters and two brothers. All of them work. They help their parents to sell balloons at the station. 12 year old Seema spends about six to seven hours at the station persuading parents of little children to buy her balloons. She earns about Rs. 8 per day. Seema has been at this work since she was six years old. When asked if she was being forced to work, Seema retorted : "Is there any alternative ? If I do not work, we will have that much less to eat". Seema has also to do her share of household chores like collecting fuel, water and cooking. The little twelve year old's working hours stretch to eleven hours a day. She is so tired by the end of the day that she longs to rest her weary body. The question of how she spends her free time just does not arise.

Seema was quite bitter about police harassment. Apparently the police scold and abuse the girls and shoo them away from the station. She also revealed that the girls who sleep behind the railway station in the open (there are 4 families living at this place) are sexually sharassed by the local ruffians. They creep close to them at night and try to molest them. Once a girl was able to catch one of them. The pavement dwellers not only thrashed the man but also blackened his face and paraded him on the streets. Seema's desire is to have a permanent shelter and better job opportunities, so that they can have security and the basics of life. She is quite pessimistic of her future — "What will the government do for us ? Society is not sympathetic to our plight, we are seen as pests and nuisance". Her mother cannot visualise their life improving in her life time nor in her daughter's. "It is a hard life for us poor but worse for a woman. All I can wish for my daughter is that she get a good man as husband".

8. Suneera

Suneera was born in Delhi, though the family originally belongs to Rajasthan (Alwar). Her parents have six children — 3 boys and 3 girls. Suneera is the eldest and is 15 years old (all her brothers and sisters are below 10 years of age).

Being the eldest child and that too a female, she has always been involved in helping her parents with household chores and other jobs. At the age of 5 years, she started taking their goats for grazing and doing other jobs like cooking, fetching water, etc.

Her parents had moved to Delhi even prior to her birth, in search of employment. Since then they have been living in Delhi. They have made their own *jhuggi* which actually is just the barest minimum for shelter. They have just adequate space at night for the family.

Suneera's parents work as white-washers. Together they earn Rs. 50 per day. When their third child and eldest son was of reasonable age to go out, he started working as a shoe-shiner. He too is able to earn between Rs. 5 to 10 per day. All the money has been utilized for meeting the growing needs of the family. The work in the house leaves

Suneera only with some time (3 hours per day) for herself which she has always enjoyed in the company of her friends—the girls who also remain at home.

As she was brought up in a city, she often watched many children going to school. She also often dreamt of going to school and one day, after gathering some courage, (she expressed this wish to her parents. She was denied permission). When she persisted in her demand the only explanation that was offered to her was that girls should stay at home. She was told that it is not safe for girls to go outside in the world. Suneera recollects that again sometime later she and her siblings sought permission to attend school. They were again denied permission by her parents who said that they did not have enough money to send them to school. She has never sought permission again.

In their leisure time, she and her friends always enjoyed playing or making clay houses like most children of her age group. Very often they watched the women of their community smoking "bidis". She admits that once she stole a bidi and tried one or two puffs. She coerced her friends too into trying it. She explains that they all coughed a lot but that they liked the taste. For a few days they continued experimenting; however, they later gave up the habit after watching on television that smoking is injurious to health. Sunnera then added with meaningful smile that she watched the television too without the knowledge of her parents who prohibited her from watching the television fearing that "bad scenes" on the television would be a negative influence on Suneera's impressionable mind.

She has maintained good health. Once she fell ill seriously and had severe pain in the stomach. It was found that she had worms in the stomach. Her parents insisted on home remedies for the condition, since private treatment was considered expensive and, in their opinion, "doctors at dispensaries don't treat the patient carefully." In her own words: "I realized that home remedies are not bad. At present I feel quite well, and only very rarely do I get stomach ache and that actually might be due to other causes like indigestion." Her minor health problems have not caused serious trouble since another sister is now old enough to help her in household work.

When she was "old" enough to handle money her parents started giving her pocket money (Re. 1 per day). Most often she spent her money buying sweets that she had always desired to buy. A times she buys other eatables too. Unlike other girls she does not spend money on trinkets or fancy items, she says, "This stomach of mine first asks for some tasty things. And thus, I never even thought of saving money to buy jewellery." Her parents often save money or buy different articles and keep them safely for her dowry.

She got engaged to a boy of her own community at the young age of thirteen. As she says, "In our families girls often get engaged by the age of 10-14 years and after they are 16-17 years old, their `*gauna*' is performed, i.e, the final `vida' or departure from the parents house."

It is quite interesting to note that a child like her, who spends her leisure time in playing with her friends making clay houses is to be married soon. She has been forced into maturity due to customs and tradition. Being a female child and that too the eldest has given her additional responsibilities. For example, instead of her parents, she has to take care of her younger siblings and care for their needs. In the absent for her parents she doesn't feel secure even at home. Often she has experienced frightening incidents when in the absence of her parents she or her friends have been teased by boys. She also recalls that one of her friends was raped by a boy of their own community when the girl's parents had gone out to work and her younger siblings were playing outside in the community. Suneera narrates that this girl has been married off early and has left for her husband's house probably to save embarassment and disreputation. Thus, Suneera believes that girls are definitely not safe and that they should remain inside their house or with their parents as far as possible. Reportedly her parents once lost some cash (Rs. 350) as there was no one in the house. This and other incidents keeps Suneera confined to the house.

It may be observed that Suneera is slowly replacing all her desires of studying with those of wanting to stay at home. Circumstances and situations have forced this child to develop only those ideas and desires that are agreeably to her family and community. Her desire to study was easily quelled with explanations. At 15 years of age she appears to believe that a woman's place is her home and that it is not her lot to pursue personal desires. She still carries hope in her heart as is apparent when she expresses her wish that she would like to send her children to study and become independent. Later on she also adds that she would like to have less children as rearing many children in today's expensive world would be a big problem and burden on the parents.

It remains to be seen whether or not her hopes will materialize.

9. Neelu

When tragedy befalls the young and the innocent, life seems to have lost its sense of fairness. This statement is best explained through the life history of young Neelu. Neelu is an 18 year-old girl whose eyes speak of all that is sad and miserable.

When barely two years of age, Neelu lost her mother. She also lost her only sibling, a brother who died within a couple of days of his birth. She was then cared for by her father and was married away at 12 years of age into what she had innocently hoped would be a better life. However, her marriage lasted but a few days her husband deserted her. The reason for his desertion was only that she was too "plain and ordinary" for him. Her young heart had to register with sorrow the news of his remarriage and soon after that the news of his death and consequently that of her widowhood.

Even before attaining adulthood in the legal sense, young Neelu has borne life experiences with a resilience and strength that would shame many an adult.

At present Neelu stays with her aged father at Sonia Gandhi Camp near Mohan Singh Market in a rented jhuggi. There are nearly 300-350 jhuggis mostly occupied by migrants from Rajasthan. A few families belong to Uttar Pradesh, Bihar and Tamil Nadu. Her immediate neighbourhood consists of families from Uttar Pradesh and Bihar.

Neelu's family hails from Jaipur. She came to Delhi with her parents when she was just one year old. Very soon she lost her mother and brother. Her father took care of her. Thus began her lonely life in Delhi. When she was 3 years old she was sent to the village to stay with her grandparents as her father found it difficult to take care of her and he able to tend to his work. For three years she was happy in the village playing with the children of her age, growing up with care and affection received from her grandparents, maternal aunts and cousin brother. However, when she was 6 years old, her father brought her back to Delhi to admit her to school.

Neelu was not happy at school. She preferred to play with her non-school going friends as compared to those who were attending school. Her father also did not force her to attend school. When she was seven years of age, her father took her along with him to the construction work site where he worked. It was then that she realized that a school was a better place for a child to be in. So she requested her father to put her back in school. Her father refused to do so, explaining that she had grown too old to attend school. Until today she regrets this deprivation of education. "Had I been to school at that time how nice it would be today is the thought uppermost in her mind. As she says, "Now I have to toil and slog in the burning heat and work for some money from morning till evening." Though she is tired of working her father forces her to work in order to supplement his income.

It is natural for a child who takes up work at the tender age of 7 or 8 years to develop a sort of fatigue or boredom. It has been so with Neelu too. She feels going to work everyday (to her type of work) is really a punishment and she is tired. There is nothing and nobody to cheer her in her routinous and and monotonous life.

Neelu began with construction work at a young age and is presently (since 2-3 years) engaged in road-making which is both tiring and tedious. She however is unable to express such sentiments aloud.

Neelu's most poignant memories are that before she could realise or understand the facts of life society had started calling her a widow. At times it was a direct remark like "She is a widow, that's why she can't put a bindi or wear bangles". "She is a widow so she should not speak to strangers for a long time." But she reacts to these comments with a sad face that is make like and stops a person from guaging her true feelings.

After she lost her husband, life was hard and tough. She had to go to work daily along with her father where she had to carry bricks, sand, mud, etc. She was paid 25 rupees a day. Sometimes she worked overtime in order to fetch more money. The work was very tiring. Payment was made once in 15 days. However, most of the labourers were in the habit of taking *udhar* (loan) in between. There was no proper account maintained and a lot of cheating and exploitation took place. Over-time work was rarely suitably compensated and a quarrel ensured between some labourers and the contractor. She along with her father and some other labourers were sacked in the bargain.

She and her father then took road construction work. At present life is very strenuous. It is lonely and consists of only hard work. Sundays are her only respite from work. Her general health is poor. She appears listless and weak. She dislikes work now. She would love to sit at home, and yearns for rest which her father disallows as he is more interested in the daily income. Also, at work, she is the only female worker. Though the men respect her and she has had no problem from them she is unhappy. She prefers her village where she is always in the midst of company and doesn't have to work either.

Neelu starts her day at 6 a.m. in the morning by making tea, fetching water, cooking and packing lunch. She leaves for her work spot at 8 a.m. along with her father. Her work place is at quite a distance from her jhuggi. At work she gets an hours's rest during lunch break and then she continues work till 6 p.m. She reaches home only at 7 p.m. She prepared supper, fetches more water, does other household chores, eats and finally sleeps. She yearns to go to bed after a whole days toil. Despite having started work from the age of 7 years she has never handled finance. She is very poor in accounting and does not know exactly how much she earns as her father collects her wages on her behalf. No money is given to her. Her father buys the essential groceries for the house and some new clothes once a year. She has two meals a day. Mostly they consist of rotis and fried chillies. The combined earnings of Neelu and her father is atleast 60-70 rupees per day; however she has no idea as to how the money is spent because besides atta and some vegetables very little else is purchased. She desires to have milk, fruits and other eatables but they are never purchased. In all there is too much work, very poor diet and barely any rest.

Neelu relates that she has seen only then movies in her life, i.e, before she was 12 years old. She also admits that once she had been to a movie alone. For the past 5 years however there has hardly been any leisure time. Her father doesn't allow her to go to watch the television in the neighbourhood for the fear that "girls will be spoilt or will go astray if they watch movies." She doesn't even have any close friends with whom she can express or confide her feelings. Neelu has learnt to keep silent and bear hardships patiently. In sorrows, difficulties and pain she has always been alone. Often it has happened that she was feeling very sick specially at the time of menstruation, but as she is unable to express herself openly to her father she continues working. Neelu is however very fond of her father as he is the only person in her family. At the same time she is very scared of him too since he reportedly beats her if she goes to watch the television. She is too scared to talk to her father. If she does not want to work or when she feels sick she is unable to express herself, since she is aware that her father wants her to earn. There were times when she was really ill and was allowed to stay away from work but such occasions have been few.

As a person she is quiet and does not understand or grasp things that are said very quickly. In reaction to this, women in the neighbourhood make fun of her and also sometimes call her *'pagal'* and pass unfair comments in front of outsiders (interviewer) saying, "she still sleeps with her father". But all these insults she bears silently without verbal response. She has learnt to ignore insults and keeps smiling. Inspite of their taunts she is helpful to the same ladies, accompanying them to the grocery shop or to answer natures call, forgetting all their unfair comments.

As she is not a healthy person she falls ill often. She complains of stomach ache and worm trouble. According to her when it is cloudy she gets pain in the limbs. When she is ill she prefers to go to a private doctor as she feels that they give good medicines. Her father also gets sick often. Neelu often gets fever and headache. She also has health hazards connected to her occupation such as headache, tiredness, loss of consciousness, etc.

Though Neelu is of a quiet nature and slow in grasping things she has some desires and has knowledge about the facts of life. She knows about the case of an unwed mother in their village. According to her, unwed mothers face problems such as banishment from their house, from their caste and finally from their community. They are also, according to her, likely to be beaten by people. On family planning she says, "I don't know much but I want to have only 2 children — a girl and a boy. Only then I can give them good education, food, clothes, etc."

Neelu has no concrete plans for her future. However, she hopes to get remarried and prays that her future life atleast would be a nice and happy one. In her own words, "I want to marry a nice boy, be secure, have nice in-laws, possess a nice house and lead a happy relaxed life where I don't have to work. "She is quick to add a tinge of realism that she has learnt through bitter experiences. "I don't know whether these things will materialise for me. Sometimes I am scared to marry and stay with in-laws. They are usually harsh, rude and are likely to ill-treat me. My husband may not like me and may leave me. My mother-in-law might beat me and may make me work." Thus at times she has a negative, dark picture about her future and one can hardly blame her for it since her life itself has been such.

She is engaged to a man for the second time. The marriage will be taking place very soon. However, she is unhappy and is unprepared for it. She feels scared and is worried to leave her father alone. She has had one bad experience with her first marriage. This keeps worrying her all the time. She now desires to be all alone in the house and claims to like loneliness.

She appears to be both a worried and sad person. She seems to have never experienced love, care, affection and understanding from any one specially in the crucial stages of her life in childhood and adolescence. There was nobody to offer advice or guide her when she attained menarche, but she seems to have managed well. She gained some knowledge from friends and neighbours. Despite her worries and fears one can see an occasional smile on her face. When she perceives that somebody is interested in her and is willing to talk and listen to her patiently then she doesn't mind sitting for hours on endless talking feeling neither tired nor bored. She openly expressed her feelings and problems which she has otherwise learnt to suppress.

She constantly displays contradicting thoughts and feelings. At times she reports feeling weak and scared. At other times she displays boldness. Her thoughts regarding her marriage and stay with in-laws also are contradicting at different points of time. At times she is unhappy, scared and pessimistic. Next moment she is emboldened and says, "If my mother-in-law or sisters-in-law fight or quarrel with me I will not keep quiet, I will speak back. I will not work in their house. If they ill-treat me, I will leave the house and come back to my father. If somebody tries to tease me I will show him my *chappal* or hit him." But she does not appear to be as bold as she sounds. She thinks she is now too old for formal education. Her only wish and desire is to have a nice husband and nice in-laws and no work to do. If her wish is fulfilled she feels her life will take on a new meaning.

Neelu's childhood experience of losing her mother and only sibling, her lonely life, rejection from her husband and consequent widowhood have each contributed to making life appear as meaningless and lack-luster. Neelu has seen only 'downs' in her life she has little interest or hope in life.

What can the society offer to such girls who have known nothing but sorrow in their lives ?

10. Champa

Champas is 11 years old and is the eldest among her siblings. Her family hails from Ajmer, Rajasthan. For the past 14 years they have been residing in a resettlement colony of Mohammedpur in New Delhi. She and her parents work as domestic help. She has all the talents, courage, confidence and intelligence which girls normally acquire through socialising and attending school.

Being a girl child and the eldest among the children she was burdended with work and responsibilities at the age of 6 years. Since her her mother too worked outside the house Champa's role in the family at an early age was that of being an assistant to her mother. Champa grew up with lot of work and hardly any time for play. Her neighbourhood consisted of many other Rajasthani migrant families. As her grandparents and maternal aunts stayed next door they too took care of her and her siblings in the absence of her parents. There were frequent quarrels taking place between their neighbours and them over day-to-day issues. Champa felt that all the quarrels were mainly due to jealously because of their better standard of living. Champa discusses the issue like a mature adult and asks, "Why can't they work like us and have an access to all the things ? Why should they be jealous of us ? We reap the benefits because we have worked hard".

She began working outside at the age of seven when she used to accompany her mother to the houses where she worked as domestic help. At the age of 10 years, she started working independently. She got to know of potential work through her mother's contacts.

The school going children of the homes where she goes for domestic help are her close friends. She loves to play during her free time with them. She says that they too are very found of her and that they don't take food without giving her some. She proudly says that they are very keen to know her dwelling place but that she herself doesn't feel like inviting them to her jhuggi. She sadly says that her only friends belong to educated rich families and have clean habits. "If I take them to our jhuggi, neighbours will touch them with dirty hands and the surroundings are also dirty. My neighbours don't know how to deal with new comers. They use bad expressions and my friends will surely feel uncomfortable". Unfortunately, Champa dislikes children of her own community and looks down with disdain at their dirt and poverty.

Champa start her day at 6 a.m. in the morning and finishes all the morning household tasks by 8 a.m. She leaves for work at this time. At noon she returns and cooks lunch. She is free until 4 p.m. Then she has to go to work again. She works in atleast four houses and earns Rs. 400 per month which she gives to her mother. Her mother through the help of one of her employers has opened a saving account in Champa's name. Champa and her mother are been careful and cautious with regard to money. Usually her mother buys clothes for her but if Champa asks for money in order to purchase something it is given readily to her. Recently her mother purchased a wrist watch for Champa from the weekly bazaar.

Champa has three meals a day with rice, roti, vegetables, milk, curd and fruits. All this is possible since her family income is above Rs. 1,300 per month. The family has a television and a fan in the jhuggi. She sees programmes on television during her free time.

Being a working girl she has experienced harassment at a tender age itself. Narrating one such incident in her life she says that approximately two years ago the priest at the nearby temple had allowed her family to take the extra food from the temple for their use. So once in two days Champa would go to the nearby temple to collect the food. The watchman of the temple was reported to be above 50 years of age. Reportedly he would pass lewd comments to Champa. One day he is reported to have proposed to her. In anger she threw her *chappal* on his face and abused him saying, "Aren't you ashamed to say that to a girl of 9 years who is young enbough to be your daughter or grand-daughter ? Don't you have wife and children ?" She later complained to the pandit (priest) of the temple. He terminated the watchman from service. In shame and sorrow the watchman begged Champa for pardon and asked her to speak on his behalf to the Priest. Champa like a mature person replied, "Had you not misbehaved this termination would not have taken place. Now you deserve it. Hereafter don't behave like this with anybody."

However, he later joined service after pleading with the priest. Being bold and courageous she is thus able to handle her day-to-day problems with confidence.

Though Champa has never been to school she, has attended non-formal classes in a nearby institute for a short time and knows how to write numbers from 1 to 100. She has learnt to write a few Hindi alphabets also. She is aware of 2 institutions where girls and women are being educated nd are taught stitching.

By watching the television Champa has attained a lot of knowledge regarding the government and currant happenings in the country. She has also learnt the rationale behind family planning. She likes slogans such as "*Hum bhi khush hamare bachche bhi khush*" and "*chota parivar sukhi parivar*". She says that if one has more children and less income it is difficult to look after the children. She would like to have two or three children in the future.

She is engaged to a boy who has studied upto the 8th class. They very fact of having an educated spounse makes her feel proud. She had a desire to study but being the eldest daughter, her parents were more particular about extra income. Though she was gifted with a quick grasping power and keen interest it was not channelised into studying.

She still has a strong desire to study. Her knowledge of reading and writing has been attained without attending formal school. She has gained a lot through short-term non-formal classes, the television and her acquaintance with middle-class school going children. All this has set her apart from other children in her behaviour, habits, ideas and thoughts. She wants to study because as she says, "I want to teach others and help others. If somebody is bad, I want to make him good, to correct and help those who exploit, make happy those who are not happy. Today, I don't know how to make it happen."

Having had neither the opportunity of attending school nor that of good living, Champa at 11 years has learnt a lot. She seems to have an intuitive knack for learning and has been able to use her limited resources to learn as much as possible. Working along with children from economically better families has taught her to identify with them and she places emphasis on hygiene, cleanliness and order. Besides, she has also learnt the concept of saving. Being naturally intelligent, she was quickly grapsed basics in reading and writing and has developed a sense of confidence and courage rarely seen in girls of her background. It however seems sad that she has developed a dislike for other children of her background. Her dislike and disapproval of poverty and squalour seems to be extended so as to include even her own unfortunate friends and relatives.

For Champa, being engaged to an educated boy is a matter of pride and joy. A matter of even greater pride is that she is accepted as a "friend" by children belonging to economically better off families. Having had access to the television, non-formal education classes etc. she has learnt the basics in reading and writing. Now it remains to be seen whether marriage will boost or end her confidence and skills. If girls like Champa direct their energies to teach basic skills such as reading and writing to the other deprived children much can be achieved. The first step towards that would of course be to equip her with better knowledge and awareness.

11. Kali

Kali is one of those unfortunate girls who grow up without either parents or siblings. She is all alone despite having paternal grandparents who have taken the responsibility of taking care of her. Her story explains how girls like Kali have to fight poverty, hunger, loneliness, insecurity, illness, lack of affection, love or guidance from elders and yet seize the opportunity to learn in the company of her peer group finding all her happiness in them.

Kali is 11 years old. She lost her father at the age of two immediately after which her mother abandoned her and got remarried. Kali, the only child to her parents was let in the care of her aged paternal grandparents. However, they offer her neither guidance nor care and affection and often spend hours away from home. They leave her alone in the jhuggi for the whole day while they spend their time in a tea shop in the neighbourhood returning home only in the evening. They have never bothered to ask her if she has any problems or desires. No questions are asked regarding her food though she is the only bread-winner, selling newspapers to feed her grandparents.

Kali's family hails from Bhilwara Chapenari in Rajasthan. She says that as there was neither water, electricity nor rains they were forced to migrate to Delhi. She has been working as a newspaper seller since the age of six years. Kali's only solace is that in her neighbourhood she has a number of relatives (both paternal and maternal). She has atleast a half dozen cousin brothers who protect her and are her friends. Though they are younger to her by a year or two they rally round her when strangers (e.g. interviewer) talk to her. Her cousin brothers proudly say, "She has nobody; that's why we take care of her and give her food."

The first six years of her life was spent in the village where she was happy playing in the fields visiting her cousins houses, playing, eating at their place. She recalls all this by saying, "It was real fun." Now the life in Delhi is different for her although a group of cousins are always around her. They hardly get time to play as all of them are engaged in new sapper selling. In the morning however (8 to 10 a.m.) she is free. At that time she either does some household work or wanders aimlessly when all the children of her age are busy lighting the *chulha* and making *rotis*. Even the morning tea is not made at home since they have it in the tea shop.

Kali has a number of friends who don't go to school and are engaged in newspaper selling. All of them are her cousins and belong to the same community (Rajasthani). She plays games such as *'luk michi'*,*'kokla,'* *'langdi'* and *'kho-kho'*. They also spend time making clay models such as *chula*, pot, horse, man, house and camel. Kali finds time to play at her work place since she and her friends sell newspapers in the same area. At work this group of friends guard and protect her in times of need.

Kali earns around Rs. 10 a day selling newspaper. She gives most of the money to her grandfather and sometimes spends a rupee or two on eats.

Kali is not a healthy child due to under nourishment and lack of care and affection. She is weak and prone to fever. At work she feels very tired. When she is ill she prefers to go to private doctors who reportedly are better because "they don't give an injection".

Kali is not a healthy child due to under nourishment and lack of care and affection. She is weak and prone to fever. At work she feels very tired. When she is ill she prefers to go to private doctors who reportedly are better because "they don't give an injection".

She feels free to talk to her *Buva* and is fond of her. She has learnt the basics in cooking from her. But as she is all alone she is not interested in cooking and she hardly cooks at home. She is neither regular nor particular in taking food as there is nobody to supervise or cajole her into eating. Most often she has just one meal in a day. Often it is her aunts who provide her with that meal.

Once a year at Diwali, she rebuilds her jhuggi alone. She decorates the house drawing colourful designs (*Rangoli*) artistically on the wall and floor. She even helps her relatives in making their jhuggis.

Kali is engaged to be married. She doesn't dress like other Rajasthani girls. She neither covers her head with a veil nor wears any silver jewellery or traditional costumes. She doesn't desire to beautify herself like other girls. She has neither desires nor goals for the future.

Kali tries to find meaning to her life through her friends. Though all her neighbours are her relatives they are all busy with their own families, work and problems. In reality, Kali is a lonely person who treads her way alone despite having relatives and friends. Though she is on the verge of attaining puberty she seems very immature in both her outlook and behaviour. Being ignorant and innocent she is growing with uncertainty and insecurity without desires, hopes or aspirations. However, the day she attains menarche, she will have to separate from her peer group and consider herself as a grown up girl. She will not be allowed to play and spend time as she does now. It will be a sad day in her life to give up her only wealth and assets in this world, i.e. her friends and learn to lead life truly alone. Being a closed and reserved person she is not able to express what she wants to be.

Kali is a girl who is growing and passing each day of her life aimlessly, earning because she has to survive, doing household work because she is a girl and because other girls do so. Her life goes on as a routine. When will the day dawn for girls like Kali?

12. Janu

Janu is a quiet, reserved young girl and is 13 years of age. She lives in a single-room house measuring 4' X 7'. This small space accommodates Janu's entire family of seven members. Her house is sparsely furnished, and adjoining courtyard forms the kitchen.

Janu's mother works at construction site and her father does white-washing work. They hail from Rajasthan and they migrated to Delhi in search of employment. Janu is the eldest of their five children and she is also reported to be their only girl child. This unique position, however, leaves a lot of burden on her slender shoulders - a burden she is barely able to carry.

For a child of 13 years, Janu has a lot on her hands. She virtually runs her house. Her day begins at 5.30 a.m. Unlike her well-to-do counterparts, Janu begins her day by sweeping the house, fetching water, washing utensils and when this is over, she settles down to cook for the family. On the completion of this task she accompanies her mother to the construction site and works for about an hour. Following this she returns home to look after her younger siblings. She grabs an hour of leisure time in the morning to spend in the company of her friends in the park. Her next chore is to collect firewood and cook the evening meal while continuing to take care of her two younger brothers. She yearns for her parents to return and eat their meal after which she is relieved of her work and can settle into sleep.

Janu has earlier worked in a house as domestic help at which time she used to earn Rs. 100 per month. However, it is over a year now that she has given up this work in order to look after the younger children. Since the time Janu was 8 or 9 years of age childhood has been snatched away from her and adulthood has been forced on her. She has few friends — girls like herself who know of no better life and who do not dare dream of brighter prospects.

From a very young age she has realized that in the society she lives, there is a lot of discrimination based on sex. She is able to recount small examples to illustrate this. For example, while she is punished for any error that she commits, her brothers are left unchecked for more serious offences. She works while her brothers play, and, while her desires are curbed and suppressed, her brothers are allowed to dream and pursue their dreams. Often her brothers too quarrel and beat her despite the fact that she does all the household work and that she is the eldest child. Usually it is she who has to listen to taunts and get beatings from her mother when she and her brothers quarrel. This discrimination she has borne patiently and without argument. Her young mind however questions and seeks an answer as to why she pays the price for mistakes done by others.

Being the only girl and the eldest in the family she has to do all the household work. At the age often she worked in a Kothi for a year and a month in a temple. Her jobs included sweeping, mopping and cleaning vessels. It was too much for her. From both the places she earned Rs. 100 per month and she promptly gave her earnings to her mother whereas her 2 brothers who were earning Rs. 10 each per day by working for a *dhaba* and tea shop rarely gave their earning to their parents. Her parents were unmindful of this. Janu's brothers were also given some household duties which they would shirk often, however, if Janu refused or did poor-work she would be beaten or abused.

Being of a curious mind she thinks and questions, but she cannot find an ear to listen to her grievances. She has any teenager's natural and normal curiosity regarding the facts of life. What she lacks is the friend or the parent who can satisfy her curiosities.

Janu is already engaged and she is to be married after a year. As regards the issue of marriage, Janu is unaware of the duties and responsibilities of a married woman. She is either unwilling to divulge the information she has or is unaware of topics such as child birth, sexual intercourse, etc. Looking at her reactions to pointed questions, one gets the impression that she has some knowledge about such matters.

Always hungry and unhappy living itself is an effort. She has learnt to suppress desires. Occasionally, she gets one rupee as pocket money which she promptly spends on eatables. Sometimes she saves money to buy bangles or *chappals* for herself. Her clothes are purchased by her mother.

Janu has kept her house neat and clean though it is too small for seven members. Her parents have occasional fights for one reason or the other with a neighbouring family. The fight takes place mainly due to disputes regarding the boundary of the house. Janu's parents also fight among themselves. She is sad and unhappy about the constant quarrel that takes place between her parents. Her father consumes alcohol and beats her mother. He also beats Janu though she is grown up. Her mother too beats her if she commits a mistake while at work.

When everybody is out at work she has to care for the house and her siblings. Due to this she is forced to remain at home all the 24 hours and hardly gets time like her other friends to go out into the open space to play. Sometimes she tries to make time to be with her friends. All the time, however, she has to carry her young brother with her, even when she plays game such as making mud houses, *'gitte'* etc. All her friends do their own household work: They go together to collect firewood.

Janu's daily diet is very poor. Being at home all the time and with no money in hand she has to remain hungry often. Depending on the availability of food in the house Janu has meals once or twice a day. Caring and feeding for two years old brother is a difficult task. Whenever he caries due to hunger, Janu has to try to satisfy him by feeding him with plain water as there is neither any milk nor any other eatables in the house. Due to lack of food and inadequate nutrition and excessive work Janu looks very weak. She recalls the days when she was working in a house at a tender age with too much work and a perpetually hungry stomach, "I used to get so tired and hungry. The employers at the house where I worked ate in front of me but never gave anything to me. That's why I longed to leave that place. The arrival of one more brother in the family helped me and compelled my parents to prevent me from working outside in order to look after my younger brother". Janu is unable to confide all these matters to anybody and has learnt to handle things at her own level.

Though Janu's friends smoke, she has never smoked because her mother doesn't smoke like most other Rajasthani women. Janu doesn't mind smoking but fears that if somebody reports this to her another then she might be reprimanded.

Janu is engaged to a boy who is a sweeper in a government office. Her '*gauna*' will take place after a year. Janu is not able to understand the concept of marriage. She has conflicting ideas but prefers to go by her parents wishes. She has never considered it her right to choose or do something of her choice. One can only presume that this young girl has had previous experiences which have taught her that she has no right to exercise choices since she is a girl. She yearns to study for the simple reason that "many children go to school". She wishes to learn sewing and she has attended classes for two weeks. These were later stopped by her mother so that she could take care of her younger brothers. She has also attended non-formal education classes in the neighbourhood which was also abruptly stopped for the same reason. But Janu still nurtures a hope to study and learn sewing. Her reasons for these desires are as yet not crystallized. Now her strongest wish is to have a "permanent" and secure house of her own where she can dwell, eat, sleep, work and live peacefully.

Often she appears to be ruminating and yet constantly in search of "something". Being reserved, she was neither frank nor open on issues such as her knowledge regarding sensitive topics such as rape. It was reported later by open of her friends that Janu had a elder sister who had been raped. The sister has been married away and is not mentioned in the family. For no fault of hers, the sister has been cut off from the family. Janu herself has not experienced a happy childhood and has received little love and affection from her parents and brothers. Being a girl child she has had to always sacrifice her desires and opportunities for the sake of her younger brothers. It is possible that Janu pays the price for the misfortune that befell her sister. Her life is a struggle and spells hard work. Inspite of her best efforts, Janu receives little attention or love from her family. It is possible that he anxiety created by the elder sister's misfortune has made the parents strict with Janu. However, it is said to see Janu paying the price for no fault of hers. Her story also tells us how a family is often unjust with members who have fallen into ill-luck (for example, her sister).

At a very tender age she has shouldered the responsibility of house keeping and looking after the siblings. In return for this she has received hearings and abuses. Her parents house for her is like a prison where she has to work and dwell without either love, affection or a kind word from her family. Before she has felt the need to do so she has learnt both cooking and the rearing of children. Janu gives the impression of concealing some unpleasant experiences. However, as she is not communicative it is difficult to ascertain this. Atleast one reason for her unhappy life can be explained in her own words, "My father consumes liquor and quarrels every night. He beats me as well as my mother". On the whole, Janu seems to be a depressed child who in her life had very little in terms of happiness. Her eyes are her most striking feature and hold a lot of pathos. She doesn't say much and lets her eyes speak for her ... and they tell a sad and lonely tale.

CALCUTTA

13. Saraswati Das (13)

Saraswati, aged 13, came to Calcutta nearly 8 years back with a one-year old sister and her parents, and took shelter under a bus stand in South Calcutta. It was poverty that drove them out from their village. She started picking up things from a nearby dumping ground. She does not remember when her father left them and went away where she does not know. Her mother and the two sisters had to continue ragpicking and maintain themselves. One day her mother too disappeared. Since then she and her sister have been living with another woman who has living with her children in an adjoining place. She now calls her mother. The woman, Moyna, looks after these two children and protects them. Saraswati specially picks up coal and metal pieces which are collected by the middleman who comes every evening. The total collection from the sale is taken by Moyna, their present mother. Saraswati has never gone to any school. She went for a few days to an IPER Holiday School for Child Workers but she could not continue there as at 10 a.m. and 4 p.m. daily the lorry carrying the load of the waste comes to the dumping ground and she has to be there if she has to get something in the teeth of strong competition from other ragpickers. But she is very eager is learn and go to school and she is very sorry that she could not attend the IPER School regularly. The only recreation she has gotis to go to a nearby temple where *bhajans* are sung on specific days. In the monsoon they are in a miserable condition and often have to stand in knee-deep water throughout the day and night as there is no high place nearby.

In winter too she has to sleep in the open street under the bus stand. Saraswati thus dislikes the winter and hates the monsoon most. As she is growing old she has to face some eveteasing from local boys but she said that she could protect herself. She has attained puberty. She is thinking of marriage but has no specific boy in mind.

14. Munna Majhi (8)

Munna, aged 8, and his 4-year-old sister Munni were living with their parents on the pavement of Convent Road in central Calcutta along with many other pavement dwelling families. The family migrated from a village near Calcutta after the serious flood of 1984. Their father was working as a porter on a daily wage basis. The two children helped their mother in picking up papers and pieces of wood from a nearby wood-cutting shop. But almost every second day the parents fought with each other over money and other matters which Munna could not understand. During their quarrels the two children were taken care of by a a neighbouring family. One day the quarrel was too serious and

Munna's father hit his mother with a rod and she died in a hospital. Now their father is in jail serving his term. Munna does not know what has happened to him or when he will come back. The two children continue picking up papers, pieces of wood, coal, metal pieces and sell them to a nearby shop. Munna buys some food from a nearby hotel and feeds his sister. In the night they sleep with the family staying in the same area. Munna is very keen and eager to go to school. But hard pressed with time and responsibility of looking after his sister he is unable to attend any school, not even a Holiday School of IPER on weekends.

15. Mungli Mondal (7)

Mungli Mondal, aged 7, lived with her mother, one elder sister and one elder brother along a swimming pool in South Calcutta. Her mother and sister worked as maidservants while her brother loafed about. Mungli did not have much attachment for anything but she showed interest in studies and joined the IPER Late-afternoon School for Street Children. Now Mungli is not alive. She died an unnatural death inside a big pipe that was kept on the side of a road by the civic authorities for installation. She was not very much missed in the evening when her mother and sister returned from work. Later when it was very late a search was started and next morning her body was found among the rain water pipes that were kept along the road. Nobody bothered much about how she died. The mother and the brother buried her body in a nearby burial ground. The family is still continuing to live in the same place. But the mother has met with an accident recently when she was hit by a bus and has been incapacitated for life.

16. Manoj Chowdhury (16)

Manoj and Saroj are two brother aged 16 years and 13 years. They sell chhatu (gram powder) on the pavement opposite to a school for the whole day. Their father, Prakash Chowdhury, earlier lived in Bihar and worked as cook in a *dhaba*. But due to the closing down of the *dhaba* and his inability.to get a job anywhere else he has come to Calcutta with his three sons and wife. They live in a room in a slum but their occupation compels them to sit on the road selling gram powder to the cart pushers, rickshaw pullers and porters all through the day. Even in the evening her sells tea and *bhajis* and the two sons Manoj and Saroj help him. Both Manoj and Saroj used to go to school at their village in Bihar but had to give up their studies when they came to Calcutta.

In spite of living in front of a school, Parkash could not afford to spare the money and time to educate his sons. But since 1984 he has been sending his elder son, Manoj, and since 1985 the second son, Saroj, to the Holiday School for Child Workers run by IPER at the school building across the road.

Both Manoj and Saroj have already attained fifth standard and are making definite progress in their studies. In spite of all their eagerness and interest they are often compelled to remain absent from school due to pressure of work. This is considerably hampering the progress of the two brothers. But it is the issue of subsistence that matters more than anything else in their life.

17. Ayub (12)

Ayub, 12, lives on the pavement of Park Circus with his mother and two younger sisters. His father died of tuberculosis long time back. His mother works as a maidservant in four houses and earns approximately Rs. 120 per month. Ayub has already worked in different places starting from tea-stalls to an ice-depot and now he is working in a roadside garage. He now earns Rs. 60 per month and contributes it towards the maintenance of the family. He is very keen to study and is presently studying at IPER Holiday School for Child Workers and is making appreciable progress. But environmental problems often keep him away from the school. The most common of them is that during the monsoon the area being very low-lying gets flooded and Ayub with his mother and sisters and their meagre belongings has to shift to some other place which is mostly the stairs in front of a shop or a portico. They often have to stand all day in the water with their belongings in their hands. During this time they live on a small single meal a day. Ayub has a strong urge to become a mechanic in the garage and if possible one day own such a garage and get a room in a slum where his mother and sister can stay under a roof.

18. Kalipada Sarkar (12)

Kalipada, 12, has nobody but his mother Kamala. His father left them long back and an elder brother who was living with them quarrelled with his mother and left them a few months back. They live along the pavement of Southern Avenue in South Calcutta. Both he and his mother live on ragpicking. He was totally illiterate. Later he joined one of the IPER Open Learning Centers where he has shown considerable interest in the last six months. He has also learned to read and write. But he is very whimsical and possible emotionally disturbed. While attending to his lessons he often runs away to his mother. Sometimes he comes very late, sometimes he is the first person to wait for the teacher.

19. Bhola (11)

Bhola, 11, lives on the pavement of Park Circus market with his father, a taxi driver, and mother who occasionally sells different types of wares in the market. Bhola works in a *chappal* repairing shop from 9 a.m. to 9 p.m. with a couple of hours' break in the afternoon. He earns Rs. 50 to Rs. 60 per month. He had an attack of polio as a child and requires a stick to walk. He is a very intelligent boy with a smile always on his face and interest for everything new. He has been attending one of the IPER Holiday Schools for the last two years and is making definite progress.

The only complaint he has got is that as he has to live on the pavement and has to use a stick as his crutch, he is often attacked by street dogs and is often bitten by them. He hates going to the hospital and getting injected for such dog bites. Bhola is waiting for a day when he will grow up and would earn more to have a room for himself and his parents where they can live peacefully.

29

PREVALENCE OF CHILD LABOUR IN INDIA: A SECONDARY DATA ANALYSIS

The problem of child labour (those below the age of 15 years) in developed countries is insignificant when compared with the problem in less developed countries. The low level of child labour in former countries was achieved mainly by laws governing the employment of children, by recognising the need to educate children and by increasing real incomes of parents due to industrial and social development. Besides, with industrial development, children were increasingly substituted by machines from the peripheral jobs, which were the children's major occupations. The welfare measures of the government in the form of free education, establishment of orphanages and homes for destitutes etc., also would have assisted in the reduction of employment of children. The near absence of child labour in the developed countries has resulted in excluding children below 15 years of age from the labour force.

Despite the significant progress made in industrial and social development, India has not yet been able to grapple with the problem of child labour.

This paper aims at providing a perspective of the situation regarding child labour in India. The term child labour applies to population of 5-14 year age group as those in the 0-4 age category are not capable either physically or mentally or participate in any meaningful economic activity. Information will be given for those States in the Indian Union with more than 10 million population according to 1971 Census (which together account for 97 per cent of the Indian population) so as to examine regional variations. Rural-urban differences in work participation will be looked into because of the existence of differences in the employment structure in the rural and urban areas. In urban areas a higher proportion of children are expected to be in schools because of better educational facilities, high disposable income of parents and awareness of the beneficial aspects of schooling and education. Sex differences also affect work participation and hence information will be given separately for males and females.

The relevant data for the study comes mainly from Census of India 1961 and 1971. This will be supplemented by information from reports based on various rounds of National Sample Survey.

Use of census data for a sensitive subject like child labour has its own limitations. For example, the preference for digits 'O' and '5' in age reporting in India is very conspicuous. This problem will be compounded for working children in whose case deliberate misreporting will be resorted to, as children below 15 years of age are not legally permitted to work in certain occupations. The resulting depression in the number of working children in the 5-14 year age group cannot, however, be gauged.

Participation rates among children would show variation even for small age differences unlike for adults who are within the working age group. Since the Census and the National Sample Survey Reports give information for broader age groups of children classified by economic activities, one has to be satisfied with the same.

Comparison between Census reports of 1961 and 1971 regarding work participation is also difficult because of differences in concepts and definitions. Besides reference periods in both Census and National Sample Survey reports for activity status etc., differ among themselves, imposing their own unquantifiable effect. National Sample Survey results are available mainly at all-India level and thus state-wise differences cannot be studied.

With all these limitations, Census and National Sample Survey reports are the sources to get information at all-India level, and for states together, on a comparable basis.

Child Population

Table 29.1 gives the child population of 5-14 year age group in India and states in 1961 and 1971. It shows that 26 per cent and 27.5 per cent respectively of 1961 and 1971 population fall into the 5-14 age group. These percentages are significant because they reveal the magnitude of the problem of child labour that would arise even if only a very small fraction of children were to be labourers. It may also be observed that except in the case of Kerala, for all other states the percentage share of child population has increased in 1971 when compared to 1961. This indicates that the incidence of child labour is accelerating almost in every state. Even a decline in fertility which can be expected over the future years will not be able to reduce this incidence to any considerable extent because (1) a decline in per couple fertility need not lead to a decline in the number of children as the number of couples in the reproductive ages itself is high and increasing and (2) falling infant and child mortality rate may nullify the effect of falling fertility.

Child Population by Activity Status

An examination of child population by activity status (Table 29.2) at the all-India level reveals that about half of them are 'dependents' (wasting time by interpretation of the term in Census parlance) and that only about one-third of them are attending schools. As far as workers among them are concerned, they accounted for 13 per cent in 1961 and 7 per cent in 1971 yielding the numbers of 14.5 million and 10.8 million

TABLE 29.1

Percentage Share of Children to Total Population for India and Selected States, 1961 and 1971

States	*1961*		*1971*	
	*Absolute number**	*Per-centage*	*Absolute number**	*Per-centage*
1	2	3	4	5
Andhra Pradesh	9225	25.64	11952	27.47
Assam	3298	27.78	4466	29.86
Bihar	12496	26.90	15772	27.99
Gujarat	5575	27.02	7635	28.60
Karnataka	6453	27.36	8213	28.03
Kerala	4678	27.67	5740	26.89
Madhya Pradesh	7913	14.44	11521	27.66
Maharashtra	10143	25.64	13585	26.95
Orissa	4369	24.90	6168	28.11
Punjab and Haryana	5631	27.73	6895	29.23
Rajasthan	5354	26.56	7385	28.66
Tamil Nadu	8057	23.92	10172	24.69
Uttar Pradesh	18890	25.61	24004	27.17
West Bengal	9041	25.86	12553	28.33
India	113980	25.97	150778	27.51

Source: Census of India 1971; Series 1, India Part II-c(ii) *Social and Cultural Tables.*
Census of India 1961, Volume 1, India Part II-c(i).
* In thousands.

respectively. Of the remaining, majority were engaged in household duties. This clearly shows that failure of the country to achieve so far, the Constitutional goals. State-wise rates for activity status vary and correspondingly the magnitude of the situation facing each state differs from that of the others.

Work Participation Rate

Table 29.3 presents the required information from 1961 and 1971 Census of India publications for India and at state level. Though figures for 1961 and 1971 are given, they cannot be compared for the overall participation rates because of definitional changes. It is obvious from the Table that rates for 1961 are invariably higher than those for 1971.

TABLE 29.2

Percentage Distribution of Children by Activity Status in Rural and Urban India, 1961 and 1971

Activity Status	*1961*					*1971*				
	Rural		*Urban*		*Total*	*Rural*		*Urban*		*Total*
	Male	*Female*	*Male*	*Female*		*Male*	*Female*	*Male*	*Female*	
Workers	16.61	12.29	5.42	2.45	12.69	11.41	4.61	4.09	1.23	7.13
Fulltime Students	35.37	14.64	60.78	45.71	30.35	36.63	18.99	61.41	51.99	33.62
Household Duties	0.33	13.20	0.22	8.85	6.13	1.96	17.79	0.36	7.71	8.46
Dependents	47.48	59.75	33.10	42.84	50.64	49.40	58.26	33.31	38.78	50.29
Others	0.21	0.12	0.48	0.15	0.19	0.60	0.35	0.83	0.29	0.50
Total (%)	100.00	100.00	100.00	100.00	100.00	100.00	100.00	100.00	100.00	100.00
Total (No. in thousands)	48904	45121	10445	9510	113980	63861	58437	14847	13633	150778

Source: Census of India 1971, Series 1, India, Part II-b(ii) *General Economic Tables.* Census of India 1971, Vol. I, India Part II-b(iii) *General Economic Tables.*

TABLE 29.3

Work Participation Rate of Children by Sex and Place of Residence, 1961 and 1971

State	*1961 Work participation rates*						*1971 Work participation rates*					
	Rural		*Urban*		*Total*		*Rural*		*Urban*		*Total*	
	Male	*Female*	*Male*	*Female*	*Rate*	*Rank*	*Male*	*Female*	*Male*	*Female*	*Rate*	*Rank*
Andhra Pradesh	27.21	20.01	9.49	5.12	20.17	1	20.36	11.81	7.06	2.63	14.05	1
Assam	12.94	11.16	5.65	1.79	11.52	9	9.86	1.15	4.39	1.33	5.37	10
Bihar	15.67	10.21	5.87	1.92	12.34	8	10.68	3.19	4.13	0.87	6.91	8
Gujarat	14.18	13.58	3.23	1.52	11.00	10	11.45	5.19	3.25	0.77	2.84	12
Karnataka	21.01	14.91	8.79	4.29	15.48	4	16.38	6.54	6.59	2.35	9.85	2
Kerala	3.36	3.03	3.45	2.70	3.19	14	2.11	1.77	1.89	2.07	1.93	13
Madhya Pradesh	21.86	20.86	4.29	2.62	18.83	3	14.28	7.64	2.91	1.17	9.65	3
Maharashtra	16.87	18.17	4.40	2.44	13.82	6	10.99	7.59	2.95	1.11	7.27	6
Orissa	19.62	10.96	7.52	3.33	14.81	5	14.21	2.34	5.59	1.49	7.98	4
Punjab and Haryana	14.17	7.27	4.02	0.80	9.36	12	10.86	0.62	3.95	0.23	5.37	10
Rajasthan	24.60	23.10	4.87	2.74	20.64	2	12.84	4.92	3.61	0.72	7.96	5
Tamil Nadu	17.41	13.00	6.82	4.33	12.60	7	11.61	5.48	3.61	2.10	7.01	7
Uttar Pradesh	14.41	7.51	5.84	0.96	10.22	11	8.78	2.56	4.78	0.48	5.53	9
West Bengal	9.10	2.48	3.12	0.31	4.99	13	8.15	1.08	2.98	0.71	4.08	11
India	16.61	12.29	5.42	2.45	12.69		11.41	4.61	4.09	1.23	7.13	

Source: Census of India 1971, Series, 1, India Part II-B(i) *General Economic Tables.* Census of India 1961, Volume 1, India, Part II-B(i) *General Economic Tables.*

Note: Percentage may not total 100 because of rounding.

Looking at the state-wise overall rates it may be seen that Kerala has the lowest rate of participation in both the years whereas Andhra Pradesh had the highest. Kerala and West Bengal with low rates in both 1961 and 1971 and Gujarat with low rates in 1971 have relatively lower incidence of child labour. Andhra Pradesh, Madhya Pradesh and Karnataka show a fairly high incidence in both the years. Overall relative ranking of the states remained almost the same during both the years.

Work Participation by Sex and Place Residence

Apart from the overall participation rate, Table 29.3 gives rates for each Census by sex and place of residence. It can be seen that with the exception in the case of rural Maharashtra in 1961 and urban Kerala in 1971, male participation rates were much higher than female participation rates. With the exception of Kerala for both the Censuses and rural Maharashtra for 1961, in all other cases the sexwise difference was quite evident. It may also be noticed that rural participation rates are higher than the comparable urban participation rates in all the cases except for Kerala males in 1961 and Kerala females in 1971.

The relative ranking of states undergoes a considerable change when sex and residence are considered. Andhra Pradesh remains the highest for all cases except for rural females in 1961. But Kerala does not have the lowest rate for females for either of the Censuses which goes to West Bengal in 1961 and Punjab and Haryana in 1971. The noticeable feature in Kerala's child work participation, apart from the low rate, is the lack of considerable difference between rural-urban rates and male-female rates for both 1961 and 1971.

Results of various rounds of the National Sample Survey, at all-India level for rural and urban areas separately *vis-a-vis* child workers are given in Table 29.4. One advantages of this data compared to Census is the break-up available for child workers by age group. (But unfortunately the same grouping pattern was not followed in the different rounds as can be seen from the Table). The results reveal that participation rate increases with age for both the sexes. They also conform that rural participation rates are higher than the corresponding urban participation rates and that the rates for males are higher than those of corresponding female rates.

The proportion of man-days spent by children belonging to the 0-9 and 5-14 age groups by sex, separately, for small cultivator households and non-cultivating wage earner households, for states, obtained from the 25th round of National Sample Survey. It was devoted to time disposition and wage rate for economically weaker sections of the rural population in India is given in Table 29.5.

In general, it appears that the children of the cultivating households spent more man-days in the labour force than those of non-cultivating wage earner households. It can be attributed to higher days spent on their own farm (not given in the Table). But exceptions are noted in Punjab, Kerala, Maharashtra and West Bengal. The reasons for these exceptions could be that the small cultivator families in these states possess only small cultivable areas of land.

TABLE 29.4

Labor Force Participation Rates of Children in Rural and Urban India by Sex and Age According to The National Sample Survey data for Specified Rounds

Round	*Duration*	*Reference period*	*Age group*	*Rural* *Male*	*Rural* *Female*	*Age group*	*Urban* *Male*	*Urban* *Female*
1	2	3	4	5	6	7	8	9
9	May—November 1955	Usual status	0-6	0.10	0.07	0-6	0.13	0.04
		One Year	7-15	29.28	16.07	7-15	11.06	5.01
10	December 1955 to May 1956	One day	0-6	0.08	0.09	0-6	0.03	0.02
			7-15	28.77	12.98	7-15	13.42	4.31
11 and 12	August 1956—August 1957	One day	0-6	0.26	0.05	0-6	0.05	—
			7-15	25.79	13.93	7-15	10.87	3.94
14	July 1958—June 1959	One week	5-11	10.75	7.14	0-11	1.39	0.81
			12-14	48.75	29.47	12-14	16.93	8.18
15	July 1959—June 1960	One week	0-11	11.12	3.48	0-11	1.11	0.63
			12-14	48.26	26.69	12-14	7.89	3.52
16	July 1960—June 1961	One week	5-9	3.28	2.40	5-9	0.52	0.73
			10-14	32.73	22.97	10-14	11.69	6.79
17	September 1961—July 1962	One week	5-9	2.02	1.16	5-9	0.18	0.11
			10-14	20.43	12.90	10-14	8.97	4.36
19	July 1964—June 1965	One week	5-9	2.84	1.99	5-9	2.93	2.74
			10-14	22.23	18.07	10-14	11.35	7.44
21	July 1966—July 1967	One week	5-9	2.63	2.77	5-9	0.38	0.22
			10-14	24.58	19.89	10-13	6.11	3.56
						14	16.75	7.59

Source: Pravin Visaria "Employment and Unemployment in India—A review of selected statistics" in *Report of the committee of Experts on Unemployment Estimates,* Planning Commission, Government of India, 1970, Appendix II.

It would thus appear that small cultivator households, rather than utilising their expected better financial position *vis-a-vis* non-cultivating wage earners, for educating their children, employ them on their own farms and add to family income. The need for adults to earn periodical cash income also could be a contributory factor for employing children on their own farm, when weaker sections have in their possession cultivable land. Side by side, the unwillingness to hire child labour due to lower productivity and/ or minimum wage legislation, might be acting as a depressant of employment of children from non-cultivating wage earner households.

TABLE 29.5

Percentage Distribution of Man-days Spent in Labour Force by Small Cultivator and Non-Cultivating Wage Earner Households in Rural Areas by Sex and Age, 1970-71

State	*Small cultivator households*				*Non-cultivating wage earner households*			
	Males		*Females*		*Males*		*Females*	
	0-9	*10-14*	*0-9*	*10-14*	*0-9*	*10-14*	*0-9*	*10-14*
Andhra Pradesh	3.34	53.81	3.60	28.35	2.87	44.79	1.02	21.84
Assam	2.14	16.34	2.08	3.30	1.76	12.27	—	4.63
Bihar	3.21	24.11	2.59	19.84	2.03	18.00	1.80	14.36
Gujarat	2.34	27.25	1.17	16.19	0.80	14.76	1.28	6.95
Haryana	3.67	18.88	2.17	9.77	—	39.04	1.63	14.74
Karnataka	2.29	45.53	1.43	28.47	0.82	32.76	0.95	35.41
Kerala	—	12.34	0.41	9.34	—	13.27	—	17.81
Madhya Pradesh	4.78	46.61	2.76	30.56	3.54	35.20	2.28	21.85
Maharashtra	3.27	28.22	2.73	25.57	5.34	30.63	3.10	33.84
Orissa	4.30	40.95	3.61	22.47	4.33	25.26	7.41	17.18
Punjab	2.01	34.26	0.82	5.20	3.58	41.68	2.73	13.90
Rajasthan	4.82	48.31	3.40	37.84	1.87	47.09	1.50	28.57
Tamil Nadu	1.63	25.83	3.41	30.72	0.29	27.38	0.31	22.91
Uttar Pradesh	1.98	27.80	4.45	22.52	1.88	23.06	1.21	13.83
West Bengal	0.90	19.23	1.71	4.50	1.71	22.89	0.68	8.03
India	2.73	30.92	2.75	21.24	2.23	28.46	1.59	19.26

Source: National Sample survey Report No. 237, *The Disposition and Wage Rate for Economically Weaker Sections of the Rural Population of India,* 25th Round July 1970 to June 1971. (All sub-rounds combined).

Female Participation Rate by Marital Status

It may appear surprising that one should consider participation rate by marital status for female children who are less than 15 years of age, especially when the legal minimum age of marriage in India for females is 18 years. But 11.75 per cent of all children in the 10-14 years age group are ever married (children in the 5-9 age group were "regarded" as never married for the purpose of the all India Table and all state Tables). This is information is available only for 1971 Census and the marital status of the children is classified into 4 categories: never married, currently married, widowed, and divorced/separated.

Work participation by marital status for female children (percentage of workers in each marital status category to the total population in the corresponding marital status within 5-14 age group) is given Table 29.6 The Table reveals that the lowest rate is for never married' group and the highest is for 'divorced/separated' group. The rate of divorced separated group is double than that of widows, the next highest group. Rural rates are higher than urban rates for each marital status category. These trends hold true for majority of the states.

TABLE 29.6

Female Child Work Participation Rates by Marital Status and Place of Residence, 1971

State	*Never married*			*Currently married*			*Widowed*			*Divorced/Separated*		
	Rural	*Urban*	*Total*	*Rural*	*Urban*	*Total*	*Rural*	*Urban*	*Total*	*Rural*	*Urban*	*Total*
Andhra Pradesh	9.66	2.26	8.20	44.93	17.97	42.86	53.42	45.00	52.88	62.92	39.02	61.62
Assam	1.14	1.31	1.14	7.71	2.79	5.36	33.33	40.00	36.36	0.00	0.00	0.00
Bihar	2.38	0.70	2.21	10.75	4.60	10.47	22.56	28.57	22.72	18.58	0.00	18.27
Gujarat	5.02	0.75	3.88	13.71	5.16	12.87	0.00	0.00	—	33.33	0.00	23.53
Haryana	0.92	0.28	0.83	4.17	1.49	3.91	20.00	12.50	17.86	0.00	0.00	0.00
Karnataka	6.09	2.19	5.18	18.11	12.80	17.56	31.97	46.67	32.82	29.03	50.00	31.94
Kerala	1.75	2.07	1.80	7.30	2.34	6.77	40.00	0.00	0.00	36.36	8.70	40.00
Madhya Pradesh	5.70	0.91	4.88	22.13	7.30	21.32	26.16	14.81	25.34	42.20	18.18	39.04
Maharashtra	6.61	1.00	5.00	31.99	10.18	29.83	34.64	12.50	33.34	46.13	33.67	44.32
Orissa	2.29	1.47	2.24	4.52	4.22	4.51	11.85	0.00	11.68	10.91	0.00	10.82
Punjab	0.17	0.17	0.17	1.12	2.26	1.30	0.00	—	0.00	—	—	—
Rajasthan	3.58	0.50	3.04	14.60	3.31	13.53	23.66	12.90	22.62	4.55	—	4.55
Tamil Nadu	5.44	2.08	4.43	19.81	10.05	17.89	60.00	0.00	40.00	38.46	33.33	37.93
Uttar Pradesh	1.77	0.41	1.55	8.96	3.04	8.73	7.54	8.58	7.57	3.28	0.00	3.23
West Bengal	0.99	0.67	0.93	33.42	3.47	3.43	43.48	14.29	29.55	83.31	9.38	68.86
India	3.86	1.13	3.32	16.11	6.33	15.53	22.54	18.40	22.22	42.83	25.19	41.35

Source: Census of India, 1971, Series I, India, Part II-B(ii) *General Economic Tables.*

Note: The particular Table in the Census which gives this information includes in the never married category children belonging to 0-4 years. Hence while calculating the rates for 'Total' and 'Never married' their number taken from Census of India 1971, Series 1, India, Part II-C(ii) *Social and Cultural Tables* was deducted.

These observations have to be qualified because of the nature of information itself. The 'never married' category includes children of 5-9 years of age unlike the rest of the groups and work participation among them is low. Therefore, one has to be cautious in attributing their low participation rate entirely to their marital status and in comparing the same with the rates for other categories of females. Similarly those with broken marriages, either through widowhood, divorce or separation, will have a tilt towards upper ages of the age class interval, where participation rate itself is high.

Besides, it has to be mentioned that the number of workers, as well as total number of children in the widowed and divorced/separated marital status category were small, depriving the advantage of large numbers.

Within each marital status, there are considerable variations among states. These variations besides being related to differences in overall female participation rates (Table 29.3) will have to be attributed to differing cultural practices prevailing in the states.

Share of Working Children in Total Workers

When the proportion of child workers to total workers is examined, it is found that the child workers from less than 10 per cent of the total workers in all the states (Table 29.7). Not much of a difference between the two Censuses in this respect is found. There are differences in male-female and rural-urban proportions. The proportion is very small in the case of urban males in all the states in both the years under consideration.

TABLE 29.7

Percentage Share of Child Workers in Total Workers by Age, Sex and Place of Residence, 1961 and 1971

State	*1961*					*1971*				
	Rural		*Urban*		*Total*	*Rural*		*Urban*		*Total*
	Male	*Female*	*Male*	*Female*		*Male*	*Female*	*Male*	*Female*	
1	*2*	*3*	*4*	*5*	*6*	*7*	*8*	*9*	*10*	*11*
Andhra Pradesh	10.88	11.01	4.74	7.44	10.27	9.11	11.52	3.66	6.50	9.04
Assam	6.58	9.85	2.21	6.04	7.40	5.91	6.39	2.19	10.38	5.66
Bihar	7.96	9.15	2.86	5.07	8.01	5.94	9.18	2.29	5.40	6.06
Gujarat	—	—	—	—	—	5.52	15.12	1.73	3.15	5.20
Karnataka	9.43	11.26	4.53	7.97	9.29	8.14	11.96	3.55	7.07	7.95
Kerala	2.03	3.94	1.98	5.58	2.65	1.30	3.34	1.13	4.99	1.79
Madhya Pradesh	8.89	10.20	2.02	4.66	8.80	7.31	10.01	1.69	4.47	7.27
Maharashtra	7.82	10.04	1.79	4.66	7.40	5.96	8.60	1.34	3.47	5.37
Orissa	8.28	9.77	2.88	5.85	8.45	7.73	9.56	2.72	6.13	7.18
Punjab	7.49	12.34	2.07	4.73	7.42	7.03	6.98	2.40	1.84	5.95
Rajasthan	11.07	14.72	2.79	7.12	11.53	7.05	14.92	2.25	5.20	7.31
Tamil Nadu	6.72	8.23	3.11	7.06	6.61	4.94	7.66	2.23	5.70	4.84
Uttar Pradesh	6.42	9.32	2.84	4.95	6.69	4.67	9.14	2.65	4.38	4.85
West Bengal	4.56	6.16	1.19	1.89	3.89	4.89	6.97	1.39	5.05	4.14
India	7.61	10.00	2.52	5.81	7.67	6.05	9.62	2.12	5.04	5.96

Source: Census of India, 1971, Series I, India, Part II-B(i) *General Economic Tables* Census of India, 1961, Volume I, India, Part II-B(i) *General Economic Tables.*

One noticeable feature observed is that the proportion of female child workers to female workers was invariably more than male child workers to male workers. This could be explained at least partially by the lesser participation of adult females in economic activities compared to adult males. In a traditional society like India, where males are given more importance mainly because of their role of bread winners and as heads of families, preference will be given to education of male children. That is, stagnation and drop-out rate will be high among female children than among male children, with the result that more male children will be attending school than female children. This means more female children will be available for work.

Presenting the same issue from a different angle would probably show that work participation by a pre-puberty female child would be more acceptable than that of an adult female, as female work participation is yet to be adopted as a norm in Indian society.

Besides, employment opportunities available for adult women and female children are many a time common, permitting substitution of adult workers to a certain extent by children. In other words, among women, substitution of adults by children is possible to a greater extent than among male workers leading to the observation mentioned above. The question that arises, therefore, is whether female children are as a class worse off than male children.

Distribution of Child Workers by Industrial Divisions

The Census reports classify workers into 10 major industrial divisions. The percentage distribution of child workers among these industrial divisions by sex and place of residence for both the Censuses are given in Table 29.8a to 29.8d.

TABLE 29.8A

Percentage Distribution of Urban Male Child Workers by Industrial Divisions, 1961 and 1971

State	*Year*	*Industrial Divisions*										
		I	*II*	*III*		*IV*	*Va*	*Vb*	*VI*	*VII*	*VIII*	*IX*
1	2	3	4	5	6	7	8	9	10	11	12	13
Andhra Pradesh	1961	6.61	8.53		8.69		17.23	16.68	3.92	13.22	1.88	23.24
	1971	4.90	14.67	7.27		0.59	6.73	24.81	4.56	23.24	3.18	10.05
Assam	1961	5.45	1.01		1.43		2.21	26.45	0.66	15.03	1.73	46.03
	1971	5.97	3.12	1.56		0.07	3.16	11.61	1.62	30.17	2.67	40.05
Bihar	1961	9.18	6.33		7.77		12.19	14.46	1.10	8.25	1.86	38.86
	1971	8.57	22.89	3.63		1.68	7.14	12.18	1.38	16.93	2.60	23.00
Gujarat	1961	18.26	4.64		3.63		10.10	16.26	1.07	9.88	2.32	33.84
	1971	8.88	12.00	5.19		0.42	3.26	25.18	3.07	24.85	2.98	14.43
Haryana	1961	—	—	—	—	—	—	—	—	—	—	—
	1971	13.42	10.73	3.31		0.04	3.08	22.32	2.89	21.53	3.44	19.24
Karnataka	1961	14.17	10.06		7.01		12.16	18.83	5.58	8.40	0.99	22.80
	1971	8.75	17.76	6.67		0.46	7.80	21.81	4.80	17.78	7.00	7.17

1	2	3	4	5	6	7	8	9	10	11	12	13
Kerala	1961	1.02	1.74		9.17		6.57	26.37	0.34	6.71	2.23	45.85
	1971	0.66	5.76	9.38		0.19	5.48	21.35	0.73	12.52	3.63	40.30
Madhya Pradesh	1961	11.24	3.67		9.49		14.77	15.98	4.39	12.59	2.54	25.33
	1971	7.99	12.05	5.92		0.87	12.31	17.28	2.22	19.80	3.65	17.91
Maharashtra	1961	5.36	8.61		9.71		8.24	17.59	2.63	12.30	3.59	31.97
	1971	3.61	16.22	4.51		0.45	4.11	22.07	3.48	27.86	3.25	14.44
Orissa	1961	6.49	5.36		6.78		11.01	10.96	0.90	9.72	2.22	46.56
	1971	6.81	14.98	7.04		0.39	5.56	11.54	0.45	20.83	4.00	28.40
Punjab	1961	18.37	4.56		5.87		11.03	20.62	2.53	7.16	2.58	27.28
	1971	12.62	13.96	3.44		0.00	2.86	30.64	1.54	17.48	2.73	14.73
Rajasthan	1961	24.33	3.10		5.98		11.33	15.35	6.41	8.33	2.44	22.73
	1971	17.71	6.69	4.25		0.63	9.79	21.33	4.34	15.17	3.43	16.66
Tamil Nadu	1961	4.95	6.93		6.91		17.52	26.33	2.63	12.90	1.29	20.54
	1971	3.38	12.71	4.47		0.11	11.31	34.56	2.72	20.08	3.61	7.05
Uttar Pradesh	1961	5.89	2.37		2.10		17.33	26.29	2.36	13.01	2.39	28.26
	1971	6.36	7.55	1.43		0.10	13.46	27.96	1.94	14.00	6.20	21.00
West Bengal	1961	1.83	2.15		7.14		5.28	22.52	1.50	14.97	3.14	41.47
	1971	2.60	7.74	1.61		0.06	6.01	21.97	1.24	27.32	3.40	28.05
India	1961	8.66	5.83		6.71		13.07	20.49	3.00	11.31	2.12	28.80
	1971	6.41	12.34	4.44		0.49	8.06	24.34	2.96	20.39	4.11	16.45

Source: Census of India, 1971, Series-I, India, Part II-B(i), *General Economic Tables*.
Census of India, 1961, Vol. I, India, Part II-B(i), *General Economic Tables*.

Notes: 1. Percentages may not total 100 because of rounding.

2. Industrial Divisions: I Cultivation,, II Agricultural Labour, III Livestock, Forestry, Fishing, Plantation etc.; IV Mining and Quarrying, V Manufacturing, Processing, Servicing and Repairs—(a) Household industry, (b) Other than household industry, VI Construction, VII Trade and Commerce, VIII Transport, Storage and Communication, IX Other Services.

3. Industrial divisions III and IV are combined in 1961.

TABLE 29.8B

Percentage Distribution of Rural Male Child Workers by Industrial Divisions, 1961 and 1971

State	*Year*	*Industrial Divisions*										
		I	*II*	*III*		*IV*	*Va*	*Vb*	*VI*	*VII*	*VIII*	*IX*
1	*2*	*3*	*4*	*5*	*6*	*7*	*8*	*9*	*10*	*11*	*12*	*13*
Andhra Pradesh	1961	29.68	29.32		13.71		20.92	0.62	0.42	0.99	0.10	4.22
	1971	26.10	43.29	21.98		0.32	2.64	1.07	0.54	1.28	0.17	2.61
Assam	1961	76.31	8.81		6.68		0.65	0.69	0.21	1.48	0.19	4.98
	1971	70.66	17.72	3.27		0.05	0.34	0.66	0.14	1.95	0.12	5.09
Bihar	1961	41.26	25.59		17.10		9.04	0.76	0.13	0.94	0.12	5.07
	1971	35.67	53.48	5.94		0.17	1.53	0.67	0.06	0.81	0.11	1.56
Gujarat	1961	62.42	20.40		3.49		8.39	0.56	0.47	0.69	0.12	3.48
	1971	47.61	42.68	4.99		0.25	1.23	1.17	0.27	0.91	0.13	0.76
Haryana	1961	—	—	—	—	—	—	—	—	—	—	—
	1971	51.45	29.55	11.53		0.20	1.63	1.80	0.71	0.66	0.19	2.28

1	2	3	4	5	6	7	8	9	10	11	12	13
Karnataka	1961	51.00	21.85		6.59		14.48	1.02	0.50	0.60	0.04	4.22
	1971	36.16	38.74	16.70		0.24	2.38	1.17	0.67	1.20	0.17	2.57
Kerala	1961	12.02	17.61		18.82		11.67	9.71	0.87	2.72	1.00	25.58
	1971	8.41	31.27	18.85		0.29	4.94	14.12	0.69	5.57	1.49	14.37
Madhya Pradesh	1961	59.61	20.49		13.04		3.67	0.21	0.29	0.36	0.03	2.30
	1971	48.27	38.68	8.67		0.08	2.21	0.42	0.19	0.42	0.04	1.02
[Maharashtra	1961	41.49	31.62		17.65		5.33	0.45	0.46	0.59	0.08	2.33
	1971	32.85	53.58	8.56		0.13	1.38	0.82	0.41	0.97	0.13	1.20
Orissa	1961	49.76	24.98		4.66		9.96	0.19	0.05	0.52	0.09	9.81
	1971	35.41	46.10	8.87		0.10	1.85	0.710	0.07	0.75	0.05	6.10
Punjab	1961	60.32	11.62		5.47		15.00	1.02	0.37	0.47	0.16	5.57
	1971	50.10	37.94	6.86		0.01	1.17	1.78	0.36	0.73	0.16	0.87
Rajasthan	1961	68.40	4.93		8.36		14.86	0.25	0.32	0.26	0.04	2.58
	1971	63.60	14.421	16.79		0.25	1.47	0.62	0.34	0.48	0.13	1.90
Tamil Nadu	1961	39.35	26.82		11.38		8.61	2.46	0.64	1.23	0.08	9.43
	1971	29.54	48.86	9.45		0.31	3.00	4.38	0.69	1.71	0.20	1.86
Uttar Pradesh	1961	69.59	16.03		0.92		9.64	0.74	0.18	0.92	0.17	4.81
	1971	57.62	32.39	1.68		0.03	2.95	1.30	0.17	0.74	0.13	2.99
West Bengal	1961	43.68	24.17		13.13		6.01	2.05	0.44	1.38	0.14	9.01
	1971	33.23	50.10	6.19		0.12	1.82	1.62	0.30	1.60	0.22	4.80
India	1961	51.40	21.16		9.85		10.51	0.86	0.33	0.80	0.11	4.98
	1971	41.22	40.21	9.83		0.16	2.07	1.28	0.33	1.00	0.15	2.51

Source: Same as in Table 29.8a.
Notes: Same as in Table 29.8a.

TABLE 29.8C

Percentage Distribution of Urban Female Child Workers by Industrial Divisions, 1961 and 1971

State	*Year*	*Industrial Divisions*										
		I	*II*	*III*		*IV*	*Va*	*Vb*	*VI*	*VII*	*VIII*	*IX*
Andhra Pradesh	1961	8.40	18.94		2.30		31.71	8.00	4.98	3.20	0.25	22.22
	1971	3.13	30.64	1.37		0.94	17.84	17.21	4.40	3.90	1.01	19.56
Assam	1961	2.96	0.82		2.18		35.59	12.05	0.05	1.55	0.09	44.75
	1971	3.88	0.60	1.28		0.00	3.16	1.88	0.13	1.54	0.03	87.50
Bihar	1961	17.00	13.62		6.60		23.24	5.38	2.87	2.07	0.49	27.86
	1971	3.65	39.86	0.83		6.11	7.34	3.99	5.53	2.17	2.47	28.00
Gujarat	1961	34.94	7.21		2.62		21.40	6.63	1.61	2.82	0.53	22.24
	1971	6.76	29.97	1.57		1.15	6.84	15.63	11.55	3.43	1.18	21.92
Haryana	1961	—	—		—		—	—	—	—	—	—
	1971	19.33	24.64	1.56		0.00	7.91	11.41	3.63	2.34	1.30	27.88
Karnataka	1961	15.88	13.32		2.67		29.81	10.17	7.21	1.64	0.04	19.26
	1971	3.60	28.17	3.86		0.63	20.18	14.16	4.79	2.55	5.94	16.12
Kerala	1961	0.77	2.83		0.36		18.39	9.67	0.14	0.81	0.17	66.86
	1971	0.06	4.01	0.11		0.32	7.27	13.50	0.13	1.14	0.22	73.24
Madhya Pradesh	1961	17.20	7.96		5.55		33.78	6.05	5.06	2.39	0.63	21.38
	1971	4.96	24.31	1.25		1.92	32.19	83.49	2.38	2.34	0.86	21.30
Maharashtra	1961	10.15	24.76		2.35		22.54	11.78	2.00	3.18	1.17	22.07
	1971	2.33	32.32	1.53		0.58	9.01	16.63	4.20	2.96	1.59	28.85

State	*Year*	*Industrial Divisions*										
		I	*II*	*III*		*IV*	*Va*	*Vb*	*VI*	*VII*	*VIII*	*IX*
Orissa	1961	2.60	3.63		5.26		18.85	7.91	1.76	7.28	3.16	49.55
	1971	0.65	14.00	2.18		1.62	10.03	5.97	0.76	7.09	8.26	49.44
Punjab	1961	31.89	2.26		1.55		24.31	7.48	2.21	1.42	0.64	28.24
	1971	1.65	7.68	0.27		0.27	21.95	19.34	2.06	6.04	1.51	39.23
Rajasthan	1961	42.89	4.30		3.95		21.14	7.67	2.30	3.04	0.11	14.60
	1971	19.17	11.36	3.27		0.70	23.01	15.15	3.10	2.87	1.04	20.33
Tamil Nadu	1961	4.82	9.03		4.26		43.23	9.61	2.47	1.49	0.30	24.79
	1971	1.71	17.78	5.59		0.13	26.56	26.00	3.13	2.75	1.75	14.60
Uttar Pradesh	1961	5.82	2.22		1.68		56.34	5.63	0.54	3.50	0.33	23.94
	1971	4.19	12.76	1.10		0.00	36.84	9.87	0.45	4.38	1.67	28.74
West Bengal	1961	1.03	3.35		1.38		25.12	15.84	1.70	2.97	0.53	48.08
	1971	0.63	5.47	0.25		0.00	6.79	8.05	0.36	2.72	1.61	74.12
India	1961	12.45	12.23		3.02		31.47	9.05	3.45	2.59	0.43	25.32
	1971	3.57	22.62	2.38		0.60	17.86	15.48	3.57	2.98	2.38	28.57

Source: Same is in Table 29.8a.
Notes: Same as in Table 29.8a.

TABLE 29.8D

Percentage Distribution of Rural Female Child Workers by Industrial Divisions, 1961 and 1971

State	*Year*	*Industrial Divisions*										
		I	*II*	*III*		*IV*	*Va*	*Vb*	*VI*	*VII*	*VIII*	*IX*
1	2	3	4	5	6	7	8	9	10	11	12	13
Andhra Pradesh	1961	34.51	43.03		2.73		11.73	0.77	0.38	0.81	0.01	6.03
	1971	15.53	67.60	4.70		0.32	4.93	2.00	0.53	0.63	0.06	3.70
Assam	1961	74.03	2.27		7.33		13.51	0.48	0.12	0.20	—	2.06
	1971	39.14	10.44	32.25		0.18	3.13	1.51	0.41	0.25	0.04	12.65
Bihar	1961	49.15	29.36		7.48		9.26	0.50	0,12	0.38	0.02	3.73
	1971	14.30	78.71	2.29		0.42	2.14	0.65	0.07	0.23	0.16	1.03
Gujarat	1961	67.58	20.50		2.15		6.32	0.30	0.42	0.20	0.02	2.52
	1971	35.910	59.05	1.70		0.38	0.82	0.76	0.44	0.15	0.05	0.75
Haryana	1961	—	—		—		—	—	—	—	—	—
	1971	49.92	31.85	6.19		0.58	2.96	4.08	1.86	0.11	0.07	2.38
Karnataka	1961	55.66	25.59		3.63		9.30	0.96	0.48	0.38	—	4.00
	1971	18.14	55.27	10.66		0.38	8.06	2.11	1.01	0.44	0.23	3.70
Kerala	1961	6.89	19.57		6.20		31.51	8.28	0.34	0.42	0.23	26.56
	1971	1.18	31.34	6.20		0.18	13.89	18.78	0.19	0.46	0.32	27.46
Madhya Pradesh	1961	67.94	22.38		3.50		3.18	0.30	0.29	0.19	0.02	2.20
	1971	35.53	57.63	1.87		0.13	3.19	1.39	0.31	0.16	0.02	0.77
Maharashtra	1961	53.69	40.18		1.18		2.72	0.23	0.35	0.20	0.02	1.43
	1971	27.59	66.69	1.50		0.12	2.37	0.62	0.41	0.15	0.05	0.80
Orissa	1961	47.79	24.44		2.26		10.95	0.43	0.04	0.56	0.02	13.51
	1971	11.24	60.17	8.09		0.93	7.125	2.05	0.40	1.03	0.14	8.83

1	2	3	4	5	6	7	8	9	10	11	12	13
Punjab	1961	81.56	4.56		0.78		7.76	0.72	0.25	0.08	0.02	4.27
	1971	11.73	39.78	2.20		0.34	14.12	21.96	1.78	0.60	0.16	9.61
Rajasthan	1961	77.80	4.02		5.56		10.02	0.14	0.21	0.12	0.01	2.12
	1971	55.26	21.36	18.26		0.28	1.50	0.45	0.37	0.11	0.08	2.33
Tamil Nadu	1961	38.93	28.82		5.53		12.62	139	0.46	0.30	0.01	11.94
	1971	14.49	60.78	9.15		0.41	6.04	5.94	0.56	0.46	0.12	2.05
Uttar Pradesh	1961	63.66	22.83		0.52		8.66	0.32	0.04	0.30	0.03	3.54
	1971	41.48	51.22	0.96		0.05	3.23	0.85	0.06	0.14	0.04	1.97
West Bengal	1961	52.69	20.13		6.37		13.30	2.37	0.11	0.53	0.04	3.96
	1971	12.90	57.15	8.72		0.32	8.56	2.89	0.18	0.56	0.29	8.43
India	1961	56.64	25.42		3.52		8.69	0.63	0.27	0.34	0.02	4.47
	1971	27.77	57.35	5.12		0.26	4.05	1.78	0.41	0.33	0.09	2.78

Source: Same as in Table 29.8a.

Notes: Same as in Table 29.8a.

It may be recalled before looking into these Tables that participation rates for 1961 are not comparable with those for 1971 because of reasons cited earlier.

Looking at Table 29.8a across the states, it may be concluded in a very broad sense that in 1971 the major industrial divisions in which urban male children were found, are 'manufacturing', 'trade and commerce' and 'other services'. In most states, these three divisions accounted for more than 60 per cent of urban male child workers. It was as high as 80 per cent in Assam. In Assam and Kerala 'other services' alone accounted for 40 per cent of employment. These three divisions were followed by 'agricultural labourers'. Then came 'cultivators', 'household industry', 'transport, storage and communication', and 'mining and quarrying' in that order. For 1961 this broad trend continues except that 'trade and commerce', and 'other services' interchange their positions; so would 'agricultural labourers' and 'cultivators'. Definitional changes may explain the lower figures in 1971 *vis-a-vis* those for 1961 in respect of 'cultivators', 'household industry' ad 'other services'.

In respect of rural male child workers, divisions 'cultivators' and 'agricultural labourers' account for the majority (Table 29.8b). The relative importance of these divisions is not uniform over states. The two groups together account for more than 80 per cent of all the rural male child workers. In Uttar Pradesh and Gujarat, this proportion reached upto 90 per cent. The noticeable exception was Kerala for which 'cultivators' and 'agricultural labourers' accounted only for 40 per cent.

Next in importance to the already mentioned divisions is 'livestock, forestry, plantation etc.' The other divisions account individually for small proportions (although there are differences between them) except in the case of Kerala where the shares of 'manufacturing other than household industry' and 'other services' are quite large (14% each) 'transport and communications', 'construction'; and 'mining and quarrying' take the three bottom positions for rural male children. The share of 'cultivators', 'household industry' and 'other services' are lower in 1971 compared to 1961 and has to be attributed to definitional changes as in the case of urban male children.

For the urban female children it may be said in general that 'other services' constitutes the major division of industry followed closely by 'agricultural labourers' (Table 29.8c). In sex states, Assam, Haryana Kerala, Orissa, Punjab and West Bengal, 'other services' accounted for single largest share, the share in Assam, Kerala and West Bengal being very high. For these six states the differences between the shares of this division and those of the share of the next major division ('agricultural labour' more often) were quite large. In other five states, Andhra Pradesh, Bihar, Gujarat, Karnataka and Maharashtra, 'agricultural labour' had the largest share. For these states, except for Karnataka 'other services' had second rank and the differences with the shares of 'agricultural labour were not as large as in the states where 'other services' had the first rank and some other divisions occupied the second rank. 'Other services' and 'agricultural labour' had the second rank in six and three states respectively. The leading position of 'other services' is maintained in 1961 in 11 out of 14 states.

Next in importance in accounting for urban female employment in 1971 were the divisions 'household industry' (first rank in 4 states, 2nd rank in 2 states and 3rd rank in 6 states) and 'manufacturing other than 'household industry,' interchanging their positions among states. Of the remaining divisions, 'construction' is of next importance to 6 states, 'trade and commerce' to 4 states, and 'cultivators' to 4 states and 'transport storage and communication' to one state, thus making it difficult to assign a rank to each of them considering all states together. 'Mining and quarrying' appears to be of least importance as source of employment for children for all states. The trend observed for 1971 holds mostly true for 1961. Reduction of workers in cultivation and household industry, and increase in agricultural labour between 1961 and 1971, as a phenomenon attributed to definitional change, are applicable to urban females also.

Looking at the details of rural female child workers (Table 29.8d) based on figures for 1971, one can conclude that 'agricultural labour' is the most important division (first in importance in 12 states—and except in Kerala accounts for more than 50 per cent of workers— second in two states and fourth in one state). Next in importance is the division 'cultivators' since except for Kerala and Punjab, cultivators follow closely or lead 'agricultural labourers'. 'Livestock, forestry etc.' and 'household industry' can be ranked 3rd and 4th in importance and were followed generally by 'other services' and 'manufacturing other than household industry' in that order. As far as other divisions are concerned, none of them had any considerable shares—only in very few cases did the share exceed even 1 per cent. However, it may be said 'construction', 'trade and commerce', 'transport, storage and communication' and 'mining and quarrying' would rank in descending order of importance.

In urban areas male children are found employed mainly in 'manufacturing other

TABLE 29.9A

Percentage Distribution of Male Child Workers by Occupational Groups and Place of Residence, 1971

State	*Place of residence*	*Occupational group (Indian Standard Occupational Classification, code number)* 40	43	52	53	54	55	62	64	65	68	75	78	79	83	84	88	89	95	99	*Total*
Andhra	Rural				—		5.53	44.61		24.74											74.88
Pradesh	Urban	7.63	11.25							7.85				6.29		7.68				8.56	49.26
Assam	Rural				23.08				23.22	6.93											53.23
	Urban	11.46	6.63	17.49	31.82																67.40
Bihar	Rural	5.12			8.27			23.13		28.96											65.48
	Urban	10.87	5.86	10.57	20.38								5.23	6.28						5.86	65.05
Gujarat	Rural	5.15						11.44		37.33											53.92
	Urban	5.60	7.84	14.98								7.13					5.84			12.11	53.50
Haryana	Rural	8.11								30.59								9.03		21.46	69.18
	Urban	8.85	6.94	11.13						5.12						7.20				14.41	53.65
Karnataka	Rural							36.18		25.23											61.41
	Urban	6.02	6.10	10.45						7.32		9.66				5.74			5.10	9.32	59.71
Kerala	Rural			15.85	6.17				6.04	17.62	5.69	12.72		5.69	12.72					5.68	69.77
	Urban		6.83	24.48	16.84						6.83		10.33							5.07	70.48
Madhya	Rural									60.39			6.89								67.28
Pradesh	Urban		6.44	12.00									9.93							10.80	39.17
Mahara-	Rural							34.17		22.08										5.37	61.62
shtra	Urban		12.63	17.96	8.93							10.13								6.10	55.75
Orissa	Rural									52.30										6.18	58.48
	Urban	9.51	7.27	11.46	16.73	5.73														18.45	69.15
Punjab	Rural							6.09		51.82								6.76		5.72	70.39
	Urban	10.16	5.87	5.67	7.60							6.06		5.38	8.00	7.18				10.95	65.87
Rajasthan	Rural							65.58		10.29											75.87
	Urban	9.22								5.73		5.47					6.31		6.12	12.56	45.41

Tamil	Rural							12.60		25.40		11.23									49.30
Nadu	Urban	16.13		5.42								16.79	5.70	7.20							51.24
Uttar	Rural	7.81					5.01	6.83		5.95		11.74								8.50	45.84
Pradesh	Urban	9.16			7.69							9.34		8.39		5.08				8.88	48.54
West	Rural			21.15				10.11	5.77	14.47			6.54								58.04
Bengal	Urban	7.00	13.74		23.17									5.46							57.90

Source: Census of India, 1971, Series 1, India, part II-B(V), *General Economic Tables.*

Notes: (a) Only those occupations with more than 5 per cent of child workers are included. Cultivators and agricultural labourers as a group are excluded (b) ISOC code expansion (40) Merchants and shopkeepers, wholesale and retail trade, (43): Salesmen, shop assistants and related workers, (52): Cooks, waiters, bartenders and related workers, (53): Maids and other housekeeping service workers n.e.c., (54): Building caretakers, sweepers, cleaners and related workers, (55): Launders, dry cleaners and pressers, (62): Farmers other than cultivators, (64): Plantation labourers and related workers, (65): Other farm workers, (68): Fishermen and related workers, (75): Spinners, weavers, knitters, dyers and related workers, (78): Tobacco prepares and tobacco product makers, (79): Tailors, dress makers, sewers, upholsterers, and related workers, (83): Blacksmiths, tool makers, and machine tool operators, (84): Machinery fitters, machine assemblers, and precision instrument makers (except electrical), (88): Jewellery and precious metal workers and metal engravers (except printing), (89): Glass formers, patters and related workers, (95): Bricklayers and other construction workers, (99): Labourers n.e.c.

TABLE 29.9B

Percentage Distribution of Female Child Workers by Occupational Groups and Place of Residence, 1971

State	Place of residence	Occupational group (Indian Standard Occupational Classification, code number)																				Total
		35	40	52	53	54	55	62	64	65	71	73	75	77	78	79	89	94	95	97	99	
Andhra	Rural						18.49	12.87		13.82			9.76		22.57							77.51
Pradesh	Urban				13.90		9.44						14.51		27.65			5.20			11.80	82.50
Assam	Rural				14.32				65.89				5.34									85.55
	Urban				31.45																	81.45
Bihar	Rural				9.17			13.20		17.09			5.12		11.03		5.55	9.46				70.92
	Urban				37.79						7.56								7.86		11.06	64.27
Gujarat	Rural							10.84		21.29			5.50				8.57	8.19			9.46	72.23
	Urban				17.03								12.29						17.77		18.48	65.57
Haryana	Rural					7.15				18.59			10.44			6.36	24.12				25.38	92.02
	Urban	6.16		7.39	14.78	7.39							6.16				8.62		6.16		17.24	73.90
Karnataka	Rural							17.14		10.90					26.23						6.14	69.08
	Urban				15.26								14.80		21.72			8.08	5.14		8.75	73.78
Kerala	Rural			33.50	5.52				5.83				23.97		7.75			8.06				84.63
	Urban			59.48	14.74								6.73		7.49							88.44
Madhya	Rural									22.32					30.77		5.87	7.22			7.00	73.18
Pradesh	Urban				12.00								5.69		35.52		5.38	5.90			10.41	74.90
Mahara-	Rural							16.73							17.60			7.93			12.40	66.66
shtra	Urban				35.55								11.12		15.76				6.22		6.45	75.10
Orissa	Rural				5.56					23.93			7.02					10.48			16.02	63.01
	Urban		6.02	5.50	24.08	8.60														6.67	23.80	74.67
Punjab	Rural					9.78				6.49			17.51			6.93	40.53				6.76	88.00
	Urban				19.85	12.21							19.24								10.69	61.99
Rajasthan	Rural							70.34		7.70											5.30	83.34
	Urban				5.76	6.40							15.01		16.03		5.73	7.59			12.54	69.06

Tamil	Rural			10.44		21.16	6.13	16.35		8.31					62.39
Nadu	Urban	9.99						35.23		6.96		18.01			70.19
Uttar	Rural		7.58			6.17		16.95	6.29	6.92	6.23		6.54	5.70	62.38
Pradesh	Urban	11.71	7.54					35.44		6.49					61.18
West	Rural	15.37			22.56					20.31					58.24
Bengal	Urban	70.61								5.19					75.80

Source: Same as Table 29.9a.

Note: (a) Same as Table 29.9a. (b) ISOC code expansion: For codes common to both males and females see, note (b) of Table 29.9a. (35): Clerical and related workers; (71): Miners, quarrymen, well drillers and related workers; (73): Wood preparation workers; (77): Food and beverage processors; (94): Production and related workers n.c.c.; (97): Material handling and related equipment operators, loaders and unloaders.

than household industry', 'trade and commerce' and 'other services' whereas urban female children are found to be engaged mainly in 'other services', 'agricultural labour' and 'household industry'. In rural areas male and female children have common industrial divisions for their employment, the evidence pointing towards agricultural and related activities (cultivators, agricultural labour, livestock, forestry, plantation etc.) and household industry. Thus there seems to be sex biased employed pattern in urban situations as compared to rural settings where such bias is lacking. In these broad generalisations one should not forget certain regional variations which can be noticed by a discerning observer. For example, more than 40 per cent of urban male children are engaged in 'other services' in Assam and Kerala. In urban areas (in majority of the states) more than 20 per cent of the urban male child workers are found in 'manufacturing other than household industry'. Again the proportion of urban female children in Assam, Kerala and West Bengal and to a certain extent in Orissa engaged in 'other services' is very large when compared to other states.

Occupational Distribution of Child Workers

According to Indian Standard Classification of Occupations, occupations are classified into eight major Divisions. They are further divided into groups with each having its own subdivisions. This information is given for all workers excluding 'cultivators' and 'agricultural labourers'.

The purpose of this section being to identify, in as much detail as possible, the occupations at which children are employed, the major divisional groupings are inadequate as they conceal the real pattern of occupational distribution. At the same time, finer subdivisions, which would have been more useful, are not available classified by age. Therefore, this section has to consider the position at group (2 digit) level only.

The state-wise occupational distribution of children by sex and place of residence for the year 1971 is given in Tables 29.9a and 29.9b. In the Tables for each state the percentage shares of those occupations, which account for 5 per cent or more of child workers by sex and residence in that state, are given. These occupations together account for the major share of employment in the respective states, except in a few cases.

Looking at these Tables, it may be generalised for all states considered together, that occupational groups, 'merchants and shop keepers', 'wholesale and retail trade', 'salesmen, shop assistants and related workers' and 'machinery fitters, machine assemblers and precision instrument makers' are male biased. Similarly female biased occupations are 'glass formers', 'potters and related workers', and production and related workers' not belonging to any specified subdivision. Occupational groups 'cooks, waiters, bartenders and related workers (both domestic and institutional)' 'farmers', (other than cultivators'), 'other farm workers', 'spinners, weavers, knitters, dyers and related workers', 'tobacco prepares and tobacco product makers, do not show much sex discrimination in employment. In addition to this, there are certain occupations which are important only for certain states or group of states. For example, plantation work in Assam, Kerala and

West Bengal is important for both sexes of children while in Karnataka, it is of significance for female children. Sweeping, cleaning etc. are important occupational activity groups employing females in Haryana, Punjab and Rajasthan, and both sexes in Orissa.

Occupations which can be distinguished by rural—urban orientation incidentally have sex bias also. That is, male biased occupations are generally urban oriented, and female biased, rural oriented.

An examination of occupational pattern in states reveals a few interesting patterns. A few exceptionally high concentrations of child workers in certain occupations in certain states need special mention. 'Maids and other housekeeping services of miscellaneous nature' employ 81 per cent and 71 per cent of urban female child workers in Assam and West Bengal. Similarly in rural Rajasthan, 'farmers other than cultivators' provide employment for 66 per cent and 70 per cent of male and female children respectively. In rural Assam, 'plantation and related work' accounts for 66 per cent of female child employment. Sixty per cent of rural male child workers serve as 'other farm workers' in Madhya Pradesh and 52 per cent each in Orissa and Punjab. In urban Kerala one finds 59 per cent of urban female child workers in the category of 'cooks, waiters etc.'

The occupation which employs a good proportion of both male and female child workers in almost all states is 'other farm workers'. Second in overall importance comes 'maids, housekeeping and other related work'. 'Farmers other than cultivators' is another group of occupations which is very important from the point of view of rural male child employment.

The importance of occupational groups 'other farm workers' and 'farmers other than cultivators' as a source of employment particularly in rural areas is not surprising, as agriculture and related activities are universally accepted as avenues for child employment. 'Spinning and weaving' is also found to be a major source of employment especially for female children. 'Tobacco preparation and tobacco product makers' were found important in Andhra Pradesh, Karnataka, Madhya Pradesh and rural West Bengal, accounting for about one fifth to one third of female child workers. In Haryana and Punjab 'glass formation and pottery work' absorbed 24 per cent and 41 per cent of female rural workers respectively. In almost all states, quite a good proportion of child workers were classified into 'labourers not elsewhere classified'.

Distribution of Child Workers by Level of Education

Information on distribution of child workers by level of education is presented in Table 29.10. It presents information from various rounds of National Sample Survey. Invariably, information from all the rounds has shown a large majority of child workers in the illiterate groups. They are followed by those in the below primary level. Considering the type of occupations in which they are working, one would not be surprised at these type of distributions.

TABLE 29.10

Percentage Distribution of Child Workers by Level of Education, Sex and Age According to The National Sample Survey Data for Specified Rounds

Place of Residence			*Age Group*	*Level of Education*							
				Illiterate		*Literate below Primary*		*Primary*		*Middle*	
				Male	*Female*	*Male*	*Female*	*Male*	*Female*	*Male*	*Female*
Urban	16	July 1960—June 1961	5-9	89.81	92.48	10.15	7.52				
			10-14	59.89	72.04	40.11	27.96				
Rural	17	Sept. 1961—July 1962	5-9	93.74	98.31	6.26	1.69				
			10-14	88.94	93.74	11.06	6.26				
Urban	19	July 1964—June 1965	5-9	42.42	43.20	49.25	50.90	8.33	5.90		
			10-14	37.86	43.57	25.03	22.62	31.49	26.94	5.62*	6.87*
Urban	21	July 1966—June 1967	5-9	84.16	79.15	12.14	14.37	3.70	6.48		
			10-13	62.84	76.15	23.08	15.48	14.08	8.37		
			14	55.04	64.25	22.90	15.33	21.90	15.10	0.16*	5.32*
Urban	22	July 1967—June 1968	5-9	90.01	82.82	8.31	15.97	1.68	0.21		
			10-13	63.80	79.07	21.94	13.76	14.12	7.04	0.14*	5.32*
			14	52.90	70.11	21.51	15.09	25.39	14.08	0.11*	—
Rural	19	July 1964—June 1965	5-9	72.03	87.05	25.55	12.83	2.42	0.12	—	
			10-14	73.40	88.53	19.41	6.92	5.41	4.18	1.78	0.37

Source: National Sample Survey Report Nos. 103, 173, 181, 190, 214.
*Middle and Secondary School Combined.

Distribution of Female Children by Marital Status

Table 29.11 presents the distribution of working female children as well as non-working female children (for comparison) into 'never married' and 'ever married' categories. 'Ever married' category was not split into 'currently married', 'widowed' and 'divorced/separated' since the latter two groups had only negligible shares. At all-India level it can be seen that while 21 per cent of working children are in the 'ever married' groups, only 5 per cent of non-working children are in this category. For the urban areas, the situation is only slightly different, though revealing lower incidence of 'ever married' children 10 per cent for working, and less than two per cent for non-working.

Significant state-wise variations are observed. The proportion of urban 'ever married' children is the lowest for Kerala (0.39%) followed by Tamil Nadu (0.81%) and Orissa (2.06). The highest rate was for Rajasthan (34.89). Other states sharing high proportion of 'ever married' urban female children are Madhya Pradesh, Bihar and Uttar Pradesh. Among rural working children, the proportion of 'ever married' is the lowest for Assam (0.85%) and the highest for Uttar Pradesh (38.70%). In the rural areas, high percentages were observed in Bihar (32.38%), Madhya Pradesh (34.24%) and Rajasthan (36.12%).

TABLE 29.11

Percentage Distribution of Female Child Workers and Non-Workers by Marital Status and Place of Residence, 1971

State	*Urban*				*Rural*				*Total*			
	Never W	*Married NW*	*Ever W*	*Married NW*	*Never W*	*Married NW*	*Ever W*	*Married NW*	*Never W*	*Married NW*	*Ever W*	*Married NW*
1	2	3	4	5	6	7	8	9	10	11	12	13
Andhra Pradesh	83.86	98.05	16.14	1.95	76.20	96.09	23.80	3.91	76.60	96.51	24.40	3.49
Assam	96.93	98.73	3.07	1.27	99.15	99.89	0.85	0.11	98.94	99.82	1.06	0.18
Bihar	77.41	95.93	22.59	4.07	67.62	91.19	32.38	8.81	67.90	91.67	32.10	8.33
Gujarat	95.90	99.41	4.10	0.59	94.68	98.17	5.32	1.83	94.74	98.50	5.26	1.50
Haryana	83.53	96.58	16.47	3.42	76.05	93.71	23.95	6.29	76.46	94.12	23.54	5.88
Karnataka	91.11	98.75	7.89	1.25	89.71	96.77	10329	3.23	89.94	97.25	10.06	2.75
Kerala	99.61	99.80	0.39	0.20	98.78	99.73	1.22	0.27	98.93.	99.71	1.07	0.29
Madhya Pradesh	74.62	96.34	25.38	3.66	65.76	90.00	34.24	10.00	66.01	91.07	33.99	8.93
Maharashtra	89.68	99.00	10.32	1.00	83.68	97.14	16.32	2.86	84.00	97.68	16.00	2.32
Orissa	97.94	99.29	2.06	0.71	96.41	98.02	3.59	1.98	96.49	98.28	3.51	1.72
Punjab	95.06	99.61	4.94	0.39	95.65	99.39	4.35	0.61	95.51	99.44	4.49	0.56
Rajasthan	65.11	93.62	34.89	6.38	63.88	89.06	36.12	10.40	63.92	89.86	36.08	10.14
Tamil Nadu	99.19	99.85	0.81	0.15	98.91	99.75	1.09	0.25	98.95	99.77	1305	0.23
Uttar Pradesh	83.02	97.42	16.98	2.58	61.30	89.63	38.70	10.37	61.97	90.79	38.03	9.21
West Bengal	92.94	97.94	7.06	2.06	89.05	97.23	9.99	2.77	89.64	97.38	10.36	2.62
India	89.82	98.19	10.18	1.81	78.76	94.69	21.24	5.31	79.42	95.37	20.58	4.63

Source: Census of India 1971, Series I, India, part II-B(ii) *General Economic Tables*.
W = Workers; NW = Non-Workers.

Besides Assam, Tamil Nadu and Kerala also had low rates (1.09% and 1.22% respectively). Though the pattern was the same for both working and non-working children, proportion showed wide variations. These variations could be reflections of cultural norms governing child marriages and also work participation of females in general and children in particular.

Conclusions and Observations

The child work participation in India was observed to be 7 per cent in 1971 as against 13 per cent in 1961. The low percentage observed in 1971 has to be attributed to exclusion of unpaid worker from the worker category. With the huge population that India has, these percentages give alarming number of child workers. Furthermore, the possibility of deliberate concealment of child labour, both by employers and parents/guardians for fear of possible unfavourable consequences of labour legislations, cannot be ruled out. Thus the magnitude of the problem of child labour in India is much more serious than what meets the eye through censuses.

The present paper highlighted the state-wise variations in the intensity of child labour prevailing in the country. The co-existence of low and high problem states within the nation proves that the country does not have to go very far to reduce the overall intensity of the problem. It is probably only a question of creating a conducive atmosphere, such as awareness of the importance of education (especially of female children) and creation of educational facilities etc. In this context, it is worth remembering that the frequently extended target year for universal child education is fast approaching.

It was also noted, to the extent possible, the industries and the occupations in which children are employed in the states. It can be seen that these are not industries or occupations of high productivity. In other words, withdrawal of child labour from the working force is not likely to cause any setback to economic activities or production. Besides, even if some activity is likely to suffer because of the withdrawal of child labour, the large number of unemployed adults available in the country can be made use of.

Data presented in this study cast doubt on the argument that a decline in the importance of agriculture and related activities (the long accepted major avenues for child employment) will reduce the extent of child labour. It would appear that children displaced from agricultural and related activities would land up as shop assistants, waiters, domestic servants etc.

The type of occupations in which children are employed raises a question worth pondering. It is often argued that children are viewed as an economic asset by poor families. On the other hand, all evidence about earnings of children (not examined in this paper) show that these earnings are meagre and that most of the children are employed in sub-human conditions. The question, therefore, is whether the meagre wage offered by the greedy employers providing only physical existence, contributes to the careless attitude of parents in forgetting their obligation towards their children and imbreeding prolifically.

It would appear that lac of strict enforcement of the legal minimum age at marriage also plays a role in child work participation. Depressing though it is, a good proportion of children both currently married and with broken marriages are found to be workers.

In low income countries like India, economic utility of children is very high (compared to high income societies), and they are expected to contribute, however meagre their contribution be, to the family income. So under these circumstances, all that can be expected is, to ease their working conditions and prevent them from working for long hours and in hazardous jobs. The apathy to enforce the protective provisions of the constitution and legislative enactments keeps the conditions of the working children in as precarious a condition as it ever has been.

From the national point of view, the loss due to child labour is of 'no small magnitude. In the hands of to-days' children lies the nation of tomorrow. They are to be equipped with health and education in order to be more useful to the nation. Unfortunately half the children are wasting their time, while a significant fraction of them are breaking their backs to earn a meagre living. Ultimately the nation will have to pay the price for negligence of children.

30

CHILD LABOUR IN INDIA: AN ANATOMY

The existence of child labour is a slur on a modern welfare state which seeks to promote the allround development of its citizens. Children are the future hope of the society. They are like buds which need to be properly nursed and well taken care of so that they bloom fully, grow into able human beings, and contribute their worth to the future development of the society. On the contrary, instead of being sent to schools and properly educated, they are made to work, it amounts to squeezing the bud before it blooms. It not only thwarts the development of children but of the society as well, since only able citizens make an efficient society. Hence child labour has been regarded as an evil in India since time immemorial. In ancient India, it was the duty of the king to educate every boy and girl and parents could be punished for not sending their children to schools, called Ashrams, which were really residential schools under a Guru (a learned sage). (Gupta, 1987, p. 1). Child labour existed only in the form of child slaves who were purchased to do some 'low and dishonourable' work. Kautilya (4th century B.C.) considered it degrading to make children work on such jobs and hence prohibited the purchase and sale of children below 8 years. (Kautilya's Arthasastra). A number of legislative measures have been taken in independent India to control the evil of child labour. Article 24 of the Indian Constitution clearly states that "no child below the age of 14 years shall be employed to work in any factory or mine or engaged in other hazardous employment". Article 39(e) states that the tender age of children should not be abused and citizens should not be forced by economic necessity to enter a vocations unsuited to their age or strength. Article 39(f) states that children should be given opportunities and facilities to develop in a healthy manner and in conditions of freedom and dignity. Article 45 states that the state shall endeavour to provide within a period of ten years from the commencement of the constitution free and compulsory education for all children until they complete the age of fourteen years. (The Constitution of India, p. 26). Despite these, however, India is presently having the highest number of child labour in the world. And, they evil appears to be rising, in stead of declining, over time. The paper makes a modest attempt to anatomise the magnitude, distribution and causes of this social evil in the country.

I

Incidence: Child labour includes all those aged 14 years or below who are engaged in some productive work, whether paid or not, within the family or outside. (Khatu, 1983, p. 69). The problem is not confined to any part of the world or sector of the economy. On the contrary, it is a global phenomenon and is quite pervasive both in time and space. Historically, the institution of child worker has existed since time immemorial. Children have been helping and working with their parents and elders since long. This is how they have been gaining skills and learning their traditional family crafts without any formal training outside. Spatially, it exists to some extent, in almost all corners of the world; the poor developing countries on the one hand and the rich developed countries on the other; the capitalist as well as the socialist countries. Sectorally, it extends from family farm and domestic activities to large factories, in the rural as well as the urban areas. Some of the important activities in which children are employed include farm, forestry, animal keeping, cooking, beedimaking, match industry, coir industry, incense making, paper bag industry, gem polishing, embroidery, newspaper selling, garment making, carpet weaving, assembling of electrical and electronic items, etc.

TABLE 30.1

Child Labour (Aged 10-14) in Some Countries of The World—1975

Countries	*Number (in thousand)*			*Percentage of Child Labour*		
	Boys	*Girls*	*Total*	*Boys*	*Girls*	*Total*
1	*2*	*3*	*4*	*5*	*6*	*7*
U.S.A.	221	106	327	2.1	1.1	1.6
China	5397	4128	9525	12.2	9.6	10.9
Sweden	2	1	3	0.6	0.3	0.4
Italy	70	44	114	3.1	2.0	2.6
Hungary	2	4	6	0.6	1.3	1.0
Egypt	426	101	527	18.2	4.5	11.5
Mozambique	220	77	297	41.8	14.5	28.1
Tanzania	334	223	557	35.9	23.9	29.9
Brazil	1054	382	1436	15.8	5.8	10.8
Peru	44	40	84	4.6	4.3	4.5
Mexico	390	91	481	10.0	2.4	6.3
Indonesia	1425	1048	2473	16.5	12.5	14.5
India	7620	7537	15157	19.4	20.7	20.0
Thailand	623	730	1353	23.0	27.7	25.4

Source: I.L.O., Labour Force Estimates and Projections, 1950-2000, 1977.

According to 1981 census, there were 13.59 million working children in India. Other estimates are on a much higher side. The National Sample Survey (1983) estimated it at 17.36 million. The Operations Research Group, Baroda, put it at 44 million, while C.W.C. (Concerned for Working Children), Bangalore (1985) kept it at 100 million. One reason for these large differences is that, while the Census counts as workers only those children who are engaged in economically productive work, the definition of child labour, according to Operations Research Group, is broader and includes all children between the ages 5-15 who are engaged in productive work, whether paid or unpaid, at any time of the day within or outside the family. Since not all works which children do are remunerated, the Group's estimate is more realistic. (Burra, 1989, p. 652). In 1975 the International Labour Organisation estimated the number of working children for different countries of the world. Some of these data are contained in Table 30.1. These estimates, it must be noted, refer only to the full time child workers and represent only the "tip of the iceberg" because other children are not usually covered in statistical surveys of the labour force. (*Children in the World,* 1979, p. 62).

Most children work without pay to supply the extra hands needed for their families' survival mostly in rural areas. Both boys and girls help in the fields and tend animals; girls help prepare food, care for younger children and carry water. As they are not full time paid employees, they are not counted as workers in statistical surveys. Even then, as shown in Table 30.1, i estimates are alarming. The total number of child workers aged 10-14 years in India during 1975 stood at 15.16 million which was the largest among the countries of the world including China. As a percentage to all children in that age group, working children came to 20.00 which was also one of the highest in the world next only to Tanzania (29.9), Mozambique (28.1) and Thailand (25.4). A further look at the table reveals that though child labour exists all over the world, it is more pronounced in the poor developing countries and less pronounced in rich developed countries. Further, both among the developed and developing countries, it is less prevalent among those countries which are more welfare-oriented. The pertinent case in point is that of the U.S.A. in relation to Sweden. Though the U.S.A. has a higher per capita income than Sweden, it has a much higher incidence of child labour. Similarly, among the developing countries, though Brazil has a six times higher per capita income than China, it has an equally higher incidence of child labour. So is the case with Thailand and India. The former has both higher income as well as incidence of child labour than the latter. Hence child labour appears to be a case of underdevelopment—economic as well as social among the countries of the world.

II

Sectorial Distribution: The sectoral distribution of child workers in India, as per 1981 census, is shown in Table 30.2. As expected, most of the child workers are engaged in agriculture which forms the largest sector of the economy employing over 68 per cent of all workers. The predominance of agriculture is even more pronounced in the case of child workers. Over 80 per cent of them are employed in agriculture. Children accompany their parents to the fields and help them in such activities as sowing, transplanting, weeding, harvesting, digging roots, collecting fruits and guarding the crops against birds and animals. Within agriculture, of the two categories of agricultural workers—agricultural labourers and cultivators—they predominate in the former. Thus, about 43 per cent of the childworkers are agricultural labourers and only 38 per cent are cultivators; where as only 26 per cent of general workers are agricultural labourers and 42 per cent are cultivators. This is primarily because of the fact that most of the child workers belong to poor landless and semi-landless household which can not afford to send their children to schools. They are forced by circumstances to work on neighbouring farms to supplement their families' incomes which are otherwise not sufficient for sustenance. Next to agriculture, child workers are most numerous in sectors allied to agriculture such as livestock, forestry and fishing. Children take out animals for grazing, wash them in streams, catch fish from waterholes and pits, participate in food gathering activities and bring small bundles of firewoods from the forests. As these activities are light in nature, children abound in them. Infact, in relative terms, these activities depict the maximum concentration of child workers. They account for 5.67 per cent of all childworkers in the country against 2.22 per cent in the case of all workers. Child workers account for 14.21 per cent of the total workers in these activities as compared to their share of 5.56 per cent in the total workers of all sectors. Cottage and household industries constitute the third important sector in which child workers are concentrated. A household industry is one which is conducted by the head of the household or members of the household at home or within the village in rural areas or within the precincts of the house in which the household lives in urban areas. About 5 lakh child workers are engaged in such industries which come to 3.63 per cent of all child workers. This percentage is slightly higher than that of general workers (3.50). A number of factors explain the concentration of children in this sector. Firstly, such industries can easily evade legal restrictions. (Rodgers and Standing, 1981, p. 7). Secondly, it is believed that human body is soft, flexible and pliable in childhood and therefore can learn with ease how to twist, bend, stretch or assume different postures as required by particular jobs. Skills are therefore best learned if learning is begun fairly early. Craftsmen and artisans ensure that their children start acquiring skills early. In hereditary crafts like carpet weaving, cotton and silk weaving with intricate designs, wood carving, embroidery, etc., training starts early. (Dube, 1981, p. 188). Thirdly, since the productivity per man in several such industries is low they can not afford to hire in adult workers. The entire family, including children, therefore work in such industries so as to make a living for them.

The relative concentration of child workers in all other sectors is much below than that of general workers. The concentration is least in the case of transport, storage and communication, followed by construction, and mining and quarrying. Table 30.3 depicts the percentage distribution of child and general workers in the three broad economic sectors: Primary, secondary and tertiary. The primary sector includes agriculture, forestry, fishing, animal husbandry, and mining and quarrying. The secondary sector covers manufacturing, processing and construction activities. All other activities are included in the tertiary sector. A look at the table reveals that the concentration of child workers both in absolute and relative terms is the highest in the primary sector. This sector engages 86.64 per cent of the child workers as compared to 71.12 per cent in the case of general workers. This is followed by the secondary sector which employs only 8.57 per cent of child workers as a against 12.39 per cent of general workers. The concentration of child labour is the minimum in the tertiary sector which accounts for just 4.79 per cent of the child labour as compared to 16.49 per cent of all workers.

TABLE 30.2

Sectoral Distribution of Child Labour in India 1981

Sector	*Number in thousand*		*% Distribution*		*% Share of child worker in total*
	All Workers	*Child Worker*	*All Workers*	*Child Worker*	
1. *Agriculture*	167249	10977	68.37	80.75	6.56
(a) Cultivator	102882	5196	42.06	38.23	5.05
(b) Agricultural labour	64364	5781	26.31	42.53	8.98
2. Livestock, Forestry Fishing, etc.	5427	771	2.22	5.67	14.21
3. Mining and quarrying	1283	30	0.52	0.22	2.34
4. Manufacturing, *Processing etc.*	26592	1074	10.87	7.90	4.04
(a) Household Industry	8573	493	3.50	3.63	5.75
(b) Other than household industry	18019	581	7.37	4.27	3.22
5. Construction	3706	91	1.52	0.67	2.46
6. Trade and Commerce	14294	265	5.84	1.95	1.85
7. Transport, Storage and Communication	6142	35	2.51	0.26	0.57
8. Other Services	19911	351	8.14	2.58	1.76
All Sectors (1-8)	244606	13593	100.00	100.00	5.56

Source: *1981 Census of India*, Office of the Registrar General and Census Commissioner, India, New Delhi.

TABLE 30.3

Distribution of Child Labour in Primary, Secondary and Tertiary Sectors—1981 (in per cent)

Sector	All workers	Child workers
1. Primary	71.12	86.64
2. Secondary	12.39	8.57
3. Tertiary	16.49	4.79
4. All Sectors	100.00	100.00

Source: 1981 Census, Office of the Registrar General and Census Commissioner, India, New Delhi.

Spatial Distribution: The statewise and sex-wise incidence of child labour in India as per 1981 census has been shown in Table 30.4. The incidence of child labour has been measured in terms of the labour participation ratio which reflects the ratio of child workers to total number of children (in %). The all-India average of the incidence of child labour comes to 5.46 in the case of male children and 2.95 in the case of female

TABLE 30.4

State-wise Incidence of Child Labour

State	*Labour Participation Ratio*				*Literacy Rate*	*Poverty Ratio (1983-84)*
	Child Labour		*Labour of All Ages*			
	Male	*Female*	*Male*	*Female*		
1	2	3	4	5	6	7
A.P.	9.70	7.29	57.12	27.02	29.9	36.4
Bihar	4.38	1.56	49.19	9.06	26.2	49.5
Gujarat	4.82	2.23	52.19	11.03	43.7	24.3
Haryana	3.93	1.11	48.94	4.69	36.1	15.6
Karnataka	8.28	4.83	53.90	18.95	38.5	35.0
Kerala	0.79	0.79	41.04	12.77	70.4	26.8
M.P.	7.41	5.31	53.52	22.35	27.9	46.2
Maharashtra	5.57	4.86	52.51	23.98	47.2	34.9
Orissa	7.40	2.45	54.38	10.70	34.2	42.8
Punjab	5.34	0.25	53.14	2.27	40.9	13.8
Rajasthan	5.27	2.72	49.92	9.32	24.4	34.3
T.N.	5.68	4.57	55.85	22.36	46.8	39.6
U.P.	4.26	0.88	50.31	5.39	27.2	45.3
W. Bengal	4.02	0.93	48.71	5.81	40.9	39.2
India	5.46	2.95	51.62	13.90	36.2	37.4

Source: *1981 Population Census of India*, for Poverty Ratio—Year Book 1986-87, Table C-11, p. 151 and 152, Ministry of Health and Family Welfare, New Delhi.

children. Further, there are large inter-state variations in the data. It varies between 9.70 and 0.79 in the case of male children, and 7.29 and 0.25 in the case of female children. The state of Andhra Pradesh has the highest incidence of child labour both for male and female children. In the case of male child workers, Andhra Pradesh in followed by Karnataka (9.28), Madhya Pradesh (7.41) and Orissa (7.40), while Kerala depicts the lowest incidence of male child labour (0.79). In the case of female child workers, Andhra Pradesh is followed by Madhya Pradesh (5.31), Maharashtra (4.86) and Karnataka (4.83), while Punjab has the lowest incidence or child labour (0.25).

III

Explanatory Variables: After glancing through the inter-state variations in the incidence of child labour, an attempt is being made to provide some explanation for these variations terms of some such key variables as the level of poverty, the level literacy and the general labour participation ratio. The goal is being sought to be achieved by working out the coefficients of correlation between these variables and the incidence of child labour. Contrary to the general notion that poverty is the root cause of child labour, the relevant data do not provide a significant correlation between the incidence of child labour and the poverty ratio (i.e. the percentage of people living below the line of poverty), the coefficients of correlation (r) being 0.2895 for male child workers and 0.3389 for female child workers. However, the existence of a positive correlation, howsoever weak, does prove that poverty provides some explanation for the phenomenon of child labour. There is significant negative correlation between the incidence of child labour and the level of literacy in the states, the coefficients of correlation (r) being -0.5375 in the case of male child workers and -0.1961 in the case of female child workers. This shows that as the level of literacy goes up in the society, the incidence of child labour comes down. The weak negative correlation coefficient in the case of female child labour is on account of the fact that the level of literacy among females in the country is still very low. From the above facts, it clearly emerges that it is not merely the economic advancement but the overall social development including education, etc., which provides the major explanation for the incidence of child labour. This is the reason why Kerala has lower incidence of child labour than Punjab, Haryana and several other states which have lower poverty ratios than it. The pattern is similar to that, as observed earlier, found in the case of different countries of the world. Finally, there is a very strong positive correlation between the level of child labour and the general labour participation ratio in the states, the coefficient of correlation being 0.8931 in the case of male child workers and 0.9415 in the case of female child workers. This reflects the fact that the incidence of child labour is highly dependent, besides other things, on the demand for labour as depicted in the general labour participation ratio. It is this which explains why the states of Punjab and Haryana have one of the lowest incidence of female child labour. Both these states have very low labour participation ratio for females.

Temporal Trend: Over time, the magnitude of child labour appears to be rising both in absolute and relative terms. In absolute number it has risen from 10.74 million in 1971 to 13.59 million in 1981. In relative terms, the percentage of child workers to total child population in the country has gone up from 4.66 in 1971 to 5.17 in 1981. The percentage share of children in the total workforce, however, has witnessed a slight decline from 5.95 to 5.56 over the same period. Further, within the category of child workers, there are divergent trends in respect of male and female child workers. Table 30.5 contains data depicting the growth of child labour in the country for males and females separately over the period 1971-81. As is evident from the table, there has been a decline in the volume of male child labour in the country over 1971-81 by 3.51 per cent.

TABLE 30.5

Growth of Child Labour in India (1971-81)

State	*Percentage increase over 1971-81*	
	Male Child Worker	*Female Child Worker*
A.P.	-3.30	29.02
Bihar	-21.44	-0.76
Gujarat	-11.18	-2.85
Haryana	-9.30	99.71
Karnataka	5.47	54.24
Kerala	-41.12	-32.56
M.P.	9.69	52.81
Maharashtra	13.43	49.05
Orissa	-8.40	84.58
Punjab	-24.21	132.62
Rajasthan	-10.05	31.78
Tamilnadu	-0.12	69.88
U.P.	-2.31	-22.68
W. Bengal	-4.88	57.86
All India	-3.51	32.23

Source: *Analysis of Work-Force in India,* Occasional Paper No. 8, of 1988, Office of the Registrar General of India and Census Commissioner, Ministry of Home Affairs, Government of India, New Delhi.

The trend of decline is uniform in all states except Karnataka, Madhya Pradesh and Maharashtra where it has witnessed an increase. The reduction in the number of young male workers is due to higher enrolment in schools. Also, some of the states have energised the restrictions on child labour. (Suri, Rele *et. al.* 1988, p. 27). In the case of female child workers, however, there has been a rise in their number by 32.23 per cent over 1971-81. This is in quite contrast to the male child workers. The trend of rise is applicable in all states except Bihar, Gujarat, Kerala and Uttar Pradesh where it has declined. The maximum percentage increase has taken place in states like Haryana, Punjab, Orissa and West Bengal which have made rapid strides in the field of agriculture and allied activities. The rapidly rising trend in the case of female child workers also reflects the backward attitude of the society towards girls. They are being regarded more as a liability rather than an asset to their parents and the family. More of them, therefore, are being made to work rather than sent to schools. The rising trend in the case of girl workers is discernible despite the fact that a lot of under-reporting takes place in their case.

IV

Causes of Child Labour: Among some of the major factors responsible for the institution of child labour in India, poverty ranks first. Most of the child workers belong to poor, landless and semi-landless families whose income is otherwise insufficient to keep the family alive. The children are, therefore, made to work to supplement the meagre income of the family. Thus in one study 97 per cent children came to carpet weaving in Kashmir due to poverty. (Ali, 1987 p. 56). In many cases in rural areas, due to extreme poverty, agricultural labourers and poor peasants take loans from money lenders and their employers by pledging their young children who work with the masters for very low or no wages till the loans is paid. Most of the village artisans and craftsmen can not make a living unless their children work with them and thereby supplement their incomes. It is primary on account of poverty that poor parents fail to send their children to schools.

From the point of view of employers, children provide cheap and convenient labour. Children are an un-complaining labour force. They can be made to do any work, for any time and for any wages. Children are paid substantially lower wages than their adult counterparts on the plea that they are less efficient, their requirements are less and they are learning the job. Thus, child workers in the carpet weaving industry in Jaipur are reported to be paid Rs. 7-8 per day as compared to Rs. 15-20 per day for adult workers. (Gupta 1987, p. 40). This keeps the cost of production low. Hence, it is in the interest of the employers to employ children instead of adults. Many industrial units are surviving because of the supply of cheap child labour. In organised industries, factory laws apply and minimum wages are paid. The earnings in several industries, such as carpet weaving, are not sufficient. Hence, labour in the organised carpet industry is becoming a problem. Many such units are closing down or giving orders to individuals working in their homes. It is young children who are being pushed to work in such units which can easily ignore legal restrictions.

Finally, children are made to work by way of learning the job. It held that children are more receptive and body organs are more pliable and adjustable at an early age. An imprint acquired in childhood is easily erased. Hence craftsmen and artisans ensure that their children start acquiring skills early. Small boys are sent away as apprentices, some of them earning a little money, or they are taught at home. The same holds good in the field of cultivation. It is argued that a cultivator's son who does not learn to handle the plough and other agricultural implement at the appropriate age will find it difficult to handle them later. This logic is also involved in the case of domestic works. It stands to reason that the tasks they have to perform should be learned at a proper age.

V

To sum up, the institution of child labour is a global phenomenon and is quite pervasive over time and space. However, it is more concentrated in poor developing countries as compared to rich developed countries of the world. Despite all public pronouncements against the evil of child labour, India is today having the largest number of child workers in the world. In relative terms also, the incidence of child labor (i.e. as a percentage to the child population) in the country is one of the highest in the world. Again, the evil is rising, rather than declining, over time, especially in the case of female child workers. Most of the child workers come from poor families which can not afford to spare their children for schooling and make their children to work so as to augment their meagre family become which are otherwise insufficient for their survival. Most of these workers are concentrated in the unorganised sector of the economy comprising farm, forestry, livestock, fishing and household industries where the productivity per man is low. Among the states, it varies between 9.70 and 0.79 in the case of male children, and between 7.29 and 0.25 in the case of female children. Andhra Pradesh had the highest incidence of child labour both for male and female children. Kerala shows the lowest incidence of male child labour, while Punjab has the lowest incidence of female child workers. The incidence of child labour is poorly, though positively, correlated with the level of poverty. It is strongly correlated with the level of illiteracy and the overall work participation ratio. The incidence is more in those areas which are not well developed both socially as well as economically. Hence the institution of child labour is essentially a case of underdevelopment, economic as well as social.

REFERENCES

1. Ali, N., *'Child Labour in the Carpet Industry of Kashmir'*, in Gupta and Voll. (1987).
2. Burra, N., (1989) 'Out of Sight, Out of Mind: Working Girls in India', *International Labour Review, Vol. 128, No. 5,* International Labour Office, Geneva.
3. *Children in the World,* (1979), A Publication of the Population Reference Bureau in Observance of the International Year of the Child, Washington D.C. 20036, U.S.A.
4. Constitution of India (1981) (As modified up to the 15th January 1980) Government of India, Ministry of Law, Justice and Company Affairs, New Delhi.
5. Dube, L., (1981), *'The Economic Roles of Children in India; Methodological Issues'*, in Rodgers and Standing (1981).
6. Gupta, M., (1987), Child Labour: 'A Harsh Reality', in (ed.) Manju Gupta/Klaus Voll, *Young Hnds at Work-Child Labour in India,* Atma Ram and Sons., Kashmere Gate, Delhi.
7. Gupta, M., (1987), 'We Cut Our Fingers but No Blood Falls...': Child Labour in the Carpet Industry in Rajasthan, in Gupta and Voll (1987).
8. *Kautilya's Arthasastra,* (1950) Translated by Dr. R. Shamasastry, Sri Raghuveer Printing Press, Mysore.
9. Khatu, K.K., (1983), *Working Children in India,* Operations Research Group, Baroda.
10. Rodgers, G. and Standing, G., (1981), 'The Economic Roles of Children: Issues for Analysis', (eds.) Rodgers, G. and Standing, G., *Child Work, Poverty and Underdevelopment,* (eds.), International Labour Office, Geneva.
11. Suri, K.C. Baur, J. and Rele, J.R., *Analysis of Work Force in India,* Occasional Paper No. 8 of 1988, Office of the Registrar General of India, and Census Commissioner, Ministry of Home Affairs, 2/A Mansingh Road, Govt. of India, New Delhi.

31

DIMENSIONS OF CHILD LABOUR IN INDIA

While once discussing about the significance of human factor in national development, the great humanist of our era, Pandit Jawaharlal Nehru, had aptly remarked: "But somehow the fact that ultimately everything depends on the human factor gets lost... in our thinking of plans and schemes of national development in terms of factories and machinery and general schemes. It is all very important and we must have them, but ultimately, of course, it is the human beings that counts, and if the human being counts, well, he counts much more as a child than as a grown up" (Quoted in Gangrade and Gathia, 1983: i). Although this statement reinforces in general terms the potentiality of human-wealth in particular, it rightly lays emphasis on the importance of a well-groomed child population, which remains as the repository of the future talents of a country. Pandit Nehru was very clear in his mind about the significance of the child, which was reflected in his policies of child welfare, and more so in his emotional attachment to the children of the world. But the fact remains that the children, the potential wealth of a country, are the most neglected and ill-nourished lot in most of the developing countries of the world, including that of our own. While about percentage of our total child population fall prey of death before they reach 5 years of age, millions of those who survive do not even get minimum familial and national support to shape themselves as healthy and effective citizens of the country. On the contrary, when they need all the warmth and affection, they get exposed to the unhygienic and half-starved world—sometimes forcibly and some other times out of compulsion—to eke out their living and to support their families.

The concept of grooming up of a healthy and well-nourished child population is not of recent origin, emanating from our new slogans of national development or recent policies of hi-tech industrialisation. In fact, the moral and ethical responsibility of giving birth and caring of a healthy child has been ingrained in the normative code of conduct of the Indian population since millennia, the reflections of which can still be seen in many of our *Puranas* and *Upanishads.* In Indian folk belief, the child carries more of a ritual value than a material value. In order to give birth to a healthy child, many rituals and associated taboos are observed right from the first knowledge of conception till the child is safely born. The kind of lowly status conferred on a barren woman despite her economic standing in rural and tribal India vividly reflects the significance of a child. Moreover, there is no denying to the fact that from the times of antiquity fill the modern times, the importance of a child has been realised as being an asset not for the family of his birth, but for his community, kin-group and the nation at large. But at the present juncture, unfortunately, the pragmatic reality seems to be different from the ethical and moral considerations. A child in destitution is envisaged to be the responsibility of no one. He is left to himself quite often. It is indeed shocking that while billions of dollars are being thrown for sophisticated arms, ammunitions, nuclear power competitions, massive space explorations, a large percentage of children in the developing world is still half-starved, clotheless and in perpetual plights, struggling for the bare subsistence. This needs no probing in the context of our country, as the incidents are glaringly open and explicit. When one enters into either a tea-stall, a restaurant, the residence of a middle-class *baboo*, a railway platform, a small-scale industry or a motor garage, one hardly fails to overlook the toiling children at their teens, serving there to just meet their daily requirement of bread. During the teens, when a child is supposed to claim all possible care for his future, physical and intellectual growth, he is seen selling his labour for maintaining himself and his family. In India, comprehensive plans have been formulated for child welfare, protective constitutional and legislative measures have been enforced, free schooling has been implemented, but the extent of child labour and child abuse has never deteriorated considerably, on the contrary, there is a proportionate rise in this trend keeping pace with the general rise in the child population of the country.

Defining Child and Child Labour

The conceptualisation of the child status leads to ambiguity, as it is guided by individual considerations. Therefore, a standard has to be accepted to determine an age-range for defining a child. The Factory Act of 1948, which is an elaborate and highly specific Act relating to child labour, makes use of 3 different concepts to classify the workers, viz., a 'child,' a 'young person' or an 'adolescent,' and an 'adult.' It has been made explicit in this Act that a person below the age of 15 years is to be regarded as a child. Therefore, any physical labour undertaken by a child of below 15 years either under compulsion of voluntarily in an organised or unorganised sector, qualifies to be called as child labour. A 'young person' or an 'adolescent,' according to this Act, refers to a person between 15 and 18 years of age, while a person above 18 years of age is referred to as an 'adult.'

Extent of Child Labour in India

It is indeed shocking to see the extent of child labour in Indian in its present stage. The Census of India Report reveals that by 1981, the number of child workers in the country was about 1,360 lakhs, while it was about 1,070 lakhs in 1971 or about 4.66 per cent of the total child population of the country. The picture seems still gloomy for the future, as the 'labour force projection' estimates the number of child workers to go upto about 3,338 lakhs of 1990 and 3,765 lakhs by 1995. This clearly means a three-fold rise of child workers between 1981 and 1990, which should concern our politicians, academicians and bureaucrats. Table 31.1, however, presents a clear picture of the extent of child labour in India.

TABLE 31.1

Number of Child Workers (5-14 Years) in India by NSSO (1977-78)* and Census (1981) Estimates

(in 000's)

Category	*NSSO (1977-78)*		*Census (1981)*	
Total Population of Children	17,19,498		17,93,136	
Total Workers	2,00,199	(11.6)**	1,35,908	(7.6)
Main/Major time workers	1,66,203	(9.7)	1,11,674	(6.2)
Marginal/Subsidiary workers	33,996	(2.0)	24,234	(1.4)

*NSSO-National Sample Survey Organisation

**Figures within parenthesis indicate the respective work participation rates

Source: Child in India: A Statistical Profile, p. 467.

In India, child labour constitutes a significant proportion of the totality of main workers According to 1971 Census enumeration, child labour constituted about 5.9 per cent of the total labour force in the country, while the total children were abut 42 per cent of the Indian population. Although slight decline is noticed in the work participation rate for main workers between 1971 and 1981, in substantive terms, the gravity of the situation has drawn everybody's attention. Table 31.2, in this context, is self-explanatory.

TABLE 31.2

Work participation Rates for Main Workers (0-14 Years) During 1971 and 1981

Area	*Male*		*Female*	
	1971	*1981*	*1971*	*1981*
All	6.65	5.46	2.63	2.95
Rural	7.56	6.30	3.05	3.53
Urban	2.75	2.46	0.82	0.88

Source: Child In India: A Statistical Profile, p. 452.

The above mentioned Table while gives us some consolation due to the declining trend of male child labour between 1971 and 1981, the situation seems much more alarming for the rising rate of female child labour in our country. This development inevitably goes against all the efforts made by the Government and many Non-Government

Organisations to particularly ameliorate the plights and tribulations of the women in general and young women in particular.

Work participations rate among children in different States reveals that while Andhra Pradesh occupies the highest position with 9.64 according to 1978 survey, in the second, third and fourth positions are the States of Rajasthan, Madhya Pradesh and Tamil Nadu respectively, followed by the Himachal Pradesh. Table 31.3 reveals a clear picture in this regard.

TABLE 31.3

Work Participation Rate Among Children (1971 and 1978) of Different States

States	*1971*	*1978 Survey*
Andhra Pradesh	9.24	9.64
Assam	3.41	2.18
Bihar	4.42	1.85
Gujarat	4.51	2.46
Haryana	2.97	1.58
Himachal Pradesh	5.01	5.40
Jammu and Kashmir	3.56	2.62
Karnataka	6.50	4.91
Kerala	1.30	0.90
Madhya Pradesh	6.11	6.51
Maharashtra	4.74	2.88
N.E. Region	4.90	5.20
Orissa	5.30	5.12
Punjab	4.16	1.92
Rajasthan	5.16	7.37
Tamil Nadu	4.58	5.56
Uttar Pradesh	3.59	1.23
West Bengal	2.69	1.80

Source: Child in India: A Statistical Profile, pp. 460-61.

Areas of Child Labour

A child may be found employed in many different kinds of activities to earn his livehood. He may be employed forcibly or voluntarily, in an organised sector or in an organised sector. Although an exhaustive list of their areas of employment is difficult to prepare and present, the common places of employment may be: carpet weaving, match making, bidi making, embroidery, incense making bamboo making, bidi making, embroidery, incense making, bamboo making, pencil making, small auto garages, construction, restaurants tea picking, rag picking, printing press metal workshop, shoe polishing, hawking, vegetable vending, stall keeping, weaning units, leather industries, coir industries, waste paper picking, envelope making, brick making, slate making and many other similar activities. The Census report of 1981, however classifies the areas of employment undertaken by the children, as revealed in Table 31.4.

TABLE 31.4

Child Workers in Different Jobs

(in 000's)

Job	*Main workers*	*Marginal workers*
Cultivation	11,169	2,424
Agricultural labour	4,013	1,183
Livestock etc.	704	67
Mining etc.	27	03
Manufacture-		
(a) Household	424	69
(b) Non household	541	40
Construction	80	11
Trade and Commerce	245	20
Transport etc.	34	01
Other jobs	327	24

Source: Child in India: A Statistical Profile, p. 449.

Causes of Child Labour

Although there is no single factor responsible for the participation of the children below 15 years of age in the highly competitive job market, poverty seems to be one of the most dominant reasons. In spite of high claims by the Government, the study by Institute of Public Opinion reveals that 41.2 per cent of the population is still below the poverty line. Therefore, child labour is no longer a medium of exploitation by is necessitated by the economic necessity of the parents and in many cases that of the child himself. Inadequate income of the parents does not fulfill the minimum requirements of the children, which, in most of the cases, inspires the children to enter into the job market.

Poverty is most often supplemented by other socio-economic factors to expose the child to manual jobs. Due to high degree of illiteracy and ignorance of the parents, the children are deprived of getting proper counselling for building up their future career, and at the time of economic necessity, the children move into the job market to eke out their, subsistence. Most of the times, a bigger family size adds to the misery of the parents to maintain the children properly, which motivates some of them to search for a job even in their teens to supplement the family income. Since education has become expensive these days, those who cannot afford to educate their children, indirectly encourage them to go for a job instead of sitting idle. As unemployment creates havoc in our country and there is no adequate provision for maintenance allowance to the unemployed, the children of unemployed parents immediately jump to the job market. Besides these handicaps of the children, the employer finds child labour as the cheapest labour, malleable and can be easily controlled. Hence, the encouragement also comes from the profit-seeking employer to engage a child to get a good return out of his investment. There are still some political considerations that encourage child labour in our country, and for which, the safeguards extended for the prevention of child labour are not implemented effectively. The foremost of these being the fact that the children are not voters, and hence, do not constitute a political pressure group; this eventually makes no politician interested to think about and solve the problems relating to child labour. Furthermore the children are mostly silent listeners or non-listener of the policies/programmes meant for them, and hence, their problems are not properly realised. The Trade Unions, which have fighting for the welfare of the workers in the country, do not bring into their fold the child workers, for which no-body pays serious attention to their plights.

Impact of Labour on the Child

Although it is said in general terms that physical labour has a tremendous impact on the growth of the child, the socio-psychological studies have portrayed the real magnitude of the problem. Labour has its impact on the physical development, general health condition and morality of a child. Physical labour and consequent work pressure make the child both weak and timid. These hinders the educational or intellectual development of a child constant suppression and physical labour easily lead a child to become a delinquent in course of time. Therefore, physical labour has a long lasting evil impact on the overall development of the children.

Government Provisions for Child Labour Prevention

Even before Independence, apprehending the problems of child labour, the British Govenrment in India had appointed the Whitley Commission and the Labour Investigation Committee, 1946 to evolve suitable remedial measures to control and prevent child labour. After independence, many Constitutional provisions and legislative enactments have been made and suitably amended from time to time to control the magnitude of problems relating to child labour. Article 24 of the Indian Constitution mentions explicitly that no child below the age of 14 shall be employed to work in any factory or mine or engaged in any other hazardous employment. Article 15(3) confers right on the States to make special provisions for women and children to protect them. Similarly, Article 23 confers a fundamental right against certain forms of exploitation. The provisions of the Indian Penal Code provide punishment for such exploitation like forced labour and this Article gives a constitutional sanction to punishment.

Under Chapter IV of the Constitution, Article 39 is clearly aimed at protecting the women and child workers. The Article reads: "The State shall, in particular, direct its policy towards securing:

(e) that the health and strength of the workers, women and men, and tender age of children are not abused and that citizens are not forced by economic necessity to enter avocations unsuited to their age and strength, and

(f) that children and youth are protected against exploitation and against moral and material abandonment."

Moreover, Articles 42 and 43 guarantee the workers to earn suitable wage, good working condition, decent standard of life and full enjoyment of leisure, and social and cultural opportunities.

Besides these constitutional provisions, atleast 13 major legislative enactments for children have been made. Without further delineation, these include, Factories Act of 1948, Mines Act of 1952, Plantation Labour Act of 1851, Merchant Shipping Act of 1958, Motor Transport Workers Act of 1961, Employment of Children Act of 1938, Apprentices Act of 1961, Contract Labour Act of 1970, Bidi and Cigar Works Act of 1966, Shops and Commercial Establishment Act under different nomenclatures in different States, etc.

A fair review of the institutional protections for child labour in the forms of constitutional provisions and legislative enactments explicitly tells about the efficiency of our Governmental measures. In spite of all the stringency to save our millions of wasted talents under the suppression of their employers, child labour continues rather more vigorously at the moment. What is, therefore, lacking is proper appreciation and internalisation of the provisions made by the Government by our citizens. Unless institutionalisation of policies and internalisation of the same by the participating population are not allowed to move simultaneously and with coherence, no programme can be successful. An example in this context can be presented. When the Ministry of Labour imposed restriction on the employment of children in the carpet industries in Uttar Pradesh, carpet weaving was consciously and cunningly reduced to cottage industry, and the children engaged there were tole to be the apprentices rather than employees. This clever maneouvre and indifference of the people eventually went in favour of the industrialists and child labour in carpet industry remained unabated.

Role of NGO's

Since the Government measures to safeguard the interest of the children failed on many fronts due to public non-participation, the role of Non-Governmental Organisations is expected to be of immense help. The effectiveness of the NGOs is attributed to two major factors: Firstly, since its workers do not belong to the Govenrment Departments, they are relatively more acceptable to the people due to their aversion towards Government Officials in some areas. Secondly, since the workers of the NGOs operate at the grassroot level, they constitute the strongest source of motivating the people by their personal interaction and involvement with the problems that the people face in their day to day routine activities. However, it is suggested by some experts that the NGOs can adopt either of the three approaches given below or a combination of them to solve the problems of the mass in general, and the problem of child labour in particular:

(a) Moralist Approach;
(b) Legalist Approach; and
(c) Paternalistic Approach.

The NGOs adopting a moralist path can strive for bringing about a new consciousness among the people through mass education and demonstration the problems involved in child labour and to familiarize the people with the constitutional provisions and legislative enactments made to effectively safeguard the interest of the children as a community. The legalist approach refers to timely and suitable legal counselling to the child labourers, their parents or well-wishers to prevent the incidence of child abuse or to ensure the child labourers to get their due as per the policy guideline by the Government. The paternalistic approach is more protective in the sense that the NGOs can rehabilitate the child labours and take the responsibility of their education and employment in due course. Whether it is one of these approaches or a judicious combination of all of them that the NGOs adopt, they are believed to be better motivators than the Government machinery with respect to any problem area including child labour and child abuse. Therefore, the role of NGOs in this respect is most significant and we have every reason to trust their success in this endeavour.

REFERENCES

Gangrade and Gathia, 1983, *Women and Child Labour in India,* Delhi: Concept Publishing House.

Govenrment of India, 1961, *Census of India,* Series, 16, Part II A, General Population Table.

Government of India, 1981, *Report of Child Labour in India,* Simla: Ministry of Labour, Labour Bureau.

Government of India, 1985, *Child in India: A Statistical Profile,* New Delhi: Ministry of Labour.

Kulshrestha, J.C., 1978, *Child Labour in India,* New Delhi: Ashish Publishing House.

Pandhe, M.K. (ed.), 1979, *Child Labour in India,* Calcutta: India Book Exchange.

32

PROBLEMS OF CHILD LABOUR IN INDIA

Children have been integral part of human labour force in all societies. With the socio-economic development and modernisation, economic role of children vanishes and child participation in labour force is curtailed to a considerable extent. But this fact has been achieved only in few western or developed countries. In most of the third world or developing countries, a large number of children continue to be at work. According to ILO estimates, in 1975, some 55 million children under the age of 15 were at work around the world. Of these, 30.5 million were in South Asia, 9.9 million in East Asia, 9.6 million in Africa, 3.3 million in Latin America and only 1.3 million in all the developed or Western countries. In India, the 1981 census listed 11.17 million children as full-time workers. In 1971 census this number was 10.75 million, indicating that the absolute number of child workers is increasing in this country.

Now an obvious question; why child participation in labour force is a menace to their development? Why must be curtail it? Work as a direct fulfilment of a child's natural abilities and creative potentialities is also conducive to its healthy growth. But work, when takenup as a means for fulfilment of some other needs, become inslaving in character and deleterious in its impact. The latter type is harmful because the energy that should have been spent on nurturing talent, capacity and power, is used for the purpose of bare survival. It becomes a total evil when the energy generated by a child is appropriated by some others and the child is left with a fraction of it, which can meet even this basic survival needs. Child labour, therefore, assumes the character of a social problem in so far as it arrests or distorts the natural growth process of a child to full adulthood. The use of children as a source of labour force, raise many other questions with demographic and economic implications. Demographically speaking, the economic contribution of children is an important contributing factors in the demand for more children and consequently leads to population growth. (Kasarda, 1971). Among other implications, child labour deprives children of educational opportunities, minimises their chance for vocation training and forces them to remain unskilled labourers with low wages as long as they are economically active. Thus, the participation of children in labour force, runs-contrary to the whole thesis of human resource development which is so essential for the over-all socio-economics development of a nation.

Our Constitution provides for protection of child workers. Article 24 lays down that, "no child below the age of 14 years should be employed to work in any factory or mine or engage in any other hazardous employment." This important legislative provision on employment of children relate to the minimum age of employment, working hours, health certification, work on dangerous machines, etc. The minimum age for employment ranges from 12 years, under the Parliament Labour Act, 1951, to 15 years under the employment of Children Act, 1938. However, none of these legislative measures are strictly enforced and some of the hazardous occupations are even beyond the purview of existing legal provisions.

On the other hand it is argued that the child labour can not be totally banned in India, solely on the grounds of child deve_opment. For a poor man, working child is a economic necessity. For the large number of people below the poverty line (37 per cent in India), meager earnings of children is a necessity of sheer survival.

This complexity of the problem of child labour is the gensis of present Chapter. It is an attempt to study various dimensions of child labour in India, its possible effects on the child development with particular reference to the education component. The data have been drawn from 1971 and 1981 Census of India.

Size and Growth of Child Population

India is a nation of youngs. According to 1981 census, nearly 40 per cent of India's population was in 0-14 years age group. Since the children below 5 are incapable of working and participating in the economic activities, it is the children in 5-14 years age-group who are focus of our attention. In 1981 census, there were 179.31 million children in 5-14 years age-group, of these 93.44 million were boys and 85.87 million girls.

TABLE 32.1

Children in 5-14 Years Age Group by Sex and Residence 1971 and 1981

(Millions)

Residence	*1971*			*1981*		
	Total	*Boys*	*Girls*	*Total*	*Boys*	*Girls*
Rural (Percentage)	121.57	63.56	58.01	139.92 (15.10)	72.99 (14.83)	66.93 (15.39)
Urban (Percentage)	28.12	14.70	13.41	39.39 (40.07)	20.45 (39.11)	18.95 (1.12)
Total (Percentage)	149.69	78.26	71.43	179.31 (19.79)	93.44 (19.39)	85.87 (20.23)

The Table shows that in both the censuses, proportion of boys in 5-14 years age-group was slightly higher than the girls. However, the population growth rate during the decade 1971-81, was some what higher for girls than the boys. In accordance with the national pattern of residence, nearly 78 per cent children were living in rural areas. Although the growth rate of child population was much higher in urban areas (two and a half time more) than the rural areas, in both the types of residence, it was lower than the national growth rate (Rural 1968 per cent, Urban 46.30 per cent) during this period.

The Concept of Child Labour

The term 'Child Labour' is variously used, meaning 'employed Child' or 'Working Child.' It signifies employment of children in gainful occupations with a view to add in the household income. However, it must be noted that children do not always work for monetary gains. It is not unusual to find them as unpaid workers, particularly in household industries. They contribute substantively in family labour. Moreover, children spend much of their time in household maintenance activities. We therefore, need a broader definition of work to include not only directly productive-paid activities, but also unpaid family labour. We may then define the child labour as that segment of child population, which participate in paid and unpaid work. Here we shall refer to census definitions. It is well known that the census of India has modified the definition of workers and non-worker from one census to another in enumerating child and adult workers. The reference period in which a person is considered as worker or non-worker has also changed from time to time. Fortunately, in 1971 and 1981 censuses of India, definitions of worker and non-workers have almost remained the same. In these censuses the stress was on the concept of main activity *i.e.*, on the economically productive pursuits in which worker engaged himself or herself for most part of the time. As for seasonal work, such as agriculture and ancillary pursuits, the main activity of a person was defined with reference to his/her work during the year preceding the enumeration. Further, if a person participated in economically productive work, not as a main activity or most part of year, he is not treated as worker but as marginal worker. Persons attending household duties, students, institutional population, etc., were not treated as workers.

TABLE 32.2

Number of Children (5-14 Years) in the Labour Force by Residence and Sex in 1971 and 1981

(Million)

Area	*1971*			*1981*		
	Total	*Boys*	*Girls*	*Total*	*Boys*	*Girls*
Rural (Percentage)	9.97	7.28	2.69	10.19 (+ 2.21)	6.68 (- 8.24)	3.51 (+ 30.48)
Urban (Percentage	0.78	0.61	0.17	0.98 (+ 25.64)	0.73 (+ 19.67)	0.25 (+ 47.06)
Total (Percentage)	10.75	7.89	2.86	11.17 (+ 3.91)	7.41 (- 6.08)	3.76 (+ 31.47)

As stated earlier, in 1981 Census of India, 11.7 million children (of 5.14 years age) were listed as workers. Of these 7.41 million (66.34 per cent) were boys and 3.76 million (33.66 per cent) were girls.

This Table gives as account of the child workers in rural and urban areas and changes in its composition during 1971-81. As evident from the Table, majority of child workers (over 90 per cent) were from rural areas. The employment pattern has remained the same during 1971 and 1981 or for boys and girls. An analysis of the change in number and composition of child workers during 1971-81 gives some interesting results. Though, at aggregate level the number of child workers has increased by 3.91 per cent, increase in rural areas was 2.21 per cent only and in urban areas 25.64 per cent. The number of boys in the labour force has declined, primarily due to the decline in their number on rural areas. In urban areas the number of the working boys has shown an increasing trend. Number of working girls has increased significantly in both the areas.

A better understanding of the extent and changes in the child labour force can be had from work participation rate, which may be defined as follows:

$$\text{Child Work Participation Rate} = \frac{\text{Number of working Children (5-14)}}{\text{Total Number of Children (5-14)}} \times 100$$

Greater significance can be introduced in this measure by making it sex and area specific.

TABLE 32.3

Child Work Participation Rate by Sex and Residence, 1971 and 1981

Area	*Proportion of Children (5-14) in the Labour Force*					
	1971			*1981*		
	Total	*Boys*	*Girls*	*Total*	*Boys*	*Girls*
Rural	8.21	11.46	4.64	7.28	9.15	5.24
Urban	2.76	4.13	1.25	2.48	3.53	1.30
Total	7.18	10.08	4.01	6.23	7.93	4.37

It is evident from the Table that the child work participation was much higher in rural areas as compared to urban areas. The activity rate of girls was appreciably lower than the boys in both the areas. The Table also shows that at the aggregate level, child work participation rate has gone down in both the areas during the period under study. This decline has mainly been due to the fail in the boy's activity rate, as in both the areas the girls participation in the labour force has increased during this period. But the increase in the girl's activity rate was not large enough to off-set the general decline in the labour force participation rate.

From the above analysis it is apparent that though the child work participation has marginally declined during the decade 1971-81, a significant proportion of children continue to work at odd jobs. It must be recognised that the proportion of boys girls (in 5-14 years age group) at work to the respective population of boys girls (in 5-14 years age group) at work to the respective population in that age group is small and does not by any means account for the large wastage and dropout that occur among primary school children, unless one assumes a larger and more rapid turn-over and intermittency of employment of children in that age group that is reflected in the figures of child workers which is on account of the general economic state of the country (Mitra, 1978).

Sectoral Distribution of Working Children

An understanding of the trend in the employment of children in various sectors can be had from the 1971 and 1981 census data.

Table 32.4 indicates certain broad differences in the employment pattern of children in rural and urban areas. In rural areas, majority of children were employed in primary sector, while in urban areas, more children were working in secondary or tertiary sectors. Another important finding is the more even distribution or urban child workers in three industrial categories. In rural areas more than 90 per cent of child labour force was concentrated in primary sector only. The activity pattern of boys and girls was broadly similar. However, there were differences in their pattern of sectoral preferences. The proportion of child labour engaged in cultivation was much higher among boys than the girls. But there were more girls as agricultural labourers than the boys. In the secondary sector, more female children were employed in household industries than the male children, whose participation was more in other (than household) industries In the tertiary sector, trade and commerce attracted more boys than the girls.

Regarding the change in the employment pattern during the decades 1971-81, the study shows a shift (though very small) from primary and tertiary sectors to the secondary sector in both the areas and for both the sexs. Decline in the child labour force in primary sector was comparatively small than the tertiary sector. Industries where decline in the proportion of child workers was more evident are; live stock, forestry, etc., in primary sector and other services in tertiary sector. Gain was mainly in the non-household manufacturing industries.

In the above analysis two factors which deserve greater attention are; (a) employment of children in non-household enterprises and (b) increase of child workers in manufacturing (other than household) industries. According to Mani Nag (1983), all the institutional changes that are related to decline of children's contribution to labour, perhaps most important one is the change from household organisation of production to modern organisation from, in which means of production are either owned or controlled by States or other non-household enterprises and the labour is supplied by the individuals

TABLE 32.4

Sector-wise Percentage Distribution of Working Children by Sex and Residence, 1971 and 1981 (Industrial Categories)

Type of Industry	Rural				Urban			
	1971		1981		1971		1981	
	Boys	Girls	Boys	Girl	Boys	Girls	Boys	Girl
1	2	3	4	5	6	7	8	9
Primary Sector								
1. Cultivator	42.45	27.78	42.93	31.13	6.46	3.32	5.87	3.58
2. Agricultural Labourers	40.21	57.34	40.33	55.14	12.40	22.37	12.14	22.57
3. Live Stock: Forestry, Fishing and Plantation.	9.83	5.13	8.04	3.90	4.45	2.43	3.52	1.81
Sub-Total	92.49	90.25	91.30	90.17	23.31	28.12	21.53	27.96
Secondary Sector								
4. Mining and Quarrying	0.17	0.28	0.21	0.30	0.40	0.81	0.21	0.25
5. Manufacturing, Processing, Services and Repairs,								
(a) Household Industries	2.07	4.04	2.56	4.35	8.02	17.96	7.95	17.35
(b) Other than household Industries	1.27	1.80	2.54	2.53	24.36	15.50	31.39	21.36

6.	Construction	0.34	0.41	0.41	0.57	2.94	3.69	3.27	3.18
	Sub-Total	3.85	6.53	5.72	7.75	35.72	37.96	42.82	42.14
Tertiary Sector									
	Trade and Commerce	1.01	0.33	1.26	0.40	20.39	3.01	19.18	2.97
	Transport, Storage and Communication	0.14	0.09	0.13	0.04	4.14	2.09	3.03	0.52
	Other Services	2.51	2.79	1.58	1.64	16.43	28.82	13.43	26.59
	Sub-Total	3.66	3.21	2.97	2.08	40.96	33.92	35.64	30.08
	Total	100	100	100	100	100	100	100	100

in exchange of monetary compensation. As the differences between centrally planned and free market forms are mainly with respect to the ownership and distribution of the means of production, they can be lumped together in the modern category, as opposed to the household organisation of production (Potter, 1983). The employment opportunities for children decline in modern organisational forms mainly because the labour contracts are with individuals rather than the households and the place of work is no longer the place of residence.

In this context, our analysis reflect on the state of economy of the country. Not only the bulk of child labour force was employed in non-household enterprises, their number has increased in certain sectors like, manufacturing non-household industries. It indicates that, though there is a sectoral transformation in the economy from household to non-household enterprises, it has not dented the child participation in labour force. Perhaps, in site of all the hazards of labour participation, working child is a economic necessity.

Working Child and Education

Though the labour-force participation of children adversely effect almost all the aspects of their development, the most important one is the schooling of children. It is reported that the major economic consequences of compulsory primary education introduced in post-revolutionary China is not the increased cost of tution borne by the parents but the lost labour the children could provide (Parish and Whyte, 1978).

The present study also shows that the proportion of workers among the children attending schools was much lower than the children not going to schools.

Table 32.5 indicates that in rural areas 48.33 per cent boys and 27.40 per cent girls were attending schools. In urban areas their proportion was 69.27 per cent and 60.43 per cent respectively, for boys and girls. It is further observed that among those who were attending schools, less than 0.1 per cent children in urban areas and less than 0.75 per cent children in rural areas, were employed in labour force either as main workers or marginal workers. On the other hand, among those boys who were not attending schools 18.75 per cent in rural areas and nearly 12 per cent in urban areas were employed as main or marginal workers. For non-school going girls these proportions were 10.56 per cent in rural areas and 3.73 per cent in urban areas, respectively.

Above analysis clearly indicates that the work participation of children, influence their educational prospects to a large extent. Almost negligible difference in labour force participation of rural and urban school going children, indicates that in the rural areas also, where generally more children take-up employment, school attendance drastically curtail the employment of children. This phenomenon is also supported by the fact that among the rural school going children, proportion of marginal workers was very small.

Conclusion

From the present study it clearly emerges that even though, the child work-participation-rate has marginally declined during the decade 1971-81, the number of children in

TABLE 32.5

Children (5-14) by School Attendance and Economic Activity (1981)

Area	Total Child Population		Children Attending Schools							
			Total		Main Workers		Marginal Workers		Non-Workers	
	Boys	Girls	Boys	Girls	Boys	Girls	Boys	Girls	Boys	Girls
Rural	7,29,93,046	6,69,32,814	3,52,74,613	1,83,39,441	38,749	7,717	2,23826	75,885	3,50,12,038	1,82,55,839
			48.33	27.40	0.11	0.04	0.63	0.42	99.26	99.54
Urban	20,445,794	18,942,012	1,14,48,666	1,14,48,666	4,848	969	4,735	1,303	1,41,53,909	1,14,48,399
			69.27	60.43	0.03	0.01	0.03	0.01	99.93	99.98
Children not Attending School										
			3,77,18,432	4,85,93,373	66,41,722	35,01,384	4,34,306	16,28,659	30,64,42,404	4,34,63,330
			51.67	72.60	17.61	7.20	1.15	3.35	81.24	89.44
			62,82,302	74,93,353	7,26,697	2,45,354	20,656	34,071	55,34,949	72,13,928
			30.73	39.56	11.57	3.27	0.33	0.45	88.10	96.27

labour force continue to increase. However, the proportionate increase in the child labour force was much larger in urban areas as compared to the rural areas. It indicates that either the conditions compelling rural children to seek employment are improving or the new entrants to the labour force are shifting from rural to urban areas.

The study also shows a marginal shift in the employment pattern of children from agriculture and services sectors to industry sector. It implies that, with the expansion of economy, child workers are being pushed from safer household enterprises to the hazardous industrial sector.

Another important finding of the study is that the education, specially school attendance of children, significantly reduces the child participation in the labour force.

From the above findings it is imperative that the legislative measures safe-guarding the interest of child workers, should be strictly enforced to curtail their entry into the more hazardous occupations. Efforts should also be made to universalise the primary education as it is most effective check on the children's entry in to the labour force.

REFERENCES

Kasarda, J.D. (1971), "Economic Structures and Fertility" *Demography,* Vol. 8, No. 3, pp: 307-318.

Mitra, Ashok (1978), "India's Population: *Aspects of Quality and Control,*" Vol. II. Abhinav Publication, New Delhi, pp. 543-553.

Nag, Mani (1983), "Fertility Response to Modernisation," in *Fertility and Family,* Proceedings of the expert group on Fertility and Family. New Delhi, 5-11 Jan. 1983, United Nations, pp. 125. 158.

Naidu, D.A. (1981), "Child Labour Participation in India: A State Wise Census Analysis," *Journal of Family Welfare,* Vol. xxvii, No. 4, June, pp. 48-59.

Narain, Vatsala (1979), 'The Assignment of work' in K. Srinivasan *et. al.* (eds.) *Demographic and Socio-Economic Aspects of Child in India.* Himalaya Publishing House, Bombay, pp. 553-570.

Parish, W.L. and M.K. Whyte (1978), *Villages and Family in Contemporary China,* University of Chicago Press. Chicago. p. 228.

Patnaik, Malabika, (1979), "Child Labour in India: Size and Occupations Distribution, *Indian Journal of Public Administration,* Vol. xxv. No. 3, July-September, pp. 668-677.

Potter, J.F., (1983) "Institutional Determinants of Fertility," in R.D. Lee and R.A. Balatao (eds.) *Determinants of Fertility in Developing Countries:* A Summery of Knowledge. Academic Press, New York.

33

DIALOGUES ON CHILD LABOUR

The Harbans Singh Report

The reaction to the Harbans Singh report on the condition of working children in the match industry in the south Indian town of Sivakasi provides us with a microcosm for understanding the entire range of responses toward child labour by government officials, social activists, and trade unionists. We begin the review of attitudes toward child labour with an interviewed with the official who was secretary of the Tamil Nadu Labour Department at the time Harbans Singh submitted his report to the government.

I asked the official, Mr. Padmanaban, to describe to me his reaction and that of other officials to the Harbans Singh report and whether any of its recommendations were implemented. Mr. Padmanaban first commented on the overall situation in Sivakasi.

"Sivakasi is a very backward agricultural area. The main industries are matchsticks, firecrackers, and litho printing. A few enterprising entrepreneurs set up these factories in the 1992s. It's a backward area and the people in it are backward. First the parents started to work in these factories and they said let the children work too., The sticks are given to the peasants and they take them to their houses to make the matches. The whole family does the work at home."

Don't children also work in the factories?

"Yes, there are some ten-to-fourteen years olds. They are the ones who don't have earning members in their family. Sometimes the father is too old to work, or if the father is working he says why not the son too. Here every man wants his son to take on the same job. If the father works in the factory he wants his son to do the same work.

"The employers also want the children. It is easy to handle the child in the factory. There are no discipline problems, no unions. Another factor is that the children have nimble fingers. They are deft. The children can do more work than the adults. And the children only get one-third or one-half of the wages adults get.

"But you have to ask," he continued, "why is the boy working in the factory? You seem, it is a question of survival. In agriculture you must work three months at least before you can get any money from what you sell, but in the factory you can get quick money. Child labour has been there for a long time. It has to be regulated. There must be a proper transportation, proper facilities, and most important, proper wages. The children should not be treated as sweat labour. There must be a proper study area for the children who leave the school to go for these jobs. And the legislation is not adequate to given them protection."

What would happen if child labour were banned?

"There are hundreds of factories there with children under fourteen. Are we going to close down these factories? The parents say `We want our children in these factories. The children must work to support their parents, especially the old parents who do not have any income. The adults do not want to work there since they can get work elsewhere, so they say send their children."

If wages were higher wouldn't adults take these jobs?

"The economic status of the factory requires that the children must work there. You must look at the problem from an economic and from a sociological point of view. It should not be viewed in isolation. We say that where the children are employed, then you organise some education for them. You make a child skilled in the factory. The child working in the factory learns how to make firecrackers and may be something else. You see, the factory owners have picked up this young material. The material has to be molded, isn't it? You have to give him some skills. Let the child have his meal in the factory. Provide toilet facilities. You enrich this boy or girl to become a really skilled worker in the factory. If you take the child out of the factory, the factory would close and no one would have work.

"A father is working there, so he will want his son to work there too. It is the same in agriculture. The father brings his son to work in the field and to help with the animals. So the father thinks that if there is unemployment on the land, why not take his ten or eleven year old to the factory? Why not train him so that his future is assumed? If I am helpless and have no land, no patronage, no political claim, and I am working in the factory, I would like my son to come to the factory so that when I retire may son can work and support the family. It is like an apprenticeship. The typical man in a backward village, he says that a ten-year-old boy is no longer a child. You may say he is a child, but the villager says that if he can walk a distance of one kilometer, go to the cinema, talk to people, and can work, he is not a child."

Why not wait until the child is older before putting him to work, I asked?

"Unemployment is so high. If I wait until my boy is eighteen, will he be assured of a job? Who will give him a job after eighteen? This does not apply to people with power or to people with some land. Then the son can get some adult to help him take up a job. But in our state fifty or sixty per cent of the people are below poverty. They earn may be two hundred fifty rupees a month. This is the compelling reason for children to work. If you put twenty thousand children in Sivakasi out of work, what will happen to their families and who will give them employment when they become eighteen and the factories are closed?"

Was the Harbans Singh report ever released to the public?

"No, it was intended as a confidential report to the government. When the government commissions a report, normally it does not make it public. The labour minister asked us what to do abut Sivakasi. I told him how can we end twenty thousand jobs. A government official has to be practical. And the minister knows that there would be a political problem if we abolished these jobs. So I should be practical, not theoretical, when I speak to the minister."

A. Social Activist's Perspective

Though the Harbans Singh report was never released, its contents were widely discussed in the press as a result of the efforts of a young activist, Smitu Kothari, who obtained access to the report and publicised its findings. Kothari went to Sivakasi, met the children and their parents, owners, managers, foremen, distributors, government officials, and leaders of the local political organisations. He photographed the children at work and in a number of articles in the popular press reported his findings. His reports confirmed and amplified what appeared in the Harbans Singh report.

The general working environment in most of these cottage industries, " he wrote, "was appalling. Cramped spaces, practically no ventilation and filthy floors were evident in about every unit we visited. Puddles of chemicals around the vats of chemicals were also evident in most units."[1]

Though Kothari visited Sivakasi six years after Harbans Singh had submitted his report to the government, he found no indication that safety conditions had improved. An accident, he reported, took place in September 1981. There was a massive explosion at the Arunchalam Fireworks on the outskirts of Sivakasi, killing thirty-two, persons including six children. A few months later, in February 1982, in a nearby village, a firecracker factory went up in flames killing six more children. The children had been stuffing explosive powder into the firecrackers when the accident occurred.

Writing about why there was child labour at Sivakasi, Kothari blamed the government's development programme. "The underdeveloped drought-prone conditions of the district have made possible the recruitment of children in a growing cottage and small scale match sector that competes with a multinational match industry," he wrote.[2] When I spoke to Kothari in his office in Delhi, where he edits a monthly magazine for activists in voluntary organisations, he went on to say that "child labour is the result of development. We have a policy that makes it impossible for people to be absorbed in the labour force. Government neglected to develop irrigation in the Sivakasi area, so it remains poor and the children inevitably become labourers." According to Kothari, various proposals to create irrigation schemes in the district were turned down by the government. He is convinced that the proposals were killed "because employers do not want to develop the region since they want to be able to employ local people at low wages." When Kamraj Nadar became chief minister of the state, he said, the government supported the Nadar factory owners who opposed the development projects. Tamil Nadu, said Kothari, has implemented a number of irrigation projects efficiently, but per capita expenditures for irrigation in Ramanathapuram district, where Sivakasi is located, is very low. "I think that the only way you can deal with the problem of child labour is to develop the land. If there is enough employment of adults they will not need to send their children to work in the factories."

Kothari is opposed to banning child labour. "When considering intervention," he wrote, "we are faced with a grim reality where we have to accept that in this situation we can, at best, humanise this development..... Displacing the 45,000 children in Sivakasi.... raises another serious dilemma. The displacement will not only affect the livelihood of their parents but will give a boost to the multinational WIMCO as the small and cottage sectors will definitely be hit by this step. An alternative could be for thee sectors to semi-mechanise their operations. Ironically, the small-scale sector has refused to use these on the plea that it would displace employment." Kothari also opposes replacing children with adults. "If.... displacement takes place, can their parents who because of economic compulsion send their children to work, work in their place? This will, of course, mean a final step in their alienation from their lands."[3]

The only really significant change that can reduce child labour," he continued, "is to launch a massive irrigation programme in the area. Not only will substantial land be made productive, parents of working children who own this land will experience economic recovery. But as was pointed out earlier, there will be tremendous resistance to this from the owners of industry." Kothari concluded on a militant note. "We can therefore conclude hat there is only a political solution to the problem. Solutions have to be conceived and activised outside the present framework. Meanwhile only a major involvement by action groups and/or trade unions, which agitate for the children's rights, can change the plight of child labour not only in Sivakasi but all over the country."[4]

What is the attitude of trade unions toward child labour in Sivakasi? In the West, union were in the forefront of the movement of abolish child labour on the grounds that adult workers were displaced by poorly aid children. I put the question to Kothari. "There are four trade unions in Sivakasi," he replied, "but none of them are interested in enforcing the child labour laws. In fact I cannot think of a single union that has taken up the cause of child labour. I think the unions don't take up the issue because there is a shortage of work in Sivakasi and the children come from the same families as the union members. Moreover, employers make the argument that the work done by children is suited for them and could not be done as well by adults. The same argument is used in the carpet industry. The firms want more children. They say there is a shortage of children in Sivakasi!"

An Industrial Relations Official

I raised the same question with Dr. P. Lakshmanan, Director of the Tamil Nadu Institute of Labour Studies in Madras, a center devoted to the teaching and training of trade-union workers and factory inspectors. For many years Dr. Lakshmanan has worked closely with trade union leaders as well as with government officials and managers. His institute is under the state Department of Labour. "The unions at Sivakasi," he said, "mainly want better wages and amenities for their members, they don't really care about child labour."

Why?

"Well, they would be unpopular with the parents of the children. The parents support the employers. Besides, the unions are not there in the cottage industries where the children work. One reason employers prefer child labour is that the children don't join unions and agitate! Children are obedient. Any type of work can be extracted from the children. You can tell a child to clean the table or go for coffee, but not an adult. Adults will be conscious of hours of work, but children will work until the employer releases them. And they are nimble. They can do some work better than adults."

I asked Dr. Lakshmanan if he thought the labour inspectors in Tamil Nadu could enforce the child-labour laws.

"If you look at the employment registers in the factories you will not see any children listed. The employers pay them cash, they do not pay any benefits, and the wages are lower than what they pay adults. So it is difficult to enforce the minimum-wage laws or get any benefits for the children. The employers send the children out when they hear that inspectors are coming. We could send the police with the inspector to surround a factory, fine the employer, and make him put the children on the register. But if we catch him, he will list the children, but then strike them off the register the net day. And if we go to court, he will only have to pay fifty or a hundred rupees. The law says there can be a fine or imprisonment, but judges will not imprison an employer. So the employer only needs to pay the fine and then he can break the law again. And if he is caught breaking the law again and we went to the court, it would take the court another six months to find him guilty and he would just pay the fine again! In Tamil Nadu last year there were three thousand seven hundred prosecutions under the provisions of the factory acts, and about three thousand five hundred convictions. The total fines came to about six hundred forty-three thousand rupees, an average of less than two hundred rupees per fine.[5] That includes all violations. There are no separate figures on child labour. Most of our labour laws are not enforced. To do that you need to change the attitudes of the employers and you must make workers aware of their statutory rights.

The various committees appointed by the government," he pointed out, "have not recommended banning child labour. What would the children do? Poor people say that there children are an asset, that they need to employ their children. If you go to parents and tell them that they should send their children to school, the parents will say that they need to send their children to work."

I asked him if anything had come to the recommendations of the Harbans Singh report a decade earlier. Had there been any improvement in the condition of the children? He said that the report called for the raising of wages for the children, setting up sheds in the villages so the children need not travel to the factories, and the establishment of nonformal education. The only improvement so far, he said, was that there was now a nonformal education programme for about 900 children.

Matches, he said, is not the only industry in Tamil Nadu with child labour. "There are children here working on the plantations, making bidis at home, and working in the hotels and small shops. So many retail and wholesale shops employ children. There are more hotels coming up here so there are now more children working."

Do you think there has been an increase in child labour in Tamil Nadu?

The percentage of children as workers is declining, but the number of children working is going up. That is because of the population increase. As the labour force grows, the number of child labourers increases. Take Sivakasi. If I am a parent, then last year I may have sent two children to work there, but now I have another child so I send him to the factory too. There are more children now in Sivakasi than there used to be."

Do you think I asked, the government will ever release the Harbans Singh report to the public?

"The report says the law is not enforced, so it would create a bad impression with the public if it were issued. Then why should the government publish the report until action is taken? And after action is taken, then the report is out of date so it is to late to publish it."

A Catholic View

Father K.N. George, director of the Madras School of Social Work, is a Catholic priest known for his strong opinions, especially on matters affecting the poor. A small, bouncy, loquacious man, Father George characterised child labour as a "necessary evil." "The wages you get in agriculture are very low. Agricultural workers are paid fourteen rupees a day. The husband and wife work, and they may have, say, three children. So they take the children to work with them. Sometimes the children get two rupees for looking after the cattle. Then there are children working in mechanic shops, in tea stalls, in hotels and garages. They work twelve hours a day or more. They don't get proper food, their clothing is inadequate and they just sleep on the ground. But at least when they work in a garage, they learn a job. Sometimes their parents work on construction projects and the children help. If we stop the children from working, they will have an empty stomach. So my view is that it is a necessary evil until the parents have enough income to support the family.

"Here in Madras there are about one thousand boys doing ragpicking, earning about four rupees a day. They get paid for the rags and the employers then sell those rags for ten rupees. We have a project to give the boys gloves and some hot food. But, I say, let the boys be a source of income for their family. I think we need to think about second-best solutions. I don't think we can enforce the legislation without hurting the families."

A Labour Ministry Official

The view that regulation and amelioration rather than abolition are what is called for was echoed by a high official in the Ministry of Labour in New Delhi, a one-time member of the International Labour Organisation (ILO) governing board and a highly influential person in the field of labour policy in India. Given the dependence of the poor upon child labour, he explained, it is unrealistic to try to end child labour at this time. But, he went on to say, the government should end child labour in dangerous industries such as firecrackers and diamond cutting. ":We should also put more effort into improving conditions in the other industries where children work. We should shift the match industry to the villages so children would not have to travel and the work would be safer. We should improve ventilation where the children work. We should provide benches for the children working on the hand looms. And we should give the working children at least one hour of education a day. The education should be provided by the employer with the help of voluntary agencies.

It would be a mistake, he explained, to have a uniform minimum-age law for employment since it couldn't be enforced. For the same reason he was opposed to making child labour in the cottage-industries sector illegal, especially since that sector hires so many children from poor families. "But we shouldn't make child labour legal either! Let us keep it this way, but we should do more to improve the education and condition of children in small-scale industries and in the cottage-industries sector."

Another View from the Labour Ministry

I asked Mrs. Girija Eswaran, the ranking official in the Labour Ministry concerned with child-labour laws and their enforcement whether she had any evidence that the enforcement of child-labour laws in Sivakasi would hurt the poor because employers would close down factories, or whether the employer would then simply hire adults." I met with the employers at Sivakasi, She said. "They are quite brazen about the use of child labour. They said that they would show me their books so I can se how little profit they make. They said that if the government ended child labour they would cut costs by mechanising rather than hire more adults. The employers know that the politicians and the parents would be in an uproar if we tried to end child labour. So they feel quite strong in dealing with the government. You know, the children are exploited by employers, parents, the unions, the politicians—they are all in collusion with the government, which does not enforce the law."

Mrs. Eswaran said that her ministry was trying to get some studies on the economics of child labour. "We need to know if companies would fail if they could not employ children." The Commerce Ministry, she said is concerned with encouraging the growth of small-scale and cottage-industries to expand employment, and they insist that many small shops would close if they could not employ children. The carpet industry, bangles, matches, and other cottage industries would be badly hurt. The ministry also points out, she added that some of these are important export industries. "They tell me that the carpet industry would collapse if children were not employed! Other countries, they say, like Pakistan, employ child labour and how could we then compete with Pakistan? The Commerce Ministry says we must look at the economics of it." In the mid 1970s, she said, India was able to expand substantially its carpet exports after the Shah of Iran had banned the employment of children in the carpet industry, pushing the price up and reducing their exports.

The Commerce Ministry, she added, was itself an employer of child labour. The Development Commissioner of Handicrafts under the Ministry of Commerce runs apprenticeship programmers to teach children to be carpet weavers. There are government training centers in Kashmir, Uttar Pradesh, and other parts of northern India. The children — they are supposed to be twelve, but many are younger—are given normal wage (200 to 300 rupees per month) while they learn to weave, and then they are given positions in small weaving workshops and in factories. Often, she said, they work on pit looms within their own home in rooms that are damp, dimly lit, and ill-ventilated.

I asked Mrs. Eswaran if she thought that the officials I had spoken to were right in thinking that it was possible to improve the working conditions for the children. "We have tried to improve conditions for children working on pit looms. The carpet is nine feet long so they put the loom into a large pit and the child sits on the cold ground. It is so wet and cold sometimes that the children get cramps in their feet. But there is nothing you can do about it since the village houses are too low to put the loom at ground level. We suggested that the employers build a loom shed, but the parents say they don't want it. They say that each hut should have its own loom since the whole family works the loom, and they each take turns. It is literally a cottage industry.

"In Firozabad," she continued, "I saw bangles made in the cottages. Little children work alongside the women. The glass is molded in the factories, and in the houses the bangles are joined with a candle. There are other parts to the process of bangle making and some of it is done in the village houses. I have been to these houses. The squalor is sometimes unbelievable.

What about enforcing minimum wages?

"In the tea plantations," she said, "the unions objected to proposals to raise the minimum wage. They think that then the employers wouldn't hire the children! If the children were not hired, the tea-plantation owners would go outside the plantation of find workers and when the children grew up they would not be able to find jobs. In the plantations it is the custom that employers hire the children of the tea-plantation workers and if a worker dies then her children are hired."

An Economist

Nasir Tyabji, an able young economist at the Madras Institute for Development Studies, examined the contribution of child labour to household income and the contribution of labour to the costs of production in the match industry. The idea of the study,, he said, was to find out whether child labour was essential to the household and to the industry. "The amount added by the child to household income seems to be small," he reported, "but it is often stable. So it can be important, especially when the parents are in agriculture. We don't have any data on the second question yet, but we think that the labour costs are not as important as people think. We don't have any evidence that the match industry in Sivakasi would go under if they couldn't hire children and had to pay higher wages to adults. But if that were the case then the excise taxes on Wimco could be raised to protect the small-scale industries. They are protected already," he pointed out.

"When all is said and done we need to ban child labour. If children were removed from the work force there would be more jobs for adults. Sivakasi has to be attacked. The problem is that the government has not been willing to deal with it."

Why? I asked.

"There are about eighteen families who control the industry and they are all tied to the politicians. When there was that bus crash and so many children were killed the government minister said he would take firm steps to end child labour. But nothing happened. It is because there is a nexus of the employers, the politicians, and the families."

Mr. Tyabji's views were exceptional. Of the dozen people I interviewed in madras, he was one of two (the other an exgovernment official also working at the Madras Institute of Development Studies) who believed that child labour should be banned at Sivakasi and elsewhere in the state. All the others said that the government should try to ameliorate the conditions of work. Though the agreed that child labour should be prohibited in dangerous occupations, they did not think child labour should be prohibited in the match industry.

A Tea-Plantation Official

"The workers," said the former chairman of the Tea Board in West Bengal, "are as attached to the land as the tea bushes. They were born in the tea estates. They live there all their lives. They die there. The mother who works in the tea gardens has no place to leave her children. She puts her child on her back and brings the child with her when she works. What is more natural then that the child wants to know what the mother is doing and wants to help her pluck-the tea. That is how the child becomes a worker. It is easy for children to pluck. Their fingers are nimble and the bushes are at their height. The child plucks the leaves and puts them into her mother's basket. Whatever the child plucks increases the pay of the mother. I would not say that the children are employed.

They are helping their parents., Then, when the child is twelve, she is given a basket of her own and earns her own wages. She is paid half of what an adult is given."

The tea plantation of West Bengal and Assam employe 21,000 children between the ages of twelve and fifteen, 14,000 adolescents from fifteen to eighteen, and 203,000 adult males and 224,000 adult females. No figures are kept on how many children under twelve—the minimum age for employment in the tea plantations—"help" their parents. Adults are paid 9.70 rupees a day, children 4.95 rupees. Workers are also given cereals at reduced rates, 20 per cent lower than the market price, and each family is given living quarters, a single living room, a kitchen space, and a common bathroom.

Until a few years ago, I was told, the owners of the plantations were responsible for providing education to the children of plantation workers. Then the government passed the responsibility onto the district boards, but the tea plantation owners must still pay for all costs at the primary school except for the teacher's salaries. Primary school, standards one through five, is, I was told, compulsory." "Yes, it is compulsory," said the former chairman of the Tea Board, "but it is not enforced in a God-forsaken place like that. By class four, most of the children drop out. When thy are nine or ten years old they are actually working and do plucking with their mothers. During the plucking season, from June through September, the mothers get additional wages on a piece basis. When it is off season the workers prune the bushes and do other work.

In the harvest season the whole family is working. In the plantation there is both recognised and unrecognised child labour, since some children are below and some above twelve years of age. During these four months there is also some additional contract labour and these workers also bring their children. Minimum wage laws do not apply to contract labourers, who are all paid by piece work. During the harvest season as much as forty per cent of the labour force may be contract labour.

"The workers call themselves coolies. That mental attitude is there, so they say, of what use is an educated child. As it is the tea industry cannot absorb all the children into the labour force. Except during the harvest season there is not enough work. About half the children in the plantations enter the labour force there, while the other half have to go outside the plantations to find work."

The secretary of the West Bengal Labour Department explained to me that the minimum age for working on the plantations was twelve, compared with fourteen in industry, because plantation work was not considered hazardous. "We in the department are willing to raise the minimum age to fourteen, but the basic problem is that the parents want to sent the children to work. The plantation unions also say that the work isn't hazardous and it adds to the income of the family."

But, I asked, don't the unions understand that if there were no child labour, more adults would be employed?

"No, they say that all the members of their families are working in the plantations now, so they would lose income if their children could not work. The practice in the tea plantations is that if a worker dies his child is then employed. If the children were not hired, the unions, say, then the owners would go outside the plantation to bring in workers, and then when the children grew up they would not be able to find jobs on the plantations. They also say there is no point in educating the children since the only jobs are in the plantations. If the children were educated where would they go to find work?"

Do all the children remains to work on the plantations?

"No, some young hill people get education and join the army—particularly the Nepalis—and some come down to the plains for employment. They take jobs in shops, become drivers, or work in repair shops. The hill people are more interested in education then the plains people. There are some good schools run by the missionaries in the hills, and a few run by the government. There are fewer schools in the plantations in the plains and most of the children there drop out of school by the third grade."

What happens to them? What kind of jobs do they get?

"Those who don't find work in the plantations go to the cities to find jobs. They work in shops serving tea and cleaning tables. There are no restrictions on the employment of children in domestic work and the middle class here hires children. There must be tens of thousands of children doing that kind of work in Calcutta. The boys or girls usually work in two or three houses during the week. They don't go to school, they only do domestic work."

A Labour Secretary on the Carpet Industry

The carpet industry is a major employer of children. In Uttar Pradesh and in Kashmir the Government of India Handicraft Board has set up apprenticeship programmes to enable children to learn to do carpet weaving at an early age. private establishments prefer to hire children. "The employers," explained the secretary of labour in Uttar pradesh, "say that the children's fingers are small. They have nimble little fingers, and they can move them faster. The children can make more knots in the carpets than adults because of their little fingers."

The secretary described the conditions under which the children work, in rooms that are crowded and have poor ventilation and bad lighting. "I complained to one manufacturer," the secretary explained, "but he said it would cost more for them to put in better lighting and windows and benches. I said that the bad lighting was hurting the eyesight of the children so he should provide better lighting. And he said that the ministry should provide eyeglasses for adults!"

Can't you do anything about it? I asked. Couldn't you prosecute him? "No, the Factory Act does not apply to these small establishments. It only covers places employing more than ten persons. So there is no statutory protection for children in factories that employ under ten people. We think the act should be amended to cover these small establishments. We can inspect factories but under the law the labour department does not have machinery to deal with the unorganised sector at all. And even in the case of factories, if an employer is found in violation, the fine is only two hundred to five hundred rupees. The case can take two years, and once the inspectors, have made the "mistake" of bringing a case for prosecution then the inspector will have to go to court many, many times to win the case. The act says there can be imprisonment for one month or a fine for violating the labour laws, but the court always makes it a fine. No one ever goes to jail for violating the labour acts.

"In the carpet industry the owners say that the costs will go up if we abolish child labour. The owners say they will not employ the adults if they cannot hire children."

Why?

"Oh, just to teach them a lesson? The carpet owners are usually high caste Hindus or well-off Muslims. They are not bothered adult poor people. Now the Commerce Ministry has set up a programme for children in the carpet industry. They are taught how to improve their carpet work, how to join the threads together and to finish off the carpets by scissors. These things are taught by the industries department. And the children are given a certificate! But these children are not made literate. They are not getting a general education. That is because the parents are greedy. So an awakening has to be brought to the parents. They need to know that an investment in the child is more important than the little income they can get from their children."

It is true, I asked, that the Commerce Ministry supports the use of child labour in the carpet industry? I was told by an official in Delhi that the ministry is concerned that if children were not employed in the carpet industry, India could not effectively compete with Pakistan and Iran in the sale of carpets and exports would fall. They also argue, I was told, that you must start teaching carpet weaving at an early age and not wait until the children are fifteen.

"Yes, that is the view in the Commerce Ministry, especially in the Handicraft Board, but I don't share those views. The other problem, perhaps the greatest problem, is the demand of the people. There were reports of poor conditions in the carpet factories in Mirzapur, and some employers were prosecuted. There was talk of closing down the factories. People in the area were scared that they would not be able to get employment for their children. There were cries in the Congress party that without work these people would not have food. But we said we should prohibit the employment of children. When we arrived in Mirzapur, the children started running away from the factory saying that the antichild labour people have come? There is not a committee under the central Ministry of Labour with labour ministers from four states looking into the question of how working conditions for children can be improved. But we should prohibit the employment of children! If the laws were enforced then employers would have to hire adults and pay fixed wages. Now we cannot get employers to pay even the minimum wages to children. The problem is that we have no field agency in this department that can enforce child-labour or minimum-wage laws. In all of U.P. we have only forty inspectors under the Factory Act to inspect then thousand factories. Thee labour inspectors deal with child labour too, but they cannot deal with the unorganised sector. Our laws are outdated.

"In rural areas employers do not even know that the employment of children is an offence. It is with the same with bonded labour. There is no enforcement agency. We found that some members of the U.P. legislative assembly had children working for them as bonded labourers under old contracts."

He does bonded labour come about?

"Suppose I borrowed one hundred rupees some years ago from a land-lord in the village. Then I work for the landlord to repay the debt. I get some payment as livelihood, and the rest of the work is for repaying the loan. And if I die before paying off the debt, then my children or grand-children must work for the landlord! Often children are sent as bonded labourers to pay off the loan. If we enforce these laws on bonded labour and child labour, there is bonded to be some class conflict."

I have met many government officials in state and central government labour departments. I told the secretary, but he was the only official I had spoken to who was so strongly opposed to child labour. How, I asked, did he come to develop such strong views on this issue?

"I belong to a scheduled-caste community in the Punjab. We had no land. We wee agricultural labourers. We had no money to spend on festivals. At nine my father took me out of school and sent me to work. I rebelled and wanted to stay in school. I even threatened suicide! So my parents agreed to let me stay in school. I was at the top of my class, so I stayed on the school and went to college. Ultimately, I entered the Indian Administrative Service. I was the oldest child and other members of my family, my younger brothers and sisters, followed me to school. I don't think my father was so poor that he had to send me to work, but it was not the custom in his family to send children to school. Many parents do not think, but just send their children out to work. If we in the government emphasise that children should not be sent to work, then they will go to school.

"Now all my children are in college. If I had listened to my father I would still be working in the village."

REFERENCES

1. Smitu Kothari, "There's Blood on Those Matchsticks: Child Labour in Sivakasi," *Economic and Political Weekly (2 July 1983), p. 1193.*
2. *Ibid.*, p. 1194.
3. *Ibid.*
4. *Ibid.*, 1199, 1200.
5. Most of the earlier acts pertaining to the illegal employment of children provided for fines of up to 500 rupees. The Child Labour (Prohibition and Regulation) Act of 1986 lays down a minimum penalty of 10,000 rupees. No data are available as to the enforcement of the new act.

34

THE MEANING AND CONSEQUENCES OF CHILD LABOUR

'What I want is FAC TS... Facts alone are wanted in life.'

—Charles Dickens, *Hard Times*

How many children work in the world today? Establishing this simple fact and much else about the meaning and consequences of child work is not as easy as it might appear. Dickens's Mr. Gradgrind would be driven to apoplexy by the plethora of estimates or guesstimates in the field. Recent commentators start with the 1979 ILO figure of 52 million. However, in 1983 ILO called this a conservative estimate. For one thing it only included full-time workers. The Anti-Slavery Society estimates that the figure is more like 100 million (1985, p. 7). Professor Roudhiba suggested in his report to the UN that 145 million working children between the age of 10 and 14 was more realistic.

The regional picture is not much clearer. Asia is thought to have the largest child worker population. India alone of officially said to have 17.36 million child workers, more than anywhere else, comprising 5.9 per cent of the total labour force—some 93 per cent of these child workers are in the rural areas (UN Seminar, 1985); and yet, other estimates for India talk of 54 million and 100 million. In Africa, 20 per cent of children under 15 are said to be working and in some African cities, children constitute 17 per cent of the total work-force. In Latin America, estimate between 12 and 26 per cent have been put forward for some countries (ILO Paper, UN Seminar, 1985).

Clearly much more rigorous work needs to be done in this area, but it is in no state's interest to have an accurate picture of the extent of child work, and only recently has the subject attracted social scientists. If we are to attain a better understanding of child work then we shall need to place it within the broader framework of the institution of childhood which has attracted the attention of historians, sociologists and anthropologists. Here one is reminded of Anna Freud's depiction of childhood as a phenomenon which taxed of defied our understanding. Nevertheless, it would be useful to explore childhood in an historical context, at least to begin with, in order to obtain a view on how we have arrived at the various perceptions of what is desirable or undesirable for children.

It was Philippe Aries in his classic *Centuries of Childhood,* who first put forward the thesis that childhood is a modern Western invention. According to Aries, 'there was no place for childhood in the medieval world' (Jenks, 1982, p. 31). The infant who could not participate in the adult world simply did not count. Only gradually in the sixteenth and seventeenth centuries do we witness, in the art of the times, the child or infant of the upper strata depicted in special dress and thereby distinguished from adults. By the eighteenth century everything to do with children's health and education had become established as a concern worthy of serious attention. By the end of that century childhood had been established by Blake and Wordsworth as a major literary theme, something which was to continue well into the nineteenth century with Dickens, Mark Twain and Tolstoy.

The seventeenth century appears then as a watershed in the evolution modern institution of childhood. 'Baby,' 'child' and 'youth' were interchangeable terms prior to the modern age. The child in medieval society was fully integrated from the earliest age into all aspect of daily life including education, work and play, Children were treated as if they were expendable, as indeed they were. Even in the early nineteenth century the English essayist Charles Lamb could remark in a letter to a friend '..... we have had a sick child, who, sleeping or not sleeping, next to me, with a pasteboard partition between, killed my sleep. The little bastard is gone' (Schorsch, 1979 p. 11). At the end of the fifteenth century the numbers seven and fourteen were already associated with childhood. Seven was the beginning of the rite of passage for boys, when apprenticeship contracts were drawn up, and by 14 schooling in reading, writing and religion was over, as was apprenticeship. Girls were even less likely to survive infancy and were regarded as a liability by medieval parents until married off as early as 12 (if a sufficiently attractive dowry could be provided). Girls were less likely to have been schooled and would remain subordinated to men throughout life. The Reformation, with its encouragement of individualism, also helped to establish the individuality of the child. By the end of the seventeenth century each child was regarded as having a soul of its own and was given its own name. This separation had its price in the growing institutional constraints on the child's freedom. Parents, the Church, moralists, and educators all came to circumscribe the world of the child, who was deemed to need both protection and a prolonged period of training.

Today we have come a long way from the romantic view of innocent childhood in which children were depicted as 'little angels' who are 'close to God.' Today childhood in industrialised countries is problematic, protracted, ill-defined, and the centre of vehement claims and counter-claims concerning 'what is best for the child.' Childhood has spawned an army of child-care professional experts in the new sciences of pedagogy, paediatrics, psychology and psychoanalysis (Ennew, 1986a). The modern conception of childhood, invented and sustained by adults, has two key features. Firstly, a rigid age hierarchy which separates children from adults. This institutionalisation of childhood is marked by special dress, games, language and literature. Secondly, the myth of childhood innocence where the child must be both happy and separated from the corrupt adult world. This becomes expressed in the child-cared family which is determined materially if in no other way to make these the best years of life.

These adult modes and prescriptions have been codified into international standards expressed in Declarations, Covenants and Charters. These date back to the early part of this century and express a protective view of childhood. In such instruments the child cannot by definition be a worker in the formal economy, but requires a protracted period of socialisation in which schooling becomes the acceptable from of 'work' for the child. Children have become in these circumstances economic dependents and liabilities. And school-days are seen as a golden age.

Nevertheless, there are physiological criteria which provide clear broad stages in childhood and its separation from adulthood. These are: infancy (0-5), pre-pubertal childhood (6-2), and post pubertal childhood (12 to adulthood or majority). The age of adulthood is now expressed by the Draft UN Convention on the Rights of the Child as 'being eighteen unless, under the law of his/her state he/she has reached his/her age of majority earlier.' In the end one returns to the simplest of all definitions of a child by chronological age which itself differs from state to state.

Children have always worked and today where families need help, in developed and developing countries, children will and do continue to work. Work has always been part of a wider set of childhood activities which is the starting point for any classification and analysis of children's economic role Here the most comprehensive conceptual framework to date is that of Rodgers and Standing. The authors distinguish ten childhood activities: domestic work; non-domestic work; non-monetary work; tied or bonded labour; wage labour, marginal economic activities; schooling; idleness and unemployment; recreation and leisure; and reproductive activities (Rodgers and Standing, 1981, pp. 2-11).

Typically, cooking, cleaning, child care and other domestic duties are under taken to some extent by children in all societies. Such duties form part of the socialisation process and cannot, according to the International Labour Organisation, be termed child labour (Blanchard, 1983, p. 18). But domestic work, as it has been defined, becomes 'social exploitation' if it denies children their right to play, to learn and to enjoy a normal childhood. Many children, especially girls, do miss educational and recreational opportunities because of a heavy domestic work burden. Though domestic work does not of itself produce in income it is economically important because it facilitates adult work, freeing parents to go out to earn money, Such domestic work can begin very early, especially in developing counters, where the starting age can be as low as five or less. Though girls often carry the heaviest burden of preparing food, cleaning the house, washing the clothes and looking after younger brothers and sisters, boys too, in countries as diverse as Peru, Jamaica and India, play their part.

Nevertheless, boys tend to do less, particularly in the case of child care, though there are examples where pre-pubertal boys share domestic duties with girls. But not all domestic work takes place within the child's own family. There are the 'maids-of-all-work' in developing countries, whom professor Boudhiba described as virtual slaves (Boudhiba, 1982, p. 46). These girls tend to come from rural areas to the home of an urban 'relative' who undertakes to look after them and provide them with an education. But they are usually being framed out to distant, if not fictional, relatives where they need not be paid for being on call virtually 24 hours a day. Being strangers to the city and isolated from their parents, they are powerless to change their position. Domestic work is not only an unrecognised form of economic contribution, it remains unappreciated as a from of child labour.

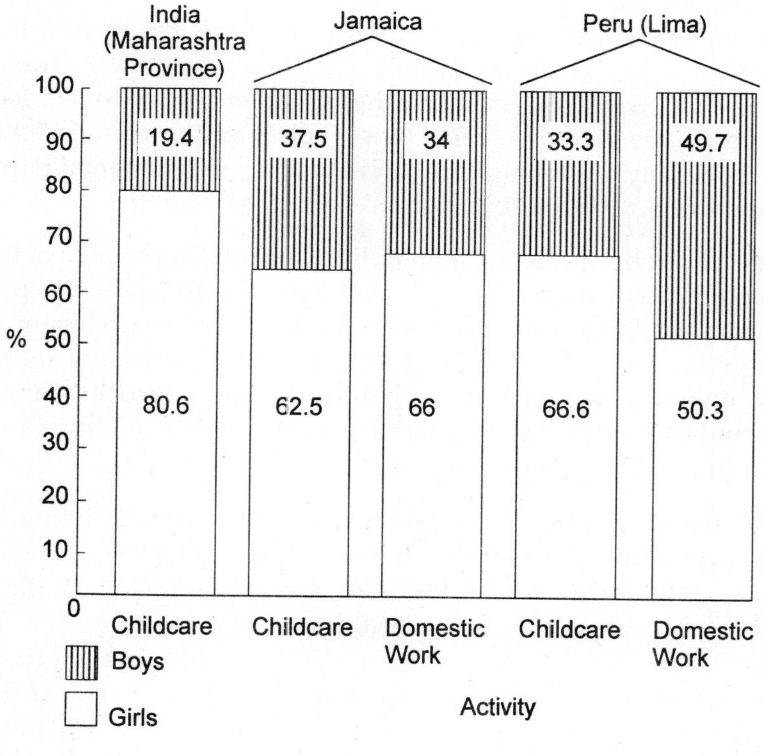

Fig. 34.1 Childcare and Domestic work performed by minors, related to sex of worker in three countries.

Sources: Ennew and Young, 1981; Ennew, 1985; Shah *et al.*, ASS, 1984, p. 146.

Non-domestic, non-monetary work forms a continuum with domestic work, especially in subsistence economies. It encompasses such time-consuming activities as looking after animals, protecting fields from pests, weeding, etc. Analytically, this category can be broken down depending on whether the production is for the family's consumption or for the market, and whether the child is working for its own benefit, or for parents, for relatives, or for strangers. This form of child work for no pay of widely viewed as the largest sector of child work in the world. At the first UN Seminar on Child Labour, delegates from developing countries stressed that this type of work expressed family solidarity and therefore was not subject to exploitative relationships. Exploitation occurs, they contended, when third parties are involved, usually in an urban context. Thus, logically, child labour cannot be a major problem. The anthropological evidence, though non-quantitative, tends to undermine this blithe assumption. The idea that rural children learn as they work and are, therefore, experiencing a traditional form of socialisation rather than exploitation, ignores the extent to which even simple societies are not integrated into cash economies and are subject to agricultural capitalism. In reality, children are involved from the age of five or six in hard labour in agrarian communities. One study of family labour among pastoralists in the Sahel has shown that children often perform much harder work than adult and such work often express a sexual division of labour: 'The boys look after the sheep, gather wood, collect fodder, draw water, sow and reap. The girl milk, cook, spin, look after the younger children. The country child is invariably a working child and work is a fundamental part of his/her existence' (Mendelievich, 1979, p. 128).

Such work demands often prelcude school attendance; besides much of the curricula is urban biased and Western oriented, which often acts a further inducement for parents to see their children working rather than wasting their time in irrelevant study. This social exploitation results in a lifetime disadvantage in the labour market for the individual child, and acts as a further mechanism for the improverishment of small peasant farmers, and the perpetuation of high levels of social inequality. Child labour is but another twist in the vicious circle of poverty.

Even the term 'cottage industry,' in which the child works at home, should not obscure the real costs to healthy child development that it often entails. In the Indian glassware industry in Moradabad, Uttar Pradesh, nearly one-quarter of the work-force are children who work in all but one of the processes, either at home, or in workshops. Long hours, heat, gases and dust, leave many children with eye injuries and lung diseases. Working as part of a family unit is, therefore, no protection if the family is subject to exploitation, as for example within plantation labour or crafts manufacture. Children working outside of their parental home on a fostering, adopted, godchild, apprenticeship basis, find themselves even more the hostages to fortune in the face of isolation and powerlessness.

To be a slave is to reach the limits of powerlessness. In Indian some children work for either a money lender or landowner as bonded labour to pay off he debts of parents or even grandparents. But this can easily become a contract for life: 'Sometimes, his parents or, when he grows older, he himself may take further loans, get deeper into debt and continue to work as a bonded labourer without any possibility of release,' (Blanchard, 1979, p. 55). This form of intergenerational debt resembles a feudal landlord-tenant relationship in which the child is pledged to work for the landlord or money lender, in order that a debt be paid off, or to obtain a loan or some other benefits. It continues in India despite attempts to outlaw it, most notably by the Bonded Labour System (Abolition) Act 1976. As many as 1000,000 bonded labourers still exist, many of them children, and not solely in agriculture, but in such cottage style industries as brick making and match manufacture.

Child-wage labour exploitation is the easiest to document and, therefore, to campaign and legislate against. But there is ample evidence that child-wage labourers continue to work even when minimum age legislation exists. It is small-scale enterprises or 'sweatshops,' often operating as subcontractors to larger enterprises, that are most adapt at avoiding the usually inadequate factory insepectorate. Child-wage labour is a feature of developed and developing countries, and one which increases adult unemployment and lowers overall wages. Children are the most subordinate and cheapest form of labour, thus highly attractive to some types of employer, be they in Britain or Bangladesh. The child-wage sector can, according to Rodgers and Standing (p. 7), be analysed in terms of the following criteria: family or individual basis; method of payment—time rate or piece—share cropping system; work with a training component and without; regular or casual work and seasonal work; legal or illegal work; work compatible with schooling and work competitive with schooling. The most difficult cases to document are those in which children earn an income in the informal (marginal) non-waged sector, such as car washing, shoe shining, market trading and garbage collecting. It also includes such illegal activities as begging, petty theft and prostitution. Economists have been reluctant to analyse the informal, as opposed to the formal, sector of the economy, and yet the two are intertwined and their activities are vital to the survival of poor people, especially in urban areas. Many of these activities take place on the street, leading to the exotic phenomenon of 'street children.' This category has been notoriously difficult to define, covering as it does children who retain contact with a family and a home to those relative few who appear totally abandoned to their 'mother the street'—the true outcasts.

The sixth child activity, schooling, is vital for future participation in the adult labour force. Premature work has been shown by a host of studies to damage permanently the child's future work prospects. Not all of those children who fail to gain access to schooling, or who drop out early, enter the labour force. Many enter 'forced idleness,' which is unemployment, a growing feature of some developed economies. Such a condition does not necessarily encourage the next activity, leisure, because poor children and youths find it difficult to gain access to leisure facilities or to pursue intellectually stimulating hobbies. Additionally, health activities such as adequate sleep, eating and cleaning, are difficult to maintain under the damaging work situations that have been well documented from Italy to Thailand (Valcarenghi, 1981, pp. 49-56 and Banerjee, 1980, p. 34).

The Minority Rights Group Report of 1985 suggested that it was through work that most child exploitation takes place. But when does child work become explorative? There have been many attempts at defining exploitation in this context, however the most comprehensive formulation has been put forward by UNICEF in its 1986 Executive Board Paper (UNICEF, 1986c, pp. 3-4):

1. *Starting full time work at too early an age*
   This happened historically in the earlier stages of industrialisation in Europe where children began work in factories from nine, eight or even five years., This is still the case today in many developing countries.
2. *Working too long* within or outside of the family so that children are unable to attend school, where it is available, or to make the most of school due to fatigue or lack of time. In some cases children still work 12-16 hours a day.
3. Work resulting in *excessive physical, social and psychological strains* upon the child as in the case of sexual exploitation in prostitution and pornography, work in sweatshops, as well as such dangerous work as military service and mining.
4. *Work and life on the streets* in unhealthy and dangerous conditions.
5. *Inadequate remuneration* for working outside of the family as in the case of child workers in carpet weaving who are paid US$ 3.00 for a 60-hour week.
6. *Too much responsibility too early* as in the domestic situation where children under ten may have to look after young brothers are sisters for a hole day thereby preventing school attendance.
7. *Work that does not facilitate the psychological and social development* of the child as in dull and repetitive tasks associated with industries like handicrafts.
8. *Work that inhibits the child's self-esteem* as in bonded labour and prostitution, and in a less extreme case the negative perception of 'street children.'

This framework accommodates the traditional view that the term exploitation has something to do with a third party who extracts a profit for instance, via exploiter/ employer and exploited/employee relationships. But, more importantly, it goes beyond it to embrace a 'social exploitation' dimension by acknowledging work in the informal sector (where the family can be the exploiter), as well as the human rights dimension recognising children's subordinate position in society.

The analysis of indices of exploitation is crucial to distinguishing child work from child labour, and therefore to the setting of priorities and policies. There has been an almost universal tendency hitherto in the literature to use child work and child labour almost interchangeably as if they were synonymous. In fact, child labour is a sub-set of child work, denoting that work which is exploitative of the child. Child work becomes child labour when it threatens the health and development of children. It is child labour, and not all child work, that one is trying to root out. After all, child work can be a positive experience and, in the best circumstance, children's work can prepare them for productive adult life. Through their work they can gain increasing status as family members and citizens. They can learn the skills of their parents and neighbours. Therefore, children's work can be an integral part of family life and can contribute to their healthy development. It can also build their confidence and self-steem. Child work can then be a painless and gradual initiation into adult life.

The dividing line between socialisation and exploitation will also reflect levels of development: a highly developed industrialised society, with adequate provision for the schooling of children, a full range of social service and minimum age and wage laws, will perceive exploitation of children differently from a primarily agrarian society with large numbers of rural workers and urban slums and shanty dwellers. And in practice they do. In the grey areas exploitation lives in the eye of the beholder.

Child labour has implications for the individual, the group and the wider society. It was in early industrial Britain that social investigators first associated child work with poor health. The health of exploited child workers in still being endangered today, some hundred years later. A WHO/Defence for children (DCI) joint report on child labour states that: 'Normal growth spurts during puberty and adolescence are adversely affected by the poor nutrient intake and increased manual work' (Shah, 1985, p. 39). In 28 countries, the average per capita intake of calories is 73 to 89 per cent of what is required, but it is lower for the poorer segments of the population, from which most working children come, even though their work raises their nutritional requirements. Working children also become more susceptible to infectious diseases, including tuberculosis, if they suffer from malnutrition, anaemia, fatigue and inadequate sleep. The report cities other physical health hazards, including bone lesions and postural deformity due to working doubled-up in carpet factories and lifting heavy weights. In modern industries other health, problems occur: 'The eyesight of young girls working for 12-14 hours a day in micro-computer factories is reported to be damaged within a period of 5-8 years' (Shah, 1985, p. 39). The report recognises much work of a more rigorous scientific nature needs to be done to determine the critical age when children are prone to health hazards, the type of work and working environments which adversely affect health, growth and psycho-social development (Shah, 1985, p. 37).

In unregulated sweatshops occupational hazards and risks are enormous. Children often work with poorly maintained and dangerous machinery and in intrinsically dangerous works situations such as mining. Even on the streets, children can be subject to the constant threat of traffic accidents and street violence. Exploitative sweatshops often have an especially pernicious effect on children's health. Excessive noise can lead to hearing loss, and hot, damp or dusty conditions to the transmission of communicable diseases. In manufacturing, children can be exposed to toxic substances, such as glue in shoe production. Even being outdoors is not necessarily an escape as many children in modern agriculture are often exposed to lethal chemical pesticides.

TABLE 34.1

Types of Child Work

Type of work	*Rural*	*Urban*
A. *Within the family (unpaid)*		
1. *Domestic/household tasks* e.g., cooking, cleaning, child-care, fetching water, cleaning utensils, washing clothes, poultry etc.	X	X
2. *Agricultural/bastoral tasks* e.g. ploughing, weeding, harvesting, herding livestock, etc.	X	
3. *Handicrafts/cottage industries* e.g., weaving, basketry, leatherwork, woodwork, household industries in the urban 'informal sector'	X	X
B. *With the family but outside the home*		
1. *Agricultural/pastoral work*		
(a) migrant labour	X	
(b) local agricultural labour (full-time or seasonal)	X	
2. *Domestic service*	X	X
3. *Construction work* e.g., buildings, roads, etc.	X	X
4. *'Informal economy'* e.g., laundry, recycling rubbish		
(a) employed by others		X
(b) self-employed		X
C. *Outside the family*		
1. *Employed by others*		
(a) tied/bounded/slave	X	X
(b) apprentices		X
(c) skilled trades e.g., carpets, embroidery, brass and copper work	X	X
(d) industries/unskilled occupations/ mines		X
(e) domestics e.g., 'maids-of-all-work'		X
(f) commercial e.g., shops, restaurants		X
(g) begging		X

Type of work		*Rural*	*Urban*
(h)	prostitution and pornography		X
2.	*Self-employed*		
	informal sector work e.g., shoe-shining, car washing, recycling rubbish, running errands, selling newspapers, etc.		

Source: UNICEF, 1986c, p. 12.

Child prostitution and pornography are increasing world-wide, as is the incidence of sexually transmitted diseases. The drug trade also uses children, both as intermediaries and countries and the children themselves often become addicted. In many cities glue-sniffing and the abuse of soft and hard drugs is endemic among street children. In developing countries large numbers of working children face the unhappy reality of increasing separation from their natural families. Poverty produces its own stress to the point that marriage and less formalised adult relationships break down. One parent or guardian leaves, or is forced to leave to find work, placing an additional burden upon the remaining single parent—often the mother — as well as the children who may be forced to work for the family's survival., Home relationships and the economic situation may continue to deteriorate to the point where the child abandons the family, or is abandoned by it. As children's contracts with their families weaken, they lose even their limited access to basic services, such as health, education and recreation. In urban areas, children who work daily no the streets may experience a freer and more adventurous lifestyle than at home, but at the same time they encounter much higher level of risk and less access to services and support.

Street children habitually faced with negative behaviour towards them have serious problems in maintaining healthy self-esteem and miss out on play and recreation essential for their social and emotional development. The opportunity cost of working for children is often a reduction in their chances of any kind of schooling. Formal education takes place during the day and during working hours. Therefore, a large proportion of working children do not attend school. Other constraints on regular school attendance include the cost of fees, books and uniforms as well as the often inappropriate nature of the curriculum. Meaningful apprenticeship might at least compensate for some of these disadvantages, but it can also be a form of exploitation in which the child acts as a servant to the craftsman on very low ay, running errands and performing menial tasks which bear no relation to the trade. The working child can then become locked into a vicious circle of deprivation and disadvantage in which the poor and unskilled child becomes a poor and unskilled adult.

As we have seen, children in rural areas can make an early work contribution. This, in turn, can positively influence fertility as the family views children as more hands rather than more months, as well as a form of social security in old age. The extent of child work in rural areas also has implications for rural emigration. As noted before, the parental use of child workers in domestic and farm activities may well allow other family members to migrate in search of seasonal or longer-term employment. Such migration usually involves male heads of households often leading to an increased work burden for the children. Conversely, lack of opportunities for child work, or a lack of adequate schooling and recreational facilities can encourage the emigration of children themselves.

Unemployment may be increased by the participation of young workers and high unemployment increases labour-force divisions. In urban industrial labour-markets, high and rising youth unemployment encourages the more affluent families to invest more in schooling, as higher qualifications are necessary to secure highwage and high-status jobs. By contrast, among the working class, high unemployment may have the perverse effect of discouraging school attendance, not only because their labour is needed to supplement family income, but due to the perception that the amount of schooling their children could obtain would be insufficient to secure a reasonable job (Rodgers and Standing, 1981, p. 35). In fact, work experience may be more useful to them in pursuit of the job they hope to obtain. This can only perpetuate labour force divisions along class lines.

The early sexual division of labour in which boys and girls often perform different work tasks encourages a 'sexual dualism' in which men have access to non-domestic wage opportunities while women are subordinated by their religion to domestic and substance farm activities. Child work can, therefore, be a mechanism by which these sex roles are learned and perpetuated. Another social outcome of child work can be seen in the commitment to a wide set of kinship obligations that the child may well carry throughout life. Child work within an extended family context is a way of socialising the child into the notion of obligations to kin which may be exploitative in nature. Child work is, thus, associated with greater inequalities of income and wealth. It is, as we have seen, both a symptom and a cause of poverty through the process of lifetime disadvantage it implies; via lack of access to schooling; through the low-wage mechanism it encourages and sustains; through the higher fertility and fragmentation of assets which it implies for the long term or where wealthy peasant families with more children can work and therefore secure more land.

Child labour is not accidental. Many children are hired because they can be paid at much lower rates than adults. In certain industries like carpet-making or electronics assembly, children are more skilful because of the dexterity of their small fingers. But children, because of their dependent position, are the most easily exploited of all workers. They are the cheapest from of labour and their situation is analogous to that of other relatively powerless groups, such as women workers and new immigrants, who accept lower wages and poor conditions of work because of the lack of organisation and their need to work. Not all child labour is therefore the result of poverty.

We have already seen the extent to which children are absorbed into the more time-intensive tasks in agrarian societies. Children are a from (perhaps the only form) of capital investment open to peasant farmers. Additionally, continuing rental obligations may force peasant families to employ all their domestic labour resources. Debt is a common mechanism that encourages this feudal-like situation and children may be the commodity traded to meet debt repayments. The growth of wage labour and capitalist relations of production has been associated in the industrialised societies with a decline in child labour in the long run. In the early stages children were used in many contexts to help further capital accumulation. It was common for whole families to b employed for a 'family wage,' especially, but not exclusively, in agriculture. In developing countries today, large industrial firms and other sizeable capitalist enterprises do not seem to make extensive use of child work, perhaps because of the skill factor or the need to respect legislation, or because of the abundant supply of youth and adult workers. Nevertheless, there is one notable exception, and that is the use of child workers in small manufacturing enterprises where it is probably under reported because of its illegality. In such enterprises children are used as cheap 'sweated' labour, frequently alongside older relatives. Such practices have been reported in both industrialised and developing countries. Here, too, child work can be a way of circumventing the potential power of trade unions as well as substituting cheap labour for higher adult wage employment.

Another correlate of capitalist relationships is the need for a wage income to pay taxes or to purchase new consumer goods, forcing many youths and children to migrate. Where farming is dominated by male workers, as in Latin America and the Caribbean, there may be a considerable amount of migration of girls and young women. Where men have been the first to move into the wage labour sector women and children have taken over domestic and subsistence work or lower forms of wage employment, such as cotton picking and weeding (Rodgers and Standing, p. 17). Landlordlessness, which itself forces children into the labour-market, is another correlate of capitalist relationships. With the growth of capitalist relations the labour-market becomes increasingly differentiated and the participation of child workers can be conducive to the formation of a subordinated workers' group. Reducing the wage for subsistence permits increased exploitation. Moreover, poor access to schooling, increasingly needed in the labour-market, perpetuates disadvantage.

The situation of child workers is also affected by economic changes, such as the world-wide recession of the early 1980s. Unemployment rates rose to 51 per cent of the urban labour force in some African countries. Latin America in particular has been significantly affected by the Debt Crisis and the harsh repayment policies advocated by the International Monetary Fund turning the 1980s into the decade of debt rather than development. The effects of these trends, including increased poverty, inequitable distribution of income, and adult unemployment directly affect children. Child work in paid-wage employment outside the family has increased as children are forced to work for their own and their families survival. This qualitative change in child work has opened up more opportunities for exploitation (ILO, 1983).

Child work is not only a response to economic processes, it also reflects the culturally determined roles and functions of children, the values by which the activities of children are judged, and the nature of the socialisation process. These two sets of factors—economic and cultural — indeed go together, though the nature of the relationship has been much debated. Child labour, then, remains a seriously neglected issue in relation to the magnitude of the problem, and though the study of child labour is hampered by several particular research problems, the real constraint lies in the universal perception of it as a low-priority concern. Nevertheless, it was in industrialised societies that the problem of child labour was first identified as a public issue with attempts as systematic investigation. The prevailing view that child labour is a thing of the past needs challenging and where better to start than in the first industrial nation, Britain.

35

CHILD LABOUR AND COMPULSORY-EDUCATION POLICIES

In 1986 and 1987 the Government of India adopted a new set of policies toward working children, which for the first time reflected the privately held views of officials in the ministries of Labour and Education. The government would no longer ban child labour (with some exceptions) but would instead seek to ameliorate the conditions of working children. The government would also endeavor to provide voluntary part-time nonformal education for working children rather than press for compulsory universal primary education. The new policies won legitimacy from several international agencies in the form of quasi-official statements and grants for specific programmes. This chapter first reviews the government's new approach toward child-labour laws, then turns to the government's new education policy.

Child-Labour Policy

The official expression of the new child-labour policy is the Child Labour (Prohibition and Regulation) Act, approved by the Indian parliament in January 1987. The act prohibits the employment of children in certain occupations and processes, while regulating the conditions of work in other jobs. Children are prohibited from employment in bidi making; carpet weaving; cement manufacturing; cloth printing, dyeing, and weaving; match manufacturing; explosives and fireworks; mica cutting and splitting; shellac manufacturing; soap manufacturing; tanning; wool cleaning; and building and construction work. The central government can add to the list upon the advice of a newly constituted Child Labour Technical Advisory Committee. The prohibition applies only to children who are not yet fourteen. The act replaces the various age limitations set in earlier acts (e.g., fifteen in merchant shipping and transportation, twelve on plantations).

The act provides for the protection of working children not employed in specified hazardous occupations and processes. It sets limits on the number of hours children can work continuously ("an interval for rest for at least one hour" after three hours of work), limits the number of days of employment ("every child employed in an establishment shall be allowed in each week, a holiday of one whole day"), and restricts the times of work ("no child shall be permitted or required to work between 7 p.m. and 8 a.m.").

Central and state governments are permitted to set rules for cleanliness in the place of work, the disposal of wastes and effluents, ventilation, temperature, dust, fumes, and so forth. Employers are required to maintain a register with the names and birth dates of all children they employ. Under the act any citizen may file a complaint with the local court if he or she believes that children under fourteen are being employed in prohibited occupations and processes—but it is necessary to produce a certificate from a government doctor that the employed children are under fourteen.

Critics of the legislation said that the government had legalised child labour. The bill did precisely that. The new act imposes no age limit on the employment of children. It simply specifies that children are prohibited from being employed only in certain occupations and processes. Even this restriction is carefully circumscribed. The act says that "nothing in this section shall apply to any workshop wherein any process is carried on by the occupier with the aid of his family." Thus, the act prohibits the employment of children in the making of matches in workshops, but not if the work is carried out in family-run workshops.

Even the regulations pertaining to conditions of work are circumscribed with the same qualification that none of these restrictions "shall apply to any establishment wherein any process is carried on by the occupier with the aid of his family or to any school established by, or receiving assistance or recognition from, the government" This latter phrase exempts government-run apprenticeship programmes to teach children carpet weaving.

The act represents the culmination of a long debate within and outside the government between those who argued that government should take steps to enforce the many laws that prohibit the employment of children and those who argued that "existing socioeconomic conditions" make enforcement unrealistic and that government should instead seek to ameliorate the conditions of work. The debate became public in 1979 with the appointment by the government of India of a Committee on Child Labour to examine "the causes leading to the problems arising out of the employment of children" and to review existing legislation. To understand the debate we must first review the policies adopted by the British and the post-independence government that have been reconsidered.

Child-Labour Laws: A Legislative History

Restrictions against the employment of children were introduced by the British in the Indian Factories Act of 1881, which imposed a minimum age of seven years. Partly under the influence of the International Labour Organisation in the 1920s and 1930s, India subsequently passed a series of acts for the protection of children. The Factories Act as amended in 1922 raised the age limit to fifteen years. The Indian Mines Act of 1923 raised the minimum age for employment in mines to thirteen years. A Royal Commission on Labour, appointed in 1933, examined the practice of parents pledging the labour of their children by taking advances in return for bonds—a practice called bonded labour. The practice was common in the carpet factories of Amritsar and the bidi factories of Madras. Though the government of India had eliminated the system of indenture, under which adults pledged their own labour on contract, the government had not banned the pledging of child labour by parents.

Subsequent acts regulated the employment of children in specific sectors of the economy, in each instance imposing a minimum age for employment. The Employment of Children Act (1938) was the first act devoted entirely to child labour. It listed occupations and processes in which children could not be employed, all of which were later incorporated into the 1987 legislation. The act similarly exempted family-run workshops. The Factories Act of 1948 set fourteen as the minimum age of employment in factories, defined as a premise employing at least ten persons where manufacturing is being carried on with the aid of power, and above twenty where no power is employed. A "fitness" certificate was required from a doctor for children over fourteen and under eighteen. No birth certificate or certificate of school attendance was required. The law also restricted the number of continuous hours of work, night work, and the use of machinery by young persons.

India's Constituent Assembly wrote into the constitution specific protections for children. Article 24 provides that "no child below 14 shall be employed in any factory or mine or engaged in any hazardous employment." Article 39 promises that the state shall direct its policy toward ensuring that "children are not abused and that citizens are not forced by economic necessity to enter avocations unsuited to their age or strength," that "children are given opportunities and facilities to develop in a healthy manner and in conditions of freedom and dignity, and that childhood and youth are protected against exploitation and against moral and material abandonment." Article 45 says that the state shall endeavor to provide by 1960 free and compulsory education for all children until they reach fourteen years of age.

A series of acts further extended protection to children: The Plantations Labour Act of 1951 prohibited the employment of children under twelve; the Mines Act of 1952 prohibited employment under fifteen; the Factories Act of 1954 prohibited the employment of adolescents under seventeen at night; and the Beedi and Cigar Workers Act of 1966 prohibited the employment of children under fourteen in any factory manufacturing bidis or cigars. These central government acts were applicable throughout the country. State governments also passed acts regulating the conditions of work for young people in restaurants, hotels, and shops, setting age limits ranging from twelve to fifteen.

In response to a United Nations General Assembly resolution proclaiming 1979 as the International Year of the Child, the government of India appointed the Committee on Child Labour to review existing legislation. The sixteen-member committee included members of parliament, representatives from institutions dealing with children, and officials of sate and central labour departments. In his inaugural speech to the first meeting of the committee the central government labour minister called for a new set of policies toward working children. He noted that the government had not enforced legislation banning child labour.

> It is not that this is not a desirable objective. . . but we have-to think of two sets of problems related with a proposal for an immediate legal ban on the employment of child labour. One set of problems can be described as economic problems, flowing from the problems of poverty. The fact remains whether an immediate prohibition of the employment of child labour will not lead to the closing of some channels of supplementing incomes for extremely poor families who live below the poverty line. . . . Another set of problems can be described as administrative problems, because you may pass a law in your wisdom, but the law has to be implemented. What is a law's worth if it is to remain imprisoned in the Statute Book? Social reform has to be practical. . . In spite of all these laws you find in some areas, especially where you have to deal with far flung areas, where the representatives of the administration can reach only with great difficulty, where there can be connivance and complicity, then it becomes very difficult to enforce a law unless conditions are such that there is a tendency to accept the sanctions of the law. Therefore, if we say tomorrow that all child labour should be abolished in this country, make it punishable, it will he very difficult to see that it is enforced.'

The Committee on Child Labour listened to this argument sympathetically. In an exceptionally frank statement, the committee in its report agreed that most of the legislation was not enforced:

> In the course of its spot inspections and discussions, the Committee got a clear impression of several inadequacies in the existing administrative setup for the implementation of various laws. The jurisdiction of individual inspectors was too extensive for them to keep a regular watch on activities within their purview. In several States one inspector was required to cover a group of several districts. He was also burdened with very wide ranging other responsibilities pertaining to labour legislation. The results of this situation were apparent. There were practically no prosecutions in most parts of the country of any violation of existing laws pertaining to child labour. In one of the States it was pointed out with pride that the first prosecution ever launched by them was only in the International Year of the Child! The Committee itself during spot inspections noticed children of very tender age working in certain factory premises in total disregard of the statutory provisions. In the course of the discussions with different interests, including officials of labour departments, it was pointed out that the entire situation was being overlooked because of certain inherent factors. There was, in fact, a vicious circle. The Labour Inspector, whenever he got a chance to book any violation, had difficulties in collecting evidence for proper prosecution. The fact of employment of a child against law was denied both by the employer and the parents of the children. Social acquiescence in the existing conditions also made it difficult to enlist support of other independent witnesses. A general sympathy was prevalent

> amongst people towards any one employed. It *was* also argued that if the child was not so employed he would really be in the streets and thus become a more dangerous hazard for the community at large. By keeping the child occupied, he was kept away from becoming a vagabond. Some also argued that since the parents also were involved in occupations, it was not possible for the child to be left all by himself in the house and the parents, therefore, preferred to make the child work in some establishment. Some even took the view that the environment in which the child was working was distinctly better than the environment in which he lives and, therefore, discouraging him from such a situation was not being helpful to him.[2]

The Committee nonetheless urged the government to strengthen its enforcement machinery and to make use of voluntary organisations and trade unions. The committee proposed that the government increase the number of prosecutions and increase the penalties, including one-year jail sentences and fines of up to 2,000 rupees. It also suggested that attention be given to creating an institutional framework for collective bargaining for working children, though the committee offered no such framework. The committee noted that the elimination of child labour would benefit employment of those in the age group of fifteen to fiftynine, but regarded such an approach as "radical and perhaps not feasible at first sight." Instead, the committee pressed for the enforcement of minimum-wage laws for adults ("If parents' earnings increase, they would be less inclined to allow their children into service"). The committee supported primary education for children but repeated the familiar argument that "serious doubts are raised about the usefulness of the present system of education," which "does not prepare them for future occupations. In fact it raises amongst children aspirations and hopes only for 'white collared' jobs. The educational curriculum must be geared to bring the maximum of skill and competence in the child keeping in view the environment in which he is living."[3]

The Committee called for a strengthening of nonformal education facilities for working children. "Employers should be urged to include education as one of the necessary ingredients of labour welfare measures in then establishment. It would also be worthwhile in the view of the committee, to impose a cess on industry to raise funds for this purpose; or alternatively to allow concessions in taxes, etc. to employers who undertake to implement educational schemes."[4]

There was a debate within the committee over whether there should be a uniform minimum age for employment and, if so, whether it should be fixed at fifteen years or less. One member of the committee, the development commissioner in charge of small-scale industries, pointed out that there was no minimum age for employment except for occupations specified by existing laws. Thus children of any age could be employed as domestic helpers, while in some sectors of the economy (plantations, shops, and establishments) the age limit was twelve. Given the economic circumstances and the fact that so many children were not in school because the type of education that is now being imparted in schools makes it completely unattractive to the parents of children particularly in the rural areas where children are considered an economic asset," he recommended that the minimum age for employment in all occupations be lowered to twelve.[5] Other members of the committee questioned whether any age limit should be imposed, except in selected hazardous occupations. The committee concluded, however, that the minimum age for entry into *any* employment should be fifteen years, that existing laws be consolidated, and that the ministry should enforce legislation relating to the employment of children.

The government rejected the recommendation that the minimum age of entry into employment be fifteen years, but agreed with those recommendations aimed at improving conditions for working children: health schemes in areas with concentrations of child labour, supplementary nutrition provided by employers to working children with tax concessions from the government, and the establishment of nonformal education for working children.6

In 1983 the planning minister, S.B. Chavan, stated the government's position that banning child labour was "not feasible due to the prevailing socio-economic constraints and exigencies."[7] The seventh five-year plan (1985-1990), approved by the National Development Council, said that since it is not feasible to eradicate child labour, the government should try to make the conditions of working children more acceptable. The plan proposed a greater role for voluntary agencies in providing child workers with health care, nutrition, and education. The abolition of child labour, it said, could only be achieved when there is sufficient improvement in the conditions of the families whose children are compelled to work.

In its annual report (1983—1984) the Ministry of Labour said that the government had accepted child labour as a "harsh reality' and that it was neither "feasible nor opportune" to prevent children from working in the present stage of economic development.[8]

In November 1985 a Bangalore-based organisation created by trade- union activists, the Concerned for Working Children (CWC), held a national seminar in Bangalore under the auspices of the central government's Department of Education in the Ministry of Human Resource Development. The seminar's final report made a distinction between "child work," which should be regulated, and "exploitation of child work," which should be prohibited. Government policy, the report said, should aim to protect the working child and make provision for the working child's educations. The CWC prepared a draft bill on child labour, which became the model for the act the government subsequently brought to parliament. The widely circulated committee proposal started with the familiar premise, "It is now a well recognised fact that high incidence of child labour is essentially a problem of development. ... In developing countries like India, the families with no or meagre income are forced to send their children to the labour market as soon as they are old enough to get out of their houses, often at the age of 4 or 5."[10] The CWC draft bill recommended that no age limit be imposed on child labour except in hazardous occupations where there would he a fifteen-year-old age limit. They recommended that wages for children be set by a government board, that the terms of employment for child workers be put in writing and sent to parents and to government inspectors, that a child labour development fund be created with funding from employers, that evening and weekend schools for child workers be created, and that child labour unions be established.

The Bangalore seminar report concluded that child labour and education had to be seen

> in relation to the power structure and the social system in which it is embedded. It is a product and a part of under-development and its vicious circle of parental poverty and of low productivity. The abiding solution can lie only in long term economic regeneration so that employers will not have to seek such minimally paid labour nor parents be compelled to drive their children to the indignities of forced labour to supplement their low incomes.[11]

The seminar participants faulted the education system as totally irrelevant, the yearly school timings inappropriate ("a full day schedule of school obviously keeps away working children"), and supported proposals for nonformal education ("it is obvious that the educational needs of working children can be best served by nonformal education"). Education for all, said the report, depended on dealing with such issues as agrarian relations, rural indebtedness, bonded labour, and the payment of minimum wages. The general thrust of the seminar was that the elimination of poverty was a precondition to the ending of child labour.

The bill drafted by the Concerned for Working Children and the revised version subsequently proposed by the government generated opposition from some activists and journalists. Dr. Neera Burra, a sociologist who had extensively researched child labour, wrote a series of sharp attacks against the proposed new policy.[12] She faulted the proposed Child Labour Bill on the following grounds:

1. The list of hazardous occupations is drawn almost entirely from the Employment of Children Act of 1938 and fails to include new hazardous occupations. Nor is it clear what criteria will be used for defining what is hazardous. Garbage picking (commonly described in India as "Ragpicking"), for example, is not classified as hazardous though thousands of children collecting scraps of iron, glass, paper, and rags often pick up bits of food to eat and are prone to tetanus and skin diseases.
2. Hazardous work is exempt if it is part of family labour, though in many industries, such as bidi making and match making, owners operate through a putting-out system, with households and small shops doing hazardous work under unsatisfactory working conditions. Under the pretext of family labour, employers can get around restrictions on the employment of children.

For children working in these small shops, no safeguards are provided at all.

3. In spite of constitutional provisions banning child labour in hazardous occupations, existing legislation his not been enforced. Is there any reason to believe that the government will enforce the new legislation?
4. The legalisation of child labour in so-called nonhazardous occupations without regard for age is a violation of articles 24, 39, and 45 of the Constitution, which ban child labour and call for compulsory schooling.

Dr. Burra went on to criticize the government's proposed National Child Labour Programme (NCLP). The proposed NCLP would provide free lunches for working children, a scheme she noted that would undermine the government's existing programme of providing free lunches to school children as an inducement to school attendance. Similarly, the provision of medical and other welfare services in the match and fireworks, industries meant that the government was inducing children to continue to work in hazardous industries (this provision was subsequently dropped).

In a hard-hitting address at a seminar on child labour in New Delhi organised by the Indian Social Institute to protest the proposed bill, Dr. Walter Fernandes, the institute's director, argued that the proposed legislation would legitimate the government's decision not to enforce existing child-labour laws in such hazardous industries as match making, carpet weaving, and bidi making. The government, he said, should first demonstrate its commitment to abolishing child labour by dealing with these industries, then move on to implement the Rural Indebtedness Abolition Act to end bonded labour. He accused the government of lacking the political will to enforce existing child-labour legislation since politicians are receiving financial support from employers of child labourers.

The concluding report for the conference urged the government to enforce existing child-labour legislation and to implement the constitutional directive for free and compulsory education until the age of fourteen. "If the constitutional directive on universal and free primary education were to be implemented, then children would automatically be away from full- time work."[13] The decline in expenditures on elementary education demonstrates, the report said, the lack of the government's concern with ending child labour.

The role of "vested interests" in not implementing the Employment of Children Act of 1938 or the constitutional protection provided to children was another theme of Dr. Burra's.

> From the urban middle class housewife to the landlord in the village, from the parents to the employers in the unorganised sector—everyone wants child labour. After all if you can pay less and get more work done, why not! The only person who suffers is the child who doesn't count. Socially minded people salve their conscience by employing children ostensibly to save them from starvation and look upon it as a social service! Whatever the CWC may have to say about

> regulating hours of work, better conditions of work, health facilities, etc. it is an impossible task. We are dealing with millions of children all over the country and not just a few in an urban slum. . . . It is totally unrealistic to think that children will benefit by this bill. It will just give a carte balance to employers and parents to exploit the poor child with the benign indulgence of the State.

The argument that child labour should be made legal in order to regulate, concluded Dr. Burra, was a false promise.[14]

Within the government, however, the overwhelming sentiment in the relevant ministries was support for the new initiative. The general manager of the Handloom and Handicrafts Export Corporation said that a ban on child labour in the carpet industry would be suicidal for exports. The HHEC is a government organisation that runs 200 training centers for children, many well below age fourteen. The union minister for labour, Mr. P.A. Sangma, said that a move to ban child labour would cause hardships to those who depended on their income and would be impossible to implement. Instead, the government proposed to make the conditions of work less arduous. The minister called upon employers in Sivakasi to support the government's 14 crore ($10 million) national child-labour welfare project, saying that "I dictate to the conscience of the industrialists to look at the problem from a humane angle." He expressed his appreciation to managers in the match industry in Sivakasi who were supporting the scheme, saying that "we realise that child labour exists because of economic necessity and because a family has to earn somewhere from somebody."[15]

India and the International Labour Organisation

The new legislation, by legalising child labour in nonhazardous employment, appeared to violate the ILO convention on child labour. But officials of the ILO, along with officials of other international organisations, expressed their support for India's new strategy of regulation rather than abolition. In November 1985 the United Nations held a seminar in Geneva "on ways and means of achieving the elimination of the exploitation of child labour in all parts of the world."[16] The seminar, organised by the Secretary General of the United Nations in cooperation with the ILO, was called at the initiative of the United Nations Commission on Human Bights. Twenty-nine countries participated, and there were representatives from the major international organisations concerned with children, including the ILO, UNESCO, UNICEF, and WHO.

The seminar subscribed to the Indian distinction between child labour and the exploitation of child labour. Speakers said that "in many developing countries, child labour was unavoidable, in particular child labour performed within the family, mostly in rural areas, in order to supplement the family's income. This type of work could not be considered as exploitative. . . . It was further observed that there were certain positive aspects of some forms of child labour. In certain particular contexts, work formed a part of the training process of the child and prepared him for adult life and did not involve exploitation."[17]

Much of the discussion at the seminar centered around the problem of how to distinguish between child labour and the exploitation of child labour, considering such issues as the age of the child, the nature of the work, whether work was essential for the survival of the child or the child's family, the conditions of safety and health in which the child worked, the working hours, and whether wages were discriminatory.

Kurt Herndl, assistant secretary general for human rights, raised four issues: (1) whether exploitation is merely the existence of child labour or whether it refers to specific exploitative elements in the employment of children. Should one, he asked, consider the employment of all children under the age of twelve by definition exploitative? (2) What is meant by a "child"? In practice, he noted, three categories are used: children under twelve, children between twelve and fifteen, and children between fifteen and eighteen. (3) How should we distinguish between labour that is dangerous, hazardous, and morally outrageous (e.g., child prostitution) and acceptable firms of child labour? (4) What would constitute the "elimination' of exploitative practices? Banning the employment of children under twelve, he reported, and the banning of child labour in all hazardous and unsafe activities is the minimum standard advocated by the ILO.

The seminar recommended that "States ... should review their legislation in the field of child labour with a view to absolute prohibition of employment of children in the following cases: employment before the normal age of completion of primary schooling in the country concerned sexual exploitation of children; night work; work in dangerous or unhealthy conditions; work concerned with trafficking in and production of illicit drugs; work involving degrading or cruel treatment." Other recommendations dealt with improving the conditions for working children. These included "undertaking development programmes aimed at achieving equitable distribution of income, generating opportunities for employment, creation of small businesses, and agrarian reforms; and abolish, wherever possible primary school fees; introduce flexible school timetables to enable children who work to receive education; . . . establish or improve medical services for school children and children at work."[18] No mention was made of introducing compulsory education.

The ILO, since its inception, has been an advocate of legislation prohibiting the employment of children. In 1919 the ILO adopted its first Minimum Age Convention, which fixed a minimum age of fourteen for employment in industry. Subsequently, the ILO approved conventions regulating the age and conditions of work of children in particular sectors and occupations. A declaration issued in 1979, the International Year of the Child, reiterated the ILO's commitment to the elimination of child labour but also declared that pending its attainment the ILO would work for the improvement of the conditions of working children. In 1983, the annual report of the director general of the ILO Francis Blanchard, was devoted to the issue of child labour. He reiterated the ILO's stance on child labour and noted the "close correspondence between school attendance rates and the incidence of child labour," which underscored the ILO's 1973 minimum-age recommendation that full-time attendance at school or participation in approved vocational orientation or training programmes should be required and effectively ensured up to an age at least equal to that specified for admission to employment." He agreed with .those who said that "child labour is embedded an poverty and it is through sustained increases in standards of living that it will be abolished," but, he went on to say, recognition of this reality must not serve as a pretext for inaction. The problem of child labour is so grave and is often manifested in forms so unacceptable that it cannot be left aside until economic conditions and social structures are fundamentally improved."[19] He urged states strictly to enforce their child labour laws and called upon member states to ratify the ILO Minimum Age Convention of 1973 which established fifteen as the minimum age of employment in most sectors, while permitting light work from age thirteen.

But other officials of the ILO and other international organisations took a position more sympathetic to the new Indian policy. In a number of widely circulated papers, Assefa Bequele, a senior research economist at the ILO from Ethiopia, argued that governments should carry out a two pronged approach of protecting children from extreme forms of exploitation while improving the conditions of employment for others. 'The close link between poverty and the incidence of child labour suggests the strong complementarity of anti-child labour policies and those aiming at employment creation and poverty alleviation."[20] Rural development programmes and income generating and income maintenance programmes were thus necessary, he wrote, for eliminating child labour. More broadly, he concluded, "changes in the structure of the present international system, including a more equitable distribution of economic opportunities among nations.. . and other changes advocated by the International Development Strategy can, by enhancing national efforts aimed at poverty alleviation and rapid growth, provide significant impetus to the struggle against child labour."[21]

To what extent the international organisations should throw their political weight behind efforts to end "exploitation" and to ameliorate child labour rather than pressing for its abolition has been an issue within the ILO, UNICEF, WHO, and the UN Commission on Human Rights. A handful of officials in each of these agencies has given considerable attention to these questions, notably Assefa Bequele in the ILO, William Cousins in UNICEF, Dr. P.M. Shah at WHO, and Abdelwahab Bouhdiba of the UN Commission on Human Rights. Among these officials there are subtle differences, but in the main they have tended to emphasise the need by governments to end the worst forms of exploitation and to ameliorate the conditions of working children rather than press for abolition. Dr. P.M. Shah, an Indian pediatrician, has pressed for programmes of health care for working children, believing that such programmes can be developed through cooperation between government agencies and employers. Officials at UNICEF have suggested that the agency give special attention to providing services to children in especially difficult circumstances, such as street children and children of refugees and immigrants. At the ILO the emphasis is on protection rather than abolition, at least for the short run. Work in hazardous and unsafe activities, wrote Bequele, should be prohibited. For other children, protective measures are advocated, including the provision of fair remuneration, strict limitation of hours of work, and the maintenance of satisfactory standards of safety and health. Steps should be taken to expand educational opportunities, including "increased access to it by the relatively deprived sectors and socio-economic groups, improvements in the quality of education so as to make it more relevant and attractive to the poor, and reducing the real cost of education to the poor."[22] Once again, the theme is incentives, not compulsion.

Thus, the Indian government's position on child labour, while not in accordance with the 1973 ILO convention (India, along with most developing countries, has not ratified the convention), has won considerable support at international conferences and among officials in the ILO.

Rajiv Gandhi's New National Policy on Education

Rajiv Gandhi's announcement in January 1985, only a few weeks after his election as prime minister, that he had asked the Ministry of Education to review the country's educational system and to propose a new national policy on education to take India into the twenty-first century was greeted with both enthusiasm and cynicism: enthusiasm that the young prime minister had made educational reform a high priority early in his administration; cynicism in that once again another committee would be appointed, whose recommendations were likely to go unheeded. Since this new education policy has relevance for our understanding of the government's policy toward child labour, we shall examine the policy and the debate surrounding it.'

In August 1985 the ministry's review, called *Challenge of Education—A Policy Perspective,* was released.[23] The 119-page document provided a host of recommendations for what it called "educational restructuring": universalising elementary education, reducing the school dropout rate, creating a network of "model schools" in every district in the country for the most meritorious children from rural areas, using new communications technologies in schools, vocationalising secondary education, expanding nonformal education for those who had not attended or completed school, delinking degrees from jobs, making education more "socially relevant," and depoliticising the universities. There followed months of public discussion on these proposals, innumerable conferences of educators, and the appointment of twenty-three task forces by the government to make detailed recommendations for specific subjects covered by the proposed National Policy on Education.[24]

While there was much criticism of the government's proposals for education, there was agreement that the *Challenge of Education* provided an extraordinary—and disarming—critique of the government's own failure to carry out the reforms and targets set by earlier government commissions. The report noted that from 1950 to 1983 there had been a massive increase in the number of primary schools, from 210,000 to 504,000, and a vast increase in the student population of the country, from 28 million in 1950—1951 to 114 million in 1982—1983, a growth rate of 4.5 per cent per annum. Most states reported more than 100 per cent enrollment of boys and 75 per cent for girls.

In a spirit of self-criticism, the report documented the following failures in educational development:

1. A quarter of the pupil enrolled in primary school are underage or over-age, and if these are excluded from the rate of growth of enrollments for 1971-1981 (2.5 per cent per annum) the growth rate is below the age-specific population growth rate. "This implies that the backlog of illiterate population in absolute terms keeps on increasing with time."[25]
2. Though there has been an increase in the enrollment of girls in primary schools, the situation in many states remains unsatisfactory. In Uttar Pradesh, India's largest state, the gross enrollment ratio (which includes underage and overage children) for girls is 49 per cent. In Jalore district in Rajasthan enrollment of girls is as low as 17 per cent.
3. While most children have a primary school within one kilometer of their home, nearly one-fifth of all habitations in India do not have schools. The schools themselves are often unsatisfactory: 40 per cent of the schools have no *pacca* (brick or cement) buildings; 9 per cent have no buildings at all; 40 per cent have no blackboards; 60 per cent have no drinking water; 70 per cent have no library facilities; 53 per cent are without playgrounds; 89 per cent lack toilet facilities; 35 per cent of the schools have only a single teacher to teach three or four different classes; "many schools remain without any teacher for varying periods of time and some teachers are not above sub-contracting teaching work to others who are not qualified."[26]
4. Nearly 60 per cent of the children drop out between classes 1 and 5. Of 100 children enrolled in class 1, only 23 reach class 8. "The magnitude of wastage is emaciating the educational development of the country."[27] While there has been a marginal decline in the dropout rate in some states, in Uttar Pradesh the dropout rate is increasing.
5. While the literacy rate has increased from 16.7 per cent in 1951 to 36.2 per cent and the number of literates has increased fourfold from 60 million to 248 million, the absolute number of illiterates has grown from 294 million at the time of independence to 424 million in 1981. There is also a glaring disparity between male and female literacy, the former being 46.9 per cent, the latter 24.8 per cent. In rural areas the literacy rate for males is 40.8 per cent and for females 18 per cent; in urban areas it is 65.9 per cent and 47.8 per cent respectively.
6. The regional variations are large, from Kerala, which has a literacy rate of 70.4 per cent, to Rajasthan, with a literacy rate of 24.4 per cent (only 11.4 per cant of the females in Rajasthan were literate in 1981). Eight states have literacy rates five or more percentage points above the national average: Gujarat, Himachal Pradesh. Kerala, Maharashtra, Manipur, Nagaland, Tamil

Nadu, and Tripura. Five states have literacy rates that are five or more percentage points below the national average: Andhra, Bihar, Madhya Pradesh, Rajasthan, and Uttar Pradesh (for state literacy rates, see Table 35.1; for school attendance rates by state, see Table 35.2).

TABLE 35.1

School Enrollments and Literacy Rates by State (per cent)

	Enrollment (1978)		*Literacy*		
	Ages 6-10	*Ages 11-13*	*Rate (1981)*	*Male*	*Female*
Andhra Pradesh	60.2	30.1	29.9	39.3	20.4
Assam	63.7	37.9	28.1[a]		
Bihar	54.4	25.9	26.2	38.1	13.7
Gujarat	69.8	56.9	43.7	54.4	32.3
Haryana	60.7	45.0	36.1	48.2	22.3
Himachal Pradesh	79.0	62.3	42.5	53.2	31.5
Jammu and Kashmir	58.3	41.4	26.7	36.3	15.9
Karnataka	75.1	47.4	38.5	48.8	27.7
Kerala	86.0	76.8	70.4	75.3	65.7
Madhya Pradesh	47.7	33.7	27.9	39.5	15.5
Maharashtra	79.4	56.2	47.2	58.8	34.8
Manipur	76.4	54.5	41.4	53.0	29.1
Meghalaya	60.3	53.5	34.1	37.9	30.1
Nagaland	70.4	628	42.6	50.1	33.9
Orissa	56.5	40.7	34.2	47.1	21.1
Punjab	93.2	64.1	40.9	47.2	33.7
Rajasthan	45.2	29.1	24.4	38.3	11.4
Sikkim	68.9	59.9	34.1	43.7	22.2
Tamil Nadu	87.6	50.7	46.8	58.3	35.0
Tripura	73.9	37.7	42.1	51.7	32.0
Uttar Pradesh	53.4	33.4	27.2	38.8	14.0
West Bengal	67.6	39.7	40.9	50.7	30.3
All India	64.1	41.7	36.2	46.9	24.8

Source: Enrollment figures from *Fourth All-India Educational* Survey (New Delhi National Council of Educational Research and Training. 1980), pp. 944—947. Data from survey conducted in 1978. Literacy figures from O.P. Sharma and Robert D. Retherford, *Recent Literacy Trends in India. Occasional Paper No.* I *of 1987* (New Delhi: Registrar General and Census Commissioner, 1987), p. *11;* the authors estimate that it will take seventy years for the goal of complete literacy to be achieved if current trends continue—Kerala will take fifteen years, Rajasthan a century.

*1971 figure.

7. India spends 3 per cent of its gross national product on education, similar to that of other countries in South Asia, but well below the percentage spent in many developing countries and well below the 6 per cent recommended by the Educational Commission in 1966. While in 1960-1961, 43 per cent of the educational budget was for primary education, by 1976 the expenditure on primary education had declined to 27 per cent. More than 90 per cent of the ex-penditure is for teachers' salaries and administration. Total expenditure per student per year by the center and the states has declined in real terms. Very little money is available for science equipment, kits, posters and charts, or books, even blackboards. (For data on expenditures on elementary education from 1951 to 1985, see Table 35.3.)

TABLE 35.2

School Attendance by State, 1981

	Age Group	*Total Attendance*	*Male*	*Female*
		(Per cent of population)		
Andhra	5—9	42	47	34
	10—14	1	52	30
	15—19	19	27	10
	20—24	5	8	2
Bihar	5—9	26	33	18
	10—14	41	55	25
	15—19	24	38	9
	20—24	8	15.	2
Gujarat	5—9	45	50	39
	10—14	61	70	50
	15—19	29	37	19
	20—24	7	10	3
Haryana	5—9	39	47	31
	10—14	55	71	36
	15-19	27	37	14
	20-24	5	7	3
Karnataka	5—9	43	49	38
	10-14	48	58	38
	15-19	23	32	14
	20-24	7	12	3
Kerala	5-9	75	75	75
	10-14	86	88	84
	15-19	44	49	40
	20-24	10	12	8

	Age Group	Total Attendance	Male	Female
		(Per cent of population)		
Madhya Pradesh	5-9	30	38	22
	10-14	41	55	25
	15-19	21	32	9
	20-24	5	9	2
Maharashtra	5-9	52	58	47
	10-14	63	73	51
	15-19	30	40	19
	20-24	7	12	3
Punjab	5-9	52	54	49
	10-14	63	69	56
	15-19	29	34	23
	20-24	6	8	5
Rajasthan	5-9	27	37	16
	10-14	40	59	19
	15-19	23	36	8
	20-24	6	11	2
Uttar Pradesh	5-9	25	32	17
	10-14	44	58	25
	15-19	26	39	10
	20-24	8	14	2
West Bengal	5-9	37	41	33
	10-14	53	60	45
	15-19	30	37	21
	20-24	10	14	5

Source: Data compiled from *Census of India. Part II-Special. Report and Tables Based on 5 Per Cent Sample Data.* Series numbers 2, 4, 5, 6, 9. 10, 11, 12. 17. 18, 22, 23 (New Delhi, 19831.

8. Educational expenditure is disproportionately lower in rural areas. In 1970-1971, when 4.9 billion rupees were spent on education in rural areas, 6.2 billion rupees were spent in urban *areas,* so that "the quality and maintenance of school and college buildings in urban areas are very much better than in rural areas."[28] Urban-rural disparities are further magnified by the presence of privately managed quality institutions in the urban areas.
9. From a share of 56 per cent in the first five-year plan, the expenditure on elementary education over most of the successive five-year plans has declined. By the sixth five-year plan (1980-1985), it was down to 36 per cent. On the other hand, between the first and sixth five-year plans the share for university

education rose from 9 per cent to 16 per cent. With 70 per cent of the total plan expenditure for education coming from the states there is great variation among the states in how much they spend on education, from as low as 40 rupees in Uttar Pradesh to 120 rupees in Kerala (with the all-India average at 68 rupees).

10. The goal of universalising elementary-school education remains elusive as the population grows. The number of children in the six-to-fourteen age group will be 174 million by 1990. Were elementary education universal in 1990, 110 million pupils would be in lower primary school, 64 million in middle primary; this would be 1.5 times and 3.2 times the present size, respectively. To achieve this increase, the number of school teachers in elementary education will have to increase from 2.9 million in 1990 at the existing level of educational growth (there were 2.2 million elementary-school teachers in 1980) to 4.4 million. The budgetary requirements for 1990, assuming no change in per capita expenditure, will have to double, from 15.4 billion rupees in 1980 to 32 billion rupees in 1990. With an 8 per cent per annum rate of inflation, the 1990 education budget at current prices will have to be more than four times the 1980 allocations.

TABLE 35.3

Expenditures on Elementary Education

	Expenditures (Rupees in Million)		
	Total Education	*Elementary Education*	*Per cent on Elementary Education*
first (1951-1956)	1,530	850	55.6
second (1956-1961)	2,730	950	34.8
third (1961-1966)	5,890	1,780	30.2
annual (1966-1969)	3,220	650	20.2
fourth (1969-1974)	8,230	2,350	28.6
fifth (1974-1979)	12,850	4,100	31.9
sixth (1980-1985)	25.230	9,050	35.9

Source: Dr. T.N. Dhar. *'Elementary Education* in *India,"* unpublished paper (New Delhi: Planning Commission, Government of India, n.d.). Sixth-plan data represents proposed outlays, not actual expenditures, which are usually lower. In the sixth plan. 30 per cent of the total plan outlays in education but only 7 per cent of the plan outlays for elementary-school education were from the central government.

In some respects what was more depressing than these hard numbers was the reference to the Education Commission of 1964—1966. Over a two-year period this commission (often called the Kothari Commission after its chairman, Professor D.S. Kothari of the University Grants Commission), made up of India's leading educationists and a number of distinguished foreign participants, with twelve task forces, scrutinised India's educational system. The central thrust of their 615-page report was its call for "a higher priority than that given so far to education in our national plans for development" and its plea for "vigorous and sustained implementation."[26]

Among the commission's strongest recommendations was that all areas country provide five years of education to all children by 1975.— 1976 and seven years by 1985—1986. Enrollments for grades 1 to 4 should rise from 37 million in 1965 to 72 million in 1975 to 76 million in 1985, while higher primary classes 5 to 8 should increase from 13 million in 1965 to 32 million in 1975 to 49 million in 1985. The goal of universal education by 1960 that had been proclaimed in article 45 of the Constitution was now to be achieved by 1985. The commission was particularly distressed at the high dropout rate in the midsixties, and it set as a target an 80 per cent completion rate for class 7. On the basis of the commission's recommendations the government of India announced a National Policy on Education in 1968. The government reconfirmed its commitment to provide free and compulsory education for all children up to the age of fourteen and to reduce the dropout rate.

As is well known, none of these targets was achieved. The Fourth All India Educational Survey conducted by the National Council of Educational Research and Training reported the following data for September 1978: 61 million children in grades 1 to 4, and 25.6 million in grades 5 to 8.[30] In other words, in 1978 there were 86.6 million children in elementary school as against the targeted 104 million for 1975.

It is not surprising, therefore, that the government's announcement in 1986 that the National Policy on Education had as its "new thrust" the achievement of universal enrollment and universal retention of children up to fourteen years of age by 1995 was greeted with skepticism. The skepticism was not unfounded, especially in the light of two programmes announced by the government. The first was the proposal for creating model district schools for high-achieving rural youth. Each district was to have a single residential high school, a Navodaya Vidyalaya, which would provide free boarding and lodging to gifted students chosen on the basis of competitive examinations. In these schools 75 per cent of the seats would be reserved for rural children and an effort would be made to ensure that one-third of the students would be girls. The schools would be well-equipped, with large playgrounds, lawns, hostels, audiovisual aids, and computers. Classes would be in English, but the children would learn the regional language and Hindi. Some children would be moved from their home district to a school elsewhere in the country as a way of promoting national integration through regional interaction.

Rajiv Gandhi was an enthusiastic supporter of the Navodaya Vidyalaya as. Speaking at a conference on education in New Delhi on 26 June 1986, he defended himself against the charge that the proposed new schools were elitist.

> The education system that we have today is more elitist than anything that we could imagine. ... It only makes good education available to those people who have not just adequate resources but plenty of resources. If you are lacking that, if you cannot afford seven thousand or ten thousand rupees a year to educate your child from the primary to secondary level then what is available to you is really a very bad, unorganised, pathetic perhaps is the only word, system. . . . We are attempting in this new education system to break this double standard and to try and bring good education to the weakest, the poorest sections of our society. The only measure of elitism that will be kept is that of the brilliance of the individual child and not of its economic background or its social background. And this elitism, I think, must be built into our society if the best in our society is to come out.

For the prime minister egalitarianism meant providing gifted rural youth without financial means the same quality education that he and others of his social class had obtained at such privately run institutions as the Doon School.

Critics of the Navodaya Vidyalayas said that the schools would divert substantial sums away from efforts to increase elementary-school education, and that the children in the schools would be recruited largely from among the more prosperous rural, landed classes. The cost of the school buildings for the Navodaya Vidyalayas is estimated at 10 billion rupees, while the annual central education budget is only 8.3 billion rupees. The annual cost of running 433 Navodaya Vidyalayas, each with 500 students, is estimated at 2 billion rupees after 1995. The director of the programme, J.N. Sharma, expressed his concern that "the scheme will die under its own financial weight." Critics noted that the national per capita expenditure on school children by the government is 150 rupees per year, while the proposed cost for each Navodaya Vidyalaya student is 9,500 to 10,000 rupees. In defense of the scheme, Mr. Sharma said: "Two per cent of children in every society are mentally superior to others. To cater to their greater appetite for learning, a free environment has to be given."[31]

The government did have a programme for the universalisation of education: Operation Blackboard and Non-Formal Education. Under Operation Blackboard 1 billion rupees was allocated in 1987 for basic amenities for village schools, or 2,200 rupees for each government-run primary school. But the major effort to bring dropouts and other nonenrolled children into the education system is to be made through the Non-Formal Education system (NFE), especially in the nine states that are regarded as educationally backward: Andhra, Assam, Bihar, Jammu and Kashmir, Madhya Pradesh, Orissa, Rajasthan, Uttar Pradesh, and West Bengal, states with 75 per cent of the country's nonenrolled children. NFE was put in place in 1979. A key objective is to provide education for working children. And Bordia, secretary of the Department of Education and previously an official in the Labour Ministry, argued that expenditures on improving the facilities of primary schools would do little to help the poor who drop out, whereas the system of nonformal education was targeted to meet the needs of working children.[32]

The intended elientele of nonformal part-time education was laid out in some detail earlier in the report of the Working Group on Universalisation of Elementary Education appointed by the Ministry of Education (1977):

(a) Children of the weaker sections like the scheduled castes, scheduled tribes, those in hilly areas, tribal areas, urban slums and other economically backward rural areas. There are a large number of children among these sections in the age-group 6-14 who have either never entered the formal school or have dropped out. They are helping the family in a number of ways and the school time does not suit them. Given the facility of schooling at a suitable time and place and with relevant curriculum, they might like to avail themselves of the educational facility and might like to rejoin the formal school system at some appropriate stage.

(b) Girls in the age group 6-14 who are not attracted by the existing programme of education being offered by the formal elementary school. These girls may generally not be interested in joining the formal school at any stage. Thus they would need an additional programme tailored to suit their requirements as housewives, mothers and citizens.

(c) Boys and girls (generally boys) in the age-group 6-14 who are employed in professions like carpet-weaving, pottery, etc. These children need only a part-time programme of general education which may be focussed around literacy, numeracy and citizenship training.[33]

NFE is to have a more flexible curriculum, one directed at the needs of working children and youth. According to the proposed programme children will move at their own pace. Classes will be held at hours that take into account the children's work schedule; and nongovernmental organisations will be encouraged to help plan the curriculum. The costs of NFE are split evenly by the central and state governments. From 1979 to 1984 the central government's expenditure on NFE totaled 777 million rupees. In 1965—1966, according to the government, 3.67 million children were enrolled in 128,000 centers around the country.

Observers of the programme noted that states had failed to match the funds that the center had budgeted, that teachers in the programme were not properly trained, that many of the centers had dosed down, that a large proportion of the children in the programme were below the age of nine an thus were supposed to be attending regular schools, and that there was no effective monitoring and evaluation of the centers.[34]

Critics were skeptical that the goal of enrolling and retaining all school- age children was achievable through the government's new policy on education. There was no evidence that the government was planning the kind of massive increase in elementary-school education expenditure that was needed to achieve universalisation. One critic said that the government was making token investments in nonformal education without any real commitment to developing the existing primary schools. Other critics regarded the district model schools, with English as the medium of instruction and classroom computers, as no substitute for mass education. One critic doubted that the government was really concerned with ending illiteracy. Professor Upendra Baxi, a well-known professor of law, wrote that "after acknowledging that in A. D. 2000 there would be 500 million illiterates in India, and that such magnitude of illiteracy is a drag on development towards the 21st century, the NEP document says that we should decide 'once and for all' after 'careful consideration whether the perception that 'removal of illiteracy is. . . an essential precondition for the meaningful participation of the masses in the process of political decision making and national reconstruction' would be 'valid for India'! In other words, the authors of the Report aren't sure! Some 'policy perspective', this!"[35]

These doubts about the very objectives of the government were reinforced by a statement made by the prime minister while in the United States that was widely quoted in the Indian press. In a prepared public address at Harvard University in October 1987, Rajiv Gandhi extolled Indian democracy for its success in a society that remained poor and whose population was largely illiterate. In the question period that followed an Indian student asked if it was not a blot on Indian democracy that so many people were illiterate years after independence. Gandhi replied: "I don't think literacy is the key to democracy.... Wisdom is much more important. We have seen—and I'm not now limiting myself to India, I'm going beyond to other countries—literacy sometimes narrows the vision, does not broaden it."[36]

In the January 1986 issue of *Yojana*, a government-run journal of education, eighteen of-India's-leading educationists critically reviewed the government's proposed national policy on education and suggested measures to universalise education and eliminate illiteracy: using the government surplus foodgrain to provide each child a kilo of rice or wheat each day of school as an insurance against dropping out, a massive increase in budgetary allocations for elementary schools, a shift in education expenditures from higher education to mass education and greater attention to nonformal education, greater attention to vocationalisation in the schools and more involvement of all development agencies in adult literacy programmes, greater educational decentralisation, a national model act on primary education, the expansion of part-time literacy centers, the creation of preprimary classes, the use of college students for literacy classes and adult education, and a greater effort to recruit and motivate dedicated teachers. None of the critics, it should be noted, proposed making elementary-school education compulsory.

Compulsory Education: A Legislative Review

As noted earlier, compulsory-education laws in India do not make education compulsory; they merely establish the conditions under which state governments may make education compulsory in specified areas. Thus, the Assam Elementary Education Act of 1974 contains a provision that "the State Government may, by notification, declare that elementary education shall be compulsory up to certain age to be prescribed in any area or areas of the State as specified in the notification. In such an area of compulsion the guardian of every child resident in such area shall. . . be bound to cause the child to attend a recognised Elementary School in such area." When this provision is in effect, "the State government may appoint the attendance authorities for the purpose of enforcing attendance in the schools." Fines are then prescribed for those who contravene the provisions of the law.[37]

Similarly, the Tamil Nadu Elementary Education Act (1920, amended in 1973) provides that "any local authority may ... resolve that elementary education shall be compulsory within the whole or a specified part of the local area under its jurisdiction," but only with the approval of the state government.[38] The Mysore Compulsory Primary Education Act of 1961 actually permits the state government to notify areas that primary education is to be made compulsory. A related set of rules (the Mysore Compulsory Primary Education Rules) specifies in detail how compulsory education is then to be enforced, including the appointment of an attendance authority, procedures for the enumeration of all children within the prescribed area, the compulsory registration of the names and birth dates of children, the publication of an enumeration register, procedures for revising and updating the enumeration register, procedures for issuing notices to parents and guardians whose children are not attending school, conditions under which children are exempt (e.g., illness or the lack of a school within a mile of their home), and, finally, penalties for foiling to send children to school. However, most other state laws merely provide that initiative for the establishment of compulsory education rests with the local authorities.

A few local governments made education compulsory. As early as 1893 compulsory education was legally imposed in a division of the state of Baroda, then a princely state led by Maharaja Sayajirao Gaekwar of Baroda. The Maharaja of Baroda was an enthusiastic supporter of universal education. He regarded his experiment with compulsory education in one division as a success, and in 1906 he made education compulsory throughout the state. Earlier, the British had debated the question of introducing compulsory education into India but concluded that it was contrary to British jurisprudence, a position that was weakened by the introduction of the principle of compulsory education in England in 1870. Some Indian and British officials argued for introducing compulsory education before the Indian Education Commission in 1882, but the proposal was never seriously considered. A proposal to introduce compulsory education was taken up in Bombay in 1906, but rejected. Shortly before World War I, Gopal Krishna Gokhale, a leading Indian liberal and Congress Party president, took up the issue in the central legislature in New Delhi. He introduced a private bill proposing that local bodies, subject to prescribed conditions, be authorised to introduce compulsory education in their areas. The bill was widely circulated and while it received some support from leaders of the Indian National Congress and the Muslim League, a majority of the central legislature, most officials, and representatives of the princely states were opposed. The government regarded the proposal as utopian on financial and administrative grounds.

In 1918 a leading nationalist, Vithalbhai Patel, introduced a bill in the Bombay legislative council permitting municipal areas of the state to snake education compulsory, with grants-in-aid to be provided by the state government. The Patel Act was passed and thereafter every state under British rule passed a similar compulsory-education law, as did many of the Indian states. By the early 1930s the principle of compulsory education was written into state law; the 1950 Constitution, in article 45, made it officially a matter of national policy.

All these laws permit, but do not require, local authorities to introduce compulsory education. To ensure that local authorities did not zealously introduce compulsion in an area that was not ready, these laws require that two-thirds of those present or one-half of the total number of members of the local authority have to approve, and that the state government also has to give its approval. The acts also specify the procedures for making education compulsory: the preparation of a census of non-attending children, the issue of notices to parents, hearings to consider exemptions, a report from the school headmaster, persuasion of parents by teachers and attendance officers, another hearing with the parents, and, only as a last resort, prosecution. Describing these acts, J.P. Naik (and his two coauthors) wrote that "the early legislators were more anxious to prevent harassment to parents than to increase attendance and, except in Baroda where simplified procedures were prescribed in the light of actual experience, these early views on the subject have continued unchanged to this day."[39]

No one need have been concerned with overzealous local bodies, for as it turned out few of them made education compulsory. In 1921—1922, when the British transferred education to Indian control, education was made compulsory in eight towns and not a single village. By 1936—1937 education had been made compulsory in 167 out of a total of 2,700 urban areas and only in a handful of rural areas. Opposition to compulsion was strongest among the officers of the Indian Educational Services, and on financial grounds state governments rejected a number of proposals from local authorities.[40]

Moreover, even when local authorities did succeed in making education compulsory, there was little enforcement. In Baroda, for example, many of the villages in which education was supposed to be compulsory had no schools, so the question of enforcement was moot. Bombay province made education compulsory for the city in 1939 but, wrote J.P. Naik,

> the municipality has consistently refused to prosecute defaulting parents on the ground of trying persuasion before prosecution.. . . Ever since 1926-1927, when a quinquennial review first discussed the results of compulsory education, the official reports have been continuously complaining that no attempts are made to enforce compulsion in practice and that it has remained, more or less, on paper. It has been said, for instance, that the census of children of school-going age is not regularly taken and that procedures adopted for it leave several loopholes for truants to escape; that attendance officers are untrained and too few to cope with the situation; that local committees are always unwilling to launch prosecutions; that exemptions are granted too freely, and that the arrangements for trying cases

under the compulsory law are generally defective, so that inordinate delays which defeat the very object of the Acts are common. The conclusion is, therefore, justified that in no area under compulsion is a vigorous attempt made to enforce it rigidly, that in several cases compulsory education exists only on paper, and that in most areas, the dividing line between voluntary and compulsory education is very thin.[41]

J.P. Naik noted that there was some enforcement in Baroda (though many villages continued to lack schools) with the result that by 1921 the literacy rate in Baroda exceeded that of Bombay and in the country as a whole was only behind Travancore and Cochin.[42] The Travancore government was perhaps the most aggressive in India in its efforts to spread elementary education. In 1935—1936 the Travancore government began a scheme of grants to pupils belonging to the backward communities. In the early 1940s a midday meal programme was introduced. And in 1945, when enrollment in primary schools (classes 1 to 5) reached 80 per cent, the government made education compulsory.[43] The dropout rate was the lowest and literacy the highest of any of the states.

The low investment in primary education before independence, the absence of primary schools in much of the country, the high dropout rate and the absence of any system of compulsory education combined to keep illiteracy at a near constant rate. Between 1881 and 1931 literacy increased from 3.5 per cent to 8.0 per cent, or 1 per cent per decade. In spite of the growth in primary schools and an increase in school enrollment between 1921 and 1931 the literacy rate during the entire decade continued to rise by only 1 per cent. A committee appointed by the government to review the growth of education in British India (the Hartog Committee) concluded that "in the primary system, which from our point of view should be designed to produce literacy and the capacity to exercise an intelligent vote, the waste is appalling. So far as we can judge, the vast increase in numbers in primary schools produces no commensurate increase in literacy, for only a small proportion of those who are at the primary stage reach Class IV, in which attainment of literacy may be expected. The waste in the case of girls is even more serious than in the case of boys."[44]

The assumption of office in seven provinces by the Indian National Congress in 1937 led to a discussion of how to expand primary education. Provincial finances were a problem, especially since Congress was committed to introducing prohibition, a policy that substantially cut a major source of government revenue. It was at this time that Mahatma Gandhi proposed his famous scheme of Basic Education. In a series of articles in his journal *Harijan* he laid out his views on how to establish mass education at low cost:

As a nation we are so backward in education that we cannot hope to fulfill our obligations in this respect in a given time during this generation if this programme is to depend on money. I have, therefore, made bold, even at the risk of losing reputation for constructive policy, to suggest that education should be self-supporting. By education, I mean an allround drawing out of the best in the child—in body, mind and spirit. Literacy is not the end of education nor even the beginning. It is only one of the means whereby men and women can be educated. Literacy in itself is not education. I would, therefore, begin the child's education by teaching it a useful handicraft, enabling it to produce from the moment it begins its training. Thus, every school can be made self-supporting, condition being that State takes over the manufacture of these schools.[45]

Gandhi's proposals were endorsed by a conference of education ministers from the seven provinces with Congress governments. A committee chaired by Dr. Zakir Hussain (later, president of India) subsequently prepared a detailed description of the curriculum for the scheme of Basic Education (or *Nai Talim*). "It is significant," commented J.P. Naik, "that during the whole discussion, there was no mention of making education compulsory as the idea of compulsion in any form was repugnant to Gandhian philosophy."[46]

A major new proposal was made in a plan called Post-War Educational Development in India (1944), prepared by Sir John Sargent, educational advisor in the Central Advisory Board of Education. The Sargent plan proposed the adoption of Gandhi's Basic Education scheme, but rejected the view that elementary-school education could pay for itself through the sale of articles produced by pupils. It called for a substantial increase in expenditures in elementary education to enable India to bring all children from six to fourteen into the school system over a forty-year period, and proposed that education during this period be made compulsory. The report noted that in areas where there was legal compulsion, there was no organised system of trained attendance officers to see that children attended school, and the courts were disinclined to enforce the law. Sargent proposed that compulsory education could be made to work if the government carried on an extensive educational propaganda campaign among parents and that it was also important to have "attendance officers who know their duty and courts which are ready to do theirs."[47]

The post-independence government regarded the Sargent plan as too conservative. The government s position was that compulsory universal elementary-school education should be achieved not in forty years (1945- 1984), but by 1960. The provision of compulsory education in the Constitution notwithstanding, successive Indian governments have sought to universalise elementary-school education but without making it compulsory. None of the states has sought to compel local authorities to make education compulsory. By the early 1950s officials within the government of India concluded that the financial resources for the establishment of universal compulsory education by 1960 were not available as a consequence of the government's decision to undertake large development projects. The first five-year plan noted that a programme to provide education for all children in the six-to-fourteen age group would require an annual expenditure of 4 billion rupees, an additional 2 billion rupees for teacher training, and another 2.72

billion rupees for the construction of buildings.[48] But the plan only provided 1.56 billion rupees for education over the five-year period.[49] Neither the Planning Commission nor the Ministry of Education proposed that the recommendation of compulsory education by the Sargent Committee be adopted. Many educators—J.P. Naik being one of them—continued to be persuaded that much of the resources for the expansion of education could still come from the Basic Education scheme proposed by Gandhi, under which schools would raise enough money from the sale of crafts produced by children to pay for the cost of teachers. Basic Education was seen by some educators not simply as an educational programme but as a financial programme to make schools partially self-supporting.

The authority to set policies, priorities, and programmes in education moved from the states to the central government as the Planning Commission and the Ministry of Education set targets and proposed financial allocations. There was little or no educational innovation by the state governments, which looked toward the center for resources and policy. Education, initially listed in the Constitution as a state subject, was subsequently transferred to the list of concurrent subjects. Though there were variations among the states in their expenditures on education, the major constraint on the expansion of elementary-school education was the limited budgetary allocations made by the central government. The allocations for elementary education declined in successive five-year plans, even as the budget for higher education grew. Whatever the rhetoric, clearly the government regarded higher education a greater priority than the establishment of mass elementary education. Education, said each of the five-year plans, is an "investment in human resources," essential economic growth. Though the plan documents alluded to other benefits from education, the planners evidently saw education primarily in the context of a development strategy that emphasised large development projects and the training of skilled workers rather than mass education. Governing elites in many other countries have had a more positive and broader view of the purpose and importance of mass education than India's governing elites.

Historical Comparisons: Advanced Industrial Countries

The nation that the children of the poor should be removed from the labour force and placed into schools is a very modern one. Until only a few centuries ago, children everywhere worked alongside their parents, learning to gather food, hunt, cultivate crops, to fetch water, collect firewood, tend the cattle, and help in the household. Only the children of the privileged classes could escape manual work, and in this they emulated their parents—priests, landlords, and rulers—whose control over wealth, knowledge, and power enabled them to educate their children to assume the same roles as their parents. There was a process of social reproduction in which educational, social, economic, and political institutions reproduced social classes.

A distinctive feature of modern societies is that they break with the principle of social reproduction. It is no longer assumed that children necessarily ought to do what their parents have done. Indeed, given the ways in which the occupational structure of modern societies constantly changes, it is essential for the continued expansion of the economy that children be educated to take jobs that are different from those of their parents. One key to such generational mobility is education. Education does not ensure occupational mobility, of course, but without education occupational mobility in modem industrial societies is exceedingly difficult.

Child labour was not created by industrialisation, nor is it the result of capitalism. It represents the persistence of traditional preindustrial conceptions of the child in relation to work and to parents. The traditional conception in most societies is that children should be socialised to contribute to the maintenance of the family. Early in life children begin the process of entering adulthood through a period of work apprenticeship. The family, not the individual, is the unit of social action as the family develops a strategy that is conducive to its collective well-being.

Child labour in nineteenth-century Europe was qualitatively different from what had preceded it. Children were employed in factories, for employers, for wages. Some worked in cottages and in tenements with their parents, who in turn were paid for the output of the household. Industrialisation increased job opportunities for working-class families. Urban working-class families dependent on daily wages sought to reduce risk through the employment of their children. Children's work became more dangerous: machines and chemicals, endangered their well-being, ventilation was poor, hours long, and wages low (though higher than what children could earn in money or in kind by working on the farm with their parents).

Even before these conditions became widespread there existed some sentiment for restrictions on the conditions under which children should be employed. As early as 1284 a statute of Venetian glass makers forbade the employment of children in certain dangerous branches of the glass-making trade, and in 1396 a Venetian ducal edict prohibited work for children under thirteen in certain trades. As Philippe Aries has documented, childhood was discovered ("invented?") in Europe in the thirteenth century, but it became more significant by the end of the sixteenth and early seventeenth centuries.[50] In the eighteenth century the concept of adolescence, as distinct from that of childhood, emerged. In time, the central concern of the family became its own children. Children became, as Viviana Zelizer has written, "priceless."[51] Children were transformed from valuable wage-earners to economically useless but emotionally priceless objects. The transformation did not occur without considerable public debate, and while the upper and middle classes held this view of their own children they did not readily apply it to the children of the poor.

It was not until the nineteenth century that, governments began to regulate the conditions of employment for children and to restrict the ages at which children could work. However, much of the earls' legislation proved to be ineffective, although the passage of the legislation itself was indicative of changing attitudes toward children and work, and toward the responsibility of the state as protector of children against employers and parents.

Attitudes toward the employment of children were closely linked to sentiments regarding their education. With the Protestant Reformation came the view that everyone ought to be able to read the Bible. Protestant churches and parishioners took on the responsibility of teaching children to read and write. Long before the state entered the field of education, civil society created its own schools. When the state created schools it was to supplement, not to replace, private education. But at some historical moment every industrialising country introduced the principle of compulsory education. Parents, no matter how poor, were not permitted to use the labour of their children in lieu of sending them to school. Children could continue to help at home, work in the fields, even be employed in factories or in putting-out shops, but for part of the day they had to attend school. How many hours of school they had to attend, and for how many years, varied from country to country, and there were differences too in what they were taught and where religion fit into the state-run, schools. But once the principle of compulsion was established as a matter of state policy, these questions became matters of public debate. Compulsory education was introduced initially for children from ages six to eight or ten. In time it was extended from primary to secondary school. As the minimum years of schooling was extended, restrictions were imposed on the employment of children: the number of hours they were permitted to work, the kind of work they were allow to do, and the minimum age for employment. The public sphere was redefining the very definition of childhood.

Every contemporary developed country underwent this process, but the manner and timing varied greatly from country to country. The pace of industrial development and urbanisation were important, but what is more striking is that mass education—and sometimes compulsory education—often preceded industrialisation and urbanisation. One might say that the conception of modernisation, at least with respect to education, sometimes preceded the reality of a modern society and economy. Mass education diffused in Japan, for example, in the eighteenth and early nineteenth centuries, and the Meiji regime imposed universal and compulsory education before the initiation of large-scale industrialisation. The state promoted education in Scotland in the eighteenth century, and both the Swedish and Prussian states moved toward establishing compulsory education and the regulation of child labour early in the nineteenth century.

Since the nineteenth century—and in some countries earlier—the major driving force for popular education was the intervention by the state to provide free tax-supported schools and to *enforce* legislation *compelling* parents to send their children to them. In Scotland, colonial Massachusetts, and in Germany, Protestant leaders, believing that education was essential to salvation, successfully persuaded governments to make education compulsory. In 1524 Martin Luther sent a letter to German municipalities insisting it was their duty to provide schools, and the duty of parents to educate their children. In Scotland a similar religious influence was exercised by John Knox. In 1647

Massachusetts passed the Old Deluder Satan Law, so-called because the preamble said that the old deluder Satan kept men from knowledge of the Scriptures, compelling local authorities to set up compulsory elementary schools. In Sweden a royal decree in 1723 instructed parents and guardians to "deligently see to it that their children applied themselves to book reading and the study of lessons in the Catechism." Failure to do so could lead to fines used for the "instruction of poor children in the parish."[52] In Europe, one country after another—Scotland, Prussia, Austria, and Sweden early; France, England, and Italy later—made education compulsory. At the end of the nineteenth century Japan became the first non-Western country to make elementary-school education compulsory, with a declaration by the Meiji government in 1872 and the promulgation of the Imperial Rescript on Education in 1890. Subsequently, other non-Western countries made education compulsory, most notably and successfully South Korea and Taiwan.

The historical cases raise three issues. The first is the question of what constituted the driving force toward literacy and universal education. Could state intervention have succeeded had not certain fundamental economic and technological changes taken place? Technological changes, so it has been argued, reduced the need for unskilled labour, and therefore of child labour. As the income of the working class increased, the parental need for the income of children was reduced. Parents were then in a position to invest in the future income of their children by entering them into the school system. While these changes do not explain state intervention, it is argued, state intervention without them would not have been possible.

While this argument appears to fit several cases it does not stand up in a comparative analysis, for there are far too many instances where states compelled education prior to a reduction in the need for unskilled labour or a rise in family income. Indeed, in many instances the reverse can be argued: a reduction in the availability of child labour increased the need for technological change, and a reduction in the employment of children increased adult employment and income. Seen from a comparative perspective, the timing of state intervention was unrelated to a country's level of development. Moreover, the diffusion of mass education sometimes preceded state intervention as well as economic development. Scotland and Sweden, for example, achieved near-universal education in the eighteenth century before either became industrialised and without state intervention. Similarly, in Japan a high level of literacy was attained prior to that country's development, though it took state intervention to achieve universal mass education. In Taiwan and South Korea the state created a system of national elementary education when per capita incomes were comparable to what they are in India today and when literacy rates were low. In contrast, industrial Britain did not make education compulsory until 1881, stymied by opposition from the Anglican church and a strong ideological tradition of voluntarism. If any generalisation is to be made of timing it is that mass literacy more often than not has preceded industrialisation. Countries of western Europe were largely literate early in the nineteenth century and Japan had a high level of literacy on the eve of the Meiji restoration. It was the high level of literacy rather than a declining need for unskilled labour that facilitated the introduction of compulsory education by the state.

Second, what was the relationship between the spread of mass education and the reevaluation of the child in relation to the family's social and economic aspirations? Did increased opportunities for mobility lead families to conclude that they should invest in their children's education rather than place them into the labour force at an early age, or alternatively, did the widespread availability of education, pressures for education from religious leaders and institutions, and sanctions by the state lead families to rethink the relationship between education and work for their children? How did it happen that children came to be regarded as "priceless," their education and well-being given precedence over that of their parents? Did cultural change—the impact of religion, liberalism, secularism—create these new attitudes toward children and thereby ease the passage into state intervention, or did changes in the economy and in the behavior of the state precede and shape family attitudes toward children?

The answer, one suspect, is surely not uniform for all societies. In some cultures parents of low income are keen on the education of their children, while in other cultures, with similar economic conditions, parents choose instead to place their children into the labour force. Moreover, in some cultures education is regarded as an intrinsic good, in others it is valued for its instrumental benefits. What is clear is that in many societies a shift does take place in which income within the family is no longer transferred from the young to the old but from the old to the young. This generational shift in income transfers is central to an understanding of the demographic transition from large to small families. Once children are viewed as a cost rather than a benefit and, to use the language of economists, as a consumerable good rather than an investment, then fertility rates decline. While not all societies with universal education have low fertility rates (other factors may intervene), all societies with low fertility rates have universal education.

Third, what was the relationship between the diffusion of mass education, the introduction of compulsory education, and the abolition of child labour? Can child labour be eliminated in a society in which education is not universal? The historical examples described here point to the links between compulsory education and child-labour laws. With the diffusion of mass education, state compulsion was introduced to deal with those children whose parents, invariably of the lower classes, chose to place their children into the labour force rather than into school. Child-labour laws proved to be unenforceable unless all children were required to attend school. Then, as the minimum age of schooling was extended, so was the minimum age for entrance into the labour force Country after country established a system of rules as to when and under what conditions children could enter the labour force, usually with work permits granted by the state. Only upon proof of age or the completion of a specified number of years in school could young people be given work permits that entitled them to seek employment.

State intervention to remove children from the labour force and require that they attend schools was often politically contentious. Many regarded it as improper or unrealistic to compel the parents of the poor to send their children to school. The notion that children ought not to work, that they ought to be in school, and that the state should assure both, was in some societies rejected by both conservatives and leftists, each from quite different perspectives. On the Left were those who argued that child labour was inherent in the system of capitalist exploitation and that parents needed the income of their children. On the Right were those who argued that industry needed low-wage child labour, that the state ought not to disrupt the social order by educating poor children beyond their station, that the education provided by schools was ill-suited to the needs of the poor, and that child labour relieved the state of caring for the poor. Still others pointed to the unenforceability of child-labour legislation and on a more philosophical level to the inappropriateness of state interference in the rights of parents.

Opposition to state intervention was thus tied to conceptions of children and work, to the question of the rights and obligations of the state versus the rights and obligations of parents, and to the character of the capitalist order itself. A review of the nineteenth-century debate is instructive for it demonstrates how powerful were the arguments—and the political forces behind them—against state intervention, and how in time they were overcome. It is striking how similar these debates were to contemporary debates in India, especially with regard to the question of whether the state should force the parents of the poor to send their children to school; and yet how different are the socio-political forces between India and those countries that did intervene on behalf of children.

The Debate

Education versus Work

One argument against compulsory education was that education would make the poor unsuited for the boring manual work that society requires. Voltaire wrote that "it is absolutely necessary that a great proportion of mankind is destined to drudgery in the meanest occupations, that nothing but early habit can render it tolerable, and that to give the meanest of people an education beyond the station in which Providence has assigned them is doing a real injury." English conservatives argued that schooling was inappropriate for the working class, whose children could better acquire skills as apprentices. To many of London's poor, elementary education seemed irrelevant since for generations the working class had been urged not to look beyond their station, with the result that parents—and conservatives who subscribed to this view—saw no practical value to education.

The British Parliament sought to reconcile education with work for the lower classes by creating a system of part-time education. The 1833 Factory Act provided that children employed in the textile industry (other industries were subsequently added) were to receive two hours of schooling, six days a week. This system of part-time education remained in place for another half century. An alternative solution was followed by the Prussian government, which emphasised vocational training for working-class children. The children of the poor were compelled to attend the *Volksschule,* where they were taught skills that would enable them to remain in the working class. It was a policy that probably contributed to the technical quality of German products. Similarly, both the Japanese and Korean governments opted for educational systems that emphasised basic vocational training at the elementary-school level.

Child Labour and Poverty

A second objection to compulsory education was that child labour is necessary for the well-being of the poor when the state is unable to provide relief. Thus, in a country with large numbers of poor people and inadequate poor laws, the state ought to promote the employment of the children of the poor rather than remove them from the labour force. From this point of view the more that could be done to place children into the work force the greater the likelihood that poverty could be ameliorated. The 1601 English Poor Law, designed to banish idleness, authorised the involuntary "binding out" of needy children as apprentices to masters. Poor-law officials paid keepers several pounds for each child taken off their hands. One of the arguments for part-time education was that the children of the poor could continue to work even as they attended school. As one of the poor-law commissioners put it, "children who have to live by their labour should be trained to labour early . . . boys should be accustomed to work at the earliest practicable age."[53]

A similar position was argued by the governor of New York, who in 1767 proudly stated that "every house swarms with children set to work as soon as they could spin."[54] New York imposed a tax on carriages to support a linen-making shop to provide employment for the poor, "especially women and children and thus lessen the burden of caring for them." And Alexander Hamilton argued for protecting infant industries, noting that "children are rendered more useful by manufacturing estabalishments than they otherwise would be."[55] One of the arguments for industrialisation was that it would uplift the poor by providing employment opportunities to women and children.

Opposition to child-labour legislation came not only from employers but from those who believed they were protecting the interests of the poor. As late as the 1920s the New York state legislature killed a proposal that cigar making in tenements should be prohibited, persuaded by manufacturers that the proposed bill would throw needy families out of work. Officials in mill towns were reluctant to enforce compulsory-education laws on the grounds that poor parents needed the earnings of their children. The same argument was used in the London School Board after education was made compulsory in 1871. Many labour and socialist., members of the board who advocated the abolition of school fees and provision of free school meals were hesitant to enforce compulsory attendance. Annie Besant, a member of the board, wrote that many families needed the income of their children. "One has to choose," she wrote, "between leaving the child ignorant or having it starve, so that one must do harm anyway. . . . It makes one heartsick."[7] One analyst of the workings of the London School Board in the 1890s noted that "it is not surprising that in prevailing social conditions those who believed more ardently in the value of educating working class children should on occasion attempt to prevent its effective execution. But this meant that the Board's teachers and officials, already under severe pressure from the right, faced opposition too on their left, thus rendering their work even more difficult."[57]

Both in the United Kingdom and in the United States, trade unions fought against the argument that the poor gained from the employment of their children. Union leaders recognised that child labour forced wages down and displaced adult workers. The Knights of Labour and the American Federation of Labour actively supported legislation for compulsory education and for banning the employment of children tinder fourteen. In the 1920s Herbert Lehman; lieutenant governor of New York and a leading member of the National Child Labour Committee, which led the campaign, noted that 125,000 children under seventeen were holding jobs in the state. If many of these "employed boys and girls remained in school," he said, "that would leave jobs for their elders to fill."[58] The following decade, in the midst of the depression, state after state extended compulsory education to age sixteen or seventeen in an effort to reduce adult unemployment by deferring children from entering the labour force.

Child Labour and Marginal Industries

A third argument was that without low-wage child labour certain industries would be forced to close, outcompeted by more efficient industries at home or abroad, and that exports would then fall and unemployment increase. This argument was particularly troublesome in the United States, where child-labour laws were passed by state governments and were not nationally uniform: It was frequently argued in state legislatures that the passage of a particularly stringent child-labour law would lead a mill to move elsewhere, usually to the south, where legislation was more lenient. Trade unions sought to counter this tendency by pressing for a constitutional amendment that would enable the federal government to pass national legislation, and when that failed they successfully pressed for such legislation under the interstate commerce clause of the Constitution.

The threat of international competition was also used against legislative reforms. In Prussia, where legislation restricted the employment of children under twelve (and in some industries for those under fourteen), the government hesitated to extend child-labour laws into industries with export markets. Much of the pressure for extending the legislation, curiously enough, came from military officers concerned that the health and physical well-being of their recruits (military service was compulsory in late-nineteenth-century Prussia) was damaged by the premature employment of children in the industrial regions of the country. In an extraordinary development, Emperor William II called for an international workers-protection conference on the grounds that the difficulties in passing child-labour legislation because of fear of international competition could be resolved only through an international agreement. In March 1890 representatives from fifteen European countries met in Berlin, where they passed numerous resolutions on the protection of children. While these resolutions were nonbinding, the conference proved to be a precursor of later efforts by the International Labour Organisation to create common international rules concerning the employment of children.

A fourth argument against state intervention to eliminate child labour came from those who believed that child labour was the result of capitalism and the technologies it created. Karl Marx, the leading exponent of this view, argued that child labour is a source of profit to employers and is thus inherent in a capitalist system of wage labour. At some length Marx described the cruelties of child labour: in steel, where children were employed at night; in glass manufacturing and in coke heaps, where young girls are "begrimed with dirt and smoke"[59] in brass foundries; in book binding; in candle factories; in the sorting of rags; and in the household production of lace. Time and again, Marx returned to two central arguments: that the new technologies increased the demand for cheap, unskilled labour; and that the decrease in the rate of profit led capitalists to increase their exploitation of labour.

As profits declined, he wrote, the capitalist buys "with the same capital a greater mass of labour power, as he progressively replaces skilled workers by less skilled, mature labour-power by immature, male by female, that of adults by that of young persons or children." Children, along with the unemployed, were part of-the "industrial reserve army." "Pauperism," he wrote in an eloquent passage, "forms a condition of capitalist production and of the capitalist development of wealth. Within the capitalist system all methods for raising the social productivity of labour are put into effect at the cost of the individual workers.., so that they become means of domination and exploitation. They transform his life-time into working-time and drag his wife and child beneath the wheels of the juggernaut of capital."[60]

Marx's documentation of the cruelty of child labour and his analysis of its causes was not for the purpose of amelioration. Marx was not interested in reform, but in drawing up a charge sheet against capitalism. He therefore dismissed as irrelevant Parliament's decision to require that children' be in school up to age fourteen before they could be employed in factories. "The spirit of capitalist production," he wrote, "emerges clearly from the ludicrous way the so-called educational clauses of the Factory Acts have been drawn up, from the absence of any administrative machinery, whereby this compulsory education is once again made for the most part illusory, from the opposition of the manufacturers them. selves education clauses and from the tricks and dodges they USE to evade them."[61]

In a letter to the leaders of the German Social Democratic movement; Marx took issue with their proposal to press the German government to prohibit child labour. "A general prohibition of child labour," he wrote, "is incompatible with the existence of large-scale industry and hence an empty, pious wish."[62] Marx also took issue with the view that parents exploited children. In 1866 the Commission on the Employment of Children issued a report saying that "it is unhappily, to a painful degree, apparent through the whole of the evidence, that against no person do the children of both sexes so much require protection as against then parents." Child labour in general and home labour in particular are "maintained only because the parents are able, without check or control, to exercise this arbitrary and mischievous power over their young an tender offspring.... Parents must not possess the absolute power of making their children mere machines to earn so much weekly wage. The children and young persons, therefore, in all such cases may justifiably claim from the legislature, as a natural right, that an exemption should be secured to them, from what destroys prematurely their physical strength, and lowers them in the scale of intellectual and moral beings."

No, replied Marx, "It was not the misuse of parental authority that created the capitalistic exploitation . . . of children's labour, but on contrary, it was the capitalist mode of exploitation which, by sweeping away the economic basis of parental authority, .made its exercise degenerate into a mischievous misuse of power."[63] For Marx, then, state intervention to abolish child labour and implement compulsory education were meaningless within a capitalist system. Only the removal of capitalism could end the evils associated with child labour.

Time proved Marx to be wrong. In one industrial capitalist count after another the participation rate of young people in the labour force declined, partly the result of a growing demand for an educated and skilled labour force, and partly the result of increased school enrollments and attendance. The growth in manufacturing technology, the associated demand for skilled workers, and the expansion of opportunities for middle-class employment all made education more attractive. At the same time, and sometimes earlier, the state itself made education compulsory.

Law Enforcement and Child-Labour Laws

A fifth argument against state intervention was that child-labour laws could not be enforced since the number of manufacturing establishments and small shops was so large. Government bureaucrats despaired of administering child-labour legislation. In New York state, for example, the Factory Act of 1886 prohibited the employment of children under thirteen in manufacturing establishments. New York then had over 42,000 manufacturing establishments with 630,000 workers, but the state legislature provided funds only for the appointment of a chief factory inspector with one assistant, no office, and no transportation! It took twenty years before the state legislature increased the number of inspectors to fifty.

To a considerable extent these objections were overcome by government-enforced compulsory-education laws. Reformers argued that compulsory education was necessary if child-labour laws were to be enforced. Reformers also noted that enforcing school laws, though by no means simple, was easier than enforcing child-labour laws and factory acts. Teachers, social workers, truant officers, school census takers—the school bureaucrats responsible for the enforcement of compulsory-education legislation—knew their community. Once a child was enrolled in the local school, truant officers could go to the child's home if the child failed to appear. Parents were also less willing or able to bribe truant officers than employers were to bribe factory inspectors. Moreover, parents of young children in the six-to-ten or six-to twelve age group were less likely to resist the pressures for compulsory education than the parents of older children.

The enforcement of compulsory-education laws was facilitated by the system of compulsory birth registration. In England compulsory birth registration was established in the 1830s, in New York state in 1853. As birth registration records became available, the task of enforcing truancy laws and issuing working papers was made easier.

On the Rights Versus Duties of Parents

Of all the arguments against state intervention to ban child-labour and impose compulsory education, the most powerful came from those who argued that the state ought not to interfere with the rights of parents to choose what is best for their children and their families. The Scots intellectuals Adam Smith, James Mill, Thomas Macaulay, Thomas Malthus, W.T. Thornton, and John Stuart Mill were responsible for developing the case for state intervention.

Adam Smith, the theoretician of the market, was the first to present systematically the case for state intervention in education. In *The Wealth of Nations,* he wrote: "Ought the public.., to give no attention, it may be asked, to the education of the people? Or if it ought to give any, what are the different parts of education which it ought to attend to in the different orders of the people? And what manner ought it to attend to them?"

Smith's answer: "In some cases the state of the society necessarily places the greater part of individuals in such situations as naturally form in them, without any attention of government, almost all the abilities and virtues which that state requires, or perhaps can admit of. In other cases the state of the society does not place the greater part of individuals in such situations, and some attention of government is necessary in order to prevent the almost entire corruption and degeneracy of the great body of the people."

Had society created such a situation? Smith argued that the division of labour had created such a situation and he explained why and with what consequences:

> In the progress of the division of labour the employment of the far greater part of those who lived by labour, that is, of the great body of the people, comes to be confined to a few very simple operations, frequently to one or two. But the understandings of the greater part of men are necessarily formed by their ordinary employments. The man whose whole life is spent in performing a few simple operations, of which the effects too are, perhaps, always the same, or very nearly the same, has no occasion to exert his understanding, or to exercise his invention in finding out expedients for removing difficulties which never occur. He naturally

> loses, therefore, the habit of such exertion, and generally becomes as stupid and ignorant as it is possible for a human creature to become. The torpor of his mind renders him, not only incapable of relishing or bearing a part in any rational conversation, but of conceiving any generous, noble, or tender sentiment, and consequently of forming any just judgment concerning many even of the ordinary duties of private life. Of the great and extensive interests of his country he is altogether incapable of judging; and unless very particular pains have been taken to render him otherwise; he is equally incapable of defending his country in war. The uniformity of his stationary life naturally corrupts the courage of his mind, and makes him regard with abhorrence the irregular, uncertain, and adventurous life of a soldier. It corrupts even the activity of his body, and renders him incapable of exerting his strength with vigour and perseverance, in any other employment than that to which he has been bred. His dexterity at his own particular trade seems, in this manner, to be acquired at the expense of his intellectual, social, and martial virtues. But in every improved and civilised society this is the state into which the labouring poor, that is, the great body of the people, must necessarily fall, unless government takes some pains to prevent it.[64]

What can government do to remove the torpor into which the labouring classes descend as a consequence of the division of labour? Adam Smith continued:

> The education of the common people requires, perhaps, in a civilised and commercial society, the attention of the public more than that of people of some rank and fortune.... (The common people) have little time to spare for education. Their parents can scarce afford to maintain them even in infancy. As soon as they are able to work, they must apply to some trade by which they can earn their subsistence. That trade too is generally so simple and uniform as to give little exercise to the understanding; while, at the same time, their labour is both so constant and so severe, that it leaves them little leisure and less inclination to apply to, or even to think of anything else.

But though the common people cannot, in any civilised society, be so well instructed as people of some rank and fortune, the most essential parts of education, however, to read, write, and account, can be acquired at so early a period of life, that the greater part even of those who are to be bred to the lowest occupations, have time to acquire them before they can be employed in those occupations.

> For a very small expense the public can facilitate, can encourage, and can even impose [emphasis added] upon almost the whole body of the people, the necessity of acquiring those most essential parts of education.[65]

The "public" can facilitate the acquisition of these "essential parts of education" by' establishing in every parish or district a little school. These can be supported in part by the public and by charitable institutions.

Does the state itself benefit from mass education? Adam Smith had no doubt:

> The state. . . derives no inconsiderable advantage from their instruction. The more they are instructed, the less liable they are to the delusions of enthusiasm and superstition, which, among ignorant nations, frequently occasion the most dreadful disorders. An instructed and intelligent people besides, are always more decent and orderly than an ignorant and stupid one. They feel themselves, each individually more respectable, and more likely to obtain the respect of their lawful superiors, and they are therefore more disposed to respect those superiors. They are more disposed to examine, and more capable of seeing through, the interested complaints of faction and sedition, and they are, upon that account, less apt to be misled into any wanton or unnecessary opposition to the measures of government. In free countries, where the safety of government depends very much upon the favourable judgment which the people may form of its conduct, it must surely be the highest importance that they should not be disposed to judge rashly or capriciously concerning it.[66]

There are thus two parts to Adam Smith's advocacy of state intervention in education. The first is that the division of labour by confining workers "to a few very simple operations" destroys the intellectual abilities of workers, and that the common 'people, left to themselves, are unlikely to remedy these defects by tending to their own education, for they lack the time and would not choose to defer entering the labour force in order to acquire an education. But the case for government attention rests on the second part of his argument, namely that there are a variety of public goods, not simply private benefits, that come from mass education. These public goods include an increase in public order by making the masses less liable to the "delusions of enthusiasm and superstition," teaching them to respect their superiors and disposing them to be critical of those who are in opposition.

A related argument, put forward by other Scots intellectuals, was that law and order were maintained as a result of popular education. Scotland, it was noted, with more education than either England or Ireland, had a lower crime rate. "The quiet and peaceful habits of the instructed Scots peasant," wrote Malthus, "compared with the turbulent disposition of the ignorant Irishman, ought not be without effect upon every impartial reasoner."[67] In the same vein W.T. Thornton suggested that state education was less expensive than maintaining prisons.

The link between education and the protection of property rights was addressed by Thomas S. Macaulay, speaking to Parliament in 1848. "It is the sacred duty of every government," he said, "to take effectual measures for securing the persons and property of the community; and that the government which neglects that duty is unfit for its situation. This being admitted. I ask, can it be denied that the education of the common people is the most effectual means of protecting person and property?"[68]

The classic liberal case for state responsibility for education—and for compulsory education—was made forcefully by John Stuart Mill in his *Principles of Political Economy* (1848) and *On Liberty* (1859), Mill argued for both state provision and compulsion in education, resting his argument on two principles: (1) that since education was necessary for a child to fit him "to perform his part well in life," parents were as obliged to provide their child with "instruction and training for its mind" as they were to provide "food for its body"; and (2) that education was necessary for "the members of the community general, who are liable to suffer seriously from the consequences of ignorance and want of education in their fellow citizen." For Mill, education for the poor was essential for self-improvement, social mobility, and citizenship, reflecting his own egalitarian socialist and democratic political philosophy.

In *On Liberty* Mill addressed the question of compulsion, since as an advocate of liberty ("A person should be free to do as he likes in his own concerns") he needed to justify state interference with individual rights. Mill argued that a person

> ought not to be free to do as he likes in acting for another, under the pretext that the affairs of the other are his own affairs. The State, while it respects the liberty of each in what specially regards himself, is bound to maintain a vigilant control over his exercise of any power which it allows him to possess over others. This obligation is almost entirely disregarded in the case of the family relations, a case, in its direct influence on human happiness, more important than all others taken together. . . . It is in the case of children that misapplied notions of liberty are a real obstacle to the fulfillment by the State of its duties. One would almost think that a man's children were supposed to be literally, and not metaphorically, a part of himself, so jealous is opinion of the small interference of law with his absolute and exclusive control over them.

Mill went on to argue that the state should compel the education of "every human being who is born its citizen," and that the state "ought not leave the choice to accept or not to accept education in the hands of parents." Mill wrote of the double duty of parents toward the children themselves and toward the members of the community who suffer from the consequences of ignorance and want of education in their fellow citizens: "It is therefore an allowable exercise of the power of government to impose on parents the legal obligation of giving elementary education to children."[69]

That those who advocated state intervention ultimately won does not mean that the policies were the result of their arguments. Mill may have had logic on his side, but the Anglican church—which feared a secular state-run compulsory-education system—had the power to impede the adoption of compulsory-school legislation for another quarter of a century. The British experience reminds us that who makes the arguments matters. The differences in when various Western countries made education compulsory and legislated and enforced child-labour laws depended on the attitudes of those within the state apparatus and upon those outside who could successfully influence state policies. The opinions of politically influential forces, the kinds of coalitions that were constructed on behalf of or in opposition to state intervention, and the institutional structure of the state appear to be more important in explaining the timing of state intervention than the level of industrial development, per capita incomes, or the prevalence of poverty.

The Policies and Politics of State Intervention

While the debate over child labour was often similar from one country to another, the political forces arrayed for and against intervention varied considerably. Religious institutions supported compulsory education in some countries, opposed it in others. Trade unions; teachers' associations; social activists; the military; political parties; and education, labour, and health ministries played varying roles. Social democrats generally fought against child labour and advocated compulsory education, but in some countries they had conservative support while in others they were stymied by conservative opposition.

The patterns of policy intervention in education also varied considerably. England, for example, with its emphasis on voluntarism in organisation, localism in administration, private financing, hierarchy in the educational system, character formation as an educational goal, social admissions, unstandardised curricula, was at one pole; France, with an emphasis on state organisation of education, centralised administration, major financing by the state, career orientation as an educational goal, meritocratic admissions, and standardised curricula was at the other.[21]

Ultimately, all the advanced industrial countries (and others) adopted a system of compulsory, universal, largely (though not exclusively) state run education, and a ban on the employment of children under fourteen, with restrictions on employment of adolescents over fourteen. Each country produced its own policies, the products of divergent interests and social values. In the pages that follow we shall outline the major policies, political forces, and social values at work in Germany, Austria, England, the United States, and Japan. In the subsequent chapter we shall consider some of the more recent, successful examples of state intervention among contemporary developing countries.

Germany

Germany and Scotland were the first European countries to establish the principle of compulsory school attendance—and they did so for the same reason. Though neither country adopted compulsory education for some time, the religious pronouncements of Luther and Knox linked the national religion to the educational duties of both the state and its citizens.

As early as 1528 the government of Saxony provided for the establishment of Latin schools in every village and town. But systematic, large-scale state intervention in education was to await the rise of the Prussian state. In 1817 King Frederick William III issued a decree ordering all children from ages five to twelve to attend school if a school existed nearby, and in 1836 the Prussian state initiated a programme of building elementary schools, leaving the local community responsible for the salary of the teachers and the maintenance of the schoolhouse. Local, secular boards answering to the state administration were formed, with the local clergy serving as superintendents and school inspectors. The clergy, keen on educating the poor to work, created industry or work schools that emphasised vocational training in workshops in which children produced .goods for sale. These schools became the dominant form of education for poor and working-class children. As noted earlier, these developed into *Volksschulen* (elementary schools). Cleanliness industriousness, and order were the values inculcated by the industry schools. By 1837 over 80 per cent of Prussia's school-age children were enrolled in some form of *Volksschule*.[71] By 1849 adult literacy in Prussia was 80 per cent, compared with 70 per cent for England and 55 to 60 per cent for France. It was equalled by Scotland and exceeded only by Sweden's 90 per cent rate.[72]

The growth of the central Prussian state was reflected in the establishment in 1817 of a new Ministry for Religious, Educational, and Medical Affairs. Beneath, and responsible to, the ministry were the district administrations, which were given extensive authority for implementing and promoting mass education. Where there was no school, the district administration was empowered to create a local school board and given the responsibility for creating an elementary school to be funded by the community. Where state or private schools existed, the district administration was responsible for the appointment of teachers and the local school inspector (usually the local clergy), approval of texts and curriculum, and the school budgets.

After the 1848 revolution the school system was placed under the direct supervision of the state, teachers became civil servants, and new regulations were issued requiring that schools emphasise religious instruction. By 1871, following the unification of the German states, school attendance was universal. Adult illiteracy for the country as a whole was only 3.4 per cent. The state paid only 5 per cent of public elementary- school costs, 75 per cent came from local communities, and 20 per cent came from school fees. Under Kaiser William II the *Volksschule* was given a central role in the fight against the growing socialist movement in Germany. Religious instruction was stressed and the ethical immorality of socialism and communism was emphasised. History instruction portrayed the positive development of the German nation and the concern by the monarchy for the well-being of the working class. Under the Prussian School Supervision Law of 1872, which governed the *Volksschulen* until the World War I, a weekly plan was decreed, requiring seven to eleven hours of religion, four to five hours of German, one to two hour, of mathematics and recitation, two hours of drawing, and six hours of sports. At the middle level there was an additional six hours of history, geography, biology, and physics.

A three-track system was developed corresponding to the three broad social classes. The lower classes sent their children to the *Volksschule,* which had eight-grades. The children in the lower classes attended school approximately twenty hours per week while the middle and upper classes received about thirty hours of instruction each week. Instruction was primarily in German language, religion, mathematics, and singing for the lower classes; and in the upper classes, drawing, natural sciences, sports, and vocational training. In rural schools with more than eighty children, the school could be divided into two half-day classes, with each class attending school about sixteen hours per week. Working-class children who attended the *Volksschule* could go on to the continuation school. These schools appeared in the last third of the nineteenth century to fill the need fur skilled workers. In 1874 the Prussian state offered to build these schools if the community in which they were located made them obligatory. The Trade Workers Protection Law of 1897 obligated all masters to send their apprentices to the continuation schools.

Parallel to the *Volksschule* was the *Mittelschule,* intended for the middle classes. By charging tuition, the working class was effectively excluded. In some communities the *Mittelschule* began only in grade 4, while for the lower grades all the children attended the *Volksschule.* In 1911 there were 1,551 *Mittelschulen* in Prussia, with 255,000 students out of a school population of 6.5 million. Graduates of the *Mittelschulen* were qualified to attend high school; graduates of the *Volksschulen* were not.

A third track was created for the wealthy: elite preparatory schools known as the *Vorschulen.* A system of high fees and high admission standards ensured social segregation. Graduates of the *Vorschule* went on to high school and to higher education before taking on elite positions in Prussian society.

The earliest official concern over child labour occurred in 1817, when the Prussian state chancellor, Von Hardenberg, sent a survey to all "high presidents" of Prussia. Von Hardenberg expressed his fear that children employed in factories would become "chained" to a particular factory for life. The result, he said, is that few workers would be available for agriculture, domestic services, construction, and other industries. He also expressed his concern that the hard labour done by working children might make them unfit to defend their country in an hour of danger. He therefore asked his "colleagues" for advice on possible countermeasures to the "enchainment of the worker in childhood."[73] as In their official replies, many of the high presidents shared the state chancellor's concern that child labour would reduce Germany's military capabilities, a theme that was to recur frequently in the debate.

In the 1820s the Prussian culture minister undertook a campaign to eliminate the inhumane treatment of children in factories. Reports were prepared on the condition of child labour in a number of provinces, but his superior, the interior minister, refused to take action in the belief that it was improper for the state to intervene in private economic matters. The culture minister persevered by sending a circular to provincial governments reminding them of their duty to enforce compulsory-education laws.

At approximately the same time, General Lieutenant von Horn sent a military report to King Frederick William III complaining that the industrial regions were failing to provide their share of conscripts. This "degenerate physical state" was attributed to excessive working hours, the noxious substances swallowed by the children, the employment of children at night, the absence of open air, and other conditions that damaged the physical growth of children. Following a discussion in the Diet of both the economic and military aspects of child labour, the Diet sent an address to the Prussian king urging that action be taken. In 1839 the king signed into law the "Regulations for the Employment of Young Operatives in Manufactories." While it did not prevent child labour, the law required that five hours of daily schooling be provided to factory children. Similar measures were adopted by other German states. In 1853 legislation was passed raising the minimum working age from nine to twelve, forbidding night work, and limiting the work day to six hours for children between twelve and fourteen, with three hours of compulsory schooling.

As in England and the United States, child-labour laws were not effectively implemented, for there were few factory inspectors, industrialists regularly circumvented the law, and even the local clergy apparently made little effort to enforce the regulations. But with the unification of the German states into a single country following the war of 1670—1871, a commission, was appointed to investigate the problem of child labour. The imperial Parliament subsequently banned the employment of children under twelve in any factory and restricted the employment of twelve-to-fourteen year olds. In subsequent legislation that further restricted the employment of children, increasing attention was paid to enforcement. More factory inspectors were appointed, employers were obligated to keep a register of all children employed in the factory, and fines were imposed on employers for violations. The enforcement of compulsory education laws also reinforced the child labour laws. While part-time child labour persisted for some time in agriculture and in the informal sector, school attendance was obligatory through the *Volksschule* and for those not going on to high school two or three years in the *Berufsschule* (trade school.)

Under pressure-from the teachers' association, an occupational census was conducted in 1898, which reported that compulsory education notwithstanding 6.5 per cent of all school-age children were employed, in textiles, cigar making, weaving, shoe making, assembling artificial flowers, and making costume jewelry and toys. The 1904 census found that of 9.2 million children under age fourteen, 1.8 million were employed, mainly in agriculture. However, the survey also reported that virtually all working children under fourteen attended school and were employed only a few hours a day. Fourteen-to-sixteen year olds could work no more than ten hours per day. Employers were required to register all young workers with the local police and to record the working hours of all their young employees.

Germany was among the more successful states in ending child labour and in establishing compulsory education because of an unusual coalition. The military and conservatives, eager to improve the health and educational skills of conscript army, were concerned that child labour would reduce Germany's military capabilities. Teachers had professional concerns for expanding education. The Protestant clergy looked upon schooling as a place for religious education. The Social Democrats were guided by ideological and humanitarian considerations. The conservatives in turn pressed for reforms in order to undermine the socialist movement. Motives and interests were mixed: concern for military prowess and national power, religious considerations. professional concerns, humanitarianism, political rivalries. In short, there were powerful political forces at work, each for its own reasons, pressing for reform against the interests and opposition of some parents and sections of the business community.

Austria

In 1897 Mr. J. Russell Endean, a member of the London School Board, visited Austria to studs' its education system. He visited the major educational institutions—*Volksschule*, *Fortbildung* (evening schools), high schools, universities, teacher-training institutes, and trade and technical schools—that made up what the emperor of Austria once termed "the admirable system of [Austrian] public education." In the preface to his published report, Mr. Endean wrote: "My object ... in the following pages is to give my fellow subjects a careful and complete resume of the Austrian system of education, so that they may see how greatly in advance of ours that system is, in all its general arrangements, and specially so in the arrangements for ensuring the best education for the masses."[74]

Whether the Austrian educational system was in fact "in advance" of the English system is beside the point—Mr. Endean used the-comparison with a competing country in the well-established manner of trying to persuade his own government to put more resources into education—but Mr. Endean's report does provide us with a useful description of the state of Austrian mass education at the turn of the century.

Mr. Endean's was particularly impressed by the ability of the Austrian government to enforce compulsory attendance in the elementary schools. He reported that education was compulsory in the *Volksschule* for both sexes from ages seven to fourteen. Because of the system of military conscription he wrote,

> the numerical history of every family in the Empire is recorded in the books of the police of the district in which the subject resides; should he remove from one commune to another, or from one province to another, one of the first duties compulsorily discharged by the head of the family, on arriving at his new residence, in to report himself to the police bureau, giving particulars of himself and family, stating number, age, sex, etc., and he must also state to which school be proposes to send his child or children, should he have any of school age. On this being done, should it be necessary to enquire if the child or children be at school, a note is sent from the school-attendance department to the Head Master or the Director of the school named—if not attending, further enquiries are made by the School-Managers, and so the question is pursued until the parent is compelled, if need be, to send his child or children to school, and thus costs to enforce attendance are

avoided. In Austria no parent is permitted continuously to set the law at defiance, as do many in this country. The police on duty are instructed to report all school-due children found playing in the streets during school hours, should there by any.[25]

The Austrian school system was financed by the provinces and local communes. Teachers' salaries were covered by the province while the cost of school buildings, furniture, and local expenses were paid by the communes. Austria had seventeen provinces, each with its own educational board made up of members of the provincial Diet, clergy of different religious denominations, and distinguished professors and teachers. The names of members of the boards were submitted to the educational minister for his approval. Members of the communal educational boards were nominated by town councils or by communal representative councils for rural districts and were under the control of the provincial educational boards.

Students who completed elementary school could continue in the *Fort-bildung*, which provided technical education "with reference to the trades of the locality in which the school is placed," or in the *Gymnasium* (high school). There were also *Gewerbeschulen* (public technical schools), where "every hour spent in the school is distinctly devoted to the acquisition of skilled knowledge under the eyes of duly - recognised master of his art," such as drawing, engineering, architecture, building, and joinery.[76] At the age of twenty, every physically qualified Austrian male entered the army for a three-year term.

Of special interest to Mr. Endean was the Imperial and Royal Inspectorate of Schools. Inspectors—all schoolmasters or professors—were appointed by the minister of education to engage in a once or twice yearly inspection of all *Volksschule.* No date was fixed for inspection and no advance notice was given to the school authorities. The inspector entered the school in the midst of its ordinary routine. "Entering unexpectedly he tells the teacher to proceed with his lesson, of which he takes special note, and of the progress of the class. . . . He sends a special report to the Education Department of the Province. His inspection or report has no effect upon the school funds, as 'payment by results' is entirely unknown."[77] A yearly conference was held of the teachers in the district, at which the inspector discussed his overall findings.

This "admirable system" was relatively new. In the latter part of the eighteenth century few Austrian children attended school. A census taken in Vienna in 1770 showed that only 25 per cent of the city's children attended school. In the surrounding rural areas, 15 to 20 per cent of school-age children were in school. The first school law was promulgated in 1774. It provided that every parish had to establish a lower primary school *(Trivialschule)* and larger towns had to establish a three-year upper primary school *(Hauptschule)*. Parish priests continued to take some responsibility for supervising local schools, but the law provided for country and provincial school commissions appointed by the government to supervise all schools.

Throughout the eighteenth and nineteenth centuries the Catholic church and state authorities fought over who should control local schools. Church officials expressed their concern that "demagogues" in state-run schools might "imbue the young, imprudent hearts, under the pretext of humanitarianism, with pernicious ideas, to disseminate these ideas even among the lowest classes and let them strike deeper and deeper roots," as Cardinal Migazii wrote to the emperor in 1793. The French Revolution made state officials fearful of the consequences of a system of mass education devoid of a religious content. The Political School Law of 1805, confirming church control over education, warned that "it is one of the chief failures of popular education not to take into account the requirements of the class of children whom it is educating and instructing, but to believe that knowledge is suitable for every class."[78]

Not until 1867, when a new constitution was written, did the state become the sole educational authority in Austria. A Ministry of Education was formed and a National Public School Law was passed in 1869 providing for a state-run system of compulsory primary education for all children between the ages of six and fourteen. The law was opposed by the church and there was considerable opposition from rural areas to its implementation. Farmers wanted only six years of compulsory education so that their children could be employed on the farms. There was also local opposition to the school taxes used to hire teachers. Strong support for compulsory education and against Catholic clericalism in the Austrian schools came from the Social Democratic Labour party. Austrian school teachers were also among the most active supporters of compulsory public education. The Social Democrats, teachers, and various liberal reformers joined together in 1905 to form the Free School organisation to promote educational reform and to press for the enforcement of the compulsory-education legislation.

As elsewhere, the issue of child labour was closely tied to the question of educational reform. While measures for the protection of working children were first introduced in the eighteenth century under Joseph II, it was not until the end of the nineteenth century that any serious legislative steps were taken to remove children from hazardous occupations. Legislation passed in 1884 and 1885 prohibiting the employment of children under the age of thirteen (under fourteen in mining), restricting night-time employment, and permitting the employment of thirteen and fourteen year olds only if they had fulfilled the legal school requirements. Subsequent studies revealed, however, that despite this legislation the employment of children was, for a time, actually increasing.

While there were expressions of concern within the state bureaucracy and among some politicians over child labour and the failure to enforce compulsory education, it was the associations of teachers, working with the bureaucracy, who took the lead in dealing with the problem. The initial focus was on ascertaining the magnitude of child labour. Studies of child labour were conducted by the Central Association of Vainnese Teachers in 1897. An official investigation of child labour was undertaken by the Central Statistical Commission of Austria in 1900. The commission made use of statistics on student admissions to schools and, with the aid of teachers, collected data on the employment of children during the school year. The Viennese Teachers Association and the Lower Austrian Regional Teachers Association subsequently did another survey of child labour. In the next decade several child-labour laws were passed, aimed at tightening enforcement procedures, restricting (but not prohibiting) employment of children under fifteen, and imposing a limit of three hours per day for the employment of children in the compulsory-school-age group.

Under a 1918 law a system of work earns was created, similar to the system of work permits established in the United States. All children of working age were required to have a work card and to undergo a physical examination by a doctor at the expense of the employer. The cards had to list the name, occupation, and dwelling of the employer and the legal guardian of the child. The law required that employers keep the work cards up-to-date and make them available to regional officials, school directors, and a variety of government officials. Regional governments were required to establish an office under the Office of Business Inspection to inforce child-labour laws. School officials were required to send yearly reports on school attendance to this office while other agencies, including voluntary organisations, were charged with reporting to the regional offices of the Office of Business Inspection illegal employment practices involving children.

In Austria it was a coalition of a centralised and conservative bureaucracy, the monarchy, the school administration, the local police, associations of teachers, and the Social Democratic Labour party that overcame the objections of Catholic clerics, parents, and the business community to create a state-run system of compulsory primary education and enforceable child-labour laws.

England

Compared to Germany and Austria, the British government moved late and slowly into education and the regulation of child labour. A combination of forces impeded state action: the Anglican church, which feared that state intervention would reduce its hold over education; dissenting churches concerned that state education might be controlled by the Anglicans; factory owners reluctant to lose the economic benefits of low- wage child labour; a political system under which local authorities had considerable autonomy, especially with regard to education; and an ideology of voluntarism that made legislators and magistrates reluctant to force parents to send their children to school. Many critics of child labour mis-takenly concluded that it was capitalism, rather than British politics, institutions, and ideology, that impeded reform. Had they looked across the channel to Germany, Austria, Sweden, and France, they might have drawn different conclusions.

As in other Protestant countries, mass education developed early in England. Prior to 1833 education in England was wholly voluntary, financed by parents, charitable organisations, and religious institutions. The Church of England formed the National Society for Promoting the Education of the Poor, an organisation committed to the diffusion of Anglican-dominated schools and opposed to state intervention. From the point of view of the Anglican church and the British upper classes, education for the poor was a religious and moral matter—to encourage church attendance; reduce crime; implant the virtues of self-help, thrift, sobriety, and cleanliness; and to condition the lower class to passively accept their station in life. No professional training was required for becoming a teacher. The essential qualification for teaching at the beginning of the nineteenth century was certification by an Anglican bishop. There was less concern for pedagogical standards than for doctrinal orthodoxy. The contrast with developments in France could not have been greater. After the French Revolution, the French government sought to break the hold of the Catholic church upon education by creating state- run primary schools, placing religious schools under state control by compelling them to follow an official curriculum, and by creating a teaching profession differentiated from other parts of the civil service and free from clerical influence. Teacher training was obligatory and all teachers were employed by the state as civil servants."[79] Education in France became state organised, state administered, and state financed.

The English reliance upon voluntarism in education, which meant largely church-run rather than state-run schools, led to the successful diffusion of literacy and education. Even without state support an increasing number of children attended school throughout the nineteenth century. It is estimated that as late as 1869 two-thirds of all school expenditures in England came from voluntary sources, parents, charitable institutions, and churches. Primary education was largely under the control of Anglican parish schools, Sunday schools supported by Evangelicals and Dissenters as well as by Anglicans, and sundry church-supported charity schools.

The spread of mass literacy was the major achievement of the system, though the number of years of schooling for the lower classes remained limited. The 1851 census report on education estimated that the average length of a working-class child's school life was about four years.[80] Twice as many boys as girls were withdrawn from school to enter employment. Still, as early as the 1830s one-half to two-thirds of working-class adults could read, and by 1870 illiteracy ceased to be a major problem in England.

The system provided appropriate forms of education for the different classes—church-run schools for the lower classes and a system of elite education that provided the upper class with a sense of their own role as an elite. There were few advocates (as there were in the United States) of a common educational system for all classes. James Mill expressed the prevailing view when he wrote that "there are certain qualities, the possession of which is desirable in all classes. There are certain qualities, the possession of which is desirable in some, not in others. As far as those qualities which ought to be common to all, there ought to be a correspondent training for all. It is only in respect to those qualities which are not desirable in all that a difference in the mode of training is required."[81]

To English moralists education and religion, the two closely related, were instruments for social order and political stability. Education was not regarded as a means of social mobility. Nor was investment in education regarded as a means of increasing the country's wealth. The major objection to child labour was that it prevented children from attending school, where they imbibed the proper values of their social class. The earliest legislation, therefore, provided for the establishment of part-time education for factory children (the Factories Act of 1833). Nine-to-eleven year old children employed in the textile industry were to receive two hours schooling, six days a week. Later legislation provided for part-time education for children in printworks, mining, lace, foundries, metal, tobacco, and other industries. The system of part-time education was intended to enable children to remain in the labour force.[82]

The British parliament appropriated funds for education for the first time in 1833. The sum was small (20,000 pounds) but it established the principle of state educational expenditures. Thereafter, liberals, utitarians, radicals, and trade unions pressed for an expanding role of the state in education. The Education Act of 1870 was another landmark. It did not impose compulsory education, but it enabled school boards to do so. In 1871 the London School Board made education for all children up to the age often compulsory. There was considerable resistance to the enforcement of compulsory education from the poor themselves, from members of the Anglican clergy on the school board, and from the magistrates whose responsibility it was to levy fines upon parents who failed to send their children to school.

A detailed study of the London School Board describes how difficult it was to force parents to place their children in school. One official wrote at the time that parents had been accustomed to "make capital out of their children as soon as the little hands could make a match box, or paint a toy, and naturally resented any interference with their supposed rights." One member of the school board, a socialist teacher, wrote in 1902 about a conversation with a mother in Leicester who had kept her daughter at home to assist with the washing. He reflected on the "painful complexity of interests involved—the mother's need of help; the child's need of education; society's claim that the child, as its ward, shall be trained to intelligent citizenship. The mother must yield; and the mother must suffer; but, alas! no commonwealth can truly gain by the sufferings of mothers."[83]

"One London magistrate," reports Rubinstein, "commented in 1899 that if as many summonses had been granted in the 1870s as the Board had wished, 'we should have had an insurrection. But most important and most significant," he continues, "magistrates refused to cooperate with the School Board because they did not believe in the value of compulsory elementary education. Conservative in their politics, upper mid- die class in their attitudes, they saw no reason to encourage the poor to rise above their station." Rubinstein describes a case involving a twelve year old, the daughter of parents described to the court as "sober, hardworking, respectable people." She was working as a nursery maid for three shillings a week. The magistrate decided that under section 74 of the Education Act of 1870 the girl's employment was a reasonable excuse for not attending school. The judge said that "she has been discharging the honourable duty of helping her parents, and, for my own part, before I held that these facts did not afford a reasonable excuse for her non attendance at school I should require to see the very plainest words to the contrary in the Act. I may add that there is nothing I should read with greater reluctance in any Act of Parliament than that a child was bound to postpone the direst necessity of her family to the advantage of getting a little more elementary instruction for herself."[84]

In 1880 Parliament enacted legislation that made education compulsory throughout the country.[85] School boards now were required to enforce compulsory education and it became a punishable offense for parents to keep their children out of school. Opposition to compulsion continued to come from parents who depended on the earnings of their children and from employers, especially farmers, who employed low- wage child labour. But reformers increasingly persuaded members of Parliament that the right of parents to dispose of the child's labour was of less importance than the needs of the child and the community for a minimum of education.[86] Many Tories who had previously been partisans of voluntary schools were now in favor of giving local authorities and school boards the power to compel attendance.

The procedure for enforcement of compulsory education in London was as follows: Defaulting parents who failed to send their children to school received an A notice. If this was unsuccessful, a *B* notice followed, in which the parents were required to attend 'a meeting with members of the school board to explain the reasons for the absence. In 1889, 96,000 A notices and 95,000 *B* notices were issued. In the same year there were 12,800 summonses. Between 1870 and 1903 the number of children attending elementary' schools in London increased from 319,000 to 549,000, a 72 per cent increase at a time when the school-age population had increased by only a third. In 1893 the minimum age of schooling was raised to eleven, then to twelve in 1899.

The enforcement of compulsory education in London was linked to efforts by the school board to make the schools more attractive. Slates were replaced by pencils, pens, and paper. Visual aids like maps and pictures were widely used. School libraries were established. There was an improvement in physical education and in sports. Manual training centers for the teaching of woodworking were created. The content of courses was upgraded. As the school board enforced compulsory education, truancy declined. Assaults on London attendance officers were less common by the turn of the century. Attendance steadily improved, from 80 per cent in 1877 to 82 per cent in 1900 and 88 per cent in 1904. Much of the increase came from children employed in small workshops and homes, the "sweating dens" of East London. For the country as a whole literacy rose for males, from 67 per cent in 1841 to 80 per cent in 1871 to 97 per cent in 1900.

Why was it possible to pass and enforce compulsory-education legislation after 1880 and not earlier? One explanation lies in the growing pressure from the labour movement, teachers, local government officials, and social reformers. These advocates of compulsory education both shaped and reflected popular sentiment that parents should not have the right to deny their children access to education in preference for immediate earnings. The new attitude was part of a broader public concern for the health and well-being of the children of the poor. And this new attitude was in turn a reflection of changes in the English class system, which had impeded efforts to legislate on behalf of children. The changing structure of the British economy also made the argument or compulsory education more appealing. The increasing demand for clerks and other white-collar workers provided opportunities for children of the working class to enter occupations different from those of their parents. Though many poor parents continued to prefer employment for their children to education, educators could now plausibly argue that parents should not be allowed to make wrong choices for their children. This is not to say that changes in the economy pushed children out of the labour force. There is no evidence that children were unable to find employment or that parents were on their own opting for education. The large number of truancy notices issued by the London School Board provide evidence to the contrary. But changes in the economy did make the reforms more palatable. Finally, the reforms were more enforceable by the 1880s because the number of children not attending school had declined substantially. The smaller the number of truants, the easier it became to enforce truancy laws.

The compulsory-education law of 1880 notwithstanding, England continued to move more slowly into child-labour reform than other European countries and the United States. Not until after World War I did England pass legislation making education compulsory for all children up to fourteen and restricting the employment of children under fourteen in factories and workshops. Other reforms affecting the children of the poor (e.g., widows' pensions) came later. The English experience thus suggests that beliefs and ideologies with regard to children and the poor played a more important role in shaping policies than any compulsions imposed by the labour market.

The United States

As in England, religious beliefs in the American colonies played a central role in the attitudes of parents toward the education of their children and in the attitudes of government officials toward the role of the state in education. As early as 1642 Massachusetts passed a law requiring all parents and guardians to see that their charges were taught to read. Five years later another law was passed requiring all towns of fifty or more families to appoint a teacher of reading and writing to be paid for by tax funds. The law also provided that towns of 100 or more families should provide a teacher of Latin grammar to prepare boys to enter college. These laws, in effect, established three principles that were to guide subsequent educational policies: that the state had the authority to compel parents to educate their children, that public moneys collected by local authorities could and should be used to establish and support schools, and that the state could require towns to establish school using local taxes.

These laws did not restrict religious institutions or other private bodies from establishing their own schools. The close ties between die established churches and civil governments in the colonies throughout the seventeenth century legitimised the growth of sectarian and other private schools. Nor did these laws require compulsory' schooling: They required that parents educate their children, not that children attend school. The distinction is an important one, for the earliest education laws permitted parents to educate their children at home. They contained no provision for compulsory schooling and its enforcement. Such legislation was not to come until late in the nineteenth century. Finally, it should be noted that the legislation in Massachusetts distinguished between elementary schools intended for the lower classes and secondary schools intended to enable the children of the upper classes to move on to the universities.[87]

While both compulsion and public education were from the very beginning part of American educational policy, it was the private sector—particularly religious institutions—that dominated the educational scene until well into the middle of the nineteenth century. Throughout the latter part of the eighteenth and early part of the nineteenth century school enrollments increased. One measure of how pervasive education had become—both, through the teaching of children by their parents and through schooling—was the level of literacy reached by the middle of the nineteenth century. Ninety per cent of the white population over twenty years of age was, according to the United States census of 1850, literate. Only Sweden compared favorably with the United States. Adult literacy for England and Wales at the time was 70 per cent, for France 55 to 60 per cent, for Prussia 80 per cent, and for Italy only 20 to 25 per cent. (Among nonwhites in the United States, however, only 20 per cent were literate as late as 1870).[88]

The commitment to education by the Puritans was based on their belief that salvation was the primary purpose of schooling. According to Puritan doctrine children were innately depraved. Education was seen as essential to remove the evil propensity of children, and discipline was the essential mechanism for placing children on the road to salvation. Religion was the first *R*, reading the second, 'riting the third, and, in colonial times, 'rithmetic was a poor fourth. First and foremost, prospective teachers had to be certified in the faith. Since the colonists were committed to education for discipline and salvation they welcomed the creation of denominational schools. The separation of church and state and the separation of religion from education were to come later.[89]

Legislation notwithstanding, in the early part of the nineteenth century not all American children were in school. It has been estimated that in 1832 two-fifths of the factory workers in New England were children. The 1870 census reported that 750,000 children between ten and fifteen years of age were working and subsequent census reports indicated that their numbers actually increased from 1870 to 1910.

The call for compulsory school-attendance legislation began in the 1820s. In the 1830s and 1840s Massachusetts, Connecticut, and Pennsylvania passed laws limiting the hours of employment of minors in textile factories. Legislation passed in Massachusetts in 1836 required that children under fifteen years of age working in manufacturing establishments were to have attended school for at least three months during the preceding year and to have obtained a certificate of attendance. In 1842 school committees were instructed by the commonwealth to enforce the law. But there is no evidence that these laws, and others that were subsequently passed by other state legislatures in the middle of the nineteenth century, were widely or strictly enforced.

There was a further spate of legislation beginning in the 1870s, in part the result of a campaign by the Knights of Labour, then the major trade- union federation in America, to press states to prohibit the employment of children. And in Massachusetts, studies conducted by the newly created Massachusetts Bureau of Statistics and Labour stimulated legislative action. In 1873 the state passed legislation requiring that all towns provide for truant officers to enforce compulsory school education laws. An 1874 law made education compulsory up to the age of fourteen, for a minimum of twenty weeks a year. In 1876 Massachusetts passed a law prohibiting the employment of any child under ten in a manufacturing or mercantile establishment and stipulating that children between ten and fourteen thus employed must have attended school for twenty weeks in the preceding year. A deputy constable was assigned to enforce the child- labour laws and in 1878 a law was passed requiring employers to keep proof of their employees' birth and school attendance on file for inspection by truant officers. Still, according to data collected by the Massachusetts Bureau of Statistics and Labour, children under ten continued to work in factories, many children ten to fifteen had not been to school for years, and factory officials often falsified records.[90]

Perhaps the most concerted effort to extend public education was in Massachusetts. The leader of the movement for school reform was Horace Mann, a lawyer, member of the Massachusetts state legislature, and, in 1837, the first secretary of the newly created state board of education. Mann became the leader of what was known nationally as the common- school movement: a movement for free, universal education to be paid for by government; schools that would provide moral instruction but would be free of sectarian religious education, that would be open io children from all religious, social, and ethnic backgrounds, and that would have trained professional teachers who had mastered their subjects. The thrust of this movement was to expand public schooling at the cost of private schooling and to provide for greater central i.e., state government as opposed to local government) control over schools in order to ensure common and minimum standards. Central to the notion of a common school was that an elementary school would serve all the children in an area. While in England school aid was seen as a means of providing education for the poor, Horace Mann argued that there should be a common provision for the education of all children, irrespective of social class. The common-school movement in America saw education as an instrument for the social integration of classes and of ethnic communities.

There were political differences over these proposals. The Democrats believed that private academies were adequate, while the Whigs wanted government intervention to improve the number and quality of private schools. Unitarians (of whom Mann was one) were for nonsectarian schools, while the clergymen of other religious groups were often opposed to the expansion of public education and deplored the creation of nonsectarian schools. Some politicians opposed state control as trespassing on the authority of local communities. Rural leaders were particularly opposed to Mann's concern for centralising education for they believed — that teachers should be accountable to the school trustees who hired them, the parents, and other taxpayers, and that the curriculum of the rural schools should be determined by the local community. The advocates of school reform wanted professionalisation: teacher training schools, the creation of a bureaucratic educational structure that would remove authority over the schools from the hands of laymen and thereby "free education from politics," and state laws that would force rural communities to consolidate one-room schools into larger entities.

By the latter half of the nineteenth century the school reformers were winning. Free schooling became widely available throughout the country. Public education rose from 47 per cent of total expenditures for schooling in 1850 to 79 per cent in 1900. Most of this money came from local tax assessments. Studies by educational historians of school attendance reveal that an overwhelming proportion of children were in school. A study in St. Louis in 1880 reported nine out of ten children in the eight-to-eleven age group were in school. Other studies show that five years of schooling were commonplace for most children. But two problems remained of concern to educators: there was a minority of children who did not attend school and a large proportion of children in their mid-teens were in the labour force . Many of the truants were poor, of immigrant stock, and non-Protestants.

Political pressure grew for enforcing compulsory education. In 1873 Massachusetts passed legislation requiring that all towns provide for truant officers to enforce compulsory school education laws. In 1876 Massachusetts passed a law prohibiting the employment of children under ten and stipulating that children between ten and fourteen must have attended school for at least twenty weeks in the preceding year. A deputy constable was assigned to enforce the child labour laws, and in 1878 a law was passed requiring employers to keep proof of their employees' birth and school attendance on file for inspection by truant officers. By 1885 sixteen out of thirty-eight states had compulsory schooling laws, and by 1900 thirty-one states required attendance from ages eight to fourteen . With the passage of compulsory education by the state of Mississippi in 1918, the process was complete for all the states.

There had been a shortage of classrooms, but by the first decade of the twentieth century accommodations had caught up with demand, the size of classes had diminished, and there was a widespread commitment to universal education. School aid to local communities was tied to average daily attendance and this reportedly stimulated local school boards to pursue truants. Journalists and reformers actively campaigned for the enforcement of compulsory schooling and child-labour laws. Attendance, however, was not universal and it took the effort of the school bureaucracies—school census takers, truant officers, and school social workers—to ensure full attendance. Their task was eased by the mechanisation of operations that previously had employed children, although it is difficult to differentiate cause and effect. As children were withdrawn from the labour market many of their tasks were mechanised. The expansion of white-collar jobs after 1890 and the increasing demand for high-school graduates who could work in offices also made school more attractive. In short, the opportunity costs of staying out of the labour market declined, while the benefits of a high-school education were increasing. The number of children in the labour force, which had increased from 1870 to 1910, declined substantially thereafter.

The 1880 United States census reported 60,000 children in the ten-to- fifteen age group employed in New York state, but large numbers of unreported children living in tenements were also employed. Nor did the census provide data on newsboys, bootblacks, peddlers, messengers, or farmer labourers. One scholar of child labour estimated that a more realistic figure would be 200,000 child labourers in the state, and he concluded that between 1886 and 1900 the percentage of children under sixteen employed in New York's factories remained unchanged at 4 per cent of the total number of factory workers.[91] The 1880 census reported that nationally a million children between the ages of ten and fifteen were employed, about one out of every six in that age group. The 1890 census reported an increase to 1.5 million children, or 18 per cent of the age group. And the 1900 census reported 1.75 million children between ten and fifteen in the labour force. Child labour had increased particularly in the South, where there had been an expansion in textile mills. Several southern states with textiles mills-North and South Carolina. Georgia, and Alabama—had neither child-labour nor compulsory-education laws until after 1900. As the economy grew in the latter part of the nineteenth century, child labour increased.

A variety of social-reform organisations set out to end child labour and enforce compulsory education: the National Child Labour Committee (NCLC), founded in 1904; the New York Child Labour Committee, the National Consumers' League (1890), and the General Federation of Women's Clubs (1890). The knights of Labour actively pressed state governments to pass laws and enforce rules prohibiting the employment of children. The American Federation of Labour, at its first annual convention in 1881, called upon states to ban the employment of all children under fourteen. Both trade-union federations advocated a constitutional amendment to permit federal regulation of child labour. At its 1892 convention, the Democratic party called for state legislation prohibiting the employment in factories of children under fifteen years of age.

The National Child Labour Committee was among the most effective of the lobbying groups, in large part because it systematically engaged in studies of particular industries and the conditions of work of children. The NCLC launched a campaign to end the employment of children in the glass industry after they completed a study that refuted many of the claims made by glasshouse operators. Employers argued that their industry was dependent upon child labour, that children under sixteen were better equipped than adults to work, that training of good glass workers had to begin at an early age, that should child labour and night work be prohibited they would be forced to close down their plants, and, finally, the familiar argument that child labour relieved the poverty of the poor. The NCLC study revealed that productivity had increased more rapidly in states that had forbade the employment of children at night, that the wages paid to children (sixty-five cents a day) were an insignificant contribution to family in come, and that the recent introduction of machinery made the employment of children both unnecessary and more costly for the manufacturer. Starting in 1905, the NCLC fought for legislation against the glass manufacturers in New Jersey, Pennsylvania, and West Virginia, but it took a decade or more to get each of these state legislatures to prohibit night work in the glass industry for those under sixteen and to impose other restrictions on employment.[92]

The NCLC and other pressure groups, by their persistent campaign for child-labour legislation, for compulsory education, and for enforcement machinery, helped to bring child labour to an end in the United States. Through the efforts of these groups the number of factory inspectors was increased and a system was created for regulating the entrance of young people into the labour market through the requirement of employment certificates. One of the most important legislative accomplishments of the NCLC was the development of the employment-certificate system in New York City between 1908 and 1915:

> While somewhat cumbersome, it represented the best thought of the day and was carefully designed to close as many loopholes as possible. When a New York City child wished to obtain working papers he first requested permission from his school principals who, after testing the child's ability to read and write, would send him to the appropriate borough office of the Department of Health. If the child had been born in New York City, he would be told to visit the Bureau of Records to obtain a birth certificate, and, if one was on file, the bureau would so certify. In the event no certificate could be found, the applicant was referred to the Employment Certificate Office (in the Board of Health) where Jeanie Minor (the agent) would counsel him about securing evidence of age. Once the child obtained acceptable proof of age he was sent back to the school principal who then issued a record of school attendance on an approved Department of Labour form. Accompanied by one of his parents, the child now returned to the Department of Health and made a formal application, counter- signed by the parents. After 1912, every applicant for working papers was given a physical examination, a decided improvement over the old system where health officers had simply to state that in their opinion the child was normally" developed for his age and could do the work he intended to do.

"Working papers," as the employment certificates were called, would be granted only to children who had completed at least six years of schooling and were fourteen years of age or, in the absence of six years of schooling, were sixteen years of age. From 1906 to 1917, between 20,000 and 47,000 employment certificates were issued each year in New York City to children between the ages of fourteen and sixteen.[93]

The NCLC campaigned to nationalize the child-labour laws. Before World War I they persuaded Congress to pass legislation overriding what they regarded as weak state laws, but the courts intervened in 1918 and 1922, declaring child labour a matter for state-government regulation. A child-labour amendment to the Constitution submitted in 1924 was never ratified. Minimum-wage standards were incorporated into the National Industrial Recovery Act (1933) and in 1938 a Fair Labour Standards Act was passed, which provided for a minimum age of fourteen for all employment during school hours in interstate commerce and eighteen for occupations classified as hazardous by the secretary of labour.

With the establishment of these state and federal laws advocates of controlling child labour then campaigned to raise the school leaving age from 14 to 16. As noted earlier, the then lieutenant governor, Herbert Lehman, who was a member of the New York City Child Labour Committee, argued that the 125,000 young people under the age of seventeen then holding jobs were displacing adults in the labour force. His efforts to raise the school-leaving age were opposed by the Catholic church, whose leaders charged that the bill was an invasion of parental rights, that it would create poverty by reducing family earnings, and that it would overcrowd parochial classrooms. The legislation was subsequently passed over the objections of the church. School attendance was required up to age sixteen in New York and in virtually all other states, and then extended in some states to age seventeen or to the completion of high school. In 1920, 62 per cent of children in the fourteen-to-seventeen age group were in school. By 1930 the figure had risen to 73 per cent, and by 1940 to 79 per cent. In 1920, 17 per cent of all youth completed high school; in 1930; 29 per cent; and in 1940, 51 per cent.[96]

The American experience with child labour and compulsory-education laws highlights the difficulties in a highly decentralised political system where labour laws were primarily matters for state governments and education was largely a local matter. The pressure from social-reform organisatians, trade unions, and educators was directed primarily at state and local governments. Not until the 1930s with the New Deal did they have much success with limited national legislation. The principles asserted by these groups—that the state had the right to intervene on behalf of children and that children are better off if they remain in school and out of the labour market at least until they are sixteen, and preferably until they complete high school—became accepted throughout the country, but not without a long political struggle.

Japan

The role played by the Japanese state in the establishment of compulsory universal education is an effective refutation of the argument that state intervention is only possible after parents no longer need to send their children into the labour force and employers no longer require low-wage child workers. Japan was well on the way toward universal literacy by the end of the Tokugawa era, prior to Japan's opening to the

West, prior to the Meiji restoration, and prior to Japan's industrialisation. By 1868 the majority of town dwellers with a settled occupation and a good proportion of farmers of middling status were literate. While Tokugawa Japan had no organised national educational system, there were thousands of small private schools. Some catered to samurai children and were financed by the governments of the fiefs, but most were unsubsidised, fee-charging private schools for the children of commoners (known as *terakoya* or parishioner schools). By 1870 perhaps half the male population of Japan could read and write simple Japanese, keep accounts, and read public documents and newspapers.

Samurai children attending fief-run schools were educated in the Confucian clasks and studied both Chinese and Japanese. It was an elite education, "learning appropriate to the world of rulers," as one Japanese official said in the 1870s explaining why the system was no longer relevant.[96] A striking feature of the fief school was that the emphasis was on the training of men who would acquire administrative and technical skills and attitudes of loyalty that would make them useful to the fief. But both in the private, commoner schools and in the fief-run schools the emphasis was on moral education and on virtue, not usefulness, as the chief goal of study. Vocational education was important, but not to the neglect of moral education with its emphasis on the virtues of filial piety, loyalty, justice, courage, benevolence, bravery, and, of course, respect for teachers.

Tokugawa schools, like those of nineteenth-century England, sustained status divisions. Commoners were excluded from the fief-supported samurai schools, while the sons of the daimyos (feudal barons) were educated at home by private tutors. In time, the status divisions within the educational system were undermined as the principle of merit increasingly entered into the Japanese economic and administrative system. The Chinese emphasis on promotion to office by examinations (in contrast with the Japanese emphasis on hereditary rank) made inroads into the Tokugawa educational system as teachers awarded recognition to achievement in school. By the middle of the nineteenth century the principle of ascription was being undermined both in the bureaucracies of the fiefs and in the schools.

The most important educational developments in Tokugawa Japan were the sheer quantity of schools that were opened, the numbers of children who attended, and the extent to which literacy became so widespread. Tokugawa leaders believed that education would make the masses more moral and obedient. The Meiji leadership was even more enthusiastic about mass education, believing that education was essential if Japan was to become a modern country with a strong military. "Henceforth, throughout the land," began a famous school regulation of 1872, "without distinctions of class and sex, in no village shall there be a house without learning, in no house an ignorant individual. Every guardian, acting in accordance with this, shall bring up his children with tender care, never flailing to have them attend school."[97]

The promotion of mass education was thus a central objective of the Meiji regime.

Between 1880 and 1900 the Japanese government increased the primary school attendance from 41 per cent of the six-to-thirteen age group to 82 per cent. In 1910, 98 per cent of the age group was attending school.[98] The Tokugawa emphasis on education suited to one's status was ended. What was retained was the Tokugawa concern for moral education, now redefined to emphasize loyalty to the emperor and to the nation rather than to the fief. The Imperial Rescript on Education, promulgated in 1890, emphasised the importance of inculcating in school the virtues of patriotism, respect for the laws, dedication to the emperor, and filial piety. Political indoctrination was a central objective of educational policy. An official ideology was developed that stressed the unique character of the "family-state" descended from a common ancestor. Filial piety was held up as a model for the relationship between the citizen and the state.[50] All elementary-school children were to take a morals course intended to foster a "national spirit" and to develop a love and reverence for the emperor, who embodied in his person the unity of the state and the people. Every school child was required to memorize and recite sections from the Imperial Rescript on Education.[99]

To ensure the inculcation of notions of national morality, the educational system was highly centralised. Prefectural schools were placed under the control of the Ministry of Education and textbooks for primary schools were prescribed by the ministry. The system proved to be efficient, both with respect to its capacity to inculcate political loyalty and submission and to create a remarkably educated population of workers and farmers.

Since the central government was not in a financial position to provide educational subsidies even for primary education, the central government ordered local governments to collect the revenues to support compulsory education. In the late 1880s the central government began to subsidize compulsory education, with the result that elementary-school enrollments soared, from 1.3 million in 1873 to 3.3 million in 1893 to 5 million in 1903.

With universal primary education and universal conscription, Japan developed both an educated army and an educated electorate. Universal manhood suffrage was established in 1925. Since the Japanese government emphasised state rather than private education at the primary- school level, Japanese children of all social classes shared the same kind of schooling for the first six years of school, reading the same textbooks, learning the same poems, acquiring the same values. The educational system also facilitated high rates of intergenerational social mobility, and thereby weakened class divisions. While social mobility would not have been possible had Japan not simultaneously experienced a high rate of economic growth, the high growth rate was itself made possible by the expansion of education, including the growth of technical and vocational education in the upper elementary schools.

There are some striking parallels between the Japanese experience with mass education and that of the countries of Europe. In Protestant Europe and in Japan the spread of mass education began prior to industrialisation and in some countries, such as Sweden, even without formal schools. Countries like Japan, Germany, and Austria that initiated compulsory education early in their industrialisation process had less of a child-labour problem than countries like England, which deferred making education compulsory until later.

Theology was an important force for compulsory education in many Protestant countries. In Japan theology was less important in the spread of mass education, but its equivalent—a concern for moral education as a means of preserving social order and political loyalty—played a significant role in shaping the state-run education system. So too did the recognition by the Japanese ruling elite of the need for mass education to build a modern state and a modern country capable of competing with the West.

Conclusions

In reviewing the circumstances that led countries to adopt compulsory education and child-labour laws one is struck by the diversity of the arguments, the diversity of the countries—industrial and preindustrial, democratic and authoritarian, parliamentary regimes and military dictatorships, centralised and decentralised—and the diversity of the political groups participating in the debates—churches, trade unions, educators, philanthropists, social activists, government officials, military officers, and political parties. The differences in the timing of state interventions are the result of these diversities.

First, Protestantism was the determining force for the early spread of education in central and northern Europe and in North America. In Austria, Germany, the United States, England, Scotland, the Netherlands, and the Scandinavian countries high rates of literacy (in some countries up to 80 per cent) were achieved in the eighteenth century even before the establishment of compulsory education and state educational systems. In Catholic and Orthodox southern and eastern Europe less than 20 per cent of the population could read. It was Protestantism that provided the moral fervor for compulsory education and the abolition of child labour and that shaped the moral content of elementary education.

Second, the notion of education as a duty was more speedily adopted as policy when it was taken up by those within the state apparatus rather than those outside. Germany, post-revolutionary France, Meiji Japan, and, as we shall see in the next chapter, the People's Republic of China, the Republic of China on Taiwan, and South Korea moved swiftly to make education compulsory because the dominant elites within the state (a party elite in some, the military in others, government officials in most), for whatever reasons, wanted education to be compulsory. England and the United States moved more slowly' because the pressures for reform came largely from outside the state structure.

Third, while mass education spread in England and the United States early on, compulsory education was not introduced until relatively late, in both cases because of the high degree of decentralisation, and in the English case also because of the concerns by the Anglican church and by the dissenting sects over the loss of control that might accompany a state- run educational system. More centralised systems, with state financing, standardised curricula, and centralised administration, are more able to create a national system of education based on compulsion than are decentralised systems, where educational financing is local (or private), where the curricula is unstandardised, and where the political ethos emphasizes voluntarism over state intervention.

Fourth, elite attitudes toward mass education in late-developing countries were motivated by considerations of national power, most notably in Japan and, as we shall see in the next chapter, among a number of currently developing countries. Among the European countries, a concern for military power was a contributing factor in Germany. In the main, however, neither considerations of economic development nor military prowess figured significantly in the spread of mass education in Western Europe and the United States. Indeed, it is striking that in much of the early debate "human resource" considerations were of little importance, compared to a concern with the broader political, social, and religious benefits of education.

Fifth, forces outside the state structure pressing for compulsory education and for the abolition of child labour were extraordinarily varied, including church groups and religious leaders, trade unionists, school teachers and educational officials, philanthropists and social reformers, and many (though by no means all) party politicians. Generally opposed were businessmen and, often, those politicians of the Left or Right who sought the support of the working poor. Where the state was tardy, societal coalitions proved to be crucial in introducing and extending compulsory-education laws and banning the employment of children.

In all these countries there eventually developed the view that the family could no longer be relied upon as the institution for the transmission of those values, attitudes, skills, and knowledge that were essential in the modern world. Teachers appointed by and financially dependent upon the state were regarded as more effective than parents in promoting whatever notions (patriotism, discipline, obedience to authority, good citizenship, hard work) the state regarded as essential. The school emerged as a unique modern institution, indeed the only institution in which, with the introduction of compulsory education, everyone in the society was required to participate. As notions of equality, merit, mobility, citizenship, and nationality became societal and state goals, the school became a favorite institution for all political persuasions. The notion of child labour was replaced with the notion of schooling as the child's work. In a fundamental sense the school as an institution was linked to the emergence of modern civil society.

REFERENCES

1. Ministry of Labour, *Report of the Committee on Child Labour* (New Delhi: Government of India, 1979), p. 54. For a review of British policies, see Rajani Kanta Das, "Labour Legislation in Indian States," *International Labour Review* 38, No. 6 (December 1928).

2. *Ibid.*, p. 39.
3. *Ibid.*, p. 42.
4. *Ibid.*, p. 44.
5. *Ibid.*, p. 49.
6. For the response of the Government of India to the committee's recommendations, see P.M. Shah, ed., *Child Labour: A Threat to Health and Development* Geneva: Defence for Children International, 1985), pp. 99-100.
7. *Deccan Herald* (17 July 1983).
8. Ministry of Labour, *Annual Report 1983-84 (New Delhi: Government of India, 1985).*
9. The Concerned for Working Children, *The Report of the National Seminar on Education for Working Children* (Bangalore: CWC, November 1985).
10. *The Concerned for Working Children Present the Child Labour (Employment, Regulation, Training, and Development) Bill, 1985* (Bangalore: CWC, 1985)).
11. The Concerned for Working Children, *The Report of the National Seminar* (Bangalore: CWC, November 1985), p. 7. The CWC put the figure of child labourers higher than had other groups. It regarded as too low the 1983 government figure of 17.3 million and the Operations Research Group estimate of 44 million, arguing that since 90 million children in the five-to-fifteen age group do not attend school, virtually all of them should be regarded as working children.
12. Neera Burra, "Old Flaws in New Child Labour Bill," *Times of India* (7 November 1986). Se also Walter Fernandes and Neera Burra, "A Law That will Not Protect," *Indian Express* (18 August 1986).
13. Walter Fernandes, Neera Burra, and Tara Anand, *Child Labour in India: A Summary of a Report Prepared by the Indian Social Institute* New Delhi: Indian Social Institute, November 1985).
14. Neera Burra, "Pay Less, Get More Work," *Hindustan Times Sunday Magazine* (19 January 1986). See also Neera Burra, "Child Labour in India: Poverty, Exploitation, and Vested Interest," *Social Action* 36 (July-September 1986), pp. 241-263; and Sheela Barse, "Legitimising Child Labour," *Indian Express* (28 July 1985).
15. *Hindu* (17 August, 25 January, and 21 April 1986).
16. *Seminar on Ways and Means of Achieving the Elimination of the Exploitation of Child Labour in All Parts of the World* (Geneva: United Nations, ST/HR/Ser. A/18, 22 January 1986).
17. *Ibid.*, p. 6.
18. *Ibid.*, p. 26.
19. *Report of the Director-General to the International Labour Conference*, 69th sess., 1983 (Geneva: International Labour Office, 1985). For a global survey of child labour, see *Conditions of Work Digest: The Emerging Response to Child Labour*, vol. 7 no. 1, 1988 (Geneva: International Labour Office, 1988). ILO conventions are conveniently summarised in *Child Labour: A Briefing Manual* (Geneva: International Labour Office, 1986). For a bibliography, see Annotated Bibliography on Child Labour *(Geneva: International Labour Office,* 1986).
20. Assefa Bequele, *Towards a Global Programme of Action on Child Labour* (Geneva: Conditions of Work and Welfare Facilities Branch, Working Conditions and Environment Department, International Labour Office, September (1985). See also Assefa Bequele and Jo Boyden, eds., *Combating Child Labour* (Geneva: International Labour Office, 1988), esp. Ramesh Kanbargi, "Child Labour in India: The Carpet Industry of Varanasi," pp. 93-108. For an ILO analysis of the Indian situation, See *Towards an Action programme on Child Labour. Report to the Government of India of an ILO Technical Mission* (Conditions of Work and Welfare Facilities Branch,

Working Conditions and Environment Department, International Labour Office, Geneva, April 1984). This report supports the Indian view that "the abolition of child labour .... is not attainable in the short run in many developing countries; millions of children will continue to be working for many years to come. Measures to regulate and humanise child labour are therefore essential during the transitional period until its elimination" (p. 1). Other international organisations have supported the Indian position. Seem, for example, Summanta Banerjee, *Child Labour in India* (London: Anti-Slavery Society, 1979), who writes that "however outrageous the presence of child workers might be to liberal sentiments, Indians will have to live with the phenomenon as long as the level of the country's economic development remains what it is now." Similar views can be found in Garry Rodgers and Guy Standing, eds., *Child Work, Poverty, and Underdevelopment* (Geneva: International Labour Office, 1981); and *Exploitation of Working Children and Street Children* (New York: United Nations Childrens Fund, 1986).

21. Bequele, *Towards a Global Programme of Action on Child Labour*, p. 51.
22. *Ibid.*, pp. 48, 49.
23. Ministry of Education, *Challenge of Education—A Policy Perspective* (New Delhi Government of India, 1985).
24. The detailed recommendations, appear in Department of Education, Ministry of Human Resource Development, *National Policy on Education 1986—Programme of Action* (New Delhi: Government of India, 1986).
25. Ministry of Education, *Challenge of Education*, p. 18.
26. *Ibid.*, p. 36.
27. *Ibid.*, p. 22.
28. *Ibid.*, p. 57.
29. National Council of Education Research and Training, *Education and National Development: Report of the Educational Commission 1964-66*, vol. 2: *School Education* (New Delhi: NCERT, 1970).
30. Research and Training, *Fourth All India Educational Survey. Some Statistics on School Education* (New Delhi, 1980).
31. Navodaya Schools—Chalking a new Path," *India Today* (15 June 1988).
32. Anil Bordia *Working Paper on Child Labour in India—Implications for Educational Planing*, ILO Asian Regional Tripartite Workshop on Practical Measures to Combat Child Labour. Bangkok, September 1966 (New Delhi: Ministry of Human Resource Development. Government of India, 1986), p. 17. This paper provides a systematic analysis of the linkage between the Child Labour (Prohibition and Regulation) Bill and the proposed National Policy on Education. As an official in both departments, Mr. Bordia Played an important role in formulating the new policy.
33. Ministry of Education and Social Welfare. *Working Group on Universalisation of Elementary Education* (New Delhi: Government of India, 1977), pp. 11-12.
34. Education for All at Snail's Pace," Overseas *Hindustan Times* (30 May 1987).
35. Upendra Baxi, "Draft Graduates for Adult Literacy," *Yojana* (January 1986), p. 66.
36. Gandhi, at Harvard, Extolls Virtues of India's Democracy," *Boston Globe* (19 October 1987).
37. The Assam Elementary Education Act, 1974 (Gauhati: Government of Assam, Education Dept., 1974).
38. The Tamil Nadu Elementary Education Act (Madras: Government of Tamil Nadu, 1973).
39. K.G. Saiyidain, J.P. Naik, and S. Abid Hussain, *Compulsory Education in India* (Paris: United Nations Educational, Scientific, and Cultural Organisation, 1952), p. 33. Naik reviews the data

on enforcement and prosecutions in the various states for 1948-1949 on pages 68-72.

40. For an account of the preindependence history of efforts to introduce compulsory education into India, see *Compulsory Education in South Asia and the Pacific. Report of the Bombay Conference* (December 1952), Studies in Compulsory Education (Paris: United Nations Educational, Scientific, and Cultural Organisation, 1954) For a postindependence analysis of the unsuccessful efforts to universalise elementary education, see John Kurrien, *Elementary Education in India: Myth, Reality, Alternative* (New Delhi: Vikas Publishing, 1983).

41. Saiyidain, Naik, and Hussain, *Compulsory Education in India,* p. 33.

42. Baroda (now call Vadodara) had a literacy rate of 68 per cent in 1981, substantially higher than the 57 per cent rate for urban India. Other cities with populations above 500,000 with literacy rates above 65 per cent included Calcutta (66 per cent), Bombay (68 per cent), Madras (66 per cent), Pune (67 per cent), Nagpur (66 per cent), Coimbatore (66 per cent), Madurai (67 per cent), Cochin (78 per cent), Ulhasnagar (66 per cent), Tiruchirapalli (69 per cent), Calicut (73 per cent), and Trivandrum (76 per cent).

43. P.R. Gopinathan Nair, *Primary Education, Population Growth, and Socio-Economic Change (A Comparative Study with Particular Reference to Kerala)* New Delhi: Allied Publishers, 1981).

44. Quoted in Shiv Kumar Saini, *Development of Education in India: Socio-Economic and Political Perspectives* (New Delhi: Cosmo Publications, 1980), p. 64.

45. *Ibid.,* p. 73. The notion of vocational training for the masses in the early years of school has been a central theme of most recommendations for educational reform in India. For a critical assessment of vocational education in the early grades, see George Psacharopoulos, *To Vocationalised or Not to Vocationalise? That is the Curriculum Question* (Washington, D.C.: World Bank, Educational and Training Department, report no. EDT31, 1986). Psacharopoulous questions the value of incorporating vocational training into general education and argues instead for separate vocational institutions or employment-based training for the higher grades. He notes that attempts to "ruralise" the curriculum as a means of enhancing farm productivity do little more than the use of a general curriculum, with its emphasis on rudimentary arithmetic and literacy, at the primary level. Moreover, an examination of a number of country studies leads Psacharopoulos to conclude that graduates from both vocational and general education streams are absorbed equally well by the labour market and that the returns from traditional academic education are greater on average than the returns to investment from vocational training.

46. Saiyidain, Naik, and Hussain, *Compulsory Education In India,* p. 132.

47. Report by the Central Advisory Board of Education, *Post-War Educational Development in India* (New Delhi: January 1944).

48. Government of India Planing Commission, *First Five Year Plan* (Delhi: Government of India, 1952).

49. Indian Committee for Cultural Freedom, *Studies on the Plan Frame* (Bombay : ICCF 1956). The authors of the report, notable economists, officials, and other intellectuals, were regarded at the time as conservatives when they criticised the plan for its attention to large-scale projects and its neglect of education and other social services.

50. Philippe Aries, *Centuries of Childhood: A Social History of Family Life* (New York: Random House, 1962). Aries provides a history of changing adult attitudes toward children, based largely upon an examination of portraits, medical treatises, and literature. A similar study in India would be useful, though it is not clear that such a study would reveal comparable changes in adult attitudes.

51. Viviana Zelizer, *Pricing the Priceless Child: The Changing Social Value of Children* (New York, Basic Books, 1985). Zelizer argues that in the late nineteenth century, as a consequence of a

variety of cultural forces rather than changes in the structure of the labour market, American children began to undergo a process of "sacralisation," that is, the separation of children from the cash nexus.

52. Egil Johansson, "The History of Literacy in Sweden, "in Harvey J. Graff, ed., *Literacy and Social Development in the West: A Reader* (Cambridge: Cambridge University Press, 1981), p. 163. By the early part of the eighteenth century more than 50 per cent of the Swedish population was literate. Similar high rates of literacy were reported in Protestant England, Scotland, and the Netherlands, all prior to the Industrial Revolution, but not in the Catholic and Orthodox regions of southern and eastern Europe. For a review of the data on the spread of literacy in Europe, see Carlo M. Cipolla, *Literacy and Development in the West* (Penguin Books, 1969).

    There is an academic cottage industry on the diffusion of literacy in Europe. The pioneering article that set the terms of much of the subsequent debate is Lawrence Stone, "Literacy and Education in England, 1640-1900," *Past and Present*, no. 42 (1969), pp. 69-119. See also harvey J. Graff, *The Literacy Myth. Literacy and Social Structure in the Nineteenth-Century City* (New York : Academic Press, 1979); John Markoff, "Some Effects of Literacy in Eighteenth-Century France," *Journal of Interdisciplinary History 17*, no. 2 (1986), pp. 311-333; Michael Sanderson, "Literacy and Social Mobility in the Industrial Revolution in England," *Past and Present*, no. 56 (1972), pp. 75-104; Lawrence Stone, "The Educational Revolution in England, 1560-1640," *Past and Present*, no. 28 (1964); Brain V. Street, *Literacy in Theory and Practice* (Cambridge: Cambridge University Press, 1984); Lawrence Stone, ed., *Schooling and Society: Studies in the History of Education* (Baltimore: The Johns Hopkins University Press, 1976); Harvey J. Graff, *The Legacies of Literacy: Continuities and Contradictions in Western Culture and Society* (Bloomington: Indiana University Press, 1987); Egil Johansson, "The History of Literacy in Sweden, "in Harvey J. Graff, ed., *Literacy and Social Development in the West: A Reader* (Cambridge, Cambridge University Press, 1981); Harvey J. Graff, *Literacy in History: An Interdisciplinary Research Bibliography* (New York: Garland Publishing Co. 1981); Michael Sanderson, *Education, Economic Change, and Society in England, 1780-1870* (London: The Economic History Society, 1983), p. 53: Phillip McCann, ed., *Popular Education and Socialisation in the Nineteenth Century* (London: Methuen, 1977); E.G. West, *Education and the Industrial Revolutions* (New York: Harper and Row, 1975); Kenneth Charlton, *Education in Renaissance England* (London: Routledge and Kegan Paul, 1965); G.A.N. Lowndes, *The Silent Social Revolution: An account of the Expansion of Public Education in England and Wales, 1895-1935* London: Oxford University Press, 1937).

53. Harold Silver, "Ideology and the Factory Child: Attitudes to Half-Time Education," in McCann, ed., *Popular Education and Socialisation in the Nineteenth Century*, p. 146.

54. Walter I. Trattner, *Crusade for the Children: A History of the National Child Labour Committee and Child Labour Reform in America* (Chicago: University of Chicago Press, 1970), p. 26. In 1789 a petition on behalf of a cottage factory in Beverly, Massachusetts, stated that it would "afford employment to a great number of children, many of whom will be otherwise useless, if not burdensome to society" (ibid., p. 26).

55. David Rubinstein, "Socialisation and the London School Board, 1870-1904: Aims, Methods, and Public Opinion," in McCann, ed., *Popular Education and Socialisation in the Nineteenth Century*, p. 244.

56. *Ibid.*, p. 245.

57. *Ibid.*

58. Trattner, *Crusade for the Children*, p. 26.

59. Karl Marx, *The Marx-Engels Reader*, Robert C. Tucker, ed. (New York: W.W. Norton, 1978), p. 353. Marx drew much of his description from the 1864 Children's Employment Commission Report. He took issue with the report's conclusions that children need to be protected by the

state against exploitation by parents, attributing instead the exploitation of children to the capitalist mode of production (see p. 415).

60. *Ibid.*, p. 799.
61. *Ibid.*, p. 523.
62. *Ibid.*, p. 541.
63. *Ibid.*, p. 415.
64. Adam Smith, *The Wealth of Nations* (New York: Modern Library, 1937), p. 735.
65. *Ibid.*, p. 737.
66. *Ibid.*, p. 740.
67. *Ibid.*, p. 113.
68. Quoted in E.G. West, *Education and the State. A Study in Political Economy* (London: Institute of Economic Affairs, 1965), p. 32. Fro Benthan the rationale for compulsory education was that it would ensure that the poor would become educated and that ordinary people would become acquainted with the law. In his *Principles of Penal Law*, Bentham wrote, "Education is only government acting by means of the domestic magistrate" quoted ibid., p. 124), Utilitarian educationists did not regard literacy as an end in itself, but as a means of reducing crime, curbing strikes and riots, encouraging church attendance, and nurturing the values of self-help, thrift, sobriety, and cleanliness. On the relationship between education and the working class in England, see J.M. Goldstom. "The Content of Education and the Socialisation of the Working Class Child, 1830-1860," in McCann, ed., *Popular Education and Socialisation in the Nineteenth Century.*
69. John Stuart Mill, *On Liberty* (1959), in *The English Philosophers from Bacon to Mill* (New York: Modern Library, 1967), p. 128.
70. This useful typology is from Michalina Vaughan and Margaret Scotford Archer, *Social Conflict and Educational Change in England and France, 1789-1848* (Cambridge: Cambridge University Press, 1971), p. 203.
71. Thomas Alexander, *The Prussian Elementary Schools* (New York Macmillan, 1918). See also Eugene N. Anderson. "The Prussian Volksschule in the Nineteenth Century, " in Gerhard A. Ritter, ed., *Enstehung and Wandel der moderned Gesellschaft* Berlin: 1970); And Gerald Strauss,: "Techniques of Indocrination: The German Reformation," in Graff, ed., *Literacy and Social Development in the West.*
72. Cipolla, *Literacy and Development in the West*, p. 115.
73. Juergen Kuczynski, *Die Geschichte der Loge der Arbiter unter dem Kapitalismus* (Berlin: Akademic-Verlag, 1969). For translation of German sources I am grateful to Jennifer Nupp and Richard Deeg.
74. J. Russell Endean, *The Public Education of Austria: Primary, Secondary, Technical, Commercial* (London: Simpkin, Marshall, and Co., 1888), preface.
75. *Ibid.*, pp. 8-9.
76. *Ibid.*, p. 27.
77. *Ibid.*, pp. 48-49.
78. *Ibid.*, On the development of the Austrian school system, see Robert Dottrens. *The New Education in Austria* (New York: John Day, 1930); and Ernst Papanek, *The Austrian School Reform* (New York: Frederick Fell, 1962).
79. Vaughan and Archer, *Social Conflict and Educational Change*, pp. 206, 211.
80. Beryl Madoc-Jones, "Patterns of Attendance and Their Social Singificance: Mitcham National

School, 1830-1839," in McCann, ed., *Popular Education and Socialisation in the Nineteenth Century*, p. 42. See also J.M. Goldstom, "The Content of Education and the Soicalisation of the Working Class child, 1830-1860," ibid.

81. Quoted in Vaughan and Archer, *Social Conflict and Educational Change*, p. 73.

82. Silver, "Ideology and the Factory Child: Attitudes to Half-Time Education," p. 157.

83. Rubinstein, "Socialisation and the London School Board 1870-1904: Aims, Methods, and Public Opinion," p. 247.

84. *Ibid.*, pp. 236, 248, 250.

85. The case for the expansion of education through compulsion was put forth by the Liberal vice-chairman of the London School Board in 1899. "We want our lower classes to be educated.... We want them in the schools and in the homes to learn the self-respect of citizens, to feel their responsibility as voters, to have the self-restraint, the thoughtfulness, the power of judging and weighing evidence, which should discipline them in the exercise of the great power they no wield by their industrial combinations and through their political action," ibid., p. 242. A particularly eloquent case for the compulsory education of the poor was presented in 1892 by a teacher in the Metropolitan Board Teachers' Association: "Poverty, however abject it may be, cannot be accepted as an excuse for keeping children from school. But a moment's thought will show that to accept poverty as an excuse would prepetuate the very conditions that are a disgrace to our boasted civilisation..... To leave them without education would be to leave them hungry and half-naked all their lives," ibid., p. 262.

86. Gillian Sutherland, *Policy-Making in Elementary Education 1870-1895* (Oxford: Oxford University Press, 1973), p. 340.

87. There is a substantial literature on the development of education in Massachusetts. The major works include Carl F. Kaestle, *Pillars of the Republic: Common Schools and American Society* (New York: Hill and Wang, 1983); Carl F. Kaestle, *The Evolution of an Urban School System:* New York, *1750 1850* (Cambridge: Harvard University Press, 1973); Stanley K. Schultz, *The Culture Factory: Boston Public Schools, 1987-1860* (New York: Oxford University Press, 1973); Carl F. Kaestle, "Ideology and American Educational History, *History of Education Quarterly* 22 (Summer 1982); Carl F. Kaestle and Maris A. Vinovskis, "From Fireside to Factory: School Entry and School Leaving in Nineteenth Century Massachusetts," in Tamara K. Hareven, ed., *Transitions:* The Family and the Life Course in Historical Perspective (New York: 1978); and Carl F. Kaestle and Maris A. Vinovskis, *Education and Social Change in Nineteenth Century Massachusetts* (New York: Cambridge University Press, 1980).

88. Cipolla, *Literacy and Development in the West*, p. 94.

89. On the spread of mass education in the United States in the nineteenth century, see Ernest E. Bayles and Bruce L. Hood, *Growth of American Educational Thought and Practice* (New York: Harper and Row, 1966); Michael B. Katz, *Class, Bureaucracy, and Schools: The Illusion of Educational Change in America* (New York: Praeger, 1975); Albert Fishlow, "The American Common School Revival: Factor or Fancy," in Henry Rosovsky, ed., *Industrialisation in Two Systems* (New York: Wiley, 1966); Robert L. Church and Michael W. Sediak, *Education in the United States* (New York: Free Press, 1976); Michael B. Katz, *The Irony of Early School Reform: Educational Innovation in Mid-Nineteenth Century Massachusetts* (Cambridge: Harvard University Press, 1968); John Perrin, *The History of Compulsory Education in New England* (Meadville, Penn., 1876). For an analysis of the spread of education that emphasises the needs of the capitalist system, see Samuel Bowles and Herbert Gintis, *Schooling in Capitalist America: Educational Reform and the Contradictions of Economic Life* (New York: basic Books, 1976).

90. Kaestle and Vinovskis, *Education and Social Change in Nineteenth Century Massachusetts*, p. 77.

91. Jeremy P. Felt, *Hostages of Fortune: Child Labour Reform in New York State* (Syracuse: Syracuse University Press, 1965), pp. 17, 35.

92. Trattner, *Crusade for the Children*, pp. 78-79.
93. Felt, *Hostages of Fortune*, pp. 103-104, 105.
94. David B. Tyack, *The One Best System: A History of American Urban Education* (Cambridge: Harvard University Press, 1974), p. 74.
95. R.P. Dore, *Education in Tokugawa Japan* (Berkeley: University of California Press, 1965), p. 3.
96. R.P. Dore, "Japan," in Robert E. Ward and Dankwart A. Rustow, eds., *Political Modernisation in Japan and Turkey* (Princeton: Princeton University Press, 1964), p. 179.
97. The last sentence of this much-cited statement is more subtly translated by Passin as follows: "While advanced education is left to the ability and means of the individual, a guardian who fails to send a young child, whether a boy or a girl, to primary school shall be deemed negligent of his duty," Herbert Passin, *Society and Education in Japan* (New York: Tearchers College Press, Columbia University, 1965), p. 211.
98. Dore, "Japan," p. 189.
99. Herbert Passin, "Japan," in James S. Coleman, ed., *Education and Political Development* (Princeton: Princeton University Press, 1965), p. 307.
100. William K. Cummings, *Education and Equality in Japan* (Princeton: Princeton University Press, 1980), p. 19. For a study that emphasises the political and ideological conflicts in the development of Japanese education, see Teruhisa Horio, *Educational Thought and Ideology in Modern Japan: State Authority and Intellectual Freedom* (Tokyo: University of Tokyo Press), 1988.

36

CHILD LABOUR, ITS NATURE AND EXTENT OF EXPLOITATION

The high incidence of Child Labour in India is not only shocking from the moral point of view. but also represents a waste of vast human resources, which instead of being improved upon through education and training is utilised in a most unproductive and wasteful manner. With 13 million infants added every year, India has achieved the distinction of having one of the world's youngest populations. The 1971 census showed that 42 per cent of the Indian population consists of children under 15 years of age. In the 1951 census it was 37.5 per cent. In 1981 there were 137 million children in India and by 2001, the number of children is expected to be 289 million or more that the total population of the U.S.S.R. This high proportion of child population in our country warrants the need for providing living conditions which will enable children to realise their full potentialities for development. It is therefore necessary for us to look after the children at least as much as we look after dams, roads and other economic aspects of our country. The children are the human capital of the nation, and if we neglect them even economic development might be difficult, therefore in nay planing in social welfare we have got to take into account the most basic section of population that is the 'Child.' Moreover, if we want to reduce expenditure on solution of social problems arising in future, provision of preventive services for even the normal children from birth is a must.

Nature of Child Labour

Historically, the economic practice of child labour signifying material contribution to the labour economy of the family dates back to the industrial revolution when the child was removed from home, field and village and placed in the factory. Since then, the demand of industry for cheap labour has grown so rapidly and the poverty of the masses become so acute that the tendency to exploit child labour increased in unprecedented manner. As a result large number of children began to be employed in organised industries at a cheaper rate. In the absence of state control over conditions of employment in any industry in India or in any legal or executive action for the protection of the child, appalling abuses came into existence and children of tender ages were exploited, as so many factory 'hands' for specialised routine jobs with no educational or vocational value and made to work for excessive long hours on few annas a day. In certain industries, employment of children continues even today in spite of various legal provisions relating to the age limit etc. The labour investigation committee pointed out that "one black spot of labour conditions in India is this illegal employment of children in certain Industries." The important fact that has emerged from the investigation is that in various industries, mainly smaller industries, the prohibition of children is disregarded quite openly and owing to the inadequacy of the inspection staff it has become difficult to enforce the relevant provisions of the law. With the passage of social legislation in due course of time the situation eased. In an enquiry conducted by the labour bureau, it was observed that "at present in the factory industries, child labour is not serious problem."

The child employment is visible in almost all industries where unskilled labour and limited physical strength could be utilised. The occupation of children may be divided into four major groups, (a) Agriculture, (b) Manufacture, (c) Trade and, (d) Domestic.

The important sources available for estimating the incidence of child labour are:

1. Census data
2. N.S.S. data
3. Agricultural and Labour enquiries

The number of child workers in 1971 census was 10.7 million as against 14.5 million in 1961. Out of 10.7 million million as child workers in 1971, 87 per cent were in primary activities.

Extent of Exploitation

Employment of children is almost non-existent in organised industries. It persists in varying degrees in the unorganised sector such as small plantations, restaurants and hotels, cotton ginning and weaving, carpet weaving, stone breaking, brick-kill, handicrafts and road building. Employment of child worker below the prescribed age is also reported to be continuing in far off places and in rural areas where enforcement of statutory provisions is more difficult.

There is shocking conditions of labour in unregulated factories and small scale industries and they are worse still in other non-industrial occupations where the child is treated as anything but human being in his own right. There is physical wreckage of the child employed as a dock labourer, beast of burden or beast of transport, domestic slave and as a victim of social vice. Serious is the mental and moral wreckage of these "future builders of the nation" Children employed in hotels, restaurants, cinemas, brothels, gambling dens, illicit liquor and drug traffic are exposed to the demoralising influence of the foulest character who tach them tc lie, cheat, gamble, use filthy language, commit thefts and generally lead them into a carer of vice and delinquency. But no accurate data of such child labour employed in domestic services are available to study the employment trend. Apparently it appears that demand of cheap labour in domestic services is growing resulting in steady increase in the child employment. Two reasons may be assigned for this unhealthy growth. Firstly, these industries are not organised and present laws are not sufficient to deal with the problem properly, secondly, inspectorate machinery is almost absent to see the implementation oft he relevant laws and access to the domestic houses is also not free from interruptions.

Evils of Child Labour

While some unhealthy work in childhood may be a social good and national gain, but child labuour is a great social ill and a national waste as "the economic necessity for wage earning to support the family deprives the child of opportunity for education, wholesome play and recreation, stunts his physical growth, interferes with the normal development of his physical growth, interferes with normal development of his personality and thwarts his preparation for adult responsibility." To the employer, child labour is profitable as the wages of children are small, their complaints are few and they accomplish in some industries and occupations as much as adults. The employer, therefore, has no hesitation in exploiting the child in his interest without considering their needs for healthy growth and development.

The constitution of India provides for protection of child workers. Article 24 lays down that no child below the age of 14 years shall be employed in work in any factory or mine or engaged in any other hazardous employment.

It may be seen from the list of needs for children from 0 to 16 that there is a need of co-ordinating and integration of various services in the field of health and nutrition, education and training and recreation and welfare. In order to provide comprehensive services to children it is necessary to have co-ordination and integration of services already existing and to supplement the existing services.

Thus the following principles are derived from the above:

1. Child is the future human capital. It must be preserved and improved.
2. Adequate preventive services should be provided to the normal child.
3. These services should be provided to all the children in the age group of 0 to 16.
4. These services should relate to the field of,
   (a) Health and nutrition,
   (b) Education and training, and
   (c) Welfare and recreation
5. The total well-being of the child should be aimed at.

The employment of children is indeed more of an economic problem than anything else. Nevertheless, it is considered denial of opportunity to children for their proper physical development and education to be an issue of a serious nature, keeping in view of larger interests of the society. While the economic difficulties are real, a way has to be found to give the child the necessary education in his more receptive years. National commission of labour feels that this can be ensured by fixing the employment hours of children so as to enable them to attend the school.

India in its constitution is wedded to the goal of child welfare; physical, psychological and moral development of children providing them care, health, education, recreation; and the reality of child labour is utter negation of all these. Child labour is in contradiction with compulsory education for all children in 5-14 years age group; it is strange that on the one hand India faces unemployment and under-employment is flourishing on the other.

The objective of this paper is to examine the extent and nature of child labour in India, identify causes, factors and conditions associated with it and effort for its eradication on the basis of several researches, experience of activists and administration that are available and to suggest measures for gradual eradication of child labour in India.

Definition

According to Child Labour Prohibition and Regulation Act of 1986, employment of children up to the age of 14 years and in case of hazardous employments up to 18 years is defined as child labour and is banned completely form the hazardous occupations, while working and living conditions of employed children in other occupations is regulated, so long as child labour is not eradicated completely form all the occupations.

According to 1981 census child labour comprises of nearly 4.24 per cent of total Indian population in the 0-14 age group, 5.02 per cent children work as main workers and 10.97 per cent as marginal workers in the labour force. According to N.S.S. round of 1983, 17.31 million children are in the labour force, of these 10% are in 5-9 age group and 19% are in 0-14 age group. Also, more girls then boys are child labourers. O.R.G. National Survey on child labour shows 44 million working children in India. Estimates of child labour are not very exact and differ because (1) most children work in unorganised sector and are scattered in rural and urban areas, (2) work as family labour, or (3) in small units, making it difficult to estimate their exact number however it is clear that the number of working children is quite large in India.

Most (91 per cent) working children in India are in rural areas, of these 86 per cent are in agriculture and related activities and about 9 per cent are in urban areas. Again most (90 per cent) working children work in unorganised sector and only 10 per cent work in organised sector of economy. Studies have shown that working children belong to lower strata-castes-communities particularly scheduled castes and also to poor and below poverty line strata of society.

In rural areas children work in various agricultural and allied activities such as sowing reaping, grazing cattle, keeping a watch on (fields) birds and beasts, collect fuel, water fishing and such other activities. In village children work as family labour in the occupation of the family alongwith other family members, or they work as part of contract family labour where men, women and children all work together, or as hired wage labour and even as bonded labour (to repay debts of parents).

In urban areas majority of children work in small factory units or households units, in shops, restaurants, hotels, in garages and petrol pumps, and domestic servants as petty hawkers, rag pickers and often in illegal antisocial activities like prostitution, in smuggling goods, liquor and drug traffic. The concentration of child labour is found in many hazardous industries such as glass making units in Ferozabad, match making and fire works units in Sivakasi in Tamilnadu, carpet weaving in Jammu and Kashmir and in the whole of Mirzapur Bhadohibelt in U.P., diamond polishing/cutting and jari in Surat, Gujarat, lockmaking in Aligarh, tea plantations in Darjeeling area. Employers engage middle men or contractors, to bring large number of children to work for them from nearby rural and interior areas. They lure them with the advance money, often pressurise parents, even kidnap children to work in these factory units. The working and living conditions is utterly inadequate; children work in unsafe surroundings, crowded, dingy places in severe health hazards. They are provided food and make-believe shelter. They are paid meagre wages or paid low piece rate, sometimes nothing is paid in the beginning as they consider them as apprentices. Children work long hours from early dawn to late night without rest periods and holidays in crowded dark dingy, unsafe surroundings adversely affecting their health and growth. There is no education or training of skills, no recreation or leisure, even home and family environment is denied to those children. According to one estimate about 40,000 children work in Sivakasi, 20,000 in fish freezing and allied work in Quilon, Kerala, 23,000 in mines near Meghalaya 6000 to 7000 in glass factory in Ferozabad, 1300 in Kerala handloom units, 50,000 to 1.5 lakh in Mirzapur Bhadohi carpet belt in U.P.

Working and living conditions are equally deplorable when children work in cities in restaurants, hostels, shops, or petrol pumps, garages etc., so many and migrant child works long hours for meagre wages, and sleep on pavements or nearly the work place in dingy dirty places with no toilet/bathing facility. Compared to this working children of agriculture and allied work are better off, there is less health hazard, no crowding and they have open air surroundings.

Exploitation

Exploitation of working children is multifold, they are paid less, made to work long hours without rest in stress and fatigue, in accident prone situations, and many studies have narrated the health hazards they are exposed to and even accidental deaths, that take place.

Again they are deprived of education, recreation, play and leisure even normal family living. When employers provide for their food and shelter, worst food and shelter is offered, to them. They remain malnourished and exposed to heat, cold dirt crowding with no bathing and toilet facility.

Causes

1. Main cause appears to be utter-poverty, unemployment on intermittent and under-employment of parents in the family. Utter poverty conditions compel parents to send their children to work.

2. Vested interest of employers is another factor; in their greed to maximise profits and minimise cost they flout factory regulations. Employers prefer children; as they are cheap labour, honest, hard working at the same time docile and meek work force; easy to control and discipline (could be beaten up) humiliated and made to work long hours without grudge; easy to hire and fire. It is found that pockets of child labour concentration are also draught prone areas and areas of high adult unemployment.

3. Parent's attitudes and socio-cultural factors are another set of factors responsible for child labour. Unaware of the needs of children and rights of children poor backward parents look upon employment of children as proper way of socialising them, making them grow and mature early. Indian tradition of home based occupation finds it natural when children are engaged in some work at an early age, so parents find it natural even when children are sent to work outside. Parents hold traditional values of patriarchal family living as they socialise boys and girls; look upon boys as bread winners and girls as house wives, so socialise girls for work and life in the domestic sphere and boys in the work-vocation of their father or some other work outside. This results into early employment in occupations of boys and girls in feminine type of work. Often orphans, children from broken homes run away to big cities and works as migrant child labour.

4. *Education:* Limited success in providing compulsory education to all boys and girls in 5-14 age group is another important factor for child labour. A child sent to school is a child saved from exploitation, again it can enter the labour market with better skill. However, present educational system fails to motivate poor parents to send their children to school or for informal education. In the study of socialisation of boys and girls among lower strata castes communities in Ahmedabad, it was found that poor parents, find limited functional value of education; they want to given only couple of years of schooling to their girls; so that they can read, write and do simple arithmetic; girls are either not sent to school at all, or sent to school for few years only. Often girls are held up at home for domestic chores, baby sitting or for household economic activity and then with drawn completely by the time they reach adolescence, training for marriage and life at in-laws family makes them confined to domestic sphere, or they work in the company of other women as self-employed or domestic workers, while poor parents want to give more education and skill for new type or jobs or occupations to their boys. School enrollment of boys is very high in urban as well as in developing rural

areas as compared to girls. And school fails to retain students, till they complete atleast secondary education. Often school curricula, quality of teaching and other activities do not equip them with skills, enabling their easy entry in the labour market. Often even three "Rs." are not properly acquired by school-going children, and, parents as well as boys feel highly frustrated. Again, the prevalence of educated unemployment dissuades them from keeping children in the school for long. Boys with some education do not like to take to earning activity of their parents in the unorganised sector, nor do they get employment in the organised sector, they just roam about or often get involved in antisocial activities. All these highly discourage poor parents from the school system. High quality of school coupled with mid day meals, free books, dress even stipends can attract and retain poor children in the school. Unless educational system is overhauled and made to suit the needs of urban and rural pool, boys and girls would continue to enter labour force at an early age.

5. Failure of legislation; governmental effect is equally responsible for child labour particularly in the hazardous occupations. Legislation remains on paper, loopholes in the law are easily availed off by the employers and children are made to work in small or household units. Governmental administrators, factory inspectors often fail to do their job successfully, with the result, children continue to be exploited as child labour.

Results of government supported ten projects for enforcing complete ban on child labour and rehabilitation (providing for their health, nutritive food, education and occupational skills) in the major hazardous industries, are keenly awaited. Allocation of sufficient funds and efficient use of these is what the government needs to do. Voluntary organisations and trade unions need to work in the eradication of child labour programmes.

Strong political will and commitment to implement time bound programme for the graded eradication of child labour combined with efforts of voluntary organisations and trade unions, together can eradicate child labour from our society.

Clear goal of total ban on child labour with time-bound programme (for first ten years upto the age of ten and later on for children up to fourteen years of age) accompanied by rehabilitation of child worker needs to be taken.

MULTIPRONG STRATEGY

1. Modify parents' attitudes with respect to need of health, education, recreation for children, inculcate appropriate values with respect to rights of children and responsibilities of parents, special strategy is needed to emphasise girls' education and vocational skill training.
2. Strengthen compulsory education (formal and informal functional education), neighbourhood schools need attract, motivate and retain children and provide vocational skills to girls and boys.
3. Provide neighbourhood child-care-creche services so that girls are not retained at home for baby sitting when mother goes to work.

4. Use mass media for creating awareness with respect to needs of children and rights of children and awareness with respect to exploitatory child labour.
5. Strengthen employment generation, minimum wage and such other programmes to provide employment to men and women in the family.
6. Reorganise implementation of legislation pertaining to child labour and plan for rehabilitation of ex-child labour.
7. Cooperation of government and voluntary organisations including trade unions, and strong activist lobby is needed to eradicate child labour completely.

REFERENCES

1. Dr. Parveen Nagia, Child labour-cause-effect syndrome Janak Publishers Delhi 1987.
2. Manju Guta and Klaus (ed.) Child labour in India Vol. 1987.
3. *Atlas of the child in India* by Moonis Raza and Sudesh Nangia Concept Publishing Co. 1986.
4. *Child labour in India* (eds.), S. Mookherjee and Pushkar Pandya, Gandhi Labour Institute 1985.
5. *Working Children in India* by Khatu K.K. et. al., Baroda Operations Research Group 1983.
6. Papers presented at International seminar on child labour, Gandhi Labour Institute December 1987.
   A. Role of activists and child labour by Nandan Reddy Bangalore.
   B. Voluntary agencies and child labour (girls) some recommendations based on SEWA experiment by Renana Jhabvala.
   C. Exploitation of child worker in lock industry at Aligarh. By Neera Barra.
   D. Child labour in Darjeeling tea industry by Mahendra P. Lama.
   E. Child labour in carpet industry in Rajasthan by Manju Gupta.
   F. Measures of improving the working conditions of children in the carpet and bangle industries. By Champakalakshmi.
   G. Handicraft child labour in Jammu and Kashmir by M.L. Pandit.
   H. Earning profile and prospects for child labour in diamond processing units—a case-study of Surat, By Kashyap.
   I. Child labour in Jari industry—some possible explanations. By Rohit D. Desai.
   J. A study of working children in Baroda city by Kamala Srinivasan.
   K. An action plan for abolition of child labour in urban areas of Gujarat by Dr. Bhaskar Vyas and Aruna Lakhani.
   L. Health hazards of child workers at petrol pump, Agate industry and glass bangle industry. By S.H. Clerk.
   M. Elementary education and child work by Parveen Nangia.
7. Kulkarni Mana N., Match making children in Sivakasi, *Economic and Political Weekly* Vol. XVIII No. 43 October 1983.
8. Amiya Rao, Silicosis death of slate workers. *Economic and Political Weekly,* Vol. 15 Nov., 1986.
9. Sharma A.M., Child labour in Indian Industry, *Indian Journal of Social Work* Vol. 40, No. 3 October 1979.
10. Usha Kanhere, *Women and Socialisation,* A study of their status in lower strata castes communities in a metropolis, Ahmedabad. Mittal Publications, Delhi, 1987.

37

LAW AND CHILD LABOUR

The Concept

In India, there is hardly any statutory provision, which defines the term 'child labour' in precise terms. Even minimum age for admission to employment in different vocations has been differently fixed by different legislative provisions mainly due to the variations in the nature of operations in which children are employed.

However, child labour, in restricted sense, means the employment of children in gainful occupations with a view to adding to the labour income of the family which are dangerous to their health and deny them the opportunities of development (Kulshreshtha, 1978: 82). Thus, the supply of child labour is governed mainly by two factors: (1) non-availability of adult labour in the family; (2) inadequate income of the family. The latter may be due to (a) inadequate number of adult workers in the family, and (b) unemployment and/or under employment of adult labourers in the family. The demand for child labour, on other hand, arises because of its lower wage cost compared to adult.

Child Labour Legislation

Laws are made for the protection and promotion of the interests of people with a view to ensuring them happy and satisfying standards of life. They derive their social sanctions from various national and international convenants. Among developing countries, India has been playing a leading role in advocating protection of children being an active member of international organisations by signing various international declarations and agreements prepared and declared by these organisations. Special mention may be made of the Declaration of Rights of Child (1959) and United Nations Conventions on The Rights of Child which has become an International Law on Sept. 2, 1990. Article 32 of this Convention deals with child labour. This section envisages fixation of minimum age for admission to employment, appropriate regulation of the hours and conditions of employment and appropriate penalties or other sanctions to ensure the effective enforcement of these provisions.

ILO on Child Labour and India's Position

India is a party to ILO and as such has an obligation to adopt the ILO Conventions on Child Labour. Till now, in respect of children and young persons, the ILO has adopted 18 Conventions concerning their minimum age for admission to employment, medical examination and night work. On these subjects nine recommendations have also been adopted by ILO.

Conventions related to minimum age for employment have been as under:

Name of Convention	*Main Provisions*	*Ratification/Non-ratification by India*
1	*2*	*3*
1. Minimum Age (Industry) Convention (No. 5), 1919.	Prohibits employment of children below 14 years of age in any public and private industrial undertaking other than the undertaking in which only family members are employed.	Ratified. Consequently Factories Act, 1948; Mines Act, 1952; Employment of Children Act, 1938; Beedi and Cigar Workers (Conditions of Employment) Act, 1966; Motor Transport Workers Act, 1961 were passed.
2. Minimum Age (Sea) Convention (No. 7), 1920.	Prohibits employment of children below 14 years of age on vessels, except those on which only the family members are employed.	Not ratified by India, mainly due to the fact that most of Indian Seaman are employed on foreign ships.
3. Minimum age (Agriculture) Convention (No. 18), 1921.	Lays down that child under 14 years should not be employed in public or private agricultural undertaking, except outside the hours fixed for school attendance.	Not ratified, because agriculture is the most unorganised sector in India.
4. Minimum Age (Trimmers and Stockers) Convention (No. 15), 1921.	Provides that young persons under 18 years of age should not be employed on vessels as Trimmers and Stockers.	Ratified and Merchant Shipping Act, 1958 was passed.
5. Minimum Age Employment (Non-industrial) Convention (No. 33), 1932.	Lays down that children under the age of 14 years who are required to attend primary schools should not be employed.	Not ratified, due to unorganised nature of labour.
6. Minimum Age (Sea) Convention (No. 58), (revised), 1937.	The convention raises the minimum age of children for admission to employment from 14 to 15 years.	Not ratified, due to reasons already given earlier in case of Convention No. 7.
7. Minimum Age (Industry) Convention (revised) (No. 57), 1937.	This Convention raises the minimum age for admission to industrial establishment from 14 years to 15 years.	Not ratified; Reasons not known.

1	2	3
8. Minimum Age (Non-industrial employment) Convention (revised) (No. 68), 1937.	This Convention has special provisions for India. Mention may be made of the provision that children under 13 years of age are not to be employed in non-industrial occupations such as shops, offices, hotels, restaurants, places of public entertainment etc.	Not ratified, due to the difficulties of review of Shops and Commercial Establishments Acts passed by State Legislatures.
9. Minimum Age (underground work) Convention (No. 123), 1965.	Provides that minimum age for working underground mines should be fixed in consultation with, employers' and workers' organisations and that such age should not be less than 16 years.	Ratified and Mines Act, 1952 was passed.
10. Minimum Age Convention (No. 123), 1973.	Lays down 16 years as minimum age for admission to employment.	Not ratified, may be due to difficulties in review of different Acts.

Besides the above mentioned Conventions, two more Conventions have been adopted by ILO.

1. The White Lead (Painting) Convention (No. 123), 1921 prohibits, the employment of male children under 18 years of age and all female children in painting work of an industrial character involving the use of while lead or sulphate of lead or other products containing those pigments. India has ratified this Convention.

2. Radiation Protection Convention (No. 123), 1968 prohibits employment of persons under 16 years in work involving ionising radiations. India has ratified this Convention.

Regarding medical examination of young persons the Conventions adopted by ILO have been as under:

Name of Convention	*Main Provisions*	*Ratification/Non-ratification by India*
1	2	3
1. Medical Examination of young persons (Sea) Convention (No. 16), 1921.	Lays down the need of medical certificate of fitness by authorised doctor from young persons under 18 years for an employment on any vessel, other than vessel upon which family members are employed.	Ratified

1	2	3
2. Medical Examination of young persons (sea farers) Convention (No. 73), 1946.	Requires the production of medical certificate attesting the fitness of young person for work for which he is to be employed at sea.	Not ratified, reasons not known.
3. Medical Examination of young persons (Industry) Convention (No. 77), 1946.	Lays down that children and young persons under 18 years (16 years in India) should not be admitted to employment in an "Industrial undertaking" without thorough examination of physical fitness and this fitness should be subjected to medical supervision until he has attained the age of 18 years (16 years in case of India) in occupation involving high health risks and re-examination of fitness until at least the age of 21 years (19 years in case of India).	Not ratified. Some provisions have been incorporated in Factories Act, 1948.
4. Medical Examination of young persons (Non-industrial occupations) Convention (No. 78), 1946.	Requires that children and young persons under 18 years should not be allowed to work in non-industrial occupations unless they have been found fit for work in question by thorough medical examination.	Not ratified, due to unorganised nature of work.
5. Medical Examination of young persons (Underground work) Convention (No. 124), 1965.	Provides annual examination of all young persons below 21 years of age for fitness for employment underground in Mines.	Not ratified, reasons not known.

Conventions related to night work of young persons have been as below:

Name of Convention	*Main Provisions*	*Ratification/Non-ratification by India*
1	2	3
1. Night work of young persons (Industry), Convention (No. 6), 1991.	Provides that young persons upto 18 years of age are not to be employed during night in any public or private undertaking.	Ratified
2. Night work of young persons (Non-industrial occupations) Convention (No. 79), 1946.	Prohibits the employment of children under 12 years in non-industrial occupation during night.	Not ratified, due to unorganised nature of work.

1	2	3
3. Nightwork of young persons (Industry) Convention (No. 90), (Revised), 1948.	Night means 12 consecutive hours. Industrial undertaking includes only mines, factories, railways and post. Lays down that young persons upto age of 18 years are not to be employed during night in any public or private undertaking.	Ratified

Apart from these Conventions, the ILO has adopted certain recommendations and resolutions for the protection of children and young persons. Mention may be made of the recommendations entitled the Minimum Age (Non-industrial Employment) Recommendation (No. 41), 1932; The Minimum Age (Family Undertaking) Recommendation (No. 52), 1937; The Minimum Age (Coal Mines) Recommendation (No. 96), 1953; The Minimum Age (Underground Work) Recommendation (No. 124), 1965; Lead Poisoning (Women and Children) Recommendation (No. 4), 1919; Unemployment (Young persons) Recommendations (No. 45), 1935 etc. and resolution adopted in 1945 which drew attention towards maintenance, health, education, employment, protection and general welfare of children and young persons.

Constitutional Provisions

The framers of Constitution realised the need for putting curbs on child labour: (Govt. of India, Indian Constitution)

Article 15(3) enables state to make special provisions for women and children.

Article 24 prohibits employment of children below 14 years of age in any factory or mine or in any other hazardous work.

Article 23 prohibits forced labour.

The chapter IV of the Indian Constitution contains specific directions in relation to welfare of child.

Article 39(e) maintains that tender age of children should not be abused.

Article 39(f) makes it obligatory on the part of the state to direct its policies towards securing opportunities and facilities for the healthy development of children.

Article 42 provides provisions for securing just and humane conditions of work and maternity relief.

Article 43 strives for a living wage, conditions of work ensuring a decent standard of life and full employment of leisure and social and culture opportunities to all workers.

National Policy for Children

The Government of India adopted a National Policy for Children through a resolution dated August 22, 1974. This policy envisaged balanced growth of children. The measures of the balanced growth of children include that:

1. No child under 14 years shall be permitted to be engaged in any hazardous occupation or be made to undertake heavy work.
2. Children shall be protected against neglect, cruelty and exploitation.

Child Labour Legislation: Brief History

(A) Before Adoption of Constitution

The Indian Factories Act, 1881 was the first legislation passed with a view to regulating the hours of work of children working in Factories. After this, various legislative enactments such as the Indian Factories Act, 1891; The Mines Act, 1901; The Factories Act 1911; Inland Steam Vessels Act, 1917; The Factories (Amendment) Act, 1922; The Indian Mines Act, 1923; The Factories (Amendment) Act, 1926; The Indian Ports (Amendment) Act, 1931; The Tea Districts Emigrant Labour Act, 1932; The Children (Pledging of Labour) Act, 1933; The Factories Act, 1934; The Indian Mines (Amendment) Act, 1935; The Employment of Children Act, 1938; The Factories Act, 1948; The Minimum Wages Act, 1948; The Employment of Children (Amendment) Act, 1949.

In this period, formation of International Labour Organisation (ILO) in 1919, release of Report of the Royal Commission on Labour (Whitley Commission) in 1931; adoption of The Minimum Age (Industry) Convention in 1937 by the 23rd Session of International Labour Conference in which a special Article (Article 7) was incorporated regarding India; submission of Report of the Labour Investigation Committee (Rege Committee) in 1946 have also affected the Child Labour Legislation.

(B) After Adoption of The Constitution

In 1950, The Constitution of India was adopted which prohibits employment of children upto 14 years; guarantees them protection against exploitation and makes provision for free and compulsory education for children. After this, various legislations related to child labour were passed. These legislations are: The Employment of Children (Amendment) Act, 1949; The Plantation Labour Act, 1951; The Employment of Children (Amendment) Act, 1951; Mines Act, 1952; The Factories (Amendment) Act, 1954; The Merchant Shipping Act, 1958; The Apprentices Act, 1961; The Motor Transport Workers Act, 1961; The Beedi and Cigar Workers (Condition of Employment) Act, 1966; The Radiation Protection Rules, 1971 made under the Atomic Energy Act, 1962; The Employment of Children (Amendment) Act, 1978; and Child Labour (Prohibition and Regulation) Act, 1986.

The other events affecting the child labour legislation during this period are: submission of Reports by Rural Labour Enquiry Committee in 1965, National Commission on

Labour in 1969; and The Committee on Child Labour in 1979; The Minimum Age Convention in 1973; Minimum Age Recommendation in 1973; adoption of National Policy on Children in 1974; declaration of 1979 as International year of child; and United Nations Convention on the Rights of Children, 1990.

Besides these Central Acts, various state legislatures have also passed Acts for regulating conditions of employment in shops and commercial establishments.

Some of the important legislations providing legal protection to child labour in various occupations are being discussed in detail in ensuring paragraphs.

The Children (Pledging of Labour) Act (Govt. of India, 1933)

From Sept., 1971, this Act has been extended to whole of India. The basic purpose of the Act is to prohibit the pleding of labour of children. For the purpose of the application of the provisions of this Act, child means a person who has not completed the age of 15 years (Section-2). The Act lays down that an agreement, oral or written, expressed or implied, made by parent or guardian of child in consideration of some payment or benefit for causing or allowing the services of a child to be utilised in any employment, shall be void (section-3). However, it is worth mentioning that an agreement without detriment to the child and made in consideration of any benefit, other than reasonable wages to be paid for the services of the child and terminable at not more than a week's notice will not be void (section-2 proviso). The Act makes provision for fine upto Rs. 50 in case of parent or guardian is found guilty of making an agreement to pledge the labour of the child (section-4), upto Rs. 200 for making with parent or guardian agreement to pledge the labour of the child (section-5) and upto Rs. 200 for employing a child whose labour has been pledged (section-6).

The Employment of Children Act (Govt. of India, 1938)

This Act extends to whole of India and aims at regulating the employment of children in certain establishments. The Act prohibits employment of children who have not completed 15 years of age in any occupation connected with the transport of passengers, goods or mails by railways; or connected with cinder picking, clearing of an ashpit or building operation in the railway premises; or connected with the work in a catering establishment at a railway station, involving the movement of the vendour or any other employee of the establishment for one platform to another or into or out of the moving train; or connected with the work relating to the construction of railway station or with any other work where such work is done in close proximity or between the railway lines; or connected with a port authority within the limits of any port (section 3(1)).

The Act permits the employment of child of more than 15 years and less than 17 years in any of the above mentioned occupations on the condition that the child is allowed a rest interval of at least 12 consecutive hours in a day which shall include at least 7 consecutive hours between 10 P.M. and 7 A.M. (Section 3(2)). However, this shall not apply to children employed as apprentices or trainees (Section 3(2), proviso).

The Act further prohibits the employment of children below 14 years of age in workshops connected with Beedi making, carpet weaving, cement manufacturing including bagging of the cement, cloth painting, dyeing, weaving, manufacture of matches, explosive and fireworks, mica cutting and splitting, shellac manufacture, soap manufacture, tanning and wool cleaning (Section 3(3)). However, if any of these processes carried on in any workshop by the occupier with the aid of his family only without employing any hired labour or in any school established, assisted or recognised by the state Government, employment of children below the age of 15 years shall not be prohibited (section 3(3), proviso). The Act also lays down that railway and port authorities to maintain registers showing names, dates of birth, rest intervals etc. of children under 17 years (Section 3(E)).

The penalty for the breach of the provisions of Act is simple imprisonment upto one month or fine upto 500 or both (Section-4). In Uttar Pradesh, the Act has been extended to the brass-ware and glass bangle industries also.

Factories Act (Govt. of India, 1948)

The Act extends to whole of India and applies to establishment employing 10 or more workers with power or 20 more workers without power (Section-2(m)).

Under this Act, 'child' means a person who has not completed the fifteenth years of age (Section 2(c). A 'Young person' is defined either a child or adolescent (Section 2(d)). Adolescents are those who have completed his fifteenth year but not eighteenth year (Section 2(b)). Thus, young persons may be divided into three categories:

(a) Those, who are under fourteen years, are prohibited from entering in employment in factories (Section 67).

(b) Persons who are between 14 and 15 years can be employed under certain restrictions laid down under section 68, 69 and 71 to 75 of the Act. These are as follows:

 (i) Such persons can work in the factory only when they have been granted a certificate of fitness and carry while they are at work, a token having reference of such certificate (Section-68);

 (ii) Certificate of fitness is issued by certifying surgeon who, after examination, certifies whether the person is fit to work in factory as a child or as an adult (Section-69);

 (iii) The Act lays down that children should not work more than four hours a day (Section-71(1)(a));

 (iv) They should not work at night i.e. twelve consecutive hours including the period from 10 P.M. to 6 A.M. (Section-71(1) (b);

(v) The period of work is to be limited to two shirts which should not overlap and spreadover more than five hours; each child has to be employed in one relay which normally will not be changed more frequently than once in a period of 30 days (Section-71(2)).

(vi) They should not be employed in two separate factories on the same day (Section 71(4)).

(vii) The employer should display a notice regarding the periods of work (Section-72(1));

(viii) Hours of work of the child workers shall be in accordance with the period of work of children displayed in the notice.

(ix) A register for child workers shall be maintained by employer (Section-73); and

(x) Inspectors have been empowered for re-examination of any such person by surgeon and he may prohibit the employment till the examination is made (Section-75).

(c) Persons between 15 and 18 years of age are employed as adults if they possess a certificate of fitness issued by the certifying surgeon and they also carry a token of such certificate (Section-68). The adolescents under 17 years of age are permitted to work at night (Section-70(1), proviso).

The Act also prohibits young persons to clean, lubricate or adjust any part of prime mover or transmission machinery while the prime mover or transmission machinery is in motion or to clean, lubricate or adjust any part of any machine if the cleaning, lubrication or adjustment thereof would expose the young persons to risk of injury from any moving part either of that machine or of any adjacent machinery (Section-22(2)). Employment of young persons on dangerous machines has been prohibited unless they have been fully instructed regarding the possible dangers and precautions and have received sufficient training in work at such machines or are under adequate supervision of experts (Section 23(1)). Employment of children in any part of the factory for pressing cotton in which cotton opener is at work, is normally prohibited (Section-27).

Apart from weekly day of rest, the Act provides that every child worker who has worked for a period of 240 days or more in a factory during a Calendar Year is entitled during the subsequent year for leave with wages at the rate of one day for every 15 days of work as against every 30 days in case of an adult workers (Section-79).

The State Government is empowered by this Act to make rules regarding maximum weights which they may be lifted by adolescent and children (Section-34(2)).

The Act prescribes penalty of imprisonment of two months or fine upto 1000 rupees or both in case of using false certificate of fitness (Section-98) and of a fine upto 1000 rupees on parent or guardian in case of double employment of children (Section-99).

Minimum Wages Act (Govt. of India, 1948

This Act makes provision for fixation of minimum rates of wages in certain employments which have been specified by appropriate Government in the schedule of the Act. The Act maintains some expressions of adult, adolescent and child as in case of Factories Act, 1948. The Act does not make any specific provisions except that it says that different minimum rates of wages may be fixed for adults, adolescents and children (Section-3). Rule 24 of the Minimum Wages (Central) Rules, 1950 provides that in the case of a child the number of hours in a normal working day shall be 4½. Thus, it can be concluded that the Minimum Wages Act provides for a work day of 4½ hours and differential rates of minimum for child workers.

The Plantation Labour Act (Govt. of India, 1951)

This Act extends to whole of India except the State of Jammu and Kashmir. All tea coffee, rubber, cinchona and cordmory plantations measuring 5 hectares or more and employing 15 or more persons and covered under this Act (Section-1 (4a). A child (below 14 years) or an adolescent between 15-18 years can not be employed for work unless he is certified fit for work by a surgeon (Section-26). The certificate of fitness is given by a certifying surgeon who certifies that the person being examined by him is fit to work as a child or as an adolescent. Certificate remains valid for a period of 12 months after which it may be renewed (Section-27). Use of a false certificate of fitness is punishable by imprisonment which may extend to one month or with fine upto Rs. 50 or both (Section-34).

This Act makes the provisions for education as the responsibility of the employer (Section-14) and so is for housing (Section-15) and medical (Section-10) and recreational facilities (Section-13).

The Mines Act (Govt. of India, 1952)

This Act covers whole of India (Section-1(2). For the purpose of the Act, mine includes all excavations where any operation for the purpose of searching for or obtaining minerals is carried out (Section-2(j)). The Act prohibits employment of persons (below 18 years) in any mine or part thereof (Section-40) and also their presence in any part of the mine above ground where any operation connected with or incidental to any mining operation is being carried out (Section-45). However, apprentices and other trainees (from 16 years to 18 years of age) may be allowed to work under proper supervision by the manager, but in case of trainees, prior approval of Chief Inspector or an Inspector is necessary (Section-40).

The Act prescribes punishment of fine upto Rs. 500 in case of employment of persons below 18 years (Section-68). For contravention of any other provision of the Act, there is provision of imprisonment upto three months or fine upto Rs. 1000 or both (Section-73).

The Merchant Shipping Act, 1958

This Act applies to sea going ships registered in India. The Act prohibits employment of children under 15 years in a ship, except in a school ship or training ship; or in ship governed by family members, or in a home trade ship of less than two hundred tons gross; or where such person to be employed on nominal wages and will be in the charge of his father or other adult near male relatives (Section-109). The Act restricts employment of a person below the age of 18 years as a trimmers or stockers in any ship, except in a school ship or training ship or in a ship which is mainly propelled otherwise than by steam. It is worth mentioning that a person more than 16 years of age may be employed to work as a trimmer or stoker on a coasting ship provided he is employed in accordance with the prescribed conditions (Section-110(2)). Young persons over sixteen years of age may be employed on other ships also in case persons above 18 years of age are not available and that two such persons are employed to do the work in place of one person over 18 years of age (Section 110(3)). Such young persons, if employed, are required to produce medical certificate (Section-111).

A list or register of young persons shall be maintained in the ship (Section-112). The Act empowers Government to make necessary rules regarding employment of young persons on and when needed (Section-113). For contravention of its provisions, the act provides a penalty of fine upto Rs. 50 (Section 436(2)), read with the table appended thereto.

The Motor Transport Workers Act, 1961

The Act extends to whole of India and covers every motor transport undertaking employing 5 or more persons. The State Governments are authorised to apply all or any of the provisions of this Act to any motor transport undertakings employing less than 5 workers (Section-1). The Act prohibits employment of persons under 14 years of age in any capacity in the motor transport undertaking (Section-21). Without the grant of certificate of fitness, an adolescent is prohibited to work (Section 22). Such certificate is required at the intervals of one year (Section-23). Adolescents can work only for 6 hours including a rest interval of half-an-hour and also between 10 A.M. and 6 P.M. only (Section-14). The contravention of the provisions of the Act shall be punishable with imprisonment upto three months or fine upto five hundred rupees or both (Section-31).

The Appendices Act, 1961

This Act extends to whole of India (Section-1) and applies to any area or to any industry in any area notified by the Central Government (Section-1(4)). The Act lays down that a person shall not be qualified for being engaged as an apprentice to undergo apprenticeship training in any designated trade unless he is not less than fourteen years of age; and satisfied such standards of education and physical fitness as may be prescribed (Section-3). The Act prescribes that in case of minor, the contract of apprenticeship has to be entered into by guardian (Section 4(1)) and it should be registered with the Apprenticeship Advisor (Section-4(2)).

According to Rule 8 of Apprentice Rule 1962, the weekly ours of work of apprentices have been as follows:

1. Total number of weekly hours—42 to 48 hours (including the time spent on Related Instructions).
2. Apprentices undergoing basic training shall ordinarily work for 42 hours per week including the time spent on the Related Instructions.
3. During the second year, apprentices shall work for 42-45 hours per week including the time spent on Related Instructions.
4. During the third and subsequent years apprentices shall work for the same number of hours per week as the workers in the trade in the establishment in which they are undergoing their training.

No Trade apprentice shall be engaged in apprenticeship training between 10 P.M. and 6 A.M. except with the prior approval of Apprenticeship Advisor who will accord the approval either in the interest of the training of apprentice or in public interest (Rule 8(2)).

The Atomic Energy Act, 1962

In 1971, The Radiation Protection Rules have been framed under Section-30 of the Act. Rule 5 prohibits the employment of persons who have not completed eighteenth year as radiation workers except with the prior written permission of the competent authority i.e. an officer or authority appointed for this purpose by the Central Government by issuing necessary notification.

The Beedi and Cigar Workers (Conditions of Employment) Act, 1966

The Act extends to whole of India except the State of Jammu and Kashmir (Section-1). It covers all industrial premises wherein any manufacturing process connected with making of beedi or cigar or both is being, or is ordinarily carried on with or without the aid of power (2 (i)). The Act prohibits the employment of children (below 14 years) in any such premises (Section-24). The employment of young persons between 14 to 18 years is prohibited between 7 P.M. to 6 A.M. (Section-25). Young persons are entitled to annual leave with wages at the rate of one day for every 15 days of work performed by them during previous Calendar Year (Section 26(1)(ii)). The Act provides penalties for breach, which may be for the first offence, with fine which may extend to Rs. 250 and for a second or any subsequent offence with imprisonment for a term which shall not be less than one month or more than six months or with fine which shall not be less than Rs. 100 or more than Rs. 500 or with both (Section-33(1)).

State Shops and Establishment Acts

These Acts were passed with a view to regulating the conditions of work of workers in Shops and Commercial Establishments. These Acts prohibit the employment of children in shops, commercial establishments, restaurants, hotels etc. The age of children varies from 12 to 15 years. Night employment of children in shops and commercial establishments is prohibited and the daily working hours are generally upto 5 hours, although they range from 3 to 7 hours a day in different states with half an hour to one hour break after 3-4 hours of work.

Besides these Acts, the Contract Labour (Regulation and Abolition) Act, 1970 and the Bonded Labour System (Abolition) Act, 1976 have considerably affected child labour in India, though their are no specific provisions under the Act pertaining to employment of children.

The Child Labour (Prohibition and Regulation) Act, 1986

This Act extends to whole of India (Section-1) and draws a distinction between hazardous and non-hazardous operations. According to the provisions of the Act, no child (below 14 years of age) can be employed or permitted to work in any occupation connected with transport of passengers, goods or mails by railways; cinderpicking, clearing of an ashpit or building operation in the railway premises; work in a catering establishment at railway stations involving the movement of vendour or any other employee of the establishment from one platform to another or into or out of a moving train; work relating to the construction of a railway station or with any other work where such work is done in close proximity to or between the railway lines; and a port authority within the limits of any port (Section-3) read with the Schedule Part-A), and some processes connecting with Beedi making, carpet weaving, cement manufacturing, cloth printing, manufacture of matches, explosives and fire works, mica cutting, soap manufacturing, schellac manufacture, wool cleaning, building and construction industry, tanning etc. (Section-3 read with Schedule Part-B). The Act empowers Central Government for making amendments in Part-A and B of the Schedule (Section-4). For purpose of getting advice for making the above mentioned amendments in the Schedule, The Central Government may appoint Child Labour Technical Advisory Committee and one or more subcommittees (Section-5).

Part III of this Act (to be enforced on such date as the Central Government, by notification in official Gazette, appoint, and different dates may be appointed for different states and for different classes of establishments) consists of the provisions of regulation of conditions of work of children. These provisions are applicable to an establishment or a class of establishments in which none of the occupations or processes referred to in section-3 is carried on (Section-6). These provisions have been made applicable in Zari making and Embroidery work carried out in Delhi and Uttar Pradesh. Precious Stone Polishing work of Gujarat and Rajasthan, and Slate and Slate pencil manufacturing of Madhya Pradesh and Uttar Pradesh by the Central Government (Notification No. S.O. 757(E) dated August 3, 1987). Child is not permitted to work in excess of such number of hours as may be prescribed for such establishment or class of establishments (Section-7(1); to work for more than three hours without a rest (interval of at least one hour (Section-7(2) and to work between 7 P.M. to 8 A.M. (Section-7(4). The occupier is also directed by this Act to prepare and maintain a register of Children employed or permitted to work (Section-11). The appropriate Government has been authorised to make rules regarding health and safety of the working children (Section-13).

The penalty for violation of the provisions of the Act has been enhanced. According to this Act, any person found guilty of violation of the provisions of the Act may be fined not less than Rs. 10,000 and not more than Rs. 20,000 or imprisonment for not less than 3 months and not more than one year or with both (Section 14(1). For repetition of the offence imprisonment shall be not less than 6 months and not more than 2 years. (Section-14(2)).

These penal provisions are also applicable in mines, factories, merchant shipping and motor transport (Section-15(2)).

Despite these legislative enactments, India has the largest work force of child labour in world. In India, child labour is spread from Kashmir handmade carpets to Tamil Nadu (Sivakasi) match factory. According to 1981 Census, the number of child labour is more than 13 millions and 17.6 millions according to the National Sample Survey and 44 millions according to the study of the Operational Research Group (ORG), Baroda. Whatever the number the fact remains that child labour is commonly seen in different places doing different kinds of activities unsuited to their health, well being and development. The reasons may be many but failure of legislation pertaining to child labour is one of the important reasons for perpetuating this situation. Legislative deficiencies are many, some of them are as follows:

1. The basic premise of child labour legislation of India has been based on the assumption that child labour is harmful and it should be eradicated, which is open to question in developing counties in general, and India, in particular, where child labour is an economic asset for poor families.
2. Various segments of economy such as factories employing less than 10 workers with use of power 20 workers without use of power; small plantations, air transport, inland vessels, fishing vessels, home ships of less than 200 tones gross, agriculture and other unorganised sectors of economy are still untouched by child labour legislation.
3. Weal enforcement machinery in form of too small inspectorate of laws related to child labour is another factor for failure of these legislations. The peculiar socio-economic environment prevailing in the country makes it difficult to eradicate child labour.
4. Due to the ignorance and illiteracy, the law is also evaded at different places and at different points of time.
5. These laws also do not meet the international standard. Regarding minimum age, Indian laws fulfil ILO standards by and large in mines and transport but they are deficient in case of other industrial and non-industrial occupations, plantations and agriculture. Regarding medical examination of Adolescents,

ILO conventions require that in occupation involving high health risks, the age upto which medical examination is required shall be at least 21 years. It is also surprising to note that there is no provision for medical examination for working in mines above ground.

6. Commenting on child labour legislation, Report of the Committee on Child Labour (Govt. of India, 1979) observed, "...historically, legislation was passed not with the focus on the employment of the children or, for that matter, persons falling under any other age group or any particular general category, but with reference to the need to regulate employment in a particular industry and when such need arose."

Thus, at the end, it can be suggested that child labour legislation should be organised and unified as well as extended to occupations in the unorganised sector, like carpet weaving, domestic work, agriculture etc. The legislation should clearly make distinction between hazardous and non-hazardous occupations for the children. In hazardous occupations it should be strictly banned and in non-hazardous occupations, steps should be taken for gradual withdrawal of children from work by providing adequate facilities of education, nutrition, medical aid and social security benefits. Lastly, it is also necessary to sponsor and promote research studies on the impact of laws relating to child labour in order to bring out the strengths and weaknesses of the existing legislations (NIPCCD, 1982, p. 10).

REFERENCES

1. Government of India (1979), *Report of the Committee on Child Labour,* New Delhi.
2. Govt. of India (1933), The Children (Pledging of Labour) Act.,
3. Govt. of India (1938), The Employment of Children Act.
4. Govt. of India (1948), Factories Act.
5. Govt. of India (1948), Minimum Wages Act.
6. Govt. of India (1951), The Plantation Labour Act.
7. Kulshreshtha, J.C., (1978), *Child Labour in India,* Ashish Publishing House, New Delhi.
8. NIPCCD (1982), *Report of the National Seminar on Child and the Law* (November 30 to December 2, 1982), Govt. of India—Indian Constitution.

38

CHILD LABOUR: STRATEGY FOR COMBATING RISKS

Introduction

India has the largest number of world's working children. Most of these children are subjected to the worst forms of exploitation and abuse. The consequences of such exploitation are social and economic deprivation, psychological drawbacks, physical strain and mental trauma. The fact that majority of working children are finding themselves in the whirlpool of fearful existence and languishing in the quagmire of apathy for the imbroglio of growing up in abject poverty, speaks well of the indifference of the people talking of an ideal social set up. The callousness towards these children facing risks right from infancy, can be considered to be the worst form of milieu a society can envisage.

In a formulation of the Action Strategy for Eradication of child labour from the World,[1] at least two positive outcomes appeared to be visible. One, that the problem of child labour cannot be viewed in isolation, because it is a symptom of the disease which is spread at various levels. Nurkse's vicious circle of poverty fits very well into the phenomenon of child labour.[2] And two, that the phenomenon of child labour, which is a consequence of the exploitative system operating at the national and international levels, not only closes the future of millions of children in the third world countries, but also restricts the developmental prospects of these countries drastically.

This plain blunt truth has long been realised by many of the developed nations of the world like UK, Norway, Sweden, France, Germany, etc., who have been able to eradicate the system of child labour prevalent in their countries, to a considerable extent. Since these countries were at a higher stage of development, it was easier for them to work on the eradication of such a menace, but notwithstanding the where-withals of many of the underdeveloped nations and the potentials at their disposal, child labour in these countries at least, to start with, can be given a more decent form than what exists today.[3] In India, as in many other developing countries, child labour is an integral part of the early stages of development of the capitalist mode of production,[4] and for a considerable extent, its incidence depends on the economic and socio-cultural values of the society. Consequently, its eradication cannot be brought by legal measures alone, but by a series of reforms within the society, mass awareness campaigns, peoples' participation and involvement and strong trade unionism.[5] The process of eradication of child labour from such countries, is a long process, involving a gestation lag of decades.

It is for this reason that the Child Labour (Prohibition and Regulation) Act, 1986, was formulated both for the purposes of regulating the services of child labour, as well as, for prohibiting children from working in hazardous occupation.[6] The Act prohibits the employment of children who have not completed their fourteenth year in specific hazardous occupations. The Act also regulates the conditions of work of children engaged in activities permitted by law, stressing the role of health and safety measures.[7]

The Child Labour Act also provides for a Child Labour Technical Advisory Committee to advise the Central Government regarding occupations in which child labour should be prohibited. Where children are employed in non-hazardous occupation, the work according to this Act, must be regulated in accordance with paragraph III of this Act, which sets standards and conditions with regard to health and safety, maintenance of registers, periods and hours of work, overtime, weekly holidays and days of rest.

Five years have passed since the implementation of the Child Labour Act. The immediate gains accruing from this strategy have been apparently reaped by a large chunk of the child labour force in the organised sector.[8] Although this sector is constantly being monitored by the government machinery, children here too are exposed to various forms of hazards and are exploited in many ways, the employers easily flouting the rules set in paragraph III of the Act. It is however, the unorganised or the informal sector, comprising numerous small activity-oriented factories and industries, the large farm sector and the services sector where children are the most exploited and subjected to various forms of risks. In the formal or organised sector, characterised by large enterprises, using highly mechanised or capital intensive technologies, the scope of children's work relatively declines, vis-a-vis, the smaller enterprises, since child workers appear redundant and uneconomical in a production system using advanced technology and a reduced labour force. Bequele (Bequele, et. al., 1988) points out that the development of capital intensive production has the effect of displacing child labour, and this may occur entirely independently of any legislative intervention. This is, by and large, true of all economies, developed, developing, or underdeveloped. But more true is the fact that the unorganised sectors in agriculture, industry and services, in much of the developing world, children's lives are at risks, and they are subjected to several forms of hazards, despite various legislations.

This paper attempts at providing a typology of hazards working children are facing. It is only in the light of this typology that the risk factor among working children can be examined in the Indian context and a strategy formulated for combating such risks.

Towards A Typology of Hazardous Occupations

Hazardous occupations in India can broadly be classified into three broad categories or groups:

1. Intrinsically hazardous occupations.
2. Environmentally hazardous occupations.
3. Occupations with natural hazards.

1. Intrinsically Hazardous Occupations

Any occupation which allows a child to come into contact with harmful substances like chemicals, dust, fire, etc., may be termed intrinsically hazardous. There are countless number of factories or industries where hazards are intrinsic to given occupations. There are studies to show that children working in such occupations are facing the worst forms of health hazards. Although such occupations are hazardous for all workers, children are more prone to such occupational hazards, because they are in the process of growing up and attaining their full physical stature, their physique is not developed to resist different forms of hazards and also because they are not trained to work with precaution. Burra (Burra, 1986) reports that 90 per cent of workers in the glass factories of Ferozabad, where about fifty thousand children are working, contact pneumoconiosis, a condition which leads to tuberculosis. In the furnaces in the glass bangle and the glass blowing industry, the temperatures range from 700°C to 1800°C. The life span of the worker is reduced by a third because of the intense heat and dust (Burra, 1987). In a study reported by Kothari (Kothari, 1983) in the fireworks industry of Sivakasi, casualties in fire accidents are a common phenomenon. In some work situations, employers prefer to use children particularly in trenches and mines which are too narrow for a adults and these jobs may have the special risk of silicosis (Pitt, 1985) Iyengar (Iyengar, 1986) writes that children mixing chemicals in the boiler room get lungfulls of toxic fumes, suffer high degrees of intense heat and run the risk of being badly injured in fire accidents. Children who stamp frames on the metal sheet too suffer from heat and toxic fumes. Delay in removing and placing the heavy frames on the metal sheets can cause the entire frame to go up in flames, resulting in instant death. In the balloon factories of Dahanu in Maharashtra, children work continuously for nine hours each day, with a day off in the week. Medical reports about the factories state that inhalation of gas and acids continuously over a period of time can burn respiratory lining and cause pneumonia, broncho pneumonia, cough, breathlessness and even heart failure (Menon, 1985). In many industries, such as powerlooms, workers suffer from byssinosis. This disease is caused by cotton dust and fibre which get embedded in the lining of the lungs and causes fibrosis of the tissue. This reduces the normal capacity of the lungs and puts pressure on the surviving tissues. A patient of byssinosis is highly susceptible to bronchitis and tuberculosis. There are an estimated fifteen thousand children working in the powerloom industry of Bhiwandi in Maharashtra (Barse, 1985). Few studies have been reported from the slate industry of Mandsaur district in Madhya Pradesh (Mitra,

1980), Beedi workers in Kerala (Mohandas, 1960), and metalware industry in Moradabad (Kulshreshtha, 1980), all of which go to show that the conditions of work are intrinsically hazardous.

2. *Environmentally Hazardous Occupations*

Although in most of the intrinsically hazardous occupations, hazards caused due to improper environment also prevail, a vast majority of occupations create hazards caused due to the working environment, rather than work itself. Children working in the carpet weaving industry are regularly exposed to such hazards (Kanbargi, 1988). Continuous squatting can lead to leg and back deformities or water retention in the knees. Constant attention paid to colour combinations and intricate designs while weaving, can lead to eye fatigue and illness. The inhalation of wool dust can, in the long run, cause breathing problems, lung infections and even tuberculosis. These risks are aggravated by other factors, such as inadequate light, the absence of windows and ventilation, dirt floors and a lack of washing facilities. In the diamond polishing industry of Jaipur, ten thousand children work in slum like situations. The places of child's work are dark and ill ventilated. (Burra, 1988). Similarly, the diamond cutters of Surat work in badly lit rooms and very soon their eyesight is affected. These children are ruthlessly retrenched at the first sign of eye fatigue (Dayal, 1985). In many of the places, the hazards get intensified because of long hours of work (Burra, 1988).

3. *Occupations with Natural Hazards*

Many of the jobs may be non-hazardous for adults, but the situations under which children have to take up these jobs, make them hazardous. Occupations like shoe-shining, restaurant service, domestic work, rag picking, working in motor garage, and various types of jobs in the rural areas like looking after grazing animals, working in the fields, carrying loads on heads, looking after the house, etc. cause various types of physical hazards. Several studies (Shukla, 1984) show that children face a lot of health hazards working in small restaurants or dhabas or as domestic servants. Working in dhabas or restaurants, children undergo a lot of physical hazards like burning of hands while serving customers, cutting of fingers while using knife for cutting vegetables. They also undergo a lot of mental hazards listening to the abuses of customers as well as employers. Similar is the case with domestic servants, who, at times, have to slog continuously since early morning to late night. Many of the children are underfed and are given leftovers. They are most often not even given a proper place to sleep and enough clothes during winters. Shoe-shine boys and children working in garages as well as rag pickers are also subjected to various forms of exploitation like physical abuse, ill treatment, etc. They are made to work for long hours for a pittance, and often at times, without any money. Children working in the farm sector have to undertake a lot of strenuous work even from a very tender age, like lifting stacks, cutting crops or grazing animals in scorching heat. These are all occupations which make children prone to several physical complications. Discussing the typology of children's activity patterns, Rodgers and Standing (Rodgers and Standing, 1981) mention about children working as bonded labourers who are pledged by their parents in lieu of debt. Such children face the worst forms of hazards.

A Strategy for Combating Risks

The above analysis reveals that children working in different occupations are faced with serious risks to their health and physical development. Children are generally required to undertake tasks for which they are entirely unprepared physically. They also have to work for abnormally long periods. The occupations described above involve both long and short-term health risks. Some of the hazards, such as damage to eyesight or physical deformity, may not be immediately apparent, but may take some years to manifest. Sometimes children labour in ignorance of the risks they are taking and sometimes they are all too aware and yet have no alternative.

The employees very rarely take into account the physical susceptibility of working children, which is entirely different from that of adults. The working conditions of children, the nature of work and the situations forcing them into work, all subject them to severe health and safety hazards. Children are more liable than adults to suffer occupational injuries owing to inattention, fatigue, poor judgement and insufficient knowledge of work processes and also because the equipment, machinery, tools and layout of most work places are designed for adults (WHO, 1987). Studies also show that child workers have far more serious health problems than adults, even though both groups are exposed to the same working environment. In addition, large numbers of child labourers are at risk mainly because of the very early age at which they commence work. Children are especially sought after in activities highly unsuited for them because of their agility and speed (Mohsin, 1991). This applies particularly in industries where technologies are simple and production labour intensive.

A strategy for combating risks among working children can be formulated, taking into congnisance the situation existing (1) at the place of work and (2) outside the place of work. In a country like India, with a high incidence of child labour in hazardous occupations, although it is not possible to implement Article 39(e) and (f) of the Constitution,[9] at least in the short run, from the unorganised sector, the government should be extremely firm in prohibiting children working in intrinsically hazardous occupations in the organised sector.

As far as environmental hazards at the working places are concerned, the minimum requirements under the Factories Act, that is, of providing proper working conditions to children, should be fulfilled. All employers, violating the Factories Act, should be taken to task.

The machines and work designs creating hazards for children should be earmarked for adults and children should be strictly kept away from the use of such machines. If the tools and layouts at work places are in any way detrimental to children's health, they should not be given to children for use, even if the economic costs of such uses are lower.

Long hours of work and monotony, causing mental fatigue among children should be discouraged. Work timings in hazardous work should be specified, and work monotony should be broken through recreations.

The strategy adopted for working children outside the place of work should start with an intensive effort of poverty alleviation among such children. This can come about through a number of measures like free meals, an integrated strategy of non-formal education, proper living conditions, regular health checkups, proper wage policy, provision of self as well as wage employment opportunities to adult workers, etc. Although these measures have been talked about almost in all studies undertaken on child labour, their serious implementation could mitigate a lot of risks children have to face.

Last but not the least, such stupendous task cannot be undertaken by government alone. The non-governmental organisations will have to go a long way in identifying the risks working children are facing. They should help the government in solving the problems of children in hazardous occupations through undertaking researches in specific problem areas, and suggesting a set of intervention techniques (Mohsin, 1992).

NOTES

1. The draft of the Action Strategy for Eradication of Child Labour from the World was prepared by Indira Hirway and discussed in the last session of an International Seminar on Child Labour, organised by Gandhi Labour Institute and Antar Bharati, in 1985.
2. This has also been discussed in the cause-effect syndrome of child labour, a part of the paper prepared by Praveen Nangia, "Elementary Education and Child Worker in India: A policy perspective", and published in a book: *Towards Eradication of Child Labour*, ed. by Hirway, Indira, et. al., Oxford and IBH Publishing Co. Pvt. Ltd., 1991.
3. Even ILO, UNICEF, etc. have come to realise that it is not possible for the developing countries like India, Indonesia, Bangladesh and many others to abolish child labour completely in the near future. However, it is definitely possible to provide a better life style for millions of working child in such countries.
4. Indian society has been undergoing a stage of transition from the precapitalist to the capitalist mode of production characterised by the culture of metropolis, high incidence of rural-urban migration, technological improvements in modes of agricultural production, growth of small scale and cottage industries, ancillary to large and heavy industries, the mushroom and haphazard growth of the unorganised sectors, etc.
5. In fact, in many of the developed societies, Workers' Union have gone a long way in catering to the interests of working children. In India, the Concerned for Working Children, a Bangalore based group has, for the first time, talked of involving children in Unions for their own welfare.
6. All occupations related to rail and road transport, bidi (cigarette) making, carpet weaving, cloth printing, dyeing and weaving, the manufacture of shellac matches, cement, soap, explosives and fireworks, mica cutting and splitting, tanning', building and construction, factories, plantations and merchant shipping, come under the banner of hazardous occupations.
7. It outlines severe penalties for those violating the provisions both of this Act and of other related legislation. However, cases of such violations are seldom reported.

8. There are nearly 40,000 child workers in the firework industries of Sivakasi, 28,000 child workers in the mines in Meghalaya, 6000 to 7000 child workers in the glass factory at Ferozabad and about 20,000 child workers in the carpet weaving industry in Bhadoi and Mirzapur.
9. According to Article 29 (e) and (f) of the Constitution of India, the state shall direct its policy towards securing: that the health and strength of workers, men and women, and the tender age of the children are not abused and that citizens are not forced by economic necessity to enter vocations unsuited to their age or strength; and that children are given opportunities and facilities to develop in a healthy manner and in conditions of freedom and dignity and that childhood and youth are protected against exploitation and against moral and material abandonement.

REFERENCES

1. Barse, Sheela (1985), 'Child Labour Hit by Powerloom Closure', *Indian Express*, Nov. 15.
2. Bequele, Assefa and Jo Boyden (1988), 'Child Labour: Problems, Policies and Programmes', in Bequele and Boyden (eds.), *Combating Child Labour*, International Labour Office, Geneva.
3. Burra, Neera (1986), 'Glass Factories of Ferozabad-I: Plight of Workers'; *Economic and Political Weekly*, Vol. XXI, No. 46, No. 15.
4. Burra, Neera (1987), 'Born to Work: Children in the Glass Industry of Firozabad' in Manju Gupta and Kalus Voll (ed.), *Young Hands at Work: Child Labour in India*, Atma Ram and Sons, New Delhi.
5. Burra, Neera (1988), 'Exploitation of Children in Gem Polishing Industry of Jaipur-I: Structure of Industry', *Economic and Political Weekly*, Vol. XXIII, January 16.
6. Burra, Neera (1988), 'When Children are Cast in Miseries Mould', *The Hindustan Times*, Feb. 14.
7. Dayal, S.B. (1985), 'Child Labour and the Nature of Ocular Morbidities: Precipitating Problems for Eye Health Care' in Naidu and Kapadia (ed.), *Child Labour and Health: Problem and Prospects*, (1985).
8. Iyenger, Vishwapriya L. (1986), 'Child Labour in the Match Units of Southern Tamil Nadu'.
9. Kanbargi, R. (1988), 'Child Labour in India: The Carpet Industry of Varanasi', in Bequele and Boyden (eds.), *Combating Child Labour*, op. cit.
10. Kothari, S. (1983), 'There's Blood on These Match Sticks: Child Labour in Sivakasi', *Economic and Political Weekly*, Vol. XVIII No. 27, July 2.
11. Kulshreshtha, D.K. and S.K. Sharma (1980), 'Child Labour in Moradabad Metalware Industry', *The Economic Times*, Oct. 19.
12. Menon, Geeta (1985), 'Health Problems of Working Children: Some Observations'; in Usha Naidu and Kamini Kapadia (eds.) *Child Labour and Health*, op. cit.
13. Mitra, Nirmal (1986), 'Slave Children of Mandsaur', *Sunday*, June 15-21.
14. Mohandas, M. (1960), 'Beedi Workers in Kerala: Conditions of Life and Work'; *Economic* and Political Weekly, July-Dec.
15. Mohsin, Nadeem (1991), 'Strengthening Hands for Agile Fingers', Seminar given at *A.N. Sinha Institute of Social Studies*, Patna, June 7.
16. Mohsin, Nadeem (1992), 'Child Labour in Unorganised Industrial Enterprises in India: The Role of NGOs', Paper Presented at an International Interdisciplinary Conference, *Children At Risk*, Norway, May 13-16.

17. Pitt, David C. (1985), 'Child Labour and Health', in Usha Naidu and Kamini Kapadia (ed.), *Child Labour and Health: Problems and Prospects*, Tata Institute of Social Sciences, Bombay.

18. Rodgers, Gerry and Guy Standing (1981), *'Child Work, Poverty and Underdevelopment'*, International Labour Office, Geneva.

19. Shukla, S. (1984), 'Little Ones Meandering in the Dark', *National Herald*, March 25.

20. World Health Organisation (1987), 'Children at Work: Special Health Risks', Technical Report Series 756, Geneva in Bequele and Boyden (ed.,) *Combating Child Labour.*

39

LEGAL FRAMEWORK

One of the major areas of protective legislation relating to children is child labour. Observations of the Whitley Commission, the Labour Investigation Committee, 1946, and various statements and observations of many social reformers on the evils of existing child labour depriving the children of education and health, influenced the framers of our Constitution. Therefore, one of the main objectives of our Constitution is the protection of children from adverse effects of their employment on their physical and mental development.

Constitutional Provisions

The provisions of our Constitution relating to children are as follows:

Article 15(3) of the Constitution lays down that, "Nothing in this Article shall prevent the State from making any special provision for women and children.."

Article 24 provides that "No child below the age of 14 shall be employed to work in any factory or mine or engaged in any other hazardous employment."

Article 23 is also relevant for present purposes. It says that traffic in human beings and beggar and other similar forms of forced labour are prohibited. Any contravention of this provision is an offence punishable in accordance with law. Thus Article 23 confers a fundamental right against certain forms of exploitation. This provisions of the Indian Penal Code provide the punishment for such exploitation and Article 23 gives a constitutional sanction to punishments.

The Chapter IV of the Constitution contains specific directions in relation to the welfare of children. Thus Article 39 provides that "the State shall, in particular, direct its policy towards securing:

(e) that the health and strength of the workers, women and men, and the tender age of children are not abused and that citizens are not forced by economic necessity to enter avocations unsuited to their age or strength, and—

(f) that children and youth are protected against exploitation and against moral and material abandonment."

Articles 42 and 43 also provide for securing just and humane conditions of work and hold out a promise that the State shall endeavour to secure, by suitable legislation, or economic organisation or in any other way, to all workers, agricultural, industrial or otherwise, work, and living wage, conditions of work, ensuring a decent standard of life and full enjoyment of leisure and social and cultural opportunities, etc.

The 'abuse' and 'exploitation' under Article 39 (e) and 39 (f) respectively indicate that these articles are wider in social content than Article 42. Article 42 relates only to working class. This will not apply to cases where a self-employed man takes the help of his family members including children, for gainful activity because of economic pressure. This problem can be solved only by a faster rate of economic growth and social justice.

Legislative Enactments

At present, there are 13 major legislative enactments which provide legal protection to children in various occupations, these are:

(i) Factories Act, 1948,
(ii) Mines Act, 1952,
(iii) Plantation Labour Act, 1951,
(iv) Merchant Shipping Act, 1958,
(v) Motor Transport Workers Act, 1961,
(vi) Dock Workers' Regulation and Employment Act, 1948
(vii) Children (Pledging of Labour) Act, 1933,
(viii) Employment of Children Act, 1938,
(ix) Apprentices Act, 1961,
(x) Bidi and Cigar Works (Conditions of Employment) Act, 1966,
(xi) Contract Labour (Regulation and Abolition) Act. 1970,
(xii) Radiation Protection Rules 1971—under the Atomic Energy Act, 1962,
(xiii) Shops and Commercial Establishment Acts under different nomenclatures in States.

From time to time, amendments have been made in most of the above statutes, because of the progressive outlook of the Governments for improving the conditions of the important legislations which regulate the working conditions of child-workers and mitigate the adverse effect of employment on their health, education and training, etc. These are as follows:

The Factories Act, 1948

The Act extends to the whole of India except the State of Jammu and Kashmir.[1] It applies to establishments employing 10 or more workers with power or 20 or more workers without power.[2]

A 'Child' under the Act, is defined as a person who has not completed the fifteenth year of age.[3] A 'young person' is defined as either a child or an adolescent,[4] who has completed his fifteenth year but not eighteenth year.[5] Thus, "young persons" may be divided into three categories.

(A) *Those who are under fourteen years.* They are totally prohibited by this Act from entering into employment in factories.[6]

In *Walker T. Ltd. V/s Martindale,* [7] it was held that the prohibition is absolute and not restricted to employment in one of manufacturing processes; thus a child employed as a sweeper to clean the floor of a factory is in contravention of the provisions of the section, even though he is not employed in any of the manufacturing processes.

The following employment are also prohibited by the Court.

(a) Sorting of groundnuts in a Courtyard near the machinery room for decorticating—*Ramanathan Vs. K.E.*[8]

(b) To employ children under 8 years in plating straw in a work room, the benefit of which, goes to the mother, was held liable to penalty—*Beedon Vs. Parrot.*[9]

(c) Oiling of parts of machinery of the Spinning Mill by a young person during meal time, though done without orders and for worker's own amusement was held in *Prior Vs. Slaithwaite Spinning Co.*[10] violation of law making the occupier liable to fine.

(B) *Persons who are between 14 and 15 years.* They can be employed under the following restrictions provided under section 68, 69 and 71 to 75 of the Act:

(i) Such persons should have a certificate of fitness issued by a surgeon and should carry a token of such certificate.[11]

(ii) The certifying surgeon should follow the procedure laid down in section 69.

(iii) They should not work at night *i.e.,* twelve consecutive hours including the period from 10 p.m. to 6 a.m.[12]

(iv) They should work not more than four and a half hours a day.[13]

(v) The period of work is to be limited to two shifts.[14]

(vi) The shifts should not overlap.[15]

(vii) Each child has to be employed in one relay.[16]

(viii) The spread over is not to exceed five hours and should also not change except once in 30 days.[17]

(ix) They should not be employed in two separate factories on the same day.[18]

(x) The employer should display a notice regarding the periods of work for such children.[19]

(xi) The Manager of the factory should maintain a register in respect of such child-workers.[20]

(xii) No such child be employed except in accordance with the notice of periods of work displayed and the entries against his name in register of child-workers.[21]

Section 75 empowers the inspectors to require any such person for re-examination by Surgeon and he may prohibit the employment till the examination is made.

(C) *Person between 15 and 18.* They are employed as adults if they possess a certificate of physical fitness issued by the certifying surgeon and they also carry to token of such certificate.[22] The adolescents under 17 are not allowed to work at night.[23]

The object of these statutory restriction over the employment of young persons is to prevent exploitation of young labourers and to provide for their safety. This was the view expressed by Chief Justice Narasimha, Orissa High Court in *Jhunjhunwalla Vs. B.K. Patnaik,*[24] where the occupier of a glass factory was severely punished for employing 14 adolescent in blowing section of the factory, which is a hazardous occupation, without a certificate of fitness required under sections 68, and 69 of the Factories Act.

His lordship further observed that section 69 deals with the procedure to be followed by the certifying surgeon when the young person is sent to him for medical examination. He has to decide whether a certificate of fitness should be issued to the young person to work in the factory as a child (Cl. (a) of section 69(2) or whether a certificate should be given for that young person to work as an adult (Cl. (b) of Section 69(2)). Section 70 (2) says that if the certifying surgeon does not grant a certificate of fitness to a young person to work in factory as 'an adult' that person should be deemed to be a 'child' for all the purpose of the Act. Reading Sections 69 and 70 together, therefore, the reasonable inference is, that if a young person is first produced before the certifying surgeon and that surgeon is unwilling to grant him a certificate to work as an adult, the deeming provision, viz., sub-section (2) of section 70, would apply that young person would then be considered to be a 'child' but even a child who has completed his 14 years is prohibited by section 68, from being employed in a factory unless he is granted a certificate of fitness by the certifying surgeon. The deeming provision cannot apply where the young person has not been produced before the certifying surgeon. Here, there is no evidence to show that in the instant case 14 workers were actually produced before the certifying surgeon by the petitioner (occupier), therefore, sub-section (2) of section 70 has no application and the petitioner was rightly convicted.

In *'Mechnitosh Vs. First Brook Book Co.'*[25] it was observed that it was the duty of the employer to ascertain by reasonable means that the applicant was of requisite age and merely the statement of child about his age should not be treated as correct.

The Factories Act also envisages that no young persons should be allowed to clean, lubricate or adjust any part of a prime mover or transmission machinery while the prime mover or transmission machinery is in motion, or to clean, lubricate or adjust any part of any machine if the cleaning, lubrication or adjustment thereof would expose the young person to risk of injury from any moving part either of that machine or of any adjacent machinery.[26] The Act further says that no young person should work at any dangerous machine to which section 23 applies, unless he has been fully instructed as to the damages arising in connection with the machine and the precautions to be observed and has received sufficient training in work at the machine, or is under adequate supervision of a person who has a thorough knowledge and experience of the machine.[27] Government of U.P., under special power, declared presses other than hydraulic presses, Milling Machines used in the metal trades, Guillotine machine, circular saw, platen-printing machines, as of dangerous character.[28]

The Act also prohibits the employment of children to any part of the factory for pressing cotton in which a cotton opener is at work, except where the feed end of a cotton opener is in a room separated from the delivery end.[29]

The State Government is empowered by this Act to make rules prescribing the maximum weights which may be lifted by adolescents and children.[30]

Besides a weekly day of rest, every child worker who has worked for a period of 240 days or more in factory during a calender year is entitled during the subsequent year for leave with wages at the rate of one day for every 15 days of work as against every 20 days in the case of an adult worker.[31]

Rest-shelters, canteens, *etc.* are also to be provided to all workers including children.[32]

The Mines Act, 1952

This Act also extends to the whole of India[33] and includes all excavations where any operation for the purpose of searching for or obtaining minerals is carried out.[34]

This Act also defines child as a person who has not completed his fifteenth year.[35] This Act not only prohibits the employment of children in mines, but also prohibits the presence of children in any part of a mine which is below-ground or in any open cast-working in which any mining operation is being carried on.[36] Even an adolescent is not allowed to work in part of a mine which is below ground. Unless he has completed his 16th year and has a medical certificate of fitness for work.[37] A certificate is valid only for 12 months.[38] The Act also says that adolescent is allowed to be employed in any mine except between 6 a.m. and 6 p.m.[39]

Like the Factories Act the provisions of canteen, whole-some food and rest shelters, *etc.* have also been made under this Act.[40]

The Plantation Labour Act, 1951

This Act covers all tea, coffee, rubber, cinchona and cardamory plantations, and using areas 10.117 hectares or more, in which 30 or more persons are employed. [41] The

Act prohibits the employment of children under 12 years.[42] An adolescent between 15-18 years cannot be employed for work unless he is certified fit for work by a surgeon.[43] Such certificate is valid only for one year.[44] Use of a false certificate of fitness is punishable by imprisonment which may extend to one month, or with fine or both.[45]

This Act is, however, more comprehensive in the sense that this act alone makes the provisions for education as a responsibility of the employer and so is for the housing and medical and recreational facilities.[46] Perhaps the legislators were moved to make all these provisions in this Act because of the fact that plantation labour is commonly known as 'family labour' as against 'individual' child labour.

The Merchant Shipping Act, 1958

The Act applies to ships registered in India. The Act prohibits the employment of children under 15 subject to certain exceptions. It also prohibits the employment of young persons under 15 as trimmers and stokers except under certain specific conditions. Such persons, if employed, are required to produce a certificate of fitness. Further the Act empowers the Government to make necessary rules regarding employment of young persons as and when the occasion demands.

The Motor Transport Workers Act, 1961

This Act applies to the whole of India,[47] it covers every motor transport undertaking employing 5 or more transport workers. The State Governments are authorised to apply all or any of the provisions of this Act to any motor transport undertakings employing less than 5 workers.[48] This Act also prohibits the employment of children under 15 in any capacity in the motor transport undertaking.[49] The adolescents are prohibited to work unless a certificate of fitness is granted.[50] Which is valid only for 12 months.[51] An adolescent can work only for 6 hours including a rest interval of half an hour and between 10 a.m. and 6 p.m. only.[52]

The Children (Pledging of Labour) Act, 1933

Previously, the Act extended to the whole of India, except Jammu and Kashmir; but after September 1, 1971, it has been extended to Jammu and Kashmir also.[53]

The Act declares an agreement, oral or written, to pledge the labour of children, whereby the parent or the guardian of a child, in return of any payment of benefit to be received, undertakes to cause or allow the services of a child to be utilised in any employment, to be void.[54]

However, an agreement made without detriment to the child and made in consideration of any benefit, other than reasonable wages, to be paid for the child's services and terminable at not more than a week's notice, is not deemed to be an illegal agreement under the Act.[55]

Child means, under this Act, a person who has not completed the age of 15 years.[56]

The Penalty provided for the breach of the law is a fine upto Rs. 200/- on the employer and Rs. 50/- on the parents.[57]

The Employment of Children Act, 1938

This Act is also applied to the whole of India. It prohibits the employment of children under 15 in any occupation connected with the transport of passengers, goods or mails by railways or connected with the port authority within the limit of any port.[58]

With the exception of children employed as apprentices or trainees, no child between the age of 15-17 can be employed or permitted to work in these occupations unless he is allowed a rest interval of at least 12 consecutive hours in a day. The period of rest is to include at least 7 such consecutive hours between 10 p.m. and 7 a.m. as may be prescribed by the appropriate Government.[59]

The Act further prohibits the employment of children below the age of 14 in workshops connected with bidi making, carpet weaving, cement manufacturing including begging of cement, cloth printing, dyeing, weaving, manufacture of matches, explosives and fire work, mica cutting and splitting, shellac manufacture, soap manufacture, tanning and wool cleaning.[60] These provisions, however, do not apply to workshops where work is done with the help of occupier's family only or to any school established, aided or recognised by any State Government. State Governments are empowered to extend the scope of the Act to cover any other employment.[61]

The Act also required the Railway and port authorities to maintain registers showing names, dates of birth, rest intervals, etc. of children under 17.[62]

The penalty for the breach of the Act is imprisonment up to one month or fine upto Rs. 500 or both.[63]

The Government of Madras has extended the Act to children working as cleaners in workshops attached to motor transport companies. In U.P. the Act has been extended to the brassware and glass bangle industries.

The Apprentices Act, 1961

The Act extends to the whole of India[64] and provides for the regulations and control of training of apprentices in trades and for matters connected therewith.[65]

The Act provides that no person shall be qualified for being engaged as an apprentice or to undergo apprenticeship training in any designated trade unless he is atleast 14 years of age and satisfies such standards of education and physical fitness as may be prescribed.[66]

If he is a minor, his guardian is required to enter into a contract of apprenticeship with the employer[67] and it should be registered with the Apprenticeship Advisor.[68]

Bidi and Cigar Works (Conditions of Employment) Act 1966

This Act also extends to whole of India.[69] The Act provides that no child should be required or allowed to work in any industrial premises[70]; the Act defines the child as a person who has not completed his fourteen years of age.[71] The employment of young persons between 14 to 18 years is prohibited between 7 p.m. to 6 a.m.[72]

The Administration of the Act rests with the State who appoint Chief Inspectors or Inspectors for the purpose. The Act provides the penalties for breach which may be imprisonment up to three months or a fine upto Rs. 500/- or both.[73]

Provisions for canteens,[74] first aid,[75] cleaning[76] and ventilation[77] are also made under the Act.

The Contract Labour (Regulations and Abolition) Act, 1970

This Act also extends to the whole of India.[78] The Act applies to Establishments and Contractors employing 20 or more workers.[79] It is not applied to establishment in which work only of an intermittent or casual nature is performed.[80] There are no specific provisions under the Act pertaining to employment of children.

A comparative study of the above statutes make it clear that the provisions providing for canteen, rest shelters, drinking water supply, conservancy services, first aid, bathing facilities, cleaniness, for workers including child workers are made in Factories Act, Mines Act and Bidi and Cigar Workers (Conditions of Employment) Act. But there are no provisions under plantation Labour Act regarding laterines, ambulance, lighting, cleaniness, etc. Regarding drinking water facilities, the scales has been laid down by the Assam, West Bengal, Kerala and Tamil Nadu Governments. The provision for first aid is made under the Act. The Plantation Labour Act alone provides for education of child workers.

At a glance, the working hours and conditions for young persons and children under some important Acts, can be seen in the table on next page.

TABLE 39.1

The Working Hours and Conditions for Young Persons and Children

Act	*Certificate of fitness*	*Max. weekly Hrs.*	*Max. daily Hrs.*	*Rest interval*	*Spread over*	*Over time*	*Night work*	*Misc.*
Factories Act, 1948	necessary	not prescribed	5 hrs. in one shift only	½ hours	5 hours	not allowed	not allowed	—
Mines Act, 1952	-do-	-do-	-do-	-do-	-do-	-do-	-do-	—
Plantation Labour Act, 1951	-do-	40 hrs.	6 hrs.	-do-	-do-	-do-	-do-	—
Motor Transport Act, 1961	-do-	-do-	-do-	-do-	9 hrs.	-do-	-do-	—

The Shops and Establishment Acts

Various State Governments have passed the Shops and Establishment Acts to regulate the working conditions of employees including child workers in shops and commercial establishments. Time to time these Acts have been amended to meet the situation. These provisions regulate the daily and weekly hours of work, rest intervals, payment of wages, overtime, pay, holidays with pay, annual leave, employment of children and young persons, etc.

All States except Andhra Pradesh have fixed the minimum age of employment at 12 years. In Andhra, it is 14 years. These Act prohibit the employment of young persons during night between 7 p.m. to 6 a.m. The hours of work for children are also fixed which vary from 3 to 7 hours a day in different States, with half an hour to one hour break after 3-4 hours.

These are important Acts, which regulate the working conditions of child labour employed in various establishments. The details of provisions of different State Acts are given in the following table

TABLE 39.2

Statewise Special Provisions for Time, Hours of Work, Etc., for Young Persons Under the Shops and Commercial Establishments Acts

State Union Territory	*Age definition*	*Permitted employment*	*Hours of work*	*Rest interval*
1	2	3	4	5
Andhra Pradesh	14-17	6 a.m. to 7 p.m.	7 per day and 42 per week, overtime work not allowed	
Bihar	12-18	7 a.m. to 7 p.m.	Children @ 5 per hrs. day and 30 hrs. per-week, young persons 7 hrs. per day and 42 hrs. per week.	One hour after 4 hrs. work.
Gujarat	12-17	6 a.m. to 7 p.m.	6 hrs. per day	½ an hour after 3 hrs. work
Jammu and Kashmir	12-18	7 a.m. to 9 p.m.	-do-	—
Maharashtra	12-17	6 a.m. to 7 p.m.	-do-	1/2 an hour after 3 hrs. work
Kerala	14-17	7 a.m. to 7 p.m.	—	—

1	2	3	4	5
M.P.	12-17	7 a.m. to 9 p.m.	5 hrs. per day	—
Karnataka	12-15	6 a.m. to 8 p.m.	-do-	—
Orissa	12-15	Employment prohibited during night (between 10 p.m. and 6 a.m.)	-do-	—
Punjab	14-18	To be fixed by Government	5 hrs. per day and 30 hrs. per week	1/2 an hour after 3 hrs. work
Rajasthan	12-15	Employment prohibited during night	3 hrs. per day	—
Tamil Nadu	14-17	6 a.m. to 7 p.m.	7 hrs. per day and 42 hrs. per week	—
U.P.	14-17	—	6 hrs. per day	—
West Bengal	12-15	Not after 8 p.m.	7 hrs. per day and 40 hrs. per week.	1 hr. after 4 hrs. work
Delhi	12-18	8 a.m. to 8 p.m. in winter, 7 a.m. to 9. p.m. in summer	6 hrs. per day	½ an hour after 3-½ hours work
Pondicherry	14-18	6 a.m. to 7 p.m.	7 hrs. per day or 42 hrs. a week	1 hour,

Source: Indian Labour Year Book, 1970, Labour Bureau, Simla 1973, page 302.

REFERENCES

1. The Factories Act, 1948, sec. 1(2).
2. *Ibid.*, sec. 2(m)
3. *Ibid.*, sec. 2(c)
4. *Ibid.*, sec. 2(d)
5. *Ibid.*, sec. 2(b)
6. *Ibid.*, sec. 67
7. (1916) 85 J.L.K.B. 1543.
8. A.I.R. 1927 Mad. 435.
9. (1871) L.R.Q.B. 718.
10. (1898) I.O.B. 718.
11. The Factories Act, 1948, sec. 68.

12. *Ibid.*, sec. 71(1)(b).
13. *Ibid.*, sec. 71(1)(a).
14. *Ibid.*, sec. 71(2)
15. *Ibid.*, sec. 71(2)
16. The Factories Act, 1948, sec. 71(2).
17. *Ibid.*
18. *Ibid.*, sec. 71(4).
19. *Ibid.*, sec. 72.
20. *Ibid.*, sec. 73.
21. *Ibid.*, sec. 74.
22. The Factories Act, 1948, sec. 68.
23. *Ibid.*, sec. 70.
24. II L.L.J. Orissa, 551. (1964).
25. (1904) 34 C.L.T. 370.
26. The Factories Act, 1948, sec., 22(2).
27. *Ibid.*, sec. 23.
28. U.P. Factories Rule, 1950, Rule 54.
29. The Factories Act, 1948, sec. 27.
30. *Ibid.*, sec. 34(2).
31. *Ibid.*, sec. 79.
32. *Ibid.*, Chap. 71.
33. The Mines Act, 1952, sec. 1(2).
34. *Ibid.*, sec. 2(j).
35. The Mines Act, 1952, sec. 2(e).
36. *Ibid.*, sec. 45(1).
37. *Ibid.*, sec. 40(1).
38. *Ibid.*, sec. 41(1).
39. *Ibid.*, sec. 40(2).
40. *Ibid.*, chap. V.
41. The Plantation Labour Act, 1951, Sec. 4(a).
42. *Ibid.*, sec. 24.
43. *Ibid.*, sec. 26.
44. *Ibid.*, sec. 27(2).
45. *Ibid.*, sec. 34.
46. *Ibid.*, sec. 5, 6, 7.
47. The Motor Transport Workers Act, 1961 sec. 1(2).
48. *Ibid.*, sec. 1(4).
49. *Ibid.*, sec. 21.
50. *Ibid.*, sec. 22.
51. *Ibid.*, sec. 23(2).

52. The Motor Transport Workers Act, 1961 sec. 14.
53. The Children (Pledging of Labour) Act, 1933, sec., 1(2).
54. *Ibid.*, sec. 3.
55. *Ibid.*, sec. 3.
56. *Ibid.*, sec. 2.
57. The Children (Pledging of Labour) Act, 1933, sec. 4.
58. The Employment of Children Act, 1938, sec. 3(1).
59. *Ibid.*, sec. 3(2).
60. The Employment of Children Act, 1938, sec. 3(3).
61. *Ibid.*, sec. 3A.
62. *Ibid.*, sec. 3E.
63. *Ibid.*, sec. 4.
64. The Apprentices Act, 1961, sec. 1(2).
65. *Ibid.*, preamble.
66. *Ibid.*, sec. 3.
67. *Ibid.*, sec. 4(a).
68. *Ibid.*, sec. 4(b).
69. Bidi and Cigar Works (conditions and Employment) Act, 1966, sec. 1(2).
70. Bidi and Cigar Works (Conditions and Employment) Act, 1966 sec. 24(b).
71. *Ibid.*, sec. 2(b).
72. *Ibid.*, sec. 25.
73. *Ibid.*, sec. 32.
74. *Ibid.*, sec. 16.
75. *Ibid.*, sec. 15.
76. *Ibid.*, sec. 8.
77. *Ibid.*, sec. 9.
78. The Contract Labour (Regulation and Abolition) Act, 1970 sec. 1(2).
78. The Contract Labour (Regulation and Abolition) Act, 1970 sec. 1(4).
80. *Ibid.*, sec. 1(5)(4).

40

CHILD LABOUR LAWS—THEIR IMPLEMENTATION

Every society has its own pattern of life suited to their livelihood. This pattern of life in the old society was regulated through its norms. Social norms and values are upheld by an approved machinery of the society to regulate and maintain the social order. In a complex society, where social system is easily broken, it becomes much more difficult to maintain the social system. In the such situations, formal law is helpful. The major functions of the legal system are (Gangrade 1982) (1) Maintenance of public order (2) Upholding rights and duties (3) Facilitating co-operation (4) Confirming legitimacy (5) communicating moral standards. Law is always helpful in protecting the poor and the needy.

In every society, old traditions, values and norms create difficulty in adopting new changes for development and growth of its members. Therefore, reformation is needed to change its old system to meet the needs for their welfare and development. Long ago, child labour was not a social problem, but with the change in social understanding, child labour needed legislative protection against their exploitation and for their proper growth and development.

To protect children from the adverse effects of employment especially on their physical and mental development, there are several laws in India. These laws are either derived from the Indian constitution or from the International Labour Organisation (ILO) recommendations, or from the declaration of the Rights of the Child unanimously adopted by the General Assembly of the United Nations on Nov. 20th, 1959.

Constitutional Commitment

India's commitment to the welfare of children is very much reflected by its constitution in the chapter on Directive Principles of State Policy. The Constitution makes were conscious of the requirements of children in need of extra care. Article 15 (3) lays down that "nothing it this article shall prevent the state from making any special provision for women and children." Article 24 proclaims that "no child below the age of 14 years shall be employed to work in any factory or mine or engaged in any other hazardous employment." Article 39 (c) provides that "the health, strength of the workers, man, women and the tender age of children are not abused and that the citizens are not forced by economic necessity to enter avocation unsuited to their age or strength." Article 39(f) enjoins "Childhood and youth are protected against exploitation and against moral and material abandonment"' Similarly, Article (45) provides that "the state shall endeavour to provide within a period of ten years from the commencement of the constitution for free and compulsory education for all children until they complete the age of 14 years."

International Labour Organisation (ILO) Efforts

Improvement of labour standards throughout the world is the basic aim of the ILO. It has paid particular attention to the protection of the employed children. It has sought to achieve its objective of protecting children by adopting international standards in the form of "conventions and recommendations." A convention seeks to create obligations of binding nature and its ratification requires complete compliance with all its provision. A recommendation, on the other hands, contains provision which are generally in the nature of guiding principles for action and may be implemented progressively and in parts. The ILO has so far adopted 18 conventions and 16 recommendation mainly in respect of children and young person in connection with their minimum age for entry to employment, medical examination before employment and work during nights. India has been able to ratify 6 of the ILO conventions concerning the employment of children and young persons in industrial and non-industrial occupations.

The United Nations declaration says that "the child by reason of his physical and mental immaturity needs special safeguards and care, including appropriate protection. The child shall enjoy the benefits of social security. He shall enjoy special protection and shall be given opportunities and facilities by law and by other means to enable him to develop in a healthy and normal manner and in conditions of freedom and dignity. In the enactments of laws for this purpose, the best interest of the child shall be the paramount considerations. The general assembly calls upon local authorities and national governments to recognise these rights, without discrimination on account of national or social origin, property, birth or other status whether or himself of his family.

Indian Statutory Provisions

1. *Statutory provisions regarding age for employment:* Almost all states regulate employment of children. The minimum age for employment differs from state to state. The relevant statutory provisions are briefly produced below:

A. *Factory Act, 1948:* The Act prohibits the employment of children below 14 years while ILO prescribes 15 years and above for employment in any factory using power and employing ten or more workers, and in a factory not using power and employing twenty or more workers on any date of the preceding 12 months. To safeguard the health of young persons between 14 to 18 years, the Act enjoins upon the employer to obtain a certificate of fitness from a surgeon and the certificate will be valid for a period of one year from the date of issue.

B. *Mines Act, 1952:* The minimum age of this Act for working in mines above ground is 15 years as recommended by ILO also. For underground employment, prescribed age limit is 16 years and above. In addition to this, a fitness certificate is also required from an authorised surgeon as in the factory Act, 1948.

C. *Plantation Labour Act, 1951:* Under this Act, a child of 12 years and below (according to ILO 14 years) shall not be employed in plantation of tea, coffee, rubber or cinchona within an area of 10,117 hectares of more and employing thirty or more persons. A child above 12 years willing to work in plantations is required to obtain a certificate of fitness which will be valid for the period of one year from the date of issue by certifying surgeon.

D. *Motor Transport Act, 1961:* Under this Act minimum age prescribed for employment in every transport undertaking employing five or more workers is 15 years and above. The ILO also recommends the same.

E. *Beedi and cigarette workers (condition of employment) Act, 1966:* Under this Act no child who has not completed his 14 years, shall be required or allowed to work in any industrial premises where any manufacturing process connected with making of beedi or cigar. Is carried on irrespective of the number of persons employed.

F. *Employment of children Act, 1938:* To prevent employment of children inhazardous and unhealthy occupations the Act prohibits the employment of children below 15 years (as suggested by ILO) in any occupation connected with transport of passengers, goods or mails by railway, or a port-authority within the limits of a port. The Act prohibits the employment of children in railway particularly in construction work, catering services, track and line work as well as cleaning and picking of ash-pits and cinders. It also prohibits employment of children below 14 years in certain less hazardous occupations such as beedi-making, carpet weaving, cement manufacture, cloth printing, dyeing, and weaving, manufacture of matches, explosives and fire works, mica-cutting and splitting, shellac manufacture, soap manufacture and canning, etc. It may be mentioned that the Government of India has another bill to regulate employment of children.

G. *Merchant Shipping Act, 1958:* This Act prohibits the employment of children below 15 years of age in any capacity, on seagoing ships, except (a) in a school ship or training ship or (b) in a ship in which all persons employed are members of one family; or (c) in home made ship of less than two hundred tonnes gross; or (d) where such person is to be employed or nominal wages and will be in charge of his father or other adult male relative.

H. *Inland Steam Vessels Act, 1917* The Act applies to steam ships ordinarily playing in inland waters. The Act does not have any provision regulating employment of children. The reason for this omission seems to be that it is an old enactment when the community was not conscious of the need to have legislation for protection of children.

I. *Radiation Protection Rules, 1971:* Under this a child below 18 years of age is not to be employed at places where radiation takes place.

J. *State Shops and Commercial Establishment Act:* For the implementation of this act, different states have their own rules regulating employment and working hours in shops and establishment, restaurants and hotels, etc., to which the Factory Act does not apply. In Bihar, Gujarat, Jammu and Kashmir, Madhya Pradesh, Karnataka, Orissa, Rajasthan, Tripura, Uttar Pradesh, West Bengal, Goa Daman and Diu and Manipur, minimum age for employment in shops and commercial establishment is 12 years. In Andhra Pradesh, Assam, Haryana, Himachal Pradesh, Kerala, Tamil Nadu, Punjab, Delhi, Chandigarh, Pondicherry and Meghalaya, it is 14 years while 15 years in Maharashtra. According to the ILO it is 15 years.

K. *The Children (pledging of labour) Act, 1933:* The act prohibits any agreement written or oral to pledge the labour of child, whereby parents or guardians of such child undertakes to cause or allow the services of the child to be utilised for any employment in return for a payment received or to be received. A child under this Act is defined as a person who is under 15 years of age.

L. *The Apprentices Act, 1961:* Under this Act, a person shall not be qualified for being engaged as an apprentice to undergo apprenticeship training in any designated trade unless he has completed 14 years of age and fulfills the prescribed standard of education and physical fitness. The minimum educational qualification is 7th standard but for some jobs it is only 4th standard.

M. *The Contract Labour (regulations and abolition) Act, 1970:* Under this act, the permissible age for the working as contract labour is 18 and above. The second important aspect of the statutory provisions for the employment of children is the number of working hours. Different Acts have mentioned different working hours. The nature of these restrictions have been mentioned below:

   1. *Hours of work:* Four and half hours per day have been prescribed for children under the Factory Act. Similarly, in Mines Act, for the adolescent who does not possess a fitness certificate from a surgeon working hour are 4 and a half per day. No limitation on daily working hours is prescribed under the Plantation Labour Act, 1951. Seven hours including rest period is prescribed in the Employment of Children Act, 1938. Different working hours have been prescribed in different provinces for the shops and commercial establishments under the state acts.

2. *Limitations on weekly hours of work:* No clear-cut limitations have been prescribed for children under the Factory Act, 1948, the Mine Act, 1952 and the Railway (Hours of employment) Rules while Forty Hours a week for an adolescent and a child is prescribed in the Plantation Labour Act, 1951.
3. *Regulation of Rest Intervals:* The provision for the rest intervals has been prescribed under the Factory Act, 1948, and the plantation Labour Act, 1951. This provision is also made under the employment of children Act, 1938, and state Shops and commercial establishments Act.
4. *Night Work:* The provision for restriction of night work by children and in some cases even by young persons is available under the Factory Act, 1948. The Mines Act, 1952, the Plantation Act, 1951, Beedi and Cigar workers (conditions of employment) Act, 1966 and the State Shops and Commercial Establishments Acts. However, these provisions very in respect of age and prohibits work during nights.
5. *Provision on Shift relays and spread over:* Under the Factory Act, 1948, it is prescribed that the period of work of children shall be confined to two shifts which shall not spread over for more than 5 hours a day. Further, children shall be permitted to work only in one shift which can be changed for not more than once in a period of 30 days provided previous permission is obtained from the chief inspector of Factories.
6. *Double Employment:* Children are prohibited from working in more than one factory on any days under the Factory Act, 1948.
7. *Holidays:* Every working child under the Factory Act, 1948, Mines, Act, 1952, Motor Transport Workers Act, 1961, and Beedi Workers, (condition of employment) Act is entitled to a weekly holiday.
8. *Safety:* Under the Factory Act, children are not allowed to work on pressing cotton where cotton opener is at work. Further the Act disallows the young person to clean lubricate or adjust any part of a prime-mover or of any transmission machinery while the prime-mover or transmission machinery is in motion or to clean, lubricate or adjust any part of any machine if it is likely to expose her or him to risk or injury from the part.
9. *Leave:* The annual leave with wages in available to the working children who have worked for more than 240 days or more during a calender year at the rate of one day for every 15 days of work performed by them under the Factory Act, 1948, the Plantation labour Act, 1951, The Motor Transport Workers Act, 1961 and the Beedi and Cigar Workers (condition of employment) Act, 1966. Provisions are different in different states for children working in the Shops and Commercial establishments.

10. *Wages:* Wages of the child workers are governed by the minimum Wages Act, 1948, and payment of Wages Act, 1936.

11. *Penalties:* Under the Factory Act, the occupier or manager of the factory is liable to be punished if found guilty of contravention of the provisions with a sentence of imparisonment upto 3 months of a fine upto Rs. 500 or with both. The adolescents using false certificates and parents or guardians permitting double employment of a child are also liable to be punished. The Employment of Children Act provides for punishment for contravention of the provisions of the Act with simple imprisonment extending to one month or fine upto Rs. 500 or with both. Children (pledging of Labour) Act, 1933 provides punishment to parents or guardians making an agreement to pledge labour of a child with a fine upto Rs. 50 and in the case of an employer with Rs. 200. Similarly, Beedi and Cigar Workers (conditions of employment) Act, 1966 provides for penalty of imprisonment upto 3 months and a fine upto Rs. 500 or both. The working hours and conditions for young persons and children are given below:

TABLE 40.1

Act	*Certificate of fitness*	*Maximum weekly hours*	*Maximum daily hours*	*Rest interval*	*Spead over*	*Over-time*	*Night work*
Factory Act, 1948	Necessary	Not prescribed	5 hrs	1/2 hrs	5 hrs	Not allowed	Not allowed
Mines Act, 1952	-do-	-do-	-do-	-do-	-do-	-do-	-do-
Plantation Labour Act, 1951	-do-	40 hrs	6 hrs	-do-	-do-	-do-	-do-
Motor transport Act, 1961	-do-	-do-	-do-	-do-	-do-	-do-	-do-

These Acts give an impression that the Government is doing its best to check the exploitation of children by employers and others, but the real picture in the field is otherwise. Various studies and reports by official and non-official organisations have pointed out a poor enforcement and gross violation of the provisions of these Acts by the employers in general and by shops and commercial establishments in particular. There have been a lot of debates on various aspects of this problem at various forums. The Law Association of Asia and Western Pacific have not been able to come out with a clear-cut opinion on the implementation of these acts. In fact, they are in a dilemma. If laws are enforced, on important supplementary family income is necessary for the survival of the family and as such laws become on absolute measures in the present Indian context. When the child labour is allowed, the unscrupulous persons and others motivated by a desire for higher profits fail to resist temptations to abuse child labour. This subject has generated a lot of heat in the minds of various segments of the population directly and indirectly concerned with this problem. The Concern expression in various forums led the Government to think about this problem more seriously.

The Labour Minister, Government of India (1985) in the meeting of the Child Labour Advisory Committee talked of prescribing severe penalty for the violation of the child labour laws. Accordingly, the Government made an amendment in the employment of Children Act, 1938 approved by both the Houses of the Parliament. If empowers the law enforcing agencies to impose a minimum of 3 months of imprisonment of a fine of Rs. 500 for contravening the provisions section 3 of the Act. The Government of India has also realised that the legislation alone cannot prevent child labour and their abuse. Consequently, the government has mooted an ideas for an all-round development of children along with special attention to their needs. It is being thought that to eliminate child labour if is necessary to focus on the total socio-economic development of those sections of society which is supplying child labour to various industries. Similarly, the Government has proposed to improve the existing working conditions of children at work. In pursuance of these ideas, two pilot projects have been launched-one a Sivakashi (Tamil Nadu) and another at Bhadohi (Varanasi / Mirzapur of Uttar pradesh). These projects are to ensure better implementation of the child labour laws, non-formal education and health care for better development of children working in these places. This is the welcome move because no amount of laws can prevent child labour and at the same time there is no full justification for the total abolition of child labour in the present existing socio-economic conditions of the country. Since the public in general and various organisations and individual concerns did not feel satisfied with measures taken by the Government to regulate child labour, the Government of India has come out with a comprehensive legislation to meet the various criticisms on this front. Accordingly, on 22nd Aug. (1986) a comprehensive bill on Child Labour (Prohibition and Regulation) was introduced in the Rajya Sabha by the Government. The bill provides that no child below 14 years shall be employed in any of the occupations connected with the transport of passengers, goods or mail by railway, cinder picking, cleaning ash-pits or building operations in the railway premises. Child labour is proposed to be banned in catering, establishments at railway stations, ports, any workshop which carries on the processes of bidi making, carpet weaving, cement manufacture, cloth printing, dyeing, weaving, manufacture of matches, explosives and fireworks.

The Bill provides that no child shall be permitted to work from 7 PM. to 8 AM or overtime. The period of work of a child shall be so arranged that inclusive of intervals for rest (at least one hour) it shall not be over more than 6 hours. The contravention of the provisions of the bill shall be punishable with imprisonment ranging from three months to one year or a fine upto Rs. 10,000 or both. Subsequent contraventions will be punishable with 6 months, imprisonment mandatory and it could be extended to 2 years. Any person can file a complaint before the court. However, some contraventions are found in this approach. As Mahajan Krishan (1986) has pointed out the approach of those opposing Child Labour was one of escapism as discussed at the workshop on Child Labour in India organised at the Indian Social Institute on August 9, 1986. He observed that the bill totally prohibited the employment of any child, who was defined as any person less than 14 in the occupations as mentioned above. But in no-where provides for the rehabilitation of these children thrown out of these jobs. The Directive Principles of State Policy do not permit the union Government to make illusory laws in social justice. By making it illegal to work in key employments which sustain the majority of Indian families without providing for alternative measures of economic justice simultaneously. The result of the bill will be that the majority of children who are employed as mentioned above will have their wages reduced further because of the additional costs their employers will have to incur for keeping the labour inspector happy to prevent prosecution.

The bill in its very intention violates the fundamental rights of the child under Article 21 to adequate nutrition, education, clothing and shelter or a decent life. It provides to prevent abusing children due to economic necessity and to provide opportunities for their proper development. This unconstitutional intention is visible from the fact that the bill does not even provide that the employer should employ a child below fourteen after having his age determined and certified by the local civil hospital or the primary health centre. Instead, under section 10 it provides for determination of such age when a dispute arises. The whole bill will fall through simply due to this provision. Since no child who is working out of "economic necessity" or his parent who send him to work because of such necessity, will be able to fight such legal disputes against an influential and relatively better - off employer. That the framers of the bill have paid no interest to even preventive measures is shown by the value they have given in terms of penalties for violating the provisions for keeping registers and putting up notices which constitute the evidentiary basis of all prosecutions. Such a violation under section 14(3) invites a penalty of only Rs. 1,000 maximum or a simple imprisonment of 1 month maximum. However, under section 14(1) the Violation of the total ban on child labour invites a penalty of a minimal fine of Rs. 10,000 with a maximum of double that amount or a minimum of three months imprisonment which can be extended to one year. If social activists and other make much noise against the labour machinery, a few token prosecutions as provided under the various Bidi Acts, with nominal fines only will get employers off the evidentary hook and thereby prevent any conviction.

Implementation

India is a country where the largest number of child workers are employed (H.T. 1985). Its constitution gives the fundamental rights to children below 14 years of age not to be employed in any factory, mine or nay hazardous employment. The constitution also requires as a fundamental principle in the governance of the country that children of tender age are not forced by economic necessity to accept employments unsuited to their age, strength and that they are given opportunities and facilities to develop in a healthy manner in conditions of freedom and dignity, and also that children and youth are protected against exploitation. Despite the constitutional commitment and statutory provisions, the social service facilities like health, education, recreation are not fully available for the proper growth and development of the child. Poverty eradication programmes sponsored by the Government may have yielded good results. But 36 per cent of the population are still below the poverty line where their minimum needs are not met. They are forced into the labour market and are not sent to schools. It is an established fact that poverty is the crux of the whole misery. In this study also, the majority of employers (77 per cent) accepted that children join the labour force due to poor economic backgrounds of their families. Their parents are not able to fulfil their responsibility to provide them with education, proper care and recreation, etc. Sometimes children are bound to accept work at the early age to meet their family expenses due to the loss of the bread winner. Out of 309 child workers, 22 (7 per cent) have lost their fathers. The general trend of the employers is to get more and more production at limited expenses. Due to varied reasons like abundance, cheaper wages, better out-put, lesser industrial relations problems, etc., employers prefer employment of children over adults.

This phenomenon can be explained by one instance. Sections 67-68 of the Factory Act, 1948, prohibits the employment of children below the age of 14 years. To keep the unit out of the purview of this Act, many employers have divided their set-up in small scale units. Moreover, there were a number of units operating without power but employing 19 employers deliberately. Since these units are not covered under the Factory Act, the employers can employ them easily. Interestingly enough in case of units not covered under the Factory Act, it has been found that not even a single unit has maintained records or registers of employment in connection with their attendance, salary paid, terms and conditions of employment. This situation is not only prevalent in U.P. but can be found in other parts of the country as well. Addressing the delegates of the two-day Bonded Labour Conference on 12th Jan. 1986 the Haryana Chief Minister said labour laws were being freely violated in the state. Over 5,000 children conducted by Singh, M. (1980) in Bombay also revels that a majority of production units were covered under the shops and Commercial Establishments Act and the remaining units under the Factory Act was found violating the laws.

When employers were asked whether they were aware of the child labour legislation, most of them (91 per cent) denied having knowledge of labour laws. This may be due to their limited knowledge and rural background whereas the remaining 9 per cent expressed their awareness. Therefore, the employers had divided their working units into different sub-units (Singh, M., 1980) and it was found that employers had very poor knowledge in urban slums areas. When the employers were asked to indicate the source of awareness of the child labour laws, 10 per cent of there were found to have awareness of the child labour legislation. They disclosed that some officers from the labour or the income tax departments came to them two times to ask about the production expenditure and the number of workers employed. Further, some of them said that the police visited one carpet industry where he caught the owner of industry who was exploiting the child workers brought from Bihar.

The provisions relating to hours of work are also violated. During the interview, a majority of the employers (58 per cent) accepted that the child workers were put to work for 8 to 10 hours per day while 31 per cent admitted that they were engaged for 10 to 12 hours per day. A majority of the (87.4 per cent) child workers accepted that they worked for 10 to 12 hours per day and 6.1 per cent worked for 13 and more hours per day whereas the Factory Act 1948 provides for 5 working hours per day. Moreover, regarding night work, the situation is worse. About 85.4 per cent child workers were found to be working during night out of which 28.8 per cent worked for one hour on an average per day, 42.1 per cent two hours, 28.0 per cent 3 hours and the remaining 1.1 per cent for 4 hours whereas the factory Act 1948 prohibits night work for children. In view of the pitiable conditions of the child labour, the Supreme Court (1986) directed the Government of Uttar Pradesh to present a Scheme to immediately absorb the child labour in the carpet industry and other non-hazardous jobs. It was also ordered that the scheme must cover the child labour in the district of Allahabad, Varanasi and Mirzapur. This order was passed on a petition submitted by the child workers who had been kidnapped from the Palamau District of Bihar, illegally confined and forced to work in the carpet units of Uttar Pradesh without food, sleep and wages.

As a number of studies, research reports and observations revealed that the child workers were poorly paid in different units. Prof. K.D. Gangrade (1983) has reported that the payment of child workers is better especially in the carpet industry. Similar view is given by the Operations Research Group, Bangalore (1983) on the basis of findings of an All-India Survey. However, the findings of this study covering 309 child workers indicate that 51.5 per cent were paid less than Rs. 150 to Rs. 300 per month and 5.8 per cent did not get in cash but in kind such as meals, clothes or sometimes a small amount as pocket money. All the employer respondents had accepted that they did not ask the child workers to produce fitness certificates from the surgeon. As far as welfare facilities are concerned the employers were asked to mention the facilities available, but none of them gave satisfactory response as they were not providing facilities such as weekly off-day, overtime casual leave, earned leave and medical leave, and recreational educational, or any other welfare, facilities. However, 78 per cent of the employer said that they had provision to give soft loan to their child workers for social and religious purposes or for family expenses as and when needed and 52 per cent of the employers reported that they had given to their employees advance, against their salaries as per their needs, but it was found that the employers who gave soft loan to the child workers, wanted to make them bound to work, in his own industry till loan was recovered. The Factory Act provides much more facilities to the child workers.

In the selected units, out of 309 child workers interviewed, 47 (15.2 per cent) were between 6 to 10 years, 96 (31.1 per cent) between 11 to 12 years and the remaining 166 (53.7) between 13-15 years at the time of data collection. The Factory Act, 1948 prohibits the employment of children below 17 years. While the child workers were asked to describe the action on the faults taken by their employers, 30 per cent said that they were threatened for any mistake and misbehaviour, 23.1 per cent were beaten and 1.6 per cent were discharged from the jobs. Mistakes by the child is quite obvious and it may be treated as a way of learning. A majority (75.7 per cent) of the child workers accepted that they met with the accident of fingers and nail abrade. Ten parents also accepted that 62 per cent suffered from headache, 41.3 from joints and stomach pain and 32.6 per cent from eye pain, but they were not given any compensation and medical aid by their employers.

41

DEMOGRAPHIC AND SOCIAL DIMENSIONS OF CHILD LABOUR IN INDIA

Introduction

An important issue in human resource development is the schooling and work participation of children. In some ways, the two activities could be competitive. If seasonal child labour is needed for agriculture, the formal education of boys may be interrupted during busy seasons. This may lead to higher drop-out rates and greater illiteracy among working boys. The schooling of girls is governed more intricately by factors such as caste, religion, family, occupation, productive and domestic roles for girls, marriage and kinship patterns.

Appropriate formal education for children is important for their physical and mental development. Future employment opportunities, income earning capacity and occupational mobility are dependent on the child's educational attainment. Lack of adequate schooling is likely to foreclose social mobility when the child grows up. For all these reasons, public policy should be directed towards the elimination of child labour and enhancement of the level of schooling of children.

Although a necessary requirement, the accessibility of schools may not be the only or even an important factor in determining the literacy rate or educational level. Even if education is free, there are other direct costs (such as, of buying school uniforms and books) that have to be borne by the parents. There are, also, indirect opportunity costs incurred, especially by poor families, in sending children to school instead of putting them to work or employing them for domestic chores. Children are often drafted to supplement the earnings of poor families. Boys may help in agriculture, take care of animals and supplement the family labour in peak season. Girls can undertake specific, though restricted, activities and can take care of the children and household, releasing the women for full-time daily labour. Such practices are bound to continue so long as the household income is inadequate to feed its members.

The Seventh Five Year Plan recognises that 'it is not feasible to eradicate the problem of child labour at the present stage of economic development.' In this article, a broad delineation of the demographic and social dimensions of child labour is made and a few relevant policy issues are raised.

Dimensions of the Problem

Child labour is usually defined as participation in gainful activity by children between the ages 5 to 14 years. Gender and industrial structure are expected to affect the child labour participation rate most sharply. To assess the dimensions of the problem, therefore, it is useful to differentiate between rural and urban areas and between males and females.

According to the 1981 census, in the rural areas, there were 6.7 million male children and 3.5 million female children working as main workers, i.e., working for the major part of the year (See Table 41.1). The child work participation rate was 9.2 per cent for males and 5.3 per cent for females based on main workers. If we include marginal workers also (working but not for the major part of the year), the participation rates are 10.0 and 7.8 for males and females respectively. Thus, nearly one out of ten male children and more than one out of twenty female children in rural areas were gainfully employed.

TABLE 41.1

Participation of Children in the Work Force by Sex

	Population (5-14 year)	*Main Workers*	*Main and Marginal Workers*	*Child Work Participation Rate (%)*	
				Main workers Marginal	*Main and Workers*
Rural					
Males	72,993	6,681	7,339	9.2	10.0
Females	66,671	3,506	5,211	5.3	7.8
Urban					
Males	20,446	732	757	3.6	3.7
Females	18,942	246	281	1.3	1.5

Sources: Report and Tables based on 5 Per Cent Sample Data, Series India, Part-II-Special, *Census of India, 1981,* New Delhi Registrar General and Census Commissioner, 1983.

Note: Figures in thousands.

In the urban areas, there were 0.7 million male and 0.2 million female children employed as main workers. If marginal workers are included, these figures are only slightly higher. The child work participation rate was 3.6 per cent for males and 1.3 per cent for female considering main workers. This was only about a third of the corresponding participation rate for each sex in the rural areas. Thus, using the census concepts and data, in 1981 the child work participation rate among males was about double that among females; and, in the rural areas, the rate was about three times as much as in the urban areas. Child work participation was substantial among rural male children and constituted one-tenth of the male child population aged 5 years and above.

To locate the segments of the population where child work participation proliferates, the child participation rates among literates and illiterates have been calculated in Table 41.2. In rural areas, the percentage child participation rate was 4.1 for males and 2.2 for females among literate children as against 13.4 for males and 6.4 for females among illiterate children. Similarly, in urban areas, the percentage child work participation rate was higher among illiterates: 7.0 for males and 2.5 for females in this group against 1.9 for males and 0.5 for females among the literates. Thus, there was some degree of association between illiteracy and work participation among children.

This association between illiteracy and work participation could be attributed to several causes. One reason is the competing demands made on children's time between school attendance and work participation. Another reason is the pecuniary means of parents to incur extra costs to send and to keep children at school. The third reason is the opportunity costs to parents in keeping children at school instead of putting them to productive work or domestic chores. Finally, this association could also be attributed to the concern for the 'quality' of their children among the relatively better-off parents. In framing policies for the reduction of child labour and universal compulsory education, it is necessary to recognise these several causes for the relationship between schooling and the work participation of children.

TABLE 41.2

Participation of Children in the Work Force by Sex Among Literates and Illiterates

	Population		*Main Workers*		*Child Work Participation Rate (%)*	
	Literate	*Illiterate*	*Literate*	*Illiterate*	*Literate*	*Illiterate*
Rural						
Males	33,290	39,703	1,358	5,323	4.1	13.4
Females	18,135	48,536	392	3,118	2.2	6.4
Urban						
Males	13,852	6,594	270	462	1.9	7.0
Females	11,466	7,476	57	190	0.5	2.5

Source: Report and Tables based on 5 Per Cent Sample Data, Series-1, India, Part-II-Special, *Census of India, 1981*, New Delhi, Registrar General and Census Commissioner, 1983.

Note: Figures in thousands.

TABLE 41.3

Child Work Participation (as Main Workers) by Sex by Major Industrial Categories

		Rural		Urban		% to Population Aged 5-14 Years				% to Main Workers Aged 5 + Years			
						Rural		Urban		Rural		Urban	
		Male	Female	Male	Female	Male	Female	Male	Female	Male	Female	Male	Female
I.	Cultivators	2,869	1,093	43	9	3.9	1.6	0.2	0.1	3.8	7.4	2.0	3.6
II.	Agricultural labour	2,694	1,925	89	56	3.7	2.9	0.4	0.3	8.2	9.7	4.7	6.3
III.	Livestock, etc.	537	137	26	4	0.7	0.2	0.1	N	15.7	18.7	3.5	4.0
IV.	Mining and quarrying	14	11	2	1	N	N	N	N	2.1	8.2	0.5	3.4
V.	(a) Household manufacturing, etc.	171	153	58	43	0.2	0.2	0.3	0.2	4.7	10.2	3.4	7.6
	(b) Other manufacturing, etc.	170	89	230	52	0.2	0.1	1.1	0.3	3.2	10.7	2.2	6.8
VI.	Construction	28	20	24	8	N	N	0.1	N	1.8	10.0	1.4	5.1
VII.	Trade and commerce	84	14	140	7	0.1	N	0.7	N	1.9	3.2	1.6	1.5
VIII.	Transport	9	1	22	1	N	N	0.1	N	0.5	2.1	0.6	0.8
IX.	Other services	105	58	98	65	0.1	0.1	0.5	0.3	1.4	5.0	1.1	3.2
X.	All industries	6,681	3,511	732	246	9.2	5.3	3.6	1.3	4.6	8.9	1.8	4.6

Source: Report and Tables based on 5 Per Cent Sample Data, Series-1, India, Part-II-Special, *Census of India, 1981* New Delhi, Registrar General and Census Commissioner, 1983.

Note: N. denotes negligible.

It is useful to identify the industrial sectors in which child work participation is rampant. In rural areas, 3.9 per cent of the child work participation of males was among cultivator families and 3.7 among agricultural labour families (Table 41.3). The corresponding rates for female child work participation were 1.6 per cent and 2.9 per cent. This is not surprising since the dominant sector in the rural economy is agriculture. For similar reasons, in urban areas, the male child work participation rate was the highest in processing and manufacturing in the non-household sector. To adjust for these structural differences, child workers as a percentage of workers aged 5 years and above was calculated for each sector. It was fund that, in rural areas, this percentage was highest for both genders in the livestock sector and next highest in the agricultural labour sector. In urban areas, this percentage did not show as large a variation among the sectors as in rural areas. Hence, we may conclude the child work participation is particularly rampant in rural areas among families working in the livestock sector and as agricultural labourers. Families working in these sectors are also among the poorest in rural areas. Therefore, there is an empirical association between child work participation and poverty.

From the Seventh Five Year Plan document, the trends in child work participation rate to the year 2000 may be surmised (see Table 41.4). Both in rural and urban areas, among males and females, these rates are expected to decline slightly but not to negligible levels. By the year 2000, the actual number of child workers would increase by about 50 per cent in rural areas and by over 100 per cent in urban areas.

TABLE 41.4

Child Labour Force Projection by Sex

	1980			*2000*		
	5+	*5-14*	*% Child Labour*	*5+*	*5-14*	*% Child Labour*
Rural						
Males	148.9	9.1	6.1	208.5	9.6	4.6
Females	66.2	5.9	8.9	93.4	6.2	6.6
Urban						
Males	44.8	1.1	2.5	101.0	3.3	3.3
Females	10.8	0.7	6.5	24.9	1.2	4.8

Source: *Seventh Five Year Plan, 1985-90,* Planning Commission, New Delhi, 1985, Vol. 1, pp. 12-13, based on NSSO: 32nd Round, 1977-78.

Note: Figures are in million.

Past Research on Child Labour

Socio-demographic studies conducted so far provide some findings on the linkage between child work participation, schooling and poverty.

Kanbargi and Kulkarni (1985) have observed that age and gender constrain the quantum and nature of the gainful and domestic activities of children. While boys aged 5 to 7 years work, on the average, for about 2 hours a day, by 12 to 14 years they work for 5 hours a day. Boys put in more time tending livestock and working on the family farm or enterprise. Girls work for longer hours in very different activities from boys, such as in food preparation and domestic chores. The daily time spent at school and in school-related activities does not increase appreciably with age for school going children but the proportion of children at school declines sharply with age. This is reflected in the apparent decline, with age, of daily time spent on schooling among all children.

With an increase in the size of land owned or livestock held, child work participation appears to increase, especially among labour-hiring families. The higher the father's level of education, the more likely are children to attend school. Scheduled caste families have the lowest school attendance rate for children whereas higher castes have higher rates. There are regional differences in child labour participation and the schooling of children.

Srikantan *et. al.* (1978) have studied child work participation in the integrated development of a command area. Their investigation shows that for the younger generation males aged 5 to 19 years, the percentage literate were much higher for dependents than for earners in the three study groups used. This suggests that early work participation perhaps prevents (regular) attendance at school and leads to more illiteracy. Similar differences were observed for girls. Again, compared to the older generation, the younger generation had less literacy among earners and more literacy among dependants. This indicates the competition between work participation and schooling so that, among dependants, youths are more literate than adults of the same sex, whereas among earners, the contrary is true. The relationship between education and work participation of children is similar. These differentials tend to confirm the competing demands made on children by work participation and schooling, both on boys and girls, and especially among poorer families.

Policy Issues

While there would be complete agreement regarding the need to abolish child labour as soon as possible, there are several policy issues as to how this should be done. Should specific measures be adopted to give family incentives to withdraw children form work and put them in school? Should there be incentives given to children at school to increase enrolments and reduce the drop-out rate? Would broad-based general measures for poverty alleviation provide better means for reducing child labour? Finally, could such measures be successfully implemented in the field?

Although the number of child workers is large in the rural areas, as a percentage of the total number of children it is only 10.0 for males and 7.8 for females. In urban areas he percentage child work participation rate is much less—3.7 for males and 1.5 for females. Most of the child workers tend to be concentrated in rural areas, among the illiterate, in the agricultural labour and livestock sectors, and generally among the poorer families. This uneven distribution aggravates the problems of child workers and their families.

Family incentives and subsidies for sending children to school are difficult to provide since the beneficiaries are widely scattered and cannot claim the benefits by themselves. Provision of direct benefits for children (like free school lunch) could be organised more easily. But the poorest families may benefit the least from such schemes in view of their lower school enrolment and higher drop out rates. In the long-run, poverty alleviation measures are the surest ways of reducing child labour in domestic and productive work. Hence measures for the reduction of child labour should be dovetailed to and supported by broader poverty alleviation and productive employment generation programmes such as the Integrated Rural Development Programme, the National Rural Employment Programme and the Rural Landless Employment Guarantee Programme.

Some studies have shown that children are exploited in specific industries (like the fireworks factories in Sivakasi). Apart from this, children are engaged in household enterprises and in domestic chores. In poorer families, this could involve heavy work and long hours (as in carpet and handloom weaving, collecting firewood, carrying water over long distances, taking care of animals, attending to children and cooking). All these activities, apart from keeping the child away from school, are likely to place a heavy strain in the health and development of the child. It would also seal the fate of the child as an unskilled low paid worker.

Legal measures for improving the working condition of children are certainly called for in specific industries that exploit child labour. However, implementation of such laws would be difficult in the small scale and traditional sectors of the economy (like fireworks manufacture and livestock rearing).

Poorer families generally have disproportionately more child workers, at least in some sectors and, at the same time, also have more children. The marginal costs of child rearing are comparatively less than the benefits derived from children by such families. It would, however, be incorrect to attribute the larger family size to the anticipated benefits to be derived from child labour. Rather, this association between fertility and child work participation springs form a set of traditional values that emphasise motherhood and a large number of children. Reduction in family size norms can take place only with a growing desire for higher quality children and increasing the costs of bringing up and educating them. If this explanation of the relationship between fertility and child work participation is accepted, then public policy should be directed more towards improving the quality of children desired so that both fertility and child work participation is would decline. Here, again, broader measures directed towards productive employment generation and female education are more likely to succeed in the long-run than specific measures for the immediate reduction of child labour.

REFERENCES

Kanbargi, Ramesh and P.M. Kulkarni. 1985, Child Labour, Schooling and Fertility in Rural Karnataka, South India, mimeo, Bangalore, Institute for Social and Economic Change.

Srikantan, K.S., B.K. Narayan and D. Vasudeva Rao. 1978, *Female and Child Work participation in the Integrated Development of a Command Area*, Bangalore, Institute for social and Economic Change.

Government of India, 1985. *The Seventh Five Year Plan, 1985-90*, New Delhi, Planning Commission.

42

CHILD LABOUR AND ITS SOCIAL IMPLICATIONS

If one desires to know a nation, he should look for it into its children. Child is not only the future of a nation and its aspirations but also, and mainly, its strength in reserve. The future of nation is best insured if its children are healthy and active, educated and informed, disciplined and trained, as well as free from social prejudices, having a scientific outlook. It is, therefore a duty cast on the society at large to protect this crop of nation from the damaging effects of excessive exposure to vagaries of climate, as well as, from social oppression and injustice.

Taking all the aspects as a whole, the child-hood is the most significant period of one's life. It is considered, and rightly so, to be the very foundation of life on which depends the entire structure-the whole personality as such. Child—the father of man—is the natural future leader of the nation in every walk of life, may it be industry, education, politics, social services, administration, defence, civil services or anything else. It is during this formative period of moulding that the life begins to acquire shape and substance, and the attitudes, behaviours, manners and emotions do get developed.

Though it was mainly in this context that the problem of child labour and its exploitation had long been the subject of sporadic concern, it has been only recently that the probable extent and incidence of this long standing phenomena could be brought to the full view of the general public.

It is indisputable that in view of the over-all and long ranging consequences of the practice and tradition of child labour that it deserves to be placed high on the list of our priorities. Then comes the question of ways and means by which this problem should be tackled, and they would, and should, very from situation to situation. However, in each and every case it is imperative that it should be preceded by collection of facts and figures, dissemination of information, understanding of the nature of the problem and a reasonably high level of social concern for mitigation of this centuries old and the most naked form of human exploitation.

Concept of Child Labour

The term 'child labour' is, at times, used as a synonym for 'employed child' or 'working child.' In this sense it is co-existensive with any work done by a child for profit or reward. But more commonly than not, the term 'child labour' is used in a derogatory sense. It suggests something which is hateful and exploitative.

Thus, child labour is recognised by the sociologists, development workers, educationists and medical professionals as hazardous and injurious to the child, both physically and mentally.

Homer Folks, the Chairman of the United States National Child Labour Committee, has defines child labour as "... any work by children that interferes with their full physical development, their opportunities for a desirable minimum of education or their needed recreation."[1]

V.V. Giri has thus distinguished the two concepts of the 'child labour's:[2]

> "The term `child labour' is commonly interpreted in two different ways: first, as an economic practice and secondly, as a social evil. In the first context it signifies employment of children in gainful occupations with a view to adding to the labour income of the family. It is in the second context that the term child labour is now more generally used. In assessing the nature and extent of the social evil, it is necessary to take into account the character of the jobs on which the children are engaged, the dangers to which they are exposed and the opportunities of development which they have been denied."

Wage labour is, as we have seen, rather too narrow a criterion. For the wider connotation we have to include in it the notion of income earning activities which is beset with problems. The main difficulty lies in determining as to what constitutes contribution to the income of families and households. We have to include in it the usual household duties, such as, cooking, fetching water, looking after the kids, etc., as indirect contribution to household income for the wider and more useful definition.

The Committee on Child Labour has, therefore, concluded in its report that "child labour can broadly be defined as that segment of the `child population' which participates in work, either paid or unpaid."[3]

It would be pertinent to add that in the case of a child, the labour is specially harmful to him because the energy that should have been expended on the nurturing of his latent powers gets consumed for purposes of bare survival. Child labour, therefore, assumes, the character of a social problem in as much as it hinders, arrests or distorts the natural growth processes and prevents the child from attaining his full bloom manhood.[4]

Thus, child labour, in a restricted sense, means the engagement of children in gainful occupations which are often hazardous to their health, and deny them the opportunities of development. Three factors should, therefore, be necessarily present in employment/

engagement of a child so as to bring it within the concept of child labour. Firstly, the child should be engaged in some gainful activities; secondly, the work to which he is exposed, must be detrimental to his natural growth; thirdly, it must deprive him of the opportunity for development. Hence, obviously, any work taken by a father from his child on his field or at his business place for long hours also gets covered by this definition, but any work done by the students at school workshops cannot be termed as 'child labour.'

The term 'child labour' applies to children engaged in all types of activities whether these be industrial or non-industrial but which are detrimental to their physical, mental, moral and social well being and development. The brain of a child develops anatomically till the age of ten, the lungs till the age of fourteen and the muscles till the age of seventeen. Anything which obstructs the natural growth of any or all of these vital organs should be considered as detrimental to natural physical growth, or even hazardous.

In India, unfortunately, there is no such statutory provision which defines the term 'child labour' in precise terms. Even the numerous legislative provisions which prescribe the minimum age for employment in different vocations do not fix any uniform age, presumably, for reasons of multiplicity in the nature of activities in which children are employed.

The minimum age for entrance into the labour market has not been precisely fixed by law or convention, either at the national or the international level. Hence, child labour should be understood in the context of given circumstance and the nature of occupation. According to generally prevalent conceptions, the child labour normally constitutes children between the age group of 14 to 17 years. But, in fact, children of even much younger age are also coerced, or forced by the family circumstances, to undertake various jobs for hire or reward, or without any economic gain whatsoever.

Magnitude of the Problem

The accurate and precise estimate of the overall magnitude of child labour, either from a qualitative or quantitative point of view, is virtually not possible due to the predominance of informal and unorganised nature of the labour market. The problem of estimating the child labour force becomes all the more complicated and complex on account of the multiplicity of concepts, modes of measurement, methods of research and the sources of information for data collection.

A report published by the Director General of International Labour Organisation in 1960 says:

> "Children and youth make up a fifth, or a fourth or even a third of the total labour force in many of the industrialising countries. Young people between 15, to 19 make up 20% of the labour force of the Egyptian Region of the United Arab Republic, and a higher percentage in many of the less developed Asian and African countries; and it should be noted that in most of the less developed areas

the great bulk of children seek to enter the labour force by the time they are 12, 13 or 14, if they have not begun to work at a much earlier age."[5]

In respect to India the report says, "About a third of the 10 to 14 year old children in rural areas and an eighth of those in urban areas are at work.[6]

The Report IV (1) of the 57th Session of the International Labour Conference, Geneva, 1972, indicates that 90% or more of the child population was engaged in the employment market in the developing regions of the world. The report has also indicate that 4,11,25,000 children of these regions, making 5.1% of the whole of 0-14 age group, were engaged in 1960; and in 1970 the number was reduced to 3,99,75,000 which formed 4% of all children. In the industrialised areas the number of child workers in the year 1960 was 40,85,000 which formed 1.4% of all children and in 1970 the number was 33,43,000, constituting 1.1% of the total number of children. Geographically, the 1960 and 1970 figures were:[7]

TABLE 42.1

Percentage of Child Workers to Child Population in Different Regions of the World in 1960 and 1970

Regions	*1960*	*%age*	*1970*	*%age*
1	2	3	4	5
Africa	60,55,000	5.2	59,92,000	4.0
North America	2,82,000	0.5	3,11,000	0.5
Latin America including Caribbean	31,59,000	3.6	31,22,000	2.6
East Asia	83,05,000	2.9	58,30,000	1.9
South Asia including India	2,39,85,000	6.8	2,53,71,000	5.4
Europe	20,70,000	1.9	16,00,000	1.4
Oceania excluding Micronesia and Polynesia	33,000	0.7	26,000	0.5
U.S.S.R.	13,21,000	2.0	10,66,000	1.5

Since the 1960s, considerable progress has been made in the reducing child labour, largely due to the expansion of primary education in developing countries. But, it is still widespread in the Third World's agricultural sector, the informal urban sector and domestic services. However, this improvement has been uneven and far from universal, leaving many millions of children exposed to premature death or maiming in dangerous jobs.

According to a recent International Labour Organisation study on the exploitation of young children in hazardous industries in the developing world, as many as 200 million children, under the age of 15, are workers, excluding those who help on family farms and small holdings.[8]

The study on child labour says that in some Asian countries the child worker under 15 years of age represents as much as 11% of the entire labour force. In parts of Africa the proportion is as high as 17% and in some Latin American countries available estimates show that from 12 to 26% of children may be working. Experts believe that there are probably at least ten million working children in the Third World.[9]

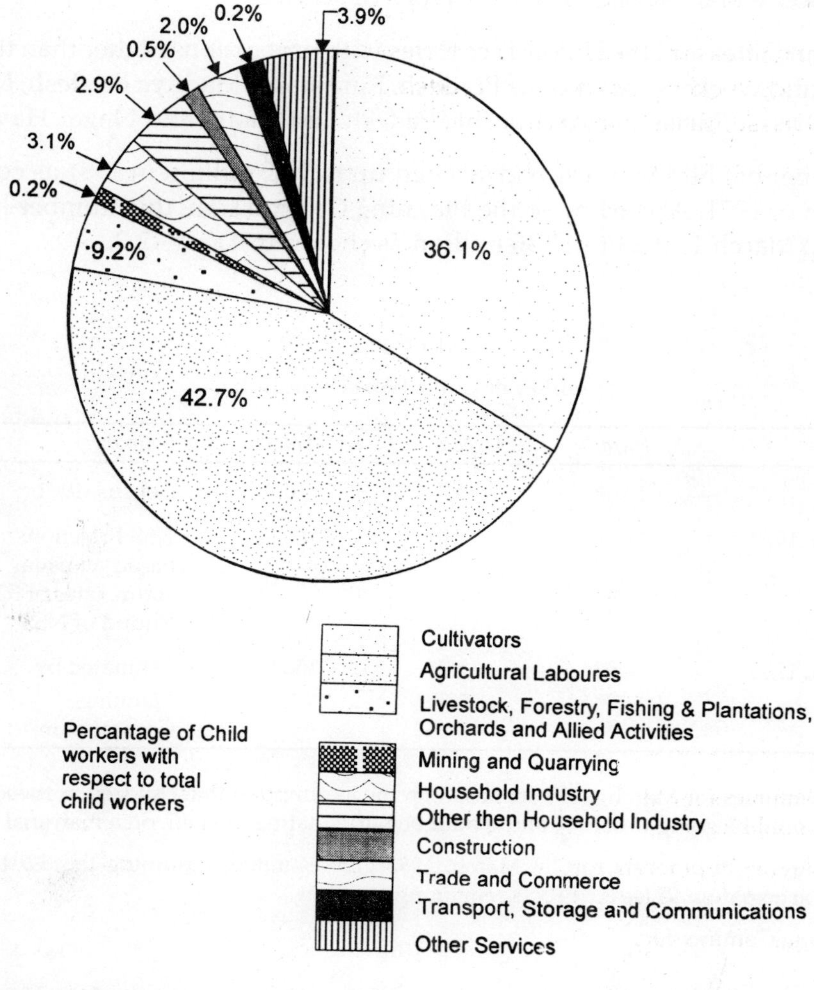

Fig. 42.1 Child Workers by Nature of Activity 1971.

The data available from the International Labour Organisation's Year Book of Labour Statistics, 1988, indicates that in absolute terms the number of child labour is the highest in India but percentage-wise it is not so.[10]

In respect to India, a general idea can be had from the census of 1971, which shows that 10.7 million children were engaged in employment. Out of them only 0.7 million, constituting 7%, were working in urban areas, the remaining 10 million, that is, 93% were employed in rural areas. 36.1% of the child labour was employed as cultivators and 42.7% as agricultural labourers. The remaining 8.2% were employed in animal husbandry, forestry, fishing, hunting, plantation and horticulture, etc., 6.1% in house-hold and industries, 2.4% in trade, commerce, transport, storage and communication, and the rest in construction work, mining and other types of services.

The Indian States and the Union Territories with proportions higher than the national average of child workers are Andhra Pradesh, Karnataka, Madhya Pradesh, Meghalaya, Nagaland, Orissa, Rajasthan, Arunachal Pradesh and Dadra and Nagar Haveli.

The number of child workers had swelled up to 14.5 million in 1981 as compared to 10.74 million in 1971. According to the Planning Commission, this number had further increased till March 1, 1983 to 17.36 million as shown in Table 42.2,

TABLE 42.2

Number of Child Workers in India

Year	*Rural*	*Urban*	*Total*	*Source*
1971	10.00	0.7	10.7	Census, 1971
1st March, 1978	14.68	1.57	16.26	NSS Projctions based on usual status rates of 32nd Round of NSS.
1st March, 1983	14.03 (15.57)	1.67 (1.79)	15.70 (17.36)	Estimated by Planning Commission.

Notes: (i) Estimates for March, 1983 are based on the assumption that children in the age-group 5-9 would be going to school and would be participating, if at all, on a marginal basis.

(ii) Figures in brackets for 1st March, 1983 give estimates assuming the 5-9 Labour Force Participation Rates (LEPR) as remaining constant.

Source: Planning Commission.

A non-governmental organisation, named as, Concerned, for Working Children (CWC), claims that 1,000 million children are at work in India, but the Operations Research Group (ORG) Baroda, puts the figure at 44 million only. However, the findings of the ORG have gained more credibility in the welfare circles since they are based on a nation-wide survey.

The Labour and Welfare Minister, Mr. Ram Vilas Paswan, informed the Rajya Sabha on March 30, 1990 that India has 1.7 crores of child labour according to the National Sample Survey of 1987-88.

Nature of Child-Work

From time immemorial it has been the practice that children were to engage themselves in some sort of work or the other, both in home and in the field. In olden days, children of tender age performed even toilsome work alongwith adult agricultural and other workers. In the mediaeval period, children used to be engaged as trainees under the guidance of their parents to learn traditional crafts of the family.

The earlier reports of the Royal Commission on Labour, the Labour Investigation Committee on working conditions of children and a number of surveys conducted by the Labour Bureau and other non-governmental agencies-all invariably focus on one point that children do light work in comparison to adult workers. But, it is no more true now. These days they do not less a hard work than their parents in order to earn enough for their family's survival.

The International Labour Organisation's report has forecast that as the modernisation of world agriculture goes ahead, the number of rural children vulnerable to exploitation may rise.[11]

The social scenario, according tot he report of Gurupadaswami Committee on Child Labour, changed radically with the advent of industrialisation and urbanisation. The Committee further says:[12]

> ".... The family members no longer worked as a team and in caste sanctioned occupations. The child had to work as an individual person either under an employer or independently without enjoying the benevolent protection of his guardian. His work place was divorced and totally dissimilar from his home. His job exposed him to various kinds of health hazards emanating from the extensive use of chemicals and poisonous substances in industries and the pollutants discharged by them. His work was reputitive, monotonous and unpromising. His hours of work stretched long but his earnings were meagre. His employer, in most of the instances, maltreated him and exploited him unscrupulously. His work environment thus endangered his physical health and mental growth."

In agriculture, children are employed not only in agricultural operations but in non-agricultural operations also. They are employed in such diverse agricultural operations as ploughing, sowing, transplanting, weeding, harvesting threshing and guarding the crops, etc.

In plantations, child labour is a part of family labour. They assist their parents in plucking of leaves and coffee berries, or collecting of latex, or they do some secondary jobs, such as, weeding spreading of fertilisers, the care of nurseries, digging of drains, etc. They are also employed to pick out stalks and coarse leaves of tea spread over the green leaves in the shadow.

There is also an increasing concern about the accident and disease incidence among child agricultural workers. Controls on hazardous insecticides and pesticides are deficient and neither the children nor their parents receive any instruction as how to use them safely. The same is true of mechanical operations.

Children in cities per form much larger varieties of activities than those in village because of the extensively diversified structure of urban economies. Often, children are employed for packing, labelling, etc., in the factories. Other industries in which children are engaged are match factories, bidi manufacturing, mica cutting, wood and cork, furniture and fixture, printing, publishing and allied trades, leather products, rubber and rubber products, machinery, transport equipment, lock, factories, gem cutting and polishing, potteries, glass bangle industries, brass work, carpet industries and personal services like laundries, dyeing and cleaning.

In Sivakasi (Tamil Nadu) match factories, children are put to work at frame filling, box filling and bundle rolling operations and at times work is carried home, Similarly, in bidi industries, children help the adults in cutting and cleaning of the leaves, and when bidies are rolled up children do the work of binding and closing of the ends of the bidies. Some children are also engaged to do the rolling work with their nimble fingers.

In pencil industries, children work amidst hazardous state dust that condemns them to early disability and death from lung diseases. Similarly, in gem cutting and polishing industries of Jaipur, Children are exposed to exploitation. During the first year of their entrance in the gem cutting and polishing, they work as helpers, learn cutting of gems on abrasive wheels and also do such jobs as cleaning of the premises, etc. After one year they learn how to shape stones by grinding facets on them. They take about four or five years to learn cutting, shaping, and drum-polishing of uncut or unshaped stones. Then they learn polishing of facetted stones on finer grinding wheels. Within next two or three years, their output is comparable to that of average adults. Mostly they work on job basis in unhealthy environment and there is absolutely no security of job.

Likewise, in potteries industry in Khurja in Bulandshahr District of Uttar Pradesh, children carry empty moulds to the worker who works on Jigger Jolly machine and carry the filled moulds out to dry in the sun. The boys who do this job are called 'phantiwalas; the 'phanti' being a piece of wood on which five or six moulds are carried. When the pots are partially dry, these children take them to the adult workers engaged on the finishing job. Thus, a weight of eight to ten kilograms, and sometimes even more than that, is carried in every round by a child engaged in these industries. This weight is too much for children of tender age, and their hands and legs often tremble after every round. The regular carrying of heavy weights by young children for long hours often causes physical deformity in them. Similarly, in brickyards, children are made to carry heavy loads which often leave them injured, weakened and even crippled.

In carpet factories of Bhadoi and Mirzapur of Uttar Pradesh, the child weaver has to work under such strenuous conditions which ultimately damage his eye-sight, and may also result into backache and other physical disabilities.

In glass-bangle industries of Firozabad of Uttar Pradesh, a large number of children work as helpers in almost every process of manufacture, such as, "Jurai" (joining of ends), "Katai" (cutting), "Jhalai" (patching), "Chunai" (sorting), "Pakai" (backing) and "Hilringold" (ornamentation). Most of these processes are extremely hazardous even for the adults, especially the blowing of the molten glass into required shapes, and expose the worker to various lung diseases. Children carry molten glass on "labyas" (a sort of iron rod) from the furnace to the adult worker and then back to the furnace for replenishment. The temperature in these furnaces ranges between 700°C to 800°C which often causes burn injuries and accidents to child workers.

Children in the age group 8-15 years are also employed in Zari-making and embroidery industry in Lucknow. They sit and work for long hours in over-crowded dingy rooms with poor lighting and ventilation. Many of them, therefore, suffer from eye diseases.

In lock industries of Aligarh, Uttar Pradesh, children are employed in almost all the processes of manufacturing and packing. They are made to work on hand-presses, polishing drums, buffing machines, electroplating devices and in spray-painting units, as well as, for filing of various components, spring-making, assembling and packing. In lock industries the available data go to show that the processes of polishing, buffing, electroplating, spray-painting and operating of the hand-presses and relatively more hazardous to the health of child workers. In Purdil Nagar of district Aligarh, Uttar Pradesh, good number of children are engaged in the manufacture of glass beeds and immitation gems, performing such jobs as that of brushing, polishing, packing and labelling. Some children and women do the drilling of beds, and string-making at their home also.

Millions of small boys and girls are engaged in the unorganised sector, comprising hotels, restaurants, canteens, wayside 'dhabas,' shops, repair workshops, and establishments of various types. They also work as hawkers, coolies, shoe-shine boys and venders. In big cities, children can be seen cleaning and washing automobiles just for a tip. The bigger the city, the higher is the persistent demand for teenagers to work as domestic servants and it is there that they are often subjected to worst types of exploitation without any means of protections-legal or social. Thee young servants are malnourished, often made to sleep on the kitchen floor and are, as a rule, not permitted to attend school. Sexual abuse is also reported to be frequent.

In a good number of occupations child worker is invariably exposed to risks of various nature because of his tender age. For instance, he is likely to suffer burn injuries while working round about big ovens, or while carrying hot beverages; the newspaper hawkers and shoe-shine boys are exposed to the risk of road accidents; rag-pickers may get cut injuries from glass pieces or broken tin cans; or the child working on construction sites alongwith his parents may sustain injuries while carrying brick or stone loads.

Interestingly, children are sometimes also employed as performing artists. They are given roles in films, and in circus they perform acrobatic feats. Magicians and jugglers use them as 'Jamura' (the helping boy) and they are also used by them for arousing public sympathy at wayside shows for alms.

Some writers and social workers are of the view that begging is a major field of operation where children are put to work. Mrs. Sengupta has observed:[13]

> "Our seething millions where child employment is rife and has become a vicious form of exploitation.... begging is becoming a real profession and there are scaring rumours that gangsters and syndicates of human beings trade in human babies and children. Certainly the mother clad in a rag and clutching a baby in her arms is a sight that is shameful, children are drugged or even, one hears, tortured, To see pavement dwellers in all their horrors living in filth, children picking up rejected and popping food mixed with filth into their mouths makes one feel desperate: but no one seems to do anything.... there should be proper deterrent action to prevent from flaunting drugged babies or little tots on the road and to use them for employment purposes."

However, it is open to serious debate as to whether begging should be considered a form of work at all, and, if not, should it not be totally prohibited for one and all.

The most nefarious, rather barbarian form of child exploitation is the practice of bonded labour. The child is handed over by the parents to the loaner as security or collateral security against small sums of loan obtained at an exorbitant rate of interest. The bonded child usually gets only a handful of coarse grain for his subsistance. He has to toil very hard and exist at the mercy of his lord for the whole of his life without the least hope of redemption. The mortgagee is usually some big landlord, money-lender or the village businessman, and the mortgager is the poor landless labourer. Though this practices is prevalent in many parts of rural India, it is predominant in Vellore district of Tamil Nadu but with a distinguishing feature that there the bonded child is allowed to stay with his parents on the condition that he must present himself at work daily at 8 a.m. The practice of bonded labour is still prevalent despite stringent laws against it which provide for imprisonment of, and imposition of fine on, the guilty.

Though strange, but it is true that the owners or managers of the lock industry of Aligarh also take in orphans as "purchased labour" and when their premises are inspected by the law enforcement authorities they try to get away on the plea that the orphan is no other a person than his own son.

Curiously, some well to do urban families, having connections in the counter-side take in some child of a poor relative, ostensibly, for supporting the child out of sympathy for the poor relatives, but he or she ends up as a domestic servant with no opportunity for education.

It has been also discovered that a sizable number of children ranging between 5 to 12 years of age had actually been kidnapped from different places to weave carpets and were forced to work for as long as 22 hours a day. These children treated like virtual slaves, were found to bear scar marks of torture. They were, reportedly, severely beaten even with iron rods, if they were difficient in work or committed errors in weaving.[14]

Thus, a closer look would go to show that child labour far from being uniform in pattern and magnitude, is by and large concentrated in certain specific activities and industries. Moreover, there appears to be considerable variance in the form, quantum and intensity of exploitation.

Child Labour and Delinquency

Basically, child labour, beggary, vagrancy and delinquency are some of the symptoms of the disorganisational process of the society. Therefore, these interrelated problems deserve to be treated and tackled within the frame work of juvenile juristical system.

Due to rapid growth of industrialisation and urbanisation, a fairly large number of people migrate from rural to urban areas in search of gainful employment or vocation. This situation greatly hampers and disrupts the stability of the traditional family life and its basic structure, and also diminishes the capability of the family to discharge effectively its responsibilities towards children. In order to supplement the meagre and irregular income of the family, children of the migrated families are left with no choice but to go to the market to sell their labour power. It not only adversely effect their physical and mental health and natural growth, and, side by side mars their future economic prospects, but also creates manifold problems of delinquency which is more frequent among children who work in street shops and as domestic servants. The child gets paid some money, howsoever meagre, for his services. It develops a feeling of independence, though wrongly in the mind of child labour. As the child is not well capable of differentiating between the good and the bad, he is likely to mis-spent the money which he had earned at a very heavy cost. Because of lack of education and proper grooming, he often trends to be impertinent at home and may even behave disobediently when asked by the parents to part with his money for the family.

The parents and other family members fast lose the control, nay, even the moral authority, over the child labour, who soon begins to imitate his adult fellow workers, mistaking them to be their ideals. The illiterate child, having freed himself from the family ties, becomes susceptible to all sorts of evil influences which may turn him into a heavy smoker, a drug-addict, a gambler, a smuggling operator, a film addict, a thief, a pick-pocket, or even a hard criminal. Such children are often seen to be in the habit of using filthy and abusive language. Some of them soon leave their home for good to live with their gangs.

These children, as a rule, leave their home very early in the morning and return to their parental shelter after sunset. The parents also return home from their work almost at the same time. Consequently, they hardly have sufficient time at their disposal to be with their children. This results into neglect of the children, and lack of supervision of, and control over, them. Guidance is conspicuous by its absence in such homes, and all the more so when the parents happen to be illiterate. Children of such homes are an easy prey for anti-social and criminal elements of the society who allure them away even for sexual misuse.

Thus grows a whole race of children, bodily and mentally ill-equipped, in a psycho-socio environment of privation and desperate struggle for existence, face to face with the predatory demands of the exploiting world. Their efforts at preparation for adulthood are cruelly shattered and crumbled by the tentacles of the monster of greed, oppression and inhumanity and by the time they acquire maturity, they are a lot of bruised and impaired individuals.

Mr. Deep Mathur hits at deep relationship between crime and child labour in the following words:

> "The relation between crime and child labour cannot be underestimated. Deprived of parental care, thee children are particularly vulnerable to exploitation for their employers own nefarious ends. Common are the stories of their involvement in the movement of illicit liquor thefts and smuggling. Moreover, the climate in which they are forced to operate, has a generous share of threats, beatings, coercion, financial insecurity and police atrocities for minor lapses. A dangerously distorted view of life begins to crystalise which ultimately poses a threat to law and order. Small wonder that a large proportion of delinquent children come from our nation's work force."[15]

Thus, it is obvious that the child labour is fruitful neither for the child himself, nor his family or the society. Therefore, in dealing with the problem of child labour and delinquency, the cost benefits, resource constraints and other considerations should not be allowed to dampen the spirit of the status because they aim to serve the larger interests of the society as such.

Desirability of Work for Children

The desirability and morality of taking work from children is still a controversial issue with extremely divergent views. Some consider all work for an earning bad for children. According to Encyclopaedia of Social Sciences:

> "Every child labourer is a called with all the needs of other children. He needs

opportunity for growth not only physical, but in mind and personality, through all the activities and experiences, which properly belong to childhood, when the business of wage earning, or of participation in self or family support, conflicts directly or indirectly, with the business of growth and education, the social evil of child labour becomes evident."[16]

The other view is that if the determinental and evil effects and consequences of work are minimised, it will be helpful for the growth and health of the child. Government of India also subscribes to this view:[17]

"All forms of work by children cannot be considered deleterious. In fact work lays an important role in the development of the child if it involves purpose, plan and freedom. The function of work in childhood should be primarily developmental and not economic; and children's work as a social good is the direct anti-thesis of child labour as a social evil."

Some claim that child labour has certain welcome implications, such as, transmission of skills, evolution of attitude to work, industrial discipline, socialisation, class consciousness and operation of labour market.[18]

In addition to this, the advocates of child labour assert that "some types of work are a source of pride, status and perhaps independence for the children themselves."[19]

Even at the time of industrial revolution there were writers who had argued that children "were better off in factories than in the streets"[20]

The Report on "Child Labour in Indian Industries" says:[21]

"Taking a global view of the situation in which India features prominently, the International Labour Organisation came to the conclusion: The problem with child labour is that it can hardly be legislated away, for its roots lie in abject poverty. Where social and economic conditions have improved, children go to school and child labour has virtually disappeared. So any society which wants its children to be free to learn and play must first free the entire population from fear of want. This means ensuring basic human needs of all people."

A good number of social thinkers are firmly of the view that the legal sanction for, and recognition of, child labour would be against the spirit of the resolution on National Policy for children which had declared the children to be the supremely important asset of the nation and asserted that child labour is also against the concept of a welfare state. They have further asserted that child labour should not be recognised by law or convention at any cost, even if the condition of the poor has not improved and the pace of economic development has not accelerated over a period of time.

It is worth noticing that the child labour reduces the opportunities of adult employment and, thus, reduces the bargaining power of adult workers. Experts claim that if all the children were withdrawn from the labour market in India, employment opportunities for at least 15 million adults would be created. Thus, the employment of child labour results in permanently weakening of the main labour force.

Child labour, it is claimed, swells the number and cost of accidents for which children are more frequently responsible than the adults. Encyclopaedia of Social Sciences says:

> "Long hours of work, late hours of night employment, continuous standing, sitting or use of single set of muscles, emphasis on the finer neuro-muscular coordinations with attendant nervous strain, indoor confinement in noisy factories and dusty trades, carrying heavy loads under the arm or lifting heavy weights, pressure of speed in the performance of simple mechanical acts, contact with industrial poisons, exposure to inclement weather are unsuitable occupations and provide harmful conditions for the growing child particularly susceptible to certain deformities and diseases."[22]

However, in the prevailing economic conditions of India, the total eradication of child labour does not appear to be feasible though much desirable. Though the ultimate aim of every society must,, undoubtedly, be complete eradication of child labour, the least we can do is to try our level best to minimise the evils of child labour and prohibit it in hazardous occupations in view of the fact that, under present circumstances, total eradication of child labour, at one stretch, would amount to inflicting unbearable sufferings on the poverty-ridden families.

The International Labour Organisation, in its report of 1980, also holds that child labour in general should be gradually eliminated because of:

(a) the physical and mental havoc wrought by it;
(b) the displacement of adult workers in effect by child workers; and
(c) the lowering of adult earning power due to its prevalence.

Employers' Viewpoint

Supporters of child labour argue and, perhaps, believe also that children who go to work at a very early age tend to acquire the habit of being industrious and labourious which is profitable for them in the long run because they become well trained workers at an early age. Many employers, exhibiting benevolent pride in their child labour force, assert that the child who starts working at a very early age soon gets to know his work and the value of money which takes him to higher success in his later life.

The National Commission on Labour was told by some of the employers that unless the fingers get trained at a very early age when they are nimble, there adaptation later on to the requirements of work would be indeed difficult.[23] The employers also agrued that handicrafts, like carpet weaving, cannot do without the child's nimble fingers, and so is the case with cottage industries like that of match sticks and fire works which save so much of foreign exchange for the country.

It is also argued on behalf of the supporters of child labour that the children of master-craftsmen get to learn their skills from their parents and then themselves develop into master-craftsmen.

The employers often advance the argument that by employing children they help them to increase the income of their families. The employment also saves them from becoming indolent and vagabonds or anti-social. Thus, they argue, it is the sympathy for the poor and the needy, rather than the desire to exploit them, which motivates them to employ children. When the employment of children increases the earnings of the family, it keeps the children away from mischief, they argue.

However, these arguments as advanced by the employers, are weightless and misleading. They look down upon the glaring fact that the practice of child labour "deprives children of educational opportunities, minimises their chances for vocational training, stunts their physical growth, hampers their intellectual development and, by forcing them into the army of unskilled labourers or blind alley jobs, condemns them to low wages all their lives."[24] No civilised nation can afford to take the risk of destroying the lives of its children who are the embodiment of all the hopes and aspirations for the country's future prosperity and progress. They represent the destiny of the nation itself.

Need of Protection Against Exploitation

By putting its child in the employment market, the family stands to suffer a great loss in economic terms also because the wages of the children are not commensurate with their work and performance. The adults are paid more for the same amount or quantity of work. Besides, the child tends not only to lose his health and opportunity for education, he pays all the more heavily by losing his potential capabilities. Hence it is an inefficient utilisation of labour power and amounts to premature expenditure of the force.

One of the most weighty arguments against child labour is that it accelerates and quantifies adult unemployment, and is indirectly instrumental for under-scaling of their wages. It has been estimated that if the children engaged in gainful occupations are ejected totally then it will, to a great extent, cure the country, automatically, of the inimical problem of unemployment, because atleast 15 million vacancies would be created thereby for the adult unemployed persons.[25]

Karl Marx had observed that the result of buying children and young persons of under age by the capitalists is physical deterioration and moral degradation.[26]

Some of the social thinkers see the source of the problem of delinquency in child labour. They say that this practice not only effects the health of children but also creates the problem of delinquency which must be paid for by the society. The child, as an individual, is the first loser, and the society, as a whole, the ultimate.

A prominent Washington merchant, S.W. Woodword, criticised the child labour by saying that, "Employment at too early an age belighted a child's economic prospects; it may be stated as a safe preposition that for every dollar earned by a child under fourteen years of age ten fold will be taken away from its earning capacity in later years."[27]

Thus, child labour is economically unsound, psychologically disastrous, physically ruinous and morally degrading.

In all respect, childhood is the most crucial period of life. It is rightly considered to be the foundation of life as the whole life depends on it. Children will in future be the leaders of industry, education, politics, social services, defence, science and civil administration. It is during this period that the moulding and shaping of the life takes place and the patterns of behaviour, ethics of conduct and the sense of moral considerations are imbibed and developed. It has, therefore, been said:

यन्नवे भाजने लग्न: संस्कारो नान्ऽयथा भवेत् ।।8।।
हितोपदेश मित्रलाभ

Meaning thereby that the behaviour patterns, attitudes, and the basic knowledge, which are imbibed during the childhood of a person, are never lost. Therefore, it is the first and the foremost duty of the parents to train and educate their children. The growth, development, understanding and comprehension of the future manpower, which is the main asset of any country, are dependent on child growth. Any investment made in the proper development of children will bring in manifold rewards in the future. For example, if we want durability of our hours, we must lay a deep and strong foundation. The latent energy and genious of a child should not be allowed to get wasted, rather it should be developed through training and proper education to ensure social, economic, scientific and cultural growth of the country.

It is the bounded duty of the country to provide for atleast free primary education for all children. One must remember that the industrialisation can wait but youth does not last long. This right to primary education must be for the present time, and not a dubious or ambiguous constitutional promise for some undefined future. The basic guarantees of our Constitution must be fulfilled here and now. As observed in Watson *vs.* City of Memluis,[28] "Vindication of conceded constitutional rights cannot be made dependent upon any theory that it is less expensive to deny than to afford them."

Therefore, so far as the projects for development of human resources are concerned, the programme for welfare of children must be given top priority. It is only in this way that children can be trained to be good future citizen, mentally alert and prosperous. We should aim at providing proper and equal opportunities for development to all children in the light of the above mentioned constitutional directives. It is only then that we can fulfil our aspirations, and achieve our objectives of social justice and equality enshrined in our Constitution.

REFERENCES

1. Quoted in *Labour Problem in America,* ed. Stein, Emanuel and Davies, Jerome, Farrar and Rinehart, Inc., New York, 1940, pp. 112-113.
2. Giri, V.V., *Labour Problems in Indian Industries,* Asia Publishing House, Bombay, 1958, p. 360.
3. *Report of the Committee on Child Labour,* 1979, p. 7.
4. *Ibid.,* p. 8.
5. Report of the Director General, International Labour Organisation; Youth and Work (Part I), 1960.
6. *Ibid.*
7. Report IV-1 of the 57th Session of the International Labour Conference, Geneva, 1972.
8. *The Hindustan Times,* New Delhi, Sept. 24, 1986, p. 11.
9. *Ibid.,* September 29, 1986, p. 6.
10. Labour Minister, Mr. Ram Vilas Paswan, in Lok Sabha on March 14, 1990.
11. International Labour Organisation's Report published in *The Hindustan Times,* May 2, 1990.
12. *Report of Committee on Child Labour,* 1979, p. 7.
13. Sengupta, Padmini: "*Child Labour as a Social Problem,*" (Unpublished).
14. Agnivesh, Swami, in his Public Interest Litigation before the Supreme Court in Bandhua Mukti Morcha vs. Union of India, AIR 1984 SC 802.
15. Mathur Deep: While They Should Have Been Playing. *The Hindustan Times,* August 19, 1984, p. 5.
16. *Encyclopaedia of Social Sciences,* Vol. III, pp. 412-413.
17. Government of India, "*Child Labour in India,*" 1954.
18. Jain, S.N., "Preventive Legal Measures in the Area of Child Labour," read at the National Seminar on Child and the Law, Organised by National Institute of Public Co-operation and Child Development, New Delhi, Nov. 30-Dec. 2, 1982.
19. Schindkrout, Enid, The Employment of Children in Kano (Nigeria), *Child Work, Poverty and Underdevelopment,* ed. Rogers and Standing, 1981, 95.
20. Hull, Terence: "Perspectives and Data Requirements for the Study of Children's Work," *Child Work, Poverty and Underdevelopment,* ed. Rodgers and Standing, 1981, 49.
21. *Report on Child Labour in Indian Industries,* 1981, p. 7.
22. *Encyclopaedia of Social Sciences,* Vol. III, pp. 412-24.
23. *Report of National Commission on Labour,* 1969, p. 386.
24. *Report of the Committee on Child Labour,* 1979, p. 9.
25. Chandra, Ramesh, "Effect of Law Income on the Size of Labour Force and Unemployment in India," *Indian Labour Journal,* 1961, p. 1164.
26. Karl Marx, *Das Kapital,* Ch. XV sec. 3-a.
27. Woodward, S.W.: "A Businessman's Views on Child Labour," *Charties and the Commons,* XV (1905-6) pp. 800-1.
28. 373 US 526.

43

CAUSES OF CHILD LABOUR

Child Labour is a socio-economic phenomenon. It is generally conceded that illiteracy, ignorance, low wages, unemployment, poor standard of living, stark poverty, deep social prejudices and appalling backwardness of the country-side are all, severally and collectively, the root causes of child labour. Mr. Madan, Deputy Director, Ministry of Labour, is of the view that "the children are required to seek employment either to augment the income of their families or to have a gainful occupation in the absence of availability of school going facilities at various places."[1]

It has been officially stated that, "child labour is no longer a medium of economic exploitation but is necessitated by economic necessity of the parents and in many cases that of the child himself."[2]

Prof. Gangrade believes that child labour is a product of such factors as customs, traditional attitude, lack of school or reluctance of parents to send their children to school urbanisation, industrialisation migration and so on.[3]

Thus, though there are many causes of child labour, it will be fruitful to study some of the principal ones in detail.

Poverty

It is an unquestionable reality that half of the population of India lives below the poverty line. The gross national product income had decreased by 5%, and per capita real income by 7% during 1979-80. According to the annual report of the Ministry of Programme Implementation for 1988-89, the poverty percentage got reduced from 48% in 1977-78 to 37 in 1984-85.[4] Out of 316 million people[5] who fall below the poverty line, 118 million children. Out of these children, 99 million are in rural areas and 19 million in urban areas.[6]

The parents of the poverty-ridden population are faced with the bewildering question as to whether they should send their children to educational institutions to learn and equip themselves with adequate knowledge in order to prepare themselves for adulthood, or to send them to the labour market augment the income of their starving families.

Widespread poverty is one of the major causes of child labour. In India, which is a developing country, poverty forces the parents to send their children to seek employment because augmentation of their income is essential for the survival of the family including the children themselves. Illness and other contingencies demand extra money in hand and the employment of children is resorted to as a quick and easily accessible way to get it.

The Institute of Public Opinion conducted a survey in 1969, which showed that 41.2% of the Indian population was below the poverty line. Half of these belong to the scheduled castes and tribes. In villages a vast majority of agricultural labour belongs to these communities.[7]

A pilot study[8] in Madras, Madurai and Coimbatore, found that about three-fourth of the children were at work to supplement their family income and 23% were working because of the death of their father or guardian.

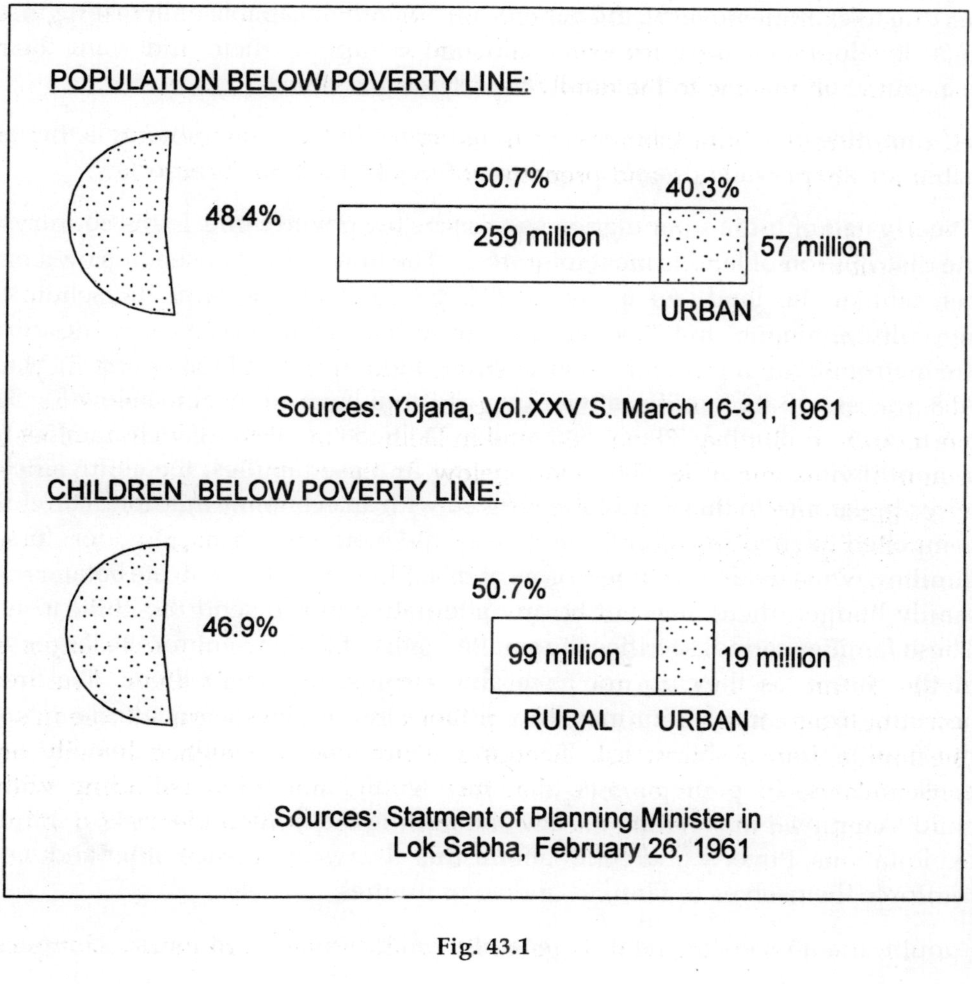

Fig. 43.1

The Bombay study[9] on working children found that low economic status of the family was the single largest factor for non-schooling of the children and their coming into the labour market.

A study on child labour in Khurja potteries[10] revealed that most of the parents of working children had less than five bighas of land. These families owned one or two milch animals which the parents tended and the children worked in the potteries of Khurja.

Our own study on child labour in Aligarh lock industries also indicated that 74.5% of the children working in those industries belonged to the families whose total monthly income was Rs. 500/- or less. 13.25% families of child labour had an average monthly income of Rs. 500/- to 800/- while 7.25% of the families of child labour in Aligarh lock industries had a monthly income upto Rs. 1000/- and only 5% of these families had an income of more than one thousand rupees per month.

Thus, due to extreme poverty, the parents are not only incapable of investing in their children's development, they are even reluctant to support them and want them to become a source of income to the family as early as possible.

The Committee on Child Labour says in its report that chronic poverty is the factor responsible for the prevalence and prepetuation of child labour. It reports:[11]

> "Nearly half of India's population subsists below poverty line. In the countryside, the distribution of land is most iniquitous. The lower 50% households own only 4 per cent of the land. As many of 27.2 per cent of the rural households are agricultural tenants and 30.4 per cent agricultural labourers. Nearly one-third of the metropolitan population lives in slums and improvised tenomant. In Madras 90.8 pre cent of the families of working children have an income below Rs. 500/- per month. In Bombay 78 per cent and in Delhi, 88 per cent of such families have a monthly income of Rs. 500/- and below. In these families, the child, since his very appearance in this world, is endowed with an economic mission. The child is compelled to shed sweat of brow to keep the wolf away from the door. In some families, when disease or other forms of disability upset the delicate balance of the family budget, there may not be any alternative but to send the child to work. These families cannot sacrifice the smaller gains of the present for the larger gains of the future, as they do not have any surplus to sustain them. The income accruing from child labour may be a pittance but it plays a crucial role in saving the family from a shipwreck. Economic compulsions weighed heavily on the consciousness of poor parents that they would not mind colluding with the child's employer in violating the law and putting the child under risks of inhuman exploitations. Poverty and child labour thus always beget each other and tend to reinforce themselves in families and communities."

No doubt, the above statement is generally valid. Poverty, of course, compels the parents to send their children to the labour market. But, it is not true for each and every society as a rule because there are some communities or societies in which, irrespective of their composition, the number of child labour is insignificant despite high levels of poverty. For example, it defies explanation that in Bihar and Uttar Pradesh which, going by the per capita income, could be termed as poor states, child labour constitutes only 4.8% and 6% of the total labour force respectively, whereas Andhra Pradesh and Karnataka, which are better off in terms of per capita income nave a higher percentage of child labour, constituting about 9% and 8% of the total labour force respectively. Another example is that of Africa. It has been noted that in regions, or amongst "Tribes," where the concept of market relationship has not yet gained any considerable ground employment of children in gainful occupation within the family or outside it is not significant at all despite the general level of existing poverty.

The above examples, though of a micro-nature, do point out that it will not be safe to consider poverty as the sole factor responsible for child labour. The concept of poverty itself is not universal. The opportunities of child employment may also vary from place to place. Moreover, there may be other overriding considerations for very poor people in not sending their children to labour market, whereas better off people may choose to make their children earn in order to further improve their living conditions, or in order to be able to save. Hence, poverty cannot be the sole cause for the incidence and magnitude of child labour.

Low Wages of the Adult

The wage structure of the adult workman has a direct bearing on the occurrence of child labour. The employer has a vested interest both ways. It is all the more so in the case of statutorily fixed minimum wage. The less an employer pays to his adult workman, the more is the exploitation and the more he stands to gain on the wage bill. The more exploited a workman is the more will be his compulsions to send his children to work, who will be paid all the more less. So, in order to ensure adequate and regular supply of cheap child labour even in violation of the protective laws, the vested interest of the employer will be to keep the wage structure of his adult workers at its lowest. This relationship of the wage structure of the adult workman—the bread earner of the family—should not be lost sight of while considering the problems of child labour.

The report of International Labour Organisation has also revealed that the problem of child labour is not problem by itself. In reality, the problem is that of maintenance of the child which is directly connected with the question of ensuring a living wage to the adult wage earner so that he may be able to maintain his family at an adequate standard.[12]

The above facts were also observed in a number of seminars, workshops and conferences on the problem of child labour, and it was felt that if the adult workmen could get a real living wage, they are likely to desist from sending their children to work.

Unemployment

The state of the unemployed is even worse than that of the poor. Low wage make a an poorer but unemployment makes him absolutely poor. It turns the weak into a cripple. Poverty dempens his spirit but unemployment kills it mercilessly. So, can one muster sufficient courage to suggest the poverty-stricken unemployed not to send his child to work? Partly employed people sail in the same boat. And, unfortunately, the curse of unemployment is an universal one. It exists in the most affluent countries, like United State of America, also, does exist child labour and its accompanying problems. In their book, 'Child Workers in America." Lumpkin and Douglas have very rightly pointed out that two-fifth of the children seek work due to the unemployment of the adult member of the family. Nearly two-third of children were at work because the adult member of the family had no employment or had some part time job, and one-third of children wanted to work due to the serious cuts in the pay of the adult.[13]

Mrs. Sengupta says:[14]

> "Labour is employed on the average for 189 days in agricultural pursuits. There are other rural employments which exist but the overall position would appear to be 100 days in the year of total unemployment. During the period of unemployment many women migrate to cities with families, and beg with babies in their arms. Thy are, therefore, employing the children from infancy for begging which is an important employment, especially now, and children of the baby group are exploited while older children are pests in every part of the city including railway stations where begging is prohibited by law but where it thrives as officials turn a deaf ear to the wails of boys and girls."

In Khurja potteries, the incidence of child labour is high due to the unemployment of adult members of the families. Ms. Burra feels that, "Bulandshahr district, although agriculturally prosperous, has little work on its mechanised arms for the bulk of rural poor who face unemployment on a massive scale. The only work available is in the potteries of Khurja.[15]

Sivakasi and neighbouring areas of the newly created Kamraj district get scanty rains. As a result, little agricultural operations are being carried out over there. This has forced the people to look for non agricultural jobs. The Sivakasi stretch has a number of match and fire-work factories where most of the operations are annual. To man these factories children are preferred because they are very hard working and cheap. This has resulted into widespread unemployment among adults.

Absence of Schemes for Family Allowance

Another direct cause of child labour, which is as causative as poverty, is the unfavourable condition at home. There may be tension and uncertainty, provoked or increased by poverty; the father may have left home; the mother may be alone; the father or mother or both may have fallen ill or become physically unfit to work, or may have died. In such families, these contingencies upest the delicate balance of the family budget, leaving the family with no alternative but to sent the children to work. These starving family would prefer a bare bread in hand today rather than go without it in the hope of buttered bread in indistinct future.

The study on child labour in Aligarh lock industries shows that 8% of children have taken up employment because they have neither mother nor father to support them, while 13% of child labour have only mother alive. On the other hand, 10.75% of children had joined this industry because they had no mother at home and the father thought that it would be better to send them to work.

However, the argument that the most of the children go to work because of the compelling circumstances in the event of loss of the bread winner is also fallacious to some degree because it is usually the head of the family himself who forces his children to go to the labour market.

The absence of statutory provisions and schemes for family allowance also adds up to the problem of child labour. In India, there are no schemes for such allowances that many help the needy families maintain an adequate standard of living, so that they may not have to send their children to the work place. Presently, such type of allowances are being given in a number of countries, such as, Australia, New Zealand, the United Kingdom, France and the Union of Soviet Socialist Republics. But, on the other hand, in our country even the amount which is paid to widows as compensation or pension is too meagre for the sustenance of their families without the help of their working children.

Migration to Urban Areas

Further, some studies have found migration to cities, due to industrialisation and urbanisation, also to be one of the factors responsible for the problem of child labour. The Delhi study shows that there is a substantial number of migrants among child workers, particularly in the field of domestic services. They also work in tea-stalls and 'dhabas.' A large number of domestic servants belonged to Almora and Garhwal district of north-eastern Uttar Pradesh, while most of those working in tea-stalls and 'dhabas,' and also those hawking evening newspapers, had migrated from Azamgarh, Basti, Gorakhpur and Gonda district of Uttar Pradesh and, to some extent, from Bihar. The rag-pickers were partly local and partly from West Bengal. The shoe-shine boys mostly hailed from Agra, Jhansi and Shahjahanpur districts of Uttar Pradesh. It is not just a coincidence that the migrant child workers invariably belonged to the relatively poor and backward regions of the country, and not the economically developed areas, such as, West Bengal, Haryana and Western uttar Pradesh.[16]

The study of Ms. Khandekar indicated that the migrant child labour in Greater Bombay was 81%, whereas the locals were only 19%.[17]

The Bombay study[18] showed that 58.2% of the child labour was the exclusive result of the internationalisation of the urban slum culture, as their families had migrated to cities before their birth. In all, there were 90% of them who belonged to migrated families. The reasons for the migration of 87% families were economic and presence of friends and relatives in the city who could help them.

Urbanisation had even allured the children to run away from their rural homes to the cities to find employment.

Large Families

Large families, with comparatively low income, cannot afford to nourish high ideals and notions about family ties. Resultingly, such types of families fail to provide a protected childhood to their children. If the family is small and well planned, there will hardly be any need of sending their children to work in order to earn whatsoever they may. The children of small and planned families can be carefully looked after and educated. But, unfortunately, the improverished and illiterate parents think otherwise. They think that when God has given the body. He will feed it also. They also consider there or four children better than having just one or two. For them, more children means more income. They argue that whereas every human body has just one mouth to eat, it has got two hands to feed it.

It means that one talented and intelligent son is far better than a hundred illiterate fools. Even millions of stars cannot dispel the darkness which just one moon can. And, so is the case with sons.

Thus, if one has just one or two children, he will be better placed to provide for them all such facilities that are necessary for their mental, physical and social growth.

Reverting to the lock industry of Aligarh, it would be worth pointing out that the children working in them mostly belonged to the families encumbered with larger number of members. Some of the families of the working children had even more than eight members. It was found that 20.25% of the families of child labour engaged in lock industry had upto three members, 50.75% families had more than four but less than six members, 15.75% families had seven to eight members and 12.25% families had more than eight members. One child labour was found to have fourteen brothers and sisters!

A Cheap Commodity

As it has already been said earlier, the employers prefer to take in children when the given job can be accomplished by them better than the adults or at par with them, and even otherwise. To them the labour power of the children is a cheap commodity. By employing them they save on the wage bills. Besides, children are apt to be docile and more obedient, and can be easily bullied into submission. They readily do all sorts of odd jobs without a whimper. The more needy a child happens to be, the less he will be paid by the employer.

Child labour is not only very cheap, it is also trouble-free since children cannot organise agitations by themselves and, being minors, the membership of trade unions is not open to them. Neither can they demand any overtime, nor the medical and other benefits.

The activeness, suppleness and agility of the child's delicate body is an additional asset to the employer, making him more desirable for employment, for he can be made to rush in and out on errand, run up and down the stairs, bend or lie down, fetch and take back things, or hand over the tools to the adult workers. He readily dos all this and much more without whimpering, protest, sense of shame or hurted ego. No adult can be expected to do all this.

In the above respect, the Committee on Child Labour has observed:[19]

> Children have less developed ego and status consciousness. They are also less affected by feelings of guild and shame. Children can be put on non-status, even demeaning jobs, without much difficulty. Children are more active, agile and quick and feel less tired in certain tasks. They can climb up and down staircase of multistoreyed buildings several times during the day carrying tea and snacks for employees of offices located in these buildings. They are also better candidates for tasks of helper in a grocer's shop or an auto-garage. Employers find children more amenable to discipline and control. They can be coaxed, admonished, pulled up and punished for default without jeopardising relations."

The study of child labour in lock industries of Aligarh also led to the same conclusions. When we interrogated the employers of child labour they said that though it was out of sympathy that they give some work to children, actually, they preferred them because they are more disciplined and controlable. Besides, they demand nothing and are cheaper.

Sometimes, when seasonal work demands additional hands, children are more in demand, for example, during harvesting seasons when adult workers are not readily available to cope up with the work in hand.

In this country, children of very young age are engaged for domestic work because they are very cheap. The middle class families, falling within low income groups, especially prefer boys and girls of the age group 8 to 14 to work in their homes as domestic servants for food and some pocket money. These employers, though educated in formal sense, appear to have the least concern for these children and their conscience hardly pricks.

Non-Existence of Provision for Compulsory Education

Non-existence of provision for compulsory education in our country is another important cause of child labour. The Child labour and non-schooling of children have a vital linkage among the poorer sections of the population. The provision of compulsory education upto a prescribed age would compel the children to attend school, leaving hardly any scope for their employment by the self-styled benevolent masters.

In India, out of 5,47,672 villages, 48,566 do not have any school, and 1,67,382 rural schools have just one teacher for each school. At most of the places, the school presents a drab and dismal picture, and holds little attraction for the child. Thus, also because of the non-availability of schooling facilities at the initial stage, a good number of children migrate to cities and towns to seek job as an alternative to the rustic and dull village life. The parents also prefer to keep their children occupied in gainful employment lest they continue to be a burden on them and be exposed to temptations of the vagarancy without knowing its ill consequences.

As a result of inadequacy in schooling facilities and lack of opportunities for education, in Aligarh lock industries 41% of the child labour were illiterate, 31% had left the school before passing the fifth standard and only 28% had studied upto middle standard.

Further, many of the parents, especially that of the rural and slum areas, cannot afford the prescribed minima of uniforms, books and stationery etc., even though education is free upto primary level. Apart from the consideration of expenses, the allurement of the child's income also plays a major role in their decision against schooling of their children. They are also not sure that schooling will really brighten up their children's future prospects. They dread uncertainty, and prefer to follow the saying that one bird in hand is better two in bush. The plight of the educated unemployed youth in our country lends support to their views.

In relation to child labour, the importance of need for compulsory education gets confirmed, though indirectly, by the report of the National Commission on Labour, 1969, when it stated therein:

> "The gradual reduction in the employment of child labour since independence is due partly to the expansion of educational facilities by the state and also to relatively better enforcement of statutory provisions relating to child labour."[20]

The main obstacle in the way of making education compulsory for all children up to a prescribed age has been rightly indicated by the above report in the following:[21]

> "An artisans cannot afford to educate his wards though education is free. For him an uneducated child is an asset; desire to be educated becomes a double liability because of (a) loss of earnings, if the child does not work, and (b) expenditure on education, howsoever small."

A similar view was also expressed by Prof. Acharji of Xavier Labour Relation Institute, Jamshedpur, in the following words:[22]

> "Books and Stationery are expensive. Will the parent choose between food and clothing, the primary needs, or purchase books for the children? For scheduled castes and tribes even these may be available free of cost, but for all poor families the question posed is immediate supplementary income and to use the children as sources rather than postpone this prospect to an uncertain date, when he will pass

his matric and may or may not get a job in an economy where millions are still unemployed. Thus, psychologically, the path of least resistance is adopted by them."

No doubt, the role of education cannot be underestimated for proper development of children. Each and every parent wants his child to become a reputed 'A' class person but the unfortunate children have neither the means for education nor they have time to spare for it. They just cannot afford to wait for a bright future tomorrow, rather than having the bread crumbs right now.

Illiteracy and Ignorance of Parents

Despite improvements in literacy rate from 5% in 1901 to 36% in 1981, the gross number of illiterates had swelled up during this period from 225 million to 445 million.[43] Most of these illiterate people belong to the lower socio-economic strata of the population. These people are only concerned with the present and have rather much at hand to worry about. So, naturally, they deliberately try to escape from the stress and strains of worrying about the future. They are pleased with what they gain by the earnings of their children. Complacently, they do not care to avail of the educational opportunities for their children, including vocational training, even if the same may be available, though such opportunities are rare for the employed children. They are also unmindful of ill effects on the health of their working children.

The study on child labour in Aligarh lock industries had revealed that about 80% of the parents of child labour were illiterate, about 12% had studied upto Vth class and only 8% of them had education upto VIII standard.

The Madras study[24] had come to the conclusion that children who were in employment, were from low literacy groups of the society. About 44% of the parents of child labour were alliterate and another 33% of them were of low literacy groups having studied upto standard V only. Therefore, a large number of parents and guardians were not aware of the importance of education. Their sole concern was the monetary aspect of their children's employment, and not the development of their intelligence in the least.

Thus, the child labour is prevalent extensively in the lower socio-economic groups because of the lack of appreciation on the part of the parents of the role of education in improving life and the living conditions.

Taking into consideration all the aspects of child labour its consequences, Addam has condemned it and predicted[25] that today's child labourers will be the paupers of tomorrow; they are the boys and girls who will grow up either without formal schooling or the knowledge of a trade; sooner or later, their youthful energies exhausted, they will become dull, shiftless and driftless.

Traditional Attitudes

Sociological factors, too, have their share of this scourge. In the rural set up, the tradition of family occupation often motivates the child to become a bread winner. For example a goldsmith's son takes to gold-smithery, or a carpenter's child prefers carpentary. It is worth noting that 15.75% of the child labour had joined the Aligarh lock industries because of their family traditions.

Other Reasons

In addition to the above mentioned factors responsible for child labour, there are several other causes too. Firstly, the provisions of the protective labour legislations are lopsided and do not cover agriculture and small scale industries. Secondly, the enforcing machineries, which are provided by the state governments, are inadequate almost every where and fail to check up on child labour The Factories Act itself is defective in many respects, mainly so because it does not apply to craftsmen on the untenable ground that they do not use power.

REFERENCES

1. Madan, G., *Review of Legal Provisions Relating to Facilities for, and Working Conditions of Employed Children—The Impact on Their Health, Education and Development*," 1975, p. 9 (Unpublished).
2. Government of India, *Child Labour in India*, 1954, p. 2.
3. Gangrade, K.D., *Child Labour in India*, Department of Social Work, Delhi University, Delhi 1978-79 (Unpublished).
4. *The Hindustan Times*, April 27, 1989 p. 10.
5. *Yojana*, Vol. XXV/S, March 16-31, 1981.
6. Statement of Planning Minister in Lok Sabha, Feb. 26, 1981.
7. Institute of Public Opinion, *Monthly Commentary on Indian Economic Condition*, Dec., 1973.
8. George, K.N., "Child Labour in the City of Madras," in National Seminar on Employment of Children in India, organised by National Institute of Public Cooperation and Child Development, New Delhi, Aug., 1977.
9. Study of Child Labour in Bombay, National Institute of Public Co-operation and Child Development, New Delhi, 1978 (Unpublished).
10. Burra, Neera, *Where Children are Caste in Misery's Mould*, The Hindustan Times, Feb. 14, 1988, p. 5.
11. *Report of the Committee on Child Labour*, 1979, p. 9.
12. *Report of the International Labour Organisation* quoted in the book "*Needs of Children*" pub. by UNICEF, p. 144.
13. Lumpkin, K.D. and Douglas, D.W., *Child Workers in America*, 1938, p. 7.
14. Sengupta, Padmini, *Child Labour as a Social Problem* (Unpublished).
15. Burra, Neera, "Where Children are Cast in Misery's Mould," *The Hindustan Times*, Feb. 14, 1988, p. 5.
16. Gangrade, K.D., *Child Labour in India*, Department of Social Work, Delhi University, Delhi, 1978-79 (Unpublished).
17. Khandekar, M., "A report on the situation of Children and Youth in Greater Bombay," Tata Institute of Social Sciences, Bombay, 1970.

18. *Study of Child Labour in Bombay*, National Institute of Public Co-operation and Child Development, New Delhi, 1978 (Unpublished).
19. Report of Committee on Child Labour, 1979, p. 10.
20. Report of National Commission on Labour, 1969, p. 386.
21. *Ibid.*
22. Acharji, N., *Child Labour in India*, (Unpublished).
23. Census of India, 1981.
24. George, K.N., Child Labour in the City of Madras," in National Seminar on Employment of Children in India, organised by the National Institute of Public Co-operation and Child Development, New Delhi, August, 1977 (Unpublished).
25. Addam, Jane, *Child Labour and Pauperism*, 1983, p. 17.

44

CHILD LABOUR: A FRAMEWORK FOR POLICIES AND PROGRAMMES

I. INTRODUCTION

This paper on child labour is concerned with three policy and programme questions: *What is to be done? What can be done? And how can it be done?*

These questions are no doubt best dealt with at a national rather than at a regional or global level, for the problem of child labour manifests itself in different forms in different countries. Similarly, the potential and feasible means of action at the disposal of national governments might be wide-ranging in some countries but very limited in others.

Looking at the child labour situation globally, one cannot deny that progress has been made in the reduction in the incidence of child labour over the last few decades. But this progress has generally been uneven. In some countries, child labour has been virtually abolished. In a large number of countries, however, it still continues to be a persistent problem. Children are also found working in a variety of work situations and under varying conditions. Some are engaged in light work and may even find their work an essential and useful aspect of growing up. But many are found working in conditions reminiscent of the cruelty and exploitation portrayed in many novels and narratives of the early years of the industrial revolution.

Inevitably, therefore, these variations and national specificities must be taken into account in the formulation of targets and policies aimed at the elimination of child labour and at the protection of working children. However, as in other areas of social concern, there are sufficient similarities in the field of child labour among groups of countries to justify a global approach to programme and policy options. In developing such an approach to programme and policy options. In developing such an approach, however, we shall try to discuss the issues in terms of regions or groups of countries with a common set of widely recognised problems and we shall indicate, where necessary, cases where a particular goal, policy, or instrument may or may not be relevent.

II. WHAT IS TO BE DONE?

The "Abolition" and "Protection" Objective

The objectives of social policy on child labour can be stated as preventing children from working and protecting them when they are found to be working. These may be referred to, respectively, as the "abolition" and "protection" goals of child labour policies and programmes. While this distinction is convenient of the identification of goals and instruments, the two cannot be viewed separately; they are, in fact, linked conceptually and must be jointly considered in policy formulation, even for low-income countries.[1]

It goes without saying that, given the economic realities in many low-income countries, the objective of the abolition of child labour cannot be attained right away. But this does not mean that the objective should be abandoned; nor does it mean that the focus of public policy in the area of child labour should be simply the provision of minimum levels of protection for those at work. Rather, it means that countries should set realistic qualitative and qualitative targets for gradually reducing the incidence of child labour but should at the same time provide for the protection of those at work. This is so for reasons:

Firstly, although the spread of education is closely linked with growth in per capita income, it is possible, as has been shown by some countries, to effect a rapid expansion of education, to bring about a considerable reduction in the incidence of child labour and to eliminate child work, at least for the very young and vulnerable, even at considerably low levels of per capita income.

Secondly, even if it was to be argued that the policies adopted in such countries should be aimed at protection rather than abolition, a sustained reduction in the incidence of child labour could be an essential condition for the success of policies and programmes aimed at providing increased protection for working children. This is so for the following reason. A high and growing incidence of child labour is likely to lead to greater child exploitation in the form of lower child wage rates, excessive and uninterrupted hours of work and physical and psychological abuse.[2] In such a situation, the protective measures society provides for its children are likely to be undermined by the forces that operate on the supply of child labour, and hence on the "child" labour market, unless offsetting measures are concurrently carried out.

Conversely, a reduction in the incidence of child labour can provide for improved terms of employment for children, such as increased earnings and improvements in the overall conditions of work, and thus support efforts to improve, promote and protect the welfare of children. This therefore means that public policy, even in low-income countries, must encompass these two dimensions and aim at: firstly, the improvement of the conditions under which children work and the protection of children from exploitation; and secondly the gradual abolition of child labour by the adoption of measures that bear on the factors that generate and sustain it.

How can we translate these objectives into concrete national policy goals and targets in countries at different levels of development?

Perhaps the best way of approaching this question is to begin with *the Minimum Age Convention 1973 (No. 138)*, which along with its companion Recommendation, 1973 (No. 146), provides general as well as specific guide-lines on when, where and under what conditions children may or may not work, and on the types of policies countries may adopt in order to pursue the objective of the effective abolition of child labour.

The major points of Convention No. 138 can be summarised very briefly as follows:

> Firstly, it requires a country that has ratified it to specify a minimum age for admission to employment or work, and to raise progressively the minimum age for admission to employment or work to a level consistent with the fullest physical and mental development of young persons. The Convention spells out that the minimum age for admission to employment or work shall not be less than the age of completion of compulsory schooling and, in any case, shall not be less than 15 years.

However, the Convention provides different age thresholds for different types of work:

(a) "The minimum age for admission to any type of employment or work which by its nature or the circumstances in which it is carried out is likely to jeopardise the health, safety and morals of young persons shall not be less than 18 years". This may be lowered to 16 years "on condition that the health, safety and morals of the young persons concerned are fully protected and that the young persons have received adequate specific instruction or vocational training in the relevant branch of activity";

(b) On the other hand, it states that national laws or regulations may permit the employment or work of persons 13 to 15 years of age on light work which is "not likely to be harmful to their health or development", and "not such as to prejudice their attendance at school or orientation or their participation in vocational training programme... "

Though it sets these guide-lines, the Convention allows flexibility in the setting of standards, sectoral coverage and the form of child involvement in economic activities. It thus provides, for example, that a country whose economy and educational facilities are insufficiently developed may initially (a) specify a minimum age of 14 years, (b) limit the sectoral scope of application, and (c) reduce to 12 the minimum age of entry into employment on light work.

It is clear that the Convention, although comprehensive, does none the less provide flexible standards and guide-lines which countries at different stages of socio-economic development can aim for and progressively raise as living standards improve over time.

The question then is: how well are the objectives and goals set in Convention No. 138 met by various countries and, where they are not, what does that imply for setting objectives for countries at different levels of development?[3]

Historical Experience and Current Situation

In the *developed countries,* universal, primary-level education is fully attained and secondary-level education nearly so. However it is also known that there are, in many of these countries, a large number of children engaged in work and employment, not infrequently for relatively long hours and sometimes under conditions dangerous to their health and safety. In the industrialised countries, therefore, the appropriate focus of public policy is the provision of protection for school-going children who work while going to school but do so for long hours and under unsafe and unhealthy conditions.

Turning to the *developing world,* which, as is well known, consists of a heterogeneous group of countries at different levels of development and with varying resource endowments and capabilities, the picture is somewhat complex and, on the whole, quite sobering. Firstly, let us look at the positive picture.

The last 20 years have witnessed considerably expansion in education and increases in enrolment rates at primary, secondary, and university levels. For example, according to UNESCO, the school enrolment ratio for children between 6 and 11 years of age in Africa doubled between 1960 and 1985—it increased from 32.7 per cent in 1960 to 65.9 per cent in 1985; in Asia, the ratio rose from 54.2 per cent to 73.6 during the same period; and in Latin America and the Caribbean it rose from 57.7 to 83.5 per cent. In certain cases, the achievement was remarkable, considering the low level of per capita income of the countries concerned. For example, some countries, such as Sri Lanka, Kenya and the United Republic of Tanzania have already achieved, or are fast approaching, universal primary education. This means that, in these countries, at least the youngest children—namely those below the age of 12 years—are by and large outside the labour force and can therefore be assumed to receive significant protection. This in itself represents remarkable progress, especially as in the early sixties the primary school enrolment ratio in these countries was extremely low.

However, the picture in many other countries is unfortunately not so inspiring. Statistics on child labour are generally unreliable and must be interpreted with caution. However, population censuses, household and labour force surveys, and school enrolment figures confirm that child labour continues to be a pervasive problem in developing countries. In some Asian and African countries the number of child workers is estimated to be in the millions and, in a large number of countries, child workers constitute a significant proportion of the children in the relevant age group and, equally important, a considerable proportion of the overall work force. Official statistics indicate that child workers constitute as much as 7 per cent of the population under 15 years of age and as high a proportion as 11 per cent of the workforce in some Asian countries. In some African countries, again according to official estimates, as many as 20 per cent of the children under 15 are reported working.

The scale of the problem may be somewhat greater than is indicated by these estimates. The latest ILO estimates[4] indicate, for example, that in 1980, about 21 per cent of the children in developing countries between the ages of 10 and 14 years were economically active, and that the figure for 1985 may be as high as 18 per cent. These estimates are no doubt high. Yet even these may well be underestimates when viewed against the statistics on school enrolment. Thus, UNESCO estimates[5] of school enrolment for recent years indicate that, for developing countries as a whole, the enrolment ratio in 1985 between the ages of 6 and 11 years was 72.7 per cent and that between the ages of 12 and 17 years was 46.0 per cent. In other words, nearly 28 per cent of the children between 6 and 11 years and about 54 per cent of those between 12 and 17 years are not in school. If these ratios are correct, and we have every reason to believe that they generally are so, they imply that as high as 28 per cent of those between 6 and 11 years of age and the overwhelming proportion of those in the 12 to 15 year age group in developing countries may well be in the labour force and therefore working.

Possible Goals and Targets

The foregoing brief observations more or less define the dimensions of the problem and the quantitative and qualitative targets that countries can set for themselves in respect of he goal of the abolition of child labour and the protection of working children. These may be briefly stated as follows:

In the industrialised countries, the goal of the abolition of child labour has been more or less attained, with few exceptions. In these countries, what needs to be done is to provide protection for children who often work while going to school but do so, not infrequently, for long hours and under unsafe and unhealthy conditions.

In the developing countries, on the other hand, there are two distinct developments and policy concerns, depending on the level of economic development and, far more importantly, on the degree of progress attained in the field of education. There are, on one hand, those developing countries which have made rapid economic progress and/or assigned special importance to educational development, and where therefore the more modest objective whereby children under 12 years of age are not working has been, or is being, rapidly reached. In many of these countries there has also been considerable progress in the absorption of those between 12 and 15 years into the educational system, though a lot more remains to be done. The goal of public policy in such countries should therefore be to raise the effective minimum age of entry to employment from around 12 years, as is now generally the case, to 15 years and thereby attain the effective abolition of child labour. These countries, especially the newly industrialising countries and those at the upper end of the per capita income pyramid, do have the resource base and the institutional capacity to attain the virtual abolition of child labour in the not-too-distant future through an accelerated development of secondary education.

On the other hand, in most developing countries especially those which by conventional social and economic indicators are at low levels of economic development, the scale of the problem is quite enormous. Children are found working in large numbers in factories, in mines, on farms and on the streets even at an early age. The modest objective of universal primary education is not yet reached and therefore even children under 12 years of age continue to be a significance proportion of the work force. Initially, therefore, the policy goal in such countries may be to prevent work by children under 12 years of age and to extend protection for those who will continue to remain at work for a long time to come.

III. WHAT CAN BE DONE?

1. Industrialised Countries

The problem of child labour in industrialised countries is principally one of inadequate protection for children who combine work with schooling. In some countries, certain sectors (e.g. agriculture) are not covered by legislation, either because work in such sectors is considered to be different from, and less dangerous than, work in industry, or because pressure groups from such sectors have succeeded in thwarting government efforts aimed at a broader extension of social protection.

In other cases, inadequacy of protection is due to problems of enforcement. These arise either because of the complexity of existing rules and regulations or from lack of a clear delineation of responsibility for their enforcement. In some countries, for example, responsibility for the enforcement of child labour laws is divided between such agencies as the Health and Safety Inspectorate, the Public Health Inspection Services, Education, and the Policy. While a theoretical case can be made for the simultaneous involvement of various agencies and community organisations in detecting and controlling the exploitation of children, in reality such an approach is rarely accompanied by—and may even have hindered—greater vigilance and regulation of child labour.

It would thus appear that the most important areas for action in the industrialised countries are the wider application or coverage of national legislation, the rationalisation of existing rules and regulations, a clearer delineation of the powers and duties of inspectorates and the reinforcement of the regulatory and enforcement services.

While action in the spheres of regulation and enforcement is certainly vital, another area of policy concern that should be given increased prominence is the dissemination of information on the laws and regulations themselves. It has been observed, not just in the developing world but also in many industrialised countries, that many employers in small enterprises are unaware of requirements of the laws and regulations and of the adverse consequences of employment on the educational performance and health of children. It is important that they are given support in the form of advisory services, improved access to information and guidance so that they can make a positive contribution to the implementation of the law and the protection of working children.

2. Developing Countriess

As was noted earlier, education statistics show that there has been significant progress in developing countries in the reduction in the incidence of child labour. Yet, this progress has been rather uneven, and this fact must be taken into account in formulating policies on child labour. There are developing countries where the objective of the abolition of child labour could be attained without too much difficulty. These include countries which have experienced significant socio-economic progress and have virtually achieved universal primary education. These countries can therefore raise the *effective* minimum age of entry to employment from around 12 years—which seems to be the case at present—to about 15 years. The single most effective instrument for doing so appears to be the acceleration of secondary education. And this is not only desirable, both as a means and as an end, but is also feasible, given the relatively advanced level of development of such countries, their resource endowments and their institutional capability. Secondly, again for the same reasons, these countries should aim at extending the sectoral coverage of their national legislation and at strengthening their enforcement machinery.

In contrast, the situation in most developing countries, especially those referred as least developed or low-income countries, is different both in terms of the size of the problem and the scope for action. In these countries, the magnitude of the task ahead and the need for greater effort have to be balanced with the real constraints facing them. There are, however, measures which even countries at low levels of development can take, the first and foremost being the provision and extension of basic protection.

Provision and Extension of Basic Protection

Although, as was noted earlier, almost all countries have adopted national laws on minimum age of admission to employment and the conditions under which children may or may not work, these laws are seldom that adequately implemented. There are several inter-related reasons for this:

- In some cases, national laws may not be sufficiently realistic. For example, their sectoral coverage may well be beyond a country's institutional and enforcement capacity.
- Enforcement is rendered meaningless by the absence of schooling opportunities. Where the educational system is not adequately developed, it is neither possible nor useful to consider total coverage or enforcement.
- In many countries, the labour inspectorate is inadequately staffed and ill-equipped in terms of material support to carry out its legal responsibilities.
- Not infrequently, the inspectorate is hampered by problems of verification. Economic units or enterprises employing children are generally unlicensed and unregistered and do not usually keep a record of their employees. Where they do, it may still be difficult to verify the ages of children, since in many

developing countries birth certificates are of relatively recent origin and thus are not widely in use.

For these and other reasons, countries initially should try to set realistic and attainable goals and they should gradually increase the scope of their legislation or raise their standards. For example, in terms of coverage, a low-income country could first focus on selected areas and sectors which are characterised by a high incidence of relatively serious exploitation of child labour. Thus, national action would initially focus on urban areas and, sectorally, on industry and mining, gradually extending its coverage to other sectors.

However, irrespective of their current level of development, developing countries should articulate certain imperatives in their national laws and should ensure that they are observed. These include the following:

First and foremost is the identification of, and the prohibition of, child work in hazardous and unsafe activities. A large number of children in many parts of the developing world are to be found working in such dangerous industries as mining, metal works, glass manufacturing, matches and fireworks, often without protection and under extremely unacceptable conditions. They are frequently the victims of burns and cuts; many are maimed and made physically handicapped; and many more contract diseases that lead to an early death or that incapacitate them for life. That children do work and have to work is sad, but that they should work in conditions demonstrably dangerous to their health and safety is totally unacceptable and must be strictly prohibited in all countries, whatever their level of development.

Secondly, a companion goal, which countries at low levels of development in particular should take as a point of departure and consider as a *minimum standard,* is the protection of the youngest and most vulnerable children. A country could thus aim—as a short-term objective—at ensuring that children under, say, 12 years of age do not work. Many countries have the capacity, and some have demonstrated that this is feasible to ban child employment before the completion of compulsory primary education or 12 years of age. Such a measure meets at least the lower age limit set by the Minimum Age Convention, 1973 (No. 138), and would almost at a stroke significantly reduce the incidence of child labour and provide protection to the youngest and most vulnerable groups. These groups can be significant in size, as data from various countries indicate.

The single most important instrument for ensuring that children under 12 years of age do not work is the expansion of primary education. The existing disparities between sectors and among socio-economic groups must be narrowed by increasing educational facilities and services in the relatively deprived sectors and by providing easier access to them for deprived socio-economic groups. The real economic cost of schooling to the poor must be reduced as much as possible. Education is a social right, and the poor must not be denied that right because of their disadvantageous economic position and the associated explicit and/or implicit costs of schooling. These costs may consist of such direct costs as school fees, the cost of uniforms and school materials, and other incidental expenses, which may appear to be small by the standards of the well-to-do but can be a significant burden on families who barely eke out a living. But probably far more important is the opportunity cost of sending children in terms of foregone earnings, and these can be substantial. Some studies show that the earnings of child workers can constitute as much as 30 per cent or more of household incomes. In such situations, families could send their children to school only at their own peril. The long-term solution obviously lies in promoting income-and-employment generating and income-support schemes. But could not society consider alternative schemes, such as school-feeding programmes and other innovative measures, in order to lighten the burden on poor families and to make it attractive for them to send their children to school rather than to work?

By initially setting modest goals corresponding to resource and institutional capabilities, a country can at least ensure that priority sectors and age groups are covered, and the planning and implementation experience required for sustained and continued effort is acquired. Such an approach makes programming much easier and more operational but it should also be accompanied by supportive measures in order to facilitate implementation and enforcement.

Firstly, it is important to identify the activities which are most hazardous and the sectors where child labour is most concentrated. The development of a flexible and competent monitoring service is thus absolutely essential.

Secondly, in view of the difficulty of tracing enterprises, an effective system of registration and monitoring should be developed and reinforced. Enterprises should also be required to keep a record of their employees and the necessary particulars.

Thirdly, enforcement should be backed up on the one hand by stiff penalties for infringing the law and, on the other, by extensive education and information campaigns, as well as by the provision of advisory and technical services for workers and employers.

Fourthly, countries should try to develop national pilot action programmes which aim at reducing child labour and providing protection. Such pilot programmes could have a comprehensive approach, with a wide geographical coverage and multiple goals and instruments. Alternatively, they could adopt a sectoral or partial approach focusing, say, on child workers in especially difficult circumstances and hazardous working conditions.

IV. INSTITUTIONAL FRAMEWORK FOR ACTION: THE ROLE OF GOVERNMENTAL AND NON-GOVERNMENTAL ORGANISATIONS

(i) Support Within Government

The degree to which social goals are taken into account and minimum labour standards are observed in the course of economic development depends on the commitment of the political leadership and the degree of political support it can rely on for the pursuit of social justice. In the absence of the necessary political pressure or support, it is fairly easy to set aside such considerations as labour rights, human rights, the promotion of equal opportunity and the like until such time (and who can say when exactly?) that rapid growth trickles down to an uplifts the poor. For these reasons, political initiatives by concerned groups within and outside government assume an especially important role.

Within government, it is well known that the "social" ministries such as education, labour, health, and welfare, often have difficulty in obtaining support for their programmes in debates on budgetary allocations. The reasons are obvious: social objectives are elusive; the economic benefits of social programmes cannot easily be demonstrated; they are considered to be a heavy charge on the budget, though other activities of prestige value may be even more so; when they do not exist, they are not missed in the sense that the negative impact of inaction is often not felt right away and is not as dramatic, as say, balance-of-payments' difficulties or a shortfall of investment.

If, therefore, the "social" ministries are to obtain a fair say in policy deliberations and decisions on priorities for resource allocation, it is important that they proceed at two levels.

They must, first of all, develop and sharpen their case on why and how social objectives and associated programmes support and promote socio-political and economic objectives. For example, they contribute to improved productivity, improved national savings, increased national self-reliance and improved industrial relations, and hence to a more stable, egalitarian and democratic order and to greater solidarity and reduction of tension.

It is also important that social programmes should be carefully designed and scrutinised for their cost effectiveness. The implementation of a specific programme in a specific area should be decided upon not just in the light of the programme's intrinsic merit but also in terms of whether or not its implementation complements or promotes other social goals. For example, the expansion of educational and welfare programmes could be carried out on a priority basis in areas with a high level and incidence of child labour. Educational reforms (or expansion) could be conceived not only in the light of their contribution to the attainment of advanced levels of learning but also for their contribution to improving the literacy, skill, use of technology and managerial level of the self-employed and petty producers in the unorganised sectors. These people, who have considerable entrepreneurial flair who make the best possible use of resources, are known to employ a relatively large proportion of child workers. Furthermore, educational reforms could be linked to labour-utilisation patterns; for example, in many countries school calendars are still based on western models but they could be adapted to suit household labour requirements during the planting and harvesting seasons. In this way, children would be able to attend school during slack periods and to assist their families during peak periods of labour.

In other words, if the social ministries are to exert greater influence on resource allocation, it is important that they convey effectively the economic case for social programmes, that they ensure that social programmes are cost-effective and that they are implemented to the extent possible in a manner that leads to the attainment of multiple social goals. The social ministries' machinery for research, planning and implementation needs to be strengthened. In addition, given the similarity of their programmes and identity of interests, the social ministries should try to establish a mechanism for ensuring that education, health, welfare and labour objectives and programmes are synchronised and effectively articulated within the government.

The subject of child labour clearly involves several ministries. In addition to the labour, education, health and welfare ministries, it touches those concerned with the implementation of income and employment generating programmes and community development programmes. The involvement and collaborative effort of these ministries is important for effective action. Therefore, in so far as local conditions require it, an inter-agency co-ordination body on child labour may be established, with a view to exerting pressure within in government and ensuring the effective and integrated delivery of services for the reduction of child labour and the protection of working children.

(ii) Non-governmental organisations

National and international, can and do play a major role in providing vital services for deprived groups, in publicising child abuse and exploitation and in promoting the interests of working children. Their role is all the more critical in situations where freedom of association and expression is discouraged and where the dimensions and severity of child exploitation are either unrecognised or deliberately concealed. Depending on the national situation within which they are operating, non-governmental organisations can carry out a number of activities.

Firstly, they can initiate and facilitate the organisation of especially vulnerable groups of workers. There are several examples of non-governmental organisations which have successfully organised communities, especially deprived groups, and helped them to protect and promote their interest. This wealth of experience could also be used to facilitate the delivery of social and economic services and to improve the socio-economic status of low-income groups, which in turn could lead to a reduction in the incidence of child labour.

Secondly, they can carry out extensive educational and information campaigns on the evils and consequences of child labour and can encourage positive action locally and nationally.

Thirdly, they cannot only play an advocacy role but can also directly identify work situations in which cruelty to children and abusive practices occur. They may also, either individually or in co-operation with other interested groups, establish a mechanism for monitoring and reporting on such practices.

Fourthly, they can extend the scope of their social and welfare services so that child workers are included among the target groups which receive direct support from them.

NOTES

1. See ILO, *Report of the Director-General*, Part I: Child labour, International Labour Conference, 69th Session, Geneva, 1983.
2. For an overview of these issues see Elias Mendelievich (ed.): *Children at Work* (Geneva, ILO. 1979) and G. Rogers and G. Standing (eds.): *Child Work, Poverty and Underdevelopment* (Geneva, ILO, 1981).
3. For a review of the relevant international labour standards and their influence and application at the national level, see ILO: *Minimum Age*. General Survey by the Committee of Experts on the Application of Conventions and Recommendations, international Labour Conference, 67th Session, Geneva, 1981. For a shorter review, see L. Swepston: "Child labour: Its regulation by ILO standards and national legislation", in *International Labour Review*, Sept.-Oct. 1982.
4. ILO, *Economically active population 1950-2025*, Vol. V, (Geneva, 1986).
5. UNESCO, *Statistical Yearbook 1985*, (Paris, 1985), tables 2-11.

45

CAMPAIGNING AGAINST CHILD LABOUR

Child labour is largely the product of poverty and underdevelopment and campaigning against it is not going to lead to its elimination over-night. Neither can the United Nations put the world to right by simply passing declarations and conventions in this field or any other. Action against child labour, if it is to be significant, must come from within states and be supported from outside. Campaigning, in the strict meaning of the word—a systematic attempt to arouse public opinion—is widely viewed as a necessary part of this process. After all, once a community reflects on the question of why children have to work and at what cost, the alternatives to child work point in the direction of those positive changes we call development. An attack on child labour is an attack on poverty and vice versa. And the first step is awareness raising of the individual, group and the society at large.

Campaigns are not new to the developing world. Both the Green Revolution in the 1960s and 1970s and the Universal Child Immunisation Campaign of the 1980s are good examples of externally inspired development initiatives. In the latter case, UNICEF was able to inspire a massive immunisation campaign in Colombia over the summer months of 1984. All media channels were utilised and some 120,000 volunteers were mobilised to achieve three-quarters coverage of the child population against five of the major childhood diseases. And the President fired the first shot in the campaign! (UNICEF, 1984 pp. 159-79) Columbia has inspired other examples of social mobilisation behind child immunisation. Could the same be achieved for child labour? One doubts it. Child immunisation is self-evidently a good thing that most, if not all, governments find it in their interest to support. Not so with child labour, which is far more political in its implications.

The political sensitivity of child labour is reflected in the poor take-up of the chief international instrument in the field — ILO Convention 138. Few governments have ratified this convention which prohibits all work under 15 years. Many governments in the development world find the instrument too ambitious given their economic reality. Indeed, many see child work in a family context as a naturally good thing—an expression of family solidarity. Besides, why should the state interfere with parental wishes? A clear echo here of nineteenth-century Britain. Not surprisingly, then, there is as yet no internationally orchestrated campaign against child labour though the ILO has called for such systematic action at this level (Blanchard, 1983, p. 37). But there have been a number of international initiatives, and the potential does exist to construct more integrated programmes in support of government action using in part lessons drawn from past campaigns. Let us now examine the main potential actors in such campaigns.

The ILO is widely viewed as the lead international agency concerned with child labour. Funded in 1919 as part of the League of Nations, it is now a unique agency within the United Nations system because of its tripartite representation of governments, employers' and workers' organisations. It is comparable to a ministry in a medium sized country with a staff of 2,000. In a startling disclosure its Director-General, Francis Blanchard, claimed that it consumed 22,000 pencils a year, 354 tonnes of paper and a million envelopes (*Gaurdian*, 15 August 1987). How many forests were destroyed on behalf of the child workers of the world must remain another little known development statistic! From the outset the ILO has attempted to regulate child labour in the short term without losing sight of the long-term goal of elimination. Its regulating and protective work has been expressed in terms of international standard setting. These international standards, or conventions, are only binding on those member states who ratify them. Once ratified, article 22 of the ILO's Constitution requires signatories to provide annual reports on their compliance, while articles 24 and 26 allow for the consideration of complaints against a state for failure to live up to the instrument in question. Perhaps an additional reason for a lack of enthusiasm for Convention 138.

The first child work convention was passed in 1919, setting the minimum age for regular industrial work, excluding family enterprise and technical schools, at 14. This Convention no. 5 was revised in 1937 when the minimum age was raised to 15.

From 1920 to 1965 minimum age conventions were adopted for the areas shown in Table 45.1.

TABLE 45.1

ILO Minimum Age Conventions: 1920-65

Occupation	*Convention*	*Minimum age*
Seamen	No. 7 1920	14
	No. 58 1936	15
Agriculture	No. 10 1921	14 (except out of school hours)
Mining	No. 123 1965	16
Non-Industrial	No. 33 1932	14 (out allows children over 12 to be employed outside of school hours on light work)

ILO conventions are usually flexible, allowing for gradual implementation and the facility for a state to grant exceptions (so called 'saving clauses'), particularly in the case of family enterprises. In 1973 the ILO replaced these conventions with Convention 138 which applies to all areas of economic activity. Convention 138, coupled with Recommendation 146, is the most comprehensive international instrument and statement on child labour:

CONVENTION 138

CONVENTION CONCERNING MINIMUM AGE FOR ADMISSION TO EMPLOYMENT

Article 1

Each Member of which this Convention is in force undertakes to pursue a national policy designed to ensure the effective abolition of child labour and to raise progressively the minimum age for admission to employment or work to a level consistent with the fullest physical and mental development of young persons.

Article 2

3. The minimum age specified in pursuance of paragraph 1 of this Article shall not be less than the age of completion of compulsory schooling and, in any case, shall not be less than 15 years.

Article 3

1. The minimum age for admission to any type of employment or work which by its nature or the circumstances in which it is carried out is likely to jeopardise the health, safety or morals of young persons shall not be less than 18.

RECOMMENDATION NO. 146

(i) National Policy

*...... high priority should be given to planning for and meeting the needs of children and youth in national development policies and programmes......

(ii) Minimum Age 7(1)

Members should take as their objective the progressive raising to 16 years of the minimum age for admission to employment or work specified in pursuance of Article 2 of the Minimum Age Convention 1973.

As with previous conventions, no. 138 contains flexible provisions and saving clauses. The ratification of Convention 138 has been disappointing. By 1979 only 13 countries had ratified it and by 1988 this figure had risen to 36.

There are those, like the UK delegate to the UN Seminar, who assert that this paltry number overstates support for Convention 138. It was Professor Boudhiba who pointed out in his report that states often seemed to ratify conventions without having the means to implement them. So, as the UK delegate asserted, what is the point of ratifying conventions one cannot implement, and then hectoring others for not doing so? At the seminar. The Netherlands took a different view, asserting that ratification of such instruments is an indication of the political will to broadly comply with their provisions, and that it was necessary to show support for the principles they embody.

Whether for or against, all that states need do as members of the ILO is to bring conventions to the attention of their relevant authorities. In the case of no. 138, the UK Government did so in 1974 by publishing a White Paper setting out general support for the convention but claiming that it could not ratify it as yet. This has remained the official UK position ever since. Indeed the UK delegate to the UN Seminar stated that UK regulations on child work complied with, if not exceeded, the provisions of Convention 138. So why not ratify? Perhaps the most telling argument against is the reporting provision — why have your country held up to international scrutiny if you can avoid it?

Nevertheless, the ILO finds consolation in the fact that most member states have adopted a minimum age standard of 14 or higher, although a smaller group of countries have set the minimum age at between 12 and 13. Additionally, more than 100 countries have ratified one or more of the ten convention prior to 197. These conventions regulate industrial employment and dangerous work much more rigorously than family enterprise and agriculture.

The ILO has hardly been zealous in following up on Convention 138. IYC (1979) provided the first real opportunity for the ILO and other agencies to focus world attention on the issue of child labour. In his declaration concerning IYC, the Director-General stated that:

(a) a child is not a 'small adult' but a person entitled to self-fulfilment through learning and play so that his adult life is not jeopardised by the having to work at an early age;
(b) governments should... take all necessary social and legislative action for the progressive elimination of child labour;
(c) pending the elimination of child labour, it must be regulated and humanised.

A number of important publications emerged from the IYC, but the ILO's attention did not become re-focused on the issue until 1983, when the Director-General's Report made a special feature of child labour. The reality behind the exhortation has meant that the ILO has not been able to obtain major donor support for its child labour activities. This state of affairs was openly pointed to by an ILO delegate to the UN Seminar who virtually pleaded with the government delegates to reverse the low priority given to the issue by member states. Understandably, then, the sensitivity with which governments view child labour has encouraged a cautious approach by the ILO. Despite its tripartite structure, it is governmental who really count. They pay the bills and they count for more in difficult economic times.

There were NGO observes at the UN Seminar who held that UNICEF ought to be the principal agency for child labour because of its specific responsibility for child welfare. In looking ahead to the adoption of a UN Convention on the Rights of the Child, some NGOs saw UNICEF as the chief regulatory agency for this instrument. Despite these lofty ambitions (flattering in one sense, but utterly naive) the political realities facing UNICEF are no less constraining, while its operating budget is less than that of Hampshire Country Council in Britain. UNICEF, unlike ILO, was established in 1946 on a voluntary basis. It began as a temporary relief operation mainly in Europe, and it was not until 1953 that its mandate to work exclusively in the developing world became firmly established. Each year UNICEF has to go to governments for support, and in particular to the US government, its largest donor. This economic reality may account for the public relations style and strategy adopted by UNICEF's Executive Director from 1982. Under James Grant, UNICEF has made the Child Survival and Development Revolution (CSDR) its main campaigning thrust. CSDR refers to a package of low-cost child health measures which UNICEF claims could have infant mortality rates if adopted world-wide. Emphasis on CSDR, and latterly on the universal immunisation goal for 1990, tends to obscure the more broadly-based development work UNICEF continues to support.

Nevertheless, at its 1984 Executive Board, UNICEF was asked, mainly at the insistence of its Scandinavian members, to review its policy on Children in Especially Difficult Circumstances. This reflected a concern that UNICEF was neglecting important child development issues in its emphasis on child survival. The report presented to UNICEF's 1986 Executive Board covered a review of working and street children; children in armed conflict and in situations of natural disaster; and those subject to abuse. The final draft paper observed:

UNICEF, within the context of existing programmes of support and in co-operation with other agencies, should advocate and support the progressive abolition of child exploitation, the protection of working children and street children, the amelioration of working conditions and the analysis of the impact of national policies on these children. While the underlying causes are basically structural — widespread poverty, underdevelopment and gross inequality—society must do more than wait for the long-term results of structural changes that it may be seeking to effect. Through extending the child survival and development strategy in response to the special needs of these children and youth, families and communities can be strengthened to decrease and/or prevent the exploitation of child work and the growth of numbers of street children. (UNICEF, 1986a, p. 11).

In a rather confused final debate, what emerged was the recognition that UNICEF should play a major role within the UN system for street children, but in terms of actions should, 'concentrate mainly one advocacy and rely primarily on governments and voluntary agencies for implementation; (UNICEF, 1986d, p. 3). Advocacy was therefore seen as UNICEF's natural role and advantage while the more sensitive campaigning work should be left to NGO's. On the funding side, the expansion of programmes would have to be left to the initiative of field offices and secure supplementary funding for 'noted projects' (projects funded not out of UNICEF's mainstream budget, but by National Committees).

The outcome of the 1986 Board was more positive than many had hoped. It was a flexible and realistic response to the situation facing UNICEF. In the child labour field, UNICEF's intention was to build on what it knew best, i.e., non-institutional programmes for street children, and gradually extending the lessons of Latin American to the new challenges of Africa and Asia. The emphasis on the 'noted projects' mechanism again builds on past policy. Some $ 2 million was raised in this way in the early 1980s, with only a small $ 500,000 commitment from UNICEF's stretched general resources. But will UNICEF campaign against child labour? Given the realities of a threatened annual budget of some $ 400 million which UNICEF has to raise each year, campaigning is too politically sensitive to contemplate. Child Survival brings in the money while UNICEF quietly goes on with its broad-based field programmes.

Many see child labour as a human rights issue so, finally, it is worth pointing to a number of United Nations pronouncements on human rights which relate to child labour:

1. The Universal Declaration of Human Rights, 1948.
2. The international Covenant on Human Rights, 1966.
3. The Supplementary Convention on the Abolition of Slavery, 1956.
4. The Convention for the Suppression of the Traffic in Persons and of the Exploitation of the Prostitution of others, 1949.
5. The Declaration of the Rights of the Child, 1959.

Additionally, regional organisations such as the Council of Europe, the Organisation of African Unity and the Organisation of American States, have their own instruments.

Since the International Year of the Child, NGOs have become an increasingly powerful force, lobbying the UN system to adhere to the principles enshrined in these instruments, and to take more effective action against child labour. NGOs like the Anti-Slavery Society, have produced some of the best documented country studies of child labour. Others, like the Geneva based Defence for Children International have taken up the human rights dimension of child labour and effectively lobbied UN agencies (particularly UNICEF) to pay more attention to the issue.

But of all the NGOs, it is perhaps the trade unions who have the greatest untapped potential for action, both at the national and international level. The Trade Union Congress of Britain produced its own educational resource on child labour in 1985, and subsequently lobbied the ILO Governing Body to follow this example by doing more in the field of public education (see Fyfe, 1985). In *Breaking Down the Wall of Silence* the

ICFTU resolved that 'free trade unions all over the world will pave the way for the eventual abolition of child labour' (ICFTU, 1986, p. 34). But the same organisation faces its own constraints in acting upon this commitment. Its resources are limited and have only permitted small-scale projects, such as a vocational education initiative in Bombay. More fundamental, though is the reality that many of its developing world affiliates are lukewarm at best, given their member's dependence on child work. The ICFTU has, therefor, gone along with the humanising strategy, which the TUC has often opposed, of ameliorative actions which deliver services, like health and education, to the child at work, or attempts at loosening the rigidities of the school system so that working children can fit education around their work schedule.

These pragmatic projects and programmes recognise the need for children to work. But to change that reality, to eliminate the necessity for children to work, is a radical shift which requires a long-term integrated international effort, and virtually everyone agrees that public education campaigns are the first necessary, but not sufficient, steps along a very long road. The Report of the Director-General of the ILO in 1983 provides the essential rationale:

> The role of information gathering and dissemination in raising public awareness of the evils of child labour and in exposing the sectors of activities where it is prevalent should not be under-estimated. In many developing countries there is a surprisingly high degree of ignorance about the consequences of child labour in general and the ill-effects of unsafe working conditions in particular. Child work is often accepted as part of the natural state of things, and the rights and needs of the child are not always fully appreciated. A great deal of effort, therefore, needs to be made to generate and promote public awareness of the consequences of child labour and the rights of the working child and to expose unacceptable conditions wherever they exist. (Blanchard, 1983, p. 23).

The Anti-Slavery Society in a report commissioned by UNICEF as part of its preparation for the 1986 Executive Board suggested that, 'Trends in the use of child labour could be reversed by public education on the needs and the rights of children' (ASS, 1984b, p. 49). The trade union movement has an enormous potential role to play in this area. As Professor Boudhiba has pointed out: 'the unions ..... would still seem not to be clearly aware of the magnitude of the question. They should be requested to include specific activity on this matter in their programmes. They are active pressure groups that can have a decisive effect on governments, employers, enterprises and public opinion (Boudhiba, 1982, p. 71).

The ICFTU in recognising the need to respond to the challenge and child labour, and in its own report to its members early in 1986, observed that: '.... public opinion was largely ignorant of the problem and must be made aware of the dangers of child labour, the damage it can cause to family life and to entire societies and economies.' UNICEF's Draft Working Paper for its 1986 Executive Board recommended that UNICEF should work to enhance government and public awareness of children in especially difficult circumstances and of possibilities for preventive and ameliorative actions (UNICEF, 1986a, p. 14). Finally, the UN Seminar on Child Labour called on governmental, international and non-governmental organisations '.... to increase awareness amongst children, parents, workers and employers of the causes and the adverse effects of child labour and the measures to combat its exploitation' (UN, 1986, p. 28).

If everyone is agreed that the raising of public awareness is the first essential step in the child labour campaign, there is little in the way of guidance on how best this can be done. Perhaps the past is our only guide. The question of whether it is possible to derive lessons from the past has, of course, long exercised historians. Many historians would now clam that this is a futile endeavour, however, for the student of child labour campaigns, the past is virtually the only reference point. And as long as one avoids attempts at drawing crude parallels between nineteenth-century Britain and the contemporary developing world, the past can provide important pointers for those wishing to conceptualise, and contruct, child labour campaigns.

The first campaigns against child labour took place in Britain just over 200 years ago over the issue of chile chimney sweeps. Prior to the 1780s, child work was taken for granted in Britain and Europe. It was philanthropists like Jonas Hanway who turned child labour into a public issue. Hanway's aim, like those of the early nineteenth century philanthropists, was not to abolish child labour but to regulate it through parliamentary action. Then, in 1803, with the foundation of the Society for Superseeding the Necessity of Climbing Boys we witness the first attempt to abolish a from of child labour. According to Hugh Cunningham, the early reformers had to overcome four major obstacles (Cunningham, 1985, p. 1). There was, firstly, the traditional assumption that it was natural for children to work and to contribute to the family economy. Secondly, that the problem was too little work for children rather than too much. Thirdly, a belief that parents had the right to do what they wished with their children, and finally the *laissez-faire* belief in the value of free labour. That these obstacles were gradually surmounted is now part of the romance which has stuck in English history textbooks for over 50 years and become as universal as the story of 1066.

What was the reality of these first campaigns and what lessons can be learnt from them? It is a long story, for it is only gradually that we witness in nineteenth-century Britain an awakening of social conscience. Then in the latter half of the century 'a veritable fury of compassion" (Thompson, 1984, p. 384) produced 'an extreme sensibility to human suffering' (Bagehot in Collins, 1965, pp. 178-9). But how was this transformation achieved? The movement to protect children from the new impersonal and systematic exploitation under industrial capitalism took over a century to achieve its goal. This campaign was never broadly based, comprising as it did a handful of enlightened professional men from the industrial north, the workers' own Short-Time Committees, and the parliamentary skills of Lord Shaftesbury. At the centre of the campaign was the task of building the evidence which proved so effective in persuading the nation of the iniquities of child labour. The first step was the raising of awareness; many people were simply unaware of the conditions of child work around them. Richard Oastler, who become one of the lading factory reformers, had to be told about child labour abuse even though he lived alongside it. As E.P. Thompson observes, 'we forget how long abuses can continue unknown until they are articulated; how people can look at misery and not notice it, until misery itself rebels' (Thompson, 1984, p. 377)

Oastler founded the Short-Time Committees which collected evidences for the Parliamentary Committees. These in turn allowed working people to speak for themselves about the abuses of child labour. The children themselves gave testimony, particularly to the Royal Commission which in 1842 examined women's and children's work in the mines. A public accustomed to the horror stories of factory work was unprepared for the stories of child miners of seven working 14 hours a day in conditions that disabled and deformed them. Victorians were particularly susceptible to accounts of sexual depravity and exploitation, which working naked down the mines encouraged—it was this more than any other feature which shocked contemporary opinion.

For the Victorians it was the potential for sexual exploitation in the expanding industries which moved them into action. The Mines Act of 1842 was passed virtually overnight. In the end it was not factory legislation, but free compulsory education, which proved the most effective child labour law. The campaign for universal schooling was much more popularly based on culminated in the passing of the Education Act of 1870. This act expressed both a changing view of childhood and the belief that the future of the nation was ultimately served best not by making children work, but by educating them.

We must examine the techniques used by the Victorian campaigners which gradually took children out of the workplace and deposited them in the classroom, and we can identify key elements in the process which altogether provide a model for contemporary campaigns. The Victorian campaign was built firstly upon detailed *investigation,* which was of two kinds: leading figures in the campaign, like Shaftesbury, had to brief themselves and raise their own awareness; then, there were the institutional investigations of the Select Committees and the Royal Commissions. Any investigation necessarily leads to *abalysis:* in the case of child labour new social investigators like Henry Mayhew were helping to provide a classification of child workers for the first time. After analysis comes the need for *public exposure,* as the first step in raising public awareness: the 1830s and 1840s in Britain became the era of the great extra-parliamentary pressure groups; the factory movement drew much inspiration from the Anti-Slavery Movement, the most powerful and effective of these in publicising its cause. It was vital that the new knowledge of the factory conditions be *dis-seminated* widely. Robert Owen, the enlightened factory owner and model paternalist (it was Owen who established the first pre-school in Britain at his new Lanark factory in 1816), clearly recognised this, believing as he did in 'the multiplication of reason by means of its diffusion.'

audience needs a transformation of abstract notions into a medium ... emotional in its appeal. Significantly, Hanway, the first campaigner, ...on child chimney sweeps, *A Sentimental History* (1785) in a deliberate ...age the emotions of the public. Climbing boys were tailor-made for the ...gners because of their high visibility (unlike factory children and child ... entered the homes of the wealthy) and because their appearance and ...nt facilitated the slave/savage analogy; when the slave analogy was extended ...y children it became a powerful emotional tool (Cunningham, 1985, p. 2). ...r writers like Charles Dickens and Charles Kingsley transformed the new knowledge ... fictional from with which a mass audience could identify. Dickens could equally lay claim to the title of the 'children's champion' of Victorian Britain. His child heroes, from Little Nell (1840) to Jo in *Bleak House* (1853), presented for the first time the child's world from within. *Bleak House* in particular became proverbial and even the 'street arabs' treasured such tattered copies of the instalments as they could lay their hands on. Dickens's vast international appeal was instrumental in assisting both the factory reformers and more particularly the campaigners for universal free schooling.

The factory movement was able to utilise the remarkable pockets of literacy within the working class. It was workers' groups who established 'reading societies' to buy the new radical newspapers, such as the *Poor Man's Advocate* and the *Voice of the People*. The movement also produced its first pamphlets in 1836, and even the illiterate were not excluded from political discourse. Ballad singers and 'patteres' presented current political issues through song and theatre, and workers would walk miles to hear a radical speaker. The growing power of newspapers is graphically revealed by the case of W.T. Stead's account in the *Pall Mall Gazette* of buying a 13-year-old prostitute. This produced such a public clamour that it brought swift parliamentary action in 1885 to raise the age of consent and curb child prostitution. Contrast this with the painstaking efforts of Josephine Butler and others throughout the 1860s and 1870s to expose the 'white slave trade' which had consistently been ignored.

Such new opportunities for the *dissemination* of information fed into the consequent activities of *mobilisation* and *pressure* for *action*. These campaigns for political action did not always succeed (parliamentary inquiries were often as not a means of diffusing discontent), but from the *evaluation* of the points of resistance a new dissemination campaign could be mounted with a fresh attempt at mobilisation.

Out of the historically important experience of Victorian Britain, we can now construct a Child Labour Campaign Model, as in figure 45.1.

1. *Investigation:* This is the first step of acquiring information through research by mass media, NGOs, trade unions, universities, government agencies, international agencies.
2. *Analysis:* The information needs processing to arrive at plausible explanations concerning causes, consequencies and measures to be taken.

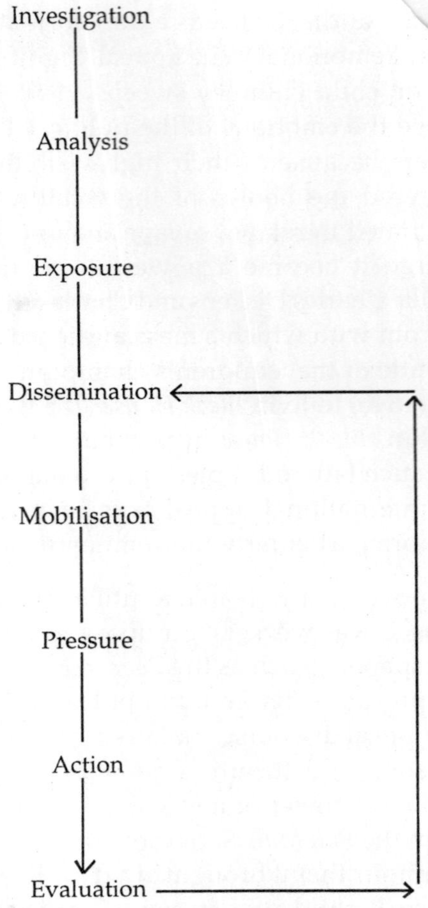

Fig. 45.1 The Child labour campaign model

3. *Explosure:* Such interpretations need a public airing through publications, etc.
4. *Dissemination:* Wider dissemination is then needed via the mass media, trade union education structures, etc., to generate greater public awareness.
5. *Mobilisation:* of those groups most likely to act, such as trade unions, NGOs, churches, etc.
6. *Pressure:* Through campaigns pressure is put on the authorities to act to eradicate the worst abuses of child labour and to protect and improve the welfare of child workers in line with intenationally agreed standards.
7. *Action:* Positive action which can be anticipated would include adoption of ILO standards, better labour inspection, punitive measures against employers guilty of the worst practices, improved provision of health, welfare, and educational services for those children most at risk.

8. *Evaluation:* All action needs evaluation, especially if, as is often the case, it is not successful the first time. Once you find out what went wrong with the campaign, you can marshal new information and 'loop back' again with a fresh attempt at dissemination and mobilisation.

Though all the elements of the models were present in the Victorian child labour campaign, they were not applied continuously either by individuals or pressure groups. Trade unions, which potentially could have activated the model, fully, had not yet developed a mass membership, and therefore the capacity for action, until after the education Acts sealed the fate of child labour. Dickens, though a genius at popular dissemination, never significantly involved himself in political mobilisation; while Shaftesbury, an expert in parliamentary pressure, kept himself aloof from popular movements.

When we look at the developing world today we see all manner of possibilities for integrated public awareness campaigns which would have been beyond the capability of those in the last century. To begin with, we only need to look at the means of mass communication available in developing countries. Perhaps for the first time large areas of the developing world have the organisation and communication structure to inform and support the majority to bring about change. Twenty years ago radios were a rarity. Today there are 8,000 radio stations in the developing world broadcasting to over one billion transistors. Twenty years ago the print media was relatively underdeveloped. Today there are 8,000 daily newspapers in the developing world. Television is also a growing force, reaching as it does some 50-60 per cent of the urban population. India has had a decade of experimentation with satellite TV to promote village education, and by 1990 almost three-quarters of its 670 million population will have access to TV. Such developments provide enormous scope for non-formal education, training and information dissemination. A number of campaigns already bear witness to this, from the spread of the Green Revolution to attempts to promote family planning, child health and adult literacy.

Equally, one can point to the educational opportunities provided by the remarkable expansion in schooling in the developing world during the 1960s and 1970s. By 1981, countries such as Sri Lanka, Tanzania, Kenya and Vietnam were achieving 100 per enrolled in formal education, making the school system one of the most important channels of communication for the vast majority of today's and tomorrow's parents. Nevertheless, this expansion makes fundamental defects. There are still major inequalities of access between urban and rural areas, and boys and girls. Drop-out rates continue to be universally high—up to 70 per cent in some cases. The absolute numbers not in school continue to rise with high birth-rates (110 million in 1960, rising to 121 million in 1975). What is also disturbing is the decline in educational expenditure (16.4 per cent of total government expenditure in 1982, reduced to 5.9 per cent in 1981) with the global recession. Despite this, primary schools, in particular, remain an important tool in any public awareness campaign against child labour as, for example, in the possibility of building child-to-child alliances.

The Green Revolution and child immunisation campaigns have shown that there is no substitute for the political will to mobilise all the possible channels of communication. Political leadership was vital in the promotion of the Green Revolution and Family Planning in Indonesia, and for the remarkable success of the Child Immunisation Campaign in Colombia in 1984. Equally significant is the growth of non-governmental organisations. India alone has 12,0000 voluntary organisations and Bangladesh, 6,000. Specifically, one can point to the growth of organised religion as a major development resource. Trade unionism, too, is on the increase in much of the developing world, albeit from a low base, and in the last decade there has been the growth of the Women's Movement. Additionally, one can mention the growth of the major youth movements of the Boy Scouts (16 million members world-wide) and Girl Guides (8 million members world-wide). To these indigenous NGOs should be added the over 3,000 NGOs in industrial countries, such as Radda Barnen and OXFAM, who are significant partners in grassroots development.

If the potential change agents and the tools for social mobilisation are in place, how can they be used in the campaign against child labour? This is the most difficult task of all because in a world where information technology has become the new wonder of the age, shamefully little is known about how to communicate information whose principal value is to the poor. Nevertheless, there are a number of initiatives which are indicative of how the Child Labour Campaign Model might operate in practice. In Kenya there is the recent WHO-sponsored Child Labour and Health Project run by Dr. Philista Onyango of the University of Nairobi. The project team engaged during 1984-5 in a number of activities which mirror the model. beginning with an investigation in eight districts in Nairobi they analysed the data and disseminated it through workshops and seminars. The project's dissemination strategy was initially aimed at parents and employers and, given the problem of illiteracy, they significantly used the medium of community drama. The team considered drama as perhaps the most powerful tool for not only presenting issues like child labour, but as a tool for collective problem analysis (Dr. Philista Onyango). The rationale behind the use of drama was its capacity both to hold the interest of large groups of parents and employers through entertainment, and to create awareness of the dangerous aspects of child labour. It was seen as vital that the people participated in this exercise through role play as part of the process of identifying the problem. This was followed by discussion out of which emerged suggested solutions. This is a good example of active learning which appears to have led to attitude shifts regarding the value of rural to urban migration (Onyango, 1986, p. 169).

The research activities of the team identified four groups which needed to be mobilised: the parents (producers), employers (consumers), the children (products) and the decision makers. Out of these the 'producers' and 'consumers' were the least likely to perceive child labour as exploitative because they benefited from it, while the official

view was that child labour law was effective and the problem did not exist. As the research team had identified child workers as school drop-outs, they decided to take school children as their target audience in the nest phase. Out of this evaluation the team 'looped back' in the model to a new dissemination strategy to ensure that every effort was made to reduce the high drop-out rate from primary schools. For despite the introduction of free primary education in 1974, five years later of the original 63 per cent of girls and boys enrolled in standard 1, only 14.76 per cent of girls and 13.85 per cent of boys were enrolled in standard 5. The project in its next phase intends to use drama in schools to create awareness of the opportunity cost of leaving school at an early stage, particularly in terms of adult employment prospects, and to try to involve children themselves in suggesting possible solutions.

In Peru, an NGO coalition co-ordinated by TIPACOM (Talleres Infantiles Procyectados a la (Comunidad) has, since the early 1980s mounted a Children's Rights Campaign mainly in the shanty-towns of Lima. Community participation was central to the strategy of creating awareness and mobilising people for action. In the shanty-town district of 3 de Mayo a Committee for the Defence of the Rights of the Child (CODEM) has been constituted by the parents and there is a similar children's committee. The aim of the committees is to investigate children's problems and to formulate possible solutions. The Committee of NGOs working in this all-year-round campaign has found direct communication through audio-visual presentations and drama the most effective channels of communication. Now, CODEM is producing its own newsletter. Though TV and radio were thought too costly by the Children's Rights Campaign, it is worth a small digression to point to the value of popular radio for the rural areas of Peru, and by extension to Latin America and the developing world. Radio is the medium best suited to the rural areas of Peru since it is both cheap and well adapted to the oral tradition of the peasantry. Recent experiments in educational radio are particularly noteworthy, such as *Tierra Fecunda* (Fertile Land) first broadcast in 1983. It has proved popular in disseminating a wide range of information not simply confined to agricultural practice. The impact achieved by *Tierra Fecunda* is evidenced by a network of over 700 correspondents throughout the country who receive 300 letters a month and about 3,000 correspondents bringing information and materials. This and similar radio programmes throughout the developing world represent an importants bringing information and materials. This and similar radio programmes throughout the developing world represent an important delivery system which could be out at the disposal of the Child Labour Campaign.

The Centre of Concern of Child Labour in Bangkok, Thailand, is a good example of an integrated approach to the raising to public awareness. Established in 1981 by an ecumenical association of Buddhists, Catholics and Protestants, the Centre operates across the activities of research, dissemination, pressure and welfare services provision. In 1982, the Centre published pamphlets containing warnings and advice for those rural families, especially in the impoverished north-east of the country, who are forced each year to send their children to work in Bangkok. The pamphlets were disseminated on a large scale to governors and governmental agencies for eventual distribution among villagers, labour officials and the media. In 1983 the Centre conducted research in Vierirem Province collecting information on children who had disappeared after obtaining work in Bangkok factories.

These grassroots organisations originating small-scale projects in the public education filed often work in isolation. There is a clear need not only to learn and, where possible, generalise from their experiences, but also to network them so that they can learn from each other. What these innovative projects generally have in common is a commitment to community participation which owes a great deal to the seminal work of the Brazilian educationalist Paulo Freire. In the early 1960s, Freire pioneered a new method of working with adult illiterates in his native north-east of Brazil. At the heart of this methodology is the concept of 'conscientisation'—the awakening of a critical consciousness in poor people. For Freire the way to break the 'culture of silence' characteristic of poor communities is through non-formal education. Indeed, Dickens's severe school-master, Mr. Gradgrind's obsession with facts, epitomizes what Friere terms the 'banking concept of education,' the aim of which is to fill people's minds with the facts and ideas of others. But to promote real awareness one needs to encourage people to think for themselves—to involve them in 'problem-posing education.' The coordinators of such programmes of education motivate through the use of the problem of poor people. These topics are typically raised in discussion groups or 'culture circles' using visual media like slides or pictures. Freire's ideas were highly influential in the 1970s but are essentially only a restatement of a precept and old as education itself; that people learn best by finding out for themselves. It was Pascal who observed that: '. . . .we are usually convinced more easily by reasons we have found ourselves than by those which have occurred to others." Freire's methodology is important because of the principles of community involvement, and starting from where people are and are not from where you wish to take them. One could envisage 'learning circles' in which a discussion starter was: 'Is it better for our children to work rather than to go to school?'

These innovative projects are highly indicative of the types of techniques and strategies which might be further elaborated. What is needed now is a move beyond these fragmentary initiatives to a more systematic and integrated global strategy. In such a strategy one can identify at least three major action programmes. They are *workshops, training manuals,* and *mass communication campaigns.* Regional and national workshops are an important activity to enable people on the ground to share experiences and ideas. If participants are carefully selected, they offer an opportunity for identifying priorities and setting an agenda of feasible actions. They also provide the elements of a future network which is vital if the learning process is to be developed. Regional workshops to encompass the Americas, Africa, and Asia would need to have representatives of governments and workers' and employers' associations. The involvement of teacher unions should be particularly encouraged, given that they straddle both the world of child welfare and organised labour. In nineteenth and early twentieth-century Britain, teacher unions were an important factor in ensuring that poor children remained in school and had access to health and welfare services. Out of these well-prepared regional meetings it is important that a future agenda of regular reporting back on national experience is built in. Any programme of national workshops ought again to retain this basic tripartite core, added to which could be relevant NGOs, health professionals, the mass media and lawyers. The latter would seem to be another neglected professional group. Lawyers have a vested interest in child labour law, but they themselves may need educating first. As Jeremy Bentham pointed out: 'Lawyers are the only persons in whom the ignorance of the law is not punished.' Again, the basic aim would be to generate a deeper awareness of the problem with the objective of working towards the constitution of a national coalition for action. Perhaps these might be designated 'Child Protection Alliances' with a prominent patron. The CLC (Child Labour Campaign) Model outlined in this book would offer a practical tool for conceptualising the design of public awareness campaigns, either at the macro level of a nationally co-ordinated movement, or at the micro level of NGOs, workers' or employers, action. The field testing of the model at both levels would be vital and the experiences of its use, with suggestions for modifications, could be shared at regular regional meetings.

The next step must be an examination of the tools for action at the community level. Here the development of training manuals, particularly, but not exclusively, for trade unions, needs exploring. Historically trade unions have not played a major role in the campaign against child labour and they continue to treat the issue as a low priority. This limited interest can and ought to be reversed through workers' education programmes, which would generate awareness of the implications of child labour for the health and development of children, their future capacity as adult workers, and its negative effects on income distribution and employment. Greater awareness of international conventions, national laws and regulations is another precondition for enhancing the capacity of workers' associations to put greater pressure on governments for action. Workers' associations do have the potential for mounting the type of integrated campaigns envisaged by the CLC model. They can play an important role in the detection and identification of child labour abuse. Through their own educational structures they can analyse this data, and then design campaigns using dissemination strategies that educate and mobilise, not only their own grassroots membership but also the general public. Workers' associations have an important role to play in organising the unorganised, especially in the informal urban sector where so much child labour is concentrated. The extension of workers' solidarity to these marginal workers, and communities would, in turn, facilitate the more effective disemination of information and knowledge, thereby opening up new possibilities in popular participation for change.

Training manuals for the literate trade union activist would make a significant contribution to the methodology of organising workers' education on a more informal and flexible basis at the community level. Such manuals would essentially be resources for tutors working with small groups of activists in workshop settings. They would function both as a resource and as a guide for people who would later run their own education programmes at the community level. As an exemplar the manual could offer a guide to co-operative learning. Active learning exercises built into manuals could increase participants' understanding of the issue of child labour, and their campaigning skills would be developed through the use and application of the CLC model.

The Trade Union Congress has already developed such a manual on child labour for its own membership (see Fyfe, 1985). The Commonwealth Trade Union Council has, through its technical cooperation programme, particularly in Africa, experience of using training manuals and preparing 'study circle' books. One can envisage the adoption of a similar methodology with other appropriate groups. The use of manuals in teacher training is a clear possibility to develop teachers' child welfare capacity, and to enable them to improve curricula so that school children themselves can be mobilised in the campaign. Schools not only need a more relevant curriculum in order to retain children, they also need more flexible working arrangements to fit in with the needs of working children. In Peru, a national organisation of working children called MANTHOC, established since 1977, has attempted to create such awareness within the teaching profession. Employers, too, could be reached through an appeal to enlightened self-interest, as it would help erode chap labour competition. Many employers in the small-scale and marginal sector might be wiling to comply with the law if they were aware of the regulations and the penalties of non-compliance. Besides, employers could be appealed to in terms of the delivery of health services to child workers. Robert Owen used the argument with other employers that it was just as important to maintain human capital as physical capital if productivity was to be maximised. Both the WHO and ILO recognised that it is possible to influence employers. There is little doubt too that a training manual resource would be an important tool for a range of NGOs to develop their advocacy function. After all training manuals provide the stimulus by which people educate themselves and develop their organisational skill.

Resource development to facilitate the mass dissemination of information and to promote awareness is the third and final element in the integrated action programme. What can be done here to reach the mass of ordinary people, in particular parents? We must look to the mass communications media, particularly TV and radio, as powerful tools of social marketing. Again there are models to act as guides in the use of the mass media for public education. The ILO in 1985 began a mass media campaign in Latin American using a series of TV sports (of 15-30 seconds duration) to promote the message of equal rights for women. The ILO has been able to obtain the agreement of governments, workers and employers to this programme, and the national TV agreed to open up prime-time slots for these 'commercials.' The TV slots use a variety of media, including cartoons, to convey messages concerning equal fights for women. The series includes 12 TV sports which are repeated for 2-3 weeks before changing to the next. Argentina was the first to adopt the package in November 1985, followed by Bolivia, and similar agreements have been signed with the majority of the countries in the

Americas Region. There is little doubt that such an approach would work equally well in urban area to deliver messages on the dangerous effects of child work, and particularly as a means of reaching those 'invisible' child workers who are employed as domestics in middle-class homes. It may well be that child domestic work (a priority concern in the field) is the most susceptible to this kind of public education campaign as so much of it rests on the attitudes and lifestyles of a group of affluent people who, unlike employers, have no collective strength.

But what of the rural areas? Here, radio takes over, and we have already seen examples of attempts to use popular radio for development purposes. There is no reason to believe that programmes could not be devised, which, rather than castigating poor people for making their children work (for of course there are exploitative parents), communicated messages concerning the health and learning needs of children and how they could organise to press for improved services. Slide-tape presentations might also be used in village meetings. Already a group of Asian NGOs, collectively called Child Workers in Asia Support Group have used sets of slides based on a comic telling the story of a child worker from India. In addition, there is a cassette, a script, a copy of the comic, a set of eight pictures and a guide on how to organise group meetings, Any audio-visual package ought to be supported by such a group leader's guide. This proposed programme of integrated activities should not simply be a top-down' process. A 'bottom-up' feedback mechanism, in which lessons at the grassroots level are fed in at the national, regional and global levels, is vital if we are to improve the art of public awareness raising in relation to the child labour problem. It is the international agencies like ILO, UNICEF and WHO who are best placed to sponsor the piloting of such an integrated programme in public education, but it will be left to governments to engage in full-scale implementation.

WORKING WOMEN AND CHILDREN

WORKING WOMEN AND CHILDREN

Volume - 5

Exploitation of Children and Welfare Measures

Editor-in-Chief

C. P. RAI

LAXMI SHIKSHAN SANSTHAN

LUCKNOW

&

ANMOL PUBLICATIONS PVT. LTD.

NEW DELHI - 110 002 (INDIA)

ANMOL PUBLICATIONS PVT. LTD.
4374/4B, Ansari Road, Daryaganj
New Delhi - 110 002

Working Women and Children

First Edition, 2000

ISBN 81-261-0658-1 (Set)

PRINTED IN INDIA

Published by J.L. Kumar for Anmol Publications Pvt. Ltd., New Delhi -110 002 and Printed at Mehra Offset Press, Delhi.

CONTENTS

VOLUME II

PREFACE

Conventionally labour force consists of persons in the age group 15 to 59 years. However, there are about 52 million child workers in the world. More than 50 million working children are from under-developed countries, where Asia alone accounts for 38 million, with concentration in South and South East Asia of 29 million. The child labour is a symptom of poverty, unemployment and illiteracy. The child labour is normally found in unorganised sectors where he is highly vulnerable to exploitation.

A common observation in India, as in many developing countries, is that a large number of children are engaged in economically productive work. Children are often employed in the rural areas, for example, to graze cattle and on the farm. In urban areas, children are engaged in, among other things, construction, automobile repairs, restaurants and domestic work. According to the 1971 Census of India, the total work of participation rate for males up to 14 years of age was 6.6 per cent; for females of the same age the rate was 2.5 per cent (Office of the Registrar General and Census Commissioner, 1977). The corresponding percentages for 1981 were 5.5 and 2.9 which, in absolute numbers, works out to be 10.7 and 11.2 million child workers in 1971 and 1981 respectively. Although the census data for the two years are not comparable, the data, nevertheless, give in idea about the magnitude of children who are working. The census data also indicate that the participation rate of children as workers in rural areas is nearly three times the rate in urban areas; whereas in 1971 the rural and urban rates were 5.3 and 1.8 per cent, in 1981 the rates for these areas were 5.0 and 1.7 per cent respectively. And the actual situation in the year 2000 A.D., has much worsened.

This book focusses on two main themes. First, Child labour: a real Position; and the second Exploitation of child labour and welfare measures.

Derived from the writings of eminent scholars in the field, this work portrays all aspects of and issues pertaining to working children and their plight and suggestions for welfare measures. We are grateful to these scholars. We also owe deep sense of gratitude to Mr. J.L.Kumar, Managing Director, Anmol Publications Pvt. Ltd., New Delhi for bringing out the work in record time.

— C. P. Rai

1

WORKING CHILDREN IN INDIA: AN OVERVIEW

"We are guilty of many errors and many faults, but our worst crime is abandoning the child, neglecting the fountain of life. Many of the things we need can wait. The child cannot. Rightnow is the time his bones are being formed, his blood is being made and his senses are being developed. To him we cannot answer 'Tomorrow'. His name is 'Today'".[1]

The above passionate words of Ganela Mistrale, the Children Nobel Laureate, reveal the deep sense of urgency for the most promising, yet the most discarded human sector. A large section of the children in poor developing countries have been denied their basic and fundamental rights of getting education and pleasures of playing and entertainment; on the other hand, these tender hands have been put to work, the conditions of which are often hazardous, unhealthy and inhuman. India, which adopted its democratic contribution in 1950 and incorporated laudatory references for the welfare of the children in its Directive Principles of State Policy, is one of the worst in this regard—the incidence of child labour is the highest here compared to any other part of the world.

Though child labour is not a new phenomenon and it has existed even in ancient times, its form have been changing. So far as the modern period is corrected, it was the industrialisation and urbanisation in the early 19th century that changed the social scenario. At this time the growth of the tea, coffee, indigo and jute industry took place. The factory and industry began taking place of handicrafts. Agriculture became more mechanised. This gave rise to landless labourers. And consequently, there was an unbroken streams of the rural poor migrating to urban centres in search of livelihood. Factory, on the other hand, required cheap and plentiful labour. Children started being employed both on farms and in factories. Because they provided a cheap and uncomplaining labour force as against adults who could be more demanding and hence more difficult to handle (Gupta, 1979).

Before we go into details into the question of child labour, it would be useful to comprehend the meaning of the term. It is used as a synonym for employed child or 'child worker'. In other words, the child labour is that segment of the child population which participates in work either paid or unpaid. Late President V.V. Giri has interpreted the term in two different ways. First, as an economic practice in which it signifies employment of children in gainful occupations. Second, as a social evil in which it is necessary to take into account the nature and extent of the job done by the children, the danger to which they are exposed and the opportunities of development which they have been denied. Further, a child labourers is differentiated from an adult labourers on the basis of age. A worker who is below the age of 14 or 15 years engaged in any productive activity whether paid or unpaid, with the family or outside, is regarded as a child labour.

Extent of Child Labour

The I.L.O. estimates that India contributes to about one-third of Asia's child labour and one-fourth of the world's working children. According to the 1981 census, workers in the age group below 14 years of age (excluding Assam) were 13.59 million. On the basis of the National Sample Survey, it was 17.36 million on 1st March, 1983. Nearly 93 per cent of the total child labour force works in the rural areas and the rest in urban areas. About 81 per cent were employed as cultivators or agricultural labourers. About 6 per cent in livestock, forestry plantation etc., and 8 per cent in manufacturing and processing and another 3 per cent in household and other services and the rest in trade, commerce and transport. These facts are revealed from Table 1.1.

TABLE 1.1

Sector-wise Distribution of Estimated Child Labour Population (%)

Sl. No.	*Sector*	*1971*	*1981*
1.	Cultivators	36.06	38.23
2.	Agricultural labour	42.71	42.54
3.	Livestock, forestry, fishing, hunting, plantation and orchard	8.24	5.67
4.	Mining and quarrying	0.22	0.22
5.	Mfg. processing servicing and repair	6.09	7.90
6.	Construction	0.55	0.66
7.	Trade and commerce	1.96	1.95
8.	Transport, storage and communications	0.39	0.26
9.	Other services	3.78	2.57
		100.00	100.00

Source: Ministry of Welfare (1985).

There are great variations amongst the states in India regarding child labour. Andhra Pradesh bears the highest incidence of child labour. It accounts for about 15% of the total child workers in the country. The rural participation rates for boys are—Andhra Pradesh (10.38%), Karnataka (16.28%), Orissa (14.45%), Madhya Pradesh (13.82%), Punjab (13.67%),

Meghalaya (13.52%) and Rajasthan (12.75%). For girls in rural areas, the participation rates are Nagaland (13.35%), Andhra Pradesh (11.47%) and Meghalaya (10.12%) The urban participation rates for boys are—Andhra Pradesh (16.69%), Karnataka (16.56%), Orissa (5.48%), J&K (4.82%), U.P. (4.80%), Punjab (4.64%), Tamil Nadu (4.53%), Assam (4.52%). The highest urban participation rates for girls are Andhra Pradesh (2.63%), Karnataka (2.36%), Kerala (2.00%). Thus, Andhra Pradesh and Karnataka has the highest rates of employment of child labour. But other States are not far behind although intensity varies.

Nature of Child Labour

According to a report prepared by the Indian Social Institute, 80 per cent of all child labour belong to the scheduled castes and tribes which have been exploited for centuries. The report of the Royal Commission on Labour, the labour investigation committee on the condition of work of children and a number of surveys conducted by the Labour Bureau and other agencies, generally point that children do light work in comparison to adult workers. In agriculture, they do work as helpers during sowing and weeding, harvesting and threshing operation, watching crops etc. In factories, they are employed for packing, pasting, labelling etc.

The salient features of child labour in India are as follows:

(i) The number of children working as child labour is growing. The bulk of child labour is employed in unorganised sector such as workers in hotels, restaurants, canteen, wayside shops or as a hawkers, newspaper sellers, coolies etc. A recent survey[2] points out that child labour is predominant in low technology traditional industries like carpet making, lock making, matches and fireworks industry, stone quarries, mines, fishing etc. There are an estimated 44 million children working, many from age of seven. This report fears that Government programmes intended to provide income generating schemes for the households such as the provision of cattle to poor families, seem likely to increase the need for the family for labour. The report also indicts the family-based cottage industries like handloom and small agro-based businesses, for increasing demand for household labour, including child labour.

(ii) A large majority of children are working as unpaid workers in farm and non-farm activities in rural areas. Children are also found as bonded labourers. The parents obtain loans and surrenders their children as security for it.

(iii) Most of the children at work are illiterate since they are initiated to the world of work quite early in life. For the same reason, they remain under-nourished, under-developed and what is worse unskilled.

(iv) A majority of those working as child labour are boys. They account for about 80 per cent of the total.

(v) Children are made to work in such hazardous occupations as construction, carpet weaving, manufacturing of machines, explosives and fire-works etc.

The conditions of work are also deplorable. A survey in Murshidabad revealed that per cent of bidi making workers are aged between 10 to 17 showing definite sign of chronic bronchitis. Several reports have came out about the large incidence of Child Labour in carpet weaving around Mirzapur and Varanasi and their deplorable conditions, significant proportion of whom are bonded.

(vi) Their houses are congested and over-crowded with hardly any ventilation or sanitary facilities. The entire *basti* is unhygienic with water-logging, dirt insects and flies which cause so many illness like typhoid, malaria, hepataties etc.

Causes of Child Labour

The main cause of child labour in India is poverty. A pilot study conducted in Madras, Madurai and Coimbatore found that three-fourth of children were at work to supplement their family income and 23 per cent were doing job because of the death of their fathers or guardians. In big cities like Bombay, Madras, Delhi etc., a large number of migrant children are seen working. A survey found that 81 per cent children were migrant in Greater Bombay whereas resident child workers were only 19 per cent.

Poverty of the household may be due to several factors: inadequate income of the family, due to unemployed adults, absence of schemes for family allowance, large family, etc. It has been found in some studies that parents force their children to take up employment because of their own earnings being very low. Further, in India, there is not allowance facility for the poor families, so that they are forced to send their children to the labour market. Impoverished and illiterate families are of the view that more children means more hands to work to bring extra money.

Absence of provision for compulsory education is another cause of child labour. Non-availability of school going facilities tend children to do some job as an alternative. National Commission on Labour (1969) states the main obstacle in the way of making education compulsory to all children upto a prescribed age in the following words: "An artisan cannot afford to educate his wards though education is free. For him, an uneducated child is an asset, desire to be educated becomes a double liability because of (a) loss of earnings if the child does not work and (b) expenditure on education howsoever small".

Migration is another cause of child labour. When family head moves from one area to another due to agricultural cycle, his wife and young children either moved with him or stay back to look after the family plot in his absence. In both cases, they seem to have bad experiences. In the urban areas, when the whole family moves from their village to the cities, they face problem of lack of shelter, hunger, joblessness etc., and it forces the children to join the labour force.

It has also been reported in some cases that in areas where green revolution is becoming a stabilised reality and wages of agricultural labourers has substantially gone up, labour families have pressed into service their child population, tempted by relatively good earnings.

Further, a large percentage of children start working because of being orphaned, dejected by parents or because of broken families and other domestic problems.

Actually child labour is both the cause and consequences of adult unemployment and under-employment. Some experts are of the view that if children were eliminated from the labour market in India, employment opportunities for at least 20 million adult unemployment workers would be increased.

Preventive Measures

Several legislations have been exacted in India for regulating child labour. Even in pre-Independence period. The Indian Factory Act 1881 fixed the minimum age for the employment of child at 9 years and working hours not more than 9 hours a day. A number of Acts passed in favour of labourers such as The Indian Mines Act. (1923), The Tea Districts Emigrants Labour act (1932), The Children (Pledging of Labour) Act (1933) and the Factories Act (1934) in which there were some provisions for the well-being of the child workers. By accepting the recommendations made by The Twenty Third Session of the International Labour Conference, 1937, India passed the Employment of Children Act, 1938, in which the employment of children under 15 years is prohibited in occupations connected with the transport of goods, passengers or mails or rickshaws.

After Independence, the Constitution of India recognised the need for granting special protection to child workers. In *Fundamental Rights*, specific provisions in regard to children have been made in part III of the Constitution. Article 24 provides categorically that no child below the age of 14 years shall be employed to work in any factory, mine or any other hazardous employment. The *Directive Principles of The State Policy* states: "(a) that... tender age of the children are not abused and their citizens are not forced by economic necessity to enter a vocation unsuited to their age or strength, (b) that children are given opportunities and facilities to develop in a healthy manner and in conditions of freedom and dignity and that children and youth are protected against exploitation and against moral and material abandonment." Some further legislation provisions were also made. The Minimum Wages Act 1948 provides for the fixation of minimum rates of wages for child workers also. The Factories Act 1948 is an important Act relating to child workers. It prohibits employment of child under 14 years of age in factories. A child who has completed the age of 14 years is not permitted to work in a factory for more than 4½ hours in any day or during night. Such workers cannot be employed in two shifts and cannot be employed in more than one factory on the same day. The Plantation Labour Act 1951 prohibits the employment of a child below 12 years of age in plantation and restricts the hours of work of a child in any plantation to 40 hours a week. The Mines Act 1952 provides for some more stringent provisions. No child below the age of 15 years can be employed in mines. Even an adolescent (between 16 and 18 years) is not allowed. Other Acts, which have some provisions for child workers' welfare, are the Merchant Shipping Act, 1958; the Motor Transport Workers Act, 1961; the Apprentice Act, 1961; the Atomic Energy Act, 1962; the Beedi and Cigarette Workers (Conditions of Employment Act), 1966; the Shops and Establishments Act in various States and Union Territories. The Government of India has also laid down the National Policy for Children in 1974. The Seventh Five Year Plan gave more weight on making the working condition of child labour better and more acceptable socially than to eradicate the problem of child labour. A partial fulfilment of the objectives stated in the Seventh Plan document, the Government of India passed the Child Labour (Prohibition and Regulation Act), 1986. The Act (a) prohibits the employment of children in certain occupations and processes of production considered hazardous and (b) regulates the conditions of work of children in the certain other occupations and production processes where they are not prohibited from working. The national policy on child labour, thus, provides for legal action, general welfare and development programme and project based plan of action for rehabilitation of children. The Government of India has been collaborating with ILO in prevention and rehabilitation of child workers in the country. The Ministry of Labour of the Government of India has signed agreements with the ILO to take up some specific projects for the rehabilitation of child labour.

This problem was also seriously taken into account in the United Nations Declaration of the Rights of the Child (1959), International Labour Organisation Resolution for the Progressive Elimination of Child Labour and Transitional Measures (1979) and also by the Resolution of the United Nations declaring 1979 as the International Year of Child. ILO's Policy on Child Labour is two fold. It required countries to carry out a series of legal and social-economic measures on the one hand and protection of children at work on the other hand.

Conclusions and Suggestions

In spite of all the development and legislative measures taken to prevent and regulate the child labour in India, the problem continues to cause alarm to all the concerned. The incidence of child labour has been increasing in the country, including in the hazardous occupations. And, therefore, there is the need for accelerating the efforts in this regard. The following points may be useful for reappraising the strategy for preventing the child labour as well as ameliorating their conditions:

(i) The existing legal framework for employment of children is rather dispersed and patchy. Some of the laws also suffer from internal contradictions. The greatest drawback of the laws is in its non-coverage. More than three-fourth of the total child workers are employed in agriculture and allied activities, but there is no law to take care of the workers employed in them.

(ii) Further, supportive measures for child labour such as removal of poverty and unemployment, ensuring minimum wages, meaningful education policy, medical and health support, proper nutrition, recreation and cultural activities, family planning, apprenticeship and vocational facilities etc., must be given much weight besides legislative measures.

(iii) The enrolment of children at primary stage should be done vigorously and alternatively. Though poverty is a major cause for child labour, but the inability or unwillingness of public authorities to spend adequate money on elementary education as well as the social background is not a less contribution factor. The fact is amply proved by the experience of Kerala. In the country only Kerala stands out as the State where not only all children are at school but the retention rate is very high; this is despite the fact that Kerala is a State with poor per capita income.[3]

(iv) The raising of public awareness and supporting community action should be given top priority in any scheme concerning child labour. Some voluntary agencies have done good work and their more involvement should be explored.

In soon, the basic strategy concerning child labour should be to gradually reduce child labour and eliminate it through improving and enforcing legislation, promoting school enrolment, raising public awareness, supporting community action and targetting hazardous environment.

NOTES

1. Quoted from Sharma (1979).
2. The Survey has been done by the Centre of Concern for Child Labour, New Delhi. See the report of the Survey in the *Hindustan Times*, New Delhi, November 15, 1992, p. 18.
3. *Ibid.*

REFERENCES

1. Government of India (1979), *National Commission on Labour*, New Delhi.
2. Gupta, Manju (1979), *Young Hands at Work: Child Labour in India*, Atma Ram and Sons, Delhi/ Lucknow.
3. Ministry of Welfare (1985), *Child Labour in India: A Statistical Profile*, Government of India, New Delhi.
4. Sharma, Alakh N. (1979), *Child Labour in Patna*, A.N. Sinha Institute of Social Studies, Patna (mimeo).

2

MAGNITUDE OF CHILD LABOUR IN INDIA: SOME POLICY PRESCRIPTIONS

No period in the history of Economic Thought has attached more importance to the protection of child labour than that of the present period. In this century, the most authoritative effort to throw light on the problems of child labour in India started with the observations made by Royal Commission on Labour. The Royal Commission on Labour stated the plight of child labour in the following words: "In many cities large number of young boys are employed for long hours and discipline is strict. Indeed there is reason to believe that corporal punishment and other disciplinary action of a reprehensible kind are some times resorted to in the case of smaller children. Workers as young as five years of age may be found in some of these places working without adequate meal intervals or weekly rest days, and 10 to 12 hours daily for sums as low as two annas in the case of those of tenderest year".[1] In 1946, Labour Investigation Committee also brought to limelight the illegal employment of children in certain Indian industries. It observed that "the important fact that has emerged from the investigation is that the various industries, mainly smaller industries, the prohibition of employment of children is disregarded quite openly and owing to the inadequacy of inspecting staff it has become difficult to enforce the relevant provisions of the law".[2] The Committee also found that legislative measures relating to child employment were not successful in ameliorating the conditions of work of child labour. However, all this was the story of child labour prior to independence. Later, India got independence and everybody expected that the various executive as well as legislative steps undertaken by the Government would be effectively implemented to protect the child fully well. But the problem of child labour still continues to be a burning problem in our country despite the four decades of planned efforts. This has constantly agitated the minds of economists, social thinkers and Jurists. In this paper, an attempt is made to assess the magnitude of the problem of child labour in India in the recent years and also to offer some policy prescriptions to mitigate the problem.

The analysis is deliberately confined to the Census data of 1981. This is mainly because the worker definition adopted in the Census of 1981 is not comparable either to that of 1971 or to the Census of 1961. The analysis is also confined to the main worker as defined in the 1981 Census. Here the main worker was defined as person whose main activity was participation in any economically productive work by his physical or mental activities and who had worked for six months (183 days) or more during the reference period. It is felt that this definition would reflect the concept of worker more meaningfully. Hence, all the marginal workers are deliberately excluded from the analysis. As regarded the statistical techniques, simple percentages are worked out.

Structure of Child Labour

The structure of child workers gives an idea of the magnitude of the problem of child labour in India in different activities. As such the statistical information relating to the activity-wise distribution of child workers is presented in Table 2.1. As can be seen from the table that around 78 per cent of the child workers are employed in the first two categories of the activity. Livestock, forestry, fishing, plantations, orchards claims the next major absorption of child labour (6.40%), followed by the 'other than household industry' category which claims 4.36 per cent. The lowest percentage of child labour is observed to be seen in mining and quarrying (0.21%) in transport, storage and communication (0.32%) and in construction activity (0.67%). The predominance of child labour in India's most important occupation viz., agriculture is understandable in view of its easier accessibility and in view of the relative difficulty involved in the enforcement of statutory provisions in the rural areas. Similarly the meagre percentage of child labour absorption in the activities relating to mining and quarrying; transport, storage and communication and construction activities may be attributable either to the hazardous nature of work process or to the lack of skills needed for the entry into the field. Thus, from the above analysis it may be concluded India's child labour lives predominantly in villages.

TABLE 2.1

Activity-wise Distribution of Child Workers, 1981

Sl. No.	*Name of Activity*	*Child Workers*	*% to Total*
1.	Cultivators	3,999,769	35.73
2.	Agricultural labourers	4,787,548	42.75
3	Livestock, forestry, fishing, plantations, orchards etc.	716,428	6.40
4.	Mining and quarrying	23,532	0.21
5.	Manufacturing and processing, servicing and repairs etc.	—	—
	(a) Household industry	432,983	3.87
	(b) Other than household industry	544,291	4.86
6.	Construction	85,415	0.76
7.	Trade and Commerce	249,205	2.23
8.	Transport, storage and communication	35,547	0.32
9.	Other services	320,826	2.87
10.	Total workers	11,195,544	100.00

Source: Census of India, 1981, Series-I, Part III-A, General Economic Tables, Table B-3.

Educational Levels and the Child Labour

The obnoxious practice of child labour could be largely traced to the socio-economic compulsion of these parents and guardians who opt their children to be employed as child labour rather than sending them to schools. As such it is interesting to analyse the distribution of child workers by educational levels in the rural and urban areas. Data relating to these variables are presented in Table 2.2. As can be seen from the table the educational levels are generally low and illiteracy persists predominantly in the child labour. However, it may be pointed out that the educational levels are higher in urban areas. It can also be observed that the percentages of male child workers are relatively higher when compared to the percentages of female child workers at all educational levels. From this two inferences can be drawn. Firstly, it may be pointed out that the Indian psychology has not changed much to break the barriers in order to get the fruits of education. Secondly, the relatively higher educational levels in the case of male children may be largely due to the higher preferences accorded to educate the male children in our society. The relatively lower educational levels in the case of female children may be also attributable to the social taboo that still exists in the minds of the vast majority of the parents and guardians of the child labour.

TABLE 2.2

Sex-wise Distribution of Child Workers by Education Levels, Rural and Urban Areas

Sl. No.	*Educational Level*	*Male*		*Female*	
		Rural	*Urban*	*Rural*	*Urban*
1.	Illiterate	5,342,133	469,128	3,117,111	195,067
		(79.75)	(63.47)	(88.93)	(77.25)
2.	Literate (without educational level)	688,782	113,162	195,723	2[illegible],572
		(10.28)	(15.31)	(5.58)	(10.92)
3.	Primary	574,730	127,725	168,601	25,241
		(8.58)	(17.28)	(4.81)	(10.00)
4.	Middle	85,659	25,681	22,721	4,132
		(1.28)	(3.47)	(0.65)	(1.64)
5.	Matriculation/Secondary	6,920	3,150	973	472
		(0.10)	(0.43)	(0.03)	(0.19)
6.	Higher Secondary/Inter-mediate/Pre-University	437	221	32	22
		(0.01)	(0.03)	(0.00)	(0.00)
7.	Non-technical Diploma or Certificate not equal to Degree	36	26	16	5
		(0.00)	(0.01)	(0.00)	(0.00)
8.	Technical Diploma or Certifi-cate not equal to Degree	47	8	9	5
		(0.00)	(0.00)	(0.00)	(0.00)
9.	Total Workers	6,698,743	739,102	3,505,185	252,514
		(100.00)	(100.00)	(100.00)	(100.00)

Note: Figures in parentheses indicate percentage to total.
Source: Census of India, 1981, Series-I, Part III-A, General Economic Tables, Table B-3.

Region-wise Distribution of Child Labour

In order to understand the magnitude of the problem of child labour employed in different regions of our country a region-wise analysis of the distribution of child workers is attempted here. Data relating to region-wise distribution of child workers are collected and these percentages are presented in Table 2.3. On the basis of the percentages of child workers to the total population the following observations can be made. Among all the regions, the highest percentage of child workers to total population emerges from Andhra Pradesh (3.28%) which is much higher than the All-India average of 1.68%. This is followed by Meghalaya (2.93%). Next in order are Madhya Pradesh (2.63%). Karnataka (2.60%). The lowest percentages of child workers to total population are registered in Lakshdweep (0.08%), Kerala (0.27%), Delhi (0.40%), Chandigarh (0.43%) and Andaman and Nicobar Islands (0.45%).

Following are some of the observations made on the basis of the percentages of child workers with respect to total workers and to total child population. The child labour forms as high as 7.75 per cent of the total workers of Andhra Pradesh while the percentages of child labour registers the lowest in the case of Lakshdweep (0.39%). It is interesting to note that even on the basis of the percentages of child workers to total child population the state of Andhra Pradesh tops the list with 8.50 per cent followed by Meghalaya (6.91%) and Karnataka (6.58%). The percentages of child workers to total child population is noticed to be very low in Lakshdweep (0.19%).

Thus, the percentages of child workers in relation to either total population or total workers or total child population are extremely high in Andhra Pradesh and extremely low in Lakshdweep. Hence, this suggests the need for conducting indepth studies to find out the reasons for these extreme variation in the child labour participation among different regions of the same country in order to launch appropriate legislative measures.

Distribution of Child Workers by Sex and Areas in the Regions

Though the involvement of child labour in economic activity is common in India, the magnitude and intensity of its sex-wise participation differs from region to region, and in the same region it differs from rural areas to urban areas. As such it is felt appropriate to analysis the distribution of child workers in different states and union territories by sex and area-wise to get better insights into the nature of child labour in India. These percentages are worked out and are presented in Table 2.4 Following are the few most important observations made from the Table 2.4. Out of the total number of child workers in India 59.83 per cent of male child workers live in rural areas while 6.60 per cent of the total male workers live in the urban areas. In the case of female child workers while 31.31 per cent of the total workers live in rural areas, 2.26 per cent only lives in Urban areas. It is interesting to observe from this table that the male child labour and female child labour combined together are predominantly confined only to the rural areas of India with the only exception of Chandigarh and Delhi. Another interesting observation from the Table 2.4 is that in most of the regions while the total percentage of male child workers in rural and urban areas combined together account for a greater proportion of the total number of the child workers, in the case of Himachal Pradesh, Manipur, Nagaland, Sikkim, Arunachal Pradesh, Goa, Daman and Diu and Mizoram the percentage of female child workers in rural and urban areas combined together account for a great proportion of the total number of the workers.

TABLE 2.3

Region-wise Distribution of Child Workers

Sl. No.	*Region*	*Percentage of Child Workers to total*		
		Population	*Workers*	*Children*
1.	India	1.68	5.03	4.26
2.	Andhra Pradesh	3.28	7.75	8.50
3.	Bihar	1.28	4.31	3.07
4.	Gujarat	1.36	4.21	3.50
5.	Himachal Pradesh	1.41	4.11	3.56
6.	Haryana	1.10	3.89	2.64
7.	Jammu and Kashmir	1.82	6.00	4.44
8.	Karnataka	2.60	7.08	6.58
9.	Kerala	0.27	1.00	0.76
10.	Madhya Pradesh	0.63	6.85	6.38
11.	Maharashtra	2.01	5.20	5.25
12.	Manipur	1.25	3.11	3.19
13.	Meghalaya	2.93	6.75	6.91
14.	Nagaland	1.89	3.98	5.14
15.	Orissa	1.95	5.97	4.93
16.	Punjab	1.07	3.64	2.90
17.	Rajasthan	1.72	5.65	4.06
18.	Sikkim	2.50	5.37	6.32
19.	Tamil Nadu	1.80	4.58	5.14
20.	Tripura	0.96	3.25	2.45
21.	Uttar Pradesh	1.14	3.90	2.74
22.	West Bengal	0.96	3.39	2.47
23.	Andaman and Nicobar Islands	0.45	1.35	1.13
24.	Arunachal Pradesh	2.37	4.78	6.02
25.	Chandigarh	0.43	1.24	1.29
26.	Dadra and Nagar Haveli	2.52	6.17	5.93
27.	Delhi	0.40	1.25	1.12
28.	Goa, Daman and Diu	0.63	2.05	1.78
29.	Lakshdweep	0.08	0.39	0.19
30.	Mizoram	0.92	2.20	2.32
31.	Pondicherry	0.53	1.83	1.44

Source: Census of India, 1981, Series-I Part III-A, General Economic Tables, Table B-3.

Thus, from the foregoing analysis it is understood that the magnitude of child labour employment differs from region to region, even in the same region intensity of sex-wise distribution of child labour also differs. The big question now is how to solve the problem of child labour in India?

TABLE 2.4

Percentage Distribution of Child Workers by Sex, Rural and Urban Areas

Sl. No.	*Region*	*Male*		*Female*		
		Rural	*Urban*	*Rural*	*Urban*	*Total*
1	2	3	4	5	6	7
1.	India	59.83	6.60	31.31	2.26	100.00
2.	Andhra Pradesh	52.79	5.26	39.60	2.35	100.00
3.	Bihar	71.34	4.19	23.63	0.84	100.00
4.	Gujarat	61.20	8.34	28.81	1.65	100.00
5.	Himachal Pradesh	40.26	1.17	58.04	0.53	100.00
6.	Haryana	74.02	6.83	18.44	0.71	100.00
7.	Jammu and Kashmir	68.05	10.74	27.85	2.53	100.00
8.	Karnataka	54.87	8.36	33.11	3.66	100.00
9.	Kerala	42.77	8.60	40.80	7.83	100.00
10.	Madhya Pradesh	56.70	3.10	38.88	1.32	100.00
11.	Maharashtra	48.83	5.62	43.28	2.27	100.00
12.	Manipur	38.22	3.62	53.34	4.82	100.00
13.	Meghalaya	56.84	1.68	39.89	1.59	100.00
14.	Nagaland	41.68	2.51	54.20	1.61	100.00
15.	Orissa	71.49	3.76	23.37	1.38	100.00
16.	Punjab	83.36	12.18	3.68	0.78	100.00
17.	Rajasthan	62.13	5.52	31.13	1.22	100.00
18.	Sikkim	38.25	4.31	54.89	2.55	100.00
19.	Tamil Nadu	45.98	10.71	37.32	5.99	100.00
20.	Tripura	69.09	2.17	25.70	3.04	100.00
21.	Uttar Pradesh	75.67	8.82	14.72	0.79	100.00
22.	West Bengal	73.50	8.33	14.51	3.66	100.00
23.	Andaman and Nicobar Islands	66.19	19.39	11.70	2.72	100.00
24.	Arunachal Pradesh	42.88	1.19	55.36	0.57	100.00
25.	Chandigarh	6.64	74.36	1.23	17.77	100.00
26.	Dadra and Nagar Haveli	50.93	2.38	44.27	2.42	100.00
27.	Delhi	5.87	80.12	2.63	11.38	100.00
28.	Goa, Daman and Diu	34.06	12.49	36.82	16.63	100.00
29.	Lakshadweep	25.81	25.81	35.48	12.90	100.00
30.	Mizoram	42.26	2.40	53.33	2.01	100.00

Source: Census of India, 1981, Series-I, Part III-A, General Economic Tables, Table B-3.

In order to solve the problem of child labour, first we should identify the causes of employment of the children. These reasons for employment of child labour may be broadly grouped into three headings (1) the attitude of the parent/guardian; (2) the attitude of employer; and (3) the attitude of the Government.

Attitude of the Parent/Guardian: The socio-economic compulsions of the parent/guardian are responsible for making the institution of child labour survivable. Though an unmistakable under current of anxiety for the future of their children is seen in some of the parents/guardians, this attitude hardly helps them to help their children in view of their poverty-stricken lives. Child labour supplements the income of the family and this is essential because the earnings of the adult workers are extremely low.

Attitude of Employer. The employer are also responsible for intensifying the problem of child labour in India. Though the employers' community prides itself in providing lawbound welfare measures, this section is not whole heartedly interested in implementing the spirit behind the legislative measures. The employer always wants to cash on the loop-holes that are there in the legislation. Hence, there is need for change in the attitude of the employers towards the upliftment of the child labour. But, this humanness is mostly lacking in most of the employers.

Attitude of the Government: Though the Government is undertaking legislative measures to protect the child labour in India these are not effectively implemented. Moreover, there is need for strengthening the existing legislation aimed at protecting the child labour to make it completely free from loop-holes.

Policy Prescriptions

Now having seen the magnitude of the problem of the child labour and also the chief reasons for its sustenance, one feels the need for launching a determined attack to solve the problem of child labour in India. The following are some of the remedial measures to rectify the problem of child labour in India.

1. The State Governments have to take concrete steps to strictly prohibit the employment of the children in occupation which have been banned under the Child Labour Act.
2. The State Governments have to suitably amend the law, if need be, so that firm action could be taken against the employers who had engaged child labour under the prohibited category of works.
3. The State Governments must activate the law enforcement machinery to see that all the legislative measures aiming at the welfare of the child labour are fully implemented in occupations, where employment of children is permitted.
4. Besides this, the Government should also provide financial assistance in the form of grants-in-aid to the voluntary bodies for imparting non-formal education, health care, nutrition and vocational training to the child labour.

5. Efforts should also be undertaken by the voluntary organisations to involve the local public and parents/guardians of child labour, so that they become aware of the efforts made by the Government for the upliftment of child labour.
6. Finally, as has been suggested by Sri V.V. Giri, a long time back extension of free and compulsory education should be given higher priority as this is the only panacea for checking evils of child labour.

After all, children are the blooming flowers of the garden of our society. Therefore, it is everyone's responsibility to protect these flowers from the damaging effects of excessive exposure to heat, cold and rains. They should be put on the right track always, as they are the seeds of future national growth.

NOTES

1. *Report of the Royal Commission on Labour*, pp. 96-97.
2. *Labour Investigation Committee Main Report*, 1946, p. 35.

3

"WE CUT OUR FINGERS BUT NO BLOOD FALLS..."

Carpet weaving was introduced into India in the 16th century by the Mughal emperors. During the reign of Akbar and Shahjahan, imperial carpet factories were established in Agra, Delhi and Lahore. With the departure of the Mughals, this craft did not get the royal patronage it required for survival. The rebirth of the Indian carpet industry dates back to the first half of the 20th century, when carpet production for export was launched on a commercial scale. India exports about 95% of its carpets, as the expensive floor covering is beyond the reach of all but the small, higher income segment of the population.

The art of carpet making has spread from Kashmir to the Southern tip of India. Uttar Pradesh produces 80% of the weavers. Rajasthan and Jammu and Kashmir take up 5% each and the rest 10%. Rajasthan produces fine and medium quality carpets ranging from 100 to 280 knots per square inch. Jaipur, Tonk, Sikar and Bikaner are the main centres for carpet manufacture. It is estimated that 6,000 carpet looms are operating in the State employing about 30,000 people. Due to the present market position, it is estimated there will be an annual increase of 10%, which means 2,000 new entrants every year.

Rajasthan, having a sheep population of about 10 million, is the leading wool producing state in the country. Annual wool production is about 14 million kilos and India is second in the world in wool production. Wool for carpet weaving comes mainly from Bikaner, Sixty per cent of the wool from Rajasthan is suitable for carpet weaving and is considered among the best in the world because of its pile flexibility.

The nomadic tribes in Rajasthan had been traditionally weaving 'namdas' and roughly finished carpets for their own domestic use. It is only in the mid 20th Century that carpet production on a large organised scale started in the State because of its export potential. Entrepreneurs from outside, mainly from Uttar Pradesh and Punjab came and set up factories for carpet production. Carpet weaving was then found to be a good source of income even for people who had traditionally not been carpet weavers.

However, these big organised factories, having between 25 to 200 looms, can hardly be seen today. Because of stringent factory and labour laws, entrepreneurs prefer to sub-contract the work into smaller units. The small production units have between 3 to 10 looms employing less than 20 people. A large number of looms have been dispersed into weavers' homes in the neighbouring villages and there is no attempt to conceal child labour.

Today, it is mainly a cottage industry, the skill of carpet-knotting being handed down from one generation to another. The small manufacturer does not have facilities for all the ancillary processes like dying, washing, finishing, packing, etc. The carpets are woven in the small sheds or in weavers' homes and then taken to the main exporter/entrepreneur who has a centralised worksite for the finishing process.

The weavers are mostly Muslims or belong to Scheduled Castes such as Khatik, Koli, Raigar, Chamar, etc. These people own small pieces of land where they barely manage to produce coarse grain, mainly due to lack of irrigation and other facilities. Those who have no land practice their traditional crafts such as slaughtering animals, making shoes, selling fruit and vegetables, weaving cloth, etc. Income from land and their traditional crafts was not enough to eke out even a bare existence for the family. In the early seventies, there was a sudden boom in the carpet industry and these people realised that carpet weaving could give them some additional income. Most of these families took to carpet weaving 12-15 years ago.

One can only make a rough estimate of the number of child workers employed in this industry because no records are kept by the employers. Being mainly a cottage industry is difficult for any surveyors to visit each and every homes are looms operate. It is, however, estimated that roughly 310 workers are employed in this industry out of which at least 0% would be children below the age of 15 years. A survey of industry is difficult if accurate data is required because most of the looms are in weavers' homes or in small sheds employing less than 20 workers. These are not registered under the Establishments Act or Factories Act and hence, technically, do not exist and no rules and laws apply to them. Labour inspectors never bother to visit them and they maintain words of the labour employed by them.

Manufacturers commission knotters in distant villages and supply them with dyed woollen yarn and a given design with specified size and quality required. Some knows own their looms, others are provided with looms by middlemen or contractors who act as a link between dealers/exporter and knotters. Sometimes, large carpet manufacturers/export in towns and cities lend weavers the money for the purchase looms and deduct the amount from their wages over a period of time. The exporter pays the middleman for the goods supplied and it is the middleman who pays the weaver according to the work produced. Usually the exporter has no direct contact with the knotter. In the rural areas, the weavers are mainly farmers so carpet knotting is a part time activity, children and adults work on the looms when they are free and especially in seasons when work in the field is less, whereas in the home the weavers work full time. Children having looms in their own houses would not be sent as hired labour on other's houses.

Most of the weavers are male and 70% would be male children between the ages of 6 to 14. Less than 10% would be girls. They work from 8 a.m. to 6 p.m. with an hour's break for lunch and usually one day off a week if working in a factory. A child earns between Rs. 8 to 15 per cay. The works on an average 20 days in the month, he earns between Rs. 150-300. From this the contractor will take his commission (14-15%) and the rest is paid to the parents. For the raw work done, an adult is paid 1½ times more. In the present structure, raw material and other overheads account for 30% and labour contributes 43%. For high quality carpets the our component may go upto 60-70%. Hence, having more children working who are paid far less than the adult wages is extremely beneficial for the manufacturer because it keeps his costs low.

The number of big, organised factory type units which are owned by big or small entrepreneurs, is fast reducing. This change started 3-5 years back. The reason given by the entrepreneurs was that government Factory and Labour Laws made running of these units very difficult. They preferred to give the work to weavers or to contractors, who got the work done in the homes of the weavers themselves. The entrepreneurs and contractors both felt that running big units was difficult also because of the erratic and irresponsible behaviour of the labour who would take huge advances and loans and then either not come regularly to work or disappear altogether or start working in some other unit without paying back the previous loan.

What is the working environment in the family run units? The houses are small, consisting of a small verandah and one or two rooms, a small courtyard with a mud floor at the back. The loom is set up either in the front verandah or in the courtyard. Since the courtyard is open, they will put up jute covering or plastic sheeting during the rains. But work gets reduced during the rainy season. In these family units, all the male members work on the loom whenever they can get spare time. A five feet loom will take there workers while a 7 ft. loom takes 4 workers. They begin work at 8 a.m. and work through the day till 5 p.m. with a break for lunch when the whole family sits down to eat together. The male children are taught by the father or elder brother to knot the carpets as early as the age of 5-6 years. The male child is then put to work on the loom every day. Initially, he will be guided by the elders but after about one year, he can work on his own. In these family units, the adult male members also work on the loom. It is not left only to the children. After all, a family may have only 1 or 2 male children. Then it is the responsibility of all the male members to contribute their labour. In these homes, the children seem much happier and relaxed, because there is less pressure on them. Some families send the child to school in the morning, making him work on the loom only after coming back in the afternoon. No women or girls work on the loom. Most of them make bandhini (tie and dye). When the parents were asked why they did not send their child to school, they would laugh and say, "What will the school teach them? Will the school give them a job? Here at least the boys learn to weave a carpet and girls learn to do bandhini. They can at least feed themselves." Payment by the contractor is made to the head of the family for the work produced on a rate agreed upon earlier. The child gets no wage separately.

The houses are small and dark with very little ventilation inside. But the courtyard is airy and well-lit. In summer, it becomes hot and in the monsoons it is wet. But the jute covering and plastic sheet is of some help if it is used. Carpet knotting needs complete concentration and there is tremendous strain on the eyes. The children work almost 8 hours a day. The wool fluff constantly gets into their lungs. The children look weak. Even the adults do not have a robust physique. They accept this as a part of their work. They agree that carpet weaving affects their lungs but feel there is no option when one has to feed oneself. In these colonies, one hardly saw any male children playing around. The sound of their laughter was not to be heard—only the sound of the knotter counting the knots came softly from inside the houses.

The second type of unit is the organised, factory type unit. The shed is set up by an entrepreneur; the loom and all other equipment is owned by him. However, the labour in most of these units is recruited through labour contractors. A labour contractor will take the responsibility of one or more looms. He finds the labour, learns the design and sees that the product is finished on time. Most of these contractors began their life as carpet weavers and hence know the craft well. They begin by working on the looms, and by the time they are 15 years or so, depending on their ability, they leave weaving and become contractors. It is in these organised units that one notices the exploitation of children much more. At least three quarters of the knotters are children. Some are as young as 5 or 6 years of age though the majority are in the age group of 8-14 years. We even noticed 3-4 children who were barely 4 years of age. They were not actually weaving but, we were told, would begin to do so in a few months after observing their elder brother at work. Their day begins at 8 O'clock. There is no question of being late. The contractor will see to it that they are on time. The children are scolded and threatened if they become slack in any way. They work non-stop till 5 p.m. or 5.30 p.m. with a break of 45 minutes to 1 hour for lunch. The children bring their lunch from home which comprises of rotis, onion and, maybe some dal. It is a frugal meal and there is no nutritional food supplied to them to give them energy for the tedious work they have to do. Running water is available, because the carpets have to be washed, but there are no toilet facilities. In case of accidents or ill health, the Seth takes no responsibility. If at all, it is the contractor who might take the child to a doctor or usually just send him home. There were no first aid boxes to be seen. The sheds are dark and poorly ventilated. The floors are usually mud floors. The looms are surface looms and the child sits crouched on the platform which is barely 1-1/2 ft. wide with his eyes fixed on the loom for hours at a stretch. They work for at least 8 hours a day. There are no windows for fresh air and the few tube lights hanging above are usually not switched on. Even if they are, they cast more shadows than give light. The children constantly breathe the wool fluff which gets into their lungs. Most of the children have an unhealthy look about them. They were working like automatons with a despondent and resigned look on their faces due to the drudgery of their work. It was as though the joys and fun of life was passing them by since they were being denied their childhood.

Children are brought by the parents or other relatives to the labour contractor when they are hardly 6 to 7 years of age. The parents feel that they will be kept away from mischief on the streets. Children may be sent for weaving because they do not work in school and are wasting their time. During the training period, they only get 25 p-50 p per day as pocket money and the parent is given Rs. 25-30 per month. After learning for one year, they begin to earn Rs. 7-8 per day.

They are paid for the unit of work produced. For the same work, an adult earns Rs. 15-20 per day. This is one of the main reasons for employing children as knotters. It keeps the cost of production down. Labour constitutes almost 45% for low quality, 60% for medium quality carpets and upto 70-75% of the cost for high quality carpets. Hence, it is in the interest of the employers to employ children instead of adults. It is true that children, having nimble fingers, work faster and are able to produce more in comparison to the adult. However, it is also true that children due to their immaturity and playfulness tend to make mistakes in their weaving which an experienced adult would not do. Women would be able to do this work but because weavers are mostly Muslims, women don't come out to work because of purdah and prefer to stay at home doing bandhini. The wages are paid to the parents of the child by the contractor, who takes a part of that as his commission. Wages are usually paid weekly and it is the parent who comes and discusses the accounts with the contractor. Often large advances and loans are taken by the parents and then the child becomes almost a bonded labourer, never able to break away from the clutches of the contractor, who forces him to work to make up the advanced money. Parents are now becoming conscious of the fact that a young adult boy can earn more by driving a cycle-rickshaw or working in jewel craft which has a big export market and high wages, or in any of the numerous industries coming up in and around Jaipur. These are organised industries where the factory laws apply and minimum wages are adhered to. The earnings from carpet weaving are much less in comparison. Hence, labour in the organised carpet industry is becoming problematic. As mentioned before, many such units are closing down or giving orders to individuals working in their homes. It is only those young children between 6-12 years of age who are too young to drive a rickshaw or work in factories who are pushed into carpet weaving and then spend their entire children as illiterates, in dark unhealthy surroundings with no time to laugh and play.

The children live in awe of the contractor. They have to produce a given amount of work everyday, between 2"-2½" on a 2 foot span. In case they weave less, their wages are cut. The parents will be angry, the contractor will be angry and the Seth will be agitated because his delivery schedules get upset. These children live in constant dread. No wonder at the slighest excuse they take a holiday. Almost every Seth or contractor, who was interviewed, admitted that the children work for only 15-16 days every month.

They stay away either for some family function or just feign illness. When we talked to the children separately or even to young contractors, who themselves were weavers earlier, they admitted that unless they took 10-15 days off every month, they would not be able to survive the physical strain of weaving. The children say, "Yes, we do miss not playing around but then half the moth we don't come to work any way—so its not so bad". The children have to sit on their haunches because that is the only position which facilitates the knotting process. Their arms and hands have to be in close contact with the threads hence sitting with legs dangling in front is not possible because the knees would come in the way and weaving quickly would be impossible. In this crouched position the stomach muscles are constantly being pressed. The leg and knee joints suffer intense pain. The eyes feel the strain from being fixed constantly on the wool and cotton yarn. Any distraction invariably means a mistake in the knotting. According to the older children, the body soon gets used to these discomforts. When we asked the reason why children were considered best for weaving of carpets, we were told by everyone, the Seth, the contractor and the older children, that it is only a child's body that can get used to the physical strain involved in this work, and soon the body does not feel it at all. If a person was to try to learn this work in adulthood, his body would not be able to adapt itself to the discomfort of sitting and working in this crouched position. We tried to sit on the bench in this position and could not do it for more than 5 minutes.

TABLE 3.1

Type of unit	*No. covered*	*Adult weavers*	*Child weavers*
Factory shed	10	70	220
Family unit	40	80	80

It can be been from the above table that organised factory types units employ three times the number of children to each adult weaver, whereas in family units the proportion is generally 1:1. In some families we saw 3 adults and only 1 child working.

What accidents occur? Who gives first àid or medical treatment? The normal answer would be a sarcastic laugh. "Our fingers get cut. We put some turmeric paste or mehendi paste and go back to work. Our fingers are bloodless—no blood falls. We don't grow, our chests don't grow, our legs loose their strength. We are incapable of doing any other work."

TABLE 3.2

Age Composition of Child Labour

Age group	*No. of children*
Below 6 years	12
6 to 8 years	70
9 to 14 years	218

Working in this environment has serious repercussions on the health of the children. This work is piece rated and hence the body is strained to its utmost to produce and fatigue is ignored. This leads to both mental and physical strain. Sitting crouched with the stomach muscles pressed, their appetite suffers. They remain aneamic and suffer from constant colds due to inhaling dust and wool fluff. Common ailments take longer to heal because of low body vitality. Most children seem to have weak eyes even though they never complain about it. When the Chief Medical Officer was contacted, he said that no special medical surveys had been conducted by the Rajasthan Government to assess the effect of carpet weaving on the health of the children. He could give me no data or information for this reason. Rajasthan has bad, worm infested water. No filtered water is usually available at the worksites. The children drank water drawn from handpumps or from earthern jars kept in a corner.

We closely examined some of the children and found that their eyes were sunken in and had a vacant, distracted look. Their legs were weak, very thin and spindly. Their chests were narrow. None of them looked in good health. A child of 14 hardly looked more than 7-8 years of age. Their growth was definitely retarded. Often we would notice a certain maturity on the face but the body would be of a child. Most children were uncomplaining—they seemed resigned to their fate.

Carpet weaving is a process which has been banned in the schedule of the "Employment of Children Act, 1938" and again in the "Child Labour Act of 1986". In Rajasthan, the Government is running 35 training centres with a grant-in-aid from the State. Initially, these had been started by the All India Handicrafts Board. Each centre is designed to train 50 trainees for a period of one year.

The trainees range from the age of 8 years to 15 years, both girls and boys. The children come at 8 a.m. and work till 5 p.m. with an hour's break for lunch. The rooms are dark, dingy and small with hardly any natural light coming in. Each child gets a stipend of Rs. 60 per month. It has been found that not more than 42% of the children trained continue to practice the craft they have learned. Hence, at least for the remaining 58%, this stipend alone seems to be the incentive to make them to through the training programme. Carpets produced here are sold through the Rajasthan Government Emporia. Hence, these can rightly be called training cum production centres, which means they undertake commercial activity. This is a typical example of a Government organisation clearly violating the Act prohibiting child labour in the carpet weaving process—an Act which has been in existence since 1938 and been reinforced by the Child Labour Act of 1986. Does the Government feel that they are only training a child and not making him work? Will a child trained at 9 years of age wait for 5 years to restart weaving or will he go straight away into the labour market for this industry.

From the above description, we can see the extent to which children are exploited in the carpet industry. The question is why do parents send their children to work? In the villages the problem was lack of other job opportunities, inadequate land holdings,

constant drought, lack of irrigation facilities and, hence, low family incomes which needed to be supplemented by a child's wages. In the towns, again, the problem was inadequate employment opportunities, low family incomes and hence tremendous economic pressure on every member of the family. Even with new industries coming up, there are not enough opportunities for male adults in the region. In India, it is considered auspicious to have sons. They are not thought of as more mouths to feed but more hands to work. Hence these young hands are put to work as soon as they can possibly manage to learn a craft, which may be as early as 6 to 7 years of age.

The truth of the matter is that child labour is cheap and convenient. Children are an un-complaining labour force. They can be made to do any work, for as much time, for whatever wages. A child who starts to work at the age of 7 or 8 is totally exhausted, mentally and physically, by the time he is 30-35. He does not have the physical strength to do laborious work and hence, his earning capacity gets reduced. To survive he then sends his child to work and this cycle goes on. The only way this evil can be mitigated is by creating an awareness; a consciousness within the society and the community as a whole so that parents, employers and the Government realiase the harm which is done to the child by stifling his natural instincts, by forcing him to work and by denying him the freedom to laugh, play and educate himself.

APPENDIX-1

Cartpet Manufacturing Centres in India

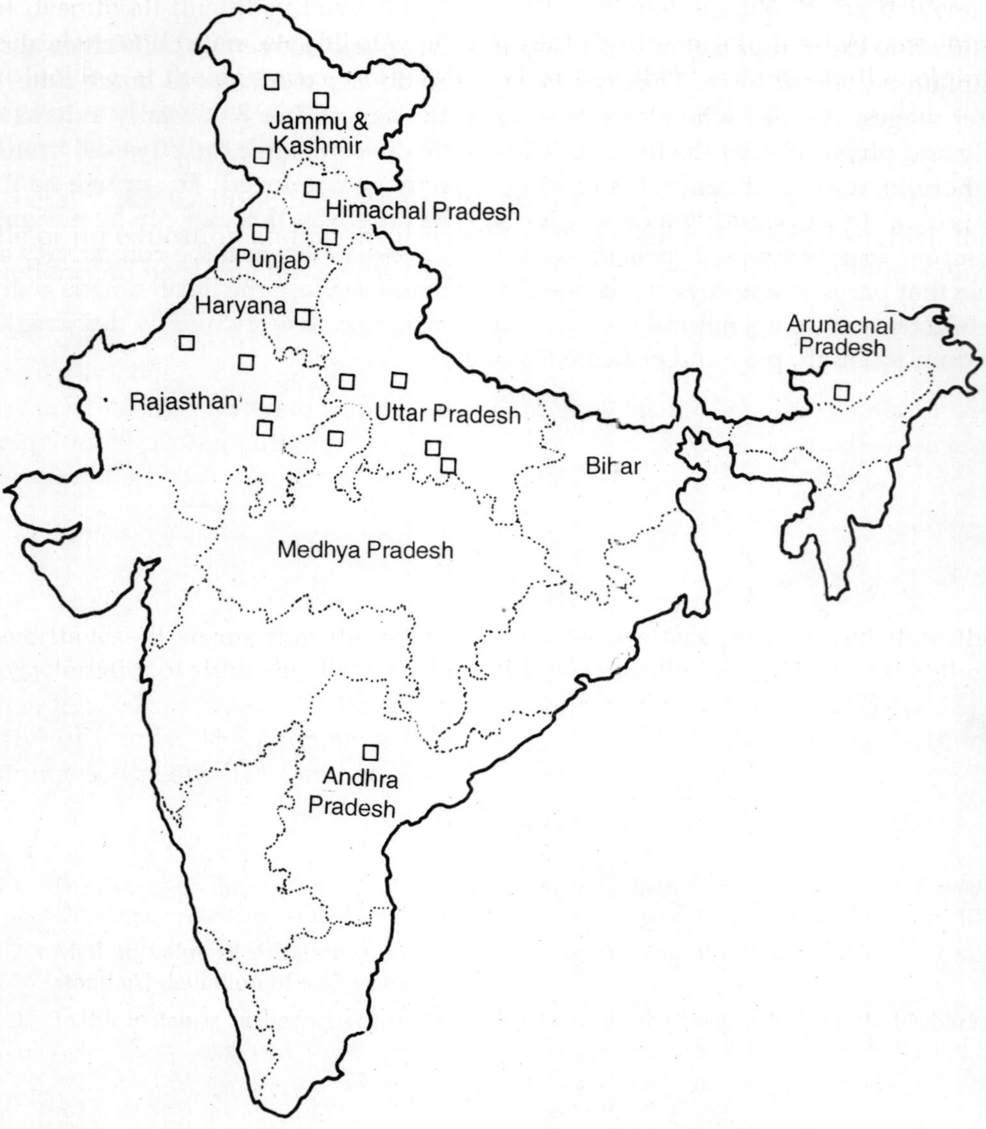

APPENDIX-2

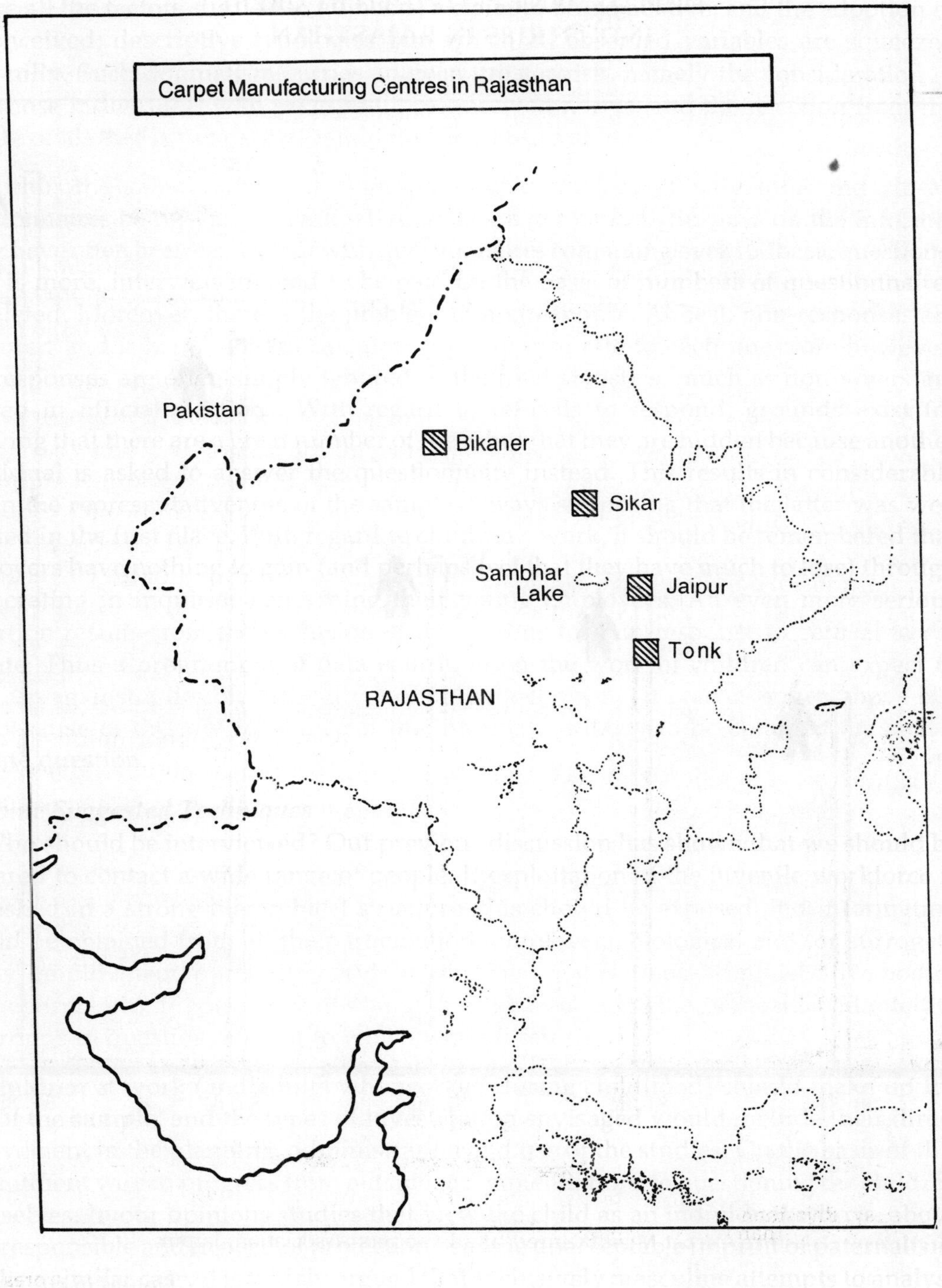
Carpet Manufacturing Centres in Rajasthan
Pakistan
Bikaner
Sikar
Sambhar
Lake
Jaipur
Tonk
RAJASTHAN

APPENDIX-3

EMPLOYMENT PROVIDED BY CRPET INDUSTRIES IN RAJASTHAN

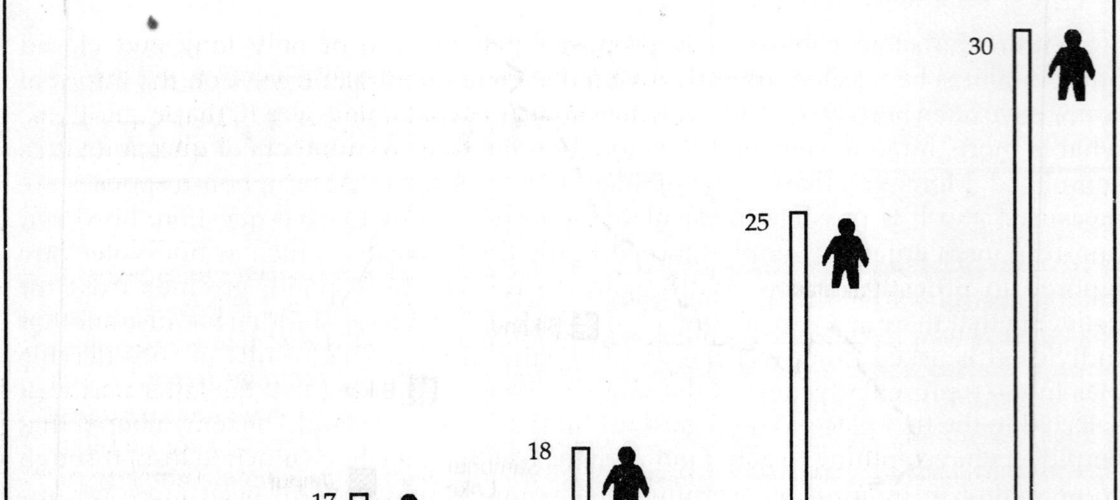

*Courtesy: Rajasthan Carpet Manufacturers and Exporters Association, Jaipur.

Figures in crores (Rs.)

APPENDIX-4

VARIOUS STAGES IN THE CARPET MAKING PROCESS SHOWING WHERE CHILDREN ARE EMPLOYED

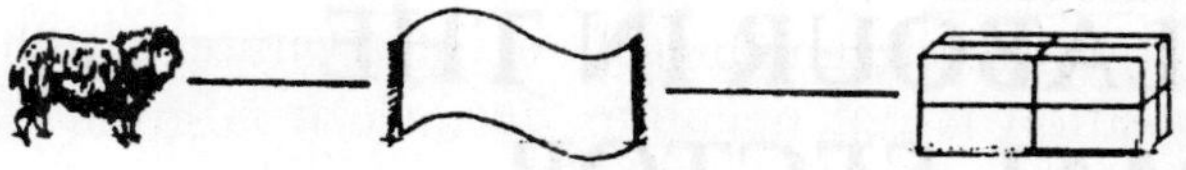

Sheep rearing	Adults and children mainly for sheep grazing
Purchasing of wool	Adults
Selling to the manufacturer	Adults
Dyeing of wool	Adults
"Individual manufacturer:"	
Making of balls	Children and Women
Setting up of loom and placing of kabli on top	Adults
Weaving	Children and adults
De-looping of carpet	Adults
Binding	Children and adults
Washing	Adults
clipping	Adults
packing	Adults

Figure 3.4

4

CHILD LABOUR IN THE INFORMAL SECTOR

A number of studies have been made by the I.L.O. and other national and international agencies covering various aspects of the informal sector. However, nothing tangible has been done so far to examine the employment conditions of children who are engaged in the informal sector for a living. This paper attempts to touch upon certain questions, relating to child labour in the informal sector like the nature and composition of the child labour force, factors that bring them in the informal sector, their wages and conditions of employment and causes for the apathy on the part of the Government for not undertaking any significant ameliorative steps.

Concept of the Informal Sector

The term informal sector in comparatively a recent field of study. This term was in fact coined by Keith Hart in his study "Informal Income Opportunities and Urban Employment in Ghana" in 1968 and since then it has gained popularity and has been used widely in studies relating to urban employment and socio-economic surveys of people in urban areas.

Initially this term meant to refer to all those who struggle hard to make ends meet, that is the urban poor in general but, in course of time, there has been a major change in the concept of this term. Although by now several definitions have appeared for this term, two of them deserve to be mentioned here. The first definition was devised for a survey done in 1969 in Bouke. It used five criteria to distinguish the informal sector from other sectors namely (a) the receipts of the enterprise should be quite small; (b) the equipment used should be rudimentary; (c) the number of workers in the enterprise should be very small; (d) low labour productivity; and (e) the fact that the entrepreneur is not actively seeking more customers. (Castell, 1971, p. 47).

The other definition was used by the I.L.O. in its wide-ranging survey of employment conditions in Kenya during 1971-72. This definition not only represented a major advance of the informal sector concept on a theoretical level, but also served to enliven the debate surrounding its nature and viability. According to this definition the activities pertaining to the informal sector were characterised by case of entry, reliance on indigenous resources, family ownership of enterprise, small scale of operation, labour intensive and adopted technology, skills acquired outside the formal school system and unregulated and competitive markets. (ILO, 1973, p. 6).

These characteristics of the Informal sector suggest and researchers agree that production units in this sector are motivated by employment generation and they have little capital and skills at their disposal. These features also imply that they are relatively more labour intensive and have low value added per worker, as compared to the formal sector.

Definition

The informal sector may be defined "to consist of small-scale units engaged in the production and distribution of gods and services with the primary objective of generating employment and incomes to their participants notwithstanding the constraints on capital, both physical and human, and knowhow". (ILO, 1981, p. 17).

Such a definition of the informal sector would also seem to provide the justification for focusing employment and development policies on this sector. It emphasises the significance of urban population growth to the emergence of the informal sector.

Nature of Activities

Informal sector activities may be discussed both in the context of a developing country as well as a developed or an industrialised one. In the developing countries again it can be discussed in the context of urban areas as well as rural areas. Here in this paper the term informal sector has been used in the context of activities in the urban areas only and that also in the developing countries like India.

Whether it is urban area or the rural areas, children are engaged in good number in the informal sector. They are engaged in a wide variety of occupations like domestic servants, hawkers, cooks, porters, cleaners, helpers in cycle repairing or scooter repairing shops, waiters in hotel and restaurants, parking cars, selling newspapers and soft drinks and collecting empty bottles etc.

Broadly speaking persons in the informal sector can be classified in three categories: (a) child labour (b) Women workers and (c) Adults and old people. Whatever may be their age or sex, the labour force engaged in the informal sector in most metropolitan and provincial towns in the developing countries may belong to the following types of economic activities:

(a) self-employed people;
(b) people employed as members of the family either manufacturing goods or providing services;
(c) people employed on occasional or intermittent basis;
(d) people employed on a clandestine or below the counter fashion which is performed outside the framework of law;

(e) wage earners in mini enterprises; and

(f) people employed in ambulant and itinerant works.

So far as child labour is concerned, they are also engaged in these categories like women and adult workers.

Nature and Composition of the Child Labour force

In most of the studies made for informal sector, it was found that children were engaged in many of the trades. In a study of informal sector in KANO (Nigeria), it was seen that more than 15 per cent of the workers were below the age of 14 years. Young people below 14 were particularly important in trade and other services like painting, mechanics, welding, electrical repair, panel beating etc. (Mabogunje and Filani, p. 108). Similarly the study of informal sector in Colombo showed that about a quarter of the participant in that sector were more or less children. The Jakarta Study (Moir, p. 108) found 18 per cent of the participants in the informal sector below 16 years of age. In another study of informal sector in Calcutta it was found that many trades were carried on mainly by child labour, like boot polishing, domestic servants, newspaper hawkers, cycle repairing shops and small tea shops and road side restaurants.

Thus the fact can not be denied that informal sector provides shelter to child labour. Their percentage may differ from one town to the other, from one country to the other depending on factors like the minimum age of employment, system of compulsory education, socio-economic conditions of the people, availability of educational and training facilities and the policy of the state on employment of children. But the fact remains that informal sector provides possibilities of employment to children who are in need of it or badly looking for a living.

Factors Responsible for Employment of Children in the Informal Sector

There are certain factors which enable children to seek employment in the informal sector in comparison to the formal sector. These factors include: (a) absence of any statutory minimum age for employment; (b) easy entry; (c) less competition among job seekers; (d) absence of any minimum requirement of education or training; (e) easy nature of work; (f) provision of food, shelter and clothing in the city by the employer; (g) absence of any minimum wage requirement; and (h) easy entry and easy exit.

These factors enable the child labour to enter the informal sector as and when they like. Broadly speaking four types of children are found engaged in informal sector.

(a) Children belonging to poor families undertaking jobs to supplement their parents income.

(b) Children who have none to support them.

(c) Children who are sent to urban areas by their parents in rural areas for earning a living.

(d) Children who run away from their families.

For the organised sector there are labour legislations which lay down minimum age for employment. The Factories Act 1948 clearly specifies that children who have not completed their fourteenth year of age, can not be employed in any factory. Further in the organised sector entry is difficult and the competition among the job seekers is quite keen. Certain level of education and training for an entry in the organised sector imperative. Since minimum wages have been statutorily laid down or prevailing wages are known, employers find it difficult to employ child labour at a reduced or a lower wage. All these factors restrict the entry of child labour in the formal sector. Since these situations are not prevalent in the informal sector and there is complete freedom of entry and exit, informal sector attracts more child labour. Studies made of informal sector for some of the cities in India like Calcutta and South Gujarat have shown that children are one of the important constituents of informal sector labour force.

Employment Conditions

No significant work has been done in India to study the employment conditions of children in the informal sector. Dearth of literature and absence of data in this regard are important handicaps in making any scientific observation. However a few studies made by the ILO and some other agencies throw some light in this regard. Most of the studies made for informal sector have shown that wages of workers in the informal sector are far from satisfactory. Children's wages are very low in comparison to wages of adults doing the same type of work. With regard to working conditions of children in the informal sector five areas seem to be significant: First, children in the informal sector not only receive lower wages but that also not regularly and in cash. Secondly their hours of work are much longer. Information received through the questionnaire show that children in the informal sector do not have any prescribed working hours. It depends on the sweet will and whim of their masters. Domestic servants, cooks, children in cycle repairing shops, vendors, child labour in tea stalls, hotels, road side dhabas, laundries, start working from early morning and continue till late night. Thirdly, they are victims of a very rough behaviour by their masters and co-workers. Ill-treatment, beating assaults and abuses are regular affairs. Fourthly, they do not enjoy a stable employment relationship. They are kicked out of their services or are terminated on flimsy grounds or even false charges. Lastly, they do not enjoy any welfare facility, social security or even leave or holidays. In totality, employment conditions of children in the informal sector are worst in comparison to the formal sector.

Absence of a Suitable Protective and Regulative Labour Legislation

The emergence of the urban informal sector as a major source of employment and income in the Third World Countries in recent years is primarily a manifestation of increasing pressure of population growth justaposed against the inadequate growth of employment and income opportunities in rural areas and small urban centres on the one hand, and in the formal and government sectors of the urban economy on the other. Rising inflation rate and growing poverty further aggravate the situation and force a number of children to enter in the informal sector for a living. Number of children in the informal sector in cities like Calcutta, New Delhi, Madras, Bombay, Kanpur, Bangalore, Ahmedabad, Patna, has fastly increased during the years. Although the Central Government and the various state governments are aware of the situation and the exploitation of the child labour in the informal sector, no significant effort has been made so far to adopt a comprehensive legislation regulating the employment conditions of child labour in the informal sector. Unless a comprehensive legislation or a legislation of a composite nature dealing with wages, hours of work, health, safety, welfare facilities, leave and holidays, social security, retrenchment, dismissal and discharge is adopted and a suitable enforcement machinery is created for this purpose, nothing tangible can be achieved.

Although it is not easy to have proper enforcement of any legislation in the informal sector, but initiative must be taken. Factors like scattered nature of undertakings, lack of records or proper information, absence of unionism,, absence of formal employer-employee relationship, literacy and ignorance among children, inadequacy of the enforcement machinery are some of the factors responsible for lack of a suitable labour legislation in the country dealing with child labour in the informal sector.

Implications for Policy

The informal sector will continue to expand in volume during the coming years. Its potentiality of generating employment and income must not be overlooked. With the growing inflation and poverty in the country, the number of child labour will continue to swell. Since their entry in the organised sector is restricted by laying down minimum age requirement, the only sector to absorb the child labour will be the informal sector. Absence of any legislation regulating their employment provides free hands to employers to use the child labour the way they like. Indeed it is difficult to enforce any legislation in the informal sector regulating working conditions. However, some start has got to be made. State can not remain as a silent spectator when the children in a large number are being exploited. To start with, the State may introduce a licensing system to employ and child labour for wage. A Directorate of Child Labour may be created. Children willing to go for wage employment must be enrolled with the said Directorate. Persons desirous to have child labour should obtain a permission or a licence from the said Directorate before they employ any child labour. Once the Directorate has the full information about all the child labour and their employing masters, it will not be difficult to enforce the provisions of any legislation in this regard. Although it is a difficult task, but it is not impossible. Since India is a Welfare State and it is committed to promote welfare of all citizens in the country, it has a moral responsibility to promote welfare of child labour too. In country like India child labour can not be abolished, but it must be regulated.

REFERENCES

1. Castell, P. (1971), For Minister du Plan and Ministere de Agriculture, 1969, *Abidjan*, No. 5.
2. ILO (1973), *Employment, Incomes and Equality—A Strategy for Increasing Productive Employment in Kenya*, Geneva.
3. ILO (1981), *The Urban Informal Sector in Developing Countries*, Geneva.
4. Mobogunje, A.L. and M.O. Filani, *The Informal Sector in a Small City: The Case Study of Kano (Nigeria)*, ILO Study, p. 83.
5. Moir Hazel, *Occupational Mobility and the Informal Sector in Jakarta*, ILO Study.

5

CHILD WORKERS AND ROLE OF NGOs—SOME REFLECTIONS

Introduction

The socio-economic profiles of developing countries indicate that the period through which these countries are passing is a dangerous catastrophe.[1] History has shown that changes among men, women and children began with a vision of an alternative to the then existing situations. Can we do something now? Could the efforts of provide help to the children in distress be elements in providing the first step towards alternatives?

These are some of the questions posed in this paper and the scenario presented provide an entry into the issue of child labour exploitation in the informal sector. A new turn in development efforts requires that we take note of what is happening to our children today.

India is often referred to in the report as a country having the largest number of working children. Of the total population some 42 per cent are estimated to be below 15 years of age and the total number of child workers according to the 1971 census report was 10.7 million, representing 4.66 per cent of the total child population and 5.9 per cent of the total labour force.[2]

Children in the informal sector includes children working in tea shops, small eating places, printing presses, cycle and vehicle repair workshops, metal workshops, etc.[3] Self-employed children such as shoe-shining boys, stall keepers, hawkers, rag-pickers are also counted in this sector. The industries, some of which are run on both, a factory and cottage industry basis, engaging child work in sizeable numbers include: carpet-weaving; bidi-making; cloth weaving; leather work; coir-making; match industries; mica; button-making; bamboo work; waste paper; reuse materials such as envelopes; brick manufacturing and slate-pencil making, etc.

With fast spreading urbanisation industries in small towns and semi-urban areas use child workers in large numbers.

Child Workers in "Industries"—Some Examples

(a) *The brick kiln industry* in Stwarigaon near Delhi, attracts poor rural families who come to work from October to June when there is no agricultural work. The labourers bring their whole families with them and live in shacks and tents on the site without education, health facilities or clean drinking water. Families are paid on a piece-work basis ranging from Rs. 18 to 21 per 1,000 bricks, so they use their children to increase the production. The father digs the clay, the children carry it is their mother who moulds it ready for drying. The family gets only one day off per fortnight. The children risk injury from the work, as well as silicosis of the lungs after three or four years of exposure to brick dust.[4]

(b) *Carpet-weaving* promoted by KVIC is one of the important cottage industries in India. States like U.P., Kashmir and Tamil Nadu are flourishing centres of carpet weaving. Varanasi, Bhadoi, Mirzapur are big centres of carpet weaving. It is estimated that in the Mirzapur belt some 50,000 workers are engaged in carpet-weaving of which nearly 20 per cent are children. In Kashmir, the state of great tourist attraction, carpet-weaving involves little girls as their tender fingers are considered to be good for making knots in the carpet. In Kashmir another back weakening and tiring work is embroidery.

(c) *The match industries* of Sivakasi, (a drought prone area) Ramanathapuram, Tamil Nadu employing thousands of children from the age of 5 of for over ten hours a day is no more a secret now.[5] Women and children predominate in this cottage industry. Children working in the match factories are mostly from harijan landless families belonging to the neighbouring areas and are paid on a piece-rate basis. These children are transported early morning between 3 and 5 A.M. every morning from the villages as far as 30 km. In Sivakasi, of a total of 1,00,000 workers, the child labour population is estimated around 45,000. Here girls seem to outnumber boys.[6]

The KVIC is connected with this cottage industry which is their principal marketing agency. What is worse is that children's utility as workers diminishes as they grow older. They are replaced by another set of young children.

(d) *In bidi-making* units the piece-rate system of wages has encouraged the use of children as helpers. Mothers bring with them 4-year old children who contribute to the mother's output and perhaps are "socialised" in the work environment.[7] In the bidi-making sector plucking tender leaves is the first activity. Then these sorted leaves are bundled as per their size and taken to the contractor's agents. This work is mainly done by women and children. In bidi-making children work in factory sheds and in their own homes on a piece-rate basis. Children between 6 and 12 years are often observed making bidi.

Similar piece-rate arrangements are found in other industries such as coir-making, carpet-weaving, brick-making, etc.

There are children working in sector that could be termed as "self-employed." In Delhi one can see children hanging around traffic intersections selling newspapers or cleaning cars. Others can be seen at railway stations and shopping centres looking for an opportunity to carry a load. During the Asian Games and before the police used to round up 35 to 40 children every day and produce them before the Child Welfare Board and the Children's Court. A study conducted by Usha Rai shows that two-thirds of those came from families earning less than Rs. 200 per month. Many children were driven away from home by step-mothers and delinquent relatives. These children are expected to not only look after themselves but also supplement the meagre family income.

However, these children do not like to be referred to as beggars. Take the case of Ramrakha. He along with six or seven children comes from Kalyanpuri resettlement colony. They are between 8-14 years of age. Ram's father sells vegetables but earns very little. So Ramrakha comes to traffic intersections by 8 A.M., when office traffic starts increasing on the road. They carefully select those road crossing where a number of cars stop at the crossing. As soon as cars stop at the red light signal they rush to clean cars and in return get few paise at the most.

Often they face humiliation as many car owners do not like them and often refer to them a beggars. By afternoon Ramrakha collect Rs. 2-3 and rushes to buy the evening newspapers which he sells up to 9 o'clock. By 10 o'clock he reaches home and hands over Rs. 4 to 5 to his mother. If the earnings of the day are less than Rs. 4 then he gets reprimanded but for earnings over Rs. 5 he gets incentives in the form of special "chattnis" or a piece of pickle.

Along with such self-employed children are the *rag-pickers* of Delhi about whom special mention is required.

The road encircling Delhi is known as Ring Road and at two sports a traveller will find vultures swooping down on garbage dumps. The Municipal Corporation trucks come and disgorge the city's garbage every day. While the vultures pick up the carcasses, groups of small children are at work among the heaps of garbage. They pick out pieces of broken glass, rust iron, used plastics, paper, cloth, and whatever little things they feel could be of some use.

Eleven year old Rakesh comes here every morning at about 8 A.M., from Trilokpuri, a "jhuggi jhopri" colony across the Yamuna, and works till 5 to 6 in the evening. In the evening he sells his collection to the "kabadiwala" (dealer in scrap, etc.). This dealer after sorting and making bundles sells the scrap to factories in Ghaziabad, Faridabad, Meerut and Kanpur.

The buying rates are 25 paise a kilo of waste paper, Rs. 2 for a kilo of plastic waste, Re 1 for a kilo of iron pieces. These rates are much lower than in other places.

A fact worth noting is that these children have well defined areas for rag-picking and encroaching is dealt with severely. The dealer is also fixed and his *modus operandi* is the same as that of a construction contractor.

Pappu, aged 12 is from another resettlement colony named Seelampur. Pappu lives with his widowed mother and an elder brother who started plying a rickshaw at the age of 15 after the death of his father.

Pappu starts from home before 7 A.M. and goes to marketing centres when the streets are swept, so that he can pick up the maximum waste. He walks around many areas all day with a load on his back. His total earnings may be Rs. 4 a day. Cuckoo, younger brother of Pappu joins the rag-picking only on holidays and in fact Pappu's earnings have helped to send Cuckoo to school.

The health of these children who work in the garbage heap with bare feet often cut by glass pieces and rust iron suffer from skin diseases and risk tetanus infections. However, they are very proud of their work as they feel that they are not beggars but earn their own livelihood.

Child rag-pickers like shoe-shine boys and others who are "self-employed" and unorganised, and have no means to increase their professional capacity are unprotected. In other cottage industries such as bidi-making, match packing, embroidery work, the child at least learns a skill but a rag-picker's fate is sealed. In Delhi, such children may number up to 5,000. What can be done for them?

Like rag-pickers, children working in small eating places also work in very exploitative conditions. Neerja Choudhury in her report (*Statesman*, 1982) his given a fine description of such children. As per this report there are 60,000 children employed in *dhabas* (eating places), tea stalls and restaurants of Delhi.

These children have to work more than 12 hours and they get only Rs. 2-3 per day with no holidays. Forced to leave poverty-stricken villages in the hope of finding money to send back to their families from the city, these children are deprived of parental affection or community support and are abused and kicked around.

According to a study by the Indian Council for Child Welfare on *Working Children in Urban Delhi* in 1977, the majority of the children employed in the dhabas of Delhi come from Bihar and U.P. They work for more than 12 hours a day and get. Rs. 26 to 50 a month and free board and lodging.

There are between, 2,00,000 and 3,00,000 registered shops and establishments in Delhi as per the Labour Commissioner of Delhi Administration. But they are not "categorised." Even if one-tenth of them are estimated as eating places, it comes to 20,000. This does not include many unregistered dhabas which employ children in large numbers according to the Child Welfare Council study.

Enforcement of law results in immediate dismissal of these children and the ultimate loser is the child and the family. In 1981 the Delhi Administration Labour Department launched 30,000 prosecutions; none, however, were related to children's wages or their hours of work. These children are often victims of homosexuality and suffer from venereal diseases.

The Child in Traditional Indian Culture

In mythological or older literary works very little reference is made to the work roles of children except that a child during his study period was to participation the domestic chores of the guru's (teacher) household as well as that of the ashram (residential school), helping out in the economic pursuits that sustained the latter. Such schools did not charge fees but the students were expected to contribute their labour towards the running and upkeep of the institution. However, the life of Krishna indicates that at the age of 6 lie was working as a cow-grazer within the vicinity of the village.

In the country, keeping watch over the crops and frightening away birds and beasts coming to feed on their fields was the children's main responsibility. Older children helped to look after siblings. In the craft/artisans sector the transfer of skills started at an early age and craftsmen's children contributed substantially to the economic endeavours of the family, the community. Till today in the villages children in the traditional craftsmen's family follow this pattern. So children are expected to learn through participation in production.

Children form an integral part of the Indian family economy. Work is not viewed as being antithetical to childhood. They learn skills through observation, imitation and assistance to the family adults. Children also shared the work environment of the adults.

This is one of the reasons why while thought his process children develop a certain sense of efficacy and competency, they are used by their parents as sureties for debts[8] and are in demand for agricultural work on contract basis—what is often referred to as "bonded labour." The law is unable to protect children in such cases as "law breakers are cleaver than law makers.[9]"

With the above background in mind the NGOs should first think what the word "child exploitation" conveys to the people. It is not easy to draw a clear line between the kind of child labour that is acceptable and what is termed as "child exploitation."

Generally, child exploitation involves the extraction of excessive profits from a child's labour (taking the term "labour" to include activities such as begging, theft or prostitution). Using a child's labour to inflict physical or mental suffering or damage on the child could also be classed as exploitation, as could work situations that deprive the child of fundamental rights such as the right to liberty or the right to be untied with its family.[10]

An interesting fact that emerged concerning child exploitation and reported in 1981 was that the extra profit derived from the employment of children—in excess of what would arise from employing adults—could amount to between $ 8 billion and $ 20 billion.[11]

The persons NGOs' work in the field of child labour could be divided into three categories:

(i) Moralist approach
(ii) Legalist approach
(iii) Paternalistic approach

The moralist approach emphasises literacy programmes, primary education schemes, etc. It seems to follow the basic Eurocentric approach, a compartmental division of education, training, production and retirement. Compulsory schooling as has been experienced has not helped much as it has neither developed the creative faculties nor provided a meaningful basis for subsequent labour market entry.

The tendency of legalism is to transform a socio-economic problem into a legal one and should be watched and analysed carefully. This does not mean that the opportunities in the legal field such as public interest litigation should not be availed of. The idea here is only to caution the NGOs. However, there have been good examples of using legal aid for the cause of working women and children at the Asiad construction sites by the Indian Social Institute, Peoples Union for Democratic Rights and Peoples Institute for Development and Training.[12]

Another excellent use of public interest litigation is by *Manushi*— a women's in the informal sector.[13]

The paternalistic point of view promotes the "protection" approach and typically argues that children are victims of lack of stable family life; lack of recreative activities; contact with delinquency; physical risks and lack of education, etc. The protectionists fail to realise the ambiguity that on the one hand, they promote informal activities, and on the other hand, try too offer solace to the exploited workers (women and children) in the informal sector. But the crux of the problem is *not of age but of exploitation.*[14]

Concluding Remarks

Several studies indicate that the plight of working children has some relationship with industrial capitalism. This gradual shift to cash crops and the growing number of landless labour also adds to the exploitation of child labour.[15]

Several cases from the informal sector point towards the need to understand the structural socio-economic situation prevailing and advocate a closer look into the deeper causes so as to grasp the nature and magnitude of children economic contribution.

Above all the NTOs working with women and children need to think in terms of a vision: what type of society in the future are our children going to inherit? On this will largely depend the global search for peace.

NOTES

1. Willy Brandi, *North-South Report—A Blue Print for Survival.*
2. K.D. Gangrade, *Children at Work* (ILO Paper).
3. Ministry of Labour, Labour Bureau. *Child Labour in India,* Simla, 1954.
4. *Anti Slavery Society Report, 1979.*
5. *India Today,* January, 15, 1983, pp. 96-99.
6. S. Das Gupta, *PIDT Personal Communication,* 1982.
7. Subhash Joshi, Nipani, *Personal Communication,* 1982.
8. Marla Sharma, *Bonded Labour,* Gandhi Peace Foundation, Delhi, 1977.
9. K.D. Gangrade quoted in *Newsweek,* January 1983.
10. UNICEF, Supplement No. 16.
11. Sub-Commission on the Protection of Discrimination and Protection of Minorities, July 1981 session.
12. Supreme Court judgement, Sept. 1982.
13. *Manushi* is a women's magazine published by women (Editor, Madhu Kishwar).
14. Alian Morice, Institute d'etude du development economique et social, Paris (France).
15. Marla and Mahajan, *Bonded Labour,* 1981.

6

WAGE EMPLOYMENT IN THE INFORMAL SECTOR

As has been mentioned earlier, we continue the discussion of wage employees in this chapter but focus more on the informal sector. The chapter has been divided into three parts. First, we sketch a profile of the informal sector as it obtains in our sample. Second, we observe some broad comparisons between the informal and formal sectors. And finally, we present an overview on wage employees in general, wherein some of their common problems, their aspirations and suggestions for remedial action are discussed.

During the survey we had enquired from the respondents about the type of undertaking they were working for. Most of the respondents fall into three major categories. First, government; second, large enterprises where more than ten people were working; and third, the small informal undertakings. The contents of this chapter are based on the above classification and we focus on the informal sector. Of the total of 2073 wage employees that were enumerated in our sample, a little more than six hundred belong to this sector, i.e., about twenty-nine per cent. Thus in this analysis the definition of the informal sector is based on the nature of undertaking as given by the respondents. There are many different ways in which the informal sector can be defined, but as elsewhere in the Report we are eschewing getting into a debate on the subject, and are focussing on the factual description based on the responses.[1]

PART I

Wage Employees in Informal Sector—A Profile

Ninety per cent of the wage employees in the informal sector were male and their average age was 31.4 years (with standard deviation of 11.25). There was hardly any variation across the slums either in terms of their sex or age. Sixty-five per cent of these employees were married persons.

In terms of educational standards, a high proportion of these employes (thirty-nine per cent) was illiterate and had no education. About twenty-eight per cent were educated up to the forth standard and another twenty-eight per cent were educated between grades five to eight. Only 3.6 per cent of the employees had received education up to the S.S.C. or above. In terms of education there were substantial inter-slum variations. Cheetah Camp had a larger group of illiterate persons (forty-six per cent). At the other extreme, Jogeshwari had not only fewer illiterate employees (only thirty per cent) but also a large number of SSCs (11 out of a total of 22 were SSCs).

In terms of job profile (see Table 6.1) the most prominent occupations that emerge are those of tailors and cutters (sixteen per cent of the sample). Next to this came the job of jari workers, prominently located in only one slum. The third major job was that of drivers. Other than these three major job categories, there were other occupations like that of carpenters, salesmen, shop assistants, shoe manufactures, helpers and unskilled office workers, etc. But the larger frequency of respondents fell in the category of 'job not identified' (twenty-to per cent).

TABLE 6.1

Distribution of Wage Employees in the Informal Sector by Type of Job

Job	*Slum*				
	Dharavi	*Cheetah Camp*	*Jogeshwari*	*Wadala*	*Row Total*
1	2	3	4	5	6
Nurses, pharmacists	2	1	0	0	3 (0.5)
Clerical workers	2	0	1	0	3 (0.5)
Drivers	15	15	12	2	44 (7.3)
Masons	0	1	1	1	3 (0.5)
Carpenters	6	6	4	1	17 (2.8)
Electricians	1	0	0	0	1 (0.2)
Welders/platers	0	1	3	0	4 (0.7)
Turners	2	1	2	0	5 (0.8)
Fitters	2	2	0	0	4 (0.7)
Machine operators	2	3	1	0	6 (1.0)
Mill workers	0	1	6	5	12 (2.0)

1	2	3	4	5	6
Tailors, cuters	22	36	40	1	99 (16.3)
Shoe makers, repairers	7	2	4	0	13 (2.2)
Compositor, printer	3	0	3	3	7 (1.2)
Painters	4	3	1	0	8 (1.3)
Jari workers	5	65	11	0	81 (13.4)
Salesmen, shop assistants	5	6	11	7	29 (4.8)
Helpers	9	8	5	0	22 (3.6)
Unskilled office workers	1	1	6	2	10 (1.6)
Building	3	1	2	1	7 (1.2)
Domestic servants	0	6	6	3	15 (2.5)
Mechanics	6	0	1	0	7 (1.2)
Supervisors	0	1	0	0	1 (0.2)
Manual labourers	4	6	5	2	17 (2.8)
Unidentified	37	46	31	4	118 (19.5)
Others	26	19	19	6	70 (11.6)
Column Total	164 (27.1)[1]	231 (38.1)	175 (28.9)	36 (5.9)	606 (100.0)

Note: *Total %.

The job profile varied from slum to slum. For example, eighty per cent of the jari workers were located only in cheetah Camp. Mill workers were mostly in Wadala and Jogeshwari. Most of the mechanics were found in the Dharavi slums. Domestic servants were again largely to be found in Jogeshwari and Cheetah Camp. This is analogous to what has been mentioned in the previous chapter, that the job profile depends a lot upon the location factors of the slum and the time period in which the migrants arrived and the slum developed. In spite of the fact that there were small, informal undertakings which, among other things, are also characterised by uncertainties, as many as twenty-four per cent of the employees described their jobs as permanent.

In terms of duration of employment, although the largest number of respondents (27%) were in the category of 1-3 years, the figure for the higher categories of 407 and 8-10 years were also 22.5 and 20.5 per cent respectively. In other words, about seventy per cent of the wage employees fell in these three categories. But the distribution was positively skewed. Ninety per cent of these jobs were reported to be full-time job. But, as has been stated above, only twenty-four per cent of the employees described their jobs as permanent. On the whole from the 'duration of employment' variable one gets the impression that there is a high concentration in the initial short duration 1-3 years category, and it slopes down gradually upto the 8-10 years category, but tapers off steeply thereafter. The perennial downward drift after high response in the categories of duration may be indicative of the rate of attrition in the initial informal sector. Wage employees might eventually be moving either into the formal sector or to some other avenues of employment.

When we classified the nature of undertakings in which these wage employees were working according to their main activity, we found that 'personal services' takes the top position with thirty-five per cent of the employees. Manufacturing and trade and commerce activities each account for twenty-three per cent of the wage employees. In other words, about eighty-one per cent of the wage employees of the informal sector were engaged in these three activities. But once again there were major or inter-slum variations in this respect. Employees working in the personal services were largely concentrated in Cheetah Camp, Jogeshwari, and Wadala in order of diminishing magnitudes. Trade and Commerce were major activities for Dharavi, Jogeshwari and Wadala residents. But most of the manufacturing units seemed to be concentrated in Dharavi and Wadala. As many as forty-one per cent of the wage employees in Dharavi were concentrated in the manufacturing sector. Interestingly enough, according to this analysis Dharavi emerges as an industrial-commercial slum with forty-one per cent of the informal wage employees in manufacturing, thirty-five in trade and commerce and with only 6.5 per cent of them working in personal service. This is in contrast with Cheetah Camp where fifty per cent of the wage employees were engaged in personal services. It is needless to caution that the profile of the slums becomes blurred when we combine both the formal and the informal sectors.

Temporary and casual employees revealed that they worked on an average twenty-three days per month and about 10.25 months per year. On an average it seems that they worked at least 236 days per year. Correspondingly their monthly mean earnings were Rs. 225 but there was too much dispersion in the distribution. However, there was not much inter-slum variation either in the number of days worked or in terms of their earnings.[2] The daily earnings worked out to be Rs. 11.44.

Eighty per cent of these employees are on their first job, and most of those who had done some kind of job earlier (n=126) also came from what could be described as the informal sector (n=72). About forty-seven per cent of them did not have to wait at all to get their first job. And in eighty-six per cent of the cases informal about the job was received with the help of friends and relatives. In terms of place of job, in eighty per cent of the cases, the venue of the job was outside the slum and they had to use some kind of transport to get there.

So far, we have confined ourselves to describing generally the main features of the wage employees in the informal sector. We notice that there are a few deviations with regard to the level of illiteracy, the number of days worked and wages per month as compared to the general picture of the wage employees which we have drawn in our proceeding chapter. With a view to bring out these distinctions into relief we compare below the two sectors in detail.

PART II

A Comparative Analysis of Wage Employees in the Formal and Informal Sectors

Let us begin the comparison of the formal and informal sectors by first looking at some of the features of the households of wage employees in the informal sector (set Table 6.2). Some aspects like education have already been discussed. Here, we wish to focus on the size of the house, the number of workers in the household, as well as the number of unemployed in the household to which the wage employees of the informal sector belong. First of all it has been observed that in three of the four slums, the informal sector wage employees come from larger households. The difference is large enough in those three slums to yield a mean household size of 5.67 (with standard deviation of 2.68) in the informal sector as compared to a mean size of 5.06 (with standard deviation of 2.14) in the formal sector. The finding can be significant from the point of view of the hypothesis that the informal sector wage employees may be "peripheral" household members who live in with some other prime earners. Or, alternatively, it could be another example of the link between poverty and a large family.[3]

Prima facie the poverty-large family link cannot be totally ruled out. Nevertheless on the basis of some other informal one cannot completely deny the other hypothesis that the wage employees in the informal sector are additional earners living in with some prime earning member. The defence of this hypothesis can, to some extent, be drawn from the fact that some other features of the households like duration of stay in Bombay/slums, etc., were overwhelmingly common in both the formal and informal sectors. Thus, the reasons for the incidence of large families in the informal sector in three of the four slums are still open to debate.

We pursued the household labour characteristics further, and found that in all the slums the number of workers per household was larger amongst the informal sector wage employees than in the formal sector. The biggest gap was noticed at Jogeshwari, while it was the least at Wadala. To some extent this may be understandable in view of the large size of the household as reported above. In order to control the variation, we corrected the number of workers for the size of household and found that in three of the four slums the difference in number of workers per household was significant, although in the informal sector it was marginally lower. But the fourth slum yielded the opposite result. But in this case it had also been observed earlier that wage employee of the formal sector had a large household size (5.72) as compared to the wage employees of the informal sector. Moreover, keeping in view the small size of N one needs to proceed cautiously in the case of Wadala.

TABLE 6.2

Household Size by Sector of Employment

Slum		*Formal*	*Informal*
1		2	3
Dharavi	M_1	4.55	5.1
	SD_2	2.15	2.21
	N_3	431	164
Cheetah Camp		5.09	6.01
		1.96	2.72
		3.26	2.31
Jogeshwari		5.14	5.96
		2.02	2.95
		448	n=175
Wadala		5.72	4.6
		2.32	2.05
		n=246	n=36

Notes: 1 M = Mean
2 SD = Standard deviation
3 N = Number of cases

We further pursued that analysis by locking at the reported unemployment of the wage employees households according to the sectors (see Table 6.3). It was found that while in the case of Dharavi, and Jogeshwari unemployment per household was reported more in the case of the informal sector; in the case of Cheetah Camp it was the other way round. Wadala did not report any unemployment in the informal sector households. We clubbed all these aspects together and arrived at a labour force participation rate of the households according to the sectors. As regards the formal sector it was found that in three of the four slums the labour force participation rate hovered around (.55) while in the case of Dharavi it was quite high (.65). In the informal sector it has greater fluctuation and varies between .5 to .63. We are ignoring here the statistics dealing with Wadala, as the number of respondents is too low to permit any generalisation.

TABLE 6.3

Household Labour Force by Sector of Employment

		No. of workers per household		*No. of unemployed per household*		*Mean Household worker*		*Mean Househld labour force*	
		Formal	*Informal*	*Formal*	*Informal*	*Formal*	*Informal*	*Formal*	*Informal*
Dharavi	M	1.7	1.82	1.27	1.4	.37	.36	.65	.63
	SD	.98	.93	.52	.65				
	N	n=431	n=164	n=92	n=45				
Cheetah Camp		1.56	1.77	1.37	1.23	.31	.29	.58	.5
		.96	1.09	.64	.52				
		n=326	n=231	n=73	n=78				
Jogeshwari		1.5	1.81	1.36	1.48	.29	.30	.56	.55
		.74	1.02	.6	.71				
		n=448	n=175	n=97	n=50				
Wadala		1.59	1.62	1.47	—	.28	.35	.54	.35
		.81	.7	1.2					
		n=246	n=36	n=75					

Notes: M = Mean
SD = Standard deviation
N = Number of cases

A comparative analysis of the occupational profile of the employees in the two sectors (see Table 6.4) reveals that most of the employees in the formal sector work in mills (12.9 per cent), building/construction (10.2 per cent), helpers (5 per cent) and manual labourers (4.1 per cent). In the informal sector the first two categories are only marginally represented. But, as might be expected, there are quite a few manual labourers (2.8 per cent) and helpers (3.6 per cent). Some of the occupational categories like fire fighters, electricians and supervisors are totally missing from the informal sector, whereas occupational categories like tailors, cutters, carpenters salesmen/shop assistants, etc., are found more in the informal sector. The most outstanding case is that of tailors and cutters, eighty per cent of whom are found in the informal sector.

Another aspect which we should like to focus upon is the wage earnings of the employees in the formal and the informal sectors. We had stated in the previous chapter that mean wages were Rs. 320.45 for all the wage employees. Now if we split the employees according to sectors, we observe that the mean wages for the formal sector are Rs. 361, while for the informal sector these are only Rs. 225. In other words wage employees in the formal sector actually enjoy thirteen per cent higher wages than the overall mean (discussed in the previous chapter), while those working in the informal sector earn to the extent of thirty per cent below this (see Table 6.5). As wages constitute the vital single statistic which captures most of the attributes of employment/job market we analyses this difference in detail.

TABLE 6.4

Occupational Profile According to Formal/Informal Sector

Non-informal sector	*Actual Number*	%	*Actual Number*	%
1	2	3	4	5
Nurses, Pharmacists	15	(1.0)	3	(0.5)
Fire Fighters	12	(0.8)		
Masons	10	(0.7)	3	(0.5)
Carpenters	12	(0.8)	17	(2.83)
Electricians	14	(1.0)	1	(0.2)
Welders, Platers,	13	(0.9)	4	(0.7)
Fitters	26	(1.8)	4	(0.7)
Machine	57	(3.9)	6	(1.0)
Mill workers	187	(12.9)	12	(2.0)
Tailors, cutters	26	(1.8)	99	(16.3)
Compositors, printers	10	(0.7)	7	(1.2)
Painters	19	(1.3)	8	(1.3)
Salesmen/shop assistants	13	(0.9)	29	(4.8)
Helpers	73	(5.0)	22	(3.6)
Unskilled office workers	35	(3.8)	10	(1.7)
Building	148	(10.2)	7	(1.2)
Domestic servants	21	(1.5)	15	(2.5)
Mechanics	13	(0.9)	7	(1.2)
Supervisors	17	(1.2)	1	(1.8)
Manual labourers	59	(4.1)	17	(2.8)
Others	196	(13.5)		
Unindentified	456	(31.4)	118	(19.5)
Column Total	1452		606	

In the preceding chapter we have pointed out the difference in wage earnings according to sex of the employee. We found that female wage employees on an average earn about fifty-six per cent of the earnings of the male wage employees. When we split the data across the sectors, we found that sexwise wage differentials prevail in both the formal and the informal sector than in the informal. But what is more disturbing is the extremely low level of mean value in the case of female informal sector wage employees. This amounts to only Rs. 134.27 per month, which is about fifty-seven per cent of the male wage employees in the informal sector, and thirty-six per cent of he male wage employees in the formal sector. Moreover, it is only fifty-eight per cent of even the female wage employees in the formal sector. So we are faced with both problems; not only is the relative difference in the earnings substantial, but the absolute level of the wages is also dismally low.

TABLE 6.5

Formal/Informal Sector Wage Differential by Sex

		Formal Sector	*Informal Sector*	*Overall*
Male Wage employees	M SD	367.96 (196.13) n=1371	234.74 (139.58) n=539	329.9 (191.56) n=1910
Female Wage employees		229.79 (143.9) n=73	134.27 (85.44) n=62	184.24 (128.61) n=135
All wage		361.0 (196.13) n=1455	224.67 (138.41) n=602	

M = Mean; SD = Standard Deviation; N = Number of cases

In terms of the age profile, we notice that the average age of wage employees in the formal sector is far lower than the age of the employees in the informal sector. As a matter of fact distribution clearly reveals that the absolute frequency in each age category keeps on decreasing in the case of the informal sector, while it follows a standard peak distribution pattern in the case of the formal sector.

The age and income break-up indicates that in the formal sector forty-seven per cent of employees earn between Rs. 300-500, and that more than half (54%) of such employees are in the age group of 35 to 39 years age cohort. On the other hand only 15.6 per cent of the employees earn that income in the informal sector. The largest number of employees in the informal sector. The largest number of employees in the informal sector is in the category of Rs. 201-300 (28%) and these are concentrated in the age cohort of 25 to 29 years (34%).

On the whole we can safely conclude that while in the case of the formal sector, there appears to be a clear relationship between the age and the wages, this is not so apparent in the case of the informal sector. In the case of the former, as we move from lower age cohorts to higher age groups, the income also rises along with it, but the relationship is not so clear in the case of the informal sector.

In terms of education, the major difference between the sectors is that the informal sector has more (39.2%) employees with no education whatsoever as compared to the formal sector employees (34.3%). Besides, there are some other interesting observations which can be made in this regard. Both these sectors seem to reward education more or less in similar ways although there are some marginal differences. Illiteracy seems to cost more in the informal sector to the extent that those within it receive only 88 per cent of the mean wage in this sector. Similar share of illiterates in the formal sector is 93 per cent. In terms of benefits of education, those who have received education upto 0-4th grade, and those who have continued with their education from 5-8th grade seem to perform more or less in the same way (see Table 6.6). In the formal sector their earnings are equal to mean wages while in the informal sector they are about 6.5 per cent more than the mean value of wages. But actually it is those who have studied upto the S.S.C. and above who make the major difference. In the formal sector they earn thirty per cent more than the mean wages, while the percentage for the informal sector is thirty-five. From this description it is clear that both sectors provide higher wages to the more educated and the behaviour of both these sectors is strikingly similar.

TABLE 6.6

Formal/Informal Sector Wage Differential by Education

Level of Education		*Mean Wages* Formal Sector	Informal Sector
Nil education	M	336.14	197.8
	SD	(194.46)	(131.9)
	N	n=496	n=236
0-4th grade		364.4	239.6
		(185.9)	(146.5)
		n=389	n=166
5-8th		356.2	239.4
		(174.4)	(129.1)
		n=432	n=172
S.S.C. and above		469.28	303.41
		(267.78)	(172.22)
		n=119	n=22
Mean wages		361.0	224.7

Notes: M = Mean
SD = Standard deviation
N = Number of cases

As a matter of fact, it is interesting to see the informal sector yielding a similar income differential owing to education as does the formal sector.

In terms of employment there are major differences between the two sectors. Formal sector wage employees are largely engaged in the manufacturing sector, service industries and in transport and communication, in descending order. As compared to this the informal sector wage employees are mostly engaged in personal services, trade and commerce and manufacturing. Thus, in terms of sectors of employment, the formal and informal sectors present a disjoined picture except for the manufacturing category which is common to both the sectors. But this link itself is rather tenuous, as the highest number of formal sector employees is found in the manufacturing category, while in the informal sector it has quite a low rating.

It is interesting to note further that there is hardly much difference in the wage payments in manufacturing, service industries or personal services in the formal sector, while some differences exist within these categories in the informal sector. Of the three categories mentioned above, trade and commerce manage to earn marginally more (5%) than the mean wage in the informal sector. Personal services on the other hand yield about ten per cent less in wages to its employees in the informal sector. But the differences are not very pronounced. For the sake of comparison we are also providing wage distribution in the case of manufacturing industries as this is a category common to both the formal and informal sectors.

As had been mentioned earlier, the number of people who have only part-time jobs are more (6%) in the informal sector than in the formal sector (1.7%). The period of waiting for the first job is positively more in the formal sector than in the informal sector. This clearly indicates that there is some 'ease of entry' in the case of the latter.

PART III

In the first two parts of this chapter we have tried to provide a brief description of the informal sector in comparison with the formal. In this part we example the difficulties, aspirations and possible avenues of assistance as these have been articulated by the wage employees in general.

Problems/Difficulties/Aspirations

About forty-four per cent of the wage employees were not satisfied with their present job (see Tables 6.7 and 6.8). The major reasons cited by them for their dissatisfaction were low earnings and uncertainty of the job in the same order. We asked them to point out the single most important reason for their dissatisfaction. Seventy-five per cent of those who were dissatisfied mentioned low earnings as the single crucial factor. When asked about their willingness to change their present job, only 28.8 per cent responded saying that they had earlier attempted once to change the job, while the rest did not respond at all. Those who had not bothered to change cited three reasons in the following order for not having attempted to do so: the first reason, unavailability of the job; the second, lack of pull; and the third was, they did not know how to set about it. It is indeed a sharp reflection on the working of the labour market of the slum-dwellers. Wage employees cited lack of influence as the major difficulty in getting a job, and this was followed by lack of skill. Earlier in the previous chapter we had considered the low skill levels of the jobs in which these wage employees are engaged, and their consequent lack of faith in skill/training, etc., as the main vehicle for improving their performance. We have noted above that either they do not possess the necessary skills and even if they do, there is no scope for them in their present job.

TABLE 6.7

Distribution of Wage Employees by Reasons for the Dissatisfaction with the Present Job

Slum/Reasons	*Low earn- ings ings*	*Long dis- tance from resi- dence*	*Poor working condi- tions*	*Job Not in tune with training*	*No pros- pects for pro- motion*	*Job uncer- tainty*	*No social secu- rity*	*Emplo- yer not behav- ing well*	*N.A.*	*N.R.*	*Total*
Dharavi	224	2	8	1	2	18	1	0	341	5	602
Cheeta Camp	253	9	3	0	1	26	0	0	265	3	560
Jogeshwari	213	1	7	1	2	13	0	8	378	3	626
Wadala	96	2	1	0	0	3	0	1	181	1	285
Total	786	14	19	2	5	60	1	9	1165	12	2073

TABLE 6.8

Distribution of Wage Employees by The Most Important Reason for Dissatisfaction with the Present Job

Slum/Reasons	*Low earn- ings ings*	*Long dis- tance from resi- dence*	*Poor working condi- tions*	*Job Not in tune with training*	*No pros- pects for pro- motion*	*Job uncer- tainty*	*No social secu- rity*	*Emplo- yer not behav- ing well*	*N.A.*	*N.R.*	*Total*
Dharavi	175	2	14	1	4	52	1	1	347	5	602
Cheetah Camp	192	7	5	0	3	40	0	0	310	3	560
Jogeshwari	190	5	7	1	2	22	0	8	390	1	626
Wadala	76	0	2	0	1	23	0	1	181	1	285
Total	633	14	28	2	10	137	1	10	1228	10	2073

All the wage employees in our sample were asked why they did not prefer to become self-employed despite the low earnings. In answer to the question about forty-four per cent mentioned financial limitations as the reason why they did not want to go into business on their own. But more interestingly, thirty-seven per cent did not wish to go in for such activity in any event. One wonders if the evidence is indicative of the slum-dwelling wage employees being averse to taking risks. But keeping in view their low earnings and their family liabilities it is understandable. When asked if the Government could help them, only fifty per cent felt positively that it could. But the remaining respondents felt otherwise. They gave reasons for their opinion. The largest number—nearly thirty-one per cent—felt that there was no need for the government to help. A few of them mentioned corruption in the government as their reason for not asking for its help. About three per cent felt that lack of their own savings was a handicap in approaching the government to ask for help.

Conclusion

We attempt here to sum up the information collected regarding wage employees in these two chapters. First of all we have so many wage employees in our sample of two thousand families, that on an average each family has slightly more than one wage employee. Most of these wage employees are full-time employees. Even among those are temporary or casual, most of the employees work sufficient number of mandays per year as to be nearly fully employed. Looking to the number of years in which these employees have been continuously engaged in their jobs, one can safely conclude that their jobs are essentially stable, and that they continue to be retained even when their technical status so often is that of a temporary/casual employee.

In terms of the nature of jobs, two thirds of them are engaged in manufacturing and service industry. The rest are engaged in trade and commerce, transport, etc. A thorough look at them reveals the crucial importance of their role in facilitating the process of industrialisation in general and urbanisation in particular.

In terms of the nature of organisations which employ them as wage employees about two-thirds belong to large-scale formal organisations and the government. Approximately thirty per cent belong to the small informal sector of the city. It is significant that large formal organisations and government undertakings have failed to provide their employees with basic minimal facilities, in spite of their being employed full-time, or near full time.

In terms of comparative analysis between the formal and the informal sectors, the major finding is that there are substantial wage rate differences between the two sectors. Formal sector wage employees get as much as sixty per cent more than the informal sector. Wage employees. Another interesting aspect has been that within the two sectors stratification according to different levels of education and sex is quite comparable. Male employees and more educated employees get higher wages in both sectors.

In terms of occupational profile the differences are mostly as expected. Some occupations like fire-fighting supervisory work, etc., do not exist in the informal sector where shop assistants, tailors, salesmen and carpenters predominate.

In terms of education, training and skill we find that the situation leaves much to be desired. Nearly one-third of the wage employees continue to be illiterate although, of late, the rate of illiteracy among the younger age cohorts has been steadily declining. It seems that in the kind of jobs wage employees are doing, the level of education is not taken into consideration when appointing the employees. But educated persons, unlike illiterate workers, certainly prefer to wait and choose more suitable jobs rather than accept whatever is immediately available. Once the employees are on a job, for a majority of them there is a very little job mobility either vertically or horizontally. Once in the job, educated people tend to earn higher wages, and certainly those who have passed the S.S.C. and above have a clear edge over the others. It should again be emphasised that this does not imply that they may find their jobs quicker or enjoy higher starts, but only that they end up earning more once they are in the job. It may be that owing to their education, once they are in a job they display greater usefulness, or versatility, hence get promoted to higher wages. But there are few with S.S.C. and above, in the sample for a reliable generalisation.

In terms of technical training/skill inculcation, very few of them had any formal training as such, or those who had such training have not necessary used it. Wage employees do not seem to place much value on training by itself, as they are aware that it may be a desirable condition but is not an essential condition for getting them a good job. In addition to training, one needs to have financial help and influence to get the jobs. But despite all this, they have some favourite occupations like being drivers, tailors, electricians and fitters, etc., all of which appear to be dream jobs for the wage employees. But looking at the age-wage profile, it is clear that there is some on-the-job-informal-training and that the earnings of employees stabilise around the mid-thirties. The differential earnings can be attributed to their experience.

Finally, it must be pointed out that because of the their acute need to earn, even with little or no education and an insufficient training/skill-base, the jobs which the slum-dwellers end up doing have as much to do with the surroundings and the nature of the slums as with the personnel job factors, etc. Actually it is the job openings during particular time phase or which the job seekers scramble in the city. They then develop their habit as close to their jobs as possible. At least such seems to be the practice during the initial settling down of immigrants in Bombay. This is one of the reasons why the occupational profile differs rather sharply from slum to slum. But in the case of old and large slums like Dharavi, this tends to change over a period of time.

It is interesting to find that there is not much inter-slum variation in terms of wages, earned per month. The range is ± 15 per cent, but the variance within each slum is also quite large which makers the comparison of inter-slum difference a bit meaningless. Nevertheless it seems that the wage differences are less pronounced than the other characteristics of slum-dwellers. Perhaps this bears testimony to the fact that the market forces tend to smother away all occupational/locational differences and price all labour fairly uniformly. The phenomenon is largely due to lack of specific education/skill/training on the one hand and an abundance of labour on the other.

NOTES

1. For details on this aspect see latest volume edited by Sethuraman, *The Urban Informal sector in Developing countries—Employment, Poverty and Environment,* ILO, 1981, Ch. 2, pp. 10-23.
2. Median value of duration of employment was five and a half years (Mean 7.2 years with standard deviation of 6.65 years).
3. In this instance, as the focus of analysis is on the wage employees, the household characteristics have been "weighted" with the number of wage employees from each household. It may marginally enhance or dampen the household attributes as the case may be, but the overall impact of weightage is only small.

7

THE EXPLOITATION OF CHILDREN IN THE "INFORMAL SECTOR"

This chapter attempts to identify the obstacles likely to be met by researchers on child labour, especially in the urban informal sector of low-income countries. The work of children raises complex problems which make a traditional research approach using sample surveys of representative groups almost valueless. The International Year of the Child, 1979, made the subject of child work fashionable; but little hard research has been one, and one has the impression that children's work plays a more significant, perhaps even fundamental, role in the economies of Third World countries than has been appreciated up to now. While there is a widespread wish to uncover and to understand the problem thoroughly, adequate data are lacking.

This chapter treats children's work from an economic standpoint, i.e. it examines the specific roles of children in different systems of production, and in the reproduction of the labour force in an underdeveloped urban environment. Particular emphasis is placed on activities often termed "marginal," even though they are widespread and essential to dependent economies. Following on from this, we shall show how research methods should have a more qualitative and anthropological content than those normally used to study adult employment. Within this framework, several areas in which data collection would be useful are proposed: work duration and pace; migration and length of schooling' acquisition of skills; training costs, earnings and, when they exist, wages; relations between the family, the child and the entrepreneur; and the State's behaviour towards the illegal employment of young people.

OBSTACLES TO EFFECTIVE RESEARCH ON CHILDREN

Many studies contain information on child labour. Although this is generally non-specific, it nevertheless frequently provides a useful picture of the periphery of the problem. Such data include:

- schooling and school attendance
- apprenticeship

— unemployment amongst school leavers
— population age and sex structure.

There are numerous studies on the so-called informal sector, a term about which we shall make some critical comments below. Among such studies it is possible to find informational on children's economic activity but, as this subject is not usually the main focus of the research, the data are incomplete. The majority of studies do not include any information at all on children, with the exception of some data on apprenticeship. A brief survey of the literature on Africa, for example, yields virtually no data. It is as tough the problem of child labour does not exist for those engaged in research on the informal sector, though they frequently recognise statistical differentiations based on sex, ethnic or national origin, length of establishment and many others. Where age is a variable, it is treated in groups (15-20, 20-25, for example) which are inappropriate with regard to children. And yet this is a problem, the extent of which is universally recognised. This, then, is the current situation, which constitutes an urgent problem, but for which investigative techniques are lacking. There are several reasons for this, which we list below.

1. The Pattern of Interests in the Work of Children

It has to be recognised that, few groups have a direct interest in tackling the problem. At the highest level, many governments avoid through investigation into certain questions, such as residual slavery or violent initiation rites. It is likely that investigation into children's work would be viewed with such reticence, at least if it were treated in terms of exploitation. There are two possible government attitudes towards the subject. Either child labour is made illegal, in which case the authorities will no doubt prefer to turn a blind eye to its continued existence; or there is no specific legislation resulting in a laissez-fair policy which relies on a conspiracy of silence. It is all the easier to maintain these negative attitudes because juvenile activities tend to be concentrated in sectors where official control is difficult.

Though it certainly should not be regarded as unique, an example of governmental resistance to investigations of the extent of child labour is the report of the Anti-Slavery Society on the work of young girls in the Moroccan carpet industry (1978) . Initially the government denied that "such practices are widespread" and opposed publication of the report (see, for example, the statement of the Moroccan Ambassador to London of 14 January 1976, as reproduced in Anti-Slavery Society, 1978, p. 63). Subsequently, in response to inquiries made in the Working Group of Experts on Slavery (established by the UN's Subcommission for the Prevention of Discrimination and Protection), the Government accepted that "large numbers of children aged under 12 years.... end up in the drafts sector." The Government reported that, while it was difficult to regulate conditions in the small-scale private carpetmaking enterprises, the available legislation had been applied in the public sector (ILO, 1981a, para 370).

Because of their institutional arrangement, intergovernmental bodies, such as the ILO and World Bank, have to be cautious in their investigations of child work in specific countries. However, the ILO has regularly brought information of the kind cited above to the attention of government authorities, and has provided assistance to governments in improving and enforcing legislation. Moreover, studies and technical co-operation activities on various aspects of child labour have been intensified in recent years, being particularly stimulated by the International Year of the Child.

It is likely that hostility, or at least a degree of non-co-operation, will be encountered from those for whom the children work. Later in the chapter we shall show how difficult it is to define these people because of the overlap between family lineage units and productive units. Whoever they are, those who use child labour know very well that the practice is disapproved, if not by the law then in unwritten social rules. For research to be successful, when the children's employers are interviewed they must see that it is not against their own interests to rely honestly and fully to the questions put to them. If this confidence cannot be achieved, they may well suspect the advent of new legislation and stricter controls and will avoid answering awkward questions.

To this note of caution of further subtlety should be added which is prompted by observations we made in Africa during interviews with a variety of people on the situation of children working in garment or metal workshops. A very frequent response was that these were not child workers but apprentices (and it was only after closer questioning that the interviewees would admit that the apprenticeships were sometimes extremely long, provided relatively ineffective training and were highly profitable for the children's employers). This is important because, while Western countries tend to define an individual on the basis of demographic criteria (e.g. age, sex), this is not universal. In the case cited above the young workers were viewed in terms of their social status (apprentices) and not in terms of their age.

Finally, a word about the children themselves. It would be an illusion to maintain that, subjectively, they have anything to gain from an inquiry into their economic activities when these are necessitated by unemployment in the family, the threat of future unemployment and an inadequate collective income. Such circumstances may lead children to carry out small-scale tasks in a more or less "informal" way. Exploitation and the ideological considerations that accompany it should not be confused: working could well impart a significant element of self-esteem to a child. It is almost certain that many children are pleased to be able to work. This raises a final obstacle, which is that the researcher may be inclined to ethnocentrism and may substitute moral prejudice for economic observation. This is particularly likely to be true if the investigator is convinced that the work being observed is ethically unacceptable, in which case communication with the group concerned would almost certainly be biased.

All the obstacles arising from the interests of these various groups can and must be overcome by applying appropriate methodologies. For example, it is probably advisable to avoid official channels; to use flexible interviewing techniques; to devise a system of reinterpretation or translation of replies; and to extend the investigation, to include everyone concerned with the child. These points will be developed later. It can be noted here that the existence of these difficulties has at least one beneficial side-effect in that they compel researchers to use new and appropriate methods.

2. The Position of the Child Relative to the Researcher and to Society

The nature of this issue can be brought out by comparing the work of children with that of women. This is comparison which can be useful, but is also risky. The constant availability of cheap labour—a necessary condition for the survival (and sometimes the prosperity) of a large number of small-scale activities — is common to these two groups. In addition, because the work of both groups often carries no social recognition, it is not paid according to the surplus value it represents. However, such analogies tend to obscure some fundamental differences because children, in their own view, are not a homogeneous group able to make themselves heard or put forward their own demands.

If the international Year of the Child and International Women's year are compared (noting in particular the various reforms and research springing from the latter), it is clear that there are two major differences in the exploitation of the two groups:

(1) Children do not constitute either a movement or a or a political force capable of initiating or controlling studies on their own situation. It is unquestionably the existence of such a movement, on an international scale, that has produced such an abundant literature on the exploitation of women in their domestic enclave.

(2) The wide criticism of he somewhat paternalistic and condescending approach to International Women's Year is infinitely more relevant to the attitudes surrounding the International Year of the Child. Moreover, it is clear that, whatever the hypotheses and proposals put forward by researchers and experts working on children, they can be sure of silence from their subjects. Progress in research on child labour tends to be held back because children are regarded as "protected" beings and not as responsible individuals. Nevertheless, it goes without saying that any programme advocating the radical and immediate elimination of children's work will run up against opposition from the children themselves, at least in the non-salaried sector.

A consequence of the differences described above is that children are not the subjects but the *objects* of study, and this marginal position on the field of inquiry has certain methodological implications — notably an ethnocentric temptation with strong moralistic or Eurocentric overtones. This temptation can be overcome only by using investigative methods in which children play an important role at least until they become an organised social group. There have in fact been instances of social struggle during which a leadership structure was created that was quite capable of initiating its own programmes: the Soweto students are an example.

A final point is that women's status is permanent whereas that of the child is temporary; this simple fact makes it difficult to follow up studies on the situation of children, as opposed to their development.

3. Problems of Definition

The question of children's work in the informal sector leads us to consider the complexity of he three terms: work, children, and the informal sector.

(a) Work

Work, defined at the most general level as a simple exertion of physical or intellectual energy, is a somewhat unclear and undiscriminating concept. For example, we are not accustomed to considering school work, domestic activity (such as fetching water) and the assistance given by an apprentice as belonging to the same economic sphere. The first question which arises is therefore: at what point should a child's activity be called work? As an initial step a certain number of discriminatory criteria, such as the following, should be applied:

- paid work/unpaid work
- productive work/non-productive work
- full-time work/intermittant work.

In order to get away from definitions that are too subjective, we would advocate studying the question of work on the basis of whether or not it constitutes exploitation. It is in fact this idea which motivated the establishment of a study programme on child labour. The notion of exploitation can accommodate original concepts and hypotheses and an examination of the concrete mechanisms behind the work of children, instead of being restricted to a simple descriptive account. We shall return to this point, but we suspect that the terms "employment" or "work" are often euphemisms for "exploitation."

The complexity of the concept of work as applied to children may be better appreciated with the help of the following example. In technical colleges a great deal of time is generally spent on making various objects as part of the requirements for officially recognised technical apprenticeships and courses. These objects may be sold either to agents or at sale organised by the college authorities. In a single productive activity there is thus sometimes exploitation of children's work, but in other cases there is no exploitation. The implication here is that a definition of work should be related not only to the activity itself but also to its economic and social context. In certain rich countries this is beginning to be recognised, leading to demands for remuneration for housework and even for studying.

(b) Child

The term "child" is difficult to define objectively. From the outset it should be remembered that the concept of childhood is a recent one, at least if it is understood in terms of the consequences of being boxed into different life-stages. It is unlikely that this kind of definition is applicable to productive activities in low-income countries because it was developed in a different context.

The word "child" can have several limits according to which of the following criteria are taken:

- — biological (puberty)
- — legal (schooling legislation and labour laws)
- — custom (status in the domestic unit, for example).

The basis of these boundaries is mainly a chronological and non-qualitative criterion, i.e. age. However, the adoption of a universal age criterion comes up against many obstacles:

- — variations from one society to another
- — the danger of a Western perception of the age above which a child becomes an adult
- — geographical variations (rural/urban) and differences according to social milieux
- — differences in age limits according to the sex of the child
- — the methodological difficulty of follow-up; each child, by definition, passes beyond whatever limit is set.

It may be thought that schooling should carry a certain weight in the definition; in our opinion this is not entirely justified because for various reasons schooling may sometimes be artificially prolonged. For the moment, we do not propose any particular age criterion. We suggest that investigation be turned towards an examination of the adaptation of the observed activity to the biological or social situation of the child. At all costs, ethnocentrism must be guarded against: to view all the work of all children as monstrous and as a black mark against underdeveloped countries cannot help to advance research. For those from underdeveloped countries, the institution of a fixed retirement age in Western societies probably seems no less absurd.

(c) The "Informal" or "Unstructured"[1] *Sector*

These terms, and associated concepts, pose many problems, and there is an abundant literature on the subject. They are commonly used to describe all small-scale activity that has little capital and a relatively large labour force and is organised in a non-capitalist way. This definition is far from satisfactory because it risks obscuring the relationship between different economic spheres through putting forward the idea of a dualistic organisation of society. In a former study, we put forward our conception of this sector as "superexploited" in economies dominated by multinational enterprises. This provides an organic rather than a descriptive definition of the activities in question. If this conception is valid, the exploitation of child labour is seen as a component of the permanent process of surplus extraction from the sector. We shall return to this later.

A fundamental point here is that those activities which are called "unstructured" are, in reality, usually highly "structured." Even though many studies show the dependent and exploitative relationship between the formal and informal economic sectors, this observation and the empirical evidence supporting it are usually ignored. Nevertheless, it is very important to know whether children are included in the networks which span the two sectors and to identify their employers. At the time this text was being completed, a newspaper article referring to the work of children in Asia offered an example of the way in which children's activities may bridge the two sectors: "Finally, many illicit street vendors of fruit and miscellaneous objects, and newspaper sellers, have to account for their earnings at the end of the day to unscrupulous businessmen who exploit them." (Viratelle, 1979). The most common fault found in purely descriptive studies is their failure to identify the centres of power and capital accumulation and an overhasty characterisation of petty activities as improvised and independent. In our opinion, the "unstructured" sector is in fact structured in two ways:

— through its submission to the dominant capitalist mode of production
— through the existence of organised groups within it.

Many small-scale urban enterprises employing numbers of children as shoe-shine boys, newspaper sellers, car washers and even beggars observe certain rules which, although not necessarily obvious, are none the less strict: admission into trades, territorial rights, and redistribution of earnings are some examples. This does not mean that there should be attempts to invent structures where they do not exist, but the theoretical and methodological orientation must be maintained, which implies that an inventory of the modes of organisation underlying activities which are apparently unconnected and improvised should be established. We were able to observe the existence of structures within the so-called "unstructured" sector in Kaolack, the second largest city in Senegal. Young people transport clients in motorcycle taxis from one point to another in this very spread-out city. To an observer, this looks like a fragmented, small-scale activity. Not at all: the vehicles are owned by civil servants and others who invest in the purchase of vehicles (often putting themselves into debt) and rent them out to the young people daily. The youngsters themselves are organised into fiercely competitive "garages" with strict rules for admission and which are protected to varying extents by the local authorities.

Finally, we recall certain characteristics of petty urban activities that have emerged from previous studies.[2] In general, petty informal activities:

— produce, at low prices and under heavy competitive pressure, value for large-scale concerns (by undertaking piece-work, subcontracting and client credit, for example);
— still under the same competitive conditions, provide goods and services for wage earners in the modern and public sectors and of the urban poor, thereby contributing towards lower wage rates; it is clear that, in less

industrialised countries (or where industry is export-oriented), the prices of informal sector products are much lower than imported manufactured goods even when both have the same use-value;

— incidentally play the role of a "reserve army," taking on the burden of job creation, and exerting an indirect pressure on salaries in the formal modern and state sectors;

— often operate in fragmented markets where capital is not interested in investing.

The consequences of these characteristics for the question which interests us here are clear: cheap and even unpaid labour is an indispensable element in the survival of many petty activities because of the high degree of competition. It is in this sense that a prior scientific and non-empirical definition of the so-called informal sector is necessary for a more profound analysis of the role of children within it.

However, the identification of the relevant trades that is needed if research is to be focused comes up against several difficulties:

— scope of the investigation: should this be limited to urban areas or, being in mind the similarity of tasks, should rural and semi-rural areas be included?

— the overlap between domestic and productive units: for instance, where "informal" productive activities are controlled by and organised around a lineage, it would probably be useless to try to determine whether a child's work arose from the household or from the enterprise.

— children work under two distinct arrangements: more or less independently, or for another individual or group who in exchange provide lodging, food and perhaps money. Both these situations must be expected and must be taken into account in the methods of investigation adopted.

The conclude this discussion of the obstacles which cannot be disregarded when examining the question of children's work in the small-scale production sector, we want to underline the fact that, in our view, these difficulties will not be overcome by initiating vast projects. The urgent and essential tasks are to formulate theoretical systems and to identify research themes; if this is not done there is a risk that the conceptual and definitional problems outlined above will persist.

THE THEORETICAL FRAMEWORK

1. Sources of Children's Work

The work of children in the small-scale production sector must, in our view, be approached through its specific and organic aspects: on the one hand children's work is one of the essential mechanisms of non-capitalist but capital-dependent economies, and on the other, it plays a special role in the extraction of surplus value and in price formation.

With respect to the potential pool of juvenile labour, we find two phenomena. The first of these is rural to urban migration. The dismantling of subsistence economies, and the advent of export-oriented plantation agriculture, has led to a considerable increase in urban populations. Children have been deeply involved in this process because their agricultural work was not longer secure following the destruction of the delicate equilibrium between subsistence and commercial production. In addition, the birth rate has not dropped. Statistics show that urban populations are relatively young, a consequence of the rural exodus of young people. Children arriving in the cities alone are usually accommodated by families who themselves face employment problems: putting these unproductive and costly individuals to work is thus a primary objective of the family with which they live. This must be seen in the more general context of urban poverty, itself partly a product of accelerated rural-urban population drift. If several members of a family are unemployed, the income contributed by a child is by no means negligible; it may even be indispensable. The position of girls in this type of situation is particularly revealing: school is for them a luxury, apprenticeship would offer nothing and the main objective is for girls to be in good employment before marriage, especially with a view to providing for the expenses of the wedding.

The second phenomenon is premature school leaving, There is widespread agreement that since the 1960s, education systems have failed to some extent, as a result of their lack of success in teaching basic skills and in opening the way to a job which justifies the years spent at school. Very few policies have been able to stop the massive wastage of schooling that can be observed in most African countries from the primary level upwards. In the hope of learning of productive trade and in the frequent absence of institutions specialising in and adapted to the multiple activities around which urban employment resolves, young people who drop out of the education system turn towards small businessmen and self-employment. Thus it is often argued that apprenticeships offer the most appropriate solution where the education system has failed to pass on basic skills. This does not mean that all apprenticeships do actually lead to acquisition of the desired qualifications and competence. On the contrary, apprenticeships seem to be above all a convenient no man's land untouched by legislation, where the small entrepreneur is in undisputed control of his apprentices, of what he teaches (or does not teach) and of the length of the apprenticeship.

2. The Economic Use of Children

It is here that, in the production system being examined, everyone becomes involved; the State, which does not take financial responsibility for training; the child's family, which does not have the means to meet the high costs of a schooling which may have no evident immediate advantages; the small businessman, of course, or the contractor (who may be a member of the family), for whom the children are an inexhaustible source of cheap, even free, labour. Since the strength and durability of the informal sector reside in its low prices, an extremely cheap workforce is an indispensable condition for its survival. It is important to note that if, other things being equal, illegal "apprentice" labour (and that of children in general) were to be instantly and completely stopped, many small production units would be doomed to immediate closure because they operate on the basis of minimum margins. Apprenticeship, seen as an unpaid labour contribution, plays an organic role in the formation of low prices in and the maintenance of a small-scale, pre-capitalist production. In the end, apprenticeship itself aggravates competition in the heart of the producers camp, and a *priori* each boss must look askance at his apprentices when the time comes for them to set up on their own. This explains a point mentioned above, i.e. the artificial prolongation of the apprenticeship period, and the fact that many apprentices complain that they are not taught their trade properly. To complete the vicious circle, the use of children for secondary and unspecialised tasks constitutes the first excuse given by bosses for not paying them. In the formal sector, apprenticeship, which is found mainly in artisanal and industrial activities, is usually more strictly controlled with regard to age, conditions of work and methods of payment.

It is true that apprenticeship is not the whole story and that it covers the older age groups only. Nevertheless, inasmuch as it results in underpaid or unpaid work (and sometimes even in work that is paid for by the apprentice), we think it entirely relevant to the subject of children's work in general.

The London-based Anti-Slavery Society's report on girls' labour in Morocco's carpet industry (Anti-Slavery Society, 1978) gives a particularly cogent example of the economic use of children. In addition, it lends support to our view of the informal sector. The report makes the following allegations:

(i) The background to girls' work in Morocco is "the economic reality which is that of dependence," as indicated in the introduction to the French text (pp. 964-966).[3] According to this introduction Morocco's economy "is still that off an underdeveloped country without an industrial infrastructure and which supplies the West with agricultural products, staple foods and items manufactured under subcontract." The introduction adds that "the increase in the number of children being exploited" is accompanied by a variety of other factors also revealed in the report, i.e. such as the decline in school attendance "which currently leaves half the rural children without schooling" and ineffectual labour legislation.

(ii) There is considered to be active or passive support by the State for this exploitation. Examples of passive support cited include the inefficiency of labour legislation surveillance mechanisms ("Work inspectors, very seldom call and generally expected to be paid for their silence" (p. 56) legislation for the protection of minors reaches only the fringes of these activities (in 'handicraft co-operatives and apprenticeship schools" women and children are not "salaried workers in the sense of the current Moroccan labour legislation" and this is admitted by the government (p. 46). Examples of active support are also given: "Government policy is to give all possible aid to exporters of rugs: wool is imported duty free ('temporary importation') on condition that it is exported in the form of rugs. Exports duty and certain taxes are waived" (p. 7). Again, "though governmental-owned factories generally conform with the law in regard to recruitment and in most respects set a high standard, the *maalema* survives in a few state factories as well as in most of those in the private sector" (p. 57). (The *maalema* system will be described below.) Finally, "More than half the working force of three state centres was made up of children under 12. In this respect the State does not abide by its own legislation, for even apprentices under 12 are illegal" (p. 9).

(iii) There is a hierarchy of control encompassing even small-scale carpet production enterprises: a number of small workshops may belong to a single owner who is sometimes foreign; marketing, particularly in Europe, is in the hands of large Western companies; small workshops sometimes subcontract, and are therefore totally dependent on modern marketing channels. This reveals the highly structured nature of the carpet industry even when carried out on a small scale. Reduction of labour costs seems to be a constant preoccupation: "Most Moroccan manufacturers consider that Morocco in now in first place for North African rugs and many did not hide the fact that low labour costs made Moroccan rugs highly competitive. In Iran, for instance, legislation forbids the employment of children under 14 and this has considerably raised the cost of Persian rugs" (p. 7).

(iv) Families existing on a subsistence income are eager to find work for their daughters. Workshops are often located near *bidonvilles* (shanty towns) or poor districts. The report also points out that "Parents play into the hands of the factory owners in their desire to see their daughters bringing in even small sum of money" (p. 10).

(v) Traditional social relations are present. Recruitment and dismissal is often in the hands of female intermediaries *(maalema)* who receive a salary from the employer; the latter thus remains within the letter of the law but does not know the age or the wages of the girls employed. The *maalema* acts as supervisor and pays the children whatever she likes (usually on a piece work basis). This paternalistic system benefits from all the advantages of work done at home but under conditions of raised productivity. The report describes the *maalema* system as "a relic of the old craftsman-apprentice structure" (p. 11). Of the state rug-making centres visited by the Society, "conditions were worst in the two centres using the *maalema* system" (p. 10).

(vi) Recruitment methods, working conditions and wages are often deplorable, although the investigators observed that government establishments were better (p. 9). Small girls are engaged from the age of 8, and there ware incredibly long working hours (up to 72 hours per week), very little or no paid holiday, measure wages (by the piece) or none at all for apprentices, undernourishment and overwork.

(vii) There is confusion between co-operative and industrial operations on the one hand and between apprentices and wage workers on the other. In the first place, the co-operatives are not groups of producers but "under-takings run by the State on commercial lines with the workers receiving some sort of remuneration for their work" (p. 47). This system encourages the extreme variations found in working conditions and wages. In the second lace, it is difficult to distinguish between "schools of apprenticeship" and "craft centres with apprentices" (p. 47): the former often function in the same way as the latter.

(viii) Finally, it is important to note that the Anti-Slavery Society visited the factories and workshops twice, in 1975 and again in 1977. Between the two visits the team "found that the situation, far from having improved, had worsened" (p. 6).

In reply to these allegations, the Ministry of Labour and Social Affairs of Morocco reported that it had instructed the labour inspectorate concerning the measures to be taken to ensure that labour legislation, and particularly provisions relating to conditions of work and occupational safety and health, were respected in undertakings in the carpet industry, and also instructed the inspectorate to inquire into conditions in the undertakings where child labour was reported by the Anti-Slavery Society since the descriptions and analysis it contains have implications far beyond the particular case of the Moroccan carpet industry. The similar role played by children for subcontractors in certain Asian countries is well known, and another Anti-Slavery society paper (Banerjee, 1979) provides some suggestive data in this regard.

3. Specific Characteristic of Child Labour

Children's work possesses a variety of characteristics within the framework of its economic role at the heart of the informal sector. In brief, we can note the following:

(i) Labour supply is plentiful because of continued high birth rates and high rural emigration. This places children in an intensely competitive environment with little bargaining power over the conditions imposed on them.

(ii) Children do not have a "right to work," and this makes the juvenile workforce easy to manipulate. The duration of employment and its regularity are determined by the unpredictable ebb and flow of orders and markets. The small businessman or trader can underemploy and child if production threatens to drop.

(iii) The illegality of much children's work makes their dismissal easy. Political and trade union organisation, which provide the only chance they have of improving their situation, is difficult because of their age, entrenched paternalistic exploitive systems and lack of social recognition of children as producers.

(iv) The unspecialised nature of the work children do implies that they may be given a wide range of tasks, depending on the production mechanisms. In addition, certain tasks are technically well suited to children and are highly profitable from the point of view of the employer; this is the case of the "little hands" in the tobacco and match industries of the Indian peninsula.

(v) Finally, some juvenile activities are particularly well adopted to clandestine and illegal operations because of children's physical and psychological characteristics, such as agility, running and hiding, the ability to keep quiet or to mislead. Although somewhat trained by subjectivity, these points should not be ignored in a study of the tasks in which child labour is concentrated.

It is not claimed that these few reflections encompass all the economic questions relating to child labour. It is nevertheless hoped that they show how these questions can be approached. While there is little doubt that exploitation of Children in the Third World appears to be concentrated in the informal sector, it is necessary to identify the practical consequences and try to locate precisely the specific niches occupied by children in the economics of developing countries.

RESEARCH THEMES AND METHODOLOGICAL TOOLS

1. The Need to Disaggreate Different Types of Children's Activity

The productive and commercial activities of children should not be treated as if they were a homogenous group.

(a) Basic distinction

We give here a number of elementary distinctions which must always be observed;

— girls' work/boys' work
— age (e.g. less than 12/12-16 years)
— permanent/intermittent work
— independent work/work for a group or individual (in terms of remuneration)
— work with a training component/unskilled work

(b) Modes of Production and Exploitation

A theoretically more fundamental disaggregation must be directed towards different mods (or forms) of production and to the particular mods of exploitation associated with them.

(i) Work in the domestic unit must occupy a separate category as, to the extent that it does not fall within the modes examined below, it is not in itself an object of exploitation. If exploitation is defined in terms of the appropriation of all or part of the product of the labour of others, there must necessarily be a product. In its narrow sense (in practice domestic and productive activities frequently overlap) domestic work is a component of the division of tasks within the family unit and is accompanied by redistribution of earnings amongst the various members. It is essentially reproductive labour, servicing family members who are part of a workforce employed elsewhere. If exploitation is present it is indirect. This point is a difficult one, and not free from ambiguity — if the domestic work of a child is taken over by a servant (of the same age perhaps) the economic characteristic of the same work change.

(ii) There is also a quasi-slavery category, that involves not only appropriation of the child's labour but also of the child directly. The existence of such social relations, which are also found in activities serving capital, is facilitated by ownership rights over children by their older relatives. This is a phenomenon typically found in child prostitution. This category of exploitation, as well as the next, cannot be explored without studies of the networks which support apparently independent activities.

(iii) A third mode of exploitation, which we shall call quasifeudal, is based on a dependent personal relationship between the child and his or her employer. The child supplies labour within a paternalistic relationship in exchange for which the employer (who could be a parent) offers protection, lodging and food. Craft and small business apprenticeships would come into his category. The use of low-paid or unpaid labour is, as already noted, the condition for the survival of the majority of small-scale urban enterprises. However, this is an inherently contradictory form of exploitation, for although the creation of a commodity involves appropriation of the child's surplus value, children's work is not socially recognised and cannot be freely sold on the labour market. It seems that it is correct to talk in terms of "superexploitation" because the juvenile labour force is not paid at the same rate as adults doing the same work, thanks to the maintenance of quasi-feudal dependency. In this category of superexploitation, child-created value is essentially extracted from the absolute surplus, that is, through protracted working hours. A characteristic of craft-type production is the low investment in equipment in relation to the volume of work undertaken. It follows that a profit will only be made if two conditions obtain: a long working day and low wages. It should also be noted that superexploitation can be found in large-scale capitalist enterprises. When this is the case (we have given an extensive example above) there is every reason to suppose that, even if work organisation is capitalist, the social relations of production are quasi-feudal (this is doubly true in the case of children because they are not usually in a position to sell their labour to the highest bidder).

(iv) In contrast to the preceding categories, commercial activities can extract value created in another location. These activities, very often undertaken by children, include street vending, a variety of trading, door-to-door sales, etc. Within this category, distinctions can be made according to the individual who receives the proceeds: either the child works for an adult who receives part of the proceeds, or the child works independently. The latter is probably much less common, over long period at least, than certain observers maintain. In order to clarify this point, research should seek to identify the commercial networks. It is possible that appropriation of sales proceeds can take the from of protection by an official or anonymous institution. The illegal character of some "marginal" commercial activities naturally favours the development of protection rackets and their possible existence should always be taken into account.

These typological suggestions are not complete. In particular, we have excluded all activities outside the small-scale urban sector, such as agricultural work or those directly and integrally absorbed into capitalism. We simply wish to insist on the necessity of introducing relevant distinctions between various children's activities not as a function of subjective empirical categories but in relation to a theoretical and economic position. Rodgers and Standing's chapter in this volume is, on this point, more rigorous and exact than our own proposals.

In summary, we strongly maintain that, in our view, child labour is, in general, characterised by the convergence of inherited social relations and an exploitation, of which the ultimate gains — whatever the intermediate processes—serve the dominant capitalist mode of production.

2. Research Themes

In this section some lines of research will be proposed which, it is hoped, will help in tackling the difficult problem of child labour.

(a) Historical analyses and their relevance in present day low-income countries

We strongly advocate a study of child labour in Europe from the beginning of the Industrial Revolution to the end of the nineteenth century. This proposal should not be misinterpreted. Such a study should not week to make comparisons through structural analogies or strained parallels with today's Third World, thereby reducing the problems of the latter to mere historical phenomena. On the contrary, a historical analysis of child labour in Western societies must be oriented towards a better understanding of the specific mechanisms operating in underdeveloped countries. During the whole period of industrialisation of Western countries, the exploitation of child labour had two aspects. First, in the absence of protective legislation, there was unconstrained use of child workers in non-capitalist activities in an attempt to slow or reverse the decline of these activities. Second, there was direct, extensive and cynical exploitation of children by capital itself (mostly in mines and the textile industry). If, however, these two aspects were to be directly applied to present-day underdeveloped countries, we should find the parallels to be weak. Public enlightenment, and the use of advanced technologies based on a high organic composition of capital (the relationship in terms of value between equipment and the wage (bill), have led to a weakening of the role (if not the number) of children working in industry; the type of exploitation experienced by children in the nineteenth-century Europe is, in the present world, being confined to sectors which are difficult to modernise (e.g. crafted carpets or packaging of "beedi" cigarettes).[4] It would therefore, be a waste of time to try and prise out a direct appreciation and understanding of current systems of child exploitation from studies of European societies up to the last century. Having said this, such a study could help in understanding the following processes:

— The evolution of the birth rate in relation to economic processes; in particular the stage of accumulation at which the birth rate began to decline and the different types of industrialisation to which family renewal strategies corresponded.

— Other demographic changes in relation to the economy, notably the mortality and marriage rates corresponding to different stages or economic development. The hypothesis underlying this suggestion is that the high turnover of the juvenile workforce, itself related to high mortality and/or early marriage, allowed superexploitation of children even beyond the physical minimum necessary for reproduction of the workforce.

The role of children in capital accumulation, in the formation of surplus value and in the domestication and proletarianisation of the peasantry.

— The significance of the introduction of compulsory schooling and legislation on hours of work and child labour; in particular, were mass schooling and the reduced productive role of children two outcomes of a single set of conditions, or did school contribute to the disappearance of child labour?

— The development of thinking on the place of the child in different social groups.

If care is taken not to fall into the trap of "Eurocentrism", this type of study will yield invaluable material which could speed the development of interpretive schemes of child labour in the Third World, and would discourage subjective or moralising approaches.

(b) Research on Government Policy Towards Child Labour

Any even modestly comprehensive research must include an analysis of all proposed or existing policy interventions as well as a detailed study of legislation in force from the point of view of both its nature and its efficacity.

The earliest recommendations for the total and world-wide suppression of children's work were made long ago. In practice, however, we have not come anywhere near this objective. Thus an analysis of the implicit and proclaimed aims of policies would be of considerable interest. In this way the somewhat vague and idealistic question: "What type of legislation?" Would be replaced by the more realistic one: "Why is there no legislation?" Or, if it does exist, "Why it is not applied?"

In this way the legal/moral/position normally adopted would be revealed as an obstacle to more scientific studies based on objective facts. Similarly, the question of whether the anomaly is the existence of children's work or the way in which children are exploited could be resolved. Another fundamental question needs to be posed at the same time: "Is it possible to eliminate child labour without changing the, economic, and social systems harbouring it, especially the dependent relationship of such systems vis-a-vis developed capitalist economies?" It would also be possible to measure the efficacity of legislation which does not correspond to the productive forces involved and to examine the difficulties experienced in applying international recommendations. Finally, such a study could test the relevance and consequences of certain more general strategies officially aimed at improving economic structures: Does rural development aggravate rural emigration? Does industrialisation in the name of capital modernisation contribute to unemployment? Is the promotion of "dynamic" artisanal activities ultimately a cause of superexploitation of children? The implications of such strategies for children are important and need to be assessed.

(c) Data collection

The collection of information needs to be structured around those hypotheses on the economic roles of children which need to be tested. The following points are intended to show that the rejection of an empiricist approach, which sometimes leads to an almost random collection of information, has methodological implications. On the basis of the hypotheses noted above, we suggest that data should be collected on the following subjects:

(1) Migration, specifically the release of labour from rural environments: nature, volume, modalities, family strategies.

(2) The effects of family structure on children's work: role of direct antecedents, other kin, the extended family; competition or reciprocity between parents and children. Inquiries should not stop at the formal parents but also include organic lines of descent.

(3) The networks, circuits and hierarchical channels that host the exploitation of children's work. The necessity of including this point has already been stressed. Data must aim to identify power and decision-making centres, financial circuits, the routes along which earnings are channelled and the beneficiaries of these earnings, the links between small non-capitalist enterprises and their suppliers, distributors and the State.

(4) The children's social origins, length of time spent working, schooling and qualifications.

(5) Working hours and conditions and their fluctuations, related to the economic needs of production and distribution.

(6) The types of task allotted to children in relation to learning skills and the degree of responsibility they are allowed.

(7) The level and type of remuneration — negative (apprenticeship fees, gift on finishing a course), zero or positive — and compared with what an adult would receive for the same work. This information must take into account the main elements relevant to the cost of the reproduction of the labour force.

(8) Mortality, specific illnesses, relative susceptibility to parasitic and viral attacks, undernourishment, the risk of occupational accidents. In order for the results of this part of the inquiry to be useful, these questions should also be directed towards the adult population who worked during their childhood. The main aim here is to establish whether, and under what conditions, the exploitation of children involves excessive physical demands and a significant reduction in life expectancy or in lifetime health status.

(9) An assessment in terms of value (with its monetary equivalent) of the additional product accruing to employers as a result of using child labour. There is no point in pretending that this would be easy but, using the methods proposed below, it would be possible to design indirect measures and make estimates.

(10) Concealed juvenile activities that traditional types of inquiry tend to ignore: domestic work, illicit street trading, trafficking and prostitution, for example. Here, more than for any other aspect of the problem, the development of a new methodology seems indispensable.

(11) Finally, the ideological positions of different groups with regard to children's work. Those of children themselves: self-esteem, fatalism, submission or rebellion to authority, expectations, perception of work in general, attitudes towards wages, interest in tasks, awareness of differences in working conditions.

Most of the proposed research themes require data that are not necessarily numerical. The choice of themes is guided by the theoretical relevance of the information, but this does not exclude purely statistical inquiry. the choice is simply based on priorities ordered according to our analysis of the causes of children's work.

3. Methodological Approaches

(a) Some Approaches to be Avoided

Direct quantitative assessment of the number of children at work is unhelpful and misleading. The information obtained through this method can reveal declared employment only and not the clandestine, illegal and occasional workforce which is, without doubt, where the core of the problem is to be found. If, in spite of this, it is necessary to have a measure of the numbers of children involved, this would have to be obtained through crops-checking, and making approximations from indirect sources such as the distribution of jobs between the formal and informal sectors; rural-urban migration; school attendance and school leaving; apprentice registration; housing, consumption and income of domestic units, etc. A combination of these sources should lead to a more satisfactory and controllable set of figures than direct enumeration. The theoretical problems connected with identifying the juvenile population at work must in any case be resolved before one attempts to establish a representative sample.

Another trap to avoid is that of exaggerated empiricism. This is characterised by an unending multiplication of questions in the absence of a system of hypotheses; a wish to reduce all the factors studied to numbers; a claim to be exhaustive; and the adoption of preconceived, descriptive typologies into which all observed variables are squeezed willy-nilly. Such dogmatism carries an even greater risk, namely the consideration of only those individuals who exemplify preconceived norms, and the rejection from the sample of all that is not easily identifiable and observable.

Within the same context, it is proposed that the use of only long and closed questionnaires be rejected. Investigative tools are not neutral. Surveys on the informal sector have often been carried out with questionnaires containing over 100 basic questions; what is more, interviewers tend to be paid on the basis of numbers of questionnaires completed. Moreover, there is the problem of nonresponse. At best, non-responses are measured and it is possible to calculate the response rate to each question; however, non-responses are often simply ignored in the final statistics, much as non-voters are ignored in official elections. With regard to refusals to respond, grounds exist for believing that there are a great number of these but that they are hidden because another individual is asked to answer the questionnaire instead. This results in considerable bias in the representativeness of the sample, always supposing that the latter was well selected in the first place. With regard to children's work, it should be remembered that employers have nothing to gain (and perhaps feel that they have much to lose) through co-operating in inquiries concerning their young employees. An even more serious distortion results from the exclusion of the reasons for non-response or refusal to co-operate. Thus a programme of data collection on the work of children can expect to come up against a double difficulty, not only for the general reasons given above but also because of the low reliability of the information likely to be obtained on such a delicate question.

(b) Some Suggested Techniques

Who should be interviewed? Our previous discussion has shown that we should be prepared to contact a wide range of people. If exploitation of the juvenile workforce is enmeshed in a strong hierarchical structure, this should be exposed and information should be obtained from all the participation (employers, biological and/or surrogate family, employment, purchasing arid distribution organisations, administrative bodies and government). It goes without saying that the inquiry methods must be adapted to the groups in question, a point to which we will return.

Children at work (and adults who worked during childhood) should make up the core of the sample, and the types of investigation envisaged would include their direct involvement in the planning, administration and use of the studies. On the basis of this commitment we can progress from outside recommendations to questioning the children themselves. In our opinions studies that view the child as an individual who is, above all, irresponsible and in need of protection bear the unacceptable imprint of paternalism. To take a similar case, it is widely argued that exclusively masculine attempts to analyse and attack women's oppression in the West entailed the takeover and re-interpretation of women's demands, with the ultimate effect of intensifying the very subordination they were purporting to attack. If this analysis is correct, it is clear that it is even more relevant to the case of children. The ILO should seize the opportunity presented to it by international concern over this question and let the children themselves speak.

A rejection of the quantitative and empiricist methods that are traditionally employed in research on the Third World need not present practical difficulties and may, on the contrary, be an advantage. The approach taken in this chapter has led to the proposal of essentially qualitative empirical material and analytical tools, but all quantification is not excluded. With this in mind, investigations should observe a certain number of ground rules:

(1) Complete coverage of the population should not be attempted. Instead there should be an analysis of a small-group of individuals chosen for their theoretical rather than numerical credentials. Selection would thus focus on an activity where child work is assumed to be frequent and organically essential to the creation of value. A thorough examination of a single activity is greatly preferable to vast surveys that try to encompass all the problems of an entire region.

(2) Adopt, whenever possible, non-directive or semi-directive interview methods in order to document the various issues raised in this chapter. In this way unexpected information can be dealt with and the interviewee can respond indirectly., perhaps while talking about other things, to the questions put forward. The greater the resistance to the inquiry (and there is likely to be considerable resistance in the case of children's work), the more appropriate this method.

(3) Attempt to introduce into the urban, small-scale activities environment anthropological methods that have proved themselves over a long period in the rural sector. An anthropological approach rests on a fundamental principal: expect to give, and lose, a lot of time. More precisely this means that, when there is no shared identity between researcher and investigator, it is better (and not much more expensive) to use participatory interview techniques which require long contact with the selected groups (cf. Devauges, 1977 and Salem, 1979, who have employed this method). It is not recommended that payment be according to interviews completed because this tends to diminish the quality of the information collected. Treatment of the results yielded by an anthropological type of inquiry combines modern (computer) and traditional (manual, content analysis) methods.

(4) Establish interpretative systems for free responses, the inevitable accompaniment to the anthropological method. In fact, such responses do not always reflect reality but can be interpreted according to certain codes. For example, if a child replies that he or she wishes (or does not wish) to

work, this information would have to be analysed (and the gap between the information and the child's precise feelings) according to whether he or she is alone or with an employer, parents, an official, etc., and according to the child's perception of the reasons for the interview. Thus a decoding system must be developed, always remembering the risk of ethnocentric interpretation, as well as the need for an extended interview (even re-interviews) and cross-checking between different assertions during the interview. Another example, for which a decoding system would be required, is the dissimulation of employers who, sensing that they are involved in proscribed or morally unacceptable social relations, tend to say that they employ children in order "to do them a favour".[5] This type of claim should be assessed in combination with other information (attitudes of parents, children, authorities, social group) and should contribute towards the formulation of interpretive keys. In general, a variety of interviewees will permit comparison and cross-checking of sources. In particular, individuals who directly exploit, in their social relations, the labour of children talk of the subject in a devious manner which can he truly assessed only in the light of the experiences recounted by others (suppliers and traders, the State, and, of course, the children).

(5) The anthropological method can be usefully combined with other approaches: analysis of legal texts and governmental declarations; administration of questionnaires to enterprises to discover sources of inputs and labour as well as the destination of the products, turnover, fiscal constraints, gross and net revenues and structure of the workforce; inquiries amongst families with regard to migratory history and the position of each member vis-a-vis productive employment, reconstruction of family life histories; and studies of investments by multinational enterprises in different sectors of Third World countries,

CONCLUSION

In conclusion, we should like to return to the subject of interventionist policies and the ideologies underlying them.

There are two approaches to the study of child labour in the informal sector. The first is concerned with supporting and encouraging certain informal activities while at the same time "protecting" the children engaged in them. This strategy is, in our opinion, ambiguous if not actually contradictory. While suppression of the most oppressive aspects of informal activities is the apparent and undeniably worthy aim, the success of such a strategy might very well intensify the problems associated with child labour. For example, policies designed to assist the most "dynamic" artisans (market protection or tax concessions, for instance) will tend to increase inequality in the artisanal sector as a whole. In addition, there is reason to believe that it is precisely these favoured artisans who systematically use the free labour of women and children. Finally, if measures for the protection of children are applied without taking into account the economic realities facing the informal sector workforce, the clandestine nature of much juvenile labour will simply grow, further aggravating children's insecurity.

The above comments indicate that this first approach, which we shall term "voluntarist", is somewhat unrealistic. The second approach, which we have attempted to outline to some extent in previous sections, is based on concrete social and economic observation and not on more or less humanitarian and Eurocentric notions.

It is true that this second approach is highly tinged with scepticism, even pessimism, as to the validity and the simple efficacity of interventionist policies, other things being equal. But our position is not negative, because it is guided by the conviction that children should collectively decide for themselves whether they work and under what conditions. Proposals to eliminate child labour, without compensation for family income lost thereby, should be viewed with great caution. Child work may not be morally natural, but it is economically natural under conditions of extroverted accumulation, economic dependence and extreme poverty. We do not agree with those who set out to eliminate child work without taking these facts into account. It would be of great interest, given this argument to examine the effects and limitations of the measures concerning children (and women as well) in the recently independent Third World countries of which the governments have followed socialist-oriented economic policies.

How should the voluntarist approach, which seems to dominate many international recommendations, be analysed? We should like to suggest that the characteristics of the latter can be reduced to three "-isms": moralism, legalism, and paternalism.

Moralism views child work as an anomaly (although the same is surely true of all exploitation of labour". From this standpoint, one could even maintain that children are unnaturally "condemned" to 10 years of schooling, if one takes into account the energy consumed both by schoolboys and street traders, for instance. The moralist conception of the problem originates in the Western division of human life into successive stages, i.e., schooling, production, retirement. The universal application of such Western criteria seems to us to be quite unacceptable.

Legalism, a corollary of the moralistic attitude, is concerned with the establishment of new regulations, recommendations and laws. Since its foundation in 1919 the ILO has been much concerned with the gradual elimination of child labour and the promotion of the well-being of children in fields within its competence.[6] At the very first session of the International Labour Conference, which was held in the year of its foundation, a Convention was adopted which fixed the minimum age for admission of children to industrial, employment at 14 years. Between 1919 and 1965 ten Conventions on minimum age for admission to employment in various economic sectors were adopted. Finally, in 1973, the Convenction concerning Minimum Age for Admission to Employment (No. 138), which replaced all the previous relevant Conventions, was adopted. It should be mentioned, however, that in 1980, seven years after the adoption of this Convention, only eight developing countries (half of them in Latin America) had ratified it. It seems to us that the tendency of legalism to transform a socio-economic problem into a legal one should be carefully watched.

Finally, in our opinion, the *paternalist* position constitutes the principal ideological basis of voluntarism. We have experienced International Women's Year and the International Year of the Child, but no-one dares propose the Year of the Proletariat because the paternalist overtones would be inescapable. The idea of a child as a human being in need of protection is ambiguous: on the one hand it is desirable that children, in common with all human beings but especially by virtue of their physical limitations, should benefit from laws forbidding their exploitation; however, to reduce the problem of child work to one of "protection" is to exclude children from any decisions about themselves and to create inferior beings. In our view, the only acceptable "protection" (and one that does not contradict the preceding paragraph) lies in giving children the right to be heard and to organise; up to now, this right has been immediately and violently repressed when children have claimed it.

The "protection" approach is based on certain presumptions about the special position of children. Typically it is argued that children are the victims of: (1) a lack of a stable family life; (2) a lack of recreative activities; (3) contact with delinquency; (4) physical risks; (5) a lack of education.[7] All these points could be applied to workers of all ages in underdeveloped countries, not just to children. The problem is not one of age but of exploitation.

REFERENCES

1. "Non-structure" is the most common French translation of "informal." The tow concepts are ideologically very similar. Much recent empirical work on the informal sector has been carried out within the ILO's World Employment Programme, See, for instance, ILO: *Employment, incomes and equality: A strategy for increasing productive employment in Kenya* (Geneva, 1972); S.V. Sethuraman: "The urban informal sector: Concept, measurement and policy," in *International Labour Review* (Geneva, ILO), July-August 1986 idem (ed.): *The urban informal sector in developing countries: Employment, poverty and environment* (Geneva, ILO, 1981).
2. See in particular M. Bienefeld and M. Godfrey: "Measuring unemployment and the informal sector," in *IDS Bulletin* (Brighton, Institute of Development Studies) 1975, No. 3, pp. 4-10, from where the following points are taken.
3. Quotations in (i) are translations from the introduction to the French edition of the Anti-Slavery Society report; elsewhere from the English version.
4. It would be truer to say that these types of industry are not interested in modernisation inasmuch as cheap labour has an intrinsic advantage for them. To take the two examples given: it may not be by chance that patterns on crafted carpets are not uniform or that "beedi" packets are conical. If production were mechanised, these characteristics would probably disappear.
5. cf. J. Charmes; *Methodologie generale des enquetes sur le secteur non-structure en Tunisie* and *Recueil d'interviews aupres de menuisiers et ebenistes de Tunis et de Sfax* (Tunis, INS, 1977).
6. ILO *Minimum age for admission to employment*, Report IV (1), International Labour Conference, 57th Session, Geneva, 1972, p. 3.
7. This list was taken from as unpublished text, but is representative of the approach.

8

THE ECONOMIC ROLE OF CHILDREN IN INDIA

I. Introduction

In relation to societies of the Third World the pehnomenon of child labour needs to be viewed and assessed in a fresh perspective. A view is gradually gaining ground that, rather than being shocked and scandalised by the employment of children in work for wages, we need to understand the nature, extent and kinds of work in which they are engaged in different parts of the world. No useful purpose is served either by condemning poverty or by invoking the need for schooling for all children within a certain age group; it is necessary instead to review the place of children in the society and to look into the culturally conceived obligations towards and expectations form them. The notion that *any* kind of work that does not constitute either play or education, in the strict sense of the terms, is always an unjust imposition on children and that this labour dispossesses them of their childhood needs to be re-examined.

India has the largest number of the world's working children. According to the 1971 census, 4.66 per cent of the total child population in India were working. Table 8.1 gives the distribution of workers in the 5-14 age group in various sectors of economic activity. The figures in Table 8.1 are undoubtedly a gross underestimation of the reality. Estimates form the data obtained in the twenty-seventh round of the National Sample Survey put the number of child workers at 15.1 million (Seal, 1979). The age-specific labour force participation rates derived from the data obtained in the sixteenth and twenty—seventh rounds of the National Sample Survey are shown in Table 8.2.

Any survey of the extent of child labour in India has to recognise that the information is widely scattered. Some government reports have provided some material, other data can be found in records and surveys, in the empirical studies of sample populations of child workers in particular localities and/or industries and occupations, in analyses of secondary data by social researchers, in newspaper reports, and in popular and other articles.

A recent survey report (Gangrade, 1979) provides basic information on the incidence and distribution of child labour in India, the occupations in which they are found, their conditions of work, and reasons for their joining the labour force. Excellent as is the report, it brings home a realisation that our knowledge of working children in India is scanty.

TABLE 8.1

Percentage Distribution of Total Boy and Girl Workers in Age Group 5-14 Among the Various Sectors of Activity, 1971

Activity	*Rural*		*Urban*	
	Boys	*Girls*	*Boys*	*Girls*
Total workers	100.0	100.0	100.0	100.0
Primary Sector				
1. Cultivation	42.41	27.58	6.46	3.32
2. Agricultural labour	40.24	57.50	12.41	22.37
3. Livestock, forestry, fishing, plantation, etc.	9.84	5.14	4.45	2.43
Secondary Sector				
4. Mining and quarrying	0.17	0.28	0.40	0.81
5. Manufacturing, processing, servicing and repairing:				
a) Household *industry*	2.07	4.06	8.02	17.96
b) Other than household industry	1.27	1.80	24.37	15.50
6. Construction	0.34	0.42	2.94	3.69
Tertiary Sector				
7. Trade and commerce	1.01	0.33	20.40	3.01
8. Transport, storage and communication	0.14	0.09	4.13	2.09
9. Services	2.51	2.80	16.42	28.82

Source: A. Mitra (1978).

Census data and other kinds of survey data have been used for a sociological understanding of the phenomenon of working children (see, for instance, Jain and Chand, 1979; Khandekar and Naik,. 1972; Mitra, 1978; Premi, 1973; Seal, 1979; Zachariah and Sebastian, 1966). It would be possible to make more use of data from the decennial Censuses, National Sample Surveys, Rural Labour Inquiry, Labour Bureau reports and also of other of official statistics of education, delinquency, .etc. It is, however, necessary to take a critical look at the lacunae in these data in order to improve the recording of children's work.

TABLE 8.11

Age-Specific Labour Force Participation Rates: 1960/61 and 1972/73

Sex	*Age*	*Participation rate*			
		Rural India		*Urban India*	
	16th round[1]	*27th round*[2]	*16th round*[1]	*27th round*[2]	
		July 160 to. June '61	*Oct. '72 to Sep. '73*	*July '60 to June '61*	*Oct. '72 to Sep. '73*
1	2	3	4	5	6
Male	5-9	3.28	2.57	0.52	0.84
	10-14	32.73	26.33	11.69	10.16
Female	5-9	2.40	1.94	0.73	0.38
	10-14	22.97	19.97	6.79	5.83

1. A person was considered as being employed if he/she had worked for pay or profit on at least one day during the reference week on some economic activity.
2. A person was considered as employed if he/she had pursued some gainful work for at least one hour or one day during the seven days preceding the date of enumeration.

Source: Seal (1979).

So far the attention given to the question of child labour in India has been somewhat perfunctory; much of the work on this subject, which borders on social inquiry and social work, is characterised by over-simplification and catch-all explanations and solutions which can be attributed, at least partially, to the presence of some underlying, inappropriate assumptions regarding childhood and its correlates. Value judgements and evaluative standards rooted in and deriving from Western experience cannot always be meaningfully superimposed on the social realities of the developing countries.

As an example of a distorted view of children's participation in productive activities and in the general economy of India, consider the following statement in the Indian Government Labour Bureau's Report on Child Labour (1954):

> In spite of protective legislation the social evil of child labour persisted in India from the early days of the industrial system. The evil still persists in the many unorganised sectors of industry and in agriculture. (p. 2)

One need hardly emphasise that it is totally misleading to associate child labour in India only with industrial development. It is true that the establishment of certain kinds of industry, the reorganisation of many cottage industries and crafts on non-familial and commercial bases, and capitalisation of agriculture, have expanded the scope for exploitation of child labour. This does not mean, however, that the involvement of children in economic activities is a recent phenomenon in India, where around 80 per cent of the population live in villages under exploitative land relations; large numbers of people exist at the subsistence and below-subsistence level; particular crafts are traditionally pursued by specific caste and ethnic groups; there is large-scale use of labour-intensive technology; means of communication and living conditions are often primitive.

Here is another vehement condemnation of child labour:

> Child labour is economically unsound, psychologically disastrous and physically as well as morally dangerous and harmful. It involves the use of labour at its point of lowest productivity and is, therefore, an inefficient utilisation of labour power. Child, labour precludes the full unfoldment of child's potentialities. It deprives him of education, training and skills which are the necessary prerequisites of earning. power and economic development. Children are the most vulnerable group in any population and in the need of the greatest social care. On account of their vulnerability and dependence, they can be exploited, ill treated and directed into undesirable channels by unscrupulous elements in the community. The State has the duty of according proper care and protection to children at all times as it is on their physical and mental well-being that the future of the nation depends. However, in view of our contemporary economic situation, the total eradication of child labour through legislation does not seem to be an immediate possibility. The only pragmatic alternative, therefore, is the dissipation of undesirable conditions and practices attendant to it. (India, National Institute of Public Co-operation and Child Development, 1977, pp. 1-2).

These examples highlight the need for a better understanding of the Indian social reality, fewer generalisations, greater conceptual clarity, and methodological refinement.

This paper begins by briefly looking at the child and work as they are depicted in Hindu tradition and sacred literature, and then goes on to examine cultural notions regarding the stages of human life placing childhood and the child in a certain perspective. Together, these suggest a way of understanding the possible roots of people's attitudes and views. Further, he contemporary patterns and extent of child labour are surveyed in a few sectors to assess its place in the family and the economy. Simultaneously, there is an attempt to assess the available sources of data in the cultural heritage and in the social science literature that could be used for developing a proper understanding of child work. Finally, some conceptual and definitional problems are raised along with some suggestions concerning approaches and methods that would be useful in studies of child labour.

II. The Child in Traditional Indian Culture

The mythology, legends and classical literature of India deal more with gods and kings than with the common people. As such, few specific references to the work roles of children from the lower strata or even average groups in society, can be easily traced. Significant inferences can be drawn, however, from general descriptions and particular episodes featuring in this literature. For example, the epics tell us that education was invariably imparted by a sage in his hermitage, traditional schools being built around venerable men of learning. Their rigorous codes applied equally to children of royal lineages and the sons of commoner families. The legendary Rama, a human incarnation of Vishnu of the Hindu Trinity and his brothers were sent by their father, the ruler of the kingdom of Ayodhya, to the *ashrama* (hermitage) of sage Vashishta, and accepted its discipline. Like all others they participated in the domestic chores of the Guru's household as well as of the *ashrama*, helping out in economic pursuits that sustained the latter, in addition to keeping up with a demanding learning schedule. Such schools did not charge fees but the students were expected to contribute their labour towards the running and upkeep of the institution.

Krishna — a latter incarnation of Vishnu and the principal hero of *Mahabharata*, another epic — though born of royal parents, had to be removed from them and the palace immediately because of the wrath of his maternal uncle who was determined to kill him. His childhood was spent in humbler surroundings, in the household of a minor chieftain of cowherds. There are graphic descriptions of how, at the age of 6, Krishna was launched by his foster-parents into the job of a cowherd and, how, like all other boys of his age, and in their company, he went out to graze cattle in the pastures in the vicinity of the village. He was fun-loving and mischievous, but there are no instances suggesting that he ever tended to shy away from work assigned to him or of his being negligent in discharging the responsibility given to him.

Nowhere does one find any mention of the desirability of, or insistence on, restricting childhood only to play and education, separating it from productive work. Among agriculturists, who then as now formed the largest part of the country's population, the children had specific tasks. Keeping watch on the crops and frightening away birds and beasts coming to feed on them was their main responsibility. Older children are shown as helping out in looking after younger children. For the children of artisans and craftsmen, education in their craft or skill started early, their families and guilds imparting to them the necessary training. From their early teens craftsmen's children started contributing substantially to the economic endeavours of the family and the community, and in general children participated in such tasks as gathering wild fruits, tubers, herbs and vegetables, shallow water fishing and, a little later, hunting.

Thus, we find children being entrusted with work that was time-consuming but not arduous. This kept them occupied and allowed the elders to pursue activities involving heavier labour and more complex skills. Children could combine recreation with the limited work roles assigned to them; in fact much of their work was looked upon as full of fun and play, and it is significant that work was never disassociated from play and education. From their early years children started learning to be, and then functioning as, participants in and productive members of the family and the community.

As children's activities were enmeshed with the activities of adults, it goes without saying that the constraints, limitations and deprivations of a particular group characterised the life of its children also. References to slavery, domestic service, and master-servant relationship in literature, particularly Buddhist literature, unmistakably point towards the presence of children toiling as slaves and servants at the mercy of their masters. Much more light could perhaps be thrown on the place of children among the lowly groups if we made a serious effort to delve into the relevant literature. In the mediaeval period also, both Hindu and Muslim affluence was characterised by the use of children as personal servants, often working as helpers and apprentices to the adults.

III. Life Stages in Indian Tradition

The notion of the division of the normal human life span into stages or phases according to age is a part of the Indian tradition. The four principal stages of life — the celibate, the householder, the anchorite, and the ascetic — are well known. These stages have been identified in other ways also. A work on the traditional system of medicine says: "There are three ages, namely, childhood, middle age, and old age. He who is less than 16 years is to be recognised as *bala,* i.e. a child. The same text adds that childhood also has three divisions one during which a child consumes only milk (i.e. a suckling baby), a second during .which the child consumes both milk and cereals, and a third during which the child lives (essentially) on cereals (Bhavaprakash, Ayurvedagrantha). It should be pointed out, however, that these stages are not identical in be different authoritative works; even the substages of childhood mentioned in the same work may overlap. But there is no doubt that each term used for these substages denotes a certain number of years and is broadly associated with degrees of maturity and the development of abilities. Also, different terms are meant to be used in different contexts (see annex to this chapter).

More commonly the human life-span is divided into childhood, youth, adulthood, and old age. It may also be divided into childhood (*balyavastha*), youth (*yuvavastha*), middle age (*praudhavastha*), and old age (*vriddhavastha*). Age as well as certain rites of passage are used as the criteria for identifying a person with a particular stage of life and not the exact calculation of years, months and days. In point of fact this is not even possible. While astrological prediction about one's future hinges on the exact moment of birth, only a few in the upper castes and classes are in a position to provide such information. For others, the recording of date and time of birth may be necessary for the preparation of a horoscope but its relevance for calculating how much time has elapsed since birth is not realised. Details of age are thus not retained for ready use, particularly in rural areas. The indifference of the common people towards proper reporting of births combines with negligence by petty officials and village Panchayat functionaries in performing their duty of recording births and deaths in a village. Information needed for civic purposes is thus hard to come by. Needless to say, specific measures against child marriage, child labour, immoral trafficking in young girls, and so on, are confronted with woefully inadequate and inaccurate information about age. Fortunately, with a few literate persons in the community, the situation is improving.

In any broad classification of the stages of life or age groups, childhood in India is understood to cover the period up to 16 years. Girls, however, are believed to attain maturity earlier. According to *Arthashastra*, for instance, a boy becomes major at the age of 16 while a girl becomes major at the age of 12. Attainment of puberty confers maturity on a girl. In common parlance the expression for menarche is "becoming mature". There is also a difference between boys and girls in respect of proper age for marriage. For girls the time between the onset of puberty and marriage is viewed as some sort of a liminal period during which the girl needs special protection. This is the period when she is capable of becoming, but must not become, a mother.

It is a common experience in Indian villages that in the first two, or three years of life a child is indulged by all. It is also a period during which the mother is able to give the child considerable attention, which is gradually withdrawn when the next pregnancy starts. An infant or small child (there are specific terms to distinguish between different periods of early childhood) should not be allowed to cry. Elders and neighbours consider it their duty to protect children from neglect and indifference. That these attitudes and reactions are informed by the prescriptions and advice contained in written traditions is indicated by the following verses from a treatise on health and medicine:

> One should not let a child cry unless it cannot be avoided such as when it has to be massaged and bathed or has to be administered medicine.
>
> "A child should be protected with special effort from the, sun, lightning, rain, smoke, fire, wind and uneven ground.

There is considerable evidence in literature, ethico-legal codes and common conceptions to suggest that the age of 16 years provides a cut-off point between childhood and youth. The following verse from *Bhagawata Purana*, a tenth-century treatise, finds its echo in many regional languages: "A son should be doted on for the first five years, he should be disciplined for the next ten years, when he is 16 he should be treated like a friend" (stanza 114, Chapter 10). The same sentiments are expressed in a saying popular in North India: "Treat your son like a king till he is five, treat him like a slave for the next ten years, and begin treating him like a friend when he is 16." This also reflects the appropriate behaviour expected of a boy at different ages.

The following observations made in an Indian village suggest that the above advice is put into practice:

As a rule infants are treated with affection. The mother nurses it whenever it starts crying indicating its desire to be fed. ... When it is 6 to 8 months old, elder sisters, female relations and male members of the household may start sharing this task with her by occasionally giving solid food to the child.

> ... On the whole, an infant is the cause of delight to the family, and it is often fondled and carried about by the elders.

> ... The situation radically changes after the child reaches the age of 5 or 6 years. Now the parents must be strong and should start disciplining it.[1]

Demarcation of life stages according to age in no way negates the idea of continuity. On the contrary, that idea is quite strong in the Indian consciousness. According to the traditional system of medicine and also the general folk conception, the prenatal period is important from the point of view of the development, both mental and physical, of the child. It is commonly believed that the mental and physical make-up of the child is influenced while it is still in the womb, by what the mother eats and also by her thoughts, feelings and actions. The outside world impinges on the child in a number of ways, in the first stage through the mother.[2]

An important aspect of the notion of continuity in human personality is the importance of practice and training of the muscles, the sense organs and various parts of, the body in performing certain activities. As mentioned earlier, it is believed that the learning process starts soon after conception. It is commonly recognised and emphasised that the human body is soft, flexible and pliable in childhood and can therefore learn with ease how to twist, bend, stretch or assume different postures as required by particular jobs. Co-ordination of limbs and balance of body, sense of timing and attuning of sense organs are relatively easier to learn at this stage. Skills are therefore best learned if learning is begun fairly early. It is not only a physical adjustment but also a mental adjustment that has to be achieved in learning skills.

Musicians start training their own children at the age of 5 or 6. Besides training the vocal chords, the sense organs need to be attuned and sensibilities need to be developed. It is commonly believed that an imprint acquired in childhood is not easily erased. An early start in music also helps a proper crystallisation of tastes and inclinations. For the same reason an early start is preferred for training in dancing.

Craftsmen and artisans hold similar ideas and so ensure that their children start acquiring skills early. The nimble fingers and keen eyesight of children are greatly valued. In hereditary crafts like carpet weaving, papier mache, cotton and silk weaving with intricate designs, woodcarving, embroidery, etc., training starts at an early age. The need for a minimum of training and practice in a skill and the idea of "catch them young" both play their part in sustaining the pattern of early involvement of children in hereditary crafts. Small boys may be sent away as apprentices, some of them earning a little money, or they may be taught at home. Anandlakshmy noted that training in the community of weavers in Banaras, famous for its embroidered silk, begins when boys are between 7 and 14 years of age. In families where there are facilities or looms for absorbing the services of the young apprentice, the boy is taught the craft at home. However, some weavers still prefer to send their Sons to another weaver for learning, believing that outsiders with no emotional ties can enforce stricter and better learning, through physical punishment if necessary (Anandlakshmy, 1970, pp. 47-48).

Training begins in a potter's household, the main production centre, as soon as children are capable of doing some light work.[3] Several distinct stages, which differ between boys and girls, have to be completed before the child is considered to have learned the craft. Children are sometime sent to relatives in distant places for special training. And while learning the major tasks of the occupation the child worker learns of other, complementary skills.

Similar ideas regarding the greater receptivity of children and pliability of their bodies operate in cultivation, where children are involved in the work of production at a fairly early age. The argument that a cultivator's son who does not learn to handle the plough and other implements at the appropriate age would find it difficult to handle them later, has sufficient strength. This logic Is also invoked in the case of domestic-work. Once it is assumed by the parents that children are to live and function more or less in the same society as their own, it stands to reason that the tasks they have to perform should be learned at a proper age.

IV. Child Work Roles in Tribal Groups and Rural Areas

1. Tribal Groups

Although most ethnographic accounts of tribal groups, at different socio-economic levels and patterns of subsistence, have little to say about children and their work roles, a few studies do offer some information on the activity patterns of children, their gradual integration into the economy, and the division of work according to sex and age. An example is this account of children's activities amongst the Kamar, a tribe of shifting cultivators, hunters, and gatherers:

> When the boys grow up and attain the age of 7 or 8 years, they get their first wooden bow and arrows of the normal type, although in size considerably smaller than those used by the adults. This adds to the status of the children who now begin to make independent efforts at hunting rabbits, squirrels, and small birds. With a little practice many of them are very successful at it.[4]

By that time, as Dube notes, the children graze the domestic animals and begin to learn basket-making; a little later they join the adults in hunting expeditions. By the time they are about 14 years of age, the children are expected to be able to take care of themselves.

Among the Dhurwa of Bastar, when a boy reaches the age of 10 he is expected to know how to handle a (wooden) plough, reap the harvest, cut and bring the fuel from the forest alone or in company — and sell and purchase articles in the market. Similarly, a girl of the same age is expected to be proficient in weeding paddy fields, harvesting, cooking meals, fetching water from the sources, taking care of her younger siblings, sweeping the house, and washing the verandah walls and courtyard of the house with cowdung.[5] It is obvious that this description only lists the work that a 10-year-old boy or girl is usually expected to do. It does not indicate exactly at what age a child starts doing a particular task.

In his restudy of the socio-economic conditions of the Chodra, a tribe in Gujarat, Ghanashyam Shah has given figures of male and female workers in different age groups for a total population of 18,223. Unfortunately, he has used broad age categories and has not taken care to distinguish between children and adults. In the "below 10" age group as many as 25 per cent of the boys and 31 per cent of the girls were workers, while in the 11-17 age groups 65 per cent of the males and 75 per cent of the females were workers.[6] Use of broad categories (which miss the required distinctions) and lack of .uniformity in the use of age categories: (making comparisons difficult) are two of the principal limitations of quantitative data in general. In a study of income-earning trends and social status of a Harijan (scheduled caste) community in Tamil Nadu, it is reported that 14.2 per cent of those below 25 years of age were land-owning cultivators, and that in the, same age group, 54.7 per cent were coolies (Vagiswari, 1972). It is impossible to get any idea about child workers contributing to these percentages, although the proportion of workers in the age groups below 25 givers an indication that there must be many child workers in the community.

Among the Kolgha of Gujarat, when boys are 6 years old they begin taking the cattle out for grazing, usually with other children. They also catch fish from water holes and pits, participate in foodgathering activities, and become wage labourers when still in their early teens.[7]

Among the Bhils of Western India, after a boy has completed his sixth year he begins harvesting crops and collecting Mohua flowers. When he grows a little older he is asked to tend the cattle in the woods and is expected to be self—supporting soon afterwards. Both boys and girls work on farms as paid labourers doing the weeding and harvesting. Sometimes the payment is in kind in the form of cloth and maize.[8]

The Jatapu are a tribe in Andhra Pradesh. Jatapu children, as a rule, are responsible for looking after the cattle, sheep and goats. When a boy is 6 years old, his father gets him one or two goats from the money-lender for grazing. The products are shared equally between the money-lender and the boy's father, the goat being returned to the owner after a certain time. Groups of children take the animals out and must wash them in the stream on their return in the evening. By the time a boy is 13 or 14, he also begins to take on agricultural work. Girls of 6 years old may be entrusted with all the household tasks such as cleaning the courtyard, getting water from the stream, and taking the animals for grazing if there are no boys in the house. A daughter helps the mother in all domestic tasks.[9]

Among the Bagatha and related tribes studied by Reddy (1971), children between 6 and 9 years of age accompany their no parents to the field to help them in such activities as sowing, transplanting, weeding and harvesting, digging roots, collecting fruit, and scaring off birds. Division of labour by sex is sharpened in the 10-14 age group when girls attend to feminine tasks in the house, field and forest, take care of infants and guard the house, while boys go along with men to the fields and forests.

In her account of the Dimasa of Assam, Danda emphasises the sexual division of work among children. Girls of about 8 years old are seen accompanying their mothers to the market with small loads on their backs. They occasionally fetch drinking water and small bundles of firewood and are taught weaving at a tender age. By the age of 14 or 15, boys have learned most of the agricultural activities and sometimes they are assigned the work of honey collection.[10]

Furer-Haimendorf's description of the participation of children in the daily activities of the household among the Gonds of Andhra Pradesh gives a clear idea of the economic roles of children in this tribal community with sedentary cultivation:

> The first serious work of children is the guarding of crops against birds and monkeys. A field whose owner neglects the watching offers a sorry sight, and a husband and a wife find it practically impossible to guard the crops throughout the 24 hours, unless they are helped by their children.
>
> While boys and girls share in the work of guarding crops, it is the boys alone who are called upon to herd the cattle.
>
> Small boys... help in collecting stubble and rubbish during the first spring ploughing and are later useful at harvest ... boys of 14 can be seen ploughing with the broad *wakur*, while the more difficult ploughing with the pointed plough (*ser*) is usually left to grown men.
>
> Girls begin helping in the household at a very early age. One can see tiny girls with small pots on their heads following their mothers or elder sisters to the well, and what at first is little but play, develops soon into a useful contribution to the volume of work which has to he done in every household.[11]

The foregoing descriptions provide us with some profiles of the participation of children in domestic and non-domestic activities of tribal household groups according to age. While the descriptions lack exactness and there are some differences in the age reported for particular activities — which may be authentic or could be subjective — there is considerable convergence in the way the, scope of children's activities is progressively widened, in the kind of assistance they provide to the parents, and in the over-all role of children in the household economy. What is not explicit are the views of children and parents towards each other in regard to the former's contribution. Nor is there any quantification of data providing us with the exact age range at which particular activities are taken up or measurement of the time contributed by children in comparison with that of their parents in various kinds of activities.

2. *Rural Areas*

It must be emphasised that even the patterns given above are not generally revealed in other accounts of tribes; they are rare in the studies of villages or individual castes. It appears that Indian scholars were preoccupied with the complex phenomenon of caste, so that most studies, whether of economy, politics, or even of kinship and religion, have revolved around that subject, and in recent, years to a limited extent around class. Even the demographic census data collected by the field worker have neglected details about children's participation in economic activities. Excepting some brief descriptions in a few village studies,[12] children do not figure at all. In many of the studies of particular caste groups or communities, children do not find a mention either because their participation in the economy was not very significant or because the focus of the scholar was different.

Children's roles and activity patterns in rural India, however, have not been completely neglected. They have found greater mention in some more recent anthropological, sociological and economic studies. Analyses of macro-level data for rural areas also provide information on the distribution of children in various occupational categories. Children figure prominently in studies dealing with the phenomenon of bonded labour, which will be discussed a little later. Programmes of community development and their evaluation, as well as educational planning and literacy programmes, have taken note of children's roles and preoccupations.

A study of the socialisation of Rajput children in a village in Western Uttar Pradesh by Minturn and Hitchcock (1963) refers briefly to their participation in economic activities. Anandlakshmy's sensitive study, mentioned earlier, of child development in two separate samples of agriculturalists — the well-to-do and the poor—and in two communities of craftmen hand-block printers and silk weavers presents patterns and processes of children's involvement in various productive activities (Anandlakshmy, 1978). Considerable quantitative data on children's activities were collected in this research project, but the report does not carry out any analyses of these data. Anandlakshmy's reporting remains essentially descriptive.

A few studies focussing on the role of women in the rural economy provide interesting data on children's participation. Thus, in a research project on women workers in the coir industry directed by Moilly Mathew, it was found that a large number of children were employed in coir making. Even school children were employed in coir making before and after school hours. In coir spinning, where the payment was on a piece-rate basis, there was a strong tendency to work long hours in order to earn as much as possible and involve children in work on a group basis.[13]

In a study of the impact of development on rural women in Western Uttar Pradesh by Jetley, as many as 83 out of 245 girls in the 6-11 age group (33.5 per cent) were reported to be engaged in economic activity and not attending school. Over 52 per cent (117 out of 222) girls in the age group 11-18 gave 'being engaged in economic activity' as a reason for not attending school, but it is difficult to calculate how many of these belonged to the 11-14 age group.[14]

In field surveys in rural Rajasthan and rural West Bengal, designed to make a realistic assessment of women's participation in the household economy, Jain and

Chand (1979, p. 2) found that children, especially from the lower-income groups, engaged in economic activity of various kinds almost with the same intensity as adults. Their findings on children were a by-product of their investigations regarding female work.

3. *Implications of Findings from Tribal and Rural Studies*

We may now take note of what emerges from studies of children's activity patterns in the various groups reviewed so far. Children form an integral part of the household economy; they receive training for work roles and gradually start making an individual contribution. Work is not viewed as being antithetical to childhood. There is, however, the notion of appropriate work for particular age groups and also of the appropriate time for learning particular skills and tasks. Learning is achieved mainly through observation, imitation and assistance to elders.

Children share the adult work environment and are observers and participants in it. In general, by between 12 and 14 years of age boys and girls have acquired the capability of doing most of the work that adults do. However, this does not mean that they are considered as adults. The lines of authority and decision-making, deference structure, initiative in productive operations, extent of control over one's and one's family members' earnings or productive capacities, and marital status have much relevance in the attainment of adulthood and do not only depend on the ability to do an adult's work.

While such boys and girls develop a certain sense of efficacy and competence, it is precisely their non-adult status which makes them so vulnerable to exploitation. They may be used by parents as sureties for debts and are in demand for agricultural work on a yearly contract basis. Their output is more or less equal to that of adults but they are paid lower wages. Preference for child workers is most common in the unorganised sector because in such jobs it is relatively easy for employers to circumvent the laws prohibiting child labour. Children may be concealed from factory inspectors during the latter's visits. Sometimes children's ages are overstated to make them eligible for employment, and on others those who would qualify for adult wages are forced to accept that they are younger than their true age. The law has proved unable to deal with such practices.

V. Child Work in Industry

Khandekar has long been interested in analysing secondary data on children and youth. She has drawn attention to the fact that in urban areas migrant families and migrant individuals account for a high percentage of child labour (Khandekar, 1970). There are few empirical studies of working children in urban areas but they highlight the unhealthy conditions in which children work, the long hours and a general lack of education (see, for instance, Barooah, 1977; George, 1977; Musafir Singh, Kaura, and Khan, 1978). Children are employed in a variety of places and occupations, including domestic service, tea stalls and small eating establishments, metal workshops, motor vehicle workshops, cycle repair shops, printing presses, household industries, provision stores, and all kinds of small shops. They also work on their own, as shoe-shiners, stall keepers, hawkers, and so on. Contributing to the family income is the most important motivation for employment, although many children also work to support themselves.

Industries in small towns and semi—urban areas provide an important avenue of employment for children.[15] Both home-based units utilising only family labour and units employing workers and apprentices rely heavily on children's labour. Labour Bureau reports supply figures of children working in such establishments and in industries as a whole, but it is doubtful if the children who work in the former are fully represented. Moreover, while conditions of work in these establishments are reported, we need to know more about the socioeconomic status and living conditions of the workers.

In her recent study, Gulati (1980) reports on the extent and nature of children's involvement in the coir industry in a few selected villages from two Talukas of the Trivandrum district. One of these Talukas, Neyyatinkara, is known for household production of coir, while the other, Chirayankil, is known for larger coir-producing units. In all 192 girls and 75 boys were studied. The proportion of school drop-outs was fairly high (48 per cent) but some children combined school with participation in coir making. Of the various operations which form part of the process of coir making, ratt rotating alone or combined with husk beating and spinning accounted for 64.7 per cent of the sample of child workers. Husk beating was also being done by many of the other children. In household production; they worked in the early hours of the .day and then contributed two hours of work after returning from school. Where the children had to go to production centres, those attending school generally worked during holidays and only those living near to the centre worked for some time after school hours. A household mainly using family labour needed its children to help in the coir-making operations; others needed the children's wages for maintenance.

Sivakasi, situated in the drought-prone district of Ramanathapuram in Tamil Nadu, has earned notoriety for its match industry employing thousands of children, from the age of 5, for over ten hours a day. Women and girls predominate in the industry, for little boys have many more avenues open to them and may go off to work in towns and cities as hotel boys, garage hands, hawkers, domestic workers and so on.

Children working in the match factories are mostly from families of Harijan landless labourers from the hinterland, and are paid on a piece-rate basis. They are transported to and from the place of work in buses, which pick them up well before daybreak and generally drop them off after 6 p .m. Two other industries in Sivakasi, making toy crackers and coloured calenders, also employ children in large numbers. It is estimated that these three industries employ about 40,000 child workers, who form more than half of their total labour force (Menon, 1979).

Carpet weaving is one of the important cottage industries of India, flourishing in the states of Madras, Travancore, Uttar Pradesh and Kashmir. This is essentially a group activity which needs different levels and types of skill and also mechanical equipment. Employment of children in activities suited to them keeps the cost of production low. They also work as apprentices. In household carpet-weaving enterprises, children are considered indispensable as helpers and as trainees who will continue the craft.

According to the Report of the Labour Bureau (1954), after the Factories Act of 1948 the industrial organisation of carpet weaving was radically changed. The work connected with weaving shifted from factories to the houses of the master weavers where laws against child labour would not apply. The looms were supervised by several master weavers who would engage about three people to work each loom, of these one or two would be children starting from the age of 10. Thus it was estimated that around Bhadohi in Uttar Pradesh, 25 per cent of the 50, 000 workers engaged in carpet weaving were children, while in Mirzapur 8,000 out of 20,000 workers were children.

In Kashmir, carpet weaving involves little children, particularly girls, in long hours of back-weakening work. Another :flourishing craft utilising child labour in this region is fine hand embroidery. It has been observed that maintenance of the same posture for hours and the intricacy of the work often leads to physical deformities and eye strain among children working in these cottage industries. (*Times of India*, 1978; S.C. Dube, personal communication.)"[16]

In and around Surat District in Gujarat, boys in their early teens are engaged in large numbers in diamond-cutting operations which can have very harmful effects on the eyes. The workers are paid well so there is no dearth of child labour in this lucrative enterprise.

VI. Debt Bondage of Children and the Impact of the Wage System

Recent research has provided ample evidence that debt bondage is still prevalent in many parts of the country. As reported by Das, in many parts of Bihar wages are available only during the 120 days required for agricultural operations; for the rest of the year the expenses of daily needs, marriages and funerals, and bribing of forest officials inexorably drive the rural poor into the clutches of the moneylender, who thus acquires an assured supply of labour.[17] In Purulia, particularly in the hilly areas and southern parts of the district, bonded labour in payment of debt is prevalent among the scheduled casts and tribes. Children of the debtor book after the cattle of the master while womenfolk work as domestic servants. But in spite of such services by the entire family, only the interest on the loan is remitted so far as the account book of the master is concerned.[18]

In Maharashtra, extensive borrowing of money for marriages, deaths and festivals, and for repaying government loans, has meant that bonded labour has become a permanent feature. It is more common in districts with a predominantly tribal population. The debtors know neither the current balance nor the interest charged and continue to be exploited, even over generations. A substantial proportion are bonded from childhood.[19]

Bhil debtors are in the power of the Gujar landlords.[20] In the tribal areas of Madhya Pradesh, agreements between debtors and creditors for paying off the debt by service are common and one finds sons working in repayment of petty loans taken out by their fathers.[21]

In Karnataka, a *Jeeta* (bonded labourer) serves his master for the petty advances he or his guardian has taken and often spends his whole life repaying the interest alone. A disabled *jeeta* servant has to send his son to do the work. Making loans of cash and food grains to labourers in the off-season is an easy way of obtaining bonded labour. In a landless family a boy may start working as a bonded labourer from the age of about 8.[21]

In Orissa, continuing indebtedness, reinforced by loans for current consumption at high interest rates from the land-lord-cum-usurer, make debt bondage of sharecroppers and agricultural labourers a feature of rural life.[23] A money-lender reduces the rural poor to the status of sharecroppers on their own land.

A variant of bonded child labour has been reported from the Kalahandi district of Orissa which reflects the dependent relationship between the rich Brahmin landlords and the Gauda (cowherd) tenants and domestic servants. The Brahmin are creditors for the Gauda, who are perennially in need of loans. One common way of clearing the debts is to sell young daughters at the age of 8 to 10 as maidservants to the Brahmin masters-cum-creditors, who then take the responsibility of marrying these girls to boys of appropriate caste when they come of age. Before then, a girl so purchased is engaged in all kinds of household chores and personal services to the members of the master's family. A Gauda family feels lucky if all its girls are thus employed, for they find it an honourable and effective way of having their daughters looked after. This is known as the system of *Gaharen Tokil* (S.L. Srivastava, personal communication).

The eight states which were surveyed for the practice of bonded, labour in 1978, in a research project jointly conducted by the Gandhi Peace Foundation and the National Labour Institute (Marla and Maharaj, 1978) were Andhra Pradesh, Bihar, Gujarat, Karnataka, Madhya Pradesh, Rajasthan, Tamil Nadu, and Uttar Pradesh. The total number of bonded labourers in these states was 21.7 lakh or 6.1 per cent of the 37 million agricultural labourers in these states. In states like Madhya Pradesh, Uttar Pradesh, Gujarat, Rajasthan, and Karnataka the percentage of bonded labourers to total agricultural labourers was much higher than the average, ranging from 7.6 per cent in Karnataka to 11.8 per cent in Madhya Pradesh. It is noteworthy that 84 per cent of bonded labourers were from scheduled castes and tribes.

In several areas fathers over 40 years of age tended to free themselves by deputing their sons into bondage. "In many cases the farmer, who is more interested in extracting the physical labour as intensively as he can, encourages the ageing bonded labourer to free himself by mortgaging his son. By and large, the bonded labour affected families are the constant sources of supply of bonded labour to the farmers for generations" (Marla and Maharaj, 1978, pp. 24-25). Often a man received a patch of land for cultivation by mortgaging his son for a paltry sum. About 21 per cent of bonded labourers in these states, taken together, were below 20 years of age. In Andhra Pradesh 21 per cent of bonded labourers were under 16 years of age, in Karnataka 10.3 per cent belonged to this age group, while in Tamil Nadu 8.7 per cent were form this age group. The case study material shows that, at the time of mortgage entry, a bonded labourer may be as young as 5 or 7 years old. It is well known that many boys customarily enter into bondage at the time of their marriage to repay the debt incurred on the occasion. Such a servant may be known as a "marriage servant," meaning that he has entered into bondage as a result, and at the time, of marriage.

Some features of the system of bonded labour particularly encourage the use of child labour:

(i) The pawning or mortagaging of a by for a paltry sum of money and for some privileges form the master;
(ii) The substitution of compulsory services (in repayment of a loan) by a son's labour;
(iii) The tacit understanding that when one person in a family is a bonded labourer, his wife and children are also expected to work.

With respect to point (iii) it has been reported that in Gujarat, for example, girls do not like to marry a Hali servant because they are thereafter expected to serve in the house of the master. In Palamau, Bihar, the system of intergenerational and family bondage ensures that there is an unbroken supply of bonded labourers for the master., In other areas also, because of persistent debt, many cases of bondage span generations.

According to the National Labour Institute—Gandhi Peace Foundation study, 78 per cent of the cases of bonded labour were of debt bondage. And more than 60 per cent of the bonded labours had mortgaged themselves for an indefinite period. The indicates that the prevalence of bonded labour had a strong foundation that technological innovations in agriculture has not weakened. Indeed, the phenomenon of bonded labour was also prevalent in agriculturally advanced regions.

According to the same study, as many as 13 per cent of the bonded labourers were working for their masters because they belonged to a particular caste or because their family had customary service relations with the master. In such obligatory relationships men, women and children in the household have to render service to the master's household. To reiterate, with the traditional service relationships in which households of barbers, washermen and agricultural labourers, among others, are attached to land-owning households, it is rarely just one member of the household who works for the patron family. Child labour becomes an integral part of such arrangements.

The piece-rate system of wages has also encouraged the use of children as helpers or as fully fledged workers. Thus, in the tea gardens of Assam, where the employment of children below 12 years of age is prohibited by law, girls under 12 years old help their mothers in plucking tea leaves during the flush season, which is every second month. A girl generally prepares the midday meal, and when she carries it to the field for the mother she remains to help, learning to pluck the leaves efficiently in the process. Each worker is paid according to the weight of leaves plucked and a little girl is able to contribute 1 to 5 kg. to her mother's basket every afternoon. As this practice is allowed by the management, future workers are being trained by the women who are currently working for them.[24] The is true of Indian tea gardens generally. On the two gardens for which data were collected by Jain, only 3 per cent of children were going to school, for, as Jain notes, "education did not equip them for working on plantations." Similarly, in the match industry mothers brought with them their 3- to 4-year-old children who contributed to the mother's output and were thereby introduced to the work environment.

The first activity in the making of leaf cigarettes is the plucking of the leaves form which tobacco is to be rolled. The leaves are sorted, made into bundles of a specific size, and then brought by contractor's agents. This work involves not only adults (mostly women) but also children, without whose help the sorting of leaves and tying them in bundles would be a slow and uneconomic process.

In the *bidi* (leaf cigarette) industry children are employed in the workplace where *bidis* are rolled, as well as in homes under the work-at-home plan. Where premises are not provided by the contractors a group of workers rent a workshop, work with the material issued to them and hand over the product to the contractor (or subcontractor). Children between 8 and 12 years of age, and sometimes even those in the 5-8 age group, are employed in these workshops. Where rolling of *bidis* is done under the work-at-home system, the children's contribution is considerable.

Such arrangements also operate in many craft enterprises such as coir making, tailoring and carpet weaving, and in activities such as brick manufacturing. Adult workers who enter contracts or wage employment in manufacturing establishments or households tend to involve children as helping hands or substitutes. It is common for gardeners, domestic servants, sweepers, washermen and farm hands to share their work with their children.

Like piece-work, contract family labour tends to demand effective use of children's work. For example, the Chamar of Western Uttar Pradesh migrate seasonally to Haryana or Punjab villages for wage labour. During the transplanting seasons families rather than individuals migrate, women being indispensable for transplanting operations. A few families of labourers together take a contract to complete the work of transplanting in particular fields. All men, women and children belonging to these households adopt one routine and work hard to finish their section, for such contracts provide additional earnings that last them during the following months.[25]

VII. The Household and Measuring Child Work

The significance of the economic role of the household has been emphasised in much of the preceding discussion of the work roles of children, whether it was with reference to the importance of training in the socialisation process, to bonded labour, to the impact of the wage system, or to the involvement of children in agriculture, handicrafts, contract labour and so on. It would be worth looking at this unit form the point of view of a research strategy to study the work roles of children. The following diagram visualises the household as a residential unit, as a resource-owning unit, and as a unit for employment; it distinguishes between the roles of children in these different contexts.

	Economic Function of Household		
	Residential unit	*Resource-owning unit*	*Employment unit*
Children's work role	Domestic work	"Productive" work	Income-earning work (in home or neighbourhood)

1. Land; livestock; craftsmen's tools.

Farming households whose members do most of the agricultural work, either on their own land or on rented land, and crafts-men who have their own tools come into the category of resource-owning units. Those households owning enough resources to hire labour do not usually depend on their children for farm work but may require their help in the very busy agricultural seasons. In some parts of India, such as in Orissa and Himachal Pradesh, school vacations coincide exactly with harvest time.

By definition a household is a residential unit. The distinction between a resource-owning unit and income-earning unit is not clear-cut, for the same household may work with its own resources and also function as a unit of employment or contract. Residential unit, resource-owning unit and employment or income-earning unit are here notionally separated, for these distinctions are worth taking into account in household surveys concerned with the nature and roles of child work.

1. Domestic Work

Children's contribution to the maintenance of the household is considerable and is also observable in households engaged in various kinds of economic activity. To present one illustration: on plantations where both the parents go out to work, children are expected to share in the household tasks at an early age. What a child does depends on the number of family members in different age groups and the ordinal position of the child. While both male and female children look after their younger siblings, girls start cooking at an early age, and their tasks generally include sweeping, cleaning utensils, fetching water form the tubewell, carrying food to the field and taking an infant sibling to the working mother for feeding. Boys tend the cattle, sell kitchen garden produce, and collect fire wood.

The problem involved in analysing domestic work are well known, but they need to be considered in the context of child work. Economists have analysed the catch-all category of "domestic work" in attempts to demarcate economic and non economic activities clearly.[26] While collection of fuel, fruit and vegetables from the forest, cow dung, etc., is accepted as augmenting the resources of the household, activities such as cooking and minding young babies are not considered to be "gainful." It needs to be kept in mind, however, that by performing indispensable household tasks and by minding younger siblings, a child *indirectly* contributes to the income-earning activity to the household by freeing the mother or older sibling for work in the fields or in the wage sector or he/she relieves the mother who can then do indispensable domestic work. Those who are involved in literacy programmes would accept that this indirect relationship of children's work with adult economic or indispensable domestic activity is recognised by the people.

In one recent time time-disposition study (Jain and Chand, 1979) activities of all family members above 5 years of age in 127) households were recorded, mainly through direct observation. In the analysis of data on children four categories of work were considered: gainful activity, child-care, home production, and school-going activity. In all, data were collected on 114 children form West Bengal and 87 children from Rajasthan. Work participation rates of children for the same regions obtained form the thirty-second round of the National Sample Survey, and also the participation rates from household census data of the project villages, were compared with the participation rates obtained through the time-disposition study. The authors concluded that "enumeration methodology" is not able to capture the work of women or children.

That study raised many important issues regarding the measurement of the economic contribution of women and children. Their research procedures also deserve scrutiny. It is doubtful, as the authors themselves admit, whether collection of time-disposition data can be managed by observation alone. If studies with larger samples are to be planned, the use of observation techniques would be still more difficult. In their research project on the role of women in rice cultivation, being conducted in villages in Tamil Nadu and West Bengal, Mencher and Sardamoni have planned a chart to be filled in by the women themselves recording the duration of their activities.[27] The two scholars have allowed considerable scope for checking by the investigators. Use of such charts, observation and interviewing may be combined for studies of children's use of time.

One of the criticisms of time-disposition studies is that measuring the work of an individual, particularly of a child, in terms of time spent is misleading. One of the questions raised, for example, is whether or not playing with a child should be considered as work. One way round this problem may be weighting the work done by any individual. but then it would be necessary to weight children's work in terms of its indispensability for the household and its indirect contribution to the economic, activity of the household.

2. *Productive Work*

As a resource-owning unit, the household depends upon its children to share in its productive work. In nearly all kinds of agrarian production, there are many activities that can be managed by children; and some of these are specifically regarded as children's work. This is the case not only in farming households but also in those of dairymen and fishermen and of craftsmen and artisans; Children are needed to make the household a viable, production unit and may be viewed as working to provide at least part of their own subsistence. As a saying among the Khasi tribe of Northeast India goes, "Every child brings its own food," meaning that what Nature offers needs to be transformed by the production process to obtain food or marketable items and that a child participates actively in this production process, thereby increasing output.

The problem of weighting children's work would again confront us. Work like grazing the cattle,, channelling water from one field to another, guarding the crops and running errands is time consuming but also essential. Until there is a total transformation of technology most of these tasks will remain.

In the work of craftsmen and artisans, co-operative endeavours make the involvement of children in craft-related activities a necessity. Depending upon the availability of tools and material and the demographic composition of the household, some children may be sent away as apprentices or helpers to .fellow craftsmen. In cottage industries run by entrepreneurs, many children whose hereditary craft is the same are employed. So much of the wage labour in these industries is an extension of the children's, contribution to the household economy.

In the region of the Khasi tribe in north-east India, a village council which owns all the rights of allocation and disposal of communal land and its resources allocates particular coal deposits to households on formal application. In the operations connected with mining, children, mostly boys, have an important role to play. While men do the digging inside the tunnel, boys carry the coal outside. In point of fact, children below 12 years old are preferred because their height permits them to walk inside the tunnel without bending or without much difficulty; they are lithe and do the running about effortlessly. In a village studied by G.B. Panda (personal communication), the village council has made special arrangements for a night school for the boys who work in the coal mines during the day. In regular mines the minimum age of employment is 15.

3. *Income-earning Activities*

Households owning no resources (or whose resources are negligible) engage in various income-gaining activities. For instance, agricultural labourers of certain kinds, sharecroppers, those engaged in making leaf cigarettes, embroidery workers and washermen all work as household units. Children are regular working members, or integral parts, of these units. The study of such units is essential if one is to understand the extent and the value of child labour.

In the households of fishermen in coastal Andhra Pradesh, activities of all members are geared to the operations connected with fishing. At the age of 12 a boy starts accompanying his father. Since the mother is occupied in selling the fish, 10-year-old girls learn to look after the household and 5-year-olds collect firewood (G .B. Panda, personal communication). Puthenkalam has described the involvement of school-going boys in fishing operations in Kerala (Puthenkalam, 1977).

As mentioned earlier the Chamar of Western Uttar. Pradesh migrate seasonally to Haryana or Punjab villages in search of employment. At harvest time only men go, while women and children continue to make ropes. Making ropes is a collective activity requiring the help of children. During the transplanting season when all household members migrate and a few households together contract to, transplant in particular fields, the children's contribution is substantial.

The sending of children to work for wages outside the home is a logical outcome of their activities within the household,. If children can contribute to the household economy by doing work appropriate to their age and are able to do an adult's job at the age of 12 or 13, they can also work on somebody else's field or loom, or be hired to do some other job. Perhaps because children's usefulness is so widely accepted, it facilitates the parent's decision to hire them out to ease the household's economic situation.

However, recognising that fact—which provides a corrective to unwarranted assumptions regarding child labour — should not blind us to the deprivations child wage-workers suffer, the exploitative character of the wage labour market, and the economy in which children are viewed as cheap labour. The study of child labour necessitates an understanding of these social phenomena.

In particular, focusing research on the household can accommodate many different kinds of inquiry and a wide variety of data. In addition, it is relatively easy to reach the individual through the household. However, the household approach may not be able to cover all kinds of child worker, so individuals, peer groups, work-places may be more practicable and promising fields of inquiry. But even here, knowing the family context would add to the richness of our understanding.

VIII. Education and Child Work

It is often assumed that there is a negative correlation between child work and formal education, an increase in school enrolment and attendance being associated with a decrease in child employment. So any extension of educational facilities for children is regarded as an effective remedy against the evil of child labour. Wherever rising school attendance and declining use of child labour appear together, it is difficult to say which is the effect and which the cause. But the high drop-out rates and low attendance rates suggest that children's presence is required elsewhere during school hours.

The case of Kerala is interesting. There the rate of literacy is relatively high, while the rate of children's employment is low. However, many people who know Kerala insist that the relatively low rate of children's employment is due largely to the availability of adults who render children superfluous in the labour market. The higher level of social and political consciousness among the masses, which is characteristic of Kerala, also acts as a deterrent to employing children when adults are available.[28]

It is erroneous to think that for the rural masses (and for the poor especially) education, is an investment towards enhancing earning capacity. Education is undeniably important for rural children, , but fresh thinking about its objectives, contents and methods is necessary. Plans of time schools and ungraded schools are already being implemented in some parts of the country. Informal schools in Tamil Nadu and, ungraded schools in Kerala essentially aim at fighting stagnation and high drop-out rates. Rather than attempt to use education as an instrument for the elimination of child labour we should aim at dying it a more functional content and make its timing and duration flexible to suit the requirements of those for whom it is intended.

So long as education has only a limited value, and so long as children's contributions continue to be essential, perhaps the most practical course would be to restrict the number of hours of work for children, improve their conditions of work, and organise schools with suitable timings and curricula that would give them the most essential ingredients of education within a short time. If we recognise the indispensability of the child's labour contribution and the desirability of education we have to think about how to combine the two.

IX. Conclusion

To conclude, we recapitulate some of the points made regarding possible research on work roles of children, and explicitly state much that was implied in the foregoing pages about appropriate research strategies.

Sections II and III discussed children and their work as depicted in Hindu religious tradition and sacred literature, and the cultural notions regarding the stages of human life, with particular reference to the definition of childhood and its various stages. Cultural phenomena should be seen as reflecting the socio-economic structure of society of earlier periods. The discussion identifies an important research area, illuminating the present with the help of the past, much of which remains to influence current behaviour.

Literature pertaining to slavery, differential, patterns of education and labour, organisation of guilds, relations between powerful and subservient groups, the duties enjoined upon castes at different levels, and so on, can throw much light on the children's status vis-a-vis work in various periods of history. This avenue for understanding the roots of people's attitudes and views may not be confined to Hindu literature; it would also be worth while to tap Islamic sources and those of other religions. Folk literature too may prove to be a rich source of information. Another source for understanding the situation in the late nineteenth and the present century is a special class of literature, known as "literature of the downtrodden". It has the merit of having sprung from poignant life experiences of persons in the lowly communities.

As mentioned earlier, some analyses of macro data have provided useful insights and contributed substantially to our understanding. . It needs to be emphasised, however, that more rigour and sophistication are required in the use of macro data and that this calls for an examination of categories and definitions and also of data collection methods'.

For instance, time-disposition studies can prove an effective tool for understanding the economic roles of children and, for placing them in a comparative framework. But we should try to increase the size of the samples for such studies and develop Improved techniques of observation, interviewing and self-reporting.

Implementation and evaluation of literacy programmes, primary education schemes and tribal boarding schools, etc., are often forced to take account of children's roles and preoccupations, but systematic studies of these roles and preoccupations remain to be undertaken. A few intensive studies of communities engaged in different types of work and with different degrees of economic viability should contribute a great deal here. Percentages and trends in macro analyses can be made more meaningful with the help of such studies. Moreover, they could contribute to an improvement of census categories and of terms used in other large-scale surveys. Such studies should be planned so that they cover the relevant cultural notions, measure the extent, character, and place of the work in the economy and also examine how adults and children view their own and each other's work.

In the wake of well publicised efforts to abolish bonded labour a number of art ides and reports, depicting the conditions of various kinds of bondage, have appeared. Although not specifically , focused on children, an indirect understanding of the compulsions under which children work as bonded labour can be obtained through these studies. The most common type is debt bondage, which often eludes legal measures designed to abolish it. It would be useful to undertake intensive studies of bonded labour focusing on children and bringing out the economic and social compulsions which lie at the root of the phenomenon of bonded child labour and the way children are made the target of the selfishness of money-lenders and landlords.

Employment of young boys and girls as attached labour, often as all-purpose servants, is also worth studying, as is domestic child labour in small towns and cities. These are sensitive areas of inquiry and would involve considerable tact and skill. A survey can give an idea of the age groups from which domestic servants are recruited, while a few representative cases of children working as domestic helps in households at different socio-economic.levels should give a fairly clear picture of this category of child worker.

After agriculture, cottage industries probably constitute the largest sector employing children. Because of deception of various kinds and the employment of children as apprentices and in home-based units, the statistics that would give a correct idea, of the dimensions of the problem are not easy to collect. But even where statistics exist, we have scanty knowledge of the homes of these children, their living conditions, their traditional occupations and the processes of socialisation they have undergone, the expectations of their parents from them, and opportunities for formal education they have had. Nor do we know much about the patterns of apprenticeship and the links between domestic units and contractors, middlemen or semi-organised establishments, i.e. about the mechanics of exploitation in many of these industries. For such studies it would be necessary to take up particular units, localities or communities for research.

Many types of work in small-scale industries and handicrafts have harmful effects on the health and growth of children engaged in them for long hours. While also affecting adults, these hazards are much greater for growing children. Risks to attaining a normal stature and posture and retaining normal eyesight are characteristic of many kinds of work in which children are required to sit and work, straining their eyes, for long hours. Tuberculosis is associated with the making of leaf cigarettes. This is an industry, like those dealing with mica, fireworks, matches, etc., with clearly harmful effects. A few incisive studies of the effects on children's health, nutrition and growth of certain types of work and their environment would fill a serious gap in our knowledge by removing vague notions and by making the association of various factors clear.

Children's multifarious activities help to make a household a relatively viable unit of production or give it a subsistence income in the case of marginal farmers, agricultural labourers, construction workers, and so on. It would be particularly interesting to study the migrant labour engaged on the construction of roads and buildings and in agricultural operations.

It is being increasingly realised that improvement in the welfare of small children and women should be attempted simultaneously. Research on child work roles, and an assessment of their contribution in terms of time and actual inputs, may be efficiently organised by combining studies of children and women. Both these categories of labour often work without wages, their contribution is generally not formally recognised, children act as substitutes for mothers at home, and both pose a problem for the definitions of gainful work and workers. Moreover, the work of both needs to be viewed in their total setting and hence calls for a household approach to research in many situations. This strategy may also be advantageous for enabling, a researcher to observe and interact with the people without having to single out a particular age group for exclusive attention from the beginning. An understanding of the attitudes of elders towards children and their work will also be facilitated by focusing on both women and children'.

This chapter does not advocate use of any particular source of data, nor of any one approach to the exclusion of others. It cautions that, in this complex area of inquiry, there are chances that some serious biases may creep in and distort our view; indicates the relevance of cultural notions, even for assessing the structural socio-economic conditions that provide the basic context for children's participation in economic activity; looks at some available data on child work in India; and offers a few suggestions on developing research strategies. In other words, what is advocated is to look for deeper causes so as to grasp the nature and magnitude of children's economic contribution, and to understand the economic and cultural causes of this phenomenon. There is a need to evolve research strategies which ensure that reality does not elude us.

ANNEX

The following terms are used with reference to child activities, roles and status in different contexts.

Arbhaka: for a new-born child.

Shishu: for a child of a few months to a year or so. It is also used to denote a child before the ceremony of first solid food giving which is generally performed at the age of 6 months to 8 or 9 months. In another source, *shishu* refers to a child under 8 years.

Bala: under 5 years. It is also used to denote a child before the performance of the tonsure ceremony... It is commonly used as a general term to refer to non-adult status.

Poganda: from the fifth to the end of ninth year, or until the sixteenth year.

Kishora: 10 to 16 or 11 to 16 years. Its feminine form is" *kishori*.

Kumara: this term is used to denote — a boy before his *upanayana*, or initiation into the learning of sacred knowledge, has been performed... Its application in this sense is restricted. *Kumara* is generally used in the sense of a minor in law. It is also used to denote an unmarried person and in a slightly distorted or interpolated form the term is also present in the regional languages. Culturally speaking, marriage confers adulthood on a person. For a girl the term is *kumari*.

It is an interesting fact that in the most northeasterly corner of India, a community known as Ramos follows a system of clear-cut distinctions in referring to persons belonging to different age groups. To quote Dhasmana: "As the children grow up they are addressed according to their age group. Children up to the age of 3 years are called *anga*. A group of children of this age group are addressed as *anga kiding*. Children between 4 to 9 years are called as *home*. Children of this age group play in the villages during the day time and wait eagerly for the return of their. parents in the evening. After they attain the age of 9 or 10 they are separated in their nomenclature and activities. The boys between. 9 to 14 are called *yapa*. They help their parents in wood cutting and other agricultural jobs. The girls, of this age group are called *Nyimum*. They look after children in the house, bring water from the water point and prepare food. The boys of the age group of 14 years to 19 or more are called *Ami mitur*. A young boy is addressed as *Ami* or *Mitur* until his fortieth year. After the attainment of boyhood a boy begins to learn the intricacies of agriculture, fishing and hunting. For some time he is an understudy to some experienced person like his father, uncle or an elder brother".[29]

Collection of terms denoting different ages and age groups, and the meanings and references implicit in them, for various Indian languages should be a fruitful area of study.

NOTES

1. S.C. Dube, *Indian village* (London, Routlege and Kegan Paul, 1955), p. 149.
2. A culmination of such beliefs is found in the story of Abhimanyu, who figures in the epic of Mahabharata. It shows that a child in the womb is capable of absorbing even systematic knowledge. While Subhadra, the mother, was being given an explanation of the Chakravyuha (an intricate army formation, impenetrable to an enemy) by her husband, Abhimanyu, the child in the womb, was listening intently. Unfortunately, midway through the narration, Subhadra fell asleep and the husband stopped the narration. Abhimanyu could learn only how to enter the *Chakravyuha* and not how to come out of it. He grew up with this incomplete knowledge which eventually became the cause of his death at the age of 16. Like a true warrior he entered the *Chakravyuha* arranged by the enemy and fought bravely till he penetrated it. But not knowing how to get out, he found himself helpless and was killed.
3. B. Saraswati, *Pottery Making Cultures and Indian Civilisation* (New Delhi, Abhinav Publications, 1978).
4. S.C. Dube, *The Kumar* (Lucknow, Universal Publishers, 1951), pp. 86-87.
5. K. Thusu, *The Dhurwa of Bastar* (Calcutta, Anthropological Survey of India, 1965).
6. G. Shah, *Socio-economic Conditions of Chodras: A Restudy*, (Surat, Centre for Social Studies, 1977).
7. T.B. Naik, M.J. Hazari, and G.P. Pandya, *The Kolghas of Gujarat: A socio-economic study and a development Plan* (Tribal Research and Training Institute, 1979).
8. S.L. Doshi, *Bhils* (New Delhi, Sterling Publishers, 1971).
9. D.L.P. Rao, *An Analysis of Kinship, Economy and Religion of Jatapus—A scheduled tribe in Andhra Pradesh*, unpublished Ph.D. disseration, Andhra University, 1970.
10. D.G. Danda, *Among the Dimasa of Assam: An ethnographic study* (New Delhi, Sterling Publishers, 1978).
11. C. von Fürer-Haimendorf, *The Gonds of Andhra Pradesh* (Bombay, Vikas Publishing House, 1979).
12. For example, S.C. Dube, 1955, *op. cit.*; A.R. Kutty: *Marriage and Kinship in an Island Society* (Delhi, National Publishing House, 1972); M.N. Srinivas: *The Remembered Village* (Delhi, Oxford University Press, 1976).
13. M. Mathew, *Women workers in the unorganised sector of coir industry in Kerala* sponsored by ICSSR (Kottayam, 1989). Indian Institute for Regional Development Studies.
14. S. Jetley, *Impact of Development on Rural Women: A Case Study from Western UP*, sponsored by ICSSR (Banaras Hindu University, 1979).
15. The industries, some of which are run on both a factory and cottage industry basis, engaging child workers in sizeable numbers include: *bidi* (leaf cigarette) making; weaving (cotton, silk, wool); embroidery; carpet weaving; hand block printing; clay modelling; pottery; candle manufacturing leather tanning and shoe making; coir making; rope making; match industry; mica; shellac; toy making; button making; bamboo work; envelope making; horn industry; cotton ginning; cleaning and pressing; bleaching and printing; and brick manufacturing.
16. I am grateful to my husband, Professor S.C. Dube, currently ICSSR National Fellow at the Institute of Educational Planning and Administration, New Delhi, who was then vice chancellor,

University of Jammu, for providing me with this information. The programme on non-formal education of the University had included, as an essential element, acquiring of basic information about the rural population in the state.

17. A.N. Das, "Of human bondage," in *Mainstream,* 1976, No. 35.
18. K. Chaudhuri, "Bonded labour," in *Economic and Political Weekly* 1976, No. 10.
19. H. Dalvi, "Maharashtra: Bonded labour continues," in *Economic and Political Weekly,* 1977, No. 22.
20. S.D. Kulkarni, "Over a century of tyranny," *Economic and Political Weekly,* 1977, No. 10.
21. R.P.S. Bhonwal, "Bonded labour," *Social Welfare,* 1976, No. 5.
22. M. Tippashetti, "Jeeta system and the law," *Social Welfare,* 12976, Nos. 5-6.
23. G. Iyer and A.N. Das, "Orissa: A case study of poverty and bondage," *National Labour Institute Bulletin,* 1976, No. 5.
24. I am grateful to Shobhita Jain, Jawaharlal Nehru University, for preparing a note on children's contribution to the household economy of the plantation workers in Assam on the basis of her data collected for a doctoral thesis under preparation.
25. This is based on a discussion with Mukul Dube of his data on migrant labour from Western Uttar Pradesh villages collected for a doctoral thesis under preparation.
26. For example, Bardhan divided domestic work into the following categories:

    (i) Household chores like shopping, food processing and cooking, washing and cleaning, child-care and attending the sick and the old in the household;

    (ii) Social and ceremonial activities;

    (iii) Collection of 'free" goods (wild fruits, vegetables, fish, small game, cowdung, firewood, grass, etc), etching drinking water, and work on garden produce (to the extent that this is not reported as work on own farm);

    (iv) Production, repair and maintenance of consumer durables for household use (sewing garments, taking care of live-stock in domestic use, improving and repairing own houses, etc.);

    (v) Involuntary idleness not reported in any other time disposition category.

    Activities (iii) and (iv) should be regarded as gainful activities; although Bardhan cautioned that some activities in (i) might also be gainful. Quoted by D. Jain and M. Chand: *Field Investigation of Rural Households: Especially their time disposition* Vol. II and III, (New Delhi, Institute of Social Studies, 1979.
27. The research project is financed by the ICSSR and is located in the Indian Statistical Institute, New Delhi.
28. My attention was drawn to this interpretation by Saradamani of the Indian Statistical Institute, New Delhi.
29. M.M. Dhasmana, *Sociology of the Ramos of Arunachal Pradesh,* Ph.D. thesis, Gauhati University, 1978.

9

CHILD LABOUR IN INDIA: A SILENT CONSPIRACY

"My salutes, to thee, oh poverty!
I am indeed blessed by your grace
I can see the whole world;
but no one sees me" ... Vedas
"... they are hanging on a thin string of survival".

One does not need to elaborate criteria, cunning measurement or probing analysis to recognise raw child labour and to understand its antecedents. This indeed much that is transparent about misery and exploitation of child labour[1]. However, not everything about child is quite so simple. Even the identification of the child labour and the diagnosis of child labour may be far from obvious when we move away from the extreme and raw poverty[2]. Furthermore, to construct an overall picture, it is necessary to go well beyond identifying the child labour which is itself a big challenge. Finally, and most importantly, the causation of child labour raises questions that are not easily answered.[3]

This paper is concerned with some practical approaches and field actions. Its main focus is on bringing out through action case studies the main issues which NGOs ought to consider while tackling the problem of child labour. The paper contains brief reports on action study efforts carried out by Centre for Concern for Child Labour (CCECL).

ACTION CASE STUDY-I

Migrant Tribal Children in Carpet Weaving in Mirzapur

I am Sama. My age is 10 years and I am from Palamu (Bihar). I came here (Mirzapur district) three months back. My master has paid Rs 300 to my father through a recruiting agent. I was promised Rs. 200 per month salary with four to five hours of work. But I get up at 5 a.m. and work till sunset. There is a lunch break hardly for half/an hour. In the morning I do not get enough time even to go to toilet. I have some stomach trouble since the last two months but the master hurls all sorts of abuses at me and says the 'job' is to be completed as he has to meet an export order.

At home we are five brothers and sisters. My father has no land and he works for a rich farmer. But he does not get enough to feed us all. I want to get away from here but how can I? The master will beat me. He even does bad act with young boys and I am afraid one night he may ... I get only Rs. 50 in a month and my master says he has already paid the money to my father. I have learnt to smoke a *bidi* here only.

The contractor in the same village has the following to say: "Children's small and nimble fingers are good and fast at tying tight knots. I have to pay less to them. I export my carpets to foreign countries."

CCFCL initiated action against this exploitation by understanding the export connection and child abuse. Major observations of our action study are (1) Carpet master weaver who acts as a middle man or a contractor, finds children of tender ages of eight to 12, very useful for the weaving work (2) Though the carpet export has increased from Rs. 90 crore per year to Rs. 120 crore in the last 10 years, the, conditions of working children have been deteriorating. (3) Trade unions are not actively associated with the various aspects of employment of children. However, journalists are helpful in exposing the exploitation of working children. (This is evident from the famous Palamu Bonded Children case which was first taken up by newspapers and subsequently by the Supreme Court of India).

(4) The local authorities and lower level of functionaries are not sensitive to children's issue and working children's problems with the result that the government schemes are not implemented well.

Some of the implications of these findings would be: (a) the schemes for child labour cannot be implemented well if protective machinery is not evolved, and (b) there is a need to break the myth of nimble finger theory and develop appropriate technology for carpet weaving.

ACTION CASE STUDY-II

Child Labour in Lock-making Industry of Aligarh Uttar Pradesh

The following observations were made by an interdisciplinary team consisting of one doctor, one lawyer and one social activist, about the child labour in the lock industry of Aligarh: (1) Majority of the lock-making children are short and thin compared to the non-working children of the same age. Most of them complained of ear trouble. (2) Most of these children belong to one particular minority community in which large number of helpless divorced women seem to depend on children's income. (3) The working hours of the children are from 7 a.m. to 6 p.m., about 60 to 65 hours a week. (4) The children who are employed mainly as contract workers, face numerous psychological problems. They also complain of fatigue, headache, ear trouble, back pain and depression as well as of accidents and injuries (there is no formal training for these children.) Since the action study is still going on we cannot give any final assessment but we can definitely state that the child labour in this industry is badly exploited. Our study shows that most children want to study further. They also want some place for entertainment

ACTION CASE STUDY-III

Nepali Child Workers in Delhi

This action study was carried out in Delhi and in the bordering areas of Nepal touching India from where the children come to Delhi. These children work as domestic servants (mainly girls) or as helpers in restaurants. Our study shows that: (1) Most of these Nepali migrants workers are in the eight to 10 years age group. (2) They enter India walking through the tough path near Pithoragarh, Uttar Pradesh and Raxsoul (Bihar). (3) These children work form 5 a.m. to 10 p.m. with some free time in the afternoon. (4) Many of these children are brought to India by their distant relatives, while some are also brought by pimps and small time racketeers wanting commission. (5) Most of them are from farmers' families who cannot afford to feed them. (6) These children are many times assaulted sexually.

An important implication of these findings is that efforts should be made for the upliftment of the families from which these labourers come. Also, there must be some procedure to record the details of migrant Nepali children to India to check their exploitation and abuse.

Our action case studies discussed above are quite revealing. It seems that rural child workers and the children working in families are almost completely neglected by policy and law makers and consequently they are exploited very badly.

The studies also show that there is no regular official channel for disseminating information to the employer and children regarding regulations concerning employment of children. The list of legal requirements, to be observed by an employer when employing children, is not publicised on television or radio - the two most powerful media totally controlled by the government. The general public is not aware of children's right let alone rights of child labour. The most common infringement of the law is the failure to notify the local authority when a child is employed.

Unfortunately, trade unions who can contribute substantially towards improving the conditions of child labour, have not shown much interest to understand this phenomenon as they are more busy in increasing perquisites and facilities of the workers in the small organised sector. The unorganised sector is almost left out by them. It is also important to note that there is no system of annual wage revision for the child workers. The most common method for increasing the income level is by increasing the working hours. There are no arrangements for systematic skill training, and there is neither any scope for them to learn new higher skills in the same work.

CCFCL Approach

The CCFCL directly works with issues of exploitation of child labour. Though

CCFCL a non-governmental organisation, was formally established in 1985, the abuse of children has for many years been of concern to CCFCL members in their individual capacity. The long-term goal of CCFCL is to work towards the elimination of child labour by the present author year 2001 AD. The present programmes of CCFCL include (1) initiating practical action programmes to improve the condition of working children; (2) Improving health, recreational and educational provisions for child labour; (3) Raising public awareness by providing information on child labour problems to the interested social action groups or authorities; (4) Creating public opinion and acting as a pressure group for child labour; (5) Promoting child labour welfare programmes among employers, trade unions and voluntary organisations; (6) Demanding and agitating for the promotion of occupational safety and health at the work places where children work; (7) Demanding strict enforcement of laws and regulations pertaining to child labour; and (8) canvassing with the policy makers for rectification of the Minimum Age Convention, 1973 (No. 138).

CCFCL is deeply influenced by ILOs convention No. 138 in setting its programme objectives. In 1985, CCFCL demanded appointment of a Protector General of child labour in India and also urged that a special clause be included in all the trade agreements to prohibit the use of child labour in export items.

The limited but valuable experience of the action programmes have taught CCFCL that some of the important measures that have been taken to abolish child labour are loan facilities for production inputs to marginalised families, maintenance allowances to helpless widows or divorced women, subsidised non-formal education and infrastructure for health care and skill formation. Child labour is a major issue for our country as these labourers are the most exploited lot. Trade unions must therefore come out strongly in favour of abolishing child labour in a time-bound fashion.

REFERENCES

1. Amartya Sen, *Poverty and Famines, An Essay on Entitlement and Deprivation* (Oxford University Press, 1982).
2. Gerry Rodgers and Guy Standing, *Child Work, Poverty and Under-development* (ILO, Geneva, 1981).
3. Gangrade and Gathia, *Women and Child Workers in the Unorgnised Sector,* (Concept, New Delhi, 1983).
4. Elias Mondelievich, *Children at Work* (ILO Office, Geneva, 1980).

Following books were also consulted to check field observations:

1. *Child Labour in India,* S. Banerjee.
2. *Newsweek,* January 24, 1983.
3. *Women Workers in the Unorganised Sector,* Nirmada Bannerjee, 1985.
4. *Children in India,* Alfred de Souza, 1979.
5. *Towards a Peoples Anthropology,* Fei Hsiao Tung, 1981.

6. *Child Labour and Health,* Usha S. Naidu and K.R. Kapadia, 1985.
7. *Proceedings of National Seminar of Child and the Law,* NIPCED, 1982.
8. *Child Labour: A Yhreat to Health and Development,* P.M. Shah, 1985.
9. *All Work and no Play: Child Labour Today;* Trade Union Congress.
10. *World Development Reports,* World Bank.
11. *The State of the World's Children,* UNICEF.
12. *Health for All: An Alternative Strategy;* ICSSR, ICMR, 1981.

10

TRADITIONS RELATING TO PROTECTION OF CHILDREN AGAINST EXPLOITATION

Universally, it is a realised and accepted fact that protection of children against exploitation is essential to their mental and physical development. The minimum age for employment of a child varies from place to place and nature of work. The problem of child labour and the protection of children from exploitation is visualised and treated in different ways in different countries. It is pertinent to discuss some such countries in the following pages.

Child Labour in England

The increase of population has been the main factor for child labour. It compelled parents to send their children to do some profitable work. In 1536, the Government of England enacted a legislation for the employment of poor children in agriculture or other crafts, between the ages 5 to 14 years.

Another important law was enacted in 1563. It was known as statute of Apprentices. The main aim was to give facilities for the training of village artisans and to provide efficiency to agricultural labourers; to fix the rates of the wages and also to make a complete industrial code to fulfil the needs of the day. Under the said law a healthy person between the ages of 12 and 60, who was not employed any where, was liable to agriculture labour, unless he had a certain amount of property. For the security of the continuation of the employment it was necessary under this Act that employment should not be made less than for a year and a notice of three months' duration was also required to terminate the services. The said Act was also applied for the purpose of training and thus apprenticeship became compulsory for all employment. The minimum age of entrance into the training was fixed at 7 years.

During the reign of Elizabeth I, in 1601, Legislation emphasised on the parents the duty to look after their children. But if the parents could not support their children, they could practise as apprentices under a local official appointed as the overseer of the poor.

During the seventeenth century many proposals were chalked out to solve the problem of poor children. Thomas Firmin, a leading and successful businessman, pondered over the possibility of achieving profit from the employment of poor children. In view of this profit he opened a combination of school, factory, whole-sale warehouse, and retail shops for the children who had attained the age of 3 and wanted to learn how to read and spin.

William III empowered the Board of Trade to make enquiry into the conditions of poor children in the year 1967. John Locke, the political philosopher and Lord Hales were appointed the members of the commission to study and to make recommendations for the betterment of poor children's conditions. In the recommendations of John Locke the children and their parents were to be given free meals for their work.

The importance of child labour was recognised when the Industrial Revolution brought new techniques in the field of manufacture of Textiles. Webbs describes:

> High up in the lonely valleys of Lancashire and Yorkshire, mills were built by the side of rushing streams, where the new machines could be driven by water power, and needed only "tending" by docile fingers, and bodies small enough to creep under the frames. The necessary operatives had to be brought from somewhere, and the cheapest source was the workshouse.... Parish officers accordingly found themselves impotuned by the agents... to recruit their staffs, who without asking any premium, carried off the children literally by cart loads, taking even infants three or four years old.... (In one such) contract between a London parish and a Lancashire manufacturer, the manufacturer undertook to receive one idiot with every twenty sound children.

Children, who were brought to the agents of mill owners, were inspected for their physical conditions. The children, selected, were taken to the mills where they were apprenticed for eight or nine years almost in slavery.

Those poor parents who had no sufficient income, were in need of the earnings of their children. As the evils of the factory system were developing in Lancashire, a resolution was passed by the magistrates in Manchester in 1784 to attract attention towards the evils. A Board of Health was set up in Manchester in 1795 to investigate the conditions of children working in factories. The said Board reported that the working conditions of children were injurious and dangerous to their health, because they got no moral and religious education or instructions as they had to work for long hours.

A Bill was introduced by a successful Cotton Spinner, Sir Robert Peel, relating to the children working in the Mills. This Bill took the form of law as "The Health and Morals of Apprentices Act," on December 2, 1802. The main provisions of this Act were: the apprentices in cotton and woollen mills, were not allowed to work at night and they were required to work only for 12 hours daily. The children up to the age of nine years were not allowed to work in factories. Provisions for sanitation, ventilation, elementary education, religious services, etc., were made under the same Act. For inspection of mills, a provision for the appointment of a clergyman and a magistrate was made by this Act, but this provision was not enforced. As this Act was not applicable to the employment of free children, many mill owners avoided the provisions of this Act cunningly by employing them.

The Act of 1802 was not effective. It merely touched the fringe of the problem. The wages of adult workers were insufficient to carry out the needs of their family without the help of their children's income. Further if the children were treated rudely, it was impossible for their parents to object to this treatment because their own employment wee also in the hands of the same employers. Sir Robert Peel introduced a bill relating to the children's work. An Investigation Committee was appointed to investigate child labour's conditions. Robert Owen worked for the imposition of a definite restriction in all types of factories.

The law was amended in 1819 to extend its application to children hired directly from their parents, but this Act applied only to the cotton mills. Children below nine years of age of 16 years were required to work only for 12 hours a day. They were prohibited to work at night *i.e.*, between 8 p.m. and 5 a.m. An interval of one and a half hours was also provided for meals.

The enforcement of this Act was also inadequate and the provisions of this Act were very cunningly avoided. However, the struggle for factory legislation continued and the law was only amended in details by the Acts in 1820, 1825 and 1830. Ultimately the Act of 1831 repealed the older Act. This Act of 1831 was applied only to the cotton factories. This Act limited the work of young persons, below the age of 18 years, to 12 hours on week days and 9 hours on Sundays. The Act also prohibited young persons under 21 years to work in the night.

The attempts of persons interested to secure a ten hours day were not immediately effective. However, some improvement was made, when the Factory Act of 1833 was passed by the Parliament. This Act was the first effective attempt as it established an inspectorate to enforce its provisions. The Act provided for the appointment of four factory inspectors who were not connected with the locality in which factories were situated. The inspectors were employed and paid by the Government and were empowered to impose fines on manufactures who broke the law. This Act applied to all textile mills except silk mills. The children below 13 years were required to work only for 9 hours a day and 48 hours a week. The night work between 8.30 p.m. and 5.30 a.m. was prohibited to young persons below 20 years. Provision for education was made which required that every child-worker should attend school for atleast two hours a day. According to this Act, two whole and eight half holidays were to be allowed in a year. Thus, the principles which were embodied by this Act, became the foundation stone of factory legislation for a long period and this was regarded as a model of factory legislation in other countries.

The employment of women and girls under ground and the employment of boys under 10 years in the pits were prohibited by the Mines Regulation Act which was passed in 1842 as an attempt to correct conditions reported by the Children's employment commission, which found children as young as 4 years working in the mines. They opened and shut the doors that guided the drift of air through the mines and filled the wagons when the men had cut and dug the coal. The children also worked as "pushers" or "hurriers" to push the trucks along from the workers at the base of the shaft.[1] The Commission was also shocked when it came to know that 8 to 9 years was the traditional age of initial employment in the mines.

In 1844, a Factory Act was passed because the earlier Act of 1833 was found imperfect. This Act was applied to all textile establishments in which machinery was used. The Act reduced the minimum age for entering in labour-fields to 8 years, whereas it was 9 years under the previous Acts. This Act provided that children between 8 and 13 years could not be employed for more than 6½ hours per day with 3 hours at school. The Act fixed the working hours for young persons between 13 and 18 years at 12 hours a day and 69 hours a week. The powers of inspectors were extended, but the power to inflict fines was taken away from inspectors. The owners who violated the provisions of the Act were to be punished by the local magistrate.

The struggle for a ten hours day also continued at this time. Therefore, Ten Hours day law was finally passed in 1847. This Act provided the maximum hours of work for women and young persons in the textile industries *i.e.*, 58 hours a week and 10 hours a day with part holiday on Saturday. The relay system became possible under the new Act as the factory day extended over a period of 15 hours from 5.30 a.m. to 8.30 p.m. using the shift system. Due to this fact it was very hard to determine whether the provisions of the Act were followed. In fact the law was avoided in many factories.

To remove the defect in the Act of 1847, another Act was passed in 1850, which limited the working day to the hours between 6 a.m. and 6 p.m. in summer and 7 a.m. and 7 p.m. in winter. Hours of work for young persons and women were provided in this Act. Later on, regulations were extended to children in 1853. The Act of 1850 was the result of complete surrender of the principle of *Laissez Fair* in respect of textile factories. In 1850, a system of inspection of mines was introduced under the Mines Act, 1842.

Further legislation was made after several years. During this period, the employers unsuccessfully attempted to get the repeal of Factory Laws. Working conditions in the establishment, where dyeing, bleaching and printing were carried on, were regulated by the Act in 1860 and 1870. In the years 1862-66, a Royal Commission which was established to investigate the working conditions in non-textile industries and textile establishments in which power driven machinery was not used, pointed out the presence of child labour, excessive hours and unhealthy conditions in the establishments. The legislation was made to remove the evils which were pointed out by the Royal Commission. In 1864, several non-textile industries came under the jurisdiction of the Factory Act.

In 1867, two important Acts were passed. First was the Factories Acts Extension Act which extended the application of the existing law to a number of industries. The second one was the Workshops' Regulation Act which made a distinction between a factory and workshop. Under this Act, a workshop was a place other than a factory in which in handicraft was carried on by any child, young persons, or women, to which the employer had access and of which he had control. Regulations which were made under this Act, were similar to the factories. However, the regulations were applied only to the places in which less than 50 persons were employed or which did not come under the definition of factories.

Again, in 1874 a few changes were made in law by passing the Factories Act of 1874 which applied to textile industries. Working hours for women and young persons were limited to 10 hours a day and 56½ hours a week. The overtime work was not allowed under this Act.

Then, one of the effective measures to limit the incidence of child labour was taken in 1876 when elementary education was made compulsory upto the age of 10 and again, provisions for free education were introduced in 1891. Further in 1899 school attendance upto the age of 12 was required.

A demand for codification arose as there were various extensions of the factory legislation at this time. As a result, the Factory and Workshops Act was passed in 1878. Under this Act all the industrial establishments were classified into five classes, namely, Textile factories; non-textile factories workshops; workshops in which neither children nor young persons were employed and domestic workshop in which only family members were employed. According to this Act, distinction between factory and a workshop was based not upon the number of persons but upon the use and non use of machinery which was driven by power.

In Britain, there were two main features of labour legislation from this time of 1914. Firstly, state protection was given to the individuals employed in gainful occupations; and, secondly, various special measures were taken to regulate the conditions of labour in hazardous trades. In 1883, rules were made under the Factory Act to regulate certain other types of works, for instance, in white lead works and bake houses. Again, in 1889 rules were made to repress the moisture in Cotton Cloth Mills. In the same year the Act was extended in its application to theatrical entertainments. In 1891, the whole subject matter was strongly reviewed by an important Act known as the Factory and Workshop Act. Under this Act minimum age for admission to employment in the factories was fixed at eleven. The power to inspect the sanitary conditions was taken from inspectors and given to local authorities. In 1895 the children below 14 years were not allowed to work at night. Their working hours were also reduced to 30 hours a week. The provisions for occupational diseases were made only in 1896.

In 1901, the Factory and Workshops Act was codified, which was a model for further development in this field. By this Act of 1901, children below 12 years of age were not allowed to work in factory or workshops. The young persons under 16 years were required to have a certificate of physical fitness. Ten hours a day prevailed in non-textile industries. Under this Act there were no holidays, but this act provided for spreading over of work. Regulations, under these Acts, applied to children between the ages of 12 and 14, to young persons between the ages of 14 and 18 years and to women above 18 years. But the provisions relating to sanitation and safety were applicable to all workers.

In the field of Coal Mines, the whole law was codified in 1911 by an Act known as Coal Mines Regulation Act. This Act forbade the employment of children and women underground. The Act of 1919 regulated the hours of underground work at 7 per shift.

The hours of work of women and young persons (persons over compulsory school leaving age, but not yet eighteen) were strictly controlled by the Employment of Women, Young Persons and Children's Act of 1920. The Children and Young Persons Act, 1933. The Hours of Employment (Convention) Act, 1936.

A consolidated Act of all the existing laws came into force on July 1, 1938 known as Factories Act of 1937. This Act fixed the working hours for women and young persons at 9 hours per day and 48 hours per week. It was also provided under the Act that the whole period of employment including meal time should not be more than 11 hours a day. The young persons under sixteen were not allowed to work after 6 p.m. and ordinarily they were prohibited from working more than 44 hours a week, unless the Home Secretary permitted in certain circumstances for 48 hours. They were also prohibited to work on overtime or shift work. Then in case of shops, the Shops Act of 1934 allowed the young person to work at 48 hours a week and this Act also regulated their overtime.

In 1944, the education Act was passed which provided that children who were within two years of compulsory school leaving age may be employed. But such employment was subject to very strict regulations. Children below 13 years were not allowed to enter into the labour market. The Act provided that the employment of children under 15 years be limited to two hours a day after school on school days. These working hours were to be fixed between 6 a.m. to 8 p.m. The local authorities were empowered to make exception to this rule and to provide the conditions of employment of children in their respective areas.

In 1946, an Act was passed, known as Coal Nationalisation Act of 1946. Under this Act, National Coal Board was put under the sole responsibility of promoting the safety, health and welfare of the employees.

The provisions of the Factories Act, 1937 were modified by the Factories Act of 1948. Under this Act, factory inspectorate, a part of Factory Department, was wholly responsible for the high standard of safety, health and welfare of the workers. The Act of 1948 regulated the hours of work for young persons aged 16 to 18 years and fixed the working hours for children under 16 at 44 hours a week. The children below 16 were not allowed to work overtime and at night. Under this Act a certificate of physical fitness for work by a surgeon was also required from the person under 16 years.

In England, the Shop Act of 1950 limited the hours for persons under 16 to 44 hours a week and for persons between 16 and 18 to 48 hours a week.

In 1954, by the Mines and Quarries Act, 1954, women were forbidden to work underground in mines. Young persons were also prohibited to work at coal mines. They were only employed when they showed the medical certificate of fitness. Both women and young persons were prohibited by the Act from heavy loads which might cause them injury.

In 1961, the Factories Act of 1961 was passed. The Act requires that a young person should have a certificate of fitness for work in factories issued by the factory doctors within seven days of his employment.[2] In addition to this provision, many specific measures are provided under the Act to safeguard the health of women and young persons by forbidding them from undertaking certain hazardous works, for example, cleaning the moving machinery.[3] They were also prohibited to do certain processes, such as, lead smelting, jute works and paint and colour manufacture. They were further required not to do dangerous processes, including asbestos manufacture, blasting operations and chromium plating. Hours of work for an employment in which the young persons and women can be employed, are also restricted to 48 hours a week. In case of persons under sixteen, work-hours were fixed at 44 hours a week.[4]

The Act also lays down that young persons and women cannot be allowed or required to work for more than 9 hours a day excluding the breaks. Further, they are required to work between 7 a.m. to 8 p.m., but persons under sixteen must end their work at 6 p.m. The Act provides that the spell of work must not exceed four and a half hours or five hours if ten minute interval is provided during the course of the spell. These provisions are applicable to all women and young persons employed in a factory. The Act also prevents the employer from using a shift system in view of the convenience of women who have domestic commitments as well as jobs.

The restrictions under Section 86 are provided for normal working hours and they are subject to rules about overtime contained in Sections 89 and 90. The maximum hours of overtime allowed under the Act are 6 hours a week, or 100 hours in any year. The actual period of work on any one day must not be more than 10 hours or the period of employment in one day must not be more than 12 hours including breaks. Further, employees should not be required to start work before 7 a.m. (as in normal working hours), but can continue until 9 p.m. or 1 pm. on Saturdays. On Sundays no one is allowed to work. The Secretary of State is empowered, under the Act, to make exemption from these provisions and to allow double day shifts.

The male young persons over 16 years may be employed on a round the clock shift system in case there is continuous process of manufacture in the establishment, but their total hours of work and hours of night work are controlled.

It is recommended by the Report on Hours of Employment of Women and Young Persons that some changes in these rules should be made, but this report does not suggest that limitations on hours and night work should be plentiful.

Again, the Children and Young Persons Act, 1963 made a general prohibition of the children more than two years below of school leaving age and laid down that bye-laws may allow the employment of such children by their parents or guardians in light agricultural or horticultural work.

In addition, the children and Young Persons Acts 1933 and 1963 do not permit the employment of children under 16 in entertainment except if the child has a licence issued by the local authority where he resides. Such licence can only be granted on condition that child's health and education do not suffer.

At present, the statutory minimum school leaving age is sixteen.[5] The legislation prohibited the employment of children who had no completed the school leaving age in any industrial establishment. Young persons and women are prohibited to work underground in mines and in certain other hazardous occupations, for example, lead manufacturing process. The national legislation limits the maximum permitted hours of work for women over 18 and young persons between 16 and 18 at 48 hours a week and 10 hours a day (9 hours a day for six day week worker) in the premises to which Factories Act is applicable. Women and young persons are not allowed at night by the national legislation.

Child Labour in America

One of the main features of colonial America was wide spread indenture. The indenture was a procedure laid down by the country to support dependent children and to guarantee that such children would not become dependent as adult in the lack of sufficient knowledge or habits to earn the means of subsistence. The employers took advantage of this situation and exploited the children as a means of cheap labour.

In Maryland, two indenture laws were enacted in 1638 and in 1793, which defined the liabilities of masters and servants, but these laws were enacted for different causes. The earlier law was enacted for the convenience and profits of the land-lords who were in need of child servants. The other law was passed as destitution grew among children forcing them to become useless members of the society.

The law of 1638 provided the rights and duties of masters and apprentices transported to Maryland for indenture. All male persons under the age of 18 were required to serve the masters until they attained the age of 24, subject to the provisions of contract. The maid servants, excluding slaves, of 12 years old or younger were required to serve for seven years and if she was above 12 years of age, she was to serve for four years. In the end of their bondage, they received something in kind from their masters.

By the law of 1793, the Justices of the Orphan's Court were authorised to cover with bondage, every Orphan child to some manufacture, mariner, mechanic, handicraftsman, or other person, as apprentices. Clothes, food and shelter were provided to the child. In addition, if possible, knowledge of reading, writing, and arithmetic was also provided to the children. The male children were required to gain knowledge of a trade.[6]

The children of very needy parents, illegitimate children and the children belonging to the other State, were also bound by the justices. It was upon parents to choose the master for their children. Such power of binding a child was also given to the trustees of the poor, if the child belonged to an alm house. Some penalty was prescribed if the bound apprentice ran away from his master. If the indentured child was maltreated, he could be removed by justice of Peace.

In Massachusetts, indenture was somewhat different. The Massachusetts Bay colony made it obligatory in 1642 that every dependent child be attached to a family where he would be engaged in an employment so that he would be self-supported. In 1672, it was required of parents to apprentice their children. The stated objectives of these requirements were to provide the child an adequate family home and preparation for work, but in practice, it was not so. Kelso states:[7]

> Cleaning off the account on the treasure's book by a long term indenture, which for practical purposes amounted to a sale of the child with no guarantee of protection, save public indignation, against enslavement and abuse, was the constant effort of the early town authorities.

In New York, the indenture took the form of law only in 1788. The Mayor, recorder, alder-man, or any two of them were authorised to bind a dependent child without the parents consent if he was found begging. The maximum age of indenture was 21 for male and 18 for a female. The disobedient apprentices were sent to the correction-house. It was the duty of the master or mistress to teach the indentured child to read and write.

In 1662, the Rhode Island General Assembly defined the philosophy of such indenture more briefly than other States by saying that it would endeavour to "Employ or put out of service, all such young able persons as are not of sufficient estate to maintain themselves or which in Idleness may be likely to become a charge on or damage to such town."[8]

In Rhode Island, the children, of the parents who were chargeable to the town; or of those who were unable to care for them properly, can be apprenticed like orphan children and children of State supported parents. Boys were apprenticed till they attained the age of 21 and girls till they attained 18 or got married.

With the introduction of machinery in textile mills, employment of children was found as a source of cheap labour. Alexander Hamilton sanctioned the new industries because he thought they would render children more early useful. As Edith Abbott pointed out:[9]

> The introduction of children into our factories was a natural consequence of the colonial attitude toward child labour, of the provisions of the early poor laws, and of philanthropic efforts to prevent children from becoming a public charge, and, above all, of the puritan belief in the virtue in industry and the sins of idleness.

In 1806, the first cotton mill was established by Samuel Slater at Pawtucket, Rhode Island. Samuel Slater employed only children between 7 and 12 years. some of them were taken from alms-house. He used the family system of employment in his mills. Such family system was also used in other States and employers left no stone unturned to attract the family with the greatest number of children.

As there were lack of educational facilities in factories where children were employed, the State took step to control child labour. In 1836, Massachusetts passed a law which made school attendance of 3 months in the preceding year compulsory precondition for permission to employ children below 15. In 1842, both Connecticut and Massachusetts fixed the maximum hours of work for children in cotton and woollen mills. The law was applicable to children under 12 years in Massachusetts and under 14 in Connecticut. In 1860 many States had passed similar legislation which prohibited the employment of children below 10 or 12 in all types of factories.

As a result of civil war, children as young as 7 were employed in the textile mills for long hours. In addition to the employment in factories, such children were similarly employed in other industries, in domestic services, and as telegraph and messenger boys.

The children from Orphanages were also employed in dangerous types of work in glass industries situated in Pennsylvania, Illinois, Ohio, New Jersey, and several other States. These industries were so dangerous that they were called boy destroying industries. Children of very young age were also employed in mines for long hours in small, dark, airless chutes.

The working conditions and reasons for exploiting the children have been very well discussed by Jeremy P. Felt:[10]

> They could help, support needy parents, develop qualities of industry, and avoid the vice of idleness. The leader of society was a self-made man. But the full implications of industrial child labour became evident. Here was no benevolent system of practical education for young people, but a programme of cheap, easily discarded labour that depressed the wages of adults and broke the spirits and bodies of children. Here were children from the age of 6 working in filthy, jam packed tenements operating dangerous machinery, or running about the streets doing everything from selling newspapers and carrying messages to procuring women narcoties.

The statistics relating to the child labour was for the first time included by the United States Census in 1870, which pointed out that there were than three quarters of a million children between 10 to 16 years in the employment and children below 10 years were also in the employment but their number was not known.

Gradually, social reformers and labour unionists aroused public attention against the evils of child labour. In 1886, American Federation of Labour, impelled by the necessity of State protection to children below 14 years by prohibiting all types of their employment. Again in 1889, Mrs. Florence Kelley, a socialist, had delivered a paper on the evils of child labour. In the same year, National Consumes League also roused the public opinion against child labour. Other organisations also took various steps to control the child labour.

By the last decade of the century, some greater protection to children was given by legislation in the Northern States. In 1891, Illinois prohibited the employment of children below 14 in mines. Such prohibition was extended to factories in 1893 which made a provision for inspection to enforce the Law. Such age limitation was extended to commence in 1897.

Similar provision to prohibit children of similar age were made in New York in 1889, but after 1893 children below 16 could not be employed. Such children could only be employed if they could read fluently and write simple sentences legibly. In 1896, it was required of New York manufacturers to have three things before employing a child, namely, a parent's affidavits regarding the age of child, a written statement from a teacher that child had attended regularly a school that provided instruction in reading and writing, etc. and a statement from the Board of Health certifying that the child has completed 14 years.

Notwithstanding these steps to limit the child labour, there were increases in number of employed children in southern States as there were absence of any protective legislation for children.

To investigate child-labour, a committee was appointed by the Association of Neighbourhood Workers on the suggestion of Felix Adler in April 1962. Robert Hunter was appointed the Chairman of this Committee.

The committee very soon collected enough of money to a point Helen Marot as full time investigator. Original object of this committee was to investigate some material so that the State would be forced to appoint a child labour commission. This New York Child Labour Committee was solely responsible for the passing of a law that became the basis for other States to make such type of laws.

In May 1903, Florence Kelley and Jane Addams read a paper on destitute children at the annual meeting of National Conference of Charities and Correction held in Atlanta, Georgia. At the same meeting Murphy read a paper on "Child labour as a national problem." Some weeks later a special committee was appointed by the New York Child Labour Committee. It consisted of W. Baldwin, Florence Kelley, Murphy and Felix Adler. By this an organisation of the National Child Labour Committee came in April 1904.

Thirty persons, who were active in making public opinion against child labour, were taken as charter members of the National Committee. Its first executive was Florence Kelley. Her book "Some Ethical Gains through Legislation," published in 1905, showed some facts relating to child labour and considered the plan for a commission for children.

Only in 1906, it was possible for the committee to introduce into Congress a bill for the establishment of a Bureau. Public hearing began after three years. During this period members were busy to raise the public opinion in and out of Congress against child labour. This fact was responsible for the White House Conference on the care of Dependent Children in 1909, which influenced the Congress to pass the children Bureau Bill.

The Children Bureau Bill, which was framed by Florence Kelley and Lillian Wald, finally passed by Congress and received the assent of President Taft in April 1912. The President appointed Julia Lathrop of Hull House as the first director of the children's Bureau.

The first federal child labour law was passed in 1916 as a result of activities of National Child Labour Committee. Administration under this law was given to the Children's Bureau. This Act prohibited the shipment in interstate commerce of goods produced in factories or mines employing children under 14 years of age (sixteen in mines), or requiring children between 14 and 16 to work more than eight hours a day or at night. This law was not applicable to agricultural pursuits, stores, offices and numerous street trades so that only 20 per cent of the working children of the United States were covered under this law.

Supporters of federal regulation failed in their subject by conservatism of the judiciary the united States Supreme Court in *Hammer Vs. Dagenhart*[11] declared the child labour law unconstitutional as an improper exercise of the power to regulate interstate commerce.

Facts of this case were, three days before the law of 1916 was scheduled to go into effect a federal district judge in North Carolina issued an injunction staying its enforcement in order to protect the rights of Reuben and John Dagenhart, aged 14 and 12 respectively, to work more than eight hours a day before reaching the age of 14. Southern Textile Mill operatives challenged the constitutionality of the 1916 Act.

The United States Supreme Court declared by a five to four vote that the commerce clause of the Constitution could not be invoked to obstruct the freedom of children and employers to make contracts within the several States. The Court was unanimous in their opinion that child labour is an evil, but the members were divided in their opinion is to the right of Congress to use its power over interstate commerce in correcting that evil. Both sides of the Court cited precedents in which Congress had used that power for the correction of social evils. The majority of the court, however, drew a distinction between a prohibition of articles harmless in themselves but prohibited as a means of regulating the conditions under which those harmless articles were produced.

Though the law was declared unconstitutional, yet the administrative method and procedures, developed by the children's bureau, provided the basis for subsequent federal legislation.

To meet the objections of Supreme Court; Congress passed another law to protect children from exploitation in industries in 1919 named as the Revenue Act of 1919. This Act provided that industry, where children were employed in violation of the standard established by the 1916 Act, would pay a tax of 10 per cent of annual net profit of that industry. During two years, considerable progress was made in the direction of alleviating the evils of child labour. But on May 15, 1922 the United States Supreme Court declared the Act unconstitutional in *Bailey Vs. Drexel Furniture Co.,*[12] the Drexel involved the question of the constitutional validity of the child labour tax law. The plaintiff below, the Drexel Furniture Company, was engaged in the manufacture of furniture in the western district of North Carolina. On September 20, 1921, it received a notice from Bailey, United States Collector of internal revenue for the district, that it had been assessed $ 6,312,79 for having, during the textile year 1919, employed and permitted to work in its factory a boy under 14 years of age and thus, incurred the tax of 10 per cent on its net profits for that year. The company paid the tax under protest, and after rejection of its claim for a refund, brought this suit.

The Supreme Court with but one dissenting opinion held that Revenue Act of 1919 was unconstitutional on the ground that it was an attempt of interfering with the right of the States to regulate labour within their jurisdiction and that real object in the legislation was too remote from its avowed object.

Due to this seriousness of the problem of the child labour reformers tried for another method for achieving federal control. That step was an amendment to the Federal Constitution. In 1924, the following constitutional amendment was passed by Congress for presentation to State legislatures:

Section I: The Congress shall have power to limit, regulate and prohibit the labour of persons under eighteen years of age.

Section II: The power of the several States is unimpaired by this article except that the operation of that laws shall be suspended to the extent necessary to give effect to legislation enacted by the Congress.

As ratification of this amendment by three fourths of State was necessary, a struggle began to secure that ratification without delay. Only a few State approved that amendment and twentyfour States came under the influence of propaganda of the associations of employers and rejected amendment. These associations attacked the amendment by charging that it was framed in Soviet Russia, that children would be nationalised by the said amendment. They further charged that Congress would enjoy, by this amendment, unrestricted powers to interfere between the rights of parents awl children. They also said that this amendment would prohibit all types of work by children under 18 years and that they could not do even domestic work.

As a result of this propaganda, only six States namely, Arkansas, Arizona, California, Colorado, Montana and Wisconsin ratified the amendment upto January 1933. After 1933, the law was codified under the National Industrial Recovery Act which prohibited the employment of children under 16 years. Such children could only be employed in agriculture and in domestic services. In a short time, this Act was declared unconstitutional in *Schechter Poultry Corp. Vs. United States*[13] by the Supreme Court on May 27, 1935. As a result of this adverse decision the progress of ratification was very slow. By now, only 24 northern States ratified the amendment, yet the ratification by 12 more States was necessary.

In 1936, Department of Labour administered the Walsh Healey Public Contracts Act, which forbade the employment of boys under 16 and girls under 18 of United States on contracts which were of more than $10,000 value. If an employer knowingly employed children under prohibited age to engage in contract work involving the manufacture, assembling, handling or shipment of materials or supplies; he was liable to pay to United States damage of $ 10 per day for each such child employed. In case of the violation of these provisions, the contracts could also be cancelled.

The Walsh Healey Act 1936 was upheld by Supreme Court in *Lukens Steel Co. Vs. Frances Perkins.*[14] Under the original Act of 1937, benefit was not provided to the growers, if they employed children under 14 or if they had taken work for more than 8 hours a day from the children between 14 and 16. These provisions were not applicable if the children's families owned at least 40 per cent of the crop when the work was done. In 1944, the Act was amended to provide for a cash benefit for those who conformed with the requirements.

As the ratification of the amendment by eight more States was required, the child labour section was included, in the Fair Labour Standard Act of 1838, by the Congress. These provisions stipulated that "no producer, manufacturer, or dealer shall ship or deliver for shipment in commerce, any goods produced in an establishment.... in the United States ...in which within 30 days prior to the removal of such goods.... any oppressive child labour has been employed."[15] "Oppressive child labour" was defined as the employment of any one under the age of 16 or between the ages of 16 and 18 by an employer, other than a parent or guardian, "in any occupation which the chief of the children's Bureau.... shall find and declare particularly hazardous for the employment of children between such ages or detrimental to their health' and well being."[16]

The chief of the Children's Bureau was charged with the following additional responsibilities:

(a) To determine by regulation and orders that the employment of children of 14 to 16 years in other than manufacturing and mining is not oppressive when it is confined to periods that will not interfere with their health and well being.[17]

(b) To establish regulations certifying that a person is: above oppressive labour age.[18]

(c) To make all investigations and inspections relative to records, wages, hours, and other conditions of employment of minors.[19]

(d) To institute any necessary legal action when unlawful practice exist relatives to oppressive child labour.[20]

The employment of minors as telegraph messengers had been exempted from the sixteen year minimum age requirement by the United States Supreme Court in *Western Union Telegraph Co. Vs. Katharine F. Len-root,*[21] which was decided on January 8, 1945.

The Western Union Telegraph Company collected in communities of origin and despatched them by electrical impulses to places of destination where they were distributed. Messengers were employed in both collection and distribution. A little under 12 per cent of the messengers, were under sixteen years of age, and about .0033 per cent were from sixteen to eighteen years of age, engaged in the operation of motor vehicles; scooters, and Tele-motors. These messengers were employed only in localities where the law of the State permitted it. It was not denied that both groups were engaged in oppressive child labour as defined by the Federal Act.

The Supreme Court held that the child labour provisions of the Fair Labour Standards Act do not embrace the work of messengers of Western Union, on the ground that the word "shipment" as used in Fair Labour Standards Act was not intended by Congress to include "shipping electrical impulses."

The provisions of Fair Labour Standards Act were similar to the Child Labour Law of 1916, but the changes had been made in the attitude of United States Supreme Court, toward federal control over Local Industry due to the changes in the personnel of the United States Supreme Court.

The changed legal philosophy can be seen when the Supreme Court reversed earlier decision of *Hammer Vs. Dagenhart in United State, Vs. Darby Lumber Co.*[22] and declared that provisions of Fair Labour Standards Act were constitutional.

In 1946, the children's Bureau was taken from the Department of Labour and given to the newly set up Social Security Department, under the Presidential reorganisation plan. The administration of Fair Labour Standards Act was taken from the Chief of Children's Bureau and given to the Department of Labour. Since that time it was the responsibility of Labour Department to administer the Act through its organs, namely Wages and Hours and Public Contracts Division and the Child Labour and Youth Employment Branch of the Division of Labour Standards.

Many changes were brought in the child labour provisions under Fair Labour

Standards Act by the amendments in 1949. By these amendments, the children under 18 employed in hazardous employment by their parents and the children were permitted by the School Law to work in agriculture during school time, were protected by the minimum wage, overtime prohibitions and child labour qualifications of the Act. Children were permitted to work in agriculture, only when the session of the school was closed. Further, the employment of children in the interstate or foreign commerce was also prohibited. On the other hand, the children employed as news boys or in performing radio and television programmes were not covered. The children employed in transportation, public utilities and communication were protected.

The definition of *Oppressive Child Labour* was raised to the age level of 16 and 18 in section relating to "particularly hazardous...employment of children... detrimental to their health and well being.[23]

The President's Commission on Migratory Labour was established by President Truman in 1950. This Commission recommended to the appointment of a Federal Committee on Migratory Farm Labour.

It also recommended the enforcement of the Sugar Act, and provisions of the 1949 amendments of child labour amendment to the Fair Labour Standards Act. It also recommended to limit the agricultural child labour under 14 out side school hours.

These recommendations were not new things, hut were the same as suggested by previous study groups. Yet the importance of the Commission was not lessened as it established some positive aims.

On August 26, 1954, a Co-ordinating Committee, under the chairmanship of the Secretary of Labour was appointed by President Eisenhower, to act as the Committee on Migratory Labour.

The Committee, following the recommendations of the Commission, made action programme for programme emphasis by its member agencies. In recent years 29 States have established Migratory Committees and some Federal programme to improve the services available to the Migrant children such as educational programme and child care centers.

In 1964, President Johnson suggested that a programme should be made to make young persons self-supporting. The provisions for a job corps, a work training programme and a work study programmes were included in the Economic Opportunities Act of 1964.

Child labour bulletin 101, under the title 'A Guide to Child Labour Provision to Fair Labour Standards Act' published by the United States Department of Labour in 1971 provides that at 16 years of age young persons may be employed in any occupation other than a non-agricultural occupation declared hazardous by the Secretary of Labour. There are no other restrictions, if not contrary to State or local law, young person of this age may be employed during school hours, for any number of hours, during any periods of time.

18 years minimum age for employment in non-agricultural occupation declared hazardous by Secretary of Labour.

16 years minimum age for employment in agricultural occupation declared hazardous by Secretary of Labour any time and for employment in agriculture during the hours schools are in session in the district where the minor lives, while working.

14 years minimum age for specified occupation outside school hours.

Employment of 14 and 15 years old youth is limited to certain occupation outside school hours only and under specified conditions of work as set forth in Child Labour Regulation No. 3 which provides that:

(a) 14 and 15 years minors may not be employed;

- *(i)* during school hours except as provided in paragraph *(b);*
- *(ii)* before 7 a.m. or after 7 p.m. except 9 p.m. from June. 1, through labour day (Time depends on local standards).
- *(iii)* more than 3 hours a day on school day.
- *(iv)* more than 18 hours a week in school week.
- *(v)* more than 8 hours a day on non-school day.
- *(vi)* more than 40 hours a week in non-school week.

(b) In the case of re-enrollees in work training programme conducted under Part B of Title 1 of the Economic Opportunity Act 1964, there is an exception to the requirement of para (a) *(i)* of this section.

Occupation in which 14 and 15 years old minors may be employed are: office and clerical work, modelling, art work, etc. Price making and tagging, packing, bagging and carrying out customer order, delivery work, clean up work, kitchen work and work in connection with cars and trucks such as dispersing gesoline and oil, courtesy service, car cleaning, washing, polishings and cleaning vegetables, fruits.

Occupation in which 14 and 15 years old minors may not be employed are: manufacturing, mining, processing occupations, public messenger service, operation or tending of Hoisting Apparatus of any power driven machinery, occupation in connection with transportation, warehousing, communication and public utilities constructions and in any occupation found and declared to be hazardous.

The Bulletin further provides that an employer can protect himself from unintentional violation of the minimum age provisions by obtaining and keeping on file an Age or Employment Certificate for such minor employee showing the minor to be of the age established for the occupation in which he is employed.[24]

Child Labour in Union of Soviet Socialist Republic

The Soviet State has also taken various steps to protect its women and children. In addition to the general protection applicable to all factory and office workers, some specific protections are provided to labour of women and children by legislation.

The employment of women and young persons under 18 in hazardous work is prohibited by Article 129 of the Code of Labour Laws. Such types of work were listed by the National Code of Labour of U.S.S.R. in 1932. Later on, these lists were changed due to the improvement in sanitary conditions of labour and removal of hazards in certain employments. A standard of maximum weight that can be lifted was made according to the Article 129 of the Code of Labour Laws. Night and overtime work by children is prohibited.

In addition, there are certain specific rules to protect children. These are:

(a) The employment of children below 16 is prohibited, but children below 15 years can be taken for educational work with the permission of a Trade Union.

(b) The young person under 18 can be employed after a medical check up. Later on he is required for medical examination not more than once a year.

(c) Maximum permitted working hours for young persons between 16 and 18 years are 6 hours a day and for children from 15 to 16 years of age are 4 hours a day.

(d) The young persons under 18 can enjoy usually holidays of one month duration, but not less than 24 working days. As a general rule summer holidays are also provided to children.

Child Labour in India

In Ancient India

The concept of child protection was not unknown to ancient India. Manu Smiriti reveals the fact that education was necessary for the children. The fathers and mothers were punished by the community if they did not send their girls and boys to the hermitage of a Guru or University after their attaining the age of eight years. *Manu Smiriti* says:

कन्यानां सम्प्रदानं च कुमाराणां च रक्षणम्।। मनु० (7।152।।)[25]

It means that it is the duty of King to made compulsory Brahamcharya to educate every girls and boys of society. In case of breach of this rule, he should punish their parents. In other words, after eight years no children should be left at home. They should be sent to Asarams *i.e.*, schools for education.

As regards child labour in ancient India, it can be said that it existed in the form of child slaves. The children of less than 8 years were purchased as slaves like articles of trade for doing low and dishonourable work. Children of slaves took birth as slaves, lived and died as slaves unless the Master liked to release them from slavery.

Kautilya pointed out that the Trade of Children as slaves was not prohibited in Mlechchas, because they were backward and uncivilised. On the other band Arya child was prohibited to become a slave

म्लेच्छानाम दोष: प्रजां विक्रेतुघातुं वा ।। न त्वेवार्यस्य दास भाव: ।।[26]

If an Arya child was sold or pledged with some one, then all the parties to the contract including the witnesses were liable to be punished. The degree of punishment depended upon the status of parties. Kautilya said:

उदरदास वर्जमार्य प्राणम प्राप्त व्यवहारं शूद्रं विक्रयाधानं नयत: स्वजनस्य द्वादशपणो ।।
वैश्यं द्विगुण: ।। ब्राहमणं चर्तुगुण: ।।[27]

It was realised by Kautilya that children were not physically fit to do dishonourable work. Taking such work from children was considered by Kautilya against humanity and shameful. Therefore, he prohibited the purchase and sale of slave children below 8 years. He said:

गृहे जात दायागत लब्ध-क्रीता नामन्यतमं दास मूनाष्टवर्ष विबंघुमकायं
नीचे कर्मणि विदेशे दासी वा सगर्माय प्रति बिहित गर्भभमेण्यां विक्रया धानं
नयत: पूर्व साहस दण्ड: क्रेतृ श्रोतणां च ।।[28]

Near the middle of the 19th century, the mechanised large scale production came into existence. That time, state regulations were lacking over the conditions of employees in any industry. The employers were free to bargain with labour. Therefore, the labour in this country was exploited by the employers for their benefits. Many children were employed in cotton and jute mills and coal mines, they were even employed for underground work. With the advent of Factory Organisation, some public attention was drawn towards the existing evils of child labour and in spite of active opposition from the employers, first protective legislation for child labour was enacted in 1881. This Act was known as the Indian Factories Act of 1881. This Act provided some protection to the children firstly by forbidding employment of children under seven years in factories and also in two separate factories on same day, secondly, by limiting their working hours to nine hours a day and thirdly, by making it compulsory that four holidays in a month and rest intervals should be given to them. In addition, the Act made the provisions for safety such as fencing of dangerous machines.

However, this Act covered only factories employing 100 or more persons. The evils continued due to the lack of enforcement machinery. In addition to these defects, the coverage was quite inadequate as it did not pay any attention to the agriculture and unorganised sectors of industries. The result of this was that child labour continued as a means of cheap labour.

In 1891, the Indian factories Act was enacted on the recommendations of a factory commission which was appointed by the Government of India in 1890. This step was an advance over the Act of 1881. Under the Act of 1891, the lower age was extended from 7 to 9 years. The upper age also exceeded from 12 to 14. Working hours were reduced from 9 to 7 hours per day. The children were not allowed to work at night. However, the exploitation increased because the attention was not paid due to the provisions of the Act due to the inadequate enforcing machinery.

Children's position in mines was also not different. Their condition was very bad. In 1901, about 5000 children were those child workers who had not completed their 12 years. In 1901 Mines Act was passed, which prohibited the employment of children under 12 years of age. The Chief Inspector of mines was empowered by the Act, to prohibit the employment of children to certain place, if he was satisfied that the employment conditions were dangerous to children's health and safety. This defective position Continued because no improvement was made to the provisions of this Act till the next mines Act.

Soon, the employers started work in factories for whole day and night, because they started to use electric power in their factories. In addition to this factor, the plague, which broke out for the first time in the industrial towns, also compelled the workers not to surrender to the old conditions of work. This position continued as there was no improvement inside the factories. But ultimately government felt that it was impossible to leave the matter in the hands of employers. It, therefore, appointed the Freer Smith Committee in 1906 and a Factory Labour Commission in 1907 to make inquiries on labour conditions in factories. Thereafter a New Factory Bill was introduced in 1909 which was enacted into law in 1911.

The Factories Act of 1911 reduced the working hours of children in factories to 6 hours a day. The Act further provided that all child workers should have in possession a certificate of age and fitness for employment. The children 'were not allowed' to work at night *i.e.,* between 7 p.m. and 5.30 a.m. and they were also prohibited to work in certain dangerous process.

The next step in the history of child labour law was the Indian Factories (Amendment) Act of 1922 which was enacted to give effect to the International Labour Conventions on the minimum age for admission of children into employment, hours of work and night work of young persons and women. The scope of factory was extended to cover any premises where 20 or more persons were employed and mechanical power was used. The Local Governments were empowered to extend the provisions to any premises where 10 or more persons were employed. For the purpose of this Act, child was defined as a person who had not completed his 15 years of age. The children under 12 years were prohibited to enter into labour, market. The children were required by this Act, to have a medical certificate as to their age and physical fitness for the employment. Their working hours were fixed by this Act to 6 hours a day with an interval of half an hour to the children employed for more than 5½ hours. The inspector was empowered to enquire from children a certificate of re-examination for continuing work. This Act also prohibited the employment of women and young persons under 18 in certain land processes. Some minor changes in this Act were introduced by an amendment in 1923.

The existing law in the area of mines was considered as inadequate and a new Mines Act was enacted in 1923 to give effect to the hours of work conventions of International Labour Organisation. This Act fixed the working hours for above ground work at 60 hours in a week, and for underground at 54 hours in a week. The Act raised the minimum employment age from 12 to 13 years.

Three years later the Indian Factories Act of 1911 was further amended in 1926 for some administrative purpose. After, two years the Mines Act 1923 was amended for regulating the hours and working condition in mines.

Again, in 1931, the Indian Factories Act of 1911 was further amended to bring certain minor changes for administrative purpose. This Act imposed certain penalities on the parents and guardians for allowing their children to work in two separate factories on the same day. Provincial Governments were empowered under this Act, to make certain regulation for taking precautions against fire.

In the same year the Indian Ports (Amendment) Act,. 1931, prescribed a minimum age of 12 years for the employment of children in the handling of goods in ports.

The year 1931, was also important in the Indian Legal History because in this year the report of Royal Commission on Labour was published. This Commission was appointed tinder the compulsion of intensive agitation to improve the condition of labour, to investigate and report on the existing conditions of labour in industrial undertaking and plantations ; and on the health and standard of living of the workers in British India. This commission found that the children as young as five years were employed to do work for 10 or 12 hours daily for very low wages. They were not provided adequate meal interval or weekly rest. Therefore, the Commission recommended that children under 15 should not be allowed to work as adult without a certificate of physical fitness. It also recommended the fixation of maximum working hours for children at 5 hours a day. It further recommended to limit the spread over for children at 7½ hours, and to prohibit work by children between 7 p.m. and 5.30 a.m.

The area of plantation was touched by the Government of India only in 1933 when it enacted the "Tea District Emigrant Labour Act." The only provision relating to children in the Act is one requiring that no child under 16 shall be employed and immigrated to the districts unless accompanied by his parent or adult relative on whom the child is dependent.

In 1933, one more step was taken to prevent exploitation of children when Children (Pledging of Labour) Act, 1933 was enacted by the Government of India on the recommendation of Royal Commission on Labour. The main aim of this act was to eliminate the evils arising from the pledging of the labour of young children by their parents for a loan or an advance.

One year after this Act, the Factories Act was completely overhauled on the basis of recommendation of Royal Commission on Labour. A new consolidated and amended Act was enacted in 1934, which was enforced from January 1, 1935. This Act prohibited the employment of children under 12 years. The children between 15 and 17 were defined as adolescent. The maximum working hours for children between 12 and 15 years were five hours a day.

In 1935 Indian Mines (Amendment) Act, 1935 regulated the working conditions and hours of work in mines. This amendment prohibited the employment of children under 5 in mines. This Amendment Act further laid down that the adolescent *i.e.*, the young person between 15 and 17 years could be employed in underground work as adult on the production of a certificate of physical fitness issued by recognised medical authorities. The working hours for such workers, according to this amendment, were 10 hours a day and 54 hours a week for above ground work and 54 hours a week and 9 hours a day were fixed for underground work.

The Factories Act was subsequently amended by Factories Amendment Act, 1935 and Repealing and Amending Act, 1937 which did not alter the general provisions of the Act.

In 1938, the Employment of Children Act 1938 was enacted in order to prevent the evils of employment of children in workshops which were not covered by Factories Act. The provisions of this Act continues till now. This Act prohibits the employment of children under 15 in Railway and Port. By the amendment of 1939 the children under 12 are prohibited to work in workshops connected with bidi making, carpet weaving, cement manufacturing, cloth printing dyeing and weaving, manufacture of matches, explosives and fire works, mica cutting and splitting, shallac manufactures soap manufacture, tanning and wool cleaning.

Various amendments took place in the Factories Act in 1940, 1941, 1944, 1945, 1946 and 1947 which, however, did not touch the provisions relating to child labour.

It is fruitful to note that before independence, the law relating to the employment of children in various sectors had failed to achieve its goal—the elimination of the evils of child labour. The Labour Investigation Committee, in its report in 1946 pointed out that the main cause for this was the inadequacy of the inspecting staff to enforce the provisions of law.

After Independence

After Independence the first step in this regard was the amendment of the Factories Act in 1948 which raised the minimum age for entering into employment in factories, to

14 years. A new section was added which specifies that the provisions of chapter, dealing with employment of young persons, are in addition to and not in derogation of the employment of children Act 1938. The minimum age for admission to the employment in workshops was also raised from 12 to 14 by an amendment in the Employment of Children Act, 1938.

Regarding the verification of child's age in case of dispute between employer and the inspector, provisions were introduced in 1949 under the Employment of Children Act.

The Indian Constitution, which came into force on January 26, 1950, laid down special protective measures for children from exploitation. The I.L.O. convention relating to night work of young person was responsible for an amendment in 1951 in the Employment of Children Act which prohibits the employment of children between 15 and 17 years at night in Railway and Port. The employers were required to maintain a register for children under 17.

In 1951, Plantation Labour Act was passed in order to prevent the employment of children under 12 years in plantation. Next year, the Mines Act, 1952 was enacted. This Act prohibits the employment of children under 15 in mines. Adolescent could be employed for underground as adult upon the satisfaction of two conditions—firstly, he must have completed his 16 years and secondly, he must have a certificate of physical fitness from a Surgeon.

In 1954, the Factories Act was again amended by the Factories (Amendment) Act, 1954 to prohibit the employment of adolescent under 17 at night. Night means, under this Act, a period of 12 consecutive hours which include hours between 10 p.m. to 7 a.m.

Again, the children under 15 are prohibited to be engaged or carried to sea to work in any capacity in any ship except in certain specific cases by an Act known as Merchant Shipping Act which was passed in 1958.

In 1961, two important Acts were passed in order to provide a legal protection to children. One, the Motor Transport Workers Act, 1961, prohibits the employment of children under 15 in Motor Transport undertakings. Second, the Apprentice Act, 1961, provides for regulating and controlling of trainees.

One of the most important steps was taken in 1966 to protect the children in Bidi industries when the Bidi and Cigar Workers (conditions of Employment) Act, 1966 was passed. This Act prohibits the employment of children under 14 in any industrial premises. Young persons between 14 and 18 are also prohibited to work at night between 7 p.m. to 6 a.m.

A report of National Commission on Labour, published in 1969 observed that child labour persists in varying degrees in the unorganised sector such as small plantations, restaurants and hotels, cotton ginning and weaving, carpet weaving, stone breaking, brick kiln, handicrafts and road building.[29]

To regulate the Labour of unorganised sector as shown by National Commission on Labour the Government of India passed an Act in 1970, known as the Contract Labour (Regulations and Abolition) Act, 1970, this Act covers all the establishments and contractors employing 20 or more workers in the whole of India. As there is no specific provision relating to child work, many children can be seen in building the houses, roads, etc. under contractors.

In 1973, the Apprentice Act 1961 was amended by Apprentice (Amendment) Act, 1973 to protect the rights of apprentice trainees. The Act prohibited undergoing Apprenticeship training of a person under 14.

In addition to these, legislative protection to child the states passed various Shops and Commercial Establishments Acts for their respective State. In these Acts the minimum age of employment on shops and commercial establishments under the respective State enactments is 12 years in Assam, Bihar, Gujarat, Madhya Pradesh, Maharashtra, Karnataka, Orissa, Rajasthan, West Bengal and Delhi and 14 years in Andhra Pradesh, Kerala, Tamil Nadu, Punjab, Uttar Pradesh and Pondicherry.

The Social Welfare Department under Central Government established a working group in April 1974 to study various aspects of child labour in the country. This working group recommended on November 15, 1974, an organisation to meet the situation and to suggest some remedies.

Notwithstanding the socio-economic limitations, an appreciable step was taken by the government to establish a National Children's Board in December 1974: Prime Minister and Secretary to the Government of India in the Department of Social Welfare, are its President and member secretary respectively. The constitutive parties to this Board are the Minister of Education and Social Welfare as working Chairman and the Minister of Health and Family Planning, the representatives of the Parliament, State Governments and Social Institutions, etc. The aims of this Board are to create public attention towards the needs of children, to review periodically the progress made in protecting the children and to recommend to prevent such gaps, etc. About the working of this Board, it was observed by Mr. Indira Gandhi, "...It would be better, if this Board instead of dealing merely with the problems side....looks at the opportunity side.... of the work for children."

A seminar from November 25 to 28, 1975 on "Employment of Children in India" was organised by the National Institute of Public Co-operation and Child Development in pursuance of the recommendation made by working group, on November 15, 1974. This seminar on November 28, 1975 recommended that the aims to protect children should be achieved by compulsory education. The seminar further recommended, firstly, for the training of children under 14 and; secondly, for creation of separate inspectorate of child labour to enforce the laws.

The above seminar further recommended that efforts should be made to evolve a

National Children's Code incorporating provisions of the Children's Act with model rules, uniform standards and norms governing employment of children in various sectors and vocations.

A proposal at the above seminar was also made to provide social security to poor families in the form of compensatory economic aid so that children could be sent to school instead of work. This idea will take sometime to be implemented due to the economic limitations.

Child Labour in Other Countries

The principle of prohibiting employment of children is an universally accepted principle. This principle has been introduced in Constitutions of many countries like Brazil, Elsalvada, Honduras. The minimum age for admission to employment varies from country to country and place to place. In the less developed countries like the near and middle east countries, the minimum age for employment is between 12 years and 14 years.

In general, it can be noted that minimum age regulations in agricultural sectors are less in comparison to other sectors of work. The minimum age regulations are either rare or in small quantity particularly in Africa, the near and middle east and Asia. They provide the rules only for plantations which are large undertakings. Thus it can be said that many children working on family farm are not protected by such minimum age regulations.

REFERENCES

1. Hammond, J. L. and Hammond, B., *The Town Labourer*, 1760-1862 (New York Augustus M. Kelly) (1967) Reprint.
2. Section 118, Factories Act, 1961.
3. Section 21, Factories Act, 1961.
4. Section 86, Factories Act, 1961.
5. Paxton, John (editor) *The Statesman's Year Book 1974-75,* Macmillion Press Ltd. 1974, London and Basingstoke, p. 77.
6. Archives of Maryland, *Proceedings and Acts of the Assembly,* Vol. 1, p. 80.
7. Kelso, Robert W., *The History of Poor Relief in Massachusetts, 1620-1920* (Boston Houghton Muflin Co. 1922) p. 168.
8. The Charter and the Acts and Laws of His Majesties colony of Rhode Island and Providence plantations in America, (1719).
9. Abbott, Edith. "A study of the Early History of Child Labour in America." *The American Journal of Sociology,* Vol. XIV, No. 1 (July 1908), p. 15.
10. Felt, Jeromy P. *Hostages of Fortune* (Syracuse: Syracuse University Press, 1965, p. VII.
11. 247 U.S. 251.
12. 259 U.S. 20.
13. 295 U.S. 495.

14. 310 U.S. 113.
15. Fair Labour Standard Act, Public Law 718, Chapter 676, Sec. 12(*a*).
16. Fair Labour Standards Act Public Law 718, Chapter 676, Sec. 3(1).
17. *Ibid.*
18. *Ibid.*.
19. *Ibid.*
20. Fair Labour Standards Act, Public Law 718, Chapter 676, See. 3(1).
21. 323 U.S. 490.
22. 312 U.S. 100.
23. *New Wage Hour Law, Fair Labour Standards Amendments of 1949*, Sec. 116(1).
24. *Child Labour Bulletin No. 101*, U.S. Department of Labour, Work Place Standard Administration, Wage and Hours Division.
25. Sarswati Dayanand, *Satyarth Prakash*, p. 79.
26. Kautilya, *Arthshastra*, Pt. III, Chapter 13, Prakaran 65-6-7.
27. Kautilya, *Arthshastra*, Pt. III, Ch. 13, Prakaran 65—1 to 4.
28. *Ibid.*, Prakaran 65-2-7.
29. *Report of National Commission on Labour* (1969), p. 386.

11

LINKING CHILD LABOUR AND FERTILITY BEHAVIOUR

Introduction

The hypothesis that the economic contributions of children make high fertility rational behaviour for households in rural, subsistence-level settings has experienced a meteoric rise in popularity. From the publication of *The Myth of Population Control* by Mamadani in 1972 (where this idea was probably first articulated) to the present, it has come to be taken almost as common-sense knowledge that it 'pays' poor peasants to have large families. This phenomenon is all the more remarkable if we consider the few empirical studies relevant to the topic which are available and which cannot yet be considered to have explored the subject adequately. Furthermore, the few studies to date have not reached a unanimous conclusion, some finding little evidence to support the hypothesis. Because of the importance that the general acceptance of this proposition could have for population policy, a critical assessment of the evidence of date is in order. This comprises the subject of this article.

Theoretical Considerations

The empirical work thus far on the topic of child labour has not been designed to collect all the data necessary to settle the question whether economic benefits accrue to peasants in less developed countries. Partly, this is due to the novelty of the topic as a subject of research. First cracks at a problem are liable to be deficient in design simply because not all important facets of the problem are immediately known. Partly, however, the topic itself is particularly difficult to deal with methodologically. We can agree with Caldwell (1983) when he states that because 'both the intimate way in which the family must be penetrated and the complexity of all the ways in which family members are of economic advantage to each other' make such research difficult. In the paragraphs which follow, I shall review conceptual and methodological considerations which empirical studies of the child labour question should encompass and be able to respond to.

The first theoretical question that must be addressed is whether or not an economic framework is valid at all stages of development. If development can be considered a multi-dimensional continuum stretching from hunting-and-gathering societies to post-industrial ones, is there a point along this continuum before which it simply makes no sense to expect fertility decision-making to be linked to economic rationality? This viewpoint was common in earlier literature (see, for instance, Bourgeois-Pichat, 1962), but several more recent studies have found that rural folk in a variety of settings give economic-type responses to queries about the value of children (Bulatao and Arnold, 1977; Vlassoff, 1979). Whether such responses really imply an economic outlook or are just convenient or result from misinterpretation of the meaning of 'value' is of course open to question. It is possible that, given a thorough reinterpretation of economic concepts, even a hunting-and-gathering society could be said to take fertility decisions based on economic rationality, but a study based on such a perspective might scarcely resemble an economic one in its usual sense and might; conceivably, it might seem more like an anthropological one.[1] On the other hand, if we accept the idea that a threshold of economic rationality (with regard to fertility) does exist along the development continuum, the problem then becomes where to place it.

A difficulty which stems from the above uncertainty is the extent to which couples in primitive societies (perhaps it is better to speak of families rather than couples) have the ability to regulate their own fertility. Little is known about this (Easterlin, 1975). Apart from fragmentary anthropological data, a crude approach to this problem can be made through the study of breastfeeding while considering the entire history of humankind, can be safely said to be the only effective means of birth control which was widespread (United Nations, 1985). (Abstinence and possibly abortion may have also been practised for fertility regulation, but very little is knows about either of these practices, except for taboos governing abstinence. Even here, however, the post-partum period of abstinence would largely coincide with the breastfeeding period.)

The most extensive body of data relating to breastfeeding, that of the World Fertility Survey, does not show that breastfeeding is currently practised in rural, less developed settings in one way as to raise the fertility of the poorer peasant classes. In fact most without exception, analysis reveals that poor peasants (measured by occupation or by education) have longer breastfeeding intervals which *ceteris paribus* results in lower fertility (United Nations, 1915). Admittedly, this kind of evidence is not conclusive, but it does not fall in the direction which would support the hypothesis under study.

If we accept that, for practical purposes, the range of populations that are likely to be subjected to empirical study including only those which have now passed the threshold of economic rationality (or at least have entered the domain of economic analysis as generally understood), then another somewhat related question arise that the socio-economic structures which are theorised to creative conditions under which children can be net economic assets still can be currently observable populations? For, even if the theory of intergenerational flows of benefits is plausible, it may have no practice significance if almost all less developed countries have now sufficiently progressed beyond the stage in which such a theory would have validity Caldwell's writings (see, for instance, Caldwell, 1983) can be questioned in this respect. Central to his intergenerational wealth flow theory is an authoritarian extended-family structure with a 'patriarch' at its centre. It is doubtful that such a model of family organisationally was ever applicable much beyond the region of sub-Saharan African as claimed by Caldwell (1978), but in the present context of social change in technology, education, urbanisation and even rural industrialisation occurring in the developing world, the authoritarian scheme seems distinctly out of place. Intergenerational wealth flows seems fit more comfortably in a situation of unconstrained resources particularly land, which again may be a feature in parts of Africa for the most part, however, abundant land where children's labour can be fruitfully employed does not fit the reality of much of the present-day developing world.

Another problem with the economic approach to fertility motivation is that studies in this genre often use the same data that analysts using sociological, cultural or even political perspectives have used. The education variable (say, years of completed schooling), is a case in point. Economic studies have tended to treat female education as a proxy for the shadow price of women's time (Mincer, 1963; De Tray, 1974), a procedure which seems to some to dilute the full significance of education (Ryder, 1973). Caldwell (1983), for instance, sees mass education as a crucial factor in ushering in fertility transition by upsetting the power structure within family units. Others view education as primarily representing 'economic class' (Hull and Hull, 1977). A recent study of ten different societies uses similar data to support the hypothesis that social prestige, not economic benefits, motivates high fertility in subsistence-level conditions while competitive sources of prestige reduces the relevance of high fertility in somewhat more developed societies which have accumulated surplus wealth (Hill, 1984).

While the foregoing observations may be of some interest in themselves, their particular relevance for the present topic is that it suggests and important question, namely, what percentage of the total motivation for procreation is due to economic factors such as child labour or security from children in old age. It seems obvious that other, competing explanations (such as, social, psychological and cultural) carry some weight as fertility determinants. That being the case, a conceivably minor share in fertility motivation might remain for the economic benefits of children, to the extent that they exist at all, once other factors are accounted for. Unfortunately, studies attempting to partition motivation between the various determinants are lacking. Thus, from a practical point of view, it is difficult to judge how important economic motives are from those studies which find that net benefits accrue to parents from child labour.

On the benefits side, a crucial methodological question concerns the definition of what constitutes a useful economic contribution from a child. I reality, economic activity is not as easily measured as the copious amount of available statistical information might suggest (e.g., see Anker, 1983). In a rural setting, some activities (such as the ploughing of a field) are easily recognised as productive economic activity, but there are a plethora of other activities, particularly among those carried out by children, which are much less clear-cut. Is guarding a grain field from birds, by shouting and hurling the occasional stone at the offenders, justifiably included as economic activity? And even if it is so deemed, can it be valuated at the same wage level as, say ploughing? One way around this problem is to view child labour, however trivial it may be, as freeing adults, usually the mother, to undertake more productive activities.[2] Children in less developed countries could be thus considered as 'time-supplying' (Lindert, 1983). Even so, it is doubtful that each unit of time 'freed' by the child should be valuated at the full market rate. All or part of this time may be spent by the adult in consuming rather than producing and, therefore, may not raise household income, although it may increase the welfare of certain family members.

Two related points concern on-the-job training and play activity. When farming technology is traditionally and changing only slowly or not at all, sons in general must learn skills from their fathers. For some activities (such as ploughing, harrowing and seeding), a fairly long apprenticeship is required. The proper classification of job-training activities is problematic since it is difficult to disentangle the productive part from the non-productive training part. No empirical studies, apparently, have attempted to make this distinction in their research designs. In low-income agricultural communities, children are also limited in their choice of leisure activities. Some child labour may occur simply because of a lack of other outlets for activity for children. While such activity is productive and should be counted as an economic contribution, it may not be expected by the parents and may not therefore be highly valued.

Thus far, we have discussed problems concerned with defining and measuring economic benefits, but the topic demands the treatment of costs as well so that net benefits can be determined. Lindert (1980, 1983) has posed three pertinent questions regarding the cost-benefits of children. First, what kind of child do parents want? This refers to the quality of children desired by parents. A common finding is that peasant (farmers are usually sensitive to the need to have educated children (Vlassoff, 1978; Bhattacharya and Brown, 1983) and to the costs that this desire implies. Costly children are less likely to ever yield net benefits to their parents and parents themselves seem to be aware of this. At any rate, the fact that children can vary significantly in their cost to parents needs to be taken into account in designing research. Past studies, far from allowing for differing costs, have in general not considered costs at all or only superficially (Lindert, 1983). Caldwell also sees rising costs, mainly due to education, as undermining parent-directed wealth flows and goes to some pains to explain why patriarchs should allow their authority to be eroded in this way (Caldwell, 1983). What he fails to appreciate, however, is that parents often actively encourage the maximum education feasible for their children.

Another pertinent is cost and benefits to whom and, related to this, who makes the fertility decisions (Lindert, 1983)? Caldwell's writings also emphasise this point, the locus of gain from child labour as well as the reproductive decisions being made by the patriarch of extended family. Obviously, the analysis of child labour in relation to fertility makes little sense if decisions are made by people other than those to whom benefits, if any, accrue. Such considerations have seldom, however, been taken into account in designing research in this topic. Usually the nuclear family has been used both as the locus of fertility decision-making and the economic unit within which costs and benefits flow.

Third, Lindert (1983) asks costs and benefits relative to what? If a couple had not had their last child, what would they have consumed instead and how would they have spent their time? These sound more like questions applicable to an advanced consumer society, but if we realise that both consumption goods and time can have negative values if the child makes positive contributions, they apply equally in less developed countries. The point is that the decision to have an extra child is not made in a vacuum but, presumably, is weighed in comparison to other, alternative consumption decisions. Studies of the benefits of child labour in less developed countries have obviously not achieved this level of sophistication. What would be required would be a quasi-experimental design in which couples were matched on a number of background characteristics differing only in the number of children they had. Patterns of consumption and time use could then be compared between the group which had an extra child and the group which did not. Only then could the relative cost (or benefit) of an extra child be calculated. Relative costs are importantly in comparisons over time or across diverse groups.

The problem of causality has been previously recognised (Vlassoff, 1979; Repetto, 1976) but a consideration of it has not generally found its way into empirical research. The question is: Do peasants have high fertility in order to profit from the work of their children or do children work because their parents have experienced high fertility? Under the first causal ordering, peasants see the economic advantages that children bring and make their fertility decisions accordingly. But the causal direction could conceivably flow in the opposite direction: peasants have many children (perhaps because they cannot control their fertility) and economic straits force them to demand work from their children *post facto* because every addition to household income helps even if the marginal productivity of children is very low. In the first case, the investigation of costs and benefits makes sense since fertility is, at least partially, a question of economic choice. In the second case, however, benefits of child labour are not relevant: child labour, although it may be observable, is not a motivation for fertility behaviour. Fertility may be high, using Easterlin's terminology (1975), because the cost of fertility regulation may be higher than the cost of surplus fertility. In empirical studies, causality can be investigated indirectly through questions about the perceived utility of child labour to parents. If parents do not subjectively value highly labour inputs from their children (as in Vlassoff, 1979), the interference can be drawn that the direction of causality runs from fertility to child labour. Direct questions about fertility motivations, such as those used in the value of children series of surveys, would seem to contamination of *post facto* reasoning on the part of respondents.

A somewhat more technical question is whether child labour during a whole year should be used in calculating benefits or whether contributions only during the agricultural peak seasons should be considered (Lindert, 1983). The problem arises when child labour is to be valued monetarily: should the peak-season wage rate or the annual average rate be used? The choice of one or the other can make an enormous difference to the total value of child labour since it often is the case that the demand for child labour outside the peak season does not exist and so wage rates are close to or at zero. It has been argued (see, for instance, Nadkarni, 1976) that even though demand is non-existent during most of the year, labour shortages exist for the short harvest season when the only practical source of labour comes from within the family, especially for poor peasants who cannot afford to compete in the labour market against wealthier farmers. While understandable, such a view may be too extreme on several grounds. First, adult labour utilisation in subsistence-type agriculture tends to be very low. For instance, a survey of 50 African countries found an average adult working year to consist of only about 1,000 hours (Cleave, 1970). With a lot of spare adult labour capacity available, the necessity of child labour even in peak seasons diminishes. On the other hand, at very low levels of technology peak activity becomes more pronounced (Mueller, 1976), so that while a labour shortage may temporarily arise it will be a short period, perhaps trivially so. For example, if the period in question is only, say, two weeks, it is easy to envisage ad hoc scheduling arrangements among farmers which would vitiate the need for child labour. Third, is the subsistence-agriculture paradigm still valid for the agricultural sector in general in less developed countries? It is common to find subsistence crops being supplemented by cash crops and technological improvements are becoming more extensive. To the extent that this is true, the peak season loses relevance.

A problem sometimes alluded to, but rarely addressed, is the economic context in which fertility decisions are made. In terms of peasant agriculture, patterns of landholding is of principal concern. At times the arguments made of the positive benefits of child labour seem more suited to a situation of 'frontier expansion' than to a context of a high rural population density and low-level agricultural technology. Studies of frontier expansion have suggested a positive link between the size of landholding and fertility (e.g., Lebergott, 1960). In the case of dense rural habitation, however, the size of holdings tends to be small and the ratio of adult labourers to land available to the household large. Opportunities to make productive use of child labour therefore are slight and, where observed, an effort should be made to gauge the extent to which child labour is simply replacing labour that could have been supplied by adult members of the household. Also, studies in less developed countries often show that richer farmers with more land make mor use of labour from their children (Stokes *et al.*, 1984; Fure, 1983; Vlassoff, 1979). These can be interpreted as demonstrating the constraint which landholding size places on child labour among peasants households.[3]

A point emphasised by Lindert (1983), but again largely ignored in empirical work, is the importance of survival rates in calculating costs and benefits of children. Taking into account mortality risks, as Lindert does with the Philippines data, will always tend to devalue benefits of children compared to their costs since benefits assume greater weight in the more distant future (using the decision to have an additional child as the reference point) while costs are most onerous in the less distant future. Thus, mortality risks which rise with time tend to reduce benefits relative to costs.

Discount rates have proven to be a controversial aspect of cost benefit calculations since the net benefit of a child, or at least whether the child 'pays back' the parents' investments in a reasonable number of years, can depend on what rate is used to discount future costs and benefits. Again, the different patterns of costs and benefits as one proceeds into the future mean that the higher the discount rate used, the less will be the valued benefits form children compared to their costs. Lindert uses a discount rate of 13 per cent on the ground that investment in an extra child is akin to investing in a fairly risky project such as education. Other writers have argued that a discount rate of zero or even a negative rate is appropriate in rural areas of less developed countries. Mueller (1976, p. 103), for example, assumes a zero rate of discount because 'peasants may not be aware of reasonably safe opportunities to earn interest on savings'. This view, however, seems extreme: money-lending has been observed even in subsistence economies and it is probably safe to say that rural banking has made inroads into the majority of rural areas.

We can agree with Caldwell (1983) when he emphasises that studies about the economic utility of children should pay special attention to ages, both of the older as well as the younger generation. One finds that children are sometimes grouped in age categories which are so broad that it becomes difficult to say something meaningful about the relation between child labour and fertility. In reality, interest in the topic is evoked by the moving image of very young children toiling in fields and carrying out onerous errands. It is not uncommon to find references to children beginning productive work as young as at age 4 years. This contrasts sharply with age groups reaching into early adulthood which are sometimes used to collapse the data. Partly, small sample size necessitates the grouping of data, but more core could be taken to achieve more meaningful categories. For instance, the educational system extant in the survey area should be used in deciding on age groups of children: once children have completed the number of years of schooling normally available to the average households, children have little to do except work for the family business. The fact that they do work after this point may mean that further educational opportunities are simply not available rather than that their labour contributions are indispensable.

Partly, however, the problem of age is that in most research to date, a cross-sectional approach has been applied to a topic that is bound up in the life-cycle of families. Costs and benefits flow between members of a family literally from the moment of birth to the time of death. If parents are assumed to be calculating costs and benefits over their whole life, then the relevant time frame would be from the time of the fertility decision until the expected death of the parents or at least until the moment when the child starts to make a net benefit. If, on the other hand, the view is that peasants need labour contributions in a more limited time frame,[4] then contributions of children only in those ages should be considered.

Finally, the importance of education in relation to the topic of the economic utility of children cannot be exaggerated. In this we can agree with Caldwell, whose more recent writings have placed greater emphasis on education as a central factor in the reversal in inter-generational flows, even though we need not ascribe its importance to 'Westernisation' (Caldwell 1983). Education impinges on child labour in several ways. First, children in school are removed from the labour market, so at one level school attendance can be used as a measure of the economic necessity of child labour.[5] But more fundamentally, where education has taken hold as it were, an important social change seems to take place. Parents begin to value their children's education more and more so that perhaps less work (either household chores or more obviously productive work) is demanded of them while more effort is made to give them the maximum education possible. As a consequence, children's costs become conscious facts and their economic benefits begin to pale in significance. On top of this there are the connections mentioned by Caldwell: more educated children may tend to be more rebellious, they may set up separate households more frequently, and they may decide more often on the use of contraception without consulting their elders. All these latter linkages, however, are long-term ones which are unlikely to be measured in field studies. They form more theoretical speculations which perhaps help to explain the fertility transition but are hard to verify empirically.

Many points have been made in the preceding paragraphs which, unfortunately, do not blend into a coherent whole. Probably, there are other criteria which empirical studies of child labour and fertility should take into consideration. Nevertheless, as a way of summarising the theoretical and methodological problem mentioned in this section a list of requirements which empirical work should encompass follows:

1. An effort should be made to verify that in the population under study, respondents in fact view fertility decisions as economic ones. Allied to this, the extent to which fertility decisions are made at all should be evaluated (i.e., if the population has 'natural fertility,' no contraceptive practice exists except for breastfeeding which is generally not consciously intended to limit fertility).
2. Data should be collected that, as far as possible, proves an economic point. That is, data which may have multiple interpretations should be avoided as measures for economic concepts or at least their multiple significations explicitly recognised.
3. The research design should also cope with the problem of the importance of economic motivation relative to other possible motivations for higher/lower fertility. For instance, comparing the fertility-child labour relationship with,

say, the influence of child deaths on fertility would help to put the economic relationship in perspective.

4. The definition of useful labour contributions needs special attention. Standard ILO or statistical office definitions should probably be avoided.[6] A useful division of children's activities may be 'time-supplying' activities—activities which are more or less equivalent to productive adult activities, and activities whose output is produced jointly with an adult.
5. The economic context of the study area needs to be incorporated into the research design. For example, child labour cannot be measured in isolation: the simultaneous activities of adult members of the household must be recorded before the value of the child labour can be gauged. The level of surplus adult labour should also be considered since conclusions about the necessity of child labour in peak seasons depends on it. Additionally, if possible, data should be collected over an entire year to avoid peak-season biases.
6. Household structure is crucial in studies of this kind and so must be considered in the research design in relation to other economic variables. The household members who benefit from child labour must be identified as well as intra-family obligations having economic implications which may extend beyond the classical definition of a household. Related to this, care should be exercised in choosing age groups targeted for study.
7. Causal direction should be tackled or at last made explicit. In a sense this is an intractable problem since fertility decisions always temporally precede child labour observations, but clever design may help to clarify the issue by connecting a series of factors. For instance, if it is found that child labour greatly expands in age groups above the end of the normally attainable educational career, child labour as a motivation for fertility is not supported since a more likely explanation is that children began to work because alternative (and more desirable) uses for time (i.e., more education) were not available.
8. Since the proper value of a discount rate has been much debated, it would be convenient for empirical studies to try to resolve the issue for the area being surveyed.

Review of Empirical Studies

Punjab, India

This early study (Mamadani, 1972) was probably the first to clearly articulate the view that peasants need high fertility for the economic benefits gained thereby. Mamadani also clearly made the connection between poverty and the economic gains of child labour, as well as those from grown-up children. Mamadani's style is polemical and the anecdotal nature of the data seriously detracts from the work as empirical or scientific (see Vlassoff, 1978, for a more detailed criticism). On the other hand, it must be said that Mamadani's study made a forceful statement of the problem and showed the usefulness of an anthropological approach to data collection.

The study, however, meets few of the criteria listed in the previous section. Respondents are viewed as basing fertility decisions (i.e., rejecting family planning) on economic considerations, but it is doubtful that the meaningfulness of fertility decision-making can be measured solely by attitudinal-type responses. Contraceptive practice was generally low in the field study area, so in a sense the respondents lacked two clear alternatives about which they could make a decision.

This is brought out clearly in a follow-up study some ten years later (Nag, 1982), in which it is shown that some of the respondents who were vehemently opposed to family planning on economic grounds had later voluntarily been sterilised: Neither does Mamadani make any attempt to weigh the importance of the economic motive for high fertility, which he believed he had unearthed, against other possible determinants. The direction of causation is not explored either except insofar as respondents themselves offered explanations of their fertility behaviour. Lastly, discounting future costs and benefits is not discussed. In fact, no serious calculation of net benefits is attempted by Mamadani. In passing, it may be remarked that the Punjab setting of the study may, in those times, have had some of the characteristics of 'frontier settlement' given the large-scale redistribution of land which occurred in the years following the partition of Punjab. To that extent, labour may have been comparatively scarce and the labour of sons more highly valued.

Bangladesh

This influential study (Cain, 1977) used data collected on the time-use of inhabitants from an agricultural village to support the conclusion that male children become net producers at an early age and more than cancel the costs they incur by 15 years. Activity is divided into 'enabling' labour and productive work, but the possibility of joint production is not contemplated. More importantly, the net result of the labour of children (such as baby-sitting and collecting fuel) in terms of adult members' activities thus enabled is not measured.

The problem of integrating the economic context into the study design is hinted at but never adequately taken into account. For example, Cain acknowledges that for the 23 per cent of households with no land, the chances of children finding wage employment were 'limited' and, at the same time, that most farming families hired labour at least occasionally. Hence, some kind of labour market must have existed in the study area which would compete with a household's supply of child labour. Cain in fact alludes to this but does not systematically attempt to link hired labour with family-supplied labour. Furthermore, as Lindert (1983) points out, the wage rates used in the study tend to exaggerate the value of child labour since peak-season rates were employed.

Also missing in this study is any reference to schooling and to how education may compete with child labour in the use of children's time. This is somewhat strange in view of the time-budget method of data collection which would have automatically gathered such information. Perhaps the short duration of the data collection encompassed too little of the school year to yield reliable results.

Cain's study has the limited aim of demonstrating that by quite an early age children become 'net-producers,' so no link is made with fertility. Thus, we do not know to what extent behaviour to limit family size was common in the village (from other sources I strongly expect, of course, that very little contraception was being practised). There is, at any rate, no way of judging whether net economic benefits from children were viewed as a reason to alter fertility behaviour. Household structure is not described in detail in the study nor is it related to patterns of child labour. Therefore, we do not know to whom benefits accrued or whether the persons who benefited also made the fertility decisions.

The calculations used to estimate net benefits are open to many criticisms. First, the only cost considered is the consumption of one food staple—namely, rice.[7] Second, no attention is paid to discount rates or to survival probabilities. Third, the productivity of children relative to adults is measured by taking peak-season rates which probably overestimate the annual relative productivity. Peak-season rates were probably used because children commanded a wage rate only at that time (Lindert, 1983). However, even here it appears that possible overestimation may have occurred by including such items as meals supplied as part of the daily wage—some meals supplied to children may really have been part of an accompanying adult's wage. Fourth, as mentioned earlier, hours worked are based on peak-season observations which leads to a further overestimation of income produced by children. Altogether these calculations lead to an overly bright picture: children produce more than they consume by 13-14 years of age and become net assets by their early twenties. Furthermore, since there are no obvious externalities to cloud this picture (since villages are largely closed economic systems), over the years Bangladesh should have grown ever more prosperous.

Indonesia and Nepal

The two related studies on Indonesia and Nepal (Nag *et al.*, 1977) which use somewhat different data collection techniques have a similar objective of trying to determine the economic value of children by measuring child labour. As in the Bangladesh study, reported economic activity is recorded and a similar distinction is made between 'directly productive' and 'household maintenance' work.

In general, except that longer periods of field study eliminated the problem of peak-season bias,[8] the same criticism can be made for these investigations as were made for the Bangladesh study. Furthermore, expressing child labour in terms of a proportion of an adult labour standard, as has been done in these studies, has the additional drawback of obscuring the possibility of adult underemployment. To the extent that adults are underemployed, child labour could be replaced without cost to the household as a whole if better uses of children's time arose. In view of the fact that few of the criteria listed in the previous section are satisfied, little confidence can be placed in the tentative conclusion reached by these studies, namely that children have net positive economic value to their parents.

Maharashtra, India

Although suffering from many of the same defects as the previous three studies, this village study (Vlassoff, 1978) differs from them in a number of respects. Much more attention was paid to the economic context of the study area and to the wide variety of arrangements by which labour was exchanged. The different interpretations which may be applied to the activity of children was also explored, although measuring productive work was probably not any more successful. Less reliance was placed on observing child labour and more on the value that fathers' perceived such labour to have. A main feature of the study was to link child labour (and old age security) with fertility and family planning behaviour, although the problem of causality, it was acknowledged, prevented definite statements from being made based on the analysis of this relationship. More weight was given to attitudinal data precisely to circumvent the causality problem, but the validity of such data is always somewhat doubtful, especially if the attitudinal questions are not subject to extensive prior testing. Like the previous studies, cost data were not collected. Finally, educational data were given prominence, mainly because it became apparent in the course of fieldwork that education of children was a prime concern of parents despite the obvious increase in costs to parents that educating their children implied.

Even though the main finding—that child labour probably does not motivate high fertility—is probably no more defensible than the opposite findings of the other studies reviewed, the chief merit of this Indian village study was to sound a warning by elucidating a number of conceptual and methodological pitfalls in this genre of empirical investigation.

West Bengal, India

This work on West Bengal (Bhattacharya and Brown, 1983) is novel in several respects. First, although the authors claim that the study group is rural (even though the village lies close to the Calcutta/Howrah urban conglomeration), economic activity was centred on a cottage industry (costume jewellery) not on agriculture. To some extent, this setting sheds some light on whether in fact child labour as a positive motivation for fertility is arguable only in less developed rural areas, as most have maintained, or whether children in urban contexts may also possibly make positive net contributions. This study shows that at least in a semi-urban setting, children work alongside adults. The study also grapples with fertility and with the direction of causality between fertility and child labour. This is done by analysing patterns of labour participation of *adults and children* to determine whether fertility rises when children begin to contribute economically or, vice versa, if children tend to make more of a contribution if fertility was comparatively high to begin with. Even though the results are not convincing, the study should be given credit for making a serious attempt to link fertility and child labour (which, after all, is the core of the research problem).

The West Bengal study also forcefully highlights the importance of education in research on child labour. According to the authors, a likely scenario goes somewhat as follows: development leads to increased educational opportunities. This, initially, may have a pro-natalist effect and lead to higher fertility. Later however, parents find that increased costs prevent them from educating all children: at least some must be removed from school to work (in the cottage industry in this case). The added income in no way compensates for the low level of education to which these children are forever more condemned. This generates an anti-natalist attitude, possibly leading to lower fertility. Although no data were collected to prove this thesis in its entirety, the study furnishes some partial evidence. It is to be recommended for bringing out the important role of education, a relationship which more influential studies have simply omitted.

Tanzania

This study on Tanzania (Kamuzora, 1984) is the only study, other than Caldwell's work in Nigeria (1977), based on African data. Basically a time-allocation survey (like the Bangladesh and other similar studies), the author uses as a starting point the idea that in Africa land is plentiful and abundant. Thus an economic context entirely distinct from the earlier Asian research is apparently being observed here. (Whether African land is really so freely available, at least without the constraint of capital investment, may be a pertinent question, but one which I am incompetent to answer.) Perhaps because the original purpose of the survey was not related to child labour, the age groups used (5-9, 10-19, 20 +) are not very illuminating. Even so, an odd finding is that boys aged 5-9 years contribute marginally more work than do youths aged 10-19 years. This leads to the thought that the definition of economic activity may have included activities that would have been classed as 'enabling' or 'household' tasks in other studies. Or, ore probably, schooling may be subtracting from the labour input of the group aged 10-19 years.

Apart from presenting a breakdown of time allocation by these broad age groups, little else is contributed to the problem of child labour and fertility. What, superficially, appears to be evidence of excess supply of labour is countered by the not altogether convincing statement that 'in a peasant economy the demand for labour determines its supply'. Although no cost data were collected, the author suggests that the preference for school attendance over child labour in a context of poverty indicates that costs outweigh benefits.

Mexico

This study on Mexico (Shumann, 1982), for which it was impossible to obtain more than an abstract, examines an *ejido* (communal village) in southern Mexico. This is the only relevant Latin American research that I know of. The study links fertility to the 'perceived relative value of children's and finds no significant relationship.

The Philippines

Of all the research reviewed here, only Lindert (1980, 1983) has taken cost data (other than presumed consumption of staple foods, as in Cain's investigation) into account as well as direct opportunity costs to parents. The overall finding is that in this setting, described as relatively 'affluent,' children are never net assets. As noted by Lindert, the net cost of parents would be even higher if less conservative estimates of costs were used or if peak-season wages (the only ones available) were not used. It must be pointed out, however, that this study uses presumed average costs, there data not being collected for individuals. It is impossible to say, therefore, for a given family whether children were or were not net assets: this may be affected by the household type, the economic context of the family or by what adults do with the time 'supplied' to them by their offspring. Nor, as in the majority of studies reviewed, is any connection made to fertility.

Karnataka, India

This recent study on Karnataka (Kanbargi and Kulkarni, 1986) is without doubt the most exhaustive analysis to date of the relationship between child labour and fertility (see also, Kulkarni and Kanbargi, 1986). Many of the problems outlined in the previous section have been addressed directly in this investigation. Foremost among these is the interrelationship between education, fertility and child labour. An integral part of the research design is concerned with confronting this problem and, in fact, a principal objective of the study is to examine how demand for labour might affect school attendance. The costs of children are not measured, but the study nevertheless is sensitive to the probable influence of costs, for instance, for schooling (even though education is nominally free in Karnataka). Third, the economic context of the study area is considered, both in the sample stratification used (dry land, wet land) and in measuring, albeit in a superficial way, the work of adult members of the family unit. Nonetheless, apparently no attempt has so far been made to use these data to compare the work contributions of children with those of adult household members.

The study is also unique in employing probability sampling covering virtually the entire state of Karnataka. This is in sharp contrast to all the other investigations reviewed here which are of the 'village study' type. Nevertheless, the study suffers from a small number of observations (comparable, in many cases, to the number of interviews recorded in the village studies), which has forced the authors at times to use rather large age groups (for instance, 5-14 years). As noted, such aggregations can confuse the analyses by uniting decidedly distinct experiences.

Some of the results of this study—the most complete to date—merit emphasis. First, no significant effect of child labour on fertility is observed. School attendance is influenced negatively by the demand for labour but the only important demand variable was the presence of young siblings in the household. This demand would obviously disappear if fertility was lower. Also worth mentioning is the finding that labour demand does not affect the amount of work contributed by non-schoolgoing children. This suggests that once rural children leave school, their work has a cultural aspect determined partly by prevailing values regarding what children should be doing at various ages. It is even possible that such stereotyping may have influenced responses regarding the number of hours of work performed by young drop-outs.

Summary

This paper addresses the popular theme that children are net positive assets in rural areas of less developed countries and that, therefore, child labour would have a positive effect on fertility. It attempts, first, to highlight the important factors about which empirical data must be gathered in order to do convincing research of this topic and, second, to show that research to date has in large part failed to do so. Among the criteria which have generally been ignored, the following were especially important: the costs of raising children, the economic context (particularly the possibility of the productive use of adults' time freed by the activity of children), the importance of education (in changing taste preferences from quantity to quality of children and in increasing costs while reducing benefits), the need to bring fertility into the research design and, at the same time, to confront the problem of the direction of causality (from child labour to fertility or vice versa?).

In view of the inadequately designed research on the topic so far, it is premature to conclude that child labour motivates high fertility in less developed countries and even less justified to claim that poor rural families need child labour to survive.[9]

REFERENCES

Anker, R. 1983, *Female Labour Activity in Developing Countries: A Critique of Current Data Collection Techniques*, Working Paper No. 136, World Employment Programme Research; Geneva, ILO.

Bhattacharyya, A. and A. Brown. 1983, *Cottage Industry and Fertility in West Bengal, India*, Paper presented at annual meeting of Population Association of America.

Bourgeois-Pichat, J. 1962. 'Social and Biological Determinants of Human Fertility in Non-Industrial Societies,' *Proceedings of the American Philosophical Society*, Vol. III, No. 3, pp. 160-63.

Bulatao, R. and F. Arnold. 1977. 'Relationships Between the Value and Cost of Children and Fertility: Cross-Cultural Evidence,' *International Population Conference, Mexico, 1977*, Liege, IUSSP.

Cain, M. 1977. 'The Economic Activities of Children in a Village in Bangladesh,' *Population and Development Review*, Vol. 3, pp. 201-28.

———. 1984. 'On the Relationship Between Landholding and Fertility,' Centre for Policy Studies, Working Paper No. 106, New Work, Population, Council.

Caldwell, J. 1978. 'A Theory of Fertility: From High Plateau to Destabilisation,' *Population and Development Review*, Vol. 4, No. 4.

———. 1983. 'Direct Economic Costs and Benefits of Children,' in R. Bulatao *et al.* (eds), *Determinants of Fertility in Developing Countries*, Vol. 1, (New York, Academic Press).

Cleave, J. 1970. *Labour in the Developing of African Agriculture*, Doctoral Dissertation, Stanford University.

De Tray, D. 1974. 'Child Quality and the Demand for Children,' in T. Schultz (ed), *Economics of the Family*, Chicago, University of Chicago Press.

Easterlin, R. 1975. 'The Effect of Modernisation on Family Reproductive Behaviour,' in United Nations, *The Population Debate: Dimensions and Perspectives*, Vol. 2, New York, United Nations.

Fure, E. 1983. 'Are Children Poor Men's Riches?' *Scandinavian Economic History Review*, Vol. 31, No. 3, pp. 161-77.

Hill, J. 1984. 'Prestige and Reproductive Success in Man,' *Ethnology and Sociobiology*, Vol. 5, No. 2, pp. 77-95.

Hull, T. and V. Hull. 1977. 'The Relation of Economic Class and Fertility: An Analysis of Some Indonesian Data,' *Population Studies*, Vol. 31, pp. 43-57.

Kamuzora, C. 1984. 'High Fertility and the Demand for Labour in Peasant Economies: The Case of Bukoba District, Tanzania,' *Development and Change*, Vol. 15, pp. 105-24.

Kanbargi, R. and P.M. Kulkarni. 1986. Child Labour, Schooling and Fertility in Rural Karnataka, South India, Mimeo, Bangalore, Institute for Social and Economic Change.

Kulkarni, P.M. and R. Kanbargi. 1986 Demand for Child Labour and Child Schooling in Rural Karnataka, mimeo, Presented at the seminar on Child Labour: Dimensions and Implications, 21-22 April, Bangalore, Institute for Social and Economic Change.

Lebergott, S. 1960. 'Population Change and the Supply of Labour,' in *Demographic and Economic Change in Developed Countries*, Princeton, Princeton University Press.

Lindert, P. 1980. 'Child Costs and Economic Development,' in R. Easterlin (ed), *Population and Economic Change in Developing Countries*, Chicago, University of Chicago Press.

———. 1983. 'The Changing Economic Costs and Benefits of Having Children,' in R. Bulatao *et al.* (eds), *Determinants of Fertility in Developing Countries*, Vol. 1, New York, Academic Press.

Miner, J. 1963. 'Market Prices, Opportunity Costs, and Income Effects,' in C. Christ *et al.* (eds), *Measurement in Economics: Studies in Mathematical Economics and Econometrics in Memory of Yehuda Grunfeld*, Stanford, Stanford University Press.

Mueller, E. 1976. 'The Economic Value of Children in Peasant Agriculture,' in R. Ridker (ed), *Population and Development: The Search for Selective Interventions*, Baltimore, The Johns Hopkins University Press.

Nadkarni, M. 1976. '"Overpopulation" and the rural poor,' *Economic and Political Weekly*, Vol. 11, No. 31, pp. 1163-72.

Nag, M. 1982. 'The Khanna Study Revisited,' *Indian Express*, 27 October.

Nag, M. *et al.* 1977. 'Economic Value of Children in Two Peasant Societies,' in *International Population Conference, Mexico 1977*, Liege, IUSSP.

Repetto, R. 1976. 'Direct Economic Costs and Value of Children,' in R. Ridker (ed), *Population and Development: The Search for Selective Interventions*, Baltimore, The Johns Hopkins University Press.

Ryder, N. 1973. 'Comment,' *Journal of Political Economy*, Vol. 81, No. 2 (Part ii), pp. 965-69.

Schumann, D. 1982. Fertility and Economic Strategy in a Southern Mexico Ejido, Doctoral Dissertation, Southern Methodist University, Dallas, Texas.

Stokes, C. *et al.* 1984. 'Access to Land and Fertility in developing Countries,' in W. Schutjer and C. Strokes (eds), *Rural Development and Human Fertility*, New York, Macmillan.

United Nations. 1985. 'Breastfeeding and Related Aspects of Post-Partum Reproductive Behaviour,' Working Paper of the Population Division, IESA/P/WP/90, New York, United Nations.

Vlassoff, M. 1978. *Economic Motives and Fertility in an Indian Village,* Doctoral Dissertation, Gokhale Institute of Politics and Economics, University of Pune.

———. 1979. 'Labour Demand and Economic Utility of Children: A Case Study in Rural India,' *Population Studies,* Vol. 33, No. 3, pp. 415-28.

NOTES

1. Parenthetically, in the usual micro-economic framework, income, prices and tastes jointly determine the demand for children. The possibility of changing tastes, however, is an aspect of the economic analysis of children which is invariably treated superficially even though it is formally present in the model.
2. The context in which this is usually framed is in the care of younger siblings by older ones. But even here, care must be taken no separate care provided solely by an older sibling from situations in which such care is provided jointly with the mother.
3. Cain (1984) interprets such findings as resulting more from differential temporary migration than from real fertility differences.
4. In the extreme, in the case of the argument that labour is required for peak-season work, the child would probably have to make a contribution during his very first year of life to be an economic asset for such peasants.
5. A regret of the research I did in Maharashtra was that I relied on the accuracy of the apparently meticulous attendance records kept by the clerk of the local (village) secondary school. Later, when they were to be used, a little independent checking proved them to be untrustworthy. Had I realised this early enough in the data collection phase of the research, I could easily have mentioned a separate and more accurate record of school attendance.
6. ILO thinking on the appropriateness of usual definitions is undergoing change in the direction of more context-oriented definitions (Anker, 1983).
7. Even here, there is an apparent calculation error for children aged 7-9 years where a daily calorific requirement of 1,201 is used. Perhaps, 1,501 was intended? At any rate, consumption is understand for this group as a result of the error.
8. This may not be entirely true in the study on Nepal since it appears that many of the observations come from a short one-and-a-half month period when vacationing students were employed as additional data collectors.
9. In fact, almost all the evidence to date shows that peasants with more land enjoy higher rates of participation from their children. Thus, the opposite may be true.

12

PARTICIPATION OF CHILDREN IN ECONOMIC ACTIVITY

Introduction

A common observation in India, as in many other developing countries, is that a large number of children are engaged in economically productive work. Children are often employed in the rural areas, for example, to graze cattle and on the farm. In urban areas, children are engaged in, among other things, construction, automobile repairs, restaurants and domestic work. According to the 1971 Census of India, the total work of participation rate for males up to 14 years of age was 6.6 per cent; for females of the same age the rate was 2.5 per cent (Office of the Registrar General and Census Commissioner, 1977). The corresponding percentages for 1981 were 5.5 and 2.9 (Office of the Registrar General and Census Commissioner of India, 1984) which, in absolute numbers, works out to be 10.7 and 11.2 million child workers in 1971 and 1981 respectively.[1] Although the census data for the two years are not comparable, the data, nevertheless, give in idea about the magnitude of children who are working. The census data also indicate that the participation rate of children as workers in rural areas is nearly three times the rate in urban areas; whereas in 1971 the rural and urban rates were 5.3 and 1.8 per cent, in 1981 the rates for these areas were 5.0 and 1.7 per cent respectively.

Given the high prevalence of labour in India, an investigation of the phenomenon can provide an insight into its various dimensions. A study of child labour is important not only because of the purported link with fertility but also for an understanding of the implications associated with it. Children often do not attend school because they have to work to augment the family income. Working children are more susceptible to ill-health and some of the work they perform can even retard their mental and physical development (Rodgers and Standing, 1981). This paper focuses on the economic participation of male and female children in the rural areas of India. Before an analysis of child labour is presented, we shall briefly review past research findings.[2]

Past Research

Among the studies that have examined child labour in rural India, the economic analysis by Rosenzweig and Evenson (1977) is of considerable interest. Supplementing the 1961 census data with other data, they found that in the districts of India adult male and female education is negatively related to per cent of male children engaged in cultivation, herding or as hired labour. In those districts where the adult female wage is higher, the proportion of female child workers is lower but the degree of urbanisation has an opposite effect. Land size and productivity have influenced child labour positively. In a similar study, using 1969-1971 rural survey data, Rosenzweig (1981) has shown that the percentage of population designated as scheduled castes is significantly and negatively associated with both the male and female child work. Increase in the adult male wage and the presence of developmental programmes in the district tended to lower the work activities respectively of the male and female children. Naidu (1981) has examined child labour in the states of India and reported a negative correlation with per capita income and average rural wage rate for adolescents. Micro data on the activities of children were collected by Kanbargi and Kulkarni (1985) from rural households in Karnataka state. Their data revealed that the number of hours children and women work are positively linked but school attendance and average rainfall in the village exert a negative influence.

Although these studies identify some of the factors that explain child labour, we take advantage of another available data set to analysis child labour by its components. In other words, child labour is separately investigated for children who are below and above 10 years of age. The reason for this is that the nature of child work in rural areas varies with the age of children (Cain, 1977; Nag *et al.*, 1980). Young boys, unlike adolescents engaged in agricultural activities, do not perform cumbersome tasks that require a great amount of physical strength. The situation is similar for girls—as they mature, they begin to participate in activities such as weeding and husking. Moreover, the difference in the work done by children who belong to landless and landed households is emphasised. Cain (1977), pp. 217, 219 mentions that 'among males aged 10 years and older, those from landless households do considerably more work than those from the landed classes' and 'poor females do considerably more directly productive work than females in the more well-to-do households.' Finally, as the review suggests, some of the relationships do not emerge from different data. Rodgers and Standing (1981) observed that in the papers by Rosenzweig, the results from the 1961 data are not replicated by the 1969-71 data. Making use of the data generated by the National Sample Survey Organisation (NSSO), this analysis on child work seeks to establish the relationships described by others and extend the earlier work done.

Hypotheses

An important independent effect on child labour is the monetary contribution of children to their family income. Children's work is usually different from that of adults and, where adult unemployment rates are high or wage rates are low, the wages earned by children are a valuable addition to family income. In the rural parts of India, since households mainly depend upon agriculture (which is sometimes that only means of livelihood), the distribution of land in a village affects the amount of work children do. With the introduction of modern techniques in agriculture, a general practice among farmers is to irrigate land by tubewells and use chemical fertilisers which substitute for child labour: children as a routine irrigate fields by drawing water from wells and collect and prepare manure for the fields. Female literacy also influences child labour. A literate mother encourages children to attend school and, conversely, discourage child labour. Caste is basic component of the social and economic structure in a village and within these structures persons belonging to the scheduled castes occupy the lowest position. Their children join the labour force at an younger age.

Data and Variables Used

The data utilised in this study are drawn from a survey conducted during 1970-71 by the NSSO (1978) among the rural households in India. For the purpose of the survey a stratified sampling design was used.[3] The households were divided into two groups: small cultivators who possessed some land for cultivation (i.e., the bottom decile of all cultivators and non-cultivators who had no land and were wage [cash and kind] earners). Data from 16,800 sampled households were published for the 61 agro-climatic regions of India.[4] These regions were formed on the basis of similarity in their population density and cropping pattern such that each region comprises about 4 or 5 districts (Bardhan, 1983). Regional data on child labour and wages are obtained from this 1970-71 survey.

Table 12.1 gives the definition of the variables used and their mean and standard deviation. As the table shows, the mean percentage of man-days children work (in their own farm or other farms, either for wages or as the exchange of labour, self or non-self employment) is strikingly less for younger children (below 10 years of age) than older ones (above 10 years of age). Also, male children in both cultivating and non-cultivating households work for longer periods than female children.[5] Similarly, both age and sex have an important bearing on wage rate. An additional wage variable considered in the analysis is that of adult females (FWAGE). Data for this are also contained in the survey. But information on other variables—females literate (FELIT), schedule caste males (MASCH), fertiliser usage (FERTZ) and land concentration ratio (CORAT)—is obtained from Bardhan (1983) who had compiled the regional data for 1970-71 from various sources. Both FELIT and MASCH data are taken from the 1971 census. Fertiliser statistics of India provide figures for FERTZ. The 1971-72 survey of NSSO contains data on CORAT. Though these organisations responsible for collecting data constantly strive to improve the quality, the data used in this article may suffer from some biases. For example, evaluation of some of the surveys pointed out that perhaps both under and over-estimation occur (Chatterjee and Bhattacharya, 1975; Suryanarayana and Iyengar, 1986; Vaidyanathan, 1986). To what extent the data used here are in error is not exactly known. However, some clues on the nature of the data can be gleaned from an analysis of the survey data.

TABLE 12.1

Variables, Sample Means and Standard Deviations (NSS Regions of India, 1970-71)

Variable	*Definition*	*Mean*	*Standard Deviation*
Independent			
MASCH	Percentage of males belonging to schedule caste	14.53	8.11
FELIT	Percentage of females literate	14.22	9.98
FERTZ	Value of fertiliser used per hectare of area (Rs.)	0.02	0.02
CORAT	Concentration ratio of land	0.62	0.10
Average Rate of Earnings Per Day (Rs.) for			
FWAGE	Females 15-59 years	1.64	0.64
MWNNC	Males below 10 years in non-cultivating households	0.27	0.46
FWNNC	Females below 10 years in non-cultivating households	0.15	0.33
MWNCU	Males below 10 years in cultivating households	0.42	0.59
FWNCU	Females below 10 years in cultivating households	0.20	0.41
MWTNC	Females 10-14 years in non-cultivating households	1.20	0.74
FWTNC	Females 10-14 years in non-cultivating households	1.09	1.02
MWTCU	Males 10-14 years in cultivating households	1.73	2.59
FWTCU	Females 10-14 years in cultivating households	0.93	0.58
Dependent			
Percentage of Man-Days Economically Active in a Week for			
MNINC	Males below 10 years in non-cultivating households	1.87	2.83
FNINC	Females below 10 years in non-cultivating households	0.91	1.50
MNICU	Males below 10 years in cultivating households	2.05	2.15
FNICU	Females below 10 years in cultivating households	1.48	1.70
MTFNC	Males 10-14 years in non-cultivating households	25.36	17.77
FTFNC	Females 10-14 years in non-cultivating households	15.53	12.59
MTFCU	Males 10-14 years in cultivating households	27.62	14.88
FTFCU	Females 10-14 years in cultivating households	16.21	9.90

Source:

Results

The results of the regression analyses for working children below the age of 10 years are presented in Table 12.2. In this table, the coefficient for each predictor variable and R^2s are shown for male and female children in cultivating and non-cultivating households. The regression coefficients express the increase or decrease in the dependent variable due to a unit increase in the predictor variable while all other variables are held constant. The square of the multiple correlation coefficient, R^2, refers to the proportion of variance in child labour jointly explained by all the predictors.

For male children in non-cultivating households, MASCH, FERTZ and MWNNC are significant at the 5 per cent level. The coefficient of MASCH indicates that the presence of scheduled castes in the regions increases the employment of children. The predictors FERTZ demonstrates a strong association of fertiliser usage with child labour and corroborates the hypothesis that modern methods of agriculture have a favourable influence on child labour. MWNNC, as expected, enhances child work. Additionally, FELIT, which is significant at the 10 per cent level, is positively related to the economic activity of young male children in non-cultivating households. The variables used in the analysis together account for a fairly high proportion of variation—33 per cent—in the dependent variable.

TABLE 12.2

Regression Analyses of Economic Activity of Children Below 10 Years in Rural India, 1970-71

Independent/ Dependent Variables	*MNINC*	*FNINC*	*MNICU*	*FNICU*
MASCH	0.18	0.01	0.07	0.02
	(3.17)+	(0.45)	(1.79)*	(0.50)
FELIT	0.12	0.02	-0.07	-0.05
	(1.93)*	(0.47)	(1.64)*	(1.16)
FERTZ	-56.75	-6.36	-12.92	10.64
	(2.12)+	(0.42)	(0.70)	(0.58)
CORAT	-5.22	-3.33	-0.72	-4.58
	(1.02)	(1.12)	(0.20)	(1.28)
FWAGE	-0.07	-0.64	-0.72	-0.03
	(0.13)	(1.99)*	(1.82)*	(0.07)
MWNNC	2.47	—	—	—
	(3.20)+			
FWNNC	—	1.39	—	—
		(3.03)+		
MWNCU	—	—	0.65	—
		(1.47)		
FWNCU	—	—	—	0.58
		(0.91)		
CONST	1.85	3.54	5.03	5.11
R^2	0.33	0.26	0.28	0.12
F	3.56+	2.48+	2.91+	0.99

Note: *Significant at the 0.10 level;
+significant at the 0.05 level. Figures in parentheses denote its values.

In the case of female children, however, only one of these variables—FWNNC—retains its importance. FWAGE exerts a weak and negative influence on female child work. Compared with males, the R^2 for females is lower, with a value of 0.26. Some of the predictor variables were substituted with others to determine if another set may better explain female children's economic activity. Of those substitutions, the variable measuring intensity with which multiple crops are produced in a region has a negative effect on female child work.[6] This result is similar to that for males and strengthens the forementioned negative relationship between mechanisation in agriculture and the utilisation of children as workers. Young children in cultivating households, nevertheless, display no statistical evidence of such a relationship. But for males below the age of 10 years, in contrast to young males in non-cultivating households, MASCH and FELIT operate negatively on the economic activity of males in cultivating households. FWAGE functions to decrease the employment of young males. At the same time, none of the variables affect female children's work in cultivating households.

The regression coefficients for children above the age of 10 years are given in Table 12.3. No significant variables emerges in the analyses for older working children in non-cultivating households. The exception is that for female children: for them, the negative effect of FWAGE predominates. Older children of both sexes in cultivating households, on the other hand, show rather interesting results. The regression analysis for males working children ($R^2 = 0.42$) reveals that three variables—MASCH, FELIT and FERTZ—are statistically significant. Two of these variables, MASCH and FELIT, maintain the same sign in the analysis of female working children. These variables, as described, also exercise considerable influence on young male children in cultivating households. Thus, regions that have a higher concentration of scheduled castes and adult females who are literate tend to discourage work by children.

While the relationship between child work and adult literacy is in the expected direction, the result for MASCH and FELIT is opposite to that observed for young males with no land. It appears that both young and adult scheduled castes possibly perform the work children in cultivating families would otherwise do. The reason for a positive coefficient for FELIT is not clear. For older males, a variable that outweighs the influence of others is FERTZ with a coefficient of 327.33. Here again, the sign of the FERTZ coefficient is different from that for younger children: the usage of fertilisers reinforces the farm employment of older children. The hypothesised negative effect of new methods in agriculture on child labour requires modification for older children. This may suggest that young children are not suitable for the demands of jobs that modern technology creates in rural areas.

Discussion

The forementioned results show that while examining child labour by age, sex and landholding, some of the variables that are significant in one analysis may turn out to be insignificant in another analysis. The analyses highlight the possibility of a change in the manner in which the same variable influences a different component of child labour. Though the results seem to a certain extent contradictory, they are not so. In fact, they are consistent with the findings mentioned in the literature.

TABLE 12.3

Regression Analyses of Economic Activity of Children Between 10-14 Years in Rural India, 1970-71

Independent/ Dependent Variables	*MTFNC*	*FTFNC*	*MTFCU*	*FTFCU*
MASCH	-0.34	-0.02	-0.64	-0.49
	(0.83)	(0.06)	(2.40)+	(2.53)+
FELIT	-0.66	-0.17	-1.41	-0.49
	(1.47)	(0.57)	(4.89)+	(2.22)+
FERTZ	136.92	-75.64	327.33	124.01
	(0.69)	(0.57)	(2.56)+	(1.33)
CORAT	21.11	24.27	14.69	-2.41
	(0.54)	(0.93)	(0.61)	(0.13)
FWAGE	-0.55	-6.29	-1.93	-5.84
	(0.12)	(1.99)*	(0.70)	(2.93)+
MWTNC	-1.99	—	—	—
	(0.45)			
FWTNC	—	0.94	—	—
		(0 46)		
MWTCU	—	—	-0.72	—
		(1.10)		
FWTCU	—	—	—	-0.17
		(0.07)		
CONST	25.48	14.12	44.10	38.90
R^2	0.06	0.17	0.42	0.33
F	0.49	1.48	5.31+	3.47+

Note: *Significant at the 0.10 level;
+Significant at the 0.05 level. Figures in parentheses denote its values.

Both the proportion of scheduled castes and female literates explain child labour across the regions of rural India. Scheduled castes, who generally have no agricultural land, send their children to work for wages. If young children can earn a higher wage, more children are attracted into the labour force. The wage contribution of children belonging to households that have some land is not as important as in the case of landless households. In rural India, a rise in the income of a husband or wife frees children to participate in activities other than those in the labour force. The results for females underscore the cross effect of the employment of children and adult wage increasing the female wage rate in the rural areas substantially decreases the economic activity of female children.[7] In regions where female adult wage is high, female children presumably spend their time in domestic work, which otherwise would have occupied the time of adult women. A particularly interesting result is that there is little evidence of the effect of land distribution on child labour, but that landholding status is an important dimension of child labour. The results also suggest the impact of modernisation in agriculture on child labour. In his analysis of child employment in Egypt, Levy (1985) also showed that mechanisation has a differential influence on children in labour force.[8] He mentioned that 'mechanisation apparently displaces mainly young children' (p. 788). This study did not separately examine child labour for landless workers.

We have also analysed child labour using other variables. For example, we attempted to understand the influence of adult employment on child work. Similarly, the influence of child labour on fertility was also assessed. In these cases, we found that there was no significant effect. Unfortunately, we could not measure some of the variables as we would have desired. For the same reason, we did not analyse child labour in the context of a simultaneous system of equations. Nonetheless, the analyses show that we can obtain meaningful results from the data.

The data we have used in this study refer to the year 1970-71 and the characteristics of children in the labour force may have undergone changes since then. The school enrolment of children has increased and fertility levels are on the decline. In spite of these and other changes, children continue to be employed in economic activities and the relationships described may still be present. Providing attractive alternatives to employment for children and improving the conditions under which adult women work can induce parents to withdraw their children from labour force.

REFERENCES

Bardhan, P. 1983. 'Regional Variations in the Rural Economy,' *Economic and Political Weekly*, Vol. 18, No. 30, pp. 1319-34.

Cain, M.T. 1977. 'The Economic Activities of Children in a Village in Bangladesh,' *Population and Development Review*, Vol. 3, No. 3, pp. 201-27.

Chatterjee, G.S. and N. Bhattacharya. 1975. 'Some Observations on NSS Household Budget Data,' in V.M. Dandekar and P. Venkataramaiah (eds), *Data Base of Indian Economy, II: Role of Sample Surveys*, Calcutta, Statistical Publishing Society.

Kanbargi, R. and P.M. Kulkarni. 1985. Child Labour Schooling and Fertility in Rural Karnataka, South India, Mimeo, Bangalore, Institute for Social and Economic Change.

Khatu, K.K., A.K. Tamang and C.R. Rao. 1983. *Working Children in India*, Baroda, Operations Research Group.

Levy, V. 1985. 'Cropping Pattern, Mechanisation, Child Labour, and Fertility Behaviour in a Farming Economy: Rural Egypt,' *Economic Development and Cultural Change*, Vol. 33, No. 4, pp. 777-91.

Nag, M., B.N.F. White and R.C. Peet. 1980. 'An Anthropological Approach to the Study of the Economic Value of Children in Java and Nepal,' in H.P. Binswanger, R.E. Evenson, C.A. Florencio and B.N.F. White (eds), *Rural Household Studies in Asia*, Singapore, Singapore University Press.

Naidu, D.A. 1981. 'Child Labour Participation in India: A Statewise Census Analysis,' *Journal of Family Welfare*, Vol. 27, No. 4, pp. 48-59.

National Sample Survey Organisation (NSSO). 1978. *Time Disposition and Wage Rate for Economically*

Weaker Sections of the Rural Population of India, No. 237, Twentyfifth Round (July 1970—June 1971), Delhi, Controller of Publications.

Office of the Registrar General and Census Commissioner. 1977. *General Economic Tables*, Census of India, 1971, Series 1, Part II-B(i), Delhi, Controller of Publications.

———. 1984. *Report of Tables Based on 5 Per Cent Sample Data*, Census of India, 1981, Series 1, Part-II—Special, Delhi, Controller of Publications.

Rodgers, G. and G. Standing. 1981. 'The Economic Roles of Children: Issues for Analysis,' in G. Rodgers and G. Standing (eds), *Child Work, Poverty and Underdevelopment*, Geneva, ILO.

Rosenzweig, M.R. 1981. 'Household and Non-household Activities of Youths: Issues of Modelling, Data and Estimation Strategies,' in G. Rodgers and G. Standing (eds), *Child Work, Poverty and Underdevelopment*, Geneva, ILO.

Rosenzweig, M.R. and R. Evenson. 1977. 'Fertility, Schooling, and the Economic Contribution of Children in Rural India: An Economic Analysis,' *Econometrica*, Vol. 45, No. 5, pp. 1065-79.

Suryanarayana, M.H. and N.S. Iyengar. 1986. 'On the Reliability of NSS Data,' *Economic and Political Weekly*, Vol. 21, No. 6, pp. 261-64.

Vaidyanathan, A. 1986. 'On the Validity of NSS Consumption Data,' *Economic and Political Weekly*, Vol. 21, No. 3, pp. 129-37.

NOTES

1. There are also other estimates suggesting that a large number of children work. In a nation-wide survey in 1980, Khatu *et al.* (1983) find that there are 44 million working children. The difference between the census and survey figure is partly due to the definitions used. Census data are presented here being official source for such information.

   Acknowledgements: This analysis was carried out when Murali Dhar Vemuri was working at the International Institute for Population Sciences (IIPS), Bombay. We are grateful to Dr. K. Srinivasan, Director IIPS, for his encouragement, help and cooperation. We are also grateful to Prof. P. Bardan for his comments.

2. Several studies on child labour have been conducted in India. For this article, we have examined those published studies that have taken into account statistical controls for understanding child labour.
3. For details regarding sampling and the collection of data, see NSSO (1978).
4. A list of the regions and their composition is contained in the survey report.
5. In an Indian household, it is common for female children to be engaged in domestic work. The NSSO data also show this.
6. The regression coefficient for multiple cropping intensity has a value of -0.13 which is significant at the 10 per cent level.
7. Se Rosenzweig (1981).
8. In addition to mechanisation, Levy described a stronger effect that cotton-growing intensity has on the employment of younger children compared with older ones.

13

REPORT OF THE WORKING GROUP ON EMPLOYMENT OF CHILDREN

The Department of social Welfare set up a Working Group on 5 April 1974 to consider various problems that arise out of employment of children. The terms of reference and composition are at Annexure I.

The first meeting of the Working Group was held on 15 November 1974 when a detailed paper on the nature and magnitude of the problem of child labour and the legal provisions relating to employment of children (age, hours of work, spread of work, nature of work, etc.), medical care, education, food, housing, recreation, etc., was circulated for the consideration of the members of the Working Group. The Group noted the data constraints and recommended that a workshop may be organised in which subject matter specialists and persons with experience of labour administration may be invited to participate.

The National Institute of Public Cooperation and Child Development organised a Seminar at New Delhi on Employment of Children in India from 25 to 28 November 1975, in which five working papers on various aspects of child employment were considered. The Seminar came up with 35 recommendations.

The recommendations were considered in detail by the Working Group which met ten times. The Working Group recognised the complexity of the problem of child labour and the difficulties in reconciling short term objectives with long term goals in the face of the current socio-economic realities in the country. While arriving at different decisions, the Working Group gave particular attention to the desirability of making the decisions as specific as possible. On certain aspects the Working Group itself came to the conclusion that the present state of knowledge did not admit more definite decisions and detailed studies were necessary so that all possible implications could be taken into consideration.

STATEMENT OF THE PROBLEM OF CHILD LABOUR

The Working Group took note of the context in which the problem of child labour has developed. In earlier times, when the family was the unit of production and universal elementary education had not been recognised as an objective, it was common for children to assist their parents by doing light tasks in agriculture, animal husbandry, household industry, etc. With industrialisation, and the emergence of a wage earning class, children became subject to economic and social exploitation by employers whose primary consideration was maximisation of profits. This was pointed out by the Royal Commission on Labour (1929-31) which described at length the extremely unsatisfactory employment and working conditions of child workers.

A number of legislations and executive orders have been passed from time to time to prevent employment of children, regulate their working conditions, etc. in the organised sectors of industry. There are, however, deficiencies in the enforcement of whatever legislative provisions exist for well-being of children. The Labour Investigation Committee (1946) noted that the legislative measures relating to child employment met with little success. The report on Child Labour in India (1954) by the Labour Bureau, Simla had also pointed out the unsatisfactory state of affairs in several industries.

The Indian Constitution safeguards the interests of children in employment. Article 24 lays down that no child below the age of 14 years shall be employed to work in any factory or mine or engaged in any other hazardous employment. Article 39 (e) and (f) lays down as Directive Principle of State Policy 'that the health and strength of workers, men and women, and the tender age of children are not abused and that citizens are not forced by economic necessity to enter avocations unsuited to their age or strength' and 'that childhood and youth are protected against exploitation and against moral and material abandonment.'

The National commission on Labour (1969) reported that the 'gradual reduction in the employment of child labour since Independence is due partly to the expansion of educational facilities by the State and also to relatively better enforcement of statutory provisions relating to child labour. Employment of children is almost non-existent in organised industries. It persists in varying degrees in the unorganised sector such as small plantations, restaurants and hotels, cotton ginning and weaving, carpet weaving, stone breaking, brick kiln, handicrafts, and road building. Employment of child workers below the prescribed age is also reported to be continuing in far off places in rural areas where enforcement of statutory provisions is more difficult'.*

Statistics on the extent of employment of children are available only to a limited extent. According to the 1971 Census, the total number of child workers below the age of 15 years is 10.74 million or 5.9 per cent of the total labour force. Most of the child workers are in agriculture, livestock raising, etc. Ninety-three per cent of the child workers are in rural areas. Chid workers constitute 4.7 per cent of the total children. In terms of rural urban differential, only 0.4 per cent of children below 15 years of age in urban areas are workers as compared to 5.5 per cent in rural areas.

* *Report of the National Commission on Labour*, Ministry of Labour, Employment and Rehabilitation, 1969, p. 386.

The Working Group is of the view that the employment of child labour under the age of 15 years is no doubt undesirable and the long term objective of preventing employment of children in order to provide them adequate opportunities for growth and development is undisputed. It is the immediate future, however, which poses a dilemma. The Working Group noted that the poor economic condition of a large segment of the population and the high dependency ratio in families necessitate for pure reasons of survival, that members start contributing to the family income early in life. The deprivation of this much-needed contribution will, in the short run, depress the net availability of food and nutrition for all members, including the children. The extent of availability of educational and other social services to occupy the child have also to be taken into consideration. On the other hand, employment of children which provides cheap labour tends to shrink the employment market for adults and depress their wages. Early entry of children into the work force is tantamount to denial of the child's rights for growth and development. Taking into consideration the existing socio-economic realities, the Working Group is of the view that the balance of advantage would lie in regulating the working and employment conditions of children, protecting them from abuse, exploitation and occupational hazards and at the same time ensuring for them opportunities for educational and other facilities required for their growth and development.

RECOMMENDATIONS

The Working Group after careful consideration of the various issues outlined in the terms of reference, makes the following recommendations:

Legal provisions relating to the employment of children in various categories of regulated jobs and the extent to which these are enforced.

(i) A comprehensive note reviewing the existing legal provision relating to employment of children is given in Annexure V. The provisions in different laws have been grouped into the following categories: (a) minimum age for employment, (b) medical examination, (c) prohibition of work in hazardous occupation, (d) hours of work, (e) prohibition of night work, (f) weekly holidays, (g) annual leave with pay, (h) minimum wage, (i) vocational training, and (j) health, safety and welfare. The note also gives the norms laid down by I.L.O. Conventions in this regard and the extent to which these have been ratified by India.

It is evident that the provisions in regard to child workers are not uniform nor do they cover all the employees in every specified industry. The hours of work, prohibition of night work, prohibition work in hazardous occupations of night work, prohibition work in hazardous occupations, weekly holidays, medical fitness requirements, etc., vary from Act to Act. The definition of a child and young person is also not uniform in the different legislations. Small establishments are left out. Children in agriculture and other unorganised industries domestic services, etc., are outside the ambit of protective legislation.

The Working Group is of the view that it is not so much the deficiencies in legal provisions or the difference in regard to provisions of different legislations which require priority consideration.

(ii) At a later stage, when the results of full and proper enforcement have been duly assessed, and the level of social and economic development indicate the desirability of amending the existing legislation, expanding its scope and coverage, or enacting of new legislation, the following action could be taken:

(a) a study in depth of each legislation should be made for which purpose relevant information may be obtained from the Labour Bureau, Simla and the Chief Inspector of Factories of States. While making the study the needs of children in regard to medical care, education, nutrition and welfare should be kept in view. The amendments should then be proposed in consultation with the Department of Legal Affairs.

(Action: National Institute of Public Cooperation and Child Development)

(b) The Seminar on Employment of Children had suggested a National Children's Code which would, on the one hand, lay down minimum standards regulations and, on the other, give enough scope to the administrative machinery to suit local conditions and requirements. This may be examined in the light of the Report of the Law Institute on laws relating to children when received and other relevant material.

(Action: Department of Social Welfare)

Facilities of medical care, food, housing, recreation and opportunities for education available to children in employment in different categories of jobs under various Acts; the health hazardous, if any, involved in such jobs and the available measures for protection against them.

(iii) Part IV of the Working Paper circulated for the first meeting of the Working Group on 15 November 1974 (Annexure II) shows the limited extent of current statutory provisions in regard to education of worker's children, medical care, canteen, housing, recreation, etc., for workers even in organised sectors. Specific statutory provisions for giving medical care, education, food, housing and recreation to child workers do not exist but the general amenities for all workers prescribed under different legislations are available to child workers as well.

The implementation of whatever statutory provision exist is unsatisfactory. The Report of the Committee on Labour Welfare has pointed out the deficiencies in this regard *Immediate action is, therefore, necessary to improve the enforcement of the provision.*

(Action: Ministry of Labour)

(iv) In view of the fast changing technology and the use of new processes, commodities, machines, etc., occupations hazardous for children need to be properly identified industry by industry and measures instituted for protecting child workers. Where research studies are necessary before such occupational hazards can be listed, this may be sponsored forthwith by the respective Ministries/Departments concerned. *It is essential to constantly review the list of occupations hazardous to children and to enforce the ban on their employment vigorously in such hazardous occupations.*

(Action: Concerned Ministries, Coordination by Ministry of Labour)

(v) The Working Group recognised the urgent need to educate the employers as well as the public about the existing legal provisions to protect the interests of children. *An educational brochure should be prepared by the Ministry of Labour* with the assistance of Ministry of Heath and Family Planning, Department of Social Welfare, etc., giving detailed information on the rationale of passing protective labour laws with regard to employment of children and indicating how the violation of such legislation would be harmful to children. *The brochure should be widely circulated among employers, trade union leaders and the general public.*

(Action: Ministry of Labour)

(vi) The Working Group recognised the need for adequate welfare services and amenities for child workers but felt that action should be initiated at a later stage when the level of socio-economic development suggests action. It is of the view that the provision of welfare services and amenities for child workers should not be confined or limited by what is envisaged in the legislations. In the organised sector, employers organisations, State Welfare Boards and voluntary organisations can step in to supplement legislative provisions. The Working Group considered the suggestion made by the Seminar on Employment of Children for the creation of a Special Fund on the lines of Welfare Funds for workers in coal mines, mica mines, etc., and by a *majority view accepted the recommendation that on appropriate statutory fund be created.* The fund should be created by imposing a levy on industries/agencies employing children and should be utilised for providing welfare services to child workers. The administrative responsibility for operating these Funds should be given to the State Labour Welfare Boards.

(Action: Ministry of Labour)

Minimum age of employment of children under all Acts at 14 years.

(vii) The minimum age for employment has been defined in several legislations (Annexure V, para 10). Some sectors like agriculture, have not been covered by any legislation at all. Where legislation exists, the minimum age for employment varies from 12 years, as in the Plantations Labour Act, 1951 to 15 years as in the Motor Transport Workers Act, 1961.

The Working Group is of the view that it is not possible at the present stage of development to have a standard minimum age of employment in all sectors of the economy. However, *it may be possible to have uniformity in particular fields and for specific purposes. Variations in this regard among different states in the same sector could be removed.* For instance, the Shops and Commercial Establishments Acts in some States prescribe the minimum age of employment as 12 years and in others 14 years. It would be desirable to have the minimum age of employment at 14 years in all the States in shops and commercial establishments. The minimum age for employment under the plantations Act should be raised to 14 years. *The Ministry of Labour may initiate immediate action in this regard.*

(Action: Ministry of Labour)

(viii) The Working Group noted Convention No. 138 on minimum age for admission to employment adopted by I.L.O. in 1973. This Convention prescribed the minimum age to be less than the age of completion of compulsory schooling and, in any case, not less than 15 years. Developing countries, may, however, initially fix the minimum age at 14 years. The Convention lays down that in the case of work which is harmful to the health, safety or morals of young persons, the minimum age should not be less than 18 years. The Convention is applicable as a minimum to mining, quarrying, manufacturing units, construction, plantations and other agricultural undertakings, producing for commercial purposes etc. *The Working Group is of the view that it is not possible for India at the present stage of development to ratify this Convention. The Government of India should, however, take it as a norm to be progressively achieved.*

(Action: Ministry of Labour)

Whether the employment of children in any category of jobs in the existing conditions of work adversely affects the growth of their personality and the opportunities of educational development, and to suggest remedies.

(ix) A major problem that faced the Working Group was the absence of empirical data on different facets of the problem of employment of children, including statistics on the nature and extent of violation of existing statutory provisions relating to children, and the extent to which certain kinds of work adversely affects their growth and development. The Working Group is of the view that *at a later stage, when action is contemplated taking into consideration the level of social and economic development, research studies should be sponsored on various problems arising from the employment of children to enable the situation to be viewed in its proper perspective.* The required action for undertaking such studies should initiate from the concerned Ministries. For instance, studies relating to child labour in railway establishments should be undertaken by the Railway Board which is the concerned administrative Ministry, Similarly, those on plantations should be undertaken by the Ministry of Commerce. The concepts, parameters, definitions, tabulation framework, etc., used in the research studies should permit comparability. This should be ensured by the Labour Bureau, Simla.

(Action: Concerned Ministries; coordination by Ministry of Labour)

(x) Parents from low income groups are sometimes compelled to make their children join the work force for economic reasons. If their incomes can be increased, they are likely to desist from sending their children to work. Cottage and small industries should be promoted in rural areas. Due care should be taken of the market aspects, so that sustained augmentation of family income is possible.

(Action: Ministry of Industrial Development)

(xi) The widespread entry of children from low income groups into the employment market was not conditioned only by economic factors. There was also lack of proper appreciation on the part of parents as to how continuance of children in education would benefit their employment prospects and improve the standard of living. *The Department of education, Department of Rural Development and the Ministry of Information and Broadcasting should, therefore, make concerted efforts to retain children in the school system by educating and motivating parents to put their children into schools that in the employment market.*

(Action: Deptt. of Education, (ii) Deptt. of Rural Development and (iii) Ministry of Information and Broadcasting)

(xii) A large percentage of children, particularly from the lower income strata, who join the school system drop out and eventually join the labour force. *The Working Group is of the view that in order to retain them in schools, a number of measures are necessary:*

(a) The school environment and the curricula should be made attractive and interesting to sustain the interests of the child. Measures like supply of books, uniforms, stationery, mid-day meals, etc., should be introduced in all schools predominantly attended by poor children. Formal education alone, however, will not be able to tackle the problem and therefore the programme of non-formal education should be suitably expanded to cover these children.

(Action: Department of Education)

(b) In rural areas, the timings and vacations of the primary and middle schools should be adjusted to suit the requirements of the agricultural cycle so that children can help their parents in their work and can also attend school regularly.

(Action: Department of Education)

(c) Certain reforms in the school system are also necessary. Vocationalisation of courses should be undertaken for children in the age group of 11 to 14 years. The services of craftsmen in the village may be utilised to impart pre-vocational training to such children. Training Institute should be set up in rural areas where children can get suitable training in skilled and semi-skilled jobs and meet the requirements for skilled and semi-skilled manpower generated as a result of introduction of technological innovation in the countryside in agriculture, etc.

(Action: Department of Education and Ministry of Labour)

(d) Children under 14 years who cannot continue in school should be trained in suitable trades. The Apprenticeship Act, 1961 provides for the training of apprentices of 14 years of age and above in different trades. The possibility of extending the provisions of this Act to selectively cover children under 14 years in certain trades needs to be examined by the Ministry of Labour.

(Action: Ministry of Labour)

(e) Many children from lower income groups whose mothers go out to work, cannot attend school because they have to look after the younger siblings. Community creches and day-care centres should, therefore, be established through voluntary effort in rural as ell as urban slum areas.

(Action: Department of Social Welfare)

(xiii) Destitute children also swell the ranks of the child labour force. Such children should be taken care of by welfare services. The Department of Social Welfare is implementing a scheme of assisting voluntary organisations for the welfare of children in need of care and protection. *The services under the programme should be expanded.*

(Action: Deptt. of Social Welfare)

(xiv) The Working conditions of children engaged in domestic services, particularly their wages, hours of work, health, food and nutrition, recreation, education, etc., needed improvement. *Voluntary organisations like Mahila Mandals, Mohalla Committee, Welfare Societies and public leaders should educate the employees and the employers so that the working conditions of young domestic servants were made as conducive as possible.*

(Action: Deptt. of Social Welfare)

(xv) The Department of Social Welfare has constituted the National Children's Board with the Prime Minister as President and the Ministry of Education and Social Welfare as the Working Chairman. Representatives of all Ministries/Departments attend the meetings of the Board. Since the Board, is the highest policy making body in this country on matters pertaining to children and oversees all aspects of development of children its advice could be sought on various issues pertaining to the employment of children.

(Action: Deptt. of Social Welfare)

Whether regulatory measures on employment of children in unorganised sectors of industry could be introduced?

(xvi) Some regulatory and promotional measures need to be adopted in small and cottage industries to improve the working and living conditions of child labour and minimise the health hazards to which they are exposed. The rules framed under the Factories Act 1948 could be used as model guidelines to the extent feasible. *To begin with, it may be enforced in industrial estates with the help of the organisers of such estates.*

(Action: Ministry of Labour
(ii) Ministry of Commerce and
(iii) Ministry of Industrial Development)

(xvii) The Working Group recognised the formidable nature of the problems involved in the enforcement of legal regulatory measures in the less organised sector as for instance, catering establishments, smaller plantations etc. It took the view that *for success in this sphere immediate action is necessary so that enlightened social consciousness should be created among both the employers and the employees through educational, and promotional efforts of organisations like the Central Social Welfare Board, Federations of Trade Unions, and voluntary agencies.*

MACHINERY FOR IMPLEMENTING PROVISIONS RELATING TO EMPLOYMENT OF CHILDREN

Legal enactments and statutory provisions safeguarding interests of child labour can be effective only if backed by adequate enforcement and inspecting machinery. The Working Group noted that the present position in this regard was unsatisfactory and considered several possibilities for improving the situation. It recommended that the following measures need to be immediately taken:

(a) The existing enforcement and inspecting machinery safeguarding the interests of child labour is inadequate and, therefore, there is a need to properly orient and strengthen it in consultation with the State Governments. The Union Ministry of Labour should, in consultation with State Governments also consider if the present norm of 150 factories per labour inspector is adequate and whether it is being followed. It is not practicable to set up a separate inspectorate for child labour.

(Action: Ministry of Labour)

(b) It is necessary to have consultations with enforcement agencies in the States (Chief Inspector of Factories, Director General of Factories' Advice Service, State Labour Departments, etc.) to ascertain the feasibility and modality of involvement of voluntary effort such as creation of cadre of voluntary inspectors and the enlistment of the help of Probation Officers who can assist the enforcement staff by visiting work sites, bringing cases of violation to the notice of the official inspection machinery, etc.

(Action: Deptt. of Social Welfare)

(c) The lapses of employers in implementing legislative and other provisions in regard to children need to be widely publicised in order to build strong public opinion against defaulters. The Ministry of Information and Broadcasting, State Directorates of Publicity and the State Labour Directorates should make use of mass media for the purpose.

(Action: (i) Ministry of Labour
(ii) Ministry of Information and Broadcasting)

(d) The Home Departments of State Government should be approached to make necessary submissions to the courts so that offences relating to child labour when proved, are given deterrent punishment in suitable cases.

(Action: Ministry of Labour)

(e) Along with the strengthening of the enforcement machinery, some of promotional measures are also necessary for safeguarding the interests of child workers. Special employment bureaux should be set up by social welfare organisations for facilitating suitable placement of children in need of work and for providing appropriate vocational guidance and training. Voluntary organisations should be encouraged to open a few such employment bureaux on an experimental basis.

(Action: Deptt. of Social Welfare)

(f) Trade unions and social welfare agencies, too, have an important role to play in protecting child labour from exploitation and in ensuring that suitable opportunities are made available to them for their development. They should organise seminars, workshops, etc., and utilise other forums for effective enforcement of the provisions relating to child workers and for steps to better their conditions. Trade unions in the country should be effectively involved in controlling the magnitude of child labour and protecting the interests of children in employment. The Ministry of Labour should try to evoke the interest and cooperation of enlightened trade unions in this work. The Department of Social Welfare should enlist the interest of voluntary social welfare agencies in this regard.

(Action: (i) Ministry of Labour
(ii) Deptt. of Social Welfare)

(g) The Central Board of Workers' Education and Small Scale Service Institutes should organise seminars particularly in the less organised sectors of industry of highlight the need for labour laws relating to children.

(Action: Ministry of Labour and Ministry of Industrial Development)

(h) Since child labour in the unorganised sector is predominantly in the rural areas, it is necessary to educate the members of Panchayati Raj bodies so that they can mobilise public opinion against exploitation of child labour.

(Action: Deptt. of Rural Development)

(i) Wherever Acts relating employment of children are properly enforced, the extent of child labour is reduced. It is, therefore, necessary for the concerned Ministries/Departments to take follow-up action for the implementation of different provisions in these Acts in States/Union Territories. The effective implementation of Children Acts also reduces the incidence of child labour and, therefore, the enforcement machinery for this legislation needs to be suitably strengthened.

(Action: (i) Ministry of Labour
(ii) Ministry of Commerce and
(iii) Deptt. of Social Welfare)

(j) The present scope of the Children's Act, 1960 should be examined with a view to make it more comprehensive so that opportunities for development are available to those children who may otherwise be obliged to work in hazardous conditions. It may also be seen whether the term 'victimised children,' under the Children's Act, 1960 may be made more comprehensive to include children who are forced to work in hazardous occupations.

(Action: Deptt. of Social Welfare)

(k) The machinery for coordination of work to safeguard the interests of children in employment was considered by the Working Group. It noted that such problems require coordinated action by a number of Ministries/Departments at the Centre as well as in the States/Union Territories. However, there should be a nodal Ministry to coordinate the work and since coordination of child welfare programme has been assigned to the Department of Social Welfare Under the Allocation of Business Rules the Working Group decided that this Department may be entrusted with coordination of work in this sphere.

(Action: Deptt. of Social Welfare)

The Working Group discussed the suggestion of the Seminar on Employment of Children for the setting up of a National Society for the Protection of the Working Child to effectively coordinate the work of Children's Aid Societies. It came to the conclusion that time was not yet ripe for the establishment of such a society.

S.Y. Ranade Chairman
Secretary to the Government of India
Deptt. of Social Welfare

MEMBERS

M.M. Rajendran
Joint Secretary
Deptt. of Social Welfare

R.S. Jain
Deputy Secretary
Deptt. of Mines

S.N. Dutt
Deputy Secretary
Deptt. of Education

R. Ramanathan
Deputy Director (Estt.)
Railway Board

T.S. Sankaran
Additional Secretary
Ministry of Labour

M.K. Mishra
Deputy Legal Adviser
Ministry of Law Justice
and Company Affairs

R.K. Sanyal
Deputy Commissioner
Deptt. of Family Planning

K.V. Iyer
Director (Labour and Employment)
Planning Commission

A.R. Dhruwasan
Senior Research Officer (SW)
Planning Commission

B. Chatterjee
Director
National Institute of
Public Cooperation and
Child Development

(Smt.) Pramila Pandit Barooa
General Secretary
Indian Council for Child Welfare

(Smt.) Meera Mahadevan
Chairman
Mobile Creches for Working Women

A.B. Bose
Member-Secretary
Director (Research)
Deptt. of Social Welfare

ANNEXURE-I

NO. 8-10/73-RPU
GOVERNMENT OF INDIA
(BHARAT SARKAR)
MINISTRY OF EDUCATION AND SOCIAL WELFARE
(SHIKSHA EVAM SAMAJ KALYAN MANTRALAYA)
DEPARTMENT OF SOCIAL WELFARE
(SAMAJ KALYAN VIBHAG)

New Delhi, the 14th January 1975
24th Pausa 1896 Saka

Subject: Setting up a Working Group on Employment of Children.

In supersession of the office order No. 8-10/73-RPU dated 5th April, 1974, it has been decided to extend the Terms of Reference and Composition of the Working Group as fallows:

Terms of Reference

(i) to review the legal provisions relating to the employment of children in various categories of regulated jobs and the extent to which these are enforced;

(ii) to study the facilities of medical care, food, housing, recreation and opportunities for education available to children in employment in different categories of jobs under various Acts; the health hazards, if any, involved in such jobs and the available measures for protection against them;

(iii) to study the possibility of fixing the minimum age of employment of children under all Acts at 14 years;

(iv) to assess, in the light of findings, whether the employment of children in any category of jobs in the existing conditions of work adversely affects the growth of their personality and the opportunities of educational development, and to suggest remedies;

(v) to consider whether regulatory measures on employment of children in unorganised sectors of industry could be introduced; and

(vi) to consider the machinery for implementing provision relating to employment of children.

Composition of Members

(i) Secretary — Chairman

Department of Social Welfare

(ii)	Joint Secretary (SW) Department of Social Welfare	Member
(iii)	Joint Secretary Department of Mines Ministry of Steel and Mines	Member
(iv)	Joint Secretary Ministry of Commerce	Member
(v)	Joint Secretary Ministry of Shipping and Transport	Member
(vi)	Additional Legal Adviser Ministry of Law, Justice and Company Affairs	Member
(vii)	Joint Secretary Ministry of Labour	Member
(viii)	Shri G.S. Madan Deputy Director Ministry of Labour	Member
(ix)	Joint Secretary Department of Family Planning Ministry of Health and Family Planning	Member
(x)	Joint Secretary Department of Education and Social Welfare	Member
(xi)	Additional Director Establish. (Specl.) Railway Board Ministry of Railways	Member
(xii)	Director (Labour and Employment) Planning Commission	Member
(xiii)	Joint Director (Social Welfare Division) Planning Commission	Member
(xiv)	President Indian Council for Child Welfare	Member
(xv)	Director Central Institute of Research and Training in Public Cooperation	Member

(xvi)	Chairman Mobile Creches for Working Women	Member
(xvii)	Director (PREM) Department of Social Welfare	Member Secretary

Sd/-

(K.R. Ramachandran)

Joint Secretary to the Government of India

14

CHILDREN AND WORK*

An ILO Policy Framework for the International Year of the Child, 1979.

INTRODUCTION

Background

On 21 December 1976, the United Nations General Assembly adopted a resolution proclaiming 1979 as the International Year of the Child (IYC) with general objectives of promoting welfare of children. The resolution calls upon the UN agencies to contribute to the implementation of the objectives of the year, the purpose for which an inter-agency advisory group was formed in early 1977.

Since March 1977, the ILO has participated in several inter-agency advisory group meetings. The nature of the discussions indicate that certain points regarding ILO policy concerning working children need to be clarified and analysed. The purpose of this exercise is to enable the ILO focal points to co-ordinate interdepartmental activities in a clearer perspective so that the ILO inputs for the preparation of the International year of the child, 1979, adhere to a coherent policy pattern.

Main Issue

It is a well-known fact that, despite the efforts made by the ILO and member State to abolish child labour, there exists a substantial number of children, particularly in developing areas of the world, who are at work, often in exploitative conditions. No doubt, they belong to the most vulnerable category for whom the IYC intends to offer intensive assistance. The immediate question would be how the ILO should confront this reality of working children and reconcile it with the long-term objective of eliminating child labour; how to harmonise the need to protect these working children with the existing ILO activities in order to relate policy action to IYC.

Scope of the Exercise

(a) The UN Secretary-General's report to ECOSOC IYC made it clear that the focus of the year was to be children and *not children and youth*. Though there is no explicit

---

*Prepared by INTERNATIONAL LABOUR OFFICE Geneva, February 1978.

reference for the age of children in that report, or in the resolution, the Preparatory Committee to ACC (May 1976) States that "the year should focus on *children from birth to about age 14 or 15,* but should not exclude the prenatal period". And this was reaffirmed at the first meeting of the IYC Advisory Group. Accordingly, the present exercise takes up ILO policies and programmes in relation to population in that age group. Also the term "children" in this paper means that age group.

(b) The ILO focal point for IYC has been assigned the responsibility to work for the year and not for the permanent ILO programmes regarding children. Accordingly, the present exercise takes up relatively modest problems which would constitute elements of an ILO policy framework for IYC.

ILO ACTIVITIES ON BEHALF OF CHILDREN: A BRIEF REVIEW

To put the problem in perspective, it might be useful to make a brief review of the policies and programmes hitherto undertaken by the ILO concerning the question of children.

Constitutional Mandate

The ILO Construction and the Declaration of Philadelphia clarify, though in simple terms the obligation of the ILO to work on behalf of children.

(a) In its preamble, the Constitution refers to the "protection of children" as one of the requisites to improve the conditions of labour.[1]

(b) The Declaration makes it obligatory for the ILO to further programmes to promote "child welfare" among nations of the world.

Principal Phases

(1) Prohibition of Child Labour

The prohibition of employment of children has been one of the basic concerns of the ILO since its creation, as manifested in the adoption of the Minimum Age (Industry) Convention (No. 5) at the first session of the International Labour Conference in 1919, which prohibits in principle the admission to employment of children *under 14.* Since then, a number of Conventions and Recommendations have been adopted by the Conference dealing with the minimum age of admission to various occupations or the earlier instruments have been revised.[2] Comprehensive stands in this field have been embodied in the Convention (No. 138) and Recommendation (No. 146) adopted by the Conference in 1973, which established an over-all minimum age of 15 years in principle, without reference to the type of work involved. Convention No. 138 explicitly reaffirms ILO policy orientation towards child labour. In its preamble, it notes the following goal: "...(of) *achieving the total abolition of child labour...*", and requests member States to "raise progressively the minimum age for admission to employment or work to a level consistent with the fullest physical and mental development of young persons".

(2) Protection of Children at Work

While promoting prohibition of child labour, the history of the ILC shows a consistent policy to protect working children from undesirable conditions of work. A series of Convention and Recommendations prohibiting certain types of work and regulating the conditions of work of *young persons* also apply to *children* either explicitly or implicitly.

(a) Night Work

The prohibition of night work for children goes back to 1919 when the ILO adopted the Night Work of Young Persons (Industry) Convention (No. 6) which prohibits the employment of young persons under 18 during the night with particular stress on the night work of those under 16. A number of Conventions and Recommendations have followed this early norm,[3] some of which explicitly refer to children *under 14.*[4]

(b) Hazardous and Dangerous Work

The first ILO adopted Lead Poisoning (Women and Children) Recommendation (No. 4) recommending member States to prohibit employment of persons under 18 years in certain work dealing with lead. It was followed by a number of standards restricting employment of young persons including, children, in certain types of work.[5]

(c) Medical Examination

Since its early days, the ILO has also adopted a number of instruments which require medical certification of fitness on entry to employment and periodical medical examinations for children and young persons.

(d) Other Working Conditions

The ILO instruments provide for stricter standards for young workers in relation to working hours, weekly rest, holidays with pay and apprenticeship.

In addition to the standard-setting activities described above, the ILO has done a considerable amount of research work and organised experts meetings and seminars on the protection of children. In the recent programme of PIACT, the ILO expresses its intention to extend specific activities for young workers in order to improve their working conditions and environment.

(3) Preparation for Employment (Vocational Guidance and Vocational Training)

Another field of the ILO's concern has been to promote the development of children's adaptability for work, or assisting children prepare themselves for future working life. This phase of ILO activity seems to be of relatively recent development, the first reference being found in the Vocational Training Recommendation, 1939 (No. 57), which states that compulsory education should provide "pre-vocational preparation for all children" as a process to "facilitate future vocational guidance". Thereafter, however, the ILO's concern for this question seems to have been rapidly enhanced. In addition to the establishment of standards, a number of expert meetings and meetings of consultants have analysed problems of vocational guidance, pre-vocational guidance and vocational training for children. Since 1940, a number of related studies and publications have also appeared on these questions. Technical co-operation programmes have also continuously developed on this subject.

A part from vocational guidance, the terminology used in these standards and other ILO documents regarding "vocational preparation" is not always consistent: number of different terms have been used such as "pre-vocational training" or "pre-vocational preparation". Such terms frequently designate schemes for children of school age (in school or out of school), in order to foster interest in work, give them knowledge on work and life, and to impart basic practical skills and related technical knowledge, as a preparatory process to entering into full vocational training.

With regard to formal vocational training, the ILO's position seems to be given exclusively to young persons above school-leaving age. The Vocational Training Recommendation, 1939 (No. 57) states that any "attempt at vocational training should be avoided" in pre-vocational preparation while the Vocational Training (Agriculture) Recommendation, 1956 (No. 101) recommends "practical courses in the use of school gardens and in homecrafts as part of school work". The Minimum Age Convention, 1973 (No. 138) also admits the vocational training of children above 14 years under certain conditions (Article 6).

In his report to the meeting of the Fifth African Regional Conference (September-October 1977), on the agenda item entitled "Education for development", the Director-General emphasised the importance of the non-formal education for young people—particularly in the rural area.

Another area that continues to be the concern of the ILO as reflected in its own technical co-operation programmes as well as those in co-operation with other agencies is specified in ILO Recommendation No. 99 concerning vocational rehabilitation of the disabled. It incorporates special provisions for disabled children and young persons. They emphasise, inter alia, that "the fundamental purpose of vocational rehabilitation services for disabled children and young persons should be to reduce as much as possible the occupational and psychological handicaps imposed by their disabilities and to offer them full opportunities of preparing for, and entering, the most suitable occupations".

(4) Protection of Children of Working Mothers

The ILO has also shown some concern for the protection of children of working mothers in relation to the question of maternity protection of working woken.

At its first session in 1919, the International Labour Conference adopted the Maternity Protection Convention, 1919 (No. 3), providing for the standards of leave before and after childbirth and nursing time. This convention was followed by a number of Conventions and Recommendations which evolved standards for facilities for nursing mothers, child care facilities and services and extended leave for child care. The Declaration and plan of Action on equality of opportunity and treatment for women workers, adopted by the 1975 Conference, called for member States to strengthen social infrastructure for child care.

This forms, however, a quite different area of policy from (1), (2) and (3) mentioned above and does not directly relate to child labour.

QUESTION OF WORKING CHILDREN

As mentioned earlier, the preparatory work for IYC has brought to light the question of children who are actually working as a most vulnerable section in society. As one of the main aims of the year is to extend programmes to the most disadvantageous groups of children, the ILO is expected to develop programme action in this area together with other agencies.

Present Situation

The ILO's efforts to build up standards concerning child labour 'have undoubtedly played a great role in stimulating and shaping national regulations concerning minimum age for admission to employment and, more generally speaking, in bringing out a wider recognition of the need to regulate the employment of children." There remain only a few countries which do not have legislation concerning minimum age or regulations on the employment of children covering industry. Considerable progress has been made in applying it to the organised sectors and many of the worst abuses connected with the employment of children have been suppressed and child labour in its classic sense of mass exploitation in mines and factories has become an evil of the past. However, child labour still remains widespread and not less disquieting in many parts of the world.

"The extent of child labour is illustrated by some estimates, the lowest of which surmises that at least 43 million aged 14 or under were economically active in 1970. More than 90 per cent of these children were in the developing regions of the world where one out of every 16 children aged between 5 and 14 was a workers." According to recent ILO estimates this number will have grown to 52 million in 1979. Among them, only 1 million will originate from developed countries; the remainder, approximately 29 million, will be from South Asia, 10 million from Africa, 9 million from East Asia and 3 million from South Asia, and 3 million from Latin America. The estimates also show that 80 per cent of these working children would be classified as "unpaid family workers". The tabulated data only shows the "tip of the iceberg" as the status of "economically active" young persons is both a controversial definitional problem and a sensitive issue with governments. Behind the statistics, it can be easily surmised that a much larger number of children are engaged in economic activities.

There does not yet exist any over-all statistical data analysing occupational distribution of these children or systematic analysis of the actual conditions of their work. But some research results indicate that the great majority of children are to be found in agriculture or in small-scale industries in rural areas, and in workshops or quasi-family undertakings in urban areas. It appears that they frequently work under conditions detrimental to their health and welfare and that they have never been to school or have been to school or have dropped out at some stage of their schooling. Nevertheless, as there are often no alternatives in many developing areas, the children who have jobs and are able to contribute to the family income are considered to be "privileged." Indeed, they are far more privileged than those children who are forced on to the streets in substantial numbers in the urban centres of developing areas.

Why Do Children Work?

Again there is no over-all statistical data analysing the reasons why children work.

Is it because of the lack of legislation? Certainly "yes" in some countries where they have no norm prohibiting child labour because they have a permissive attitude towards child labour and it is taken for granted that children work. However, there are only a few such countries at present. As noted before, in almost all countries, including developing countries, the legislation concerning minimum age for admission to employment or regulations about the employment of children exists and at least covers industry. Is it then because of the ineffectiveness of enforcement of such legislation? Again, "yes" for in many countries, an inspection system is not adequately developed. And more so because legislation often excludes traditional workshops, quasi-family undertakings, petty commerce, street trades and agriculture where the majority of children work, and because the enforcement of legislation, if any, is extremely difficult in these sectors.

However, while part of the problem certainly derives from inadequate legislation and insufficient enforcement, a far more basic cause for children to work would be the poverty of the family. A child goes out to work as a wage earner, apprentice or a bound worker in order to contribute to the family income or to, at least, lighten his family's burden of supporting him. Also, another widespread cause for child labour would be the general low standard of development of the areas or the countries where there are little educational facilities and very little, or no industry. The only possibility of work is in subsistence farming or fishing and petty commerce in which the family undertakings depend on the work of the entire family and its members. There, children may not have any school to attend; instead they are counted as indispensable manpower in their parents' undertakings. At least they can learn vocational knowledge and skill for the trade, there being no other way of learning.

Ignorance, negligence or indifference of the society towards the question of child labour should also not be overlooked. Reforms in the past, in many countries, originated in the recognition of the misery of child labour and awareness of the public opinion for the betterment of the situation.

If this is indeed the reality, the strategy to eliminate child labour should include, in the first instance, an attack against poverty and underdevelopment. Efforts should be made to increase family income so that children would not have to work to make ends meet in the household economy, and also in the promotion of development of communities so that children would have proper access to educational opportunities. This might be considered the fundamental prerequisite for the elimination of child labour. These elements would be part of the over-all plan of development in which the entire UN system is involved, and for the ILO this would form a component of the Basic Needs Strategy, the Programmes of Rural Development and the World Employment Programme.

The ILO strategy should also include programmes to promote awareness among people including employers, trade unions and parents towards a wider recognition of the problem and a deeper understanding for its improvement.

What do They Need?

If children work, and they do, policies must be planned on how to meet their needs. What are their needs?

First, they should no doubt be protected from exploitation and from the hazardous conditions of work which would endanger their physical and mental development. They should be ensured of safety and health in their working place; they should be kept from night work; they should not be carrying heavy loads; they should be ensured of limited working hours and sufficient weekly rest periods and holidays and their individual physical condition and fitness for the job should be cared for, etc. This would mean adequate provisions in national legislation, which adhere to the standards set by the ILO, and its effective enforcement. Also it would mean incentives to encourage employers to improve general working conditions and environment of the working place. Further, it would be necessary to have programmes to bring about a proper recognition of the needs of children among parents and the general public.

Children should also have access to educational opportunities, to at least get the basic education and, hopefully, the basic vocational education which would develop there potentiality to be capable workers and responsible citizens. Where there are schools the working hours should be so regulated that the children are able to attend classes. Where there are no schools, provision of some informal education should be made. Provision of such educational facilities falls naturally under public authorities; the responsibility of ensuring children's access to such facilities involves parents and employers.

Provision of educational facilities, especially development of the free compulsory education system is of basic necessity in order not only to give children adequate learning but also to keep them from working: for staying out of school and engaging in work are often two sides of the same coin.

Needs of Children by Categories

For designing programmes, "working children" could be classified in the following four categories: children in wage-earning employment; children bounded with artisans; children living and working in family as "unpaid family workers" and children working and schooling.

Working children in each category have their own specific problem and needs, in addition to the general problem and needs as observed above.

(a) Children in Wage-Earning Employment

These are the ones who are the most easily exposed to the danger of exploitation and hazardous conditions. Much depends on the discretion of the employers. The employers should be urged to ensure adequate conditions of work for the children by enforcement of legislation and administrative advice. Also, parents should be encouraged to make their children leave work and go to school, if the economic situation so allows. However, the children are often employed in small scale industries, petty commerce and domestic service, to which labour legislation, if any, would not usually apply. Labour administration alone would have limited influences in this field and co-operation with other administration of social services is imperative, in fact-finding and publicity work as well as relief work for individual cases.

(b) Children Bounded with Artisans

The same danger of exploitation and hazardous conditions is to be found with them, more so as they are often bound by an advance paid to their parents and, as they often live with their patrons, their duty often includes service for the family of their patron. However, this type of work can promise a future for the children, the definite future as artisans. Employers or patrons should be urged future as artisans. Employers or patrons should be urged to provide children with adequate training as well as improved conditions by enforcement of legislation and administrative advice. Setting standards of work and training by organisations of employers would also be encouraged. Such standards should include children's access to school. Obscurity of their conditions of working and living, however, would be the first question to face.

(c) Children As "Unpaid Family Workers"

They are supposed to form the majority of working children, engaging mostly in agriculture. The danger of exploitation is usually less than in category (b), as they live in family and parental care and their work is not formally controlled. They can also learn, by doing, skills needed for a craft. Their main deprivation seems to be lack of educational opportunities, not to speak of the lack of vocational preparation for employment in modern sectors. Too often they are deprived of schooling, simply because there are no schools.

Provision to open schools should be of prime importance. Informal educational facilities such as classes by co-operation of voluntary organisations could replace formal school education. Measures for children of this category would be most directly related to the development programmes in general, where co-operation of various agencies would be necessary.

(d) Children Working and Schooling

Some children have a working and a schooling life combined. They are privileged in the sense that there are schools to attend and that their parents allow them to go. Some of them are really privileged in that they do engage in light work of their own choice on a part-time basis while attending the ordinary school of primary education, which is usually allowed by the national legislation as well as under certain conditions by exceptional clauses contained in ILO standards. But the majority would be those concerning minimum age who engage in regular work and still want to attend school. Their school attendance often cannot but be on a part-time basis because their working hours prevent them from full-time attendance. On the other hand, those children who work after full-time schooling are in danger of exhaustion because of the double burden. Ensuring schooling hours, should come first. In order to ensure schooling hours and to limit the total amount of the burden, regulation of working hours would be inevitably required. Also climate and practice for ensuring adequate schooling hours among employers and parents should be developed.

ILO POLICY FRAMEWORK FOR IYC

The above observations seem to lead to the following suggestions:

ILO Policy orientation

ILO policy programmes for the coming years, including 1979, the International Year of the child, could be based on the following guidelines:

(1) Prohibition of Child Labour

The ILO would promote programmes to prohibit child labour with a view to achieving the total abolition of child labour which is its basic long-term goal. Specifically it would promote ratification and application of Convention No. 138 and other Conventions on minimum age still in force. It would also encourage member States to promote labour inspection and other measures to eliminate child labour.

(2) Protection of Children at Work

The ILO would strengthen its programmes to protect children who work. In addition, it would also continue to promote statutory control of their work, introduce measures to ameliorate their working and living conditions and improve their access to educational opportunity. Within this framework, ILO's Basic Needs Strategy would explore the needs of working children as part of its research programmes.

To meet their needs, however, does not or should not mean to preserve child labour. On the contrary, the basic ILO policy objective is to eliminate this. The protection of the children by meeting their needs is, therefore, to be considered something of a "transitional programme" which would extinguish itself when child labour has become abolished eventually. Nevertheless, at present and in the foreseeable future, an adequate protective policy would play an indispensable role for the welfare of the needy children who have to work, unless such work is contrary to ratified ILO Conventions on minimum age, in which case the priority objective would be, of course, the implementation of these Conventions. Also, it would function as an effective step to accelerate the progressive prohibition and to achieve eventually the total abolition of child labour by producing a climate in favour of children and developing conditions to enable achievement of such goal.

(3) Attacking the Basic Causes of Child Labour

The basic causes for child labour being underdevelopment and ignorance, the ILO would develop programmes to attack the basic economic and social causes. Particularly, the ILO would continue to develop its programmes of employment-generating projects and of rural development to tackle poverty and underdevelopment. It would also develop research and publicity programmes on child labour in order to clarify the problems of child labour and to promote awareness of the problem among member States as well as among other international agencies.

(4) Provision of Vocational Preparation for All Children

The policy to develop children's adaptability for future work life by providing adequate preparation, is a most positive approach on behalf of children. The policy, which is of relatively recent development, would be enhanced in future in parallel with the growing concept in the ILO of "development of human resources" or with increasing emphasis put on quality of human life in planning for development in general. The ILO would attempt to evolve programmes to promote vocational guidance and selected types of pre-vocational training, both formal and informal for all children both in out of school. In these programmes, special consideration would be given to girls so that they would have equal opportunities with boys in conformity with the principles set forth in the Human Resources Development Recommendation, 1975 No. 150). Special care would also be taken of problems of disabled children to receive education and training best suited to their age, abilities, aptitudes and interests in line with the vocational Rehabilitation (Disabled) Recommendation, 1955 (No. 99). The ILO would place particular emphasis on developing operational activities by technical co-operation projects in co-operation with UNESCO and UNICEF. Such strategy of the ILO might be symbolically expressed and supported by the concept "Today's children are tomorrow's workers".

(5) The ILO would also continue to be concerned with child care facilities and services of working mothers, by including such components in its programmes concerning "maternity protection for working mothers" and "strengthening social infrastructure"

in various countries. This policy orientation would be enhanced in parallel to the increase of participation by working mothers in the labour force and the progressive concern by the public in this question. Though this policy does not fall directly in the area of the ILO, it is obvious that this would also contribute to the "welfare of children", wherever the ILO is concerned and the IYC is particularly interested.

ANNEXURE 1

Children and Work, 1979

Area	*Total active (millions)*	*Unpaid family workers**	
		Per cent of total active	*(millions)*
World	52.0	80	41.2
—More developed regions	1.3	40	0.5
—Less developed regions	50.7	80	40.6
South Asia	29.0	80	23.2
East Asia	9.1	70	6.4
Africa	9.7	95	9.2
Latin America	3.1	65	2.0
Europe	0.7	50	0.4
USSR	—	—	—
Northern America	0.3	10	—
Oceania	0.1	85	0.1

* Includes workers on own account.

Source: ILO, Bureau of Statistics.

REFERENCES

1. "The Minimum Age Convention, 1973 (No. 138) permits the employment or work of children of 13 to 15 years of age in light work, if such work does not prejudice their attendance at school (Article 7).
2. Minimum Age (Sea) Convention, 1920 (No. 7); Minimum Age (Agriculture) Convention, 1921 (No. 10); Minimum Age (Trimmers and Stokers) Convention, 1921 (No. 15); Minimum Age (Non-Industrial Employment) Convention, 1932 (No. 33); Minimum Age (Non-Industrial Employment) Recommendation, 1932 (No. 41); Minimum Age (Sea) Convention (Revised), 1936 (No. 58); Minimum Age (Industry) Convention (Revised), 1937 (No. 59); Minimum Age (Non-Industrial Employment) Convention (Revised), 1937 (No. 60); Minimum Age (Coal Mines) Recommendations, 1953 (No. 96); Minimum Age (Fishermen) Convention, 1959 (No. 112); Minimum Age (Underground work) Convention, 1965 (No. 123).
3. For example, night work of Children and Young Persons (Agriculture) Recommendation, 1921 (No. 14)*; Night Work of Young Persons (Non-Industrial Occupations) Convention, 1964 (No. 79)*; Night Work of Young Persons (Non-Industrial Occupations) Recommendation,

1946 (No. 80); Night Work of Young Persons (Industry) Convention (Revised), 1948 (No. 90) and Wages, Hours of Work and Manning (Sea) Convention (Revised), 1958 (No. 109).

4. Those marked with an asterisk in footnote 2 above.
5. They include: White Lead (Painting) Convention, 1921 (No. 13); Radiation Protection Convention, 1960 (No. 115); Conditions of Employment of Young Persons (Underground Work) Recommendation, 1965 (No. 125); Maximum Weight Convention. 1967 (No. 127); and Benzene Convention, 1971 (No. 136).

15

CHILD LABOUR—A HARSH REALITY

With an increasing rate of industrialisation and modernisation the incidence of child labour, in all the developing countries has been growing alarmingly. It is a socio-economic and development problem of varied dimensions and great significance particularly from the futuristic point of view. When India is poised to enter the 21st century after a short while—an era of total modernisation of industry and agriculture—the problem of child labour is growing both extensively and intensively.

Child labour in India has been in existence all through the ages. While in the past, children worked in the family occupations that were determined by the caste system, more as apprentices or understudies to the head of the family or any other elderly craftsman within the family, clan or caste, and the work was a part of the process of socialisation of the child, in the contemporary society the children are employed as wage labourers. The child as a wage labourer is purely a phenomenon of industrialisation and modernisation. And as viewed by the National Commission on Labour (1969) the employment of children is more of an economic problem than any thing else.

The basic attributes of work are purpose, plan and freedom. The function of work in childhood is primarily developmental and not economic. The work as a direct fulfilment of child's natural abilities and creative potentialities is always conductive to his healthy growth. When work is taken up as a means of a direct fulfillment of child's natural abilities and creative potentialities he is enormously benefitted. But when the work is taken up as a means of survival it becomes enslaving in character and deleterious in its impact. And when the business of earning or of participation in self or family support conflicts directly or indirectly with the business of growth and education the result is child labour. It rather assumes the character of a social problem in as much as it hinders, arrests or distorts the natural growth process. To state it differently, child labour refers to an economic practice and signifies employment in the so called gainful, occupation to the labour of the family. Its extent is normally measured by the qualitative standards; only an age line differentiates it from adult work and employment.

Many attempts have been made to define the term child labour but without much success. It generally refers to an employment of a child in a gainful occupation with a view to supplement labour income of his family. The United States Child Labour Committee viewed child labour as "any work by children hat interferes with their full physical development, their opportunities for a desirable minimum of education or their needed recreation." According to late Shri V.V. Giri, the former President of India and a labour leader of repute, the term child labour has two basic elements; (i) employment of children in gainful occupations with a view to adding to the labour income of their families; and (ii) purposeful oppression and exploitation of working children leading to deprivation of their legitimate opportunities for growth.

The term child labour basically means the children below the age of fifteen who are employed for hire or reward in occupations that are injurious to their physical, mental, intellectual moral and social development due to oppression and exploitation inherent in that employment.

The term child labour, hence, does not include the children in the age group 5-15 who are working for an hour or two to earn additional pocket money, the children who help their parents on family farms or occupations, and the youngster doing household chores. The term child labour instead encompasses the young boys and girls working in small industries, enterprises, in tasks that are repetitive and involve handling of microscopically fine wires, assembling of minute or tiny parts ultimately resulting in loss of eyesight with in few years of Employment or resulting in physical disabilities, the farm-hands, the cowherd and shepherd boys who are subordinated to work for day and night, the children, working in factories and mines the bonded children, the children employed as seasonal and cheep labour in pesticides-soaked fields, the children working in numerous small industrial workshops and service establishments including hotels and other types of eating places, the self-employed depending on the middlemen for a reward for their labour, the children in street trades practically ubiquitous in all the developing countries. These are the children who are forced to live a premature adult life, working long hours for low wages under conditions damaging to their physical and mental development, sometimes separated from the families, frequently deprived of meaningful educational and training opportunities that could open up for them a better feature.

Magnitude of the Problem

India has earned the dubious distinction of having the world's largest child labour population. It has about one-third of the total child labour population this planet has. Even China which has largest child population does not have such a big number of child workers. According to the official estimates based on a sample survey conducted in 1983 there were 17.36 million working children below 14. The Operations Research Group, Baroda in 1984-85 estimated that there are 44 million child workers in India. These figures only refer to the working children who have been recognised and counted. The number of children who are not covered by any ecensus enumeration or sample surveys, who are outside the scope of the term 'worker' as defined by Census, and whose employment and work is disguised and clandestine is enormous. Furthermore, two-fifth of the total India's child population live in conditions adverse to survival.

Using the percentage calculation of the Census and sample surveys and the Operations Research Group, as well as other estimates, the number of working children in 1987-88 would be 55 million. Thee sources also tell us that the population of children in the age-group 5 to 15 is 26.2 per cent of the total population, which means that there are 196.2 million children in the age group 5 to 15. And if we accept the observation that two-fifth of the total Indian child population live in conditions adverse to survival and that another 5 to 10 per cent of the children seek employment not because of economic compulsions but because of their parents' desire to get them employed in supposedly fuerative jobs while they are still young or to prevent them from becoming delinquents, we may safely estimate that more than 100 million children are most likely supplementing their family incomes or supporting themselves through wage labour. In fact, an international voluntary organisation called BALAI estimated in 1985 that there were more than 110 million child workers in India.

Add to this disturbing phenomenon of huge number the incidence of child labour has been increasing year after year. Another disturbing phenomenon of child labour is that in recent years the children from the neighbouring countries like Nepal and Bangla Desh are sneaking into the child labour market in cities like Delhi, Calcutta, etc., making the problem still more complex.

Sectors of Child Employment

The National Commission on Labour observed that 'the high incidence of child labour is.... mostly in agriculture, plantations and shops and in the small scale and unorganised sectors. It is not entirely absent even in the organised sector of Industry. Children are still employed in mica mines.... (p. 34). According to the report of the Director General of I.L.O., the sample enquiries suggest that in India as many as 87 per cent of the 10-14 years old children in rural areas and about one-eighth of those in urban areas are at work (p. 9-10). Chemical producing industries probably employ large number of them. Similarly food, non-metalic, mineral products, tobacco, match factories, tea factories, mica factories, and beedi manufacturing employ children in large numbers.

In other words, children are employed in all the three sectors, viz. agriculture, manufacturing industries and services. More than 80 per cent of the child workers in India are employed in agriculture and allied occupations including the plantations while the remaining are engaged in different occupations and umpteen number of activities in towns and cities of all sizes either on a full-time or part-time basis. To mention a few of these, children are employed in domestic services, hotels and restaurants and other eating places, the automobile workshops had fuelling stations, small factories, workshops and repair shops (that are not covered under the Factories Act, 1948), beedi and agarabatti rolling, garment manufacturing, shoe making and shoe shining, transport, fireworks and match factories, zari and zaradosi industry, carpet weaving, handloom and power-looms, food processing, food packing and labelling, packing of consumer articles, cycle repairing, box making basket making, brick kilns, construction industry, rag picking, street trades like vegetable and fruit vending, sale of lottery tickets, the traditional occupations like carpentry, tailoring, pottery, hair trimming and dressing, laundry retail outlets, load carrying, news paper selling and distributing, clubs and cinema houses, etc, etc. The list is rather endless. As a matter of fact, it is rightly observed that "there is no occupation/activity where a child is not employed."

Why Child Labour and Child Employment?

Child labour is essentially a development problem. It is a product of the existing socio-economic conditions in any given society. Hence, the basic causative factor for increasingly large number of working children in India (and other developing countries (too) has been extreme and widespread poverty of the masses. The complexity of the problem increases when it is coupled with adult unemployment and under-employment, inadequate and intermittent nature of income, low standard of living and mass illiteracy and ignorance.

Chronic poverty, however, is the strongest single factor responsible for high incidence, prevalence and perpetuation of child labour. A child from a poverty stricken family seeks work, according to I.L.O. Surveys, in order "to reduce to the greatest extent possible the poverty in which he is living and thus to help him to satisfy his basic needs. Even the smallest payments in cash or in kind are welcome in the poverty-stricken home in which, as a rule, he lives. Moreover, the child is led to believe that he must work from an early age through solidarity with the family group, so as to compensate as much as possible for the economic burden that he represents and to share in the maintenance of his family, which is usually a very large one. Today, very many children in the developing countries consider it quite normal that they should continue the family tradition of not attending school and of beginning work at a tender age, irrespective of the degree of poverty of the family. Another reason why children work is the parents' wish to keep their children occupied and off the streets, so that they do not get up to mischief, that is, tempted to draft into vagrancy with al its consequences. Of course, this argument is valid only when the child finds a job indoors and cannot be put forward when he is sent to work on the streets in the first place."

"Children may also feel obliged to work because they are doing badly at school and because there is no other alternative. If the parents are able to let the child go to school for only a few years, it is likely that he will encounter more difficulties during his years at school than a child from a better-off family. However, in many cases the parents prefer to send the child out to work rather than to school, either because there is no school within a reasonable distance of the family home, or because they cannot do without the income the working child brings in, or because they cannot meet the costs of sending the child to school, or again because they cannot see what use schooling would be to him."

"Another direct cause of child employment is the situation at home. There may be tension and uncertainty, provoked or increase by poverty; the father may have left home; the mother may be alone, the father or the mother, or both, may fall ill, or become physically unfit, or die. However, the argument that the children are obliged to work because of the disappearance of the breadwinner is often fallacious because it is generally the head of the family himself who sees to it that his children go out to work.:

"Again, when a rural family migrates to the town, the adults are straight-away faced with a new and unknown environmental and labour situation. As a result of the instability and insecurity that this causes, the children are often set to work so that the family may survive" (I.L.O.: 1979: 8-9).

It is a well-known fact that half of the Indian population subsists below the poverty line. In the country side the distribution of land is highly inadequate and inequitous. The lower 50 per cent of the households own only 4 per cent of the cultivable land. As many as 27.2 per cent of the rural household are agricultural tenants, while 30-40 per cent are agricultural labourers. Nearly one-third of the urban population live in slums and improvised slum tenements in metropolitan cities. In these families the child since his very appearance in this world is endowed with the economic mission of earning a living for himself and his family. These families cannot sacrifice the smaller gains of the present for the larger gains of the future only because they do not have any surplus to sustain themselves. The income accruing from child employment may be a pittance, but it plays a crucial role in saving the family from shipwreck. Economic compulsions weigh so heavily on the conscience of the poor parents that they do not mind colluding with the employers in violating law and putting the child under risks of inhuman exploitation. Poverty and child labour thus always beget each other and tend to reinforce themselves.

"The growth of industrial and urban based production, the rapid rate of rural-urban migration and the parallel growth in urban adult unemployment have led to increased child labour in urban based activities. Many child workers are therefore engaged in wage or semi-wage employment in industrial or semi-industrial production and outside the orbit of the family. As a result, many of them are subjected to abusive employment practices and, worse still, are forced to work under conditions which are dangerous to their health and physical and mental development" (I.L.O.: 1983: 10).

Another important reason for high incidence of child labour is lack of faith among the poor people in the existing education system. Most parents despite themselves being illiterate make a definite choice between education for the child and a job. Such parents feel that if the child goes to school there is no guarantee of a job on completing his/her education; but if the child enters a job and receives training in a trade/occupation he would be assured of a job on completion of that training. For these people the present education system has no relevance. Instead employment for their children before they reach the age of majority is more meaningful and preferable. Furthermore, traditionally in Indian society occupations were determined by birth and the children were expected to learn their fathers' craft. Even today in industries like carpet weaving in Uttar Pradesh and Jammu and Kashmir, or in zari and zaradosi industry in Surat region of Gujarat, children are employed to undergo training—no adult without a training is employed and training is provided only when the person enters the trade as a child. It may be noted that the Government of India has opened training centres in Varanasi-Bhadoi districts of Uttar-Pradesh to provide training to the children wanting to enter the carpet weaving industry on a monthly stipend of Rs. 100/-.

Exploitative Working and Employment Conditions

While child labour is an economic compulsion for the parents, it provides economic advantages to the employers. Children are fund working in all types of industrial and service establishments in urban areas both in the formal and informal sectors and also in commercial agriculture. Often they are working for low wages and for excessively long hours. Vulnerable, flexible and non-organised, the child workers are used for reducing the labour cost and maintaining competitive advantages and as a means of adapting and responding to economic uncertainties and fluctuations in demand (I.L.O.: 1983:11).

The conditions under which the children work vary widely across activities and as between rural and urban, between agriculture, industry and service sectors. The rural environment under which children work in agriculture and related fields either in self-employment or on wages represents more a problem of access to, or denial of educational opportunities rather than immediate threats to their health and overall physical development. The child workers are not subjected to unhygienic working conditions or the exploitation or strict supervision of the employer as one would find in the industry sector. Only those children who are working under a debt bondage are subjected to exploitation of all kinds.

In urban non-agricultural activities, however, the child workers are confronted with more difficult conditions of work. In addition to denial of schooling and recreation more often their working conditions pose serious threats not only to their physical growth but exposing them to various types of occupational health hazards and cutting short their working life and often life itself. The self-employed children, like the rat pickers, are exposed to the exploitation of the middlemen to whom they must sell their collections. They handle not only dirty a harmful materials but also hazardous items like broken glasses, rusted metal, etc.

In carpet industry the children enter the job at the age of 5 to 7 and continue to work. Particularly in the Varanasi-Bhadoi region, majority of the children employed in the carpet industry are migrants from other districts of Uttar Pradesh and Bihar. They work and live in the loom sheds, which are hut like structures lacking light and ventilation. The rooms are ill-lighted, the floors are damp and mud or dung smeared. The lower half of their body has to be in damp pits to keep the height of the roof low; or otherwise they are required to work squatting on the floor in the same posture the whole day. The studies reveal that these children are paid wages ranging from Rs. 25/- per month to Rs. 500/- and more depending on their skills and age. Skin and eye diseases are quite common among these children due to unhygienic working and living condition and continuous concentrations in putting knots as per the design requirements. Many children were employed under debt bond age till recently; they were kept under lock and key by the master weavers.

In the glass and bangle industry, the children work in improvised factory sheds handling molten glass, and, even where they are assigned comparatively light work, such as packing, pasting, labelling, etc., it is done in the atmosphere of factory temperature of 40° to 45° centigrade.

In the diamond cutting industry, the children work in small rooms ill-ventilated and ill-lighted and they handle machines. The children are also subjected to dust, fumes and noise.

In the zari industry, there are two types of work involved one is making the zari and the other is making of zaradosi articles. The zari making is a household occupation where the entire family takes part. The zaradosi workshops normally employ children both as workers and apprentices; the children work in the sheds of the contractor. The observation reveal that all these children suffer failing eye sight at a very young age and become of little use as zaradosi workers when they attain adulthood. In fact, the prospects of marriage of a girl is stated to increase if she is proficient in zari making.

In the match industry, children work at factories, large and small, as well as at home. Children are employed in making of the match box, filling up of the frames with splints before dipping them in the chemical. In the factories children work for long hours and get paid a piece rate basis .

In the cashewnut industry female children constitute a sizeable portion of the labour force which is, in fact, predominantly female. As in carpet industry, young girls are preferred because of the nimble fingers and delicate wrists supposed to be the prerequisites of high' efficiency and productivity. The piece-rate wages prevalent force them to work for long hours but at lower rates of wages. Besides wage exploitation, all workers in general and the girls in particular employed in shelling section are affected by the continuous handling of the roasted nuts. Over a period of one or two years their finger skin gets whitish and gives the look of luekoderma. As a matter of fact, they must retire from work before they are to get married and sit at home for quite a few months till the skin regains its normal colour and look since some stigma is attached to employment in a cashewnut factory and decolourisation of the skin bordering on the incurable skin disease of leukoderma.

In hotels and eating places like the Dhabbas the children are required to work for 12 to 15 hours a day without rest and holidays doing all kinds of jobs. In construction and brick kiln industries the children are required to lift heavy head loads besides working for long hour. The only satisfying aspect of child labour in construction industry is that majority of them work along their parents.

As a matter of fact, few will disagree about "the prevalence and severity of exploitation of child labour: the employment of children in tasks or under conditions that jeopardise their physical and mental well-being, the extraction of profits from child labour, by paying low wages, to learn, to enjoy a normal childhood. What makes such exploitation especially offensive and serious is that children are far more vulnerable than adults in physical, psychological and organisational terms and hence far more susceptible to extreme subordination than any other category of workers" (I.L.O.: 1983: 12).

Excessive Hours of Work and Low Wages

Exploitation of child workers in terms of wages paid in all industrial occupations and to some extent in some other occupations in all the developing countries is common and widespread. While economic compulsions force the parents to send their children to work and accept whatever wages are paid the child labour provides economic advantages to the employers. Hence, when the employers are approached by poor parents for some job for their children/wards its is provided. Once in employment, his labour is exploited to the maximum possible extent. Normally no wages are paid to the child workers during the first few months of employment, and only normally wages for some more months. This is the period when the child workers are kept as apprentices and under 'probation.' They will not be paid their wages till such time the employer is convinced that the child workers has learnt the job and could do it more productively. And when they start receiving wages it is invariably low. This seems to be the important reason for the wide-spread use of child labour, particularly in small scale industrial establishments, the informal and unorganised sectors as well as agriculture.

It is observed that the status of children as regards payment has remained more or less the same from 1950 till date in India. Whatever wages the child workers receive is too less for their subsistence. In certain cases, the minimum wages fixed by the Government are paid and in most other cases such payment is circumvented. The maximum wages ever paid to working children are normally in diamond cutting industry ranging from Rs. 20 to 30 per day. The lowest, is, however, in the unroganised sector and in employments like domestic services and agriculture, where a child worker is paid rarely above Rs. 30/- per month.

"Children are also subjected to methods of remuneration, such as piece-rates that place undue strain upon them and are vulnerable to abuses, such as unjustified deductions" (I.L.O.: 1983: 13) as could be found in cashewnut processing, beedi, and agarabatti rolling industries in India.

Unduly long hours of work is another major form of exploitation of child workers. Children in agriculture, manufacturing industries and service sectors are found working for long and, not infrequently, excessive hours. In agriculture and domestic services children below 15 are put to excessively long hours of work varying from eight to twelve or more. And an official survey conducted by the Ministry of Labour, Government of India covering the factories employing children found that, in 44 out of 50 cases, daily working hours of children varied between six to eight as against the four and a half hours prescribed under the Factories Act, 1948. Further, more night work is not uncommon, especially in small workshops, hotels, and eating places, street trades, etc., Children are also not provided with sufficient rest intervals and holidays.

Hazardous Work and Unsafe Working Conditions

The most important single cause for concern is the danger to their life and health posed by the hazardous occupations they are employed in or by the unsafe working environment in many agricultural and industrial establishments where they are employed. In commercial agriculture, the child workers are exposed to dangerous machinery, constant physical effort and contact with chemical products such as fertilisers and pesticides. In construction, where children are often used for fetching, carrying and similar tasks, they are vulnerable to false, to injuries from falling objects, to damage from lifting of heavy weights and other types of accidents. Their lack of training and experience in handling tools, their short span of concentration, the use of unguarded machinery, the unsafe use of electricity, the shortage of gloves, goggles and other protective equipment and the insalubrious state of work-places resulting from dust, fumes, lack of hygience, poor lighting and inadequate ventilation are all potential sources of accidents and diseases. Such dangers are compounded by fatigue due to excessive hours of work, undernutrition, and the physical weakness of children. Children are also required to undertake more hazardous tasks such as creeping under the moving parts of dangerous machines to clean them, holding welding parts together without any protection: or 'dirty work' such as cleaning with solvents, cleaning sewers; or glueing leather and foot wear products, etc, (I.L.O.: 1913: 14).

Physical Abuse and Other Psychological Problems

Children in some work situations are exposed to physical and mental abuse, which may take several forms. But perhaps the worst is that which involves separation from parents, isolation sometimes amounting to virtual imprisonment and physical cruelty as could be found in the carpet weaving industry in the Varanasi-Bhadoi region in India. Child workers in agriculture and domestic service and small hotels are often contracted out for long and often permanent separations from their parents, or under debt bondage. Many employer-indulge in harsh practices such as beating and starvation. Where children are separated from their parents and live with adult fellow workers in hotel employment are subjected to homosexsuality by the adult workers or the employer himself.

In addition to these forms of exploitation, there are also other kinds of deprivations from which child labourers suffer, including the absence of clear and written contractual agreements the dearth of feeding programmes, health care facilities and other welfare services, and the lack of insurance and social security. The effects of all these, together or separately, on the physical and mental development of the working child can be far-reaching and often irreversible.

Exploitation of child workers in India and other developing economies has been extensive and intensive mainly because they do not have a legal existence. The child workers are denied all statutory protection that are available to adult workers.

Impact of Work on Child

Research studies in India and other countries have revealed that the working children not only become premature adults, but their physical and mental growth are stunted. In employments like commercial agriculture, mines, construction, zari and zaradosi industry, carpet weaving, powerloom sector, fireworks, match industry, workshops and small factories and in jobs requiring handling of microscopically fine wires and assembling in tiny parts, children are required to work under dangerous conditions that often cause physical injuries, loss of eye sight, skin diseases, respiratory problems and lung diseases and some times the life itself. The existing labour legislations do not provide for any kind compensation for employment injuries suffered by the working child. On the contrary, when a child becomes disabled due to employment injuries is mercilessly thrown out of employment. Thus a child sent to labour market to earn a livelihood for himself or supplement the family income becomes a dependent on the family and the community for the rest of his life. This is the most unkind aspect of child labour.

The working children are denied not only their right to education, training and better career opportunities, but also their joyful childhood which any normal child should have, Widespread use of child labour has not only created situations of acute exploitation but also his increase the social costs to the community. It is a fact that a large number of children below 15 either do not go to schools or drop out from the schools at an early age to take up jobs. This has led to the under development in skills and premature exposure to occupational and health hazards and the resultant stultification of the growth of personality of the child. Some of them become useless for other jobs in their adulthood because they take up jobs in childhood out of compulsion.

Employment of children in odd jobs such as carrying and lifting heavy loads, working in constant chemical polluted plants, performing acts of various nature in unhygienic conditions, night work, continuous standing, meticulous attention with fixed posture for long hours, indoor confinement in noisy industrial environment, exposure to dust and heat, contact with industrial chemicals and poison, cumulative fatigue, lack of adequate sleep, etc., result in physical and mental development of child. Moreover, the improper growth of personality of the child causes many problems of adjustment in adult life besides poor occupational skills. It leads to a low level of employability which again is a factor that militates against the full utilisation of manpower in the industrialisation of the country.

Consequences of Child Labour

The grave concern for child workers arises primarily out of the implications for his health, physical, educational and intellectual development and for his lifetime opportunities, which are influenced by several factors. For instance, the implications for health and physical development depend on factors such as the nature and intensity of the work and the working conditions. The impact on education and intellectual development and lifetime opportunities hinges on the skill-intensity of the work concerned and the availability of possibilities for scooling and training. In other words, the welfare implications of economic activity by children must be viewed in the light of the socio-economic context within which children grow and work.

In traditional and semi-urban societies, "child work is viewed as a rehearsal for adult life. It is regarded as a way of preparing and training the child for the tasks of adulthood. As such, it can be a relatively painless initiation and transition. Given the absence of or the limited opportunities for vocational training, it performs an indispensable function in transmitting skills and in facilitating social adaptation. In addition, since children often work under the supervision of their parents, they do benefit from some from of protection. Child work of this kind is not generally characterised by exploitative practices (I.L.O. 1983: 15).

Safety and Health

The effect of poor and unsafe working conditions on child workers can be direct and visible. These take the from of fatal accidents or accidents that result in deformities. Although statistics on occupational accidents are not available, it may be stated that the incidence of occupational accidents among child workers is high. "Less dramatic but no less serious are the occupational health risks-which are often intertwined with socio-economic-related health problems and may be detected only after a long gestation period-to which working children are exposed. The vulnerability of the children is increased by the high incidence of malnutrition and under-nourishment. When children are required to perform heavy work activities that use up scarce reserve of energy, an imbalance arises between their energy needs and supply thereby weakening them further making them less resistant to dehabilitating diseases: (I.L.O.: 16).

In the unregulated small scale factories and hotels also major health and safety problems are faced by the working children. In glass factories for instance, the child workers are known to suffer from heat stress and run the risk of sustaining cuts and burns. In carpet weaving they are known to work doubled-up, squatting on planks, and as a consequence suffer from bone deformities in the lower limbs or water formation in the knees, or loss of eye sight. Child workers employed in mechanical and automobile repair workshops and small foundries children work in crowded, poorly ventilated, polluted and noisy surroundings. In many small scale industries they work with machinery, tools and equipment designed for use by adult workers. Hence, in such employments the risks of accidents is increased when they are not trained in the methods of handling those machines and equipment and are not provided with safety devices.

"Excessive noise leads to hearing loss; excessively hot, damp or dusty conditions are also likely to create a milieu which favours the transmission of communicable diseases such at tuberculosis. Some diseases—such as rheumatic fever-may have long-lasting effects on the cardio-vascular syrtom. Gastro-intestinal diseases thrive and spread in the absence of potable water and toilet facilities. Prolonged exposure to chemical or toxic substances such as lead, mercury and benzene can also have serious consequences" (I.L.O.: 16).

Education and Intellectual Development

Child labour besides causing concern for the safety and health also affects the working children in the long run by depriving them the opportunities to education and training. "Child participation in labour force clearly reduces the potential for schooling and educational development. Children from poor families obviously do not have as much access to education as those from wealthier families. Even where educational facilities are available such children cannot take sufficient advantage of them, either because their parents cannot afford the direct and indirect costs of schooling or because they cannot accept its opportunity cost. The chances of benefitting from education diminish even further when they work, the more so the greater the degree of drudgery of the work. Given the low educational or skill content of many of the jobs in which working children are involved the possibilities for acquiring remunerative or satisfying skills become still more remote. Children thus find themselves locked in unskilled, low-paying, unpleasant and unsafe work situations and permanently disadvantaged in the labour market" (I.L.O.: 17).

Unemployment and Poverty

Ordinarily child labour is regarded as a means of improving incomes or at least of somewhat restraining deterioration in incomes and consumption levels. It is rather obvious that the wages earned by the child could be good contribution to the family income and be viewed as a means of alleviating poverty. But at the macro level child labour is normally associated with higher levels of adult unemployment and greater inequality of income and wealth. It is argued that the "levels of adult unemployment may be raised by the participation of children. The employment of children may also help to maintain low wages for the labour force as a whole since, as cheap labour, they can be substituted for adults. Hence, through its impact on both the level of unemployment and the wage rate, employment reduces the total income share of working households and thus leads to increase in the degree of income inequality within society. It is further argued that child labour can also accelerate differentiation and wealth inequality through its effect on demographic behaviour. The micro-economic theory of fertility and empirical evidence suggest that child labour has a positive influence on fertility, Children in agrarian societies, in particular, are economically valuable to their parents in at least two ways: as a source of labour contributing to the household economy, and as a source of social insurance and support in old age. The economic value of children therefore favours larger families. But this inturn leads, in the longer run, to greater sub-division sand fragmentation of land and possibly also to landlessness. At the same time, to the extent that child labour is readily available for employment by wealthier peasants it leads to greater differentiation within the peasantry" (I.L.O.: 17-18).

Finally, it is argued that there is the impact "on access to schooling and subsequent performance in the labour market. Manual work or work that involves little skill acquisition is likely to leave children permanently disadvantaged in the labour market. Aside from the repercussions on health and on physical and mental development and the impact of these on the child's future performance, such employment conflicts with and is often carried out at the expense of schooling—and this at a time when education has increasingly become a major vehicle for access to opportunities for earning more satisfactory incomes and rising to better jobs." (I.L.O.: 18).

Child labour, therefore, is a harsh reality rooted in poverty widespread adult unemployment, low rate of literacy and other problems of economic growth and development. The fact that this problem does not exist in developed countries reinforces the thesis that it is rather impossible to eradicate the problem in any society/economy so long as the larger problems of poverty, unemployment, and illiteracy are not removed, which, in fact, need long term measures. However, a few effective steps could be taken in the intermediate and immediate future to gradually reduce the incidence of child labour, to prevent the exploitation of working children by the unscrupulous employers, and to provide congenial working conditions, and more importantly, to enable the working children to acquire better skills and efficiency to be better adult workers, which is so vital for faster development and to enter the 21st century.

Child labour has evoked a deep concern among all those who link the future of the country to the present of the child. But almost all of them only seek to prohibit the employment of children through legislative enactments and strict enforcement of the laws passed by the State. Various committees and commissions appointed by the Government of India since Independence to study the conditions of labour in general and that of child labour in particular, have only recommended strict enforcement of the existing laws dealing with the employment of children, or consolidation of all the existing legislations into a single comprehensive one with uniform definition and provisions. Recommendations of the National Committee on Child Labour (1979), and the Committee of State Labour Ministers on Child Labour (1983) are examples in this regard. These Committees recommended, on the one hand, the enactment of a comprehensive legislation prohibiting the employment of children, and, on the other, to provide for some welfare measures to reduce the incidence of child labour.

The National Committee on Child Labour recommended, inter alia, (a) comprehensive educational facilities for child workers and to include education as a part of labour welfare measures to be adopted by employers, (b) arrangements for non-formal education in areas where there is a concentration of working children, (c) periodical medical check-up to be linked with national health schemes, and (d) arrangements for recreational and cultural activities in areas where there are large number of working children. These recommendations are based on only some broad observations instead of an indepth study of the problems of the working children.

The Annual Report of the Ministry of Labour, Government of India for 1983-84 states that the government has accepted child labour as a "harsh reality." Despite the provisions of restrictive labour laws, the practice continues unabated because the exploitation of children offers financial advantages to employers and an economic compulsion to the parents. Hence, it feels that it would be neither feasible or opportune (emphasis added) to prevent children from working in the present stage of economic development. The Report calls for an improvement in the working conditions and facilities of education, extra nutrition and health care for the children.

But a genuine concern for working children should go beyond welfare measures and improvement of the working conditions. Our concern should be the regulation of child labour in different occupations and its abolition in hazardous jobs through legal and educative measures, on the one hand, and, on the other, to make provisions for formal and non-formal education, vocational training, career development, health and welfare of the working children, and improvement of socio-economic conditions of the families of the child workers. Only well planned long term measures would help eliminate child labour.

But any attempt to evolve and accept such measures needs a detail empirical survey on the problem, for such a kind of problem has different dimensions that differ from one society to another, one region to another and from one time to another. More and more research studies are needed in a country like India to understand the casual factors of the problem of child labour and to design effective measures to eliminate the problem in the long run, but more importantly, to check its uncontrolled growth.

The National Committee on child Labour also pointed out that 'al future action in respect of child labour would depend on how intensively children employed are studied and remedial action determined thereafter.' Therefore, the committee recommended that more studies to gather information and data about working children and their working conditions be taken up and sponsored (Recommendation 5:1:P.50).

This survey of the urban working children was taken up not only in response to the recommendation of the National Committee on Child Labour but also with the following objectives:

1. to understand the profiles of working children and the factors that force their parents/families to send them to labour market;
2. to study the employment and working conditions of child labourers so as to identify the areas of exploitation;

3. to know the forms and extent of exploitation of child workers so as to design remedial measures;
4. to ascertain the interests of the working children in continuing their education, vocational training and career interests as well as to know their willingness to pursue education, and vocational training;
5. to develop action projects to help the working children and their families to improve their working and living conditions in the short run which would help to reduce the incidence of child labour and its elimination in the long run; and
6. to suggest legislative measures to regulate the employment and working conditions and provide for education and development of working children.

Methodology of the Study

Although quite a few studies on the problem of child labour are conducted in the country and one or two in Bangalore city, it was decided to make this an exploratory-cum-descriptive study. But considering the non-availability of a sample frame, the huge population of working children, and the objectives of the study, it was decided to employ the non-probability method of sampling consisting of 600 children employed in different occupations as wage labourers. There 600 child workers were selected by the field investigators from the small sale industrial and commercial establishments, automobile workships and fuelling stations retail trade, hotels and restaurants, domestic services, construction and allied occupations, the unskilled jobs and other miscellaneous occupations.

To begin with, it was decided to collect the data with the help of the active members of the Bangalore Labour Union Bangalore—a union of unorganised sector workers—many of whom were child workers. As such a few briefing sessions were held to explain to them the interviewing techniques and methods of data gathering and recording. But except for one, they did not take up the task since they could not gain confidence in this new task. Consequently, graduate volunteers had to be recruited on payment of an honourarium per interview.

Although the detailed interview schedule was prepared for data collection in the initial stage of the study, it could not be used when the field investigations progressed when it was found that the children and their employers were not very much willing to go on record and the interviewers themselves faced the problem of using a structured lengthy schedule. Hence, the volunteers were asked to collect the data picking up relevant portions from the schedule and thus converting it into an interview guide, but more in the form of case history.

With a view to increasing the reliability of the data, the volunteer investigators were permitted to contact the working children living in and around the suburbs where the volunteers themselves had their residences, and from any other areas where they could get immediate and encouraging response from the employers of children. Yet the volunteer—investigators could not cover the entire city of Bangalore. Therefore, this sample and interviewer bias had to be offset by a large sample.

Data Processing and Analysis: Altogether 653 working children engaged in different occupations and from different parts of the city were interviewed. But only 600 of the case studies were chosen for final analysis taking into account the completeness and quality of the data. The data were processed on ORG computer in the Indian Institute of Management, and analysed statistically used the Chi-square test of hypothesis.

16

THE EFFECTS OF CHILD LABOUR ON THE CHILD

The impact of Child Labour — Physical, Psychological, Social and Economic Implications

A critical assessment of the various effects of child labour on the child is of vital significance to this study. It must be borne in mind that any negative impact labour has on children is the logical result of the inhumane nature of their employment. The primary reason for children's employment, from the employers' viewpoint, is that it is cost efficient in the overall scheme of maximum profits. Understandably, child labour is not entirely without any positive features; this arises from some common elements that are characteristic of both the labour and work processes discussed previously. However, the risks arising from child labour far outweigh any of its advantages; consequently, these need addressing.

Child employment has differential impact on children based on factors such as geographic location, type of occupation, sex and age of the child.

Studies show that in urban areas, children are exploited more and undergo greater privations than their counterparts in the rural sectors (Mendelievich, 1979). With increasing mechanisation of agricultural methods, many farmhands are displaced and are forced to move with their families to nearby cities in search of a better life; this phenomenon augments the numbers of children in the urban labour force. Generally, it is found that the child employed in a family undertaking, whether in agriculture or industry, is exploited less than the wage earning child.

In some sectors, girls have to keep longer employment hours than boys. In domestic service, the Labour relations between the employer and employee are arbitrary and authoritarian. It has been found that in many cases, domestic servants are exploited beyond endurance, sometimes suffering physical and psychological abuse (Mendelievich, 1979: 37). The employer maintains an ambiguous status in relationship to the maid servant. The employer may appear both paternalistic (or maternalistic as the case may be) and contemptuous towards the servant. The young girl may or may not be allowed the privilege of taking a break between her chores; this is dependent on her employer's prevailing disposition. In many households these girls are victims of physical harassment and sexual exploitation. She is servile and treated akin to a chattel. Any remuneration of her services is paltry, and in most cases she does not get to enjoy her labour's returns, as they are paid directly to her family or relatives.

There are again the differences that exist between the self-employed child and wage-earning child in service for an employer. In terms of operating independently, fixing and earning a wage, hours of work, kind of work and so on; children who are self-employed experience a greater degree of freedom than those children who labour for an employer. They are, however, only relatively free, for they are constantly sought after and harassed by financial dependents like family. Their freedom is a precious one; of it is contingent upon various other factors. For instance, in general, self employed children have irregular income patterns. Since most of these children are engaged in some form of street trading, their incomes are dependent on several factors: location of their pitch, season of the year, time of the month, the demand for the goods on sale, the purchasing power at the disposal of the buyer, percentage of the profits that the children are allowed to retain if they re working for a third party and various other related factors. Frequently, these children also operate form within very hazardous environments; if theirs is a mobile occupation like newspaper sales or shoe shining; or if they are engaged in street trading of some sort, they are out until late at night, exposed to the weather, to the dust and dirt of city streets, to traffic hazards, and are in constant danger of being detained by the police on grounds of vagrancy. In view of these conditions, Edward N. Clopper (1970) based on a study conducted in the U.S. in the early years of this century concluded that there was a direct relationship between child labour and delinquency, that besides factors such as poor home conditions and lack of schooling, child labour was a major cause of delinquency.

The manner in which the children are treated and the conditions under which they toil are usually left to the employer's whims and fancies; he decides on employment conditions arbitrarily and unilaterally. In many cases, there is not even a formal contract of employment that ensures the protection of the child; the employer hires and fires at will. Conditions of labour and rate of wages are subject to many abuses. Press reporters have observed four year olds labouring for sixteen hours a day in the math factory. In various employment sectors, children are employed on a 6-7 day-a-week basis; and in domestic services, the child has virtually no breaks except the hours of rest earned at night (Menon, 1979: 11).

The inequity of remuneration pattern is very severe. Quite often children who work for their family undertakings receive no payments for their services, since their family income considered to be one indivisible whole. This is also the case when families are employed by third parties — the children take part in the employment, but the family receives the total earnings and the children are deprived of enjoying what might only a mere token of the fruit of their labours. This inequity is even more phenomenal in the case of apprentices who in reality perform ancillary tasks to their employers, and do not instead acquire the skills of the trade as they intend to. In this instance, the children are basically unpaid employees.

As wage earners, their wages are derisory tokens in relation to the value of their output. It is always an unfair sum compared to that received by an adult doing the same job (Mendelievich, 1979: 40; Indian Ministry of Labour: "Report of the Committee on Child Labour," (1979). Of course, the employers are quick to justify this practice by arguing that the child is lacking in experience; the child has no financial obligations towards the maintenance of the family; the costs of training the child can be recovered only by a proportionate cut in the child's earnings.

The following passage best describes the physical conditions of labour for those children (*Encyclopedia of Social Science*, 3:412-424, in Ministry of Labour Report on Child Labour, 1979).

> *Long hours of work, late hours of night employment, continuous standing, sitting or use of single set of muscles, emphasis on the finer neuro-muscular coordinations with attendant nervous strain, indoor confinement in noisy factories and dusty trades, carrying heavy loads under the arm or lifting heavy weights, pressure of speed in the performance of simple mechanical acts, contact with industrial poisons, exposure to inclement weather- are unsuitable occupations and provide harmful conditions for the growing child peculiarly susceptible to certain deformities and diseases.*

Since these children are employed in the non-formal sector, labour unions ignore their rights. Children are also less likely to change their jobs providing employers with a great deal of power over them — a quasi parental power (*U.N. Chronicle*, 1989: 45)

It is found that there is a causal relationship between different types of labour and the attendant ailments and accidents the children experience. Children are employed in big numbers in plantations; child employment is seen as part of the employment of the family group. While parents perform heavier tasks like felling trees and ploughing, their children assist them in picking leaves and coffee berries, or collecting latex; or, the children do secondary jobs such as weeding, spreading fertilizer, caring for nurseries, digging irrigation canals, drains and other such ancillary activities. It has been observed that on some plantations, children are employed for 40 hours per week, as compared to 54 hours for adults, but the wages paid to children are labour half that paid to adults. They work in fair weather and in foul, under the scorching summer sun and in the torrential monsoon rains. It is reported that during 1971, out of the total of 0.8 million plantations employees, as many as 51,982 were children . According to the Committee on Labour Welfare (1969) and the survey of Labour Conditions of Plantation Workers (1961-1962), the services provided for these plantation employees and families are inadequate and leave much to be desired. A great majority of the families live in small hutments made of bamboo and thatched roof. The sanitary facilities in these labour camps defy any sanitary health standards. The Survey of Labour Conditions found that

about 5 per cent of tea estates, 14 per cent of the rubber plantations and 1 per cent in coffee plantations provided lavatories at the job sites. Most of the primary schools in Assam's tea gardens are one-teacher schools and their attendance varies anywhere between 14 to 45 students.

One of the large employers of children in India is the Beedi industry (Beedis are indigenous cigarettes). In 1959, there were about 0.2 million children engaged in beedi manufacturing alone; they helped to roll tobacco leaves and assisted the adult employees with cleaning and cutting the leaf and sealing the ends. A survey conducted in the town of Murishidabad revealed that about 9 per cent of employees between the ages 10-14 suffered symptoms of chronic bronchitis and 10 per cent of the boys were anemic. The study also found sufficient indication to suspect a high incidence of tuberculosis among beedi employees as a result of having started employment at a young age, long hours of employment, excessive overcrowding and the peculiar posture adopted while on the job which was detrimental to the healthy development of the respiratory organs of the child.

Firozabad, the seat of the glass bangle industry in the India, is another employer of children. Glass bangles are fancy glass bracelets decorated with colourful beads, mirrors and sequins that are in great demand among Indian women. Children are employed at various stages of manufacture, in preparing different and plastic dyes, in engraving patterns and the further decoration of these bangles. The factories run for about 8 months in the year and function mostly at night. Children between 8-14 years from one-fifth of the total labour force employed in this industry. They are underpaid and labour in dehumanizing environments. They are paid a daily wage of about Rs. 3 for an eight hour day. The temperature inside the factory averages about 40-45 degree centigrade, which makes working in summer unbearable. Seven out of ten factories in Ferozabad have no first aid boxes. Many employees suffer from asthma, bronchitis and many eye diseases. Firozabad ranks high in the incidence of tuberculosis among industrial cities.

Handloom and carpet weaving industries provide many employment opportunities for the utilization of child labourers. The carpet weaving industry of Jammu and Kashmir employes some 6500 children of 8 to 10 years of age, requiring them to work 8 hours a day for Rs. 80 per month. The children are packed into sheds with hardly any standing space, in long rows behind giant looms feverishly picking warp and wool and following the craftsman's instruction issued in military fashion. The air is heavy with wool and cotton fluffs and many of these young lungs are subject to asthma and primary tuberculosis as a result.

Children are also employed in Zari making (manufacture of gold and silver threads) and the embroidery industry. Out of an estimated 45,000 children employed in Lucknow, nearly one-sixth were between 8-15 years of age. The Committee on Child Labour reported that many children suffered varying forms of eye diseases, from having to work in over-crowded rooms with poor lighting and ventilation.

The Committee report on the precious stone polishing industry in Jaipur typifies the exploitative nature of child employment. Jaipur, known for its gem industry, employs 10,000 children , all of whom work in slums or miserable hovels. The employers engage brokers who procure these children for a pittance. It is found that due to the nature of jobs such as polishing and cutting gems, these children develop eye defects prematurely; they are ruthlessly fired at the first signs of eye fatigue. Consequently, many of these children are not only unemployed but also unemployable by teenage.

In Sivakasi, the home of match making, children as young as four years of age are required to be at the factory until 7 a.m. until 6 p.m. There are an estimated 50,000 children employed in this industry and the Committee found that there was no organized system of transportation for these children from their homes to the factory sites; instead it was up to the children to rise up in the early hours of the morning to catch the factory bus. Invariably, these ramshackle buses carry a dangerous overload of children . In recent years, there have been reports of treacherous accidents where all the children on the bus have been killed. Since these factories pay the children on a piece rate basis (when the wages paid are in proportion to the task done and not on the basis of time spent on the job), it is not uncommon to see the children helplessly slog on to maximise output within available time. Many were found to be frail and anemic. There was no medical assistance available to them and often even ill children come to the factory. They work on box making, box filling, labelling and band roll pasting. Despite their best effort for the day, their returns were meagre.

Child labourers are also found in the "informal sector", including restaurants, tailor shops, domestic services, street vending, car parks, garbage collecting, building construction, machine tools and repair shops all under dehumanizing employment conditions.

The plight of the garbage collecting child in the informal sector is an account unto itself. These scrap collectors and rag pickers are engaged in the most dangerous, degrading and degenerate business of all. For the most part, these children come from poverty stricken, scheduled caste (disadvantaged minority groups), slum families. Their vary physique and nature of dress reveals this aspect of their backgrounds. From dawn until dusk, they are involved in scrounging dust bins and garbage dumping grounds for waste materials like paper, tin, plastics, rubber, coconut shells, iron glass pieces and in the process even left-over food. Since they wear no protective devices like masks, gloves or boots, they contract skin diseases and infections, and often receive bruises and outs on their hands and bare feet. Cuts from iron and glass make they susceptible to tetanus and festering wounds. But these children are indispensible to many an operation in the urban economy. Several production enterprises are based on the recycling of these wastes and hence rely heavily on these children for their supplies. They are paid about Rs. 5 a day barely enough for one meal. But in the absence of other options, they will come again tomorrow, to heap their "finds" on machines that will grind out their employer's profits.

There is no further point in belabouring the appalling conditions child labourers suffer; suffice it to say that these conditions prevail, and the damages done to every child's mental and physical being are irreparable losses.

The milieu of these children outside their job environments contributes to the confluence of factors that influence their growth and development; hence this aspect of their existence needs discussion. Their housing conditions call for considerable improvement. They often live in decrepit, squalid conditions, with noisome sanitary installations, should they exist. These conditions are far more pronounced in the urban centres. It is not unusual to find ten to fourteen members of a family huddling together in one room. In general, the walls are made of beaten tin sheets and the roof of thatched palm leaves. One only has to speculate on the quality of human relationships under such cramped circumstances. In many instances, the father is usually unemployed, or if employed, only seasonally so. Many fathers are also alcoholics and gamblers. The mother may or may not be employed and there are several children in the house including toddlers and infants, who demand her undivided attention. The house is also a refuge for the many relatives who come from the rural areas in search of a better life. All of the family members' earnings combined is still insufficient to insure a three square meal day for all. Inevitably, the child's growth and development is bound to be affected by such an environment.

There are those children who cannot afford the luxury of even such an environment; they are nobody's children, caught in the rural-urban drift. They will rest their heads wherever they find themselves at day's end. Their search for relief from the grinding poverty of their homes and their desire to make something of themselves compelled them to leave their hope-less lives in the rural sectors. These children will sleep on the pavement and sometimes even in the kitchen of the hotel or restaurant where they are employed.

Few children benefit from spending their early years in low level positions in wage labour or informal sector activities because their labour is largely unskilled under harmful conditions. Such labour has little social value since the child is far from the influence of family and community supports. Those children who work as apprentices under skilled craftsmen may have a better chance at advancing their future.

As a class of labourers, these children have no organised body to protect and lobby for their rights. In spite of the perpetually disastrous conditions under which they labour, there are no social assistance or insurance policies to protect the child. The plight of the self-employed children is not any better, for, in case of an accident or a physical malady of occupational origin, the child is obviously not covered by any from of social protection, since in the majority of cases, his employment is in violating of minimum age regulations. In the event of some mishap, the child and his parents have to suffer the irreversible consequences.

The most sophisticated instruments of measurement fall short of being able to depict accurately the toll child labour exacts from the children . The moral ills suffered by child labourers are numerous. When children become wage-earners, many are thrown into an adult world unprepared; they develop prematurely an adult consciousness and view of life. They cease almost at once to be children and, consequently, one finds that these children are quick to devise ways and means to outwit their employers and co-workers. They are likely to become arrogant, wayward, defiant, and devious. Often these children probably experience conflicting feelings since they receive mixed messages from their superiors and authorities. On the job, they are differentially treated as juniors, and underpaid in comparison to their adult counterparts; while at their homes with their families, they are regarded as full-fledged men and women as soon as they become wage earners.

Child labour can be a disorganizing factor in the family, especially in the families of children who go away to spend most of their waking hours at their job. When one takes into account that children as young as three years of age are taken away in employment, one is left to wonder about the sources of nurturance which are so essential to the child's developmental process. School and recreation are luxuries that these children have never enjoyed. For lack of any healthy exercise of mind and body, a gradual atrophy of the child's person is likely to set in and in a few years, the developmental process is retarded. The danger lies in treating the child as a pocket size version of an adult. From an ethical and evolutionary standpoint, every child should be accorded the right to an extended period of infancy and childhood. In the industrial and commercial sectors the child is ill-prepared to deal with some of the complex and intricate web of human relationships that emerge. He is the object of adult jokes and ridicule. He may be ill-treated and left out of adult conversations. Often the child has to continue working when his adult counter-parts are taking a break.

Edward Clopper in his book *Child Labour in the City Streets,* cites three possible effects that child labour may have on children. He classifies them under three headings: material, physical and moral deterioration (Clopper, 1970: 128-129). By material deterioration, he suggests that the child acquires a distaste for regular employment; his chances of acquiring the skills for a trade are very limited and he tends to join a class of casual labourers. Physical deterioration results from keeping late hours, excessive fatigue, exposure to the elements, irregularity of sleep and meals, use of additives (cigarette, coffee and alcohol), and sexually transmitted diseases. Under "moral deterioration," Clopper suggests that the child may be encouraged to play pranks and truant; he may fall prey to cheap thrills on the street; he may drift into delinquency, and be led into the underworld of crime.

Injuries that child labour inflicts upon the children are atrocious, but there are injuries child labour inflicts on society. In fact, child labour often retards any form of technological advance that would otherwise be possible. Manufacturers, by employing children , are often able to retain and perpetuate methods of manufacture which are unnecessary and antiquated. The typically indigenous industries like beedi, match production and textile manufacture for instance, are made possible through the cheap availability of child labour, Greed for profits alone make it necessary for the exploitation of tender fingers to curl tobacco leaves, to paste stickers on matchboxes, and to spin cotton in a textile mill. The same tasks can be carried out by mechanical means; instead, ingenuity and innovative skills are allowed to lie dormant because the labour of women and children is cheap and plentiful.

The productivity of children in most societies is at once exploited and an important source of dignity. While children may have been viewed as less than valuable or fully human, as economic assets their economic roles made them socially valuable and promoted some degree of interdependence. Industrialisation demeaned and debauched the productivity of children as well as men and women to the point that all social and economic value they possessed was eclipsed by the horror of their employment conditions. While advocates against child labour were motivated by the humanitarian impulse, child labour laws removed all opportunities to produce from young people. Children with little recognised intrinsic worth now have little extrinsic value beyond their potential for future success (Wineman, 1984: 122).

17

FROM CHILD LABOUR TO CHILD WORK

To date, the diagnosis and treatment of issues concerning child labour have been superficial, where the underlying value premise is that children should be excluded from participating in any economic activity. There is little consideration for the social and economic conditions of these children who along with their dependent families have few options but to labour.

An alternative approach rests on the clarification of basic concepts that are essential for the adequate analysis of child labour as a social problem, concepts such as work, labour and child. The discussion is possible because of earlier contributions of historians, philosophers, sociologists and theologians who have devoted considerable thought to the subject.

Differentiating Work and Labour

In contemporary discussion, the term "work" and "labour" have been used interchangeably and synonymously, although a studious critic discerns a semantic different that has existed throughout.

German philosopher Hannah Arendt in her book *The Human Condition* (University of Chicago Press, 1958, pp. 79-80), offers an etymological explanation of the distinction inherent in these terms.

> *The distinction between labour and work which I-propose is unusual. The phenomenal evidence in its favour is too striking to be ignored, and yet historically it is a fact that apart from a few scattered remarks, which moreover were never developed even in the theories of their authors, there is hardly anything in either the pre-modern tradition of political thought or in the large body of modern theories to support it. Against this scarcity of historical evidence, namely, the simple fact that every European language, ancient and modern, contains etymologically unrelated words for what we have come to think of as the same activity, and retains them in the face of their persistent synonymous usage.*

Arendt shows that the Greek language distinguishes between Ponein and Ergazesthal, the Latin between Labourare and Facere or Fabricare which have the same etymological root, the French between Travailler and Ouvrer, the German between Arbeiten and

Werken. Arendt goes on to state that in all these cases, only the equivalents for "labour" have an unequivocal connotation of pain and trouble. The German Arbeit initially applied only to farm labour carried on by serfs and not to the work of the craftsmen, which was called Werk. The French Travailler replaced the older term Labourer and is derived from Tripalium, a kind to torture. Similarly we find two different concepts in Hebrew, Ashaw which is the equivalent of work (meaning to make, to create, to perform efficiently) and Amhal (which stands for labour or toil and suffering).

Differentiating work and labour is determined by the particular social context, the quality of the various interactions and dynamics present in the production process. Both labour and work are born out of the ubiquitous human need to survive and much of the ambiguity that exists centres around this commonality. Those elements that make labour and work apparently synonymous are:

(a) Both work and labour are organised human responses to design ways of securing resources and satisfying human needs for sustenance.
(b) These processes involve an exchange between human beings and the "natural" world.
(c) Both work and labour require human effort — an exercise of body and mind.

The distinction between work and labour is to be found in a critical overview of the climate in which these processes operate and the quality of the relationships in operation. Historically, socio-political, scientific and technological developments have led to a radical transformation of work into labour. The transformation evolved from a simple to a complex pattern.

Work

Work is process intrinsic to life at all levels, be it plant, animal or human. Since living organisms are not self contained, from the very moment of their existence they engage in interactions and exchanges with the larger world around them. Any process aimed at bridging the gap between needs originating in an organism and resources in the organism's environment satisfying those needs may be termed "work." Therefore, work is a natural process: work insures survival and to cease to work is to cease to live.

Several multi-dimensional aspects emerge from this conception of "work." From a historical perspective, it is noted that "work" is a cumulation of past and present human capacities. Past human capacities are manifested in products of pastwork in all the advances made in the fields of art, science and technology through discoveries, inventions, sophisticated tools and instruments required to carry on simple and complex work processes in the present. Work in the present, therefore, is contingent upon work of the past and in that sense workers of the present are inextricably interlinked with workers of the past (Gil, 1979: 86).

Pope John Paul II remarks on this aspect of work in his encyclical (Pope John Paul II,

On Human Work — Laborem Exercens, Office of Publishing Services, Untied States Catholic Conference, 1981):

> *it is true that man eats the bread produced by the work of his hands — and this means not only the daily bread by which his body keeps alive but also the bread of science and progress, civilisation and culture.*

Work is a critical process to human existence and thus has serious implications to the development of self-image, self-esteem and identity. It is a crucial ingredient of social relations, self-discovery, self-expression and self-realisation.

The world and all therein in its pristine and primordial from is not yet at the disposal of humans. Trees and rocks are not yet houses, neither are wild plants and animals food and cotton is not yet a garment. In order that these raw materials are made available so that human needs can be met, we resort to transforming this natural world into an available world. It is the *raison d'etre* for the many social and economic processes that ensue.

The creation of an available world is a response to the urgent need to survive that is inherent in human beings everywhere. According to Remy Kwant (Kwant, 1960), there are two dimensions to this process. It is a service, rendered to society; and it is also the means of support of the individual. It is a "service" because the "available world" that has been created has to be maintained by the participation of human beings. It is a "support of the individual," because the "available world" is necessary for each individual whose participation in the production process enables him or her to share in the benefits of the system. Work thus by its very nature fosters interdependence. Geography, history, culture, diverse and various human needs and varying human gifts and skills bring about this interdependence beginning with the local level and extending simultaneously to global categories in a concentric manner.

Accountable control is another aspect of the work process. The worker is invested with accountable control when he or she is an active participant in the decision making that takes place at the workplace. We qualify control as accountable control since in the absence of accountability, control and authority becomes autocratic and abusive and the production process ceases to be work. Work is an enjoyable, wholesome activity when one claims the work as one's own. Such a sense of ownership is critical to worker commitment to her/his own work and the work of others.

As has been the case with many social processes historically, socio-political change and scientific and technological developments have transformed the original character of "work," thus, today, "work" assumes different meanings.

> *Throughout human history, social, psychological, economic, political, and ideological developments, as well as developments of science and technology, have resulted in increase complexity of work processes and work organisations, in specialisations in the division of labour, and in refinements of criteria of access to, and preparation for, different work roles.*

These developments regarding work became important factors in the emergence of systems of social stratification, the distribution of all kinds of rights, the cricumstances of living, the quality of human relations, and the overall existential milieu of human societies.

(Gil, 1979:86)

The emergence of the caste system in India is an example of social stratification determined by occupational stratification. Work in this system is assigned status, which each status being imputed higher or lower, superior or inferior valuation. The original nature of work has undergone change so that today it is difficult to distinguish between work and labour.

Labour

When individuals are engaged in the production process, not primarily to meet their physiological and psychological needs, but to meet the profit-motivated needs of the employer, the process they are engaged in may be called "labour." Work becomes labour when the individual's capacity to produce a surplus beyond the value of the means of existence is capitalised upon by the employer. Labour denies the producer an opportunity for self-direction and control.

Currently, labour characterises the nature of employment settings in most economies. Therefore it is important for our further understanding that the interplay of dynamics in such settings be examined.

As a result of the evolution of social policy, ownership and control of productive resources became concentrated within a small segment of our society through processes involving "legitimate" expropriation of the majority. The expropriated majority now has access to work only when it serves the interests of those in control of our societal wealth, and they do not enjoy a right to work in a real sense. Decisions of owners of productive resources in our society tend to be shaped by considerations of profit and further accumulation of capital. Accordingly, they perceive an unconditional right to work as contrary to their interests, since a surplus of idle individuals tends to depress wages, to increase profits, and to check inflation, given the dynamics of the existing institutional order. Restricting access to work selectively is, therefore, a social policy favoured by many owners of productive resources.

(Gil, 1979: 87)

Thus, we see clearly why under the existing structure of ownership and control of productive resources, only the 'privileged' are 'protected' from the labour process, while others are excluded from participating in the production process. The exclusion of women, children and other disadvantaged groups is a good example.

While work is a natural human response to survive and therefore a healthy and socially desirable process, labour denies the producer an opportunity for self-direction and control, the insalubrity of which makes it a pernicious social process.

Given this nature of 'labour,' it follows then that one should be protected from engaging in labour and encouraged to undertake work. Exploration of this possibility with reference to children engaged in production is the underlying objective of this study.

The Work-Labour Continuum

Work as described above is an almost utopian ideal under present day conditions in most societies. However, one does observe another phenomenon in operation in the larger production setting: a Work-Labour Continuum.

Since labour and work are contingent upon the context and scope of operation, there is a continuum that has the pure forms of work and labour at the extreme points and a combination of both processes in varying degrees are to be found at intermediate points. At the operational levels we do not find people engaged exclusively in work due to the pervasion of the economic system that constricts the occurrence of work, but it is possible to find production settings that manifest a learning towards work.

Family work is based on kinship relationships where the norm dictates a sense of communal contribution towards sustenance. Paid labour is based on a contractual understanding entered into between the employer and the employee. Modernised agriculture and industry introduces the concept of paid wage labour within organised and planned rural development without an attempt to understand the relationship of work and family in rural cultures.

In the present market economies, production settings that portray the "labour" pattern are more the norm than the exception. Form the employer's standpoint, the employment of the individual is seen as acquisition of capital for further profit. It is the potential for this profit that motivates employers to exploit the productive capacity of men, women and children.

Defining 'Child Labour' and 'Child Work'

The distinction between the concepts of labour and work facilitates the further understanding of the working child in contrast to the labouring child.

In most developing societies, a *child* is the progeny of parents. Despite patriarchal and hierarchical patterns in these cultures, one observes a certain wholistic continuation between male and female, between infancy, adulthood and old age. Thus, while societies in which male dominated systems and structures perceive adulthood as the ultimate stage in the cycle of human development because of its productive potential, many other cultures in the world left out of the experiences of Western economic, political and social systems do not see childhood as an inferior version of or as a waiting period for adulthood. Not do they see old age as a recession from the centre stage of life. On the contrary, each stage of life in these cultures is seen as precisely that, a stage, a point in the continuum of the whole. Hence conventional forms of legal or cultural age criterion is irrelevant to the definition of children. However, for the purpose of this study, we consider children between age 8-14.

The standard laid down in the International Labour Organisation Minimum Age Convention sets the general minimum age for admissions to employment as being fifteen years. When we consider this minimum age of employment, and the possibility that upto 44 million child may be caught in the labour force, India is left with the largest number of child labourers in the world. If one is to measure human progress by the extent that children's rights are protected, then India's children are a searing indictment against the country's progress.

Clearly, there are reasons why the child labour force in India swells. For many, the child's earnings are a much needed supplement to the total family income (Bromley and Gerry, 1979-52) and in many families where death or accident has incapacitated the family members, the child's earnings are the mainstay for the family's survival. It is also assumed that by learning a trade, a child achieves proficiency at an early age. From the employer's perspective, child employment is cost efficient as maximum output is obtained at minimum input. We were informed by a senior official in the Ministry of Labour at New Delhi that many industries like the carpet weaving industries in Kashmir and Assam would collapse in the absence of the availability of nimble fingers of little children. Employers who argue that the employment of children increases the earnings of the family and keeps the children of the streets only reflect the collousness of a free enterprise system where the earnings of family and the conservation of human resources are not the responsibility of an individual employer. It is a weak argument when one considers that some of these very jobs by design lead the children to the streets.

We do not oppose children *working* in fact, from a social and economic standpoint it may very well be a viable alternative for all the children who are driven to inhumane conditions of labour today. The provision of work settings which foster the development of children, and which are unexploitative, is of utmost importance in alleviating the problems that beset the children and their kin.

Our suggestion for an alternative approach rests on the earlier differentiation of work and labour. *Child Labour* is the employment of children and the extraction of their productivity for the economic gain of another, with debilitating ramifications on the psychological and physical development of the child.

The *working child*, on the other hand, enters work arrangements that offer freedom and independence. Working children cease to be mere means to another's ends; instead, they actively participate in decision making and the appropriation of resources and in that sense the whole work process is a learning experience, entered into willingly. This is the basic difference between a labouring child and a working child, and all further discussion stems from this basic distinction.

18

NGO EFFORTS IN PROGRAMMING FOR WORKING AND STREET CHILDREN*

GRASS ROOT ORGANISATIONS

In the course of this study, we came across only nine NGOs working with street and working children. The common features in this programme are that they have health and nutrition components, non-formal education, vocational training, recreational facilities and some also have counselling and saving schemes. But they vary from one another in their philosophies, approaches and strategies. The NGO's may have common activities but their implementation strategies differ. Most of the NGO's (like SEWA, Ankur, DCCW, Rag Pickers Project—Jahangirpuri, Prabhatara, etc.) are working primarily with working children and not necessarily with street children. There are three organisations who are making concerted efforts in working with street children and they are Theatre Action Group, ICCW and Butterflies.

SEWA

SEWA started work with child rag-pickers in 1981 at East and West Nizamuddin, Minto Bridge, South Extension and Maharani Bagh. As most of the children were illiterate, SEWA began with their non-formal education; they also started job placement services, health and hygiene and saving scheme. The response was very good, so much so that they were at one time interacting with 2000 children. Five years prior to this study they received funds from the Ministry of Labour, Government of India, to expand and strengthen their work. It also meant SEWA had to incorporate certain activities and implement programmes according to the dictates of the government. After the first instalment of funds, SEWA decided not to accept the second instalment. SEWA approached Plan International to fund their programmes. According to the Director, "it was an unfortunate decision. Today we run our programmes to suit Plan International objectives and in the bargain we have lost sight of our goals and objectives. Earlier we had a good rapport with the community, but today it is just implementation of programmes without

**Working and Street Children in Delhi,* NLI, Noida.

their participation." The sponsorship—a major programme of Plan International covers children who live with families; therefore they lose out on destitute street children. SEWA hopes to go back to their earlier approach which is primarily involving community/group participation, once their Plan International project comes to an end. Today SEWA works with 700 families of regpickers at East and West Nizamuddin, Maharani Bagh, South Extension, R.K. Puram (Sector-I) and Turkman Gate. They have a staff of forty. Majority of the workers are women, with 2% of them from the community.

DELHI COUNCIL FOR CHILD WELFARE (DCCW)

DCCW has been working with child ragpickers at Seemapuri for the last four year. There are 80 children on the rolls out of which 65 are regular and 25 of them are girls. Their activities are non-formal education, vocational training in weaving (very soon they will be having tailoring and potery) and a noon meal. There are facilities for bath and toilet too. The children are paid an incentive of Rs. 2 per day if they come to the center and remain there for two hours. DCCW is not keen to expand the programme is at it of low priority to them. They also mentioned it has been a frustrating experience working with these children, as at no given time there is a regular group. Children keep coming as and when they like and quite often there are a new faces. Therefore, according to DCCW it has been difficult to plan any new activity for the want of regular numbers. DCCW would offer their present premises to any NGO wanting to work with street and working children or even take over the present activity.

RAGPICKERS PROJECT—JAHANGIRPURI

"Development, Justice and Peace" (DJP) is the development cell of the Catholic arch diocese of Delhi. They have been working in Jahangirpuri for over ten years. DJP has a large community health and adult education programme in this resettlement colony. Two years ago, they started work with 600 families who are ragpickers. Presently the programme is geared towards children but at a later date parents will also be motivated to participate in the programme. Last year, DJP approached Ministry of Labour for funds, and the Ministry was keen to support them but finally it did not work out as the government's scheme did not concur with DJP's approach. An educational programme was started as the children demanded to be taught the 3 R's. The children are so keen to study that they pay Rs. 5 per month without the knowledge of their parents. About 200 children participate in the study classes. The two teachers are from the community and their salary is paid from the fees collected from the children. The children are being motivated to join open-schools. They also have recreational facilities, medical care and health education. Six months ago a saving scheme was started, which is also very popular with the children. In the near future, DJP hopes to start a center for girls.

PRABHATARA—PROGRAMME FOR WORKING CHILDREN

The programme was started four months ago. The organisation works with pavement dwellers residing near Bhikaji Cama Place and R.K. Puram. Most of them are migrants from Rajasthan. The children either pick rags or sell balloons, dusters and newspapers. None of them has been to school but all of them are keen to study. Since there is such an interest in learning, Prabhatara has started a literacy class twenty-five to thirty children participate in this activity. The children are willing to buy their slates, books and pencils. In the next six months Prabhatara hopes to initiate health care and education programme and also a saving scheme. They have only one staff but hope to hire one more in the near future.

THEATRE ACTION GROUP (TAG)

TAG started their work early in (January, 16) 1988 and is working with unlicensed collie boys. TAG has a programme for street children at New Delhi Railway Station. Although there are about 1000 such boys at the station, it is not easy to strike a rapport with them, as they are suspicious of adults. About 14 boys regularly come to the meeting place which is a community hall opposite the station. In the mornings break-fast is given to them which consists of three slices of white bread and one boiled egg. The boys pay Rs. 2 for it out of which Rs. 1 is saved on the boy's behalf. Two of them saved over Rs. 100; this gave an incentive for others to save more. While the boys have breakfast the Hindi newspaper is read aloud to them and sometimes there are discussions on certain news items. In the evenings they have formal literacy classes, recreation and discussions of their problems. TAG hopes in the future to work with street girls, but for which they need girl workers. TAG has only one male worker.

INDIAN COUNCIL FOR CHILD WELFARE (ICCW)

ICCW initiated a programme for street children at Nabi Karim in early 1988. Most of the boys are working as helpers in various metal and mechanical workshops. ICCW hopes to have a literacy class, vocational training and health care. They have started a cycle repair course and about 16 boys are participating in it. The boys are enthusiastic and are keen to learn a skill. ICCW has not been in a position to expand their programme as they did not have a regular staff. Recently a trained social worker was appointed to work at Nabi Karim. It is hoped that in the coming months more children would be motivated to participate in their programme and also further activities would be planned to suit the needs of the children. ICCW is also trying to work with the UBS programme coordinator to see if UBS programme could be extended to include these working children.

BUTTERFLIES—PROGRAMME FOR STREET CHILDREN

Butterflies also began its programme in February 1988. They work with destitute street children. At present they are working with the coolie boys of INA market (about 30) and the street vendours and shoe blacks at Connaught Place (about 20). Butterflies has a non-formal education programme, recreational activities and a saving scheme. They hope to eventually form a credit union for these children. Couple of boys who are school drop-outs have been motivated to join the open school. Butterflies would be collaborating with the Don Bosco fathers and a few schools in expanding their programme to cover a larger population of street children. They have already made contact with the coolie boys at the New Delhi railway station and one of them has volunteered to organise the group at the station and also in planning and implementing the programme. Butterflies would also be making efforts to identify street girl children. The organisation has a small team now but hopes to get more members in a couple of months.

Working with street children is quite difficult and challenging. It is very difficult to have target numbers as one is working with a floating population. Activities have to be need-based and designed to suit the interest of an individual rather than a group.

In August 1987, an NGO Forum for street and working children was constituted. As of today they have a membership of 28 NGOs. The Forum functions as an interest group for working and street children for initiating action in this area, as well as for sharing experiences and providing guidance to others. It also promotes cooperation and coordination amongst NGOs, individuals and government departments having programmes for working and street children. Another function of the Forum is to create awareness about the issues which need to be addressed regarding working and street children, the possible interventions and the problems related to working in this area amongst government departments, NGOs and the public. The Forum also publishes every quarter, a new latter on issues pertaining to street and working children.

ANNEXURE-1

HIGH CONCENTRATION OF CHILD LABOUR

A report brought out by the Human Rights Cell of the Banaras Hindu University (BHU) has revealed high concentration of child labour in saree industry of Varanasi, the systematic exploitation and ill-treatment of children employed in it, shocking conditions of work and in many cases a definite element of bondage.

The report, which was based on a sample survey conducted by Prof. R.K. Misra, Head of the Human Rights Cell, BHU was submitted to the National Human Rights Commission recently. The Commission proposes to study the measures and strategies indicated in the report in order to help in working out a plan of action.

The report puts the estimated number of children engaged in saree manufacturing in and around Varanasi at about one lakh. This includes the girls working inside the house during the pre-weaving and post-weaving stages.

According to the report the community traditionally associated with the saree manufacturing has evolved over the generations a sub-culture and a mindset, which promotes and legitimises exploitation of labour and whose worst suffers are children.

The survey found that economic compulsion of the parents was not the main factor behind high incidence of child labour in saree industry. Less than 50 per cent child workers gave poverty or the need to assist the parents as the reason for taking up employment. It was further found that 75 per cent of the employed children shared no responsibility or only a marginal responsibility regarding their families.

Starting at the age of six or seven years, these children are made to work for long hours extending up to 10 hours a day in unhealthy, ill-ventilated, ill-lighted and at times damp room. Even the basic amenities are lacking, rest and leisure are denied, health care is not even thought of, and there is no concept of leave or weekly off. The wage are low and an entrant may start at no more than Rs. 150 per month which may not go beyond 300 until the child attains the age of 13 or 14 and becomes a full-fledged weaver.

One of the reprehensible aspects of the industry, according to the report, is the practice of parents taking an advance (ranging usually from Rs. 2,000 to Rs. 5,000) from the employer against the services of their children. No interest is charged and the employed is not at all keen for the recovery of the amount. According to the well-established practice, the services of the child cannot be withdrawn so long the dues are not cleared by the parents or by a surrogate employer-creditor who is prepared to clear the dues. There is a definite element of bondage involved in this practice.

The report is emphatic about urgency of comprehensive research and an action plan having purposeful educational-*cum*-vocational training as its core supplemented by efforts to change the mindset, review of laws, publicity of laws, and activisation of enforcement machinery.

In the Saree industry, child labour system is self-perpetuating and the exploitation of children is by remote control. The child worker is ill-treated and ill-paid by the master-weaver who himself is not the beneficiary of this exploitation because the master-weaver remains under the clutches of the Mahajan or Goddidar and receives no more than sustenance wages (on piece rate basis) out of which he is not in a position to pay fair wages to the child worker assisting him.

ANNEXURE-2

SPARING A THOUGHT FOR THE SLUM CHILDREN ON DIWALI

They are the "have nots" of society. They do not have proper clothes to wear, food to eat, beds to sleep in and some do not even have homes to go back to. These slum children live within a social structure which prefers to burn up lakhs of rupees on fire-crackers rather than provide them with a proper childhood.

Their wistful eyes can melt many a heart, and it seems almost 'criminal' to ask them what they are doing for Diwali. "We cannot afford to celebrate Diwali," said 11-year-old Yashoda, resident of a slum in east Delhi. "Fire-crackers are too expensive to buy. *Bapu ke pas faltu kharch ke liye paisa nahin hai* (Father does not have money to waste)," she adds.

"*Man to karta hai* (I do feel like doing it)", confesses nine-year old Heera, shyly. "We are five sisters. If we spend on *patakhas,* how will we manage our next meal? Diwali is only for the rich," she said.

Heera's mother realises the longing and desire her children are hiding beneath the bravado of practicality. "It is the middle of the month and we have already paid our dues. There is no money left to indulge ourselves during Diwali. We all have desires but we have no money to buy anything for our children during Diwali," she says.

"Diwali does not only mean playing with crackers," butts in Raja, a skinny seven-year-old, residing in a slum in Jamuna Pushta. "*Hum puja karenge, diya jalayenge aur doosron ko maze karte dhekhenge* (We will pray, light diyas and watch others having fun)", he said.

Like every year this year too he plans to 'scrounge' around the neighbourhood looking for unused *patakhas* and *phool jharis* and then celebrate Diwali.

"When rich people can spend so much on something so temporary, why can't they give us a box of patakhas", asks Kiran, a 13-year-old domestic servant. Somewhere along the difficult path of life, Kiran has forgotten what a festival means.

"My father is perpetually drunk. As it is we have difficulty in making both ends meet. *Patakhe to mere ghar me jalenge jab bapu ko daru nahin milega,* (There will be fire works in my house if Bapu fails to get his alcohol). I'll just watch other children enjoy themselves and satisfy myself," she added on a wistful note.

Ratna's mother works in a *memsaab's* house. "Every year my mother gets a new sari during Diwali but she always keeps it aside for my wedding. We cannot afford *patakhas* but we get lots of leftover sweets from other houses," she says gleefully.

Her mother standing nearby pointed out that when she could not afford to buy her daughter new clothes for Diwali how could she think of wearing a new sari.

"My brother will get us patakhas on Tuesday," says five-year-old Maitreyi confidently, unaware that Diwali is on Monday. *"We will make gobar ke ghar and play around it. You please come too," she says with an innocent smile on her face.*

Their innocence breaks ones heart. After all they may live in slums, they may be poor. They may be dirty and grimy but they are just children, in this case probably children of a lesser God, with small dreams, hoping to spend Diwali in the only way they can afford to.

ANNEXURE-3

CHILD LABOUR PROBLEMS NEED PEOPLE'S MOVEMENT

Can a socio-economic problem like child labour be solved by mere platitudes and pledges? Deliberations at a national workshop recently gave the impression that words have magical powers and they can solve any problem. The workshop organised by the Union Labour Ministry with much fanfare was attended by District Collectors of the country.

The limitation of the objective had been specified in the nomenclature of the workshop itself. It was meant to eliminate child labour in 'hazardous' occupation only. That means other sectors can freely use child labour.

Even in its limited objective what the workshop can practically achieve is worth watching. It is estimated that over 17 million children are working as child labourers. Over 90 per cent of the country's child labourers are concentrated in Andhra Pradesh, Madhya Pradesh, Maharasthra, Uttar Pradesh, Karnataka, Bihar, Tamil Nadu, Gujarat, Rajasthan, Orissa and West Bengal. Many of these child labourers are working in hazardous occupations.

The workshop discussed various aspects and methods to eliminate child labour in hazardous occupations. Plans and schemes were announced.

An amount of Rs. 34.40 crore has been allotted towards child labour elimination programmes in 1995-96. A national authority has been established under the chairmanship of the Union Labour Minister with the objective of coordinating child-relating programmes implemented by various ministries.

So far so good. The participants have returned to their respective districts after so many yawns, and cups of tea. Many might have been forgotten the whole affair because of their busy schedules. But it is the duty of the Non-governmental Organisations to remind them of their responsibilities. As a well-meaning official put it, they should 'hammer the sleeping authorities.'

The non-effective nature of government measures—read bureaucratic—is evident in the very definition of 'hazardous'. Only 'direct' and 'affecting' hazards were considered. The occupations which have bad effects in the long-run were not enlisted. Even if all such hazardous occupations are covered, the same does not ensure that the problem is over. There might be bureaucratic lethargy, misuse of funds, industries' non-cooperation and general lack of awareness among the public. So what is required is a widespread campaign. A national workshop should be a beginning only. There should be follow-up actions and vigilance, both by government agencies and non-governmental organisations.

This workshop and its resultant actions are aiming only at elimination of child labour from the organised sector. There are loopholes in this sphere too. Take, for example, the hand-knotted carpet industry. Human rights activists allege that 70 to 80 per cent workforce in the carpet knotting industry is child labour. Though the industry points out that it is an exaggerated figure, there is no denying the fact that a considerable portion of carpet workers are children below the age of 14 years. If the functioning of the carpet industry is taken into consideration, it becomes clear that the very nature of the industry defies any government control. The so-called manufactures or exporters are not the actual manufacturers. Some of them collect export orders and depute contractors or loom owners to manufacture carpets. Loom owners are scattered in villages and most of them work from their own homes. They may employ children or involve their own children in making carpets. In such a situation, it is impossible to implement a government scheme for elimination of child labour which is identified as a hazardous occupation.

Employment of children in the unorganised sector is much more rampant and their working condition is pathetic. Small children work in roadside *dhabas*, automobile workshops, small shops and houses. They are paid a pittance for long hours of arduous work.

Take, for example, the situation prevailing in Delhi. According to a UNICEF study published in April 1992, as many as one lakh children are working as domestic servants in Delhi and about 40,000 children are working as porters and labourers. Besides, there are 30,000 children shop assistants and the same number of child labourers in *dhabas* and shops. The number of child ragpickers, newspaper sellers and others are 1,80,000. About 20,000 children are working as scooter and car repair workers. This gives a mind-boggling total figure of four lakh child labourers. That is, 18 per cent of the National Capital's total population of children have to work for their livelihood. Among them, 14 per cent are girls.

It is also estimated that children form 5.55 per cent of the total work force in unorganised sectors like agriculture. Besides these characteristically unorganised sectors, small units of both hazardous and non-hazardous industries are also not under the purview of government's elimination scheme.

The collectors' workshop held in the cosy interior of Vigyan Bhavan did not take the pligth of child labour in unorganised sector into consideration.

In short, the child labour problem is a grave one. It can't be solved by rhetoric or rituals. It needs a comprehensive and pragmatic approach involving the government machinery, non-governmental organisations and people as a whole. It needs a people's movement.

19

WHERE ARE CHILDREN WORKING?

There are broadly four kinds of child labour. First are those children who work in factories, workshops and mines. They are usually to be found in semi-urban and urban areas in both the unorganised and organised sectors. Second, are those children who are under bondage to their employers, whether in agriculture or industry. The third category of working children are the street children—those who live on and off the streets—and are to be found in the service sector of semi-urban and urban India. Children who work as part of family labour in all the contexts of agriculture, industry, home-based work, etc. belong to the fourth category. These are not exclusive categories, they are often combined in different ways.

Demographic Profile

According to the 1981 Census, there are 263 million children aged fourteen years or under in India comprising 39.5 per cent of the total population of the country. Nearly 78 per cent of the child population is in the rural areas. The share of males in the child population is 51.64 per cent (Census Commissioner and Registrar General, 1981). Approximately 11.2 million children are notified as main workers and 2.4 million as marginal workers. Main workers are those involved in full-time economic activity and marginal workers are those who are not working full-time. Table 19.1 below gives the percentage of children zero to fourteen in the workforce (all ages) according to the 1981 Census.

Interestingly, a comparison of the work participation rate (WPR) of male and female children shows that between 1971 and 1981 there has been an increase in the WPR of girls as compared to boys. (The WPR of children is the percentage of child workers to the total child population. There is an increasing trend in sending more girls then boys to work. Sumanta Banerjee says, girls outnumber boys in many sorts to work. There are twice as many girls as boys working in mines and in quarrying and also in factory work (Banerjee 1979: 26).

Table 19.2 gives the WPR of girl workers (main) by sex for both the 1971 and the 1981

Census, showing in increase in the WPR of girls and a decrease in the WPR of boys. However, some observers have noted that female participation rates tended to be under-estimated in the 1971 Census since women respondents did not consider household work as productive work (Nayyar 1987: 2207).

TABLE 19.1

Percentage of the Workforce Aged Under 15 Years, 1981

	Persons	*Males*	*Females*
1	*2*	*3*	*4*
1. Main Workers			
Total	5.02	4.17	8.35
Rural	5.78	4.88	8.86
Urban	2.12	1.80	4.58
2. Marginal Workers			
Total	10.97	19.34	9.38
Rural	11.32	21.29	9.59
Urban	5.02	5.59	4.56

Source: *Census of India 1981:* 'Report and Tables based on 5 per cent Sample Data', Series-I, Part II, Special, pp. 2-3.

TABLE 19.2

Work Participation Rates for Child Workers (Main) by Sex, 1971 and 1981

	Males		*Females*	
	1971	*1981*	*1971*	*1981*
Total	6.65	5.46	2.63	2.95
Rural	7.56	6.30	3.05	3.53
Urban	2.75	2.469	0.82	0.88

Source: *Census of India 1981:* 'Key Population Statistics based on 5 per cent Sample Data', Paper 2 of 1983, Series-I, India, p. 26.

The definitions used by the *Census of India, 1991,* for main and marginal workers were the same as in the 1981 Census. However, there was a significant change in the 1991 Census in that, for the first time, an effort was made to compute unpaid work on farms or in family enterprises so that women and children's work could be better reflected (*Census of India 1991,* Series-1, Paper 3 of 1991: 4). Thus, participation in any economically productive activity also included unpaid work on farms and in family enterprises (ibid.: 5). However, since the 1991 Census figures are provisional, only broad figures are available and data on the number of child labourers are yet to be published.

The Operations Research Group (ORG), an organisation involved with market and social research, was commissioned by the Ministry of Labour to undertake an All-India Child Labour Sample Survey in 1980-1. They surveyed about 40,000 households spread all over the country using questionnaires. These households were spread in 238 urban centres and 805 rural centres in seventy-seven districts excluding the north-east. Their survey was conducted zone-wise rather than state-wise. According to them:

> A working child is that who was enumerated during the survey as a child falling within the five to fifteen age bracket and who is at remunerative work may be paid or unpaid, and busy any hour of the day within or outside the family.... The estimated working children in our country are around 44.0 million. Out of these about 21.0 per cent are in urban areas and the rest are rural based (Khatu *et al.* 1983: 69).

Other than the decennial Censuses and the National Sample Survey no other report, except for that of ORG, appears to have any systematic data base for their estimates on child labour. According to a 1991 UNICEF report, 'Going by the official "medium projection" of a total population of 820 million by 1990, the number of children of the preschool age, three to six years, would be over 60 million; and those of the primary school age, six to eleven years, would exceed 100 million' (UNICEF 1991: 48). If the figures for the age group eleven to fourteen years are added, the figure goes well above the 100 million mark. The report clearly states that 'as of 181, there was an estimated 75 million children between six to fourteen years out of school (of the total population of around 140 million in that age group)' (ibid.: 57). According to the UNICEF report, 'most of the children of school age who are not at school may be expected to be put to some work, in the home or outside, unpaid or paid in cash or kind. India has probably more working children than any other country' (ibid.: 60). It will be seen that estimates range from 13.59 million (Census Commissioner and Registrar General 1981), to 17.36 million (NSS 1983) and 44 million (Khatu *et al.* 1983). The differences in the estimates of child labour are partly attributable to the differences in the definitions employed as also the year in which any estimate was made. While it is true that one needs to have a roughly accurate estimate of the size of the problem, I would argue that the different definitions used above are not useful from the point of view of analysing the problem and understanding its varied dimensions. Such an understanding would be the first step towards framing policies and devising programmes for different categories of child labour.

Child Labour

Table 19.3 a list of industries and occupations with estimates of the numbers of total workers as also child workers. In some cases, figures are not known since the writers of the articles from which this information has been gleaned have not mentioned any figures. Even where the figures have been mentioned, they represent estimates arrived at by different writers on the basis of local interviews and discussions and not necessarily on the basis of household surveys. However imperfect these statistics might be, they indicate the diversity of industries and the range of geographical locations where child labour is to be found.

Apart from factories and workshops, children are also employed to work in mines. One report says that:

> ... in Meghalaya, children work in mines of private companies, in trenches ninety centimetres wide and one metre high, where adults could only 'crawl'. As soon as their size is no longer profitable, they are thrown on to the streets (*The Indian Worker*, 4 April 1980: 3).

A report on child labour in Rajasthan (Thanga Raju 1977: 369) pointed out that children in the age-group of five to fourteen comprised about 4.5 per cent of the total labour force in the mining and quarrying industry in that State.

Bonded Child Labour in Industry

Mode of Recruitment and Retention in The Workforce

This is clearly the harshest form of child labour as very small children, sometimes only eight or nine years old are separated from their parents for life.

A large segment is made up of those children whose parents pledge them to factory owners or their agents or middlemen in exchange for small consumption loans (Juyal *et al.* 1985: 73; Ganguly 1984; Singh *et al.* 1980; Menon 1979; GOI 1981: 18).

These children work for long years for the industrialists, and are paid at well below the minimum wage. Loan repayment calculations are engineered to the severe detriment of their illiterate parents. The industries in which this type of transaction is widespread are the *beedi* industry in the States of Andhra Pradesh, Madhya Pradesh and Tamil Nadu (Mehta 1983: 15; Mohandas 1980), the carpet industry of Mirzapur-Bhadohi in the State of Uttar Pradesh (Prembhai 1984; Gangrade and Gathia 1983: 4-5; Ninan 1984a, b, c, d, e; Devi 1984a, b; and Chowdhury 1984a, b), the match industry of Sivakasi in the State of Tamil Nadu (Sarma 1979: 346; Menon 1979; *The Indian Worker*, 17 September 1979: 4), the slate industry of Mandsaur in the State of Madhya Pradesh (Rao 1980: 1883, Singh 1986: 159) and the silk industry of Varanasi in the State of Uttar Pradesh (Juyal *et al.* 1985: 84). One difficulty in assessing the numbers of children bonded to industries is that most journalistic accounts are descriptive rather than quantitative.

Beedi Industry

Of all the industries employing children, the *beedi* industry in India and the carpet industry of Mirzapur-Bhadohi-Varanasi are the most notorious. In the report of the Task Force on health prepared for the National Commission on Self-Employed Women, *beedi* workers in Tamil Nadu told of their pitiable condition where they had to mortgage their children in order to survive. One middle-aged woman told Prayag Mehta, the then Director of the National Labour Institute.

> I have mortgaged my seven-year-old girl, and eight-year-old boy to a Sheth three years ago for a loan of Rs. 200 (Rs. 100 on each child). Two years later, my husband was mortgaged to the same Sheth for a loan of Rs. 200. My two children and their father roll 4000 *beedis* a day. They work al the time for the master. Their total wage should be at least Rs. 20 a day. However, the Sheth has been paying them each Rs. 2.50 a day, out of which he deducts half the money every day (Mehta 1983: 15).

Another woman said:

> All of us are forced to mortgage our children. What else can we do? When we mortgage other items to the Sheth, we lose control over those items, like our utensils and jewellery. We don't have these any more. We have only children. When we mortgage them, we lose control over them, as we lose control over other items (*ibid.*: 15-16).

Saroja, another woman, said:

> Our grand-children are also mortgaged. We are like bonded labour. We are slaves. We just give birth to children and then leave them to work for the moneylenders. We can ask no questions. We have to follow them like slaves. Husband, children and grand-children all work in this way. All are slaves (*ibid.*: 16).

Mehta writes:

> In voices choked with emotion, they described how mercilessly their children are beaten by the moneylender employers. Most of the children are very young when mortgaged. It is difficult for them to work all the time. Sometimes they do not go. The Sheth then beats them severely. Their fingers are injured by caning (ibid.).

Most of the mortgaged children said that they became bonded over very small sums of money. They had in fact paid back both the principal and the interest but since they and their parents are illiterate, they did not understand the basis of calculation. Even after ten or fifteen years of work, when they want to leave, the employers demand the principal and the interest.[1]

If the *beedi* industry is oppressive, the conditions of children in the carpet industry are worse.

Carpet Industry

Gangrade and Gathia's study of carpet weavers in Varanasi reveals that:

> To keep the production cost low the middlemen often suggest to the families to engage children under twelve years of age. They even pay advances of Rs. 400 to Rs. 500 for some family function and thus tie the child to work for them indirectly (Gangrade and Gathia, 1983: 4-5).[2]

In some cases, the parents ask for advances against the child. But there is ample evidence that often employers take advantage of the poverty of the families and offer large loans against children knowing that the parents will never be able to pay off the debt. Sevanti Ninan, writing about child weavers in Bhadohi in Uttar Pradesh, says:

> The latest 'Carpet Bulletin' which is published from this region moans that advances are killing exporters. But the proprietor of one of the bigger units in Bhadohi, Ratin Chand and Sons, says candidly, 'they don't need advances, we thrust it upon them' (Ninan, 1983).[3]

The carpet industry has become notorious for its bonded child labour Kapoor 1992; Dasgupta 1992; McDonald 1992; *Times of India,* 4 August 1992; *Financial Express,* 11 August 1992). Even the Uttar Pradesh Government report on child weavers admits to the incidence of bonded children (GOUP 1986b: 3).[4]

Prembhai, a social activist who was appointed Commissioner by the Supreme Court to investigate the incidence of child bonded labour in the carpet industry, found that out of a sample of 858 children who were interviewed, 414 or 48 per cent had received small loans from their employers. Eighty-three per cent of the children had received about Rs. 500 which had been adjusted against wages after a few months (Prembhai 1984: 53). Many of them had in fact worked for more than five years. Preambhai's interviews established that out of the 858 children from Bihar, 572 or 67 per cent had to do free work for employers such as grazing the cattle, working in agriculture, fetching water from the well and other odd jobs over and above the time spent on weaving (ibid.: 62). Prembhai says: 'If they tried to escape or go to another loom owner who promised better payments, they were caught, brought back and punished' (*ibid.:* 63).

Many children were kidnaped to weave carpets (ibid.: 90; *down to Earth,* 15 September 1992: 50-1). According to Juyal, about 50 per cent of the hired child labour force, which is two-thirds of the total labour force, has been sold to the loom-holders (Juyal 1987: 30).

Prembhai visited Chhichori village in Palamau district of Bihar which is located twenty kilometres from the district head-quarters, Daltonganj. The children and the parents were interviewed in depth. The investigation revealed that:

> ...in all thirty-two children were taken away from this village in four batches by Shiva Kumar (barber) and his brother Sudama Thakur of the same village. Shiva Kumar Thakur was working with Shri Pannalal, the carpet loom owner of village Belwaria (Mirzapur) and acted as his agent. He lured the children distributing toffees, making promises of showing cinemas, etc. He recruited them for Pannalal and his brother on the false promises that the children will be given food (three meals per day) plus clothes and Rs. 10 to 20 per day as wages. Most of them were taken without the consent and knowledge of their parents. Shiva Kumar had warned them not to tell the parents about their going with him to cinema or otherwise (Prembhai 1984: 89-90).

An important fact that came out of this investigation was that at least eleven children were studying in the local school. Parik Ram said that he was promised by Shiva Kumar that every afternoon after 4 o'clock, arrangements would be made for education. He was also told that he would be given three good meals, clothes and Rs. 20 a day as wages and that if he were to feel unhappy, he could go back home. Other children—Mogul, Kodu and Virendra—were similarly lured and taken to Belwaria village.

Koiler Bhuian, aged ten, said that he and other children were forced to work from dawn to late at night. Petromax lamps were used for night-work. All the children were locked up at night and when they went out for their morning ablutions in the open field, they were escorted by two persons. Koiler Bhuian said:

> I tried to escape three times but I was caught and severely beaten. My feet and hands were tied together and I was slung onto a jackfruit tree in front of Pannalal's house. I was tied with a rope and repeatedly lifted and thrown on the ground. I was beaten with sticks and shoes and sometimes even with an iron *panja* (the fork used for weaving). Once my thigh was branded with a hot iron rod when I tried to escape and was caught. Four other children were also branded: Shyam Mochi in the armpit, Munni on the hand, Inder Mochi and Vinod on the led (*ibid*.: 91).

Seven children were taken in the third batch: Inder Mochi, Rajchani Bhuiya, Vinod Bhuian, Vijai Bhuiya, Nathuni Thakur and Anil were between seven and eleven and Madan looked about fourteen years. These children reported that they were often beaten with a bamboo if there was any fault in weaving, that they were only given one or two *rotis* (whole wheat bread) for food, and were beaten up if they asked for more. Shiv Kumar and Sudama Thakur threatened to set their houses on fire and beat them if they disobeyed. When some of them tried to escape, they were captured and severely beaten (*ibid*.: 92).

Some of the parents went to the village where these children were working and asked the loom-owner to release their children. But the loom-owners demanded Rs. 500 for the release of each child against the cost of food consumed as well as the yarn the children were supposed to have damaged while they were learning. As the parents had no money, they had to return home without the children. Many parents had sold all their possessions in order to be able to purchase a bus ticket to come to get their children back. Many of them found that their children had disappeared and in some cases were later told that the child had died (*ibid*.: 91-101).

This is not merely the story of thirty-two children but of hundreds and thousands of them, many of them kidnapped or lured away or pledged by their parents for paltry sums of money. Most of them are kept in captivity, tortured and made to work for twenty hours a day without a break. Little children are made to crouch on their toes, from dawn to dusk everyday, severely stunting their growth during formative years. Social activists in the area find it hard to work because of the strong mafia-like control that the carpet loom owners have on the area. Any whisper of an investigation of child weavers means that the children are just whisked away from the area (Proceedings and Resolution of First National Workshop on *Eradication of Child Labour in Carpet Industry* 1991). According to the Anti-Slavery Society, which made a representation to the United Nations Working Group on contemporary forms of slavery in Geneva, there are about 100,000 children employed to work in the carpet industry in conditions of slavery (Puri, 1984).

Most of the children working in the carpet industry belong to the Scheduled Castes and Scheduled Tribes and many of them come from the perennially drought-prone areas of Bihar, particularly from districts like Palamau. They are children of landless labourers, many of whom have been deprived of their lands by the landlords of the village. Ironically, in spite of the conditions of semi-slavery in which these children were working, after they were restored to their parents, they returned to work for the same masters. Mahasveta Devi, a social activist, interviewed some parents who had knowingly sent their children to the looms. One person was brutally frank and said: 'We cannot feed our children. What is the use of keeping them with us and seeing them die? Let them earn a living, let them eat' (Devi 1984a: 751).

Glass Industry

I was told by many workers that a large number of children were working as bonded slaves in glass factories. In Chandwar village, just outside Firozabad, there is a *pakai bhatti* (a unit where bangles are baked in layers on metal sheets covered with silica sand). Two little boys work here. One was about twelve years old and the other was eight years. Their job was to arrange bangles on the trays which the *pakaiwala* (the person who places trays of bangles into the furnace and also strokes it) would put into the furnace. The heat was unbearable as the temperature soared to 800°C. These two boys have been left behind by their parents. The older boy was studying in school till a few months prior to my interview. When his father had an accident working on a thresher and lost his arm, the boy was withdrawn from school and brought to Firozabad. His father had taken an advance from the *thekedar* (contractor) and the boy was to pay off the loan from his wages.

The other boy comes from Tundla village in Agra district. His father left his little boy behind for an advance of Rs. 500 from the *thekedar*. On being asked whether he had any brothers and sisters, the boy put his head down and started crying. The old man sitting next to him explained that the boy was feeling homesick as his father had just come a few days ago to collect the child's wages and had gone back to the village. These two boys live alone in the *pakai bhatti* unit and cook their food on the silica-covered trays.

Other Industries

Slate Pencil Industry: Cases of bonded labour have also been reported in the slate pencil industry of Mandsaur in the State of Madhya Pradesh where, according to journalist and activist Amiya Rao: '...the owners use the same technique as rich landowners do to keep their labour as bonded slaves—they advance them, even force upon them, large sums of money...' (Rao 1980: 1883)[5]

Handloom Industry: Even the 1981 report of the Government-appointed Gurupadaswamy Committee recognised that in Kanchipuram in Tamil Nadu, a large number of children in the age-group of seven to fourteen years were working on looms and had been pledged into work on a long-term basis (GOI 1981: 18)[6] Juyal, writing about the Varanasi silk industry, holds that it is a common practice for workers to take advances from the employers and in exchange put children to work (Juyal *et al.* 1985: 84).

Recruited by Contractors

Brass Ware Industry: There are many methods of recruiting children. A very common way is through contractors or middlemen. In the brass ware industry of Moradabad, I was told by village officials that while adults go on their own in search of work, children are recruited by *dalals* (middlemen/broker), who usually belong to the village and who are paid a commission for bringing child workers. *Thekedars* and workshop owners prefer children because they are easy to control. The middlemen look for out children. Their parents are offered an advance of Rs. 100 or the equivalent of a month's wages. If a parent takes an advance, the child has to work whether he likes it or not. If he plays hooky, the wages of other children from the same village are cut some control is maintained in this way. Parents of the children who belong to the town are induced into sending them to work by the lure of an advance of about Rs. 500. This lump sum payment is a big incentive for parents and it is adjusted against a child's wages over a few months.

Pottery Industry: I asked several children working in the pottery industry of Khurja how they came to know that work was available in the potteries. Fazal, a ten-year old boy said:

> *Thekedars* come to the village and say they want children so we know that there is work. Often the *thekedars* don't want to give the work to adults. We are young, we can work fast and we don't get tired so easily (Burra 1987: 23).

Glass Industry: In industries where large numbers of workers need to be recruited—sometimes on a daily basis—a special role is assigned to workers entrusted with the task of recruitment. Usually a former worker himself, the *jagaiya* (the person whose responsibility it is to wake up workers on night shifts. He is also the man who recruits labour for the factory owner) of the glass industry is on the monthly pay-roll of the factory-owner and, though he has a status superior to that of the ordinary worker, he is not really part of the management structure. The term *jagaiya* means the one who wakes others up; he came to be so designated when the glass factories functioned only at night and he had to go around waking up the workers to report for duty. Today, he visits the local labour markets in Firozabad to select those lucky ones who will have work for the day. Familiar with the community, he ensures that the same workers do not get continuous employment and thus claim rights; on occasion, he can be bribed by those in dire need of work (Burra 1988).

Match Industry: In the match industry of Sivakasi, village contractors are employed and they transport children from their homes to the factories. The contractors perform multiple functions: they wake up the children in time to board the buses, they ensure repayment of advances given by match units to workers and they act as the eyes and ears of the factory owners to report new arrivals in the village who may have come to create trouble for the entrepreneurs by organising the labourers (MIDS 1985: 59-60).

In the match industry,

> Inquiries showed that the factories engage agents to procure child labour. Often money is advanced to children rather than their parents—and this keeps them bound to the employer (Sarma 1979: 346).[7]

In a study conducted in the Sivakasi match factories in Tamil Nadu, Kulkarni reported one woman as saying: '...the child in the 'womb' is pledged to the factory, and consumption and maternity loans are obtained on the undertaking that the child born, girl or boy, would work for the factory!' (Kulkarni 1983: 1855).

Bonded Child Labour in Agriculture

Where bonded labour is widely prevalent as in the States of Rajasthan, Uttar Pradesh, Bihar, Orissa and Andhra Pradesh, child bonded labour is an inter-generational phenomenon. The pattern that emerges is that usually a father or grandfather has taken a loan. After slaving for many years, when the man becomes too old to work, his master demands that the young son of sons be sent to replace the father and, around the age of ten, the young child is introduced into the system of bondage. Sadhu and Singh (1980: 42) quoting a National Labour Institute study on bonded labour showed that 21, 10.3 and 8.7 per cent children below fifteen years were bonded in Andhra Pradesh, Karnataka and Tamil Nadu respectively.

Most of the child bonded labourers in the rural areas are sons of bonded labourers. In most cases by having a male member of the family working as a bonded slave, the family becomes impoverished and for survival send younger sons into bondage. As Marla says:

> First, the boy has to tend cattle, and later he has to perform the complicated agricultural operations. As long as he is young and strong, once mortgaged by his family to the landlord, he becomes the private property of the master, a thing with human flesh and blood that can be easily manipulated according to the whims of the landlord's family (Marla 1977: 46-7).

In some areas of India, like Andhra Pradesh, Orissa and Bihar, child bonded labour is widespread. According to a study done in Andhra Pradesh by the Rural Wing of the National Labour Institute, child bonded labour known widely as *Jeeta Gadus* or *Jeeta* (a term used to refer to bonded labourers mainly in south India) was widely prevalent in the villages of Sidipet, Medak and Gogipet *talukas* (an administrative unit of the district).

These children were tied to moneylenders and local landlords. In some villages it was found that landlords were using primarily child labour (NLI Rural Wing, 1977: 539).

There are regional variations in the profile of bonded labour. Thus, according to the National Survey on bonded labour conducted by Marla, in Andhra Pradesh 20 per cent of the bonded labourers in the state were under the age of fifteen years (Marla 1981: 44). In Orissa children below the age of fifteen years make up 20.5 per cent of the total bonded labourers in the State (*ibid.*: 93). In Rajasthan, 17 per cent of the bonded labourers are twenty years old or younger (ibid.: 104). And in Tamil Nadu 10.6 per cent of the bonded labourers belong to the age group of eleven to fifteen years (ibid.: 113). It is only with respect to Gujarat that it was found that no bonded labourer identified was younger than twenty years (*ibid.*: 62).

Children become bonded for the smallest thing. In Bihar, Ramlakhan Bhuiyan of Ramkanda village borrowed Rs. 100 to buy clothes and has been working since he was the height of a man's thigh. He was about twenty years when this story appeared (Mundle 1976: 725). A similar story is that of Ram Lakhan who sold himself for Rs. 10. That was eighteen years ago when he was hardly five years. His parents had died and he had nothing to eat or wear. So he asked the village moneylender to lend him Rs. 10. The orphaned boy was given the loan but on condition that the labour of his life belonged exclusively to the moneylender till he paid his debt (Mundle 1976: 653).

In a study of a Karnataka village, Sudha Rao found that the *jeeta*, servants who belonged to the peasant, Harijan and artisanal castes were all under fourteen years and invariably from families which had incurred debt. According to her, 8 per cent of the total households in the village had *jeeta* servants (Rao 1984: 769).

A newspaper report documents how tribal children in Raipur district in the State of Madhya Pradesh are mortgaged to landlords at the age of seven years. For a sum of about Rs. 200 given at the time of marriage, the young man becomes a full-fledged bonded labourer since he will never be able to repay that sum. In course of time, his children are also mortgaged and the story repeats itself (*Indian Express* 11 April 1984; *M.P. Chronicle* 17 April 1984). A more report pointed out that there were about 2000 child bonded labourers in the Raipur district of Madhya Pradesh alone (Chanthanom 1989: 4).

It is a characteristic of feudal agrarian relations that families of agricultural labourers are bonded to their masters for several generations. The bonded child labourer is bonded not so much because he is a child as much as because he is a member of a bonded family. Commonly a family takes a loan, is charged interest at usurious rates and provides services to the landlord and his family in order to pay off the debt. The bonded family is hardly paid any wages but is given something in kind for its bare sustenance. When the father is old or dies, the young sons of the family step into their father's shoes and the cycle continues (Murthy *et al.* 1985: 2). One estimate has it that nearly 7.5 million children below the age of fourteen years were in bondage (*The Times of India*, 1 July 1989).

While there are different estimates of child bondage in India, the then Minister of State for Labour announced in 1980 in Parliament that a random sample survey in a hundred villages in ten states estimated that the incidence of bonded labour was 22.4 lakhs (1 lakh = 100,000) and 66 per cent of the bonded labourers belonged to the Scheduled Castes and 18.3 to the Scheduled Tribes (*The Indian Worker*, 29 December 1980: 3) The states of Andhra Pradesh, Bihar, Orissa, Rajasthan and Uttar Pradesh are all known to harbour bonded child labour.

Street Children

Street children constitute the third category of children who work for survival, and are largely found in semi-urban and urban metropolitan centres. These children find themselves on the street because they have either run away from their families, or been abandoned or kidnapped. They usually live in public places such as railway stations, bus stops and footpaths and are without the protection of their families. They may be self-employed such as shoeshine boys, newspaper vendors, ragpickers, hawkers and vendors, or they may work in establishments like *dhabas* (small way-side eating places), as domestic servants and *coolies* (porters), or as casual labourers on construction sites, as helpers in shops, and so on. Not all children who work in urban metropolitan centres fall into the category of street children for there are many children who work as part of family labour, or return to the womb of the family in the evenings. It is estimated that in Delhi, 400,000 children are child workers and 100,000 are street children (UNICEF n.d.: 17). In the city of Hyderabad, it is estimated that there are 30,000 street children (Rao and Malik 1992: 2). A study undertaken by Ghosh in 1992 estimated that there would be between 75,000 to 100,000 street children on the streets of Calcutta (Ghosh 1992: 1). There are an estimated 25,000 street children in the city of Madras (Arimpoor 1992: 8) and in Bangalore city, Nandana Reddy estimates that there are about 45,000 street children of whom 25,000 are homeless (Reddy 1992: 3). It is their aloneness which makes street children particularly vulnerable to the anti-social elements of the city and places them into a special category for purpose of programme and policy (Prasad 1982; Ganguly 1984; Rai 1984; Anklesaria 1984; Mehta 1983; Shukla 1984).

There is very little authentic data about how many such children there are in different places. But the most significant fact about them is their physical separation from their families. In the town of Aligarh in Uttar Pradesh, I had an opportunity to interview a few children in the Children's Observation Home without any adult being present and over a period of a few days. A couple of stories will bring out the plight of such children.

Rasheed and Baheed are two brothers aged thirteen and eight years respectively. They were picked up under Section 3 of the U.P. Children's Act, 1951, which says that any child found alone in a public place can be caught by a policeman and taken in protective custody. Rasheed and Baheed were escaping from their respective employers in Lucknow when they were apprehended by the police at the Aligarh Railway Station. They were hoping that their father would rescue them.

The two brothers have been on the run for several years. Their father is a vegetable vendor in Lucknow. He used to beat his children in an alcoholic rage: Rasheed and Baheed decided to run away from home. They went to the Lucknow railway station and slept on the platform. They swept the trains occasionally and earned a little money. One day a man came to them and asked if they were hungry and wanted food. The boys were revenous and were taken by the man to a nearby hotel where he let them eat to their hearts' content. After they finished their meal, he told them to pay for the food or work for him. Rasheed and Baheed had no choice but to agree to work. The man even offered to pay them Rs. 200 a month and give them food. But when they arrived at the hotel, they were locked up in a back room. For two months, they worked from 6 a.m. to 10 p.m. with out wages. They had to wash the plates and vessels, and sweep the floors, but were never allowed to serve clients. For that work, the hotel owner employed adolescents who were trusted.

Rasheed said there were two other boys between the ages of seven and nine years who were held captive like him and his brother. One day, they were hatching a plan to escape, when an older boy overheard them and reported the matter to the *malik* (employer/owner). The *malik* was furious, he beat them up badly and made them go without any food that day. But Rasheed did not give up hope. One day he recognised a client who belonged to his neighbourhood. He braved the wrath of the employer and approached him. He asked the man to inform his father that they were being held against their wishes. A few days alter the father arrived. The *malik* tried to tempt the father with Rs. 100 so that he would leave the boys behind but the father refused. The children managed to escape from this *dhaba* owner. But when they went home, they had to face physical violence again from their father everytime they did not want to work. They found the work at the bakery very hard as the baker made them carry heavy trays of baked goods on their heads from the bakery to the shops. In despair they ran away once again back to the railway station where they swept the floors of the compartments in moving trains and earned some money. From their savings, they bought the various items they needed and managed to earn Rs. 20 a day. One day they got off at the Aligarh station to have lunch and were picked up by the police.

Physical abuse was one of the main reasons that children gave for running away from home. Often, the children I talked to, understood the cause of parental rage—extreme poverty and hunger. Raju, who was nine years old belonged to Farakhabad district of Uttar Pradesh. His father used to beat him up. When asked why he had left home, the answer was, '*Mazboori se.*' Raju's family were Khatiks or of low caste and made *beedis* for a living. His father was heavily in debt and they rarely had food to eat. According to Raju:

> My father would fly into a terrible rage and hit me. We were heavily indebted to the *seth* (a term used to describe the rich, a term often used for landlords, owners of workshops and factories) from whom my father had borrowed Rs. 1000 to buy goats. When the goats died and he fell ill, we had to borrow more money. If we

> (my mother, father and I) worked morning and night we could make *beedis* worth Rs. 250. But the *seth* would take away half the *beedis* saying that they were damaged. After cutting the interest, we rarely had Rs. 200 left for food. Sometimes we got one meal in two days. I know my father was taking out his frustration on me.

When Raju's father got desperate, he would beat the boy. One day Raju decided to work in a road-side hotel. Whatever he earned he gave to his mother. But one day, a truck driver came and offered him a job at his hotel from Rs. 8 a day. Thinking that the hotel was close by, Raju got into the truck. The unscrupulous man took him to Etah district a few hundred miles away. Escaping from one ruthless employer to another, the boy is now in the Aligarh Observation Home since August 1986 and he knows his father will never come for him. It is now some years since he left home. The memory of abject poverty is very vivid on his mind. His memory of his home is very hazy. Raju will remain in custody till he is eighteen or unless he runs away from the Home as many children do.

Working Children

Children who work as part of family labour make up the fourth and last category mentioned. They will be referred to as working children. These children are to be predominantly found in agriculture where they help their parents in a number of ways. Male children in rural areas begin helping parents at five or six years of age and are inducted full-time into agricultural work by the age of nine or so. Grazing cattle, collecting fuel and fodder, farm activity, household chores, looking after younger siblings and, accompanying parents to work-sites elsewhere are some of the tasks they have to perform (Kishwar and Horowitz 1984: 69-103).

A number of working children are also found in home-based work, helping their parents (Kulshreshta and Sharma 1980; Juyal *et al.* 1985; Hasan 1978). Such home-based work could be for a number of industries such as the *agarbatti* (incense sticks) industry spread out in the States of Andhra Pradesh, Madhya Pradesh, Maharashtra and Gujarat (Jhabvala and Sebstadt 1980-1: 29; Krishnakumari 1985), the garment industry in West Bengal (*Shramshakti* 1988: xl), the coir industry in the State of Kerala (Gulati n.d.) and the *beedi* industry in the States of Tamil Nadu, Karnataka, Andhra Pradesh, Gujarat and Maharashtra. It is typical of home-based, piece-rate work that the rate payable to the adult per unit of output is so low that the parents are compelled to put their children to work in order to barely survive (Bhat 1987).

Working children are often to be found amongst migrant families at construction sites, sugar factories, brick-kilns, mines and plantations where circumstances do not permit the parents to leave the children behind in their homes. The children of migrants form a very large percentage of the non-domestic, non-monetary child labour force (Pichholiya 1980: 106; Sud 1985). Malabika Patnaik's study (1979: 674) reveals that 'as many as 80 per cent of the children of migrants are workers. This is four times higher than the rate among the settled population.' Similar accounts are given by Khandekar (1970: 53) and Sebastian (1979: 181-98). Ghanshyam Pardesi (1985) writes that children below the age of fourteen years work in the Udaipur marble mines. This is also the case in Madhya Pradesh where Arindam Sengupta tells us that in the unorganised kilns, quarries and mines, women and children form a majority of the work-force. In the limestone kilns and quarries in and around Katni in north-eastern Madhya Pradesh, 70 to 80 per cent of the workers are women and children. They are engaged in back-breaking work, carving out chunks of stone from the earth, breaking them up and then carrying them in baskets to the edge of the pit. They have to climb about 100 feet (Sengupta 1983: 80-1).

In the plantation sector, the then Minister of State for Labour, Mr. J.B. Patnaik, told the Parliament that the proportion of child labour in all the tea plantations had risen from 4.9 per cent to 8.4 per cent (*The Indian Worker*, 31 March 1980: 10). He gave no explanation for this. A more recent study undertaken by Sharit Bhowmik, pointed out that under the Plantation Labour Act, children above the age of twelve years could be legally employed as permanent workers. According to Bhowmik, 'the plantation industry thus enjoys the dubious distinction of being the only industry in the organised sector which legally permits the employment of child labour' (Bhowmik 1992: 2287). Bhowmik quotes from the Tea Board of India statistics according to which, the total number of child labourers were 54,899). The bulk of child labour lies in the plantations of Assam and West Bengal. In Assam there were 42,458 child labourers and in West Bengal there were 10,676 children employed. The tea growing states of South India, on the other hand employed very little child labour. Only 433 children were reported employed in the plantations of south India (*ibid.*).

Working children are also affected by the rigidity and inflexibility of the schooling system. The schooling schedule does not allow children to take time off during sowing and harvesting seasons. Nor does it allow children to re-enter the school system at times convenient to them and their families. The subsistence economy of rural India forces poorer households to utilise the labour of their children whether it is for agricultural operations or for households chores, which releases adults for a more directly productive activity (Khatu *et al.* 1983: 69). According to a report on child labour written by Patel and Alagh (n.d.: 17), about 52 per cent of the child workers from rural labour households worked as agricultural labourers. Another study reported that the proportion of child labour in agriculture to the total child labour force in the country has gone up from 80.35 per cent in 1961 to 87 per cent in 1971 (Murthy *et al.* 1985: 15). The major part of the child labour force, therefore, is to be found in the agricultural sector. The figures were calculated from the 1961 and 1971 censuses. Murthy, Ramaiah and Sudarshan point out that the capacity for child labour in non-agricultural sectors is very low.

Another subgroup falling into this category is made up of children, particularly girl children, who accompany their mothers working as part-time domestic servants. The vulnerability of the female child to sexual abuse in the setting of the urban slum pressurises the parents to see that she is never alone.

It is necessary to point out that the categories employed are not water-tight compartments and many children could be classified as belonging to more than one category. For example, the children who work in certain industries like the glass industry of Firozabad and the carpet industry of Mirzapur-Bhadohi in the State of Uttar Pradesh, and the match industry in Sivakasi in the State of Tamil Nadu could be classified under the first category of child labour where children work in factories, workshops and mines. Equally, since some sections of the child population working in these industries have been pledged by their parents against loans taken by them (Kulkarni 1983: 1855; MIDS 1985: 59-60; Burra 1988), they could also be considered as belonging to a subgroup of bonded child labour. Again street children who operate in the urban environment without the shelter of their families can also be looked at as children who are working and necessarily a part of the labour force. However, a distinction here must be made: while all street children are part of the labour force, it is not as if all child labourers are street children, for many of the children in the cities live with their parents and work in a variety of contexts; at home and outside it as well. Despite these definitional problems, these categories are useful not only from an analytical point of view but also from the policy perspective. Programmes to deal with their specific disabilities and the contexts in which they are set will vary according to category.

NOTES

1. See also *New Age*, 4 September 1986: 6; Purushotham 1983: 18-23.
2. See also Ninan 1984a, b, c; Devi 1984a, b; and Chowdhury 1984a.
3. See also Das 1985: 3.
4. See also Chowdhury 1985; Tiwari 1985.
5. See also Singh 1986: 159.
6. See also *The Times of India*, 7 September 1981.
7. See also Menon 1979; *The Indian Worker*, 17 September 1979: 4.

20

WAGE-STRUCTURE OF CHILD LABOUR

Child labour force in the informal sector is mainly employed as a wage-workers. Besides, some of them may be working independently as own-account workers such as balloon-sellers, shoe-shine boys and hawkers in variety of informal sector activities. This chapter mainly focuses on the children working as wage-workers in the informal sector. Such workers, like other workers in the informal sector, are not protected either by legal regulations or by strong trade unions. This deprives them not only of the legal minimum wage but often other benefits such as minimum standard of safety, medical care, security of service and right of legal redress. Consequently, the wages of the workers in the informal sector in general and of the children in particular tend to be very low.

Most of the informal sector enterprises employ illiterate or semi-illiterate workers who have neither any trade experience nor any skills. Moreover, a significant proportion of the labour force is comprised of children.

This chapter, concentrates mainly on the socio-economic characteristics of the working children,* their living conditions, nature of their employment, sources of obtaining their first job, mode of payment of wages inter-industry and intra-industry mobility, working conditions, job satisfaction and the level of wages.

In all 95 children working as wage-workers were interviewed. It was found that three of them were working in the formal sector while 92 were found to be working in the informal sector enterprises. The following analysis, thus, concentrates on those working in the informal sector activities only.

Socio-economic Characteristics

Table 20.1 contains data relating to age, sex, marital status and educational level along with the migrant status of the working children and the provision of electricity in the house/place of living of the working children.

---

*Only those children have been considered who were working as wage-working.

TABLE 20.1

Socio-economic Characteristics of the Working Children

Socio-economic Characteristics	*Number of working children* Male	*Female*	*Total*	*Per cent*
Age in years)				
Below 8	—	—	—	—
8-9	1	—	1	1.09
9-10	6	—	6	2.52
10-11	8	—	8	8.69
11-12	9	—	9	9.78
12-13	21	—	21	22.83
13-14	46	1	47	51.09
Total	91	1	92	100.00
Median age		13.02		

Sex	*Number*	*Per cent*
Male	91	98.91
Female	1	1.09
Total	92	100.00

Marital status	*Male*	*Female*	*Total*	*Per cent*
Married	—	—	—	—
Unmarried	83	1	84	91.3
Others*	8	—	8**	8.7
Total	91	1	92	100.00

Educational Level

General Education	*Number*	*Per cent*
No formal education	46	50.00
Primary	40	43.48
Middle	6	6.52
Above middle	—	—
Total	92	100.00

Migrant status	Number	Per cent
Migrant	25	27.17
Non-migrant	67	72.83
Total	92	100.00

* Married but 'Gauna' has yet to take place.

** All these working children were emigrants.

Type of Residential Accommodation Used by the Working Children

Status of House	Migrant	Non-migrant	Total	Per cent
Owned	1 (2.00)	49 (98.00)	50 100.00)	54.35
Rented*	—	14 (100.00)	14 (100.00)	15.22
Neither owned** nor rented	4 (100.00)	—	4 (100.00)	4.35
Provided by the employer	13 (76.47)	4 (23.53)	17 (100.00)	18.48
Rented and shared	7	— (100.00)	7 (100.00)	7.6
Total	25 (27.17)	67 (72.83)	92 (100.00)	100.00

Provision of Electricity in the House/Place of Living of the Working Children

	Number	Per cent
Electrified	68	73.91
Not electrified	24	26.09
Total	92	100.00

* Includes children living with their parents in rented house.

** Includes children living with their parents/relatives in free accommodation without paying any rent for this accommodation.

Note: Figures in parentheses are percentages.

As regards the type of residential accommodation, it was found that 54.35 per cent of the working ch:ldren lived with their parents in owned houses; 15.22 per cent lived with their parents in rented accommodations; 7.6 per cent shared the rented accommodation.

Those who shared the accommodation were migrants. Nearly one-fifth of the working children were provided accommodation by their employers. A small percentage (4.35) of them were also living in such accommodation which was neither owned nor rented. Such workers were living either with their relatives without sharing any rent or in a religious place (Temple in one case). A few were living with their parents who were provided accommodation free of rent by their employers. Nearly one-fourth of the working children did not have the facility of electricity in their houses or place of living.

Ninety-nine per cent of the working children were male and only one per cent female. Though a large majority (91 per cent) of the working children were unmarried, yet 9 per cent of them were married but 'Gauna'* had not taken place so far. It was true mainly in the case of migrants. As regards the age distribution of the working children, it was found that 7.61 per cent of them were between the age of 7 and 10 years and 18.47 per cent between 10 and 12 years. Nearly three-fourth (73.92 per cent) of the working children were between the age of 12 and 14 years. The median age was 13 years. The distribution of working children in terms of level of educational showed that half of them had never gone to school. Out of the remaining 50 per cent, 43.5 per cent had schooling upto primary and the remaining 6.5 per cent upto middle standard. No formal education and low level of education shows that a majority of the parents of the working children are desirous of having money in place of education of their children.

Nearly three-fourth (72.83 per cent) of the working children were natives and the remaining 27.17 per cent migrants.

Analysis of the data shows that none of the working children was engaged in agriculture and transport industry. It was perhaps due to the nature of occupations in such industries which could not absorb any of the working children. Table 20.2 contains information regarding the type of enterprises in which the working children were employed. The data reveal that 38.05 per cent of the working children were engaged in the service industry which included domestic servants and utensil cleaners, assistants in different types of repair works (car-repairing and cleaning, motor-cycle and bicycle repairing, tailoring, store repairing, electric impliances repairing and dyeing, etc.) and newspaper-sellers. Trade was another important industrial category which employed 31.52 per cent of the total number of working children. This category included in addition to small business shops and establishments, *dhabas* (eating places), hotels, tea and sweetshops, etc. Manufacturing is the next important industrial category in terms of the number of working children "employed (28.26 per cent), where the children were working as helpers in manufacturing of plastic goods, leather goods, furniture and iron girls, etc. Besides, a few were also found to be engaged in packaging, wrapping and printing activities. Construction was the least important category in terms of wage-employment to children., In this category, only two children were found to be working

---

*Marriage ceremony has taken place but the bride is living with her parents.

as casual labourers.

TABLE 20.2

Distribution of Working Children by Different Industrial Categories

Industrial Category	*Number of working children*			
	Migrant	*Non-migrant*	*Total*	*Per cent*
Manufacturing	3 (11.54)	23 (88.46)	26 (100.00)	28.26
Construction	—	2 (100.00)	2 (100.00)	2.17
Trade including hotels and restaurants	15 (51.72)	14 (48.28)	29 (100.00)	31.52
Community, social and personal services including repairs services	7 (20.00	28 (80.00)	35 (100.00)	38.05
Total	25 (27.17)	67 (72.83)	92 (100.00)	100.00

Note: Figures in parentheses are percentages.

Size of the Enterprise

The information sought about the size* of enterprises in which the working children found jobs is given in Table 20.3. It may be mentioned here that no such information was collected from the construction workers because of the nature of their job.

It is evident from the data in Table 20.3 that about 79 per cent of the enterprises in the informal sector were employing upto 4 workers. It may be mentioned here that 7.59 per cent of these employed only one worker and all of them except one were households employing domestic servants. 37.97 per cent of the enterprises employed two workers, 20.25 per cent three workers and 12.66 per cent four workers. The proportion of the enterprises employing five or more workers was 21 per cent. Though, 11.39 per cent had employed five workers. Yet, 5.06 per cent also employed six workers. Only 4.35 per cent enterprises employed 7 to 9 workers. It is clear from the table that the number of enterprises decreases with the increase in its size except in the case of enterprises employing one worker. The mean size of the enterprises worked out to be 3.25 workers.

*Size of an enterprise in terms of workers includes the employer also.

TABLE 20.3

Distribution of Enterprises by their Size and the Industrial Category

Industrial Category	*Number of workers employed (size of enterprise)* 1	2	3	4	5	6	7	8	9	*Total*
Manufacturing	—	5 (25.00)	4 (20.00)	2 (10.00)	3 (15.00)	3 (15.00)	1 (5.00)	—	2 (10.00)	20 (100.00)
Trade including hotels and restaurants	—	13 (50.00)	5 (19.23)	3 (11.54)	4 (15.38)	—	—	—	1 (3.85)	26 (100.00)
Community, social and personal services (including repair services)	6* (18.18)	12 (36.36)	7 (21.21)	5 (15.15)	2 (6.06)	1 (3.03)	—	—	—	33 (100.00)
Total	6 (7.29)	30 (37.97)	16 (20.25)	10 (12.66)	9 (11.39)	4 (5.06)	1 (1.27)	—	3 (3.00)	79** (100.00)

Median Size 3.25

* 5 of these children were domestic servants.

** Excludes construction workers as they work on casual basis.

Note: Figures in parentheses are percentages.

Table 20.4 shows the sex-wise distribution of workers by the industrial categories. It can be observed that 56.03 per cent of the labour force in the informal sector enterprises was of adult male. There was no adult female in such enterprises. Remaining 43.97 per cent were children below the age of 14 years, out of which only 1.56 per cent were female.

The data contained in table reveal that the highest percentage of child labour was in trade which accounted nearly half of the labour force (47.5 per cent) engaged in this activity. No female child was found to be working in trade. Service industry employed 45.98 per cent as child workers. The percentage of female child-workers was 1.15. But for the domestic work, there was no female child in any other occupations of this industry. The percentage of children was lowest in manufacturing industry (38.64 per cent of its total labour force).

Out of total working children, 35.4 per cent were employed in service industry, 34.51 per cent in trade and the remaining 30.09 per cent were employed in manufacturing industry. Thus, comparatively a higher proportion of working children was employed in trade and services. "The main reason for employment of children in these enterprises besides their being cheap labour, is that they can do nearly as much work per unit of time as adults."[1]

The placement of child labour in trade including hotels and restaurants, tea stalls, sweet-shops and other shops and establishments is preferred by the employers because:

1. these establishments mostly serve the lower and middle class of society which has low purchasing power, and the entrepreneurs of these establishments charge a comparatively low price of their goods;
2. child labour is easy to handle and does not create problem for them;
3. the children do not hesitate while doing petty jobs such as picking up of used utensils, cleaning of tables, washing of floors and utensils, etc.;
4. being energetic, the child workers carry tea and snacks more quickly from one place to another;
5. child labour may also be used to attend the personal needs of the owners and perform the other household jobs as and when urgency arises.

Thus, in employing child labour in such establishments the employer not only gains in terms of cheap labour but also gets nearly as much work per unit of time as adult worker.

Nature of Employment

The data on the nature of employment of the sampled working children are presented in Table 20.5. It can be observed from the data in the table that a large majority of the working children (86.96 per cent) was employed on regular and full time basis. The

TABLE 20.4 (A)

Sex-wise Distribution of Workers by the Industrial Category

Industrial Category	*Workers employed*							
	Adults			*Children*			*Per cent*	*Grand Total*
	Male	*Female*	*Total*	*Male*	*Female*	*Total*		
Manufacturing	54 (61.36)	—	54 (61.36)	31 (35.23)	3 (3.41)	34 (38.64)	30.09	88 (100.00)
Trade including hotels and restaurants	43 (52.44)	—	43 (52.44)	39 (47.56)	—	39 (47.56)	34. 51	82 (100.00)
Community, social and personal services including repair services	47 (54.02)	—	47 (54.02)	39 (44.83)	1 (1.15)	40 (45.98)	35.40	87 (100.00)
Total	144 (56.03)		144 (56.03)	109 (42.41)	4 (1.56)	113 (43.97)	100.00	257 (100.00)

Note: Figures in parentheses are percentages.

TABLE 20.4 (B)

Sex-wise Distribution of Workers by the Industrial Category

Industrial Category	*Number of units*	*Employment per unit*						*Grand Total*
		Adults			*Children*			
		Male	*Female*	*Total*	*Male*	*Female*	*Total*	
Manufacturing	20	2.7	—	2.7	1.55	0.15	1.70	4.40
Trade including restaurants	33	1.30	—	1.30	1.18	—	1.18	2.48
Community, social and personal services including repair services	26	1.8	—	1.8	1.5	0.04	1.54	3.34
Total	79	1.82	—	1.82	1.38	0.05	1.43	3.25

proportion of working children employed on casual basis was only 4.34 per cent. Regarding the placement of working children into different industrial categories, it was observed that in construction both the child workers were working on casual basis. In manufacturing 88.46 per cent of the working children were full-timers, and the remaining 11.54 per cent were part-time workers. The part-timers were school-going children and were engaged in the occupational of wrapping of toffees and packaging of Photo-films after school time. In services, 88.57 per cent of the working children were working on regular and full-time basis and the remaining 11.43 per cent were found to be working on part-time basis. Here again, most of the part-timers were school-going children who were engaged in the work of selling newspapers and domestic work. Sofaras trade is concerned, 89.65 per cent of the working children were regular full-time workers, 3.45 per cent part-time and remaining 6.9 per cent were working on casual basis. Out of these casual workers one was employed in a hotel-cum-tea-shop, the other was employed on a 'rehri.' Thus, the nature of employment of working children is mostly regular and full-time. However, those working on part-time basis were school-going children, explaining thereby that perhaps the economic necessities compels the families to send their children to work.

TABLE 20.5

Distribution of Working Children by the Nature of Employment and the Industrial Category

Industrial Category	*Nature of employment*				*Total*
	Regular full-time	*Regular part-time*	*Casual*	*Contractual*	
Manufacturing	23 (88.46)	3 (11.54)	—	—	26 (100.00)
Construction	—	—	2 (100.00)	—	2 (100.00)
Trade including hotels and restaurants	26 (89.65)	1 (3.45)	2 (6.9)	—	29 (100.00)
Community, social and personal services including repair services	31 (88.57)	4 (11.43)	—	—	35 (100.00)
Total	80 (86.96)	8 (8.70)	4 (4.34)	—	92 (100.00)

Note: Figures in parentheses are percentages.

Trade Skill and Experience

When the question on trade skill and experience was put to the respondents, it was found that all the working children in the informal sector had no previous skills and were being trained while on their job.

Sources of Obtaining the First Job

As and when a household decides to send some of its children to work, the household has to seek the help of some agency in getting information about the availability of job. Newspaper advertisements and employment exchanges which are the main sources of information in the formal sector and in large enterprises fail to help these households because of statutory restrictions. However, for the informal sector job-seekers (children or any member of the household) have often to seek the help of their relatives friends. In some cases self-help can also bring fruit. The data concerning the main sources information in obtaining the first employment to children are given in Table 20.6. The data shows that 91.3 per cent of the working children got their first job through relatives and friends. The contribution of relatives was 64.13 per cent and that of friends 27.17 per cent. Self-help contributed in the case of 8.7 per cent.

As among the various sources of information in obtaining the first job relatives were found to be the most important source in the case of all industrial activities in which the children were employed. The contribution of friends was on the next place. In construction out of 2 children one got his first job through self-help while the other through relatives. In the case of trade and manufacturing self-help contributed 13.79 and 7.69 per cent respectively; while in services, this contribution was the least (2.86 per cent). Thus, formal sources of information did not contribute at all in providing information about the availability of jobs to the working children. Relatives and friends and to some extent self-help seem to be the major sources of information in obtaining the first job in the case of working children.

Mode of Payment of Wage

Children can be paid their wages either in cash or in kind or in both. In the formal sector of the economy, wages are mostly paid in cash but in the informal sector they may be paid in cash or in kind or in both. The data relating to the mode of payment of wages to the working children in the informal sector are given in Table 20.7. It can be observed from the data in the table that the payment of wages 'partly in cash and partly in kind' was the most popular mode of payment (58.7 per cent). The payment of wages in cash was the next important category (22.82 per cent). However, 18.48 per cent of the working children' also received their wages exclusively in kind. Thus, though the adult workers in the informal sector may be paid either in cash or 'partly in cash and partly in kind', the possibility of payment of wages exclusively in kind cannot be ruled out in the case of working children. In construction and manufacturing' the important mode of payment of wages was cash. However, in manufacturing 46.15 per cent of the workers were also paid 'partly in cash and partly kind.' In construction, both the working children were paid in cash. In the case of trade payment of wages 'penalty in cash and partly in kind' was the most important mode of payment. Here, 86.2 per cent of the working children were paid 'partly in cash and partly in kind.' In service industry, both partly in cash and partly in kind' as well as exclusively in kind were the major modes of payment of wages to the working children. Some 11.43 per cent of the working children in this industry also received their wages in terms of cash. In service industry the working children who were paid exclusively in kind (two tea plus food) were the new entrants. They were

TABLE 20.6

Source of Information in Obtaining the First Employment by the Industrial Category

Industrial Category	*Sources in information*					*Total*
	Relatives	*Friends*	*Newspaper Advertisement*	*Employment exchange*	*Self-help*	
Manufacturing	15 (57.69)	9 (34.62)	—	—	2 (7.69)	26 (100.00)
Construction	1 (50.00)	—	—	—	1 (50.00)	2 (100.00)
Trade including hotels and restaurants	17 (58.62)	8 (27.59)	—	—	4 (13.79)	29 (100.00)
Community, Social and personal service including repair services	26 (74.28)	8 (22.86)	—	—	1 (2.86)	35 (100.00)
Total	59 (64.13)	25 (27.17)	—	—	8 (8.7)	92 (100.00)

Note: Figures in parentheses are percentages.

expecting to get wages in terms of cash in addition to kind very soon.

An attempt was also mode to find out whether the payment of wages was daily, weekly or monthly basis. The data in this respect are presented in Table 20.8. The data in the table reveal that practice of payment of wages in the case of majority of working children (56.22 per cent) was monthly. However, 31.52 per cent of the working children were also getting their wages on daily basis. Two thirds of the daily paid working children were in service industry.

TABLE 20.7

Distribution of Working Children by the Mode of Payment of Wages and the Industrial Category

Industrial Category	*Mode of payment of wages*			
	Cash	*Kind*	*Cash and kind*	*Total*
Manufacturing	13 (50.00)	1 (3.85)	12 (46.15)	26 (100.00)
Construction	2 (100.00)	—	—	2 (100.00)
Trade including hostels and restaurants	2 (6.90)	2 (6.90)	25 (86.20)	29 (100.00)
Community, social and personal services including repair services	4 (11.43)	14 (40.00)	17 (48.57)	37 (100.00)
Total	21 (22.82)	17 (18.48)	54 (58.70)	92 (100.00)

Note: Figures in parentheses are percentages.

The practice of payment on weekly basis was prevalent in manufacturing, where 11.54 per cent working children were covered by this practice. Some 15.38 her cent of the working children employment in manufacturing were also being paid at irregular intervals. It may be mentioned here that practice of payment of wages on daily basis was prevalent mostly in service industry. It was so because out of 19 cases, 14 were paid in kind (in terms of tea plus food). The practice of payment of wages on monthly basis appeared to be the commonest except in construction.

The data relating the distribution of working children by the persons who receive wages on behalf of the working children are shown in Table 20.9. The data in the table reveal that an overwhelming majority of the working children 82.61 per cent) received their wages themselves. In the case of 17.39 per cent, parents or relatives received wages on behalf of the working children. In trade, this tendency was relatively more common where on behalf of nearly 35 per cent of the working children, either the relatives or parents received wages.

TABLE 20.8

Wage Payment Practice by the Industrial Category

Industrial Category	*Wages paid*				*Total*
	Daily	*Weekly*	*Monthly*	*At irregular intervals*	
Manufacturing	3 (11.54)	3 (11.54)	16 (61.54)	4 (15.38)	26 (100.00)
Construction	2 (100.00)	—	—	—	2 (100.00)
Trade including hotels and restaurants	5* (17.24)	—	24 (82.76)	—	29 (100.00)
Community, social and personal services including repair services	19 (54.29)	1 (2.86)	12 (34.28)	3 (8.57)	35 (100.00)
Total	29 (31.52)	4 (4.35)	52 (56.52)	7 (7.61)	92 (100.00)

*These children were paid in terms of kind only.

Note: Figures in parentheses are percentages.

Inter-Industry and Intra-Industry Mobility

The data on inter-industry and intra-industry mobility of the working children are contained in Table 20.10. It is apparent from the table that out of 92 working children, 40 (43.5 per cent) reported either inter-industry or inter-industry mobility. Among these 40 workers 27 (67.5 per cent) experienced intra-industry mobility while the rest 32.5 per cent experienced inter-industry mobility. Thus, though the intra-industry movement of working children is more popular, yet the tendency to move from one industry to another is also quite significant.

It can also be noticed that intra-industry movement of working children was more pronounced in the case of trade (76.47 per cent), services (64.71 per cent) and in manufacturing (60 per cent). The data further reveal that only one working child moved out of agriculture and joined manufacturing. In manufacturing, out of 5 working children, 3 moved in the same industry and 2 outside the industry who joined trade. In construction, there was no movement either in inter or intra-industry. In trade, out of 17 working children 13 joined trade, 3 services while the remaining one joined the construction with his father, who was a mason, to learn this work, because his previous job was finished. In services out of 17 working children 11 remained with in the same industry, 5 accepted a job in manufacturing while the remaining one joined trade. Thus, trade and services seem to be the most attractive categories for working children to move.

Table 20.11 presents the data concerning the distribution of the working children by the percentage increase in their monthly wages as a consequence of mobility. It can be observed from the data that out of 40 working children who changed their jobs, 15 (37.5

per cent) experienced either a decline in their wages or no gain at all. Out of these 15 children, 7 had a decline in their wages, while the remaining 8 experienced on gain at all. Such workers were those who had to change their jobs either due to the ill-treatment by their employers or termination of the previous job by the employer. Thus, these working children had to accept same level of wages or even less than the wages paid in the previous job. Nearly two-thirds of the working children experienced an increase in their wages. Out of these 25 working children, 6 experienced increase in their wages less than 40 per cent. Three children experienced this increase between 40 to 80 per cent, 5 between 80 to 120 per cent and 7 working children experienced increase in their wages between 120 to 200 per cent. 4 workers were such who experienced even more than 200 per cent increase in their wages, mostly all such working children were those who moved inter-industry and joined trade and services.

TABLE 20.9

Distribution of Working Children by the Person who Receives Wages on Behalf of the Working Child

Industrial	*Payment of Wages*			*Total*
Category	*To the child himself*	*To parents*	*To relatives*	
Manufacturing	23 (88.46)	2 (7.69)	1 (3.85)	26 (100.00)
Construction	2 (100.00)	—	—	2 (100.00)
Trade including hotels and restaurants	19 (66.52)	5 (17.24)	5 (17.24)	29 (100.00)
Community, social and personal services including repair service	32 (91.43)	3 (8.57)	—	35 (100.00)
Total	76 (82.61)	10 (10.87)	6 (6.52)	92 (100.00)

Note: Figures in parentheses are percentages.

The mobility of working children to inter- or intra-industry is not only once, but they change their jobs number of times. Table 20.12 shows job-wise mobility of the working children. Out of 40 children who changed their jobs, 30 (75 per cent) had their second jobs, 8 (20 per cent) 3rd job, while in the case of the remaining 2 children it was their 4th job.

An attempt was also made to look into the reasons which prompted mobility among working children. These are listed in Table 20.13. It can be observed from the data in the

TABLE 20.10

Inter-Industry and Intra-Industry Mobility of Working Children*

From the Industrial category	*To the industrial category*					*Total*
	Agriculture and livestock	*Manufacturing*	*Construction*	*Trade*	*Services*	
Agriculture and livestock	—	1 (100.00)	—	—	—	1 (100.00)
Manufacturing	—	3 (60.00)	—	2 (40.00)	—	5 (100.00)
Construction	—	—	—	—	—	—
Trade including hotels and restaurants	—	—	1 (5.88)	13 (76.47)	3 (17.65)	17 (100.00)
Community, Social and personal services including repair services	—	5 (29.41)	—	1 (5.88)	11 (64.71)	17 (100.00)
Total		9 (22.5)	1 (2.5)	16 (40.00)	14 (35.00)	40 (100.00)

* Some children changed more than one job and industry. Here the mobility is shown in terms of the last two jobs held.

Note: Figures in parentheses are percentages.

TABLE 20.11

Distribution of Working Children* by the Percentage Increase in their Wages and the Type of Mobility

Type of mobility	*Percentage increase in wages per month*								*Total*
	Decrease in wages	*No. change*	*Less than 40*	*40-80*	*80-120*	*120-160*	*160-200*	*200+*	
Inter-industry mobility	4 (30.78)	1 (7.69)	1 (7.69)	—	2 (15.38)	2 (15.38)	—	3 (23.08)	13 (100.00)
Intra-industry mobility	3 (11.11)	7 (25.93)	5 (18.52)	3 (11.11)	3 (11.11)	2 (7.41)	3 (11.11)	1 (3.7)	27 (100.00)
Total	7 (17.50)	8 (20.00)	6 (15.00)	3 (7.5)	5 (12.50)	4 (10.00)	3 (7.5)	4 (10.00)	40 (100.00)

* Some children changed more than one job. In their case the difference in income was calculated between the last two jobs held.

Note: Figures in parentheses are percentages.

table that among the various reasons prompting mobility those relating to economic factors were the most important (37.50 per cent). More than 60 per cent of the working children who changed jobs due to this reason moved in the intra-industry. Did not get along with the employer (ill-treatment/irregular payment of wages, compulsion to attend the personal needs of the employer) was the next important reason for mobility of the working children. Almost all these children also moved within the same industry. Some 17.50 per cent of the children moved from their previous job either due to better working conditions (previous job was difficult/not understanding the previous work) or due to more favourable location. Termination of job was also one of the reasons for the mobility of the working children in 10 per cent of cases. One child worker had to move from one job to another since his previous employer used to give his whole wages to his father who was a drunker. The new employer has opened his saving bank account.

TABLE 20.12

Job-wise Mobility of the Working Children

At present working in industrial category	*Number of times moved*			
	2nd job	*3rd job*	*4th job*	*Total*
Manufacturing	6 (66.67)	2 (22.22)	1 (11.11)	9 (100.00)
Construction	—	—	1 (100.00)	1 (100.00)
Trade including hotels and restaurants	12 (75.00)	4 (25.00)	—	16 (100.00)
Community social and personal serivces including repair services	12 (85.71)	2 (14.29)	—	14 (100.00)
Total	30 (75.00)	8 (20.00)	2 (5.00)	40 (100.00)

Note: Figures in parentheses are percentages.

Working Conditions for Child Labour in the Informal Sector

In the In the formal sector the workers enjoy formalised working conditions including fixed working hours. They are also protected in respect of their wages. The informal sector workers on the other hand do not enjoy fixed working hours. The working hours vary from one occupation to another depending upon the nature of occupations. For example, in the case of sweets-manufacturer (Halwai, Tea shop, dhaba etc.) the working children have to work for much longer hours as compared to those working in grossery

shops and other shops and establishments. The data on the average number of hours worked per day by the working children in the informal sector enterprises are given in Table 20.14. The data shows that only 8.7 per cent of the working children in the informal sector worked for less than 8 hours which is the normal practice for adult workers in the formal sector. Some 33.7 per cent of the children worked between 8 to 10 hours, 30.43 per cent between 10 to 12 hours, 27.17 per cent worked even more than 12 hours a day. This shows that the working children placed in the informal sector enterprises do not enjoy any uniform practice of working for fixed hours. This is so, because the informal sector enterprises follow no uniform practice of working for fixed hours.[2]

TABLE 20.13

Distribution of Working Children by the Type of Mobility and the Reasons for Moving

Reasons for moving	*Type of mobility*			
	Inter-industry	*Intra-industry*	*Total*	*Per cent*
Got a higher starting salary	5 (33.33)	10 (66.67)	15 (100.00)	37.50
More favourable location	—	2 (100.00)	(100.00)	5.00
Better working hours/ conditions/previous job was difficult/not understanding the previous work	2 (40.00)	3 (60.00)	5 (100.00)	12.50
Did not get along the Employer (illtreatment/irregular payment/ compulsion to attend the personal needs of the employer	3 (23.08)	10 (76.92)	13 (100.00)	32.50
Job terminated/job finished	2 (50.00)	2 (50.00)	4 (100.00)	10.00
Others*	1 (100.00)	—	1 (100.00)	2.50
Total	13 (32.5)	27 (67.5)	40 (100.00)	100.00

* One child worker had to move from one job to another since the pervious employer used to give his whole wages to his father who was a drunker. The new employer has opened his saving bank account.

Note: Figures in parentheses are percentages.

TABLE 20.14

Distribution of Working Children by the Average Number of Hours Worked Per Day and the Industrial Category

Industrial category	*Average number of hours worked*						
	Less than 4	*4-6*	*6-8*	*8-10*	*10-12*	*12-15*	*Total*
Manufacturing	— (11.45)	3	— (46.15)	12 (38.46)	10 (3.85)	1 (100.00)	26
Construction	—	—	—	2 (100.00)	—	—	1 (100.00)
Trade, including hotels and restaurants	—	—	4 (3.45)	6 (20.69)	6 (20.69)	16 (55.7)	29 (100.00)
Community, social and personal services including repair services	3 (8.57)	1 (2.86)	—	11 (31.42)	12 (34.29)	8 (22.86)	35 (100.00)
Total	3 (3.26)	4 (4.35)	1 (1.09)	31 (33.07)	28 (30.29)	25 (27.17)	92 (100.00)
		(8.70)					

Note: Figures in parentheses are percentages.

The analysis of the data also indicated that the practice of working less than 8 hours existed only in the case of manufacturing and services. All such workers were part-timers and almost all of them were school-gaing children. In manufacturing nearly half of the children found, to be working between 8 to 10 hours a day, while 42.31 per cent worked even for 10-15 hours a day. In construction the formal sector norm of 8 hours a day was practised. In trade, more than half of the children (55.17 per cent) worked between 12-15 hours per day while 41.38 per cent worked between 8-12 hours a day. In services, 34.29 per cent of the working children were found to be working between 10-12 hours a day, 31.42 per cent between 8-10 hours a day. In services, nearly one-fourth of the working children attended to their work more than 12 hours a day. They included mostly the domestic servants.

An attempt was also made in the case of working children to know the distance of place of work from the place of living. The data are depicted by Table 20.15. No such information was collected from the working children engaged in construction because of nature of their work. The data in the table reveal that out of 90 working children 32.22 per cent were found to be living at the place of work, or very close to the place of work, 22.23 per cent at less than 1 kilometer and 25.56 per cent had to cover the distance of 1 to 2 kilometer to reach their place of work. Not only this, 18.89 per cent of the working children had to cover the distance of more than 3 kilometers. It may be mentioned here that those who lived away from their place of work had to reach there and go back to their houses on foot.

TABLE 20.15

Distribution of Working Children by the Distance of Place of Work from Place of Living and the Industrial Category

Industrial category	*Living at the place of work/ quite near*	*Distance covered in kilometers*				*Total*
		Less than 1	*1-2*	*2-3*	*3+*	
Manufacturing	8 (30.77)	7 (26.92)	9 (34.62)	2 (7.69)	—	26 (100.00)
Trade, including hotels and restaurants	11 (37.93)	9 (37.03)	5 (17.24)	3 (10.35)	1 (3.45)	29 (100.00)
Community, social and personal services including repair services	10 (28.57)	5 (14.29)	9 (25.71)	8 (22.86)	3 (8.57)	35 (100.00)
Total	29 (32.22)	21 (23.33)	23 (25.56)	13 (14.45)	4 (4.44)	90* (100.00)

*Excludes construction workers because of nature of their work.

Note: Figures in parentheses are percentages.

TABLE 20.16

Distribution of Working Children by Rest-Interval and the Industrial Category

Industrial category	*Length of rest-internal*			*Total*
	No rest	*Upto ½ hour*	*½ to 1 hour*	
Manufacturing	11 (42.31)	9 (34.61)	6 (23.08)	26 (100.00)
Construction	—	—	2 (100.00)	2 (100.00)
Trade including hotels and restaurants	27 (93.1)	1 (3.45)	1 (3.45)	29 (100.00)
Community, social and personal services including repair services	23 (65.71)	9 (25.72)	3 (8.57)	35 (100.00)
Total	61* (66.31)	19 (20.65)	12 (13.04)	92 (100.00)

*Includes 8 part-time working children.
Note: All these working children did not have any fixed length of rest intervals.
Figure in parentheses are percentages.

As regards the rest interval of the working children Table 20.16 depicts that 66.31 per cent of the working children did not get any rest time, out of which 57.31 per cent were full-timers, 20.65 per cent got upto ½ to 1 hour interval. The remaining 13.04 per cent workers got ½ to 1 hour rest. None of these working children had any fixed length of rest interval. In manufacturing, 57.69 per cent of the workers were given rest intervals. Next important category in which children had rest time was services (25.72 per cent). In trade, only a negligible percentage (6.9) were given rest interval.

The working children were also asked to state if they got their wages for the period of absence from work. Reply of almost all the children was that they had to loose their wages if they absented from duty. Only a very small number of working children (5) replied that their employers were kind enough not to cut their wages for absence only in the case of illness. Thus, on the whole, the working children were governed by the rule 'no work no pay.'

Level of Earnings

The distribution of working children by level of wages in different activities has also been computed and is shown in Table 20.17. It can be seen from the data that out of 92 working children 82.61 per cent received less than Rs. 300 per month. Nearly 45 per cent of the working children were receiving even less than Rs. 150 per month. Only 17.39 per cent of the working children were earning more than Rs. 300 per month.

In trade, wages paid to the children were higher as compared to other industrial categories. The mean wage was lowest in service industry (repair works).

TABLE 20.17

Distribution of Working Children by Monthly Wages and the Industrial Category

Industrial category	*Wages per months (Rs.)*									*Total*
	*30**	*30-60*	*60-90*	*90-120*	*120-150*	*150-180*	*180-240*	*240-300*	*300+*	
Manufacturing	1	2	4	2	1	6	7	1	2	26
	(3.85)	(7.69)	(15.38)	(7.69)	(3.85)	(23.08)	(26.92)	(3.85)	(7.69)	(100.00)
Construction	—	—	—	—	—	—	2	—	—	2
							(100.00)			(100.00)
Trade include hotels	—	—	—	—	3	2	5	6	13	29
and restaurants	(10.34)	(6.9)					(17.24)	(20.69)	(44.83)	(100.00)
Community, social and										
personal services inlcu-	7	8	5	7	1	1	3	2	1	35
ding repair services	(20.00)	(22.86)	(14.28)	(20.00)	(2.86)	(2.86)	(8.57)	(5.71)	(2.86)	(100.00)
Total	8	10	9	9	5	9	17	9	16	92
	(8.7)	(10.87)	(9.78)	(9.78)	(5.43)	(9.78)	(18.48)	(9.78)	(17.39)	(100.00)

	Mean Wage	Model Wage
Manufacturing	153.46	149.00
Trade	252.93	309.25
Services	93.86	37.50

Percentage of children earning less than legal minimum wage (for an adolescent) = 93.48

* Most of the working children in this category were those who were getting wages in kind (only two tea).

Note: Figures in parentheses are percentages.

As regards the number of working children having more than one job to earn extra income, it was found that only 2 workers were found to be working for extra time. One worker, who was a part-time worker on a Rehri used to collect rags after that time and the other worker who was employed in printing press used to watch the Rehri of hawkers in the Sabji mandi early in the morning, for which he used to get Re. 1 per Rehri.

Since there are no fixed hours of work for the children working in the informal sector, there is no question of over time payment. However, in manufacturing in the case of plastic melting industry it was found that these children sometimes worked overtime during night and got wages for this extra time in some cases 50 paise per hour, while in small cases Re. 1 per hour.

Job Satisfaction

Information on job satisfaction is contained in Table 20.18. The data show that 33.7 per cent of the working children were not satisfied with their present job in terms of income as well as working conditions. In manufacturing and trade employed in other than hotels the proportion of working children who were not satisfied with their job was higher than that of services. In construction, no worker was satisfied with his job. In services, the proportion of the working children satisfied with their job was surprisingly high. This was so, because most of these children are employed in repair works in which they were interested. For example, cycle-repair, motor-cycle repair, etc. were of interest to children as they expected to become mechanic in the near future. The other category of the working children who felt satisfied was of those engaged as domestic servants because they were given better food and shelter than what was available in their own houses.

TABLE 20.18

Distribution of Working Children by Job Satisfaction and the Industrial Category

Industrial category	*Number of working children*			*Total*
	satisfied	*not satisfied*	*not replied*	
Manufacturing	14 (53.85)	10 (34.46)	2 (7.69)	26 (100.00)
Construction	—	2 (100.00)	—	2 (100.00)
Trade including hotels and restaurants	17 (58.62)	11 (37.93)	1 (3.45)	29 (100.00)
Community, social and personal services including repair services	25 (71.43)	8 (22.86)	2 (5.71)	35 (100.00)
Total	56 (60.87)	31 (33.7)	5 (5.43)	92 (100.00)

TABLE 20.19

Distribution of Working Children by the Reasons of Job Dissatisfaction and the Industrial Category

Industrial category	*Reasons of job dissatisfaction*						*Total*
	Job is not secure	*Low wages*	*Work place is far from residence*	*Do not like the employer*	*Do not like the working conditions*	*Others*	
Manufacturing	—	2 (20.00)	1 (10.00)	1 (10.00)	6 (60.00)	—	10 (100.00)
Construction	2 (100.00)	—	—	—	—	—	2 (100.00)
Trade including hotels and restaurants	1 (9.09)	6 (54.55)	—	1 (9.09)	3 (27.27)	—	11 (100.00)
Community, social and personal services inclu-ding repair services	—	7 (87.5)	—	—	—	1* (12.5)	8 (100.00)
Total	3 (9.68)	15 (48.39)	1 (3.22)	2 (6.45)	9 (29.04)	1 (3.22)	31 (100.00)

* Not understanding the work.

Note: Figures in parentheses are percentages.

An attempt was also made to find out the reasons of dissatisfaction which is shown by Table 20.19. It is clear from the table that half of the dissatisfied children (48.39) per cent were dissatisfied due to low wages. Next important reason of dissatisfaction in order of preference was worse working conditions (specially in manufacturing). Thus, 35.52 per cent of the children were dissatisfied due to ill-treatment by the employer and uneven working conditions. 9.68 per cent were dissatisfied due to non-security of their job. One worker was dissatisfied due to not understanding the work.

It can be noticed that in manufacturing three-fifths of children (60 per cent) were dissatisfied due to uneven working conditions. Sometimes children have to work even during night, specially in plastic melting work. In this work the children are to remain standing in the water throughout night to wash the degenerate of plastic. Besides, they have to work in stink. In the survey, it was found that one of such children got serious lungs disease and remained in the Rajindra Hospital for its cure. Lastly, it was suggested by the doctor to leave this job. Now he has joined packing works. In furniture and manufacturing works, it was replied by the children that when an urgent order to prepare some chairs, stools and other household articles was received, they had to work during whole night. In trade and services also, low wages dominated the reason for dissatisfaction. In trade, the dissatisfied working children were employed at small tea shops, establishments or rehris. In services, dissatisfied working children were those working as apprentices without being paid any thing in cash, but in kind only.

TABLE 20.20

Distribution of Dissatisfied Working Children by Mobility in Future and the Industrial Category

Industrial Category	*Type of mobility*		*Total*
	Looking for a better job in a similar occupation	*Looking for a better job in different occupation*	
Manufacturing	2 (20.00)	8 (80.00)	10 (100.00)
Construction	—	2 (100.00)	2 (100.00)
Trade including hotels and restaurants	7 (63.64)	4 (36.36)	11 (100.00)
Community, social and personal services including repair services	4 (50.00)	4 (50.00)	8 (100.00)
Total	13 (41.94)	18 (58.06)	31 (100.00)

Note: Figures in parentheses are percentages.

It is worth mentioning that all these children were looking for a better job in a similar or different occupation. Table 20.20 shows that 58.06 per cent of the working children were looking for a better job in a different occupation, while the remaining 41.94 per cent in a similar occupation. The data in the Table show that in manufacturing four-fifths of the working children were looking for a better job in different occupation, while in trade most of the children were looking for a better job in a similar occupation. In case of services, this ratio was fifty-fifty. In construction all the working children were looking for a better job in a different occupation.

The data in Table 20.21 show retirement benefits and paid weekly holidays available to the working children in the informal sector. It is evident from the data that none of the working children in the informal sector enterprises enjoyed any finding benefits such as security of service, retirement benefits (gratuity, pension, etc.) and bonus etc.

Insofar as the weekly holidays are concerned, the data show that none of the working children in construction, 91.43 per cent in services, 86.21 in trade and 65.39 per cent in manufacturing were not entitled to any paid weekly holiday.

TABLE 20.21

Distribution of Working Children Enjoying Retirement Benefits and Paid Weekly Holidays and the Industrial Category

Industrial Category	*Total number of working children*	*Number of children enjoying retirement benefits*	*Paid weekly holiday*	*Per cent*
Manufacturing	26	—	9	34.61
Construction	2	—	—	—
Trade including hotels and restaurants	29	—	4	13.79
Community, social and personal services including repair services	35	—	3	8.57
Total	92	—	16	17.39

As regards the trade union of the working children in the informal sector enterprise, it was found that there was no such trade union.

NOTES & REFERENCES

1. Vishwa Mittar, *Growth of Informal Sector in Punjab's Urban Economy: A Case Study of Patiala City* (Patiala, 1984), unpublished Ph.D. Thesis, p. 226.
2. *Ibid.*, p. 242.

21

MIGRATION AND CHILD LABOUR

The influx of migrants brings with them number of children to help their parents or relatives in raising their level of earnings by employing them in variety of activities of the urban economy. The child labour, which faces restrictions to entry in the formal sector activities, is comparatively more easily absorbed in the informal sector activities, which are not guided by the legal restrictions. Therefore, it would be interesting to study the socio-economic characteristics of the working children belonging to the migrants. The data for the purpose highlight: How many and what type of children are migrating and from what areas? How did they come to Patiala? Why did they come at all and what are the reasons of their migration? What was their age and educational level at the time of migration? How many of them were employed before migration? Do they enter similar or different occupations on arrival? And finally, how much they remitted and the purposes to which the remittances were put?

The survey covered 110 working children out of which 35 (31.82 per cent) were migrants and the remaining 80 (68.18) per cent) natives. The data in Table 21.1 reveal the distribution of migrant-working children by the previous place of residence. It is revealed that out of 35 working-children only two (5.71 per cent) migrated from within the State and remaining 33 (94.29 per cent) migrated from outside and state. More than three-fourth (82.86 per cent) of the migrant-children were from rural areas.

TABLE 21.1

Distribution of Migrant Children by the Previous Place Residence

Previous place of residence	*Urban*	*Per cent*	*Rural*	*Per cent*	*Total*	*per cent*
Within the State	2 (100.00)	33.33	—	—	2 (100.00)	5.71
Outside the State	4 (12.12)	66.67	29 (87.88)	100.00	33 (100.00)	94.29
Total	6 (17.14)	100.00	29 (82.86)	100.00	35 (100.00)	100.00

Note: Figures in parentheses are percentages.

Distribution of working children by age and migrant status (Table 21.2) shows that the migrant children were comparatively younger than the non-migrant children. Their median ages were 12.93 years and 13.06 years respectively.

TABLE 21.2

Distribution of The Working Children by Age-group and Migrant Status

Age (in years)	*Migrant-status*		
	Migrant	*Non-migrant*	*Total*
Below 8	—	1 (1.33)	1 (0.91)
8-9	—	1 (1.33)	1 (0.91)
9-10	2 (5.71)	5 (6.67)	7 (6.36)
10-11	5 (14.29)	4 (5.33)	9 (8.18)
11-12	4 (11.43)	7 (9.33)	11 (10.00)
12-13	7 (20.00)	17 (22.67)	24 (21.82)
13-14	17 (48.57)	40 (53.34)	57 (51.82)
Total	35 (100.00)	75 (100.00)	110 (100.00)
Median age	12.93	13.06	13.04

Note: Figures in parentheses are percentages.

The data relating to the age of the migrant children on arrival by the place of previous residence (Table 21.3) show that nearly half (48.57 per cent) of the migrant children were below the age of 10 years, 31.43 per cent between 10 and 12 years and the remaining 20 per cent were between 12 and 14 years of age at the time of migration. Thus, child migration at a very tender age seems to be common from the rural areas and also from outside the State.[1]

It is further seen (Table 21.4) that most of the children were recent migrants. One-third of them had migrated since 1 year or less, 17.14 per cent since 2 years and 25.72 per cent since three years. Nearly 23 per cent of them had migrated since 4 years of above.

TABLE 21.3

Distribution of Migrant Children by the Previous Place of Residence and Their Age on Arrival

Age on arrival (in years)	*Previous place of residence*				*Total*
	Urban	*Rural*	*Within the State*	*Outside the State*	
Below 8	2 (33.33)	4 (13.79)	1 (50.00)	5 (15.15)	6 (17.14)
8-10	1 (16.67)	10 (34.48)	—	11 (33.33)	11 (31.43)
10-12	3 (50.00)	8 (27.59)	1 (50.00)	10 (30.31)	11 (31.43)
12-14	—	7 (24.14)	—	7 (21.21)	7 (20.00)
Total	6 (10000)	29 (100.00)	2 (100.00)	33 (100.00)	35 (100.00)

Note: Figures in parentheses are percentages.

TABLE 21.4

Distribution of Migrant Children by the Period of Migration

Years since in-migrated	*Number of children*	*Per cent*
1 or less than 1	12	34.29
2	6	17.14
3	9	25.72
4	2	5.71
5 +	6	17.14
Total	35	100.00

As regards the sex-wise migration, it was found that there was no female migrant child. Thus, child migration seems to be sex selective. It is so because the migrants do not allow their daughters to migrate with them or with the relatives and friends. However, if the migrants move along with their families, the female children were allowed to work as domestic servants. But this exertion cannot be proved for want of adequate data.

Further, eight children were married but their 'Gauna' had not taken place so far. The remaining children were unmarried. This shows that child-marriage is still common in some parts of the country.

TABLE 21.5

Distribution of Working Children by Educational Level and Migrant Status

General education	*Migrant Status*		
	Migrant	*Non-migrant*	*Total*
1	2	3	4
No formal education	21 (60.00)	35 (46.67)	56 (50.91)
Primary	11 (31.43)	35 (46.67)	46 (41.82)
Middle	3 (8.57)	5 (6.66)	8 (7.27)
Above middle	—	—	—
Total	35 (100.00)	75 (100.00)	110 (100.00)

Note: Figures in parentheses are percentages.

The educational levels of the children by their migrant status (Table 21.5) shows that 60 per cent of the migrant children had received no formal education, 31.43 per cent had studied only upto primary level and the remaining 8.57 per cent upto middle standard. No child had received education above the middle standard. It is natural because the children migrate at a very young age and so they have to abandon their education. In the case of non-migrant children nearly half (50.91 per cent) of them had received no formal education, 41.82 per cent had studied upto primary and the remaining 7.27 per cent upto middle standard. No child had received education above middle. Thus, non-migrant children were more literate (49.9 per cent) as compared to migrant-children (40 per cent).

The information on the main activity of children during the year before migration (Table 21.6) shows that only 17.14 per cent of the migrant children were employed at the time of migration at their place of origin. The remaining were either unemployed (45.72 per cent) of students (28.57 per cent). Some 8 per cent were unable to work.

Distribution of working children by the employment status and migrant category (Table 21.7) shows that both the migrant and the non-migrant children were engaged mostly as wage-workers. But, the proportion of wage-workers was higher among the non-migrant working children as compared to the migrant children. However, one-fifth of the migrant and 5.33 per cent of the non-migrant children were also found to be working as own-account workers. They were hawkers, shoe-shine boys, balloon-sellers, peddlars, etc. This clearly shows that children of migrants, who cannot get wage-employment at the place of destination get them absorbed in self-employment activities.

TABLE 21.6

Distribution of Migrant Children by Previous Place of Residence and Their Main Activity in the Year Before Migration

Main activity in the year before migration	*Number of children*	*Per cent*
Employed	6	17.14
Unemployed	16	45.72
Student	10	28.57
Others*	3	8.57
Total	35	100.00

* Includes children unable to work.

Distribution of working children by industrial category and migrant status (Table 21.8) shows that among a variety of industrial categories, migrant children were concentrating mainly on trade including hotels and restaurants (51.43 per cent) and community social and personal services including repair services* (28.57 per cent). The non-migrant working children were concentrating mainly in community, social and personal services including repair services** (37.27 per cent) and manufacturing (34.67 per cent). Trade attracted only 20 per cent of the non-migrant children.

TABLE 21.7

Distribution of Working Children by The Employment Status and Migrant Category

Employment status	*Migrant Status*		
	Migrant	*Non-migrant*	*Total*
Wage worker	25	67	92
	(71.43)	(89.33)	(83.64)
Own-account worker	7	4	11
	(20.00)	(5.33)	(10.00)
Unpaid family worker	3	3	6
	(8.57)	(4.00)	(5.45)
Others*	—	1	1
		(1.34)	(0.91)
Total	35	75	110
	(100.00)	(100.00)	(100.00)

* Beggar.

Note: Figures in parentheses are percentages.

Thus, the migrant children absorb themselves in all types of jobs which would provide them salaries, while the non-migrant children besides earning for their family seem to be desirous of learning technical know-how. The latter mostly engage themselves in various types of repair works.

As regard the type of accommodation occupied by the migrant children (Table 21.9), it was found that one-fifths of the migrant children were found to be living with their parents and 14.29 per cent with relatives. Nearly two-fifths of them were provided accommodation by their employers. Another one-fourth of the migrant-children were sharing the rented accommodation. However, one child who was a balloon-seller had no fixed place of living. He used to sleep on foot-path.

Reasons for Migration of the Migrant Children

Pull as well as push factors are responsible for migration of people to urban areas. Attraction of city life and comparatively higher income opportunities are among the pull factors and inferior conditions of living in the sending areas along with lack of work opportunities are among the push factors responsible for migration. Besides,

* Most of them were working as domestic servants.

** Most of them were engaged in repair works.

another push factors may be on work is that the economic compulsion of parents may induce them to send children on work to the nearest or even far off urban centres. The adverse financial position of parents compels them to borrow from the village money-lender, who charges exorbitant interest rates on the loans advanced to the villagers. A pressure from the side of money-lender to repay the debts is likely to compel the parents to send their wards to cities to earn, since no work is available in the village. Thus, financial factors in addition to large family size with low family income seems to be responsible for child migration. Lack of interest in studies, non-availability of work in the village and liabilities (social and well as financial) are other factors responsible for child migration. Information has been sought from the working children to enlist the various factors responsible for their move to the city. These responses are contained in Table 21.10.

TABLE 21.8

Distributing of Working Children by The Industrial Category and Migrant Status

Industrial category	*Migrant Status*		
	Migrant	*Non-migrant*	*Total*
Agricultural and livestock	1 (2.86)	—	1 (0.91)
Manufacturing	3 (8.57)	26 (34.67)	29 (26.36)
Construction	—	2 (2.67)	2 (1.82)
Transport	3 (8.57)	—	3 (2.73)
Trade including hotels and restaurants	18 (51.43)	15 (20.00)	33 (30.00)
Community, social and personal services including repair services	10 (28.57)	31 (41.33)	41 (37.27)
Others*	—	1 (1.33)	1 (0.91)
Total	35 (100.00)	75 (100.00)	110 (100.00)

TABLE 21.9

Distribution of Migrant Children by the Type of Accommodation Occupied in the City

Type of accommodation	*Number of children*	*Per cent*
Living with parents	7	20.00
Living with relatives	5	14.29
Living in accommodation provided by the employer	13	37.14
Rented but shared	9	25.71
Others*	1	2.86
Total	35	100.00

* No fixed place of living.

The analysis of the data in the Table reveals that the economic factors dominate the decision for the migration. Debts and financial liabilities of the family, to follow family and lack of work at the place of origin were amongst the most important reasons of migration. To seek better employment and to learn some technical or repair works were the other reasons responsible for child migration. Maltreatment on the part of step-mother and drunkard father and lack of interest in studies were also responsible in the case of 11.43 per cent and 8.57 per cent of the children respectively. Charm of the city life was the least important factor in stimulating child labour to city since only one child reported that he migrated to the city because of the charm of the city life. In fact, this child was a run-away child who came here with a person of his village without informing his parents about his move. Another child migrated along with his parents form an adjoining state due to political reasons. He joined as wage-worker in a manufacturing unit and had to leave his studies.

TABLE 21.10

Distribution of Migrant Children by Reasons of Migration

Reason of migration	*Number of children*	*Per cent*
1	2	3
1. Debts and financial liabilities of parents	27	77.14
2. To follow family (parents or relatives live here)	26	74.28
3. Lack of work at the place of origin	25	71.43
4. Economic compulsion of parents	9	25.71

1	*2*	*3*
5. To get better employment	6	17.14
6. To learn Technical or repair works	6	17.14
7. Discouraging behaviour of parents (parents and step-mother's behaviour, etc.)	4	11.43
8. Lack of interest in studies	3	8.57
9. Liked the city life*	1	2.87
10. Others**	3	8.57

* This child was a run away child.

** Two children migrated due to the death of both father and mother while the another one migrated with his family from Haryana (Panipat) to Patiala due to political reasons.

Note: The percentages do not add upto 100 because some children gave more than other reason of migration.

Means of Migration

Children being in their tender age are mostly unaware of the urban life if they belong to rural area and if they belong to urban area they are not well informed about the living conditions in the urban area of destination. Children rarely dare to move alone and some body has to accompany them to the place of destination. The other difficulty in their case is to find a job themselves. It is doubtless that most of the children are mostly sent to the place of destination by their parents (willingly or unwillingly). Usually, children do not move alone towards the place of destination. They, generally move along with the parents, relatives and friends, employers, contractors and only in a few cases at their own. The data relating to the persons accompanying the child during migration was collected and are presented in Table 21.11.

TABLE 21.11

Distribution of Migrant Children by the Means of Migration

Means of migration	*Number of children*	*Per cent*
Came with parents	10	28.57
Came with relatives	15	42.86
Came with villagers/friends	7	20.00
Came at their own	3	8.57
Total	35	100.00

It is seen from the data in the Table that most of the children moved along with their parents or relatives and friends. However,, 8.57 per cent of them came at their own.

Sources through which the migrant children obtained their first employment in Patiala has also been investigated. These sources are given in Table 21.12.

TABLE 21.12

Distribution of Migrant Children by Employment Status and the Source Through Which They Obtained Their First Employment in the City

Source	*Employment status in the first job in the city*					
	Self-employed		*Wage workers*		*Total*	
	Number	*Per cent*	*Number*	*Per cent*	*Number*	*Per cent*
Relatives and friends	9	90.00	24	96.00	33	94.29
Advertisements/employment exchanges	—	—	—	—	—	—
Self-help	1	100.00	1	4.00	2	5.71
Total	10	100.00	25	100.00	35	100.00

The data in the Table show that the most important source through which migrant children obtained their first employment in Patiala was "Relatives and friends'. Self-help was another important source in this respect. Advertisement and employment exchanges—the two important formal sector sources of information were of no avail to these children.

As regards the period of waiting for the first job after migration, it was found that almost all the migrant children obtained a job within a few days (less than 10 days). This is due to the reason that either parents or relatives and friends of these children are already living here. They helped them in getting employment. Moreover, most of these children being sponsored migrants, job was quickly found for them. This shows that migrant children were being absorbed quickly in the urban labour market.

The information on type of assistance provided to these children by their relatives or friends was also collected and is given in Table 21.13.

TABLE 21.13

Distribution of Migrant Children by the Type of Assistance Provided by Relatives and Friends Living at the Place of Destination

Type of assistance	*Number*	*Per cent*
Stayed and lived with them	32	96.97
Assisted with money	14	42.42
Provided food	30	90.90
Helped to get employment	33	100.00
Total number of migrant children who receivec. assistance	33	

Note: The percentages do not add upto 100 since each migrant child has listed more than one type of assistance.

Out of 35 migrant children, 33 had relatives and friends living in Patiala City. These children received assistance in one form or another from them. Thirty-two (96.97 per cent) lived with their relatives and friends during the period they had to wait till they found employment. Some of them (12 children) are also still living with their relatives and friends. All the children were helped by their relatives and friends in getting employment. Ninety per cent of the migrant children were provided with food till they found employment. However, 42.42 per cent also received help in terms of money too. Thus, prior contacts with the area of destination tend to help the children to migrate to a particular area.[2]

Ownership of Land and House at the Place of Origin

It may be expected the most of the migrant children belonging to non-agricultural households will not be owning any land at their place of origin. But, those who belong to the agricultural households in the rural areas may be having some agricultural land.

The data on ownership of agricultural land by the families belonging to the migrant children at their place of origin are given in Table 21.14.

TABLE 21.14

Distribution of Migrant Children by Ownership of Agricultural Land by Their Families at the Previous Place of Residence

Land owned at previous place of residence (acres)	*Number of children*	*Per cent*
No land	22	62.86
Less than 2	2	5.71
2-5	4	11.43
5-7	7	20.00
Total	35	100.00

The data in table shows that nearly two-thirds of the families belonging to the migrant children did not own any agricultural land at the place of origin. Further, none of the families belonging to these children owned land more than 7 acres. It may be mentioned here that mostly the land owned or cultivated was of inferior quality (less productive) so for farming is concerned (as was told by many respondents).

Nearly one-seventh of the families belonging to these migrant children did not own houses at the place of origin. In the remaining cases only mud-houses were owned by the parents of the migrant children.

Only 6 children were reported to be employed during the year before migration. The information regarding the children who were employed before and after migration is given in Table 21.15.

TABLE 21.15

Distribution of Migrant Children Who were Employed Before and After Migration by Their Employment Status

Employment status during the year before migration	*Employment Status in the first employment in the city*			*Total*
	Unpaid family worker	*On account worker*	*Wage worker*	
Unpaid family worker in agriculture	—	—	2 (33.33)	2 (33.33)
Own account worker	—	—	—	—
Wage worker	—	—	4 (66.67)	4 (66.67)
Total	—	—	6 (100.00)	6 (100.00)

Note: Figures in parentheses are percentages.

The data in table show that two children were working as unpaid family workers at the place of origin and another four were employed as wage-workers. After migration, all the six children were found to be engaged in the informal sector as wage-workers. In fact, the children who were employed as wage-workers at the place of origin were paid very low wages and they migrated to the place of destination to get higher wages.

Link With Native Place

Two factors such as contribution to the family income through remittances and visit to place of origin are important to explain a migrant worker's link with his native place. To ascertain in the strength of the link with native places the data were collected and are presented in Table 21.16.

TABLE 21.16

Distribution of Migrant Children by Number of Visits Paid to the Native Place During Last Year (1984)

Number of visits paid to the native place during 1984	*Number of children*	*Per cent*
None	29	82.86
One	3	8.57
Two	1	2.86
More than two	2	5.71
Total	35	100.00

It is found that a very high proportion (82.86 per cent) of the migrant children did not visit the place of origin during the year. Few of them (8.57 per cent) did visit once. Another 8.57 per cent visited the place of origin more than one time. The observation should be considered carefully since many of the migrant children were recent migrants and in the case of some others very little amount was left after making remittances. These two reasons mainly prohibited the children to pay a visit to their native places. Thus, it is difficult to conclude that the link of the migrant children with the native places were not so strong.

Remittances and the Child Labour

The purpose of child-migration is to receive a part of the income of children by the sending areas. Migrant children often save a portion of their income for sending it back home. The remittances may be used by the recipients for meeting their consumption or investment needs. In many cases, remittances may also be used for paying off debts. Thus, the socio-economic transformation of the receiving areas may take place through remittances. In fact, the size and frequency of remittances may have some economic impact on the areas of origin. However, the size and frequency of remittances is constrained by the type of migrants, their level of income and the nature of the job in which the migrants are employed as well as the number of visits, a migrant pays to his place of origin.

During the survey, it was found that 17 children were sending remittances. Their proportion amongst the migrant children worked out to be 48.57 per cent. The classification of data by the level of remittances is given in Table 21.17.

TABLE 21.17

Distribution of Migrant Children Sending Remittances by the Level of Remittances

Level of remittances (Rs. per month)	*Number of children*	*Per cent*
Less than 80	6	35.29
80-100	7	41.18
100-150	3	17.65
More than 150	1	5.88
Total	17	100.00

Per cent of migrant children sending remittances	=	48.57
Remittances as percentage of cach + kind earnings	=	36.46
Remittances as percentage of only cash earnings	=	60.41
Mean level of remittances	=	Rs. 104.11 p.m.

Since the migrant children were paid both in cash and kind, the proportion of income earned in cash being sent home was calculated and is given at the foot of the

Table. It was found that 60.41 per cent of the cash earnings was being remitted by the migrant children. Further, on an average one-third of the migrant children were sending less than Rs. 80 per month of the place of origin. Only 6 per cent of them were able to send more than Rs. 150 per month. This is so, because of the low level of earnings of migrant children. The mean level of remittances was Rs. 104.11 per month.

The distribution of migrant children sending remittances by their employment status and industrial category, is shown in Table 21.18.

The data in the table show that the most important industrial category so far as remittances are concerned is trade, where nearly three-fourth of the migrant children employed were sending remittances. In manufacturing 66.66 per cent of the migrant children were involved in the act of remittances. In Transport, 33.33 per cent of the migrant children were involved in the act of remittances. In Transport, 33.33 per cent of the migrant children were sending remittances, while in services this proportion was only 10 per cent. Thus, nearly half of the total migrants were sending remittances. Out of the total migrants sending remittances nearly three-fourth were employed in Trade, 11.77 per cent in manufacturing and remaining 5.88 per cent were employed in transport and agriculture each. Out of 17 migrant children who were sending remittances only one belong to urban areas and 16 belonged to rural areas and outside the state (Table 21.19). Thus, nearly all the remittances were made to the rural area and that too outside the state. Another finding of this analysis is that more than half (55.17 per cent) of the migrant children belonging to rural area and only 16 per cent to the urban areas, were sending remittances.

TABLE 21.18

Distribution of Migrant Children Sending Remittances by the Employment Status and Industrial Category

Industrial activity	*Number of children*	*Employment status of the children sending remittances*			
		Wage worker	*Own account worker*	*Total*	*Per cent*
Trade including hotels and restaurants	18	12 (80.00)	1 (50.00)	13 (76.47)	72.22
Manufacturing	3	2 (13.13)	—	2 (11.76)	66.66
Community, social and personal services including repair services	10	1 (6.67)	—	1 (5.88)	10.00
Transport	3	—	1 (50.00)	1 (5.88)	33.33
Agriculture and livesstock	1	—	—	—	—
Total	35	15 (100.00)	2 (100.00)	17 (100.00)	48.57

Note: Figures in parentheses are percentage.

TABLE 21.19

Distribution of Migrant Children Sending Remittances and the Place of Origin

Place of origin	*Number of migrant children sending remittances*				
	Total number of migrants	*Within the state*	*Outside the state*	*Total*	*Per cent*
Urban	6 (17.14)	1 (100.00)	—	1 (5.88)	16.67
Rural	29 (82.86)	—	16 (100.00)	16 (94.12)	55.17
Total	35 (100.00)	1 (100.00)	16 (100.00)	17 (100.00)	48.57

Note: Figures in parentheses are percentages

Table 21.20 shows the distribution of migrants who sent remittances by their present employment status. The data in the table show that 60 per cent of the wage-workers were sending remittances while 28.57 per cent of the own-account workers were able to send remittances. This shows that the wage-workers, (specially employed in trade) were mostly involved in sending remittances.

TABLE 21.20

Distribution of Migrant Children who Sent Remittances by their Present Employment Status

Employment status	*Total number of migrant children*	*Migrants sending remittances*	*Per cent*
Wage-workers	25	15	60.00
Own-account-workers	7	2	28.57
Total	32*	17	53.12

* Excludes three unpaid-family-workers.

The uses to which the remittances of the children are put are depicted by Table 21.21.

It can be seen from the data in the table that the remittances by children were mostly used for consumption purposes. For paying off debts by the parents of these children (64.70 per cent) was another important use to which the remittances were put. To meet the medical expenses of parents and education of other children in the family at the place of origin was also one of the uses in the case of 17.65 per cent each. However, in 23.52 per cent cases the remittances were used to purchase necessary articles for the marriage of their sisters.

TABLE 21.21

Use(s) of Remittances by Households of the Migrant Children at the Place of Origin

Uses of remittances	*Number of households*	*Per cent*
1. Food, clothing and other household necessities (consumption purposes)	17	100.00
2. For paying of debts	11	64.70
3. To meet the medical expenses	3	17.65
4. For education of other children in the family	3	17.65
5. For marriage of sister(s) (to purchase necessary articles)	4	23.52
Total	17	

Note: Total of percentages do not add upto 100.00 because in some cases the remittances by the children were put to use by their parents for more than one purpose.

NOTES AND REFERENCES

1. Vishwa Mittar, *Growth of Informal Sector in Punjab's Urban Economy: A Case Study of Patiala City* (Patiala, 1984), unpublished Ph.D. thesis, p. 271.
2. Similar conclusions have been drawn by Vishwa Mittar, *Growth of Informal Sector in Punjab's Urban Economy: A Case Study of Patiala City* (Patiala, 1984), unpublished Ph.D. thesis, p. 289.